AMERICA

PATHWAYS
—TO THE—
PRESENT

Civil War to the Present

About the Authors

Andrew Cayton, Ph.D.

Andrew Cayton is Professor of History at Miami University in Oxford, Ohio. Born in Cincinnati, Ohio, he is the grandson of a high school history teacher. Dr. Cayton received his B.A. with high honors from the University of Virginia and his M.A. and Ph.D. from Brown University.

Dr. Cayton is an early American historian, whose specialization is political and social history. He is the author of *The Frontier Republic: Ideology and Politics in the Ohio Country, 1780–1825* and coauthor of *The Midwest and the Nation: Rethinking the History of an American Region.*

Dr. Cayton received the 1993 Outstanding Teacher Award from the Ohio Academy of History and the 1992 Distinguished Educator Award from the College of Arts and Sciences at Miami University. He lives in Hamilton, Ohio, with his wife, Mary Kupiec Cayton, and daughters, Elizabeth and Hannah.

Elisabeth Israels Perry, Ph.D.

Elisabeth Israels Perry serves as the Director of the Graduate Program in Women's History at Sarah Lawrence College, in Bronxville, New York. She previously taught U.S. women's history at Vanderbilt University, in Nashville, Tennessee. She received her B.A. and Ph.D. in history from the University of California at Los Angeles.

Dr. Perry's period of specialization is the late nineteenth and early twentieth centuries. Her greatest scholarly interests are women's history and reform movements. She is the author of *Belle Moskowitz: Feminine Politics and the Exercise of Power in the Age of Alfred E. Smith.* She is the coeditor of *The Challenge of Feminist Biography: Writing the Lives of Modern American Women.*

Dr. Perry has received major grants from Fulbright, the National Endowment for the Humanities, and the American Council of Learned Societies. She has directed three NEH Summer Seminars for secondary school history and literature teachers.

Allan M. Winkler, Ph.D.

Allan M. Winkler chairs the Department of History at Miami University of Ohio. He received his B.A. from Harvard University, his M.A. from Columbia University, and his Ph.D. from Yale University.

Dr. Winkler's specialization is twentieth-century social and political history. He is the author of eight books, including *The Politics of Propaganda: The Office of War Information, 1942–1945; Modern America: The United States from the Second World War to the Present; The Recent Past: Readings on America Since World War II;* and *Home Front U.S.A.: America During World War II.* His most recent book, published in 1993, is *Life Under a Cloud: American Anxiety About the Atom.*

Dr. Winkler began his teaching career in the Peace Corps in the Philippines, where he worked at the elementary and secondary level as well as at the college level. He has taught at Yale University and the University of Oregon, and has also held the Bicentennial Chair in American Studies in Helsinki, Finland and the John Adams Chair in American Civilization in Amsterdam, in the Netherlands.

PRENTICE HALL

A Division of Simon & Schuster
Englewood Cliffs, New Jersey 07632

ISBN 0-13-8025886

Printed in the United States of America

1 2 3 4 5 6 7 8 9 02 01 00 99 98 97 96 95 94

Program Reviewers

Teacher Advisory Panel

Alfred B. Cate, Jr. Central High School, Memphis, Tennessee
Pamela Gray Tustin High School, Orange County, California
Robert Durkin Washington Irving High School, New York, New York
Richard Hryniewicki Cudahy High School, Wisconsin
Phillip James Lincoln-Sudbury High School, Sudbury, Massachusetts
Gerald F. Krows Moore High School, Moore, Oklahoma
Jayne Rotsko Ipswich High School, Ipswich, Massachusetts
Gloria S. Sesso Half Hollow Hill East, Dix Hills, New York
Jerome L. Ruderman Frankford High School, Philadelphia, Pennsylvania

Student Review Board

Brenda Borchardt Cudahy High School, Cudahy, Wisconsin
Rebecca A. Day Moore High School, Moore, Oklahoma
Lena K. Franks Frankford High School, Philadelphia, Pennsylvania
Phillip Payne Moore High School, Moore, Oklahoma
Brooke J. Peterson Lincoln-Sudbury High School, Sudbury, Massachusetts
Jeramogi Carreé Todd Central High School, Memphis, Tennessee

Historian Reviewers

Parentheses indicate area of specialization.

Elizabeth Blackmar Department of History, Columbia University,
   New York, New York (social and urban history)
Donald L. Fixico Department of History, Western Michigan University, Kalamazoo,
   Michigan (American Indian history, American history Reconstruction to the present)
Mario Garcia Department of History, University of California,
   Santa Barbara, California (Latino history)
Gerald Gill Department of History, Tufts University, Medford,
   Massachusetts (African American history, twentieth-century history)
William M. King Afroamerican Studies, Center for Studies of Ethnicity and
   Race in America, University of Colorado at Boulder, Boulder, Colorado
   (Afroamerican history, twentieth-century U.S. society and culture)
Huping Ling Division of Social Science, Northeast Missouri State University,
   Kirksville, Missouri (Asian American history)
Melton A. McLaurin Department of History, The University of North Carolina
   at Wilmington, Wilmington, North Carolina (nineteenth-century social history)
Roy Rosenzweig Department of History, George Mason University,
   Fairfax, Virginia (nineteenth and twentieth-century social and cultural history)
Susan Smulyan Department of American Civilization, Brown University,
   Providence, Rhode Island (twentieth-century history)

*Prentice Hall and the authors are grateful to our reviewers, who provided valuable assistance in making
this textbook one that meets the needs of American history teachers and students. Teacher and student reviewers
read chapter manuscript. Historian reviewers read chapters with content that corresponded to their
areas of specialization.*

The *Pathways* Team

*The editors, designers, marketers, managers, electronic publishing specialists, copyeditor, production and manufacturing buyers, page production
manager, and advertising and production manager who made up the* Pathways *team are listed below.*

Alison Anholt-White, Gabriella Della Corte, Robert G. Dunn, David Graham, Barbara Flockhart, Jeffrey M. Ikler, Dorshia I. Johnson,
Linda D. Johnson, Russell Lappa, David Lippman, Nancy Rogier, Luess Sampson-Lizotte, Holly Schuster, Amit Shah, Virginia Shine,
Diane Shohet, Marisa Sibio Shuff, Martha G. Smith, L. Christopher Valente, Pearl B. Weinstein, Naomi Y. Wilsey, David R. Zarowin

CONTENTS

OVER ★ THERE

SPECIAL FEATURES

Viewpoints

Two opposing or contrasting viewpoints on major historical topics

Links Across Time

Examples of how events and ideas have shaped life in the past and in the present

**Biographical sketches of both famous and
ordinary Americans and their impact on society**

TIME & PLACE: A GEOGRAPHIC PERSPECTIVE

**An in-depth look at the links between
geography and history**

History might not have Happened This Way

**Examples of how decision makers—both political
leaders and ordinary citizens—shaped history**

American Album

**Artifacts from the exhibitions and collections at the
Smithsonian Institution National Museum of American History**

The Way It Works

**Detailed drawings that illustrate key historical events
and advances in technology**

105-horsepower, six-cylinder engine

Driver

Commander

One of four Lewis machine guns

One of two 57-mm pedestal-mounted guns

Armor plating

Pressed steel track plate

HISTORIAN'S TOOLBOX

Historical Evidence

Maps

Maps (continued)

Graphs, Charts, and Tables

Bridging Past and Present

The construction of the Brooklyn Bridge between 1869 and 1883 is one of America's great stories. The story of this bridge also tells us a lot about the subject of history and why this subject is so fascinating and important.

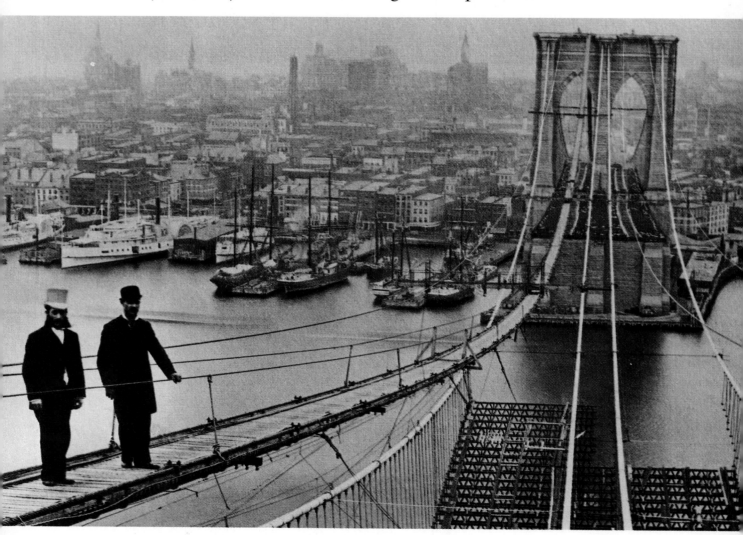

Because other, shorter suspension bridges had failed before the Brooklyn Bridge was begun, the outcome of this project remained in doubt until its completion. Two engineers check the progress of the bridge's construction in 1881 (above), and workers cut and tie cables in 1882 (right).

HISTORY IS FULL OF UNEXPECTED OUTCOMES

John A. Roebling designed the Brooklyn Bridge and began its construction. He never knew the results of his effort, however. At the very beginning of the construction in 1869, a boat crushed his foot, and two weeks later he died from tetanus.

John Roebling's unfortunate story illustrates something about history that we may overlook. We know what John Roebling never knew—that his plan succeeded and that the Brooklyn Bridge still stands today. When we read about the events of the past, we can easily forget that the participants in the drama did not know how things would turn out. They had no more idea about the outcome of events than you now have about the outcome of today's events.

John A. Roebling

HISTORY REVEALS THE CAUSES OF EVENTS

People knew they needed a bridge to connect Manhattan Island with Brooklyn for more than half a century. Why was the bridge not begun until 1869, and why was it begun by John Roebling? History does not always give one sure answer about how and why an event took place. But historians can tell us about important earlier incidents that led to the event.

The East River, which the Brooklyn Bridge would eventually cross, flows swiftly and runs deep. The river served as a major route

for large ocean-going ships and could not be blocked with a low bridge. The best type of bridge to span this river would be a suspension bridge, and it had to be almost 1,600 feet long. No one had ever constructed a long-span suspension bridge until John Roebling built one in 1846 across the Ohio River at Wheeling, West Virginia. The bridge that made him famous and captured the public's imagination, however, was the one that stretched more than 1,000 feet across Niagara Falls.

Roebling's technical success was not the only reason the Brooklyn Bridge got built when it did. Residents of Manhattan had used ferry boats to travel back and forth between Brooklyn and Manhattan. Although traveling by ferry took much longer than crossing a bridge, a bridge would cost the taxpayers more money than they wished to invest. In the winter of 1866 to1867, however, the cold weather halted ferry service and isolated Manhattan. The residents now were ready to pay for their bridge.

Fireworks mark the opening of the Brooklyn Bridge on May 24, 1883 (below). The bridge, which was completed by Washington Roebling (inset) after his father's death, marked a turning point in history. It began an era of bridge building that greatly improved transportation in the United States.

History reveals that many key events of the past have had a lasting impact on the present.

Emily Roebling, Washington Roebling's wife, carried his instructions to work crews at the bridge when an accident disabled Washington.

HISTORY MIGHT NOT HAVE HAPPENED THIS WAY

What happened when John Roebling died only a few weeks after beginning the bridge? Was only one outcome possible? When you turn the pages of a history book, you may feel that historical events were destined to turn out a certain way; in other words, history had to have happened the way that it did. But, if people had made different decisions and taken different actions, history might not have happened that way. Historians examine the options people had and the reasons they chose a certain path. From the study of history, we learn that many individuals, making personal choices and selecting among options, determine the course of events.

With the sudden death of the most-respected bridge builder of the time, the fate of the bridge—which many doubted could be built—was in question. The project might have been abandoned, or the corrupt political leader of New York, Boss Tweed, might have put one of his cronies in charge. Instead, John Roebling's son, Washington Roebling, carried on after his father's death.

Washington Roebling proved an able successor to his father, although an 1872 accident disabled him physically. Washington Roebling spent the last eleven years of the project confined to his apartment in a wheelchair. He watched the progress of the construction through his apartment window, while his wife, Emily Roebling, carried his instructions to the work crews at the bridge.

HISTORY IS EVERYONE'S STORY

The Roeblings did not build the bridge alone. The muscle, sweat, and skill of hundreds of laborers, many of them foreign born, were crucial. These workers toiled under hard and dangerous conditions. Some died in the process. Bankers and financiers, together with national and city politicians, also played major roles in building the bridge.

Historians, however, cannot tell everyone's story. They must focus on the people and events they feel are most important. Some historians choose to tell the story of a few famous people—political, military, and industrial leaders. *America: Pathways to the Present* chooses instead to weave the stories of ordinary women and men from many backgrounds and occupations together with the stories of the famous.

HISTORY HELPS US UNDERSTAND THE PRESENT

The building of the Brooklyn Bridge was a turning point in history. Its success led to a boom in bridge building that made the crossing of major waterways a casual, everyday event throughout the country. The Brooklyn Bridge is an important path to the present, but it is only one of many events that, when studied historically, can lead us to a better understanding of the United States today. History reveals that many key events of the past have had a lasting impact on the present.

Obviously, most of the people you will read about in this book died long ago. As a result, their dreams and actions may seem remote to you. But the people of the past once walked and talked, hoped and dreamed, cried and laughed like you. And many of the things they did—from the bridges they built to the games they played—still affect us today.

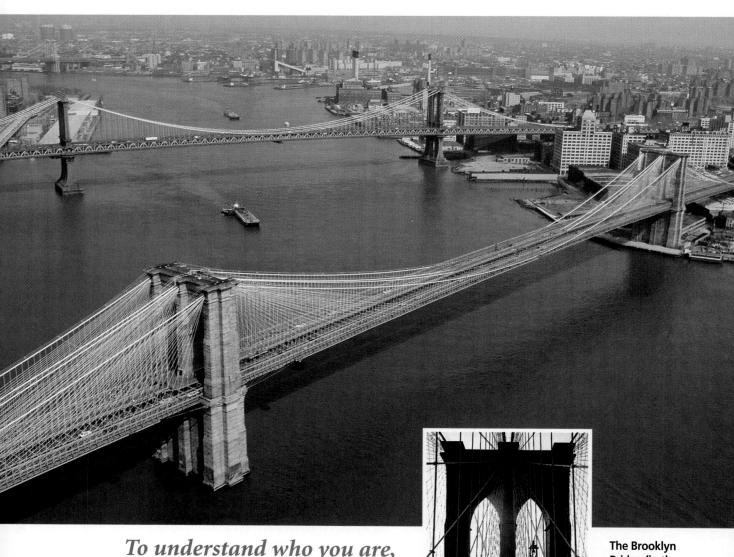

To understand who you are, you first have to know about those people whose beliefs and experiences shaped your life.

The Brooklyn Bridge (in the foreground above and in the inset) remains an important part of the life of New Yorkers today.

THE PAST IS DIFFERENT FROM THE PRESENT

Studying the past is like studying a foreign country; the people there often do things differently from us. In America's past, its people sometimes did things quite differently than we do today. For example, Americans once had a very different view of what *equality* meant.

When historians examine our country's past, they focus on the realities of people's lives at that time. They try to help us understand why people in the past made the choices they did. History is not always pleasant or uplifting. The stories of the past do not always have happy endings. Sometimes they are very violent and disturbing.

We need to be honest about these events, and also to try to understand them and assess their meaning. Your job as a history student is to make a connection with them, to find out what you do and do not share with them and to engage them in conversation as a means of gaining a better understanding of both them and yourself.

UNITED STATES HISTORY SHOWS THEMES

As we study the past, we see certain themes of history emerging. Among them are a desire for personal freedom and respect for the dignity of all human beings, and a belief in political democracy and faith in the idea of self-government. There is also a fundamental notion of social equality, and faith in our ability to improve our environment so that as many people as possible can enjoy a decent standard of living. These themes, which run throughout this book, are described on pages 6 and 7.

Disagreements about how to balance these themes provide much of the energy of American history. Americans agree that liberty is an important goal, but they also believe that it should be balanced with the need for social order. Americans know that the two goals of liberty and order constantly clash, but that each is important to the success of the other. Similarly, how do we balance the need for change with the need for stability? How do we balance economic growth with the need to preserve the environment? How can we share the benefits of prosperity with everyone without reducing the standard of living for many?

WHY STUDY HISTORY?

Knowing about the past can help you understand the present. You know this from personal experience. To understand who you are, you first have to know about those people whose beliefs and experiences shaped your life.

Studying history also keeps the memory of these people and their experiences alive. Learning the history of the nation is like learning the history of a family. Historians feel a sense of obligation to the people who came before. Studying history is their way of saying, we remember you, as we hope people will remember us.

History reminds us of the continuity of the human experience. We may dismiss the past as irrelevant, to conclude that dead people and past events have little to do with us. But that would be a mistake. The present is linked to the past. History is not about memorizing a series of dates and events; it is an active, imaginative journey during which you share experiences with people from the past. These people may speak, think, and dress differently from you, but they still share universal concerns and a wish for a better future. To study history is in a very real sense to participate in history itself.

Themes in American History

Much of what you learn about American history can be better understood if you view events as part of a larger pattern. The themes listed on page 7 apply to all periods of American history and can help you link events across time.

A jazz band poses for a photograph in the 1930s (above). A huge audience listens closely to rock and folk music at Woodstock in 1969 (inset). American culture—the special expression of ideas, attitudes, and feelings through various art forms, manners, and morals—is one of the important themes in American history.

REFORM MOVEMENTS

People in the United States have frequently taken action in grass-roots movements to right perceived wrongs and to secure improvements in the quality of life.

VALUES

A variety of religious, ethical, and moral beliefs have propelled and guided the quest of Americans for a just and ordered society.

ECONOMICS

Americans have searched for new and better ways to make a living and have struggled to define government's role in this pursuit.

TECHNOLOGY

Americans' ability to develop new skills and tools and to increase their knowledge of the physical world has greatly affected the way they live and work, and has led to a high standard of living.

ENVIRONMENT

The geography and available resources of the continent have affected the actions of Americans. Similarly, the actions of Americans have affected the environment and physical landscape.

DIVERSITY

The United States throughout its history has been made up of a gathering of many peoples from throughout the world. Americans have both benefited from and encountered problems with this diversity.

UNITY AND CONFLICT

Americans have developed unique political systems and laws that affirm a shared commitment to certain goals, such as individual rights and equality. Nevertheless, groups with differing views on how to achieve these goals have sometimes clashed.

AMERICAN CULTURE

In every period of their history, Americans gave special expression to their views in forms such as art, literature, films, music, manners, and morals.

AMERICAN DEMOCRACY

The concepts of democratic representation, equality under the law, and freedom from discrimination have been gradually broadened to include previously excluded groups.

THE UNITED STATES AND THE WORLD

America's relationships with other countries have been influenced at different times by a sense of mission, by values, and by self-interest.

The Nation's Beginnings to 1860

"A people without a history
is like wind on the buffalo grass."
–Proverb, Teton Sioux

The rich and varied histories of several groups of people shaped the growth and direction of our nation. When the colonists overthrew British rule in the American Revolution, the new nation they created was already a multicultural society. As the nation grew, it struggled to achieve a balance between liberty and order. In the early 1800s, the United States seemed to be a nation in constant motion. With the migration of Americans to the newly acquired territories in California and Oregon, the United States stretched from sea to shining sea.

The excitement of government by the people is captured in this 1815 painting, "Election Day in Philadelphia," by John L. Krimmel.

Encounters and Colonies
To 1754

*F*ive hundred years ago, a few frail ships crossing the waters of the Atlantic Ocean first brought Europeans to Native American shores. Africans torn from their homelands soon followed. After a period during which Native Americans and Europeans alternately dominated and resisted one another, the Europeans overwhelmed Native Americans and took hold in North America.

Events in the United States

800–1000
Navahos migrate to the Southwest from the fringes of North America.

1000 Norsemen under Leif Ericson land on the coast of North America.

800	900	1000	1100	1200

Events in the World

800 Charlemagne crowned emperor of Romans.

1095 European Christians set out on the First Crusade to capture Palestine from the Muslims.

REVIEW UNIT

Pages 12–18

Three Lands on the Atlantic

Each of the three main culture areas around the Atlantic Ocean had a long history of its own before they all began to interact with one another in the late 1400s. Though these cultures had many similar customs and beliefs, certain differences among them would later lead to a violent clash of values.

 Pages 19–23

The Atlantic World Is Born

The voyage of an Italian navigator was the prelude to centuries of trade and tragic conflict among Native Americans, Europeans, and Africans. In these years new societies would be built and old ones swept aside.

 Pages 24–29

European Settlement and Native American Resistance

After 1492, the Spanish, English, French, and Dutch invaded the Americas, devising various ways to exploit its natural wealth. Meanwhile, Native Americans fought against them, determined to preserve their way of life.

 Pages 32–37

Life in Colonial America

For England in the mid-1600s and early 1700s, the colonies were a reliable source of raw materials and a prime place to sell English goods. Eventually, however, the colonies grew and prospered with little direct interference from the English government. As they grew, a distinct colonial culture emerged.

 Pages 38–42

African Americans in the Colonies

Although they had no rights in the highly unequal world of colonial America, African Americans actively shaped society from very early times.

		1598 Spain claims territory of New Mexico.	*1630* European settlers found the Massachusetts Bay Colony.	*1680* Pueblo people expel the Spanish from New Mexico.	*1750* Number of enslaved African Americans in the British colonies passes 236,000.
	1492 Columbus sails from Spain and lands on islands in the Caribbean.				

1300	**1400**	**1500**	**1600**	**1700**	

1271 Marco Polo journeys to China.			*1591* End of the Songhai Empire in West Africa.	*1648* The Taj Mahal is completed in India.	*1762* Catherine the Great becomes ruler of Russia.

Three Lands on the Atlantic

SECTION PREVIEW

Each of the three main culture areas around the Atlantic Ocean had a long history of its own before they all began to interact with one another in the late 1400s. Though these cultures had many similar customs and beliefs, certain differences among them would later lead to a violent clash of values.

Key Concepts

- By the 1400s, the region that would become the United States was inhabited by many diverse cultural groups linked by trade.
- Competition among the highly structured societies of Europe encouraged the people of that region to look overseas for trading opportunities in the 1400s.
- The kingdoms of West Africa were complex and wealthy cultures, with an extensive trading system that stretched from the Guinea coast to North Africa.

Key Terms, People, and Places

kinship network, clan, hierarchy, patriarchal society, lineage; Guinea, Songhai

Native American artists in what is now Gallatin County, Kentucky, sculpted in stone the spare, crisp lines and curves of this face.

Archaeologists theorize that beginning as much as 40,000 years ago, people migrated eastward from Asia to a land where humans had never lived before—the Americas. The people who descended from these migrants are today generally referred to as Native Americans, because their ancestors were the first to be native to, or born on, the American continents. In fact, the Native Americans' own legends say that their people have lived in the Americas since the creation of the earth.

Over the centuries after their arrival, Native Americans grew in number and fanned out across North and South America. As they went, they gained hard-won knowledge about how to live on the land, weaving new societies and building on old traditions to meet the demands of their times. Their language branched and evolved until groups who spoke its separate offshoots often could not understand one another. Empires rose and fell among them; skills and crafts sprang into being, only to vanish and revive again.

During these thousands upon thousands of years, the wide Atlantic and Pacific oceans generally isolated the Americas from people elsewhere in the world. Those other people, too, were forging societies and building cultures. Then, in the late 1400s A.D., the Atlantic Ocean ceased to be a barrier and became instead a highway on which the three main cultures around the Atlantic Ocean—Native American, European, and African—came into contact with one another. The similarities and differences among their beliefs and their ways of life at once began to profoundly affect the interaction among them. This section compares and contrasts the beliefs and the ways of life of these three cultures before contact.

America: A Flourishing World

By the late 1400s, when the encounter among the Atlantic cultures began, some eight to ten million people may have lived in what is now the United States. Some scholars contest these figures, claiming they should be as low as 700,000 to 800,000. The map on page 13 shows that whatever the size of this population, it included a dazzling number of distinct groups. The map also indicates how these groups can be categorized by region, reflecting differences in the way they adapted their way of life to the local environment.

Social Organization and Spiritual Life No matter how Native Americans adapted to the land in which they lived, whether they hoed the soil in the dry Southwest or stalked buffalo on the Great Plains, they generally looked to the

Native American Culture Groups and Trade Routes, c. 1500

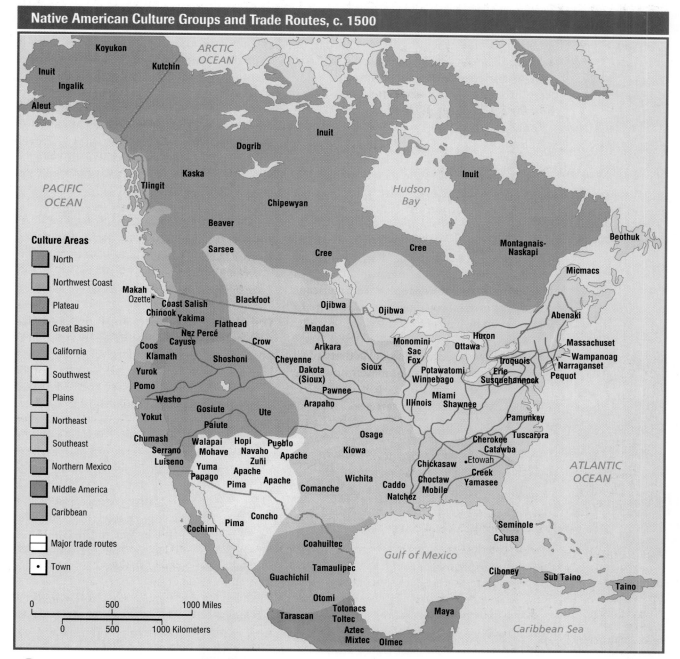

Culture Areas

- North
- Northwest Coast
- Plateau
- Great Basin
- California
- Southwest
- Plains
- Northeast
- Southeast
- Northern Mexico
- Middle America
- Caribbean
- Major trade routes
- Town

0   500   1000 Miles

0   500   1000 Kilometers

ARCTIC OCEAN

PACIFIC OCEAN

Hudson Bay

ATLANTIC OCEAN

Gulf of Mexico

Caribbean Sea

Koyukon, Kutchin, Inuit, Ingalik, Aleut, Dogrib, Kaska, Tlingit, Chipewyan, Beaver, Sarsee, Cree, Cree, Montagnais-Naskapi, Beothuk, Micmacs, Makah, Ozette, Coast Salish, Chinook, Yakima, Flathead, Blackfoot, Ojibwa, Ojibwa, Abenaki, Nez Percé, Cayuse, Crow, Mandan, Huron, Ottawa, Massachuset, Coos, Klamath, Shoshoni, Arikara, Monomini, Sac, Fox, Iroquois, Wampanoag, Narraganset, Pequot, Yurok, Cheyenne, Dakota (Sioux), Sioux, Potawatomi, Winnebago, Erie, Susquehannock, Pomo, Pawnee, Miami, Shawnee, Washo, Gosiute, Arapaho, Illinois, Pamunkey, Yokut, Ute, Osage, Cherokee, Tuscarora, Paiute, Catawba, Chumash, Walapai, Hopi, Pueblo, Kiowa, Etowah, Serrano, Mohave, Navaho, Apache, Chickasaw, Creek, Luiseno, Zuñi, Yamasee, Yuma, Apache, Wichita, Choctaw, Mobile, Papago, Pima, Apache, Comanche, Caddo, Natchez, Cochimi, Pima, Concho, Coahuiltec, Seminole, Calusa, Tamaulipec, Guachichil, Ciboney, Sub Taino, Taino, Otomi, Totonacs, Toltec, Tarascan, Maya, Aztec, Mixtec, Olmec

Geography and History: Interpreting Maps

The map shows only some of the groups thriving in North America in the 1400s. The trade routes, too, are only a selection; nearly any waterway or path served as a potential path for trade. *In which region is a small number of culture groups spread out over a large area? Why?*

family to fulfill many of their social needs. Their families provided them with many of the services we expect today from governments, churches, and private organizations, including medical care, child care, settlement of disputes, and education.

For the Native American, the family usually meant not just parents and children, but a **kinship network**. This was a group of relatives, or kin, such as parents, children, grandparents, aunts, uncles, cousins, and those who had married into the family.

One kind of kinship network is today referred to as a **clan.** A clan was formed of groups of families who were all descended from a common ancestor. The Lenape people of the mid-Atlantic seaboard, for example, had at least three clans. The diagram below illustrates how the Lenape clans gathered together for ceremonies that had social, religious, and political significance.

Ceremonies such as these, which reinforced social ties, were vital to the social organization of Native Americans. Furthermore, like Africans and Europeans, Native Americans believed that misfortunes, such as military defeat, disease, or bad harvests, happened to people who ignored rituals. For this reason, whether they were planting crops, falling in love, or burying their dead, Native Americans strictly followed traditional rituals. Failure to do so was an invitation to disaster.

Peaceful Trade One traditional activity of all Native American groups, no matter how large or small, was trade for food or goods within their group and outside it. They traded not only for items they needed or wanted, but also to demonstrate hospitality and friendliness. Even basic economic transactions took on a social dimension, because sharing was a sign of respect. Such trading customs began thousands of years before the collision of the Atlantic cultures and continued long afterward. A French priest, Father Joseph François Lafitau, noted in 1724 that the Native Americans

have traded with each other from time immemorial. . . . The feasts and dances which they have when they go to deal with other tribes [groups] make their trade an agreeable diversion. . . . Their way of engaging in trade is by an exchange of gifts.

The Native American View of Land Use
Although Native Americans might give away possessions as gifts, they never traded away land. In their view, the land could not be owned. They believed that people had a right to use land and could grant others the right to use it too. But to sell land outright, as people in other countries did at the time and as we do today, was unthinkable to Native Americans. Chief Joseph, a leader of the Nez Percé people in the late 1800s, expressed the age-old Native American view:

T he country was made without lines of demarcation [boundary lines], and it is no man's business to divide it. . . . The earth and myself are of one mind. The measure of the land and the measure of our bodies are the same. . . . I never said the land was mine to do with it as I chose. The one who has the right to dispose of it is the one who has created it.

Central post This post was a symbolic link to the sky, home of the Creator.

Carvings These carvings represented twelve sky spirits.

Entry at east This entry symbolized birth.

Oval Floor The shape represented the back of the turtle that was believed to form the earth.

Wolf clan

Drummers

Turtle clan

Turkey clan

Circle of men

Circle of women

Exit at west This exit symbolized death.

In a ceremony woven of prayer, chanting, and dance, clans of the Lenape gave thanks to the Creator. The longhouse and all within it reflected relationships in the universe. For example, men sat within a circle of women, who headed the clans.

This difference in views about how land should be used would lead to violent disagreement between Native Americans and Europeans when the two cultures met.

The Nations of Europe

The meeting of the three Atlantic cultures was brought about by the Europeans, who were the first to cross the Atlantic Ocean. One aim in particular motivated them to do so: the desire to win wealth through trade. Their trade, however, was very different from Native American trade, and arose in the context of a very different society.

The Importance of Land Europeans in the 1400s depended heavily on farming for survival, but land was scarce and people were numerous. In fact, for centuries Europe had had more people than it could feed with the crops it grew at that time. Thus land was valued because owning land meant being powerful. Relatively few people owned and controlled land; these few—the wealthy—did little work. Instead, they made the people who farmed their land pay rent or give over part of their crops.

By contrast, the working poor made up about 50 percent of the total population of Europe; the very poorest group varied between 10 and 20 percent. Most of the working poor were farmers, or peasants, growing crops such as wheat on land they did not own. Halfway between the rich and the poor was a middle class of craftspeople, who made goods, and merchants, who exchanged goods for money.

A World of Ordered Levels Europeans explained this world of contrasts—of great wealth, middling wealth, and enduring poverty—as part of a **hierarchy**, or system of many levels in which each level has power over the levels beneath it. Europeans believed that everything, from the universe to the average household, was ordered in hierarchies. At the head of most European hierarchies was a father figure. In the Christian religion, the most common faith in Europe at that time, God was considered the supreme Father. Most governments, too, had a parentlike ruler at their head—sometimes a queen, but most often a king. In

European families, whether wealthy landowners or poor peasants, each individual father ruled over his dependents—his wife, children, and, in some cases, servants or apprentices. This type of male-dominated social organization is called a **patriarchal society**, or patriarchy. By contrast, Native American societies were often led by men and women together, and few were organized into hierarchies.

The Household Kinship provided the focus for the daily life of Europeans, as it did for Native Americans and Africans. In England, for example, the most important social unit was the family and its household. In the English household, at least at the level of farmers and tradespeople, everyone performed economic activities for the good of the whole. Unlike most modern

Using Historical Evidence For Europeans in the 1400s, the household was a center of production. In this household workshop, a family works together. *How do the tasks the family is engaged in serve their common good?*

American homes, the primary purpose of the English household was production rather than consumption. In other words, people worked long hours in and around the house to provide for their basic needs. They did not consider the house as simply a place where they could use and enjoy products made elsewhere.

The survival of the household depended upon the willingness of all its members to put aside their individual interests for the good of the whole. In this respect, European households were like Native American families.

Europe's Traders Look Outward During the 1400s, competition for trade grew more intense in Europe, encouraging queens, kings, and merchants to look outward for new sources of wealth. England offers a good example of the increasing energy of European trade. The people of this nation developed an extensive trade with the rest of Europe during the 1300s and 1400s. They shipped lead and tin from English mines, and hides, wool, honey, and butter from English farms. Furthermore, they added value to raw materials by turning them into more finished goods. Increasingly, traders shipped out woolen cloth produced by English spinners and weavers instead of raw wool. During the two centuries after 1350, the percentage of total wool exports shipped in the form of cloth surged from 4 percent to 60 percent. In the bustling ports of Spain, France, and Portugal, English traders exchanged these goods for wines, fruit, silk, spices, silver, and gold.

The English were not alone. Merchants from all over Europe were scouting for new markets. Around 1520 an anonymous English poet gave this pessimistic assessment:

W e Englishmen behold
Our ancient customs bold
more preciouser than gold
be clean cast away,
And other new be found, the which
(you may understand)
that causeth all your land
So greatly to decay. . . .
Other lands advanced be,
And buy and sell among us free;
And thus our own commodity

Doth clean undo our self . . .
French ware hither is brought,
And English handcraft goeth to nought.

This fierce competition illustrates a crucial difference between the way Europeans and Native Americans conducted trade. Unlike Native Americans, Europeans tended to see trade as a simple material exchange that did not create further social obligations between people. As in the case of many other differences between cultures, neither view was right or wrong. In this particular case, however, just as in the case of varying views about land use, the difference would lead to bitter misunderstandings when Europeans and Native Americans finally encountered one another across the Atlantic.

MAKING CONNECTIONS

What evidence do you see in your own life of nations competing for trade?

The Trading Kingdoms of Africa

With so much pressure for new markets and new products, it was no wonder that Europeans began to look overseas for trading opportunities. Africa had always been the major source of gold for Europeans, and India offered exotic spices that fetched a good profit. The Portuguese, under the direction of Prince Henry the Navigator, began raiding and trading on the western coast of Africa as early as 1434. One of their navigators, Bartolomeu Dias, rounded the southernmost cape of Africa in 1488, and by 1498 another, Vasco da Gama, had forged beyond Africa and on to India. At this time, trade in the area of the most contact between Europeans and Africans, West Africa, was concentrated in two areas: the coastal forests and the drier region beyond the coast.

The Forest Kingdoms The coastal region of West Africa that became the focus of trade between Europeans and Africans stretched from Morocco in the north to the Congo River in the south. In the center of this long swath was the area of heaviest interaction, generally called

Guinea. In the 1400s, Guinea was home to three energetic forest kingdoms: Oyo, Ife, and Benin.

Trade was vital to Guinea long before interaction began across the Atlantic Ocean. In Benin, for instance, merchants traded farm products, works of art, and goods forged from African iron, which at that time was probably superior to any in the world. Trade was controlled by the Oba, or king, who had a very high status among his people. From a central city, also called Benin, he ruled all of the surrounding forest land, waging war, directing agriculture, and regulating commerce through administrators and local leaders.

The ruling classes in Guinea were generally groups made up of people who identified closely with one another because they shared a common ancestor. This type of kinship network is called a **lineage.** (Native American clans are a form of lineage group.) These leaders dealt with their people primarily through local headmen, who usually were also the heads of similar kinship networks.

In fact, lineages were the major social units in this part of Africa. Most societies in Guinea were made up of people who lived in towns and supported themselves primarily through farming. Usually, most of the people in a town in Guinea belonged to the same lineage. Even in larger urban areas, people probably lived close to their families, since the lineage provided them with social support when they needed it.

For spiritual support, the people of Guinea relied on religious beliefs that varied considerably from one group to another. Generally their beliefs included a Supreme Being who created other, lesser gods or spirits. These spirits inhabited everything, from animals to trees and stones. The people of Guinea believed that humans, too, were living spirits both before and after death. In short, the world was full of spirits of all kinds. Like Native Americans and Europeans, Africans believed that the goodwill of more-than-human forces must be won through prayer and ceremony.

A Golden Empire South of the Sahara Beyond the coastal forests, in the grasslands south of the Sahara, lay another area of African trade in the late 1400s. Called **Songhai,** it was one of the largest empires in the world at the time. Its capital city alone, Tombouctou, had a population of some 100,000. Leo Africanus, an African who visited Songhai at this time, enthused about its trading power, saying, "It is a wonder to see what plentie of Merchandize is daily brought hither and how costly and sumptious all things be."

Songhai's traders obtained goods such as gold and ivory from the forest kingdoms. The forests also supplied another popular trade item, kola nuts, used to flavor a beverage that was the first version of the colas people drink today. The traders carried these goods north across Songhai, paying heavy fees to Songhai's ruler, and then on across the Sahara in caravans of as many as 12,000 camels. On their return trip from North Africa, Songhai's traders brought salt, weapons, cloth, horses, books, and paper. The books were often destined for Tombouctou, with its world-renowned university and some 150 schools, or for the other cities of Songhai that boasted university centers— Gao, Walata, and Jenné.

The person who profited most from this trade was Askia Muhammad, the ruler of Songhai. To rule over his domain, which extended over much of western Africa, Askia directed a highly developed system of paid officials. This hierarchy made the organization of Songhai society similar to that in Europe but unlike the family-centered Native Americans. Askia's officials administered laws, kept the peace, collected taxes, and monitored

The Oba, attended by servants holding symbols of power, is offered trade goods by Portuguese traders (background) in a bronze plaque of the 1500s.

The Baule people of West Africa made this pendant, over three inches long, from the gold for which their region was well known.

An engraving from the 1800s captures a moment repeated countless times through the centuries: a caravan arrives at the city of Tombouctou.

diplomatic exchanges with other nations of the world. Under Askia's direction, they ran a sophisticated banking system. They also oversaw great royal estates that produced food or manufactured goods.

Slavery in Africa As in some parts of Europe and North America, a more grim item of trade than food and goods could be found in Africa as well. This was human life—in the form of people kidnapped from one region of Africa to another and enslaved. In a sense, the entire trading system was built on enslaved people, not only because they were sold as goods themselves, but also because they produced or gathered many of the other goods that were exchanged,

from gold to kola nuts. They also carried goods through parts of West Africa where animals were not an effective means of transport.

In Africa, people who had been cut off from their lineage were the most likely to be enslaved. They included prisoners of war (probably the greatest source), orphans, criminals, or other people torn from their homes or rejected by society. Generally, slaves were adopted into existing kinship networks.

In their new lineages, enslaved people filled a wide variety of positions, playing a major role in African life. After the collision of the Atlantic cultures, they would also be forced to go to the Americas, where they would take part in creating the new societies that would someday arise there.

SECTION 1 REVIEW

Key Terms, People, and Places
1. Define (a) kinship network, (b) clan, (c) hierarchy, (d) patriarchal society, (e) lineage.
2. Identify (a) Guinea, (b) Songhai.

Key Concepts
3. Give two reasons Native Americans traded goods.
4. Why did Europe look overseas for trading opportunities in the 1400s?

5. Give evidence to show that Benin was a complex and wealthy kingdom.

Critical Thinking
6. **Formulating Questions** What questions would you have asked of an English couple in the 1400s to determine how well their household fit the patriarchal model?

The Atlantic World Is Born

SECTION PREVIEW

The voyage of an Italian navigator was the prelude to centuries of trade and tragic conflict among Native Americans, Europeans, and Africans. In these years new societies would be built and old ones swept aside.

Key Concepts

- For Native Americans, one effect of contact with Europeans was death from disease.
- Europeans competed among themselves to settle and exploit the Americas.
- After interaction began among the Atlantic cultures, millions of West Africans were transported against their will to the Americas.

Key Terms, People, and Places

Atlantic World; Christopher Columbus

Shortly before sunrise on Friday, August 3, 1492, three ships set sail from the seaport of Palos, in the Spanish kingdom of Castile. Before the crews lay the ocean and a great enterprise—"the Enterprise of the Indies," as their commander called it—the challenge of finding a new route to the Indies, or Asia.

A Voyage of Encounter

The expedition was Spanish, but its commander, **Christopher Columbus,** was not. He had been born into a family of woolen weavers in Genoa, Italy. Stubborn and moody, he had devoted most of his forty-one years to mastering the craft of navigation and to dogging European monarchs to win financing for this very voyage.

Going West to Reach the East Not until January 1492 had Isabella, Queen of Castile, finally granted Columbus his wish. Dubbing him High Admiral of the Ocean Sea, Isabella authorized him to make contact with the people of "the lands of India." As the admiral later explained, Isabella and her husband, King Ferdinand, had "ordained that [Columbus] should not go eastward by land in the usual manner but by the western way which no one about whom we have positive information has ever followed."

Columbus knew that the earth was a sphere. As daunting as the trip was, he was not afraid of falling off the planet when he sailed westward, as later legend suggested. However, Columbus *was* gambling when he assumed he could reach the Indies, or Asia, by sailing west across the vast expanse of the ocean. It was a gamble he would have lost, because he had underestimated the size of the planet. The expedition had neither food nor water enough to sail all the way to Asia.

The Encounter Begins Fortunately for Columbus and his crew, in mid-October he encountered the islands of the Caribbean Sea and the Native Americans on them, the Tainos. The Tainos greeted the newcomers with gifts—much astonishing Columbus, who was not familiar with the Native American view of trade as an exchange of gifts. In 1493 Columbus wrote about the Tainos to Isabella and Ferdinand:

They are so ingenuous [innocent] *and free with all they have, that no one would believe it who has not seen it; of anything that they possess, if it be asked of them, they never say no; on the contrary, they invite you to share it and show as much love as if their hearts went with it.*

Technology developed for long sea voyages, like this compass of 1580, guided Columbus west across the uncharted Atlantic Ocean.

Whales and flying fish, suggesting the hazards of the Atlantic, alarm the crew of a lively Portuguese caravel in this painting from 1594.

Columbus's voyage was significant because it was one of encounter, not discovery. After all, the Americas had long since been discovered by others, the Native Americans. Centuries earlier, other little-known explorers had also found their way across the waters to the Americas and had even settled there.

But with Columbus's crossing in 1492, a regular, permanent exchange began among the people of the Americas, Africa, and Europe, involving goods and people, ideas and diseases. This exchange brought into existence a world of encounter—the **Atlantic World.**

MAKING ❌ CONNECTIONS

Is it still accurate to speak of an Atlantic World today? Why or why not?

The Impact of the Encounter on Native Americans: Disease

For the people of the early Atlantic World— whether Native Americans, Europeans, or Africans—life expectancy was much lower than it is today. In their era, minor illnesses or wounds could suddenly become fatal due to poor hygiene and medical practices. Exchange across the Atlantic only made this problem worse, for it brought together people who had been isolated from one another and had no resistance to one another's diseases.

Diseases Strike Native Americans Europeans had already experienced a severe decline in their population due to plague and other diseases. They brought a similar disaster with them when they arrived on the American continents. Passing germs through even the most casual contact, explorers and soldiers infected Native Americans with smallpox, typhus, measles, and other deadly diseases.

The Effects of Disease Once Europeans reached the Americas, disease spread ahead of them, carried by the extensive Native American trading system. Inca Garcilaso, the son of a Native American woman and a Spanish captain, described what explorers found in 1540 when they first reached Talomeca, a town of the Creek Native American group in what is now Georgia. It had five hundred houses, a temple with eight separate halls, and was ringed with outlying towns—all vacant. Garcilaso explained:

> The Castilians found the town of Talomeco without any people at all, because the recent pestilence [disease] had raged with more virulence [strength] and cruelty in this town than in any other of the entire province. [Near] the rich temple, it is said they found four longhouses filled with bodies from the plague.

As people of European descent pushed westward across the North American continent over the next three hundred years, the diseases they brought repeatedly ravaged Native Americans.

The Impact of the Encounter on Europeans: Struggle and Exchange

"God saw fit to send the Indians smallpox," said one European about 1525. The diseases that struck Native Americans seemed to some Europeans to be a sign that God intended Europeans to conquer the Americas. And conquest was exactly what Europeans planned, for

three reasons. The first was to obtain land, which was scarce in Europe. The second was to convert the vast natural resources of the Americas into goods that could be traded. The third reason was to "bring to the worship of [Christ] and the profession of the Catholic faith [the] residents and inhabitants" of the Americas, in the words of Pope Alexander VI in 1493.

Competing for Empire At the urging of Pope Alexander, in 1494 Portugal and Spain agreed to the Treaty of Tordesillas. Under the treaty, any lands not already claimed by other Christians would be divided between the two countries by an invisible line around the world. Spain was assigned rule over what lay west of the line, including most of the Americas. Portugal was left with control over the rest, including Brazil and its route around Africa.

For centuries, Spain and Portugal were able to control and exploit much of the regions they claimed. Soon, however, the people of other nations grew eager for their share of the wealth. France, England, and the Netherlands began to move into North America in the 1500s and 1600s (see Section 3). Although these nations fought bitterly among themselves for control of

A Native American in Mexico drew this picture of a victim of smallpox comforted by a healer. The squiggle symbolizes spoken words.

| 1650 | 1700 | 1750 | 1800 | **Links Across Time** | 1850 | 1900 | 1950 | 2000 |

Navigating the Ocean

Early sailors sighted the sun on an astrolabe to find their latitude (above). Today they rely on a geopositioning instrument that reads signals from satellites to give a ship's position by night or day (left). *What advantage does the new technology offer?*

Native American lands, on the whole they felt confirmed in the certainty that European culture was superior to any in the world, and that Europeans were meant to rule all others.

The Exchange of Cultures The culture that Europeans brought to the Americas included languages, laws, and customs. Europeans also introduced crops, such as wheat, and domesticated animals, such as the cow and the horse. The settlers who followed the conquerors brought with them European technologies, including the firearm and the wheel.

But exchange across the Atlantic was not one-sided, as the chart below shows. One American plant, the potato, quickly became the new food of the poor in Europe, bringing an end to the repeated famines Europe had suffered. Another, manioc, became the chief food throughout much of Africa.

Europe's wealthy also benefited from the exchange. In the first century after Columbus's voyage, the amount of gold and silver in Europe's economy increased eight times over, boosted by ore from the mines of the Americas. This new wealth ignited Europe's economy and quickly made it the richest on earth.

The Impact of the Encounter on Africans: Slavery

When Europeans began to exploit the natural resources of the Americas, they found they needed a large amount of labor to do so. They turned to West Africa to supply it, and West Africans soon were swept into their own encounter with the Americas, suffering violence and displacement for centuries after Columbus's voyage.

The Independence of West Africa Regular interaction between Europeans and Africans had begun even before the voyage of Columbus. Throughout the late 1400s, the Portuguese had been moving down the African coast in search of new markets. They found that from Songhai to the forest kingdoms, West Africans had a well-developed economy, and could control European trade within their countries. Furthermore, the Africans were able to defeat virtually all European efforts to conquer them, both then and over the next four centuries.

As time went on, Europeans realized that although they could not seize the land of Africa, they could seize another valuable resource—the West Africans themselves. Settlers in the Americas were beginning to grow crops such as sugar and tobacco to send to Europe. European slave traders supplied the labor needed on large farms by tapping into the existing West African slave trade.

As early as the 1400s, Europeans took up stations on the West African coast. To these outposts European governments and trading companies shipped various goods to be exchanged for enslaved people.

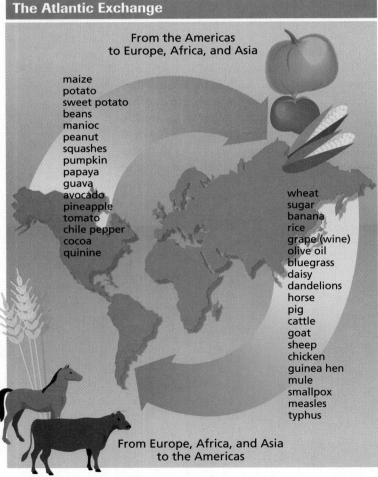

The Atlantic Exchange

From the Americas to Europe, Africa, and Asia

maize
potato
sweet potato
beans
manioc
peanut
squashes
pumpkin
papaya
guava
avocado
pineapple
tomato
chile pepper
cocoa
quinine

wheat
sugar
banana
rice
grape (wine)
olive oil
bluegrass
daisy
dandelions
horse
pig
cattle
goat
sheep
chicken
guinea hen
mule
smallpox
measles
typhus

From Europe, Africa, and Asia to the Americas

Interpreting Charts
Exchanges across the Atlantic went both ways and included valued crops, domesticated animals, and diseases. *In which direction did the listed diseases move?*

The Growth of the Slave Trade Facts and figures on the impact of slavery on West Africa remain a matter of controversy. Some researchers estimate that during the 1500s some 275,000 West Africans were transported involuntarily across the Atlantic Ocean. By contrast, they say, the 1700s saw 6,050,000 transported. Estimates of the total number of West Africans abducted from their homeland and taken to North and South America range from 9,300,000 to 11,500,000 or more. The removal of such a huge number of people over several centuries seriously affected some African societies. The Aja-speaking people in Guinea, for example, were completely destroyed. Europeans also set in motion grim wars between African societies to obtain slaves to sell. New empires equipped with guns sprang up and overran the old kingdoms.

Mere numbers, however, cannot portray the full horror of slavery for West Africans. Slavery had existed in Africa before the encounter of the Atlantic cultures, but Europeans gave it a very different face in the Americas. African slavery was based on the belief that people who had been enslaved were inferior to their masters because they were not connected with their master's lineage. Among Africans (and Native Americans), captives taken in war might later be adopted into a lineage and regain at least some freedom. Such adoption shows that the basic humanity of enslaved people was recognized in Africa. In the Americas, European masters believed that enslaved people were inferior simply because they were of a different race. Because slavery was based on race, enslavement in the Americas usually offered enslaved people no hope of regaining

their freedom. Thus their masters forever denied that enslaved people were humans, with desires and dreams of their own.

In the aftermath of the encounter across the Atlantic Ocean, vast changes tested the ways of life and the values of people on four continents. Out of that collision the society of the United States would eventually emerge—a society still struggling to understand cultural differences that had their origin on separate continents hundreds of years ago.

Viewpoints
On Celebrating Columbus Day

The five-hundredth anniversary of Columbus's voyage to the Americas inspired a spirited debate over whether a celebration was appropriate to mark the event. *What broader issue, other than the celebration of Columbus Day, is revealed in the viewpoints below?*

For a Celebration of Columbus Day
"Celebrate Columbus? Not if that simply means backslapping and flag waving. But it can mean more: taking stock of the long, fascinating record, noting that inevitable conflict resulted in losers as well as winners and produced a mixture of races, customs, and habits never before seen in the world."
Journalist Paul Gray, *Time*, October 7, 1991

Against a Celebration of Columbus Day
"Yes, Christopher Columbus was the first European to sail to America in recorded history. But Columbus set into motion a sequence of greed, cruelty, slavery and genocide that, even in the bloody history of mankind, has few parallels. He organized an extermination of Native Americans."
Essayist Hans Koning, *The New York Times*, August 14, 1990

SECTION 2 REVIEW

Key Terms, People, and Places
1. Define Atlantic World.
2. Identify Christopher Columbus.

Key Concepts
3. How did European disease affect Native Americans?
4. What changes did contact with the Americas bring to Europe?

5. What effect did the Atlantic slave trade have on West Africans?

Critical Thinking
6. Distinguishing False from Accurate Images Is it true or false to say that Columbus discovered the Americas? Explain your answer.

European Settlement and Native American Resistance

SECTION PREVIEW

After 1492, the Spanish, English, French, and Dutch invaded the Americas, devising various ways to exploit its natural wealth. Meanwhile, Native Americans fought against them, determined to preserve their way of life.

Key Concepts
• Native Americans experienced some success in slowing the Spanish invasion of New Mexico.
• The Native Americans of the Chesapeake Bay area resisted English settlement during the 1600s, but were sharply reduced in number.
• The French and Dutch colonies in the Northeast were based on mutual trade with Native American groups, but in New England the English fought to replace the Native American way of life with their own.

Key Terms, People, and Places
conquistador, *encomienda* system, colony, presidio, *congregacion*, indentured servant, Reformation, religious toleration; Popé, Powhatan, Puritans, Metacom

A silent witness to the Spanish attempt to conquer Florida, this soldier's helmet was lost in the 1500s at Palm Beach and discovered in recent times.

A fter the American, European, and African cultures collided in the 1400s, the Spanish were first to invade the Americas. They had three reasons for conquest: to spread the Christian religion, to gain wealth, and to win fame or improved social standing. In short, they fought for God, gold, and glory— and perhaps the love of gold most of all. The thirty-four-year-old Hernán Cortés, one of the **conquistadores,** as the Spanish conquerors were called, spoke for many when he said in 1519: "I and my companions suffer from a disease of the heart which can be cured only by gold."

The Spanish Settle in the Americas

The Spanish conquistadores ruthlessly destroyed much of the culture they found in the Americas. They did not try to replace it completely, however, by driving out the Native Americans. Instead, they attempted to force Native Americans into Spanish culture. One method the Spanish employed to accomplish this was known as the *encomienda* **system.** Under this system, Native Americans were required to farm, ranch, or mine for the profit of an individual Spaniard. In return, the Spaniard was supposed to see to their well-being. The *encomienda* system was a version of the social system of Europe, where the wealthy controlled land worked by the poor.

By the 1550s, the Spanish had numerous well-established **colonies.** Colonies are areas settled by immigrants who continue to be the subjects of their parent country. These Spanish colonies formed a large empire on the islands of the Caribbean Sea, and in Mexico, Central America, and South America. In order to protect the colonies, the Spanish built defensive bases in Florida—for instance, at St. Augustine—and in what they called New Mexico. (Spanish New Mexico included parts of what is now Arizona and Texas. See the map on page 25.)

The settlements that dotted the south and west of the land that is now part of the United States were really just **presidios,** or forts, manned by a few soldiers. But the survival of these Spanish outposts was due not to the soldiers, but to the faith of a few dozen Franciscans. These priests, members of a Catholic order dedicated to the work of St. Francis of Assisi, settled

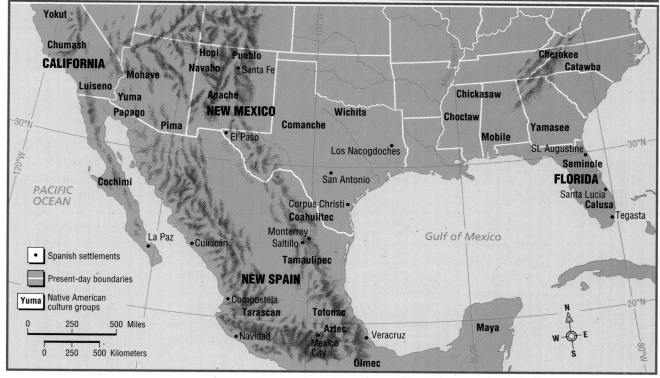

Spanish Settlements and Native American Groups in the South, 1500s–1600s

Yokut

Chumash

CALIFORNIA

Luiseno

Mohave

Yuma

Papago

Pima

Hopi   Pueblo

Navaho   • Santa Fe

Apache

NEW MEXICO

• El Paso

Rio Grande

Comanche

Wichita

Cochimi

PACIFIC OCEAN

La Paz   • Culiacán

Monterrey

Saltillo •

Coahuiltec

Corpus Christi •

San Antonio

Los Nacogdoches

Cherokee

Catawba

Chickasaw

Choctaw

Mobile

Yamasee

St. Augustine

FLORIDA

Santa Lucia

Seminole

Calusa

• Tegasta

Gulf of Mexico

Tamaulipec

NEW SPAIN

• Compostela

Tarascan

• Navidad

Totonac

Aztec

Mexico City

• Veracruz

Olmec

Maya

• Spanish settlements

Present-day boundaries

Yuma Native American culture groups

0   250   500 Miles

0   250   500 Kilometers

N   E   W   S

30°N   120°W   100°W   30°N   20°N   90°W   80°W

🌐 **Geography and History: Interpreting Maps**
An adviser to the Spanish king in the 1500s remarked: "It is towards the south, not towards the frozen north, that those who seek their fortune should bend their way; for everything at the equator is rich." *Cite evidence from the map to show that Spanish settlers followed this policy.*

throughout Florida and New Mexico. They established dozens of missions—headquarters for their work of converting Native Americans to Christianity. With the help of soldiers, the priests forced the Native Americans into settled villages called *congregacions,* where they were made to farm and worship like Catholic Europeans.

MAKING CONNECTIONS

The Spanish combined force and persuasion to settle Native Americans in *congregacions.* How would you expect the Native Americans to react?

Native American Resistance to the Spanish

Fighting by Native Americans against the Spanish was generally disorganized. But in New Mexico, following years of drought that weakened Spanish power, the Pueblo people united and expelled the Spanish in what is called the Revolt of 1680.

The Background of the Revolt The Spanish had established outposts along the Rio Grande, including a capital at Santa Fe in 1610. By the 1670s, widespread sickness and drought had reduced the Pueblo population to 17,000 people. Seeking to reverse this decline, the Pueblo began to turn back to their traditional religious practices, which the Spanish denounced as witchcraft and tried to stamp out. Then a brilliant medicine man named **Popé** rallied the disheartened Pueblos and some Apaches. Popé blamed the Spanish for all the Native Americans' miseries. One Pueblo witness, Jeronimo, later reported Popé's claim that when the Europeans were gone, the Pueblo *would gather large crops of grain, maize [corn] with large and thick ears, many bundles of cotton, many calabashes [squash] and watermelons.*

The Revolt Drives out the Spanish In August 1680, the 2,350 Spaniards in New Mexico suddenly were confronted with a well-coordinated revolt by more than 8,000 warriors. The Native Americans killed 375 colonists and 21 of 33 priests outright, destroyed missions, and drove the Spanish out of Santa Fe. By early September, when the surviving Spanish gathered near El Paso, they numbered around 1,500.

It took the Spanish years to reestablish themselves along the Rio Grande. They did not retake Santa Fe until 1696. During this time, however, the Pueblo still declined rapidly in number, under increasing attack by the neighboring Apache and Navaho people. By 1706 the Pueblo population had shrunk to only 9,000. In the 1700s they accepted Spanish rule to gain protection.

In forming this new connection, however, both sides compromised. The Pueblo became Catholics who continued to practice traditional rituals. They acknowledged Spanish authority, but governed their own local affairs. The *encomienda* system was abolished altogether. Ultimately, the Spanish and Pueblo forged a new bond in which their dependence on each other overcame mutual distrust.

The Jamestown Settlement

The English arrived in the Americas with an attitude toward conquered peoples that was even more harsh than that of the Spanish. Believing it was best to remake completely any culture they conquered, they did not practice the forced blending of European and Native American societies that was taking place in the Spanish colonies. For the English, conquest would be all—or nothing.

A Colony near the Chesapeake Bay In 1607 the English established their first successful settlement, Jamestown, about 60 miles from the mouth of the James River in the Chesapeake Bay region, in a colony they called Virginia. Unfortunately, the site they chose was a mosquito-infested swamp, and the settlement was very nearly a complete disaster. In its first decade, disease and starvation were common; the settlers even resorted to cannibalism. By 1624, of the approximately 6,000 Europeans who had migrated to Virginia over the preceding sixteen years, only about 1,300 remained alive.

Native American Reaction The Native Americans in the Chesapeake region, who numbered about 8,000, did not stand by idly while foreigners invaded their land. Shortly after the arrival of the English, about 200 Native Americans attacked. Only an English cannon forced them to retreat.

The leader of the Native Americans in the region, **Powhatan,** had every reason to distrust the settlers' intentions. The Spanish had captured his brother, Opechancanough, in the 1560s. Opechancanough had visited Spain twice, lived for a time in the capital of Spanish Mexico, and accompanied Spanish expeditions to the Chesapeake area. In 1570 he returned to his own people. During his years with the Spanish, Opechancanough came to know and despise the goals of European settlers—which included exploiting the labor of the Native Americans and the natural wealth of their land.

In spite of initial conflicts and continuing mutual suspicion, an uneasy peace was eventually established between the Native Americans and the English. Both sides tried to keep this peace. In fact, during the times of the settlers' worst problems, the Native Americans saved the newcomers by supplying them with food and fresh water. But in March 1622, relations between the two peoples broke down altogether. At that time Opechancanough planned and led a brilliantly coordinated surprise attack on Jamestown. It was only partially successful. Still, 347 of the English lost their lives—more than 10 percent of the population of the settlement at that time. Within days, the settlers killed as many or more Native Americans in retaliation.

Powhatan's people mounted their last major act of armed resistance against the English in the Chesapeake area in 1644. It failed. During the attack, Opechancanough, still active and defiant at nearly 100 years of age, was shot through the back in the streets of Jamestown.

Two years later, the Native Americans agreed to make a regular payment to the English in return for a guarantee of some land. By 1669, however, there were only 2,000 Native Americans left in the Chesapeake region.

The Tobacco Colony

During the early years of their settlement, only one thing saved the Virginia colonists from failing altogether: growing tobacco for sale. In 1616, Virginians sent 2,500 pounds of the weed to England; by 1640, Virginia and its neighboring colony Maryland, which had been established in 1632, were sending home 3 million pounds a year.

To produce tobacco, planters needed people to work the fields. During the first sixty years after the founding of the colony, they turned primarily to **indentured servants** from England. These were people who had to work for a master for a period of time, usually seven years, under a contract called an indenture. In return for their work, their master paid the cost of their voyage to Virginia and gave them food and shelter. Some indentures promised a piece of land to the servant at the end of the indenture period. Historians estimate that between 100,000 and 150,000 men and women came as servants to work in the fields of Virginia and Maryland during the 1600s. Most of them were eighteen to twenty-two years of age, unmarried, and poor.

Few of the indentured servants lived long enough to claim their land at the end of their service. Exposure to the climate and diseases of the Chesapeake Bay killed them in horrendous numbers. Just as discouraging was the fact that it became harder to make a fortune after the first years of the tobacco boom. Early and wealthy settlers had taken the most fertile and easily accessible land. Driven by this land shortage, in 1676 a man named Nathaniel Bacon raised an unauthorized force of planters and indentured servants to drive the Native Americans farther west. His action quickly evolved into a rebellion against the established government, and was put down forcefully.

After Bacon's Rebellion, those in power saw that they needed a more controllable source of labor. Accordingly they began to buy enslaved West Africans brought across the Atlantic Ocean by slave traders. As discussed in Section 5, these enslaved Africans had a major effect on the culture and economy of the Southern Colonies, beginning in the 1700s.

Europeans and Native Americans in the Northeast

In 1608 a French explorer, Samuel de Champlain, founded the town of Quebec on the St. Lawrence River in what is now Canada. Perched on heights above a narrow stretch of the river, Quebec was a prime location for a trading settlement. Similarly, the Dutch—people from the Netherlands—established New Amsterdam

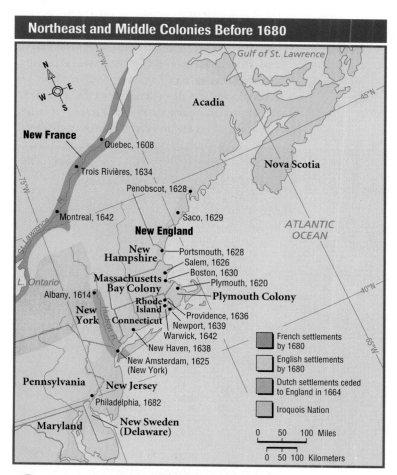

Northeast and Middle Colonies Before 1680

French settlements by 1680

English settlements by 1680

Dutch settlements ceded to England in 1664

Iroquois Nation

Geography and History: Interpreting Maps
Native Americans and Europeans quickly became dependent upon one another. While Native Americans controlled vast stretches of woodland, European settlement was at first limited to coastal and river areas. *How did the location of the Iroquois help make them powerful?*

(now New York City) in 1626 to control trade along the Hudson River. Later, Fort Orange (Albany), founded in 1624, became the center of their trade with the Native Americans.

The Fur Trade Both the French and the Dutch traded knives, beads, and guns for furs that could be sold in Europe. These furs were to the French what tobacco was to the English in Virginia and Maryland. As the Dutchman Adriaen Van der Donck noted in 1655,

> The Indians, without our labour or trouble, bring to us their fur trade, worth tons of gold, which may be increased, and is like goods found.

Unlike tobacco growing, the fur trade did not require elaborate farms or towns. Rather, it depended on forming trading ties with Native American hunters and trappers, and on leaving alone the forests and streams that formed the animals' natural habitats. Because the French depended on Native American trapping, Native Americans in areas of French contact remained more powerful than those in Virginia. Yet they were greatly weakened by disease and by wars they fought to control the fur hunting grounds.

One group, the Iroquois, was particularly successful at both war and trade. In the mid- to late 1600s, the Iroquois engaged in a series of struggles called the Beaver Wars, in which they pushed the Hurons and other Native American groups out of their homelands to an area west of the Great Lakes. The Iroquois occupied the area between the French to the north and the Dutch and the English to the east and south. The Iroquois were thus in a perfect position to tip the balance of power among European colonists in the Northeast. For instance, the Iroquois were allies of both the English and the Dutch even after 1633, when the English entered the region that is now Connecticut and New York and began to compete with the Dutch for control of the area. And the Iroquois retained their powerful position into the early 1700s, finding it easy to accept the transition when the English took over the Dutch colony of New Netherlands completely.

Puritans in New England In 1630, while the French and Dutch were building trade links with Native Americans, the Great Migration—a wave of English migration across the Atlantic Ocean—began to reach the shores of New England. Immigrants had come to New England before then—the most familiar today is the group known as the Pilgrims, who settled at Plymouth, Massachusetts, in 1620. The Pilgrims, however, numbered only 102 people when they landed. By contrast, a total of 1,000 settlers braved the Atlantic crossing in 1630 to found the new Massachusetts Bay Colony. By 1643 the colony's population had increased to 16,000 people living in twenty towns, including its capital, Boston.

The Great Migration had its origin in a major change in Christianity that began a century earlier. At that time a powerful religious movement, the **Reformation,** swept over Europe in a protest against what was seen as the corruption and inadequacy of the Catholic church. The Reformation gave birth to a new form of the Christian religion, known as Protestantism. In England, most of the population became members of a new Protestant national church, the Church of England.

Using Historical Evidence David, Joanna, and Abigail Mason posed for this portrait about 1670. Like other Puritan children, they could expect to live twice as long as children in colonies where life was harder. *What evidence of prosperity do you see in this painting?*

Despite this change in the English church, some people still believed that its worship remained too similar to Roman Catholic worship. They wanted to "purify" the English church from within, and so they were called **Puritans.**

The term *Puritan* has come to be associated with cheerlessness and hypocritical morality. Contrary to this image, Puritans were people capable of affection and merriment as well as deep religious devotion. They did, however, insist that social order begins with personal order. Well-ordered families in well-ordered towns in well-ordered colonies: that was the Puritan ideal. Though the Puritans came from England to escape persecution, or harassment, for their beliefs, they themselves did not believe in the principle of **religious toleration**—the idea that people of different religions should live in peace. This would have run counter to their ideal of an ordered society, and to their belief that they alone possessed the truth. They punished dissidents—people who disagree with a political or religious system—by banishing or hanging them.

King Philip's War In order to create their dream of an ordered society, Puritans transformed the landscape of New England. They replaced forests with fields, cultivated wheat, barley, and corn, and raised domestic animals like cows and pigs rather than relying on wild deer or beaver. Their population grew rapidly: by the 1670s they totaled some 45,000 people living in about ninety towns. All of these changes threatened the livelihood of the Native American groups in the Northeast. Most of these people belonged to the Algonquian culture and lived by hunting game, gathering plants for food, and growing crops—a way of life that required sixteen to twenty times as much land per person as the way of life practiced by Puritan farmers.

"You know," recalled Miantonomo, leader of the Narraganset people, in 1642,

> Our fathers had plenty of deer and skins, our plains were full of deer, as also our woods, and of turkies, and our coves full of fish and fowl. But these English having gotten our land, they with scythes cut down the grass, and with axes fell the trees; their cows and horse eat the grass, and their hogs spoil our clam banks, and we shall be starved.

In the spring of 1675, the leader of the Wampanoag people, **Metacom**—also known by his English name, King Philip—could no longer bear seeing the newcomers destroy the world of his people. He rallied Native Americans throughout southern New England and defended the Native American way of life—much as the Pueblos were doing in the Southwest and Powhatan's people had done in the Virginia colony.

In proportion to the number of people involved and their possessions, no war in American history cost more in lives and property than King Philip's War, as the conflict was called. In the end, however, the Puritans won. With the final defeat of Metacom and his allies, the English conquest of New England was virtually complete.

Native Americans fought on both sides in the war that sprang up in 1675. This medal was presented to those who helped the English.

SECTION 3 REVIEW

Key Terms, People, and Places
1. Define (a) conquistador, (b) *encomienda* system, (c) colony, (d) presidio, (e) *congregacion*, (f) indentured servant, (g) Reformation, (h) religious toleration.
2. Identify (a) Popé, (b) Powhatan, (c) Puritans, (d) Metacom.

Key Concepts
3. What was the effect of Native American resistance in New Mexico?

4. How did the Native Americans of the Chesapeake Bay area respond to invasion by the English?
5. How did the French and Dutch in the Northeast differ from the English in their relationship with Native Americans?

Critical Thinking
6. **Identifying Central Issues** North America was a difficult, dangerous place for both the Spanish and the English. Why did they want to move there?

The Decision to Use Enslaved Africans for Labor

Time Frame:	Mid- to late 1600s
Place:	The Chesapeake Bay area
Key People:	English gentlemen planters
Situation:	In the 1600s, planters in the Chesapeake Bay searched for a steady source of labor to work their fields. Their decision about where to obtain that labor would have a profound effect on the future United States.

To English colonists in early Virginia, the possibilities for making money seemed almost limitless. They had nearly all of what we now call the three factors of production. Backers in England had put up one of these factors, the investment money, or capital, needed to begin the settlement. Virginia offered the second, abundant land. Only one factor was missing: someone to do the work of clearing forests, plowing fields, and harvesting crops.

Labor Options

As gentlemen, the planters had no intention of performing physical labor, since in the social structure with which they were familiar, such labor was a badge of lower social status. They wanted to create a society in which they could live off the labor of others.

Nor did the planters consider simply hiring workers, the way we would today. The notion of laborers working for a certain number of hours for a wage is a fairly modern one. People in the 1600s generally did not view labor itself as something that could be bought or sold.

What other choices did the planters have? In the beginning, they planned to use Native Americans. They knew that the Spanish had successfully forced Native Americans to work in mines to the south. Moreover, Native Americans already were living in Virginia and knew the land and climate. The English had great confidence in their ability to persuade Native Americans to work for them in exchange for the advantages offered by the supposedly superior civilization of Europe.

Another potential source of labor was indentured servants from England. They proved inexpensive, because disease and grim working conditions killed close to two thirds of them before they could take possession of the land promised in their indentures.

Planters discovered a third option when a ship landed a group of enslaved Africans in Jamestown in 1619, an event that is depicted in the painting below. But it was not an option they seized on immediately. Forty years later, fewer than 1,700 Africans lived in Virginia and Maryland; sixty years later, in the 1680s, Africans totaled only around 4,000.

Weighing the Choices

The decision about which form of labor to use was not made suddenly and dramatically. Over the decades the choice grew clear. Native Americans demonstrated by an active resistance that they would have no part in the plans of the English. Moreover, European disease soon severely reduced Native American populations, conclusively canceling that option.

GOALS	Find a cheap and reliable source of labor to exploit the natural resources of the Chesapeake Bay area.		
POSSIBLE ACTIONS	Use Native Americans	Use English indentured servants	Use enslaved Africans
ADVANTAGES/ DISADVANTAGES	• Difficulty in obtaining and controlling laborers due to resistance • Failure of labor supply due to decrease in Native American population	• In the early and mid-1600s, low cost of labor due to short life of indentured servants; need for constant supply because of high death rate • Ease of communication and interaction due to shared language and customs • In the late 1600s, increased cost due to increased life span • Possible political disturbances	• In the late 1600s, a lower cost than indentured servants to obtain and maintain • Steady supply due to immunity to European disease and hardiness to warm climate • Problems in communication and interaction due to language and customs different from English

At first, English landowners clearly preferred the second option—English indentured servants. Indentured labor cost landowners little, especially if the servants died young. Furthermore, indentured servants already shared the language and customs of the planters. By contrast, enslaved Africans were expensive to purchase and came from a culture unfamiliar to the English. For this reason slavery contributed such a small part to the Chesapeake labor force that the practice was not legally recognized until 1660.

In the last few decades of the 1600s, however, English gentlemen began to buy large numbers of slaves from Africa. By 1700, there were 20,000 enslaved Africans in Virginia. Another 100,000 were imported by 1750. What brought about this reversal in established practice? Why did so many individual planters make the conscious decision, at approximately the same time, to replace indentured servants with enslaved Africans?

Part of the answer is strictly economic. By the middle of the 1600s, better diets and improved working conditions meant that white servants were living longer—and demanding their promised 50 acres. The high early death rate that had made indentured servitude cheaper than slavery was disappearing. At the same time, many planters were increasingly able to afford enslaved Africans. It became cheaper to buy and support an African laborer for the duration of his or her lifetime than it was to support an indentured servant for seven years and then give him 50 acres.

Part of the reason for the shift was political. Bacon's Rebellion revealed the tensions between rich planters in the Chesapeake area and those who were less fortunate. The gentry began to see enslaved Africans as a more stable and less unruly source of labor than indentured servants.

They imagined enslaved people simply would become a permanent part of the lower order in the hierarchical society of the colonies. Their assumption was that Africans would never expect their freedom, would never expect any land, and would never expect to have any say in running the colony.

During the 1700s, slavery became well established throughout the English colonies. It had never been inevitable, however. It was a deliberate choice among three options made by powerful men in order to secure their economic and political position.

EVALUATING DECISIONS

1. Why were planters forced to give up the idea of using Native Americans for labor?
2. Why did planters in the Chesapeake Bay area prefer indentured labor in the early years?

Critical Thinking

3. **Recognizing Ideologies** Summarize the key assumptions made by wealthy planters in deciding to use African labor.

Life in Colonial America

SECTION PREVIEW

For England in the mid-1600s and early 1700s, the colonies were a reliable source of raw materials and a prime place to sell English goods. Eventually, however, the colonies grew and prospered with little direct interference from the English government. As they grew, a distinct colonial culture emerged.

Key Concepts

- Although England flirted with the idea of strictly regulating its colonies in order to increase its power and wealth, on the whole it let them develop on their own in the early 1700s.
- As they grew, the colonies in each region developed very different economies and societies.
- Colonial Americans organized their society according to a belief in inequality.
- As British settlers migrated west, tension increased among Native Americans, the French, and the British, as all competed for the same territory.
- A religious movement called the Great Awakening indirectly challenged the colonial acceptance of inequality.

Key Terms, People, and Places

mercantilism, balance of trade, salutary neglect, triangular trade, gentry, Great Awakening

Playing their part in trade by buying finished goods from the parent country, customers in the colonies ordered English cloth from this sample book.

B y the late 1600s and early 1700s, English-speaking people had established a cluster of colonies on the Atlantic coast of North America, as shown in the map on page 33. England prized these colonies for two reasons: they were suppliers of food and raw materials, such as tobacco, rice, and lumber, and they were avid buyers of English goods. These activities—supplying materials and buying goods—dovetailed neatly with a new European economic theory called **mercantilism,** which supposedly explained how a nation could increase its wealth and thus its power.

Mercantilism at Work

According to the theory of mercantilism, a country should get and keep as much bullion, or gold and silver, as possible. For England, France, and other countries without mines like those Spain controlled in the Americas, the only way to obtain more bullion was to have a favorable **balance of trade**—that is, to export more goods than were imported. Mercantilist Thomas Mun, writing in 1664, explained the theory this way:

> A s the treasure [money] *which is brought into the Realm by the balance of our foreign trade is that money which only does abide with us, and by which we are enriched; so by . . . money thus gotten (and no otherwise) do our Lands improve.*

To boost its balance of trade, mercantilists believed, a nation should have colonies where it could buy raw materials and sell products. The colonies should not be allowed to sell products to other nations or even to manufacture goods. The right to make goods for sale was reserved exclusively for the parent country, since manufacturing was a major source of profit. In 1660 the English king, Charles II, approved a stronger version of a previous law called the Navigation Act, which, together with other legislation, brought the colonial policy in line with these mercantilist goals.

However, after the end of the rule of the next king, James II, the British government rarely tried to interfere directly in colonial business. By the 1700s legislative bodies, such as the House of Burgesses in Virginia and the assemblies in other colonies, had gained extensive power over local affairs. Most of these assemblies consisted of an upper house of prominent colonists appointed by the king and a lower house elected by voting landowners. Even in colonies owned by the king, laws could not go into effect without the consent of the free men of the colony or their chosen representatives.

Why did the British government allow its colonies such freedom in governing them-selves—far more than was found in Spanish or French colonies? Part of the answer lies in the English traditions of strong local government and weak central power; part of it lies in the fact that the British government lacked the resources and the bureaucracy to enforce its wishes. Then, too, colonists recognized the authority of the king and Parliament without being forced to; most were proud to be British subjects.

Finally, the economy and the politics of the colonists served the interests of Great Britain very well. The British realized that the most salutary, or beneficial, policy was to neglect their colonies. Thus, later historians would call British colonial policy during the early 1700s **salutary neglect.**

MAKING CONNECTIONS

Can you think of ways in which the policy of salutary neglect might backfire on the British and harm their interests in the colonies?

The Expanding and Diverse Economies of the Colonies

While the Spanish colonies continued to rely on mining silver and growing sugar, and New France still focused on the fur trade, the British colonies of eastern North America developed diverse economies.

Staple Crops in the Southern Colonies In the Southern Colonies—Virginia, Maryland, South Carolina, North Carolina, and Geor-gia—the economy was based on growing crops that were in constant demand. Such crops are called staples. In Virginia and North Carolina, the staple crop was tobacco; in the warm and wet coastal regions of South Carolina and Georgia, it was rice. In the early 1730s, these

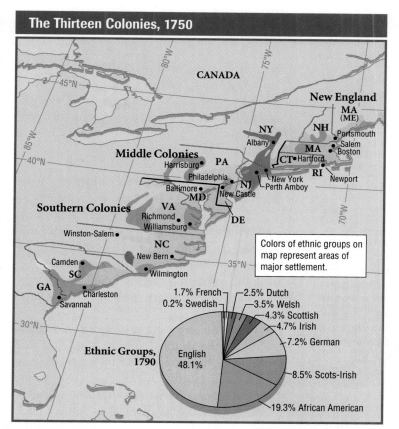

The Thirteen Colonies, 1750

Colors of ethnic groups on map represent areas of major settlement.

Ethnic Groups, 1790
- English 48.1%
- 19.3% African American
- 8.5% Scots-Irish
- 7.2% German
- 4.7% Irish
- 4.3% Scottish
- 3.5% Welsh
- 2.5% Dutch
- 1.7% French
- 0.2% Swedish

Geography and History: Interpreting Maps
English settlements in North America in the 1700s generally clung to the Eastern seaboard and its rivers. In this narrow band, however, lived a wide variety of ethnic groups. *Which was the largest group after the English?*

two colonies were exporting 16.8 million pounds of rice per year; by 1770 the number was 76.9 million. Meanwhile, the number of pounds of tobacco exported per year by Vir-ginia, Maryland, and Delaware rose from 32 million in 1700 to 83.8 million in 1770.

Throughout the Southern Colonies, enslaved Africans supplied most of the labor on tobacco and rice plantations. Virginia planters began to purchase large numbers of Africans in the mid-1600s. In 1650, Africans in Virginia numbered only about 500, which accounted for 3 percent of the colony's population. By 1700, enslaved Africans totaled 16,000, or 28 percent of the colony. About 1750, the figure was 40 per-cent. In South Carolina, Africans outnumbered Europeans throughout the 1700s. In 1730, for example, 60 percent of South Carolina's popula-tion was of African heritage.

To produce staple crops, planters needed huge amounts of land and labor but very little else. As a result, the Southern Colonies remained a region of plantations strung out along rivers and coastlines. Except for the cities of Charles Town (Charleston), South Carolina, and Williamsburg, Virginia, the South had few towns and only a small group of people who could be called merchants.

A Mixture in the Middle Colonies From Maryland north to New York, the economy of the Middle Colonies was a mixture of farming and commerce. The length of the Delaware and Hudson rivers and the tributaries that fed them allowed colonists to move into the interior and establish farms on rich, fertile soil. There they specialized in growing grains, including wheat, barley, and rye.

But commerce was just as important as agriculture in the Middle Colonies. New York and Philadelphia were already among the largest cities in North America. Home to growing numbers of merchants, traders, and artisans—craftspeople such as printers, bakers, and furniture makers—the streets of these cities teemed with people in the business of buying and selling goods. As the map on page 33 shows, the Middle Colonies had many different ethnic groups. In contrast, most of the residents of Massachusetts were still of English descent, while most people in the South were either of African or of English descent.

Agriculture and Trade in New England In the 1700s the New England Colonies were a region of small, relatively self-sufficient farms and of towns dependent on long-distance trade. Unlike the merchants of Philadelphia and New York, those in Boston, Salem, and Newport, Rhode Island, did not rely heavily on local crops for their commerce. Instead, they had long since developed a business of carrying crops and goods from one place to another—a "carrying trade." They might haul china, books,

In the unequal society of the colonies, a white wig, or hair powdered to look like one, was the hallmark of a gentleman.

and cloth from England to the West Indies in the Caribbean Sea; transport sugar back to New England, where it was usually distilled into rum; trade rum and firearms for slaves in West Africa; and then carry slaves to the West Indies for more sugar. This trade between three points in the Atlantic World—the Americas, Europe, and Africa—was called the **triangular trade.**

Everyday Life in the Colonies

In general, colonial American society was dedicated to the belief that people were not equal. Almost all Americans of European descent, for example, accepted slavery as a normal part of life. Nearly all colonists also assumed that women were not equal to men. Some may not have liked these assumptions, but colonial society offered little opportunity for debate over such issues. In the words of one New Englander, "ranks and degrees" were as much a part of this world as "Mountains and Plains, Hills and Vallies."

The Gentle Folk Colonial clothes, houses, and manners offer the best evidence of this belief in inequality. **Gentry**, or men and women wealthy enough to afford others to work for them, set themselves apart by their clothing: wigs, silk stockings, lace cuffs, and the latest fashions in suits, dresses, and hats. Ordinary people wore plain breeches and shirts or dresses. Wigs were an unmistakable sign of status, power, and wealth.

"Gentle folk," a colonial term for the gentry class, were the most important members of colonial society; to be considered "gentle," one had to be wealthy. For English colonists, the foundation of real wealth was land. Although adult, single women and free African Americans could legally own land, almost all landowners were white men.

From New Hampshire to the Carolinas and Georgia, small groups of landowning men in each colony dominated politics. Lawyers, planters, and merchants held most of the seats in the colonial assemblies, or lawmaking bodies.

Women in Colonial America The colonial belief in inequality defined the status of colonial women, including the wives and daughters of gentlemen. Within the households of colonial

America, husbands exercised nearly unlimited power. English law, for example, permitted men to beat their wives without fear of prosecution. Most women, either as underage daughters or as wives, were legally the dependents of men, could not own land, and thus could not vote or hold office or serve on a jury. Even adult, single women—widows, for instance, who took ownership of land from their late husbands—did not have any political rights, although they could conduct business.

In practice, however, men and women depended heavily on one another. In colonial America, women juggled a number of duties that contributed to the well-being of the household and also of the community. Women took chief responsibility for the tasks that kept a household operating, such as cooking, gardening, washing, spinning thread, weaving cloth, cleaning, and sewing. They supported one another by helping in childbirth, sharing equipment and tools, and applying community pressure on offenders in cases of domestic abuse. Women also assisted in whatever work their husbands did, from planting crops to managing the business affairs of the family. And they trained their daughters in the traditional responsibilities of women.

Women sometimes took on these multiple duties before marriage. One example is Eliza Lucas Pinckney of South Carolina, who as a teenager managed her father's plantations in the late 1730s and early 1740s. This responsibility fell to Pinckney because, as she wrote to a friend, "Mama's bad state of health prevents her going thro' any fatigue," and her father, the governor of the Caribbean island of Antigua, was usually absent. As she wrote to her friend:

I have the business of 3 plantations to transact, which requires much writing and more business and fatigue of other sorts than you can imagine, but lest you should imagine it too burdensome to a girl at my early time of life, give me leave to assure you I think myself happy that I can be useful to so good a father.

Using Historical Evidence Prudence Punderson, a Connecticut housewife, created this symbolic view in needlework of the life of a colonial woman. The symbols, from right to left, indicate birth, work, and death. *What three symbols would you choose to sum up your own life? How do they differ from the symbols Punderson chose?*

Pinckney was more than just a stand-in for her father. She was one of the people responsible for promoting the growing of indigo, a type of plant used in making a blue dye for cloth, which became a major staple crop in South Carolina.

The Nature of Work in Colonial America By the mid-1700s, life was better for most Europeans in North America—even those who were not of the gentle class—than it would have been in Europe. American colonists ate better, lived longer, and had more children to help them with their work than their European counterparts. Still, whether these working people were skilled artisans in cities or small farmers in the countryside, they had to labor very hard to keep themselves and their families alive.

Everyone in a household—husbands, wives, children, and servants—worked to maintain the household by producing food and goods. In fact, the basic goal of the household was to maintain itself. While men grew crops or made goods such as shoes, guns, or candles, the rest of the household was equally busy. Many women sewed and spun cloth, made butter, and tended small gardens and animals. Children helped both parents from an early age. Almost all work was performed in or around the home; the separation between work and home with which we are familiar today did not develop until the 1800s. Even artisans worked out of shops in the front of their houses.

The First Movement West

Less than 150 years after the times of starvation and trouble at Jamestown, the British colonies in North America had become economic successes. Colonial settlers, with the forced cooperation of enslaved African Americans, had transformed the Atlantic colonies into a world of prosperous farms, towns, and plantations. Though it may be hard to believe, British colonists had begun to feel crowded, especially in New England.

By the middle of the 1700s, English settlers began moving into the interior of North America. Scots-Irish (Scottish people who had settled in Ireland) and Germans settled central Pennsylvania and the Shenandoah Valley of Virginia. Farther to the north, people were spreading into the Mohawk River valley in New York and the Connecticut River valley in what is now Vermont. They were migrating in search of land on which they could stake their independence and maintain their households.

Just ahead of the English migrants were Native Americans, including the Delaware and the Shawnee. They were moving west, too. Though heavily involved in trade with the Europeans, they preferred forest life to farm life. By the mid-1700s, disease and war over trade had taken a toll on Native American cultures; the Iroquois, for example, were no longer as strong militarily as they had been in the 1600s. Native Americans nonetheless remained powerful players in the development of American colonial society. And they remained adept at playing on the rivalry between the French in Canada and the British in New York and Pennsylvania.

The relentless intrusion of the English alarmed the French as well as the Native Americans. By the early 1750s, it was clear that some kind of explosion was rapidly approaching. The most likely setting was western Pennsylvania. There the interests of the colonies of Pennsylvania and Virginia were in conflict with both the Native Americans and the French. Whoever controlled the forks of the Ohio River, the place where the Allegheny and Monongahela rivers meet to form the Ohio, would have a considerable strategic advantage over everyone else.

Religious Tensions Within the Colonies

While tensions built along the outer edges of the British colonies, unrest was also increasing within them. Nowhere was this more obvious than in colonial religious life.

In the early 1700s, many ministers believed that the colonists had fallen away from the faith of their ancestors. In the 1730s and 1740s, they led a series of revivals that especially touched women of all ages and young men. This revival of religious feeling is now known as the **Great Awakening.**

The purpose of the preachers who brought about the Great Awakening was to remind people of the power of God and—at least in the beginning—of the authority of their ministers. In a well-known fiery sermon, "Sinners in the Hands of an Angry God," revivalist Jonathan Edwards appealed to his congregation:

> O sinner! Consider the fearful danger you are in: it is a great furnace of wrath, a wide and bottomless pit, full of the fire of wrath, that you are held over in the hand of that God, whose wrath is provoked and incensed as much against you, as against many of the damned in hell. You hang by a slender thread.

As time went on, however, the Great Awakening did more than revive people's religious conviction. It energized them to speak for themselves and to reject the traditional authority of ministers and books. As George Whitefield, one of the most famous and popular revivalists, said,

> The Generality of Preachers talk of an unknown, unfelt Christ. And the Reason why Congregations have been so dead, is because dead Men preach to them.

People flocked not to the established ministers but to wandering preachers, who told of the ability of all people to have a personal relationship with Jesus Christ. According to these preachers, the infinitely great power of God did not put Him beyond the reach of ordinary people. The message these ministers spread was that faith and sincerity

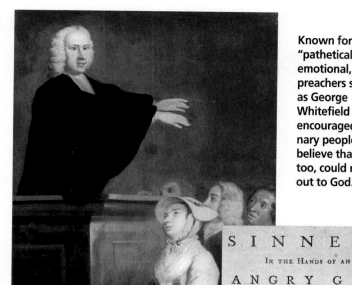

Known for their "pathetical," or emotional, style, preachers such as George Whitefield (left) encouraged ordinary people to believe that they, too, could reach out to God.

SINNERS
IN THE HANDS OF AN
ANGRY GOD.
A
SERMON
Preached at ENFIELD, July 8th, 1741.
At a Time of great Awakenings; and attended with remarkable Impressions on many of the Hearers.

By JONATHAN EDWARDS, A.M.
Pastor of the Church of CHRIST, in NORTHAMPTON.

Amos ix. 2, 3. *Though they dig into Hell, thence shall mine Hand take them; though they climb up to Heaven, thence will I bring them down. And though they hide themselves in the Top of Carmel, I will search and take them out thence; and though they be hid from my Sight in the Bottom of the Sea, thence I will command the Serpent, and he shall bite them.*

"The bow of God's wrath is bent, and the arrow made ready on the string." Such was the warning of God's power contained throughout Jonathan Edwards's fiery sermon.

were the major requirements needed to understand the Gospel.

In the end, the Great Awakening became a challenge to the social and political order of British North America. If ordinary people did not need a hierarchy of ministers to help them know God, perhaps the hierarchy of gentle folk was not so necessary either. And if people could figure out how to worship God on their own, couldn't they figure out how to govern themselves as well?

SECTION 4 REVIEW

Key Terms, People, and Places

1. Define (a) mercantilism, (b) balance of trade, (c) salutary neglect, (d) triangular trade, (e) gentry, (f) Great Awakening.

Key Concepts

2. What were the English colonies supposed to do for the parent country, according to mercantilist theory?
3. Describe the economies of the Southern Colonies, the Middle Colonies, and the New England Colonies.
4. Describe the basic belief on which colonial American society was based and its effect on society.
5. How did Native Americans and the French react to westward expansion by British settlers?
6. Why was the Great Awakening an indirect challenge to the fundamental colonial belief in inequality?

Critical Thinking

7. **Recognizing Ideologies** Eliza Lucas Pinckney wrote that she was happy just to be of use to her father. What does this suggest about her attitude toward herself?

African Americans in the Colonies

SECTION PREVIEW

Although they had no rights in the highly unequal world of colonial America, African Americans actively shaped society from very early times.

Key Concepts

- Slave traders removed Africans from their homelands by force and transported them across the Atlantic Ocean.
  - People of African descent enslaved in South Carolina and Georgia were especially successful in preserving many of their cultural traditions.
  - African Americans in Virginia and Maryland created a unique blend of European and African cultures and established stable family systems.
- The lives of African Americans in the New England and Middle colonies varied like the economies they supported with their labor.

Key Terms, People, and Places

Middle Passage, low country

Continuing traditions established in Africa, enslaved African Americans made and played this banjo and fiddle in North America.

Not counting Native Americans, about one out of every five people living in British North America by the middle of the 1700s was of African descent. As in the case of all immigrants, the experiences of African Americans in the colonies varied depending on where they lived.

Although there was no typical African American experience in the colonies, for many African men, women, and children, interaction with colonial society began when they were uprooted from their homeland and sold into slavery. One African who later told his story from the beginning was Olaudah Equiano.

AMERICAN PROFILES

Olaudah Equiano

Olaudah Equiano was born around 1745 in the country of Benin. He wrote in his autobiography decades later that the land of his youth was "uncommonly rich and fruitful" and "a nation of dancers, musicians and poets." As a child, he learned "the art of war" and proudly wore "the emblems of a warrior" made by his mother. When Equiano was ten, his world was shattered. Two men and a woman kidnapped him and one of his sisters while their parents were working. Separated from his sister, Equiano was enslaved to a series of African masters. About six months after he was kidnapped, Equiano found himself facing a still greater trial. Taken to the coast, he was sold again and put aboard a British slave ship bound for the Americas. In his autobiography, he wrote:

> The first object which saluted my eyes when I arrived on the coast was the sea, and a slave ship which was then riding at anchor and waiting for its cargo. These filled me with astonishment, which was soon converted into terror when I was carried on board. . . . Indeed such were the horrors of my views and fears at the moment that, if ten thousand worlds had been my own, I would have freely parted with them all to have exchanged my condition with that of the meanest [lowest] slave in my own country.
>
> Equiano's Travels, 1789

During the **Middle Passage,** the name given to the part of the triangular trade that went between Africa and the Americas bearing enslaved Africans, Equiano witnessed many scenes of brutality. Although historians differ on the actual figures, from 10 to 40 percent of the Africans on a slave ship might perish in a

"No eye pities; no hand helps," said a slaver describing the condition of his human cargo. An eyewitness painted this scene aboard a slave ship in 1846.

crossing. Sick with fear about where they were being taken, they were forced to endure chains, heat, disease, and the overpowering odor caused by the lack of sanitation and their cramped, stuffy quarters. As Equiano wrote, "Many a time we were near suffocation from the want of fresh air, which we were often without for whole days together." Conditions were so grim on Equiano's voyage that two people committed suicide; a third was prevented from doing so and then whipped.

Occasionally enslaved Africans physically resisted during the Middle Passage by staging what the slavers called "mutinies." The heavily armed and manned slave ships were evidence that the slavers lived in continual fear of Africans striking out for their freedom. No mutiny took place aboard Equiano's ship, although statistics about the British slave trade show that a rebellion occurred every two years on the average. Many of these were successful.

Equiano's ship finally arrived at a port on the island of Barbados, in the West Indies, where the crew put up the Africans for sale at a public auction. Most went to work and die in the sugar plantations of the West Indies. Equiano noted how the sale separated families, leaving people grief-stricken and alone.

I*n this manner, without scruple, are relations and friends separated, most of them never to see each other again. I remember in the vessel in which I was brought over, in the men's apartment there were several brothers who, in the sale, were sold in different lots; and it was very moving on this occasion to see and hear their cries at parting. O, ye nominal Christians [Christians in name only]! might not an African ask you, Learned you this from your God, who says unto you, Do unto all men as you would men should do unto you?*

In 1766 Equiano was taken to Virginia, where he was eventually able to buy his freedom. Migrating to Great Britain, he found work as a barber and a personal servant and became active in the antislavery movement.

Treating humans as property led to unspeakable cruelties. This branding iron was used to mark an owner's initials on enslaved Africans.

Equiano's case was unusual. Relatively few enslaved Africans ever regained their freedom. The very uniqueness of his story illustrates, however, how the experiences of Africans varied

This authentic watercolor painted on a South Carolina plantation in the late 1700s documents a dance form and musical instruments that have been linked to the Yoruba people of West Africa.

greatly in colonial times. Slavery was legal everywhere, but the number of enslaved people in each region and the kind of labor they performed made for significant differences in African American life from one place to another. African Americans, moreover, not only survived slavery but preserved and adapted elements of their original cultures. Through the process of negotiation that occurs in all human relationships, they were often able to better their situations—even in spite of the intentions of their masters.

MAKING CONNECTIONS

Give examples of negotiation in society today, both between individuals and between groups.

Africans in South Carolina and Georgia

Much of the seaboard region of South Carolina and Georgia is formed by a coastal plain called **low country.** Planters found the low country excellent for the cultivation of rice and indigo. Enslaved people there labored under particularly brutal conditions. Charles Ball, an African American observer whose account was published in 1836, describes the situation as it had existed for well over a century:

> *The general features of slavery are the same every where; but the utmost rigor of the system, is only to be met with on the cotton plantations of Carolina and Georgia, or in the rice fields which skirt the deep swamps and morasses of the southern rivers.*

By contrast, North Carolina was more suited to tobacco farming, and so the lives of enslaved people in that colony were similar to the lives of African Americans in the other tobacco colonies, Virginia and Maryland.

African Americans in South Carolina and Georgia made up the majority of the population, and they generally had regular contact with only a handful of colonists. As a result, they were able to exercise greater control over their day-to-day existence than those enslaved in other colonies and to preserve many of their cultural traditions. Many had come to South Carolina and Georgia directly from Africa. They still practiced the crafts of their homeland, such as basket weaving and pottery, and they continued making the music they loved and telling the stories their parents and grandparents had passed down to them. In some cases, they kept their culture alive in their speech. The most well-known example is the Gullah language, a combination of English and African. As late as the 1940s, speakers of Gullah were using four thousand words from the languages of more than twenty-one separate groups in West Africa. African Americans even preserved the African manner of burial.

Strong African kinship networks helped people not only survive slavery but also preserve their traditions. Family relationships remained of supreme importance. When they had no relatives or only a few, enslaved Africans created new relationships with one another by acting as substitute kin. In these relationships, people behaved as if they were brothers or sisters or aunts or uncles, though in fact they were not.

The skills and knowledge that African Americans brought with them to South Carolina and Georgia also profoundly affected the lives of their masters. African Americans had superior knowledge of cattle herding and fishing, as well as great skill in the use of semi-tropical herbs. Because many had grown rice extensively in their homelands, they generally had vital, practical know-how about its cultivation. Without this knowledge, to say nothing of African American labor, it is doubtful that the colonies that came to depend on rice as a staple could have survived.

In these and many other ways, the African American majority in South Carolina and Georgia made the best of a horrible situation. Forced to come to North America, they found strength in each other's company and in the memory of their African origins. In the low-lying areas along the South Carolina and Georgia coasts, Africans worked not only to raise rice but to make the environment as much their own as their masters'.

Africans in Virginia and Maryland

The way enslaved people lived in Virginia and Maryland differed sharply from the way of life of African Americans in South Carolina and Georgia, in three ways. First, enslaved people in Virginia and Maryland made up a minority rather than a majority of the population and relatively few had come directly from Africa. Second, the work they performed was different. Cultivating tobacco, the major crop, did not take as much time as growing rice, so slaveowners put enslaved African Americans to work at a variety of other tasks. And third, African Americans in Virginia and Maryland had more regular contact with European Americans. The result was greater integration of European American and African American cultures than in South Carolina and Georgia.

Virginia planters could not afford to buy many slaves, so they encouraged enslaved African Americans to raise families. Thus colonists in Virginia and Maryland tended to allow fuller development of African American family and community life than those colonists from the rice plantations of the low country. It was economically advantageous for tobacco planters to allow such social interaction.

In the latter half of the 1700s, African Americans in Virginia and Maryland laid the foundation for stable family units and blended the customs of African and European origin. They mingled the African and the European in everything from food and clothes to religion. Meanwhile, some enslaved men in Virginia worked away from plantations as artisans or laborers in Richmond and other towns. As long as they sent back a percentage of their wages to the plantations, they lived relatively independent of their master's control. They were, however, still subject to harsh laws that controlled what they could do, and their children were born enslaved.

Slavery in New England and the Middle Colonies

About 400,000 African Americans lived in the Southern Colonies by the late 1700s, compared to about 50,000 in the New England and Middle colonies combined. The lives and work of African Africans in these colonies north of Maryland reflected the region's mixed economy and its varied ways of life. They had considerably more freedom to choose their occupations than did African Americans in the Southern Colonies.

Estimated African Population of the Colonies, 1690–1750

Year	New England Colonies	Middle Colonies	Southern Colonies
1690	905	2,472	13,307
1700	1,680	3,361	22,476
1710	2,585	6,218	36,063
1720	3,956	10,825	54,058
1730	6,118	11,683	73,220
1740	8,541	16,452	125,031
1750	10,982	20,736	204,702

Source: *Historical Statistics of the United States*

Interpreting Tables
The growth in the number of African Americans, although relatively small in the 1600s, jumped considerably in the early 1700s. *In which group of colonies did the number of African Americans increase most sharply?*

This doll—perhaps made by an African American for one of his or her children—was found in the attic walls of an old house.

Throughout the 1700s, most African Americans in the north worked on farms, either in the fields or as cooks, housekeepers, personal servants, or artisans. They also worked in the forests as lumberjacks. Because shipbuilding and shipping were major economic activities in the New England and Middle colonies, some African American men worked along the seacoast. As dockworkers, merchant sailors, fisherman, whalers, and privateers, their labor contributed to the growth of the Atlantic economy. Others, men and women, worked in cities, in manufacturing and trading or as servants in the homes of wealthy families.

Laws and Revolts

Beginning about 1680, all the colonies passed laws controlling the activities of African Americans. Generally, enslaved African Americans could not go aboard ships or ferries or leave the town limits without a written pass; in some colonies they were forbidden to gather even for a dance. Punishment by whipping, banishment to the West Indies, and death were the norm for crimes ranging from owning hogs and carrying canes to disturbing the peace and striking a white person. In New York, for instance, any African American found traveling alone more than 40 miles from Albany could be put to death. In Virginia, runaways caught at night were by law supposed to be cut into pieces. Many of these laws also were applied to free African Americans and to Native Americans.

Harsh conditions sparked forceful resistance. In New York City, where the population in 1740 was 16 percent African American, brutal laws were passed to control African Americans. These led to rebellions in 1708, 1712, and 1741. After the rebellion of 1741, thirteen African Americans were burned alive in punishment. In the colonies as a whole, African Americans undertook about forty-seven documented revolts during the sixty years from 1740 to 1800.

Thus slavery became part of the new kind of society that grew up in North America, built on inequality but also built, as all societies are, on relationships between ordinary people. The next section shows how new tensions would emerge in that society during the 1700s, due to western expansion and religious upheaval.

SECTION 5 REVIEW

Key Terms, People, and Places
1. Define (a) Middle Passage, (b) low country.

Key Concepts
2. How did African Americans respond to conditions on the Middle Passage?
3. In general, how did the lives of enslaved Africans in Virginia and Maryland differ from the lives of those in South Carolina and Georgia?
4. How were enslaved people generally employed in the New England Colonies?

Critical Thinking
5. **Identifying Central Issues** How was the African American family in the 1700s affected by slavery?

Expressing Problems Clearly

The ability to express a problem clearly means being able to describe the nature of a situation or a question that is difficult, puzzling, or open to debate. When you express a problem clearly, you are taking the first step toward understanding and solving it.

In 1780, seven free African American men from Dartmouth, Massachusetts, protested to the State Legislature that they were being subjected to taxation without representation. The following excerpt is adapted from a manuscript in the Archives Division of the Massachusetts Historical Society.

Read the excerpt. Then use the following steps to practice expressing problems clearly.

1. Analyze the information. When you are confronted with a problem, study the information available. (a) Read the excerpt. What information was given by the free African Americans to support their petition?

2. Identify the basic concepts involved. Problems usually arise out of a specific set of circumstances. They often revolve around a concept or general principle, too, such as fairness. To identify the concept, try to express the problem in terms of what the petitioners wanted. (a) What benefit did the authors want to gain for themselves? (b) Why did they think they had cause to submit their case?

3. Identify the function of the supporting details. With any problem, details often are presented that may not be basic to the problem itself. (a) What details support the petition?

(b) What details in this excerpt did not relate to the basic issue of taxation without representation?

4. Express the problem clearly. Now that you have identified the main area of dispute and stripped away the irrelevant details, you are ready to express the problem clearly. How would you describe the problem outlined in the excerpt?

"The petition of several poor negroes and mulattoes who are inhabitants of the Town of Dartmouth humbly shows that we, being chiefly of the African extract and by reason of long bondage and hard slavery, have been deprived of enjoying the profits of our labor or the advantage of inheriting estates from our parents as our neighbors the white people do, having some of us not long enjoyed our own freedom. Yet of late, contrary to the invariable custom and practice of the country, we have been and are now taxed both in our polls and that small pittance of estate which through much hard labor and industry we have got together to sustain ourselves and families withal. We apprehend it therefore to be hard usage and . . . doubtless (if continued will) reduce us to a state of beggary, whereby we shall become burdens to others if not timely prevented by the interposition of your justice and power. Your petitioners futher show that we apprehend ourselves to be aggrieved, in that while we are not allowed the privilege of freemen of the state having no vote or influence in the election of those that tax us. Yet many of our color (as it is well known) have cheerfully entered the field of battle in the defense of the common cause. . . .

That these, the most honorable court, we humbly beseech they would take this into consideration and let us aside from paying tax or taxes or cause us to be cleared, for we have been a people that was fair [free] from all these things ever since the days of our forefathers. Therefore we take it as a hardship that we should be so dealt by now in these difficult times. For there is not to exceed more than five or six that has a cow in this town. Therefore in our distress we send unto the peacefulness of the people and the mercy of God that we may be relieved, for we are not allowed in voting in the town meeting, nor to choose an officer. Neither there was not one ever heard in the active Court of the General Assembly the poor despised miserable black people. . . .

We most humbly request therefore that you would take our unhappy case into your serious consideration and in your wisdom and power grant us relief from taxation while under our present depressed circumstances."

Petition to the State Legislature of Massachusetts, February 10, 1780

Chapter Review

Understanding Key Terms, People, and Places

Key Terms
1. kinship network
2. clan
3. hierarchy
4. patriarchal society
5. lineage
6. conquistador
7. *encomienda* system
8. colony
9. presidio
10. *congregacion*
11. indentured servant
12. Reformation
13. religious toleration
14. mercantilism
15. balance of trade
16. salutary neglect
17. triangular trade
18. gentry
19. Great Awakening
20. Middle Passage
21. low country

People
22. Christopher Columbus
23. Popé
24. Powhatan
25. Puritans
26. Metacom

Places
27. Guinea
28. Songhai
29. Atlantic World

Terms For each term above, write a sentence that explains its relation to the culture of the Native Americans or to the colonization of the Americas.

Matching Review the key terms in the list above. If you are not sure of a term's meaning, review its definition in the chapter. Then choose a term from the list that best matches each description below.
1. a system of many levels in which each level has power over the levels beneath it
2. a system in which Native Americans were required to work for an individual Spaniard, who was supposed to care for their well-being in return
3. groups of Native American families descended from a common ancestor
4. men and women in the colonies wealthy enough to afford others to work for them

True or False Determine whether each statement is true or false. If it is true, write "true." If it is false, change the underlined person or place to make the statement true.
1. The people of <u>Guinea</u> included Native Americans, Europeans, and Africans.
2. Askia Muhammad ruled the empire of <u>Songhai.</u>
3. <u>Popé</u> led a revolt against the Spanish in 1680.
4. New England settlers defeated Wampanoag leader <u>Powhatan</u> and his allies in King Philip's War.

Reviewing Main Ideas

Section 1 (pp. 12–18)
1. How did Native Americans view land use?
2. How was European society organized in the 1400s?
3. Describe how the empire of Songhai participated in African trade in the late 1400s.

Section 2 (pp. 19–23)
4. Why were European diseases brought to the Americans so deadly to Native Americans?
5. What was the significance of the Treaty of Tordesillas?
6. How did attitudes toward slavery differ among Africans and Europeans?

Section 3 (pp. 24–29)
7. What was the role of the Franciscans in helping the Spanish outposts in North America to succeed?
8. Describe the Pueblo Revolt of 1680.

9. How did the attitude of English settlers toward conquered peoples differ from that of the Spanish?

Section 4 (pp. 32–37)
10. What was the British government's policy toward the colonies after the rule of King James II ended?
11. Describe the colonial view regarding equality.
12. Why did English settlers begin moving into the interior of North America by the middle of the 1700s?

Section 5 (pp. 38–42)
13. Give four reasons why African Americans in South Carolina and Georgia were able to preserve many of their cultural traditions.
14. How did the employment of enslaved African Americans in the New England and Middle colonies reflect the geography and economy of the North?

1. **Expressing Problems Clearly** The birth of the Atlantic World represented the collision of three distinct cultures. What values, beliefs, and customs differed among the cultures? Choose one way in which the cultures differed, and explain why this difference might have led to misunderstanding and conflict.
2. **Identifying Assumptions** What the Spanish settlers called rebellions by Native Americans, some modern historians call armed struggles for liberation. What assumptions underlie each of these terms?
3. **Making Comparisons** During the 1700s, the gentry class in the English colonies set themselves apart from other people by their clothes, houses, and manners. Is there a gentry class in the United States today? If so, does this group set itself apart in its dress, manners, and possessions?

1. **Evaluating Primary Sources** Review the primary source excerpt on page 39. What does the quotation reveal about the way slave dealers viewed the African people they had brought to the Americas?
2. **Understanding the Visuals** The needlework on page 35 presents a symbolic view of the life of a colonial woman. Examine the needlework to discover the symbols it includes. Based on your reading of Section 4, what additional symbols would you add that represent the status of women in colonial America?
3. **Writing About the Chapter** Write a diary entry from the point of view of one of the following people in colonial America: (a) a member of the gentry, (b) an enslaved African American, (c) a woman, (d) an ordinary worker. First, make a list of the ways in which you might spend a typical day. Note any feelings you might have toward the way you spend your day, as well as reasons for why you live as you do. Next, write a draft of your entry, in which you explain your typical day in as much detail as possible. Revise your entry, making sure that your details reflect the times in which your character is writing. Proofread your entry and draft a final copy.
4. **Using the Graphic Organizer** This graphic organizer uses webs to compare and contrast characteristics of Native American, European, and African societies. (a) Using the right side of the graphic organizer, summarize the view of land held by each society. (b) Using the left side, determine the two societies in which the family fulfilled a social function. (c) Working on a separate sheet of paper, create your own graphic organizer comparing and contrasting Native Americans, Europeans, and Africans in terms of religion and trade.

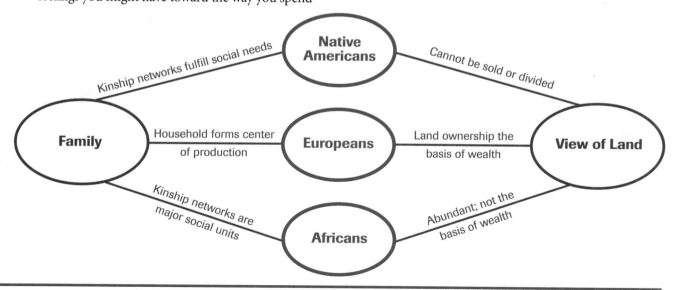

From Colonial to Constitutional Government

1754–1789

*S*truggling *for their rights and protesting against what they saw as British wrongs, colonists in the Americas demanded and won their independence from Great Britain. The new nation they formed, however, seemed to many Americans to be prone to disorder and instability. Thus, in the 1780s a group of well-educated, well-organized men worked to establish a powerful central government under a written constitution.*

Events in the United States

1754 The French and Indian War begins.	**1759** The British defeat the French at Quebec.		**1766** Colonists riot to protest the Stamp Act.	**1770** The Boston Massacre increases British-colonial tensions.

1754	1758	1762	1766	1770

Events in the World

1756 The French and Indian War spreads to Europe.	**1762** Catherine the Great becomes ruler of Russia.		**1769** Scotland's James Watt makes a steam engine capable of running other machines.

Pages 48 – 54
Colonial Issues and Independent Ideas

Under the pressure of new debts from a war between France and Britain, the British government tried to make its colonies pay what it cost to govern and protect them. In doing so, the British sparked deep anger and resentment among many colonists.

Pages 55 – 61
The War for Independence

Americans won their independence militarily by outlasting the British in one of the longest and costliest wars in American history. It was a true people's war—though not all Americans fought on the same side.

Pages 62 – 67
Government by the States

Many Americans were pleased with the highly democratic state created during the American Revolution. But a sizable number of citizens lobbied hard for a stronger national government.

Pages 68 – 74
The Constitutional Convention

During the summer of 1787, delegates fashioned a Constitution that forever sealed the people's right to direct their government.

Pages 76 – 81
Making a New Government

With political skill and persuasive argument, the Federalists managed to win approval of the Constitution. They then labored to make the United States government as impressive as possible, choosing talented officials and planning an elaborate national capital.

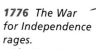

1776 The War for Independence rages.
• The Continental Congress signs the Declaration of Independence.

1781 British General Lord Cornwallis surrenders at Yorktown.

1787 The Constitutional Convention is held in Philadelphia.
• Shays's Rebellion begins.

1790 Rhode Island becomes the last of the original 13 states to ratify the Constitution.

1791 The Bill of Rights is ratified.

1774 **1778** **1782** **1786** **1790**

1778 English explorer James Cook lands on Hawaii.

1781 Peruvian leader Tupac Amaru II leads a revolt against Spanish rule in Peru.

1789 The French Revolution begins, taking its inspiration from the American Revolution.

Colonial Issues and Independent Ideas

SECTION PREVIEW

Under the pressure of new debts from a war between France and Britain, the British government tried to make its colonies pay what it cost to govern and protect them. In doing so, the British sparked deep anger and resentment among many colonists.

Key Concepts

• During the French and Indian War, Americans became increasingly aware of how different they were from the British.

• The pattern of events between 1763 and 1775 led many Americans to believe the British were using taxation as an excuse to deprive Americans of their rights.

• Writings of the 1770s established new and radical principles of freedom and equality in American government and society.

Key Terms, People, and Places

American Revolution, War for Independence, depression, boycott, Declaration of Independence, popular sovereignty; minuteman, George Washington, King George III, Thomas Paine, Thomas Jefferson

Colonists who poured their tea from this pot bolstered their resistance to the Stamp Act, a British tax law that led to the War for Independence.

On the morning of April 19, 1775, about 70 men stood on the green in the center of Lexington, Massachusetts. They were **minutemen**—local residents organized as a defensive force who had pledged to respond in a matter of minutes when called to action. They had been waiting since 2 A.M. for the British force that was to march through Lexington on its way to destroy a store of military supplies in neighboring Concord.

A little after dawn, British major John Pitcairn led between 700 and 800 British regulars into Lexington, outnumbering the minutemen ten times over. Pitcairn took a position behind the Americans and ordered them to give up their guns. The captain of the minutemen told his men to go home. Some began to leave; others stood their ground.

Exactly what happened next will never be known. Both British and Americans denied shooting at each other first. In any case, the British soldiers were soon firing into the American ranks and using their bayonets. Within minutes, eight dead Americans lay on Lexington Green and another nine were wounded. The victorious British regrouped and marched on toward Concord.

This brief encounter was the beginning of an eight-year war between the British government and thirteen of its North American colonies. To win their independence, the colonies would organize themselves into a loose confederation called the United States of America. The war and the political and social changes that accompanied it are called the **American Revolution.** The war itself is called the **War for Independence.** But before you read about the Revolution, you must first understand what motivated several dozen farmers and artisans to stand on a green in the middle of the night and defy the authority of their king.

The Background to Revolution: The French and Indian War

During the early 1700s, the tension between the Native Americans and the French on one side and the colonists and the British on the other had gradually built toward a clash. In 1754, an inexperienced, twenty-one-year-old officer from Virginia named **George Washington** tangled with French forces near the forks of the Ohio River. It was the first skirmish of a major war that lasted until 1763, called the French and Indian War because the British and their colonists waged it against the French and their Native American allies. While Native Americans fought on both sides, many tended to ally themselves with the French in the beginning. They saw the French as less likely to disrupt their way of life, not only because fewer French had come to North America, but also because the French were not trying to transform Native American lands into another Europe.

After several French successes, the British finally began to win the war. The year 1759 proved decisive. British brigadier general James Wolfe led his troops by night over a goat path up the steep heights of the city of Quebec. There his men defeated the enemy and forced the surrender of the capital city of New France.

With the fall of Quebec, the war was virtually over. In the Treaty of Paris, signed in 1763, the French turned over all of Canada to the British. A century and a half after the founding of Jamestown and Quebec, the British were the only Europeans governing the American continent outside New Spain.

But the French and Indian War had several bad side effects that severely strained British-American relations. For example, the arrogance of many royal officers insulted colonial gentlemen like George Washington. The behavior of British troops, moreover, struck many New Englanders as immoral. Their bad language horrified men who believed that God determined the outcome of events depending on the religious sincerity of those involved. And it seemed to ordinary colonists that the British were dealing with their colonial governments and local merchants in a high-handed manner—suggesting that the British considered the colonists to be inferior. This angered Americans, who felt they had every right to be treated like full-fledged citizens of a great empire, especially while they were helping protect that empire.

MAKING CONNECTIONS

Describe in two sentences how the Atlantic World changed from the founding of Jamestown to the end of the French and Indian War.

Using Historical Evidence By distorting space and time, the painter of this view of the British attack on Quebec was able to illustrate several events at once. *What British actions are shown?*

The Issues That Led to the War for Independence

In protecting Americans with troops and ships during the French and Indian War, Great Britain had built up huge debts. It only made sense that the colonists should pay their share of the cost of running the Empire so that Britain could pay off those debts. Besides, the British knew that the colonists were well off; their collective standard of living was higher than any in Europe. Britain, in particular, was in the midst of a serious **depression,** or economic slump.

An End to Salutary Neglect In 1763 George Grenville, the chief minister under the British king, **George III,** began a series of changes in British policy designed to deal with debts from the French and Indian War. From the point of view of the British, they were doing nothing wrong. After all, according to the theory of mercantilism, the colonies existed to serve the interests of the parent country.

In early 1764, under Grenville's leadership, the British Parliament passed a law called the Sugar Act, which was intended to raise money from the colonies by a change in the tax on molasses, a product that was widely used at that time. The act signaled an end to Britain's salutary neglect of its colonies. Now Britain would deliberately interfere in local matters, disrupting old traditions and accepted customs. Colonists who were involved in overseas commerce, including southern tobacco and rice planters as well as northern merchants, were especially displeased with the change in policy.

Grenville's government also dealt with another serious problem by issuing a law called the Proclamation of 1763. This proclamation closed the trans-Appalachian region, the area between the crest of the Appalachian Mountains and the Mississippi River, to all settlement by colonists. Parliament reasoned that if there were no settlers in the region, no money would be required to protect them from Native Americans. Colonists who had been eager to migrate westward did not like these limits on their movement.

The Stamp Act Crisis The growing anger over British government actions finally exploded in 1765 after Parliament's passage of the Stamp Act. Grenville intended this law in part to raise money for the defense and support of the American colonies. It required that all legal documents and printed materials—newspapers, for example—should have an attached paper stamp bought from the government. The stamp simply showed that a required fee had been paid. The modern practice of putting a paper stamp on a piece of mail is similar.

Grenville consulted with agents of the colonies and gave them time to suggest alternatives. His consideration for colonial feelings won him no friends, however. News of the Stamp Act created a firestorm of protest in the colonies. Merchants and artisans joined together in a **boycott**—a form of protest in which people refuse to buy goods or services. Colonial legislatures, and a special Stamp Act Congress, met to argue that colonists were free-born Englishmen and Parliament could not tax them without their consent. They had no representatives in Parliament, they pointed out, and so Parliament had no right to decide what kind of taxes they should pay. In other words, there should be no taxation without representation.

Interpreting Charts

In the time line below, events before the War for Independence are charted as cause and effect. They combine to form a series of provocations and tragic miscommunications on both sides. *In what years did delayed effects of the Quartering Act occur?*

1764	1765	1766	1767	1768	1769

Some events are shown out of order within their proper year to clarify cause and effect.

Parliament passes and strictly enforces **the Sugar Act** to raise money to pay for the cost of administering the colonies.

↓

Colonists respond with written protests, occasional boycotts, and cries of **"No taxation without representation."**

The Stamp Act requires the purchase of tax stamps, which are to be attached to all printed goods.

↓

Colonists protest violently. Delegates of nine colonies meet in New York as **the Stamp Act Congress** and prepare a Declaration of Rights and Grievances. **Boycott** of British goods begins.

The Quartering Act requires the colonies to quarter, or provide food and lodging for, British soldiers.

↓

Most colonial legislatures refuse to pay for supplies required by the Quartering Act.

The Stamp Act is repealed at the urging of British merchants, who are feeling the effects of colonial boycotts.

The Declaratory Act reminds colonists that Britain keeps the right to make laws in the colonies.

↓

Even though colonists rejoice at the repeal of the Stamp Act, they continue to resist other British-imposed laws like the Quartering Act.

The Townshend Duties require colonies to pay minor import duties on tea, glass, lead, oil, paper, and painter's colors.

↓

John Dickinson encourages protests against the Townshend Duties by writing the first of twelve "Letters from a Farmer in Pennsylvania," which are published in all but four of the colonies' newspapers. **Colonies boycott British imports again,** cutting trade in half.

The **New York Assembly is suspended** for the colony's refusal to comply fully with Quartering Act.

The British government orders troops to be stationed in Boston to enforce the Townshend Duties.

↓

Boston colonists refuse to quarter British troops.

The British governor of Virginia dissolves the Virginia Assembly for its resolution against British taxes and other protests.

↓

Virginia, Maryland, and South Carolina agree not to import certain British goods.

British Action

Colonial Action

JOIN OR DIE

British merchants, too, howled in protest as they saw their trade with the colonies threatened by the boycott. In the face of such a torrent of opposition and the virtual refusal of colonists to buy the stamps, Parliament backed down. Grenville was forced from power, and new British leaders repealed the Stamp Act in 1766.

The Colonists Resist "Slavery" The triumphant colonists quieted down. But the issues raised by the Stamp Act would not go away. Could Parliament tax Americans without representation in Parliament? Did the rights that English law gave to free men in England also belong to free men in the American colonies?

In 1767 Parliament reasserted its authority by placing taxes on certain imported goods, including lead, glass, and tea. These Townshend Duties, named after the chief British financial official, Charles Townshend, also provoked protests and a boycott. Once again, Parliament eventually backed down, repealing all the taxes in 1770—all the taxes, that is, except for one that

Parliament kept to save its pride: the tax on tea. As a result, tea became a symbol of British injustice, and many Americans refused to drink it.

By 1770, growing numbers of Americans were convinced that British politicians were engaged in a deliberate plot to rob them of their personal independence through taxation. Protest groups that had formed during the Stamp Act crisis—"Sons of Liberty" and "Daughters of Liberty"—complained that the British were taxing them in order to take away their property and make them into what amounted to slaves. This was something many people, whether gentlemen, farmers, or artisans, believed they simply could not tolerate. In the words of John Dickinson, a Pennsylvania lawyer,

Colonists saw the "cursed stamp" as a symbol of enslavement to the British crown.

T*hose who are* taxed *without their own consent, expressed by themselves or their representatives, are* slaves. *We are* taxed *without our own consent, expressed by ourselves or our representatives. We are therefore—SLAVES.*

1770	1772	1773	1774	1775

In Boston, British troops come to the aid of a fellow soldier and fire into an angry mob. Five colonists are killed.

⬇

Colonial propagandists quickly dub the riot the "Boston Massacre."

⬇

British officials in Boston move troops to quarters outside the city to ease tensions.

⬇

Parliament repeals Townshend Duties, but retains tea tax.

⬇

Colonists **end boycott** begun in 1767.

The British government orders that governors and judges in Massachusetts are now to be paid by Britain, removing them from the colony's control.

⬇

In response to the new salary arrangement, Samuel Adams forms the **Boston Committee of Correspondence** to alert Massachusetts and "the world" to the "infringements and violations" of the rights of colonists in Boston.

⬇

The Gaspée, a British revenue cutter, aggressively patrols the Rhode Island coast in order to control colonial smuggling.

⬇

To protest the harsh treatment of legitimate traders as well as colonial smugglers, Rhode Island colonists burn the *Gaspée.*

➡

Parliament passes **the Tea Act** in an attempt to save the East India Company from bankruptcy and to reassert its right to tax.

⬇

A group of Boston patriots destroy a shipment of tea in a protest known as **the Boston Tea Party.**

In response to British investigation of the *Gaspée* affair and to the aggressive British enforcement of customs regulations, Virginia's House of Burgesses appoints a **Provincial Committee of Correspondence** to inform all the colonial provinces of the actions of the British Parliament.

The Coercive Acts, called the **"Intolerable Acts"** by the colonists, are passed in response to the Tea Party:
- **The Port Bill** closes Boston's port until payment is made for the destroyed tea.
- **The Massachusetts Government Act** effectively imposes a new form of government on the colony.
- New provisions to **the Quartering Act** force colonists to quarter British soldiers in private homes, if necessary.
- **The Administration of Justice Act** gives royal officials in Massachusetts the right to trial in a court outside the colony.

Four thousand troops are sent to Boston to enforce these acts.

⬇

In Philadelphia, delegates from all of the colonies except Georgia meet in the **First Continental Congress.** It creates the **Continental Association** to boycott British goods and sends a petition of grievances to the king, outlining what it considers the rights of the colonists and their assemblies.

British troops march to Concord, Massachusetts, to seize and destroy colonial munitions being stored there.

⬇

Colonial and British troops clash in the **Battle of Lexington.** The **Second Continental Congress** meets in Philadelphia to address revolutionary war aims and appoints George Washington commander-in-chief of the Continental Army.

2 A mob, drawn by news of trouble, floods into the street from a nearby square.

3 Responding to a call for help, a British captain brings seven soldiers from headquarters.

4 Attacked by the mob, soldiers fire on citizens, killing five.

1 Boys throw ice at a sentry guarding the Customs House.

Paul Revere, a silversmith and Patriot, used the so-called Boston Massacre as the subject of anti-British propaganda (left). His engraving shows the end result—troops firing on citizens—but omits the events leading up to the shooting (above). A handful of soldiers attacked by hundreds of angry citizens fired without orders; they and their commanding officer were charged with murder but later acquitted.

More British actions followed. British troops occupied Boston in the late 1760s to protect officials enforcing the Townshend Duties. Tensions between soldiers and townspeople exploded in the Boston Massacre on March 5, 1770. An African American, Crispus Attucks, and four other colonists were killed.

Then, in 1773, the British government announced that it was going to sell millions of pounds of tea at discounted rates directly to the American public. To the colonists, the move seemed a way of trying to buy their acceptance of the detested tea tax. In harbors up and down the Atlantic seaboard, ships loaded with tea were turned away. Some residents of Boston, in a protest now known as the Boston Tea Party, threw the cargoes of several ships into the harbor.

Losing all patience, Parliament passed the Coercive Acts in 1774 to punish the colony of Massachusetts. Among other things, these acts—called the Intolerable Acts by colonists everywhere—virtually shut down individual town governments and the colonial legislature. These strong measures only confirmed American suspicions that the British were moving to take away their freedoms and their property.

Local Committees of Correspondence, groups formed to coordinate protest throughout the colonies, met to elect delegates to the First Continental Congress. The delegates discussed the proper reaction to the Coercive Acts. Their efforts to find a peaceful solution failed. In July 1775, after the war had erupted at Concord and Lexington, the Second Continental Congress agreed to a statement they called *A Declaration of the Causes and Necessities of Taking Up Arms*. It stated that the members were "resolved to die Free men rather than live Slaves."

The Continental Congress was only putting into words the belief that had brought the farmers and artisans of eastern Massachusetts to the green at Lexington that April. It was the conviction of the Congress and the minutemen alike that at some point they had to take a stand against the pattern of enslavement they saw in the actions of the British, whom they perceived as corrupt, immoral, and power hungry. They did not consider themselves radicals or revolutionaries; they were simply protecting their way of life, their land, and their households.

The Ideas That Led to the War for Independence

From the beginning, the American Revolution was more than a rebellion or a war for independence. The Revolution itself began long before the war and continued long after the war had ended. It announced the creation of a new society committed to such powerful ideas as equality and democracy. Although the immediate accomplishment of the Revolution was simply to preserve the power of white men of the "gentle" class, its long-term significance lay in changing people's thinking about the world. During the time of the Revolution, Americans acquired the habit of challenging authority and asserting their rights—a habit they have never lost.

Two Documents Spread Democratic Ideas One of the chief documents that expressed and developed the ideas of the Revolution was *Common Sense,* published in 1776. Written by **Thomas Paine,** a recent immigrant from England, this pamphlet reached hundreds of thousands of readers of all social classes. Democratic in both style and substance, it was a direct assault on the whole idea of government by kings and aristocrats. What good were kings? asked Paine bluntly. "Of more worth is one honest man to society, and in the sight of God," he said, "than all the crowned ruffians that ever lived."

The other great democratic document of 1776 was written by an American aristocrat, or member of the gentle class, named **Thomas Jefferson.** In June 1776, after the colonies had been at war with Britain for over a year, the Continental Congress decided that it was high time to issue a statement declaring that the colonies were cutting their ties with their par-

ent country. This is the document we now call the **Declaration of Independence.**

The Congress appointed a committee of five, including Jefferson, to write the declaration. The committee depended upon Jefferson to compose the first draft. So successful was he that his fellow committee members proposed very few changes. Jefferson drew largely on a theory of government devised by earlier European political thinkers, including the Englishman John Locke. These theorists believed that people had natural rights—rights that belonged to them simply because they were human, not because kings or governments had granted these rights to them. According to this theory, originally people had been completely free of government. In order to gain increased safety and comfort, they had joined together in a community. They had then given certain individuals the power to govern the community, forming a social contract. If a ruler failed to act in the best interests of those he governed, he was breaking the social contract. In that case, the people had the right to revolt and choose a new form of government.

Jefferson wrote that governments get their power from "the consent of the governed," implying that ordinary people can and should govern themselves. This idea is now called **popular sovereignty**.

What the Declaration Accomplished On July 4—the date Americans now celebrate as Independence Day—all thirteen colonies joined in accepting the declaration. With that vote, they ceased being colonies and officially became a new nation, the United States.

But the Declaration achieved more than just proclaiming the existence of the United States of America. It also announced that both popular sovereignty and equality were basic principles of American government and society. As the declaration stated:

W*e hold these truths to be self-evident, that all men are created Equal, that they are Endowed By their Creator with Certain unalienable rights* [rights that cannot be taken away], *that among these are Life, Liberty, and the pursuit of happiness.*

A Declaration by the Representatives of the UNITED STATES OF AMERICA, in General Congress assembled.

When in the course of human events it becomes necessary for one people to dissolve the political bands which have connected them with another, and to ~~assume~~ assume among the powers of the earth the ~~equal~~ separate and equal station to which the laws of nature & of nature's god entitle them, a decent respect to the opinions of mankind requires that they should declare the causes which impel them to the separation.

We hold these truths to be self-evident: that all men are created equal & independent; that from that equal creation they derive rights inherent & inalienable, among which are the preservation of life & liberty, & the pursuit of happiness; that to secure these rights, governments are instituted among men, deriving their just powers from the consent of the governed; that whenever any form of government shall becomes destructive of these ends, it is the right of the people to alter or to abolish it, & to institute new government, laying it's foundation on such principles & organising it's powers in such form, as to them shall

Using Historical Evidence The Declaration of Independence, said Thomas Jefferson (above), was "an expression of the American mind." The suggestions of other members of the drafting committee are marked on his first draft. *How did Jefferson correct the phrase "for a people"? Why did he make this change?*

Together the Declaration of Independence and *Common Sense* defined the basic principles of the new American nation. The United States was to be a nation in which ordinary citizens would run their own government. Both documents also attacked the age-old notion that some people were better than others simply because of the circumstances of their birth. People born rich or in long-established families should have no more rights than people born poor or of unknown parents. As the later history of the United States shows, the idea that all people were equal—and thus should have equal rights—would prove very contagious.

The Declaration accomplished a great deal, but it did not make the colonists independent of Great Britain. Before that could happen, they would have to fight a long and difficult war.

SECTION 1 REVIEW

Key Terms, People, and Places
1. Define (a) American Revolution, (b) War for Independence, (c) depression, (d) boycott, (e) Declaration of Independence, (f) popular sovereignty.
2. Identify (a) minuteman, (b) George Washington, (c) King George III, (d) Thomas Paine, (e) Thomas Jefferson.

Key Concepts
3. What effect did the French and Indian War have on the American colonists' view of the British?

4. Describe three British actions the colonists interpreted as signs of a British intention to take away their liberty.
5. What ideas did Thomas Paine attack in *Common Sense*?

Critical Thinking
6. **Determining Relevance** By 1770 many Americans thought the British were trying to take away their freedoms. Did it matter whether or not they were right? Explain your thinking.

The War for Independence

SECTION PREVIEW

Americans won their independence militarily by outlasting the British in one of the longest and costliest wars in American history. It was a true people's war—though not all Americans fought on the same side.

Key Concepts
- Despite the size and experience of the British military, the British did not have a superior position at the start of the war any more than the Americans did.
- The forces of the United States continued to fight against the British despite repeated losses.
- The Americans, with the help of the French, ended the war by trapping Cornwallis's army at Yorktown.
- Many American groups, including Native Americans and African Americans, experienced violence and hardship during the war.

Key Terms, People, and Places
Treaty of Paris, inflation; Patriots, Loyalists, Tories, Marquis de Lafayette, Baron von Steuben

As important as all the talk of self-government was, it would remain only talk if Americans could not win their independence. The British were not willing to let thirteen colonies go their way without a fight, especially when those colonies were prosperous. It took the Americans eight years, from 1775 to 1783, to accomplish their goal of freedom. Not only was the War for Independence the longest war in United States history after the Vietnam War, but it was the only one to be fought throughout the entire nation.

Advantages and Disadvantages

After scattering the rebels—or **Patriots,** as the Americans preferred to call themselves—from Lexington Green on April 19, 1775, the British forces continued on to Concord. (See Section 1.) There they fulfilled their mission by burning some rebel war supplies. As the British returned to Boston, however, Patriots from nearby towns gathered along the route and sniped at them from behind stone walls and other cover by the roadside. The easy British victory at dawn had become an exhausting and costly defeat by evening, as the British tallied 273 wounded or killed, compared to only 95 Patriots.

Still, the British had several reasons for believing that they would easily crush the rebellion in their American colonies. After all, Great Britain was the most powerful nation on earth. It had the richest economy, the largest navy, and an experienced and confident military. Almost a decade earlier, its armies and ships had defeated France in North America and Europe and added India as well as Canada to its Empire.

American Disadvantages The Americans, on the other hand, had no navy, no army, and no real government. They were not only disorganized, they were divided by state, by region, and by differing political goals. They even were split along racial lines. In the South, the British offered freedom to enslaved African Americans who would fight against the rebels. Throughout the colonies, Native Americans were outraged by American attacks against them and believed that their best interests lay in supporting the British, who were trying to prevent settlement in the West.

Furthermore, a great many colonists, called **Loyalists**—or **Tories,** after the majority party in Britain's Parliament—preferred to remain loyal to King George, even if they disagreed with the policies of his officials. John Adams estimated that one third of Americans were rebels, one third Tories, and one third neither. Tories tended

In a gesture symbolizing America's self-reliance, George Washington, the commander of the United States forces, declined to accept these elegant silver pistols captured from British Major John Pitcairn.

to be either merchants or well-established people with connections to the British government. They might also be freed slaves, Scots-Irish people in the backcountry, and other people who preferred to be ruled by the British rather than by colonial gentlemen. About 80,000 people left the United States during the war rather than give up their allegiance to the British Crown.

British Disadvantages The British had their own problems, however. The war was not popular in Great Britain. Many of the British resented paying taxes to fight the war and sympathized with the Americans. In addition, the British had to fight against an enemy that was thousands of miles away across an ocean, spread out over a huge territory, difficult to identify, and without any visible organization that could be attacked. As Americans would discover two centuries later in Vietnam, winning battles and having superiority in training are not enough when your opponent constantly shifts ground—and will not give up.

The Battle of Bunker Hill

The British began the war assuming that they could crush the rebellion by simply "showing the flag." They would remind people in New England of the power and authority of their government. They would intimidate them into surrender. The best example of this strategy was the battle for Breed's Hill near Boston in June 1775. (It has come to be called the Battle of Bunker Hill, after a nearby hill.)

After pursuing the British on their return from Concord in April, the Patriots—a varied group of white and African American artisans, farmers, and others—had surrounded Boston. But they were so disorganized that they could not agree on what to do next; in fact, they were unable to feed themselves and keep their camps around Boston in order.

Meanwhile, the British under General Thomas Gage sat in Boston, well supplied and protected by the British navy in the harbor. In early June, the Americans extended their lines north of Boston to the hills in Charlestown. General Gage decided to take advantage of this move to overawe the rebels and send them home. He ordered a massive frontal assault by some 2,200 troops on the Patriot camp at the top of Breed's Hill.

After landing by ship, the British had to march uphill for about a mile. They began their attack at about 3 P.M. on a sunny day. It was a magnificent sight. Hundreds of soldiers in scarlet coats moved forward up the slope, accompanied by drums and bagpipes and carrying battle flags in an impressive display of discipline and power.

When the British neared the American line, the rebels fired a ragged but deadly volley into their ranks. Without cover on the open hillside, the British were an easy target for this withering fire. Their proud army staggered and retreated. According to one anonymous Englishman,

> *O*ur light-infantry were served up in companies against the grass fence [a defensive barrier], *without being able to penetrate. . . . Most of our grenadiers and light-infantry . . . lost three fourths, and many nine tenths of their men. Some had only eight or nine men a company* [about 100 men] *left; some only three, four, and five.*

Embarrassed but still determined, the British troops attacked again. Again, the rebels stopped them. Again, the British attacked. This time the rebels, out of ammunition, retreated in disarray. The British troops, having picked their way through the bodies of dozens of wounded and dead comrades, overran the American position and took the hill.

The Battle of Bunker Hill was a British victory. But it came at too high a price. Of the 2,200 men Gage sent into battle that day, 226 were killed and another 828 were wounded. In other words, the number of casualties, or dead and wounded combined, was close to 50 percent, more than the British could bear. Above all, the battle demonstrated that the Americans would not be intimidated easily.

In early July, the general appointed by Congress, George Washington, assumed command of the American troops and brought greater discipline to the army. The siege of Boston continued throughout the fall and winter until the

A minuteman using shoot-and-run tactics killed the British officer who carried this sword during the retreat from the Battle of Concord on April 19, 1776.

BOSTON

CHARLES TOW

Americans dragged cannon they had captured in New York into position on the hills south of Boston. Faced with the possibility of deadly bombardment, the new British general, William Howe, evacuated Boston on March 17, 1776.

MAKING ✕ CONNECTIONS

Even in this early period of the war, the British and Americans constantly alternated between attacking and retreating. As you read on, notice how this general pattern continues. Who would be most likely to win such a war, and why?

War for Morale, 1776 to 1778

The British fleet took General Howe, his army, and thousands of Loyalists to Halifax, Nova Scotia, where they regrouped. In late summer, Howe launched an attack on New York City. The British had decided to concentrate on the Middle Colonies because the population of those colonies included more Tories, who could support them. In a series of large and small battles, Howe trounced Washington's poorly trained, poorly equipped, and poorly organized army.

An American volunteer, Michael Graham, later recalled one of these battles in August 1776.

I *t is impossible for me to describe the confusion and horror of the scene that ensued: the artillery flying with the chains [of the gun carriages] over the horses' backs, our men running in almost every direction, and run which way they would, they were almost sure to meet the British. . . . And the enemy huzzahing when they took prisoners made it truly a day of distress to the Americans.*

The Crisis By October the British had captured New York City and driven Washington's army all the way to Pennsylvania. Men were deserting Washington in droves; between the summer and winter of 1776, Washington's army shrank from 20,000 to about 6,000. The entire cause was on the verge of collapse.

In December 1776, Thomas Paine issued a paper he called *The Crisis*, which began with these words:

T *hese are the times that try men's souls. The summer soldier and the sunshine patriot will, in this crisis, shrink from the service of their country; but he that stands it NOW, deserves the love and thanks of man and woman. Tyranny, like hell, is not easily conquered; yet we have this consolation with us, that the harder the conflict, the more glorious the triumph. What we obtain too cheap, we esteem [value] too lightly: It is dearness [expensiveness] only that gives every thing its value.*

The Surprise Attack on Trenton Although the "summer soldiers" may have deserted, Washington still had some Patriots to form an army that next winter. He had the daring to put them to good use, too, as he broke the rules of

In a costly attempt to overawe American forces, waves of British troops climb Breed's Hill toward the waiting enemy.

war by ordering a surprise attack on the enemy in their winter quarters. On Christmas Eve, 1776, Massachusetts fishermen rowed Washington and 2,400 men across the Delaware River to New Jersey. At dawn, they attacked Trenton, as shown on the map below, and captured the mercenaries, or hired soldiers, whom Great Britain had brought from the German state of Hesse; a few days later, the Patriots fought a small battle at Princeton. Then Washington retreated to Pennsylvania.

The significance of Trenton was immense, if only because it shored up sagging American morale. It was hardly a great military victory, and George Washington was far from a great general—in fact, he lost most of the battles he fought during the war. He was, however, a great leader. He inspired people to follow him, and he recognized when to act boldly and decisively. Furthermore, he gradually came to understand that winning individual battles meant little compared to just hanging on and being ready to strike when the British made a mistake. Despite all the victories the British won in 1776, they could not win the war because they could not put Washington out of business.

The War for Independence, 1775–1781

Americans force the surrender of 5,000 British troops at Saratoga. The victory wins new allies for the United States—the French.

George Rogers Clark, with less than 200 soldiers, secures the West by capturing Vincennes.

George Washington boosts morale with a surprise attack on Trenton.

Washington and the French trap the British at Yorktown, ending the war.

General Nathanael Greene wears out the British in the South with cautious but determined warfare.

Quebec 1775
CANADA
Montreal
ME (part of MA)
Ft. Ticonderoga 1775
NY
Saratoga 1777
NH
Concord 1775
Lexington 1775
Bunker Hill 1775
Albany
MA Boston
White Plains 1776
Ft. Detroit
CT
RI
PA
Princeton 1776
Trenton 1776
Germantown 1777
Philadelphia
Brandywine 1777
Brooklyn Heights 1776
New York
Monmouth Court House 1778
MD
DE
VA
Yorktown 1781
Richmond
ATLANTIC OCEAN
1778 Vincennes
1779
Ohio R.
LOUISIANA
Guilford Court House 1781
NC
Cowpens 1781
1781
Wilmington
Kings Mt. 1780
Camden 1780
SC
1780
Charleston 1780
GA
Savannah

Legend
- British troop movements
- British victory
- American victory
- Indecisive battle
- Forts
- Territory claimed by Spanish

West Florida
East Florida
New Orleans

0   200   400 Miles
0   200   400 Kilometers

Geography and History: Interpreting Maps
Because the movements of United States forces were so often a reaction to British advances or retreats, only British movements are shown here. The major battles of the early part of the war took place in the North, but the focus shifted gradually southward. *Locate battles that took place in 1775, 1777, and 1781.*

The War Turns at Saratoga The next summer brought only mixed success for the Americans. Howe brushed aside Washington's army and captured the American capital of Philadelphia. But at Saratoga in upstate New York, a hastily organized army of Americans defeated a British army moving south from Canada in October 1777. Many historians call this victory the turning point of the war, for it convinced many people that the Americans would win if they could just hold on.

Among those persuaded was the French government. At the urging of Ambassador Benjamin Franklin, the French joined sides with the Americans. Not only did this mean money and supplies, it also meant that the British had to protect themselves in Europe. The French officer the **Marquis de Lafayette,** who fought alongside the Americans, later persuaded the French to assist with an army of 6,000 men.

Another European was also vital to the American cause: the Prussian officer **Baron von Steuben.** During a bitter winter at Valley Forge, Pennsylvania, he drilled Washington's troops and wrote a book of regulations that brought much-needed discipline to the Continental Army.

In the same year, 1778, the British abandoned Philadelphia and marched back across New Jersey toward New York City. At Monmouth Court House in New Jersey, Washington's army, now better equipped and better trained, caught up with the rear guard of the British and fought them to a standstill. After years of disorganization, the American army now had the discipline that made it a unit fit to be reckoned with.

Fighting the War to an End

While they continued to occupy New York, the British turned their primary attention to the South. There they hoped to demoralize the Americans by freeing slaves and laying waste the countryside. In 1780 the British captured Charleston, South Carolina. They then used the city as a base of operations, winning several battles.

The war, always an ugly business, was especially vicious in the South. Most of the southern war was fought by Americans against Americans, as Tories and Patriots clashed. At the battle of King's Mountain in South Carolina in 1780, where the Tories suffered a defeat, all the combatants were Americans. Elsewhere in the western part of the South, other Patriot forces dealt the British several losses.

Meanwhile, the British general Lord Cornwallis marched from South Carolina toward New York. Harassed but not defeated by small American armies commanded by Nathanael Greene and the Marquis de Lafayette, Cornwallis decided to transport his army to New York by ship in the summer of 1781. Marching his forces to the Virginia coast, he took up a position at Yorktown, near the point where the York River enters the Chesapeake Bay.

Washington, who was in camp near New York City, again acted boldly; he left the middle states and moved his army quickly south. There, together with the recently arrived French army, he laid siege to Yorktown in September. Luckily for the Americans, a French fleet turned back a British fleet off the coast of Virginia, and Cornwallis was trapped by a force twice the size of his own. On October 19, 1781, he had the "mortification," as he put it in a later letter to his superior, of surrendering his army to Washington and the French.

As the war moved into the southern states, it became increasingly hard fought. The commander of the British troops in this cavalry skirmish, Colonel Banastre Tarleton, was known as "the Butcher" for killing his prisoners.

A wife of one of the American soldiers, Sarah Osborn, was present at the surrender. Over fifty years later, she recalled that the British forces

> marched out beating and playing a melancholy [sad] tune, their drums covered with black handkerchiefs and their fifes with black ribbons tied around them, into an old field and there grounded their arms and then returned into town again to await their destiny.

The "melancholy tune" the British played was a song popular at the time called "The World Turned Upside Down." And that it was; the world would never be the same again. Faced with rising opposition at home, a new British government began negotiations that resulted in the signing of the **Treaty of Paris** in September 1783. Under this treaty, George III was no longer sovereign, or ruler, in his thirteen former colonies. Instead, the people were sovereign, although exactly which people that meant and how they would rule remained to be determined. In any case, it was not just white men, but all kinds of people who had fought the War for Independence.

A People's War

The British lost their colonies because Americans—or at least some Americans—had the determination to outlast them, even in the face of repeated military defeats. Like all wars, the War for Independence affected many people. Perhaps 200,000 men or more served at one time or another in the American cause.

The American Soldier's Experience Most of the fighting was carried out by young, relatively poor men. They and their officers were paid badly, if at all, and poorly fed and clothed. Washington wrote: "You might have tracked the army . . . to Valley Forge by the blood of their feet." In 1780 a soldier named Joseph Plumb Martin described their situation:

T he men were . . . exasperated [irritated] beyond endurance; they could

not stand it any longer. . . . What was to be done? Here was the army starved and naked, and there their country sitting still and expecting the army to do notable things while fainting from sheer starvation.

Occasionally their various frustrations boiled over into unrest, as in the case of the brief mutiny in January 1781 by a unit known as the Pennsylvania Line.

African American men—about five thousand of them—also experienced the life of a soldier, in the fighting on both sides. Women, too, both white and African American, served the cause they believed in, whether rebel or Tory. Many followed husbands, lovers, or fathers into battle, cared for them, and nursed them. These women formed an unofficial but vital part of the army, which could not have functioned without them. And a few actually fought side by side with men. The most famous was Deborah Sampson, who disguised herself as a man, took the name Robert Shurtleff, and served in the Continental Army from May 1782 to October 1783. Her husband later became the only man to be granted a pension as the "widow" of a veteran.

The Civilian Experience of the War The war affected civilians too. The British navy blockaded the seacoast and severely disrupted American commerce. Measured in the British monetary unit of pounds sterling, the combined value of American imports and exports fell from about £4,600,000 in 1775 to £200,000 in 1777. Exports of tobacco and rice in particular fell markedly. Occupation by British soldiers damaged cities such as New York. In fact, half of the 21,000 people who lived in New York before the war left the city.

Nearly everyone felt the pinch during the war. Often needed goods were scarce. Even when goods were available, it was not always possible to purchase them, due to **inflation**, or a steady increase in prices over a period of time that reduces people's ability to buy goods. In Massachusetts, for example, the price of a bushel of corn rose from less than one dollar in 1777 to almost eighty dollars in 1779. Congress issued paper money (called Continental

This woodcut was published in 1779 with a poem in which a Daughter of Liberty described civilian hardships during the War for Independence.

dollars) to pay for military expenses. But inflation soon made the money of little value. In 1777 it took three Continental dollars to equal one dollar in gold; by 1778, it took seven; one hundred in 1780; and almost a hundred and fifty in 1781. This decline in value gave rise to the expression "not worth a Continental." In the long run, the War for Independence stimulated economic development. But its short-term impact was harsh.

The Native American Experience of the War
Not all of the pain of the war was economic. In the middle and southern states especially, rebels and Tories treated each other savagely; they harassed each other, destroyed property, and killed hundreds of people. But the group most hurt by the war was the Native American population. At first, the Iroquois tried to stay out of what Mohawk sachem Little Abraham called "a family affair" between Britain and its colonies. The war, however, provided an excuse for Americans on the New York frontier to settle the question of control in the region. Angered by American attacks on their villages, the Iroquois joined the British in 1777. Under the able leadership of another Mohawk sachem, Joseph Brant, they launched several devastating raids in New York and Pennsylvania. In 1779, Americans under the command of General John Sullivan retaliated with raids of their own. Meanwhile, in the South, Virginians and Carolinians sent repeated expeditions to attack the Cherokee for supporting the British. For most Native Americans, the American victory in 1783 was a serious blow, the meaning of which would only become clear in the next two to three decades.

The War for Independence was a long and brutal war, complete with betrayals and corruption, torture and terrible violence. But it confirmed the commitment of many white Americans to the cause of independence. Now that they had won, however, they faced the difficult challenge of defining exactly what their victory meant.

Despite the brilliant leadership of Joseph Brant (above) and others, Native Americans suffered great hardships during the long war.

Georgia's Nancy Hart was said to have shot one of the six Tories who broke into her home, wounded another, and held the rest prisoner until her husband returned—to help her hang them.

SECTION 2 REVIEW

Key Terms, People, and Places
1. Define (a) Treaty of Paris, (b) inflation.
2. Identify (a) Patriots, (b) Loyalists, (c) Tories, (d) Marquis de Lafayette, (e) Baron von Steuben.

Key Concepts
3. Give two advantages and two disadvantages of the British at the beginning of the War for Independence.

4. Explain how the victory at Saratoga led to final victory at Yorktown.
5. What was the overall effect of the war on Native Americans?

Critical Thinking
6. **Checking Consistency** How can it be true that Washington was a poor general but a great leader?

Government by the States

Many Americans were pleased with the highly democratic state and national governments created during the American Revolution. But a sizable number of citizens lobbied hard for a stronger national government.

Key Concepts

- Before 1788 the national government was weak and the state constitutions were powerful.
- A group of men called the Nationalists believed that the new nation's many problems could be solved only by a strong national government.
- Shays's Rebellion persuaded many that the United States was on the brink of dangerous disorder.

Key Terms, People, and Places

confederation, Articles of Confederation, legislative branch, executive branch, judicial branch, unicameral legislature, bicameral legislature; Nationalists

A testimony to changed attitudes, this bowl made by diehard revolutionary Paul Revere honors a general who crushed a rebellion against increased taxes in 1787.

O n December 23, 1783, a month after watching the British army leave New York forever, George Washington performed perhaps the most remarkable act of his life: he voluntarily gave up power. Having helped Americans achieve their freedom from a king, he did not want to become another ruler over them. In an act of formal resignation that astonished the world, he gave up his commission as commander of the American army.

Washington's resignation highlighted a new dilemma for the American people. Could they enjoy their freedom without the strong, unified, national government symbolized by Washington's leadership? Could they keep their new liberty and maintain order at the same time? In short, what kind of government should a free people have?

Would a dictatorship—the very government Washington was afraid of creating—be able to solve the problems of the United States today more easily than a democracy? Explain.

Government in the Early United States

George Washington had become powerful in large part because a single military authority was needed to win the War for Independence. The Congress that approved the Declaration of Independence in 1776 was nothing more than a loose collection of representatives from thirteen separate states. Almost no one imagined creating a powerful national government. After all, Americans were rebelling against an imperial government that had tried repeatedly to strengthen its power over them.

Instead, many people saw Congress as only a necessary wartime inconvenience. The white men who had a voice in government thought of themselves as citizens of individual states rather than as citizens of a nation. It is significant that in referring to the United States, most Americans in those times wrote "the united States are" rather than "the United States is," as people do today. They believed that the nation as a whole was less important than its thirteen parts. It was not a nation as much as it was a **confederation**—an alliance of states formed to coordinate their defense and their relations with foreign governments.

The Articles of Confederation To govern the United States, the Continental Congress created a set of laws called the **Articles of Confederation.** Although written in 1776, the Articles were not approved until 1781. Under the Articles, the government consisted of a legislature, or group of representatives from the states who gathered

Both the stern general and his officers were overcome by emotion on the day Washington left the army. With his resignation, the nation was left without strong leadership.

to conduct business. The gathering of the legislature was called a Congress. This Continental Congress passed laws and tried to make sure they were enforced. Thus it combined the functions of a **legislative branch**—the part that makes laws—and an **executive branch,** the part that executes or puts into action the laws passed by a legislature. The Articles made no attempt to create a **judicial branch,** the part of government that judges whether laws have been broken; that job was left to the states.

Under the Articles, states could send as many representatives to Congress as they wished. But each state had only one vote in Congress. It took nine votes, not just a simple majority, to pass any measure dealing with money and unanimous approval to amend or change the Articles. Congress also did not have the power to tax—a serious disadvantage that forced the national government to beg funds from the states. Nor did Congress have any coercive power, the power to force the states to do what it wanted.

These and other defects in the Articles made the United States government weak. But that was exactly what most Americans wanted their national government to be. As late as 1783, the author of the Declaration of Independence, Thomas Jefferson, put forth the argument that "the constant session [meeting] of Congress cannot be necessary in time of peace." Congressional representatives, Jefferson stated, should "separate and return to [their] respective states, leaving only a Committee of the states, [and thus] destroy the strange idea of their being a permanent body."

State Constitutions

Far more important than the Articles in the country's early years were the individual state constitutions—the sets of laws that established the governments of the states. Not every state adopted a new constitution during the Revolution, but most did. The most revolutionary was the

Weaknesses in the Articles of Confederation

One vote for each state, regardless of size
Congress powerless to impose and collect taxes or duties
Congress powerless to regulate foreign and interstate commerce
No separate executive to enforce acts of Congress
No national court system to interpret laws
Amendment only with consent of all the states
A 9/13 majority required to pass laws
Articles only a "firm league of friendship"

Interpreting Tables
The weaknesses of the Articles aroused concern both at home and abroad. "All respect for our government is annihilated [destroyed]," Thomas Jefferson reported from France. "The present is justly considered an alarming crisis," added an observer in the states. *Choose one weakness listed in the chart and explain why it would hurt the nation.*

Pennsylvania Constitution of 1776. Under this state constitution, all white men twenty-one or older who paid taxes—not just gentlemen—were allowed to vote. In itself this was a radical innovation.

The writers of the Pennsylvania constitution went still further, however. They took care to make the legislature the most powerful part of the government, because the legislature was the body most directly responsible to the people. The representatives in the legislature were very responsive to the people's wishes, since they stood for election every year. Their terms of office—like those of officers in the executive branch—were limited, so that no one could hold power too long. Furthermore, the representatives served in a **unicameral legislature**—that is, a legislature with just one house, or group of representatives. No other house balanced its power, as is the case in a **bicameral legislature,** a legislature with two houses. Thus the voters of Pennsylvania had great control over their own government. This was a truly radical government structure in a time when most nations were still ruled by kings and queens.

While other state constitutions did not go as far as Pennsylvania's, most made popular sovereignty a central principle of government. The men who wrote these early constitutions believed it was more important to protect the people from their government than it was to protect the government from the people.

Criticism of the New Constitutions

Some Americans did not like either the Articles of Confederation or the new state constitutions. Their numbers increased as the years passed. More and more gentlemen worried that the American Revolution had given too much power to the "people"—in other words, those who were not of their own class. As a general rule, democracy involves more conflict of opinion and apparent disorder than other systems of government, and these critics worried that such freedom was incompatible with an orderly, smoothly functioning society.

They had plenty of disorder to point to. By 1786, three years after Washington's resignation, the nation still owed about $50 million—a huge sum at that time—to foreign countries and to its own citizens for the expenses of the War for Independence. Debt everywhere was such a problem that some state governments were distributing cheap paper money to help their citizens pay off their loans. This was creating economic chaos.

All the states were desperately looking for ways to raise money. States with good seaports heavily taxed goods bound for neighboring states—whose citizens were outraged at the taxes. Land sales also became an issue. In the Treaty of Paris in 1783, the United States had gained political control over the vast area between the Appalachian Mountains and the Mississippi River. The states, disregarding the rights of Native Americans in the territory, quarreled bitterly among themselves over which should be able to profit by the sale of this land.

A considerable number of American gentlemen believed that much of this disorder had arisen because the people had too much power in their state legislatures. As noble as this kind of democracy might be, these critics thought, it was not always the best way to run a government or a society.

The Nationalists Fear That the Government Is Too Weak By the early 1780s, a group of men called **Nationalists** were working to make the national government stronger, so that it could

Are you in debt? Print money to pay your bills. Many states resorted to this tactic during the War for Independence and the years afterward.

counterbalance what they saw as the unpredictable behavior of the states. The Nationalists were former military officers, members of Congress, merchants, planters, and lawyers, and many whose names are now familiar: George Washington, Benjamin Franklin, James Madison, and Alexander Hamilton.

In the 1780s, Nationalists expressed their views about the dangers of a weak national government and too much democracy both in private correspondence and in letters written for publication in newspapers. They pointed out that Congress sometimes did not have enough members in attendance to do anything. They warned that the lack of a national court system and national economic policies would create tension and chaos. They feared that the United States would not command respect from the rest of the world and that Americans would be treated badly abroad.

Most of all, however, they worried that Americans' fondness for challenging authority and for asserting individual rights was getting out of hand. For this reason, the Nationalists called the years from 1781 to 1787 the Critical Period—which they perceived as a time of social disorder and indecision about how to govern the new nation. Fisher Ames of Massachusetts put it this way:

Every man of sense must be convinced that our disturbances have arisen more from the want of [government] power than the abuse of it.

Most Americans did not agree with this view. The new state constitutions and the Articles of Confederation were doing exactly what they were supposed to be doing: keeping government close to the people. So what if government was disorderly? So what if mistakes were made? Better to have mistakes under the government of the people than efficiency under the rule of tyrants. Besides, Congress under the Articles had won the War for Independence and worked out a treaty with Great Britain. Those were no small accomplishments.

The Nationalists Argue from History
Because the Nationalists, a relatively small

Though the Revolution was over, many Americans were still challenging authority. In this engraving, a crowd puts an end to a county meeting by throwing a government official into a brook.

group, were generally successful men with a standing in society that they wanted to protect, some historians have concluded that they were essentially looking after their own interests when they called for a stronger national government. To a certain extent, that is exactly what they were doing. But they were also well educated in European history. They knew that nearly every European nation of any size that had tried a republican government—a government of the people—had failed, ending in chaos and then tyranny. This had happened to the Roman Republic, over 1800 years before their time; it might, the Nationalists reasoned, happen to the United States as well. They believed history had demonstrated that people were not naturally wise enough to have so much power over their own affairs. Concluded George Washington as he surveyed what he considered the disorder of the times: "We have . . . had too good an opinion of human nature in forming our confederation."

The Nationalists See America as a Model
Finally, the Nationalists agreed with Thomas Paine that America was a model for the world. It would be irresponsible, they believed, to allow the nation to fall into disagreement and

Viewpoints
On the United States as an Independent Nation

Long before the Critical Period, the question of the United States' future was debated on both sides of the Atlantic. **What major concern is expressed in the British viewpoint below?**

European Opinion

"I [see] *insurmountable causes for weakness that will prevent America from being a powerful state.* . . . In short, such is the difference of character, manners, religion and interest of the different colonies that if they were left to themselves, there would soon be a civil war from one end of the continent to another."

Andrew Burnaby, British clergyman, in *Burnaby's Travels Through North America*, 1775

Colonial Opinion

"*Let us view* [America] *as it now is*—AN INDEPENDENT STATE *that has taken an equal station amid the nations of the earth.* . . . *It is a vitality* [living thing] *liable, indeed, to many disorders, many dangerous diseases; but it is young and strong, and will struggle* . . . *against those evils and surmount them.* . . . *Its strength will grow with its years.*"

Thomas Pownall, former governor of Massachusetts, in *A Memorial Most Humbly Addressed to the Sovereigns of Europe on the Present State of Affairs, Between the Old and the New World*, 1780

violence. If they did, wrote Englishman Richard Price in 1785,

> the fairest experiment ever tried in human affairs will miscarry; and . . . a REVOLUTION which had revived the hopes of good men and promised an opening to better times, will become a discouragement to all future efforts in favor of liberty, and prove only an opening to a new scene of human degeneracy and misery.

Indeed, as you have seen, it was Washington's profound understanding of history and his regard for this greater cause that led him to give up his command to civilian authorities so promptly. He did not want to play the role of Julius Caesar of ancient Rome—a general who became a symbol of tyranny by replacing a republican government with a dictatorship.

Shays's Rebellion

In 1786, Nationalists managed to arrange a meeting of the representatives of the states in Annapolis, Maryland, to discuss the economic problems caused by the Articles of Confederation. But only twelve delegates from five states attended. There simply was not much interest in revising the Articles. All that the Nationalist leaders could obtain was a promise to try again. They called for another meeting in Philadelphia in the summer of 1787.

Between the time of the convention in Annapolis and that in Philadelphia, dramatic changes occurred—including the outbreak of armed rebellion in Massachusetts. The uprising became known as Shays's Rebellion after its leader, Captain Daniel Shays, a veteran of the War for Independence.

The Causes of the Rebellion At its root, Shays's Rebellion was a struggle over debts and taxes. In the 1780s, Massachusetts was in a serious economic depression, yet it owed money both to private lenders and to the national government for the expenses of the War for Independence. In 1786 the legislature voted the heaviest direct tax in the history of Massachusetts to that time. Furthermore, the legislature decreed that the tax had to be paid in specie, or gold or silver coin, which was scarce, rather than in paper money. In taxing their citizens so heavily, public officials were driven by a desire to honor the state's debts and by pressure from merchants to whom much of the money was owed.

Already suffering hard times, citizens now had to come up with specie to pay heavy taxes. Many refused to do so, and the rebellion was under way. Throughout rural areas of Massachusetts, but especially in the west, citizens drove off tax collectors and protested the new taxes with petitions and public meetings. When the courts rejected their petitions, the rebels closed them down. Crowds of protesters reacted violently when the state legislature refused to repeal the taxes.

Historians argue about exactly who supported the rebellion. In fact, people often chose sides for purely personal or local reasons. Still, it is safe to say that in Shays's Rebellion many citizens were reacting violently to the direct interference of merchants and politicians in their lives. They were very mindful that part of the reason they had fought the American Revolution was to keep a distant government from imposing taxes after an expensive war. Unlike the government and the merchants they fought, they believed that the growth of state power was a bad development.

The Aftermath of the Rebellion Even in this case of open rebellion, Congress could only look on helplessly, unable to provide any assistance. It had no money to raise an army and no way to force the states to give it money. Finally the government of Massachusetts managed to gather an army and send it to the western part of the state, where it dispersed the rebels in January 1787. The unrest soon quieted down. Many rebels and their families left Massachusetts for Vermont, New York, or Ohio.

The significance of Shays's Rebellion lived on, however. This significance was twofold. From the perspective of the rebels, the rebellion demonstrated a continuing commitment to defy the authority of any government when that government acted against the people's wishes. From the perspective of the Nationalists, Shays's Rebellion was an example of the kind of civil unrest that was coming if they did not act soon. It confirmed their worst fears that Americans would sacrifice social order for individual liberty. A Pennsylvania doctor, Benjamin Rush, wrote after Shays's Rebellion:

Liberty and order clashed in Shays's Rebellion, as protesters—shown here blocking a courthouse—refused to pay taxes, and the government insisted that laws be obeyed.

T*he same enthusiasm now pervades all classes in favor of government that actuated us* [put us in action] *in favor of liberty in the years 1774 and 1775.*

The rebellion did indeed convince many well-educated and prominent Americans that they had to act. In May 1787, delegates began to arrive in Philadelphia—in a trickle at first, but after a week or so in sufficient number to begin the business at hand. In the words of one key participant, James Madison, that business was to "decide forever the fate of republican government."

SECTION 3 REVIEW

Key Terms, People, and Places
1. Define (a) confederation, (b) Articles of Confederation, (c) legislative branch, (d) executive branch, (e) judicial branch, (f) unicameral legislature, (g) bicameral legislature.
2. Identify Nationalists.

Key Concepts
3. What were three weaknesses of the Articles of Confederation?

4. Why did the Nationalists call the years between 1781 and 1787 the Critical Period?
5. What is the twofold significance of Shays's Rebellion?

Critical Thinking
6. **Checking Consistency** Why did the Nationalists believe that disorder during Shays's Rebellion was not justified, although disorder was justified during the American Revolution?

The Constitutional Convention

SECTION PREVIEW

During the summer of 1787, delegates fashioned a Constitution that forever sealed the people's right to direct their government.

Key Concepts

- James Madison was a central figure in the gathering of Nationalists at the Constitutional Convention in Philadelphia.
- A key question in the debate about the new government was whether each state would have equal representation in the legislature or whether larger states would have more power than smaller states.
- The founders of the Constitution blended popular sovereignty with restrictions that limited the power of the people.

Key Terms, People, and Places

Virginia Plan, veto, New Jersey Plan, Great Compromise, Three-fifths Compromise, separation of powers, system of checks and balances, Electoral College; James Madison

During the Constitutional Convention, Benjamin Franklin often wondered if the decoration on the chair in which Washington sat represented a sunset or a sunrise—and whether the convention would be an end or a new beginning for the United States.

T he delegates to the convention in the summer of 1787—that is, most of them—did not leave Philadelphia until they had written a new set of rules by which the nation was to be governed, rules which today Americans refer to simply as the Constitution. It begins with this Preamble:

W e the People of the United States, in Order to form a more perfect Union, establish Justice, insure domestic Tranquility, provide for the common defence, promote the general Welfare, and secure the Blessings of Liberty to ourselves and our Posterity, do ordain and establish this Constitution for the United States of America.

Over the years, Americans have come to see the first three words of the Constitution, "We the People," as the most important. Everything else in the document follows from the basic assumption that in the United States the people will govern themselves.

The men who wrote the Constitution, however, were not as interested in protecting popular sovereignty as they were in restraining it. Notice that among their purposes they listed forming "a more perfect union," because the union of states was far from perfect. They wanted to "insure domestic tranquility," or peace within the nation, because Shays's Rebellion had shown how weak the safeguards of tranquility were. Finally, they wanted "to secure the blessings of liberty" for themselves and for those who would come after them, because they were afraid they might lose their liberty if chaos broke out.

The Constitutional Convention was by no means a gathering to make the final refinement of a successful government; instead it was a rescue mission for one that might well be failing. According to the most influential member of the convention, **James Madison,** the idea was to find a way to "at once support . . . the national authority, and leave in force the local authorities" only to the extent that the local authorities could be useful without interfering with the national government.

AMERICAN PROFILES
James Madison

Madison, like many of the fifty-five men who attended the convention in Philadelphia during the summer of 1787, was a relatively young man. He was only thirty-seven; half of the delegates were over forty-two. Aside from being gentlemen of about the same age, the delegates had little in common. They were from a wide variety of backgrounds. A few were very rich, but some had no more than a comfortable living. Many were well educated and familiar with the theories of European political thinkers. Few, however, had spent as much time on the specifics of a possible government as had Madison. In his home at the foot of the Blue Ridge Mountains he spent evening after evening poring over books of history, government, and law. By the time of the convention, Madison had already invested a year of thought in the form of new government.

James Madison (above) looked like a boy even at age thirty-seven. The Nationalist Fisher Ames described him as "little and ordinary," but added, "his language is very pure . . . and to the point."

The "Father of the Constitution," as Madison came to be called, grew up on a plantation in Orange County, Virginia, where he studied European political thought under a Scottish tutor. Although Madison was an unassuming man, he always retained something of an intellectual edge over his peers due to natural inclination and his intensive training.

Madison's studies of philosophy had led him to believe that people are naturally selfish creatures driven by powerful emotions and personal interests. That did not mean there was no hope for order in society, however. European theorists had argued that through proper government, humans could take control of themselves and their world and improve the condition of both. Constitutions established political structures that encouraged the best in people while restraining their worst tendencies. A dream of devising just such a constitution was exactly what would bring James Madison to the Philadelphia Convention.

Even after he entered public life, Madison was never comfortable with crowds and their politics. He did not marry until he was forty-three, but when he did he found a good match in the lively and cheerful Dolley Todd, a twenty-six-year-old widow. They were happily married for forty-two years.

Supporting his life of productive leisure and domestic happiness, however, were several dozen enslaved people. Madison, like many of the Framers of the Constitution who owned slaves, considered slavery immoral. And like them, he was unable to bring himself to do anything about this contradiction. Madison knew that if he had been born a slave, he could not have become a successful public man. He would not have had the opportunity to accomplish what he did in the Virginia legislature and at the Continental Congress, or at the convention itself.

Madison made it his business to attend every meeting of the convention. During these sessions, he could be seen busily taking the notes that later would become our best record of the proceedings. The delegates were intentionally secretive; they allowed no reporters to attend and kept silent when questioned by outsiders. They even posted sentries to keep curious onlookers away from the windows of the room where they met. Only in secrecy, they believed, could they speak their minds freely.

Inside that room, the Assembly Room of the Pennsylvania State House (now called Independence Hall), was a colorful and exciting scene. There sat the members of the Convention, representing every state except Rhode Island, which had declined to send delegates. All the summer long, the members came to Philadelphia and went away again; never were the full fifty-five participants present at once. They stayed until family or business called them home—or until the sweltering heat of the city summer, with its smell and its infinite number of flies, drove them away.

Divisions and Compromises at the Convention

The major division at the Constitutional Convention in 1787 was between those who wanted to abandon the Articles of Confederation and those who merely wanted to amend them. Nearly everyone agreed on the need for a stronger national government, but some saw no need to start from scratch. Madison and others who wanted truly significant changes were able to dominate the proceedings by bringing a plan with them. Their **Virginia Plan** became the focus of discussion against which all other ideas were weighed.

The Convention Is Divided The Virginia Plan called for the creation of a bicameral, or two-house, national legislature. Each state would send representatives in proportion to the number of its citizens. A state with a large population would have more representatives in both houses than a state with a small population—and thus have more voting power in the legislature. The proposed government would also have an executive branch and a judicial branch, as well as the right to tax its citizens, thus correcting serious shortcomings of the Articles of Confederation. It would also have the power to **veto**, or overturn, any act of a state legislature—an idea that frightened some because it would give the national government greater power than the states.

Opponents of the Virginia Plan, many of whom were from smaller states, were afraid they would have no power in the new government. So they proposed an alternative, the **New Jersey Plan.** Like the Virginia Plan, this plan would give Congress the power to tax and would create executive and judicial branches. It preserved a feature of the Articles of Confederation that the big states did not like, however: every state would continue to have an equal vote in a unicameral Congress, no matter how large the state population. The New Jersey Plan ensured that the states would remain the most powerful governments in America.

The Convention Compromises On July 2, the convention voted on whether representation in the legislature should be based on population. The vote was split and the convention deadlocked. For a while, matters seemed hopeless. Then, over a period of several days, a solution emerged, one that is now called the **Great Compromise.** The legislative branch would be made up of two houses, as called for in the Virginia Plan. But in one house—the House of Representatives—each state would have a number of representatives that corresponded to the size of its population. In the other house, the Senate, every state would have an equal number of representatives.

An observer noted that the streets outside the Pennsylvania State House during the convention were filled with people of "every rank and condition in life, from the highest to the lowest, male and female, of every age and every color. . . . There seemed to be some of every nation under heaven."

As they signed the Constitution on September 17, 1787, the delegates put an end to the divisions of opinion that had made the work of the convention difficult.

The Great Compromise, approved on July 16, included the answer to another crucial question. How should the enslaved people who were so numerous in the southern states be counted? If they were all included in the count of the general population, the southern states would have great power in the House of Representatives. If they were not counted at all, the southern states would be weak in the House. The delegates adopted a formula that became known as the **Three-fifths Compromise.** Under this plan, all enslaved people would be counted, but then the total would be multiplied by three fifths.

The Three-fifths Compromise did not mean that enslaved African Americans would be allowed to vote, however, or that their interests would be represented in Congress. They, like Native Americans, were excluded from participating in the government, although in this early period some free African Americans in some states could vote.

Although many features of Madison's plan survived these compromises, the delegates never went as far in strengthening the national government as Madison would have liked. For example, they refused to give Congress the right to veto state legislation. So upset with such revisions was Alexander Hamilton, a key Nationalist delegate from New York, that he left the convention. Madison, too, was disappointed, but he stayed in Philadelphia.

MAKING CONNECTIONS

Slavery became an increasingly divisive issue in the United States, eventually becoming one of the causes of the Civil War—a period when the Constitution failed to hold the nation together. What problems do we face today that the Founders were unable to foresee?

The Outlines of the New Government

After further debate over the exact provisions of the Constitution, the convention turned the document over to a Committee on Style on September 9. It then approved the final draft on September 17, 1787. Although the delegates provided a way to change the Constitution,

The American System of Checks and Balances

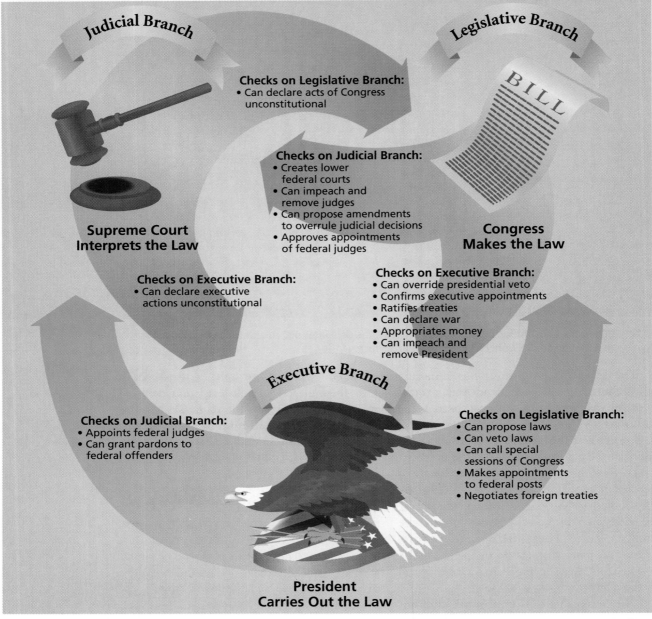

Judicial Branch

Checks on Legislative Branch:
• Can declare acts of Congress unconstitutional

Checks on Judicial Branch:
• Creates lower federal courts
• Can impeach and remove judges
• Can propose amendments to overrule judicial decisions
• Approves appointments of federal judges

Legislative Branch

BILL

Supreme Court Interprets the Law

Congress Makes the Law

Checks on Executive Branch:
• Can declare executive actions unconstitutional

Checks on Executive Branch:
• Can override presidential veto
• Confirms executive appointments
• Ratifies treaties
• Can declare war
• Appropriates money
• Can impeach and remove President

Executive Branch

Checks on Judicial Branch:
• Appoints federal judges
• Can grant pardons to federal offenders

Checks on Legislative Branch:
• Can propose laws
• Can veto laws
• Can call special sessions of Congress
• Makes appointments to federal posts
• Negotiates foreign treaties

President Carries Out the Law

Interpreting Charts
"You must first enable the government to control the governed," wrote Madison, "and in the next place, oblige it to control itself." The control Madison meant is found in the system of checks and balances in the Constitution. *How does the executive branch check the judicial branch?*

which has been amended twenty-seven times, this written plan of government has remained basically the same for over two hundred years.

The delegates created what some began to call a federal government, in which power was shared among state and national authorities.

The Constitution called for a **separation of powers** among the three branches. That is, powers of government at the national level would be divided among legislative, executive, and judicial branches. In addition, each branch would be able to check, or stop, the others in certain ways. For instance, the President, as the head of the executive branch, could veto acts of Congress. This executive power was balanced, however, by Congress's power to overturn the veto with a two-thirds vote of both houses. This government structure is known today as the **system of checks and balances,** illustrated in the chart on page 72.

The New Congress By dividing power between the state and national governments and among the three branches of the national government, the delegates had ingeniously constructed a government that both preserved and limited popular sovereignty. A comparison of the House of Representatives and the Senate further demonstrates their aims.

Because voting in the House of Representatives was based on population, the House was the part of government most directly responsible to the people. Therefore, its members were all to be chosen every two years. If the people wished, they could change the membership of the House quickly.

They could not do the same with the Senate. According to the process outlined in the Constitution (later changed), members of state legislatures would elect senators for six-year terms. Only one third of the Senate would come up for reelection every two years. Thus it was harder for the people to have a direct and sudden impact on the membership of the Senate.

Why did the convention make the Senate more removed from the people? The authors of the Constitution felt that in this way the Senate would be less likely to follow the whims of the crowd. Because no law could be passed unless approved by this more elite body of representatives, the people could not force the passage of bad laws. Furthermore, the writers of the Constitution wanted to make sure that the Senate could be trusted with certain powers, such as giving advice and consent to the President, a responsibility they did not grant to the House of Representatives. They did, however, decide that bills about raising and spending money should be introduced in the House of Representatives alone, because the large states were afraid of losing their influence over money matters.

The House of Representatives and the Senate, when combined as the Congress of the United States, became the most powerful legislative body in the nation. Only the Congress could coin money, deal with other nations, declare war, raise an army, provide for a navy, and regulate commerce. In a sweeping statement now known as the Elastic Clause because it fits so many situations, the Constitution declares that the Congress can

make all Laws which shall be necessary and proper for carrying into Execution the foregoing Powers, and all other Powers vested by this Constitution in the Government of the United States, or in any Department or Officer thereof.
Article 1, Section 8, Clause 18

The President of the United States The Constitution created a strong executive officer, the President of the United States. His term was to be only four years, but he could be reelected as many times as the people wished.

Again, the writers of the Constitution placed a shield between the government and the people by making the election of the President complicated. Voters were to choose electors to do their electing for them. Each state would have as many electoral votes as it had members of Congress. Whoever received the majority of the votes in the meeting of the electors—the **Electoral College**—would become President.

Members of the convention knew that George Washington was likely to be the nation's first President. They believed, however, that it would be difficult for presidential candidates after him to win the required majority—Washington was unique in being popular nationally. Thus the convention provided for the House of Representatives to be the final decision makers. If the Electoral College failed to produce a clear majority for one candidate, the choice would go to the House of Representatives. There each state would have one vote, and the representatives would continue to vote until one of the candidates received a majority.

The Electoral College was a device to allow the people to feel as if they were participating in the choice of their President, while ensuring that

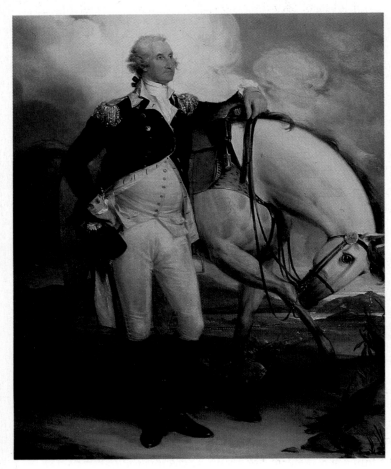

The Framers expected that Washington would be the only future candidate for President who would be nationally known and thus able to be elected by a clear majority of the voters.

tory—in the elections of 1800 and 1824. But in 1787 many assumed that it would happen often.

The Constitution gave the President enormous powers. He was to be commander-in-chief of the armed forces. In the system of checks and balances, he also had the power to veto acts of Congress.

Federal Courts The President, again with the advice and consent of the Senate, would also choose judges for the national court system. These judges would hold office for life, as long as they did not act dishonorably. The choice of judges was one step removed from the people—that is, the President, indirectly chosen by the people, chose the judges. In addition, removing judges was made difficult so that the people could not directly control them. Although the Constitution called for one Supreme Court and several lesser ones, the details were left purposely vague. In later years, Congress developed the court system to fit the nation's needs.

This, then, was the outline of the new government as set forth in the Constitution, completed by the delegates in three months of intense work during the summer of 1787. They agreed to submit their new document to state conventions for approval rather than directly to the people. And they required the approval of only nine of thirteen states to make the Constitution legal. Supporters of the new Constitution knew that winning approval for it would not be easy. The following section tells the story of their struggle to make sure that the document they had crafted in debate and compromise became the law of the land.

electors or members of Congress would make the actual selection. Or so the writers of the Constitution thought. As it turned out, a deadlock of the electors has only occurred twice in American his-

---

SECTION 4 REVIEW

Key Terms, People, and Places
1. Define (a) veto, (b) the Great Compromise, (c) Three-fifths Compromise, (d) system of checks and balances, (e) Electoral College.
2. Identify James Madison.

Key Concepts
3. Describe James Madison's view of government.
4. What were the differences between the Virginia Plan and the New Jersey Plan?

5. How did the authors of the Constitution keep the people from directly electing the President?

Critical Thinking
6. **Testing Conclusions** A commentator in the late 1800s said that in making the Constitution, the Founders built "a machine that would go of itself." Cite some features of the structure of the Constitution that have made it adaptable to the changing needs of the nation.

Identifying Central Issues

Identifying central issues means recognizing the problems at the core of a piece of information. Usually, all the problems a writer discusses are connected in some way with the central issues. Thus it is vital to be able to recognize central issues—and to be able to judge them without being swayed by the way they are expressed.

The excerpt below is part of an article that appeared in a newspaper in Rhode Island, the only state that did not send delegates to the Constitutional Convention. It is a parable—a story in which a lesson is set forth in symbols. In a parable, the symbols are chosen specifically to influence the reader's understanding of the central issues being discussed.

First read the excerpt, and then use the following steps to identify the story's central issues.

1. Identify the subject of the excerpt. Refer to the excerpt to answer these questions. (a) What is the subject of the excerpt? (b) On what date did the parable appear in the newspaper? (c) Given the subject and the date of the excerpt, to what historical period or event do you think the writer of the parable is referring?

2. Examine the excerpt to determine the meaning of its symbols. A symbol is something that stands for or suggests something else. Review the excerpt, and then answer these questions. (a) Who or what do you think the parents and the sons in the parable represent? (b) What historical period or event is represented by the events in the parable that occur between the building of the house and the addition to the house? (c) Who or what do you think the three rooms of the dwelling represent? (d) Who or what do you think the "thirteenth son" represents?

3. Summarize the message or main idea, and identify the central issue of the excerpt. (a) What central issue does the excerpt from a 1787 newspaper article address? (b) Explain how the parable illustrates this point. (c) What point does the parable make about the consequences of failing to participate in a common effort?

Philadelphia, August 25, 1787

The conduct of the United States, with respect to their governments, may be illustrated by the following story:—An old man arrived, after a long and dangerous voyage, upon the coast of America, with a family consisting of a wife, a few choice old servants, and *thirteen* sons. As soon as they landed, they joined and built a large and commodious dwelling-house, where they lived in safety for several years. The sons, however, grew weary of the company of their parents, and each of them built a cabin for himself, at a distance from the family mansion-house. They had not lived long in this way, before they began to suffer many difficulties and wants. . . . At last *twelve* of them met by agreement upon a plain, and agreed to petition their father to be admitted again under his protection. The venerable [honorable] old man opened his doors to them, and they again became members of his family. They first joined in repairing and fortifying the old mansion-house. They, moreover, added *two* more rooms to it, for the separate use of the old man and his wife, in order thereby to preserve their dignity and authority. From this time the whole family became respectable, happy, and prosperous . . . .

The *thirteenth* son, who refused to accompany his brothers to his father's house, after living a miserable life . . . by himself in the woods, was found *hanging* . . . to the limb of a tree near his cabin.

—*Providence Gazette and Country Journal,* Vol. 24 (Saturday, September 8, 1787), p. 2

Making a New Government

SECTION PREVIEW

With political skill and persuasive argument, the Federalists managed to win approval of the Constitution. They then labored to make the United States government as impressive as possible, choosing talented officials and planning an elaborate national capital.

Key Concepts

• The Federalists based their argument in favor of the Constitution on the nation's need for a strong, energetic government. The Anti-Federalists feared strong government under the proposed Constitution more than they feared the direct rule of the people.

• The Bill of Rights was designed to protect Americans against the power of the national government.

• The nation's first Congress and the executive branch under President Washington tried to set an impressive tone for the new government.

Key Terms, People, and Places

ratify, Bill of Rights, cabinet, administration; Federalists, Anti-Federalists, Alexander Hamilton; District of Columbia, Washington

As the debate on the new Constitution spread across the land, its supporters rallied around a new symbol—a ship with full sails, ready to ride the winds of the future.

T oday, many Americans seem to assume that approval of the Constitution was a foregone conclusion. In actuality, the proposed government was highly controversial. Had the Constitution been put to a vote in 1787, it is extremely doubtful that a majority of Americans would have voted for it.

Arguments for and Against the Constitution

Supporters of the Constitution were called **Federalists** because they stood for a strong federal government—a form of government with powers divided between a central government and several regional governments, or states. The Federalists had all been Nationalists, but not all Nationalists were now Federalists. The Federalist leaders included Washington, Madison, and Alexander Hamilton of New York—the man who had left the Convention in disgust, but now had decided to throw his support behind the Constitution. Federalists argued that even if there were problems with the document, it had to be approved.

The Federalist The most influential statement of their reasoning was a series of eighty-five essays now called *The Federalist,* published in a New York City newspaper. The authors were Hamilton, Madison, and John Jay, a Nationalist from New York. The purpose of *The Federalist* essays was simply to convince the members of the New York state convention to agree to the Constitution.

In the essays, Hamilton and Madison explained the need for the Constitution and how the federal government would work. They called for "a republican empire." In the 1700s the word *republican* did not refer to a political party. It referred to a government by the people. Because most previous empires had been governed by lone rulers, an empire governed by the people was a striking idea.

Indeed, because the country was so big, wrote Madison in *The Federalist* Number Ten, no one faction—what is called a "special interest group" today—would be able to control the government. Instead, the United States would referee the conflicts of interest that could not be avoided in a democracy. Madison argued that the strength of the federal system was not in preventing regional or economic or religious interests from fighting with each other, but in keeping any one of them from getting the upper hand for long. Without the Constitution, argued the Federalists, the United States would degenerate into anarchy—lack of government—and civil war.

Anti-Federalists: Against the Constitution

By contrast with the Federalists, the opponents of the Constitution, who were called **Anti-Federalists,** were certain that the new government would be the death of American liberty. They had widespread support in the areas that had less commerce, particularly the lands distant from the Atlantic Ocean and major rivers. People in these areas had less need for the leadership and laws of a strong national government.

The Anti-Federalists condemned the Constitution as a betrayal of the American Revolution. What was the President but a king? Had people fought and died in the long war against Great Britain to create another government that ruled them from a distance and could tax them and regulate their affairs even more than the British had ever attempted to do?

While the Federalists feared the people more than government, the Anti-Federalists feared government more than the people. Many objected not only to the presidency, but to the new federal court system. They also worried that those governments closest to the people—the local and state governments—would be crushed by this new giant of a federal government.

MAKING CONNECTIONS

Think over what you know about the federal government today. Were the Anti-Federalists right to be afraid that it would gain too much power? If you answered yes, suggest additions to the Constitution to protect the people. If you disagree, give evidence to support your answer.

How the Federalists Won Ratification

Most Americans probably agreed with the Anti-Federalists. But the Federalists had several advantages in their campaign for ratification of the Constitution. First, they played on the feeling of many that the Articles of Confederation needed to be reformed. Second, they made the Anti-Federalists look as if they were merely neg-

United we stand—Divided we fall!

ative critics with no constructive plan of their own to offer. Third, the Federalists were a well-organized national group in regular contact with each other. The Anti-Federalists tended to be men with only local and state power who could not coordinate their activities on the national level. Fourth, the Federalists had George Washington, a national hero who was universally expected to be the first President.

For the Constitution to replace the Articles of Confederation, nine states had to **ratify,** or approve, it. Several states—Delaware, New Jersey, and Connecticut—ratified it quickly. They were relatively small states and their citizens expected advantages in being part of a large federal structure. Georgia, too, approved the Constitution promptly. The Georgians feared a war with Native Americans and wanted a national government to ensure they would have federal help. In Pennsylvania, conservatives had won power and were revising the state constitution of 1776; they readily agreed to the new federal government. These states acted in December 1787 and January 1788. Then Massachusetts narrowly voted to ratify. Maryland and South Carolina soon fell into line. The honor of being the ninth state went to New Hampshire, although the Federalists there had to delay the vote until they had a majority.

Even with the approval of nine states, everyone knew the new nation would not be able to succeed unless the highly populated states of Virginia and New York joined in. Loud debates—and some maneuvering that might not have been entirely honest—produced Federalist victories by slim margins in the voting in both these key

Nine states had to approve the new Constitution before it became law. This cartoon shows the states as pillars, with nine upright and a tenth being raised.

states during the summer of 1788. North Carolina had rejected the Constitution but finally reversed itself and agreed to ratify it in November 1789. In May 1790 Rhode Island similarly reversed an earlier vote of rejection and became the last of the original thirteen states to say yes.

The Bill of Rights

The states did adopt the Constitution—but the voting was close, and they might easily have rejected it. What turned the tide in close states like Massachusetts, Virginia, and New York? While the persuasive skills of men such as Madison and Hamilton had an impact, by far the most important factor was the Federalist offer to add immediately several changes to the Constitution. Congress proposed them in September 1789. And in December 1791 the resulting ten amendments became part of the document. They are known today as the **Bill of Rights.**

The Argument Against the Bill of Rights

Most Federalists saw no need for these amendments. Members of the Constitutional Convention had talked about protecting freedom of speech, the press, and religion. But they decided such provisions were unnecessary, largely because they were establishing a government of, for, and by the people. Under the Constitution, the people and the government were the same. So why did the people need to protect their rights from themselves? Most Americans, however, did not buy this clever argument.

The Argument for the Bill of Rights

To many Americans, the new federal government seemed a potentially tyrannical force in their lives. They wanted protection from it. Thomas Jefferson, who generally approved of the Constitution, urged Madison to agree to explicit protection for freedom of religion and of the press as well as from armies and unjust courts.

The Bill of Rights	
1st Amendment	Guarantees freedom of religion, speech, press, assembly, and petition
2nd Amendment	Guarantees the individual states the right to maintain a militia
3rd Amendment	Restricts the manner in which the federal government may house troops in the homes of citizens
4th Amendment	Protects individuals against unreasonable searches and seizures
5th Amendment	Provides that a person can be tried for a serious federal crime only if he or she has been accused of that crime by a grand jury; protects individuals against self-incrimination and against being tried twice for the same crime; prohibits unfair, arbitrary actions by the federal government; prohibits the federal government from taking private property for public use without paying a fair price for the property taken
6th Amendment	Guarantees persons accused of crime the right to a swift and fair trial
7th Amendment	Guarantees the right to a jury trial in cases of civil suits heard in federal courts
8th Amendment	Protects against cruel and unusual punishment and excessive bail
9th Amendment	Establishes that the people have rights beyond those stated in the Constitution
10th Amendment	Establishes that all powers not guaranteed to the federal government and not prohibited to the states are held by each of the states, or the people of each state

Interpreting Tables
The Bill of Rights was intended to protect Americans from the powerful government the Constitution created. The Third Amendment, for instance, ensured that the government could not put citizens on trial without a jury drawn from the people themselves. *Which amendment protects the people from government interference in their religion?*

A bill of rights is what the people are entitled to against every government on earth . . . and what no government should refuse, or rest on inference [leave unstated].

So strong was the Anti-Federalist demand for a Bill of Rights that Madison and other Federalists gave in to it. In fact, it was this concession of the Federalists—their agreement to amend the Constitution to protect certain basic freedoms—that was the key to their victory. Without the promise of a Bill of Rights, several states probably would not have ratified the Constitution.

The New Government

In the elections that took place in the fall of 1788, most of the people elected to Congress were Federalists. George Washington of Virginia and John Adams of Massachusetts were chosen as President and Vice President. The selection of Washington was unanimous. But the work of strengthening the government had only just begun.

Few groups have ever had grander plans for the United States than the Federalists. Having created a Constitution to secure the republic from too much influence by the people at large, they moved to make their vision of a great "republican empire" come true.

The Leader of the New Republic Washington became President in New York City on April 30, 1789. He was dressed in a brown broadcloth suit made in Hartford, Connecticut, and white silk stockings. A committee of newly elected members of Congress escorted him to Federal Hall. There, on a small porch in front of thousands of people crowding nearby streets and rooftops, he took the oath of office and kissed a Bible. The crowd roared its approval.

In addition to great popularity, Washington also had formidable tasks. The United States had a huge debt, no permanent capital, and no federal officers beyond the elected members of Congress and the President and Vice President. Immediately, Washington began to appoint

officials, including the **cabinet**—the heads of the major departments of the executive branch. For attorney general, he chose Edmund Randolph of Virginia; for secretary of war, the able Henry Knox. The choices to head the state and treasury departments were even more crucial.

Secretary of State Thomas Jefferson Washington chose Thomas Jefferson to be secretary of state—the official who would manage the nation's relations with other countries. Jefferson was not particularly well known in 1789, despite the fact that he had been the principal author of the Declaration of Independence. Jefferson had been the American ambassador to France from 1785 to 1789, in touch with events in the United States only through correspondence with friends like James Madison. He would one day become the third President of the United States.

Jefferson had a passionate commitment to human rights—and yet he owned enslaved people. Jefferson well knew that slavery was wrong. Few white planters wrote more

With enthusiastic hopes for their new government, Americans cheered the inauguration of Washington on April 29, 1789.

The campaign buttons of modern times are the offspring of these buttons commemorating Washington's inauguration.

eloquently about it as a moral evil; and yet he could never bring himself to free more than a few of his enslaved workers. As a planter, his livelihood depended on their labor. He would not discard his prejudices and risk losing the personal independence that slave labor brought him, even for the principle of democratic equality.

Washington chose Jefferson to be secretary of state because he had experience dealing with France, still the closest ally of the new republic. But in the bargain he also got a man who would become one of the President's most ardent critics. While Jefferson approved of the Constitution, he never trusted the new government.

Treasury Secretary Alexander Hamilton

Like Jefferson, Treasury Secretary **Alexander Hamilton** was relatively young (only thirty-four) and intellectually brilliant. Washington entrusted Hamilton with control of the largest department in the government and with responsibility for finding a way to pay off the huge debt the nation still owed from the War for Independence. In contrast to Jefferson, who disliked government and remained idealistic about the people, Hamilton was a practical fellow who believed that governmental power, properly used, could accomplish great things. He had every intention of making his time in the federal government an active one.

Jefferson and Hamilton were on a collision course. But in the first months, even years, of the new government, matters went fairly smoothly. The adoption of the Constitution occurred at the same time as a general recovery from the economic problems brought on by the war. Americans were happy to have the question of their national government resolved. They were eager to move on to other things.

Formalities of the New Government

During the first four years of Washington's **administration,** or term in office, the government was preoccupied with matters both large and small. Washington and his officials were doing things no one else had done before. No one knew exactly what the Supreme Court was supposed to do. No one knew exactly how Congress and the President should deal with each other.

President Washington was doing what he could to make his government impressive. His appearance and personality helped. Washington was tall (more than six feet) and physically imposing, especially on horseback. He was also solemn and reserved, a very private man. The President lived in a formal, if not extravagant, manner, believing that it was necessary to command the respect of the citizens of the United States as well as the rest of the world. Soldiers escorted his carriage, which was pulled by six horses. He and his wife Martha held regular Friday afternoon parties, or levees, to entertain government officials and ambassadors. Every year, government officials celebrated the President's birthday with elaborate ceremonies and pageantry. To many, such parties and ceremonies made Washington seem like a king with a court.

Planning a Capital City

The efforts to make the new government awe inspiring went beyond recruiting talented officials and holding formal ceremonies. The United States needed an impressive capital, too. It got one, as a result of the Residence Act of 1790, which specified that the capital would be a 10-square-mile tract of land on the Potomac River near Washington's home at Mount Vernon, Virginia.

This federally governed area was to be called by the grand name of the **District of Columbia.** (The name **Washington** was not used for the capital city itself until 1799, after President Washington had died.) On Jefferson's recommendation, George Washington appointed an African American mathematician and inventor, Benjamin Banneker, to the commission in charge of surveying the city. Pierre Charles L'Enfant, a French artist and architect who had fought for the United States during the War for Independence, developed the city plan. L'Enfant designed a capital with broad streets, public

Changes to the Capitol

T he Capitol in 1800 was no more than one wing in a muddy wilderness (left). Today, with two wings and a dome, the Capitol dominates the Washington skyline (above). *Describe in your own words the impression the Capitol gives today.*

walks, a mansion for the President, a pedestrian mall, and the Capitol, which would house Congress. Although the federal government moved to the District of Columbia in 1800, it took decades longer to realize the L'Enfant plan in its entirety.

Washington, D.C., with its great boulevards, marble buildings in the Roman style, and public monuments, is the most obvious legacy of the Federalists' grand plans for the United States. They meant to display the power and majesty of their new national government. Washington,

D.C., was the symbol of the strong federal government they had lobbied for throughout the 1780s and outlined in the Constitution of the United States.

Some Americans, however, found the Federalists' interest in ceremony and grandeur disturbing, not to mention expensive. And, as the next chapter discusses, in the 1790s they would unite in growing numbers behind Secretary of State Thomas Jefferson to protect what they believed was the true legacy of the American Revolution—liberty.

SECTION 5 REVIEW

Key Terms, People, and Places
1. Define (a) Federalists, (b) Anti-Federalists, (c) ratify, (d) Bill of Rights, (e) cabinet, (f) administration.
2. Identify Alexander Hamilton.
3. Identify (a) District of Columbia, (b) Washington.

Key Concepts
4. Explain why Anti-Federalists objected to the Constitution.
5. Why did Federalists think the Bill of Rights was

unnecessary?
6. Why did Washington promote formality in his administration?

Critical Thinking
7. **Formulating Questions** If you had been trying to decide whether to ratify the Constitution, what questions would you have asked the Federalists? Explain how the questions you suggest reveal your view of government.

Chapter Review

Key Terms
1. American Revolution
2. War for Independence
3. depression
4. boycott
5. Declaration of Independence
6. popular sovereignty
7. Treaty of Paris
8. inflation
9. confederation
10. Articles of Confederation
11. legislative branch
12. executive branch
13. judicial branch
14. unicameral legislature
15. bicameral legislature
16. Virginia Plan
17. veto
18. New Jersey Plan
19. Great Compromise
20. Three-fifths Compromise
21. separation of powers
22. system of checks and balances
23. Electoral College
24. ratify
25. Bill of Rights
26. cabinet
27. administration

People
28. minuteman
29. George Washington
30. King George III
31. Thomas Paine
32. Thomas Jefferson
33. Patriots
34. Loyalists
35. Tories
36. Marquis de Lafayette
37. Baron von Steuben
38. Nationalists
39. James Madison
40. Federalists
41. Anti-Federalists
42. Alexander Hamilton

Places
43. District of Columbia
44. Washington

Terms For each term above, write a sentence that explains its relation to the War for Independence, the Constitutional Convention of 1787, ratification of the Constitution, or the United States government in its first years.

Word Relationships Three of the terms in each of the following sets of terms are related. Choose the term that does not belong and explain why it does not belong.
1. (a) Declaration of Independence, (b) Treaty of Paris, (c) Bill of Rights, (d) War for Independence
2. (a) minuteman, (b) executive branch, (c) judicial branch, (d) legislative branch
3. (a) Great Compromise, (b) Virginia Plan, (c) confederation, (d) Three-fifths Compromise

Section 1 (pp. 48–54)
1. What policies did the British begin during the 1760s to deal with debts from the French and Indian War?
2. What actions did the colonists take to protest the Stamp Act?
3. What basic principles were defined in the pamphlet *Common Sense* and the Declaration of Independence?

Section 2 (pp. 55–61)
4. What were some of the disadvantages that Americans had to face at the beginning of the Revolution?
5. What did the Battle of Bunker Hill and the attack on Trenton demonstrate about American troops?
6. How did the French help the Americans win the war?
7. What groups were most severely affected by the war?

Section 3 (pp. 62–67)
8. Give evidence to prove that before 1788 the national government was weak while the state governments were powerful.
9. What were the goals of the Nationalists?
10. What effect did Shays's Rebellion have on the 1787 Philadelphia Convention?

Section 4 (pp. 68–74)
11. Describe the kind of constitution that James Madison envisioned when he came to Philadelphia.
12. How was the question of whether larger states would have more power than smaller ones finally resolved?
13. How does the Constitution limit popular sovereignty?

Section 5 (pp. 76–81)
14. Why did the Federalists support the Constitution?
15. Explain the statement: "While the Federalists feared the people more than government, the Anti-Federalists feared government more than the people."

1. **Identifying Assumptions** What did the Three-fifths Compromise suggest about how the Framers of the Constitution viewed enslaved African Americans?
2. **Identifying Central Issues** Imagine that you had been a delegate to the Constitutional Convention. Would you have been a Federalist or an Anti- Federalist? Explain your choice.
3. **Identifying Alternatives** If you were commissioned to design a new United States capital, how would it be similar to or different from L'Enfant's plans for Washington, D.C.? Explain your thinking.

1. **Evaluating Primary Sources** Review the primary source excerpt on page 66. What sentiment is the speaker expressing? How did sentiments such as this help to bring about the Philadelphia Convention?
2. **Understanding the Visuals** Contrast the painting of Washington's resignation on page 63 with the description of Washington's character on page 80. Does the painting support Washington's reputation as a reserved man? Explain your answer.
3. **Writing About the Chapter** The year is 1789. Write a letter to one of the Framers in which you express your opinion on the Constitution. First, create a list of what you see as the positive aspects of the document. Then, list the negative features. Note any suggestions you have for improvements. Next, write a draft of your letter in which you offer your ideas. Revise your letter, making certain that each idea is clearly explained. Proofread your letter and make a final copy.
4. **Using the Graphic Organizer** This graphic organizer uses a tree map to organize information about reasons for the Constitutional Convention. (a) How is the problem of a weak Continental Congress related to Shays's Rebellion? (b) What was the main source of tension between the states? (c) On a separate sheet of paper, create your own tree map about the new government in the first years after the Constitution was written, using this graphic organizer as an example.

Reasons for the Constitutional Convention

Continental Congress Is Weak
- No power to tax despite huge war debt
- No coercive power
- Need nine votes to make a decision rather than a simple majority

Individual States Unable to Work Together to Solve Problems
- States each issue their own paper money
- States tax goods shipped to other states in a desperate attempt to raise money
- States quarrel over who will profit from sale of western land

Nationalists Fear Failure and Disorder
- Warn of dangers of weak government
- Fear that Americans' fondness for challenging authority will get out of hand
- Want the United States to be a model of successful revolution
- See the years 1781–1787 as a "Critical Period" that tests the Revolution's success

Shays's Rebellion Erupts
- Shows that Americans will continue their commitment to defy government
- Fuels fears of growing civil unrest

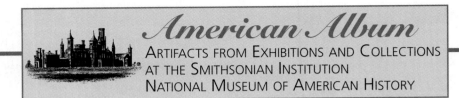

AFTER THE REVOLUTION

Life was not the same for everyone following the Revolution. How people lived their life varied depending on where they lived, their wealth, their ethnic background, their gender, and whether they were free or enslaved. This diversity can be seen in the familiar objects of everyday life. *What do these objects tell you about people's lives?*

◄ LIBERTY JUG
This practical creamware jug celebrates the nation by listing the populations of the new American states.

◄ BLACKSMITH'S ANVIL AND HAMMER
Most everyday objects were handmade by artisans using fairly simple tools, such as an anvil and hammer. A blacksmith heated metal until it was glowing and soft, then shaped it with a hammer on the anvil.

▼ GRAVESTONES These matching stones mark the graves of a husband and wife who were born in Africa. Brought to America to work as slaves, they eventually purchased their own freedom.

◀ GRIDIRON One of the most common household objects, a gridiron was used to broil foods over coals in an open fireplace. Almost all cooking utensils were designed for use in a fireplace.

▶ SAMPLER A sampler recorded the decorative stitches learned by well-off young girls. Poor girls used sewing to earn money for the family.

▲ DAIRYING This engraving titled "Straining and Skimming" shows an idealized view of two women preparing dairy products from whole milk.

◀ FREEDOM SUIT A young man learned a craft by apprenticing to a master craftsman. Because apprentices were bound for years to one master, the new clothes that some received at the end of training were called a "freedom suit."

◀ NATIVE AMERICAN OBJECTS This cradle board and dolls were made by Iroquois people, a group in upstate New York. White settlers overran most of the Iroquois lands shortly after the Revolution.

▶ RESPECT FOR THE LAND This engraving from an 1876 magazine shows the popular link between American liberty and hardworking farmers.

VENERATE THE PLOUGH

From Jefferson Through Jackson
1789–1860

*D*uring the early republic, the nation grew dramatically, and its jostling, young population faced new challenges on every side. In national politics, white men who had a say in government continued to focus on the question of how much power the national government should have. In economic matters, a revolution transformed the way Americans worked, lived, and bought and sold products. Meanwhile, settlers were streaming constantly over the Appalachian Mountains, creating new states in lands that had been home to Native Americans.

Events in the United States

1790s Native Americans form alliances to resist encroachment onto their land.

1801 The House of Representatives elects Thomas Jefferson as the nation's third President.

1810s A Second Great Awakening revives religion in the United States.

1820 The Missouri Compromise forbids slavery in certain areas of the nation.

| 1789 | 1796 | 1803 | 1810 | 1817 |

Events in the World

1791 Haitians revolt against French rule.

1802 Nguyen Anh unites a country in Asia and calls it Vietnam.

1815 Brazil declares its independence.
• Napoleon is defeated at Waterloo.

1824	1831	1838	1845	1852	1859

1828 Andrew Jackson wins the presidency.

1837 The United States government forces the Cherokee to move west.

1840 New England mills produce 323 million yards of cotton cloth.

1850 The population of New York City reaches half a million.

1824 Simón Bolívar becomes emperor of Peru.

1835 English becomes the language of government in India.

1839 The first photographs are taken in France and Britain.

1848 German Karl Marx publishes The Communist Manifesto.

1854 Charles Dickens publishes Hard Times.

The Election of 1800: A Turning Point in History

SECTION PREVIEW

With the election of 1800, American leaders peacefully accomplished the nation's first transfer of power from one party to another.

Key Concepts
- Under the program of Treasury Secretary Alexander Hamilton, the national government won increased support by taking over the debts of the states.
- Spurred on by a fear of war, the Federalists passed laws restricting freedoms—and the Jeffersonians reacted angrily.
- White American men had a choice between liberty and order in 1800, and they exercised it by electing Thomas Jefferson as President.

Key Terms, People, and Places
political party, first American party system, excise, tariff, Whiskey Rebellion, precedent; Jeffersonian Republicans

In 1800, during widespread enthusiasm over a turn away from Federalism and back to the republican principles of 1776, an unknown artist painted Liberty feeding the American eagle.

Today politics in the United States is dominated by two major **political parties.** These are groups actively involved in the political process of the nation, which run candidates for offices in order to establish and control government policies. One party is the Republican party; the other is the Democratic party. The Republican party came into being in the 1850s, but the first form of the Democratic party became active in the United States in the 1790s, when Thomas Jefferson and other critics of George Washington's administration formed an alliance of widely different people to oppose the Federalists. Originally these critics were called Republicans or Democratic Republicans because they stood for a more democratic republic. To avoid confusing them with the modern Republican party, historians call them **Jeffersonian Republicans.** This group, along with the Federalists, formed what today is known as the **first American party system.**

Hamilton Acts to Strengthen the Government

In an effort to expand the role of government under the Constitution, Hamilton won congressional approval for the national government to take on the debts incurred by the states during the War for Independence. This decision may seem strange at first. The United States already had a huge debt of about $50 million. Why would Congress want to add to this burden?

The Reasons Behind Hamilton's Program
The answer is simpler than one might think. Most of the state and national debt was owed to European banks and American merchants and speculators, or people who take a financial risk in the hope of future profit. Hamilton knew that these creditors, or lenders, were interested in keeping alive and well whatever government owed them money. If the individual states owed them money, Hamilton reasoned, they would care about the states. But if the United States government owed them the money, they would be less interested in the individual states and more concerned with the future of the United States as a whole.

Creditors accepted this plan because Hamilton outlined a regular budget and set up a regular payment scheme. Two measures would help to raise money to pay off the debts. In 1791 Congress made whiskey the target of a new **excise,** which is a tax on a product manufactured within a country. Then, in 1792, Congress created a tax on foreign goods imported into the country, a type of tax called a **tariff.** Hamilton put some of this tax money into a special fund used to pay creditors. He did not intend to pay them off right away; if he did, they would have no reason to care what happened to the United States. Instead, the government paid them interest—a percentage of the money they were owed. To handle these complicated financial matters, Congress also established the Bank of the United States in 1791.

Hamilton thus transformed the debts of all American governments into what amounted to a long-term investment in the United States government. The national debt had been a weakness in the 1780s. Now, even though it totaled over $80 million, it had become a source of strength.

Opposition to Hamilton's Plan Many believed the Federalist program, coupled with the elegant style of Washington's presidency, smacked of aristocracy and monarchy, an all-out assault on the hard-won liberty of the American people. Secretary of State Jefferson had fierce arguments with Hamilton over the treasury secretary's plans. At the end of 1793, Jefferson formally resigned. From his home at Monticello, however, he remained involved in politics by corresponding with other critics of the administration.

Resistance to Hamilton's economic program was growing beyond the small group of men active in national politics. As early as 1793, artisans and professional men were forming what were called Democratic Societies to oppose the Federalists. These Jeffersonian or Democratic Republicans included slaveholders, planters, commercial farmers, and people distant from urban areas. They objected to the interference of the national government in local and state affairs. And they disliked taxes.

In western Pennsylvania and other frontier areas, many people took their dislike a step further and refused to pay the excise tax on whiskey. Whiskey was not just a traditional beverage—it was one of the only products farmers could make out of corn that could be transported to market without spoiling. In 1794, farmers who opposed the whiskey tax in western Pennsylvania closed courts and harassed tax collectors. But President Washington and Secretary Hamilton were determined to crush what was called the **Whiskey Rebellion.** In the summer of 1794, they marched 12,000 soldiers across the Appalachian Mountains as a show of force. The rebellion quickly dissolved.

MAKING CONNECTIONS

Contrast the response of the national government during the Whiskey Rebellion with its response during Shays's Rebellion. What accounts for the difference?

Liberty vs. Order

From the very beginning of the United States, international politics intruded on life in the new nation. In 1789 the people of France started a revolution of their own, overthrowing their king and establishing a new government. Frightened that the lower classes in their own nations might also revolt, European governments, led by that of Great Britain, rallied against the French. The French fought back. In 1793 a full-scale war broke out, beginning a series of conflicts called the Wars of the French Revolution, which continued off and on until 1815.

Impact of the French Revolution The issue of the French Revolution sharply divided Americans. Federalists tended to oppose it, seeing it as an example of a democratic revolution gone wrong. The Jeffersonians generally embraced the French Revolution as an extension of the American Revolution. Controversy raged over which side the new nation should support—its old enemy, Britain, or its old ally, France. In 1794 the Federalist government, believing that the long-term interests of the United States would be served better by an alliance with Britain than with France, reached an agreement called the Jay Treaty with Great Britain. Many Americans saw it as a betrayal of revolutionary ideals.

In the midst of this storm of bitter feelings, President Washington chose not to run for a third term. He thus set a **precedent**—a custom followed in later times though not a written law. Washington's precedent was followed until 1940, when President Franklin D. Roosevelt ran for a third term.

Washington's Vice President, John Adams, ran for President against Thomas Jefferson in 1796. Adams gained a majority of electoral votes; Jefferson finished second. In accordance with the election system established by the Constitution, Jefferson became the new Vice President. President Washington left office in a bit of a huff, warning the nation about the dangers of factionalism—the struggle between factions, or parties.

The War Crisis and the Election From the beginning of the Adams administration, the United States began to drift toward war with France. By 1798 France and the United States were involved in what amounted to an undeclared war, firing on and seizing one another's ships on the high seas.

The Federalists took advantage of the war crisis to press even stronger measures through Congress. Among these were an increase in the size of the army, higher taxes to support the army and navy, and the Alien and Sedition Acts of 1798. Under the Alien Act, the President gained the right to imprison or deport citizens of other countries residing in the United States. Under the Sedition Act, persons who wrote, published, or said anything "of a false, scandalous, and malicious" nature against the government of the United States or its agents were subject to heavy fines and imprisonment. The Federalists used the Sedition Act to muzzle their critics.

John Adams (above), an outspoken and decisive Federalist President, was driven out of office after only one term when the Federalists and Jeffersonian Republicans clashed in the election of 1800.

Both Federalists and Jeffersonian Republicans were angry by the late 1790s. Congressmen were physically assaulting each other in the House of Representatives. Crowds taunted President Adams, forcing him to enter the presidential residence in Philadelphia through the back door. In Virginia, Jeffersonians drank a toast calling for "a speedy death to General Washington."

As the presidential election loomed, pitting John Adams against Thomas Jefferson and other candidates, many people believed that the future of the nation was at stake. Would the nation tilt toward what Jefferson called "the Spirit of 1776," the ideal of liberty found in the Declaration of Independence, or toward the Spirit of 1787, the emphasis on order stated in the Constitution?

The Election of 1800

The personal attacks and negative campaigning of elections today are nothing new. The election of 1800 was truly a nasty campaign. When the dust had settled and the balloting was over in December 1800, Jefferson won the popular vote. He was unable to get a majority in the Electoral College, however. Despite the fact that the Jeffersonians had won most of the seats in the new Congress, the old House of Representatives—which was mostly Federalist—had to decide who would be President. Even before the voting began in the House on February 11, 1801, it was clear that no candidate could get a majority immediately. Margaret Bayard Smith, the wife of a newspaper editor, later described both the scene at the Capitol and her own feelings as she awaited the news:

*I*t was an awful crisis. The people, who with such an overwhelming majority had declared their will, would never peaceably have allowed the man of their choice to be set aside. . . . A *civil war must have taken place. . . . Crowds . . . from the adjacent county and cities thronged to the seat of government and hung like a thunder cloud over the Capitol. . . . That night I never lay down or closed my eyes. As the hour drew near its close, my heart would almost audibly beat.*

On February 17, only a few days before the end of Adams's term, the House of Representatives finally elected Jefferson as the third President of the United States on the thirty-sixth ballot. Wrote Margaret Smith: "The dark and threatening cloud which had hung over the political horizon rolled harmlessly away."

New Jersey law allowed women to vote until 1808. During the crucial election of 1800, they helped Jefferson win the state and sent a full slate of Jeffersonian Republicans to Congress. When the election had to be decided in the House of Representatives, New Jersey was one of eight states that stood by Jefferson throughout the balloting.

A Revolution Without Violence

Washington, D.C., in 1801 seemed very much like the Federalists' plans in general: grand and unfinished. The new capital designed by L'Enfant with broad boulevards and Roman buildings was little more than a swamp with muddy, rutted roads and half-completed structures. Here, on March 4, 1801, Thomas Jefferson took the oath of office administered by Adams's appointee, Chief Justice John Marshall.

With this inauguration, the Federalist leaders of the young republic proved that they could do what so many leaders in other times and places have found so difficult. Although few on either side could forget their bitter disagreements and personal hatreds, the Federalists did step down and let the Jeffersonian Republicans take over. Whether they stood for the Spirit of 1776 or the Spirit of 1787, Americans had proved that they could transfer power from one party to another—and do it peacefully.

SECTION 1 REVIEW

Key Terms, People, and Places
1. Define (a) political party, (b) first American party system, (c) excise, (d) tariff, (e) Whiskey Rebellion, (f) precedent.
2. Identify Jeffersonian Republicans.

Key Concepts
3. What was the major goal of Hamilton's financial program?
4. Why did the Federalists pass the Alien and Sedition Acts, and what did they use the Sedition Act for?
5. Why was the election of 1800 a turning point in the history of the United States?

Critical Thinking
6. **Recognizing Ideologies** How does the Sedition Act reflect the Federalists' position in the controversy between those who favored liberty and those who favored order?

The Lasting Impact of the Election of 1800

The real winner of the election of 1800 was the Constitution of the United States, simply because it survived. As late as February 16, several representatives were heard to proclaim they would "go without a constitution and take the risk of civil war" rather than vote for "such a wretch as Jefferson." In the end, however, Americans accepted Jefferson's political victory and the changes it brought to their national government. In doing so, they established the peaceful exchange of power that we take for granted today.

Trimming Federal Power

Jefferson considered the election of 1800 to be more than just a peaceful transfer of power. He called it "as real a revolution in the principles of our government as that of 1776 was in its form." As President, Jefferson hoped to establish

a wise and frugal [minimal] *Government, which shall restrain men from injuring one another, shall leave them otherwise free to regulate their own pursuits of industry and improvement, and shall not take from the mouth of labor the bread it has earned.*

The Jeffersonians did reverse much of what the Federalists had done. They reduced taxes and severely cut the size of the federal bureaucracy and the armed forces.

Even if he had wanted to, however, Jefferson could not have destroyed the work of the Federalists completely. He let the Bank of the United States that Hamilton had created continue to function, knowing that its twenty-year term would run out in 1811. And Jefferson was unable to reduce the power of the judicial branch of the government, which he believed was a stronghold of Federalist attitudes. In

1800 Despite Federalists' fears, "Mad Tom" Jefferson does not pull down the federal government, as this cartoon predicts.

1880s–1890s Candidates for President continue to broaden their appeal to the people.

1800	1840	1880

1824 A smooth transfer of power occurs even though the House of Representatives elects John Quincy Adams as President in defiance of the popular vote for Andrew Jackson.

fact, in a clever decision in the case of *Marbury* v. *Madison,* Chief Justice John Marshall was able actually to increase the strength of the courts by establishing the power of judicial review. This power enables federal courts to review laws and if necessary declare them unconstitutional.

Continuing Federal Power

Despite some success in cutting the government, foreign policy forced Jefferson to apply federal power more than he wished to. When Europeans went back to war in 1805, French warships began harassing American ships trading with Britain, and British ships interfered with American ships trading with France. Jefferson, like other Americans, was outraged by these acts and believed that they should be punished. At his insistence, Congress passed the Embargo Act of 1807, halting all commerce with Europeans. Refusing to use military force—both on principle and because the United States had no real navy—Jefferson instead tried economic pressure to force both the British and the French to back off.

Many Americans hated the embargo—particularly New Englanders who made their living through trade. They now smuggled goods to Great Britain and other countries in defiance of the President and Congress. With the authority of the national government at stake, Jefferson had no alternative but to use his gunboat navy and federal agents to enforce the law. Jefferson's popularity evaporated as the hated embargo dragged on into 1808.

A Political Revolution

Ironically, the unpopularity of the embargo merely reinforced the central policy of Thomas Jefferson's presidency: that government should not interfere in the lives of citizens. In spite of the embargo, Jefferson left behind a relatively weak national government. Not until the federal government boosted its power during the Civil War (1861–1865) would the United States reject Jefferson's model of a frugal government. And even today, Americans who sympathize with Jefferson's beliefs continue their campaign for reduced federal power. The election of 1800 was indeed a political revolution with lasting impact.

REVIEWING THE FACTS

1. What was the "real winner" of the election of 1800?
2. How did the failure of the Federalists influence later politics?

Critical Thinking

3. **Distinguishing Fact from Opinion** When Jefferson called the election of 1800 a revolution, was he stating a fact or voicing an opinion? Explain your reasoning.

1941 Demonstrating continued national unity despite party differences, Congress approves President Roosevelt's call for a declaration of war.

1920   **1960**   **2000**

1992 The forty-second change of Presidents follows the pattern for a smooth transition set after the election of 1800.

Life in the New Nation

SECTION PREVIEW

During the first part of the 1800s, Americans pushed westward, and they knit the land together in a network of refreshed religion, new communication, and commerce fueled by bold inventions.

Key Concepts

- Americans settled and transformed the trans-Appalachian region of the United States with unprecedented speed and thoroughness.
- Inventions such as the cotton gin and improvements in transportation allowed rapid economic development, while a revolution in communication changed the social and political life of the new nation.
- A new awakening of religious life encouraged the participation of all—men and women, rich and poor, and people of all races. Thus, religion became more democratic.

Key Terms, People, and Places

Northwest Territory, black codes, Missouri Compromise, Industrial Revolution, Second Great Awakening, evangelical movement; Andrew Jackson, Eli Whitney

The main reason that the United States grew explosively during its early years was that Americans had so many babies. One of them lay in this cradle about 1800.

Tens of thousands of people migrated west of the Appalachian Mountains in search of better living conditions. Others came up with inventions that dramatically improved production, transportation, and communication. Still others focused on improving their spiritual life by bringing a new democratic liveliness to religion. But alongside this booming expansion and change there remained the continued enslavement of African Americans and the ongoing devastation of Native Americans.

The Settlement of Trans-Appalachia

The population of the United States grew explosively during the period before 1830, as the graph on page 95 shows. About 2.7 million people lived in the original thirteen states in 1780. By 1830 there were 12 million people in 24 states. During the 1780s, the population increased by more than 40 percent, the greatest increase by percentage in the country's history. The number of Americans was roughly doubling about every twenty years.

Starting in the 1770s, Americans of both European and African descent migrated over the Appalachians into the Ohio, Mississippi, Tennessee, and Cumberland river valleys. In a matter of years, cities developed at key points such as Cincinnati, St. Louis, Memphis, and Chicago. Territories became states, and farms and plantations appeared in place of forests and meadows. As Morris Birkbeck, a traveler who described his journey over the Appalachians, wrote in the spring of 1817:

O*ld America seems to be breaking up, and moving westward. We are seldom out of sight, as we travel on this grand track towards the Ohio, of family groups behind, and before us, some with a view to a particular spot, close to a brother perhaps, or a friend who has gone before, and reported well of the country.*

W**hile Jeffersonians and Federalists debated the proper role of the national government, ordinary Americans were rapidly developing the new nation.**

In 1787, when the United States Constitution was being written, only a few hundred Europeans were living north of the Ohio River. By 1830 there were hundreds of thousands of Americans of European and African descent living in the three states and two territories in the region.

National Policy and the West

In the late 1700s, the United States government had tried to influence the nature of western expansion. The Land Ordinance of 1785 provided for the regular survey and sale of Native American land northwest of the Ohio River, called the **Northwest Territory,** or the Old Northwest, to distinguish it from the present-day Northwest. The Northwest Ordinance of 1787 established a process by which territories, as lands in the West were called, could become states.

Under President Jefferson, the national government continued to play a key role in the development of the trans-Appalachian west. More dramatic was the Louisiana Purchase of 1803. Although he had doubts about whether the Constitution permitted him to do so, Jefferson accepted when French emperor Napoleon Bonaparte offered to sell France's claim to a vast area of Native American land (see the map on page 885). The purchase nearly doubled the size of the United States. But its most immediate impact was to give American settlers unrestricted access to both the most important waterway in the center of North America—the Mississippi River—and the most important city, New Orleans.

MAKING CONNECTIONS

The migration into the trans-Appalachian region has been called a repopulation or resettlement. Why?

The War of 1812

The War of 1812, which Congress declared in June of that year, also had a great impact on trans-Appalachia. The direct cause of the war was the ongoing interference with American shipping by the British navy. Western Ameri-

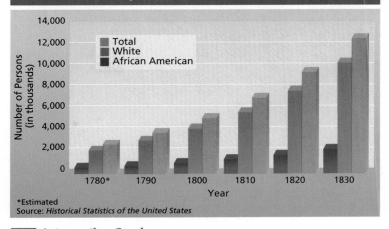

United States Population Growth, 1780–1830

*Estimated
Source: Historical Statistics of the United States

Interpreting Graphs
The census, a national head count taken every ten years, recorded the startling population growth of the United States. *Which group grew more rapidly, white or African American? About how much did the total population increase between 1780 and 1830?*

cans were also irritated by continuing British support of Native American resistance; many dreamed of conquering Canada.

With only a small army and navy, the United States was in no position to challenge Britain, which was then one of the strongest nations in the world. Not surprisingly, things did not go well for the Americans. A planned invasion of Canada from Michigan failed in the summer of 1812. In 1814 a virtually unopposed British army burned most of Washington, D.C., including the Capitol and the White House.

American forces had more success in the western region. In the summer of 1813, Master Commandant Oliver Hazard Perry and a small fleet of ships defeated a British flotilla in the Battle of Lake Erie and gained control of the Great Lakes. In October 1813, William Henry Harrison defeated a combined force of Native Americans and British soldiers at the Battle of the Thames. In Alabama, **Andrew Jackson** won the Battle of Horseshoe Bend in March 1814 against the Creeks and other Native Americans.

The greatest American victory, the Battle of New Orleans, took place in January 1815. Ironically, this occurred after the United States and Great Britain had negotiated the Treaty of Ghent, bringing the War of 1812 to an end. Still, the victory of Jackson's 4,500 volunteers

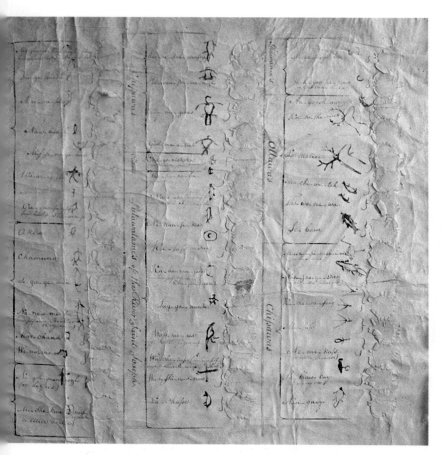

Using Historical Evidence Forced to sign away their rights to Ohio in the Treaty of Greenville (above), Native Americans made their mark beside the English spelling of their names. *What Native American groups are identified in the vertical headings?*

at Miamitown (now Fort Wayne, Indiana) in 1790. Then they overran an expedition commanded by Northwest Territory governor Arthur St. Clair, inflicting one of the biggest defeats ever suffered by a United States army.

The Native American alliance, however, soon was deserted by the British. Worse still, they now faced a tougher foe in General "Mad Anthony" Wayne, who trained and equipped a new national force, the Legion of the United States. In 1794 Wayne led the Legion to victory over the Native Americans at the Battle of Fallen Timbers in what is now northwestern Ohio. As a result of this battle, in the next year the Miami, Delaware, Shawnee, and other Native Americans were forced to accept the Treaty of Greenville, in which they lost the southern two thirds of Ohio. The treaty also compelled them to acknowledge that the Ohio River was no longer a permanent boundary between their lands and lands settled by Americans of European descent.

Many Native Americans resisted European cultural as well as military dominance. A major exception were the Cherokee, who lived in eastern Tennessee, western North Carolina, and northern Georgia. Led by men of mixed Native American and European American heritage, such as John Ross, the Cherokee adopted a policy of accommodation. They devised legal and political systems that blended Cherokee and European traditions and in 1827 declared themselves an independent nation. Many Cherokee adopted the notion of private property and became farmers and artisans.

over 11,000 British regulars greatly boosted American morale. The Battle of New Orleans ended the war on a high note—and made a national hero out of Andrew Jackson.

Native American Resistance

The battles of the Thames and Horseshoe Bend basically brought to an end the Native American resistance to American expansion east of the Mississippi River. These battles formed the final chapter in a long struggle dating back to the early 1790s, when many Miami, Delaware, Shawnee, and others had come together and created a sizeable opposition in this region. Assisted by the British in Canada and led by warriors such as Little Turtle and Blue Jacket, they smashed a United States army

African Americans and Slavery in the Trans-Appalachian West

Not all of the Americans moving west of the Appalachians were of European heritage. One recent historian has estimated that owners forcibly relocated some 98,000 enslaved African Americans from Virginia and Maryland between 1790 and 1810. When the people brought directly from Africa or from the West Indies are added in, some 194,000 African Americans were among the multitudes of people who settled Kentucky, Tennessee, and the Gulf Coast states. Another 144,000 followed between 1810 and 1820.

North of the Ohio River, slavery was technically illegal, in accordance with the Northwest Ordinance of 1787. But laws called **black codes** kept African Americans there under the authority of white Americans. Indentured servitude, too, was used as a means to exploit African American labor without resorting to enslavement.

More powerful than the willingness to exploit African Americans, however, was the prejudice that led new settlers to try to keep African Americans out of their territories and states altogether. Many Americans of European descent living in Ohio, Indiana, and Illinois did not want African Americans in their states, not only because of bias, but because of their fear that African Americans would take up land and take away jobs. As a result, stiff requirements for African American settlers kept the African American population north of the Ohio River very small.

The Missouri Compromise

Americans in the early republic agreed that slavery was legal south of the Ohio River and illegal north of it. But by 1819 the case of Missouri, which did not lie on either side of that river, led to a lengthy debate in Congress.

The issue seemed simple: should Missouri be admitted to the Union as a slave state—a state where slavery was legal? Several members of Congress from the North objected to this. They were not simply concerned about the liberty of African Americans; they also worried that another slave state might increase the power of the southern states in the national government. Members of Congress from the South replied that the national government had no business dictating to states what they could and could not do. They feared that if the United States could forbid slavery in Missouri, it would soon do so elsewhere.

After months of bitter debate, Congress reached what is now called the **Missouri Compromise,**

which was signed into law in 1820. Under the agreement, slavery would be permitted in Missouri; at the same time, Maine was carved out of what had been northern Massachusetts and admitted to the union as a free, or nonslave, state. This arrangement would balance power in the Senate between North and South. Furthermore, Congress agreed that as the United

Hundreds of thousands of enslaved African Americans settled in the West with their owners. This sketch by Louis Miller shows a group on the march from Virginia to Tennessee.

The Missouri Compromise, 1820

OREGON COUNTRY (Occupied by U.S. and Great Britain)

Unorganized Territory

CANADA

MICH. TERR.

MEXICO

36°30' N Missouri Compromise Line

ARK. TERR.

States formed by Missouri Compromise

Free states and territories closed to slavery

Slave states and territories open to slavery

ME VT NH NY MA RI CT PA NJ DE MD IL IN OH VA MO KY NC TN SC ATLANTIC OCEAN GA AL MS LA FLA. TERR.

PACIFIC OCEAN

0 150 300 Miles

0 150 300 Kilometers

Geography and History: Interpreting Maps
Under the terms of the Missouri Compromise, a new free state, Maine, was carved out of Massachusetts to balance the new slave state, Missouri. Congress also agreed that in the future, only states south of 36° 30' N latitude would be slave states. Southerners figured that cotton would not grow north of this line. *Which would cover more land under the compromise, the new free states or the new slave states?*

States expanded westward, states north of 36° 30' N latitude would be free states, and states south of that line would be slave states, as the map on page 97 shows.

Improvements of All Kinds

While many Americans were conquering and developing the West, others were finding ways to conquer distances and save time. Many of their inventions stemmed from a development in Great Britain known as the **Industrial Revolution.** This revolution was a major change in the economy due to the increased use of machines powered by sources other than humans or animals. The British jealously guarded this new technology, making it against the law for anyone knowledgeable in the design of industrial machines to emigrate to another country.

Textile Improvements In 1789, however, an English textile worker named Samuel Slater defied British law and brought the Industrial Revolution to the United States. Working from memory, he duplicated British machinery that quickly and efficiently spun cotton fibers into thread. Slater's water-powered spinning mill at Pawtucket, Rhode Island, was only the first of many. Throughout the 1790s and into the 1800s, New Englanders were building mills at the many waterfalls of their region.

The boom in milling cotton was fed by another new invention, the cotton gin. Devised by New Englander **Eli Whitney** while visiting a Georgia plantation in 1793, the gin easily separated the seeds from cotton fiber. A worker could clean 1 pound of cotton per day without a gin; with a gin operated by water power, he could clean 1,000 pounds. Profit per pound of cotton skyrocketed, and with it the amount of cotton planted for harvest. The bales of cotton produced in the South rose from 6,000 in 1792 to 146,000 by 1805 and 334,378 by 1820. As profits grew, so did the demand for slave labor. The cotton gin, shown at left, was largely responsible for the continued growth and economic success of the slave labor system. It also fed the southern fever to move to undeveloped lands in the West, where sure wealth was the reward of anyone who put large acreage into producing cotton.

Steam Power The boom in cotton was helped by another innovation, the steamboat—a boat driven by the power of steam produced by burning coal or wood. By the 1820s, dozens of steamboats traveled on American rivers, reducing the costs of transportation and commerce.

People today are so used to rapid travel that they may find it hard to understand the significance of the steamboat. Before this invention, the speed at which humans could travel had not changed much in centuries. In the 1700s it still took as long to travel from Rome to London as it had taken in the time of the Roman Empire. Now the steam engine created a revolution in transportation. Soon it would be adapted for travel on land—by railroads—and for use as a power source in factories and mills.

Canals People were not only overcoming river currents; they were creating their own rivers in the form of canals. If rapids or waterfalls interrupted the easy flow of commerce, or if moving

Planters had been looking for a way to clean the seeds from the short-fiber cotton that grew well in the South, and Eli Whitney's cotton gin filled that need.

5 The **clearer** brushes clean cotton fibers off the cylinder.

2 The **movable bar** forces raw cotton against the grate.

1 The **hopper** holds raw cotton.

6 The **clearer compartment** catches cleaned cotton.

3 The cotton seeds are too large to pass through the **grate.**

4 Teeth on the **cylinder** catch cotton fibers and pull them through the grate. Cotton seeds are left in the hopper.

goods from one river to another was vital, the solution was to build a canal. In the early 1800s, there was a virtual frenzy of canal building, much of it by states, some by private investors.

The most successful of these projects was the Erie Canal, which opened in 1825. Built by the state of New York, this 363-mile ditch linked the Hudson River and Lake Erie. But it affected an even wider area. Farmers in the Great Lakes region could now ship their products to markets as far away as New York City and beyond.

Communications Americans in the early republic also enjoyed improvements in communication. Here the federal government took the lead. There were only 75 post offices in the United States in 1790; by 1830 there were 8,450. Regular mail delivery made communication with distant places more efficient than ever before. It also created a national network of information, since the mail carried newspapers, magazines, and books. Newspapers in themselves made information available to large numbers of people; they were to the early 1800s what television was to the late 1900s. The way Americans experienced their world would never be the same again.

The Democratization of American Religion

In the early 1800s, a new wave of religious revivals called the **Second Great Awakening** swept the United States. Like the First Great Awakening in the 1730s and 1740s, this revival was an **evangelical movement,** stressing preaching instead of rituals, and emphasizing that people could be saved for a happy life after death if they believed in Christ and the Bible. This movement was democratic—its members believed that anyone could participate and experience salvation if he or she chose to do so.

Among the denominations, or religious subgroups, that experienced the most growth during the Second Great Awakening were Baptists, Methodists, and Disciples of Christ. Methodists in particular attracted large numbers of converts in the late 1700s and early 1800s. With a well-developed organization and an insistence on the idea that anyone could achieve salvation, Methodists grew into one of the largest Christian denominations in the United States in the 1800s.

Women and children were the main participants in the religious awakening of the early

Using Historical Evidence Camp meetings were a scene of excitement and energy. *Describe the reactions of the crowd to the speaker at this meeting.*

1800s. Within the new church community, women organized sewing circles and women's auxiliaries, or clubs. They also formed local and regional reform societies to help widows and orphans, to convert people to Christianity, and to improve the living conditions for mothers.

In addition to participating in this enlarged community, women exercised increasing power over the selection of ministers within the churches. The successful minister was generally one who consulted frequently with the women in his congregation. Evangelical religion energized women living in the changing world of the early republic. Through religion, women shared a sense of spiritual equality with men, even if their political power was limited. Religious work gave them wide outlets for their talents, offering them an opportunity to influence the moral development of their communities.

African Americans and Democratic Religion

In the 1700s, Methodist and other evangelical congregations were often multiracial; Americans of both European and African heritage often worshiped God together. Indeed, American Protestantism owes much to African religious traditions, such as the call-and-response, in which the congregation responded as a whole to a statement made by one member.

In many communities of enslaved people, a rich combination of Christian and African spiritual traditions was emerging. Along the coast of South Carolina, enslaved African Americans transformed Christian worship services into a mutual activity of both preachers and congregations. When they incorporated

This lantern lit the way to a meeting at a religous camp during the great reawakening of religious life that took place during the early 1800s.

their own traditional African beliefs, such as the belief in possession by spirits, they gave an entirely new dimension to the worship.

Enslaved people also adopted Christian ideas and stories that condemned their bondage and offered some hope of rescue. African American hymns, or spirituals, became powerful testaments to the confidence of enslaved people that some day, in heaven if not on earth, they would be liberated.

Although some white Methodists and others in the late 1700s did attack slavery, most whites were uncomfortable with multiracial worship, especially as African Americans became more assertive about sharing in democratic liberty. In the North, this tension produced another distinctively American denomination, the African Methodist Episcopal Church (AME).

Like other Americans, great numbers of African Americans turned to evangelical religion because they believed their souls were at risk; their faith was profound and genuine. But Methodism and other Protestant denominations also offered the framework of community and assurance that what mattered in the United States was not wealth or color, but what civil rights leader Martin Luther King, Jr., would later call "the content of one's character."

The democratic power of evangelical Christianity was enormous. This power did not overcome prejudice based on race or establish real equality. Still, revivals reinforced in the field of religion what the American Revolution had begun in the world of politics. Though the United States was far from achieving full social equality and popular sovereignty, there was no getting away from the fact that Americans were defining themselves as a nation in those very terms.

Key Terms, People, and Places
1. Define (a) Northwest Territory, (b) black codes, (c) Missouri Compromise, (d) Industrial Revolution, (e) evangelical movement.
2. Identify (a) Andrew Jackson, (b) Eli Whitney.

Key Concepts
3. What area did Americans settle in the early 1800s?

4. Describe improvements in communication in the new nation.
5. Why was the Second Great Awakening democratic?

Thinking Critically
6. **Making Comparisons** Compare and contrast the First Great Awakening and the Second Great Awakening.

SECTION 3

Changing Households and New Markets

SECTION PREVIEW

In colonial times, people had focused on how to keep their households operating. For many people in the early republic, that focus gave way to a determination to make money—as much and as quickly as possible.

Key Concepts
- During this period, the meaning of work changed. Instead of an activity that kept households running, labor became something to be bought and sold.
- The growing power of banks reflected the increasing importance of credit and money.
- As manufacturing increased, more and more households purchased goods that once had been produced in the household.

Key Terms, People, and Places
Market Revolution, entrepreneur, capitalism, capital, household economy, commodity, centralize

With a growing population, expanding territory, and constantly improving transportation and communication, the United States in the early 1800s was experiencing a vast change and increase in its market for goods. Americans purchased more and more goods, rather than making those goods themselves. And rather than trading one kind of goods for another, Americans used money—both cash and credit—to get what they needed. This change in the way people made, bought, and sold goods is now called the **Market Revolution.**

With enormous enthusiasm, American men during this period began to devote themselves to the business of making money. Everywhere, north and south, they went in pursuit of what they called "the main chance"—their opportunity to strike it rich. Among the most endearingly deceptive of these go-getters was writer Mason Weems.

AMERICAN PROFILES

Mason Weems

Born in Maryland in 1759, Weems was the youngest of nineteen children. He chose the ministry as his career and was ordained an Anglican priest in 1784. For the next several years, he was rector of a parish in Maryland.

In the early 1790s, "Parson" Weems abandoned the ministry and took up printing pamphlets and selling books. He was little more than a peddler until he linked up with the Philadelphia publisher Matthew Carey in 1794. Working as an agent for Carey, Weems traveled as far north as New York and as far south as Georgia.

Weems's big break came with the death of George Washington on December 14, 1799. Smelling the possibility of profits, the parson already had begun a biography of America's most well-known man. Within a month of the President's death, Weems, barely able to restrain himself, wrote to Carey:

I 've got something to whisper in your lug [ear]. *Washington, you know, is gone!*

In the early 1800s the banking industry was a powerful force that helped bring changes to the way things were made and sold. One such change—illustrated on this bank note—was that people began to work for a living outside their homes.

Millions are gaping to read something about him. I am very nearly primed [ready] *for 'em.*

In order to improve his chances of making money, Weems "enlivened" his biography with "interesting and entertaining" anecdotes, or brief, engaging stories. His attitude seems to have been that it mattered little that these anecdotes were not true. The idea was to sell books, and if a writer had to embroider the truth to create sales, well, that was the price of profit.

Mason Weems went from poor peddler to wealthy best-selling author overnight.

The scheme worked. First published in 1800, Weems's *Life and Memorable Actions of Washington* went through twenty-nine printings before the author's death in 1825. The total today is more than eighty. Meanwhile, Weems's anecdotes found their way into other histories. In one of these anecdotes, six-year-old George Washington is accused by his father of damaging a cherry tree.

L*ooking at his father, with the sweet face of youth brightened with the inexpressible charm of all-conquering truth, he bravely cried out, "I can't tell a lie, Pa; you know I can't tell a lie. I did cut it with my hatchet."*

Generations of Americans grew up believing in this story. As far as we know, the incident never happened. But we do know that Weems made a lot of money when he invented it.

The Nature of Work Changes

Mason Weems was a businessman who devoted his life to finding that competitive edge that would bring him a profit. This type of person—known as an **entrepreneur**—was becoming much more common in the United States at that time. An entrepreneur is someone who takes on business risks for the sake of profit. Entrepreneurs thrived in the economic system beginning to flourish during this time. In this system,

known as **capitalism,** manufacturing is controlled by private corporations and by individuals competing for profit. This system takes its name from the term *capital.* **Capital** is a supply of wealth that can be used to produce goods and make money. Capitalism was not new, strictly speaking, but during the early 1800s, it rapidly expanded. And as it did so, the nature of work itself began to change.

The Household Economy Declines In the 1600s and 1700s, the **household economy** had dominated North American life outside the major seaports. In this type of economy, people's business consists of simply keeping their households running. Colonial Americans grew their own food and made their own clothes, soap, and other necessities. Their goal was not to get rich but to have enough property to be able to live comfortably and independently.

To be sure, most Americans in the 1600s and 1700s sold products—from extra crops to eggs to cloth; and many bought items they could not make for themselves, such as books and glass. But such buying and selling did not dominate their lives. Work was something done for and within the household. It was not at that time a **commodity,** something to be bought and sold.

When most Americans work today, they are essentially selling their time and labor. Their employers buy their services. To a great extent, the idea of selling labor in order to earn money dates from the early nineteenth century. As more and more people moved and then moved again, as the United States became a nation of strangers, Americans changed their economic habits. Whether they labored in workshops, mills, or offices, people started to work for a specific number of hours each day and for a specific amount of money.

As time passed, families produced fewer and fewer of the things they needed; instead, they bought those items from stores or other individuals. By 1830, goods such as soap and clothes were commonly made outside the homes where they were used. The people who

Changing the Workplace

When entrepreneurs centralized work during the early 1800s, they drastically changed the way most Americans spent their days. Rather than working at home or on the farm to keep their households running, people increasingly reported to a factory or mill each day where they labored in exchange for a wage.

Today, the workplace for the majority of American workers is neither the factory nor the farm, but the office. A small but increasing number of these office workers, however, are opting to turn back time. Instead of leaving their homes for the workplace each day, they are working for their employers at home—or telecommuting—as part of what some people describe as "a work-at-home revolt." Personal computers, modems, FAX machines, answering machines, and copiers are only some of the high-tech tools that permit workers to perform their jobs from their homes. Today it is estimated that 3 to 6 million people telecommute at least one day a week. That number is expected to increase to some 25 million by the year 2000. *What features of the household economy of the 1700s and the market economy of the 1800s are combined in the new work-at-home jobs?*

made goods—whether in their own homes, in workshops, or in factories—were not the same as the people who used them.

Centralizing Work Making goods in workshops and factories was a logical development of changes in the way things were made. Increasingly entrepreneurs would **centralize** manufacturing by making all tasks involved in producing something happen in one place. Centralizing work dramatically increased production. One centralized industry in New England, the cloth-making mills, produced 4 million yards of cotton cloth in 1817; by 1840 the amount was 323 million yards. Often, however, entrepreneurs hired noncentralized workers—women working at home—to cut and sew the cloth into clothing.

MAKING CONNECTIONS

How would our lives in the United States today be different if households still produced most of what they needed?

Banks Spark Economic Growth

The Market Revolution brought new businesses to the forefront of American life. Banks quickly rose to the top as the most influential of the new organizations, because they provided the credit and the cash necessary for entrepreneurs to buy land or to invest in moneymaking schemes.

The first real banks appeared in the United States in the 1780s and 1790s. By the 1830s, hundreds of them had cropped up. Banks could be found in remote rural areas as well as in the middle of cities. Some Americans favored them because banks meant money, available to borrow. Others saw banks as the source of the problems that came with debt and economic depression.

Banks generally were started by groups of private investors. Although states had to give banks legal standing by issuing each of them a charter, they did not strictly control the banks. As a result, many banks made bad loans—loans to people who could not repay them—and most banks did not have additional money on hand to back up their transactions. Still, as long as they had the confidence of their customers, banks sparked economic growth by putting money into people's pockets.

Money in the early republic was not what it is today. The United States government did not issue paper money. Most people preferred to deal in specie, or coin, mainly of gold or silver. Specie was scarce, however, and difficult to carry around. The most common form of money was bank notes—pieces of paper that banks issued to their customers, who then used the notes to pay for goods and services. Similar to modern-day checks, bank notes were promises to pay specie on demand. The problem with these notes was that their value was unpredictable. Imagine selling something and receiving in payment a $100 check that might really be worth anything from $50 to $200, depending on the time and place you tried to cash it.

Despite the shortcomings of their notes, banks fueled the development of the American economy. They provided the loans that allowed Americans to buy millions of acres of federal land in the West and to invest in various moneymaking schemes. Although people continued to rely on money borrowed from private individuals, they turned increasingly to banks. And banks—because they tended to act together—caused wild economic booms and severe depressions such as the Panic of 1819.

Americans Learn to Buy

As the Market Revolution continued, Americans began to buy more and more goods. In colonial America, only the houses of the wealthiest planters and merchants had been full of goods. But in the 1800s, the relatively simple homes of the 1700s gave way to much more elaborately decorated and furnished homes. In many ways, families were defined more by what they bought than by what they sold.

By the middle of the 1800s, the homes of middle-class Americans were positively cluttered with purchased items. Middle-class families bought reproductions of paintings to hang on their walls; china and silverware to eat with; fine materials and silks to make clothing; and more expensive furniture. Parlors—rooms similar to modern living rooms—became a necessity in every home. Families entertained guests in their parlors, which were filled with knick knacks and furniture, in order to display their good taste and material comfort. When they did not have guests in the house, many people preferred to spend time in their kitchens. How could anyone relax in chilly parlors stuffed with goods?

Some Americans avoided or resisted the Market Revolution. But whether they liked it or not, Americans were affected by a growing acceptance of the idea that making money was a good thing. This straightforward pursuit of capital set Americans of the 1800s apart from their colonial ancestors.

A general commitment to capitalism did not mean economic development was the same everywhere, however. By the 1830s, different sections of the United States were developing in different ways. In particular, the economy and societies of the North and South were growing more and more distinct.

SECTION 3 REVIEW

Key Terms, People, and Places
1. Define (a) Market Revolution, (b) entrepreneur, (c) capitalism, (d) capital, (e) household economy, (f) commodity, (g) centralize.

Key Concepts
2. What was the impact of the Market Revolution on households?

3. What positive effect and what negative effect did banks have on the United States between 1815 and 1845?
4. What changes did increased purchasing of goods bring to American homes?

Critical Thinking
5. **Predicting Consequences** How might bringing workers into one central place affect family life?

Sectional Divisions Arise

SECTION PREVIEW

The North remained largely a land of farmers, now producing cash crops for the city market. In the South, much of the region's wealth was built on a peculiar relationship between capitalists and their workers—slavery.

Key Concepts

- Farmers in the Old Northwest encouraged both the growth of cities and an increasingly complicated system for supplying them with farm goods. In the Northeast, workshops and factories manufactured the goods households were no longer producing.
- Like the North, the South was a dynamic, capitalist society, but its staple crops required little processing or handling before they were shipped directly to markets outside of the South.
- Enslaved people occasionally rebelled as a group, but most resistance consisted of small rebellions in daily relationships.

Key Terms, People, and Places

section, capitalist; Denmark Vesey, Nat Turner; North, Northeast, Old Northwest, South

I n the early 1800s, Americans became more and more aware that their nation was divided into **sections,** regions distinguished from one another by economic and cultural differences. The two main sections during this period were the North and the South.

The Northern Section

The **North** itself was made up of two parts. One was the **Northeast,** composed of New England, New York, New Jersey, and Pennsylvania—an area that had once been the New England and Middle colonies. The other was the region north and west of the Ohio River, called the **Old Northwest** to distinguish it from the Northwest of today. It included land that is now Ohio, Indiana, Illinois, Michigan, Wisconsin, and part of Minnesota.

The Old Northwest Farmers in the Old Northwest produced large quantities of corn, wheat, and other grains for sale as far away as Europe. Mostly they worked with the assistance of family members or young men hired to help out during harvests.

Grains were profitable crops, but they tended to spoil. Farmers had to deliver them to market quickly or turn them into a product that would not go bad. For example, corn could be used to raise pigs. Pigs could then be slaughtered and sold not just for meat, but also for fat—which was used to make soap—and bristles, which were useful in brushes. Similarly, wheat and other crops could be fed to cattle. Farm families also sold wheat, oats, barley, and corn to brewers and distillers, who transformed these crops into beer and whiskey, products that were easy to store and transport.

To process and market farm products, farmers depended on urban centers and specialized personnel, including bankers, operators of slaughterhouses and distilleries, and merchants. From Pennsylvania west into Iowa, small towns dotted the landscape, ringing the central urban areas they supplied, such as Cincinnati, St. Louis, and later Chicago. The reputations of these cities reflected their primary business. Cincinnati, for example, was known as "Porkopolis." Some 162,000 hogs were slaughtered there in 1835.

In the early 1800s, farmers sent flour, meal, pork products, whiskey, and other products by river to New Orleans to be sold in the islands of the Caribbean Sea, the eastern United States, and Europe. The market for these goods

A woman going to work in one of the busy mills of the North carried her noonday meal in this tin and wood lunch pail.

Overhead shaft

Dressers

Looms

Spinning frames

Main shaft

Main drum

Mill wheel

Water flow

Clean, cheap power drove the textile mills of New England. Though at first mill builders relied on a system of huge wooden gears to harness river power, they soon adopted the system of belts shown here. On the first floor, cotton was spun into thread; on the second, thread was woven into cloth; on the third, the cloth was dressed or finished.

driven power looms in Waltham and Lowell, Massachusetts. To operate these mills, they hired young unmarried women from New England farms, promising them a regulated and moral environment as well as a predictable income. The women were generally pleased to be able to earn money to put aside before they married. They made about $3.25 for a seventy-three-hour week in the 1830s; after deducting $1.25 for room and board, the average woman made about $2.00 per week. Part of the reason the mill owners hired women laborers was because they could be persuaded to work for about half the pay that men would have demanded. Women made up the bulk of factory employees until the 1840s, when immigrant Irish men, unable to find better-paying jobs, took their places.

Women millworkers usually lived in boarding houses run by the mill owners. Six days a week, twelve hours a day, from dawn till seven at night, they tended the grinding, clattering machines. In the evening they might attend lectures or classes, or gather in sewing or reading circles. Although the work was boring, the women valued the strong friendships they developed with their co-workers.

expanded even more during the 1820s and 1830s, when canals created an economic lifeline through the Great Lakes to New York City.

The Mills of the Northeast The pork, beef, and beer of the Old Northwest were sold into a market where many people no longer raised their own food. Although most people in the Northeast still lived on farms, many others now worked in the factories supplying the cloth, shoes, and other goods that households had once made for themselves.

After the War of 1812, businessmen in Boston financed huge new mills with water-

Into the Cities The Northeast was full of young people looking for work. Unable to support themselves as farmers in the Northeast, where the population had outgrown the available land, some went west. But thousands went to cities. In 1810 only about 6 percent of Americans lived in cities. By 1840 about 12 percent lived in cities, an increase shown in the graph on page 107.

The largest cities in colonial North America had had no more than 30,000 residents. By contrast, in the early United States, the population of New York City (meaning Manhattan only) increased sharply—from about 33,000 in 1790 to about 124,000 in 1820, and then to about 516,000 by 1850. The population of Boston and Philadelphia also increased, as did that of smaller places such as Baltimore.

Work had changed in the northern cities, and with it an entire way of life. Colonial households had been more than the homes of families; they had also served as schools, hospitals, welfare centers, and support agencies. Many Americans may not realize that the government services of today were first established to help fill the gap left when the household lost importance. As the household economy broke down, people no longer supplied the same care to their families within the home. Men, and women as well in many cases, no longer worked in the household, and older members of the family often lived alone. Thus, the residents of northern cities were largely on their own, without households to support them in times of trouble.

In the cities, the growing number of poor people were concentrated in areas where housing was cheap. The Five Points area in lower Manhattan, for example, was notorious for its run-down buildings divided into apartments by the 1830s. Two decades later, a group of middle-class Methodist women described Five Points as

> *miserable-looking buildings, liquor-stores innumerable, neglected children by scores, playing in rags and dirt, squalid-looking women, brutal men with black eyes and disfigured faces proclaiming drunken brawls and fearful violence.*

Cities were simply unable to handle the tremendous increase in their populations. They lacked sewage systems and reliable supplies of fresh water. Police and fire services were primi-

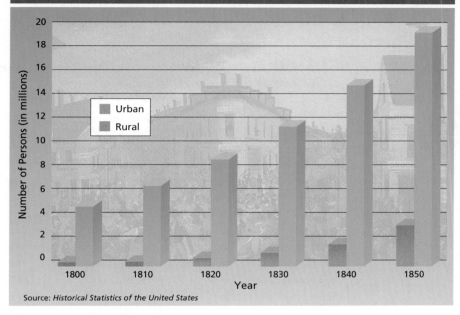

Urban and Rural Populations of the United States, 1800–1850

Source: *Historical Statistics of the United States*

Interpreting Graphs

The scene in the background of this graph is the Five Points area of Manhattan about 1830. *How many Americans lived in cities in 1830? In 1850? What was the increase in urban population during the years 1830 to 1850?*

tive at best. When disease struck, disaster followed. In 1832 and 1833, cholera, an intestinal disease carried by contaminated water, swept along the rivers and canals of the United States, leaving thousands dead or weakened in its wake.

MAKING CONNECTIONS

Were the problems of cities in the early 1800s similar to those of cities today? If so, how?

Owners and Workers Clash

Owners of factories and businessmen in general began to see the relationship between themselves and their employees in strictly economic terms. As **capitalists,** they supplied the capital that built the factory or started the business. They then paid for the labor of the people who worked for them. Beyond that, the employees were on their own. The Lowell mill owners were the exception. Most employers believed that if workers lived in poor housing, had little to eat, or dressed in rags, it was of no concern to the employer. In a society where buying and selling goods and labor determined so much, human welfare mattered little.

Workers had a different viewpoint. Work was no longer a rewarding focus of personal life, as it had been for most colonial Americans. People looked instead for increased wealth to take the place of that reward. And rather than attacking capitalism itself, workers focused on problems that arose in their specific situations, including long hours and low wages. In 1834, for example, one out of every six women in Lowell went on strike when employers announced a 15 percent wage cut in response to poor sales.

Such strikes were the only real weapon workers had. They had become an American tradition as early as the 1700s, when sailors and dockworkers went on strike. Shoemakers also made use of the tactic in the first decade of the 1800s. But between 1834 and 1836, 168 strikes took place in the United States, mainly for shorter hours and higher pay.

In 1834, during this period of intense labor activity, the first national labor organization, the National Trades Union (NTU), was formed. Close to 300,000 people belonged to the NTU and other unions in the 1830s, a large number for that period.

The early flowering of unions was short-lived, however—killed by economic depression and court rulings that outlawed labor organizations. All the same, the stage was set for later labor activity. By the 1840s, the North had a booming and complex economy. It was increasingly a region of cities and towns, banks and factories, a place with growing tensions between middle- and working-class people. More and more, the market linked people together or pushed them apart. The market was redefining northern society.

The Southern Section

Like the North, the South remained overwhelmingly agricultural. The area considered the **South** consisted of what is now Delaware, Maryland, Virginia, West Virginia, North Carolina, South Carolina, Georgia, Kentucky, Tennessee, Alabama, Mississippi, Louisiana, and Arkansas. Its primary products were staple crops such as cotton, tobacco, sugar, and rice. Cotton especially was immensely profitable, by far the most valuable single product of the United States in the 1800s. No wonder southerners commonly remarked, "Cotton is king," and called their section the Cotton Kingdom.

Most of the staple crops of the South did not require the same kind of processing that was needed to transport the grains of the Old Northwest long distances. Properly cared for, cotton and tobacco would not spoil before they reached distant markets in the Northeast and Europe. In 1860 King Cotton made up two thirds of the total value of American exports; tobacco made up one tenth.

A Dynamic Farm Economy The South had an economy not unlike that of a colony. Its residents produced staple crops and raw materials that were processed and sold elsewhere. They did not develop as many towns and industries as did northerners. The region remained one of farms and open countryside. In the mid-1800s, travelers were struck by how empty the region seemed compared to the increasingly crowded and bustling North.

Yet the South had as active an economy as any part of the United States. White southern men saw in cotton what Parson Weems saw in his biography of George Washington—a ticket to wealth. Southern farmers and planters were just as much developers and entrepreneurs as the factory owners and business people of the North.

Southern Cities Although it was not as town-centered as the North, the South did have cities. New Orleans in Louisiana, Charleston in South Carolina, and Richmond in Virginia had many of the same problems that troubled New York City and Boston. Southern cities, however, were fewer in number, smaller in population, and were growing more slowly. They served the needs of plantations.

The southern cities were also home to large numbers of free African Americans. By 1850, of the 3.7 million African Americans in the United States, 12 percent were free. Some lived in the North, but most resided in southern cities or rural areas away from the large plantations. Generally, free African Americans were older and better educated than enslaved African Americans.

Whether in the North or South, free blacks were usually very poor. Excluded from better-paying jobs, they worked as laborers, servants, cooks, laundresses, and barbers. And although they had their freedom, they enjoyed almost none of the privileges of American citizenship. They could not vote or hold office, for example.

The Slavery System

A planter had to have three things in order to profit from growing cotton, tobacco, sugar, and other agricultural products. The first was land—lots of it. The second was relatively easy and inexpensive access to markets. This requirement meant that the most profitable plantations were located along rivers. Finally, white southerners needed labor to grow crops such as cotton. Enslaved African Americans often supplied this labor.

Most white southerners did not own enslaved people. In 1830, slaveholders made up only 36 percent of the white population. All the same, because of their wealth, slaveholders did possess great influence in politics, society, and of course, the economy. And the South would have been very poor without the African American workers who built its economy. They made up more than half of the population of South Carolina and Mississippi in 1860, and two fifths of the population in Florida, Georgia, Alabama, and Louisiana.

Life on Small and Large Farms The life of enslaved Americans varied depending on circumstances. The typical slaveholder owned only a few African Americans. On small farms, enslaved people often worked side by side with their owners and their families. They sometimes ate together and slept in the same house. Close personal relationships sometimes developed; but, just as often, enslaved workers endured all manner of cruelties without a larger community to turn to for support and protection.

Most enslaved Americans, however, did not live on small farms. Because a few white men owned most of the enslaved people of the South, most enslaved African Americans lived on plantations. There they had the benefits of a sizeable community of people, usually including twenty or more African Americans. But plantation life had serious drawbacks in contrast to life on a small farm. Labor could be harsher, for example. Plantation workers frequently toiled in gangs under the supervision of foremen and slave drivers.

For enslaved women in particular, life could be extremely difficult. In addition to bearing and caring for their own children and taking care of their households, they cooked and served food, cleaned houses and clothes, and labored in the fields. Especially hard work was required of them at harvest time in the late summer and fall. In addition to the drudgery of plantation life, they also had to endure rape or the threat of rape by slave owners.

Slavery as an Economic Relationship Whether enslaved people lived closely with their owners or not, their relationship was always affected by the fact that slavery was based on economics. Owners exploited enslaved humans in order to get work done; they saw enslaved people as property that performed labor. In a bill of sale from 1811, an

Using Historical Evidence Five generations of an African American family—all enslaved—posed for this photograph outside their plantation home in 1862. *Describe their living conditions. Could this photograph be used as evidence of conditions during the 1840s? Explain your thinking.*

Viewpoints
On Slavery

Because the economy of the South depended on slave labor, southerners began to defend the institution against a growing antislavery movement. *In the quotations below, how does the viewpoint of the formerly enslaved man conflict with the southerner's viewpoint?*

In Defense of Slavery

"A merrier being does not exist on the face of the globe than the Negro slave of the United States. They are happy and contented, and the master is much less cruel than is generally imagined. Why then . . . should we attempt to disturb his contentment by planting in his mind a vain and indefinite desire for liberty—something which he cannot understand?"

Professor Thomas R. Dew, William and Mary College, address to the Virginia legislature, 1832

In Opposition to Slavery

"I thank God I am not property now, but am regarded as a man like yourself. . . . You may perhaps think hard of us for running away from slavery, but as for myself, I have but one apology to make for it, which is this: I have only to regret that I did not start at an early period."

Henry Bibb, who escaped from slavery with his family, in a letter to his former master, 1844

---

enslaved woman named Eve and her child, at a price of $156.00, are listed between a plow for $1.60 and "Eight Fancy Chairs" for $9.25. Such treatment of humans as property was the essence of slavery.

Or consider the situation of one enslaved man, Moses Grandy. He happened to be standing in the street when he saw his wife go by in a group of enslaved people who had been sold to a slaveholder named Rogerson. Grandy later recalled:

Mr. Rogerson was with them on his horse, armed with pistols. I said to him, "For God's sake, have you bought my wife?" He said he had: when I asked him what she had done, he said she had done nothing, but that her master wanted money. He drew out a pistol and said that if I went near the wagon on which she was, he would shoot me. I asked for leave to

shake hands with her, which he refused, but said I might stand at a distance and talk with her. My heart was so full that I could say very little. . . . I have never seen or heard from her that day to this. I loved her as I love my life.

Enslaved African Americans Resist

Like working-class people in the North, enslaved people in the South fought back on occasion. One open resistance in the early 1820s was led by **Denmark Vesey**, an African American in Charleston, South Carolina. Having bought his freedom with a lottery jackpot, he supported himself as a carpenter. A preacher at the local African Methodist Episcopal Church, Vesey was well read and determined in his principles. He quoted the Declaration of Independence and the Bible in his arguments against slavery. He was impatient with African Americans who would not stand up to whites. According to the report of his conspiracy, when he saw an enslaved person step aside to allow a white man to pass him on the street, Vesey

would rebuke him, and observe that all men were born equal, and that he was surprised that anyone would degrade himself by such conduct; that he would never cringe to the whites, nor ought anyone who had the feelings of a man. When answered, We are slaves, he would sarcastically and indignantly reply, "You deserve to remain slaves."

Vesey and several allies, including the African-born Gullah Jack, planned to take over Charleston in July 1822. About eighty participants were to act in six units arranged by African origins.

But Vesey was betrayed by some of his followers. The governor of South Carolina called out five companies of troops in June, and the rebellion was smashed before it could get started. Before the end of the summer, thirty-five African Americans were hanged, including Vesey, and another thirty-seven were banished from South Carolina.

Nat Turner, a well-educated, thirty-one-year-old African American preacher who believed he acted with divine inspiration, also planned a rebellion. In 1831 he led about seventy enslaved people in southeastern Virginia in an uprising. The rebels killed fifty-five whites. Eventually, local militia captured most of the rebels. The state of Virginia hanged about twenty of them, including Turner. Crowds of frightened and angry whites rioted and slaughtered about a hundred African American bystanders who had no part in the plot.

The aborted Vesey and Turner rebellions led to harsher slave laws. Virginia and North Carolina passed laws against teaching enslaved people to read. Criticizing slavery in speech or writing was forbidden. Whites throughout the South became extremely frightened of possible rebellions. In South Carolina, Edwin C. Holland wrote that enslaved African Americans were

the barbarians who would, IF THEY COULD, become the DESTROYERS of our race.

Yet rebellions of enslaved people in the region were rare. More commonly, enslaved people resisted slavery in less dramatic fashion. Some ran away, though when caught, they might be forcibly returned. Others refused to work at the pace established by their owners, pretending not to hear or understand. Yet another form of resistance was stealing or destroying property.

Though slavery was based on a need for labor, like the relationship between entrepreneurs and workers in the North, it obviously

encouraged different attitudes toward labor. The separation between work and home transforming the North did not occur in the South because most people, enslaved or not, continued to work at or near home. Thus, the Market Revolution took different forms in the North and South. Both regions were active, expanding capitalistic societies. But the North was a world of farms and cities, banks and factories, while the South was a world of farms and plantations producing cotton and other staples. The North adopted new technologies eagerly, the South more slowly. These differences laid the foundation for serious conflict in the 1850s and 1860s.

An eclipse of the sun in 1831, claimed enslaved African American Nat Turner, was a sign that "I should arise and prepare myself, and slay my enemies with their own weapons." This etching depicts his capture.

SECTION 4 REVIEW

Key Terms, People, and Places
1. Define (a) section, (b) capitalist.
2. Identify (a) Denmark Vesey, (b) Nat Turner.
3. Identify (a) North, (b) Northeast, (c) Old Northwest, (d) South.

Key Concepts
4. How did agriculture in the Old Northwest encourage the growth of cities?
5. Explain why, despite the South's use of slave rather than free labor, that region can be considered as capitalist as the North.
6. Describe the most common forms of rebellion among enslaved people.

Critical Thinking
7. **Making Comparisons** You have read that the economy of the South was like that of a colony. Was the economy of the North also like that of a colony? Explain your response.

The Age of Jackson

During his presidency, Andrew Jackson worked to clear a path to success for white men. His time in office was dedicated to that effort, no matter what the cost to his enemies or his victims.

Key Concepts

- National Republicans such as John Quincy Adams and Henry Clay argued that government power should be used to promote economic development. Jacksonian Democrats strongly opposed this role for the national government.
- Despite his opposition to a strong national government, President Andrew Jackson opposed one state's attempt to strike down a federal law.
- Jackson refused to support the Cherokee when the state of Georgia seized their land.

Key Terms, People, and Places

American System, second American party system, secede, Trail of Tears; John C. Calhoun, Henry Clay, National Republicans, Jacksonian Democrats

A new clash between political parties began in the election of 1824. During the campaign, supporters of candidate John Quincy Adams distributed this decorated box.

O n July 4, 1826—the fiftieth anniversary of the Declaration of Independence—Thomas Jefferson and John Adams both died. This remarkable coincidence was just one among many signs that the generation that had brought the United States into being no longer was leading administrations and holding membership in Congress. Two years before, in 1824, James Monroe had ended his second term in office. In 1824, for the first time in the brief history of the nation, none of the presidential candidates could boast of having been a leader during the Revolution.

The Election of 1824

The four main candidates in the election of 1824 were John Quincy Adams of Massachusetts, John C. Calhoun of South Carolina, Henry Clay of Kentucky, and Andrew Jackson of Tennessee.

The Accomplishments of Adams The son of Abigail and John Adams, John Quincy Adams had become a Jeffersonian Republican nearly twenty years earlier when he was a senator. He had made his reputation as a diplomat, a role that suited him. While he was well educated and highly ethical, he was also considered to be cold and formal. While serving as secretary of state under Monroe, he had negotiated the Adams-Onís Treaty of 1819, by which the United States acquired Florida from Spain.

Another legacy of Adams's diplomatic career was the Monroe Doctrine of 1823, which Adams largely wrote. During the 1820s, every Spanish colony in the Western Hemisphere except Cuba and Puerto Rico had won its independence. The Monroe Doctrine warned European governments to stay out of the Americas and allow the new nations to develop on their own.

But neither the government nor the merchants of the United States had any intention of leaving the former Spanish colonies alone. The new countries possessed huge markets that attracted Americans. Moreover, the United States did not have the armed forces necessary to make the Monroe Doctrine anything but a paper declaration of policy. Still, the policy was a bold one for a young nation whose Capitol had been burned to the ground by a foreign army only a decade earlier. And much of the credit went to John Quincy Adams.

Calhoun and Clay: South and West Born in South Carolina, **John C. Calhoun** had served in the United States Congress and as Monroe's secretary of war. A brilliant man, Calhoun had been an early supporter of national economic policies. But in the 1820s, he was beginning to shift toward defending southern sectional interests, which required protection of both slavery and the agricultural exports the slavery system produced, especially cotton. He withdrew from the race when he saw a chance to become Vice President. Besides, another candidate, William H. Crawford of Georgia, was already representing southern interests.

Henry Clay, a former speaker of the House of Representatives and a United States senator from Kentucky, was the most dynamic and colorful politician of his generation. "Harry of the West," as he was called, was a slaveholder and a man of great passions. He wanted to be President, and he was willing to make a political deal if it would improve his chances at a later time.

Jackson's Candidacy Catches Fire Finally, there was the wild card—Andrew Jackson. Jackson had served in the Senate in the 1790s and was a wealthy plantation owner near Nashville, Tennessee. Yet his fame rested not on these eminent positions in government or society, but mainly on military exploits like his victory at New Orleans in 1815. Jackson's iron will and his impulsive, passionate personality made him enormously popular. Those same characteristics also worried many people who saw him as a poorly educated and ill-tempered military chieftain.

As 1824 progressed, Jackson's candidacy caught fire. Like Jefferson, Jackson believed in the common people, whose support he rapidly gained. The general won the majority of the people's votes, but neither he nor any other candidate received a majority of votes in the Electoral College. Thus the House of Representatives had to choose a President from among the top vote-getters. That left Jackson and Adams as the main rivals—and Adams won a majority of votes in the House.

But Jackson and his followers believed that Adams's victory was the result of what they called "a corrupt bargain" with Clay. They charged that Clay, in return for giving Kentucky's votes to Adams, had been given the post of secretary of state. Adams and Clay

Jackson Forever!
The Hero of Two Wars and of Or'eans!
The Man of the People!
HE WHO COULD NOT BARTER NOR BARGAIN FOR THE
PRESIDENCY!
Who, although "*A Military Chieftain,*" valued the purity of Elections and of the Electors, MORE than the Office of PRESIDENT itself! Although the greatest in the gift of his countrymen, and the highest in point of dignity of any in the world,
BECAUSE
It should be derived from the
PEOPLE!
No Gag Laws! No Black Cockades! No Reign of Terror! No Standing Army or Navy Officers, when under the pay of Government, to browbeat, or
KNOCK DOWN
Old Revolutionary Characters, or our Representatives while in the discharge of their duty. To the Polls then, and vote for those who will support
OLD HICKORY
AND THE ELECTORAL LAW.

Using Historical Evidence This poster praises Andrew "Old Hickory" Jackson for honoring the constitutional election system in 1824 even though it cost him the presidency. *How does the poster describe Andrew Jackson?*

both denied the accusation, but a great many Americans believed it.

MAKING CONNECTIONS

In the election of 1824, the candidate chosen by the majority of American voters was denied the presidency. Such a result is still possible today. Do you think the Constitution should be changed so this can no longer happen? Why or why not?

Two New Parties Face Off

While Jackson plotted to get his revenge in the next election, President Adams and Secretary of State Clay tried to establish a federal policy of actively intervening in the economy of the nation. In 1825 Adams said:

> The spirit of improvement is abroad upon the earth. . . . Let us not be unmindful that liberty is power; and that the tenure [holding] of power by man is . . . upon condition that it shall be exercised . . . to improve the condition of himself and his fellowmen.

To Improve the Nation Simply put, Adams believed that the national government should

Second American Party System

National Republicans/Whigs	Jacksonian Democrats
Example: John Quincy Adams	Example: Andrew Jackson
Federal government should take a leadership role	Federal government should remain as inactive as possible
Federal government should support internal improvements, such as roads and bridges	The individual states should be responsible for internal improvements
For national bank	Against national bank
Tended to be middle-class or well-established Protestants	Tended to be ambitious slave-holders, small farmers, non-Protestants, and working class

Interpreting Tables
Both National Republicans and Jacksonian Democrats agreed on the goals of the American system, but disagreed on how to reach those goals. *How did each party want to bring about internal improvements?*

take the lead in developing the economy. The new administration was proposing what Secretary Clay called an **American System.** Under this system, the government would support internal improvements, including roads, canals, bridges, lighthouses, universities, and many other projects. The purpose of the improvements was to encourage the development of American industries. In addition, the government would put a high tariff, or import tax, on goods brought into the United States. This tariff would make foreign goods more expensive and encourage Americans to buy goods manufactured in the United States.

The Election of 1828 Few politicians quarreled with the goal of making American industries stronger. But many believed, as did Andrew Jackson, that the United States government had no business taking such an active role in the economic development of the nation. They argued that Americans wanted the national government to leave them alone, and that society and the economy actually would work better without government interference.

Both Jackson and Adams had once been Jeffersonian Republicans, the party that had quarreled with Federalists, largely over constitutional issues. Now the stupendous changes of the Market Revolution were pushing economic issues to the forefront of the debate, and once again politicians were choosing sides.

The supporters of Adams and Clay began to call themselves **National Republicans.** They believed they were true to the Jeffersonian spirit of improvement. The followers of Jackson called themselves Democrats, a shortened form of Democrat-Republicans, the old name of the Jeffersonian Republicans. Historians often refer to them as **Jacksonian Democrats.** Members of this party believed that they were true to the Jeffersonian commitment to frugal, or minimal, government. This new face-off in politics, in which the National Republicans challenged the Jacksonian Democrats, is now known as the **second American party system.** It is summarized in the table at left.

Some clever state politicians, including New York senator Martin Van Buren, agreed with Jackson's opposition to a powerful national government. They joined together in supporting Jackson when the election of 1828 rolled around. In this election, voters realized that their choice would determine the role the national government would play in their lives. As a result, more than twice as many men voted in 1828 than had voted in 1824, and most of these new voters threw their support to the man of the people, Andrew Jackson. With this sizable following, Jackson trounced Adams.

Federal Policy in the Age of Jackson

Like Jefferson, Andrew Jackson tried not to do much as President. He used his veto power to keep the government as inactive as possible, rejecting more acts of Congress than the six previous Presidents combined. Typical was the Maysville Road Veto of 1830. Congress had voted money to build a road from the Ohio River at Maysville across Kentucky to Lexington, but Jackson vetoed the bill. He did not object to the road; he just thought the state of Kentucky, not the national government, should build it.

Jackson Defends the Spoils System For many years, victorious office seekers had appointed their friends and supporters to public office in their administrations. This practice, known as patronage, became official when

Andrew Jackson took office. He dismissed more than two hundred previous presidential appointees and nearly two thousand other officeholders and replaced them with Jacksonian Democrats.

Patronage under Jackson became known as the spoils system. In this case, the spoils, or booty taken from a conquered enemy, were government jobs for party supporters. Jackson defended the system on the grounds that any intelligent person could perform the duties required and that "rotation in office" would prevent a small group from controlling the government. His support for the spoils system contributed to Jackson's image as the champion of the common man.

The Bank War The defining moment of Jackson's presidency came in 1832. The President had a deep personal hatred of the Bank of the United States. He had lost money to the first bank in the 1790s, and he had never agreed with the establishment of the second bank in 1816. Like many Americans, Jackson believed the Bank of the United States was a "monster" institution. He held it responsible for the Panic of 1819 and the hard times that had followed.

Under law, the Bank of the United States could only operate until 1836, unless Congress

extended the life of the bank by issuing it a new charter. Supporters of the bank, including Senator Henry Clay, Senator Daniel Webster of Massachusetts, and the president of the bank, Nicholas Biddle, decided to recharter it four years early, partly to embarrass Jackson. They expected that he would offend his followers by allowing the bank to continue.

The Bank of the United States already had survived one challenge. In a complicated scheme to hinder the bank, the state of Maryland had tried unsuccessfully to make the bank pay a tax, and then imposed a large penalty when it failed to do so. The national government claimed the fine was illegal, and the dispute reached the Supreme Court in 1819. In *McCulloch* v. *Maryland*, Chief Justice John Marshall went to the heart of the issue by declaring the fine illegal and the bank itself constitutional. The powers of the federal government were greater than those spelled out in the Constitution, Marshall said. He based his argument on Article I, Section 8, which states that Congress has the right "to make all laws necessary and proper" for carrying out the powers granted it under the Constitution. Thus Congress had the power to create such a bank if it wished. Furthermore, Chief Justice Marshall stressed that

Using Historical Evidence In this cartoon, Andrew Jackson drags Henry Clay behind him as he attacks the monster national bank. *How has the artist suggested that the danger is imaginary?*

because the national government had created the bank, no state had the power to tax it. "The power to tax is the power to destroy," he pointed out. No state could destroy by taxes what the federal government under the Constitution had created.

In 1832 the supporters of the Bank of the United States acted without understanding the popularity of the President or the unpopularity of the bank. Jackson vetoed the act of Congress that rechartered the bank, dooming it to close in 1836. The President justified his action as a protection of the rights of ordinary citizens. In a lengthy veto message, he attacked the bank as a tool of greedy aristocrats:

> I t is to be regretted that the rich and powerful too often bend the acts of government to their selfish purposes. Distinctions in society will always exist under every just government . . . but when the laws undertake . . . to make the rich richer and the potent more powerful, the humble members of society—the farmers, mechanics, and laborers—who have neither the time nor the means of securing like favors to themselves, have a right to complain of the injustice of their Government.

The National Republicans thought they could use the issue of Jackson's veto against him in the election of 1832. They changed their name to the Whigs, after the party in the British Parliament that had opposed the king during the 1700s, and ran Henry Clay for President. Criticizing Jackson's veto, however, was a mistaken strategy. As in 1828, Jackson won the election by a huge margin.

The Nullification Crisis

During his second administration, Jackson proved equal to yet another challenge. Supporters of the American System had passed the Tariff of 1828, which put a high tax on imports in order to encourage manufacturing within the United States. Most manufacturers, however, were in the North, and southerners did not like paying higher prices for goods to help northerners make a profit. They called the Tariff of 1828 the Tariff of Abominations, after the term *abomination*

The issue of nullification burst on the national scene in 1830, in a debate on the subject between Massachusetts senator Daniel Webster (standing) and South Carolina senator Robert Hayne (seated, hands before him). Webster rejected nullification, claiming it would make the Constitution "a rope of sand" that would not hold the states together.

used in the Bible for something especially horrible or monstrous. In 1832, after passage of yet another tariff act, South Carolina declared the tariffs "null, void, and no law, nor binding upon this State, its officers or citizens." In doing so, it raised the question of nullification: did a state have the right to nullify, or declare illegal, a law passed by Congress? South Carolina also went further by threatening to **secede,** or withdraw, from the United States if its nullification was not respected.

You might expect that Jackson would be sympathetic to South Carolina. After all, he was a supporter of "negative" government, or using government power to protect the people from the government itself. He had put federal power to work attacking politicians he considered corrupt and laws that he thought would prevent the people from fully enjoying their liberty. Thus he had acted to destroy the Bank of the United States. Furthermore, he understood southern issues; he was a slaveholder himself. Yet South Carolina's nullification outraged him.

Why would a believer in negative government take offense when a state asserted its rights? The explanation of this seeming contradiction is simple. President Jackson believed that in defying the laws of the United States, South Carolina was defying the will of the people. That he would never allow.

At Jackson's urging, Congress passed the Force Bill in 1833, which compelled the state of South Carolina to collect the Tariff Act duties. The President threatened to send 50,000 troops to the defiant state. But Henry Clay engineered a compromise that ended the crisis. Congress reduced some of the import duties, and South Carolina cancelled its Nullification Act—although as an act of continued defiance it nullified the Force Bill at the same time.

The Trail of Tears

President Jackson also used federal power negatively to support the relocation of the Cherokee, Choctaw, Creek, Chickasaw, and Seminole peoples to what is now Oklahoma. He had a deep prejudice against Native Americans and believed that they would prevent white people from moving west and opening up land for cotton production.

Many Americans shared Jackson's prejudice against Native Americans. In 1829 Georgia seized Cherokee land for cotton growers. After appealing to the United States Senate with little result, the Cherokee appealed directly to the American people in 1830. In that appeal, the Cherokee said:

> The people of the United States will have the fairness to reflect, that all the treaties between them and the Cherokee were made . . . for the benefit, of the whites. . . . We wish to remain on the land of our fathers. We have a perfect and original right to remain without interruption. . . . The treaties with us and laws of the United States made in pursuance of treaties, guaranty our residence. . . . It cannot be that the community we are addressing, remarkable for its intelligence and religious sensibilities, and preeminent [admired] for its devotion to the rights of man, will lay aside this appeal.

Two years later, Chief Justice Marshall, in the case *Worcester* v. *Georgia,* ruled that Georgia's action was unconstitutional and should not be allowed. But Jackson and Georgia ignored the Supreme Court, which had no power to enforce its decision. In 1837 and 1838, the United States Army gathered about fifteen thousand Cherokee and forced them to migrate west.

On this nightmare journey, which has come to be called the **Trail of Tears,** about one out of every four Cherokees died of exposure or disease. In an added outrage, the $6 million spent by the federal government to relocate the Cherokee was charged against the $9 million

A navy ship bore this figurehead of Andrew Jackson in 1834. In an action typical of the strong political feelings of the time, someone sawed off the head soon after the carving was fastened in place.

William Henry Harrison was known as "Tippecanoe" because he had fought in the battle by that name. Whigs in 1840 campaigned for him and running mate John Tyler with the slogan "Tippecanoe and Tyler too."

that the Cherokee had been forced to accept for their lands.

The Age of Jackson Ends

Jackson's presidency was marked by his strong personality, his unsinkable courage—and his quick temper. To many Americans, he seemed a larger-than-life figure, a tough, stubborn man who embodied the spirit of the frontier.

After two terms, Andrew Jackson left the presidency. The next President, Martin Van Buren, whom Jackson had supported as a candidate, was not as popular as the general. The Panic of 1837 struck during his term. In this severe depression, caused in part by the end of the national bank, thousands of people lost their jobs and poverty grew worse in American cities.

When the next election year arrived in 1840, the depression was still dragging on. The Whigs did what they could to imitate the Democrats. They chose William Henry Harrison as their candidate for President, a military hero like Jackson. They boasted that Harrison, too, was a plain man of the people, and that he had lived in a log cabin. In fact, he was the son of an aristocratic family and had grown up in a mansion. It was a fierce campaign, and over 80 percent of eligible voters cast ballots. Many voted in hopes that a change might end the depression.

Harrison defeated President Van Buren, only to be defeated in turn by illness. He caught a cold while giving a lengthy inaugural speech and died of pneumonia a month later. Vice President John Tyler, who took over as President, was more of a Jacksonian Democrat than a Whig, and his term was largely one of fruitless quarreling between the parties.

Much as Whigs and Jacksonians quarreled, however, they almost all agreed that an essential ingredient of American liberty was the right to compete and to make money. Politicians argued about the effects and the course of the Market Revolution. But rare was the political leader who did not believe that it had brought unparalleled economic and social progress to the United States of America.

SECTION 5 REVIEW

Key Terms, People, and Places
1. Define (a) American System, (b) second American party system, (c) secede, (d) Trail of Tears.
2. Identify (a) John C. Calhoun, (b) Henry Clay, (c) National Republicans, (d) Jacksonian Democrats.

Key Concepts
3. What was the main difference in outlook between National Republicans and Jacksonian Democrats?

4. Why did Jackson oppose nullification?
5. Why did Jackson fail to support the Cherokee when Georgia took their land?

Critical Thinking
6. **Formulating Questions** What questions would you have asked a politician during the Age of Jackson to determine whether he was a Whig or a Jacksonian Democrat?

Determining Relevance

etermining relevance means discovering whether a logical connection exists between one item of information and another. If relevance does exist, you can use one item to learn about the other. For instance, you have seen that the Market Revolution led to increased opportunities for making money. You have also seen that a new political party system developed in the 1820s because politicians and voters were keenly interested in the role government should play in improving ways to make money. So you know that the Market Revolution is relevant to an understanding of American politics during this period.

Use the tables on this page and the following steps to practice determining the relevance of different pieces of information.

1. Identify the main purpose of each table. Study each table, including titles and headings. (a) What purpose does Table A serve? (b) What is the purpose of Table B? (c) What is the purpose of Table C?

2. Determine the relevance of the tables. Examine each table in the light of a specific need. (a) Imagine you want to find out how people who favored slavery voted in 1828. Which tables would be relevant? (b) Imagine you want to know which candidates in 1824 favored tariffs. Which tables would be most relevant? (c) Imagine you have used Table A to find the total votes cast for Jackson and Adams

in 1828. Now, however, you want to know how each section of the country voted in that election. Which table would now be relevant to your needs?

3. Use your understanding of the relevance of the tables to support an observation. (a) Using the relevant tables, support the statement that western states tended to be against the national bank. (b) Generally speaking, northerners favored the American System of tariffs and internal improvements more than southerners because the North had more industry. Explain how the tables support this generalization. (c) Imagine that you want to demonstrate to someone that in an election the popular vote is often closer than the vote in the Electoral College. Explain how the tables could be used to demonstrate this.

A. Presidential Elections, 1824 and 1828

Year	Candidate	Political Party	Votes Cast		
			Popular	Electoral	House of Representatives
1824	John Quincy Adams	No distinct party designations	108,740	84	13
	Andrew Jackson		153,544	99	7
	Henry Clay		47,136	37	0
	W. H. Crawford		46,618	41	4
1828	Andrew Jackson	Democratic	647,826	178	No vote needed
	John Quincy Adams	National Republican	508,064	83	

Source: *World Almanac & Book of Facts, 1993; Historical Statistics of the United States*

B. State Electoral Votes Cast for President, 1828

	Slave States		Free States		
	South	West	North	West	Total
Number of States	9	3	9	3	24
Number of Electoral Votes	86	28	123	24	261
Number of Democratic Electoral Votes	77	28	49	24	178
Number of National Republican Electoral Votes	9	0	74	0	83

Source: *Historical Statistics of the United States*

C. Candidate Profiles

Issue	Adams	Jackson
Slavery	Against	For
National Bank	For	Against
Protective Tariffs	For	Generally against
Federally Funded Internal Improvements	For	Against
Voting Rights for Propertyless Workers	Against	For

Chapter Review

Understanding Key Terms, People, and Places

Key Terms.
1. political party
2. first American party system
3. excise
4. tariff
5. Whiskey Rebellion
6. precedent
7. Northwest Territory
8. black codes
9. Missouri Compromise
10. Industrial Revolution
11. Second Great Awakening
12. evangelical movement
13. Market Revolution
14. entrepreneur
15. capitalism
16. capital
17. household economy
18. commodity
19. centralize
20. section
21. capitalist
22. American System
23. second American party system
24. secede
25. Trail of Tears

People
26. Jeffersonian Republicans
27. Andrew Jackson
28. Eli Whitney
29. Denmark Vesey
30. Nat Turner
31. John C. Calhoun
32. Henry Clay
33. National Republicans
34. Jacksonian Democrats

Places
35. North
36. Northeast
37. Old Northwest
38. South

Terms For each term above, write a sentence that explains its meaning.

Matching Review the key terms in the list above. If you are not sure of a term's meaning, review its definition in the chapter. Then choose a term from the list that best matches each description below.
1. a new wave of religious revivals that took place in the early 1800s
2. group that runs candidates for political offices
3. a supply of wealth that can be used to produce goods
4. something that can be bought and sold

True or False Determine whether each statement is true or false. If it is true, write "true." If it is false, change the underlined name to make the statement true.
1. Denmark Vesey invented the cotton gin.
2. Nat Turner led an uprising of enslaved people in Virginia in 1831.
3. Andrew Jackson supported the spoils system.

Reviewing Main Ideas

Section 1 (pp. 88–91)
1. How was Alexander Hamilton able to change the national debt from a weakness to a strength?
2. Briefly explain the significance of the election of 1800.

Section 2 (pp. 94–100)
3. What was the effect of the Louisiana Purchase on the westward expansion of the United States?
4. Describe how steam power improved transportation in the first half of the 1800s.

Section 3 (pp. 101–104)
5. How did the meaning of work change during the first half of the 1800s?
6. Why were there more banks in 1830 than in 1780?

Section 4 (pp. 105–111)
7. What products did the farmers of the Old Northwest produce in the early 1800s?
8. What did the growth of factories and textile mills suggest about the role of the household?
9. Why did factory owners and workers clash during the early 1800s?

Section 5 (pp. 112–118)
10. What was the importance of Jackson's veto of the rechartering of the Second Bank of the United States?
11. Why might one expect Jackson to be sympathetic to South Carolina's attempt to nullify federal tariffs?
12. Describe the situation that led to the Trail of Tears.

1. **Identifying Assumptions** Today we expect a peaceful transfer of power when Americans vote to change political parties in a presidential election. Why were people unable to make this assumption in the election of 1800?

2. **Determining Relevance** During the early republic, rapid population growth and constant migration created a nation of strangers. Are we a nation of strangers today?

1. **Evaluating Primary Sources** Review the primary source excerpt on page 116. Give evidence from the quotation that Jackson deserved his reputation as a "man of the people."

2. **Understanding the Visuals** Describe in your own words how the cotton gin on page 98 operates.

3. **Writing About the Chapter** It is 1830, and you are visiting the United States from abroad. You have visited once before, in 1783. Write a letter to your family at home describing the changes that you observe in American society. Create a list of the changes that you have observed between the two visits, as well as the things that have remained the same. Next, divide your lists into categories, such as "changes in the role of women," "new inventions," and "life for African Americans." Write a draft of your letter in which you compare your observations from your two visits, organized according to the categories you have chosen. Revise your letter, making certain that each idea is clearly explained. Proofread your letter and draft a final copy.

4. **Using the Graphic Organizer** This graphic organizer uses a web to organize information about the Market Revolution. Webs often can describe the attributes of a historical era. In this web, dotted lines show connections among these attributes. (a) Explain the connection between the development of centralized work and the decline of the household economy. (b) Create your own web map about Section 5, using this graphic organizer as an example.

Reform and Expansion
1815–1860

*I*nspired by religious revivals that emphasized the importance of character and the possibility of personal change, in the early 1800s many Americans participated in a variety of reform movements. Meanwhile, thousands of Americans began pushing westward into Texas, New Mexico, California, and Oregon—invading land where Native Americans and Mexicans had lived for centuries. The tensions that resulted from these encounters led eventually to conflict with Native Americans and a war with Mexico.

Events in the United States

1817 The American Colonization Society forms to return African Americans to Africa.

1821 Stephen Austin founds a colony of American settlers in Texas.

1831 Abolitionist William Lloyd Garrison founds *The Liberator, an* antislavery newspaper.

1815	1820	1825	1830	1835

Events in the World

1816 Argentina declares its independence.

1822 The American Colonization Society founds the West African nation of Liberia.

1830 Greece becomes an independent state.

1841 Catharine Beecher publishes A Treatise on Domestic Economy.

1848 A gold rush begins in California.
• The Mexican War ends.

1851 Maine bans the manufacture and sale of all alcoholic beverages.

1861 Kansas becomes a state.

1865 Maria Mitchell becomes the first professor of astronomy at Vassar College.

1840	1845	1850	1855	1860	1865

1840 Female delegates are excluded from the World Anti-Slavery Convention in London.

1845 Irish potato famine spurs immigration to the United States.

1859 Charles Darwin publishes The Origin of Species.

Reform and Abolitionism

SECTION PREVIEW

Dismayed by a wide variety of social problems, many middle-class Americans banded together in the mid-1800s in an effort to improve life in the United States. Among these activities was an antislavery movement.

This banner celebrates the founding of William Lloyd Garrison's famous antislavery newspaper, *The Liberator.*

Key Concepts

- Middle-class reformers believed that improving individual character was the first step in improving society as a whole.
- Free African Americans, at the forefront of the antislavery movement, began to build momentum against slavery during the early 1800s.
- The antislavery movement increasingly divided the North and South.

Key Terms, People, and Places

Transcendentalism, temperance movement, abolition, gag rule; Lyman Beecher, Henry David Thoreau, Horace Mann, Dorothea Dix, William Lloyd Garrison, Frederick Douglass, Harriet Tubman; Liberia

A s the United States moved through the Great Awakening in the early decades of the 1800s, Americans began to look at the nation they were creating and take action to guide its growth.

Religion and Philosophy Inspire Reformers

The impulse to reform what exists grows out of a vision of a better way of life. For early reformers, religion and philosophy supplied this new vision.

Evangelical Reformers The evangelical ministers of the Second Great Awakening preached that humans have the power to choose to act rightly, not only in accepting Jesus Christ but in other personal decisions. In their view, those who correctly use this power to choose have "character," meaning they exercise self-restraint and follow God's laws. As reformers, these ministers sought to end all practices that worked against self-restraint.

One such minister was **Lyman Beecher.** The son of a blacksmith, Beecher attended Yale University and became a popular preacher in Boston. In 1832 he moved to Cincinnati to become president of the Lane Theological Seminary. Beecher, like other revivalists, feared that "the vast extent of territory, our numerous and increasing population, . . . diversity of local interests, the power of selfishness, and the fury of sectional jealousy and hate" threatened the future of the United States. How, he wondered, could such a huge, loosely organized nation survive the rapid and far-reaching changes of the Market Revolution? The answer, he and others believed, lay in the work of improving the individual. In other words, people of good character would make a country of good character.

The Transcendentalists Another group of reformers was more philosophical than religious in outlook. Relatively few in number—and centered mainly in New England—the followers of **Transcendentalism** believed that the most important truths in life went beyond, or "transcended," human understanding. Transcendentalists prized self-reliance and the questioning of authority—ideal qualities for reformers. One Transcendentalist, Ralph Waldo Emerson, went so far as to ask, "What is man born for but to be a Reformer?" Another Transcendentalist, **Henry David Thoreau,** demonstrated the importance of individuals reforming their own lives. In 1846, Thoreau refused to pay taxes to support the Mexican War because he saw the war as a government plan to extend slavery. Rather than be a part of that plan, he went to jail, which was the penalty for not paying taxes.

The Major Reform Movements

The young United States had many ills that attracted the attention of reformers—widespread use of alcohol, a crying need for a system of basic education, and the problems of crime and mental illness. The first of these, consumption of alcohol, was the target of the most successful middle-class reform of the era.

The Temperance Movement Americans were drinking more alcoholic beverages per person during the early 1800s than at any other time in American history. And reformers believed that only Americans who did *not* drink—who were "temperate," or moderate, in their habits—could be in control of themselves and thus be free to develop their character and contribute to their nation. In 1842 a thirty-three-year-old lawyer named Abraham Lincoln illustrated this viewpoint clearly when he said he looked forward to the

happy day when . . . the victory shall be complete—when there shall be neither a slave nor a drunkard on the earth. . . . How nobly distinguished that people who shall have planted and nurtured to maturity both the political and moral freedom of their species.

The campaign against alcohol began about 1815 and became known as the **temperance movement.** By 1834 the American Temperance Society boasted 7,000 local organizations with 1,250,000 members. They urged people to take pledges to abstain from alcohol, lobbied distillers and distributors of alcohol, established alcohol-free hotels and boat lines, encouraged employers to require their workers to sign antidrinking pledges, and worked for political candidates who promised to ban the sale of alcohol.

The temperance movement had a significant impact on Americans' drinking habits. Between the 1830s and the 1860s, the per capita, or per person, consumption of distilled spirits in the United States dropped dramatically, as the table at right shows.

Improving Public Education

The failure of individual character, reformers believed, was partly due to a lack of good public education. Beginning in the 1820s, many working-class and middle-class citizens started to demand tax-supported schools. Despite opposition from some taxpayers, the movement for educational reform gained strength in the 1830s. It owed much of its eventual success to **Horace Mann,** a Massachusetts lawyer who became that state's first secretary of the Board of Education in 1837. Under Mann's leadership, Massachusetts pioneered school reform. He began a system of graded schools, uniform curricula, and teacher training. Using Massachusetts as a model, educational reformers led movements to establish public schools in other states. By the 1850s most northern states had established free public elementary schools, and by the beginning of the next decade the number of public high schools in the United States had risen to three hundred. Progress toward public education lagged far behind in the South, however. In addition, access to public education tended to be better in urban than in rural areas.

Even where public schools did exist, some groups remained blocked from using them. Girls, for example, often were discouraged from attending school, particularly if they wished to continue their education after learning to read and write. More frequently, towns and cities barred free African Americans from entering local public schools. In places where African Americans could attend public schools, such as Boston and New York, they often were segregated in inferior schools.

Opportunities for women and African Americans in higher education were even more

Alcohol Consumption in the United States, 1800–1860

Year	Gallons Consumed Per Capita
1800	6.6
1810	7.1
1820	6.8
1830	7.1
1840	3.1
1850	1.8
1860	2.1

Source: *The Alcoholic Republic: An American Tradition,* by W. J. Rorabaugh

Interpreting Tables
Per capita, or per person, consumption of alcohol in the United States is shown on this table. *What evidence of the impact of the temperance movement does this table illustrate?*

This 1857 photograph shows a class at a school in Massachusetts. Teachers of the time tended toward strict discipline and drill to teach their students.

School* Enrollment, 1840–1870

*Primary, secondary, higher
Source: *American Education, The National Experience, 1783–1876,* by Lawrence A. Cremin

Interpreting Graphs
Thanks to the efforts of Horace Mann and other educational reformers, school enrollment in the United States increased rapidly in the mid-1800s. *What group do you think is most represented by these figures?*

limited. Although sixteen states funded some kind of higher education by 1860, few students at these schools were female or African American. Several private colleges, such as Oberlin, Amherst, and Dartmouth, did open their doors to a small number of African American students, and three black colleges—Avery, Lincoln, and Wilberforce—were founded during this period. In addition, Oberlin, Grinnell, and several other private colleges were coeducational. For the most part, however, white males were the only students welcome at public universities.

The Work of Dorothea Dix A Boston schoolteacher named **Dorothea Dix** paid a visit to a Massachusetts jail in 1841. She discovered men and women, young and old, sane and insane, first-time offenders and hardened criminals all crowded together in deplorable conditions. Many of the inmates she met were dressed in rags, poorly fed, and living in unheated cells.

Shocked, Dix spent the next two years visiting every prison and poorhouse—a place where very poor people lived supported by public funds—in Massachusetts. In the report she prepared for the Massachusetts legislature, Dix

"I come to present the strong claims of suffering humanity," wrote Dorothea Dix in her report to the Massachusetts legislature.

related in vivid detail the appalling conditions and mistreatment she had witnessed. Her powerful testimony convinced Massachusetts lawmakers to pass legislation to improve conditions in prisons and poorhouses. Dix also persuaded them to establish a separate public institution for the mentally ill, arguing that "To confine the insane to persons whose education and habits do not qualify them for this charge is to condemn them to mental death."

As a result of Dix's campaign to have the mentally ill treated as patients rather than criminals, fifteen states established special hospitals for the mentally ill. Few individual reformers in United States history have been as effective as Dix.

The Antislavery Movement

Of the many reform movements that sprang up between 1820 and 1860, the **abolition,** or antislavery, movement created the most widespread controversy, both outside the movement and within it.

Colonization Typical of this controversy was the reaction to one abolitionist proposal, colonization, a program to return free blacks and emancipated slaves to Africa.

Convinced that African Americans would never achieve full participation in American society, in 1822 some antislavery advocates founded the country of **Liberia** in West Africa as a homeland for African Americans.

Although a free African American named Paul Cuffe had been one of the originators of the idea of colonization, the plan offended most African Americans. They were interested in improving their lives in the land they considered their home, the United States, not moving to a continent they had never seen. At an 1817 meeting in Philadelphia, three thousand free African Americans shouted their opposition to such schemes with a roar that threatened to "bring down the walls of the building," according to one report. Thanks largely to such opposition, colonization was a failure. As of 1831, only about 1,400 African Americans had migrated to Liberia.

Radical Abolition As they demonstrated in rejecting colonization, African Americans wanted not to dodge the issue of slavery but to end the practice immediately. For African Americans, the movement to end slavery had a personal dimension and an urgency that white people could never fully understand. By 1829, nearly fifty African American antislavery groups had formed throughout the nation. In that year, a forty-four-year-old free African American named David Walker captured their sentiments in his *Appeal to the Colored Citizens of the World.*

Walker's essay was an eloquent and angry denunciation of slavery and the nation that tolerated it. He did not mince words. White Americans had made African Americans into "the most wretched, degraded and abject set of beings that ever lived since the world began." Throwing the words of the Declaration of Independence in the faces of whites, Walker not only demanded equality but also spoke of the right of revolution.

Walker wanted neither charity nor condescension, but to be treated as a human entitled to the opportunities the United States had to offer. He hoped that white people would cooperate so that all Americans could "live in peace and happiness together." But if they would not

Free and Enslaved African American Population, 1820–1860

Source: *Historical Statistics of the United States*

Interpreting Graphs
The population of both free and enslaved African Americans rose sharply in the early 1800s. *Which rose more rapidly?*

listen, he warned them, then "we must and shall be free I say, in spite of you . . . for America is as much our country, as it is yours."

Although David Walker died in the streets of Boston in 1830, possibly murdered by poisoning, his *Appeal* marked a shift in the antislavery movement to a more aggressive tone and approach. During the 1830s, many African American and white members of the movement embraced this more militant form of abolitionism. One was a white Bostonian named **William Lloyd Garrison,** who in 1831 began publishing *The Liberator,* an antislavery newspaper supported largely by free African Americans. Garrison denounced moderation in the fight against slavery. He proclaimed to the world his commitment to ending slavery:

I am in earnest— I will not equivocate—I will not excuse—I will not retreat a single inch—AND I WILL BE HEARD.

With the support of both white and African American abolitionists, Garrison also founded the American Anti-Slavery Society in 1833. As the decade progressed, more middle-class northern whites became sympathetic to the cause of the immediate abolition of slavery. By 1835 the American Anti-Slavery Society had some 1,000 local chapters with roughly 150,000 members. Agents traveling throughout the North for the society distributed more than one million antislavery tracts, or informational pamphlets, every year.

One of the most influential members of the American Anti-Slavery Society—and probably the most powerful African American abolitionist—was a self-educated man named **Frederick Douglass.** Born in Maryland around 1817, Douglass spent the first twenty-one years of his life in slavery before escaping to the North in 1838. After settling in New Bedford, Massachusetts, Douglass became a full-time agent for the American Anti-Slavery Society. Douglass condemned slavery in eloquent speeches that he delivered in both the United States and Great Britain. In 1847 he parted ways with Garrison and founded his own antislavery newspaper, called *The North Star.*

Once enslaved, Frederick Douglass often denounced the "murderous traffic" of the slave trade in his abolitionist speeches.

The Underground Railroad Given the intense passions stirred by the issue of slavery and the fierce commitment of many abolitionists, it is not surprising that divisions appeared in the antislavery movement. Some abolitionists favored indirect action to end slavery and some favored direct action, whether legal or illegal. The underground railroad, for instance, was daringly illegal. It was actually not a railroad at all, but a network of men and women "conductors" who helped runaway enslaved persons escape to the North and then into Canada. (See "Time and Place: Routes to Freedom," on pages 130–131.) African Americans made up the majority of the railroad's volunteers. One of them was a courageous formerly enslaved woman named **Harriet Tubman,** who repeatedly risked her life to lead runaway enslaved persons to freedom. She was known as "the Black Moses" among African Americans because her calling, like that of Moses in the Bible, was to lead her people to freedom. Tubman boasted later in life: "I never run my train off the track, and I never lost a passenger." Her work enraged southern slave owners, who offered a $40,000 reward for her capture.

MAKING CONNECTIONS

Individuals and religious groups that participated in a "sanctuary movement" in the 1980s ignored immigration laws in order to prevent Central American political refugees from being returned to countries where they might be tortured, imprisoned, or murdered. Was this activity comparable to the underground railroad? Explain your thinking.

Resistance to Abolitionism

Abolitionists, though vocal, remained a minority in the early 1800s. In the North, merchants worried that the antislavery movement would further sour relations between North and South and consequently hurt trade between the two regions. White workers and labor leaders feared competition from free African American workers willing to accept lower wages. Even northerners who opposed slavery did not necessarily want free African Americans, whom they viewed as socially inferior, living in their communities.

Northern opposition to the antislavery movement sometimes became violent. Hostile opponents often booed abolitionists to drown out their messages or used physical threats to prevent them from speaking. William Lloyd Garrison narrowly escaped death in 1835 at the hands of an angry Boston crowd. Abolitionist editor Elijah P. Lovejoy was not so lucky. When he tried to prevent the members of a hostile mob from destroying his printing press in Alton, Illinois, in 1837, they shot and killed him. Many who were not normally sympathetic to the abolitionist cause were angered by Lovejoy's brutal murder.

Not surprisingly, most southerners were outraged by the criticisms the antislavery movement leveled at the institution of slavery. Attacks by northern abolitionists such as Garrison, together with Nat Turner's 1831 rebellion, made many southerners even more determined to defend the institution of slavery. During the 1830s, it became increasingly rare and dangerous for southerners to speak out in favor of freeing enslaved people.

Public officials in the South also joined in the battle against abolitionism. Southern postmasters, for example, refused to deliver abolitionist literature. In 1836, moreover, southern representatives in Congress succeeded in passing the so-called **gag rule,** which for the next eight years automatically tabled all antislavery petitions and thus prevented them from being read in the House.

In provoking these responses, abolitionism was gradually building a fire that would sear both North and South. It had other unexpected consequences too, as the next section shows, for it inspired women to reach out for new freedoms of their own.

"There's two things I've got a right to . . . death or liberty." So said Harriet Tubman (far left), shown here with a group of formerly enslaved people whom she led to freedom.

SECTION 1 REVIEW

Key Terms, People, and Places
1. Define (a) Transcendentalism, (b) temperance movement, (c) abolition, (d) gag rule.
2. Identify (a) Lyman Beecher, (b) Henry David Thoreau, (c) Horace Mann, (d) Dorothea Dix, (e) William Lloyd Garrison, (f) Frederick Douglass, (g) Harriet Tubman.
3. Identify Liberia.

Key Concepts
4. Why did middle-class reformers of the early 1800s place so much emphasis on individual character?
5. Why did most free African Americans reject the idea of colonization?
6. What steps did white southerners take to resist abolitionism?

Criticial Thinking
7. **Drawing Conclusions** What does the northern response to the abolition movement suggest about racial attitudes in American society as a whole during this era?

Routes to Freedom

*On a map, the routes of the underground railroad look like a confused tangle of
lines streaming from the slave states of the South to the freedom of Canada. What
logic lies behind that apparent confusion?*

The underground railroad was not strictly a railroad, nor was it underground: it was a network of routes, including paths, roads, rivers, and real railways, that led fugitives out of slavery in the South. Geography can help explain the routes marked out by the railroad.

Geographers use themes in their study, much as a workman uses tools. Two of these themes are place—including the physical characteristics of the land—and regions. The routes of the underground railroad depended on certain physical features and regional attitudes in the United States.

> "It is evident that there exist some eighteen or nineteen thoroughly organized thoroughfares through the State of Ohio for the transportation of runaway and stolen slaves."

Physical Features Lead Out of the South

Several physical features of the South provided relatively protected routes for fugitives traveling to underground railroad connections in the free states. In the West, the valley of the Mississippi River was a natural escape route. Some enslaved people even managed to book riverboat passage northward and reach the underground railroad routes of western Illinois. The Mississippi pathway was dangerous, however, because it constantly brought fugitives into contact with potentially hostile white people.

The east coast, by contrast, boasted a physical feature that offered protection from human pursuers, but posed serious natural dangers. This was the string of low-lying swamps stretching along the Atlantic coast from southern Georgia to southern Virginia. Fugitives who traveled north through the swamps—and survived the hazards of poisonous

snakes and disease-bearing mosquitoes—linked up with one of the eastern underground railroad routes to Canada shown on the map on page 131.

But the physical feature that had the greatest impact on the choice of a southern route was the Appalachian mountain chain. Its narrow, steep-sided valleys, separated by forested ridges, stretch from northern Georgia into Pennsylvania. The Appalachians affected the routes to freedom in two ways. First, their forests and limestone caves sheltered fugitives as they avoided capture on their way north. Second, the Appalachians acted as a barrier that deflected western runaways northward into a region of intense underground railway activity.

Regional Attitudes

This busy region was formed by Ohio and parts of the states on either side of it, Indiana and Pennsylvania. As a whole, the region shared a long boundary with two slave states, Virginia and Kentucky.

Once the fugitives crossed into Ohio, they found themselves in a region with an attitude toward

Frederick Douglass established a print shop in Rochester that became a depot.

John Brown led fugitives on a midwinter journey from Missouri to Canada via Chicago.

Portuguese fishermen and Native Americans of the Shinnecock group helped transport escaped enslaved persons from Long Island to New England.

Dorchester County was the birthplace of Harriet Tubman. She rescued about 300 enslaved persons on 19 trips to the South.

The home of Presbyterian minister John Rankin in Ripley was one of the most active depots.

Levi Coffin, a Quaker, helped more than 3,000 enslaved persons to escape.

Harriet Beecher Stowe maintained a depot in Walnut Hills.

Slaveholders looked upon the underground railroad as organized theft.

Seminole in Florida offered safe havens for escaped enslaved persons.

The underground railroad

Slaveholding states

Swamps

1850 boundaries

0   150   300 Miles

0   150   300 Kilometers

slavery very different from the one in the region they had left behind. Southern Ohio was home to many Quakers, Covenanters, and others who volunteered their houses as depots, or stations, on religious principles. There, too, lived free African Americans, as well as whites who had moved out of the South because they opposed slavery. In the north and east of the state, many whites had roots in New England and shared its antislavery views. The photograph on page 130 shows the sort of lengths such people took to aid African Americans. This cupboard slid back to reveal a hiding place where several fugitives might conceal themselves if necessary.

The sympathetic attitude of residents throughout much of the Ohio region caused a headache for southern slave owners. "It is evident," an anonymous writer declared indignantly in 1842, "that there exist some eighteen or nineteen thoroughly organized thoroughfares through the State of Ohio for the transportation of runaway and stolen slaves." To the east of Ohio, regional attitudes were similar.

Southern Illinois, however, was a dangerous region for fugitives, because it had been settled by southerners and remained proslavery. Often sympathizers in that area simply ticketed fugitives on a real railroad, the Illinois Central, for swift transit to Chicago. From there they continued on toward Canada, following the North Star as it shone in the night sky and marked their route to freedom.

GEOGRAPHIC CONNECTIONS

1. What physical features in the South offered fugitives protection from pursuers? What dangers also lurked in those areas?
2. Why did so many of the underground railroad routes run through Ohio?

Critical Thinking

3. **Demonstrating Reasoned Judgment** If you had been an enslaved person escaping from the South, which route to freedom would you have taken? Explain your reasoning.

Women and the Working Class

SECTION PREVIEW

Although middle-class women were expected to devote their energies to home, family, and community in the early 1800s, many women were not content with this work. Meanwhile, many people resented interfering reformers who told them how to live their lives.

Key Concepts

- The reform movements of the 1830s and 1840s provided American women with new opportunities to speak and act publicly.
  - Inspired in part by the abolitionist movement, some American women started a women's rights movement in the 1840s.
  - More concerned with economic survival than social reform, working-class people resented reformers' efforts to impose values with which they did not necessarily agree.

Key Terms, People, and Places

suffrage, cult of domesticity; Catharine Beecher, Lucretia Mott, Elizabeth Cady Stanton, Sojourner Truth; Seneca Falls

Awareness of the plight of women who were enslaved, as shown in this antislavery logo, made many white abolitionist women begin thinking about women's rights.

Women played a prominent role in almost every reform movement of the first half of the nineteenth century, from temperance to antislavery. In spite of the enormous contribution they made to these movements, their participation was often highly controversial. Middle-class women at this time were expected to raise and educate their children, create a nurturing home, entertain guests, serve their husbands, do community service, and engage in such genteel activities as needlework. Participating in politics or public meetings with men was considered shocking and unladylike. Even a successful public figure like Dorothea Dix found it necessary for a man to present her findings to legislatures.

The cultural attitudes of the period were reinforced by laws. For example, women did not enjoy **suffrage,** or the right to vote, at this time. In most states in the early 1800s, moreover, married women could not own property, make a will, or keep the wages they earned outside the home. During the 1840s, some women began to be angered by these forms of legal discrimination, as well as by attempts to block their participation in public life. Others, however, continued to promote a role for women as reformers in the home.

AMERICAN PROFILES

Catharine Beecher

One of the most visible advocates of a domestic role for women was **Catharine Beecher** (1800–1878), who tried to win respect for women's contributions as wives, mothers, and teachers. Daughter of the revivalist Lyman Beecher and sister of both the novelist Harriet Beecher Stowe and the prominent Presbyterian minister Henry Ward Beecher, Catharine Beecher grew up in a family devoted to moral improvement and public service.

Born on Long Island in New York, Beecher attended school in Connecticut, and began teaching in 1821. Teaching was considered a proper occupation for a young woman because it was an extension of the role of mother. In 1823, a year after her fiancé was drowned at sea, Catharine and her sister Mary Beecher started the Hartford Female Seminary.

While teaching, Catharine Beecher also started writing about and lobbying for the education of females. Beecher's most popular and influential work was *A Treatise on Domestic Economy,* first published in 1841. In the *Treatise,* Beecher sought to help middle-class women adjust to a new world where they were consumers more than producers and where they were having fewer children. Aside from offering practical advice and household tips, she wrote on a positive note about the contributions that women could make in a capitalistic society.

Beecher did not believe that women should move beyond the realms of family and education. In her view, being a mother and a wife should give women their focus in life. Women's work remained as central to the overall economy as it had been in the 1600s, but in different ways. Although middle-class women no longer milked cows or planted vegetables, they were not supposed to become idle or lazy. In fact, it was precisely because they had primary responsibility for the home and the family, Beecher argued, that women were so important.

Everyone knew, wrote Beecher in her *Treatise,* that "the success of democratic institutions . . . depends upon the intellectual and moral character of the mass of the people." Everyone also agreed that "the formation of the moral and intellectual character of the young is committed mainly to the female hand." Here, then, was the reason why women were so critically important to the welfare of the United States:

> The mother forms the character of the future man; . . . the wife sways the heart, whose energies may turn for good or for evil the destinies of a nation. . . . Let the women of a country be made virtuous and intelligent, and the men will certainly be the same. The proper education of a man decides the welfare of an individual; but educate a woman, and the interests of a whole family are secured.

Catharine Beecher helped to establish notions about the role of American women that continue to be held by some segments of American society today. Women were power-

In her *Treatise on Domestic Economy,* Catharine Beecher argued that women should play the central role in managing the household and raising children.

ful, but only privately, in their duties as mothers and wives. Some historians refer to this as the **cult of domesticity,** or the belief in the importance of women's role in the home.

Beyond the Private Sphere

As influential as Catharine Beecher was, many northern middle-class American women in the first half of the 1800s did not limit themselves to the home and charitable work. Increasingly, women challenged traditional attitudes by becoming involved in political activities.

Women who participated in the abolition movement saw obvious parallels between the plight of enslaved African Americans and the status of women. Neither group could vote or hold office, and both were denied the full rights of American citizens. Although white and African American women had been aware of these constraints for decades, the religious revivals and reform movements of the early 1800s heightened their sense of women's potential and power.

In addition to raising their consciousness, abolitionism provided women with a political platform from which they could assert their power. In 1836, for example, South Carolina–born abolitionist Angelina Grimké demanded that the women of the South fight slavery. Although women could not make laws, she said, they could still influence those who do: "If you really suppose you can do nothing to overthrow slavery, you are greatly mistaken. . . . You can read. . . . You can pray. . . . You can speak. . . . You can act." Both black and white women began to attend meetings, gather petitions, give public talks, and write pamphlets and books.

The Seneca Falls Convention In the 1840s, two American abolitionists, **Lucretia Mott** and **Elizabeth Cady Stanton,** took their search for human rights one step further by organizing the first convention in history to discuss the question of women's rights. Held at **Seneca Falls,** New York, in 1848, the convention issued a *Declaration of Sentiments* signed by sixty-eight women and thirty-two men. Only one African American, Frederick Douglass, was present.

The *Declaration,* written by Stanton, deliberately echoed the form and language of the Declaration of Independence. In addition to protesting women's lack of legal and political rights, it also attacked the double standard that society held for men and women:

> T he history of mankind is a history of repeated injuries and usurpations [violent seizing of power] *on the part of man toward woman, having in direct object the establishment of an absolute tyranny over her. . . . Because women do feel themselves aggrieved* [offended], *oppressed, and fraudulently deprived of their most sacred moral rights, we insist that they have immediate admission to all the rights and privileges which belong to them as citizens of the United States.*

Although the vast majority of Americans ignored or dismissed the Declaration, the Seneca Falls convention marked the beginning of the organized movement for women's rights in the United States.

Sojourner Truth Speaks Out for Women

African American women also were inspired and empowered by the movement for abolition. Among the most famous of these were three former enslaved women: Harriet Tubman, famous for her activities in the underground railroad; Harriet Brent Jacobs, author of the 1861 book *Incidents in the Life of a Slave Girl;* and **Sojourner Truth.**

Truth, whose original name was Isabella Baumfree, was born in Ulster County, New York, in 1797. Freed in 1827, she initially found work as a domestic servant in New York City but soon became involved in a variety of religious and reform movements of her day. She took the name Sojourner Truth in the early 1840s because she believed her life mission was to travel around the nation telling the truth about slavery and God.

Although she never learned to read or write, Sojourner Truth became a powerful spokesperson in the antislavery cause. She also became one of a small number of African

Elizabeth Cady Stanton (left) issued a manifesto declaring that "all men and women are created equal."

Sojourner Truth is pictured on the right. Her commanding presence and powerful speaking style captured people's attention at many antislavery and women's rights meetings.

American women in the 1840s and 1850s who were active in the movement for women's rights. No black women attended the Seneca Falls convention, and only a handful came to most other women's rights conventions. For most black women, abolition was the more pressing issue. Truth, however, was often in attendance at these meetings, reminding white women that their African American sisters also had a place in the movement for women's rights.

MAKING CONNECTIONS

Just as the women's movement of the 1840s was inspired by the abolitionist movement, the women's movement of the 1960s was inspired by the civil rights movement. Why do you think these two movements for racial justice, separated by more than a century, encouraged the rise of movements for women's rights?

A Foundation for Change

The activities of such reformers as Elizabeth Cady Stanton and Sojourner Truth did not bring about a sudden, fundamental change in the status of American women. Nevertheless, reformers did succeed in gradually expanding the opportunities available to American women outside the home.

Whereas no seminary or college in the United States admitted women in 1820, by 1890 more than 2,500 women a year were graduating from American colleges and universities. Thanks in part to the benefits of education, women began appearing in professions from which they previously had been excluded. After becoming the first woman to earn a medical diploma, Elizabeth Blackwell began practicing medicine in New York City in 1850 and seven years later founded the first school of nursing in the United States. Astronomer Maria Mitchell, pictured above, was not only a member of the American Academy of Arts and Sciences but also became the first professor of astronomy at newly founded Vassar College for women in 1865.

Women also excelled as writers, editors, and publishers. Margaret Fuller, the editor of an important philosophical journal, also wrote an 1845 book *Woman in the Nineteenth Century,* in which she criticized cultural traditions that restricted women's roles in society. And as editor of the popular magazine *Godey's Lady's Book,* Sarah Josepha Hale published articles about women's issues for almost fifty years.

In spite of fierce opposition, the women struggling for equal rights would not be silenced. In the piercing words of Sojourner Truth:

> *The women are coming up, blessed be God, and a few of the men are coming up with them. But man is in a tight place, the poor slave is on him, woman is coming on him, and he is surely between a hawk and a buzzard.*

The Lives of Southern Women

Just as southerners bitterly resented the criticisms and activities of the abolitionists, they did not welcome the advice of northern reformers who prodded them to give more rights to women. The reasons behind this were both economic and social.

While the North became increasingly industrial and urban in the early 1800s, the South remained primarily agricultural and rural. In fact, the great majority of southern whites in the 1830s and 1840s were farmers who depended on the cash crop of cotton for their living. In most areas of the South, the household remained an important economic unit. Less affected by the Market Revolution that was changing the character of the North, many southern families, both rich and poor, continued to blend work and family activities. They saw little need for restructuring family life. Furthermore, because farms and plantations were often miles apart, opportunities to participate in public organizations and community meetings were rare.

Social relationships remained quite traditional in the South, especially with regard to matters of gender. Whether small farmers or wealthy planters, southern males viewed themselves as the rulers of their domains. Southern plantations, in particular, were classic examples of patriarchal systems. The master of the plantation exercised power over all of his dependents, including women, children, and enslaved African Americans.

A few southern white women saw parallels between their position in this patriarchal system and that of the enslaved. South Carolina's Mary Boykin Chesnut confided to her diary that her husband was "master of the house. To hear is to obey. . . . All the comforts of my life depend upon his being in a good humor." Chesnut went so far as to comment that "there is no slave . . . like a wife."

Reform and the Working Class

Like southerners, working class people viewed reformers as meddlers and moralists who had no business interfering in the lives of others. The large size of this working class was a result of the Market Revolution of the early 1800s. Some members of the working class were people born in the United States who had moved from farms to cities to find factory jobs. Many, however, were immigrants who came to the United States during the dramatic surge in immigration that took place between 1830 and 1860. The graph on page 137 shows this increase.

Although some of the new immigrants arrived from Scandinavia and England, most came from Ireland and Germany. Because the system of slave labor in the South limited economic opportunities in that region, the great majority of these immigrants settled in the North. Forced out of their homeland by the disastrous potato famine of the mid-1840s, Irish immigrants tended to settle in northeastern cities and take manual labor jobs in factories or on canals or railroads. German immigrants, on the other hand—many of whom had fled political oppression after the failure of the European revolutions of 1848—bought farmland in the Midwest or settled in northern cities such as New York, Philadelphia, Cincinnati, Chicago, and Milwaukee.

Religious differences immediately created tension between middle-class reformers and working-class immigrants. Nearly all of the Irish immigrants and many of the German immigrants were Roman Catholic. Reformers strongly disapproved of the Catholic religion. They believed that the emphasis Catholicism placed on ritual and the authority of the Pope and bishops made it impossible for individuals to think for themselves and to find their own salvation.

For their part, working-class immigrants found that the evangelical Protestant version of character-building and self-improvement were unnecessary luxuries. They were much more concerned with putting food on the table and

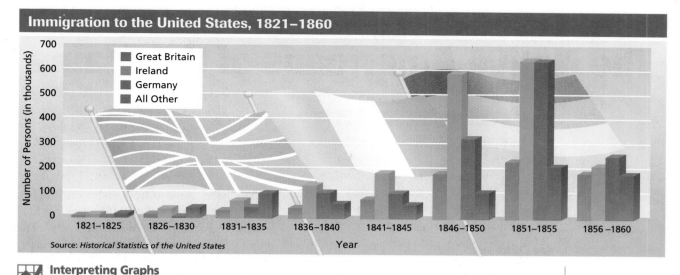

Immigration to the United States, 1821–1860

Number of Persons (in thousands)

Legend:
- Great Britain
- Ireland
- Germany
- All Other

Years: 1821–1825, 1826–1830, 1831–1835, 1836–1840, 1841–1845, 1846–1850, 1851–1855, 1856–1860

Source: *Historical Statistics of the United States*

Interpreting Graphs

Seeking to escape famine and revolution in Europe, several million immigrants came to the United States in the 1840s and 1850s, changing the character of the United States population in the process. *Which nation sent the largest number of immigrants to the United States in the period from 1846 to 1855?*

keeping a roof over their heads than with debating issues of morality.

Whether immigrant or native born, working-class people valued different things from most middle-class reformers. Because they had so little power in their working lives, working people wanted to do as they pleased in their leisure time. Alcohol often played an important role in their social lives. Men drank in taverns that were the center of neighborhood society. Women bought beer to enjoy with neighbors on the steps of tenements. The idea that drinking alcohol was an inherently immoral act was a strange one in their view, and they resented temperance activists who preached to them about its evils.

In the end, what many middle-class reformers wanted, particularly evangelical reformers, was for working-class people to become like them. They sought an end to drinking and gambling, a celebration of hard work, and a form of religion that encouraged self-improvement rather than devotion to tradition. Reformers hoped that public schools, together with laws that restricted drinking and gambling, would transform working-class men and women into the middle-class idea of model citizens. What working people wanted was to be left alone to live their lives as they wished.

Thus, in the 1840s tensions increased between the middle class and the working class, as well as between North and South. For the time being, the existing political system was capable of containing these strains and stresses. But another factor would soon heighten tensions still further and put the nation at risk: ongoing expansion to the West.

SECTION 2 REVIEW

Key Terms, People, and Places
1. Define (a) suffrage, (b) cult of domesticity.
2. Identify (a) Catharine Beecher, (b) Lucretia Mott, (c) Elizabeth Cady Stanton, (d) Sojourner Truth.
3. Identify Seneca Falls.

Key Concepts
4. How did the reform movements of the 1830s and 1840s advance the cause of women's rights?
5. Who organized the Seneca Falls convention?
6. Why did the working class and reformers clash?

Critical Thinking
7. **Making Comparisons** Compare and contrast the achievements and failures of the antislavery and the women's rights movements.

The Native Americans of the Plains

SECTION PREVIEW

"Whether the horse was originally a native of this country or not it is out of my power to determine," wrote explorer Meriwether Lewis in 1806. In fact, the horse was not native to the plains, and its introduction to Native Americans completely transformed the lives of some.

Key Concepts

- The arrival of the horse changed the lifestyle of many Native Americans on the Great Plains.
- Nomadic cultures tended to increase the power of Native American men and weaken the influence that women had exercised in more settled villages.
- Contact with traders brought disease to Native Americans who lived on the Great Plains.

Key Terms, People, and Places

nomad; Meriwether Lewis, William Clark, Sacajawea; Continental Divide, Great Plains

The flags and horses on this Sioux beaded vest indicate increasing contact among Native Americans, Europeans, and the United States.

E ven before the United States had completed the purchase of Louisiana from France in 1803, a curious President Jefferson was making plans to send an expedition west to explore the nation's new territory. Jefferson hoped this expedition would both establish the political boundaries of Louisiana and gather information about the territory's natural resources that might prove useful for future economic development. In addition, as Jefferson related in an 1806 speech that revealed much about his attitude toward Native Americans,

I . . . sent our beloved man, Captain Lewis, . . . to go up the Missouri river to get acquainted with all the Indian nations in its neighborhood, to take them by the hand, deliver my talks to them, and to inform us in what way we could be useful to them.

Explorers **Meriwether Lewis** and **William Clark** set out from St. Louis, Missouri, in May 1804 with a small "Corps of Discovery." The roughly fifty men who participated in the expedition journeyed up the Missouri River and over the **Continental Divide,** which is the ridge of the Rocky Mountains that separates rivers that flow west from rivers that flow east. They then journeyed down the Columbia River to the Pacific Ocean before returning east more than two years later. The nation received with much interest the scientific samples, maps of the mountains and rivers of the territory, and information about the Native Americans in the region that the group brought back.

Lewis and Clark's well-organized expedition was a remarkable achievement, but it was not a journey into unsettled territory. Many thousands of Native Americans lived west of the Mississippi River in the early 1800s. In fact, the expedition owed some of its success to one of these Native Americans—a Shoshone woman named **Sacajawea,** who served as translator and guide for the two explorers.

Lewis and Clark were by no means the first white people that Native Americans west of the Mississippi had encountered. Both animals and technology from Europe had been affecting Native

German botanist Frederick Pursh drew and classified this evening primrose from a specimen collected by Meriwether Lewis.

American societies of the **Great Plains**—the vast grasslands that lie between the Mississippi River and the Rocky Mountains—for almost two centuries.

This Navaho wall painting shows the Spanish bringing horses and other animals into the Southwest. Horses quickly spread north onto the Great Plains.

The Coming of the Horse

One of these European animals, the horse, had a profound impact on the everyday lives of the Native Americans of the plains. The Spanish brought horses to their colonies in New Mexico, and Native Americans acquired them through trading, raids, and the carelessness of the Spanish. By the mid-1700s, horses had spread as far north as the Missouri Valley, the Dakotas, and parts of what are now Oregon and Washington.

Before the arrival of the horse, Native Americans had generally utilized only one domesticated, four-legged animal—the dog, which was useful for hunting and fighting. In contrast, the horse not only improved transportation and communication, but it also changed virtually every aspect of Native American life, from the nature of warfare to the division of labor between men and women.

The Horse Affects Farming and Commerce

Many Native Americans took advantage of the horse without allowing it to transform their cultures. The Pawnee, Mandan, and other Native American nations continued to live primarily as farmers, hunters, and gatherers. As in most Native American societies, the women in these villages did most of the farming, while the men were responsible for the hunting.

The Mandan resided in several villages along the Missouri River in the present-day Dakotas. French men visited them as early as the 1730s, bringing manufactured goods, including blankets, jewelry, tools, and guns. They exchanged these goods for beaver pelts and buffalo hides. By the late 1700s, the Mandan had become part of an international trading system, functioning as both middlemen in the fur trade and discriminating consumers. This trade had a far greater impact on their way of life than did horses.

The Pawnee, on the other hand, became somewhat more mobile than the Mandan following the arrival of the horse. They began to use horses to travel from their homes in the river valleys onto the plains for semiannual buffalo hunts. Although these hunts became an important part of the year, the Pawnee always returned to their villages afterward, where they continued to farm, hunt, and gather.

The Rise of the Nomads

Other Native Americans rode the horse to an entirely new way of life. They became **nomads**—people who migrate constantly instead of living permanently in a particular place. Carrying their possessions on the backs of horses, they followed the vast herds of buffalo that crisscrossed the Great Plains.

By 1800 the Native Americans of the Great Plains had used horses to hunt the buffalo for more than half a century. During that time they discovered a multitude of purposes for the buffalo. According to James R. Walker, a doctor who lived for a time among the Oglala Sioux, Native Americans used

> their hair for making ropes and pads and for ornamental and ceremonial purposes; the horns and hoofs for making implements and utensils; the bones for making soup and articles to be used in their various occupations and games; the sinews for making their sewing thread and their stronger cords such as bowstrings; the skins for making ropes, tipis, clothing . . . ; the flesh and viscera [intestines] for food.

Most of the nomads who lived on the Great Plains in the early 1800s were recent immigrants to that region. The Crow had long lived on the plains, but the Cheyenne, the Sioux, the Comanche, and the Blackfeet all migrated to that area after horses made it possible for them

Alfred Jacob Miller's painting illustrates the nomadic life many Native Americans of the plains adopted after the arrival of the horse. Using the *travois* shown, dogs could pull 40-pound loads five or six miles a day.

to live on the move. Although the seemingly endless herds of buffalo drew them to the plains, these Native Americans also moved westward to avoid the wave of settlers who were pushing toward the Mississippi River and beyond.

MAKING CONNECTIONS

Horses had an enormous impact on the way many Native Americans lived. What technological advances of the early 1800s had a similarly significant impact on East Coast inhabitants of the United States?

Changing Roles for Men and Women

While there were significant variations from group to group, the nomadic Native Americans of the plains did share some characteristics. Because they depended heavily on skilled riding, hunting, and fighting, which only men learned formally, nomadic societies granted men higher status than women. Men had to be aggressive warriors in dealing with other Native Americans as well as in hunting buffalo. In the early 1800s, Native Americans often conducted raids on one another to obtain horses or to subdue rivals.

Men also benefited because in nomadic life, social and political structures tended to be more fluid than in farming villages. Wealth was determined by the number of horses one had,

and power by the skill and daring one showed in battle or during the hunt.

A young Cheyenne named Wilkis remembered when his uncle taught him how to hunt buffalo and gave him the following advice:

Ride your horse close up to the buffalo, as close as you can, and then let fly the arrow with all your force. If the buffalo turns to fight, your horse will take you away from it; but, above all things, do not be afraid; you will not kill buffalo if you are afraid to get close to them.

Eventually Wilkis became exactly what a grown man was supposed to be according to Cheyenne culture: "I was a good hunter; I had a herd of horses, and had been to war, and been well spoken of by the leaders whose war parties I went with."

Women were generally less influential and less well off in nomadic cultures. Because these Native Americans rarely stayed in one place long enough to farm the land, women's responsibilities now involved activities created by a horse-centered culture. For the most part, women spent their time either preparing for the hunt or drying buffalo meat and tanning buffalo hides after it was over.

Female influence in agricultural villages had rested, in part, on the fact that women remained at home and ran the village when the men left for long periods of hunting and fighting. After Native American nations such as the Sioux and Comanche had adopted a nomadic way of life, however, women followed their husbands and fathers on an endless buffalo hunt. Power that had previously resided in the female-oriented village now rested in the male-dominated hunting parties.

The Decline of Village Societies

Before the arrival of the horse, the Native Americans of the Great Plains lived in relative harmony. But as the 1700s wore on, the nomadic Native Americans engaged in a series of destructive raids on more settled Native American groups. To the south, the Comanche drove the Apache and Navaho west into New Mexico. In the North, the Sioux—in alliance with the Arapaho and Cheyenne—emerged as the dominant Native American group by the early 1800s.

Caught between white Americans who were pushing from the east and their nomadic neighbors to the west, agricultural Native Americans suffered greatly. The diseases brought by white settlers added to the tragic effects.

No group was hit harder by European diseases than the Mandan. From a population of close to 10,000 in the mid-1700s, the number of Mandan already had fallen to a total of around 2,000 by June 1837. By October, after the smallpox hit, only 138 were left. American artist George Catlin later claimed that, in addition to disease, another reason the Mandan died in such large numbers was because they were trapped in their villages.

The Mandans were surrounded by several war-parties of their more powerful enemies the Sioux, at that unlucky time, and they could not therefore disperse upon the plains, by which many of them could have been saved.

By the mid-1800s, about 75,000 nomadic Native Americans dominated the Great Plains. In addition, roughly 84,000 Native Americans from the East, forced to relocate by the United States government, lived in what is now Oklahoma. These two groups constituted about 40 percent of the Native American population of North America.

Until the 1840s, their relationship with white Americans had been uneasy but distant, consisting mainly of occasional contacts with fur traders or explorers. But that was about to change. The revolutionary impact of the horse on the people of the Great Plains seems slight when compared with the changes brought by wave after wave of white settlers from the East.

Artist George Catlin lived with and observed the Native Americans of the plains for many years, producing more than 500 sketches and paintings of the Native American way of life. The above painting is entitled *Buffalo Chase—Single Death*.

SECTION 3 REVIEW

Key Terms, People, and Places
1. Define nomad.
2. Identify (a) Meriwether Lewis, (b) William Clark, (c) Sacajawea.
3. Identify (a) Continental Divide, (b) Great Plains.

Key Concepts
4. How did the horse affect Native Americans?
5. Why did Native American women lose power in Native American societies that became nomadic?

6. According to George Catlin, why did European diseases have a worse effect on Native American village societies than on nomadic Native Americans?

Critical Thinking
7. **Predicting Consequences** In making it easier for the Native Americans of the plains to follow and kill buffalo, how did the arrival of the horse also make their way of life more vulnerable?

Hispanic North America

When a stream of American traders and settlers began to move into Texas, New Mexico, and California, tensions with Mexico grew.

Key Concepts
- Spain tried to strengthen its northern colonies in California, New Mexico, and Texas in the late 1700s.
  - Harsh conditions on the California missions led to the death of thousands of Native Americans.
  - In New Mexican society, patriarchal authority was weak and the power of women was relatively strong.
- The American immigrants who moved into Texas established an independent republic in 1836.

Key Terms, People, and Places
secularize; Stephen Austin, William Travis, Antonio López de Santa Anna, Sam Houston; Monterey, Santa Fe, the Alamo

These Spanish mission bells were rung at religious services to indicate key points in the Mass.

The United States government assumed that the Louisiana Purchase would remain part of "Indian Country." But thousands of migrating Americans had other ideas. By the 1830s, many white settlers already were pushing west into Indian Country.

In the North, the stream of migrants was so large and steady that it led to the rapid creation of three new states: Iowa (1846), Wisconsin (1848), and Minnesota (1858). Long before these states came into the Union, however, many Americans in the southern part of the United States were moving west along the coast of the Gulf of Mexico.

The Spanish Attempt to Strengthen Their North American Empire

The Spanish commitment to the conquest of what is now the southwestern United States had always been weak. After the Pueblo revolted against Spanish settlers in present-day New Mexico in the late 1600s, this commitment grew even weaker. In the 1700s, surrounded by increasingly powerful nomadic Native Americans, the Spanish remained confined to a string of small towns along the Rio Grande and in present-day Texas.

Spanish weakness in New Mexico and Texas reflected the larger weakness of the empire as a whole. No longer the most powerful nation in Europe, Spain in the late 1700s faced growing threats to its North American territory from other European nations, including the British, the French, and the Russians from the northern Pacific Coast.

To confront these various threats, the Spanish government attempted to establish better relations with the Comanche and Apache. As a result of these efforts, they were able to achieve a somewhat fitful peace with these Native American groups.

Securing California More dramatic was the Spanish effort to secure the area that is now the state of California, which they feared would fall into the hands of either the British or the Russians. In the late 1700s, Spanish soldiers and priests established a network of missions and presidios, or forts, along the rugged California coastline. Eventually they created a chain of twenty-one missions running north from San Diego to San Francisco.

From the Spanish perspective, the colonizing efforts in California were a great success. While their settlements in New Mexico and Texas remained small, the presidios and missions in California were dynamic, thriving places. Enthusiastic and controversial Franciscan missionaries such as Father Junípero Serra devoted themselves to converting Native Americans to Christianity. In addition to becoming visible symbols of Spanish authority and centers for missionary activity, the California outposts became lively centers of trade.

The missions thrived largely, however, as a result of Native American labor, and the priests who ran these communities were often harsh taskmasters. Because whippings and confinement in irons awaited those who refused to work, some Native Americans chose to leave when opportunities to escape arose. Moreover, the Native Americans who tended the cattle and sheep, farmed the land, built the missions, and wove clothing usually received only food, clothing, and shelter in return for their efforts. Poor living conditions and inadequate medical care contributed to devastating epidemics among the Native Americans on the missions. Between 1769 and 1848, the population of Native Americans in California fell from about 300,000 to about 150,000.

While the number of Native Americans declined, the number of Mexicans grew. Settling along the coast, usually around the missions and presidios, these Mexican colonists re-created the strong extended families that were often found in Spain and Mexico at that time. **Monterey** was the capital of the territory of California, although important settlements also were located at Santa Barbara, San Diego, and Los Angeles.

New Mexico Grows Meanwhile, change also had come to New Mexico. Thanks to long stretches of peace and increased attention from Spain, the Mexican population in the region increased from 3,800 in 1750 to 19,000 by 1800. Unlike eastern North America, however, the powerful nomadic Native Americans and the harsh landscape of New Mexico made it impossible for large numbers of people to spread out over the countryside in small farms. As a result, many people earned a living as craftspeople and traders in large settlements such as Albuquerque.

Population growth and an increase in commercial activity affected social relationships among those living in New Mexico. The authority of parents, particularly fathers, grew weaker. Residents of New Mexico who were not members of the landed aristocracy, or the segment of the wealthy class that owned land, began to choose their own husbands and wives; in the past they had been expected to accept their parents' choice of a partner.

Women in this region enjoyed considerable independence. Wives were able to run businesses, divorce their husbands, own property, and sue in courts of law. In fact, women actually lost rights and influence when New Mexico became part of the United States in 1848.

Oriana Day's painting of the California mission of San Carlos Borromeo depicts Franciscan friars leading a religious procession in the early 1800s. The Native American pictograph shown above captures another view of a Spanish mission.

Yesterday's Trails, Today's Highways

The trails that Native Americans, fur traders, missionaries, and others carved in the landscape (left) became today's superhighways. The photo above shows a group of would-be pioneers who recently reconstructed the journey along the Santa Fe Trail. *Why do you think yesterday's trails have become today's highways?*

Mexican Independence Affects Its Territories

Mexico won its independence from Spain in 1821, after thirteen years of war and economic devastation. Although California, New Mexico, and Texas, then part of Mexico, were far from the fighting, independence still had an effect on their residents. As citizens of Mexico, the men in these territories were now free to elect representatives to the new government in Mexico City.

Because Mexico's new government was hostile to the Roman Catholic church, it **secularized** the missions, meaning it put them under the control of the state rather than the church. By the 1830s, only a handful of priests remained in northern Mexico. In addition, economic reforms designed to bolster the Mexican economy actually widened the gap between rich and poor in Mexico's northern territories. But these reforms also encouraged trade with the United States.

American Economic Influence in New Mexico, California, and Texas

In 1821 William Becknell, a nearly bankrupt American, brought a load of goods from Missouri to the New Mexican capital of **Santa Fe,** where he sold them for mules and silver coins.

Other Americans followed, taking advantage of the commercial opening created by Mexican independence and economic reforms. The high quality and low prices of American goods virtually destroyed New Mexico's trade with the rest of Mexico.

By the early 1830s, caravans of wagons traveled regularly between Independence, Missouri, and New Mexico along the Santa Fe Trail. According to one of the most active American merchants, these caravans shaped the character of Sante Fe: "Instead of the idleness and stagnation which its streets exhibited before, one now sees everywhere the bustle, noise, and activity of a lively market town."

American fur traders and merchants exploited economic openings in other parts of Mexico's northern territories. New Englanders who sailed around South America to reach the West soon dominated the trade with California in fur, cattle hides, and tallow, a waxy substance used to make candles. In return, Californians bought finished goods from the New Englanders. According to one resident of Monterey in the 1840s, "There is not a yard of tape, a pin, or a piece of domestic cotton or even thread that does not come from the United States."

Long before the United States conquered the Mexican provinces of Texas, New Mexico, and

California militarily, it had conquered them economically. By loosening the regulations affecting trade with American merchants, the Mexican government ensured that the commercial ties of its northern provinces would be with the United States, rather than with its own merchants. More important, stronger commercial ties encouraged some Americans to seek new opportunities in Mexico's northern territories.

Texas Wins Independence

Nowhere was the influx of Americans into Mexican territory more apparent in the 1820s than in Texas. **Stephen Austin,** carrying out the plan begun by his father, Moses, received permission from the Mexican government to found a colony of about 300 settlers in east Texas. Austin, twenty-nine years old and a member of the Missouri territorial legislature, led the first organized group of American settlers into Texas in 1822. By 1824, some 2,000 immigrants were living in Austin's colony.

When Americans first started moving into what is now eastern Texas, the new Mexican government adopted a liberal colonization policy. The Mexican Colonization Law of 1824 promised American immigrants cheap land, the protection of the Mexican government, and a four-year tax exemption if they settled in Texas.

Soon other agents were arranging contracts for hundreds of Americans to settle in Texas. By 1830 about 7,000 Americans lived there, more than twice the number of Mexicans in the territory. Worried that they were losing Texas through immigration, Mexico passed a law in 1830 prohibiting any more Americans from settling there. Equally important, they outlawed the importation of enslaved people. Still, Americans continued to flow across the border.

MAKING CONNECTIONS

Many Americans in the 1820s and 1830s migrated to Texas following reports of fertile soil for growing crops. Today, many Mexicans attempt to immigrate to the United States. Do these two groups of people share similar reasons for wanting to settle in a new land?

Tension Erupts into War By 1835 more than 30,000 Americans and 3,000 enslaved African Americans lived in Texas. As their numbers swelled, these Americans demanded more political freedom. In particular, they wanted slavery to be guaranteed under Mexican law. They were divided between those led by Stephen Austin, who preferred to work within the Mexican system, and those led by a hot-tempered lawyer from Alabama named **William Travis,** who wanted to fight for independence.

Events in Mexico City soon helped Travis's supporters gain the upper hand. When the vain and ambitious General **Antonio López de Santa Anna** declared himself dictator of Mexico, supporters of an independent Texas became even more determined to break away. American settlers united in the cause of independence, and in March 1836, they formally declared the founding of the Republic of Texas.

Santa Anna responded to this defiance of Mexican authority by leading an army of several thousand men north to subdue the rebellion. The Mexican leader won early victories at **the Alamo,** a fortress built on the ruins of a Spanish mission in San Antonio, and at Goliad. At the Alamo, fewer than 200 Texans defended an abandoned Spanish mission for twelve days while inflicting heavy casualties on 4,000 Mexican troops. Before his death, Travis sent this plea for help "to the People of Texas and all the Americans in the World":

F*ellow citizens & compatriots, I am besieged by a thousand or more of the Mexicans under Santa Anna. . . . I call on you in the name of Liberty, of patriotism & everything dear to the American character to come to our aid, with all dispatch. . . . If this call is neglected, I am determined to sustain myself as long as possible & die like a soldier who never forgets what is due to his own honor or that of his country.*

Bowing to his father's dying wish, Stephen Austin established the first colony of American settlers in Texas in 1822.

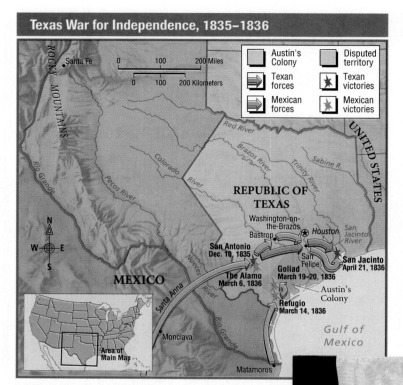

Texas War for Independence, 1835–1836

Austin's Colony	Disputed territory
Texan forces	★ Texan victories
Mexican forces	★ Mexican victories

ROCKY MOUNTAINS

Santa Fe

0   100   200 Miles
0   100   200 Kilometers

UNITED STATES

Red River

Brazos River

Sabine R.

Trinity River

Colorado River

Pecos River

Rio Grande

REPUBLIC OF TEXAS

Washington-on-the-Brazos
Bastrop
Houston
San Jacinto River

San Antonio
Dec. 10, 1835

San Felipe
San Jacinto
April 21, 1836

MEXICO

The Alamo
March 6, 1836

Goliad
March 19–20, 1836

Austin's Colony

Nueces River

Santa Anna

Refugio
March 14, 1836

Rio Grande

Gulf of Mexico

Monclava

Matamoros

N
W   E
S

Area of Main Map

Geography and History: Interpreting Maps
The Mexican government refused to recognize the boundaries of the republic Texans established. The Texas flag (right) reflected the new nation's informal name: the Lone Star Republic. *What formed the southernmost edge of the disputed territory?*

Texas Fighters Turn the Tables Still confident of victory, Santa Anna divided his force to finish off the Texan rebels, thousands of whom were fleeing eastward in what became known as the Runaway Scrape. Just when all seemed lost, more than 900 Texans regrouped at the San Jacinto River under **Sam Houston,** a strong-willed former governor of Tennessee. There they surprised the careless and arrogant Santa Anna. Rallying to cries of "Remember the Alamo! Remember Goliad!" they routed the Mexican troops in a matter of minutes. The map on this page illustrates the war for independence.

In retaliation for the Alamo and Goliad, the Texans killed several hundred of their prisoners and forced Santa Anna to sign a treaty recognizing the Republic of Texas. The Mexican government later denounced that treaty but did not contest it militarily. In the fall of 1836, the citizens of Texas elected Sam Houston as their first president.

By the end of the 1830s, with almost no help from the United States government, American traders and settlers had established a firm presence from Texas to California. They also had succeeded in prying away a large piece of territory from Mexico. As Americans continued to push west during the next decade—and the Mexican government continued to fume over the loss of Texas—tensions between Mexico and the United States grew to the point that war once again became a possibility.

The deaths of the courageous Alamo defenders—including William Travis and the legendary frontiersman Davy Crockett—and the massacre of 371 prisoners captured by the Mexicans at Goliad, enraged and energized Texans to mighty actions for their cause.

SECTION 4 REVIEW

Key Terms, People, and Places
1. Define secularize.
2. Identify (a) Stephen Austin, (b) William Travis, (c) Antonio López de Santa Anna, (d) Sam Houston.
3. Identify (a) Monterey, (b) Sante Fe, (c) the Alamo.

Key Concepts
4. Why did the Spanish try to reform their empire and colonize California in the late 1700s?
5. Were the California missions successful? Explain.

6. In what ways would the American conquest of New Mexico have a negative impact on women there?
7. Why did the Americans in Texas want their independence from Mexico?

Critical Thinking
8. **Making Comparisons** How were the attitudes of Spanish missionaries toward the Native Americans of California similar to the attitudes of many white Americans toward Native Americans at the time?

The Conquest of the West

SECTION PREVIEW

The Mexican War extended the nation's boundaries from the Atlantic to the Pacific. At war's end, the discovery of gold in California transformed a stream of western-moving settlers into a flood, resulting in growing tensions with many Native American groups.

Key Concepts

- In the 1840s thousands of Americans began to migrate to Oregon and California along a variety of long and difficult western trails.
- After a war with Mexico, the victorious United States received about two fifths of Mexico's territory.
- The push of western migration after the Mexican War and the discovery of gold in California increased friction between Native Americans and white settlers.

Key Terms, People, and Places

Oregon Trail, manifest destiny, Gadsden Purchase, Wilmot Proviso; Joseph Smith, Brigham Young

W hile some Americans were pushing into Texas in the early 1820s, others were drawn by stories they heard of a beautiful land beyond the Rocky Mountains. This vast territory, known as the Oregon Country (now called the Pacific Northwest), stretched from northern California to the southern border of Alaska.

To the Oregon Country

Although a variety of Native American groups had lived in Oregon for centuries, by the early 1800s four different nations—the United States, Great Britain, Russia, and Spain—claimed rights to the territory. Ignoring the Native Americans who already lived there,

the United States and Britain signed a treaty in 1818 agreeing to joint occupation of the territory. Distracted by other problems, Russia and Spain withdrew their claims to the area in the mid-1820s. By that time, the small but growing number of Americans who had made their way into Oregon were beginning to spread the word of what they had found there.

Routes to Oregon Merchants from New England, traveling by ship, first traded for furs with the Native Americans of Oregon in the late 1700s. After Lewis and Clark completed their expedition in 1806, fur traders such as Jedediah Smith and James Beckwourth began to roam the Rocky Mountains in search of animal pelts. Dubbed mountain men, these hardy trappers discovered Native American trails that led through the Rockies to California and Oregon, including the route that came to be known as the **Oregon Trail,** shown on the map on page 148.

Starting in 1843, groups of mainly white families from the midwestern states met at a small town in western Missouri called Independence—the beginning of the Oregon Trail. From there they began a grueling, 2,000-mile trek across the Great Plains and the Rocky Mountains.

The beauty of the plains and mountains impressed many pioneers, but it made the trip

This journal recorded the adventures of one pioneer who braved the western trails to find a new home and a new life.

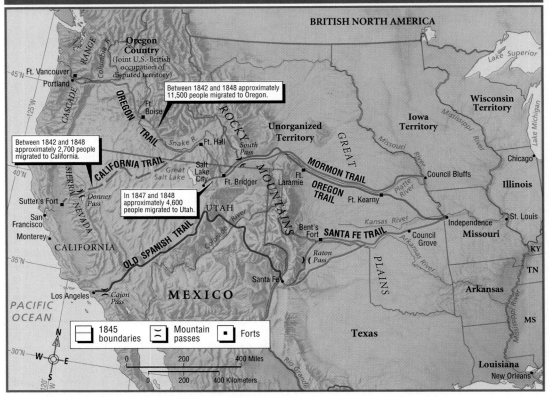

The Overland Trails to the West, 1840s

BRITISH NORTH AMERICA

Oregon Country
(Joint U.S.-British occupation of disputed territory)

Between 1842 and 1848 approximately 11,500 people migrated to Oregon.

Between 1842 and 1848 approximately 2,700 people migrated to California.

In 1847 and 1848 approximately 4,600 people migrated to Utah.

Ft. Vancouver
Portland
45°N
125°W
CASCADE RANGE
Columbia R.
Ft. Boise
OREGON TRAIL
CALIFORNIA TRAIL
Snake R.
Ft. Hall
South Pass
ROCKY MOUNTAINS
MORMON TRAIL
Ft. Laramie
OREGON TRAIL
Ft. Kearny
Platte River
GREAT PLAINS
Missouri River
Council Bluffs
Iowa Territory
Wisconsin Territory
Mississippi River
Lake Michigan
Lake Superior
Chicago
Illinois
St. Louis
Unorganized Territory
Great Salt Lake
Salt Lake City
Ft. Bridger
40°N
SIERRA NEVADA
Donner Pass
Sutter's Fort
San Francisco
Monterey
CALIFORNIA
35°N
OLD SPANISH TRAIL
Colorado River
UTAH
Bent's Fort
SANTA FE TRAIL
Kansas River
Arkansas River
Council Grove
Independence
Missouri
KY
TN
Raton Pass
Santa Fe
MEXICO
PLAINS
Arkansas
MS
Mississippi River
Los Angeles
Cajon Pass
PACIFIC OCEAN
30°N
120°W
Texas
Louisiana
New Orleans
Rio Grande

1845 boundaries | Mountain passes | • Forts

0   200   400 Miles
0   200   400 Kilometers

N S E W

Geography and History: Interpreting Maps
Thousands of settlers headed west along various overland trails in the 1840s, facing dry, barren country in some parts of the journey and tall, rugged mountains in others. *Along what important river did the final leg of the Oregon Trail run?*

no less long and difficult. Getting the heavy covered wagons across rivers, through muddy bogs, and up steep hills was exhausting, back-breaking work. And conditions for travel were often terrible in other ways as well, as an anonymous 1852 pioneer made clear:

To enjoy such a trip along with such a crowd of emigration, a man must be able to endure heat like a Salamander, mud and water like a muskrat, dust like a toad, and labor like a jackass. He must learn to eat with his unwashed fingers, drink out of the same vessel with his mules, sleep on the ground when it rains, and share his blanket with vermin, and have patience with musketoes. . . . It is a hardship without glory, to be sick without a home, to die and be buried like a dog.

In fact, the journey via the Oregon Trail was so difficult that some decided to bypass it altogether by sailing from the Atlantic coast of the United States around the tip of South America and up the Pacific coast of North America. The majority of migrants, however, traveled across the overland trails.

Movies and television westerns would have us believe that pioneers and Native Americans were constantly fighting with each other. In fact, they spent more time trading than fighting. White travelers received food and other necessities from Native Americans in return for clothing and tools. It was not until the 1850s that serious conflict developed. Far more deadly to white settlers than any threats from Native Americans were diseases such as cholera, which killed as many as 10,000 pioneers—or about 4 percent of the total—between 1840 and 1860.

Oregon Becomes United States Territory By 1845 more than 5,000 Americans had moved to the Oregon Country. When American settlers in the territory began to outnumber the British in 1843, they drew up a temporary government to be used until Oregon came under the jurisdiction of the United States. Three years later, in the Treaty of 1846, the United States and Great Britain agreed to divide the Oregon Country along the 49th parallel. Because of the growing threat of war with Mexico, this peaceful solution proved to be in the nation's best interest.

War with Mexico

As the surge of migrants from the United States into western territories gained momentum in the 1830s and 1840s, some Americans began to dream of a continental empire stretching from the Atlantic to the Pacific. These Americans believed that the United States had a divine mission to spread liberty across the continent. John L. O'Sullivan, a New York journalist, coined the phrase *manifest destiny* for this idea of continental expansion. He said that it was the nation's manifest, or obvious, destiny "to overspread and to possess the whole of the continent." Soon manifest destiny became a rationalization for expansion. Unfortunately, Americans were not the only ones who believed that it was their destiny to possess the West, as quickly became clear when the United States added Texas to its growing list of states.

Annexation of Texas After winning independence from Mexico in 1836, many Texans assumed that the United States would quickly absorb their new republic. Americans were far from united on the question of annexing Texas, however. Southerners and supporters of slavery were eager to carve one or more slave states out of the Texas territory. Northerners feared that the addition of even one slave state would shift the balance of power in Congress and the Electoral College to the South. Many people in both the North and South worried that annexation would lead to war with Mexico.

In the early 1840s, northerners and Whigs held up the annexation of Texas while southerners and Democrats scrambled to find some

way to push it through Congress. When Democrat James K. Polk, running on an expansionist platform, won the presidency in 1844, the tide began to shift. In February 1845, before Polk even took the oath of office, Congress approved annexation. After Texas voters added their approval in December of that year, Texas became the twenty-eighth state in the Union.

War for Territory Years before the United States annexed Texas, the steady influx of Americans into Mexico's northern territories had led to growing friction between the two nations. After Congress approved annexation

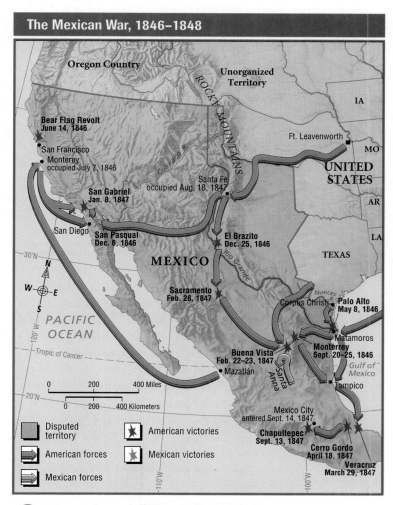

The Mexican War, 1846–1848

Geography and History: Interpreting Maps
Many Americans, including President Polk, viewed the Mexican War as an opportunity for the United States to expand its boundaries across the continent. *Looking at this map, what information can you use to make a judgment about who probably won the war?*

Viewpoints
On Expanding into Mexican Territory

Strained relations between North and South intensified when the United States annexed vast Mexican territories in 1848. *How is the spirit of the times reflected in the following viewpoints?*

Pro-Annexation

"The pretense that the annexation has been unrightful and unrighteous is wholly untrue and unjust to ourselves. If Texas became peopled with an American population, it was on the express invitation of Mexico herself. . . .What, then, can be more preposterous than all this clamor by Mexico against annexation as a violation of any rights of hers, any duties of ours?"

John L. O'Sullivan, editorial in *United States Magazine and Democratic Review*, 1845

Anti-Annexation

"They [who favor the Mexican War] have succeeded in robbing Mexico of her territory. And they are rejoicing over their success under the hypocritical pretense of a regard for peace. Had they not succeeded in robbing Mexico of the most important and most valuable part of her territory, many of those now loudest in their cries of favor for peace would be loudest and wildest for war. . . . We are not the people to rejoice. We ought rather blush and hang our heads for shame."

Frederick Douglass, African American leader of the antislavery movement, editorial in *North Star*, March 17, 1848

in early 1845, Mexico immediately broke off diplomatic relations with the United States. Continuing disagreements about the southern border of Texas signaled further trouble ahead.

President Polk and other southern Democrats wanted much more from Mexico than Texas. Polk had dreams of acquiring the entire territory stretching from Texas to the Pacific. In a provoking action, he sent two thousand American troops under General Zachary Taylor into southern Texas to support the American claim that the Rio Grande was the official American-Mexican border. Since the Mexican government claimed that the Nueces River, located quite a few miles further north, was the border, it considered Taylor's movements an invasion of Mexican territory. Tensions between the two nations escalated rapidly. Meanwhile, an American expe-

dition under the command of Captain John C. Frémont moved into California, probably under orders from the President to stir up trouble.

When Mexican troops engaged in a skirmish with Taylor's forces in early May 1846, Polk had the excuse for which he had long been waiting. Expressing outrage at the loss of "American blood on American soil," the President pushed for an immediate declaration of war. Despite some opposition, Congress gave it to him on May 13, 1846.

The war lasted less than a year and a half. Overcoming some resistance by Mexicans, American settlers and troops soon took control of California and New Mexico. Meanwhile, General Taylor had taken the war into Mexico itself. After crossing the Rio Grande, Taylor won a series of victories, leading finally to the Battle of Buena Vista in February 1847. The battle ended in victory for the Americans, ending the war in northeastern Mexico.

Pressing for complete victory, Polk dispatched forces under General Winfield Scott to take Mexico City. After fierce fighting, Scott captured the Mexican capital on September 14, bringing the war to an end.

With the defeat of its troops and the fall of the country's capital, the Mexican government was at the mercy of the United States. In the 1848 Treaty of Guadalupe Hidalgo, Mexico not only recognized the Rio Grande as the border of Texas but also gave up New Mexico and California—more than two fifths of its territory—to the United States. In return, the United States government paid Mexico $15 million and agreed to cover debts owed to United States citizens.

Five years later, in 1853, the Mexican government sold 30,000 square miles of what is now southern New Mexico and Arizona to the United States for $10 million. Known as the **Gadsden Purchase,** this land eventually provided a route for the southern transcontinental railroad. The table on page 151 shows the square miles added to United States territory from 1800 to 1860.

The Wilmot Proviso Another serious consequence of the Mexican War was that it brought the question of slavery to the forefront of American politics. The central issue that confronted Congress was what to do with the vast territory acquired by the United States from Mexico. Northerners did not want the balance of power in the United States to tip to the South and did not want to compete with plantation owners moving west, whose use of slavery drove wages down. As a result, northerners' fear of additional slave states was strong. Partly in response to Whig criticisms of the war, Pennsylvania Democrat David Wilmot attached an amendment to a military appropriations bill in 1846. The **Wilmot Proviso** stated that slavery would not be permitted in any of the territory acquired from Mexico.

Although Congress defeated the proviso, Wilmot laid bare tensions between the North and South. Eventually, the issue of slavery in the western territories would contribute to the outbreak of war between the sections. Americans could sidestep the question of slavery within existing states, but they had to confront the issue directly whenever they created new territories and new states.

Mormons Settle Utah

At the time of the Mexican War, the Mormons, one of the largest groups of migrants to head west in the 1840s, were finding a new home in present-day Utah. Mormons, or members of the Church of Jesus Christ of Latter-day Saints, had been looking for a permanent home ever since **Joseph Smith** founded the religion in western New York in 1830. Harrassed by neighbors who were suspicious of their beliefs, the Mormons moved to Ohio, then to Missouri, and finally to Nauvoo, Illinois.

Although the Mormans initially prospered in Illinois, relations with neighbors deteriorated after Smith revealed in 1843 that the Mormons accepted polygyny, a practice in which a family includes one husband and several wives. After a hostile mob killed Smith and his brother in 1844, the Mormons were forced to move on once again.

The religion's new leader, **Brigham Young,** decided that the Mormons' only hope was to live beyond the borders of the United States of that time. He and other leaders chose the Great Salt Lake Basin as the Mormons' new home, largely because it was located nearly a thousand miles from other Americans.

Starting in 1847, hundreds of Mormons left their temporary camps in Iowa for new homes near the Great Salt Lake. Within three years, more than 11,000 Mormons had settled in the region. By 1860, about 30,000 Mormons lived in Salt Lake City and more than ninety other towns in present-day Utah.

Despite many difficulties, these settlements were orderly and prosperous. The Mormons skillfully irrigated their desert region and devoted themselves primarily to farming.

At first the leaders of the Mormon church established their own system of government. With the end of the Mexican War, however, Utah became an official territory of the United States and Brigham Young its first governor. Utah eventually entered the Union in 1896 as the forty-fifth state.

Expansion of the United States, 1800–1860	
Year	Square Miles
1800	888,811
1810	1,716,003
1820	1,788,006
1830	1,788,006
1840	1,788,006
1850	2,992,747
1860	3,022,387

Source: *Historical Statistics of the United States*

Interpreting Tables
The United States more than tripled in size between 1800 and 1860. *During what decade did the largest expansion occur?*

MAKING CONNECTIONS

How was the Mormons' decision to establish a settlement in Utah in the 1840s similar to the Puritans' decision to found the Massachusetts Bay Colony in the 1620s?

The Gold Rush in California

Though settlers moving west like the Mormons often dreamed of fertile farmlands, others dreamed of instant wealth, especially after the discovery of gold at Sutter's Mill in California in January 1848. As the lumps of gold were displayed from town to town, they began to realize what the discovery meant. Walter Colton, mayor of Monterey, describes how the news affected his community:

The family who had kept house for me caught the moving fever. Husband and wife were both packing up; the blacksmith dropped his hammer, the carpenter his plane, the mason his trowel, the farmer his sickle, the baker his loaf, and the tapster his bottle. All were off for the mines. . . .

This gold miner was one of many who traveled to California to find his fortune.

Western Migration and Native Americans

The gold rush had a tremendous impact on life in California. For Native Americans, the influx of thousands of white immigrants was a disaster. The tens of thousands of miners forced Native Americans to work—the men in the mines, the women in their households. Disease and forced labor reduced the Native American population in California from roughly 150,000 in 1848 to 35,000 by 1860.

The Native Americans in California were not alone in their fate. The United States took little notice of Native American rights to the West. Until the Mexican War, the United States had proclaimed all land west of the 95th meridian to be "Indian Country." Along the so-called Permanent Indian Frontier, running from Minnesota to Louisiana, the United States Army built a series of forts. As growing numbers of Americans migrated beyond this frontier line, however, the United States established military posts farther and farther west.

Nomadic Native Americans proved to be the most successful at resisting the government's efforts to control them. By the end of the 1850s, both the United States government and the Plains Indians saw military action as their only option for dealing with each other. Increasing numbers of white Americans wanted to carve farms out of the rugged lands beyond the Mississippi River. Native Americans wanted to follow the buffalo on the wide-open plains as they had for decades. With neither side willing to yield or compromise, violence was the only possible outcome in this conflict between cultures.

Newspapers in the eastern United States were soon full of the exciting news, and people touched by gold fever rushed west by the thousands. California had 14,000 residents in 1848. Within a year, 100,000 people were living in the state, and by 1852 that number had reached 200,000.

A majority of the new immigrants were unmarried men. In fact, only 5 percent of the "forty-niners" who went to California in the 1849 gold rush were women or children. African Americans, both enslaved and free, were also part of the gold rush. Enslaved people worked as servants or searched for gold on their owners' work crews. Some free African Americans became independent miners.

SECTION 5 REVIEW

Key Terms, People, and Places

1. Define (a) Oregon Trail, (b) manifest destiny, (c) Gadsden Purchase, (d) Wilmot Proviso.

2. Identify (a) Joseph Smith, (b) Brigham Young.

Key Concepts

3. What posed the greatest threat to those American settlers who migrated to California and Oregon on the western trails?

4. What did Mexico give up in the Treaty of Guadalupe Hidalgo?

5. What was the impact of the gold rush on California?

Critical Thinking

6. Making Comparisons How was the attitude of the United States government toward Mexico's northern territories similiar to its attitude toward the area designated as "Indian Country"?

Formulating Questions

An important aspect of critical thinking is being able to formulate questions as you read. Asking questions about what you read helps you to focus on the facts. Formulating questions can help you gain insight into the material you read and thus sharpen your understanding of that material.

To formulate good questions, keep in mind the question words used by reporters: *Who? What? When? Where? Why?* and *How?* The first four words help you gather the basic facts. The last two help you to interpret those facts.

The box to the right shows a selection of epitaphs, or inscriptions, found on gravestones along the Oregon Trail. Estimates of the number of people who died range from 20,000 to 45,000. Use the following steps to formulate questions about the epitaphs. By asking questions, you can discover when people lived, how long they lived, and sometimes how they died.

1. Identify the topic. Identify the people, the years in which they lived, and, if possible, how they met their death. To guide your understanding, first think about who would be traveling on an overland trail. (a) What questions can you formulate about the ages of the people who died on the Oregon Trail? (b) What questions can you ask to identify the causes of death?

2. Identify a point of view. Who do you think wrote the epitaphs? Evaluate how people were remembered by those who knew them. (a) What questions can you formulate about the Winslow epitaph? (b) What questions can you formulate about the Martess marker?

3. Locate the important details. Study the grave markers to see what clues they offer about the historical period. Use the information about the time period, how the people died, and how those they left behind felt to help you understand what life was like on the Oregon Trail. (a) What questions can you ask to discover the dangers of traveling on the Oregon Trail? (b) What questions would you ask the people who survived?

Died: Of Cholera

(This was the most frequent epitaph found on grave sites along the way.)

Mary Ellis
Died May 7th, 1845
Aged two months

(This epitaph was found on a piece of plank standing up from a grave site, its letters traced by a red-hot piece of iron.)

Marlena Elizabeth Martess
Died Aug. 9th, 1863
Born July 7th, 1862
Friends nor physician could save her
from the grave

(This epitaph was followed by a plea to all who might pass to keep the grave in good repair.)

IN MEMORY OF GEORGE WINSLOW
who died on this great highway June 8, 1849
and was buried here by his comrades. . . . This
tablet is affectionately placed by his sons,
George Edward and Orrin Henry Winslow.

Rachel E. Pattison
Aged 18
June 19, '49

(This was a rock, hand-lettered.)

Rebecca Winters,
age 50 years

(This was crudely carved on a wagon wheel, which served as the grave's headstone.)

In Memory
of Charles Hatch HO
Died June 12, 1850

(Scratched on this carved tombstone is "Killed by Indians.")

Pioneer Grave of
John D. Henderson
Died of Thirst
August 9, 1852

Unaware of Nearness of the Malheur River Leaving Independence, Missouri, in May 1852, Mr. Henderson and Companion Name Unknown, Had completed Only Part of the Journey When Their Team Died. They were Compelled to Continue on Foot Carrying Their Few Possessions. The Twenty Miles of Desert Separating the Snake and Maleur Rivers Proved too Great a Struggle for the Weary Travelers

(This marker replaced a stone that gave Henderson's name and date of death.)

Chapter Review

Understanding Key Terms, People, and Places

Key Terms
1. Transcendentalism
2. temperance movement
3. abolition
4. gag rule
5. suffrage
6. cult of domesticity
7. nomad
8. secularize
9. Oregon Trail
10. manifest destiny
11. Gadsden Purchase
12. Wilmot Proviso

People
13. Lyman Beecher
14. Henry David Thoreau
15. Horace Mann
16. Dorothea Dix
17. William Lloyd Garrison
18. Frederick Douglass
19. Harriet Tubman
20. Catharine Beecher
21. Lucretia Mott
22. Elizabeth Cady Stanton
23. Sojourner Truth
24. Meriwether Lewis
25. William Clark
26. Sacajawea
27. Stephen Austin
28. William Travis
29. Antonio López de Santa Anna
30. Sam Houston
31. Joseph Smith
32. Brigham Young

Places
33. Liberia
34. Seneca Falls
35. Continental Divide
36. Great Plains
37. Monterey
38. Santa Fe
39. the Alamo

Terms For each term above, write a sentence that explains its relation to the reform movements from 1815 to 1860 or to the settlement of lands beyond the Mississippi River.

Matching Review the key terms in the list above. If you are not sure of a term's meaning, review its definition in the chapter. Then choose a term from the list that best matches each description below.
1. the belief in the importance of women's role at home
2. the right to vote
3. the belief that the United States had a divine mission to spread liberty across the continent
4. to transfer control from the church to the state

True or False Determine whether each statement is true or false. If it is true, write "true." If it is false, change the underlined person or place to make the statement true.
1. Under the leadership of Horace Mann, Massachusetts pioneered school reform.
2. Lucretia Mott and Elizabeth Cady Stanton organized a women's rights convention at Seneca Falls, New York.
3. Frederick Douglass published an antislavery newspaper called *The Liberator*.
4. Stephen Austin became the first president of the Republic of Texas.
5. Monterey was the capital of the territory of California.

Reviewing Main Ideas

Section 1 (pp. 124–129)
1. What were some of the social reforms undertaken by reform-minded citizens?
2. What approaches were favored by abolitionists before 1830?

Section 2 (pp. 132–137)
3. Give examples to show that the cultural attitudes toward women in the United States were reinforced by laws in the early 1800s.
4. In what ways did women begin to challenge traditional values in the period between 1815 and 1860?

Section 3 (pp. 138–141)
5. How did men acquire greater status than women in Native American nomadic societies?
6. Give two reasons that help explain why Native American village societies declined in the early 1800s.
7. Which Native American groups became dominant on the Great Plains?

Section 4 (pp. 142–146)
8. Why were the California missions able to thrive?
9. What was the ultimate effect of the increasing immigration of Americans into Texas?

Section 5 (pp. 147–152)
10. Briefly describe a typical overland journey to Oregon during the period of western expansion.
11. What were three consequences of the Mexican War?

1. **Making Comparisons** How did the views of Catharine Beecher differ from those of other women, such as Lucretia Mott and Elizabeth Cady Stanton, in the women's rights movement? What different voices can you identify in the women's movement today?

2. **Distinguishing False from Accurate Images** Briefly describe the popular image of the Native American as portrayed in television westerns and movies. What groups of Native Americans is this image based on? What groups does it ignore?

3. **Recognizing Ideologies** While the United States referred to the conflict with Mexico as the Mexican War, Mexicans called the war the North American Invasion. What do these different names suggest about each country's perspective on the war? Was the war in fact an act of aggression on the part of the United States?

1. **Evaluating Primary Sources** Review the primary source excerpt on page 134. Explain how the excerpt attacks the double standard that society held for men and women. What other groups in American society have sometimes been treated with a double standard?

2. **Understanding the Visuals** Look at the table on page 151. Why might John O'Sullivan see this table as visual evidence that the nation was following his concept of manifest destiny?

3. **Writing About the Chapter** It is 1849. You have just received a letter from your cousin in California urging you to come west. Write a response in which you explain why you will or will not make the journey. First, make a list of the reasons that support your decision. Also note the reasons that support the opposite point of view and why they fail to persuade you. Next, write a draft of your response in which you explain your intention to travel or to remain at home; use examples from the chapter to support your decision. Revise your response, making sure that you have clearly and persuasively explained your ideas. Proofread your response and draft a final copy.

4. **Using the Graphic Organizer** This graphic organizer uses a web map to organize information about nomadic groups of Native Americans on the Great Plains. In this web, dotted lines are used to show connections between ideas. (a) Why does the graphic organizer show a connection between the two animals central to nomadic culture, the horse and the buffalo? (b) Explain the other connections suggested by this graphic organizer. (c) On a separate sheet of paper, create your own web map about Spanish missions in California, using this graphic organizer as an example.

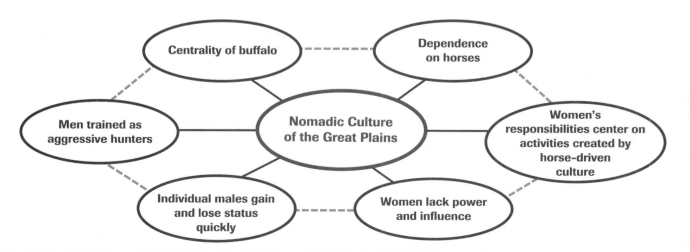

A Review of Key Ideas
Covered in Chapters 1–4

The Nation's Beginnings to 1860

Most Americans think of the early history of the United States as remote, far removed from the issues and concerns we face today. What could Native Americans, European settlers, and enslaved Africans who lived hundreds of years ago—people long since dead and in most cases forgotten—have to do with our lives now?

The people who lived hundreds of years ago established the character of American society and developed the basic principles that define the United States.

The answer is: a great deal. The people who lived on this continent hundreds of years ago established the character of American society. They developed the basic principles that define the United States. They shaped the environment and economic structures in fundamental ways. Focusing only on the recent past is like watching the last few moments of a movie: you miss the excitement that comes from understanding who the characters are and why they are in the situation in which you see them.

Cultural Encounters Through the 1700s

Long before Europeans and Africans arrived in North America, Native Americans occupied the continent. They were not all alike. They were divided into societies that spoke different languages, wore different kinds of clothing, ate different foods, and lived in different kinds of shelters. These Native American groups traded with one another and sometimes fought one another. Like all human societies, they were intent on protecting themselves and their way of life.

The Europeans Arrive The arrival of Spanish, English, French, and Dutch settlers in the 1500s and 1600s disrupted Native American societies. New diseases killed tens of thousands of Native Americans, and

increased trade and complicated new political pressures sparked devastating wars between the European settlers and Native Americans and among the Native Americans themselves.

The establishment of European colonies, however, also continued and strengthened the cultural diversity long present in North America. European nationalities were different from one another just as Native American groups were. For example, different European nationalities had different expectations about what their colonies should become. The English were interested in transforming, or completely changing, the environment into a version of their homeland. The Dutch and the French, on the other hand, tended to concentrate on extracting natural resources like fish and furs. These different expectations go a long way toward explaining why Europeans dealt with Native Americans in different ways.

Diverse Societies By the early 1700s, distinctive societies had emerged in North America. In some areas they were unique combinations of European and Native American ways of life. In New Mexico, the armed resistance of the Pueblo people had forced the Spanish to accept a mixed culture. In Canada, the French had established a colony dependent upon the fur trade, which could not operate without the cooperation of Native Americans.

In New England, English Puritans had worked to create a stable world, built around patriarchal households, social order, religious devotion, and intense soul-searching. In the place of Native American villages and hunting grounds, the Puritans had established fields, cattle pastures, small towns, and even a few sizable cities.

In the Southeast, other groups of people from England had fashioned colonies structured around the production of staples, or key crops, such as tobacco and rice. But instead of small farms and towns, they had developed plantations, or large, relatively self-sufficient farms, to produce quantities of their staple crops for European markets.

The English people in the Southern Colonies needed labor to work their plantations, and this need brought another diverse group of people into the land that would someday become the United States. These new arrivals, West Africans, did not choose to migrate. They were enslaved and brought by force to the Americas. Though they had to endure exploitation and degradation, they brought economic success to the Southern Colonies and made important contributions to American agriculture, architecture, music, and religion.

A New Nation Emerges, 1754–1800

In the second half of the 1700s, colonists of British descent emerged as the most powerful group in North America, in part because they were also the most numerous. Even as early as the mid-1700s, many British colonists had felt increasingly crowded along the Atlantic seacoast and wanted to expand into the interior of the continent. In 1754 the colonists' need for more land led to a war between Great Britain and France for the control of their territories in North America. This conflict—known as the French and Indian War—was settled in 1763, several years after a decisive British victory. Although French-speaking people remained in Canada and the Great Lakes region, after the war the French government was no longer directly involved in North America.

As this early seal shows, the United States promised a *novus ordo seclorum*— "a new order for the ages"— and a new era of liberty.

The Colonists Demand Equal Treatment British colonists were jubilant at defeating the French, but they were also disturbed at the way British officials and soldiers had behaved toward them during the war. They were even more upset during the remainder of the 1760s and during the early 1770s when the British government tried to tax them to offset the cost of defending and governing the North American colonies.

Colonial gentlemen were particularly angry. Many of them thought the British were not allowing them the full rights of Englishmen—that the British were treating them as inferiors. Some colonists believed the British government intended to tax them into slavery, making them completely dependent on Great Britain.

These fears made sense in British colonial society. Most colonists believed that human beings were fundamentally unequal and that some people were more important than others. White gentlemen—men with enough property to be independent—dominated colonial societies. Women, servants, and enslaved people were considered to be secondary to white gentlemen. They had roles to play in society, but no real power.

Respected at home, colonial gentlemen saw no reason why they should be slighted by the British government. The colonists reacted at first by petitioning for their rights and finally by fighting for them. After a year of armed clashes with the British, in 1776 the colonists declared their independence and created a new nation—the United States.

In the course of a war that lasted until 1783, the people of the United States did indeed win their independence. But they faced even greater challenges than that. In bringing about the American Revolution, they had broken away from Britain, and now they had to define what kind of a nation they were.

What would their basic principles be, the beliefs they shared that made them into one nation?

New Principles As it turned out, the American Revolution was a rejection of many of the basic principles of colonial society. In documents such as the Declaration of Independence and Thomas Paine's *Common Sense*, Americans announced their commitment to new ways of organizing and governing their society. Some of their new ideas came from the protests of ordinary people. Some came from religious and intellectual traditions. Still others were formed in the heat of the Revolution. Wherever those ideas came from, they became the new principles of American society. They included popular sovereignty, which was the idea that governments get their power and authority from the consent of the governed. In the United States, "We, the People" rule. Another basic principle was social equality, the idea that people are on some level fundamentally equal to one other. As Thomas Jefferson wrote in the Declaration of Independence, "all men are created equal" and "are endowed by their Creator with certain inalienable rights," including the right to "life, liberty, and the pursuit of happiness."

Liberty vs. Order In the late 1700s and early 1800s, the meaning of these revolutionary ideals was hotly debated in the emerging arena of American politics. Over and over again, people returned to the question of how to balance liberty and order, freedom and stability. How far should Americans carry their new principles?

One group in the 1780s, called Federalists, were concerned that the Revolution had gone too far. In the Constitution of the United States, written in 1787 and ratified in 1788, they tried to emphasize order. They gave the country a strong national government, with a President, Congress, and court system, in order to ensure "a more perfect union." Many people criticized the Constitution for making the national government too powerful. In fact, to overcome this criticism, the Federalists had to agree to a set of amendments to the Constitution, called the Bill of Rights, guaranteeing specific freedoms.

In the 1790s Federalists tried to turn the United States into an orderly and prosperous empire. They took over the debts of the states, strengthened the military, raised taxes, and followed a generally pro-British foreign policy. Many Americans objected to the strong actions of the Federalists. Led by Thomas Jefferson of Virginia, they organized what would become the Democratic party and attacked the Federalists as men who preferred order to liberty.

In 1800 Jefferson and his followers won a key presidential election. The victory of the Jeffersonian Democrats meant that the Federalists would never control the national government again. For the next sixty years, despite the efforts of such diehard Federalists as Supreme Court Chief Justice John Marshall, the United States would have a relatively weak national government.

A Time of Rapid Change, 1800–1860

Nowadays Americans like to think that they are living in times of change unlike anything in the history of the nation. But in the first half of the 1800s, too, change was rapid, bewildering, upsetting, and exciting. Part of this change was due to simple expansion. The United States doubled its claims to North American territory when it completed the Louisiana Purchase in 1803. When Native Americans became Great Britain's allies against the United States during the War of 1812, the young nation defeated them and forced them to give up a vast expanse of land. Continuing the process of conquest and development, by the mid-1800s Americans had extended their claims from the Appalachian Mountains to the Great Plains and from the Great Lakes to the Gulf of Mexico.

Other changes were equally swift. The population of the United States had been doubling every twenty years towards the end of the 1700s. During the early 1800s, it continued to grow at a wild rate. Society and the economy were transformed by the Market Revolution. In this gradual but drastic change, the United States moved away from a household economy—one centered around keeping the household going—to a money economy centered on buying and selling goods in the marketplace. People came up with hundreds of money-making, labor-saving inventions, such as the cotton gin and the steamboat. Transportation and communication improved dramatically as Americans built canals, roads, and railroads. Cities such as New

York and Philadelphia suddenly became huge metropolises. The United States was full of hustle and bustle, filled with people moving around in search of better places to live or developing new ways to do things or make a living.

The Contradictions of Equality

Despite all this change, the United States remained a nation troubled by serious problems and contradictions. Of these, slavery was the most obvious. Although African Americans lived in a republic committed to equality and popular sovereignty, most of them were still subjected to the unequal conditions of slavery. African Americans themselves were fully aware of this contradiction and pointed it out at every opportunity.

The problem was that the Constitution gave enslaved people no rights. In fact, it suggested that an enslaved African American was only three-fifths of a human being and that liberty was something reserved for white men. Yet this was contradicted by the language of the Declaration of Independence, which said that all men were created equal. By the 1830s, growing numbers of white northerners, encouraged by African Americans, were coming to the conclusion that slavery was morally wrong and should be abolished. Meanwhile, in the South, slaveholders responded to attacks on slavery by developing elaborate racial and religious justifications for it.

As for Native Americans, it had become clear by the 1830s that whites would not allow them a place in American society. After decades of resistance and some efforts at accommodation, worn down by disease and by the sheer number of white settlers, Native Americans in the East were forced by the United States government to relocate west of the Mississippi River. In the West, the Native Americans of the Plains, such as the Sioux, would continue to resist United States expansion for decades.

The Market Revolution transformed the nation's society and economy. As shown on this bank note from the early 1800s, the nation moved away from a household economy to a money economy centered on people working for a living outside their homes—in factories and workshops.

North vs. South Even the two main sections of the nation, North and South, became contradictions of each other. More rural than the North, less industrial and populous, dependent on enslaved people for labor, by the 1840s the South increasingly seemed like a different kind of America.

This difference raised a serious issue. Convinced it was their "manifest destiny" to rule North America, Americans had expanded across the Mississippi River and put down roots in what is now Texas, Oregon, and Utah. In 1846, with a view to acquiring more land, the United States had declared war on Mexico. Eighteen months later, Mexico was forced to give up a third of its territory, including Texas, New Mexico, and California. Now, which kind of America should the new land become—should it be like the South, or like the North?

According to the Missouri Compromise of 1820, slavery should have been legal throughout most of this new territory. But many northerners were now so opposed to slavery that they would no longer accept the Missouri Compromise. They insisted that slavery should never be expanded to any other states. Southerners, realizing that their way of life was threatened, angrily insisted on their right to create new states in which slavery would be legal. There was no getting around this clash of values. The contradictions built into American principles and the American way of life would have to be resolved, one way or another.

Division and Uneasy Reunion
1848–1877

"A house divided against itself cannot stand. I believe this government cannot endure permanently, half slave and half free."

—Abraham Lincoln, 1858

*L*ong before the simmering tension between North and South exploded into war in 1861, the United States had come to resemble a "house divided." A series of fragile political compromises in the early 1800s had served only to slow rather than end the growing strain between the two regions. Although the North ultimately prevailed in the Civil War, and Lincoln achieved his dream of preserving the Union, his goal of healing the nation's regional and racial rifts ended with his assassination. The period of Reconstruction that followed the war left a legacy of bitterness, resentment, and broken promises.

This 1865 photograph of Richmond, Virginia, taken by a colleague of photographer Mathew Brady, shows that the Civil War smashed the nation's cities as well as ravaging its battlefields.

The Coming of the Civil War

1848–1861

*B*y the 1850s, deep distrust divided northerners and southerners. Worse still, many Americans no longer believed that government could settle their differences. Under the strain of conflict between North and South, the great web of law, compromise, and tradition that had held the United States together for over seventy years snapped. The nation broke apart and began its darkest and most painful trial: the Civil War.

Events in the United States

1848	1850	1852	1854
	1850 Congress passes the Compromise of 1850. • Senator John Calhoun dies.	**1852** Harriet Beecher Stowe's Uncle Tom's Cabin becomes an instant best-seller.	**1854** The American, or Know Nothing, party is formed.

Events in the World

1848 Revolutions sweep Europe. • Franz Josef becomes Emperor of Austria.	1850 The Taiping Rebellion begins in China.	1851 The Great Exhibition is held at the Crystal Palace in London.	1852 The South African Republic is established.	1853 The Crimean War begins between Turkey and Russia.

162

Pages 164–168

Two Nations?

In the 1850s growing numbers of Americans were convinced that the North and South were moving in different directions. Each side saw the other as a threat to the American way of life.

Pages 169–175

New Political Parties

A compromise during the 1850s failed to end disagreement over slavery in the territories. Meanwhile the second American party system broke down as new political parties arose, aimed at solving the challenging issues of the time.

Pages 177–181

The System Fails

A series of violent clashes between antislavery and proslavery forces between 1856 and 1860 brought the United States to the boiling point. Americans on each side of the slavery issue became convinced that the other side was acting against law and morality.

Pages 184–187

A Nation Divided Against Itself

Secession spread like wildfire through the southern states when Abraham Lincoln captured the presidency. While politicians and the people debated how to respond, the first shots were fired, and the broken nation plunged into war.

1856 Debate over slavery erupts into violence in Kansas.

1857 The Supreme Court supports slave owners in the Dred Scott decision.

1859 John Brown, abolitionist, leads a raid against Harpers Ferry, Virginia.

1860 Republican Abraham Lincoln is elected United States President.
• South Carolina secedes from the Union.

1861 The bombardment of Fort Sumter signals the start of the Civil War.

1856	1858	1860	1862	1864

1857 Indian soldiers revolt against the British in the Sepoy Rebellion.

1860 English novelist George Eliot publishes The Mill on the Floss.

1863 The open hearth process for producing steel is developed in France.

Two Nations?

SECTION PREVIEW

In the 1850s growing numbers of Americans were convinced that the North and South were moving in different directions. Each side saw the other as a threat to the American way of life.

Key Concepts

- Some historians believe that serious conflict between the North and the South was unavoidable, while others believe better leadership might have prevented it.
- *Uncle Tom's Cabin* helped convince northerners that slavery was immoral and a threat to middle-class families and character.
- Southerners charged that northern capitalists exploited their workers.
- Material differences between the North and South contributed to the growing gulf between these sections.

Key Terms, People, and Places

Civil War, Union; Harriet Beecher Stowe, George Fitzhugh

A spool of thread spun in a mill and a boll of raw cotton symbolize the difference between the industrial power of the North and the agricultural strength of the South in the 1850s.

B etween 1861 and 1865, the southern and northern states clashed with one another in a violent conflict that Americans call the **Civil War.** The result of the war would decide whether the **Union,** as the unified nation was called, would continue unbroken or be shattered forever. This war continually sparks our interest because it is the only time in our history when Americans became so frustrated and disillusioned with their political and legal systems that they saw war as the only way to resolve their differences.

Historians and the Civil War

Some historians have suggested that the Civil War could have been avoided. If the United States had elected better leaders and established stronger political institutions, they believe, wild-eyed extremists on both sides would never have been able to force the nation into war. The reason most of these historians believe that the differences between North and South could have been settled is that they think American society in the middle of the 1800s was relatively similar everywhere. They emphasize that whether in Alabama, Oregon, Indiana, or Massachusetts, Americans were all essentially capitalists who believed strongly in democracy in all areas of life.

Other historians—especially more recent ones—do not accept the idea that American society was similar everywhere. They tend to emphasize differences, including differences between regions, racial groups, and classes in society. These historians do not claim that the actual events of the Civil War could only have happened in one particular way. But because they focus on differences, they believe that the North and South were going in such different directions before 1860 that some kind of major conflict was bound to happen.

This textbook combines both views. While the text has stressed the general commitment of Americans to democratic government, social equality, and capitalism (see Chapters 2 and 3), it has also pointed out growing regional differences in economic and social structures (see Chapters 8, 9, and 10).

Many Americans during the early 1800s noticed the differences between North and South. They said that the two great sections amounted to distinct nations within the United States. And the key difference between North and South—to which all the other differences were connected in some way—was slavery. It was certainly true that nearly all white Americans, including many white abolitionists, were deeply prejudiced against African Americans, believing them to be inferior to white Americans. But prejudiced or not, by the 1850s many

Christian Americans had become convinced that slavery violated the basic principles not only of the United States but also of the Christian religion. These people were mostly members of the middle class who belonged to the highly democratic Protestant faiths that had been on the rise since the Second Great Awakening. They strongly believed an individual should be able to make choices and develop character. For them, therefore, slavery was simply an evil that could not be tolerated.

The troops that struggled on both sides when the Civil War began were *not* fighting to end slavery or to save it. They were fighting about whether the South would remain part of the United States. Yet the issue of slavery was one of the main differences between North and South that brought on the war.

Uncle Tom's Cabin and the Case Against the South

Without question, the most popular statement about the impact of slavery on white Americans both in this world and the next was a novel by **Harriet Beecher Stowe,** the sister of Catharine Beecher. This book, *Uncle Tom's Cabin,* was published in 1852 and became an instant bestseller. With over 300,000 copies in print in the first year of publication, it sold millions and was translated into twenty languages.

Today, many readers are offended by Stowe's portraits of the enslaved Uncle Tom and his wife, Aunt Chloe. Stowe seems to us to have been condescending and biased in describing them. In fact, "Uncle Tom" has become an insulting nickname for an African American man who passively accepts unequal status. But Stowe intended to portray Uncle Tom as a Christian man: he was simple, passive, and nonthreatening. Her Uncle Tom was

a large, broad-chested, powerfully made man, of a full glossy black, and a face whose truly African features were characterized by an expression of grave and steady good sense, united with much kindliness and benevolence [goodwill]. *There was something about his whole air, self-respecting and dignified, yet united with a confiding and humble simplicity.*

Because there was no reason to fear such a person, the brutal treatment Uncle Tom received from his master seemed all the more intolerable.

But Stowe did not depend only on the sharp contrast between a kindly enslaved person and his cruel master to make her case against slavery. She also tried to show that slavery was opposed to ideals many northerners cherished: the cult of domesticity, or the importance of women to society, and the ideal of the family. In the novel, the neat, orderly world of Uncle Tom's cabin, formed around his happy family, comes to a tragic end when Uncle Tom's owner has to sell him. Eventually Uncle Tom falls into the hands of another slaveholder, Simon Legree.

By contrast with the saintly Uncle Tom, Simon Legree is everything Stowe's audience in the North feared and despised: an unmarried, anti-Christian, heavy-drinking brute who cares only about satisfying his desires and his greed. Not only does he rape the enslaved women of his plantation, but in the end he beats Uncle Tom to death with a whip. It was not a mistake that Stowe made Legree a northerner who lived in the South. She wanted to show how slavery could corrupt even those born outside the system.

To balance these stark images of the

Harriet Beecher Stowe's novel *Uncle Tom's Cabin* offered antislavery forces new encouragement in resisting the slavery system. It inspired songs, plays, a card game, and a children's version (top). An African American family, the Webbs (bottom), toured the North reading the book to audiences.

immoral effects of slavery, Stowe wrote powerful scenes in which northern women influence their husbands to do what is right. Thus she brought the controversy over slavery into the confines of the home, which she saw as the woman's sphere. For instance, in one scene set in a house in Ohio, a wife persuades her husband, a senator, to take no action to prevent some runaway enslaved people from continuing their escape to Canada. When her husband tries to "reason" with her, she replies,

> I don't know anything about politics, but I can read my Bible; and there I see that I must feed the hungry, clothe the naked, and comfort the desolate; and that Bible I mean to follow.

Her husband argues that to help runaway enslaved people would involve breaking the law. But the wife steadily replies:

> Obeying God never brings on public evils. I know it can't. It's always safest, all round, to do as he bids us.

Although it was fiction, Stowe's book had as powerful an effect in her time as Thomas Paine's *Common Sense* had in his. It presented northern readers with a single, vivid picture of both slavery and the South that they could understand and adopt as accurate, even if it was in fact exaggerated. As they sat in the privacy of their parlors reading *Uncle Tom's Cabin,* many northerners became convinced that slavery would be the ruin of the United States. They worried not just about the impact of slavery on African Americans, but about its impact on whites and American society in general. Of this they were sure: they would never allow the United States to become a land full of Simon Legrees.

Cannibals All! and the Case Against the North

While immensely popular in the North, *Uncle Tom's Cabin* was virtually banned in the South. Southern intellectuals and politicians saw it as a book of insulting lies. They admitted that there were some masters who treated enslaved people badly. But the South was hardly home to thousands of Legrees. White southerners had their own exaggerated view of slavery: to them, plantation households were like happy patriarchal families.

But southerners did more than protest what they saw as northern insults. Many began to justify the South and attack the evils they saw in the North. They claimed that most planters took a personal interest in the welfare of the enslaved people who labored for them, providing them with the basic necessities of life. Industrialists, on the other hand, took no personal responsibility for workers and did not care that the meager wages workers were paid could not buy decent food, clothing, and shelter. Most southerners

Southern writers promoted the myth that slavery "raised Africans from savagery" and "civilized" them. These before-and-after pictures are from a pamphlet titled *Bible Defence of Slavery*.

THE NEGRO IN HIS OWN COUNTRY.

THE NEGRO IN AMERICA.

believed that northerners were so intent on making a profit that they had no concern whatever for the human needs of their workers.

Perhaps the most direct statement of this point of view appeared in a book by **George Fitzhugh** published in 1857, titled *Cannibals All!* Attacking northern industrialists, whom he saw as no better than cannibals, Fitzhugh wrote:

You, with the command over labor which your capital gives you, are a slave owner—a master, without the obligations of a master. They who work for you, who create your income, are slaves, without the rights of slaves. Slaves without a master!

Outraged by the hypocrisy of antislavery northerners, Fitzhugh exclaimed:

What is falsely called Free Society is a very recent invention. It proposes to make the weak, ignorant, and poor, free, by turning them loose in a world owned exclusively by the few (whom nature and education have made strong and whom property has made stronger) to get a living.

White southerners argued that they were the true heirs of the American Revolution. They believed that their patriarchal households possessed an order, a grace, a sense of liberty, that Bible-thumping, middle-class reformers and capitalists could not begin to understand. On this point southerners were agreed: they were not about to let northerners, whom they saw as self-righteous, tell them how to live.

MAKING CONNECTIONS

Suggest how the North might use the Declaration of Independence to argue for ending slavery and the South might use it to argue for resisting northern interference.

Material Differences Between North and South

The differences between North and South were not simply a product of exaggerated fiction

and propaganda. Hard facts also told the story. They showed that the North was becoming still more urban, still more industrial than the South. Its population, two and a half times as large as the population of the South, was becoming even larger and more diverse, as Irish and German immigrants crowded into swelling cities. Of the ten largest cities in the United States in 1860, nine were located in the North.

Like immigration, new technology had a heavier impact on the North than on the South. The biggest technological change was the appearance of railroads. Railroads, developed in Great Britain in the 1820s, were the quickest, most efficient form of transportation the world had ever known. They made canals pointless in a matter of years.

By 1840 about 3,000 miles of track spanned the United States. African American and Irish immigrant workers added another 5,000 miles during the 1840s. It was in the 1850s, however, that the railroads truly came into their own. Over 20,000 miles were laid in that decade.

During this railroad boom, remote places suddenly became the centers of bustling commerce. The small trading village of Chicago grew incredibly. Why? Because railroads made Chicago a central location through which people both to the east and to the west shipped goods such as corn, wheat, and other cereals.

The railroads, however, primarily affected the North. In 1860 the North had 70 percent of the railroad tracks in the United States. The

Though the North was still largely a land of farms, increasingly its landscape resembled this late-1850s print of Bridgewater, Massachusetts, in which a thundering train passes smoking forges casting metal goods and machinery.

Picking Cotton: Humans vs. Machines

Picking cotton by hand (immediate right, in a photograph from the 1800s) required many workers. Modern mechanical cotton harvesters (far right) need only a few operators. *How might the slavery system have been affected if harvesting machines had been available to pick cotton in the early 1800s?*

South had tracks, and they produced great cities such as Atlanta, Georgia. But southern planters and farmers still tended to rely on transportation by water for their staple crops.

Like the railroad, another invention, the telegraph, also magnified differences between North and South. This early form of electronic communication allowed people to send messages over wire by means of coded pulses of electricity. Because telegraph wires were strung along the ever-growing network of railroad tracks, the communications revolution in the North advanced more quickly than in the South.

Railroads and improved communications nourished the booming industries of the North. In 1860 the North had 110,000 factories, compared to 20,000 in the South; it produced $1.5 billion worth of goods, compared to the South's $155 million. In fact, in terms of numbers, the South outdid the North in only two notable ways: it had more enslaved people and it had more cotton.

Unquestionably, in 1860 the North and the South had much in common. They both had been born in the same revolution and cherished that tradition. They both believed in and practiced capitalism. Even on the issue of the status of African Americans, whites in both North and South displayed tremendous prejudice. But despite these similarities, they differed greatly in their beliefs about what American society should be.

SECTION 1 REVIEW

Key Terms, People, and Places
1. Define (a) Civil War, (b) Union.
2. Identify Harriet Beecher Stowe.

Key Concepts
3. Describe the two main views historians hold about the causes of the Civil War.
4. What effect did *Uncle Tom's Cabin* have on northern views of slavery?

5. Describe George Fitzhugh's criticism of northern capitalists.
6. Describe the material differences that had arisen between the North and the South by 1860.

Critical Thinking
7. **Checking Consistency** Northerners and southerners each accused the other of exploiting labor. Explain how both sides were guilty of this practice.

New Political Parties

SECTION PREVIEW

A compromise during the 1850s failed to end disagreement over slavery in the territories. Meanwhile the second American party system broke down as new political parties arose, aimed at solving the challenging issues of the time.

Key Concepts

- Because it failed to deal with the real problem, the Compromise of 1850 was only a temporary solution to the problem of slavery in the territories.
- In the early 1850s, the second American party system came to an end as Americans abandoned the Whig party because it no longer addressed pressing issues.
- In the North, a tremendous increase in immigrants led frightened middle-class and working-class Americans to join new political parties to protect their interests.
- The Kansas-Nebraska Act of 1854 established that the people of those territories could decide for themselves whether they would have slavery.
- The Republicans won voters by campaigning against both immigrants and slavery.

Key Terms, People, and Places

Compromise of 1850, Fugitive Slave Act, states' rights, nativism, naturalization, Kansas-Nebraska Act, the Slave Power; Democratic party, American party, Know Nothings, Stephen Douglas, Republican party

S o what if there were differences between North and South? Certainly the differences were bound to cause conflict, but did they have to lead to a four-year war that would kill hundreds of thousands of people? The answer to this question requires an understanding of politics in the 1850s. The war came *when* it did and *how* it did because politicians could not resolve the question of slavery. The rest of this chapter explains that political breakdown.

The Compromise of 1850

Politicians might have been able to keep slavery from tearing the nation apart if Americans had not conquered the trans-Mississippi West. This newly acquired land forced an old question back into politics. That question, first raised by the Missouri Compromise of 1820, was whether or not slavery would be allowed in the territories.

The Slavery Question Grows Heated In theory, the Missouri Compromise had taken care of this problem by establishing 36° 30' N latitude as a permanent boundary between free and slave states. But northerners were unwilling to accept this boundary after the United States acquired a large part of Mexico in the Mexican War. They feared that the new territory would be divided into several slave states, thus giving the South a majority vote in the United States Senate and perhaps in the Electoral College.

Southerners were equally firm in insisting that the national government had no business telling its free citizens they could not take their property to the territories if they wanted to. And property, after all, was what they considered enslaved people to be.

After the Treaty of Guadalupe Hidalgo, the issue of slavery in the territories grew more and more controversial. Though tempers flared and threats flew, Whigs and Jacksonian leaders tried to downplay the issue. Zachary Taylor, a Whig, was elected President in 1848 by avoiding any discussion of slavery in his campaign.

A banner of one of the new political parties of the 1850s—the Republicans— shows John Frémont, candidate for President in 1856, and proclaims the Republicans' refusal to allow slavery in the territories.

But after Taylor died in 1850, President Millard Fillmore found the slavery issue unavoidable. Americans had been thronging into California, especially after the gold rush of 1849, and some decision about slavery there had to be made. In 1850, Fillmore and Congress struggled to put together a deal between the two rival parts of the nation.

A Solution Is Proposed This package of laws, called the **Compromise of 1850,** was designed to balance the interests of the two sections, North and South. The table at right lists the provisions of the compromise. Under the proposal, Congress would admit California as a free state; in return, the people of the territories of New Mexico and Utah were to decide for themselves whether slavery would be legal. Congress also would abolish the sale of enslaved people, but not slavery itself, in Washington, D.C. To win southern approval for this change, the compromise also called for Congress to pass the **Fugitive Slave Act.** This law ordered all citizens of the United States to assist in the return of enslaved people who had escaped from their

The Compromise of 1850
Admitted California as a free state
Allowed citizens in New Mexico and Utah territories to determine for themselves the legal status of slavery
Abolished the sale of enslaved people, but not slavery itself, in Washington, D.C.
Passed the Fugitive Slave Act, which required all citizens to assist in the return of enslaved persons who had escaped from their owners and which denied jury trials to runaways

Interpreting Tables
The Compromise of 1850 was not one but several laws, all of which dealt in various ways with a common issue. *What was that issue?*

owners. It also denied a jury trial to enslaved people who had escaped.

Debate over the compromise dragged on for months. On March 4, 1850, the United States Senate gathered to hear the opinion of John C. Calhoun of South Carolina. As it turned out, Calhoun's speech was one of the great summaries of the southern view of the crisis.

During the debate that led to the Compromise of 1850, all the great speakers of Congress had their say. Among them was Henry Clay, shown here in February 1850 as he warned that a failure to compromise would lead to "furious" and "bloody" war.

AMERICAN PROFILES

John C. Calhoun

Many in the Senate felt great emotion when it was Calhoun's turn to present his views. Everyone knew that the senator was ill and that he probably did not have long to live. So weak was he that he asked James Mason of Virginia to read his speech. But even fading away, Calhoun was still one of the most respected members of the Senate, and people waited in suspense to hear what he had written.

A Champion of the South
Born on March 18 in 1782, the sixty-seven-year-old John Caldwell Calhoun had devoted much of his public life to South Carolina and the United States. For four decades, he had been one of the towering figures in Washington, the equal of Henry Clay and Andrew Jackson. Member of the House of Representatives (1811–1817), secretary of war (1817–1824), Vice President of the United States (1825–1832), secretary of state (1844–1845), and senator (1832–1843, 1845–1850), Calhoun was deeply committed to the Union.

Devoted though he was to the United States, Calhoun was even more devoted to his principles. He had once written:

M*y politics, I think I may say with perfect truth, has . . . been founded on certain fixed principles; and to carry them into effect has been my highest ambition.*

One of Calhoun's principles was a belief in liberty and in fighting anything that threatened it. In the 1820s, it became clear to Calhoun that control of the United States government by the North was a threat to the southern way of life and to liberty as he understood it. Though trained as a lawyer, he was also a gentleman planter and the owner of Fort Hill, a 500-acre plantation in South Carolina and the home of about seventy enslaved people. Therefore Calhoun worked tirelessly throughout the 1830s and 1840s to protect slavery and to keep the North from controlling the federal government. He had great influence among those who believed in **states' rights.** According to this theory, states have the right to nullify acts of the federal government and even to leave the Union if they wish to do so.

"The Greatest and the Gravest Question"
As the speech began, Calhoun—through Senator Mason—stated the problem the nation faced.

I *have, Senators, believed from the first that . . . the subject of slavery would, if not prevented by some timely and effective measure, end in disunion [of the United States]. . . . It has reached a point when it can no longer be disguised or denied that the Union is in danger. You have thus had forced upon you the greatest and the gravest question that can ever come under your consideration: How can the Union be preserved?*

The "great and primary" cause of the crisis, Calhoun said, was that the North now had

the exclusive power of controlling the Government, which leaves the [South] without any adequate means of protecting itself against . . . encroachment and oppression.

Calhoun was certainly right about this. Over the years, the North had indeed gained power—not only through its greater wealth, but also through its larger population, which gave it more representatives in Congress and more votes in the Electoral College. It also had gained a new understanding of the principle of liberty. Many of its residents no longer would tolerate slavery in any state. Both North and South were now accusing each other of betraying basic American principles, including liberty, unity, and the sharing of power among the states.

The South—Upholder of the Constitution
In his speech, Calhoun made clear that the

Using Historical Evidence John C. Calhoun (left) was once called "the cast iron man." *Find Calhoun in the picture on page 170 by comparing that picture with this portrait.*

South did not want to part ways with the North. But he also stated that the South would not give up its liberty to save the Union:

> The South asks for justice, simple justice, and less she ought not to take. She has no compromise to offer, but the Constitution; and no concession or surrender to make.

Today Americans believe that slavery is morally wrong, because it robs people of their liberty. Calhoun and other white southern planters believed that *stopping* slavery was morally wrong, because it interfered with their liberty to own enslaved people as property. And government, they believed, should protect this basic liberty. Southern planters believed that if the federal government intended to reduce their rights or threaten their property, then it was no longer a government worthy of their respect. From the point of view of Calhoun, it was the northern section of the country, not the southern section, which was twisting the Constitution and the intentions of the Framers. The ringing finale of his speech made this clear:

> I have exerted myself . . . with the intention of saving the Union, if it could be done; and if it could not, [with saving] the section . . . which I sincerely believe has justice and the Constitution on its side.

Although Calhoun warned that the crisis required more drastic measures than mere compromise, his speech did not persuade members from the North. Congress eventually passed the Compromise of 1850.

As Calhoun had foreseen, southerners were not satisfied with the compromise, although the legislation did bring a brief calm to the nation. In reality, it solved nothing beyond determining that California would be a free state. Part of the compromise, the Fugitive Slave Act, actually made the situation worse by infuriating many northerners—including Harriet Beecher Stowe, who expressed her outrage in *Uncle Tom's Cabin.*

Less than a month after Mason read Calhoun's speech on the floor of the Senate, John

Calhoun was dead. His prophetic words and his death proved a fateful beginning for the decade of the 1850s—a time when politics in the United States changed dramatically.

The End of the Second Party System

During the early 1850s, the second American party system broke down. True, the **Democratic party** remained, the descendant of the Jeffersonian Democrat-Republicans and the Jacksonian Democrats. The Democratic party has survived many periods of crisis like the early 1850s because it has always been a collection of diverse groups. But the Whig party was not so diverse, and by the end of the 1850s it had largely disappeared. The slavery issue badly hurt the Whigs, because many of their northern voters were middle-class evangelical Protestants who were disgusted with the politicians' fondness for compromise.

Another reason the Whigs faded away was that the old issues that had divided political parties in the 1830s now seemed largely resolved. Why argue about banks? The United States was prosperous and expanding. The men at the center of the Jacksonian-Whig struggles—Jackson, Clay, Webster, Calhoun—were either dead or dying. Political parties seemed to be lumbering onward only to keep their hold on government jobs and contracts.

Rutherford B. Hayes, a Whig living in Cincinnati, Ohio, and a future President of the United States, argued in the fall of 1852 that the old parties were irrelevant.

> The real grounds of difference upon important political questions no longer correspond with party lines. . . . Politics is no longer the topic of this country. Its important questions are settled. . . . Government no longer has its ancient importance.

In the election of 1852, won by the indecisive Democrat, Franklin Pierce, a few voters seemed very interested in the outcome. The time had come for a new generation of leaders to come forward, and during the 1850s, they did emerge. Whether they would be able to deal with the new issues facing the nation was another question.

The Rise of the Know Nothings

Slavery and disillusionment with politics were not the only issues that brought down the Whigs. The equally powerful issue of **nativism** also played a part in the end of the party. This was a movement to ensure that people born in the United States, who considered themselves "natives," received better treatment than immigrants. Between 1846 and 1854, close to three million Europeans arrived in the United States. Many middle-class evangelical Protestants were particularly disturbed by the Catholic immigrants among them, most of whom had come from Ireland and Germany.

Dislike of Catholics followed a pattern. Many of the same people who objected to slavery in the South also objected to Catholicism. They knew that the Catholic religion was organized into a hierarchy reaching from churchgoers through priests, bishops, and cardinals, up to the Pope, whose word was law. Protestants believed that this hierarchy did not allow for individual free choice. They worried that "Papal Power"—the power of the Pope—would interfere with the rights of citizens in a democracy.

Fear about immigrants led in 1849 to the formation of a secret nativist society called the Order of the Star-Spangled Banner. Within a few years, its membership totaled around a million. The order insisted on complete secrecy from its members, who used passwords and special handshakes. They always replied to questions about the organization with the answer "I know nothing." In 1854 nativists went public by forming a political organization, the **American party.** It pledged to work against Irish Catholic candidates and for laws requiring a longer wait before immigrants could become citizens through the process of **naturalization.** Because it was closely associated with the Order of the Star-Spangled Banner, the American party came to be called the **Know Nothings.**

Know Nothings claimed that they were committed to "the great work of Americanizing Americans." Strongly opposed to Catholicism, they called on

every American and naturalized protestant citizen throughout the Union, to use his

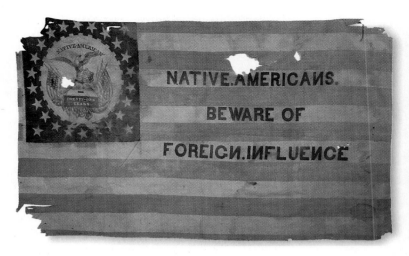

utmost exertions to aid the cause by organizing and freeing the country from that monster [Catholicism] *which has long since made its appearance in our midst and is only waiting for the hour to approach to plant its flag of tyranny, persecution, and oppression among us.*

The Know Nothings did very well in local elections in northern states. Their main supporters were middle-class Americans worried about the moral impact of immigration, and Protestant working men who were fearful of losing jobs to Irish and German immigrants.

MAKING CONNECTIONS

The term *know-nothingism* also was used later, during the 1900s, to describe a political attitude that included fear of foreigners. What evidence can you offer that this attitude can still be found in the United States today?

The Kansas-Nebraska Act

As if the growing turmoil among the parties was not promising enough trouble for the nation, a Democratic politician again raised the dangerous issue of slavery in the territories. This man, Senator **Stephen Douglas** of Illinois, had two conflicting ambitions. First, he wanted Chicago to benefit from the development of the West. The sooner the territories of Kansas and Nebraska became states, the sooner railroads

The Know Nothings called themselves "Native Americans"—by which they meant Americans born in the United States—and whipped up fears against immigrants.

Stephen Douglas champions popular sovereignty in this 1858 cartoon. Douglas believed that slavery in the territories no longer would be a national issue if it were decided by voters in the territories themselves.

could be built across them to link Chicago with the West.

But Douglas also wanted to run for President. To do that, he needed the support of southern Democrats. Pushing statehood for Kansas and Nebraska was not the way to gain supporters in the South, because under the terms of the Missouri Compromise of 1820, Kansas and Nebraska would become free states. The North would then become still more powerful, and southerners would see Douglas as an enemy.

So Douglas tried to score points with both northerners and southerners. His **Kansas-Nebraska Act,** introduced in the United States Senate in January 1854, proclaimed that the people in a territory should decide whether slavery would be allowed there. What Douglas was saying, basically, was that the nation should forget the boundary of 36° 30' N established by the Missouri Compromise and rely on popular sovereignty. In fact, "popular sovereignty" became a slogan bandied about in the debate over slavery in the territories. As Douglas wrote to a southerner in April 1854:

> The great principle of self-government is at stake, and surely the people of this country are never going to decide that the principle upon which our whole republican system rests is vicious and wrong.

Douglas knew that the Kansas-Nebraska Act would make southerners happy, because it raised the possibility that Kansas and Nebraska might become slave states, which would have been impossible under the Missouri Compromise. But he also figured—incorrectly, as it turned out—that northerners would not object to relying on popular sovereignty to make the decision. He was positive that because agriculture on the Great Plains would not support cotton or slavery, the people of Kansas and Nebraska would peacefully choose to be free states.

Instead of applauding the bill, as Douglas expected, northerners were outraged by it. Northern members of Douglas's own party, the Democrats, denounced Douglas for what they saw as a sellout to **the Slave Power**—the South.

And after Congress passed the Kansas-Nebraska Act, Douglas found out just how wrong he was about a peaceful vote in the territories.

The Rise of the Republican Party

In the uproar over the Kansas-Nebraska Act, the Whig party finally faded from the scene. It had little to offer in the furious debate over slavery. A new organization arose to deal with this very issue. It was the **Republican party,** the direct ancestor of today's party by the same name. While the Know Nothings were against "Papal Power," the Republicans were dedicated to stopping the Slave Power. Yet both believed that Catholics and slaveholders were deliberately working together to destroy American liberty.

The Republicans Gain Support The new Republicans drew their support almost entirely from the North and from Protestant middle-class and working-class voters. The party had several factions. The extremist faction included voters strongly opposed to the Fugitive Slave Act and slavery in the territories. The moderate faction was made up of antislavery voters who wanted to abolish slavery in federal territories but not interfere with the practice where it already existed. Yet another faction was composed of former Whigs still committed to a strong national government that would lead in the development of a national economy. Farmers, professionals, small business owners, craftworkers, hardworking middle-class people—these were the Republicans.

New parties appear frequently in American history. Few last very long. In the mid-1850s, however, the disappearance of the Whigs and the emotional issues of nativism and slavery produced two strong parties, the Know Nothings and the Republicans, competing for the same kinds of voters. The table on page 175 summarizes the views and supporters of these parties, as well as the Democratic party.

In the end, the Republicans survived and the Know Nothings did not. The Republicans succeeded by adopting the nativist ideas of the American party. They drew voters away from the American party, making their own party a single powerful force opposed both to slavery and Catholicism.

Political Parties of the 1850s

Party	Views	Supporters
Democrats (North)	Favored deciding issue of slavery in the territories by popular sovereignty	A variety of backgrounds, but particularly northern voters in urban areas and Catholics; some of those born in South who had moved to Old Northwest
Democrats (South)	Favored expanding slavery in territories	Those living in southern areas undergoing growth in economy and population
Republicans	Opposed to slavery, supported nativist movement	People in New England and people born in New England living in the Old Northwest; Protestant English, Scots-Irish immigrants; former American party followers
American Party	Known as "Know Nothings"; anti-Catholic, fearing "Papal Power"; nativist, favoring a longer naturalization period for immigrants; antislavery	Supporters were generally middle-class, northern Protestants born in the United States

Interpreting Tables
During the 1850s, three major parties jostled for power in the North, but only one major party represented the South. *Why did the Republicans lack support in the South? What views did the Republican party share with the American party that enabled it to win over American party members?*

The Election of 1856 Neither the American party nor the Republican party, however, won the election for President in 1856. The Democratic candidate, James Buchanan, became President, with the backing of southerners. Though an inconsistent politician, Buchanan would do what he could to repay the South for its support. He pledged to stop "the agitation of the slavery issue" in the North.

The American party candidate in the election, former President Millard Fillmore, had little chance of success. He was undistinguished and appealed to few. But the Republican candidate, John C. Frémont, drew a surprising number of votes, particularly in northern states such as Massachusetts, New York, and Ohio. Lack of political experience often helps candidates when voters are disgusted with politics, and Frémont had never been a politician. In addition, he was a hero of the Mexican War and a dynamic figure.

The Republicans had more going for them, however, than a colorful candidate. They received many of their votes from northerners fearful about the slavery issue and about what was now going on in the Kansas Territory. People there were quarreling about whether Kansas would become a free state or a slave state. And all of a sudden they were not just talking about it—they were shooting at each other.

SECTION 2 REVIEW

Key Terms, People, and Places
1. Define (a) Compromise of 1850, (b) Fugitive Slave Act, (c) states' rights, (d) nativism, (e) naturalization, (f) Kansas-Nebraska Act, (g) the Slave Power.
2. Identify (a) Democratic party, (b) American party, (c) Know Nothings, (d) Stephen Douglas, (e) Republican party.

Key Concepts
3. Give two reasons why the Compromise of 1850 failed to solve the issue of slavery in the territories once and for all.

4. Why did many Americans lose faith in the second American party system in the early 1850s?
5. What led to the founding of the American party?
6. How did the Kansas-Nebraska Act propose to settle the issue of slavery in the territories?
7. How did the Republicans gain support in the 1850s?

Critical Thinking
8. **Identifying Alternatives** If you had been Calhoun, what changes to the Constitution would you have proposed to ensure that the South remained as powerful as the North?

Analyzing Political Speeches

Political speeches are as old as government itself. Their goal has always been to persuade listeners to take a particular view. Such speeches can be about almost anything—what candidate citizens should vote for, what new law they should support, what action the government should take, or what policy it should adopt. They can serve as valuable evidence about people and events in history.

Political speakers use a variety of techniques to win over their listeners. Sometimes they appeal to the self-interest of their audience: "See how doing what I propose will make your life better." Sometimes they appeal to their listeners' social conscience: "See how doing what I propose will benefit the community or the nation as a whole." Often they appeal to patriotism.

Use the following steps to analyze the excerpts from a political speech that Henry Clay made to the Senate at the time it was considering whether to adopt the Compromise of 1850.

1. Identify the main topic of the speech and the speaker's stand on it. Recall what you already know about the speaker and his political philosophy. Skim through the speech to get a general idea of the speaker's topic and aims in making the speech. (a) What is the main topic of the speech? (b) Cite evidence in the speech that Clay believes the compromise will work. (c) What is Clay's stand on the measure?

2. Analyze the techniques the speaker uses to persuade listeners. Of course, political speakers appeal to the minds of their listeners. But because they know that an appeal to the emotions can influence their listeners as well, they also appeal to the feelings of their audience. Evaluate the speaker's persuasiveness and how he or she achieves it. (a) What does Clay tell his listeners to disregard and forget? (b) Give evidence that Clay appeals to reason in his speech. (c) Give evidence that Clay appeals to his listeners' feelings of patriotism. (d) How would you evaluate Clay's persuasiveness in this speech?

3. Study the speech for clues to what the historical period was like. (a) What does the speech tell you about how serious the tensions between North and South seemed to people at that time? (b) What does it tell you about the style of speeches during that period? (c) Compare and contrast this speech with any modern speeches you may have heard or read.

To the Senate, July 22, 1850

I believe from the bottom of my soul that this measure is the reunion of the Union. And now let us disregard all resentments, all passions, all petty jealousies, all personal desires, all love of place, all hungering after the gilded crumbs which fall from the table of power. Let us forget popular fears, from whatever quarter they may spring. Let us . . . think alone of our God, our country, our conscience, and our glorious Union; that Union without which we shall be torn into hostile fragments, and sooner or later become the victims of military despotism, or foreign domination. . . .

What is an individual man? An atom, almost invisible without a magnifying glass—a mere speck upon the surface of the immense universe—not a second in time, compared to immeasurable, never-beginning, and never-ending eternity; a drop of water in the great deep, which evaporates and is borne off by the winds; a grain of sand, which is soon gathered to the dust from which it sprung. Shall a being so small, so petty, so fleeting, so evanescent [quick to disappear], oppose itself to the onward march of a great nation? . . . Let us look at our country and our cause; elevate ourselves to the dignity of pure and disinterested patriots, wise and enlightened statesmen, and save our country from all impending dangers. . . . What are we—what is any man worth who is not ready and willing to sacrifice himself for the benefit of his country when it is necessary?
—Henry Clay, United States senator from Kentucky

The System Fails

SECTION PREVIEW

A series of violent clashes between antislavery and proslavery forces between 1856 and 1860 brought the United States to the boiling point. Americans on each side of the slavery issue became convinced that the other side was acting against law and morality.

Key Concepts

- From 1856 to 1858, the Kansas Territory became what amounted to a battlefield for conflict between northern, antislavery forces and southern, proslavery forces.
- In a decision on the *Dred Scott* case, the Supreme Court held that the Constitution protected the rights of slave owners to take enslaved people anywhere in the United States.
- During a senatorial campaign in Illinois in 1858, the North gained a new spokesperson for its antislavery views, Abraham Lincoln.
- An uprising led by abolitionist John Brown deepened the division between the North and South.

Key Terms, People, and Places

Dred Scott v. *Sandford*, Lecompton constitution, Panic of 1857; free soiler, John Brown, Charles Sumner, Chief Justice Roger Taney, Abraham Lincoln; Harpers Ferry

T ension in Kansas began in 1854, when the Kansas-Nebraska bill became law. Antislavery organizations in the Northeast then decided to take action. If the question of slavery in the territories was going to be resolved by voting, they would have to make sure antislavery forces were in the majority there. They set up so-called Emigrant Aid societies and in 1854 and early 1855 sent some 1,200 New Englanders to Kansas to fight against the Slave Power. Like others who were committed to making the territories free, the new settlers were called **free soilers.**

Meanwhile, proslavery settlers in Missouri organized secret societies to oppose the free soilers. Many crossed into Kansas to vote illegally in territorial elections. By 1855 Kansas had—only twenty miles apart—an antislavery capital at Topeka and a proslavery capital at Lecompton.

The First Blood Flows

In 1856 tensions escalated into open violence. The clashes began on May 21 when a group of southerners, with the support of a proslavery federal marshal, looted newspaper offices and homes in Lawrence, Kansas, a center of free-soiler activity.

"Bleeding Kansas" The action of the proslavery looters stirred a swift response from Connecticut-born and Ohio-raised **John Brown,** a stern evangelical who believed that he was a chosen instrument of God. He led several New Englanders by night to a proslavery settlement near Pottawatomie Creek. There, Brown and his men roused five men from their beds, dragged them from their homes, and killed them with swords in front of their families.

The looting in Lawrence and Brown's reaction to it sparked a summer of murderous raids and counterraids throughout Kansas, shown on the map on page 178. The violence won the territory a grim nickname: "Bleeding Kansas." Nor was the bloodshed confined to Kansas; it also spread to the nation's capital.

"Bleeding Sumner" On May 19 and 20, Senator **Charles Sumner** of Massachusetts had given a fiery speech titled "The Crime Against Kansas." Sumner, a leading Republican and one of the most powerful antislavery voices in Congress, bitterly attacked southerners for forcing slavery on the territory. In particular, he charged Senator Andrew Butler of South Carolina, a popular southern politician, with having

During the late 1850s, Americans increasingly turned to violence in an effort to resolve their differences over slavery. Abolitionist John Brown had a blacksmith make a thousand of these pikes to arm enslaved people for a revolt.

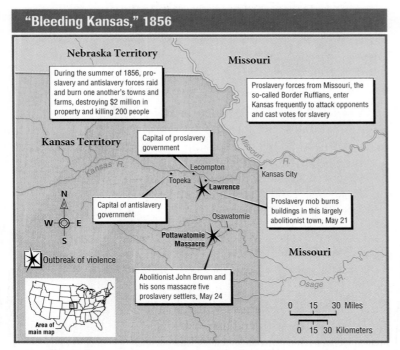

"Bleeding Kansas," 1856

Nebraska Territory

During the summer of 1856, pro-slavery and antislavery forces raid and burn one another's towns and farms, destroying $2 million in property and killing 200 people

Missouri

Proslavery forces from Missouri, the so-called Border Ruffians, enter Kansas frequently to attack opponents and cast votes for slavery

Kansas Territory

Capital of proslavery government

Lecompton

Topeka   Kansas City

Kansas R.   Lawrence

Capital of antislavery government

Osawatomie

Proslavery mob burns buildings in this largely abolitionist town, May 21

Pottawatomie Massacre

N / W–E / S

Missouri R.

Missouri

Osage R.

✹ Outbreak of violence

Abolitionist John Brown and his sons massacre five proslavery settlers, May 24

Area of main map

0   15   30 Miles
0   15 30 Kilometers

Geography and History: Interpreting Maps
Outsiders from both slave and free states meddled aggressively in Kansas politics. In one election, 5,000 proslavery men from Missouri crossed the border to vote. The final tally totaled four times as many votes as there were registered Kansas voters. *How far is the abolitionist stronghold Lawrence from the Missouri border?*

I . . . gave him about 30 first rate stripes. Toward the last he bellowed like a calf. I wore my cane out completely, but saved the head, which is gold.

Sumner survived the caning, but it took him four years to return to the Senate. In fact, he was never completely healthy again.

Northerners were outraged by Brooks's action. To them it seemed that if a southern member of Congress could beat a United States senator in the middle of the Senate without punishment, then the North was at the mercy of the South. The caning became a symbol of the arrogance and brutality that northerners imagined was typical of southerners.

Southerners, however, saw the caning as a justified response to a terrible insult against their honor. When Brooks resigned his seat in the House to give the voters in his district an opportunity to express their opinion, he was immediately reelected. Furthermore, people across the South voiced their support by sending him canes—including one inscribed "Hit him again."

A Breakdown of the System As bad as the violence in Kansas and the Senate was for the people who experienced it, its larger significance was to reveal the general breakdown of respect for law and the political process. Wrote the New York *Evening Post* shortly after the "Bleeding Sumner" incident:

Violence is the order of the day; the North is to be pushed to the wall by it, and this [southern] plot will succeed if the people of the free states are as apathetic [uninterested] as the slaveholders are insolent [boldly disrespectful].

Confusion Over Law

In March 1857, the Supreme Court added to the breakdown of trust in the law by handing down one of the most controversial decisions in its history, ***Dred Scott* v. *Sandford.*** The suit had started when Dred Scott, an enslaved man living in Missouri, had filed suit against his owner. Scott argued that because he and his

chosen a mistress to whom he has made his vows, and who, though ugly to others, is always lovely to him; though polluted in the sight of the world, is chaste [pure] in his sight . . . the harlot, Slavery.

Preston Brooks, who was both a member of the House of Representatives and Butler's nephew, was indignant at Sumner's remarks and determined to defend the honor of the South. Normally, he would have challenged Sumner to a duel; but since Brooks did not consider Sumner a gentleman worthy of respect, he planned to punish him as he might have disciplined a misbehaving dog.

Two days after his speech, Sumner was sitting at his desk in the Senate reading mail. Brooks approached him and began beating the senator with his cane. Sumner tried to protect himself, even pulling his desk out of the floor in the process. Southern senators standing nearby made no move to help him. Recalled Brooks:

Using Historical Evidence Preston Brooks raises his cane to strike Senator Charles Sumner in this lithograph by Winslow Homer. *Was this lithograph a piece of northern or southern propaganda? Explain your interpretation.*

This meant that Congress had to protect slavery throughout the Union. It had no power to ban slavery anywhere, including the territories. Taney declared that the Missouri Compromise, which had forbidden slavery in some territories, "is not warranted by the Constitution, and is therefore void."

Today we find the *Dred Scott* decision offensive because of its refusal to recognize the rights of African Americans. But it had the value of being direct and honest. Taney stated that the writers of the Declaration of Independence and the Constitution did not intend those documents to apply to African Americans. The Framers, said Taney, believed African Americans "had no rights which the white man was bound to respect." Therefore no legal basis existed in 1857 for granting any rights to African Americans, even those who were freed. Although Taney's analysis of history was accurate, it was also racist.

Antislavery forces were disgusted with the *Dred Scott* decision. It meant the national government had no power to keep slavery out of the territories. President Buchanan, however, supported the Court's decision for that very reason. He and many other white Americans hoped that now the national government would not be required to deal with the slavery issue.

wife, Harriet, had once been taken into states and territories where slavery was illegal, the couple was in fact free. By a vote of seven to two, the justices ruled against the Scotts.

Dred Scott **Supports Slave Owners** In his written opinion on the case, **Chief Justice Roger Taney** stated that as an African American, Dred Scott was inferior and without rights. Thus he was not a citizen of the United States and could not sue anyone.

Scott could not be considered free, the Court determined, simply because he had once stood on free soil. As an enslaved person, Scott was property. Taney noted that "the right of property in a slave is distinctly and expressly affirmed in the Constitution." Furthermore, under the Fifth Amendment, Congress had to protect the right of the slave owner, not the enslaved person. Said Taney:

N o word can be found in the Constitution, which gives Congress a greater power over slave property, or which entitles property of that kind to less protection than property of any other description. The only power conferred [granted] is the power coupled with the duty of guarding and protecting the owner in his rights.

The Lecompton Constitution Events soon proved, however, that the political fight over slavery had not ended. In Kansas, too, confusion arose over the law. In the fall of 1857, a small proslavery group elected members to a convention to write the constitution required for statehood. Called the **Lecompton constitution,** it was as proslavery as its namesake, the proslavery capital. The majority of people in Kansas were opposed to slavery and refused to even vote on the constitution when it was offered for their approval. President Buchanan, hoping that the problem of slavery in Kansas would go away as soon as the territory became a state, endorsed the Lecompton constitution.

Though Buchanan was a Democrat, his blatant disregard for popular sovereignty and the rule of law was too much for northern Democrats to swallow. Democratic leader Stephen Douglas spoke sharply against the Lecompton constitution and criticized Buchanan for accepting it. Congress returned the constitution to Kansas for another vote, and the people now soundly defeated it.

A New Spokesperson Emerges

Senator Douglas denounced the Lecompton constitution in part out of principle and in part because he had to be responsive to public opinion. He faced a difficult reelection campaign in Illinois in 1858, where opinion on slavery was sharply divided.

A short, stout man, Douglas was known popularly as "the Little Giant." Like many whites in the 1850s, he believed that white Americans were superior to African Americans. He went even further, however, and tolerated slavery, because he believed in the absolute right of white citizens to choose the kind of society and government they wanted.

Though Douglas was one of the most influential senators in the nation's history, today people generally remember him only because of the man the Republican party nominated to run against him, **Abraham Lincoln.** The campaign drew nationwide attention when Douglas and Lincoln met in a series of seven debates on the issue of slavery in the territories.

Most Americans know that Abraham Lincoln was born poor in Kentucky and educated himself. But they generally do not know that he later worked for railroads and other corporations as a highly paid lawyer in Springfield, the capital of Illinois. He had served one term in Congress in the 1840s. In 1858, now nearly fifty years old, Lincoln was a solid member of the upper middle class.

Lincoln shared many of Douglas's views on African Americans. During the campaign against Douglas, he stated: "I am not nor ever

have been in favor of bringing about in any way the social and political equality of the white and black races." He did not even propose forbidding slavery in the South. He hoped that by confining slavery to the states in which it already existed, it would eventually die out.

Yet Lincoln, like millions of other northerners, knew that slavery was wrong. For him, it was not just a matter of whether the slave states would have equal power in the Senate. He considered slavery a moral issue. During the campaign against Douglas, he quoted both the Bible and the Declaration of Independence to justify his stand.

*T*he Savior [Jesus Christ] . . . said, "As your Father in Heaven is perfect, be ye also perfect." He set that up as a standard, and [whoever] did most towards reaching that standard attained the highest degree of moral perfection. So I say in relation to the principle that all men are created equal, let it be as nearly reached as we can.

In a now-famous speech in Springfield in June 1858, Lincoln insisted:

A house divided against itself cannot stand. I believe this government cannot endure, permanently half slave and half free. I do not expect the Union to be dissolved—I do not expect the house to fall—but I do expect it will cease to be divided. It will become all one thing, or all the other.

Though Lincoln gained a large following, Douglas won the election. All the same, the tall, gaunt lawyer from Springfield earned a reputation for eloquence and moral commitment that would serve him and the Republicans well in the presidential election of 1860.

MAKING CONNECTIONS

You have read that Lincoln considered slavery a moral issue. Why would this stand anger and offend southern planters more than if Lincoln had considered slavery only a political issue?

John Brown's Raid

Other factors increased tensions in the late 1850s. One was an economic downturn called the **Panic of 1857.** Another was the continuing growth of the American population. Many people were uneasy; there was a sense that Americans were at sea, that their country was growing and changing so rapidly that it could be controlled no longer.

John Brown, however, was not one to resign himself to the twists of fate. He would control his own destiny and that of his nation if he could. On October 16, 1859, three years after his nighttime raid along Pottawatomie Creek in Kansas, Brown attacked the federal arsenal at **Harpers Ferry,** Virginia (now West Virginia). With him were twenty-two men, including two African Americans—Shields Green and John Anthony Copeland, a college student. Supported by abolitionists in the North, Brown and his followers hoped to seize the weapons in the arsenal and give them to enslaved people. They had a dream of a massive uprising of enslaved Americans that would end slavery, punish slaveholders, and lead the United States to moral renewal.

Alerted to the attack, United States troops under the command of Colonel Robert E. Lee bore down on Harpers Ferry and surrounded Brown and his men in the arsenal. The troops killed half of Brown's men—including two of his sons—before the rest surrendered. Convicted of treason against the state of Virginia, John Brown was sentenced to be hanged by the neck until dead.

Just before his execution, Brown wrote a brief note. Although he had failed as a soldier, his final message proved him a prophet:

Behind John Brown's "glittering, gray-blue eyes" lurked a cool willingness to break the law in order to end slavery.

I *John Brown am now quite* certain *that the crimes of this* guilty land will *never be purged* away; *but with Blood.*

Northerners hailed Brown as a martyr to the cause of justice and freedom. Southerners denounced him as a terrorist and a tool of Republican abolitionists. In short, his raid and his trial only deepened the division between North and South.

As the year 1860 began, it was clear that the majority of northerners would not accept leadership associated with what they called the Slave Power. And southerners now determinedly announced they would not accept leadership by Republicans, who were opposed to the slavery system. The next presidential election was looming. How could the Union possibly survive it?

SECTION 3 REVIEW

Key Terms, People, and Places
1. Define (a) Lecompton constitution, (b) Panic of 1857.
2. Identify (a) free soiler, (b) Charles Sumner, (c) Chief Justice Roger Taney.
3. Identify Harpers Ferry.

Key Concepts
4. Cite examples of disorder in Kansas in 1856.

5. Whose rights were upheld in *Dred Scott* v. *Sandford?*
6. Make a general statement about Abraham Lincoln's position on slavery.
7. What was the greatest impact of John Brown's raid?

Critical Thinking
8. **Testing Conclusions** Explain why the title of this section is "The System Fails."

The Dred Scott Decision

Time Frame:	March 1857
Place:	Washington, D.C.
Key People:	Dred and Harriet Scott, Chief Justice Roger Taney
Situation:	In the 1850s, as controversy raged over slavery, the Supreme Court was faced with a tough question: Did enslaved people become free when they were taken into territories where slavery was against the law?

In the 1830s, a white man from Missouri named Emerson took the Scotts, an enslaved African American couple, into the state of Illinois and the federal territory of Wisconsin. Under the Missouri Compromise of 1820, slavery was illegal in both places. After living with their owner in these free areas, the Scotts returned to the slave state of Missouri. The husband, Dred Scott—shown in the painting on this page—sued for his family's freedom in 1846. He argued that the act of setting foot on free soil had made him and his wife, Harriet, free people.

The Court's Options

When the Court finally began considering the case, the justices had to decide between two approaches to the question. They could issue what is called a *narrow ruling,* responding to the legal arguments Dred Scott had made and stating simply whether or not he was free. Or they could issue a *broad ruling,* in which they considered whether the laws involved in the case were constitutional.

Only One Option in a Narrow Ruling The Court could not really use a narrow ruling to declare Scott free. Too many issues would be left unresolved if they did so. After all, the Constitution and federal laws had always upheld the rights of property owners. The Court could not inter-

fere with that right without reexamining the Constitution at length.

The Court could, however, use a narrow ruling to declare that Scott was still enslaved. This decision had already been made by the lower courts that had considered the case. The Supreme Court could simply support their decision.

The Broad Ruling Options The justices did not *have* to make a broad ruling. But throughout its history, the Supreme Court has used certain cases to examine laws and determine if they are constitutional. The justices might well believe it was time to reexamine laws about slavery. Their broad ruling might declare Scott free or declare him enslaved.

Weighing the Options

By setting Scott free, the Court would place human rights above the right of slaveholders to own human property. African Americans and abolitionists would have enthusiastically welcomed this decision. But for

GOALS	Determine whether Dred Scott was free; make a decision about the larger issue of slavery		
POSSIBLE ACTIONS	**Rule broadly for Scott**	**Rule narrowly against Scott**	**Rule broadly against Scott**
POSSIBLE RESULTS	• Will place human rights above the right of whites to own enslaved people • Will please African Americans and abolitionists • Will make it easier for enslaved people to escape slavery • Will anger southerners	• Will please southerners and slave holders • Will probably not surprise the majority of northern white people • Will keep the compromises in place, reducing chance of violence	• Will jar compromises over slavery • Might extend slavery into the territories • Would win wide support among white southerners • Might alarm large numbers of white northerners

many whites in the 1850s, the choice was not so clear.

A majority of the Court justices, including Chief Justice Roger Taney, were southerners. Taney himself hated slavery—and proved it by setting free the enslaved people he owned. But he knew that setting Scott free would make it easier for enslaved African Americans everywhere to win their freedom. This would cause a violent backlash from southern slaveholders threatened with the loss of their labor force. And Taney also knew that the Constitution and federal laws had always upheld the right to own property. Setting Scott free would be interfering with that right. So the real question was not whether the Court would rule for Scott. Instead, the question was whether the Court would rule narrowly, or whether it would rule broadly and reconsider federal laws about slavery.

If the Court ruled against Scott narrowly, it would please southerners and slaveholders by making it impossible for slaves to become free simply by entering free territory. And most northern whites would not be surprised by one more court decision that supported slavery. A narrow ruling would not disturb the compromises made over the years between slave states and free states, such as the Missouri Compromise and the Compromise of 1850.

If the Court ruled against Scott broadly, reexamining previous laws, they might jar that fragile web of compromise. They might even use the power of the Court to extend slavery into places where it was not currently legal. Southerners would approve of this, but northerners would be outraged.

When the Court decided the case on March 6, 1857, all nine justices wrote separate statements of their opinions. Taney's was the most influential, however, and the majority of the justices agreed with him. He did not set Scott free. And he combined both a narrow and a broad ruling in his statement on the case.

In the narrow part of his ruling, Taney pointed out that only citizens could sue others. Scott, Taney claimed, could not sue anybody because the Framers of the Constitution had never intended African Americans to be considered citizens.

In the broad part of his ruling, Taney emphasized that the Constitution protected the right to own property, and no federal law could break the Constitution. The Missouri Compromise of 1820 was a federal law that interfered with the right to own property—that is, enslaved people—in certain parts of the United States. Therefore the Missouri Compromise was unconstitutional.

Taney and his colleagues may have hoped that their bold ruling would end the controversy over slavery once and for all. Unfortunately, it only increased tensions.

EVALUATING DECISIONS

1. Why could a narrow ruling not free Scott?
2. Why did Taney decide Dred Scott could not sue?

Critical Thinking

3. **Checking Consistency** If Taney hated slavery, why did he not declare Dred Scott a free man?

183

A Nation Divided Against Itself

SECTION PREVIEW

Secession spread like wildfire through the southern states when Abraham Lincoln captured the presidency. While politicians and the people debated how to respond, the first shots were fired, and the broken nation plunged into war.

Key Concepts
- The Republican candidate for President in 1860, Abraham Lincoln, carried no southern states and almost all of the northern states.
- Finding that the North was able to elect an antislavery President despite his complete rejection by the South, southern states left the Union one after another.
- Fort Sumter in South Carolina became a symbol of federal authority. Its bombardment by southern forces was the final challenge that brought on the Civil War.

Key Terms, People, and Places
John C. Breckinridge, William Henry Seward, Constitutional Union party, secessionist, Jefferson Davis; Border States, Lower South, Confederate States of America, Fort Sumter, Upper South

CHARLESTON

MERCURY

EXTRA:

Passed unanimously at 1.15 o'clock, P. M. December 20th, 1860.

AN ORDINANCE

To dissolve the Union between the State of South Carolina and other States united with her under the compact entitled "The Constitution of the United States of America."

We, the People of the State of South Carolina, in Convention assembled, do declare and ordain, and it is hereby declared and ordained,

That the Ordinance adopted by us in Convention, on the twenty-third day of May, in the year of our Lord one thousand seven hundred and eighty-eight, whereby the Constitution of the United States of America was ratified, and also all Acts and parts of Acts of the General Assembly of this State, ratifying amendments of the said Constitution, are hereby repealed; and that the union now subsisting between South Carolina and other States, under the name of "The United States of America," is hereby dissolved.

THE

UNION

IS

DISSOLVED!

Proudly declaring its independence, South Carolina was the first state to secede from the Union.

AAmericans justifiably pride themselves on the peaceful transfer of power from one group of people to another through the electoral process. This process set the new nation apart from others from the early days of the republic. But the success of the American political system depends on the willingness of the losers to accept government by the winners, at least temporarily. Only once—in 1860—has a large group of people refused to accept the outcome of a national election. The result was that the Union failed and the United States broke into two nations.

The Election of 1860

Differences between northern Democrats and southern Democrats finally ripped the Democratic party apart in the summer of 1860. For ten days and 59 ballots, delegates to their national convention sat in Charleston, South Carolina, unable to choose a presidential candidate. When they met again in Baltimore, the Democrats made the division official. Northerners nominated Stephen Douglas of Illinois and southerners chose **John C. Breckinridge,** the current Vice President. He was committed to an aggressive policy of expanding slavery in the territories.

By contrast, Republican **William Henry Seward** of New York was committed to an aggressive policy of ending slavery. Although he was the leading candidate for the Republican nomination when the delegates met in Chicago, they were worried that he was too extreme to attract the voters they needed. They also wanted to ensure victory in Pennyslvania, Indiana, and Illinois, states the Republicans had not won in the presidential election of 1856. But another candidate, Abraham Lincoln, seemed to have more moderate views on slavery than Seward. He could certainly win in his own state, Illinois. They nominated him.

Southerners, however, had heard too much extreme language from the Republicans to trust them. In 1859, for instance, one Republican declared that his party intended

to check the Slave Power in its aggressive march, to roll back the black and threatening wave of Southern oppression, to teach the Slave Power that it will have absolute need of its utmost efforts to preserve its existence within its present boundaries, without grasping by robbery and bribery the territories of other governments in order to aggrandize and perpetuate [increase and continue] *slavery.*

Less extreme were those who formed the **Constitutional Union party.** These moderates were mostly southerners who had belonged to the Whig party, along with a few politicians from the **Border States**—Delaware, Maryland, Kentucky, and Missouri. They chose John Bell of Tennessee, a moderate slaveholder, as their presidential nominee.

The November election was essentially two elections, one in the South between Bell and Breckinridge and one in the North between Lincoln and Douglas. The Republicans won a majority in the North, carrying every free state (except New Jersey, which they split with the Douglas Democrats). Breckinridge, meanwhile, won North Carolina, Arkansas, Delaware, Maryland, and the states of the **Lower South**—Texas, Louisiana, Mississippi, Alabama, Florida, Georgia, and South Carolina. Bell carried three border states, Tennessee, Kentucky, and Virginia. Douglas took Missouri.

In the nation as a whole, Lincoln received 180 electoral votes out of 303. These 180 electoral votes were the majority he needed to win the presidency. But he received only 40 percent of the popular vote; Douglas was second with 29 percent, Breckinridge third with 18 percent, and Bell received 13 percent. Contributing to Lincoln's failure to achieve a majority was the fact that he got no votes in the Lower South. His was a decisive victory, but a sectional one.

Viewpoints
On the Southern Secession

Lincoln's election in November 1860 led South Carolina to plan secession. *What issues, according to the following viewpoints, divided the northern and southern states?*

For secession

"In January next we shall take leave of the Union and shall construct with our sister Cotton States a government for ourselves. Whether the other Slave States will join seems very uncertain at least for the present. The condition of affairs at the North since the election of an Abolitionist for President makes it necessary for us to get away as quickly as possible."

E. B. Heyward, South Carolina cotton planter, letter to a friend in Connecticut, dated November 20, 1860

Against secession

"I am for the preservation of the Union; I desire to witness no separation of the States; I have a pecuniary [financial] interest both in the South and in the North. . . . The whole country has just emerged from the exercise of its constitutional and long-established functions, in the choice of a President of the United States. . . . Men of South Carolina, keep to your pledges, and retain your honor and self-respect. No harm will come to you. Mr. Lincoln and his party are your safest and best friends. They will do what is right."

Anonymous northern merchant, letter to the editor, *New York Tribune,* November 22, 1860

MAKING CONNECTIONS

Consider the major role southerners had played in the nation's history from its beginnings. Name some southern revolutionaries, Framers, Presidents, and influential members of Congress. Contrast that heritage of government power with the situation after the election of 1860.

The Lower South Secedes

Southerners were outraged that a President could be elected without any southern votes. The government of the nation, it seemed, had passed completely out of their hands. Planters and others who backed slavery called for the South to secede. They refused to remain in a Union run by the antislavery Republicans. That party, wrote an Augusta, Georgia, newspaper editor,

> *stands forth today, hideous, revolting, loathsome, a menace not only to the Union of these states, but to Society, to Liberty, and to Law. It has drawn to it the corrupt, the vile, the licentious [immoral], the profligate [extremely wasteful], the lawless. . . . It is a fiend, the type of lawless Democracy, a law unto itself, its only Lord King Numbers, its decrees but the will of a wild mob.*

The **secessionists**—those who wanted the South to secede—argued that since the states had voluntarily joined the United States, they also could choose to leave it. They believed it was an absolute necessity to do so. Typical of the secessionists was Edmund Ruffin of Virginia. He stated that because the Republicans were "a northern sectional party, and majority" in charge of the federal government, they could act constitutionally and legally "to produce the most complete subjection and political bondage, degradation, and ruin of the South."

South Carolina left the Union officially on December 20, 1860. Over the next few weeks, so did six other states of the Lower South. In early February 1861, delegates from the seven states met in Montgomery, Alabama. There they created a new nation, the **Confederate States of America,** also called the Confederacy, shown on the map below. As their president they elected Senator **Jefferson Davis** of Mississippi.

The War Starts

The question on everyone's mind as the winter dragged on was what the national government would do about the secession of seven of its member states. President Buchanan, as usual, did nothing. Meanwhile, he and the President-elect heard plenty of advice.

Lincoln's Options Some politicians proposed compromises with the South, but few people supported compromises anymore. More serious was a recommendation to allow the seceding states to go in peace. Many opposed this option, including those who believed strongly in the political value of the Union. Northern business people also objected, fearing that profits from their business with the South would be lost.

The third choice was to insist that the southern states return to the Union. After all, how could the United States function as a country if its members could come and go as they pleased? Many northerners, including Stephen Douglas, favored this option, despite the very real chance of war.

The only man in the nation who had the power to make the decision about the government's response left his home in Springfield, Illinois, in early 1861, bound for the White House. Abraham Lincoln believed secession was wrong. He was also strongly committed to stopping the expansion of slavery. But rather than focus on the reasons behind the South's secession, the President-elect emphasized his responsibility to enforce the laws of the United States. On March 4, 1861, Lincoln took the oath of office, swearing, as all Presidents must, to "preserve, protect, and defend the Constitution of the United States."

Fort Sumter, Symbol of the Union As he spoke those words, the attention of the nation was on **Fort Sumter,** a federal fort in the harbor of Charleston, South Carolina. A federal ship sent to supply the fort had been turned back by Confederate forces in January. Now several dozen federal soldiers under the command of Major Robert Anderson were

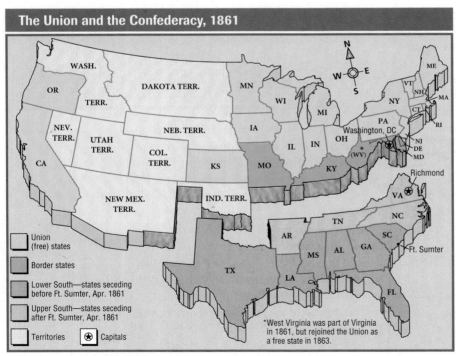

The Union and the Confederacy, 1861

Union (free) states

Border states

Lower South—states seceding before Ft. Sumter, Apr. 1861

Upper South—states seceding after Ft. Sumter, Apr. 1861

Territories

Capitals

*West Virginia was part of Virginia in 1861, but rejoined the Union as a free state in 1863.

Geography and History: Interpreting Maps
When South Carolina seceded, one Unionist sarcastically observed that the state was "too small for a republic and too big for a lunatic asylum." South Carolina was soon joined by other states, however—making the Confederate republic one of the largest in the world. *Name the states that seceded after the surrender of Fort Sumter.*

running out of supplies. If Lincoln did not resupply the fort, it would have to surrender.

Lincoln, along with much of the North and South, saw Fort Sumter as a vital symbol of the Union he had sworn to preserve. Refusing to recognize the Confederate government, on April 6 Lincoln told the governor of South Carolina that he was sending provisions to Fort Sumter. On April 10, before the supplies could arrive, Confederate president Davis ordered General P.G.T. Beauregard to demand that Fort Sumter surrender. If Anderson refused, Beauregard was to take it by force.

Anderson did refuse, and on April 12, 1861, Beauregard opened fire on the fort. After a twenty-four-hour bombardment, Anderson ordered the Stars and Stripes hauled down and surrendered Fort Sumter to Confederate troops.

By firing on federal property, the Confederate states had committed an undeniable act of open rebellion. As the defender of the Constitution, Lincoln had no choice but to respond. When he called for volunteers, southerners saw his action as an act of war against them. The **Upper South**—Virginia, North Carolina, Tennessee, and Arkansas—now joined the Lower South in the Confederacy. This left the four border states torn between two hostile nations.

Eighty-four years after the Continental Congress had declared the independence of the United States of America, the nation had come apart. Union with slavery was not possible.

Some in the South called the war the Second War for Independence. Although in the end it did not win independence for the South, the war would indeed prove a second American

Revolution. It would transform the United State as few other events ever have.

But no one in either North or South knew that in 1861. As men marched and women waved good-bye, they expected a short and glorious war. The South was going to teach the North that it could not interfere with the rights of free Americans. The North was going to teach the South that it could not abandon the federal Union the Framers had created. Neither northerners nor southerners imagined the horror that lay ahead of them, or the vastness of the changes they were bringing upon themselves.

As Confederate guns battered Fort Sumter (at the center of the harbor), some onlookers felt excitement and others feared for the future.

SECTION 4 REVIEW

Key Terms, People, and Places
1. Identify (a) John C. Breckinridge, (b) William Henry Seward, (c) Constitutional Union party, (d) secessionist, (e) Jefferson Davis.
2. Identify (a) Border States, (b) Lower South, (c) Confederate States of America, (d) Upper South.

Key Concepts
3. Summarize the results of the election of 1860.
4. How did the Lower South view the election of 1860?

5. Explain the importance of the surrender of Fort Sumter.

Critical Thinking
6. **Recognizing Ideologies** Some thirty different names have been used for the Civil War since 1861. You have read that some southerners called it the Second War for Independence. The North called it the War of the Rebellion. Explain how each name reflects the point of view behind it.

Chapter Review

Key Terms
1. Civil War
2. Union
3. Compromise of 1850
4. Fugitive Slave Act
5. states' rights
6. nativism
7. naturalization
8. Kansas-Nebraska Act
9. Slave Power
10. *Dred Scott* v. *Sandford*
11. Lecompton

constitution
12. Panic of 1857

People
13. Harriet Beecher Stowe
14. George Fitzhugh
15. Democratic party
16. American party
17. Know Nothings
18. Stephen Douglas
19. Republican party

20. free soiler
21. John Brown
22. Charles Sumner
23. Chief Justice Roger Taney
24. Abraham Lincoln
25. John C. Breckinridge
26. William Henry Seward
27. Constitutional Union party

28. secessionist
29. Jefferson Davis

Places
30. Harpers Ferry
31. Border States
32. Confederate States of America
33. Lower South
34. Fort Sumter
35. Upper South

Terms For each term above, write a sentence that explains its relation to the events leading up to the Civil War or the changes in political parties that occurred in the 1850s.

Matching Review the key terms in the list above. If you are not sure of a term's meaning, review its definition in the chapter. Then choose a term from the list that best matches each description below.
1. the theory that states have the right to nullify acts of the federal government
2. legislation proclaiming that the people in a territory should decide whether slavery would be allowed there
3. an economic downturn that increased tensions between North and South before the Civil War
4. the movement to ensure people born in the United States received better treatment than immigrants

True or False Determine whether each statement is true or false. If it is true, write "true." If it is false, change the underlined person or place to make the statement true.
1. Members of the <u>Constitutional Union party</u> were mostly southern moderates who had been Whigs.
2. <u>Stephen Douglas</u> gave a fiery speech entitled "The Crime Against Kansas."
3. <u>Harriet Beecher Stowe</u> attacked northern industrialists in the book *Cannibals All!*
4. After a twenty-four-hour bombardment, <u>Harpers Ferry</u> was surrendered to Confederate troops.

Section 1 (pp. 164–168)
1. Why did slavery seem threatening to northerners?
2. Describe George Fitzhugh's view of the North.
3. Describe technology's effect on North and South.

Section 2 (pp. 169–175)
4. Why was the Compromise of 1850 a failure?
5. Why did the Whig party fade away?
6. What issues helped the Republicans in the 1850s?

Section 3 (pp. 177–181)
7. Why was Kansas called "Bleeding Kansas"?

8. How did Lincoln and Douglas differ in their views?
9. Why did John Brown's raid lead to a greater division between the North and the South?

Section 4 (pp. 184–187)
10. You have read that Lincoln's victory in the election of 1860 was "a decisive victory, but a sectional one." Explain this statement.
11. Why did Lincoln's election prompt secession?
12. Explain why Lincoln was forced to respond to the attack on Fort Sumter.

1. **Predicting Consequences** What economic difficulties would the South have faced if Lincoln had allowed it to leave the Union peacefully?
2. **Determining Relevance** The idea that states have the right to secede did not spring out of nowhere. What other beliefs concerning government that you have read about are related to it?

3. **Demonstrating Reasoned Judgment** Lincoln was elected only by voters from the North. How might voters in other regions of the United States respond today if a President were elected on the basis of winning, for example, only the South and the West? What challenges might a President encounter if he or she had only regional appeal?

1. **Expressing Problems Clearly** Review the primary source excerpt on page 180. Why did Lincoln believe that the United States could not endure if it was half slave and half free?
2. **Understanding the Visuals** Examine the before-and-after pictures of the life of enslaved Africans on page 166. How does the artist try to show that slavery "civilized" Africans?
3. **Writing About the Chapter** You are a newspaper reporter assigned to cover the violence in Kansas in 1856, John Brown's raid on Harpers Ferry, or the surrender of Fort Sumter. First, review the description in the chapter of the event you have chosen. Consider whether you will write your story from the viewpoint of a southern or a northern reporter.

Next, write a draft of your story in which you describe the event. Revise your story, making certain that it is vivid and that it reflects a clear point of view. Proofread your story and draft a final copy.

4. **Using the Graphic Organizer** This graphic organizer uses a multiflow map to show the sequence of events immediately preceding the outbreak of the Civil War. (a) What examples of a cause-and-effect relationship does the map suggest? (b) What details from the map demonstrate the breakdown of the democratic system of government? (c) On a separate sheet of paper, create your own graphic organizer about the series of clashes between antislavery and proslavery forces between 1856 and 1860, using this graphic organizer as an example.

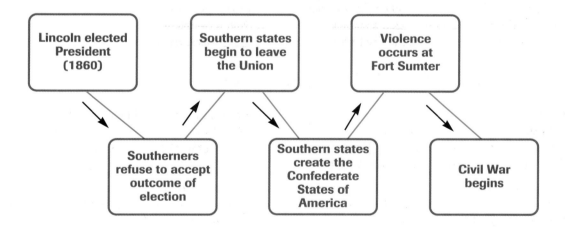

The Civil War
1861–1865

*F*or four years, the Civil War raged between the North and the South. Though the South was the main battleground, death and sorrow reached into the North as well. Hundreds of thousands of Americans were killed or maimed, and billions of dollars of property was destroyed. During this great conflict, African Americans won their freedom, and the Union was preserved, despite bad feelings that endured on both sides. The United States also became a completely new kind of nation, in which the federal government proved to be a powerful presence in the lives of the people.

Events in the United States

1861 The Confederacy defeats the Union at the First Battle of Manassas.

1862 Grant leads the Union to victory at the Battle of Shiloh.
• Congress passes the Homestead Act.

1860	1861	1862

Events in the World

1860 Garibaldi wins military victories that lead to the unification of Italy.

1861 Czar Alexander II abolishes serfdom in Russia.

1862 The independence of the African nation of Zanzibar is recognized.

1863 Lincoln proclaims freedom for enslaved people in the Confederacy.

1864 Sherman leads Union forces in capture of Atlanta and Savannah.
• Lincoln wins reelection.

1865 Lincoln is assassinated.
• Lee surrenders to Grant at Appomattox.
• The 13th Amendment abolishes slavery.

1863	1864	1865	1866

1863 The International Red Cross is founded in Switzerland.
• Civil war begins in Afghanistan.

1864 The Taiping Rebellion ends in China.
• Prussia defeats Denmark in a brief war.

1865 Paraguay declares war on Argentina, Brazil, and Uruguay.
• Transatlantic telegraph cable is completed.

The First Two Years of the Civil War

SECTION PREVIEW

In the first two years of the war, Union armies tried again and again to capture the Confederate capital but were driven back by bolder and more skillful generals. Union forces did succeed, however, in blockading the coasts of the South and seizing control of the great river valleys of its midwestern states.

Key Concepts

- Both new technology and political pressure greatly affected the tactics of the war.
- In the western part of the Confederacy, northern forces captured most of Kentucky, Tennessee, and the Mississippi Valley.
- Both the North and South resisted attempts to invade their territory in the East.

Key Terms, People, and Places

shell, canister, war of attrition, Anaconda Plan, gunboat; Stonewall Jackson, George McClellan, Ulysses S. Grant, Robert E. Lee; Manassas, Shiloh, Antietam

More than 90 percent of all battle wounds in the Civil War were caused by bullets—many of them by the new, more accurate type shown here.

"Forward to Richmond! Forward to Richmond!" thundered the *New York Tribune* in July 1861. With the secession of the Upper South from the Union, the Confederate states had shifted their capital from Montgomery, Alabama, to Richmond, Virginia. Now northern newspapers demanded immediate action from the volunteers assembled after the surrender of Fort Sumter.

Southerners were just as eager to fight. Wrote the editor of the *Richmond Examiner*:

> The idea of waiting for blows, instead of inflicting them, is altogether unsuited to the genius [nature] of our people. The aggressive policy is the truly defensive one.

Like northern troops, southern soldiers had volunteered for short periods of service. And like their brothers in the North, they were in a hurry to get the war over.

The Battle of Manassas

Public pressure for action had its effect in July 1861, when a large Union army tried to march to Richmond and collided with a Confederate army. This first major battle of the war was called both **Manassas**—the name of a nearby town—and the First Battle of Bull Run, after a small river in the area. Many Civil War battles have two names, one given by the South and the other given by the North. The South tended to connect a battle with the nearest town, the North with some physical feature close by the battlefield.

General Irvin McDowell had brought 30,000 Union troops about 30 miles west from Washington, D.C., to attack a southern army under General P.G.T. Beauregard—the officer who had captured Fort Sumter. On the morning of July 21, McDowell sent thousands of poorly trained men on a 10-mile march to strike at the left side of the Confederate army.

Confederate spies, including several women, sighted the Union troops, whose advance was no secret anyway. A huge crowd of civilians had traveled out from Washington behind the army to picnic and watch the battle.

The Confederates were well prepared. Although at first the Union troops nearly broke Beauregard's army, the southerners held their positions. The fighting was fierce: by the time it was over, nearly 5,000 men were killed, wounded, or missing.

In the afternoon, fresh Confederate troops were brought in by railroad—a technology now used in war for the first time—and streamed into the fight. Exhausted, the Union soldiers quit the battle. McDowell ordered a retreat.

But the day was not over. As they turned back, the Union soldiers ran into the crowds of sightseers who had followed them. The result was total confusion. Soldiers and civilians were caught in a tangle of wagons and horses on the narrow road. Terrified that Confederate forces would catch them, troops and picnickers broke into a panic. The army disintegrated; by nightfall it had become a mass of men running headlong for the safety of Washington.

The Tactics of the War

Battles are not always won or lost by dramatic chance events, split-second decisions, or the skill and heroism of one or two individuals. On some occasions, however, such factors do matter. At Manassas, for example, an intensely religious and energetic Confederate officer named Thomas Jonathan Jackson made his troops stand as solidly as a stone wall during a Union attack. He stopped the Union advance and earned the nickname **Stonewall Jackson**.

Though armies need extraordinary soldiers like Stonewall Jackson, more often victory depends on two less colorful factors—organization and training. At Manassas, both armies were poorly organized and trained, and the generals soon realized it. For example, neither McDowell nor Beauregard had a good staff of officers to deliver orders to the battlefield quickly and efficiently. And once the soldiers received their orders, they did not always have the training to know what to do.

Technology Influences Tactics Though both sides quickly learned their lesson about organization and training, they failed to learn that the old ways of fighting a war did not work anymore. Europeans had fought wars for centuries by attacking the enemy's capital city or gathering their forces for one big battle that would decide everything. Cannons and muskets in early times were neither accurate nor capable of repeating fire very quickly. To overwhelm the enemy, generals relied on masses of men moving across open fields.

Almost all the generals of the Civil War had been trained at the United States Military Academy at West Point, New York. They shared a belief in the old-fashioned tactics of gathering their forces in one place, attacking a position with massed troops, and driving the enemy

Viewpoints
On the Purpose of the Civil War

Throughout the years of quarreling between North and South, southerners protested repeatedly that northerners were trampling on their rights, including the right to own slaves as property. *How did the war aims of each side, as described in the viewpoints below, reflect this part of their quarrel?*

The Aims of the South
"We have vainly endeavored to secure tranquillity and obtain respect for the rights to which we were entitled. . . . If . . . the integrity of our territory and jurisdiction [legal authority] be assailed [attacked], it will but remain for us with firm resolve to appeal to arms."
President Jefferson Davis, Inaugural Address, February 18, 1861

The Aims of the North
"This war is not waged upon our part in any spirit of oppression, nor for any purpose of conquest or subjugation, nor purpose of overthrowing or interfering with the rights or established institutions of those [seceding] States, but to defend and maintain the supremacy of the Constitution and to preserve the Union, with all the dignity, equality, and rights of the . . . States unimpaired [undamaged]."
House of Representatives, Crittenden Resolutions, July 25, 1861

away. The most vital position to attack, they believed, was the enemy's capital. The generals of both North and South had seen such tactics work well in the Mexican War.

In the Civil War, however, American generals gradually had to confront a new technology that had made this strategy suicidal. Gun makers had learned that a long piece of lead with a rounded tip—a bullet—did not drift as it flew, like the older type of ammunition, which was a simple lead ball. They also had discovered that a spiral groove—called rifling—cut on the inside of a gun barrel would make a fired bullet pick up spin and travel in a nearly straight line. These new, more accurate rifles, as they were called, also could be reloaded rapidly. Cannons, too, had been improved. Instead of relying on simple iron cannon balls to smash their targets, gunners had more deadly options. They could fire a cannon **shell** that exploded in the air over the enemy or burst after it hit, or a

Advantages and Disadvantages of the North and South

	Northern States*	Southern States
Population	21.5 million	9 million
Railroad Mileage	21.7 thousand miles	9 thousand miles
Manufacturing		
Number of Factories	110.1 thousand	20.6 thousand
Number of Workers	1.17 million	111 thousand
Value of Products	$1.62 billion	$155 million
Finance		
Bank Deposits	$207 million	$47 million
Specie	$56 million	$27 million
Agriculture		
Corn (bushels)	446 million	280 million
Wheat (bushels)	132 million	31 million
Oats (bushels)	150 million	20 million
Cotton (bales)	4 thousand	5 million
Tobacco (pounds)	229 million	199 million
Rice (pounds)	50 thousand	187 million
Livestock		
Horses	4.2 million	1.7 million
Donkeys and Mules	300 thousand	800 thousand
Milch Cows	5.7 million	2.7 million
Beef Cattle	6.6 million	7 million
Sheep	16 million	5 million
Swine	16.3 million	15.5 million

* Includes border states

Source: *The American Heritage Picture History of the Civil War,* edited by Richard M. Ketchum

Interpreting Tables
Northerner William T. Sherman warned a southern friend in 1860, "You are bound to fail." *Which advantages would allow the North to raise a larger, better equipped army than the South?*

canister—a special shell filled with lead balls about the size of bullets. Canisters turned cannons into the equivalent of giant shotguns. To cross an open field against such weapons was an act of madness. Some Union and Confederate officers never realized this, though it was clear as early as the first battle at Manassas. Others eventually realized that it was slaughter to send soldiers against bullets, shells, and canister fire, but they continued to do so anyway.

Politics Influences Tactics Why did Civil War generals continue to use the old tactics? The reason is that Americans in both North and South were impatient; they wanted to win and win today, not tomorrow or next year. The people demanded instant results from their politicians, and the politicians demanded instant results from their generals.

The Confederacy would have had the greatest chance of success if it had worn down the Union in a **war of attrition**. In this kind of war, a weaker army inflicts small but continuous losses of soldiers and material that gradually add up to an unbearable burden for the other side. The table at left shows that the North had tremendous resources. But such an advantage does not always mean victory, as the British had learned during the American Revolution.

Although Confederate president Jefferson Davis apparently recognized the wisdom of waging a war of attrition, his citizens would not let him adopt it. To fight a war of attrition, the army of the weaker side often has to avoid direct confrontations. It has to be able to retreat out of the enemy's way, even if it means giving up territory temporarily. Southerners, however, insisted that their government defend the entire Confederacy. The result was that the South had to stretch its precious soldiers and equipment in a thin line from Virginia to Texas. Its war goal was basically to keep attacking armies out of the Confederacy.

The goal of the North was to conquer the South, but northerners, too, would have been better off avoiding direct confrontations. General Winfield Scott, the hero of the Mexican War and the commander of the United States Army in 1861, knew this well. Scott's recommendation called for Union forces to surround the Confederacy and slowly squeeze it to death. Northern ships could cut the South off from the rest of the world, especially cotton markets in Great Britain and Europe. Union riverboats and armies could cut the Confederacy in two at the Mississippi. This plan would make the best use of the North's advantages—its superiority in population and industry, its more extensive railroads, and its navy.

In the end, the North did make use of Scott's plan. But when word of the strategy was leaked to northern newspapers, they ridiculed it, calling it the **Anaconda Plan**, after a type of snake that coils around its victims and crushes them to death. In 1861 and 1862, most Americans still had dreams of a short war. Much as Manassas horrified soldiers and humbled officers, the political pressure for a quick victory remained strong. This public clamor for results led to more battles like Manassas. They were fought mainly between the two capitals, Richmond and Washington, which lie only 100 miles apart.

The North Begins to Strangle the South

The day after Manassas, President Lincoln appointed **George McClellan** to command the major Union army in the East. This was the Army of the Potomac, named after the river that flows past Washington.

General McClellan was a master organizer. He spent months preparing his men for battle and ensuring that they would have enough food and weapons. McClellan was a favorite with his men because he watched out for their welfare, but he was unpopular with Lincoln and northern politicians, who wanted results.

Though McClellan took no action, other Union officers did. Along the Confederate seacoasts, the United States Navy succeeded in retaking several important federal forts and in setting up a blockade of enemy ports. The great industrial and economic strength of the North came into play as the government built and bought the first of more than six hundred ships it would add to its navy. The anaconda had begun to flex its muscles.

The War on the Rivers In order for the North to squeeze the South, however, Union forces had to gain control of the midwestern part of the Confederacy. Conflict did take place even farther west, in Missouri, Texas, and Oklahoma, which was then called the Indian Territory, but the war in the midwest of the Confederacy is generally referred to as the war in the West. This region, shown on the map on this page, includes Tennessee, Arkansas, Mississippi, and Louisiana. It was a land of waterways, all leading to the Mississippi River. Whoever controlled the rivers would control commerce and military movements throughout the region. Knowing this full well, Confederate forces built Fort Henry on the Tennessee River and Fort Donelson on the Cumberland River, both in the state of Tennessee.

The Civil War in the West, July 1861–May 1863

Map legend:
- Union states
- Confederate states
- Union forces
- Confederate forces
- Union victories
- Union blockade

Geography and History: Interpreting Maps
Union generals in the West such as Grant (shown below) focused their attention on the Mississippi River. "That Mississippi ruins us, if lost," worried southern observer Mary Boykin Chesnut in 1862. *What two key cities on the Mississippi had the Union captured by the summer of 1862?*

But this type of fort was a leftover from an older time. A new and deadly technology, the **gunboat,** made such forts largely useless. The typical gunboat—shown in the illustration on page 196—was basically a small floating fort fitted with rifled cannons. Built to navigate even shallow rivers, driven by steam power, and often protected by iron armor, it brought the destructive power of Union cannon shells deep into the Confederacy.

Under the command of a tough Union general, **Ulysses S. Grant,** gunboats quickly pounded Fort Henry into surrender in February 1862. Not long after, following three days of shelling by gunboats, Fort Donelson surrendered unconditionally—earning U. S. Grant the nickname "Unconditional Surrender" Grant.

Gunboats gave Union forces a great advantage in river warfare. One Union naval commander was reported to have preached a Sunday sermon to his sailors in which he said, "Let not your heart be troubled. Ye believe in God; believe also in gunboats."

The Cumberland and Tennessee rivers now formed Union highways into the heart of the midwestern Confederate states. Nashville soon fell to the Union, and by April General Grant had pushed south nearly to Mississippi and Alabama.

The Slaughter at Shiloh On April 6, however, a southern army unexpectedly struck Grant's forces near Shiloh Church in Tennessee. The Confederates won the first day of this Battle of **Shiloh,** driving the Union troops back nearly into the Tennessee River. But Grant, displaying the determination that would see him through many a crisis in the years ahead, refused to give up. "Retreat?" he scoffed to his doubting officers after the first day. "No. I propose to attack at daylight and whip them."

With the help of reinforcements, Grant was as good as his boast. The North won the battle on April 7. But some 13,000 Union men and 10,000 Confederates had been killed, wounded, or captured. It was the bloodiest single battle that had taken place on the American continent up to that time. Wrote one Tennessee soldier after Shiloh:

> I never realized the "pomp and circumstance" of the thing called glorious war until I saw this. Men . . . lying in every conceivable position; the dead . . . with their eyes open, the wounded begging piteously for help.

The Battle of Shiloh showed northern civilians once again that the Confederacy would not

collapse overnight. But it also stopped the South from regaining western Tennessee and its river highways.

Action on the Mississippi While Grant was breaking into the Confederacy in Kentucky and Tennessee, Union gunboats and troops were taking many of the Confederate posts on the Mississippi River. In late April 1862, a naval squadron commanded by an iron-willed, sixty-year-old captain named David Farragut forced the surrender of New Orleans, Louisiana. Less than two months later, on June 6, the Union navy also seized Memphis, Tennessee. This city, too, was located in a key position on the Mississippi River.

Slowly, in battle after battle, the Union was putting the Anaconda Plan into operation. In early 1862, Union forces had captured 50,000 square miles, taken control of 1,000 miles of navigable rivers, and seized New Orleans, the largest city in the South. A southern observer, Mary Boykin Chesnut, wrote of her concern about the growing pressure on the Confederacy. Sentences stitched together from her diary over the course of April and May 1862 tell the grim story:

> Battle after battle—disaster after disaster. . . . The power they are bringing to bear against our country is tremendous. . . . I have nothing to chronicle [tell] but disasters. . . . The reality is hideous.

Only two major posts on the Mississippi River now remained in Confederate hands—Vicksburg, Mississippi, and Port Hudson, Louisiana. If northern forces could find some way to capture them, the entire Mississippi River valley would be under Union control.

MAKING CONNECTIONS

You have read in previous chapters that the South was dependent on its rivers, especially the Mississippi River, to transport cotton for sale abroad. What effect would closing the Mississippi to Confederate boats have on the South's effort to win the war?

The War for the Capitals

Though Union action on the seas and in the western river valleys was actually far more significant than capturing Richmond, the North was still obsessed with making a quick end of the war by taking the enemy capital. By the spring of 1862, George McClellan had built a huge, well-equipped army. But he was reluctant to move. President Lincoln supposedly became so frustrated with his commander that he quipped: "I will hold McClellan's horse if he will only bring us success."

McClellan's Troops Invade Virginia McClellan thought that going to Richmond through Manassas again would be a mistake. So in the spring of 1862, he moved the Army of the Potomac by ship to the peninsula near Yorktown, Virginia. He inched his troops forward until, by the end of May, he was within a few miles of Richmond (see the map at right).

McClellan had about 100,000 soldiers—twice as many as the Army of Northern Virginia, the Confederate force near Richmond. But the South had two brilliant military leaders.

The first was General **Robert E. Lee**—the man who had captured John Brown at Harpers Ferry in 1859. Lee took over as the leader of the Confederate forces when General Joseph Johnston was wounded in late May. Lee was an experienced officer, a leader of great courage and intelligence, and a highly dignified and moral man. He had once called slavery "a moral and political evil," but he fought for Virginia because—like many Americans of his day—he felt more loyalty to his state than to the Union. Like all great generals, Lee wanted well-trained men and well-thought-out plans. But he also understood that victory often depends on a willingness to take chances.

The other brilliant leader was General Stonewall Jackson. He drove his men hard and

could move his army with a speed that baffled the enemy. While McClellan was creeping close to Richmond, Jackson dashed north of the capital and carried out a series of lightning attacks on Union forces in the Shenandoah Valley in the Blue Ridge Mountains of Virginia. Lincoln was alarmed. Would Jackson attack Washington? To Lincoln and the North, the slippery rebel seemed to be everywhere at once, and his 17,000 men seemed to be three times that number. The Union secretary of war, Edwin M. Stanton, ordered 50,000 Union troops to pursue Jackson instead of joining McClellan. After Jackson had thoroughly confused and alarmed the enemy, he slipped his forces away to help General Lee.

A Union general with the determination of Grant might well have taken the Confederate capital. But McClellan was not Grant. In the Seven Days' Battles, fought from June 25 through July 1, 1862, the outnumbered southerners wore out McClellan's great army and

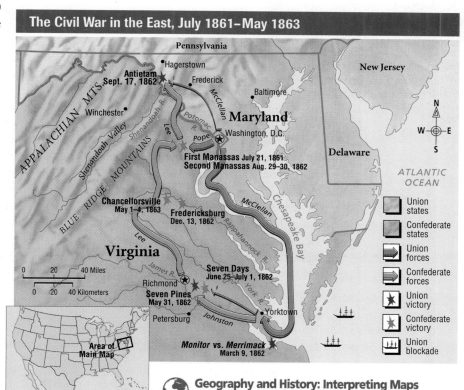

The Civil War in the East, July 1861–May 1863

Pennsylvania

Hagerstown

Antietam
Sept. 17, 1862

Frederick

Baltimore

APPALACHIAN MTS.

Winchester

Shenandoah Valley

BLUE RIDGE MOUNTAINS

Maryland

Washington, D.C.

New Jersey

Delaware

ATLANTIC OCEAN

N W E S

First Manassas July 21, 1861
Second Manassas Aug. 29–30, 1862

Chancellorsville
May 1–4, 1863

Fredericksburg
Dec. 13, 1862

Rappahannock R.

Chesapeake Bay

Virginia

0   20   40 Miles
0   20   40 Kilometers

Richmond

Seven Pines
May 31, 1862

Seven Days
June 25–July 1, 1862

York R.

Yorktown

Petersburg

Johnston

Monitor vs. Merrimack
March 9, 1862

Area of Main Map

Legend:
- Union states
- Confederate states
- Union forces
- Confederate forces
- Union victory
- Confederate victory
- Union blockade

Geography and History: Interpreting Maps
McClellan's extreme caution was his own worst enemy. "No one but McClellan would have hesitated to attack," said Confederate general Joe Johnston during McClellan's slow advance toward Richmond before the Seven Days' Battles. *What action did Lee take after winning the Seven Days' Battles?*

Both Robert E. Lee (left) and Stonewall Jackson (right) believed in a strategy once described by Jackson: "Never fight against heavy odds if . . . you can hurl your own force on only a part . . . of your enemy and crush it."

sent it limping for safety. Again the human cost was nearly unbelievable: some 30,000 Americans were killed or wounded.

The Confederacy Attacks

Now that Richmond had been saved, Lee tried to exploit the situation by invading the North. Any show of southern strength could have great benefits, because Great Britain was watching events closely, waiting for a sign that the Confederacy could stand on its own two feet. If Britain could be persuaded to recognize the Confederate States as an independent nation, its assistance in the war would be enormous. Furthermore, a successful invasion of the Northeast might force the United States to end the war.

For a few months, as Lee, Jackson, and other excellent Confederate generals fought their way into Maryland, the Confederacy seemed about to win its independence. But that hope faded on September 17, near Sharpsburg, Maryland, when McClellan's reorganized army met Lee's forces in the Battle of **Antietam.** It was the bloodiest day of the entire war: close to 6,000 soldiers were killed and 17,000 wounded. Neither side won a clear victory. All the same, Lee's heavy losses forced him to turn back to Virginia.

The War Becomes a Stalemate

After Antietam, McClellan was replaced. The Union army again tried to take Richmond. In December 1862, General Ambrose Burnside led 110,000 men against Lee's 75,000 men, who were well entrenched along the Rappahannock River near Fredericksburg, Virginia. The Union forces were soundly defeated.

In early May 1863, another Union general, Joseph Hooker, clashed with Lee at Chancellorsville, Virginia. Outnumbered as usual, Lee broke two rules of good generalship: he divided his forces, and he attacked a larger army, rather than waiting to be attacked. He sent Stonewall Jackson and his men on a long, risky march to strike Hooker from behind. The strategy worked brilliantly. Lee thrashed the Union army, though it was twice the size of his own.

Among the many Confederate dead was Stonewall Jackson, who was wounded by his own men in the confusion and died a week later. The North lost about 17,000 men and gave up its lingering hopes for a short war.

In fact, it seemed to northerners that the war had reached a stalemate. In the East, huge Union armies had now failed four times to reach Richmond. In the West, Grant was stuck in the Mississippi Valley, trying to find some way to capture Vicksburg and open up the Mississippi River to Union warships.

But the stalemate would not last long. Ulysses S. Grant was indeed a determined man—as determined as Lee was brilliant.

SECTION 1 REVIEW

Key Terms, People, and Places

1. Define (a) shell, (b) canister, (c) war of attrition, (d) Anaconda Plan, (e) gunboat.
2. Identify (a) Stonewall Jackson, (b) George McClellan, (c) Ulysses S. Grant, (d) Robert E. Lee.
3. Identify (a) Manassas, (b) Shiloh, (c) Antietam.

Key Concepts

4. Give examples of the way in which new technology and political pressure affected the Civil War.

5. What gains did Union forces make in the western part of the Confederacy in the first two years of the Civil War?
6. Why did the war in the East seem like a stalemate by early 1863?

Critical Thinking

7. **Identifying Central Issues** If you had been the president of the Confederacy, how would you have defended your nation against the Anaconda Plan?

War Brings Change

SECTION PREVIEW

During the Civil War, national government in both the North and the South became a powerful presence in the lives of ordinary people. Meanwhile, African Americans in the United States armed forces earned long-overdue respect fighting for the freedom of enslaved people in the South.

Key Concepts

- The Confederate government held great power over its citizens, but had difficulty uniting the efforts of its stubbornly independent states.
- President Lincoln limited the rights of the citizens of the North during the war.
- Republicans in Congress passed legislation that later allowed the United States to become a major economic power.
- President Lincoln enlarged the purpose of the war from just saving the Union to abolishing slavery as well.
- During the Civil War, many African Americans set themselves free, and many also fought to free others.

Key Terms, People, and Places

draft, writ of *habeas corpus*, Internal Revenue Act of 1862, greenback, Pacific Railroad Act of 1862, Emancipation Proclamation, contraband; Copperhead, Radical Republican

---

The Civil War forever changed the relationship between Americans and their government and gave a new meaning to American citizenship. These changes began as both the South and the North responded to the demands of the war.

The Confederacy— Strong and Weak

The branches and powers of the Confederate government were very similar to those of the strong, federal government of the United States. But the men who framed the Confederate constitution also made certain that it explicitly recognized slavery and states' rights. The resulting tension between a strong federal government and strong state governments caused many difficulties for the South during the war.

Strong Federal Power President Jefferson Davis and his government in Richmond faced severe challenges. Unlike their northern counterparts, they had to create a government from scratch and do it while fighting a major war. They lacked money, officials—even furniture for their offices.

Furthermore, like the government in the North, the government of the Confederate States had to persuade an intensely independent and democratic people to sacrifice their personal interests for the common good. But in the South, the problem was even more difficult, because the challenge was to turn rebels into citizens, to forge loyalty to a new government out of disloyalty to an old one. And because the South had fewer people, less money, and less industry than the North, the Confederate war effort required making use of all available human and economic resources.

To meet these needs, the Confederate government passed **draft laws** in April and November of 1862. A draft is a legal means of forcing people to serve in the armed forces. The Confederate draft laws were the first in American history. Under these laws, all white men between eighteen and thirty-five had to fight for the Confederacy, except those who owned a certain number of slaves. Men who were already in the armed forces had to remain there for another three years. Though forcing people to fight for their own independence was a contradiction in terms, the Confederate government had no choice.

Through their own efforts, including outstanding courage in battle, Americans brought dramatic changes to their lives during the Civil War. Medals of Honor like this one were awarded to many, including twenty-one African Americans.

served. About 87,000 paid a fee to avoid the army, and about 74,000 hired substitutes. The rest either moved to Canada or the West, or were exempted from service for some reason such as physical disability.

In response to emergencies created by the war, Lincoln also extended government power into the lives of the people by denying them basic rights. He interfered with freedom of the press by sending the army to shut down newspapers that criticized the policies of his administration. He also suspended the **writ of habeas corpus,** a basic civil liberty protected by the Constitution. This writ is a court order directed to an officer holding a prisoner in jail. It commands the officer to demonstrate to the court that the prisoner is being held for good reason. The Constitution allows suspension of the writ during a rebellion. Lincoln, like President Davis in the South, suspended the writ in various parts of the country. He could then imprison anyone who interfered with the war effort without having to justify his actions. As Secretary of State William Seward told the British ambassador:

> I can touch a bell on my right hand and order the imprisonment of a citizen in New York; and no power on earth except the President can release them.

Lincoln's suspension of the writ of *habeas corpus* was no idle threat. Over 13,000 Americans who objected to federal policies were held in northern prisons without trial during the war.

Permanent Increases in Federal Power

The draft, limits on freedom of the press, and the suspension of the writ of *habeas corpus* were temporary measures in response to the war. Other changes were permanent. Now that southern Democrats had left Congress, Republicans

In addition to directing the use of human resources, the Confederate government also took control of the economy of the South. It determined such matters as the production of wool, cotton, and leather and seized control of southern railroads from private owners. Such actions gave the government of the Confederacy far more power over the lives of its citizens than the government of the Union had ever had.

The South's Weakness: States' Rights
Working against this strong federal control was a fierce southern commitment to states' rights, which harmed the war effort in countless ways. For example, Lee's soldiers often had no boots. The state of North Carolina had boots enough to supply the entire Confederate army—but reserved them for the use of its own troops.

Temporary Increases in Federal Power

Like the central government of the Confederate states, the federal government of the United States also dramatically increased its power during the Civil War. In March 1863 it, too, passed a draft law. The northern draft was weaker than the southern law. Out of 776,000 northern men ordered to report for service in the course of the war, only some 46,000 actually had little opposition. They were able to pass several major laws during the Civil War that would have a lasting impact on the United States.

New Tax Laws Many Republicans, including Lincoln, were former Whigs and as such had supported a strong national government that would promote business. Faced with the need to raise money to pay for the war, they passed a tariff that not only would bring in cash, but also would protect American industries from foreign competition.

Other tax measures were aimed mostly at raising money just to wage war. In 1861 the Republican-controlled Congress passed the first federal tax on income in American history. It collected 3 percent of the income of people making more than $800 a year. Then, in the **Internal Revenue Act of 1862**, Congress created taxes on items such as liquor, tobacco, medicine, and newspaper ads. The act even established a stamp tax. While almost all of the taxes ended with the war, the Bureau of Internal Revenue created by Republican legislation became a permanent part of the federal government. It is now known as the Internal Revenue Service (IRS) and is responsible for collecting taxes from individuals and corporations.

Changes in the Nation's Finances In 1863 and 1864, Congress reformed the nation's banking system. Since 1832, when Andrew Jackson vetoed the rechartering of the Second Bank of the United States, Americans had relied on state banks, which issued their own bank notes. Believing that this system was too disorganized, Republicans created a national currency, called **greenbacks** after their color. Though greenbacks were only bank notes, the banks that issued them were chartered not by the states but by the federal government—and the government guaranteed their value.

Promoting American Expansion During the war, President Lincoln also signed several laws that had a powerful impact on the nation's expansion. The **Pacific Railroad Act of 1862** permitted the federal government to offer public land and money to several companies in return for the construction of a railroad from Nebraska to the Pacific Coast. As a result of this act, transcontinental railways would soon link East and West. The Homestead Act of 1862 granted 160 acres of federal land to settlers who lived on the grant and improved it for a period of five years. Under the Morrill Act of 1862, money from the sale of public land was to be used to fund an agricultural college in each state. Many of these colleges later developed into the great universities of the Midwest. The Morrill Act also established the Department of Agriculture to promote farming in the nation.

The Impact of Republican Legislation This Republican legislation as a whole laid the political and economic foundations for the emergence of the United States as the most powerful industrial and agricultural nation in the world. For decades, southern Democrats from Thomas Jefferson to Andrew Jackson had limited the way the federal government could direct the development of the nation's economy. Now, with southerners out of the picture, Republicans made the Civil War Congresses among the most active in American history. They created what amounted to a modified version of the American System promoted by Henry Clay and John Quincy Adams in the 1820s. In the process, they also created a cozy relationship between capitalists and the United States government.

MAKING CONNECTIONS

After the Civil War, people seldom used the term *Union* or used expressions such as "the United States *are*." They were more likely to refer to "the nation" and to say "the United States *is*." Explain how the Republican policy of making government bigger and more powerful helped bring about this change in attitude.

Reaction to Republican Legislation

Because Democrats were in the minority in Congress, they could not stop Republicans from passing such laws. Opponents of the Republicans on the streets of the nation, however, still could raise up their voices in protest. In July 1863, mobs in New York City vented their rage at the draft in one of the worst riots in American history. At least 105 people died during four days of looting and destruction. The rioters attacked draft offices, federal property, and the offices of prominent Republican newspapers.

Many members of these mobs were Irish Catholics, who had been targets of Republican nativism for years. But in many ways, the rage of the rioters had more to do with racial prejudice than federal or Republican power. The rioters believed that they were being drafted to fight a war that would benefit only African Americans. A total of eleven African Americans died in the riots, dozens were beaten, and a home for African American orphans was burned to the ground.

Antiwar Democratic politicians—called **Copperheads** after a type of poisonous snake—played on northern racial fears. They wrote editorials and gave speeches warning that Republican policies would bring a tide of African Americans to the North, freed by Union armies. These freed slaves, said Copperheads, would take jobs away from whites. Using such scare tactics, the Copperheads won many congressional and state elections in 1862.

The Emancipation Proclamation

While Copperheads were attacking Lincoln because of his sympathy for African Americans, others were angry with him for not taking a strong stand *against* slavery. They included African Americans such as Frederick Douglass and **Radical Republicans** such as Charles Sumner. The Radical Republicans were a wing of the Republican party made up of abolitionists and others hostile to the South.

During the early part of the war, President Lincoln continued to insist that the struggle was about the Union, not about emancipation, or freeing enslaved people. In fact, he promised not to interfere with slavery where it already existed; he did not want to create new enemies in slave states such as Maryland and Kentucky.

Despite Lincoln's focus on restoring the Union, eventually he realized that he could not achieve his purpose without emancipating the enslaved people of the South. In July 1862 he decided to move toward this goal by writing a proclamation to be issued at a time when the Union cause seemed to be winning. Lincoln's **Emancipation Proclamation** stated that as of January 1, 1863, all enslaved people in the areas in open rebellion against the government would "be then, thenceforward, and forever free."

On September 22, five days after Lee and his army abandoned the battlefield at Antietam and retreated south, Lincoln issued his proclamation. It had no immediate effect on enslaved people because they were still under southern control. But it was a promise that they would be free when the North won the war. Just as Lincoln had made slavery in the territories a moral issue during the campaign of 1858, he made slavery in the South a moral issue now. The war was no longer just about the political question of whether the Union would survive. It was about the moral question of whether slavery would fail. As Lincoln told Congress in December 1862:

Fellow-citizens, we *cannot escape history. . . . The fiery trial through which we pass, will light us down, in honor or dishonor, to the latest* [last] *generation. . . . We hold the power, and bear the responsibility. In giving freedom to the slave, we assure freedom to the free. . . . We shall nobly save, or meanly lose, the last best, hope of earth.*

Using Historical Evidence This cartoon of 1863 echoes Lincoln's warning that "the enemy behind us is more dangerous to the country than the enemy before us." *Explain the symbols in the cartoon.*

African Americans Free Themselves

The Emancipation Proclamation had a practical as well as a moral effect. The Proclamation encouraged enslaved African Americans in the South to set themselves free by moving to territory controlled by Union troops. Actually, they had been doing so since the beginning of the war by means of an unusual feature of the laws of war.

The Contraband Rule During war, the property of the enemy may be seized and declared **contraband**. It then becomes the property of the government. Early in the war, a clever Union general, Benjamin F. Butler, realized that if enslaved African Americans were supposedly the property of the enemy, they too could be considered contraband. The federal government, as their legal owner, could then declare them free. "We," General Butler insisted, "do not need and will not hold such property."

It was a strange irony. Slaveholders had always stubbornly insisted that by law enslaved people were only property. That legal status was now helping enslaved African Americans set themselves free, and they did so by the thousands. After one raid into Mississippi in 1864, a Union general reported: "We bring in some 500 prisoners, a good many refugees, and about ten miles of Negroes." As they left slave plantations, which depended on their labor, African Americans severely weakened the Confederacy.

African Americans Fight for Freedom Once they were free, many African Americans took advantage of another provision of the Proclamation, which allowed them to enlist in the armed forces of the United States. Now they could fight to free others who were still enslaved. The sight of African American soldiers marching across the South was a nightmare come true for white slaveholders. But for African Americans the chance to fight against slavery was a milestone in their history, and 85 percent of the African Americans eligible to fight did so. These African

Americans in the armed forces eventually totalled nearly 180,000 soldiers, almost 10 percent of the Union fighting force.

Many of the African American soldiers were from free families in the North; some were college educated. But close to 119,000 had once been enslaved. During the war, more than 68,000 were killed or wounded, and 21 won the Medal of Honor, the nation's highest award for courage in combat. One of these was William Harvey Carney, a member of the 54th Massachusetts Regiment.

African Americans (top) escape slavery by following the Union army as it retreats across the Rappahannock River in Virginia in 1862. At bottom, a boy named Jackson sheds the rags of slavery to wear the uniform of a drummer.

AMERICAN PROFILES

William Harvey Carney

Occasionally it happens that people who are otherwise unknown achieve a success so remarkable that it flames brightly in the shadows of the past. Such was the case with Sergeant William Harvey Carney.

Carney was born in 1840, but no one is sure where. It was in either New Bedford, Massachusetts, or Norfolk, Virginia. About his family the record is silent. When the Civil War began, he was just another unknown American.

Many years after his heroic actions in the Civil War, William Harvey Carney posed for a photographer. He achieved widespread fame for his refusal to let the American flag touch the ground during battle.

Carney Joins the Regiment In February 1863, a little over a month after the Emancipation Proclamation became official, Carney enlisted in Company C of the 54th Massachusetts Regiment. Hundreds of African American men from all over the northern states signed up with the regiment at the same time.

Carney soon rose to the rank of sergeant. He could not rise higher because, with few exceptions, only whites could be officers. The commander of the 54th Regiment was Colonel Robert Gould Shaw. Despite his youth—he was only twenty-five years old in 1863—Colonel Shaw was an experienced veteran of Antietam. Reserved but kind, he inspired great loyalty in his men.

Even though they wore the blue uniform of the United States, Carney and his fellow soldiers had to endure all kinds of insults. Not only were they paid less than white troops, they were denied adequate supplies and equipment. Overcoming these challenges, the 54th became a disciplined and proud unit.

When the regiment was sent to South Carolina in June, Shaw was eager to get his men into battle. Though as a veteran he knew the horrors of the new kind of warfare, he also knew the 54th had something to prove, something bigger than battlefield courage.

The Charge on Fort Wagner On July 18, 1863, as part of the Union attack on the city of Charleston, the 54th Massachusetts led the assault on Fort Wagner on Morris Island. The regiment was assigned to charge the fort under cover of darkness. The members of the 54th would have to advance along an open beach, easy targets for as many as twenty cannons within the fort and other Confederate artillery elsewhere. In addition to shells and canisters, these guns could fire bursts of grapeshot, or small pellets, and shells filled with shrapnel, a form of larger metal fragment. The 54th would be armed only with rifles and bayonets—a type of long knife fastened onto their gun barrels.

At 7:45 P.M., Carney, Shaw, and the rest of the regiment set out. The advance went well until they approached within about 300 yards of the fort. At that point a savage burst of fire slashed through the ranks of the regiment. Dozens were wounded or killed instantly.

But the rest charged on. They hurled themselves through or over one obstacle after another, including a ditch filled with 4 feet of water. Suddenly they found themselves at the base of the parapet, the main defensive wall of the fort. Not even this could stop them; they climbed it in the darkness and set the flag of their regiment at the top.

As the men of the 54th swarmed over the parapet, the Confederate defenders met them in full force. Shaw was shot dead instantly. Color Sergeant John Wall, whose job it was to carry the flag of the United States, was also hit. But before the symbol of liberty could touch the ground, Sergeant Carney seized it and planted it next to the regimental flag.

Defenders and attackers were now locked together in fierce hand-to-hand combat, which raged along the wall for close to an hour. Carney was wounded in both legs, his right arm, and his chest. But he refused to stop fighting or to let the enemy cut down the flag. When the remaining members of the regiment were ordered to pull back from the fort to a position some 700 yards away, Carney carried the flag with him. The 54th held its new position until it was replaced by other troops at 2:00 A.M. on July 19.

The Aftermath of the Assault Of the 600 members of the 54th who had charged Fort Wagner, 259 were dead, wounded, or missing. Sergeant Carney was taken to the field hospital. Other wounded soldiers saw the flag he still carried in his hands and broke into a ragged cheer. "The old flag never touched the ground, boys," he assured them.

Not much is known about Sergeant Carney's life after the charge on Fort Wagner. He reappears in history only once, in 1900. In that year he was awarded the Congressional Medal of Honor for his bravery on the evening of July 18, 1863.

The attack on Fort Wagner was a military failure. But the exploits of the 54th Regiment, widely publicized in the North, had a dramatic impact on white attitudes toward African American soldiers. Wrote a reporter for the *New York Herald*:

I saw them [African Americans] *fight at Wagner as none but splendid soldiers, splendidly officered, could fight, dashing through shot and shell, grape, canister and shrapnel, and showers of bullets, and . . . when they did retreat [it was] by command and with choice white troops for company.*

The success of the 54th Regiment proved what abolitionist Frederick Douglass had written in August 1863:

Once let a black man get *upon his person the brass letters, U.S.; let him get an eagle on his button, and a musket on his shoulder and bullets in his pocket, and there is no power on earth which can deny that he has earned the right to citizenship.*

African Americans wearing the brass letters *U. S.* took a step closer to citizenship as they proved their courage. "Nobody knows anything about these men who has not seen them in battle," boasted one of their officers.

Union troops finally took Fort Wagner seven weeks after the charge of the 54th. One of them, Corporal Henry S. Harmon, wrote soon afterwards:

I am proud to say that I am a member *of the 3d United States Colored Troops, and I hope that I am not considered boasting when I say so. Our career has not been unmarked by loss of human life. We have had ten of our number killed and I cannot say exactly how many wounded. . . . When you hear of a white family that has lost father, husband, or brother, you can say of the colored man, we too have borne our share of the burden. We too have suffered and died in defense of that starry banner that floats only over free men.*

SECTION 2 REVIEW

Key Terms, People, and Places
1. Define (a) draft, (b) writ of *habeas corpus,* (c) Internal Revenue Act of 1862, (d) greenback, (e) Pacific Railroad Act of 1862, (f) Emancipation Proclamation, (g) contraband.
2. Identify (a) Copperhead, (b) Radical Republican.

Key Concepts
3. In what way was the Confederate government both strong and weak?
4. What civil rights did Lincoln suspend during the war?

5. Give an example of Republican legislation and explain how it gave permanent support to economic development.
6. How did the Emancipation Proclamation change the war aims of the Union?
7. How did African Americans bring slavery to an end?

Critical Thinking
8. **Testing Conclusions** Lincoln came to believe that the Union could not survive if slavery was preserved. Give evidence to support this conclusion.

Using Letters as Primary Sources

When people write letters, they report firsthand about something of interest to them. For this reason, letters are a valuable source of historical evidence. Not only do they present factual information about a subject, but they also give clues to the attitudes of people in a particular historical period.

Use the following steps to analyze the historical evidence in the letters on this page.

1. Lay the groundwork for analyzing the letters by asking who, when, where, and what. (a) What clues do the letters give about the identity of the writers? (b) To whom were the letters written? (c) When were they written? (d) Where were they written? (e) What are the topics of the letters?

2. Analyze the information in each letter. Study the letters to identify their main points. (a) What specific problems does the writer of Letter A describe? (b) What tasks does the writer of Letter B perform?

3. Study each letter to see what it reveals about conditions and attitudes during the period in which it was written. (a) What general difficulties did farm wives face when their husbands were away at war? (b) Summarize what conditions were like for the wounded after Civil War battles. (c) Generalize about the contribution to the war effort made by women during the Civil War.

A *Lowndes County, Alabama, June 1, 1862*

Dear husband, I now take my pen in hand [to] drop you a few lines to let you know that we are all well as common and I am in about the same health that I was when you left. I hopes these lines may find you the same. The boys [her sons] has come home to see me on a furlough [leave from the army] and stayed 10 days. They started back yesterday to the camp. . . . John, my corn is out now and I have not drawed [harvested] any thing yet but I hope I will. My crop is nice but Pane [a hired man] has quit and left my crop in bad fix, but the neighbors says they will help us. You said you wanted me to pray for you. As for prayers, I pray for you all of the time. I pray for you nearly every breath I draw. . . . Your baby is the prettyest thing you ever saw in your life. She can walk by herself and your little grandson is pretty as a pink and grows the fastest in the world. You must come home and see all of your babies and kiss them. I have got the rye cut. . . . Your old mare is gone blind in one eye and something is the matter with one of her feet so she can't hardly walk. Your hogs and cows is coming on very well. I want you to come home for I want to see you so bad I don't know what to do. I must come to a close by saying I remain your loving wife until death. You must write to me as soon as you get this letter. Goodbye to you.

Lucy Lowe to John P. Lowe

Adapted from Katharine M. Jones, *Heroines of Dixie*, 1955

B *Gettysburg, Pennsylvania, July 8th, 1863*

My Dear Cousin, I am very tired tonight; have been on the field all day. . . . There are no words in the English language to express the sufferings I witnessed today. The men lie on the ground; their clothes have been cut off them to dress [bandage] their wounds; they . . . have nothing but hardtack [biscuit] to eat only as Sanitary Commissions, Christian Associations [volunteer workers], and so forth give them. . . . To give you some idea of the extent and numbers of the wounds, four surgeons, none of whom were idle fifteen minutes at a time, were busy all day amputating legs and arms. I gave to every man that had a leg or arm off a gill [measure] of wine, to every wounded in the Third Division, one glass of lemonade, some bread and preserves and tobacco—as much as I am opposed to the latter. . . . I would get on first rate [remain in good spirits] if they would not ask me to write to their wives; that I cannot do without crying, which is not pleasant to either party.

Cornelia

Cornelia Hancock, *South After Gettysburg*, 1956

Turning Point: The Siege Of Vicksburg

SECTION PREVIEW

The tide of war turned in the summer of 1863. Southern forces led by Robert E. Lee invaded Pennsylvania. At the same time, northern forces led by Ulysses S. Grant surrounded Vicksburg, Mississippi, in an attempt to wrest control of the Mississippi River from the Confederacy.

Key Concepts

- While Grant spent months trying plan after plan to capture Vicksburg, its residents prepared their defenses.
- In July 1863 Lee was forced to go on the offensive and attack Union general Meade at Gettysburg, Pennsylvania.
- The siege of Vicksburg was a new and extremely destructive kind of warfare directed against civilians as well as soldiers.

Key Terms, People, and Places

Pickett's Charge, siege, total war; William Tecumseh Sherman, George G. Meade; Vicksburg, Gettysburg

---

W hile the armies clashed in the East, a Union army in the West struggled to capture the city of **Vicksburg,** Mississippi. Along with another fortress at Port Hudson, Louisiana, this Confederate stronghold prevented the Union from taking complete control of the Mississippi River.

Vicksburg seemed safe from attack. Not only was the city built on hills high above the Mississippi River, but its defenders had built fortifications along the bank to the north, creating an extended platform from which they could rain cannon shells down on Union ships. A Union officer later described the location as

a long line of high, rugged, irregular bluffs, clearly cut against the sky, crowned with cannon which peered ominously [threateningly] from embrasures [openings] to the right and left as far as the eye could see. . . . The approaches to this position were frightful.

Rail lines to the east linked Vicksburg with the state capital at Jackson 50 miles away. The railroad brought regular supplies and formed a route for quick reinforcement in case of attack.

Vicksburg was not just a military prize. It was the second largest city in Mississippi, with upward of 5,000 people, including about 1,400 enslaved and 31 free African Americans. A major regional commercial center with strong ties to the North, Vicksburg had been against secession. But the city had become defiant in 1862 as Union sailors under David Farragut had swept into the Mississippi Valley, and soldiers under Brigadier General Benjamin Butler had taken control of New Orleans. Vicksburg's military governor, James Autry, had refused to surrender, saying:

M *ississippians don't know, and refuse to learn, how to surrender to any enemy. If Commodore Farragut or Brigadier-General Butler can teach them, let them come and try.*

Grant Is Determined

The Union general who now faced the task of teaching Vicksburg this lesson was Ulysses S. Grant. This rough-hewn midwesterner was exactly the kind of general the Union needed.

The Anaconda Plan called for the North to capture the Mississippi River in order to "clear out and keep open this great line of communication" for northern armies. This powder flask was issued to a sailor serving on the Mississippi.

In order to capture Vicksburg, Navy gunboats under Rear Admiral David Porter had to sail past the city at night under heavy fire. "It was as if hell itself were loose," said one observer. Porter himself, with grim humor, remarked: "It was really a jolly scene."

He did not just march armies around, like McClellan. He won battles with them. After the Battle of Shiloh, northern politicians and newspaper editors criticized Grant for his tremendous losses. "I can't spare this man," Lincoln responded bluntly: "He fights."

Like Robert E. Lee, Grant was willing to bend the normal rules of generalship when the time came to do so. But unlike Lee, Grant did not win battles through sheer brilliance—though from time to time he did show flashes of military genius. Instead Grant won mostly through determination. One of his fellow officers once described Grant as the kind of person who

habitually wears an expression as if he had determined to drive his head through a brick wall, and was about to do it.

Banging on a Brick Wall In December of 1862, Grant sent General **William Tecumseh Sherman** and several thousand men to attack Vicksburg. But Grant was unable to link up with Sherman as planned, and the effort failed. Next, Grant tried digging a canal from one part of the Mississippi River to another to bypass Vicksburg altogether, but the canal did not work. Another similar idea called for digging a

connection to the nearby Red River, but this too, proved unworkable. Next Grant tried a scheme to attack Vicksburg from the north by sending gunboats down another river, the Yazoo. Still no success. In yet another plan, Grant sent Sherman and the gunboats on a third roundabout river route. This campaign swiftly became a trap from which Sherman's forces barely escaped alive.

As an early spring came to Vicksburg in 1863, the people of the city took heart from Grant's repeated failures. But they also improved their defenses. One of the biggest businesses in the town was cave building. Twenty dollars would buy protection from bombardments—a one-room hole in the ground. Fifty dollars bought several rooms and timbered supports. In March 1863, one woman described the city as "so honeycombed with caves that the streets look like avenues in a cemetery."

Grant Moves Then, in mid-April, Grant settled on a clever but dangerous plan. He had known all along that the best way to capture Vicksburg was to attack from the land side. But he had not been able to reach that side from his position north of the city, because Vicksburg was protected by the swamps and backwaters of the Yazoo River. Now Grant decided to send his army south of the city. From that position, he would be able to march inland and attack it on the land side, as shown in the map below.

The plan had many risks. To get south of Vicksburg, the men could march overland on the western bank of the Mississippi River, a safe but difficult route. But the gunboats and transport ships Grant needed would have to make a mad dash by night past the guns of Vicksburg. And once his soldiers were south of the city, they would be cut off from their supplies.

The army marched; the ships fired up their steam engines and raced through the hail of Vicksburg's cannon shells. In late April the navy and army successfully linked up south of the city. The confidence of the white people of Vicksburg gave way to tension and fear. Some packed up and left while they could.

On April 30, Grant headed northeast toward the capital at Jackson. For twenty days, in one of the most ingenious and skillful campaigns of his career, the general and his men raided their way through west-central Mississippi, keeping the enemy in a constant state of confusion. They captured their first objective, the city of Jackson, and burned it to the ground. Vicksburg's supply line was now cut off. Then Grant's forces headed straight for Vicksburg. Confederate defenders tried to stop them on their way, but the Union army hurled them back on the city. By mid-May, Grant's troops were at Vicksburg's doorstep, chasing the Confederates into the safety of the town.

Grant's determination had brought him to the land side of Vicksburg. But the people of Vicksburg were determined too. They settled down behind their defenses to wait. Grant did not have his victory yet.

The Battle of Gettysburg

Meanwhile, back in the East, another major battle was shaping up. Lee had just defeated Hooker at Chancellorsville. During June 1863, he moved his troops into the North once again. This time he pushed as far as Pennsylvania. His plan was to cut off Washington, D.C., from the rest of the Union and win recognition for Confederate independence.

Once again, the Union army pursued Lee's forces, which were surging toward Harrisburg, Pennsylvania, a key rail center. On July 1, just west of the little village of **Gettysburg,** Union troops clashed with units of the Confederate army as Lee attempted to concentrate his forces. Within hours, tens of thousands of Union and Confederate troops poured into the area. So began the Battle of

Lincoln called capturing Vicksburg "the key" to winning the war; Jefferson Davis said the Confederate stronghold was "the nailhead that holds the South's two halves together." Ulysses S. Grant spent eight months trying to take the city.

1 Grant's camp at Millikens Bend Dec. 1862–Apr. 1863

2 Route of Grant's army past Vicksburg Mar. 29–early Apr.

3 Route of Union navy past Vicksburg Apr. 14 & 22

4 Navy ferries army to eastern bank, Apr. 30

5 Vicksburg to Jackson rail line cut, May 13

6 Grant captures and destroys Jackson, Mississippi, May 14

7 Grant defeats Confederate forces at Champions Hill May 16

8 Siege of Vicksburg begins, May 22

Raymond

Auburn

Cayuga

Grant's Route

Rocky Springs

Crystal Springs

Pine Bluff

New Orleans & Jackson R.R.

Mississippi R.

Hard Times Landing

Grant's route

Bruinsburg

Gettysburg, a struggle that would drag on through three terrible days.

On July 1, the first day of the battle, the Confederates pushed the Union troops through Gettysburg and into defensive positions along a ridge south of the town. The new Union commander, General **George G. Meade,** decided to defend this high ground and force the Confederates to attack.

On July 2, Lee sent repeated shock waves at one part of the Union battle line after another. He tried to capture high ground in two places—Little Round Top and Culp's Hill—so that he could fire down on the enemy. Both of these efforts were pushed back by outnumbered Union troops. Though the Union line stretched for miles along the ridge, Lee could not break it anywhere.

On July 3, Lee ordered a direct attack on the center of the Union line. Known as **Pickett's Charge** after George Pickett, one of the generals who led it, it was a classic confrontation between the old and the new kind of warfare. More than 14,000 Confederates marched the better part of a mile across open ground under withering fire from Union cannons firing shells and canisters. Then they charged up a rise toward the Union guns. Only a few reached the federal lines and fought hand-to-hand with Union troops; most were cut down, and the survivors were captured or forced to retreat.

The next day, July 4, Lee's army, which had suffered 28,000 casualties, left the battlefield and headed south. The exhausted Army of the Potomac, which had 23,000 men dead, wounded, or missing, did not follow the Confederates. Lee and his men escaped, but they would never go on the offensive again.

MAKING CONNECTIONS

Who was usually more successful in the Civil War battles you have read about, the defenders or the attackers? Why was this so?

Vicksburg, Too, Is Determined

Back at Vicksburg, Grant had found he could not take the city by direct attack. A **siege** would be necessary—a form of prolonged attack in which a city is surrounded and starved into surrender. Sieges have been a common form of warfare since ancient times, but at the siege of Vicksburg, the new cannon technology changed them forever.

When Union cannons began to fire on Vicksburg's residents from land and river, it was the first burst in a bombardment that would average about 2,800 shells a day. One civilian, Emma Balfour, described how she barely managed to escape into a shelter:

W*e went into a cave for the first time. . . . Just as we got in several machines [shells] exploded . . . just over our heads, and at the same time two riders were killed in the valley below us by a twenty-four pound shell from the east side, so . . . we were between two fires. As all this rushed over me and the sense of suffocation from being underground, the certainty that there was no way of escape, that we were hemmed in, caged—for one moment my heart seemed to stand still—then my faith and*

Confederate troops in George Pickett's charge at Gettysburg temporarily broke the Union line in the action shown here, at a crook in a stone wall called the Angle. After the charge, General Lee told Pickett to re-form his division to repel a possible counterattack. "General Lee," exclaimed Pickett, "I have no division now."

courage rose to meet the emergency, and I have felt prepared ever since and cheerful.

The conflict between the North and South had now become **total war**. In this form of war, opponents strike not only against one another's soldiers, but against civilians and the entire economic system of the enemy.

Total War in Vicksburg Hour after hour, day after day for forty-seven days, the people of Vicksburg endured the relentless pounding of three hundred Union guns. As May dragged into hot June, the schedule of the shellings took over everyday life. The people of Vicksburg could not sleep except during pauses in the vast uproar of the guns. They could not always eat when they were hungry or bathe when they were dirty; they had to wait until the shells that rocked their city gave them a few minutes' peace.

But the worst fear of the unfortunate residents of Vicksburg was not the shelling; it was starvation. Food had already been low when Grant surrounded the city, and now no new supplies could reach them. For weeks they had continued to hope that a southern army would come to their rescue. That hope died at the end of June, when they were reduced to eating small portions of rotten meat and moldy rice.

The Turning Point On July 3—as Pickett's men were charging the Union lines at Gettysburg—the Confederate officer in command at Vicksburg, General John C. Pemberton, met with Grant to discuss the terms of a surrender of the city. The next day, the Fourth of July, 1863, Vicksburg was turned over to the Union.

On the night of July 4, the red glare of rockets lit the sky over the Mississippi River, in celebration of the Union victory in Vicksburg and the eighty-seventh birthday of the United States. A band played festive music. Some of the people of Vicksburg wept; others made the best of the situation, grateful to have food to eat. African Americans greeted the Union troops with rejoicing. For them, the day they had long looked for had come at last.

Five days later, Confederate forces at Port Hudson, Louisiana, surrendered the last Confederate post on the Mississippi River. Though the war would continue for two more years, the Mississippi River would remain under the control of the Union navy. The Confederacy had been cut in two.

Josiah Gorgas, a Confederate officer, wrote in his diary about the tremendous turn of events in early July:

> Events have succeeded [followed] *one another with disastrous rapidity. One brief month ago we were apparently at the point of success. Lee was in Pennsylvania, threatening Harrisburg, and even Philadelphia. Vicksburg seemed to laugh all Grant's efforts to scorn. . . . It seems incredible that human power could effect such a change in so brief a space. Yesterday, we rode on the pinnacle of success— today absolute ruin seems to be our portion. The Confederacy totters to its destruction.*

SECTION 3 REVIEW

Key Terms, People, and Places
1. Identify (a) William Tecumseh Sherman, (b) George G. Meade.
2. Identify (a) Vicksburg, (b) Gettysburg.

Key Concepts
3. What quality distinguished Grant as a military leader and allowed him to capture Vicksburg?
4. What were the two most significant events that occurred during the conflicts at Gettysburg and Vicksburg on July 3, 1863?
5. What was new and unusual about the siege of Vicksburg?

Critical Thinking
6. **Identifying Central Issues** Why were the Battle of Gettysburg and the siege of Vicksburg turning points in the Civil War?

The Lasting Impact of the Siege of Vicksburg

Together with the Union victory at Gettysburg, the fall of Vicksburg ensured the ultimate defeat of the Confederate States of America. But Vicksburg was more than a turning point in the Civil War. It also marked the beginning of a new age in warfare, the age of total war.

Grant's Warfare The tactics that Grant used at Vicksburg were not completely new. In ancient times, armies had burned farmlands and besieged cities, hoping to starve enemies into surrender. But for the most part, wars after the 1600s had been little more than duels between massed armies or fleets. Battles had been limited to one or two days in length. At the end of the battle, whichever side had suffered the worst losses retreated.

Grant refused to limit his fighting in this way. He did not just attack the Confederate army; he attacked anyone and anything that stood between him and victory. That included civilians. He knew well, when he purposefully destroyed Vicksburg's supply line to Jackson, that civilians would soon go hungry as a result. He also knew that the thousands of shells he poured onto Vicksburg would fall among innocent residents of the city.

But Grant's goal was to convince the enemy that defeat meant more than the loss of a distant army. It meant an unacceptable loss of the comfort and security of daily life. Sherman later explained:

> War is cruelty, and you cannot refine it. . . . We are not only fighting hostile armies, but a hostile people, and must make old and young, rich and poor, feel the hard hand of war.

For this goal, the new weapons—accurate cannons and explosive shells—were ideal. But simpler

1863 Union cannons at Vicksburg introduce a new age of total warfare.

1940–1945 Nazi warplanes and rockets heavily damage London during World War II.

1900   **1920**   **1940**

1915 German submarine sinks the Lusitania, a civilian passenger ship, during World War I.

1945 Large parts of Tokyo are destroyed by American firebombs.

forms of destructive power also worked. In the years after Vicksburg fell, the armies of Grant and Sherman used little more than fire and crowbars to bring large-scale destruction to Georgia, South Carolina, and Virginia.

Such tactics, however, made healing the nation after the war much more difficult. The people of Vicksburg, for example, did not officially celebrate the Fourth of July until 1945, evidence of the enduring anger and bad feelings Grant's total warfare had created.

Americans Wage Total War American troops in the twentieth century would repeatedly find themselves in situations similar to the siege of Vicksburg. In later wars, too, their mission would be to bring the superior numbers and resources of the United States to bear on a well-entrenched enemy. These wars included World War II (1941–1945), the War in Vietnam (1965–1973), and the Persian Gulf War (1991). The United States and other nations would find new technologies for this purpose that would make the horror of Grant's cannons and gunboats seem puny. And more often than not, this warfare would leave in its wake a massive loss of civilian life and destruction of property.

The purpose of this destruction was to persuade the enemy that the struggle was simply not worth the cost. After Vicksburg, civilians were as much a part of war as soldiers; starvation as much of a weapon as the rifle; and victory required not just the surrender of a few troops but the complete demoralization and destruction of vast civilian populations.

The success of Grant at Vicksburg was due to his use of modern warfare—a combination of technology and total war. The people of Vicksburg would not be the last to have to decide whether it was worth losing everything just to hold on to the hope of a later victory.

REVIEWING THE FACTS

1. Why did Grant and Sherman resort to total warfare against the South?
2. In what later wars was the principle of total warfare applied?

Critical Thinking

3. **Distinguishing False from Accurate Images** Americans sometimes think of the Civil War as an old-fashioned war. How is this image false?

1960s–1970s United States planes use napalm (jellied gasoline) to burn Vietnamese villages.

1991 Dictator Saddam Hussein forces Kurds in Iraq to flee to refugee camps.

1960   1980   2000

1991 American bombs and missiles disrupt life in Baghdad during the Persian Gulf War.

A New Birth of Freedom

SECTION PREVIEW

Northern armies gradually pounded the weakened but persistent South, pushing it toward surrender. As the Civil War came to an end, the conflict became more than a struggle over the Union. It became instead a redefinition of the American nation.

Key Concepts
- In the Gettysburg Address, Lincoln redefined the United States, emphasizing that democracy existed to preserve freedom and equality.
- In 1864 Sherman carried total war into Georgia, while Grant threw attack after attack at Lee's army.
- Lincoln won reelection in 1864, demonstrating that he had the nation's approval of his war policy and his stand against slavery.
- Lee, finally hemmed in by Union forces, surrendered to Grant at Appomattox, Virginia.

Key Terms, People, and Places
Gettysburg Address, Thirteenth Amendment; Philip Sheridan, John Wilkes Booth; Atlanta, Savannah, Petersburg, Appomattox Court House

"I give thanks to the Almighty," said Lincoln when he was reelected in 1864, "for this evidence of the people's resolution to stand by free government and the rights of humanity."

A fter the Battle of Gettysburg, the people of the North decided that all the Americans who had perished there should be honored with burial in a new cemetery. President Lincoln was invited to "make a few appropriate remarks" at the dedication ceremony in Gettysburg on November 19, 1863.

The Gettysburg Address

The main speaker, Edward Everett of Massachusetts, vividly described the Battle of Gettysburg in a grand, two-hour oration. Then the President spoke for two minutes in his high-pitched voice. Simply, eloquently, Lincoln explained the meaning of the Civil War—and redefined the meaning of the United States.

Lincoln began his speech, now known as the **Gettysburg Address,** by reminding his listeners that in 1776 the American people had

brought forth upon this continent a new nation conceived in liberty and dedicated to the proposition that all men are created equal.

The Civil War, said Lincoln, was a test of whether any nation dedicated to freedom and equality can survive. Freedom and equality, he stressed, were what the Union dead had been fighting for. Americans should now resolve that

these dead shall not have died in vain; this nation, under God, shall have a new birth of freedom; and that government of the people, by the people, for the people, shall not perish from the earth.

Lincoln spoke with a wisdom ahead of his time. Americans in 1863 did not like his speech; they thought it was too short and simple. But in the years since then, people have come to appreciate that Lincoln's words marked a dramatic new definition of the United States. Freedom and equality no longer belonged to a few, as they had in 1776. They were the right of everyone. Democracy and the Union did not exist to serve the interests of white men; they existed to preserve freedom for all. Lincoln's speech marked a great milestone in the gradual expansion of liberty to all people in the United States—an expansion that still continues today.

Sherman Burns and Grant Hammers

Grant's success in 1863 convinced Lincoln that he had found a leader who could win battles. The President called the general to Washington to assume overall command of the northern armies.

Lincoln's Call Is Repeated

In his Gettysburg Address, Lincoln called for Americans to rededicate themselves to the principle that all people are created equal and so should have equal rights. One hundred years later, on August 28, 1963, the African American leader Dr. Martin Luther King, Jr., gave a speech echoing Lincoln's call for "a new birth of freedom." Pointing out that African Americans did not have full political and economic rights even a full century after the Emancipation Proclamation, King said, "We must face the tragic fact that the Negro is still not free." King repeated Lincoln's call for a new dedication to the ideals of the Declaration of Independence, saying, "I have a dream that one day this nation will rise up and live out the true meaning of its creed: 'We hold these truths to be self-evident—that all men are created equal.'"

As a result of the actions of King and others, Congress passed laws to protect the civil rights of African Americans. These laws were a giant step toward the new freedom called for by Lincoln and King. *Does the United States live up to the ideals of the Declaration of Independence today? Explain your answer.*

Grant brought with him a new plan for winning the war. He would fight Lee's army repeatedly until he exhausted it. And he would send General Sherman into Georgia to do the same to the other major Confederate army there.

Sherman's March to the Sea As it turned out, Sherman could not catch the army he was sent after. Instead he beseiged **Atlanta,** Georgia, and captured it in September 1864. Then he proposed a new plan of his own. He would march his troops from Atlanta to the sea, gathering the food he needed from the land and destroying everything he could not take with him. He told Grant:

If we can march a well-appointed army right through [Jefferson Davis's] territory, it is a demonstration to the world, foreign and domestic, that we have a power which Davis cannot resist.

With Atlanta in flames behind him, Sherman set out for the seacoast city of **Savannah,** Georgia. Cutting a sixty-mile-wide swath across the red earth of the state, he burned the harvest, plundered plantations, uprooted railroad tracks, and smashed bridges, factories, and mills. By December 22, he had reached the coast and captured Savannah. He had succeeded in his purpose—to make the people of Georgia "so sick of war that generations would pass away

before they would again appeal to it." But his march would also make the hatred between North and South still more difficult to heal.

Grant Hammers at Lee Meanwhile, Grant and the Army of the Potomac were pressing toward Richmond, relentlessly hammering at Lee's force, the Army of Northern Virginia. Outnumbered nearly two to one, Lee fought a series of defensive battles that held back the Union advance. But Grant refused to retreat to a distant camp to reorganize, like other Union generals before him. Each time Lee stopped him, Grant simply moved his army to the left and attacked again. "I propose to fight it out on this line if it takes all summer," he told Lincoln. Though northerners were enthusiastic about Grant's determination, they were horrified at its cost: by early June, 65,000 of Grant's men were dead, wounded, or missing.

Unable to reach Richmond or break Lee's army, Grant took his forces south of the Confederate capital in June 1864. There he came to a halt, threatening **Petersburg,** Virginia, the railway center that supplied Richmond. Lee followed, and the armies faced each other once again. The bloody standoff at Petersburg dragged on well into the next year.

The Election of 1864

While Grant and Sherman were fighting their battles on southern soil, Lincoln had a

Though Sherman issued orders that civilians were not to be harmed during his march to the sea, one of the soldiers who followed him wrote: "The cruelties practiced on this campaign toward the citizens have been enough to blast a more sacred cause than ours."

The End of the War

The Confederacy was still holding out. Its leaders tried everything—even signing up enslaved people as soldiers. But the women and men of the South were sick of war. By the end of 1864, more than 50 percent of the soldiers in the Confederate armies had deserted.

The map on page 217 shows the last stages of the war. The standoff at Petersburg continued through March 1865. Then Union general **Philip Sheridan** won a battle that cut off Lee's supplies and put him and his army in danger of being surrounded. Lee's men, already starving, were deserting by the dozen. His only possible hope was to abandon Petersburg and Richmond and try to link up with other Confederate forces to the south.

Again General Sheridan moved, cutting off the retreat of Lee's exhausted men with his swift, horse-mounted troops. Hemmed in by Sheridan and Grant and with no other alternative, Lee sent word that he wanted to discuss surrender.

On Sunday, April 9, 1865, Grant and Lee met in the town of **Appomattox Court House,** Virginia. Lee was as dignified in defeat as he had been courageous and skillful in battle. Grant proved as generous in victory as he had been relentless in war. The two men agreed to the terms of the surrender and were enemies no more.

What Was Lost and What Was Won

Five days later, President and Mrs. Lincoln went to the theater in Washington, D.C. In the middle of the performance, a young actor named **John Wilkes Booth** broke into the presidential box overlooking the stage and shot the President in the head. He then leapt down onto the stage and escaped.

Federal officials immediately began to hunt Booth down. They soon learned he was a member of a group of southern sympathizers who had plotted to murder all the high officials of the federal government. Within days, the army tracked Booth to a barn in Virginia; he died of wounds he received resisting arrest. Several other conspirators were caught and hanged.

political battle of his own to attend to in the North. As the election of 1864 drew near, it seemed very likely that he would lose. The nation was weary of the war, and the Copperheads were calling for peace negotiations.

When Sherman captured Atlanta, however, the mood in the North changed. Lincoln, running against Democratic candidate General George McClellan, won the election with 212 out of 233 electoral votes.

By reelecting Lincoln, voters showed their approval not only of his war policy, but of his stand against slavery. Three months later, in February 1865, members of Congress joined him in that stand and passed the **Thirteenth Amendment** to the Constitution. It was ratified by the states and became law on December 6, 1865. In a few simple words, the amendment ended slavery in the United States forever.

MAKING CONNECTIONS

Why could the northern states not ban slavery in the Union earlier than the 1860s?

Lincoln did not die instantly; he lingered until the morning of April 15, though he never regained consciousness. When he perished, the South lost not only its most powerful opponent, but also the man who would probably have become its most powerful friend and protector. Lincoln had already begun to insist that the reunion of the nation after the war should be based on fairness and mercy, not hatred and vengeance. The President, too, now became a victim of the war that had divided the nation.

Like Lincoln, many of the soldiers on both sides did not live to return home. Some 360,000 Union and 258,000 Confederate soldiers died of disease, wounds, or poor medical treatment. Few other wars in history have had so great a human cost.

Lincoln knew well that neither side could truly win such a terrible war. In his Second Inaugural Address he said:

> Both [North and South] read the same Bible, and pray to the same God; and each invokes His aid against the other. . . . The prayers of both could not be answered; that of neither has been answered fully.

The South did not win the independence for which it struggled. The North did not achieve the easy victory that it had hoped for. Instead both sides suffered bitterly.

But if both North and South lost by the war, they both also gained by it. They gained an undivided nation that would go on to become the most powerful country in the world, a democracy that would continue to seek the equality Lincoln had promised for it. And they gained new fellow citizens—the African Americans who had broken the bonds of slavery and claimed their right to be free and equal, every one.

The Final Battles of the Civil War, 1863–1865

Geography and History: Interpreting Maps
After one Civil War battle, a Union general said about the Confederate troops: "I doubt if any soldiers in the world ever needed so much cumulative evidence to convince them they were beaten." The same could be said of the South as a whole. *What were the two main movements of Union forces that brought the war to an end?*

SECTION 4 REVIEW

Key Terms, People, and Places
1. Define (a) Gettysburg Address, (b) Thirteenth Amendment.
2. Identify (a) Philip Sheridan, (b) John Wilkes Booth.
3. Identify (a) Atlanta, (b) Savannah, (c) Petersburg, (d) Appomattox Court House.

Key Concepts
4. How did Lincoln describe the Civil War in the Gettysburg Address?

5. What plans did Sherman and Grant follow in their campaigns during 1864?
6. What did Lincoln's reelection demonstrate?
7. Why was Lee finally forced to surrender?

Critical Thinking
8. **Making Comparisons** Compare and contrast the condition of the United States at the time of President Lincoln's death with its condition at the time of Washington's first presidency.

Valley of War

One of General Stonewall Jackson's most deadly weapons was a piece of paper eight and a half feet long—a detailed map of the Shenandoah Valley. What made this valley the focus of repeated fighting during the Civil War?

Great generals closely study the geography of the land where they are fighting and use it to their advantage. Like geographers, they pay careful attention to location—the relationship one place has with another. And like geographers, generals are interested in human movement across the land. Finally, military planners also study the characteristics of a place. A look at all three of these themes in geography—location, movement, and place—shows why the Shenandoah Valley played a crucial part in the Civil War.

"The Valley of Humiliation"

The Shenandoah Valley is a corridor about 150 miles long and 25 miles wide between the Blue Ridge Mountains and the Alleghenies. (See the map on page 219.) It stretches from Harpers Ferry in what is now West Virginia to the James River in Virginia. During the Civil War, its location made it mostly useless to northern armies. For them, the valley led nowhere—into rugged hills away from their main target, Richmond. But for southern armies, the valley led close to Washington, D.C. When a Union army pressed toward Richmond, a Confederate army would prowl through the Shenandoah, threatening Washington and drawing troops away from the main Union force.

Hoping to put an end to this threat, northern generals repeatedly tried to take control of the Shenandoah during the early years of the war. Even though they did win parts of it at times, they were soon forced to give up their conquests. One key town in the upper Shenandoah Valley, Winchester, changed hands 72 times between 1861 and 1865. The Shenandoah was soon known to northerners as the Valley of Humiliation.

A Corridor for Travel

Swift and decisive movement was the secret of the Confederate military strategy. Simply because Shenandoah was a valley, it formed an excellent corridor for movement. Its slopes, though forested, were not too steep or rocky for troops on foot or horseback. Furthermore, the Valley Pike, the main road through the Shenandoah, allowed even a large army like that of Robert E. Lee to travel rapidly from the heart of Virginia to the borders of the North. And the many gaps in the Blue Ridge mountain chain allowed southern forces like those of Stonewall Jackson to duck easily in and out of the Shendandoah Valley as it suited their purposes.

One key town in the Shenandoah Valley, Winchester, changed hands 72 times between 1861 and 1865.

"A Barren Waste"

The special characteristics of the valley also made it valuable to the South. For example, the population of the valley was mostly sympathetic to the Confederacy, so Union invaders had to endure constant attacks by armed but unofficial raiders. But a still more beneficial characteristic of the valley—for the South, at least—was its splendid pastures and fields, which supplied the Confederate army in Virginia with meat and grain.

The commander of Union forces, General Grant, decided in the summer of 1864 that this source of supply had to be shut down once and for all. He determined that the harvest in the valley should be so completely destroyed that "crows flying over it for the balance of the season will have to carry their provender [food] with them." He later gave these specific instructions to General Phil Sheridan: "Do all the damage to railroads and crops you can. Carry off stock of all descriptions, and Negroes so as to prevent further planting. If the war is to last another year we want the Shenandoah Valley to remain a barren waste."

Sheridan carried out these orders to the letter. In the fall of 1864 he wrote Grant:

I have destroyed over 2,000 barns filled with wheat, hay, and farming implements; over 70 mills, filled with flour and wheat; . . . and have killed and issued to the troops not less than 3,000 sheep. . . . The people here are getting sick of the war.

Grant answered: "Keep on, and your good work will cause the fall of Richmond."

In the spring of the next year, Grant's words came true. As one Confederate soldier wrote,

There are a good many of us who believe that this shooting match has been carried on long enough. A government that has run out of rations [food for its army] can't expect to do much more fighting.

Early in April 1865, Lee abandoned Richmond and surrendered. In some respects, the war had been lost months before—in the Shenandoah Valley.

GEOGRAPHIC CONNECTIONS

1. How did the location of the Shenandoah Valley make the valley useful to the South?
2. Why did Grant want to make the Shenandoah Valley "a barren waste"?

Critical Thinking

3. **Identifying Central Issues** Why do military planners study human movement over the land?

219

Chapter Review

Understanding Key Terms, People, and Places

Key Terms
1. shell
2. canister
3. war of attrition
4. Anaconda Plan
5. gunboat
6. draft
7. writ of *habeas corpus*
8. Internal Revenue Act of 1862
9. greenback
10. Pacific Railroad Act of 1862
11. Emancipation Proclamation
12. contraband
13. Pickett's Charge
14. siege
15. total war
16. Gettysburg Address
17. Thirteenth Amendment

People
18. Stonewall Jackson
19. George McClellan
20. Ulysses S. Grant
21. Robert E. Lee
22. Copperhead
23. Radical Republican
24. William Tecumseh Sherman
25. George G. Meade
26. Philip Sheridan
27. John Wilkes Booth

Places
28. Manassas
29. Shiloh
30. Antietam
31. Vicksburg
32. Gettysburg
33. Atlanta
34. Savannah
35. Petersburg
36. Appomattox Court House

Terms For each term above, write a sentence that explains its relation to the Civil War.

Matching Review the key terms in the list above. If you are not sure of a term's meaning, review its definition in the chapter. Then choose a term from the list that best matches each description below.

1. a form of prolonged attack in which a city is surrounded and starved into surrender
2. a court order commanding a jail officer to demonstrate that a prisoner is being held for a good reason
3. a small floating fort fitted with cannons
4. a legal means of forcing people to serve in the armed forces
5. national currency created by Republicans

Word Relationships Three of the people and places in each of the following sets are related. Choose the name that does not belong and explain why it does not belong.

1. (a) George McClellan, (b) Stonewall Jackson, (c) William Tecumseh Sherman, (d) Ulysses S. Grant
2. (a) Vicksburg, (b) Shiloh, (c) Antietam, (d) Manassas
3. (a) Atlanta, (b) Savannah, (c) Petersburg, (d) Gettysburg

Reviewing Main Ideas

Section 1 (pp. 192–198)
1. Why did Civil War generals use outmoded tactics?
2. How was the Anaconda Plan put into action?
3. Briefly summarize Union efforts to capture the southern capital of Richmond.

Section 2 (pp. 199–205)
4. What challenges did the new Confederate government face?
5. Why did Lincoln suspend the writ of habeas corpus?
6. What was the permanent effect of the absence of southern Democrats from Congress during the war?
7. What document gave a new moral purpose to the Union's war effort?

8. Who set African Americans free during the Civil War?

Section 3 (pp. 207–211)
9. How did the residents of Vicksburg spend their time while Grant tried unsuccessfully to capture the city?
10. What was the result of the Battle of Gettysburg?
11. In what ways was the siege of Vicksburg total war?

Section 4 (pp. 214–217)
12. Explain how the Gettysburg Address redefined the concept of freedom for Americans.
13. What were the immediate and the long-term effects of Sherman's march to the sea?
14. Briefly describe the events of 1865 that led to Lee's surrender.

1. **Distinguishing False from Accurate Images** At the end of the Civil War, General William Tecumseh Sherman was called a traitor to the North because of his generosity to the defeated troops of the South. Yet many people today misjudge Sherman and mistakenly believe he was full of hatred for the South. How did this false image arise?

2. **Formulating Questions** Create three questions to ask William Harvey Carney that could lead to a greater understanding of the role of African Americans during the Civil War.

3. **Identifying Central Issues** How was the charge on Fort Wagner and Pickett's Charge typical of the way in which many Civil War battles were fought?

1. **Evaluating Primary Sources** Review the primary source excerpt on page 202. Explain Lincoln's statement that "in giving freedom to the slave, we assure freedom to the free."

2. **Understanding the Visuals** Examine the painting of Pickett's Charge on page 210. How can you tell that the Confederate forces are about to overrun the enemy lines?

3. **Writing About the Chapter** You are a newspaper reporter filing a story about one of the following events of the Civil War: the Battle of Manassas, the Battle of Vicksburg, the dedication ceremony at Gettysburg, or the surrender at Appomattox Court House. First, make a list of your observations at the event you have chosen. Include your perceptions of the physical setting of the event, the people involved, and the event's significance. Next, write a draft of your story in which you describe the event as you observed it. Revise your story, making sure that details are vividly and clearly described. Proofread your story and draft a final copy.

4. **Using the Graphic Organizer** This graphic organizer uses a flow map to show causes and effects of the Civil War. (a) According to the organizer, what forces clashed in the 1860s? (b) Explain the connection between the Declaration of Independence and the results of the Civil War. (c) On a separate sheet of paper, create your own graphic organizer about events of 1861–1865, using this graphic organizer as an example.

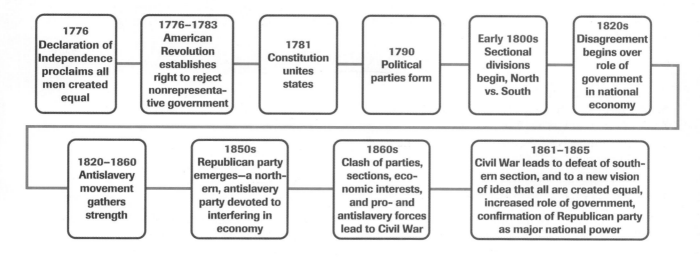

1776 Declaration of Independence proclaims all men created equal

1776–1783 American Revolution establishes right to reject nonrepresentative government

1781 Constitution unites states

1790 Political parties form

Early 1800s Sectional divisions begin, North vs. South

1820s Disagreement begins over role of government in national economy

1820–1860 Antislavery movement gathers strength

1850s Republican party emerges—a northern, antislavery party devoted to interfering in economy

1860s Clash of parties, sections, economic interests, and pro- and antislavery forces lead to Civil War

1861–1865 Civil War leads to defeat of southern section, and to a new vision of idea that all are created equal, increased role of government, confirmation of Republican party as major national power

American Album
ARTIFACTS FROM EXHIBITIONS AND COLLECTIONS
AT THE SMITHSONIAN INSTITUTION
NATIONAL MUSEUM OF AMERICAN HISTORY

LIFE AT WAR

When Union and Confederate soldiers set off to war in 1861, both sides expected it to last only a short time. They soon realized that the struggle would not be settled quickly and that they would have to adapt to long months at war. As in most wars, much of what the soldiers did was boring and uncomfortable. Their routine consisted mainly of training for battle, securing food, idling with their fellow soldiers, and traveling. Soldiers far preferred these daily discomforts and boredoms, however, to the deadly horrors they faced from fierce battles, diseases, and infections. More than 600,000 died—the most Americans ever to die in a war. Four of every ten men who went off to the Civil War were killed or wounded. *Why do you think soldiers were willing to pay such a high cost for their side's cause?*

▲ BOWIE KNIFE Many Confederate soldiers carried Bowie knives—named after frontiersman Jim Bowie.

▲ CONFEDERATE UNIFORM John Mosby, a Confederate scout and guerrilla leader, wore this jacket. Mosby and his Partisan Rangers often operated behind enemy lines in Virginia and Maryland.

▲ BULLET IN SHOULDER BELT PLATE
The soldier who wore this shoulder plate was very lucky. The plate saved his life by stopping a musket bullet.

▲ CIVIL WAR MUSKET
Many soldiers during the war used a musket, but the rifle soon replaced it as the standard army weapon. A rifle was easier to load, more accurate over long distances, and misfired less often.

▲ FIELD CUTLERY Soldiers carried utensils like these with their mess tins. Getting food to the soldiers was a problem that slowed down both armies.

▲ MESS TINS A soldier carried his own eating implements with him. These mess tins took up little space when put away and could be carried easily inside a soldier's pack.

◄ HARD TACK
Although not very tasty, this chewy bread was very nourishing, lasted a long time without spoiling, and was easy to carry.

◄ BOTTLE OF QUININE
Many soldiers suffered from the disease of malaria. Quinine relieved some symptoms, but did not cure soldiers of the disease.

► REGIMENTAL FLAG
This flag commemorates some important battles by an African American regiment. About 180,000 of the 2,000,000 Union soldiers were African Americans.

▲ FIELD HOSPITAL More soldiers died from disease and from infections caused by wounds than were killed in battles. Many women served their cause by working in field hospitals.

Reconstruction
1863–1877

*I*n the years following the Civil War, the people of the United States plunged headlong into accelerating social and economic change. For the formerly enslaved people of the South, freedom opened a new world in which they were at liberty to travel, rebuild relationships, and seek control over their working lives. Yet the fate of African Americans was still intertwined with the will of whites, some of whom respected them and some of whom did not. In the end, most white Americans proved unwilling to commit themselves to full racial equality. Reconstruction transformed the nation, but it failed to fulfill the promise of northern victory in the Civil War.

Events in the United States

1865 The Civil War ends as the last Confederate forces surrender.

1866 The Ku Klux Klan is founded in Tennessee.

1868 Congress impeaches but does not convict President Johnson.

1869 The Wyoming and Utah territories grant women the right to vote.

1863   1865   1867   1869

Events in the World

1865 Englishman Lewis Carroll publishes Alice's Adventures in Wonderland.

1867 The Dominion of Canada is established.

1869 The Suez Canal is completed in Egypt, joining the Mediterranean Sea and the Gulf of Suez.

Pages 226–231
The Meaning of Freedom

The Civil War was over and slavery was dead. Now liberty swept through the South in the wake of Union armies, and African Americans seized it with enthusiasm, exploring the meaning it held for every aspect of their lives.

Pages 232–236
Three Plans for Reconstruction

The meaning of freedom was clear to the freed people of the South. For Congress, however, the end of the Civil War raised many difficult questions about how to rebuild the nation. The result was a series of acts and amendments that redefined citizenship and attempted to create a new social order in the South.

Pages 237–241
Reconstruction in the South

Republicans stormed the South, bringing ambitious ideas about improving the political and social rights of African Americans. Their policies did lead to significant gains, but they soon found their efforts undermined by a campaign of terror and violence.

Pages 243–245
The Retreat from Reconstruction in the North

The Radical Republican blueprint for Reconstruction was based on a grand dream of social equality and justice. But economic and political changes brought by the war led the Republicans to forsake their commitment to this dream in favor of a cozy relationship with business leaders.

1876 Republican Rutherford B. Hayes wins the presidential election despite losing the popular vote.

1877 The Compromise of 1877 ends military occupation of the South.

1872 President Ulysses S. Grant wins reelection.

1875 Congress passes a Civil Rights Act.

1871	1873	1875	1877

1871 The unification of Germany is completed.

1872 Japan introduces universal military service.
• Germany expels the Jesuits.

1873 Slave markets and exports of enslaved people are abolished in Zanzibar in Africa.

1874 The Ashanti War ends in African Ghana.

1876 Korea becomes an independent nation.
• Serbia declares war on Turkey.

1877 First Kaffir War begins in South Africa.
• First tennis championship held at Wimbledon.

225

The Meaning of Freedom

The Civil War was over and slavery was dead. Now liberty swept through the South in the wake of Union armies, and African Americans seized it with enthusiasm, exploring the meaning it held for every aspect of their lives.

Key Concepts
- Enslaved African Americans took up their freedom with a readiness that surprised white slaveholders.
- To formerly enslaved African Americans, freedom meant the ability to move, to organize, to educate themselves, to participate in politics, to own land, and to decide what to do with their labor.

Key Terms, People, and Places
Reconstruction

Freedom for African Americans meant—among other things—the freedom to worship. After the Civil War, African American churches in the South gained hundreds of thousands of new members. This photograph shows a woman ready to preach.

I n June 1869, A. D. Lewis, an African American citizen of North Carolina, sent a letter to Governor William W. Holden. In it, Lewis describes a dispute he had had with a certain Dr. A. H. Jones.

I was in my field at my own work and this Jones came by me and drove up to a man's gate that live close by . . . and ordered my child to come there and open that gate for him . . . while there was children in the yard at the same time not more than twenty yards from him and just because they were white and mine black he would not call them to open the gate. . . . I spoke gently to him that [the white children] would open the gate. . . . He got out of his buggy . . . and walked nearly hundred yards right into my field where I was at my own work and double his fist and strick me in the face three times and . . .

cursed me as a dumb old Radical. . . . Now governor I wants you to please write me how to bring this man to justice.

It is not known whether Governor Holden ever answered Lewis. But the letter does say a lot about **Reconstruction,** the period of United States history in which the nation tried to adjust to the new conditions created by the Civil War.

In his letter, Lewis mentions himself, his work, and his land in terms that reflect true self-respect. Not only was he outraged by the physical injury Jones did him by striking him in the face, he was offended that Jones had insulted his dignity by giving orders to his child. Clearly, Lewis saw himself as an American citizen with legal rights. He must have believed that the legal system would protect him from assault; otherwise, he would not have written to Governor Holden at all.

Lewis's attitudes and expectations suggest a tremendous change in the American South. No longer were African Americans merely property that could be ordered about at the whim of a white owner. Now they were free citizens whose status—under the law, at least—was equal to that of white people. This change would have a profound impact not just on the southern economy, but on every aspect of the southern way of life.

Breaking Down Slavery

In 1865 the states ratified the Thirteenth Amendment to the Constitution, thereby abolishing slavery. Long before this amendment had been written and proposed, however, African Americans across the South had begun to anticipate its arrival. Whites in the North may have struggled to decide what the Civil War was all about, but African Americans had a clear purpose in mind. They sought nothing less than the abolition of slavery, and they directed their efforts toward that goal.

During the war, African Americans in the South often simply ceased paying any attention to the authority of their owners as soon as Union troops were reported to be nearby. They had no doubt they were free. Indeed, the Emancipation Proclamation and the Thirteenth Amendment merely made legal what was already fact throughout the South. As a northern journalist had observed as early as November 1862, slavery was "forever destroyed and worthless, no matter what Mr. Lincoln or anyone else may say on the subject."

The enthusiasm with which African Americans threw off the shackles of slavery actually surprised many whites. Slaveholders often reported feeling deserted or insulted by people they had once considered to be like family members. One nineteen-year-old woman, Susan Bradford, observed with regret the change in the behavior of the enslaved people who had formerly worked for her family: "Never before had I [heard] a word of impudence from any of our black folk," she wrote. Then she added with great understatement, "they are not ours any longer." The bonds that she presumed had linked her to "her people" were gone.

Symbols of the new working relationships between African Americans and white Americans after the Civil War, these two cowhands posed side by side in the 1860s.

R*ight off colored folks started on the move. They seemed to want to get closer to freedom, so they'd know what it was like—like it was a place or a city.*

In the end, many freed people returned to live on or near their old plantations. Yet the excitement of being able to move freely was memorable.

The movement of freed people was not aimless; many traveled with a purpose, for freedom also meant reuniting families. Freed people sometimes walked hundreds of miles looking for relatives separated by the slave trade. Many were successful in their quest. Reconstruction brought together families that had been broken apart by slavery and testified to the deep emotional ties among African Americans. For a time, at least, many African American women worked less time in the fields and devoted more of their attention to home and family.

MAKING CONNECTIONS

Recall what you have read about the treatment of enslaved African Americans. How accurate are white slaveholders' claims that they looked upon African Americans as members of their family? Explain your answer.

What Freedom Meant to African Americans

It was, of course, difficult for white slaveholders such as Susan Bradford to understand the impact of freedom on people who had been enslaved. To the "freed people," as they were called, freedom meant the basic things that whites took for granted. It meant, for example, the freedom to go wherever they wanted. Thus free African Americans often traveled away from the plantations on which they had worked and lived. A formerly enslaved African American from Texas recalled:

New African American Organizations Freedom encouraged the formation of new African American organizations. The most visible of these were churches. Across the South, freed people withdrew from congregations with both white and African American members and formed their own churches. They also started

As freedom opened new possibilities for social participation during Reconstruction, these African Americans in New Orleans formed a choir to raise money for an orphan's home.

thousands of voluntary organizations, including mutual aid societies, temperance clubs, debating clubs, drama societies, and trade associations.

Education Freedom also meant education. Historians estimate that 90 percent of adult freed people were illiterate in 1860. Slave codes had often prohibited teaching enslaved people to read and write. In 1862 a wealthy free African American woman from Philadelphia named Charlotte Forten had gone to Port Royal, South Carolina, to teach African Americans. She later described the enthusiasm she found.

> I never before saw children so eager to learn. . . . Coming to school is a constant delight and recreation to them. . . . Many of the grown people [also] are desirous of learning to read. It is wonderful how a people who have been so long crushed to the earth . . . can have so great a desire for knowledge, and such a capability for attaining it.

After the war, freed people continued eagerly to seek the ability to read and write. Many were taught by white school teachers—often young women—who moved to the South in an effort to help African Americans after the war. Many freed people, however, were self-taught.

African Americans also organized to set up and support schools for higher education.

Between 1865 and 1870, thirty African American colleges were founded. By 1870 those colleges had spent over $1 million in their effort to improve the education of African Americans.

Political Involvement With the end of the Civil War, African Americans thoughout the South organized to claim their rights as citizens. They held state conventions and rallies. Although they discussed economic issues, the most common themes were political ones. They wanted the political rights of citizenship: to vote, to hold office, to serve on juries. As Section 3 will show, their participation in politics during Reconstruction was substantial.

Land Ownership Finally, freedom for African Americans meant control of land and labor. It meant the right to own property, the ability to pursue whatever line of work they chose, and the power to determine what they produced.

Freed people throughout the South also sought the redistribution of land. They argued that they were entitled to the land on which they had lived, even though it belonged to white people. After all, freed people argued, enslaved people had cleared the land originally and farmed it for generations.

The most radical experiment in land redistribution occurred in coastal South Carolina and Georgia. With the arrival of General William Tecumseh Sherman and his forces in late 1864, this land came under the military rule of the United States Army. Under pressure from African Americans and Radical Republicans in Congress, General Sherman issued Special Field Order No. 15 on January 16, 1865. Sherman reserved the Sea Islands of Georgia and a 30-mile-wide strip of coastal land south of Charleston for eligible African American families. Each would receive 40 acres.

The Union general saw this order as a war measure; it was intended to punish slaveholders and to help the growing numbers of poor and starving African Americans following his army across South Carolina. By June 1865, roughly 40,000 African Americans were living on 400,000 acres of the land Sherman had set aside for them.

In spite of Sherman's program—and in spite of the dire need of the many freed people following virtually every Union army—very little land in the South was redistributed. Once the war was over, the United States refused to continue the kind of forced change in land ownership that Sherman had pioneered. In addition, freed people generally lacked the money and could not get the credit they needed to buy land from whites. Those who did buy land, however, were able to take a first step toward economic and psychological independence. A white northerner visiting the South in the fall of 1865 gave this summary of what owning land meant to freed people:

> *The sole ambition of the freedman at the present time appears to be to become the owner of a little piece of land, there to erect a humble home, and to dwell in peace and security at his own free will and pleasure. If he wishes to cultivate the ground in cotton on his own account, to be able to do so without anyone to dictate to him hours or system of labor, if he wishes instead to plant corn or sweet potatoes—to be able to do that free from any outside control. . . . That is their idea, their desire and their hope.*

These new desires and hopes of African Americans often clashed with the plans of southern whites. The story of the people of White Hall plantation illustrates how both whites and African Americans had to adjust to the realities of life in the South after the Civil War.

AMERICAN PROFILES

The People of White Hall Plantation

The family of Richard and Louisa Arnold was unusual in the mid-1800s. For decades before the Civil War, they had divided their time between a home in Rhode Island and a rice plantation they owned near Savannah, Georgia. Born in the North in 1796, Richard Arnold was both a businessman and a planter. He had purchased his plantation, which he called White Hall, in 1824. He and his wife, Louisa, and their seven children typically spent their summers in the North and their winters on the plantation. They were among the 360,000 white northerners who lived and worked in the South in 1860.

The Arnolds had divided opinions on secession. Louisa favored it, as did most of their children, but Richard opposed it, and the Arnolds spent most of the war in Rhode Island. Richard did, however, sell White Hall to his son Thomas, a Confederate supporter, so that the Confederacy would not seize it. Thomas managed the plantation during the Civil War, but abandoned it as Sherman's army approached in December 1864.

Thanks to Richard Arnold's opposition to secession and his political connections in the North, White Hall was declared exempt from Sherman's Special Field Order No. 15. In November 1865, Thomas went back to the plantation to begin rebuilding it. The Arnolds were lucky. Their money and influence had saved them from losing their plantation, as many southern planters had.

A Postwar Plantation Thomas was shocked by what he found upon his return to White Hall. The war damage to the mansion concerned him, but still more troubling was the new attitude of the African Americans who had long resided at White Hall. These were the formerly enslaved workers whom the Arnolds, like many other white southerners, had called "our people."

Thomas reported to his father that the freed people were unreliable and unfriendly. None of them would even speak to him. In order to get them to work, Thomas brought a Union colonel to "the settlement," the former slave quarters. There the federal official told the thirty or forty assembled African Americans that they would be wise to trust Arnold and agree to work at his plantation for wages. But, Thomas reported,

> *Batteast [one of the African Americans] spoke up in behalf of the whole plantation and said they had made up their minds never to work for me again, the Col. told them that they were very foolish and asked Batteast what he intended to do, that they must vacate. [Batteast answered] he did not know, but that God would point out the way.*

For generations, whites such as the Arnolds had assumed that they shared some sort of a common relationship and affection with their enslaved workers. Thomas Arnold was not the only one who saw that illusion shattered. This has been called "the moment of truth"—the time when white slaveholders finally realized that they did not have the affection and respect of the enslaved people who had worked for them, because slavery and affection could not exist side by side.

Some African Americans did continue to work willingly for their former masters. Forty-five-year-old Amos Morel and his wife Cretia went to Newport, Rhode Island, in 1865 to be with the Arnolds. They came back to White Hall with Thomas in November and went to work rebuilding White Hall into a plantation. Thomas appreciated what he saw as the loyalty of Morel, who he said was "true as steel."

New Working Relationships Richard Arnold purchased White Hall back from his son and resumed the cultivation of rice. In 1869 the place produced a million pounds of the crop; in the early 1870s, it was one of the largest rice plantations in the South. But though rice fields could be rebuilt, plantation life could not. The assertiveness and defiance shown by most of the Arnolds' former enslaved workers did not end. Many freed people had no desire to return to work in swampy fields for the benefit of whites. This was not the meaning of freedom.

The Arnolds had money, however, and spent it freely. They paid $1,700 in wages in May and June of 1867—a generous amount in those days—and spent a total of $60,000 on planting during that year. It was hard to resist good money in hard times. Even so, the Arnolds often had to rely on work gangs of Irish laborers or African Americans who were so deeply impoverished that they had no choice but to work in the rice fields.

The wages paid by the Arnolds gave their African American workers new power. In 1871 Amos Morel took his savings and bought more than 400 acres of land. He then sold pieces of it to other former enslaved workers. Later he bought more than a hundred acres for his daughter. These purchases and sales were a mild form of land redistribution compared to Sherman's famous order. But they were a beginning.

New Living Relationships In many respects, the end of slavery intensified white prejudice against African Americans. Many whites refused to accept freed people who asserted their equality. For instance, Nina Arnold, a relative of Richard Arnold, visited White Hall in 1868. She was shocked when the old nurse of the family, an African American, kissed and hugged her as an equal.

The old prejudices were severely tested in 1870 when the Arnolds gained new neighbors—William and Ellen Craft, who bought the nearby Woodville plantation. The Crafts were African Americans who had escaped slavery in Georgia before the Civil War and gone to England. Now they had returned to their homeland. They made Woodville into a center of education and vocational training for African Americans. Their efforts to empower freed people further widened the gap between the expectations of African Americans in the area around Whitehall, who sought a better life,

A visitor to White Hall sketched the mansion in 1842 (bottom). Though no picture survives of the slave quarters at White Hall, a traveler drew the children's nursery at Cherry Hill (top), another plantation of Richard Arnold's.

Using Historical Evidence A northerner touring the South in 1866 reported, "the whites seem wholly unable to comprehend that freedom for the Negro means the same thing as freedom for them. They . . . believe that they still have the right to exercise over him the old control." *How does this postwar photograph support that observation?*

and former slaveholders, who wanted a return to the old social order.

That return never came about. A Georgia doctor noted: "The revolution of our social fabric is too great, the entire upheaval and overthrow of all the foundations of our society too universal not to affect everybody." Richard Arnold died in 1873. The debts of his estate eventually forced the sale of his land in Georgia. A son-in-law bought White Hall in 1877. The vast rice plantation where white masters had once forced African Americans to work without pay in the fields now became a hunting and fishing preserve for the rich.

Within fifteen years of the end of the Civil War, the ways of the Old South were truly gone from White Hall forever. Most other plantations throughout the South remained working farms, but they too were dramatically changed. Though prejudice remained and white men still held great power over African Americans, the world of slavery had come to an end, destroyed by the combined efforts of the United States armed forces and African Americans eager to assert their independence. In its place was a new order that was still emerging, as will be discussed in the sections ahead.

SECTION 1 REVIEW

Key Terms, People, and Places
1. Define Reconstruction.

Key Concepts
2. How did African Americans react to the prospect of freedom even before the Civil War ended?
3. What did freedom mean to African Americans after the end of the Civil War?

4. Give evidence of the distrust between whites and freed African Americans at White Hall plantation.

Critical Thinking
5. **Demonstrating Reasoned Judgment** What does the exchange between A. D. Lewis and Dr. A. H. Jones, as described in Lewis's letter, suggest about problems facing freed people?

Three Plans for Reconstruction

SECTION PREVIEW

The meaning of freedom was clear to the freed people of the South. For Congress, however, the end of the Civil War raised many difficult questions about how to rebuild the nation. The result was a series of acts and amendments that redefined citizenship and attempted to create a new social order in the South.

The battle between Congress and President Andrew Johnson over Reconstruction reached its lowest point in 1868 when Congress tried to remove Johnson from office. Tickets to the proceedings were in great demand.

Key Concepts
• The Freedmen's Bureau took the first steps to help African Americans freed during the war.
• Lincoln was able to stop a harsh measure passed by Congress that would have made Reconstruction more difficult.
• By refusing to accept moderate changes, white southerners increased northern support for Radical Reconstruction.
• The Fourteenth Amendment clearly defined American citizenship in a manner that included African Americans.
• The Fifteenth Amendment guaranteed all citizens the right to vote.

Key Terms, People, and Places
Freedmen's Bureau, pardon, Fourteenth Amendment, Military Reconstruction Act of 1867, impeach, Fifteenth Amendment; Andrew Johnson

Freed people recognized that land, education, and the vote were keys to building a new social order in the South. Meanwhile, politicians in Washington, D.C., were struggling with the many questions raised by the defeat of the Confederacy. What steps should the United States government take to protect the liberties of African Americans? How, and on what terms, should the defeated Confederate states be returned to their former role in the Union? In other words, how should the federal government reconstruct the nation? These issues dominated national politics during the Reconstruction years.

Helping Freed People

One of the more insistent questions confronting the United States government was how to help the former enslaved people. The defeat of the Confederacy brought freedom, but also uncertainty. Without education and jobs, freed people faced continued poverty.

In spite of unrelenting prejudice against African Americans, many whites were committed to helping freed people build new lives. From the time of the Emancipation Proclamation in 1863, the Republican party had defined itself as an organization committed not only to ending slavery, but also to bringing some measure of justice to African Americans.

It was in this spirit that Congress established the **Freedmen's Bureau** in March 1865. The purpose of the bureau was to provide aid to freed people and help them make the adjustment to freedom. Under the leadership of General Oliver O. Howard, the bureau gave out clothing, medical supplies, and millions of meals to refugees of the war, both African American and white. Its most significant work, however, came in the establishment of schools for African Americans. With the help of the bureau, over 250,000 African Americans received their first taste of formal education.

Lincoln's Reconstruction Plan

Another central question facing the United States was how to put the nation back together after the war. In December 1863, while battles were still raging, President Lincoln had proposed a moderate Reconstruction policy. Lincoln offered a **pardon**—an official forgiveness

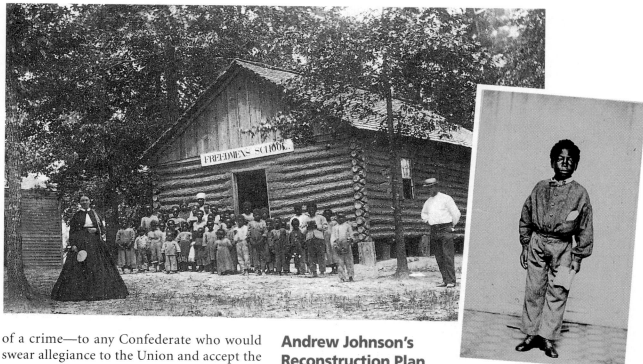

of a crime—to any Confederate who would swear allegiance to the Union and accept the end of slavery. Confederate military and government officials and those who had killed African American prisoners of war were excluded from Lincoln's offer. When 10 percent of those who had voted in the 1860 election had taken the oath in their state, that state could hold a constitutional convention. After the delegates to the convention had written a constitution endorsing the Thirteenth Amendment, their state could be returned to its proper place in the Union. Lincoln's plan did not require the new constitutions explicitly to ensure African American rights.

Radical Republicans wanted terms that would be much more difficult for southern whites to accept. They wanted to change southern society in order to ensure the rights of African Americans. They also wanted to punish the white South severely for its secession.

With the help of some moderate Republicans, Radical Republicans passed the Wade-Davis Bill in July 1864. Under this legislation, the terms a Confederate state had to meet in order to return to the Union were almost impossible to fulfill. Lincoln refused to sign this legislation. Because Congress had closed for the session after passing the bill, Lincoln's refusal to sign it amounted to a veto of the bill.

Andrew Johnson's Reconstruction Plan

For the next several months, Lincoln and Congress remained at odds over Reconstruction. But in April 1865, John Wilkes Booth's bullet both killed one President and made a new one—former Vice President **Andrew Johnson**.

Johnson Is Moderate Before the war, Johnson had been a Democratic senator from Tennessee. He was the only southerner to remain in Congress after secession. As a gesture of reconciliation toward the South, the Republicans placed him on their ticket with Lincoln in 1864.

Born in Raleigh, North Carolina, Johnson came from a poor family. He became a tailor and learned to read and write with the help of his wife. Johnson then entered politics, where he won success in mountainous eastern Tennessee.

Proud of his humble origins, Johnson had a profound hatred of rich planters and found strong support among poor whites. But to the dismay of Radical Republicans, Johnson was quite forgiving of former Confederates. He made most Confederates eligible for pardons in return for taking an oath of loyalty to the United States. In 1865 Johnson granted 13,000 pardons. He also favored easy terms under which the Confederate

Above left: A teacher and students pose outside a freedmen's school. *Above right:* To show appreciation for northern aid, Freedmen's Bureau workers sent northern benefactors a photograph of a student wearing his new school clothes and holding a book. They labeled it *"After your boxes came!"*

states could return to their place in the Union. Under Johnson's plan, states were instructed to hold constitutional conventions. The delegates at each state convention were expected to write a new state constitution that would void secession, abolish slavery, ratify the Thirteenth Amendment, and stop payments of the state's war debts. The convention could then call an election for state offices and members of Congress.

Southern Defiance Had the South fully accepted Johnson's terms, Reconstruction might have ended earlier. Instead, once southern state governments were established, they acted to weaken Johnson's plan. For example, they quickly enacted black codes, laws that severely restricted the rights of freed people. Some black codes imposed curfews on African Americans and authorized labor contracts that were little better than legalized slavery. Black codes also included vagrancy laws, under which African Americans who were not working—vagrants, under the law—could be arrested and forced to work in order to pay off their fines. The effect of the vagrancy laws, too, was to reestablish slavery by a different name.

Some southern whites also used violence in an effort to regain power over African Americans. In addition to countless individual acts of violence, serious riots erupted in several cities. In May 1866, angry whites killed forty-six African Americans in Memphis, Tennessee. At the end of July of that year, thirty-seven African Americans and three white sympathizers died in a riot by whites in New Orleans.

MAKING CONNECTIONS

Are you surprised by the South's defiant rejection of efforts at Reconstruction? Explain why or why not.

The Radical Plan for Reconstruction

President Johnson and Congress disagreed about how to respond to southern resistance to Reconstruction. In March 1866, Congress passed a Civil Rights Act in order to ensure equal rights for African Americans in spite of the black codes. Johnson vetoed it. Congress overrode his veto. It then switched course and proposed the **Fourteenth Amendment** to the Constitution, which became law two years later.

Protecting Citizen's Rights The Fourteenth Amendment said that everyone born or naturalized in the United States was a citizen and that no state could restrict his or her rights. More specifically, no state could

> *deprive any person of life, liberty, or property, without due process of law, nor deny to any person within its jurisdiction the equal protection of the laws.*

The amendment also provided for the punishment of states that did not permit African Americans to vote. In an effort to limit the President's power to pardon, it gave

Radical Rule of the South

- States of the former Confederacy
- Boundaries of military districts
- 1870 Date of readmission to the Union

Geography and History: Interpreting Maps
In April of 1865, Abraham Lincoln expressed a wish that the nation should put the southern state governments "in successful operation, with order prevailing and the Union reestablished, before . . . December." Under Radical rule, however, many of the former Confederate states did not rejoin the Union for years. *Which state was the first to rejoin the Union? Which states rejoined in 1870?*

Congress alone the power to let former Confederates hold public office. And it forbade any payments of Confederate war debts and any payments to slaveholders to make up for the loss of their slave labor.

Controlling the South White southern defiance contributed to significant Republican gains in the 1866 congressional elections. As a result, Radicals now had enough strength to impose their own conditions—and inflict punishment—on the white South.

The new Congress passed the **Military Reconstruction Act of 1867.** This legislation divided the South into five military districts that were to be governed by northern generals, as shown in the map on page 234. All qualified voters, including African American men, but excluding voters who had supported the Confederacy, had to be allowed to vote for delegates to create new state constitutions. Southern states had to guarantee equal rights to all citizens, permit African Americans to vote, and ratify the Fourteenth Amendment.

Controlling the President At the same time, Congress attempted to limit the power of President Johnson. It passed the Tenure of Office Act, which dealt with the President's power to hire and fire government officials.

Under the Constitution, the Senate has to offer "advice and consent" when the President wants to hire certain government officials. The Constitution does not limit the President's power to dismiss those officials. The Tenure of Office Act, however, said that if a President wanted to fire an official who had earlier been approved by the Senate, the Senate also had to approve of the firing. This act effectively removed the President's power to build an administration to his own liking.

Johnson and the Congress quickly came into conflict over the Tenure of Office Act. The President tried to fire Secretary of War Edwin Stanton, a Radical Republican. Arguing that the President's action was unconstitutional, the House of Representatives voted to **impeach** him—to charge him formally with wrongdoing in office. Under the Constitution, officials impeached by the House are then tried by the

Viewpoints
On Voting Rights for African Americans

The effort by Radical Republicans to extend voting rights to African Americans in the South was hotly debated in the 1860s. **Summarize the main arguments given in the two viewpoints below.**

In Favor of Voting Rights for African Americans
"If impartial suffrage is excluded in rebel States, then every one of them is sure to send a solid rebel representative delegation to Congress, and cast a solid rebel electoral vote. They . . . would always elect the President and control Congress. . . . I am for negro suffrage in every rebel State. If it be just, it should not be denied; if it be necessary, it should be adopted; if it is a punishment to traitors, they deserve it."
Thaddeus Stevens, Radical Republican (Pennsylvania), speech in the House of Representatives, January 3, 1867

Against Voting Rights for African Americans
"Most of the whites are disenfranchised [not legally able to vote] and ineligible for office, whilst the Negroes are invested with [granted] the right of voting. The political power is therefore thrown into the hands of a mass of human beings who, having just emerged from a state of servitude [slavery], are ignorant of the forms of government and totally unfit to exercise this, the highest privilege of a free people."
Henry William Ravenel, South Carolina planter, journal entry for February 24, 1867

Senate, which by a two-thirds majority can convict the official and remove him or her from office. Following this procedure, the Senate tried Johnson in the spring of 1868.

In the end, seven Radicals refused to vote for conviction. As a result, Congress fell one vote short of the two-thirds majority needed to convict. The results of this trial established the precedent that only the most serious offenses could lead to the removal of the President of the United States.

The Last Reconstruction Legislation

The final major piece of Reconstruction legislation was the **Fifteenth Amendment,** proposed in February 1869 and ratified in March 1870. (Congress did pass a Civil Rights Act in

Reconstruction Legislation

Legislation	Date	Purpose
13th Amendment	Submitted and ratified 1865	Abolishes slavery in the United States
Freedmen's Bureau	1865 and 1866	Provides services for war refugees and freed people, including food, medical aid, education
Civil Rights Act of 1866	1866	Gives citizenship to African Americans; gives federal government the power to protect African American rights
14th Amendment	Submitted 1866, ratified 1868	Defines citizenship to include African Americans; guarantees due process of law and equal protection under law
Reconstruction Acts	1867	Establish Radical Reconstruction
15th Amendment	Submitted 1869, ratified 1870	Guarantees that voting rights will not be denied on the basis of race
Ku Klux Klan Acts	1871	Seek to outlaw organizations aimed at denying African Americans their rights
Civil Rights Act of 1875	1875	Protects African American rights in public places

Interpreting Tables

During Reconstruction, the federal government struggled to create a new social and political order in the South. *Which amendment ended slavery? Which guaranteed that voting rights would not be denied on the basis of race?*

1875, guaranteeing African American rights in public places, but the act was largely unenforced.) The Fifteenth Amendment stated that no citizen could be denied the right to vote "by the United States or by any State on account of race, color, or previous condition of servitude."

The table on this page shows this amendment as well as other Reconstruction legislation.

The Fifteenth Amendment was inspired in part by the presidential election of 1868. Republican Ulysses S. Grant won a narrow victory that was made possible by the votes of African Americans in the South. The Fifteenth Amendment aimed at ensuring that African Americans would be free to vote in future elections—presumably for Republican candidates. As Chapter 11 reveals, however, southern states eventually found ways to deny African Americans the vote.

Another development linked to Reconstruction legislation was the growing consent of the Supreme Court. In a case known as *Texas* v. *White* in 1869, the Court recognized the right of Congress to reconstruct the governments of the former Confederate states. This decision demonstrated a startling new support for federal power.

Together, African Americans and Congress had redrawn the political and social boundaries of the United States. Many southern whites cooperated with this transformation. Others, however, resisted these changes. If the white South had accepted defeat more gracefully, Radical Republicans likely would not have become as powerful as they did. If the white South had given in to the more moderate plans of Lincoln and Johnson, Reconstruction in the South, as described in the next section, might have been dramatically different.

SECTION 2 REVIEW

Key Terms, People, and Places
1. Define (a) pardon, (b) Fourteenth Amendment, (c) Military Reconstruction Act of 1867, (d) impeach.
2. Identify Andrew Johnson.

Key Concepts
3. What was the Freedmen's Bureau?
4. Why did Lincoln refuse to sign the Wade-Davis Bill?
5. Describe two ways in which southern whites tried to regain the power they had had over African Americans.

6. How was the South to be governed during Reconstruction under the plan of Radical Republicans?
7. What was the purpose of the Fifteenth Amendment?

Critical Thinking
8. **Predicting Consequences** Based on what you have read so far, how effective do you think the federal government will be in creating a new and lasting social order in the South after the Civil War? Explain your answer.

Reconstruction in the South

SECTION PREVIEW

Republicans stormed the South, bringing ambitious ideas about improving the political and social rights of African Americans. Their policies did lead to significant gains, but they soon found their efforts undermined by a campaign of terror and violence.

Key Concepts

- A combination of different groups, including African Americans as well as white northerners and southerners, provided support for the Republican party in the South.
- State governments in the South during Reconstruction took major steps in civil rights, education, and economic development.
- New forms of enforced labor replaced the slave system in the South.
- The initial success of Reconstruction led to a backlash of violence against African Americans and Republicans.

Key Terms, People, and Places

debt peonage; carpetbagger, scalawag, sharecropper, tenant farmer, Ku Klux Klan, Rutherford B. Hayes

I n order for Reconstruction in the South to be effective, two conditions had to be met. First, Republicans had to hold office on the state level. Second, federal officials had to be willing to use their power to support them. For a while, these conditions existed, and Republicans were able to bring about significant change in the South. In the end, however, that success led to a violent resistance that reversed many of the gains of Reconstruction.

Republican Support in the South

Significant problems faced the Republican plan for Reconstruction in the South. After all, the party had had virtually no support in the region before the mid-1860s. And it was unlikely to win large numbers of converts among whites in the post–Civil War years.

White Republicans in the South For these reasons, the Republicans depended for their support in the South on African Americans and on people who are now known as carpetbaggers and scalawags. Both of these terms were originally insulting names given to these groups by southerners. **Carpetbaggers** were northern Republicans who moved to the South after the Civil War. Their name referred to a kind of suitcase, and it implied that these northerners had hastily migrated into the region to take advantage of the political situation. Carpetbaggers were mainly former Union army officers and Freedmen's Bureau officials.

Scalawags, a term that means "rascals," were southern whites who became Republicans. They tended to be men who had been Whigs, who were interested in economic development, or who lived in the more isolated areas. Many scalawags were poor.

African Americans in Office African Americans were key, though underrepresented, members of the Republican party in the South. Determined to win their share of political power, they organized to promote the interests of their community. In 1865 the African American state convention addressed these words to the people of South Carolina:

N ow that we are free men, now that we have been lifted up by the providence of God to manhood, we have resolved to come forward, and, like MEN, speak and act for ourselves.

Many of the northerners who flooded the South hoping to profit from post-war turmoil carried their belongings in cheap suitcases called carpet-bags. These bags became a symbol of northern rule of the South.

Sixteen African Americans served with distinction in Congress between 1870 and 1877. One of them, Robert B. Elliot (standing, left), spoke eloquently in response to former Confederate vice president Alexander Stephens in the debate over the Civil Rights Act of 1875. "What you give to one class you must give to all," he said. "What you deny to one class, you shall deny to all."

Between 1867 and 1869, approximately 1,000 men attended state constitutional conventions throughout the South. Some 265 of them were African Americans; at least 107 were former slaves. Many were veterans of the Union army, ministers, artisans, farmers, and teachers.

African Americans held high office in the South during Reconstruction, though the number of such officials was small relative to the African American population. African Americans were, after all, a majority in Louisiana, Mississippi, and South Carolina. One African American, P.B.S. Pinchback, briefly served as governor of Louisiana. Six African Americans were lieutenant governors, and several others held high state office. Meanwhile, sixteen African Americans went to Congress, and Hiram Revels, an educator and minister, became a United States senator from Mississippi in 1870. Mississippi also sent former sheriff Blanche K. Bruce to the Senate in 1874.

In addition, 600 African Americans were members of various state legislatures and hundreds of others held local offices. While some were illiterate—70 percent of African Americans could not read or write in 1880, compared to under 10 percent of whites—many were educated and virtually all were capable of making informed judgments about major issues.

Many southern whites criticized the presence of African Americans in Reconstruction governments. They accused African American officials of being corrupt or incompetent. In reality, the South's African American officials appeared to have been no worse and no better than their white counterparts. Many served with distinction.

MAKING CONNECTIONS

African Americans are still underrepresented in government. What does this fact suggest?

Republican Policies

State governments controlled by Republicans did bring change to the South. They committed state governments to systems of public education, although these systems were divided along racial lines. They passed civil rights legislation that guaranteed African Americans access to transportation and hotels, though this legislation was largely unenforced. In addition, they repealed black codes and removed restrictions on African American workers.

Economic Development Republicans focused much of their effort on improving economic conditions. Some argued that lasting change could not come to the region without land redistribution. In other words, African Americans would never gain equal rights and economic independence until they owned property. Most white Republicans, however, were unwilling to take such a step, which would have involved taking the land of planters and giving it to people who had been enslaved. This would have violated southerners' constitutional right to security of private property.

Instead, most white Republicans concentrated on economic development. Advocating "the gospel of prosperity," they contended that the key to better times was more railroads,

Atlanta Rises from the Ruins

"We have utterly destroyed Atlanta," wrote a Union soldier in 1864. "I don't think any people will want to try and live there now." The ruin of the central train station is shown at left. Yet by 1887 the commercial district (above) was booming. ***Basing your answer on the evidence here, what do you think was the key to Atlanta's rebirth?***

banks, and businesses. Southern governments aided in this development with grants, paid for out of higher taxes. But while thousands of miles of railroad track were laid, government aid did little to improve general economic conditions. Most African Americans, and not a few whites, remained mired in poverty.

Voter Anger Republican rule alienated many white voters. Taxes and state debts increased because of expenses such as grants to railroads. As in the North, state officials sometimes accepted bribes, leading to charges of corruption. In addition, the policies seemed to do little to improve economic conditions, though in fact few policies would have made much difference in the war-scarred southern economy. Moreover, worldwide demand for cotton was falling. The 1875 cotton crop equaled that of 1859 in terms of size, but not in profits.

Changes in Southern Agriculture

Devastated by the Civil War, southern planters never recovered the dominance that

they had enjoyed before the war. Some sought to re-create the past by finding ways to preserve slavery in a new form. As the economic journal *De Bow's Review* argued in 1868,

> We do not mean . . . slavery such as that which has been recently abolished, but some form of subordination of the inferior race that shall compel them to labor, whilst it protects their rights and provides for their wants.

Debt Peonage To achieve this end, planters signed former slaves to labor contracts. Under the terms of these contracts, planters advanced money to laborers in return for signed promises from the workers that they pay all debts before they moved on. Planters then found ways to increase workers' debts while keeping them ignorant of any escape. Year after year, laborers remained bound to work off debts that always got larger. Though slavery was dead, in **debt peonage,** as this system of forced labor came to be called, the South brought some aspects of the slave system back to life.

An African American couple, possibly sharecroppers or tenant farmers, pose with their children in front of their Florida home—a humble house, but the dwelling of free people.

As part of their campaign of terror, the Ku Klux Klan left miniature coffins like these—containing written death threats—at the doors of African Americans and their white supporters.

Sharecropping Many freed people wanted no part of contract agreements for their labor. In order to make money from their fields, white landowners began to rent their land to African Americans and poor whites. In one common system, farmers called **sharecroppers** grew a crop on land owned by someone else. In return for the use of the land and supplies such as seed and fertilizer, the farmer gave one third to one half of the annual crop to the landowner. Others, called **tenant farmers**, paid cash for the rental of land. They typically agreed to sell their crop to a local merchant, who gave them use of tools and supplies in advance of harvest.

By 1880 one third of the white farmers in the South were sharecroppers or tenant farmers. Where African Americans had grown 90 percent of the cotton before the Civil War, whites now cultivated 30 to 40 percent.

African American sharecroppers and tenant farmers enjoyed more practical freedom than they had possessed as enslaved people. They controlled their own schedules, determined where they lived, and worked without white supervision.

Yet the sharecropping and tenancy systems had serious drawbacks. Low cotton prices that had troubled landowners also made it hard for sharecroppers to earn enough money to survive.

Many had to borrow from local stores for food and supplies, creating debts that grew larger and larger every year. Thus sharecroppers and tenant farmers were trapped in a continuous effort to pay off their debts, just like farmers working under the system of debt peonage.

Whites Attack Reconstruction

From 1868 through 1871, many southern whites launched a counterrevolution against the changes of Reconstruction. The intensity of their violence was a tribute to how far the changes brought by the Republicans had gone. In other words, whites turned to terrorism because Reconstruction was proving successful in transforming the South.

The Ku Klux Klan At the forefront of the campaign was the **Ku Klux Klan,** an organization that began as a social club in Tennessee in 1866. Although Klan members often wore elaborate disguises, including white hoods and robes, members were well known locally. Leaders included planters, merchants, lawyers, and occasionally ministers. Many were former Confederate officers. The oath each member took included a promise to "defend the social and political superiority" of whites, to vote only for white candidates, and to protect whites against what the Klan called the "aggressions of an inferior race."

The goal of the Klan during Reconstruction was to intimidate both African Americans and sympathetic whites so that they became silent and submissive. To keep freed people from voting or asserting themselves, hooded men surrounded the homes of prominent African Americans and harassed and abused them. Whippings were common. So was murder.

In 1871 Thomas Allen, a freed person, told a congressional investigating committee in Atlanta that he had been warned against voting. He and his friends felt safe only in cities, noting that

in a great many places the colored people call the white people master and mistress, just as they ever did; if they do not do it they are whipped.

As northern anger mounted against southern violence, Congress passed the Enforcement Acts, or the Ku Klux Klan Acts, in 1871. In the next year, the United States used its considerable military and judicial power to break the Klan. But by that time, southern whites had already achieved much of their goal of "redeeming," or winning back, the South from Republican rule by thoroughly intimidating scalawags, African Americans, and carpetbaggers.

Meanwhile, Radical Republicans were beginning to lose their grip on power nationally. In the 1872 presidential race, a group of Republicans known as the Liberals refused to support Grant, whom they viewed as corrupt and incompetent. Although Grant easily trounced Democrat Horace Greeley, the division of the Republicans weakened the party. In the future, Republicans would focus more on winning elections and less on their ideals of justice and equality.

The Compromise of 1877 Final "redemption" for southern whites came in 1877. In the presidential election of 1876, Republican **Rutherford B. Hayes** lost the popular vote to Democrat Samuel Tilden. The electoral vote was in dispute, however. Hayes claimed to have won the presidency based in part on his victories in Florida, Louisiana, and South Carolina, states still under Republican and federal control. Yet another set of returns sent to Washington, D.C., by the Democrats showed Tilden as the victor in those states, and thus in the presidential race.

Congress established a special commission to resolve the crisis. The commission—whose members included more Republicans than

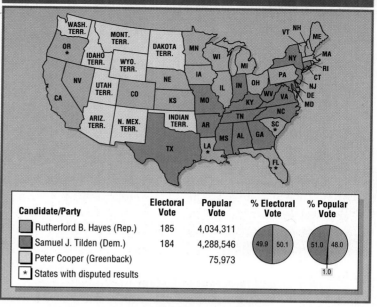

Presidential Election of 1876

Candidate/Party	Electoral Vote	Popular Vote	% Electoral Vote	% Popular Vote
Rutherford B. Hayes (Rep.)	185	4,034,311	49.9 / 50.1	51.0 / 48.0
Samuel J. Tilden (Dem.)	184	4,288,546		
Peter Cooper (Greenback)		75,973		1.0
* States with disputed results				

Geography and History: Interpreting Maps
In the election of 1876, the electoral votes in three states under federal control were disputed, but eventually went to Hayes when he promised to end Reconstruction. *In which states were results disputed? What would have been the result if even one more state had gone to Tilden? Whom did the majority of Americans favor?*

Democrats—named Hayes the victor, as shown in the election map on this page. Democrats, however, still had enough strength in Congress to reject the commission's decision. But a political deal cleared the way for Hayes's victory. In the Compromise of 1877, Hayes promised that as President, he would remove federal troops from all southern states. Southern Democrats would regain complete control of the region. In return, Democrats would allow Hayes to claim a victory he had not clearly won.

SECTION 3 REVIEW

Key Terms, People, and Places
1. Identify (a) carpetbagger, (b) scalawag, (c) Ku Klux Klan, (d) Rutherford B. Hayes.

Key Concepts
2. What groups formed the basis of support for the Republican party in the South during Reconstruction?
3. What kinds of legislation did Republican state governments in the South pass during Reconstruction?

4. In what ways were debt peonage, sharecropping, and tenant farming alike?
5. How did pressure from southern whites lead to a reversal of Reconstruction?

Critical Thinking
6. **Recognizing Ideologies** What does the Compromise of 1877 suggest about the motives of Republicans in controlling the South?

How Maps Show Change Over Time

An important task of historians is to identify change over time. One far-reaching change that took place in American life after the Civil War was the breakup of plantations and the dispersal of freed people. Maps can give important clues to such developments, what changes took place, where they occurred, how extensive they were, and how long they took.

The historical maps below give you an opportunity to identify the changes that occurred over time to 2,000 acres of land in the post–Civil War South. Use the following steps to identify the changes for which the maps provide evidence.

1. Identify the location, time period, and subject matter covered by the maps. To discover what data these maps offer, answer the following questions: (a) What specific area of land do the maps show, and where is it located? (b) What dates are given on the maps? (c) What physical features do the maps show?

2. Analyze the key to determine the type of data that it provides. A map key can help you understand the data in a map. Map keys use symbols and colors to illustrate specific data and to locate the data on a map. (a) What do the colored squares repre-

sent in the map on the left? (b) What do the colored squares represent in the map on the right? (c) How is the symbol for a church distinguishable from the symbol for a school?

3. Analyze the data in the maps. Now compare these maps to draw conclusions about the change over time that they indicate. (a) Over what period of time has the change taken place? (b) How has the location of the dwellings on the plantation changed during this period? (c) What new buildings have been added? (d) How do you explain the changes noted in (b) and (c) above?

The Barrow Plantation, Oglethorpe County, Georgia

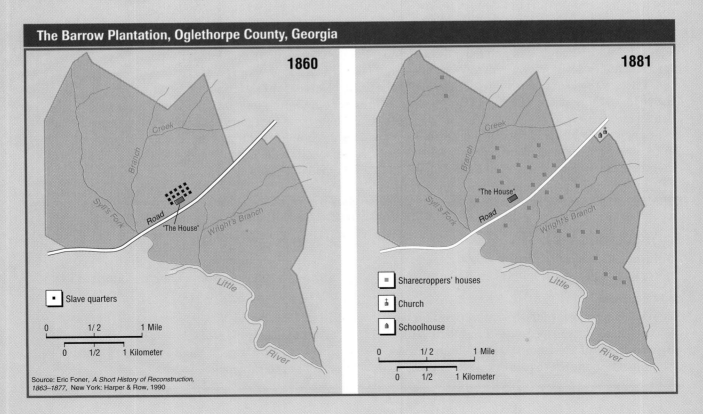

1860

Creek
Branch
Syd's Fork
Road
"The House"
Wright's Branch
Little
River

■ Slave quarters

0   1/2   1 Mile
0   1/2   1 Kilometer

1881

Creek
Branch
Syd's Fork
Road
"The House"
Wright's Branch
Little
River

■ Sharecroppers' houses
✝ Church
⌂ Schoolhouse

0   1/2   1 Mile
0   1/2   1 Kilometer

Source: Eric Foner, *A Short History of Reconstruction, 1863–1877,* New York: Harper & Row, 1990

The Retreat from Reconstruction in the North

SECTION PREVIEW

The Radical Republican blueprint for Reconstruction was based on a grand dream of social equality and justice. But economic and political changes brought by the war led the Republicans to forsake their commitment to this dream in favor of a cozy relationship with business leaders.

Key Concepts
- As industry boomed during and after the Civil War, close ties between business leaders and government officials led to widespread corruption.
- Republican governments became increasingly unwilling to serve the needs of African Americans and others among the nation's powerless.

Key Terms, People, and Places
Crédit Mobilier, United States Sanitary Commission

W hile southern whites were finding new ways to resist Reconstruction, Republicans in the North were also making adjustments to new postwar realities. Increasingly, they chose to ally themselves with leading industrialists rather than African Americans and the poor and powerless in the farms and cities of the North.

Becoming an Industrial Power

The Civil War had an enormous impact on the American economy. The need to arm, clothe, and supply hundreds of thousands of men in the early 1860s stimulated the growth of industries and made the organization of corporations more efficient. Because Republicans were willing to use government to promote economic development, they created a close relationship between corporations and politicians that lasted throughout the century.

As Chapter 8 will discuss, business boomed in the United States in the later part of the 1800s. Fueled by war profits and prodded along by a new generation of business leaders, industrial production in the United States rose by 75 percent between 1865 and 1873. In 1873 the United States reached a new milestone: it now had more industrial workers than farmers. The nation ranked second only to Great Britain as an industrial power.

Railroads set the pace for much of this economic development, in part because railroad companies worked hard to influence state and federal government policies. Governments responded with grants of land and money to pay for costly railroad projects. Politicians at all levels worked closely with influential railroad entrepreneurs; many received favors or illegal payments in return.

The most notorious example of corruption involving railroads was the **Crédit Mobilier** scandal. Crédit Mobilier was a dummy corporation created by the stockholders of the Union Pacific Railroad to oversee construction of that railroad in the 1860s. The shareholders in both corporations were the same. In effect, the owners of the railroad created Crédit Mobilier so they could pay themselves—with federal government grants—to build their own railroad. Crédit Mobilier often billed the Union Pacific for work it never performed. Many members of Congress, too, were involved in the scandal. They received shares in Crédit Mobilier in return for their acceptance of the scheme.

The Union Pacific Railway across the continent was begun with these tools on December 2, 1863. As industries like the railways grew, the nation's politicians abandoned social issues and concentrated on economic growth.

During the Civil War, American women threw themselves into public work, only to see their cause ignored by Republicans as Reconstruction ended. This wartime Sanitary Commission worker displays the writing paper, knitted stockings, and other items that cheered Union soldiers.

In general, bribes and other forms of corruption like Crédit Mobilier succeeded in getting corporations what they wanted. Between 1862 and 1872, the United States granted over 100 million acres of federal land and millions of dollars to corporations.

MAKING CONNECTIONS

Imagine that Henry Clay and Andrew Jackson had lived to see the industrial boom after the Civil War. Make a brief comment on the boom from the viewpoint of each of these politicians.

The Republicans Abandon Social Issues

Though government rarely hesitated to aid railroads and other corporations, it was increasingly reluctant to take action for less powerful groups, including African Americans, women, farmers, and factory workers.

African Americans Remain Powerless It is true that in the North, Republicans increased the role of government in civil rights. African Americans won the right to vote and to testify in court. In some places, states passed laws to ensure that African Americans had equal access to hotels and public transportation. In general, however, African Americans in the North—still only 2 percent of the population—remained poor and politically powerless.

The Postponement of Women's Rights Long before the Civil War, women had been prominent as members of the abolitionist movement. During the war, women in both the North and South had further increased their public visibility. For example, 200,000 northern women served in the **United States Sanitary Commission,** formed in 1861. It coordinated local organizations dedicated to providing medical aid and other assistance to soldiers. After the war, many women served in societies to assist freed people, and close to a thousand women went south to teach African Americans. The patriotic work of these women demonstrated the value of women's labor and proved their ability to make vital contributions outside the home.

Feminists such as Elizabeth Cady Stanton and Susan B. Anthony sought far-reaching changes in relationships between men and women. Their primary focus was on the right to vote, however. Lydia Maria Child told Charles Sumner in 1872:

> If I were to give free vent to all my pent-up wrath concerning the subordination of women, I might frighten you. . . . Suffice it, therefore, to say, either the theory of our government is false, or women have a right to vote.

Despite some sympathy from Radical Republicans, the quest for woman suffrage made little progress during Reconstruction. True, Wyoming and Utah territories did grant women the vote in 1869. But they did so for reasons that had little to do with their interest in women's rights. Wyoming wanted to attract female settlers, and Mormons in Utah wanted to increase their power by registering Mormon women as voters.

Unhappy Farmers and Working People Republican failure to satisfy the demands of suffragists paralleled their failures with farmers and working people. As Chapter 9 will show, strong protest movements arose in the late 1800s on the nation's farms. Much of this protest reflected farmers' desire for government regulation of railroads. Most Republicans did not support such regulation.

Working Americans also challenged Republicans to extend more rights to them during this era (see Chapter 8). These workers again focused on the goals of free labor, equality, and independence to which

PUCK.

THE "STRONG" GOVERNMENT 1869—1877.   THE "WEAK" GOVERNMENT 1877—1881.

Using Historical Evidence In the left frame of this Reconstruction cartoon, President Grant, supported by "carpet bag and bayonet rule," rides on an oppressed South. In the right frame, President Hayes plows under the carpet bag. *How did the cartoonist show the effect of each government on the South? What was the bias of the cartoonist?*

Republicans had been committed in the 1850s. Indeed, directly comparing the labor movement to the antislavery movement, Boston machinist and labor leader Ira Steward pointed out that just as the motive for enslaving someone is to get his or her labor for nothing, similarly,

> *the motive for employing wage-labor is to secure some of its results for nothing; and, in point of fact, larger fortunes are made out of the profits of wage-labor, than out of the products of slavery.*

The Significance of Reconstruction In 1877 Reconstruction came to an end. In most respects, it had been a tragic failure. Despite the many positive changes that took place, the nation had squandered the opportunity to achieve true equality and social justice. As an African American woman noted, "There is no redress [help] for us from a government that promised to help all under its flag." It would be close to a century before African Americans and whites would truly achieve the legal and political freedoms that were supposedly guaranteed by the legislation of the Reconstruction period.

SECTION 4 REVIEW

Key Terms, People, and Places
1. Identify (a) Crédit Mobilier, (b) United States Sanitary Commission.

Key Concepts
2. Explain the impact of the Civil War both on the American economy and on the relationship between federal government officials and business leaders.

3. How did the Republicans respond to the concerns of African Americans, women, and working people during Reconstruction?

Critical Thinking
4. **Checking Consistency** The text states that African Americans had many political rights, yet they still lacked power. Explain this apparent inconsistency.

Chapter Review

Understanding Key Terms, People, and Places

Key Terms
1. Reconstruction
2. Freedmen's Bureau
3. pardon
4. Fourteenth Amendment
5. Military Reconstruction Act of 1867

6. impeach
7. Fifteenth Amendment
8. debt peonage
9. Crédit Mobilier
10. United States Sanitary Commission

People
11. Andrew Johnson
12. carpetbagger
13. scalawag
14. sharecropper
15. tenant farmer
16. Ku Klux Klan
17. Rutherford B. Hayes

Terms For each term above, write a sentence that explains its relation to Reconstruction and the post–Civil War period.

True or False Determine whether each statement is true or false. If it is true, write "true." If it is false, change the underlined term to make the statement true.
1. The Fourteenth Amendment declared that no citizen could be denied the right to vote.
2. Sharecroppers were southern whites who became Republicans.
3. The Crédit Mobilier supported the use of violence against African Americans and sympathetic whites.

4. Lincoln offered to impeach any Confederate who would swear allegiance to the Union and accept the end of slavery.

Matching Review the key people in the list above. If you are not sure of a person's importance, review his or her significance in the chapter. Then choose a person from the list that best matches each description below.
1. After a disputed presidential election, he promised to remove federal troops from all southern states.
2. The only southerner to remain in Congress after secession, as President he favored easy terms toward Confederates after the war.

Reviewing Main Ideas

Section 1 (pp. 226–231)
1. What do Susan Bradford's observations (page 227) reveal about the response of white southerners to the enthusiasm with which African Americans embraced freedom?
2. How did freedom affect the travel and education of formerly enslaved African Americans?

Section 2 (pp. 232–236)
3. How did the Freedmen's Bureau help African Americans freed during the war?
4. What was Lincoln's Reconstruction plan and how did it differ from that of the Radical Republicans?
5. How did white southerners respond to Andrew Johnson's plan for Reconstruction?
6. Explain how the goals of the Fourteenth and Fifteenth amendments were similar.

Section 3 (pp. 237–241)
7. Give evidence to show that African Americans made significant political contributions in the South after the Civil War.
8. Describe some of the steps taken by Republican state governments in the South in the areas of civil rights, education, and economic development.
9. In what ways did white southerners try to replace the slave system?
10. Why did southern whites launch a violent counter-revolution against Reconstruction?

Section 4 (pp. 243–245)
11. What was the result of the relationship between business and government after the Civil War?
12. Explain how the concerns of the Republican party shifted after the Civil War.

1. **Making Comparisons** Evaluate Reconstruction from the point of view of: (a) a former Confederate; (b) a Republican entrepreneur living in the North; (c) an African American living in the inner city at the end of the twentieth century.

2. **Demonstrating Reasoned Judgment** Several wars fought by the United States have been followed by periods of prosperity. Suggest reasons to explain this fact.

3. **Recognizing Ideologies** Imagine that you could interview an enslaved African American and a white slave owner living during the Civil War. Describe how their visions of what the South should be like after the war might differ.

1. **Evaluating Primary Sources** Review the primary source excerpt on page 229. How does the freedman's dream of the kind of life he wants compare with the life goals of many Americans today, as you understand them?

2. **Understanding the Visuals** Examine the cartoon on page 245. Explain the different uses to which weapons are put in each panel of the cartoon.

3. **Writing About the Chapter** Imagine that the Civil War has just ended and you have a brilliant plan for rebuilding the South and reuniting the country. Before sending your plan to the President, first review the three plans for Reconstruction described on pages 232–236 and make a list of their main points. Then make a list of the points of your plan and describe how they are similar to or different from those in the other plans. Note any flaws you see in the three plans and point out how your plan will avoid these flaws. Next, write a draft of your plan in which you explain your ideas. Revise your plan, making certain that each idea is clearly explained. Proofread your plan and draft a final copy.

4. **Using the Graphic Organizer** This graphic organizer uses a tree map to organize main ideas and supporting details about the ways in which formerly enslaved African Americans experienced their new freedom. (a) Which details support the idea that education flourished among African Americans after the Civil War? (b) What conclusions can you draw from the details given under the heading *Land Ownership*? (c) On a separate sheet of paper, create your own graphic organizer about the Republican retreat from Reconstruction, using this graphic organizer as an example.

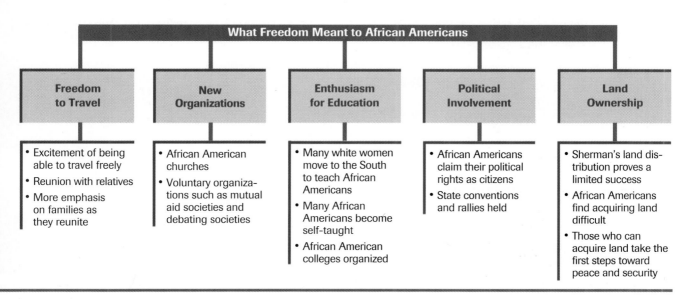

What Freedom Meant to African Americans

Freedom to Travel	New Organizations	Enthusiasm for Education	Political Involvement	Land Ownership
• Excitement of being able to travel freely • Reunion with relatives • More emphasis on families as they reunite	• African American churches • Voluntary organizations such as mutual aid societies and debating societies	• Many white women move to the South to teach African Americans • Many African Americans become self-taught • African American colleges organized	• African Americans claim their political rights as citizens • State conventions and rallies held	• Sherman's land distribution proves a limited success • African Americans find acquiring land difficult • Those who can acquire land take the first steps toward peace and security

Expansion: Rewards and Costs 1860–1920

*"Mark the spirit of invention everywhere, thy rapid patents,
Thy continual workshops, foundries, risen or rising,
See, from their chimneys how the tall flame-fires stream."*
—Walt Whitman, from "Song of the Exposition," 1872

*T*he explosive growth that Whitman celebrates in these lines sparked a transformation of the United States after the Civil War. The promise of new opportunities attracted thousands of settlers to the West, set off a dramatic wave of immigration, and swelled the populations of cities. Although expansion brought important rewards, such as technological advances, those rewards came with a price. Urban poverty, child labor, and the displacement of Native Americans were some of those costs.

This photo of an excursion party at Devil's Gate Bridge in Utah captures both rewards and costs of the nation's growth.

The Expansion of American Industry

1865–1900

*A*fter the Civil War, a revolution of new inventions and ideas transformed the United States. Industrial expansion meant new products and conveniences for consumers and business and new sources of wealth for business owners. Industrial growth also put men and women to work, but at the price of a poorer quality of life. As the century came to a close, tensions between workers and employers worsened, finally exploding in a series of violent strikes and confrontations.

Events in the United States

1866 National Labor Union is organized in Baltimore, Maryland.

1869 The transcontinental railroad is completed.
• The Knights of Labor are founded.

1877 Edison patents the phonograph.
• The railroad strike of 1877 erupts in Pittsburgh.

1880 Andrew Carnegie begins the establishment of Carnegie libraries.

1865	1870	1875	1880

Events in the World

1868 Austrian Johann Strauss II composes "The Blue Danube" waltz.

1876 Korea becomes an independent nation.

1880 Chile fights the "Pacific War" against Bolivia and Peru.

1883 *Railroads adopt standard time zones.*
• *The Brooklyn Bridge is opened.*

1890 *Congress passes the Sherman Antitrust Act.*

1894 *Pullman workers strike.*

1900 *Western Union sends 63 million telegraph messages.*

1885	1890	1895	1900

1885 *French scientist Louis Pasteur admin-isters the first successful rabies vaccination.*

1891 *Building of a railroad across Siberia, in Russia, begins.*

1895 *Italian physicist Guglielmo Marconi invents a wireless tele-graph system.*

1899 *Boer War begins in South Africa.*

A Technological Revolution

A revolution was coming. Not a political revolution—but a technological revolution that would change forever the way people worked, played, traveled, and communicated.

Key Concepts

- Technological change and an explosion of new ideas transformed American life in the post-Civil War years.
- The nature of doing business changed as a result of developments in communications and transportation.
- Changes in transportation and building methods transformed the nation's landscape.

Key Terms, People, and Places

transcontinental railroad; Thomas A. Edison, Alexander Graham Bell; Brooklyn Bridge

Inventions such as this Singer sewing machine changed daily life for many Americans.

Americans today flip a switch for light, turn a faucet for water, and communicate in many ways with people they never meet face to face. It is hard to imagine life without these conveniences. In 1865, however, no one had to wonder what such a life was like.

Daily Life in 1865

Indoor electric lighting did not exist in 1865. Instead, the rising and setting of the sun dictated the rhythm of work and play. After dark, people lit candles or oil lamps if they could afford them; if not, they simply went to sleep, to rise at dawn with the first light.

Imagine summers without the benefits of refrigeration. Ice was available in 1865, but only at great cost. Sawn out of frozen ponds during the winter, blocks of ice were packed in sawdust and stored in ice houses for later use.

Communications also were agonizingly slow. In 1860, most mail from the East Coast took ten days to reach the Midwest and three weeks to get to the West. An immigrant living on the frontier would wait months for news from relatives in Europe.

Daily Life Transformed

By 1900, this picture of daily life had changed dramatically for millions of Americans. A combination of factors made this change possible.

The post-Civil War years saw tremendous growth in new ideas and inventions. Between 1790 and 1860, the Patent and Trademark Office of the federal government issued just 36,000 patents. In contrast, in the thirty years between 1860 and 1890, it issued 500,000 for new inventions, such as the typewriter and the phonograph.

While new inventions flooded the patent office, European investors and American business leaders, using profits gained during the Civil War, began to invest heavily in these inventions. This combination of American ingenuity and financial backing created new industries and expanded old ones. By 1900, the industrial productivity and overall standard of living in the United States was in many ways the envy of the world.

The Advent of Electric Power

The blossoming of American ingenuity in the late 1800s had a profound effect on daily life for millions of people. For example, scientists began developing new uses for petroleum, including fuels such as gasoline that would help power new forms of transportation and machinery in the decades ahead.

Electricity, a miracle of light and power, provided another essential energy source. It made possible many significant advances in the nation's industrial development and in people's eating, working, and even sleeping habits.

A Master of Invention The work of **Thomas A. Edison** helped make electricity more widely available. Born in 1847, Edison grew up tinkering with electricity. While working for a New York company, he improved the stock tickers that sent stock and gold prices to other offices. When his boss awarded him a $40,000 bonus, the twenty-three-year-old Edison left his job and set himself up as an inventor.

From his so-called invention factory in New Jersey, Edison and his staff produced "invention to order." Though he had never received any formal science training, the young genius claimed that he could turn out "a minor invention every ten days and a big thing every six months or so." Within a few years, he owned hundreds of patents. Edison's favorite invention, introduced in 1877, was the phonograph, which recorded sounds on metal foil.

Edison also experimented with electric lighting. His goal was to develop affordable, practical, in-home lighting to replace oil lamps. Starting around 1879, Edison and his fellow inventors tried different means of producing light. A key to their search was finding a material that would glow without quickly burning up when charged with an electric current. After experimenting with various threadlike filaments, the team finally found a workable substance. When this filament was placed in a glass bulb, it glowed, Edison said, with "the most beautiful light ever seen."

Edison's ideas were later adapted and improved upon by others. Lewis Latimore, the son of an escaped slave, patented an improved method for producing the filament in bulbs. He worked in Edison's laboratories, where his ingenuity helped develop additional improvements in electricity. He later wrote a landmark book about electric lighting.

Until the early 1880s, anyone using electricity needed their own generator. Hoping to provide affordable lighting to many customers, Edison developed the idea of a central power station. To attract investors, in 1882 Edison built a power plant that lit eighty-five buildings in New York City. Investors were impressed, and Edison's idea spread. By 1890, offices across the country were using electricity to power lamps, fans, printing presses, and other appliances.

Westinghouse and Alternating Current Edison at first used a form of electricity called direct current to transmit power from his stations. Direct current was expensive to produce, however, and could travel only a mile or two. In the 1880s, George Westinghouse began to experiment with alternating current, which could travel longer distances more cheaply. In addition, Westinghouse used a device called a transformer to produce voltage levels that made home use of electricity practical.

By the early 1890s, financiers built on the Edison and Westinghouse inventions to create the General Electric and Westinghouse Electric companies. These companies' inventions helped spur the growth of electricity. By 1898 nearly three thousand power stations were lighting two million light bulbs across the land.

Electricity's Impact on Daily Life The use of electric current in households revolutionized many aspects of daily life. To take but one example, electricity made possible the refrigeration of foods, reducing food spoilage and the need for ice houses.

Electricity also transformed the world of work and created new job opportunities. For example, foot pedals drove the early sewing machines, which had been introduced in the 1850s. Electrified in 1886, sewing machines enabled the rapid expansion of the ready-made clothing industry. Many of the country's new immigrants, especially women and children, found work making clothing in factories powered by electricity. In addition, many women stopped making their own clothing.

For all its impact, electricity's benefits were not evenly distributed. Rural areas especially went without electricity for many decades. Even where electricity was available, many could not afford its conveniences.

Electricity provided power that made postwar industrial development possible. In turn, electric companies such as General Electric, whose ad appears here, grew into large industrial corporations.

MAKING CONNECTIONS

Think of a modern convenience that you rely on. What benefits does this item bring to your life? Are there any drawbacks associated with this item?

Improving Transportation Systems

As the Civil War ended, steam-powered ships still provided much of the nation's transportation. During the mid-1800s, however, improvements in railroad travel created interconnecting links on land. Shrewd industrialists seized upon the opportunities offered by these links to make money and stimulate industrial growth.

The Railroads Before the Civil War, most of the nation's thirty thousand miles of track were in short, unconnected lines, almost all of them east of the Mississippi River. Because no system of standard signals existed and brakes were unreliable, train travel was dangerous. Moreover, track width, or gauge, varied among railroad lines. Goods and passengers had to be moved to different cars on different lines, resulting in costly delays and inconvenience.

Matters improved after the Civil War. The most spectacular development came on May 10, 1869. On that day, entrepreneur Leland Stanford drove the golden spike that completed the first **transcontinental railroad.**

The project had begun in 1862, when the absence of southern legislators during the Civil War enabled Congress to agree on a route across the continent. Prior to the war, sectional differences over location of the route had prevented such agreement. Government involvement was vital, for only with federal funding could the massive project be completed. Thus, the government granted huge loans and land grants to two companies. One, the Union Pacific, began work in Omaha, Nebraska, and built toward the West. The other, the Central Pacific, headed east out of Sacramento, California.

Immigrants built the transcontinental line using their bare hands. Irish men on the Union Pacific line used shovels and pickaxes to dig and level rail beds across the Great Plains at the rate of up to six miles a day. Testimony to the backbreaking nature of this work was the railroad saying that there was "an Irishman buried under every tie." Chinese workers shipped in from across the Pacific Ocean by the Central Pacific Railroad chiseled, plowed, and dynamited their way through the rock, ice, and snow of the Sierra Nevada range. Workers took pride in their labor. One work crew set a record for putting down track—an amazing ten miles in one day.

Finally, after seven years of grueling labor, the two crews approached one another in what is now Utah. At a place called Promontory Point, Stanford raised his hammer to drive the final golden spike while a telegraph operator beside the track tapped out a message to crowds throughout the country: "Almost ready now. Hats off. Prayer is being offered. . . . Done!"

Problems and Solutions on the Railroads
Even after such improvements, train travel remained inconvenient for many. Cornelia Adair, an Englishwoman visiting the United States in 1874, recalled the following details about her journey:

> We were obliged to wait all Friday, the afternoon and evening, at Cheyenne [Wyoming]. *The Kansas-Pacific Railway has quarreled with the Union-Pacific, and makes the diabolical arrangement that people must get up at two in the night to go from Cheyenne to Denver [Colorado], and then no sleeping car.*

In addition to their inconvenience and lack of comfort, the railroads aroused the distrust and fear of many. One story of the early railroad days raged against the dangers of train travel, reporting

Time Zones and the Growth of the Railroads, 1870–1890

Pacific Time

Mountain Time

Central Time

Eastern Time

GREAT NORTHERN

NORTHERN PACIFIC

CENTRAL PACIFIC

UNION PACIFIC

& SANTA FE

ATCHISON TOPEKA

SOUTHERN PACIFIC

TEXAS AND PACIFIC

ILLINOIS CENTRAL

PENNSYLVANIA

SOUTHERN RAILWAY

CENTRAL

N.Y.

CANADA

Seattle
Tacoma
Portland
Butte
Fargo
Duluth
Boston
San Francisco
Salt Lake City
Cheyenne
Denver
Omaha
Chicago
Pittsburgh
New York
Philadelphia
Washington, D.C.
Richmond
Kansas City
St. Louis
Los Angeles
Pueblo
Albuquerque
Memphis
Atlanta
El Paso
Ft. Worth
Dallas
Savannah
San Antonio
Houston
New Orleans

PACIFIC OCEAN

ATLANTIC OCEAN

MEXICO

N
W E
S

Railroads built by 1870
Railroads built, 1870–1890

0   250   500 Miles
0   250   500 Kilometers

Geography and History: Interpreting Maps
Following the Civil War, railroads expanded rapidly across the United States. Workers such as those pictured here performed the dangerous, backbreaking construction. The growth of the railroads made necessary the introduction of standard time zones. *In what ways did the nation's growing transportation system help promote industrial growth?*

it is bad enough when the train kills pigs and cows and horses, but if little children get on the track accidental it will run over them too, and even old folks going to church in their buggy. It's enough to make your blood run cold.

From the folk tale
"Railroads Ain't No Good"

In spite of its supposed and real dangers, train travel continued to expand and improve. Steel rails replaced iron rails, track gauges and signals became standardized. In 1883, the railroads helped introduce standardized time zones to improve scheduling nationwide (shown on the map above). Prior to that time, most towns set their clocks independently, creating much confusion.

Railroads also took steps to improve safety. George Westinghouse developed more effective air brakes. Granville Woods invented a telegraph system for communications to and from moving trains, thus reducing collision risks.

Rail improvements made life easier not only for passengers but also for businesses that shipped goods. By the end of the century, shipping costs had dropped: in 1865, shipping a barrel of flour from Chicago to New York cost $3.45; in 1895, it cost 68 cents.

The Power to Communicate

In the late 1800s, thousands of people left their homes in Europe and the eastern United States to seek a new life in the West. Imagine their despair at leaving loved ones. Would they ever hear from family and friends again? By 1900, thanks to many advances in communications, such feelings of isolation had diminished.

The Telegraph Samuel F. B. Morse's invention of the telegraph signaled the start of the communications revolution. Using a code of short and long electrical impulses to represent letters of the alphabet, Morse sent his first message in 1844.

After the Civil War, several telegraph companies joined together to form the Western Union Telegraph Company. In 1870, Western Union sent 9 million telegraph messages over 112,000 miles of wire. By 1900, it owned 933,000 miles of wire and was sending 63 million messages a year. Like many companies born in the late 1800s, Western Union still operates today.

The Telephone In 1871, **Alexander Graham Bell** of Scotland immigrated to Boston, Massachusetts, to instruct the hearing impaired. After experimenting with an electric current to transmit sounds, he achieved a "talking telegraph" in 1876. In 1884, Bell and a group of partners set up the American Telephone and Telegraph Company, which still exists today.

Although the first telephone lines could connect only two places, such as a home and a business, soon central switchboards with operators linked homes and businesses in entire cities. President Rutherford B. Hayes had a telephone installed at the White House in 1878. By 1900, 1.5 million telephones were in use.

The Power to Build Things

Throughout the mid-1800s, the nation depended on iron for railroads and for frames for large buildings. But in the 1850s, Henry Bessemer in England and William Kelly in Kentucky independently developed a new process for making steel, a metal that is lighter, stronger, and more flexible than iron. Engineers had long known the benefits of steel, but its high cost had made its widespread use impractical. The Bessemer converter—the name commonly used for the new technology—made possible the production of affordable, plentiful steel. A new age of building was dawning. Perhaps no construction project so exemplified that new age as the building of the Brooklyn Bridge.

The "Greatest Bridge in Existence" As New York City's status as a business center rose, so did its population, many of whom settled in the nearby city of Brooklyn. But the only way to

| 1650 | 1700 | 1750 | 1800 | **Links Across Time** | 1850 | 1900 | 1950 | 2000 |

New Ways to Communicate

When Alexander Graham Bell patented the first model of his telephone in 1876, businesses everywhere flocked to buy the new invention. As technology moves into the twenty-first century, a new communications revolution is taking place. The picture telephone technology shown here allows modern businesses to speak with and to see the party whom they have called. *How might a company benefit from picture telephones?*

Water Shaft Earth was removed by scoops inside these shafts. Water in the shafts prevented loss of air pressure.

Supply Shaft These shafts allowed workers to get supplies to the work area.

Air Lock These chambers let workers enter and leave the caisson without a loss of air.

Boom Derrick

Granite Blocks

Timber Caisson Each tower was built atop a timber shell, or caisson, under which workers removed earth.

The Brooklyn Bridge included two massive towers, one of which is shown being built here. As workers removed earth beneath the tower and piled granite blocks above it, the tower sank into the ground. When completed, the two towers supported the steel cables that in turn held up the span.

In the dank space under the caisson, workers shoveled earth into the water shafts for removal.

travel between Brooklyn and Manhattan was by ferry across the East River, often impassable in winter due to ice or gales. Could a bridge high enough to clear river traffic be built across such a large distance? Engineer John A. Roebling, a German immigrant, thought it could.

Roebling envisioned a suspension bridge with thick steel cables suspended from high towers to hold up the span. At 1,595 feet long, his **Brooklyn Bridge**—which was completed by his son Washington following his death—would be the longest bridge yet built.

A Symbol of American Ingenuity Sixteen years in the making, the bridge opened on May 24, 1883. President Chester A. Arthur attended the opening ceremony. At nightfall, crowds gasped as a switch was thrown, and electric bulbs strung along the bridge lit up the darkness and shimmered on the river below. Just as suddenly, the lights went out, heralding a magnificent fireworks display. The city celebrated. Indeed, the entire United States celebrated, its ingenuity confirmed for all the world.

Inventions, faster transportation, daring construction—to this list of examples of American ingenuity should be added the new thinking evident in the American business world in the late 1800s. Changes brought about by that business, however, came with a price, as the next section shows.

SECTION 1 REVIEW

Key Terms, People, and Places
1. Identify transcontinental railroad.
2. Identify (a) Thomas A. Edison, (b) Alexander Graham Bell, (c) Brooklyn Bridge.

Key Concepts
3. What were some of the factors that helped spur economic development after the Civil War ?
4. How did electricity change daily life?

5. How were effective transportation and communication systems important to economic development?

Critical Thinking
6. **Determining Relevance** Consider the dominant transportation method in the United States before the Civil War. How might railroads have provided a broader, more widespread network than this earlier transportation method?

Using Cross-Sectional Maps

Sometimes it is necessary to use more than one type of map to understand the look of a particular piece of land. Cross-sectional maps show how an area of land would look if viewed from the side. The cross-sectional map below shows the changes in elevation along the route of the first transcontinental railroad, completed in 1869. These changes in elevation appear on the map as sharp spikes and deep depressions. Physical-political maps show the earth's surface as if viewed from above. The physical-political map below gives a bird's-eye view of the vast horizontal distances covered by the railroad.

Steep terrain, snowstorms, floods, and heat all posed great challenges to the workers who built the transcontinental railroad, but the greatest challenges arose from the changes in elevation. Use the following steps to study the cross-sectional map.

1. Study the region shown in the maps. (a) Which landforms on the physical-political map correspond to those on the cross-sectional map? (b) Does the cross-sectional map show all the land area on the political map? Explain.

2. Analyze the information shown in the cross-sectional map. (a) What were the highest and lowest elevations of each railroad route? (b) Where did the sharpest and the most gradual changes occur? (c) Write a paragraph comparing the length and elevation changes of the Central Pacific and Union Pacific routes.

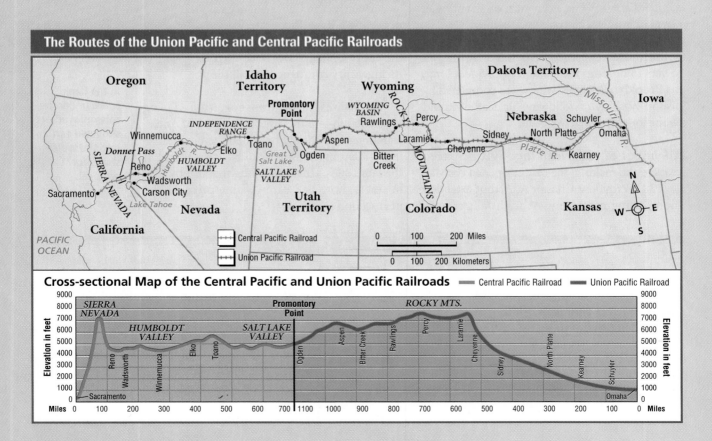

The Routes of the Union Pacific and Central Pacific Railroads

The Growth of Big Business

SECTION PREVIEW

The late 1800s saw the emergence of giant enterprises that controlled vast material and human resources. Big business produced staggering wealth for its owners and for the country. It also prompted controversy and concern over its methods.

Key Concepts

• Only large businesses had the resources needed to exploit new inventions.
• Industrialists were both hated for their ruthlessness and admired for their good works and willingness to take risks.
• Big business sought to control competition through various forms of consolidation.

Key Terms, People, and Places

social Darwinism, monopoly, cartel, trust, horizontal consolidation, vertical consolidation, economy of scale; Andrew Carnegie

T he period of invention and discovery following the Civil War set the stage for great industrial growth. But it would take more than ingenuity to bring about the transformation of the United States. Without large outlays of money, inventors could not build great factories, market their new products, or create profitable businesses. To succeed, business leaders had to pool funds and resources into large companies. Thus was born the age of "big business."

Robber Barons or Captains of Industry?

Historians have adopted the terms *robber barons* and *captains of industry* to describe the powerful industrialists who established large businesses in the late 1800s. Each term conjures up strikingly different images, and debate still rages over which is more fitting.

Captains of industry suggests that the business leaders served their nation in a positive way. This view credits them with increasing the availability of goods by building factories, raising productivity, and expanding markets. Furthermore, by creating more jobs, the giant industrialists enabled many Americans to buy their new goods. They also founded and funded many of the nation's great museums, libraries, and universities, many of which still thrive today.

The term *robber barons,* on the other hand, implies that the business leaders built their fortunes by stealing from the public. According to this view, they drained the country of its natural resources and corrupted public officials to interpret laws in their favor. At the same time, these industrialists ruthlessly drove their competitors to ruin and paid meager wages, while forcing their workers to toil under dangerous and unhealthy conditions.

Industrial growth required the contributions of workers and also of business owners, as this illustration suggests.

AMERICAN PROFILES

Andrew Carnegie

Andrew Carnegie (1835–1919) is a fascinating example of an American industrialist of this era. Born in Scotland, Carnegie's father was a skilled weaver. But when industrial growth in Great Britain replaced the need for skilled craft workers, Carnegie's family faced hard times. As a result, they came to the United States in 1848, settling near Pittsburgh, Pennsylvania. Only thirteen years old, Carnegie immediately went out to work.

Carnegie's first job was in a cotton factory at $1.20 a week. Determined to do better, he read avidly to improve himself. When his father's death in 1855 made young Andrew his family's chief earner, his quest for advancement became urgent.

Andrew Carnegie's success in business enabled him to surround himself with comfort. Here he relaxes at his private golf cottage.

After a stint as a telegraph operator, at age eighteen Carnegie won the post of secretary to the superintendent in the Pennsylvania Railroad Company. When Carnegie's boss went off to the War Department during the Civil War, the young Carnegie took over his job.

Forging a Great Enterprise Now well paid, Carnegie began to invest widely. The invention of Henry Bessemer's steel-making process had convinced Carnegie that steel would soon replace iron in many industries. During the early 1870s, Carnegie built two blast furnaces that made pig iron, the material from which steel is made.

Despite a nationwide economic depression in 1873, Carnegie systematically cut his steel prices until he had driven his competitors out of the market. Together with a partner, Henry Clay Frick, Carnegie then took control of the entire steel industry, from the mines that produced iron ore to the ovens and mills that made pig iron and steel. He even took control of the shipping and rail lines necessary for transporting his products to market.

Carnegie as a Public Figure While expanding his business, Carnegie became a major public figure. Through books and speeches, he preached a "gospel of wealth." The essence of his message was simple: People should be free to make as much money as they can. After they make it, however, they should give it away. As he wrote in 1889, "The man who dies . . . rich dies disgraced." Never leave wealth to heirs, he warned, or they will fail to learn how to survive on their own. Never leave it to others to administer, for they will never follow your instruc-

tions. Give it away yourself, he advised, not as charity but as philanthropy, gifts to institutions or to the public that help humankind.

By the turn of the century, Carnegie had built about three thousand free public libraries, supported artistic and research institutions in Pittsburgh, Washington, D.C., and New York City, and set up a fund to study how to abolish war. In these and other ways, Carnegie distributed some $350 million.

Still, not everyone approved of Carnegie's methods. Workers at his steel plants protested vigorously against his company's labor practices. (See Section 4.) Many others questioned the sincerity of his good works. In one satire by humorist Finley Peter Dunne, a fictitious Irish bartender describes what might happen if a beggar asked Carnegie for food:

> Th' pan-handler knocks an' asts f'r a glass iv milk an' a roll. "No sir," says Andhrew Carnaygie. "I will not pauperize this onworthy man. . . . Yet it shall not be said iv me that I give nawthin' to th' poor. Saunders, give him a libry."

Others admired Carnegie for achieving great things through hard work. He saw himself as "improving the conditions of all" by lowering costs for the masses. In an essay titled "Wealth and Its Uses," he wrote:

> It will be a great mistake for the community to shoot the millionaires, for they are the bees that make the most honey, and contribute most to the hive even after they have gorged themselves full.

Social Darwinism

In statements such as these, Carnegie revealed support for social Darwinism, a popular theory of the late 1800s. This theory applied to society Charles Darwin's theory of evolution, first published in 1859. According to Darwin, all animal life had evolved by a process of "natural selection" through which only the fittest survived to reproduce.

Applying this idea to the struggle between workers and employers, **social Darwinism** held that society should do as little as possible to interfere with the process by which people succeed or fail. If government and other institutions would stay out of the affairs of business, those who were most "fit" would survive—that is, succeed and become rich. Society as a whole would benefit from the success of the fit and the weeding out of the unfit.

Many Americans agreed with the great industrialists that the nation's prosperity depended on a *laissez-faire*, or "hands-off," approach to the economy by the government. As a result, government neither taxed the profits of businesses nor regulated their relations with their workers.

MAKING CONNECTIONS

Based on your understanding of the *laissez-faire* approach of government, what do you predict might happen to those business owners who were less powerful?

Competition in the Age of Big Business

Industrialists used whatever means necessary, fair or foul, to gain a competitive edge over their rivals. They paid as little as they could for raw materials, labor, and shipping. They also sometimes created monopolies and cartels to gain control over competition.

Monopolies and Cartels In order to create a **monopoly,** a business bought out its competitors and all of its patents. The business would thus eliminate all competition for its product, and it could then charge any price it wished.

Toward the end of the 1800s, federal and state governments passed laws to prevent certain monopolistic practices. Those laws did not prevent or destroy all monopolies, however, in part because political leaders were unwilling to attack powerful business leaders.

Cartels are loose associations of businesses making the same product, usually formed in secret. The goal of a cartel is to reduce the harmful effects of competition on the businesses

PUCK.

THE PROTECTORS OF OUR INDUSTRIES.

Using Historical Evidence Some Americans were offended by the argument that business leaders protected jobs. *What does this cartoon suggest about the relationship of workers to business leaders?*

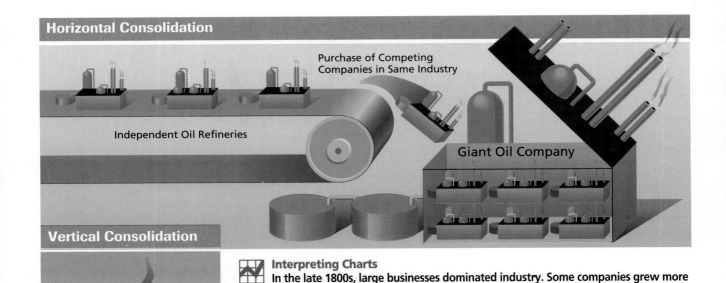

Horizontal Consolidation

Purchase of Competing Companies in Same Industry

Independent Oil Refineries

Giant Oil Company

Vertical Consolidation

A to Z Meat Industries

A-Z MEAT

Purchase of Companies at All Levels of Production

Delivery Wagons

Meat Packing Plants

Cooled Warehouses

Refrigerated Railroad Cars

Slaughterhouses

Cattle

Interpreting Charts
In the late 1800s, large businesses dominated industry. Some companies grew more powerful through vertical consolidation. By controlling all phases of production, they could lower the costs of making their product and charge less than their competitors. Other companies grew more powerful through horizontal consolidation, in which companies simply bought competitors in their field. *What problems might a business face when trying to compete with a company with a vertical monopoly? With a horizontal monopoly?*

involved. Members agree to limit the supply of their product because when supply is low, a product's price tends to increase or remain high.

From the point of view of manufacturers in the 1800s, cartels had disadvantages. During hard times they tended to fall apart. To achieve a more reliable arrangement, Samuel Dodd, a lawyer for oil magnate John D. Rockefeller, invented the trust.

The Standard Oil Trust Born in 1839 in Richford, New York, Rockefeller became rich from a grain and meat partnership during the Civil War. By 1870, he had formed the Standard Oil Company of Ohio. Oil had become a major industry following Edwin L. Drake's 1859 success at Titusville, Pennsylvania. There Drake proved the possibility of extracting oil from under the ground through wells.

As Rockefeller's company sold more oil, he was able to undersell his competitors. In addition, he persuaded his railroad friends to give him illegal refunds on part of the cost of transporting his oil. Because Rockefeller paid less to ship oil than his competitors did, Standard Oil's prices were lower.

Rockefeller soon had enough money to buy out his competitors. But the law stood in his way. State laws prohibited one company from owning the stock of another, since such monopolistic practices reduced competition and therefore "restrained" free trade.

Samuel Dodd's idea of the trust got around this ban. In 1882, the owners of forty companies agreed to turn over their assets to a board of nine trustees. In return, they were promised a share of the profits of the new conglomerate. The board of trustees, which was controlled by Rockefeller, managed the companies as a single unit called a **trust.** Because the companies were not legally merged, no laws were violated. Rockefeller's trust controlled almost all of the nation's oil-refining capacity.

Trusts proved an effective means of limiting industrial competition. As a result, many Americans began to demand that their leaders in government take action to break up the giant conglomerates. In 1890, the federal government responded by passing the Sherman Antitrust Act. This law aimed to combat restraint of trade or commerce caused by trusts.

The act, however, proved ineffective for nearly fifteen years because the federal government rarely enforced it and its vague wording made it hard to apply in court. When officials did invoke the act, they often used it against labor unions on the grounds that their actions restrained trade.

Vertical and Horizontal Methods of Industrial Control Rockefeller's approach to consolidation—the creation of one giant business from many smaller enterprises—was **horizontal consolidation.** This method involved bringing together many firms in the same business.

Other industrialists practiced **vertical consolidation,** a method by which they gained control of all phases of a product's development. Andrew Carnegie used this method in the steel business. By controlling all phases of steel production, Carnegie could lower his costs and drive competitors out of business. Carnegie could charge less because of a phenomenon called **economy of scale.** As he expanded his enterprises and produced more goods, his cost per item went down.

Public Reaction to Big Business

Few people truly liked trusts and other large business organizations. They knew that such associations did not have consumer or worker interests at heart. In 1873, this anonymous resident of Lynn, Massachusetts, recalled

It is only too evident that the cause now at work in Lynn may render it rich and prosperous as a city, but with a population of overworked, underpaid hirelings, hopelessly dependent upon employers who act upon the good old rule, the simple plan—that they may take who have the power, and they may keep who can.

But mergers were the wave of the future. By the turn of the century, the mammoth companies that contributed to the United States' enviable levels of wealth and productivity were in place: American Telephone and Telegraph, Swift and Armour, General Electric, Westinghouse, and DuPont are examples.

Rapid industrial growth did lead to strains on the economy. The gigantic markets of big business were subject to sudden fluctuations. When markets became glutted with goods, businesses had to lower prices in order to sell them. They then cut wages and laid off workers.

Other causes of strain included panics, widespread fears that heavily indebted businesses might not be able to pay their debts. When investors rushed to sell stock in affected businesses, stock prices fell and companies went bankrupt. Panics were often followed by depressions, periods of severe shrinking of economic growth. The resulting factory closings and unemployment meant widespread misery.

Unemployment was only one concern of the nation's workers. Indeed, their lives provide a sharp contrast to those of Carnegie, Rockefeller, and their fellow industrialists.

Periods of Economic Depression
1873 to 1879
1882 to 1885
1893 to 1897

The late 1800s were marred by a series of depressions.

SECTION 2 REVIEW

Key Terms, People, and Places
1. Define (a) social Darwinism, (b) monopoly.
2. Identify Andrew Carnegie.

Key Concepts
3. For what reasons were large enterprises necessary for the economic development of the late 1800s?
4. Why did manufacturers form cartels and trusts?

5. What is the difference between vertical and horizontal consolidation?

Critical Thinking
6. **Identifying Assumptions** You have read that government recognized the need to control conglomerates. What does this recognition assume about the nature of businesses?

Industrialization and Workers

SECTION PREVIEW

For millions of men, women, and children, industrialization was a blessing and a curse. It gave them jobs—but at what cost?

Key Concepts

- Industrial growth depended on the labor of millions of workers.
- Men, women, and children, both native born and immigrant, met the great demand for labor.
- Harsh working conditions inflicted physical and emotional harm.

Key Terms, People, and Places

piecework

Children workers such as these labored long hours under hazardous conditions in the late 1800s.

Natural resources, inventive minds, risk-taking industrialists—all played central roles in the nation's industrial expansion following the Civil War. This expansion would not have been possible, however, without a growing work force that labored long hours for low wages.

The Growing Work Force

Fourteen million people arrived in the United States from abroad between 1860 and 1900. Most came in the hope of finding work in the booming industrial centers of the United States. The government often encouraged these job-seekers by sending recruiting agents abroad. As described in Chapter 10, however, their reception in the United States and its workplaces was not always warm.

In a population shift almost as dramatic as this immigration, some eight or nine million native-born Americans fled poor economic conditions on the nation's farms to move to its cities during the late 1800s. (See graph at right.) Factory work, in spite of its low pay and long hours, lured most of them.

Until the end of the century, few African Americans took part in this internal migration. Although some moved into cities in the South, the better job opportunities there were closed to them.

A Hard Life for the Factory Laborer

For those who labored in the factories, work was a family affair. Every family member worked in some way. Because wages were low, no one person could earn enough to sustain a household. Children often left school at the age of twelve or thirteen to work. Girls sometimes took factory jobs so that their brothers could stay in school. If a mother could not make some money working at home, she might also take a factory job, leaving babies with older siblings or neighbors. If an adult breadwinner became ill, died, or could not find or keep a job, children as young as six or seven had to bring in cash or go hungry.

Shifts in Nonagricultural and Agricultural Labor Force, 1860–1900

*Mining, construction, manufacturing only
Source: Historical Statistics of the United States

Interpreting Graphs
In the late 1800s, more and more Americans found jobs in industry. *What was the effect of this development on agricultural employment?*

Using Historical Evidence John Furguson Weir's painting "The Gun Foundry" (1866) presents a vivid image of the nation's industrial might. *What does the painting suggest about the conditions faced by workers?*

Other than private charities, there were no support systems such as today's government welfare programs for families in need. For example, unemployment insurance—payments for workers who are laid off from their jobs—did not exist. In addition, legislators in the late 1800s resisted the idea of creating broad programs of public work to relieve the miseries created by economic crises.

Even charity was of limited help. When an economic crisis hit, charity workers had to spread out their limited resources by making relief more difficult to get. They insisted that applicants prove themselves "worthy," which meant sober and in agreement with the charity's standard of morality.

MAKING CONNECTIONS

Consider the lack of government aid for the poor in the late 1800s. How might the concept of social Darwinism have influenced government policies toward public aid?

The Industrial Laborer at Work

In the 1860s the ordinary work day was about twelve hours, and the work week was six days or longer. By the turn of the century, a ten-hour day prevailed, but in some industries, workers were told "If you don't come in on Sunday, you can forget about Monday." Good jobs were too hard to come by to ignore such a warning.

In many industries, employers paid workers a fixed amount for each finished piece they produced—for example, a few cents for a garment or a number of cigars. This system of **piecework** meant that those who worked fastest and produced the most pieces earned the most money. Piecework favored young and strong workers; older or less able workers suffered.

Increasing Efficiency In the 1880s, management engineer Frederick Winslow Taylor developed time-and-motion studies to get workers to produce more in less time. Taylor's idea was to make the most efficient use of all motion and activity. Workers hated and resisted Taylor's ideas because they imposed an outside control on the way they did their work. They also feared that any increased efficiency caused by Taylor's methods would result in layoffs or a lower rate of pay for each piece of work.

By the early years of the twentieth century, Taylor had used his studies as the basis of an entire system of so-called scientific management in which

> The work of every workman is fully planned out by the management at least one day in advance, and each man receives in most cases complete written instructions, describing in detail the task which he is to accomplish, as well as the means to be used in doing the work . . . and the exact time allowed for doing it.
>
> Frederick Winslow Taylor, *The Principles of Scientific Management*, 1911

Industrial growth created jobs for African Americans, though opportunities were limited. For example, these three men were hired for the low-paying job of carrying bricks. White men got the higher-paying jobs as masons.

Taylor's ideas were just one method of improving efficiency. Employers often increased the speed of factory machines or added to workers' loads, especially in hard times. Yet workers' pay did not increase, and their health and safety suffered. When a Fall River, Massachusetts, textile company increased the number of each worker's looms, one woman complained, "They gave us twelve looms, I didn't see that we could make it out alive at all."

Hardships of Factory Work Bosses seldom visited the factory floor where their workers toiled. Workers seldom saw a finished product. Called hands or operatives, they were viewed as cogs in a huge system performing only a small piece of the system's work. One factory manager in 1883 declared,

> I regard my people as I regard my machinery. So long as they can do my work for what I choose to pay them, I keep them, getting out of them all I can. What they do or how they fare outside my walls I don't know, nor do I consider it my business to know.

Discipline was strict. A worker could be fined or fired for being late, answering back, refusing to do a task, talking, or other minor offenses. The work was boring, and the noise of the machines was deafening. Lighting and ventilation were poor. Fatigue, faulty equipment, and careless training resulted in frequent fires and accidents. In 1882, the average number of workers killed on the job each week was 675—compared with about 200 today. Worse, there was no system to provide income to workers injured on the job. The courts in the late 1800s held that a worker who sued an employer had to show that the employer was responsible for causing the injury. This was usually impossible.

Despite the harsh conditions, employers suffered no shortage of labor. Thousands of Irish, German, and Italian immigrants, for example, built the Brooklyn Bridge. The nation's factories were likewise jammed with men, women, and children, many desperate for the opportunity to earn even meager wages.

Industry's Impact on Women and Children

Employers in industry excluded women from the most skilled and highest-paid jobs. Of course, not all men had good jobs, either. But factory owners usually assigned women to the operation of simple machines. More complex machines required machinists and engineers. These were almost always men, for only they had access to training in such fields.

Women enjoyed almost no chances for advancement in factory work. In the garment industry, for example, running the machines that cut out patterns from large stacks of fabric was defined as a man's job. It paid much more than work reserved for women, which usually consisted of performing only one part of the process of sewing a garment.

Children also suffered in the factory system. Today, the use of child labor is strictly regulated by law. In the 1880s, however, children comprised over 5 percent of the industrial labor force. In many households, children's wages meant the difference between going hungry or having food on the table.

Growing children suffered especially from the hazards of the workplace. Working in unhealthful factories or mines, living on inadequate diets, and performing monotonous, dangerous work, many children became stunted in both body and mind. As social commentator Jacob Riis noted, such work left them

grown to manhood and womanhood, just where it found them, knowing no more, and therefore less, than when they began,

Many children went to work in factories and mines. This group of boys were employed in the dangerous, unhealthy work of coal mining. The grime that covers their faces also clogged their lungs, leading to disease.

and with the years that should have prepared them for life's work gone in hopeless and profitless drudgery.
  Jacob Riis, *Children of the Poor,* 1892

The practice of child labor would come under attack in the early 1900s. By 1912, three fourths of the states would have laws limiting the presence of children in the workplace.

SECTION 3 REVIEW

Key Terms, People, and Places
 1. Describe piecework.

Key Concepts.
 2. What was the reason that prompted most immigrants to come to the United States in the late 1800s?
 3. What made life for working people so difficult in times of economic hardship?

 4. What efforts did industrialists make to increase efficiency in factories?

Critical Thinking
 5. **Identifying Central Issues** Review the quotations by Taylor and the factory manager in this section. What do their statements reveal about their views of working men and women?

The Great Strikes: A Turning Point in History

Many American workers sought relief from their difficult lives through labor unions. What they found in the late 1800s was strong resistance from big business and only fleeting success.

Key Concepts
- The gap between rich and poor widened in the late 1800s.
- Labor unions organized to improve the wages and working conditions of workers.
- Violent strikes marked relations between labor unions and business owners in the late 1800s.

Key Terms, People, and Places
socialism, collective bargaining, scab, anarchist, Pullman strike; Pinkerton; Haymarket Square, Homestead

Workers in many industries formed unions in the late 1800s.

Industrialization brought changes and great wealth to the United States. These changes, however, did not bring contentment or prosperity to the nation's working people. Indeed, as the rich grew richer during this era, these workers became increasingly bitter over their own daily struggle for a decent standard of living. During the last quarter of the nineteenth century, working men and women began to take their complaints directly and forcefully to their employers. The resulting turmoil marked a turning point in American history.

The Widening Gulf Between Rich and Poor

The 1890 census revealed that the richest 9 percent of Americans held nearly 75 percent of the national wealth. The nation's workers, *but the workers were poor* however, did not need the census to tell them that they were poor. Able in the best of times to earn only a few hundred dollars a year, workers were well aware of how the elite lived, and they resented it.

Poor families had little hope of relief when hard times hit. Some suffered in silence, trusting that tomorrow would be better; others became politically active in an effort to improve their difficult lives. A few of these individuals were drawn to the idea of socialism then gaining popularity in many European industrialized countries.

Socialism in the Industrial Age

Socialism is an economic and political philosophy that advocates collective or government ownership of factories and property. One goal of socialism is to distribute broadly a society's wealth. In the late 1800s, socialism was strongly influenced by the ideas of Karl Marx, a German philosopher who criticized the capitalist economic system and predicted its eventual overthrow by workers.

Endorsing socialism in the late 1800s was dangerous, however. Most Americans disagreed with socialist theory. They felt that socialism threatened the deeply rooted American ideals of private property and free enterprise—the right of people to compete freely and succeed to whatever extent they can. Most wealthy people also rejected socialism. They would not give up what they owned without a fight. Even though workers had numbers on their side, wealthy Americans knew that if workers tried to bring socialism to the United States by force, the federal government would respond with military action to preserve the nation's economic and political system.

Using Historical Evidence Many workers lived in crowded boarding houses, such as the one shown at left. Many wealthy industrialists, on the other hand, enjoyed great personal wealth and luxurious comforts. *How would you expect workers to respond to the contrast between rich and poor?*

The Return of Labor Unions

Socialism itself never achieved a significant following in the United States in the nineteenth century. But the limited appeal of its themes did reflect a growing discontent among the nation's workers. Many of these men and women looked instead to labor unions as a way to improve their standard of living.

Early Labor Unions The early years of industrialization had spawned a few labor unions, organized among workers in certain trades, such as construction and textile manufacturing. But these early unions had not lasted long.

Unions resurfaced after the Civil War. These groups were initially designed to provide help for their members in bad times. Soon they became the means for channeling workers' demands for shorter workdays, higher wages, and better working conditions. The increasing emphasis on protest led to growing opposition to unions among employers.

Unions grew significantly in the 1860s and 1870s. Indeed, labor activists began trying to organize nationally based unions. One, the National Labor Union formed in Baltimore in 1866, nominated a candidate for the presidential election of 1872. This union, however, failed to survive an economic downturn that began the following year. Indeed, unions in general suffered a steep decline in membership as a result of the depression.

The Knights of Labor Another early national union, The Noble Order of the Knights of Labor, was formed in Philadelphia in 1869. The Knights hoped to organize virtually all working men and women into a single union. Membership included farmers, factory workers, and white-collar workers. The union actively recruited African Americans, of whom sixty thousand joined.

Under the dynamic leadership of former machinist Terence Powderly, the Knights pursued broad social reforms. These included equal pay for equal work, the eight-hour day, and an end to child labor.

The leadership of the Knights did not generally advocate the use of strikes, and they did not emphasize higher wages as their primary goal. The majority of members, however, often differed with the leadership. In fact, it was a strike that helped the Knights achieve their greatest strength. In 1885, when unions affiliated with the Knights forced railroad owner Jay Gould to give up a wage cut, membership quickly soared to 700,000. Yet a series of failed strikes quickly followed, dampening enthusiasm in the Knights. They had largely disappeared as a national force by the 1890s.

The American Federation of Labor A third national union, the American Federation of Labor (AFL) followed the leadership of Samuel Gompers, a London-born cigar maker. Formed in 1886, the AFL differed from the Knights of Labor by seeking to organize only skilled workers in a network of smaller unions, each devoted to a specific craft. Between 1886 and 1892, the AFL gained some 250,000 members. Yet they still represented only a tiny portion of the nation's labor force.

In theory the AFL was open to African Americans. Local unions, however, often found ways to exclude African Americans from their membership. Gompers also opposed women members because he believed that their participation in the work force drove wages down.

> We know to our regret that too often are wives, sisters and children brought into the factories and workshops only to reduce the wages and displace the labor of men—the heads of families.
>
> Samuel Gompers, *Labor and the Employer*, 1887

Gompers and the AFL were primarily interested in issues of wages, hours, and working conditions—so-called bread-and-butter unionism. They sought to force employers to participate in **collective bargaining,** in which workers nego-

Viewpoints
On Labor Unions

The Senate Committee on Education and Labor held a series of hearings concerning the relationships between workers and management in 1883. The committee heard these opposing views about the need for labor unions. *What is the major argument presented in each of the two viewpoints below?*

Testimony of a Labor Leader

"The laws written [by Congress] and now in operation to protect the property of the capitalist and the moneyed class generally are almost innumerable, yet nothing has been done to protect the property of the workingmen, the only property that they possess, their working power, their savings bank, their school, and trades union."

Samuel Gompers, founder of the American Federation of Labor in 1886

Testimony of a Factory Manager

"I think that . . . in a free country like this . . . it is perfectly safe for at least the lifetime of this generation to leave the question of how a man shall work, and how long he shall work, and what wages he shall get to himself."

Thomas L. Livermore, manager for the Amoskeag Manufacturing Company, Manchester, New Hampshire

tiate as a group with employers. The Federation believed that workers acting as a group had more power than a worker acting individually. To strengthen its collective bargaining power, the Federation advocated a "closed shop" that employed only Federation members.

Growing Friction Between Labor and Employers

Not surprisingly, employers disliked and feared unions. They preferred to deal with employees as individuals instead of in powerful groups. Employers took measures to stop unions, such as forbidding union meetings and firing union organizers. They even forced new employees to sign "yellow dog" contracts that exacted a promise never to join a union or to participate in a strike. Some business leaders refused to recognize unions as the workers' legitimate representatives. Wrote one company president:

Rights and interests of the laboring man will be protected and cared for—not by the labor agitators, but by the Christian men to whom God has given control of the property interests of the country.

George F. Baer, mining
company president, 1902

Unions, of course, demanded more than recognition. The competing interests of labor and employers would not be easily reconciled.

MAKING CONNECTIONS

Consider the statement above by George F. Baer. How does it relate to the idea of social Darwinism discussed in Section 2?

The Railroad Strike of 1877

The nation's first major episode of labor unrest occurred in the summer of 1877 in the railroad industry. The strike began when the Baltimore and Ohio Railroad announced a wage cut of 10 percent, the second cut in eight months. Railroads elsewhere imposed similar cuts, along with orders to run "double headers," trains with two engines, twice as many cars—and an increased risk of accident and worker layoffs. Violent reactions against these moves among railway workers spread rapidly across Pennsylvania and Ohio and on to Chicago, Illinois, and St. Louis, Missouri. When the local militia in Pittsburgh refused to stop the unrest, employers called in troops from Philadelphia, who fired on the demonstrators, killing and wounding many. A crowd of twenty thousand angry men and women reacted to the shootings by setting fire to railroad company property. President Rutherford B. Hayes then sent in federal troops, a move that stopped the riots but caused more deaths.

From the 1877 strike on, employers relied on federal and state troops to repress labor unrest. A new and violent era in labor relations had begun.

Strikes Rock the Nation

The period 1881–1900 was one continuing industrial crisis in the United States. An amazing

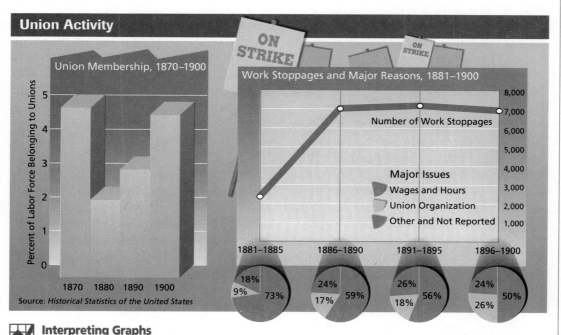

Union Activity

Union Membership, 1870–1900

Work Stoppages and Major Reasons, 1881–1900

Number of Work Stoppages

Major Issues
- Wages and Hours
- Union Organization
- Other and Not Reported

Source: *Historical Statistics of the United States*

1881–1885: 18% / 9% / 73%
1886–1890: 24% / 17% / 59%
1891–1895: 26% / 18% / 56%
1896–1900: 24% / 26% / 50%

Interpreting Graphs
A severe economic depression helped cause a steep decline in union membership in the 1870s. But the 1880s and 1890s saw growth in the numbers of members and in work stoppages. *What trends can you identify in the causes of work stoppages in the late 1800s?*

24,000 strikes erupted in the nation's factories, mines, mills, and yards during those two decades alone. Out of this ongoing turmoil, three major incidents of industrial warfare overshadow the rest.

Haymarket, 1886 On May 1, 1886, several workers' groups mounted a national demonstration for an eight-hour work day. "Eight hours for work, eight hours for rest, eight hours for what we will," ran the cry. Strikes then broke out in a number of cities. At Chicago's McCormick reaper factory, police broke up a fight between strikers and **scabs,** strikebreakers who replace striking workers and allow a company to continue operating. The police action caused several casualties among the workers.

In protest, **anarchists** called a rally for the evening of May 4 in Chicago's **Haymarket Square.** Anarchists are political radicals who oppose all government on the grounds that it limits individual liberty and acts in the interests of the wealthy, ruling classes. In an effort to whip up the anger of the workers, anarchist newspaper editor August Spies wrote

> You have endured the pangs of want and hunger; your children you have sacrificed to the factory-lords. In short, you have been miserable and obedient slaves all these years. Why? To satisfy the insatiable greed, to fill the coffers of your lazy thieving master!

At the May 4 event, someone threw a bomb into a police formation. Seven policemen died, and in the ensuing riot, police and citizen gunfire resulted in dozens of deaths on both sides. Investigators never found the bomb thrower, yet eight anarchists were tried for conspiracy to commit murder. Four were hanged. Another committed suicide in jail. In the belief that the convictions were the result of public

The violence of the Haymarket incident, depicted here, troubled many Americans.

hysteria rather than evidence, Governor John P. Altgeld of Illinois later pardoned the remaining three anarchists.

To many unionists, the Haymarket anarchists forever would be heroes. To employers, they remained vicious criminals determined to overthrow law and order. In many people's minds, unions were associated with violence and radical ideas. The Knights of Labor especially suffered from this public reaction.

Homestead, 1892 Continued labor unrest renewed fears of social revolution. It was in this environment that labor strife struck Andrew Carnegie's enterprise.

A union of iron and steel workers associated with the American Federation of Labor had negotiated a labor contract with Andrew Carnegie's steel company. In the summer of 1892, while Carnegie was in Europe, his partner Henry Frick tried to cut wages for company workers. The union at the Carnegie plant in **Homestead,** Pennsylvania, called a strike.

Frick, perhaps with Carnegie's support, was intent on crushing the union. On July 1, Frick called in the **Pinkertons,** a private police force known for its ability to break strikes. Under cover of darkness, three hundred Pinkertons moved up the Monongahela River on barges. When strikers fired on them from the shore, deaths and injuries occurred on both sides.

At first many Americans sympathized with the workers. Then anarchist Alexander Berkman tried and failed to assassinate Frick. Although Berkman was unconnected with the strike, the public associated his act with the rising tide of labor violence.

Eventually, the union acknowledged defeat and called off the strike. Homestead reopened under militia protection. "I will never recognize the Union, never, never!" Frick cried. Meanwhile, Carnegie, who had always claimed to support nonviolent unions, remained silent about the entire affair. Carnegie Steel and its successor (U.S. Steel) remained nonunionized until the late 1930s.

Pullman, 1894 Like the strike of 1877, the last of the great strikes also involved the railroad industry. This strike also completed a turning point in the federal government's involvement with labor-employer relations.

Sleeping-car maker George Pullman considered himself one of the era's most benevolent industrialists. He built a town for his workers near Chicago that boasted a school, bank, water and gas systems, and comfortable homes.

Conditions in the town, however, took a turn for the worse during a depression in 1893. Pullman laid off workers and cut wages 25 to 40 percent. Meanwhile, he kept rent and food prices in his town at the same levels. In May 1894, a delegation of workers went to him to protest. Pullman's response was to fire three of the workers. When the American Railway Union called a strike, Pullman refused to negotiate and shut down the plant.

The founder of the American Railway Union was Eugene V. Debs, a popular labor organizer from Indiana. By June 1894, Debs had encouraged 120,000 railway workers throughout the region to join in the **Pullman strike.** Though Debs had instructed strikers not to interfere with the nation's mail, the strike led to the complete disruption of western railroad traffic, including the delivery of the mail.

Railroad owners turned to the federal government for help. Arguing that the mail had to get through—and citing the Sherman Antitrust Act—Attorney General Richard Olney won court orders forbidding all union activity that halted railroad traffic. President Grover Cleveland sent in troops to ensure that strikers obeyed the court orders. Twelve deaths and many arrests resulted from ensuing violence.

Debs, who refused to obey the court orders, was jailed for six months. Its leadership in dis-

Eugene Debs was a tremendously successful labor organizer in the late 1800s. Later, Debs would combine his energetic style and his belief in socialism to conduct several unsuccessful presidential campaigns as the leader of the Socialist party.

array, the American Railway Union and its strike fell apart.

The Pullman strike and its outcome set an important pattern. In the years ahead, factory owners appealed frequently for court orders against unions. The federal government regularly responded to these appeals, denying unions recognition as legally protected organizations. This official government opposition helped limit union gains for over thirty years.

SECTION 4 REVIEW

Key Terms, People, and Places
1. Identify (a) socialism, (b) scab, (c) anarchist, (d) collective bargaining, (e) Pullman strike.
2. Identify (a) the Pinkertons, (b) Haymarket Square, (c) Homestead.

Key Concepts
3. How did industrial growth in the late 1800s affect the distribution of wealth?

4. Explain the purpose and goals of labor unions.
5. How successful were labor unions in the late 1800s?

Critical Thinking
6. **Recognizing Bias** Many labor unions did not include or effectively represent the concerns of women or minorities. What does this fact suggest about their view of worker rights?

The Lasting Impact of the Great Strikes

The federal government adopted a hands-off approach to business and its relations with its employees throughout much of the 1800s. By the turn of the century, however, government had become a central player in the ongoing struggle between business and labor unions.

The Great Strikes of the late 1800s marked the turning point for this fundamental change in government policy. Since that time, the federal government has regularly involved itself in business-labor relations. The government's position has been either more probusiness or prolabor, depending on the changing circumstances of the day. Over time, while supporting law and order, it has tried more and more often to encourage the two sides to negotiate their grievances.

After the Great Strikes

After the strikes of the late 1800s, many business owners felt little need to deal with unions. They were confident that in the event of labor unrest, government would come to their aid with guns or court orders. Labor, meanwhile, continued its struggle without any government protection. Unions enjoyed no legal right to strike, picket, bargain collectively, or recruit members without interference or threat of losing their jobs.

Some employers did conclude that it was better to work with unions than to fight them. Most, however, remained hostile, while continuing to enjoy the support of the federal government for the first three decades of the twentieth century.

1932 As the economy crumbles and millions lose their jobs, the government begins to consider offering more support to workers.

1903 The Women's Trade Union League forms to urge women to join unions, since male-dominated unions seldom recruit women members.

1900   1920   1940

1935 With President Roosevelt's support, the Wagner Act is passed, guaranteeing workers' rights to join unions and bargain collectively.

How the Depression, the New Deal, and World War II Affected Labor

In the 1930s, the federal government again intervened in labor-business relations. Now, however, government took a more prolabor position.

The Great Depression of the 1930s had a deep impact on American attitudes toward business and labor. Sympathy for the cause of labor—and distrust of business—increased among the public and in the federal government. In 1932, Congress passed the Norris-LaGuardia Act, which included provisions that limited the power of the federal courts when acting against unions.

President Franklin Roosevelt's administration also supported several prolabor laws. The most significant was the Wagner Act of 1935, which protected labor's right to organize and to bargain collectively. After more than thirty years of hostility, the federal government was now officially recognizing unions as legitimate organizations.

The federal government again adjusted its position on labor issues following World War II. Postwar prosperity in the United States led labor to seek a greater share of the nation's wealth. The result was a record number of strikes, which aroused national concern. In 1947, the Taft-Hartley Act introduced a number of new restrictions on union activity. For example, the law set guidelines for government response to strikes that involved matters of public health and safety.

Government and Labor in Recent Years

In recent years, the federal government has continued to regulate and monitor the activities of labor unions. In 1981, President Ronald Reagan ordered the firing of striking members of the Professional Air Traffic Controllers Organization, whose walkout violated federal law. And, in the late 1980s, the Justice Department pursued racketeering charges against the Teamsters' Union in response to allegations of widespread corruption and links to organized crime in that union. In settling the charges in 1989, the Teamsters agreed to reform the process by which the union elects its leaders.

REVIEWING THE FACTS

1. For what reason did business choose not to negotiate with unions in the early 1900s?
2. What events helped shape government's approach to labor in the 1900s?

Critical Thinking

3. **Making Comparisons** Summarize the difference between the federal government's approach to labor in 1900 and today.

1947 Unions seek a greater share of the enormous postwar prosperity in a wave of strikes. Congress passes Taft-Hartley Act to curb union power.

| 1960 | 1980 | 2000 |

1962 President John F. Kennedy issues an executive order that protects federal employees' right to organize and bargain collectively, but not to strike.

1993 The Teamsters union hopes to begin a new era following settlement of its dispute with the federal government over charges of corruption.

Chapter Review

Understanding Key Terms, People, and Places

Key Terms
1. transcontinental railroad
2. Brooklyn Bridge
3. social Darwinism
4. monopoly
5. cartel
6. trust
7. horizontal consolidation
8. vertical consolidation
9. economy of scale
10. piecework
11. socialism
12. collective bargaining
13. scab
14. anarchist
15. Pullman strike

People
16. Thomas A. Edison

17. Alexander Graham Bell
18. Andrew Carnegie
19. Pinkerton

Places
20. Haymarket Square
21. Homestead

Terms For each term above, write a sentence that explains its relation to the technological revolution or the rise of big business in the late 1800s.

Matching Review the key terms in the list above. If you are not sure of a term's meaning, review its definition in the chapter. Then choose a term from the list that best matches each description below.
1. the theory that society should not interfere with the process by which people succeed and fail
2. the result of a business buying out all of its competitors
3. loose associations created by businesses making the same product
4. a system by which employers pay workers a fixed amount for each piece they produce
5. an economic and political philosophy that advocates collective or government ownership of factories

True or False Determine whether each statement is true or false. If it is true, write "true." If it is false, change the underlined person or place to make the statement true.
1. Layoffs and a drop in wages led to the <u>Pullman strike</u> near Chicago.
2. <u>Thomas A. Edison</u> lowered his prices, drove competitors out of business, took control of the steel industry, and then devoted himself to philanthropy.
3. When Henry Frick cut wages at the Carnegie steel plant in <u>Pinkerton</u>, Pennsylvania, the union responded by calling a strike.
4. Violence erupted in Chicago's <u>Haymarket Square</u> when someone threw a bomb during a rally to support striking workers.
5. <u>Alexander Graham Bell</u> set up an "invention" factory in New Jersey.

Reviewing Main Ideas

Section 1 (pp. 252–257)
1. How did each of the following contribute to the technological revolution of the late 1800s: (a) Thomas A. Edison, (b) George Westinghouse, (c) Alexander Graham Bell.
2. Describe the problems that existed on the early railroads and five developments that helped solve them.

Section 2 (pp. 259–263)
3. Explain what is meant by the age of big business.
4. Describe how industrialists could be seen as both captains of industry and robber barons.
5. How did Samuel Dodd's idea of the trust get around laws against monopolies?

Section 3 (pp. 264–277)
6. The growth of industry depended on the movement of millions of people to the nation's industrial centers. Where did most of these workers come from?
7. How did the growth of industry affect women's lives?
8. What were some of the hazards faced by factory workers in the late 1800s?

Section 4 (pp. 268–273)
9. Describe the growth of early labor unions.
10. How did the federal government respond to the Great Strikes of the late 1800s?
11. How did the federal government respond to unions in the years following the Pullman strike?

1. **Making Comparisons** How have the inventions of the past thirty years changed daily life for you? Imagine that it is the year 1900. How have the inventions since the Civil War changed your daily life?

2. **Identifying Assumptions** During the late 1800s, many people began to associate labor unions with violence and radical political ideas. Why did people make this association?

1. **Evaluating Primary Sources** Review the first primary source excerpt on page 260. How does Finley Peter Dunne ridicule Andrew Carnegie's actions as a philanthropist? What underlying concern is being expressed?

2. **Understanding the Visuals** Choose two visuals from the chapter that demonstrate the inequality of labor and business in the late 1800s and explain why you think they demonstrate the point.

3. **Writing About the Chapter** It is 1900. Write a letter to the editor of your local newspaper. Describe the harsh conditions endured by factory workers and recommend changes that factory owners and the government could make that would help improve conditions. First, choose several examples from the chapter that document the difficult life of the factory worker. Then, list some possible improvements. Next, write a draft of your letter, in which you offer your evidence and your suggestions. Revise your letter, making sure that you have expressed your points clearly and forcefully. Proofread your work and draft a final copy.

4. **Using the Graphic Organizer** This graphic organizer uses a multi-flow map to organize information about the friction between labor and employers in the late 1800s. Multi-flow maps can show the causes and effects of events in history. In this map, the red box on the left shows the major cause of unrest, and the boxes on the right show the effects. (a) Based on what you have read in the chapter, why did labor unions grow significantly in the 1860s and 1870s? (b) Based on the multi-flow map, what were the effects of the railroad strike of 1877? (c) On a separate sheet of paper, create your own graphic organizer about the technological revolution using this graphic organizer as an example.

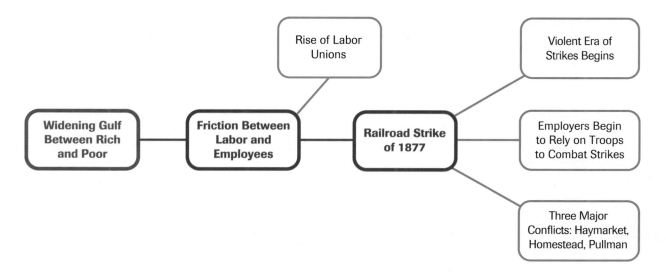

Rise of Labor Unions

Violent Era of Strikes Begins

Widening Gulf Between Rich and Poor

Friction Between Labor and Employees

Railroad Strike of 1877

Employers Begin to Rely on Troops to Combat Strikes

Three Major Conflicts: Haymarket, Homestead, Pullman

Looking to the West
1860–1900

*A*fter the Civil War, Americans accelerated their conquest of the lands west of the Mississippi River. The story of that conquest is one of hard-working farm and ranch families and determined miners. It is a tale of the bravery of those who left all behind to try a new life and of the difficulty of working the dry land. Born of these weighty realities, however, is an American myth. This myth focuses on only white Americans and ignores the story of the realized hopes of some African Americans and Asians—and the crushed hopes of others. It also ignores the tragic tale of those from whom the West was taken—the tale of the near destruction of Native American people and their cultures.

Events in the United States

1862 Congress passes the Morrill Land-Grant Act and the Homestead Act to give away public land.

1866 Oliver H. Kelly founds the Grange, an organization for farmers.

1874 Gold lures miners to Dakota's Black Hills.
• J. Glidden invents barbed wire.

1860	1864	1868	1872	1876

Events in the World

1861 Charles Dickens publishes Great Expectations.

1868 Imperial capital of Japan moves to Tokyo.
• Bones of Cro-Magnon are found in France.

Pages 280–283
Moving West
The West promised new opportunities for those who would brave its loneliness and hardships. Though settlers often found more toil than wealth in the West, many found freedoms unavailable to them elsewhere.

Pages 284–287
The Conquest of the Native Americans
Western settlers thought they were building a new life in a new land. But the land was not new at all. Much of it was ancient homeland to a number of Native American groups.

Pages 288–291
Modernization, Mining, and Ranching
The West was home for thousands of years to Native Americans. But modern farming methods, discovery of mineral deposits, and ranching soon made the West attractive to many others, including big business.

Pages 294–298
Populism
By the late 1800s, American farmers were feeding the nation and the world, yet they were increasingly concerned about feeding themselves. Declining incomes created fertile ground for a farmers' protest.

Pages 300–303
Frontier Myths
From modern rodeos to cowboy boots to novels immortalizing the prairie farmer, the wild West captures the imagination. But this image leaves out many other experiences that also helped shape the nation.

1881 *Helen Hunt Jackson publishes* A Century of Dishonor, *protesting Native Americans' treatment.*

1885 *Annie Oakley joins Buffalo Bill's "Wild West" show.*
• *Unauthorized fencing of public land is outlawed.*

1889 *The federal government opens Indian Territory to settlers.*

1893 *Frederick Jackson Turner delivers the "Turner Thesis."*
• *Colorado adopts women's suffrage.*

1900 *Congress passes a gold standard.*

1880	1884	1888	1892	1896	1900

1880 *Rodín's sculpture* The Thinker *is exhibited.*
• *Chile begins war with Bolivia and Peru.*

1885 *Belgian king Leopold II takes possession of the Congo in Africa.*

1891 *Famine strikes Russia.*

1898 *Marie and Pierre Curie discover radium and introduce the term radioactivity.*

Moving West

SECTION PREVIEW

The West promised new opportunities for those who would brave its loneliness and hardships. Though settlers often found more toil than wealth in the West, many found freedoms unavailable to them elsewhere.

Key Concepts
- Big business controlled much of the land in the West.
- Settlers from the United States acquired land in the West from big business or government grants.
  - Women and African Americans found unique opportunities in the West.
  - Life in the West meant difficult work and required cooperation among settlers.

Key Terms, People, and Places
Morrill Land-Grant Act, speculator, Homestead Act; Exoduster

Only the settlers' most cherished possessions made the trip west.

As the nation swelled with new inventions and businesses during the late 1800s, it also expanded across the continent. The story of this expansion is one of rugged frontier families, big businesses, and bold individuals who were willing to take a chance on the unknown.

Seeking Opportunity in the West

By the Civil War, Americans already had settled areas west of the Mississippi and along parts of the West Coast. Following the war, they began filling in the areas in between—the Great Plains, the Pacific Northwest, the Southwest. To most people in the United States, this land was "the West."

Americans and Europeans wanted to settle in the West for many reasons. Most hoped for a new start in life—a chance to own a farm and be their own boss, a goal that seemed increasingly unattainable in the East. Others were fleeing racial prejudice or, for some Europeans, compulsory military service in their homelands.

Big Business Takes Its Share Much of the western lands to which people were flocking belonged to big businesses—railroad, road and canal, timber, and mining companies. These companies had received huge grants of land from the federal government and made a profit from selling the land to others. When the railroads sold to farmers who worked the land and needed to transport their goods to the cities, the railroads profited even more.

To lure settlers, companies sent agents to Europe who spoke glowingly of immigration to the United States. Businesses also sent out imaginative ads, many of which stretched the truth. One brochure from a western land office falsely described Dakota as a paradise where

> *mocking birds and gorgeous paroquets [parakeets] and cockatoos warble musical challenges to each other amid the rich foliage of the sweet-bay and mango trees.*

Disposing of Government Lands Settlers also bought land as a result of the **Morrill Land-Grant Act** of 1862. This act, plus various other land grants, gave 140 million acres of western lands to state governments. States could then sell the land to fund agricultural colleges. The states sold their land grants at fifty cents an acre to bankers and land **speculators,** people who bought up large areas of land in the hope of later selling it for a profit. Indeed, when settlers began to move westward and demand for land increased, speculators could sell their holdings at five to ten dollars an acre.

The government also gave land directly to settlers through the 1862 **Homestead Act**. This act offered American citizens and immigrants who planned to be citizens 160 acres of public land each for a ten-dollar registration fee. After building a house and living and farming on the land for five consecutive years, the settler could claim ownership.

Thousands of homesteaders benefited from the Homestead Act. Many others, however, could not afford the filing fees, the expense of moving to and setting up a homestead, and the costs of farm machinery. Moreover, most city folk had no farming experience. In the end, experienced farm families migrating from nearby states or from Europe were the most likely homesteaders. Even they had trouble finding good claims near transportation—necessary if they were going to ship their goods to market—for the government gave the railroads much of the land near their tracks. Speculators controlled many other desirable lands.

The Homestead Act also was plagued by fraud. The goal of the act was to give land to people who would then live on it. To prove continuous residence, the government required homesteaders to build permanent shelters on their claims. But speculators simply wheeled portable cabins from plot to plot or built miniature shelters on several plots and then filed phony claims. Land office agents seldom verified them, as distances were too great. Besides, they made their living from the filing fees that those who staked claims were required to pay.

By 1900, individual homesteading families had filed 600,000 claims for 80 million acres. Meanwhile, over six times as much public land had gone to business interests.

Opportunity for African Americans

Some homesteaders went West to escape violence and exploitation. In the late 1870s, southern African Americans planned a mass "Exodus," similar to the biblical account of the Israelites' flight from Egypt to the promised land. For this reason, these settlers called themselves **Exodusters.** At an 1875 meeting of ministers in New Orleans, one Georgia preacher elaborated on what the African American settlers hoped to find farther north:

Homesteading gave people a chance to become landowners—a dream that had been beyond the reach of most African Americans in the South and East.

Homesteaders burned dried buffalo or cattle dung, corn cobs and stalks, even bundles of grass to keep warm.

Sod also covered the roof, which leaked terribly.

Breaking and turning the thick sod was hard work.

Wind was an abundant energy source. Homesteaders often built windmills to power their water pumps.

Three-foot strips of sod—"Nebraska marble"—were stacked to make the walls.

Soddies were filthy inside. Bugs and mice were frequent visitors.

All grown members of the household worked the gardens and fields.

Wells could be several hundred feet deep.

The geography of the West made homesteading a challenge. Timber was often scarce, so settlers built their first shelters out of the endless expanse of sod. The idea for the "soddy" was borrowed from Native American groups of the region.

We will get what we make, our crops or their value . . . ; and may not have to work on the railroad or levees in chain gangs when we are not guilty of any crime, and not to be whipped as if we were dumb brutes; not hated because we are black.

Life was not easy for the almost fifty thousand Exodusters who migrated to Kansas. Some came with money and property, but many did not. Even after finding work, only a few earned enough for a homestead. For those who did, winters were harsher than in the South, and the resettled farmers lacked experience with the crops, such as wheat and corn, widely grown in Kansas. In addition, the Exodusters could not completely escape racial hatred: Kansas, like other western lands, had an active Ku Klux Klan. In spite of these difficulties, Exodusters with farming skills managed to

make a living and in general met with better treatment than they had in the South.

Cooperation in the West

In the West, obtaining even the basic necessities could be a struggle. If settlers were not near water, they had to use buckets or cisterns to collect rainwater for drinking, bathing, and cooking. Such water supplies often carried "prairie fever" or typhoid, so wells were preferable. But until the 1880s, when well-digging machinery became available, settlers had to dig by hand, and groundwater generally lay much deeper in the West than in the East.

Working the tough prairie sod also required backbreaking labor. Even after that work was done, men often had to travel far afield to earn cash for their families' survival while they waited for their crops to come in. Meanwhile, women produced most of the articles that families needed, such as clothing, soap, candles, dairy products, and preserved foods. Wrote homesteader Mary Henderson of Oklahoma of her work on a single day, "I made sausage, rendered lard, molded 4 lbs. butter, halfsoled 3 pairs of shoes, and tonight had to iron [daughter] Agnes a dress."

Settlers relied heavily on each other as they built new communities from the ground up. Families cooperated in raising houses and barns, sewing quilts, husking corn, and providing many other forms of support. "Occasionally a new comer has a 'bee'," noted Howard Ruede about his experience on a Kansas homestead in 1877,

The neighbors for miles around gather at his claim and put up his house in a day. Of course there is no charge for labor in such cases. The women come too, and while the men lay up the sod walls, they prepare dinner for the crowd, and have a very sociable hour at noon.

MAKING CONNECTIONS

You have read about the cooperation among homesteaders in the West. Can you identify and describe similar examples of cooperation in your community today?

A Frontier for Women

Although most homesteaders went West as families, women were able to file claims on their own. Homesteading alone—whether by a man or a woman—was an enormous challenge. Some people, however, such as Wyoming settler Elinore Pruitt Stewart, saw great benefits in the challenge.

It really requires less strength and labor to raise plenty to satisfy a large family than it does to go out to wash, with the added satisfaction of knowing that their job will not be lost to them if they care to keep it. . . . Whatever is raised is the homesteader's own, and there is no house-rent to pay.
  Letters of a Woman Homesteader, 1909

Even for those women who were married, the requirements for getting land through homesteading—continuous residence on a claim for five years—often meant long periods of solitude. Such lonely experiences increased western women's eagerness for opportunities outside the home. Some western women campaigned to improve women's professional opportunities, in areas such as business, medicine, and law.

Western women launched successful city and state campaigns for the vote. In 1887 two Kansas towns, Syracuse and Argonia, passed woman suffrage. Syracuse then elected an all-female town council, and Argonia the nation's first female mayor. By 1914, women were voting in eleven states, all but one of which (Illinois) were west of the Mississippi.

For American settlers in the West, hard work was a small price to pay for the opportunity to build a new future. The homesteaders' opportunity, however, represented a threat to Native Americans there.

SECTION 1 REVIEW

Key Terms, People, and Places
  1. Describe speculators.
  2. Identify (a) Morrill Land-Grant Act, (b) Homestead Act, (c) Exodusters.

Key Concepts
  3. What group controlled most of the land in the West?
  4. How did Americans acquire lands in the West?

  5. Describe some of the hardships homesteaders endured.

Critical Thinking
  6. **Distinguishing False from Accurate Images** In your opinion, was the West a land of opportunity? Cite information from the section to support your answer.

The Conquest of the Native Americans

SECTION PREVIEW

Western settlers thought they were building a new life in a new land. But the land was not new at all. Much of it was ancient homeland to a number of Native American groups.

Key Concepts

- American expansion into the West led to the near destruction of the Native American nations there.
- When reformers sought to "civilize" surviving Native Americans, their cultures and traditions were all but lost.

Key Terms, People, and Places

squatter, boomer, sooner; George Armstrong Custer, Chief Sitting Bull, Chief Joseph; Wounded Knee

The late 1800s brought the destruction of many vibrant Native American cultures. This war shirt is made of deer hide, cloth, and fur.

For generations, many Americans have envisioned the West as a wild, empty expanse, freely available to those brave enough to tame it. But the West was not empty. Others had laid claim to it centuries before.

The Second Native American Removal

In the 1830s, President Jackson removed Native American groups living in the East to lands west of the Mississippi. By the end of the Civil War, the remaining Native Americans on United States land lived throughout the Great Plains and the West. Others were crowded into Indian Territory in present-day Oklahoma.

Following the Civil War, the railroads began pushing their way deeper into the West. With each rail laid, the Native Americans' chances for survival became bleaker. The Plains soon swarmed with settlers, many of whom felt justified in taking Native American lands because they could produce more food and wealth than did the Native Americans.

Many Native Americans, on the other hand, saw the oncoming settlers as invaders. They wanted to continue to live off their lands as they had for centuries, preserving long-held customs and honoring ancient burial grounds.

A Pattern of Conflict

When settlers from the East began to move westward in the mid-1800s, some Native Americans did not find the newcomers threatening and initiated friendly contacts. Others, however, resisted violently. Many groups, realizing that they were outgunned and outnumbered, signed treaties that sold their lands and accepted federal government demands that they live within reservations set aside for them.

But many of these agreements fell apart, sometimes because not all the members of a group supported them. In addition, Native Americans' and settlers' concepts of owning land differed. When Native Americans signed treaties, they often did not realize that settlers would not let them continue using the land. Isolated acts of violence on both sides set off cycles of revenge and counter-revenge.

The Final Destruction One by one, Native American groups fell. (See the map at right and the Illustrated Data Bank in the reference section.) From the 1860s to the 1880s, the Navaho and the Apache of the Southwest were forced onto reservations, starved, or killed in battle. In the 1860s and 1870s, the Cheyenne were destroyed. The first blow came in 1864, with

Colonel John M. Chivington's massacre of men, women, and children in a peaceful village at Sand Creek in present-day Colorado. Some reports put the number of dead as high as 450. After two more wars in 1868 and 1876, the Cheyenne finally surrendered in 1877.

Sitting Bull and the Fall of the Sioux One of the leaders in the destruction of the Cheyenne was Lieutenant Colonel **George Armstrong Custer**. Following that encounter, Custer turned to the Sioux people living in what is now South Dakota. A number of these Sioux had joined **Chief Sitting Bull** and left their Black Hills reservation. In June 1876, Custer moved his cavalry toward the Little Bighorn River in what is now Montana. There he met a larger-than-expected Sioux force. In the clash that followed—the Battle of Little Bighorn—

Custer and the unit he commanded were all killed. Sitting Bull became a fugitive, finally returning to a Sioux reservation five years later.

Following Sitting Bull's death, soldiers of the Seventh Cavalry tried to arrest a group of the chief's followers in 1890. While this was taking place, someone fired a shot. The soldiers then opened fire, killing over two hundred unarmed Sioux in what later became known as the massacre at **Wounded Knee**.

AMERICAN PROFILES

Chief Joseph

The Nez Percé inhabited a large area in what is now Idaho and the eastern sections of Washington and Oregon. In the 1850s and 1860s, some Nez Percé signed treaties agreeing

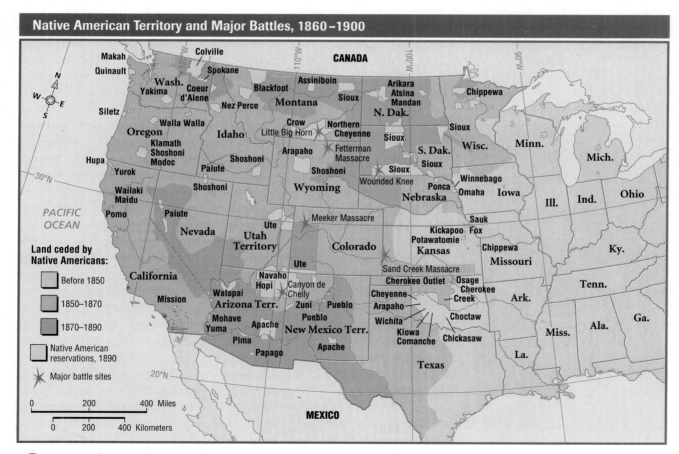

Native American Territory and Major Battles, 1860–1900

Land ceded by Native Americans:
- Before 1850
- 1850–1870
- 1870–1890
- Native American reservations, 1890
- ✳ Major battle sites

🌎 **Geography and History: Interpreting Maps**
Though Native Americans won occasional victories in isolated battles, they were vastly outnumbered and defeat was sure to follow. *What pattern can you see in the location of the remaining Native American reservations in 1890?*

to sell their lands to the government. But the largest group, which lived in the Wallowa Valley at the crossroads of the three states, refused. As the chief of this group lay dying in 1871, he made his son and successor, Joseph, swear never to sell their homeland.

Fulfilling that promise proved impossible. After pressuring **Chief Joseph** (1840–1904) for five years, General Oliver Otis Howard finally ordered him and his people to leave Wallowa Valley for a reservation in Idaho. Faced with the threat of superior force, Chief Joseph felt he must give in. Before he could do so, however, a group of Nez Percé youths attacked some settlers who had been accused of stealing Nez Percé horses. The Nez Percé and the United States government were now at war.

Chief Joseph wanted to stay and fight, but his advisory council thought that they could escape. Pursued by soldiers, the Nez Percé fled. Eventually, Chief Joseph's group reached Montana. Exhausted, they set up camp at Big Hole Basin, but in a surprise 4:30 A.M. raid, United States soldiers attacked, killing men, women, and children.

The Nez Percé who escaped looked to Canada as their last hope for freedom. On September 30, 1877, less than forty miles from Canada, Colonel Nelson Miles's cavalry charged them. Heavily outnumbered, Chief Joseph had no choice but to surrender. "I am tired of fighting," he is reported to have said.

Chief Joseph led his Nez Percé on a dramatic flight from United States troops. To his great sadness, he never returned to his homeland.

T he old men are dead. The children are freezing to death. Hear me, my chiefs! My heart is sick and sad. From where the sun now stands, I will fight no more forever.

Chief Joseph, 1877

The government sent Chief Joseph's people to Indian Territory. There, due to heat and malaria, many more Nez Percé died, including all of Joseph's children. In 1885 Chief Joseph and the remaining Nez Percé were allowed to leave the territory for a reservation in present-day Washington state, but the federal government did not allow them to return to their beloved Wallowa Valley.

The Destruction of Native American Cultures

As United States soldiers defeated Native American groups, many aspects of Native American cultures also disappeared. The peoples of the Great Plains, for example, relied on the buffalo for food, clothing, shelter, fuel, and tools. By the 1870s, the great buffalo herds began to disappear, hunted by the railroads to feed their workers and by settlers to clear the range, to satisfy a craze for hides, and for sport. The federal government encouraged the slaughter to wipe out the Plains peoples' food supply, a policy that later destroyed the Native Americans' ability to build new lives on reservations.

Some white Americans found such treatment horrifying. Inspired in part by Helen Hunt Jackson's 1881 publication *A Century of Dishonor*, a national "Indian rights" movement arose. Protesting what she saw as the government's broken promises and treaties, Jackson said, "It makes little difference . . . where one opens the record of the history of the Indians; every page and every year has its dark stain."

As sincere as reformers were, however, most believed that Native Americans needed to be "civilized." Christian missionaries, who ran schools on the reservations, shared this belief.

Other reformers sought to break Native American traditions by requiring Native Americans to farm individual plots. With the Dawes Act of 1887, the government broke up communal villages and gave separate plots to each Native American family headed by a male. Much of the land was not suitable for farming, and many Native Americans had no interest or experience in agriculture. Many simply sold their lands to speculators: between 1887 and 1934, the amount of land owned by Native Americans shrank by 65 percent.

Does the reformers' desire to "civilize" Native Americans reveal a bias? If so, what is the bias?

The Fate of Indian Territory

Relocation into Indian Territory had been difficult for the nearly seventy groups who were removed there, but worse was to come. Following the Civil War, a flood of whites began to enter the territory. Some worked for Native American landowners as tenants or sharecroppers. Others were **squatters,** people who move onto land that does not belong to them.

Although Native Americans protested and the government tried to stop them, squatters continued to come. Other would-be settlers—so-called **boomers**—pressured Congress to allow legal settlement in the territory. In 1889 Congress responded, opening for homesteading nearly two million acres of lands in Indian Territory that had not yet been assigned to Native Americans. At noon on April 22, soldiers signaled with their pistols and hundreds of homesteaders, called **sooners** if they had sneaked in earlier, rushed across the border to stake claims.

A long the line as far as the eye could reach, with a shout and a yell the swift riders shot out, then followed the light buggies or wagons and last the lumbering prairie schooner and freighters' wagons, with here and there even a man on a bicycle and many too on foot,—above all a

Viewpoints
On Land Use

As more and more settlers pushed into the West, it became clear that they and the Native Americans held different attitudes toward the land. *Which of the attitudes expressed below do you think is more common today?*

Respecting the Environment

"The ground says, The Great Spirit has placed me here to produce all that grows on me, trees and fruit. The same way the ground says, It was from me man was made. The Great Spirit, in placing men on the earth, desired them to take good care of the ground and to do each other no harm."
                    Young Chief of the Cayuse, on opposing selling land
                                           in Washington Territory, 1855

Conquering the Environment

"To open the greatest number of mines and extract the greatest quantity of ore, to scatter cattle over a thousand hills, to turn the flower-spangled prairies . . . into wheatfields, . . . to force from nature the most she can be made to yield . . . is preached by Western newspapers as a kind of religion."
                              Britain's Lord James Bryce, after visiting
                                          the American West in the 1880s

great cloud of dust hovering like smoke over a battlefield.
                                   Newspaper Reporter, 1889

As a result of pressures bearing on Native Americans in the late 1800s, many native populations disappeared. Others survived, slowly increasing their numbers and restoring the memory and practice of their customs.

SECTION 2 REVIEW

Key Terms, People, and Places
1. Identify (a) George Armstrong Custer, (b) Chief Sitting Bull, (c) Chief Joseph, (d) Wounded Knee.
2. Define (a) squatter, (b) boomer, (c) sooner.

Key Concepts
3. How did the extension of the railroad increase the pressure on Native American lands?
4. Why and how did the "second great removal" occur?

5. What was the result of the decision to allow settlement in Indian Territory?

Critical Thinking
6. **Distinguishing False from Accurate Images**
   Many people in the mid-1800s believed that Native Americans used their land "only" for hunting and subsistence farming. Find information from the text to prove that this belief was untrue.

Modernization, Mining, and Ranching

SECTION PREVIEW

The West was home for thousands of years to Native Americans. But modern farming methods, discovery of mineral deposits, and ranching soon made the West attractive to many others, including big business.

Key Concepts
- Modernization, mechanization, and "big business" methods transformed agriculture in the West.
- Mining and ranching in the West and Southwest provided opportunities for some.
- Big business practices came to dominate mining and ranching industries.

Key Terms, People, and Places
bonanza farms, cash crops, long drive

American ranchers borrowed techniques and equipment—such as these spurs—from Mexicans of the Southwest.

The spread of the United States into the West involved many challenges. Two stand out. The first was coming to terms with the native populations already living there, which Americans achieved by conquest. The second challenge lay in making the land fruitful. Inventors and industrialists solved this problem and reaped great riches as a result.

Modernization of Farming on the Great Plains

Despite the misinformation sent out by western land offices and the railroads, the Great Plains was not a farmer's paradise. Rainfall was unpredictable, and never enough. Tough prairie grass, which had thick roots that plunged deep into the earth, plagued farmers who struggled to break its iron grip on the soil. Grasshoppers, locusts, and boll weevils ruined crops and destroyed property. But the same inventiveness that had helped spur industrial expansion in the East helped overcome such difficulties in the West.

Mechanization on the Farm In many of the best farming areas of the East, 80 acres of farmland could provide a farmer with a living. Because the dry climate in parts of the West reduced the land's productivity, a farmer there needed 360 acres—one reason for the Homestead Act's limited success. Because western farms had to be so large, farmers welcomed any mechanical means to reduce the time and effort needed to work the land.

During the 1870s, improvements in farm implements multiplied. Soon farmers were riding behind a plow and plowing several furrows at once. Other inventions included harrows equipped with spring teeth that dislodged debris and automatic drills to spread grain. By 1880, farmers were using automatic grain binders and, later, a "header" drawn by six horses, which cut off the heads of standing grain. Steam-powered threshers arrived on the scene by 1875 and cornhuskers and cornbinders by the 1890s.

Manual vs. Mechanical Harvesting		
Method	Hours Required Per Acre Per Person	Maximum Acreage Harvested
Manual	61	7.5
Mechanical	3	135

Interpreting Tables
Mechanization meant a dramatic increase in the amount of crop a worker could harvest. *By what factor did mechanization reduce the amount of labor necessary for harvesting?*

Irrigation Then and Now

In the late 1800s, some homesteaders in the dry regions of the United States used wind-driven pumps to draw water from the ground. The water was then fed into ditches and out onto their fields. Many farmers in the same regions today use enormous systems that draw water from deep in the earth. The quarter-mile-long arms of these sprinklers rotate like the hands of a clock, creating a large irrigated area. *How have such technologies increased the productivity of the land?*

Agricultural Knowledge Grows Congress established the Department of Agriculture in 1862 as part of the Morrill Land-Grant Act. In the 1880s and 1890s, the department was gathering statistics on markets, crops, and diseases that affected agriculture. It set up divisions to study forestry, the animal and dairy industries, and fruit and vegetable growing.

Working together, government agricultural departments and agricultural colleges funded the work of experiment stations and held institutes that offered entertainment and inspiration to farm families. They also published materials that explained crop rotation, hybridization (the crossing of different plants to produce new varieties), and the preservation of water and topsoil.

The Big Business of "Bonanza" Farms New machines and agricultural knowledge in the late 1800s increased enormously the amount a farm could produce (see chart on page 288). Entrepreneurs who owned large areas of land now hoped to reap a "bonanza" by supplying food to the rising populations of the East. They began applying to farming the same organiza-

tional ideas then taking hold in industry. As one observer noted,

> I t is no longer left to the small farmer, taking up 160 acres of land, building a log cabin and struggling to secure himself a home. Organized capital is being employed in the work, with all the advantages which organization implies. Companies and partnerships are formed for the cultivation precisely as they are for building railroads, manufactures, etc.
>
> *Commercial and Financial Chronicle, 1879*

Bonanza farms—farms controlled by large businesses and managed by professionals—promised enormous profits to investors. They specialized in single **cash crops** raised for and readily sold at market. But these farms had their down side, as well. When the market became glutted with the enormous quantities of food they produced, prices fell. Small-scale farmers suffered the most, but even corporate giants felt the blow.

By the late 1800s, machines such as those shown in this detail from an advertisement of the time performed many harvesting tasks.

The Impact of New Farm Machinery Grain binders, threshers, and the like did not always lead to prosperity for farmers. Machines could not protect farmers against insect plagues or bad weather. Moreover, once farmers had invested in machines, they had to produce only the crop for which the machines were designed. If prices for that crop dipped, farmers could not pay off their debts. Such dips in prices were a common problem for many farmers. Wheat, for example, sold at $2.06 a bushel in 1866. By 1895 it had dropped to 51 cents. Even bonanza farmers suffered.

MAKING CONNECTIONS

Can you think of other inventions during the late 1800s that had negative, as well as positive, effects on people?

It is unlikely that this man struck it rich panning for gold. Far more successful were those who "mined the miners," or sold goods to the fortune-seekers.

Boom and Bust Strike the Mining Frontier

"Gold!" The word alone conjures up the image of a lucky prospector striking it rich. In reality, such individuals were rare and largely a phenomenon of short rushes, such as the California gold rush of 1849. By the late 1850s and early 1860s, most of the precious metals that remained in the West lay deeply buried. Only huge companies could afford the large investments in machinery, mine shafts, and tunnels required to reach these riches.

"Pikes Peak or Bust!" Still, thousands kept coming. In 1859, rumors of gold strikes in the area of Pikes Peak, Colorado, brought on a stampede of wagons with the words "Pikes Peak or Bust!" scrawled on their sides. Also in 1859, Nevada's famed "Comstock Lode," a large silver strike, brought on another rush. Gold and silver strikes throughout the West lured thousands of fortune hunters over the next several years. One of the later strikes in the Black Hills of Dakota in 1874, brought a stampede that led to conflicts with Sioux living there.

Mining communities brought together people of all colors, ethnic backgrounds, and levels of education. Asians, especially men from China who had tired of railway work, often became miners. Clara Brown, who had been enslaved in Virginia, saved enough to buy her freedom and journeyed to Colorado in 1857 to cook and wash clothes for miners. She saved enough to invest in the mines and become one of Colorado's richest citizens.

Miners worked and played hard. Widespread gambling and drunkenness gave mining towns reputations for vice. Actually, most towns settled down quickly. With sufficient population and the arrival of big companies that gave communities stability, territorial government and statehood followed.

The Mining Boom Ends A handful of miners actually struck it rich in the West, but most did not. When prospectors finally realized that all the precious metal was gone, they straggled home, leaving most mining cities deserted ghost towns. Large corporations still brought up copper, tin, and deeply buried gold and silver deposits. Like so many other industries, mining became the realm of big business.

The Cattle Frontier

When American settlers began to arrive in Texas in the early 1800s, they learned the cattle ranching ways of the Mexicans living there. It was not long before Americans had adopted Mexican ranching equipment and dress, and Texas longhorn cattle as their own.

During the 1860s and 1870s, the cattle ranching industry boomed in the West. The destruction of the buffalo and removal of Native Americans to reservations emptied the land for grazing cattle. And the extension of railroads into the West provided a means of shipping cattle to markets across the country.

Entrepreneurs, using techniques borrowed from the industrial East, began to develop profitable large-scale cattle businesses, complete from cattle ranges to stockyards. Individual cattle drivers did not do as well. These workers, about a fifth of whom were African American or Mexican, were responsible for the **long drive**— the moving of cattle from distant ranges to busy railroad centers that shipped the cattle to market. Cowboys often led their cattle along well-known cow trails like the Goodnight-Loving and the Chisholm trails.

The long drive was hard, dangerous work and required braving rough, muddy trails, pounding thunderstorms, and attacks by cattle thieves. Stampedes were another danger. Recalled one cowboy of his experience in a stampede, "We found 341 dead cattle, two dead horses, one dead cowboy and two more with broken legs after the herd had passed." Yet cattle drivers and cowboys earned low wages, in the 1870s about thirty dollars a month.

The End of an Era The cattle boom ended in the mid-1880s as a result of several factors. One factor was Joseph Glidden's 1874 invention of barbed wire, which he claimed was "Light as air. . . . Cheaper than dirt. All steel and miles long. The cattle ain't born that can get through it." As a result of this invention, farmers could fence their land and keep out grazing cattle that had caused much conflict between farmers and ranchers. Thus the open range on which ranchers had freely grazed their huge herds began to disappear. The final death knell of the cattle boom sounded when cold winters, dry summers, and cattle fever destroyed many herds and bankrupted thousands of ranchers. Cattle ranching survived, but on a much smaller scale and with new breeds of cattle that largely replaced the Texas longhorn.

Charles Russell's painting "Jerked Down" (1907) illustrates the dangerous work of the cowhand. The open range on which such scenes took place began to disappear with the introduction of barbed wire fencing in the 1870s. The new invention was featured in ads like the one above.

SECTION 3 REVIEW

Key Terms, People, and Places
1. Describe (a) cash crops, (b) long drive.

Key Concepts
2. How were farms modernized in the late nineteenth century?
3. What was bonanza farming? Who used it?
4. What was the impact of mechanization on farming?

5. In the later mining "booms" of the nineteenth century, did many individuals "strike it rich"? Why or why not?
6. Describe the ranching industry in the late 1800s.

Critical Thinking
7. **Identifying Central Issues** Briefly describe the benefits and drawbacks of new farm machinery and knowledge.

The End of the Open Range

In the last half of the nineteenth century, farmers and ranchers battled over the way that land would be used on the vast western plains. How did this struggle begin, and what was its outcome?

For thousands of years before the first European settlers arrived, Native Americans hunted great bison herds on the vast expanse of grasslands between the Mississippi River and the Rocky Mountains. In the 1800s, however, settlers began to move into the West and drove Native Americans off the land. The new settlers then began to battle with one another over the way this land would be used.

Linking Land Use and Resources

The map on page 293 shows land use in the American West today. Land use is the primary economic activity that takes place in a region. Many categories of economic activity are related to a region's natural resources and climate. Farming, for example, takes place most successfully in a region with good soil, enough water, and a long growing season.

Generally, a single economic activity, or land use, dominates a region. One reason for this is that different economic activities sometimes interfere with one another; for example, if farmers clear trees from land, those trees are not available for forestry. Also, when an economic activity makes intense use of the land and employs many people, it tends to crowd out other land uses.

Free-ranging cattle and cattle being driven to market trampled unprotected crops, and the treeless, stoneless prairie supplied no material from which to build fences to keep them out.

The Growth of Open-Range Ranching

At the beginning of the 1800s, few people looking for land to settle saw a use for the western plains. Until the 1850s, most Americans from east of the Mississippi River hurried through the plains on their way farther west.

The first Americans to settle on the plains made use of the seemingly limitless grasslands to raise cattle. Cattle ranchers were especially attracted to Texas with its herds of free-roaming longhorns. The ranchers fed their cattle on the available grass and watered them in the open streams and rivers that meandered through the plains. Then the ranchers rounded them up for market.

The ranchers' biggest problem was the great distance that separated their cattle and their customers in the cities of the Northeast. Although the journey could be dangerous, the big demand and the high prices paid for beef convinced cattlemen to take the risk and drive their cattle several hundred miles north to the railroads. The first of these long drives went from Texas to Sedalia, Missouri, in 1866.

As the railroads extended west and south, the distance between grazing land and the railroads decreased. "Cow towns" sprang up on the Great Plains next to the rail lines. Ellsworth, Wichita, and Dodge City in Kansas, Cheyenne and Laramie in Wyoming, and other towns processed millions of head of cattle during the late 1870s and early 1880s.

The Arrival of the Sod Busters

Farmers soon discovered that beneath the grassy surface of the prairies was not sand but as much as six feet of fertile topsoil. The prairie grasses,

Livestock raising
Commercial farming
Forestry
Manufacturing and trade
Little or no activity

Less than 20" annual rainfall

More than 20" annual rainfall

however, imprisoned this topsoil with a layer of dense roots called sod. Before land could be farmed, the tough, centuries-old sod had to be broken up. Although "sod busting" required the most advanced and expensive plows, farmers arrived by the thousands, encouraged by the federal government and the railroads to make the West their home.

The first homesteaders found that, among other obstacles, open-range ranching threatened their hard-earned farms. Free-ranging cattle and cattle being driven to market trampled unprotected crops, and the treeless, stoneless prairie supplied no material from which to build fences to keep them out. Barbed wire, introduced in 1874, solved this problem but created another.

The Range Wars

Angered by the farmers' attempts to fence off the land, some ranchers started to enclose huge areas. The ranchers' illegal fences sometimes cut farmers off from roads and water supplies. Farmers fought back by cutting the barbed wire and seeking government help. The ranchers mended their fences and protected them with gunfire.

Soon, even cattlemen with fenced ranches were crowded out by the farmers. Farmers could make a living with much less land than cattle ranchers. Because the federal government had a land policy that tried to benefit the largest number of people, it helped the many small farmers more than it helped the few cattle ranchers. Government land-use laws increasingly made open-range ranching impossible. Finally, several years of unusual weather all but destroyed the herds.

GEOGRAPHIC CONNECTIONS

1. In what way were the railroads essential to the success of both ranching and farming on the western plains?
2. Why did the federal government support land-use laws that favored farmers over ranchers?

Critical Thinking

3. **Synthesizing information** The western plains receive less than half the rainfall of those parts closest to the Mississippi River. How does this difference in rainfall help explain the land-use pattern shown on the map?

Populism

By the late 1800s, American farmers were feeding the nation and the world, yet they were increasingly concerned about feeding themselves. Declining incomes created fertile ground for a farmers' protest.

Key Concepts
- Farmers began to protest their plight at the close of the century.
- A political movement called populism flashed on the scene and quickly faded out.

Key Terms, People, and Places
deflation, currency policy, the Grange; Populists, William Jennings Bryan

Many Americans favored the use of silver to increase the nation's currency supply in the late 1800s.

I n 1869 journalist Henry George arrived in New York City from the West Coast. Side by side with the city's great "palaces of the princely rich," he saw so much poverty that he wondered how such inequality could exist. In his 1879 book, *Progress and Poverty,* he warned that

> S o long as all the increased wealth which modern progress brings goes but to build up great fortunes, to increase luxury and make sharper the contrast between the House of Have and the House of Want, progress is not real and cannot be permanent.

Throughout the United States, many other people also began to ask: how could so much progress be surrounded by so much poverty? Farmers were especially vocal in raising this question.

The Farmers' Complaint

Many farmers in the late 1800s were suffering from a long-term decline in crop prices that had begun after the Civil War. New farm machinery and agricultural technologies had increased their yields, but the resulting over-production had glutted markets, causing prices to fall. Moreover, international competition for markets had increased.

These developments worried the nation's farmers. For solutions, they looked to the federal government's economic policies.

Farmers and Tariffs Tariffs impose duties, or taxes, on imported goods. These taxes discourage people from buying imports by making them more expensive. Thus, the sale of goods produced at home is promoted. In the late 1800s, tariffs also brought money to the federal government, which at the time did not tax people's incomes.

Americans in the late 1800s were divided on the benefit of tariffs. Industrialists claimed that protecting American-made goods protected factory jobs—and their own profits. But because tariffs eliminated foreign competition, they also led to higher prices on the goods that workers had to buy.

Farmers resented the high prices of manufactured goods, but they did not want foreign farm produce to enter the United States "duty free." On the other hand, tariffs on farm imports prevented foreigners from earning the American currency they needed to buy American crops. Thus, tariffs hurt American farmers in two ways: by raising their living expenses at home and by lowering what they could earn abroad when exporting their crops.

Whenever the government raised tariffs to benefit industry, farmers protested. They felt that government was favoring manufacturers located in the North and Northeast. Yet tariffs were not the chief concern of the agriculture industry in the late 1800s. The dominant issue for many farmers was "free silver."

Goldbugs, Greenbackers, and Silverites In theory, an increase in the supply of money should tend to produce inflation, a widespread rise in prices on goods of all kinds. In the years following the Civil War, however, the nation's money supply shrank as the federal government took out of circulation the paper money that had been issued during the war. As a result, the nation experienced a prolonged period of dropping prices called **deflation.**

Deflation hurt farmers, whose income and ability to pay off their debts depended on high prices for their crops. Deflation helped bankers and other lenders, however, because the dollars repaid to them could buy more goods than the dollars they had lent out.

Currency policy, the federal government's plan for the makeup and quantity of the nation's money supply, thus emerged as a major issue in national politics. Supporters of inflation pushed for increasing the amount of money in circulation. Supporters of deflation wanted tight money, or less currency in circulation.

In 1873 the supporters of tight money won a victory. Until that time, United States currency had been on a bimetallic standard; that is, currency consisted of gold or silver coins, or United States treasury notes that could be traded in for gold or silver. In 1873 Congress put the nation's currency on a gold standard in an effort to prevent inflation and secure economic stability. This move reduced the amount of money in circulation.

Conservative "goldbugs" were pleased. Many of them were big lenders, and they liked the idea of being repaid in currency backed by gold. But "silverites," mostly silver-mining interests and western farmers, were furious. They claimed that the end of silver as a monetary standard depressed the prices of farm produce. "Greenbackers" also entered the debate. They argued for more paper money, which was not redeemable in gold or silver, as a means of causing inflation.

Free Silver Economists at the time were vague about the impact on crop prices of currency amounts and standards. Nevertheless, farmer protest in the 1870s revolved increasingly around the call for free silver—the unlimited coining of silver dollars as a means of increasing the money supply.

T he dollar of our daddies,
  Of silver coinage free,
Will make us rich and happy,
Will bring prosperity,

went a popular rhyme. Silver did make a limited return to the currency supply in the late 1870s—but not as the free silver promoted by many western interests. In the 1890s, most of the farm protest centered on this hope.

Organizing Farmer Protest

Because farmers lived far from one another and tended to be self-reliant, they resisted efforts at organization. In the late nineteenth century, however, improved communication and transportation systems made united action among the nation's farmers more practical. This, coupled with the widespread economic problems facing many farmers, led to the development of several powerful farm protest groups.

The Grange In 1866 the Department of Agriculture sent Oliver H. Kelley on an inspection tour of southern farms. Disturbed by farmers' isolation, the following year he founded the Patrons of Husbandry, or the **Grange,** a term that came from a word meaning "farm."

The Grange soon began helping farmers form cooperatives with the intent of saving money by buying goods in large quantities. The Grange also pressured legislators to regulate the businesses on which farmers depended—for example, grain elevators that stored the farmers' crops and railroads that shipped it. The railroads, which gave better rates to eastern industrialists, received the brunt of farmers' anger.

Although the Grange was popular, by the mid-1870s farmers were turning to other political outlets. A Greenback party, which focused on currency issues, elected fourteen members to Congress in 1878. Its power quickly faded, however, as more and more farmers adopted the free silver position in the currency debate.

Farmers' Alliances Farmers' Alliances followed the Greenback party in the 1880s. The Alliances launched harsh attacks on monopolies, such as those that controlled the railroads.

Using Historical Evidence Farmers' Alliances provided an important channel for farmer protest and political action in the late 1800s. This illustration comes from a book of songs for these organizations. *What do the images on this songbook cover reveal about the ideals of the Farmers' Alliances?*

Farmers' Alliance." Formed in 1886 in Lovelady, Texas, the group had a quarter of a million members by 1891.

A series of natural disasters gave special urgency to Farmers' Alliance programs. The Mississippi River flooded in 1882. During 1886 to 1887, twenty-one consecutive months of drought in Texas impoverished 30,000 people. Terrible blizzards, which killed thousands of cattle, struck the West in 1887. The federal government's unwillingness to respond to these disasters alienated sufferers.

The Government Responds
During this era, the Democrats and Republicans produced a series of genial but undistinguished Presidents (see Chapter 10). Some had been influenced by promises of support from the era's powerful business interests. In return, these Presidents protected American industry, whose interests often ran counter to those of western and southern farmers.

At the same time, the country was deeply divided over the issues of the day, including the tariff and currency policy. In every election from 1876 to 1892, no candidate won a majority of the popular vote. Only rarely did a President command a party majority in Congress.

Thus, the federal government seemed incapable of responding to farmers' concerns. It did, however, take some actions. In 1887 Congress passed the Texas Seed bill, which appropriated money for seed grain to aid drought victims. But Democratic President Grover Cleveland vetoed the bill, expressing a then commonly held view that "though the people support the government, the government should not support the people." Cleveland did sign the Interstate Commerce Act of 1887, which regulated the charges paid to move freight, such as farmers' crops, between states. Although the act did not control the monopolistic practices of the railroads that so

Alliance lecturer Napoleon B. Ashby accused the nation's big business millionaires of having made their fortunes by preying upon "the mighty rivers of commerce which the farmers have set flowing."

The Farmers' Alliance in the South, a grassroots organization begun in Texas in the mid-1870s to fight cattle thieving and fraudulent land claims, grew into an especially powerful group. The themes it emphasized found support among many of the nation's farmers: federal regulation of the railroads, a greater circulation of currency, state departments of agriculture, antitrust laws, and farm credit.

Farmer's Alliances held special importance for women, who served as officers and won support for women's political rights. Kansas lawyer Mary Elizabeth Lease, whose voice was said to have "hypnotic qualities," was one of their most popular speakers.

African Americans worked through a separate but parallel "Colored

Mary Elizabeth Lease won fame as a Farmers' Alliance speaker.

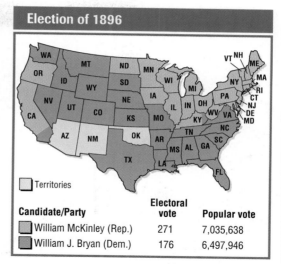

Election of 1892

Candidate/Party	Electoral vote	Popular vote
Grover Cleveland (Dem)	277	5,554,414
Benjamin Harrison (Rep.)	145	5,190,802
James Weaver (People's)	22	1,027,329

Territories

Election of 1896

Candidate/Party	Electoral vote	Popular vote
William McKinley (Rep.)	271	7,035,638
William J. Bryan (Dem.)	176	6,497,946

Territories

Geography and History: Interpreting Maps
In their first presidential election, the People's party ran poorly against both the Democrats and Republicans. In 1896, they shared candidate William Jennings Bryan with the Democrats. *What pattern can you identify in the limited success of the Populists in the presidential elections of 1892 and 1896?*

angered farmers, it did establish the principle that Congress could regulate them. Cleveland's successor, Republican Benjamin Harrison, approved the Sherman Antitrust Act in 1890. As discussed in Chapter 8, this act was meant to curb the power of trusts and monopolies. But during its first decade, enforcement was lax.

MAKING CONNECTIONS

Recall Cleveland's statement that government should not support the people. Is this opinion widely held today? Use examples from current events to support your conclusion.

The Populists Push the Farmers' Program

In 1890 the various small political parties associated with the Farmers' Alliances began to enjoy success at the ballot box, especially in the South. In 1892 the Alliances founded the People's party, a new national party that demanded radical reform in United States economic and social policies. The **Populists,** as followers of the new party were known, called for an increased circulation of money; a silver stan-

dard; and a graduated income tax, which would place a greater tax burden on wealthy industrialists and a lesser one on farmers. The Populist party also called for government ownership of the country's transportation system—which was central to farmers' livelihoods—and communications system. In an effort to attract urban support, they also endorsed an eight-hour work day and opposed the use of Pinkertons as strikebreakers. Finally, they broke through deeply rooted racial prejudice to form a united front of African American and white farmers. As one of the party's most eloquent leaders, Georgian Tom Watson, explained:

Now, the People's Party says to [whites and African Americans], "You are kept apart that you may be separately fleeced of your earnings. You are made to hate each other because upon that hatred is rested the keystone of the arch of financial despotism [absolute power] which enslaves you both. You are deceived and blinded that you may not see how this race antagonism perpetuates a monetary system which beggars both.

The idea that the poor of different races shared a common cause was unique to populism, but the idea enjoyed only a brief life

VOL. 31 NO. 779   SEPTEMBER 19 1896   PRICE 10 CENTS

Judge

THE SACRILEGIOUS CANDIDATE.
No man who drags into the dust the most sacred symbols of the Christian world is fit to be president of the United States.

Using Historical Evidence This cartoon shows William Jennings Bryan wielding the crown of thorns and cross of gold—images that he used in a famous speech. *Is this cartoon presenting Bryan in a positive or a negative light?*

during this period of American politics.

During the 1892 campaign, populism generated great excitement among its followers. But the party's presidential candidate, Iowan James B. Weaver, barely won a million votes. Democratic candidate Grover Cleveland returned to the presidency.

Back in office, Cleveland alienated labor when he put down the Pullman strike. He angered farmers with his support for a gold standard, and manufacturers when he tried to lower the tariff. The 1893 Depression, which had started before he took office, threw millions out of work. When marchers promoting Populist ideas flocked to Washington in 1894, Americans troubled by the great industrial strikes, such as Pullman, added "hayseed socialists" to their list of frightening agitators.

Bryan's "Cross of Gold"

Other Populists looked ahead to the 1896 presidential campaign. In an election that focused mainly on currency issues, the Republicans ran William McKinley on a gold-standard platform. **William Jennings Bryan,** a former silverite congressman from Nebraska and a powerful speaker, captured the Democratic nomination. He overwhelmed his party's convention with a plea for free silver. Using images from the Bible,

he stood with head bowed and arms outstretched and cried out at the climax of his speech,

Y*ou shall not press down upon the brow of labor this crown of thorns. You shall not crucify mankind upon a cross of gold!*

Although the Populists were interested in many issues besides free silver, the impact of Bryan's speech was so great that he captured the Populist nomination, too.

Bryan lost the election, carrying the Democratic West and South but not one of the urban and industrial Midwest and northern states. In these states, factory workers feared that free silver might cause inflation, which would eat away the buying power of their wages. Thus, despite populism's broad appeal, it could not bridge the ever-widening gap between America's cities and farms.

Populism's Legacy

By 1897 McKinley's administration had raised the tariff to new heights. In 1900, after gold strikes in South Africa, the Canadian Yukon, and Alaska had added more than $100 million worth of gold to the world's supply, Congress again passed a gold standard. To the surprise of many farmers, crop prices began a slow rise that would last until 1920. The silver movement died, as did populism.

Many of populism's goals, however, did not fade away. In the decades ahead, other political thinkers applied populist ideas to urban and industrial problems. In so doing, they launched new reform programs that shifted the course of United States history.

SECTION 4 REVIEW

Key Terms, People, and Places
1. Describe (a) deflation, (b) currency policy.
2. Identify: (a) Populists, (b) William Jennings Bryan.

Key Concepts
3. What were farmers' objections to tariffs?
4. What was the farmers' position on the currency question?

5. By what means did farmers organize to protest and present their views?

Critical Thinking
6. **Drawing Conclusions** Populism appealed to people in many parts of the country. How can you explain, then, the failure of the Populist party to win the presidential election?

Drawing Conclusions

Drawing conclusions means finding out an answer or forming an opinion based on information that is suggested but not stated directly. When you read about history or any subject, it is important to be able to draw conclusions. Then you can go beyond what is presented in textbooks and other sources and form new insights about a historical period or event.

Use the following steps and the two passages from the late 1800s that appear on this page to practice drawing conclusions.

1. Study the facts and ideas that the author presents. Read the two passages below, and then answer the following questions about them. (a) What facts does Washington Gladden present to describe the farmers' problems? (b) What factors does Mary Elizabeth Lease cite to explain the farmers' problems as she perceives them?

2. Make a summary statement as a conclusion about a group of details. A statement that summarizes the major points of an argument is one type of conclusion. Clarify each person's position by summarizing the basic information contained in the two passages. Then answer the following questions. (a) From passage A, what can you conclude about the farmers' plight? Would farming be more profitable if farmers worked as hard as laborers?

Or, are the farmers' problems beyond their control? (b) From the information in passage B, what can you conclude about the government's response to the problems the farmers are experiencing? Explain your reasoning.

3. Decide whether or not you can draw a conclusion based on what is stated. If an argument does not contain sufficient information, it is possible to jump to a faulty conclusion. Comparing the information in the two passages should raise some questions in your mind. As you answer these questions, you are deciding whether you have enough information to draw conclusions. (a) Given what you read in both passages, what conclusion can you draw about the relationship between farmers and the Populist party? Explain your answer. (b) Based on Lease's ideas in passage B, what conclusion can you draw concerning the ideas of the Populist party and the ideas of the major political parties?

Passage A

"The business of farming has become, for some reasons, extremely unprofitable. With the hardest work and with the sharpest economy, the average farmer is unable to make both ends meet; every year closes with debt, and the mortgage grows till it devours the land. The Labor Bureau of Connecticut has shown, by an investigation of 693 representative farms, that the average annual reward of the farm proprietor of that state for his expenditure of muscle and brain is $181.31, while the average annual wages of the ordinary hired man is $386.36."

—Washington Gladden, Congregational minister, 1890

Passage B

"The parties lie to us and the political speakers mislead us. We were told two years ago to go to work and raise a big crop, that was all we needed. We went to work and plowed and planted; the rains fell, the sun shone, nature smiled, and we raised the big crop that they told us to. . . . Then the politicians said we suffered from over-production. . . . We want money, land, and transportation. We want the abolition of the national banks, and we want the power to make loans direct from the government. We want the accursed foreclosure system wiped out."

—Mary Elizabeth Lease, Populist leader

Frontier Myths

SECTION PREVIEW

From modern rodeos to cowboy boots to novels immortalizing the prairie farmer, the wild West captures the imagination. But this image leaves out many other experiences that also helped shape the nation.

Key Concepts

• By the turn of the century, Americans believed that the American frontier no longer existed.
• Myths and misconceptions influenced American understanding of the frontier.
• Myths about the West still linger in the American imagination.

Key Terms, People, and Places

Frederick Jackson Turner

In the popular imagination, the sheriff's badge is a symbol of justice—wild West style.

T he 1800s were coming to a close, and what had seemed unimaginable a few decades before was happening. The American frontier seemed to be disappearing and an era of special meaning seemed to be ending. But what, exactly, did the era mean? The answer to that question is surrounded by many myths—and is responsible for many of the nation's most cherished images of itself.

The West at the Close of the Nineteenth Century

One by one, areas of the West became territories. Residents then wrote constitutions and applied for statehood. With these developments came the perception that the opportunities of the frontier were fading. As early as 1880, American observers of the West noticed ominous signs of change. The number of tenant farmers—who rented rather than owned land—had risen, along with the number of large farms owned by corporations. Many farmers were deep in debt. "Free" lands were harder to find. In 1890 the superintendent of the census announced the end of the frontier. The country's so-called "unsettled area has been so broken into by isolated bodies of settlement," he declared, "that there can hardly be said to be a frontier line."

This census official exaggerated somewhat. Homesteading continued into the twentieth century. Besides, many western areas that were not suited to agriculture remain sparsely settled still.

Turner's Frontier Thesis Nevertheless, by the 1890s it was clear that an era of special meaning in the history of the United States was closing. In 1893 a young historian named **Frederick Jackson Turner** delivered a speech in which he addressed this issue. He claimed a central role for the frontier in forming the American character.

The West Joins the Union

State	Year of Admission
California	1850
Oregon	1859
Kansas	1861
Nevada	1864
Nebraska	1867
Colorado	1876
North Dakota	1889
South Dakota	1889
Montana	1889
Washington	1889
Wyoming	1890
Idaho	1890
Utah	1896
Oklahoma	1907
New Mexico	1912
Arizona	1912

Interpreting Tables
In the late 1800s and early 1900s, one western territory after another achieved statehood. *Why do you think that the interior of the country was settled later than most of the West Coast?*

The West had forced its Anglo-American and European settlers to shed their old ways and adapt, innovate, and invent, he said. To the frontier, Turner claimed, "American intellect owes its striking characteristics," which he described as

That coarseness and strength combined with acuteness [keen insight] and inquisitiveness [curiosity]; that practical, inventive turn of mind, quick to find expedients [ways to achieve goals]; that masterful grasp of material things, lacking the artistic but powerful to effect great ends; that restless, nervous energy; that dominant individualism, working for good and for evil, and withal that buoyancy [liveliness] and exuberance which comes with freedom.

To Turner, it was the frontier that had produced the highly individualistic, restless, and socially mobile American, the person ready for adventure, bent on self-improvement, and committed to democracy.

Turner's Critics The Turner thesis, as his view came to be called, made certain assumptions that historians have since modified. Turner defined settlers as whites of European heritage and saw no difference in the experiences of women and men. He did not consider the importance to the West of African Americans or of the immigrants from Japan and China.

Nor did Turner consider the impact of settlement on Native American and Spanish-speaking inhabitants. Moreover, Turner played down the heavy involvement of government subsidies and of big business in bringing about American achievements in farming, cattle ranching, and mining. And finally, he ignored the extent to which immigrants made use of the many institutions and traditions they brought from their homelands in building farms and contributing to the nation's productivity.

Frontier Realities

A far more complex view of the West now prevails. This view more accurately reflects the reality of the settlement of the West.

The Real Western Settler The West did appeal to the restless, adventurous man, but it also appealed to adventurous women. While many women went west reluctantly and suffered deeply from the pressures of dislocation and deprivation, others not only survived but thrived on the frontier.

Still, the West was hardly a land of unlimited opportunity for either men or women. Boom inevitably led to bust, especially when prices fell for the commodities settlers relied on to make it big. Rare among those who made it big were African Americans, Asians, Mexicans, and single women.

Western settlers were not always eastern whites. Chinese and African American railway workers went into mining and established businesses in western towns. Chinese and Japanese settlers farmed the West Coast; about nine thousand African Americans worked as cowhands on ranches, where they generally suffered less discrimination than in other work. Thousands of Exodusters settled the West. The prosperity that western settlement brought to the United States could not have been achieved without the efforts of many groups.

A Limited View of Democracy The frontier nurtured certain democratic values. These found expression in strong legislatures, short terms for elected officials, and other institutions of popular control over government. Yet many settlers rode roughshod over the rights of the Native American populations they displaced. On the West Coast, white settlers treated Asian immigrants with scorn, segregating them

Frederic Remington's 1902 painting *The Cowboy* reveals that a romanticized image of the American West was well in place in the early twentieth century.

into neighborhoods and prohibiting them from owning land.

The Impact on the Land Although in the popular mind the settlement of the West meant progress, the costs to the environment were high. Settlers treated the vast natural resources of the West as if they were limitless. Railroad tunnels destroyed mountains. The construction of huge mines scarred the land and depleted forests. Overcultivation eroded fields, and wanton slaughter nearly wiped out the buffalo.

The Influence of Frontier Myths on National Identity

Despite today's deeper understanding of the history of the American West, frontier myths linger on. Through literature, film, and song, they continue to influence how Americans think about themselves.

Using Historical Evidence William F. "Buffalo Bill" Cody became famous by playing up the myths of the American West. This 1890 poster promoted his "Wild West" show. *What does the poster tell you about Cody's presentation of the West?*

Creating the Myths The romantic image of the American cowboy began developing as early as the 1870s, popularized in the dime novels of writers like Edward L. Wheeler. In *Deadwood Dick, The Prince of the Road: or, the Black Rider of the Black Hills,* Wheeler painted a hero who was, at various times, outlaw, miner, gang leader, or cowboy and who dealt out righteous justice against evil.

M*ounted upon his midnight steed, and clad in the weird suit of black, he makes an imposing spectacle as he comes fearlessly up. Well may he be bold and fearless, for no one dares to raise a hand against him. . . .*

Close up to the side of the coach rides the daring young outlaw, his piercing orbs peering out from the eye-holes in his black mask, one hand clasping the bridle-reins, the other a nickel-plaited seven-shooter.

Scenes like these kept alive the idea that the West saw little else but stage robberies and killings. And though Wheeler's Deadwood Dick did exist, the real cowboy of that name was no outlaw. He was an African American named Nat Love, who drove cattle north from Texas for twenty years. Entering a rodeo contest in Deadwood, a Dakota Territory mining town, Love won several roping and shooting contests. In his autobiography, Love wrote, "Right there the assembled crowd named me 'Deadwood Dick' and proclaimed me champion roper of the Western cattle country."

In 1883 William F. ("Buffalo Bill") Cody began his Wild West shows, contributing further to frontier myths. These colorful events drew thousands of paying spectators to steer-roping contests, rodeos, and staged battles between "good" cavalry regiments and "bad" Native Americans.

Writers transformed other real figures from the West, such as Wild Bill Hickock and Calamity Jane, into larger than life characters. Here's Wheeler again:

"Who was that chap?" asked Redburn, not a little bewildered.

"That?—why that's Calamity Jane!"

"Calamity Jane? What a name."

"Yes, she's an odd one. Can ride like the wind, shoot like a sharp-shooter, and swear like a trooper. . . . Owns this coop and two or three other lots in Deadwood; a herding ranch at Laramie; an interest in a paying placer claim [mine] near Elizabeth City, and the Lord only knows how much more."

"But it is not a woman?"

"Reckon 'tain't nothin' else."

This sketch helped create the stereotype of the woman who had to act masculine and be "mean with a pistol" in order to survive in the West. Deep down, however, she was always a "real" woman.

The "Strenuous Life" of the West Most stereotypes from the West were of men. The West was the place where a young man could find freedom and opportunity. He could lead a virtuous life and resist the forces of civilization that were making him soft. Many writers praised the West for having toughened the bodies and souls of young men. In his histories of the West, future President Theodore Roosevelt urged American men to experience the "strenuous life" of the West before they became too weak from the comforts of modern civilization.

Some male themes appealed to women. In 1912 Juliette Low founded the American Girl Scouts in part because she feared that civilization had made girls too soft. Citing as models the ingenuity and hardiness of women homesteaders, she made the scouting techniques of tracking, woodcraft, and wilderness survival the core of her program.

MAKING CONNECTIONS

Consider what you have read about the myths of the West. Have you encountered examples of these myths in television, movies, or other media in your lifetime? Explain.

The Myths of the West Today

Frontier myths have left permanent marks on the nation's character. How many classic American songs arose from the cowboy era? "Home on the Range," where the buffalo roam, "Sweet Betsy from Pike" or "Don't Fence Me In"—all give rise to enduring images of wide open spaces and freedom from the confines of civilization. When Americans hear these songs, they celebrate the richness of their land and the courage of their ancestors. They celebrate the truth that many endured the dangers of a hostile environment and piercing loneliness to "stake a claim" for the future. They set aside for a moment the knowledge that the buffalo are almost gone, that range settlements displaced and nearly destroyed Native American peoples, and that farmers and their barbed-wire fences brought an end to the open range for ranchers and their cattle.

Such were the realities. But who can discount the significance of myths to the spirit of a nation?

The belief that the frontier was disappearing prompted a move to conserve land in the West. Conservationist John Muir and President Theodore Roosevelt, pictured here in 1903, helped lead this conservation effort.

SECTION 5 REVIEW

Key Terms, People, and Places
1. Identify Frederick Jackson Turner.

Key Concepts
2. What did observers mean when they said that the frontier was "closed" in the late 1800s?
3. What is the Turner thesis and what are some criticisms of it?

4. Describe some of the myths of the American West.
5. How have the myths of the American West been perpetuated?

Critical Thinking
6. **Distinguishing False from Accurate Images**
   Briefly summarize the reality of the American settlement of the West for all groups involved.

Chapter Review

Understanding Key Terms, People, and Places

Key Terms
1. Morrill Land-Grant Act
2. speculators
3. Homestead Act
4. squatter
5. boomer
6. sooner
7. bonanza farms
8. cash crops
9. long drive
10. deflation
11. currency policy
12. the Grange

People
13. Exodusters
14. George Armstrong Custer
15. Chief Sitting Bull
16. Chief Joseph
17. Populists
18. William Jennings Bryan
19. Frederick Jackson Turner

Places
20. Wounded Knee

Terms For each term above, write a sentence that explains its relation to the settlement of the West, its impact on Native American culture, populism, or myths about the frontier.

Matching Review the key terms in the list above. If you are not sure of a term's meaning, review its definition in the chapter. Then choose a term from the list that best matches each description below.
1. people who bought up large areas of land to sell later at a profit
2. the federal government's plan for the makeup and quantity of the nation's money supply
3. the act giving western lands to state governments
4. the organization that promoted farmers' interests

True or False Determine whether each statement is true or false. If it is true, write "true." If it is false, change the underlined name to make the statement true.
1. African American homesteaders, who called themselves <u>Populists,</u> traveled West to escape exploitation in the South.
2. Historian <u>William Jennings Bryan</u> wrote about the importance of the frontier in forming the American character.
3. <u>Chief Joseph,</u> leader of the Nez Percé, fled with his people as far as Montana before being attacked by United States soldiers.
4. One of the leaders in the destruction of the Cheyenne was <u>Chief Sitting Bull.</u>

Reviewing Main Ideas

Section 1 (pp. 280–283)
1. Why did settlers want to move west? What additional reasons did African Americans have for moving west?
2. Describe some of the ways settlers relied on each other.
3. What campaigns did women start in the West?

Section 2 (pp. 284–287)
4. Explain how the Native American concept of owning land differed from that of the settlers.
5. Describe the pattern of conflict between the United States government and Native Americans.
6. By what means were Native American cultures destroyed in the late 1800s?

Section 3 (pp. 288–291)
7. What challenges did western land and climate pose for farmers?

8. What ethnic groups might have lived in a western mining town?
9. Describe several factors that led to the cattle ranching boom of the 1860s and l870s.

Section 4 (pp. 294–298)
10. Why did the nation's farmers suffer from a decline in crop prices in the late 1800s?
11. Describe the currency policy debate of the late 1800s.
12. How did farmers protest their fate in the late 1800s?

Section 5 (pp. 300–303)
13. What was the message of Frederick Jackson Turner's frontier thesis?
14. In what ways was Turner's thesis inaccurate?
15. What has been the impact of frontier myths on the national identity?

1. **Formulating Questions** Based on what you have read in the chapter, write four questions to ask new homesteaders about their life in the West.
2. **Distinguishing False from Accurate Images** Myths about the frontier led people to believe that the West was a lawless place where everyone could strike it rich. (a) What myths and stereotypes do we have about various regions of the country today? (b) To what extent do you think these stereotypes are accurate?

1. **Evaluating Primary Sources** Review the primary source excerpt on page 289. The excerpt states that farms owned by big business have many advantages. (a) What might be some of these advantages? (b) How might such large farms affect the small farmer?
2. **Understanding the Visuals** Scan the chapter and choose several visuals that illustrate some of the realities and the myths about the West. Write a paragraph that explains what the realities and myths were and how these visuals illustrate them.
3. **Writing About the Chapter** Imagine that the 1892 election is rapidly approaching. Create an informational flyer urging voters to support the Populist party. First decide why voters should support the Populists. Then write a draft of your flyer explaining your point of view. Anticipate and reply to any potential objections to the Populist platform. Revise your flyer, making certain that your writing is informative and persuasive. Proofread your flyer and draft a final copy.
4. **Using the Graphic Organizer** This graphic organizer uses a tree map to provide information about developing the West. (a) Based on what you have read in the chapter, how did mechanization and new agricultural knowledge lead to the growth of bonanza farms? (b) According to the graphic organizer below, what role did big business play in the development of the West? (c) On a separate sheet of paper, create your own graphic organizer, showing the effects of westward expansion on the Native American groups living in the West.

Developing the West

Agriculture	Mining	Ranching
• Mechanization • New agricultural knowledge • Bonanza farms	• Gold rushes • Mining towns • Growth of corporations	• Large-scale ranches • Cattle drives • End of the cattle boom

Politics, Immigration, and Urban Life

1877–1920

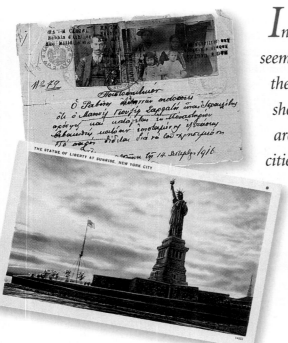

THE STATUE OF LIBERTY AT SUNRISE, NEW YORK CITY

*I*n the late 1800s and early 1900s, the United States seemed in constant motion. Millions of people were on the move. Immigrants arriving from foreign shores and Americans migrating from rural areas both found new homes in the nation's cities. The urban crowding, poverty, and crime that resulted shocked many people. Reformers suggested various ways to address these problems. But the federal government, troubled with its own corruption and undistinguished leadership, failed to address the challenges faced by its citizens every day.

Events in the United States

1882 Congress passes the Chinese Exclusion Act.

1886 The Statue of Liberty is erected in New York Harbor.

1892 The federal government opens an immigrant reception center on Ellis Island.

1894 Coxey's army of the unemployed marches on Washington.

1875 **1880** **1885** **1890** **1895**

Events in the World

1881 Czar Alexander II of Russia is assassinated by revolutionaries.

1889 The Eiffel Tower is constructed for the Paris Exposition.

1896 Ethiopia repels an Italian invasion.

Pages 308–313

Politics in the Gilded Age

In the years after Reconstruction, the United States changed from a nation of farms into one of growing businesses, factories, and cities. Yet despite such changes—and sometimes because of them—many problems festered. Among them were corruption in government and business and a series of Presidents who seemed unable to address the nation's problems.

Pages 314–319

People on the Move

The dreams of the immigrants who came to the United States in the late nineteenth century might have seemed more golden than gilded. Millions left oppression, persecution, and poverty behind to begin new lives as Americans. Most found not streets paved with gold, but unfamiliar roads that they navigated with difficulty.

Pages 320–324

The Challenge of the Cities

As immigrants from Europe and Asia arrived on American shores, most pinned their hopes on the nation's cities. Bustling, noisy, and straining at the seams, the cities were places where the new became neighbors with the old and where progress lived next door to poverty.

Pages 326–329

Ideas for Reform

The flood of newcomers added colorful diversity to the nation's cities in the late 1800s but, at the same time, contributed to a host of problems. Shocked by social, economic, and political conditions in the cities, religious and social groups pushed programs for change.

1901 President William McKinley is assassinated by an anarchist.

1907 Japanese immigration to the United States is limited.

1910s Hundreds of thousands of African Americans migrate from the South to northern cities.

1900	1905	1910	1915	1920	1925

1905 Albert Einstein develops his special theory of relativity.

1910 Japan annexes Korea.

1913 The first woman magistrate takes office in England.

1918 A worldwide influenza epidemic kills more than twenty million people.

Politics in the Gilded Age

SECTION PREVIEW

In the years after Reconstruction, the United States changed from a nation of farms into one of growing businesses, factories, and cities. Yet despite such changes—and sometimes because of them—many problems festered. Among them were corruption in government and business and a series of Presidents who seemed unable to address the nation's problems.

Key Concepts

- Unfair business practices led to new government regulations.
- Republicans and Democrats were divided on issues such as tariffs, the currency question, and political reform.
- Political leaders instituted reforms to end corrupt government practices, but these proved largely ineffective.

Political campaigns such as William McKinley's presidential bid aroused wide interest in the late 1800s.

Key Terms, People, and Places

Gilded Age, laissez-faire, blue laws, Pendleton Act, Interstate Commerce Act; Jacob S. Coxey

Many labels have been used to describe the post-Reconstruction era (1877–1900) in the United States. The most famous is the **Gilded Age,** a term coined by writer Mark Twain that implies a thin layer of glitter over a cheap base. Other labels for the period included the Tragic Era and the Dreadful Decades. All of these terms present an unflattering picture of this era. The decades earned their reputation because of widespread corruption in government and business, as well as the failure of the era's Presidents to solve the persistent economic, social, and political problems plaguing the nation.

The Political Landscape in the Late 1800s

The United States faced great challenges as it emerged from Reconstruction. Industrial expansion raised factory and farm productivity, but economic cycles of boom and bust, low wages for workers, and rising farmer debt contributed to feelings of deep discontent among most working people. Others, such as speculators in stocks and land, quickly rose "from rags to riches." Corruption tempted business and political leaders, who also hoped to achieve such dreams of power and wealth. A dissatisfied public demanded reform.

Laissez-Faire Policies In the late 1800s, businesses operated largely without government regulation. This **laissez-faire**, or hands-off, approach to economic matters holds that government should play only a very limited role in business. Supporters of this theory maintain that if government doesn't interfere, the strongest businesses will succeed and bring wealth to the nation as a whole.

In the late nineteenth century, most Americans accepted this philosophy in theory. In practice, however, many supported government involvement when it benefited business. For example, champions of the laissez-faire approach favored high tariffs on imported goods. They argued that raising the prices of imported goods discouraged people from buying them, thus helping American businesses, and eventually the economy, to grow. American businesses also willingly accepted government land grants and subsidies—payments made by the government to encourage the development of certain key industries, such as railroads.

Business giants during the Gilded Age supported friendly politicians with both legal and illegal contributions of money. Between 1875 and 1885, the Central Pacific Railroad (CPR) reportedly budgeted $500,000 annually for bribes. CPR cofounder Collis P. Huntington explained, "If you have to pay money to have the right thing done, it is only just and fair to do it."

The Spoils System Another controversial practice in American politics at the time was the spoils system. Under the spoils system, those who were elected to public office were free to appoint friends and supporters to government jobs, regardless of their qualifications—or their honesty. The use of this system became widespread during the presidency of Andrew Jackson, and by the Gilded Age its impact on government had reached a crisis point.

The spoils system appealed to many politicians because it ensured a flock of supporters in future elections. Both Democrats and Republicans handed out jobs to pay off the people who had helped them get elected. But the system led to corruption when dishonest appointees used their jobs for personal profit.

Political Parties During the Gilded Age, the numbers of Democrats and Republicans in the United States were about equal, but the characteristics of their members were quite different. The two parties also held starkly different positions on the major issues of the day.

Republicans controlled New York state, New England, and the upper Midwest. In general, they favored a tight money supply backed by gold, high tariffs to protect American business, generous pensions for Union soldiers, and government aid to the railroads. They also wanted to restrict immigration and enforce **blue laws**, which prohibited certain personal behaviors, such as drinking alcoholic beverages on Sundays.

As a rule, the Democratic party attracted those in American society who felt—and sometimes were—less privileged. These groups included northern urban immigrants, laborers, and southern planters and western farmers. Democrats claimed to represent the interests of ordinary people and favored free silver as a means of increasing the money supply and raising farm prices. Democrats typically opposed blue laws.

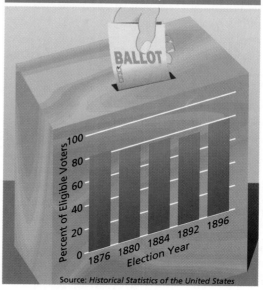

Voter Participation in Presidential Elections, 1876–1896

Source: *Historical Statistics of the United States*

Interpreting Graphs
Voter turnout was high in the late 1800s compared to earlier eras. By 1920, it had dropped below 50 percent and never again rose as high as 65 percent. *What factors might help explain the high turnout in the late 1800s?*

Presidents and Reforms

Because the two parties had roughly equal numbers of supporters during the Gilded Age, presidential candidates needed almost total support of the members of their party in order to win an election. Candidates generally avoided taking strong stands on political issues in order not to offend potential supporters. They preferred, instead, to "wave the bloody shirt," which meant they focused on their Civil War records. Once in office, however, each of the era's Presidents did exercise a degree of leadership on the major issues of the day. Indeed, the era witnessed some important reforms of the spoils system, the railroads, and trusts.

Hayes Addresses Currency and Patronage
After his election in 1876, the honest and practical Rutherford B. Hayes faced the money supply debate. Those who favored soft money—the term used to describe an increase in the currency supply—supported the passage of the Bland-Allison Act of 1878. This act favored those

with high debts, such as farmers and business owners who had borrowed money. It required the federal government to purchase and coin more silver, increasing the currency supply and causing inflation. If prices went up, farmers would make more money for their goods and would more easily pay off debts incurred earlier.

Although Congress passed the act, Hayes vetoed it because he opposed the inflation it would create. Congress overrode Hayes's veto. Nevertheless, Hayes's Treasury Department limited the effectiveness of the act by buying only the minimum silver it required. The Treasury also refused to circulate the silver dollars that the law required it to mint.

Hayes was the first President to turn away from the practice of patronage. He did not have congressional support for his actions, even from members of his own Republican party, but he did what he could through executive orders and appointments. Hayes appointed qualified political independents to cabinet posts, outlawed the practice of forcing federal employees to make campaign contributions, and fired those employees who were not needed.

Garfield Assassinated in Office In 1880 the Republican party had three factions. The Stalwarts, followers of New York senator Roscoe Conkling, defended the spoils system. The Half-Breeds followed Maine senator James G. Blaine and tried to balance the need for reform of the spoils system with loyalty to the party. Independents opposed the spoils system altogether. They were sometimes called "googoos," a derisive term that was short for *good government.* In the 1880s, when independents left the party to support a Democrat, they also became known as *Mugwumps.* An Algonquin word for "renegade chief," the term stuck when a newspaper editor joked that it really meant "unreliable Republicans," men whose "mugs" were on one side of the fence and "wumps" on the other.

Hayes had announced at the beginning of his presidency that he would not seek a second term. In 1880, Republicans selected James A. Garfield, a member of Congress from Ohio, as their presidential candidate. Because Garfield was linked to the Half-Breeds, who were only somewhat loyal to old-time Republican policies, the vice-presidential slot went to Chester A. Arthur, a Stalwart.

In the 1880 election, Garfield won a narrow victory against Democratic candidate General Winfield S. Hancock. His term was cut short, however, by an assassin's bullet. On July 2, 1881, a deranged lawyer named Charles Guiteau shot Garfield as the President walked through the Washington, D.C., railroad station. When he fired his fatal shot, Guiteau cried out, "I am a Stalwart and Arthur is President now!" Garfield suffered for nearly three months before dying.

It turned out that Guiteau was a loyal Republican and a disappointed office seeker. He felt that his loyalty had earned him a job under the spoils system, and he became enraged when Garfield passed him over. Guiteau's violent act aroused public outrage at the spoils system.

A GREAT NATION IN GRIEF

PRESIDENT GARFIELD SHOT BY AN ASSASSIN.

THOUGH SERIOUSLY WOUNDED HE STILL SURVIVES.

THE WOULD-BE MURDERER LODGED IN PRISON.

THE PRESIDENT OF THE UNITED STATES ATTACKED AND TERRIBLY WOUNDED BY A FANATICAL OFFICE-SEEKER ON THE EVE OF INDEPENDENCE DAY—THE NATION HORRIFIED AND THE WHOLE CIVILIZED WORLD SHOCKED—THE PRESIDENT STILL ALIVE AND HIS RECOVERY POSSIBLE.

Arthur Ends Patronage With Garfield's death, Vice President Chester Arthur succeeded to the nation's highest office. During the Hayes administration, Arthur had benefited from the practice of patronage. He had been appointed to a high-paying job in the New York Customs House because of his support of Senator Roscoe Conkling. Once in office, however, he urged Congress to support reform of the spoils system. With Garfield's assassination fresh in the nation's mind, President Arthur was able to garner legislative support for his ideas, and the **Pendleton Act** became law in 1883.

The act empowered three civil service commissioners to classify government jobs and test applicants' fitness for them. It also stated that federal employees could not be required to contribute to campaign funds and could not be fired for political reasons.

Democrats Take Over In the 1884 presidential campaign, the key issues were high tariffs, unfair business practices, and unregulated railroads. The Republicans nominated the eloquent James G. Blaine, a former secretary of state and senator from Maine. The Democratic party chose the genial Grover Cleveland, former mayor of Buffalo and governor of New York. In spite of the serious economic issues of the day, the campaign focused mostly on scandals.

Had James G. Blaine received railroad stock options in return for favorable votes while he was in Congress? No one could prove it. Had Cleveland fathered an illegitimate child when a bachelor in Buffalo? Cleveland admitted it was true. Republicans jeered, "Ma, Ma, where's my Pa?" to which the Democrats responded, "Going to the White House, ha, ha, ha!" In spite of his admission, Cleveland won the election, thereby becoming the first Democrat elected to the presidency since 1856. Cleveland did appoint Democrats to office but avoided giving in to the spoils system. He tried to ensure that his appointments were based on merit.

An advocate of tight money, Cleveland was acceptable to most business interests. Yet he opposed generous pensions and high tariffs, and he took back from the railroads and other interests 81 million acres of land grants on which they had failed to fulfill their obligations. Cleveland also supported regulation of the powerful railroads. He believed that fierce competition among the various railroad lines led to practices, such as secret rebates to high-volume shippers, that hurt small businesses.

Railroad Abuses Lead to New Regulations

Railroad regulation had begun in 1869, when Massachusetts officials investigated rate abuses in that state. By 1880, fourteen states had railroad commissions to look into complaints against railroad practices. Such practices included awarding stock to legislators in return for favors and manipulating the state legal system to win court challenges against rate abuses. In 1877 the Supreme Court decision in *Munn* v. *Illinois* allowed states to regulate certain enterprises within their boundaries. Lawyers for the railroads responded with the argument that, under the Constitution, states could not regulate interstate commerce. Because railroad traffic often crossed state lines, only the federal government could regulate their activities. With this argument the railroads were successful and continued to pursue their disputed practices.

Pressure mounted on Congress to take action to curb railroad company abuses. In 1887 the legislature passed the **Interstate Commerce Act**. The act required that rates be set in proportion to the distance traveled and that rate schedules be made public. The act also outlawed the practice of giving rebates and favors to powerful customers. It set up the nation's first regulatory board, the Interstate Commerce Commission (ICC), to enforce the act.

Unfortunately, the act failed to give the commission the power necessary to set rates, rendering it largely ineffective. To enforce its rulings, the ICC had to take the railroads to court. But of the sixteen cases involving the ICC that came before the Supreme Court between 1887 and 1905, the Court ruled against the ICC fifteen times. Still, the creation of the ICC established the precedent that private enterprise was subject to government control.

Using Historical Evidence This cartoon expresses the widespread concern about the harmful effects of monopolies in the late 1800s. *How do the images in this cartoon communicate such a message?*

MAKING CONNECTIONS

How did the passing of the Interstate Commerce Act weaken the policy of laissez-faire?

Efforts to Regulate Tariffs

The White House again found itself with a new tenant when Cleveland lost the 1888 election to Republican Benjamin Harrison. Tariffs provided a focal point for the campaign. Cleveland favored a minor reduction; Harrison campaigned for an increase, a position that won him much business support and, ultimately, the presidency.

Among President Harrison's achievements was the signing of the Sherman Antitrust Act in 1890, described in Chapter 8. Like the Interstate Commerce Act, however, this seemingly bold action failed to curb the power of the largest corporations until well after the turn of the century.

Meanwhile, Harrison also took actions that favored business. In 1890 he approved a huge tariff increase, and he supported legislation on behalf of special business interests. Although he was considered a conservative regarding the public treasury, he was liberal when it came to veterans' pensions. He ate up the last federal surplus in United States history with huge new pensions for the dependents of Civil War soldiers.

In the election of 1892, with many new immigrants swelling Democratic party rolls, and campaigning for lower tariffs, Grover Cleveland was returned to the presidency. By the time his term was over, however, many people were more disillusioned with government than ever before.

Cleveland's Second Term Cleveland's second term started badly. To begin with, he inherited Harrison's treasury deficit. Also, Americans were experiencing the worst depression the country had yet seen. Millions of people lost their jobs or had their wages slashed, yet government offered no help to those out of work. In 1894 **Jacob S. Coxey**, a wealthy Ohio quarry owner turned Populist, demanded that government create jobs for the unemployed. He then called for a march on Washington. "We will send a petition to Washington with boots on," he declared.

Many small "armies" started out on the protest march, but only Coxey's arrived. Police arrested him and a few others for illegally carrying banners on the Capitol grounds and for trampling the grass. Based on the tune of "The Star-Spangled Banner," a song created by Coxey's supporters mocked their government's vigilance in protecting the lawns of the Capitol while ignoring the pleas of the nation's poor.

*O h, say, can you see, by the dawn's early light
That grass plot so dear to the hearts of us all?
Is it green yet and fair, in well-nurtured plight,
Unpolluted by the Coxeyites' hated foot-fall?
Midst the yells of police, and swish of clubs through the air,*

We could hardly tell if our grass was still
   there.
But the green growing grass does in triumph
   yet wave,
And the gallant police with their buttons
   of brass
Will sure make the Coxeyites keep off the
   grass.

Anonymous, 1894

In his second term, Cleveland managed to anger not only the unemployed, but almost every group in his party. He angered labor when he sent federal troops to Chicago at the time of the Pullman strike of 1894. He angered farmers by repealing the Silver Purchase Act and returning the country to a gold standard. Having alienated so many fellow Democrats, Cleveland failed to win his party's nomination in 1896.

A Republican Returns to the White House

The Populists had emerged as a political power during the economic hard times of the early 1890s and had made gains in the elections of 1894. But in 1896 William Jennings Bryan, the presidential candidate they shared with the Democrats, lost to Republican William McKinley. Supported by urban workers and the middle class, McKinley won the election with ease.

A new tariff and the gold standard brought Republicans an even more decisive victory against Bryan in 1900. As the economic depression of the 1890s began to loosen its grip, the Republicans claimed credit with their slogan, "A Full Dinner Pail."

Coxey's Army, shown above, marched through many villages on its way to Washington to demand federal action to resolve the nation's economic problems.

McKinley did not live long enough to enjoy the effects of the growing prosperity. On September 6, 1901, a mentally ill, unemployed anarchist named Leon Czolgosz hid a gun in a bandaged hand and shot President McKinley as he greeted the public at the Pan-American Exposition in Buffalo. When McKinley died a few days later, national hysteria followed.

In the public mind, dangerous ideas, many of them associated with foreign people—or those with foreign names such as Czolgosz—were threatening the country. Those blossoming fears would have a profound impact on the nation's huge and growing immigrant population, as the next section describes.

SECTION 1 REVIEW

Key Terms, People, and Places
1. Identify (a) Interstate Commerce Act, (b) Jacob S. Coxey.
2. Define (a) laissez-faire, (b) blue laws.

Key Concepts
3. For what reason(s) is the post-Reconstruction period in national politics referred to as the Gilded Age?
4. Describe the business practices that led to government regulation. What regulations were passed in the Gilded Age, and how effective were they?
5. Describe how the spoils system worked and what action the government took to control it.

Critical Thinking
6. **Determining Relevance** For what reasons do you think political reformers believed that a civil service law could help wipe out corrupt government practices?

People on the Move

SECTION PREVIEW

The dreams of the immigrants who came to the United States in the late nineteenth century might have seemed more golden than gilded. Millions left oppression, persecution, and poverty behind to begin new lives as Americans. Most found not streets paved with gold, but unfamiliar roads that they navigated with difficulty.

Key Concepts

· Economic hardship and political and religious persecution led immigrants to the United States in the late 1800s.

· Patterns of immigration changed in the late 1800s, and Americans distinguished between "old" and "new" immigrants.

· Immigrants experienced many difficulties during their voyage to the United States and after their arrival.

Key Terms, People, and Places

steerage; Ellis Island, Angel Island

Millions of immigrants shipped their belongings and their dreams to the United States in the late 1800s.

As politicians steered their way through the nagging economic and political problems of the late nineteenth century, fascinating human dramas were unfolding far from the spotlight of Washington, D.C. Played out in the nation's gritty ports and grimy back streets, these dramas told tales of triumph and tragedy, with millions of heroes and more than a few villains. These were the stories of the nation's immigrants.

Worldwide Patterns of Movement

In the late 1800s, people in many parts of the world were on the move, from farms to cities and then on to other countries. Immigrants from around the globe were fleeing crop failures, land and job shortages, rising taxes, and famine. Some were also escaping religious or political persecution.

Immigrants to the United States The United States received a huge portion of this migration. In 1860 the resident population of the United States was 31.5 million people. Between 1865 and 1920, close to 30 million additional people entered the country. Some of these newcomers dreamed of making fortunes, or at least of getting free government land through the Homestead Act. Others yearned for more personal freedom. In the United States, they had heard, everyone could go to school, young men were not forced to serve long years in the army, and democratic government meant equality and participation for more people.

In the late 1800s, steam-powered ships could cross the Atlantic Ocean in two to three weeks. By 1900 the crossing took just one week. Even this brief journey, however, could be an ordeal for those who could not afford cabins, and most could not. The majority of immigrants traveled in **steerage**, a large open area beneath the ship's deck with inadequate toilet facilities, no privacy, and poor food, but where tickets cost as little as $15.

The Golden Door Immigrants entered the United States through several ports. Those from Europe might come through Boston, Philadelphia, or Baltimore; those from Asia might enter through San Francisco or Seattle. More than 70 percent of all immigrants, however, came through New York City, which came to be called the "Golden Door."

Throughout most of the 1800s, immigrants arriving in New York entered at the Castle Garden depot near the southern tip of Manhattan. Then, in 1892, the federal government opened a huge reception center for steerage passengers on **Ellis Island** in New York Harbor, near where the Statue of Liberty had been erected in 1886. The statue, a gift of France, celebrated "Liberty Enlightening the World." It became a world symbol of the United States as a place of refuge and hope.

Ellis Island Receives European Immigrants

Information about the number and origins of the nation's immigrants is not exact. For example, officials often misidentified their countries of origin. Also, about a third of all immigrants were "birds of passage"—usually young, single men who worked for a number of months or years and then returned home. Until 1907 Mexican immigrants were not counted. Historians estimate, however, that about 10 million immigrants, mostly northern Europeans from countries such as England and Germany, arrived between 1865 and 1890. In the 1890s, the pattern of immigration shifted dramatically, and most immigrants came from the countries of southern and eastern Europe and the Middle East. Between 1890 and 1920 about 10 million Italians, Greeks, Slavs, Eastern European and Russian Jews, and Armenians arrived.

Arriving in America Before the 1880s, decisions about whom to allow into the country were left to the states. Then, in 1891, the federal government created the Office of the Superintendent of Immigration to determine who was "fit" for life in the United States and who was not. The next year laws required all new immigrants to undergo physical examination, and applicants could be denied admission on medical grounds. Those found to have contagious illnesses such as tuberculosis faced quarantine or even deportation. Those with trachoma, an eye disease that was common among immigrants, were automatically sent back to the country they had just left. Fiorello La Guardia, who later became mayor of New York City, worked as an interpreter at Ellis Island. "It was harrowing to see families separated," he remembered in the book *The Making of an Insurgent.*

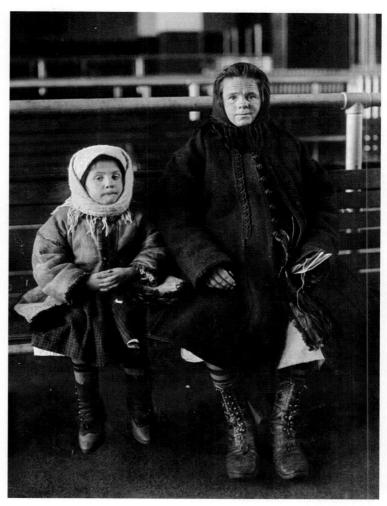

*S*ometimes, if it was a young child who suffered from trachoma, one of the parents had to return to the native country with the rejected member of the family. When they learned their fate, they were stunned. They . . . had no homes to return to.

These recent arrivals on Ellis Island contemplate a bewildering yet promising future in their new homeland.

After their physicals, immigrants showed their documents to officials and then collected their baggage. If they had the address of a friend or relative, they took a ferry, boat, or train to find them. Those who were on their own had a harder time. Crooks hung around ports with fake offers of lodgings and jobs, stealing money and baggage from the unwary.

Where the Immigrants Settled Immigrants often settled near their ports of entry. A significant number of immigrants did move inland, than men. Men tailors, for example, working 14 hours a day, 6 days a week, earned $6 to $10 a week. Women seamstresses, doing the same work, earned half that amount. Women domestic servants earned $4 to $10 a month, working 16 hours or more a day and more than 6 days a week.

MAKING CONNECTIONS

How does the treatment of men and women immigrant workers in the nineteenth century compare to the way men and women in the workplace are treated in the United States today?

From Asia to the United States

Most of the immigrants who entered the United States on the West Coast came from Asia. These people, whose cultures differed greatly from those of both Americans and Europeans, faced a unique set of challenges.

In the 1800s, railroad companies recruited about a quarter of a million Chinese workers. Like the indentured servants of the colonial era, the Chinese had to work for their companies until they had paid the cost of their passage and upkeep. Americans called these workers "coolies," a corruption of the Chinese word for "unskilled laborer." Many Chinese paid their debts, settled down, and began to work in other fields, including mining, farming, fishing, factory work, food preparation, and laundering. But the group as a whole had difficulty freeing itself from ethnic stereotypes.

White people ridiculed Chinese dress and their custom of wearing long pony tails, or *queues*. Many Americans condemned them for what they saw as the squalor of crowded Chinese neighborhoods—conveniently disregarding the discrimination and exploitation that helped create such conditions.

Because the Chinese accepted low wages, unions worked to keep them from coming to the United States. Using pseudoscientific evidence, anti-Asian movements fostered racist attitudes. One newspaper's remarks from 1870 were typical:

Chinese immigrants brought distinctive styles and customs to the United States. Traditional dress and shops helped them feel at home—but also set them apart from other Americans, who often had little tolerance for differences.

however, often seeking communities established by previous settlers from their homelands.

In this way, large settlements of Poles and Italians formed in Buffalo, Cleveland, Detroit, and Milwaukee. Chicago—a port, railroad hub, and center for the garment, grain, lumber, and livestock industries—attracted a diverse group of immigrants. Some immigrants continued on to the mining towns of the West. Only 2 percent went to the South, primarily because the area did not offer newcomers enough jobs or land. Louisiana recruited Italian farm laborers, however, and Florida also sought foreign-born agricultural workers.

Once settled, immigrants looked for work. There were never enough jobs, and employers—often immigrants themselves—took advantage of the "greenhorns." They paid them less than other workers and paid women less

The Mongoloid [Asian] blood is depraved and debased blood. The Mongoloid type of humanity is an inferior type—inferior in organic structure, in vital force or physical energy, and in the constitutional conditions of development. On this point all anthropologists and ethnologists are agreed.

In reality, some scientists of the time agreed with such incorrect views and many did not. Nevertheless, Congress responded to popular demand by passing the Chinese Exclusion Act in 1882. The act prohibited Chinese laborers from entering the country. It was renewed in 1892 and 1902, and then made permanent. The act was not repealed until 1943.

The act did not prevent entry by those who had previously established residence or who had family already living in the United States. In 1910 the government built a detention center on **Angel Island** in San Francisco Bay, where immigrants' claims of prior residence or relationship to citizens received lengthy examination.

Two hundred thousand Japanese had arrived on the West Coast by 1920, many via Hawaii, which the United States annexed in 1898. Most Japanese settled in the Los Angeles area, and soon they were producing much of southern California's fruits and vegetables.

The success of Japanese immigrants aroused the jealousy of some who gave them the derogatory nickname "The Yellow Peril." In 1905 California's political leaders urged, and two years later won, restrictions on Japanese immigration. This was accomplished when President Theodore Roosevelt made a so-called gentleman's agreement with Japanese officials, who agreed to limit Japanese emigration. In 1913 the California legislature passed an Alien Land Law, which banned noncitizen Asians from owning farmland.

From South to North

In 1902 Congress passed the Newlands National Reclamation Act to stimulate the irrigation of southwestern lands. Over the next decade, irrigation turned millions of acres of desert into fertile farmland in Texas, Arizona, and California.

The new farmland meant new jobs. About 5 percent of Mexico's population, fleeing poverty and debt, entered the United States through El Paso, Texas. The 1909 Mexican Revolution increased the flow. Later, when the Immigration Restriction Act of 1921 limited immigration from Europe and Asia, labor shortages made Mexicans more needed than ever. By 1925 Los Angeles had the largest Spanish-speaking population in any North American city outside of Mexico.

Viewpoints
On Cultural Ties

Many people held opinions on how immigrants could best adjust to their new lives in the United States. Some thought they should give up their own language and customs as quickly as possible; others thought they should hold on to their heritage. **Do you think that immigrant children or their parents had an easier time adjusting to their new lives? Why?**

On Breaking Cultural Ties

"We wanted to be Americans so quickly that we were embarrassed if our parents couldn't speak English. My father was reading a Polish paper. And somebody was supposed to come to the house. I remember sticking it under something. We were that ashamed of being foreign."

Louise Nagy, a Polish immigrant, 1913

On Preserving Cultural Ties

"We ate the same dishes, spoke the same language, told the same stories, indulged in the same pleasures [as in Syria]. . . . To me the colony [neighborhood] was a habitat so much like the one I had left behind in Syria that its home atmosphere enabled me to maintain a firm hold on life in the face of the many difficulties which confronted me in those days."

Abraham Ribahny, on his neighborhood in New York, 1893

AMERICAN PROFILES
The Immigrant Experience

Facts and figures tell only a part of the story of immigration in the United States. The drama behind the figures is best revealed in the accounts of ordinary people, whose lives and experiences reflect the struggles and triumphs of living day to day in a new land.

Sadie Frowne, Polish Immigrant Young Sadie Frowne lived an unremarkable life in her native Poland. Her mother kept a grocer's shop and worked in the fields with her husband. Sadie, too, worked hard, scrubbing floors and washing dishes, even as a six year old.

When Sadie was ten, however, her father died, shattering the fragile structure of the family's livelihood. Unable to earn enough to buy food, Sadie and her mother looked to the United States, where they hoped to build a new life. Sadie's aunt, who already lived in New York City, encouraged them and took up a collection among her friends to pay for their passage to the United States. Sadie was thirteen years old when she and her mother set out on their immigration journey.

The Frownes' crossing, which took place in 1898, lasted twelve days.

Treasured items from home, such as this stuffed bear and set of spoons, helped provide a link between an immigrant's old and new lives.

There were hundreds of other people packed in with us, men, women and children, and almost all of them were sick. . . . We thought we should die, but at last the voyage was over, and we came up and saw the beautiful bay and the big woman with the spikes on her head and the lamp that is lighted at night in her hand.

Once in the United States, Sadie found a job as a live-in servant. Her mother found employment as a garment worker. Tragedy struck again, however, when Sadie's mother contracted a fatal case of tuberculosis, a disease then raging through the crowded neighborhoods of New York City.

Now that she was alone, it was more important than ever that Sadie work. Sadie managed to get a new job as a skirtmaker earning $4 for a six-day week. With this income, she found a room that she shared with another young woman for $1.50 a week.

By keeping her weekly expenses down, Sadie was now able to set aside a dollar a week for "clothing and pleasure" and another dollar for savings. She went to school at night to learn English. She also worked to improve her sewing skills, found a better job, and moved to a nicer place in Brooklyn.

With constant work, sacrifice, and determination, Sadie was living out the dream of millions of immigrants. It was a dream of simple comforts, modest prosperity, and the chance for a better life.

A Japanese Picture Bride Tameji Eto came to the United States from Japan in 1904. After working as a farmhand, he became a foreman for the Pacific Coast Railroad Company and then leased land for his own farm.

Having achieved some security, Tameji began to think of settling down and starting a family. Because few Japanese women had emigrated to the United States, Tameji's thoughts turned to Take, the sister of one of his school friends back in Japan. He wrote her family to ask permission to marry her.

Nineteen-year-old Take had no memory of Tameji, but her parents insisted that she accept his proposal. Because such arranged marriages were typical among the Japanese at that time, Take accepted her fate. Clutching Tameji's photograph, her only means of identifying her future husband, she sailed for the United States.

On board ship, Take met other "picture brides," women whose marriages had been arranged through the exchange of photographs across the Pacific Ocean. Like her companions, Take spent the voyage trying to adapt to strange foods and wondering about her future.

After her arrival and a ten-day quarantine for an eye infection, Take finally met Tameji. Luckily, he looked like his picture, "straight and tall with lots of hair," and he also seemed kind. Together they set out for the frontier town of Grand Arroyo, California.

These Japanese picture brides looked with both hope and apprehension to life in a new land with new husbands they had never met. As part of their traditional dress, many Japanese wore a type of footwear called *geta*, shown below.

Take took up the challenge of daily chores on the frontier and the repeated cultivation necessary to farm their semiarid land. "It was not easy," she later told one of her eight children,

> but it was my future as well as [Tameji's], and I wanted to be a part of it. Father never demanded I work so hard. I did it because it was necessary and I wanted to.

The Etos' hard work paid off, and by 1919 they had enough money to buy their own farm. Because of the Alien Land Law, however, they had to buy land under the name of a white friend.

After some difficult years, the farm did well. While caring for her children, Take cooked for a farm crew of forty to fifty men. Finally, after fifteen years of hard work, the Etos felt they could afford a journey back to Japan to see their parents.

The Etos found their success on the American frontier. Opportunities there were greater for many immigrant groups, who faced discrimination in urban areas. Still, most immigrants found homes in one of the nation's large cities. Their impact on urban life in the United States was profound.

SECTION 2 REVIEW

Key Terms, People, and Places
1. Identify Angel Island.

Key Concepts
2. Why were so many people "on the move" in the late nineteenth century?
3. Why did so many people want to come to the United States?

4. How did most immigrants travel to the United States, and where did they enter the country?
5. Where did the "new" immigrants come from?

Critical Thinking
6. **Recognizing Bias** For what reasons do you think Asians were treated more harshly than immigrants from Europe?

The Challenge of the Cities

SECTION PREVIEW

As immigrants from Europe and Asia arrived on American shores, most pinned their hopes on the nation's cities. Bustling, noisy, and straining at the seams, the cities were places where the new became neighbors with the old and where progress lived next door to poverty.

Key Concepts

- American cities expanded upward and outward with the arrival of tremendous numbers of new residents.
- Increased movement of people within the United States added to urban problems caused by immigration.
- The growth of American cities contributed to corrupt political practices at the local level.

Cities such as Chicago, pictured on this postcard, grew upward and outward in the late 1800s.

Key Terms, People, and Places

suburb, ghetto, political machine, political boss, Tammany Hall; William Marcy Tweed

---

While millions of immigrants from around the world were settling into the cities of the United States, growing numbers of Americans were also on the move. Between 1880 and 1920, 11 million Americans left behind the economic hardship of their farms and headed for the opportunities of the cities. This migration within the country, combined with the new immigrants, significantly affected the nation's growing urban centers.

Americans on the Move

Young women were among those who took part in the migration from rural to urban America. As factories produced more of the goods that farm women had once produced, the need for women's labor on farms declined.

Mechanization in agriculture also reduced the need for male farmhands. In 1880 about 72 percent of the population lived on farms. By 1910 that figure was down to 54 percent. Today it is about 3 percent.

Many African Americans also were among the internal migrants. In 1870, fewer than a half million of the nation's 5 million African Americans lived outside the South. By 1890, partly as a result of increased segregationist policies and racial violence in the South, 12 percent of the region's rural-dwelling African Americans had moved into nearby cities, and 150,000 had left the South altogether. Then, in the 1910s, after the boll weevil destroyed cotton crops and floods ruined Alabama and Mississippi farmlands, several hundred thousand more African Americans migrated to northern cities.

How Cities Grew

The arrival of large numbers of newcomers from within and outside the nation radically changed the face of the nation's cities. Between the Civil War and 1900, many features of modern city life first appeared— noise, skyscrapers, traffic jams, slums, air pollution, and sanitation and health problems.

Before the Civil War, cities were small in area—rarely more than 3 or 4 miles across. Most people lived at or near the place where they worked, and they moved about on foot.

Public, horse-drawn streetcars, introduced in the 1850s, changed this pattern somewhat. Those people who could afford the fares moved outside the cities, establishing new communities in the **suburbs**, or areas surrounding the cities. Cable cars and electric trolleys (Richmond, Virginia, had the first in 1888), elevated trains, automobiles (first appeared in 1893), and subways (Boston had the first in 1897), made commuting much easier and speeded suburban growth.

Cities grew upward, too. Before the Civil War, no building stood more than five stories high. Steel girders and steam-driven elevators—developed in 1861 by Elisha Graves Otis and electrified by the 1890s—permitted the construction of skyscrapers. The first skyscraper, which was 535 feet high, appeared in Chicago in 1885. Today, the world's tallest building is Chicago's Sears Tower, which is 1,454 feet high.

As a result of expansion, cities developed specialized areas. Banks, financial offices, law firms, and government offices located in one area and retail shops and department stores in another. Industrial, wholesale, and warehouse districts formed a ring around the center.

MAKING CONNECTIONS

Recall the discussion in Chapter 9 about the impact of technology on farms in the late 1800s. How might those same developments have contributed to the growth of cities?

Growing cities lured migrants from within the United States, too. This woman found work as a porter in a subway, itself a product of urban expansion.

Urban Living Conditions

Some working-class city dwellers moved into housing especially built for them by mill and factory owners. The rest found apartments wherever they could, mostly in buildings converted into multifamily units after being abandoned by middle-class residents who moved to the suburbs. Speculators also built many cheap tenements. These were originally apartment buildings that housed several families, but they came to be identified as dirty, run-down, and overcrowded slums.

Poor Conditions in the Slums Before long, because of poverty, overcrowding, and neglect, the old residential neighborhoods of cities gradually declined. Trees and grass disappeared beneath the new, cheaply built tenements. Soot from coal-fired steam engines and boilers made

| 1650 | 1700 | 1750 | 1800 | Links Across Time | 1850 | 1900 | 1950 | 2000 |

City Garbage

As cities grew in the late 1800s, so did sanitation problems. More people meant more garbage and more sewage. When the English writer Rudyard Kipling visited New York, he found "a generous scatter of filth and more mixed stinks than the winter wind can carry away."

In crowded tenement houses, people often threw their garbage out of the windows, until the narrow alleys were heaped more than a foot deep. Garbage in other areas was collected and loaded on barges to be dumped in the ocean.

Today, many cities in the United States face serious problems in safely and effectively managing the garbage they generate. Experts estimate that the amount of waste generated in the United States in 1995 will reach 200 million tons, or 4.2 pounds of garbage per person per day. Increasingly, landfills in large cities have reached their capacity and have been closed. *What solutions to the garbage problem are being used by many towns and cities today?*

the air seem dark and foul even in daylight. Hundreds of families crammed into spaces meant only for a few. Open sewers and backyard privies attracted rats and other disease-spreading vermin. In 1905 journalist Eleanor McMain quoted a university student who visited a block of tenements in New Orleans' Italian district and described them as "death traps,"

closely built, jammed together, with no side openings. Twenty-five per cent of the yard space is damp and gloomy. . . . Where the houses are three or more rooms in depth, the middle ones are dark, without outside ventilator. . . . There is no fire protection whatever.
Eleanor McMain, "Behind the Yellow Fever in Little Palermo"

The student went on to describe "the worst features," the toilets. Only 35 of the 144 families in the block he visited had separate toilets. Sometimes, six or seven families shared only one. He found not a single bathtub in the entire block.

Contagious diseases such as cholera, malaria, tuberculosis, diphtheria, and typhoid raged in such conditions. Epidemics, such as the yellow fever that swept through Memphis, Tennessee, in the late 1870s and through New Orleans, Louisiana, in the early 1900s, took thousands of lives. Children were especially vulnerable. In New York City, in one district of tenements, 6 out of 10 babies died before their first birthday.

Fires, such as those that struck Chicago in 1871 and Boston in 1872, were devastating in these crowded neighborhoods. Once a fire started, it leapt from roof to roof, leaving thousands homeless. Crime and vice also flourished, fed by the poverty and hopelessness of the slums.

Ghettos Some urban neighborhoods became **ghettos,** sections of cities in which certain ethnic or racial groups lived. Many immigrants wanted to live near others of their ethnic group because of the comfort of familiar language and traditions. These ethnic neighborhoods strongly reflected the culture of the homeland. Wrote one tenement-house inspector after visiting Philadelphia's "Little Italy,"

The black-eyed children rolling and tumbling together, the gaily colored dresses of the women and the crowds of street vendors all give the neighborhood a wholly foreign appearance.
Emily Dinwiddie, "Some Aspects of Italian Housing and Social Conditions in Philadelphia," 1904

In the crowded cities, many immigrants were forced to live in cramped, unsafe apartments. Such conditions troubled many Americans.

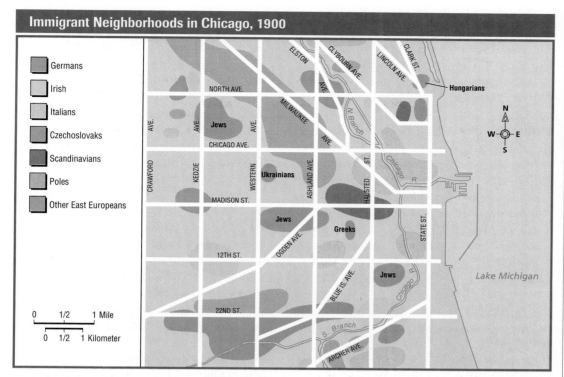

Immigrant Neighborhoods in Chicago, 1900

Germans
Irish
Italians
Czechoslovaks
Scandinavians
Poles
Other East Europeans

Geography and History: Interpreting Maps
As this map of Chicago shows, immigrants often settled in communities that had been established by others from their homeland. Thus, ethnic neighborhoods developed in many cities. *What advantages and disadvantages might ethnic neighborhoods have offered their residents?*

Dinwiddie's enjoyment of the neighborhood did not lessen her distress at the crowded conditions and poverty that she saw.

Other ghettos were neighborhoods that were segregated by necessity. Usually threats from whites were enough to maintain them. San Francisco's Chinatown had well-known street boundaries: "From Kearny to Powell, and from California to Broadway," recalled one resident. "If you ever passed them and went out there, the white kids would throw stones at you."

Still other ghettos were created by real estate restrictions known as covenants, which prevented the sale or rental of property to certain groups of people. Covenants often prevented African Americans, Mexicans, Asian Americans, and Jews from buying land or houses in the better sections of towns.

The Results of Rapid Urbanization

When the middle and upper classes left the cities for the suburbs beginning in the late 1800s, the gap between the well-to-do and the poor widened. Because many of the poor were foreign-born or people of color, the gap was not just economic, but ethnic and racial as well.

A few cities preserved areas for the most wealthy residents near the city center, such as Boston's Beacon Hill, Chicago's Gold Coast, or San Francisco's Nob Hill. Often, people living in these neighborhoods also owned country estates and were quite isolated from the nearby poverty. As Beacon Hill resident and future Massachusetts senator Henry Cabot Lodge recalled, it was not until the Boston fire of 1872 had rendered thousands of tenement dwellers homeless that he became aware of "how the other half lived."

Political Divisions Urban political divisions stemmed from social divisions. As cities expanded, pressure increased on officials to improve police and fire protection, sewage disposal, electrical and water service, transportation systems, and health care. To deliver these services, cities raised taxes and set up offices.

Various groups vied for control of city politics. Some groups represented the remaining middle and upper classes. These groups tended to be well educated and of old immigrant stock. Others were made up of new immigrant and working-class groups.

The Rise of Political Bosses Out of these clashing interests, city **political machines** arose. These were unofficial organizations designed to keep a particular party or group in power. Usually a single, powerful **political boss** presided over them. Sometimes the boss held public office. More often he handpicked others to run for office and then helped them win. An army of ward leaders, people who each administered a city district, assisted the boss by handing out city jobs and contracts and by doing favors for residents. In return, residents supported the machine ticket on election day.

Machines controlled jobs in all administrative offices. They gave their leaders access to graft, or money passed "under the table" in return for favors, such as the granting of a city contract for work.

Many people blamed the success of political machines on the large number of urban immigrants. They thought that the immigrants' lack of education and sophistication made them vulnerable to corrupt political practices. Immigrants did tend to vote for the boss and the followers of his political machine, but this was often because the machine members made up for the lack of a public welfare system. As one Boston ward leader explained,

Using Historical Evidence This bank features a figure who, when coins are placed into his hand, deposits the money into his pocket. *What message is this bank sending about political machines?*

*I*s somebody out of a job? We do our best to place him and not necessarily on the public payroll. Does the family run in arrears [in debt] with the landlord or the butcher? Then we lend a helping hand. Do the kids need shoes or clothing, or the mother a doctor? We do what we can, and since as the world is run, such things must be done, we keep old friends and make new ones.

Martin Lomasney, *Boston Globe,*
December 2, 1923

Cincinnati's George B. Cox, a former saloon owner, was an unusual example of a fairly honest political boss. A Republican, in 1879 he won election to the city council. Although he used this post to guarantee election victories and business contracts for the party faithful, he worked with local reformers to improve the quality of police officers and city services. He remained in power for almost twenty years.

One of the more notorious bosses of that time period was **William Marcy Tweed.** Tweed was the most powerful politician of **Tammany Hall,** the political club that controlled New York City's Democratic party. He amassed huge amounts of money through various methods, including graft and fraud. But the brilliant political cartoons of German immigrant Thomas Nast helped bring Tweed down by exposing his methods to the public. Convicted of crimes in 1873, Tweed eventually died in jail. Under new leaders, however, Tammany Hall dominated New York politics for another half century.

SECTION 3 REVIEW

Key Terms, People, and Places
1. Identify (a) Tammany Hall, (b) William Marcy Tweed.
2. Describe suburb.

Key Concepts
3. What inventions and developments contributed to the growth of cities?
4. How did slums develop?
5. Describe three ways that ghettos developed.

6. How did the growth of cities and urban problems contribute to the rise of political machines and political bosses?

Critical Thinking
7. **Identifying Assumptions** The text states that many immigrants settled among their own people in ethnic ghettos. What does this fact suggest about the immigrants' experience of new life in the United States?

Reading Tables and Analyzing Statistics

Statistical tables present large amounts of numerical data clearly and concisely. The patterns suggested by statistics must be carefully analyzed, however, and their sources evaluated for reliability. Statistics should be verified by other historical evidence.

Use the following steps to read and interpret the data below.

1. Determine what type of information is presented, and decide whether the source is reliable. The title of the table and the labels for the rows and columns tell you what information is presented. The source is usually found below the table. (a) What is the table's title? (b) How many decades are covered? (c) What is the source of the statistics in the table? (d) Can the data be used as historical evidence?

2. Read the information in the table. Note that the table provides the total number of immigrants for each region for a given five-year period. (a) Between 1871 and 1875, how many immigrants came from Asia? (b) Between 1881 and 1885, which region provided the largest number of immigrants? The smallest?

3. Find relationships among the statistics. You can use the data in this table to compare the immigrant populations among different regions or to trace changes in one region's immigration pattern over time.

(a) Which region had the largest total number of immigrants between 1871 and 1920? (b) During which decade did the region called America show the sharpest drop in its number of immigrants? (c) Which region on the table showed the largest increase in its number of immigrants from 1871 to 1920?

4. Use the data in the table to draw conclusions. Between 1891 and 1900, the unemployment rate in the United States averaged 10.5 percent. Between 1901 and 1910, it averaged 4.5 percent. Using the data in the table, what conclusions can you draw about the relationship between the unemployment rate and the immigration rate for those time periods?

Estimated Number of Immigrants to the United States, by Region, 1871–1920

	North-western Europe	Central Europe	Eastern Europe	Southern Europe	Asia [1]	Americas [2]	Africa	Oceania
1871–1875	858,325	549,610	15,580	37,070	65,727	193,354	205	6,312
1876–1880	493,866	254,511	24,052	39,248	58,096	210,690	153	4,602
1881–1885	1,193,819	1,128,528	63,443	120,297	60,432	403,977	331	4,406
1886–1890	1,131,844	729,967	157,749	211,399	7,948	22,990	526	8,168
1891–1895	745,433	762,216	251,405	314,625	19,255	14,734	163	2,215
1896–1900	392,907	432,363	270,421	389,608	51,981	24,238	187	1,750
1901–1905	761,527	1,121,234	711,546	1,050,721	115,941	63,774	1,829	6,134
1906–1910	807,020	1,365,530	1,058,024	1,260,424	127,626	298,114	5,539	6,890
1911–1915	652,189	1,027,138	978,931	1,137,539	123,719	528,098	5,847	6,126
1916–1920	201,304	23,276	33,547	322,640	68,840	615,373	2,596	7,301

[1] No record of immigration from Korea prior to 1948 [2] No record of immigration from Mexico for 1886 to 1893
Source: *Historical Statistics of the United States*

Ideas for Reform

SECTION PREVIEW

The flood of newcomers added colorful diversity to the nation's cities in the late 1800s but, at the same time, contributed to a host of problems. Shocked by social, economic, and political conditions in the cities, religious and social groups pushed programs for change.

Key Concepts
- One reform movement sought to limit immigration into the United States.
- Some reformers sought to control the behavior of the nation's immigrant class and city dwellers.
- Other reforms focused on helping the needy by providing charity and social services.

Key Terms, People, and Places
social gospel movement; Jane Addams, Ellen Gates Starr; Hull House

The crusade against alcohol was one example of ideas for reform in the late 1800s.

I n 1890 New York City had as many Italians as Naples, Italy; as many Germans as Hamburg, Germany; twice as many Irish as Dublin, Ireland; and twice as many Jews as Warsaw, Poland. In other cities around the country, immigrant populations were also large. Added to these numbers were many Americans drawn to the cities from the countryside. The steady stream of people to the cities brought serious urban problems that needed solutions.

Controlling Immigration and Behavior

Some reform groups felt that the problems of the cities stemmed from the presence of so many immigrants. Others objected to the habits of certain immigrants. These groups hoped to accomplish change by adopting reforms intended to "control" undesirable social behaviors. They believed that by enacting strict controls, the cities' problems of inadequate housing, pollution, crime, and corruption could be solved.

Reformers who were interested in this approach pursued their goals in two ways: by seeking limits on immigration and by trying to outlaw certain behaviors. In these ways, reformers hoped to return the nation to what they believed was a past of purity and virtue.

Nativism In the 1880s, nativism, the movement to restrict immigration that first began in the 1850s, reappeared. The movement's first success came with the passage in 1882 of the Chinese Exclusion Act. Nativist leanings, however, were not restricted to anti-Asian feelings.

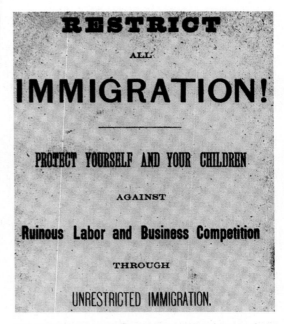

RESTRICT ALL

IMMIGRATION!

PROTECT YOURSELF AND YOUR CHILDREN

AGAINST

Ruinous Labor and Business Competition

THROUGH

UNRESTRICTED IMMIGRATION.

This 1885 brochure reflects the concern that employers would hire immigrants, who would work for lower wages, instead of native-born Americans.

In the Midwest, the American Protective Association called for the teaching of only American culture and the English language in schools and for tighter rules on citizenship and employment of all "aliens." Nativists across the country fanned public hysteria about the threat that foreigners presented to the country.

Nativists won another victory in 1885 when Congress repealed the contract labor law, which had allowed the recruitment of workers from abroad after the Civil War. Even after the law's repeal, the practice continued illegally. During periods of labor unrest, companies often brought in foreign workers to replace striking employees. These actions served to increase antiforeign feelings among workers.

Upper-class nativism found expression in the Immigration Restriction League, organized in 1894 by some recent graduates of Harvard College. Republican senator Henry Cabot Lodge gave the League a voice in Congress.

The League hoped to exclude "unfit" immigrants by forcing them to pass literacy tests. Its main targets for exclusion were the so-called "new" immigrants from southern and eastern Europe, whose cultures differed significantly from the members of the League.

Prohibition Along with nativism, the temperance movement saw a revival. Three organizations dominated the movement in the late nineteenth century—the Prohibition party (1869), the Woman's Christian Temperance Union (1874), and the Anti-Saloon League (1893). All of these prohibition groups opposed drinking on the grounds that it led to terrible personal tragedies.

Prohibition groups also opposed drinking because of what they saw as the links between saloons, immigrants, and political bosses. Immigrant men often used saloons as "social clubs" where they could pick up information about jobs as well as socialize. To prohibitionists, however, saloons formed the center of a subversive movement to take over the United States. "Foreign control or conquest is rapidly making us un-Christian, with immorality throned in power," wrote Prohibition party supporter A. A. Hopkins in 1908. Had foreigners used "armies and fleets," Hopkins cried,

they could not have achieved greater control. Such views won many followers.

Purity Crusaders As urban populations grew, vice—whether in the form of drugs, gambling, or prostitution—became big business. Vice was not unique to the cities, but large urban populations made vice highly visible and very profitable. Then as now, many residents fought to rid their communities of illegal and immoral activities.

"Purity crusaders" led the way. In 1873 Anthony Comstock founded the New York Society for the Suppression of Vice. The following year he won passage of a law that prohibited sending through the United States mails materials deemed obscene, including those that described methods to prevent unwanted pregnancy. The Comstock Law, as it came to be known, slowed the distribution of information about birth control for decades.

Other purity crusaders attacked political machines on the grounds that machine-controlled police forces actually profited from vice. Police were known to demand payment from gamblers and prostitutes, for example, in return for ignoring illegal activities. Periodically, purity forces joined with other reformers, campaigned on an antivice platform, and threw machine candidates out of office. Usually the machines returned to power in later elections, however, by ridiculing the superior tone of many purists and by arguing that morals were personal issues.

Using Historical Evidence The caption on this *Judge* cartoon reads "Uncle Sam is a man of strong features." *What does the cartoon suggest about the artist's view of immigration?*

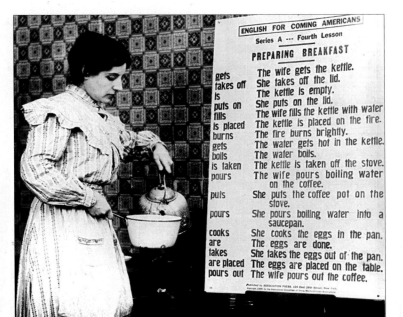

English for Coming Americans

Series A --- Fourth Lesson

PREPARING BREAKFAST

gets	The wife gets the kettle.
takes off	She takes off the lid.
is	The kettle is empty.
puts on	She puts on the lid.
fills	The wife fills the kettle with water
is placed	The kettle is placed on the fire.
burns	The fire burns brightly.
gets	The water gets hot in the kettle.
boils	The water boils.
is taken	The kettle is taken off the stove.
pours	The wife pours boiling water on the coffee.
puts	She puts the coffee pot on the stove.
pours	She pours boiling water into a saucepan.
cooks	She cooks the eggs in the pan.
are	The eggs are done.
takes	She takes the eggs out of the pan.
are placed	The eggs are placed on the table.
pours out	The wife pours out the coffee.

Published by ASSOCIATION PRESS, 124 East 28th Street, New York.
Copyright 1909, by the International Committee of Young Men's Christian Associations.

Some reformers focused their efforts on helping immigrants adjust to life in the United States. This immigrant is learning English—and the American way of life.

MAKING CONNECTIONS

Do you think the idea of nativism relates to the concept of social Darwinism? Explain.

Helping the Needy

Other reformers, moved by social conscience or religious idealism, were developing a "helping" approach to social change. They argued that the middle and upper classes should take responsibility for poverty and try to improve social conditions. Although their methods had limitations—and in fact sometimes attempted to control individual behavior—their primary goal was to help the needy.

The Charity Organization Movement In 1882 Josephine Shaw Lowell founded the New York Charity Organization Society (COS). The COS tried to make charity "scientific" and kept detailed files on those who received help. In part, COS leaders wanted to prevent the duplication of efforts, but they also wanted to help only those they considered the "worthy" poor. This attitude sometimes led to unkind treatment of the needy or to humiliating demands for "proof" of poverty.

Some charity reformers interfered in the lives of immigrants. One clergyman who worked in a southern Italian neighborhood claimed that social workers "burst" into homes of immigrant women and "upset the usual routine of their lives, opening windows, undressing children, giving orders not to eat this and that, not to wrap babies in swaddling clothes." Many COS members wanted immigrants to adopt American, middle-class standards of child-raising, cooking, and cleaning, no matter how strange to residents' cultural backgrounds. While some immigrants found this intrusive, others were grateful for the advice and assistance they received.

The Social Gospel Movement In the 1880s and 1890s, urban churches began to provide social services for the poor who now surrounded them. They also tried to focus prohibition and purity campaigns in new directions. Instead of blaming immigrants for drinking, gambling, and other destructive behaviors, they pointed out the unfortunate circumstances that drove people into such activities.

Soon, a social reform movement developed within religious institutions. Called the **social gospel movement,** it sought to apply the gospel of Jesus directly to society. In 1908, followers of such views formed the Federal Council of the Churches of Christ, an organization that supported improved living conditions and a larger share in the national wealth for all workers. Other religious organizations, such as the Society for Ethical Culture and Jewish synagogues, adapted the social gospel ideal for their own denominations.

The Settlement Movement Thousands of young, educated women and men put the social gospel into practice in an innovative reform program called the social or neighborhood settlement movement. Settlement houses offered social services, believing that charity in the form of money given by well-meaning outsiders never really helped the poor. Idealists decided that in order to find out what would be most helpful, they had to live in poor neighborhoods to witness the effects of poverty firsthand.

In 1889, inspired by a settlement movement in London, **Jane Addams** and **Ellen Gates Starr** bought the dilapidated Charles Hull mansion in Chicago, renovated it, and then opened its doors to their immigrant neighbors. At first, Starr and Addams simply wanted to get to know them, offering help when needed. Soon, they began anticipating and responding to the needs of the community as a whole.

Over the decades that followed, Addams and Starr turned **Hull House** into a center of constructive activities and programs. At Hull House, neighbors could attend cultural events, take classes, or display exhibits of crafts from their home countries. The settlement set up child-care centers, clubs and summer camps for boys and girls, playgrounds and vacation recreation programs, employment and legal aid bureaus, and health-care clinics. It also launched investigations of city economic, political, and social conditions. These actions provided a foundation for many social reforms in the future.

Settlements like Hull House sprang up across the country. Each settlement was unique. The Henry Street Settlement, founded by Lillian Wald on New York's Lower East Side, was originally a nurses' settlement. Wald's plan was to develop a system to offer home care to the poor. Its programs soon expanded to resemble many of those at Hull House.

Other settlements opened up in African American communities. Missionaries founded settlements, in part to gain converts but also to apply social gospel ideas in practical ways. Hundreds of college graduates, especially women excluded from many other professions, became settlement workers.

By 1910, more than four hundred settlements existed. Most were supported by donations and staffed by volunteers or people willing to work for low wages and free room and board. Except for leaders, such as Addams and Wald, most workers spent only a few years in these jobs. Many went on to professional careers in social work, education, or government, but few ever forgot their settlement experience. "I don't know that my attitude changed," wrote one former settlement worker, "but my point of view certainly did, or perhaps it would be more true to say that now I have several points of view." The settlements' ability to widen perspectives on social conditions and close the gap between social divisions may have been their most lasting contribution.

Judith Lathrop (left), Jane Addams (center), and Mary McDowell (right) were a few of the pioneers of the settlement house movement. *Inset:* Reformers offered help to newcomers by watching over their children while they worked.

SECTION 4 REVIEW

Key Terms, People, and Places
1. Identify (a) Jane Addams, (b) Ellen Gates Starr, (c) Hull House.

Key Concepts
2. What were the overall goals of the followers of nativism and prohibitionism?
3. Describe some activities of the purity crusaders.

4. Describe the charity organization, social gospel, and settlement movements.

Critical Thinking
5. **Testing Conclusions** The text states that the "helpers" sometimes sought to control people's behavior at the same time they helped them. Can you find examples to support this statement?

Chapter Review

Key Terms
1. Gilded Age
2. laissez-faire
3. blue laws
4. Pendleton Act
5. Interstate

Commerce Act
6. steerage
7. suburb
8. ghetto
9. political machine
10. political boss

11. Tammany Hall
12. social gospel movement

People
13. Jacob S. Coxey
14. William Marcy Tweed

15. Jane Addams
16. Ellen Gates Starr

Places
17. Ellis Island
18. Angel Island
19. Hull House

Terms For each term above, write a sentence that explains its relation to politics, immigration issues, urban challenges, or reform movements in the Gilded Age.

Matching Review the key terms in the list above. If you are not sure of a term's meaning, review its definition in the chapter. Then choose a term from the list that best matches each description below.
1. a hands-off approach to economic issues
2. the movement to restrict immigration
3. the large, open area beneath a ship's deck in which immigrants often traveled
4. a section of a city inhabited mostly by people of one ethnic or racial group

5. unofficial organizations designed to keep a particular party or group in power

True or False Determine whether each statement is true or false. If it is true, write "true." If it is false, change the underlined person or place to make the statement true.
1. At <u>Angel Island</u>, neighbors could attend cultural events or display crafts from their home countries.
2. Populist <u>William Marcy Tweed</u> demanded that the government create jobs for the unemployed.
3. <u>Jane Addams</u> renovated a dilapidated mansion in Chicago and opened its doors to neighborhood immigrants.
4. Most Asian immigrants entered the United States at <u>Ellis Island.</u>

Section 1 (pp. 308–313)
1. What practices bred corruption in American business and politics during the Gilded Age?
2. Describe three economic or political issues that concerned voters during the Gilded Age. What stands did the Republican and Democratic parties take on these issues?
3. What important laws were passed at the national level during the Gilded Age?

Section 2 (pp. 314–319)
4. What conditions in their homelands caused people to immigrate to the United States?
5. How did patterns of immigration change during the late 1800s?
6. What hardships did immigrants face during and after their arrival in the United States?

Section 3 (pp. 320–324)
7. What factors accounted for the tremendous expansion of American cities during the late 1800s?
8. Describe some of the urban problems created by the flood of immigrants and people from within the United States who settled in the nation's cities.
9. What were the advantages and disadvantages of political machines and bosses for urban residents?

Section 4 (pp. 326–329)
10. Describe some of the actions nativists took to restrict immigration.
11. How did purity crusaders attempt to control the behavior of the nation's immigrants and city dwellers?
12. How did the settlement movement seek to help the poor?

1. **Formulating Questions** Imagine that you are interviewing a young adult of the 1890s who is thinking about immigrating to the United States. What five questions would you ask to determine whether he or she is making a well-informed decision?

2. **Making Comparisons** Blue laws that restrict the operation of stores and the sale of liquor on Sundays are still enforced in some parts of the United States. Do you think that the arguments for and against these laws are the same as those used in the late 1800s?

3. **Identifying Assumptions** During the late 1800s, reformers sought to help immigrants by providing charity and social services. Many reformers also wanted immigrants to adopt American standards and customs. Do you consider the Americanization of immigrants a worthwhile objective? Why or why not?

4. **Drawing Conclusions** You have read that before 1890, most immigrants to the United States came from northern Europe. In the 1890s, the pattern shifted so that most immigrants came from southern and eastern Europe and the Middle East. In 1891 the Office of the Superintendent of Immigration was created to determine who was "fit" to live in the United States; all those admitted to the country were required to pass a physical examination. What conclusions can you draw from these facts?

1. **Evaluating Primary Sources** Review the primary source quotation on page 329. What does the speaker mean by now having several points of view?

2. **Understanding the Visuals** Section 4, page 326, states that "Reformers . . . pursued their goals in two ways: by seeking limits on immigration and by trying to outlaw certain behavior." Find two visuals from Section 4 that illustrate these two methods.

3. **Writing About the Chapter** Reread the profiles of Sadie Frowne and Tameji Eto in Section 2. Then write a fictional profile of a late nineteenth century immigrant. Describe the reasons your character is leaving his or her home country and the experiences he or she might encounter in the United States. Note how your character's experiences are similar to or different from the experiences of other immigrants.

As you write your profile, make sure that you have included enough details to make your account realistic. Proofread your profile and draft a final copy.

4. **Using the Graphic Organizer** This graphic organizer, which shows the results of the rapid expansion of American cities during the late 1800s, uses dotted lines and arrows to show connections between ideas. (a) According to the graphic organizer below, what was the first result of the growth of cities? Based on your reading, why do you think urban problems led to the widening gap between rich and the poor? (b) On a separate piece of paper, fill in the blank boxes with two important examples of urban problems during this era. (c) Create your own graphic organizer about politics during the Gilded Age.

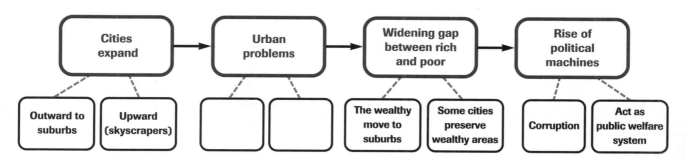

Cultural and Social Transformations
1870–1915

*A*long with the growth of industry and urban areas in the late 1800s came a host of other changes. More children began to attend school, and college became an attainable goal for a growing number of students. A recreation industry, which borrowed heavily from African American culture, emerged to meet the needs of the new urban workers. Yet some segments of society remained mired in the mud of old discriminatory attitudes, refusing to grant such groups as women and African Americans an equal chance at success.

Events in the United States

1870 Fewer than half of all American children attend school.

1873 Boston University opens its doors to women professors.

1883 Joseph Pulitzer buys the New York World.

1890 National American Woman Suffrage Association is founded.

| 1870 | 1875 | 1880 | 1885 | 1890 |

Events in the World

1872 Japan begins universal military service.

1884 All adult males win the right to vote in Great Britain.

Pages 334 – 337
The Expansion of Education

Education was a lofty goal that was out of reach for most nineteenth-century Americans. As the century came to a close, however, more and more Americans, including women and minorities, gained the opportunity to learn and grow.

Pages 338 – 342
Recreation for the Masses

The growing urban working class took its recreation seriously in the late 1800s. Entertainment and sports became new industries that careened onto the American scene and collided with more restrained values.

Pages 343 – 346
The World of Jim Crow

White society proved quite resourceful at finding ways to repress African Americans in the years after Reconstruction. Yet many African Americans demonstrated an even greater will to rise above the discrimination and hate.

Pages 348 – 351
The Woman Question

Much had changed for women in the late 1800s—new jobs, new educational opportunities, new roles in the home. Yet much stayed the same, including continued economic and political inequality. This contradiction fueled great debate at the turn of the century.

1896 The Supreme Court legalizes segregation in Plessy v. Ferguson decision.

1903 The movie The Great Train Robbery is a huge popular success.

1910 The National Association for the Advancement of Colored People (NAACP) is founded.

1915 The Supreme Court declares grandfather clauses unconstitutional.

1895 **1900** **1905** **1910** **1915**

1896 First modern Olympic Games take place in Athens.

1903 Emmeline Pankhurst founds the Women's Social and Political Union in Britain.

1910 Sun Yat-sen founds the Nationalist People's party in China.

1913 Russian composer Igor Stravinsky revolutionizes music with The Rite of Spring.

The Expansion of Education

SECTION PREVIEW

Education was a lofty goal that was out of reach for most nineteenth-century Americans. As the century came to a close, however, more and more Americans, including women and minorities, gained the opportunity to learn and grow.

Key Concepts
- Opportunities for public education expanded after the Civil War.
- Opportunities for higher education also expanded in the late 1800s.
  - The wider availability of higher education had a powerful impact on women and African Americans.

Key Terms, People, and Places
Booker T. Washington, W.E.B. Du Bois

Beginning in the late 1800s, a growing number of Americans sought the benefits of education.

A mericans had long understood that a democratic society functioned best when its citizens could read and write and communicate effectively. By the late 1800s, however, an education had became more than just a worthy goal. For a growing number of Americans, it was a necessary first step toward economic and social success. In recognition of this fact and in response to public demand, educational opportunities expanded.

Public Schools Gain More Students

By the time of the Civil War, more than half of the nation's white children were receiving some kind of formal education. A high school diploma was still the exception, however: even in 1870, only 2 percent of all seventeen-year-olds graduated from high school. Only a tiny elite went on to college. Because most children had to help their families earn a living, many left school at an early age.

The vast majority of American children had to make do with the basic skills acquired during a few school years, each of which lasted just a few months. As the United States became more industrialized and urbanized in the postwar era, young people began to realize that they needed more than basic skills to advance in life. Parents began pressuring local governments to increase school funding and lengthen the school year. At the same time, reformers pressured state governments to limit child labor. By 1900, thirty-two states had passed compulsory school laws that required children eight to fourteen years old to attend school.

Although unevenly enforced, these laws had a powerful effect. In 1870 overall school enrollment was less than 50 percent of all American children—including fewer than 1 in 10 African Americans. Fewer than 72,000 went to the nation's high schools. By 1910 enrollment was nearly 60 percent, and more than 1,000,000 students were studying in the nation's high schools.

Immigrants and Public Education Immigrants especially treasured American public education. In the mid-1890s, the Russian immigrant father of author Mary Antin was proud to send his children to a Boston public school, convinced "there was no surer way to their advancement and happiness." Adults attended school at night to learn English and civics to qualify for citizenship.

In teaching American standards of cleanliness, thrift, patriotism, and hard work, public schools promoted assimilation of immigrants into the American way of life. In playing games like baseball or basketball or cooking traditional American foods in home economics classes, immigrant children became Americanized and began to forget their native cultures.

Some parents resisted Americanization. Many Greek Orthodox and Eastern European Jewish parents sent their children to religious schools to learn about their cultural heritage in their native languages. Polish parents in Chicago in the early 1900s sent their children to

Roman Catholic schools where they learned about Polish history and religion in Polish but studied American history, bookkeeping, and algebra in English.

Immigrants also made their own contributions to American culture. As they shared customs and habits from their homelands, they enriched their new country. Thus, immigrants and Americans each benefited from exposure to one another.

Uneven Support for Schools Though state and local government support for education was expanding, not everyone benefited equally. Compared to white schools, schools for African Americans received less money—sometimes half as much. Writing of her upbringing in Durham, North Carolina, in the 1910s, civil rights activist Pauli Murray remembered vividly the contrast between "what we had and what the white children had."

W e got the greasy, torn, dog-eared books; they got the new ones. They had field day in the city park; we had it on a furrowed stubby hillside. They got wide mention in the newspaper; we got a paragraph at the bottom. . . . We came to know that whatever we had was always inferior.

African Americans were not the only group to receive a separate but unequal education. For example, beginning in the 1890s, Mexican Americans in parts of the Southwest were shuttled off to schools separate from and less well funded than those for white children. Many Asians in California were sent to separate schools. And by 1900, only a small percentage of Native American children were receiving any kind of formal schooling.

MAKING CONNECTIONS

What do today's students learn about the role of diverse cultures in American life? How are these lessons different from what students learned in the late 1800s?

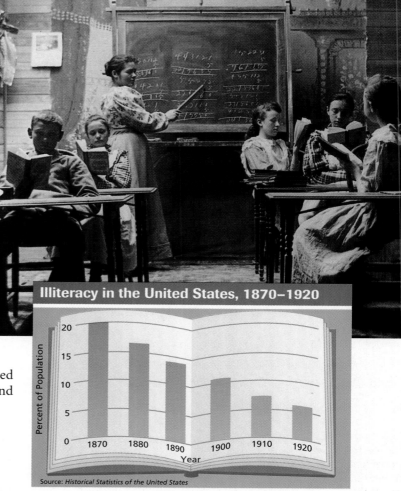

Illiteracy in the United States, 1870–1920

Source: *Historical Statistics of the United States*

Interpreting Graphs
The expansion of education meant more students in classrooms, such as this one in Nebraska in 1895. It also meant jobs for women, who filled many teaching posts. *How does the change in the nation's literacy rate reflect the growth of education between 1870 and 1920?*

Higher Education Expands

Between 1880 and 1900, more than 250 new American colleges and universities opened, and college enrollment more than doubled. Wealthy capitalists often endowed institutions of higher learning. For example, in 1885 Leland Stanford, the entrepreneur who had helped build the transcontinental railroad, and his wife, Jane Lathrop Stanford, founded Stanford University. John D. Rockefeller made donations to the University of Chicago that eventually totaled $40 million.

After the Civil War, middle-class women called for greater educational opportunities. In response, educators and philanthropists established private women's colleges with high

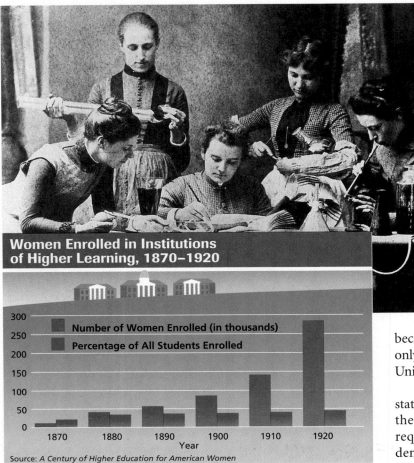

Women Enrolled in Institutions of Higher Learning, 1870–1920

- Number of Women Enrolled (in thousands)
- Percentage of All Students Enrolled

300
250
200
150
100
50
0

1870   1880   1890   1900   1910   1920
Year

Source: *A Century of Higher Education for American Women*

Interpreting Graphs
The women in this 1880 Smith College chemistry class were among the first to benefit from new higher education opportunities. *Did women achieve equality with men in the percentage of enrolled students?*

Bates, had been coeducational since long before the Civil War. Some colleges also accepted African Americans. In the postwar years, they were joined by institutions such as Cornell and Boston University; the latter announced in 1873 that it welcomed women not only as students but also as professors.

Schools founded for African Americans after the Civil War, such as Fisk and Howard, accepted both women and men. Women's numbers remained small, however, because most of the scholarships that made college study possible went to men. Anna Julia Cooper, an Oberlin graduate who later became an educator, estimated that there were only thirty black college women studying in the United States in 1891.

Women had to fight for full access to most state-funded institutions. For example, in 1863 the coeducational University of Wisconsin required women to stand until all male students had found seats. After 1867 Wisconsin directed women into a "Female College." In 1873, however, when women refused to attend segregated classes, the university was forced to reestablish coeducation.

academic standards. The first was New York's Vassar College, which opened in 1865.

Pressure also increased on men's colleges to admit women in the 1880s and 1890s. Rather than do so, some schools founded separate institutions for women that were related to the men's schools. Tulane in Louisiana became the only major southern university to take this step when it established Sophie Newcomb College in 1886. Shortly thereafter, Columbia in New York opened Barnard (1889), Brown in Rhode Island started Pembroke (1891), and Harvard University in Massachusetts established Radcliffe (1894).

Opportunities for men and women to study together—coeducation—also increased. A number of religiously based colleges, including Oberlin, Knox, Antioch, Swarthmore, and

Who Went to College?

Even with the new opportunities, only a tiny proportion went to college at the turn of the century. Because in the 1890s annual family incomes averaged under a thousand dollars, parents were hard pressed to meet college costs. A few fortunate and gifted students won scholarships or worked their way through college.

Because most scholarships went to men, women had a harder time obtaining a college education. Even those who could afford the cost faced prejudice against educating women. Parents feared that college made daughters too "independent" or unmarriageable or brought them in contact with "unacceptable" friends. When Martha "Minnie" Carey Thomas finally persuaded her Quaker father to allow her to take the Cornell University entrance exams, he said to her, "Well, Minnie, I am proud of thee, but this university is an awful place to swallow thee up."

African Americans and Higher Education

African Americans also had to fight prejudice in institutions of higher learning. In 1890 only 160 African Americans were attending white colleges. Many more were studying at the nation's African American institutions. By 1900, for example, more than 2,000 students had graduated from thirty-four African American colleges.

Foremost among these graduates was **Booker T. Washington.** Born into slavery in 1856, Washington began his studies at Hampton Institute in Virginia in 1872. His education there inspired him to develop a similar institution for African Americans in Tuskegee, Alabama. Washington taught his students skills and attitudes that he thought would help them succeed in an environment of increasing violence and discrimination. He told his students to prepare for productive, profitable work. Washington urged them to bring their intellect "to bear upon the everyday practical things of life, upon something that is needed to be done, and something which they will be permitted to do in the community in which they reside." African Americans could win white acceptance, he predicted, by succeeding in those occupations that whites needed them to fill.

Washington spelled out his approach in a speech he delivered in 1895 at the Atlanta Exposition. In addition to appealing to many African Americans, his ideas relieved those whites who had worried that educated blacks would be difficult to manage. Whites began to consult him on all issues concerning race rela-tions, and President Theodore Roosevelt invited him to the White House in 1901. Washington's autobiography, *Up From Slavery* (1901), became a classic, and he became a dominant force in the African American community.

W.E.B. Du Bois led the next generation of African Americans in a different direction. Born free in Massachusetts, Du Bois graduated from Tennessee's Fisk University and then in 1895 became the first African American to earn a Ph.D. from Harvard.

Du Bois rejected Washington's message, which he mockingly called the Atlanta Compromise. Instead, Du Bois argued that the brightest African Americans had to step forward to lead their people. He urged those future leaders to seek an advanced liberal arts education. Only when they had developed "intelligence, broad sympathy, knowledge of the world that was and is, and of the relation of men to it," he wrote, would they be equipped to lead "the Negro race." In writings such as *The Souls of Black Folk,* Du Bois urged blacks not to define themselves as whites saw them, but to take pride in both their African and their American heritages.

Expanding Opportunities While the Washington–Du Bois debate raged, college opportunities continued to grow. By 1915 the college experience was still special but no longer unheard of for most Americans. Families of only middling income began to aspire to a college education for their children. This wide availability of advanced education would distinguish the United States from other industrialized countries.

Though W.E.B. Du Bois (top) and Booker T. Washington were both influential African Americans, they differed greatly on how blacks might best benefit from education.

SECTION 1 REVIEW

Key Terms, People, and Places
1. Identify (a) Booker T. Washington, (b) W.E.B. Du Bois.

Key Concepts
2. What were the educational possibilities before the Civil War? How did this situation change after the war?
3. Why was education so important to many immigrants?

4. What kinds of higher educational opportunities were available after the Civil War, and with what results?

Critical Thinking
5. **Predicting Consequences** How would you expect the increase in educational opportunities to have affected women and African Americans?

SECTION 2

Recreation for the Masses

SECTION PREVIEW

The growing urban working class took its recreation seriously in the late 1800s. Entertainment and sports became new industries that careened onto the American scene and collided with more restrained values.

Key Concepts

- A new mass entertainment and recreation culture emerged in the late nineteenth century.
- The new culture borrowed heavily from African American musical styles.
- Popular amusements stimulated conflict between the working class and those who wanted to maintain existing moral codes.

Key Terms, People, and Places

vaudeville, yellow journalism, minstrel show, ragtime, jazz, Victorianism

Basketball and other sports were popular forms of recreation at the turn of the century.

I n rural America, time spent in play was considered time wasted. Only after the harvest was in or at times of special celebration would rural people allow themselves leisure activities, such as family and community get-togethers. These activities tended to be free—people provided their own food and music.

In contrast, working-class city residents worked by the clock. After long hours on the job, they wanted fun things to do. To meet the need for inexpensive entertainment for the masses, a commercial recreation industry emerged.

Popular Amusements in the Late 1800s

Of all the places where working people gathered in the late 1800s, saloons were the most popular. Denver (population 133,859) had nearly five hundred by 1900; New York City (population 3,437,202) had an estimated ten thousand. Besides providing entertainment, saloons served as places for forging neighborhood and ethnic ties and political alliances. Most of their customers were men. More popular with women were dance halls and cabarets, where patrons watched musical shows and danced the latest dances.

Trolley parks—amusement parks built at the end of trolley lines—were popular with the whole family. Moving pictures also appeared during this era. *The Great Train Robbery,* released in 1903, was a huge success and demonstrated very clearly the commercial possibilities of movies. By 1908 the nation had eight thousand nickelodeons—theaters set up in converted stores or warehouses that charged a nickel admission—showing slapstick comedies and other films to as many as 200,000 people daily.

Sports As leisure time expanded in the late 1800s, sporting events became a favorite pastime. Boxing and horse racing were widely enjoyed spectator sports, but baseball was by far the most popular.

By 1860, groups such as fire fighters, police officers, and teachers had formed baseball clubs in many American cities. When audiences for these games grew, entrepreneurs enclosed fields and charged admission. Teams formed into leagues and began to play championship games. In the 1870s, the sport's best players were paid. The most popular leagues, though open to Native Americans and white immigrants, excluded black players. Even the best African Americans had no alternative but to play in segregated leagues until the late 1940s.

What Americans loved most about baseball was the speed, daring, and split-second timing of the game. Pitcher Christy Mathewson commented, "The American public wants its excitement rolled up in a package and handed out quickly." Baseball fulfilled that desire. Popular writer Mark Twain remarked on the game's need for precision: "In baseball, you've got to do everything just right, or you don't get there."

Baseball and football, another sport that achieved great popularity in the late 1800s, were exclusively men's games. Women, too, took up sports. Ice-skating had long been a favorite recreation of women. The national bicycling fad of the late 1800s also became popular among women. And because this sport required practical clothing, it helped to liberate women from some of the restrictive clothing styles of the day. "For muscle-play, freedom is the first requisite," a doctor advised in an 1896 article entitled "Bicycling for Women: The Puzzling Question of Costume." Women athletes had to abandon corsets, which wrapped tightly around their torsos and restricted breathing. Thanks to cycling, as well as to sports such as golf and tennis, shirtwaists—or ready-made blouses—that were tucked into shorter or split skirts, became socially acceptable.

Women students also played basketball, an indoor game invented in 1891 to keep athletes fit during winter. On the assumption that stiff competition and hard physical exertion were unhealthy for women, recreation specialists devised less demanding rules for them. Women athletes also learned gymnastics and swam, although social standards required them to wear black cotton stockings under short dresses or bloomers.

Vaudeville

Inexpensive theatrical performances attracted large crowds in this era. **Vaudeville,** a type of variety show that first appeared in the 1870s, was the most popular. Vaudeville performances consisted of comic sketches based on ethnic or racial humor, song-and-dance routines, and ventriloquists, jugglers, and trapeze artists.

Vaudeville was strictly for the family. Theater owners insisted on keeping everything on a "high plane of respectability and moral cleanliness." A "Notice to Performers" posted on the backstage wall of a prominent vaudeville house in 1899 stated that

Such words as Liar, Slob, Son-of-a-Gun, Devil, Sucker, . . . and all other words unfit for the ears of ladies and children, also any reference to questionable streets, resorts, localities, and bar-rooms, are prohibited under fine of instant discharge.

Like baseball, vaudeville came to be seen as typically American in character. It appealed to men and women of all ages and classes. Like much of what is on television today, vaudeville was entertainment for the masses.

Newspapers

For city residents, newspapers always had been a vital source of information. In the late 1800s, they became a popular form of entertainment. Taking advantage of new production methods, publishers created larger and more interesting publications. They introduced new features, such as comics, sports sections, Sunday editions, women's pages, stories "hot off the wires," and graphic pictures.

Between 1870 and 1899, newspaper circulation soared from 2.8 to 24 million copies a day. Competing heatedly with one another, publishers urged reporters to discover fresh news

Sports were important to both men and women in this era. Baseball was a well-established spectator sport by 1886, when the picture of the team above was taken. Bicycling provided women with exercise, entertainment—and liberation from restrictive clothing.

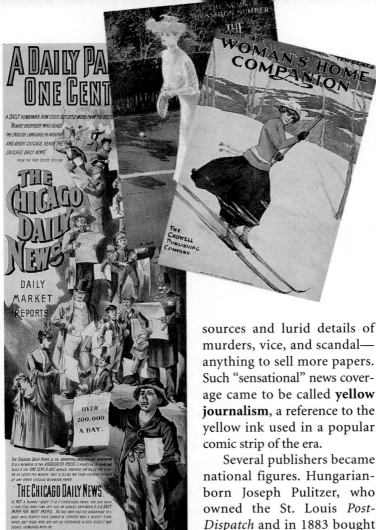

sources and lurid details of murders, vice, and scandal—anything to sell more papers. Such "sensational" news coverage came to be called **yellow journalism**, a reference to the yellow ink used in a popular comic strip of the era.

Several publishers became national figures. Hungarian-born Joseph Pulitzer, who owned the St. Louis *Post-Dispatch* and in 1883 bought the New York *World*, hoped to "expose all fraud and sham, fight all public evils and abuses." Californian William Randolph Hearst used his father's gold-mining millions to put out the even more sensational New York *Journal*.

Yellow journalism also troubled many. Critics charged that the "yellow press" intruded into private lives, invented facts, and sensationalized the ordinary with exaggeration.

Absorbing and Transforming African American Culture

As the mass entertainment culture expanded, it absorbed many forms of African American art. In the process, the culture transformed them in order to meet the tastes of white audiences.

The Negro Spiritual In 1871 nine Fisk University students went on a singing tour to raise money for their struggling school. When the Fisk Jubilee Singers began to concentrate solely on spirituals, they excited such interest that triumphal tours of the United States, England, and Europe resulted. Britain's Queen Victoria was so impressed that she had a group portrait of them painted.

In the process of making the spiritual acceptable to white audiences, the Fisk group and others like it transformed the musical form. It acquired characteristics of the European musical tradition with which whites were familiar. This new spiritual became identified as an American art form, as opposed to a purely African American one.

Minstrelsy Other forms of African American culture were also absorbed into the white entertainment world. The **minstrel show** began when white actors discovered they could captivate audiences with exaggerated imitations of African American music, dance, and humor. The shows perpetuated racist stereotypes, generally portraying African Americans as foolish imitators of a white culture they could not understand.

White actors in minstrel shows performed in "blackface"—they blackened their faces and hands and painted on wide grins. African Americans also performed in blackface, as minstrel jobs were often the only stage work they could get.

Minstrelsy peaked between the 1840s and 1870s, but even afterward every major town had a minstrel show. It survived long into the twentieth century, in vaudeville and the movies.

The music of ragtime composer Scott Joplin remains popular today.

Ragtime and Jazz A type of music known as **ragtime** originated among black musicians playing in saloons in the South and Midwest in the 1880s. Consisting of melodies with shifting accents over a steady, marching-band beat, it became a rage in the 1890s. Ragtime composer Scott Joplin, who came from

St. Louis, Missouri, became famous for his "Maple Leaf Rag" of 1899.

Jazz grew out of the vibrant musical culture of New Orleans, a city with a popular marching-band tradition. After the Civil War, African American bands experimented with new styles of playing, including "raggy" rhythms and call-and-response forms in which singers or instruments respond to a single leader. They also played jazzed-up versions of familiar melodies, such as hymns or the mournful "blues" songs of southern sharecroppers.

New Orleans jazz styles from the 1890s slowly worked their way northward through towns along the Mississippi River. By 1915, thanks in part to the success of the phonograph, jazz—and the dances associated with it—was becoming a national passion.

MAKING CONNECTIONS

How do the attitudes about African Americans as reflected in minstrel shows relate to such issues as slavery and unequal government support for the education of African Americans?

Popular Amusements and Their Critics

Middle- and upper-class city residents had long found much that was offensive in popular amusements. Since well before the Civil War, for example, they had attacked saloons for wasting workers' time and money and helping to cause family abuse. Now, critics charged dance halls and trolley parks with promoting an unsupervised mixing of the sexes. Women especially were at risk of dire consequences associated with unrespectable amusements, critics worried.

Such concerns about the proper behavior of women are examples of **Victorianism,** a term that refers to moral ideas associated with Britain's Queen Victoria, who reigned from 1837 to 1901. Many middle- and upper-class Americans accepted the Victorian morals that dictated proper behavior. They believed that self-control was essential to social progress. Thus, they held personal behavior to a high standard, requiring perfect manners, hard work, sobriety, and, above all, restraint in relations between men and women.

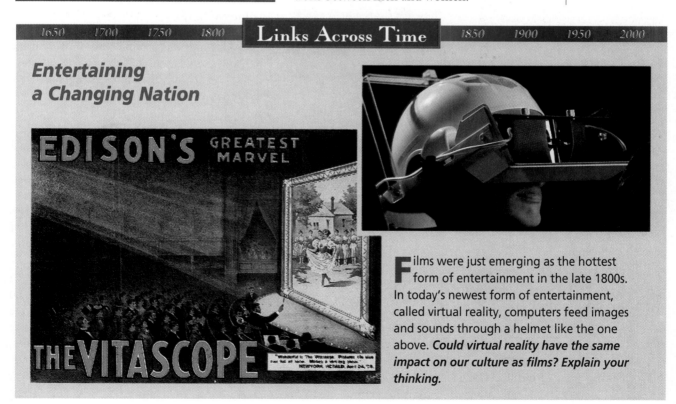

Links Across Time

1650　1700　1750　1800　1850　1900　1950　2000

Entertaining a Changing Nation

Films were just emerging as the hottest form of entertainment in the late 1800s. In today's newest form of entertainment, called virtual reality, computers feed images and sounds through a helmet like the one above. *Could virtual reality have the same impact on our culture as films? Explain your thinking.*

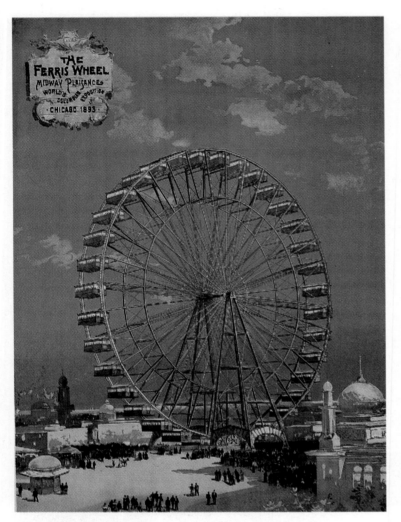

The 1893 World's Columbian Exposition in Chicago reflected many aspects of American society during this era. The ferris wheel demonstrated a fascination with recreation and amusement. The White City, some of which appears at bottom right, represented an idealistic dream of urban perfection. In another example of social norms for the time, women had a separate building to showcase their accomplishments—it was segregated from the fair's other exhibits.

When critics raised alarms about the moral impact of places of popular amusement, some Victorians proposed extreme action, such as closing down all "evil resorts." Many working-class and immigrant people resisted such attempts. For them, such commercial "resorts" were often their sole sources of amusement. In the end, a compromise evolved.

After the turn of the century, city governments began to license public amusements, requiring them to adhere to health, safety, and liquor codes, and to uphold certain standards of behavior. Kansas City, for example, tried to ban "close dancing." A regulation from 1913 read, "The lady should place her right hand on her partner's arm and not on his shoulder, and partners should keep their bodies free from each other."

Other places tried to encourage moral behavior by providing "wholesome" recreational alternatives in carefully monitored social settings. Settlement houses and voluntary associations sponsored properly chaperoned dances. Educators added activities such as social dancing to their physical education programs. The urban park movement, which had begun in the 1850s, accelerated during this period. By the late 1800s, most cities had gardens for strolling, ponds for boating, baseball diamonds, skating rinks, and even dance pavilions.

By the turn of the century, a balance had emerged between the desires of the masses to amuse themselves and of more elite groups to preserve old codes of behavior. Public amusements, however, would remain a prime area of contention between diverse ethnic, racial, class, and generational groups in the decades ahead.

SECTION 2 REVIEW

Key Terms, People, and Places
1. Describe (a) vaudeville, (b) minstrel show.

Key Concepts
2. Why did mass entertainment and recreation emerge in the late 1800s, and what forms were most popular?
3. What was the role of sports in the entertainment of the masses in the late 1800s?
4. What was yellow journalism?
5. What forms of African American music were absorbed into white culture?
6. What was the basis for the criticism of public amusements, and what was the result of this criticism?

Critical Thinking
7. **Drawing Conclusions** How did the growth of cities help make possible the growth of the entertainment and recreation outlets discussed in this section?

The World of Jim Crow

SECTION PREVIEW

White society proved quite resourceful at finding ways to repress African Americans in the years after Reconstruction. Yet many African Americans demonstrated an even greater will to rise above the discrimination and hate.

Key Concepts

• White society found a number of ways to discriminate against African Americans after Reconstruction.
• The African American community produced several responses to white discrimination.
• Many African Americans achieved great success in spite of the obstacles placed before them.

Key Terms, People, and Places

poll tax, literacy test, grandfather clause, Jim Crow, lynching, de facto discrimination, National Association for the Advancement of Colored People (NAACP); Madam C. J. Walker

Within a few years after the end of Reconstruction in the 1870s, African Americans began to see many of their newly won freedoms disappear. In the South, they were prevented from exercising their voting rights and were subjected to segregation laws and random violence. Discrimination was also rampant in the North. Despite these developments, African Americans in this era reached high levels of achievement and founded powerful organizations for self-help and protest.

Post-Reconstruction Discrimination

At the same time that white Americans were claiming elements of black culture as their own, racial discrimination and violence were making life harder for African Americans. Booker T. Washington's belief that white Americans would accept hard-working African Americans into equal citizenship was proving too optimistic.

Southern whites, who in the past had always had slavery to repress African Americans, now faced a new situation—free blacks. Whites responded with increasingly vicious methods of oppression.

Voting Restrictions In many southern communities, whites were concerned about the possible impact of African American voters. To deny the vote to blacks—and many lower-class whites with whom African Americans might join forces—southern states employed several tactics during the 1890s. They required voters to own property and to pay a special fee, or **poll tax;** both requirements were beyond the financial reach of most African Americans. Voters also had to demonstrate minimum standards of knowledge by passing **literacy tests.** These tests were rigged to keep African Americans from voting. For example, blacks might be asked questions that were too difficult for most people to answer. White people were given much easier tests.

To ensure that the literacy tests did not keep too many whites from voting, states passed laws that exempted men from certain voting restrictions if they had ancestors who had been allowed to vote before black suffrage. Such laws are examples of **grandfather clauses,** by which groups are exempted from a law if they met certain conditions before that law was passed.

Segregation Also during this period, many states instituted a system of legal segregation that further degraded African Americans. This system was called **Jim Crow,** after a minstrel song-and-dance routine.

Although Jim Crow laws usually are associated with the South, they first appeared in the 1830s, when Massachusetts allowed railroad companies to separate black and white passengers. But it was in the South that Jim Crow became firmly established in many facets of

This hood was part of the costume of the Ku Klux Klan, an organization that began to terrorize African Americans in the late 1800s.

Adoption of Voting Restrictions in the South, 1889–1908					
Year	Poll Tax	Literacy Test	Property Test	Grand-father Clause	Other*
1889	FL				TN, FL
1890	MI, TN	MI			MI
1891					AR
1892	AR				
1893					AL
1894					SC, VA
1895	SC	SC			SC
1896					
1897					LA
1898	LA	LA	LA	LA	
1899					NC
1900	NC	NC	NC	NC	
1901	AL	AL	AL	Al	
1902	VA, TX	VA	VA		VA
1903					TX
1904					
1905					
1906					
1907					
1908		GA	GA	GA	GA

*Registration, multiple-box, secret ballot, understanding clause
Source: *The American Record: Images of the Nation's Past,* Volume Two, edited by William Graebner and Leonard Richards

Interpreting Tables
As shown above, southern states began to adopt voting laws in the late 1800s. Though the laws varied in their techniques, the effect was always the same—African Americans were denied the vote. *Which states had the widest variety of voting restrictions?*

daily life. The laws began to appear in the South a few years after the end of Reconstruction and were solidly in place by 1900.

Jim Crow dominated almost every aspect of daily life by the early 1900s. The laws required the separation of blacks and whites in schools, parks, public buildings, hospitals, and on transportation systems. African Americans and whites could not use the same public toilets or water fountains. They could not sit in the same sections of theaters. Facilities designated for blacks were always inferior.

The Supreme Court legitimized Jim Crow. In 1883 the Court overturned the Civil Rights Act of 1875, ruling that the Fourteenth Amendment did not prevent private organizations from discriminating against others. *Plessy* v. *Ferguson* (1896) legalized separate facilities for African Americans, as long as they were considered to be equal to those provided to whites. The ruling in *Plessy* proved hard to enforce, and schools and other facilities in the South were rarely if ever made truly equal.

Violence The most horrible feature of the post-Reconstruction decline in conditions for African Americans was **lynching.** The term refers to a mob's illegal seizure and execution of a suspected criminal or troublemaker. Sometimes victims were merely individuals who were unlucky enough to be in the wrong place at the wrong time. The seizure sometimes included a mock trial, torture, and even mutilation before the victim—usually a man—was hanged and riddled with bullets. Those who carried out these horrors were rarely pursued or caught, much less punished.

Conditions in the North Decline Many African Americans, though realizing that life in the North was not perfect, moved there in part to escape legal segregation. What they found instead was **de facto discrimination,** or discrimination in fact instead of by law. Through the widespread cooperation of whites, who enforced unwritten agreements to discriminate against African Americans, public areas, schools, housing, and employment were effectively segregated.

African Americans also experienced occasional lynchings in the North. In addition, bloody race riots occurred in 1900 in New York City and in 1908 in Springfield, Illinois—the city where Abraham Lincoln had practiced law in the early 1800s.

MAKING CONNECTIONS

White Americans seemed to be simultaneously repressing African Americans and embracing aspects of their music and culture. Give a possible explanation for how these two developments could have occurred at the same time.

African Americans Respond to Discrimination

As conditions for African Americans deteriorated, black leaders began to seek new approaches to race problems. For example, Bishop Henry M. Turner of the African Methodist Episcopal church advocated black pride and emigration to Africa. Others criticized Booker T. Washington and his silence on such issues as lynching. Such attacks ignored Washington's quiet support for legal cases against segregation and his financial support for civil rights and African American business activity.

In 1905 a number of outspoken African Americans came together under the leadership of W.E.B. Du Bois to denounce all political, civil, and economic discrimination against African Americans. Meeting in Niagara Falls, Canada, they vowed never to accept "inferiority," bow to "oppression," or apologize "before insult." "We do not hesitate to complain, and to complain loudly and insistently," they warned.

The Niagara Movement, as this group came to be called, gained only about four hundred members and won few concrete victories. But it formed the nucleus of a group that a few years later was joined by concerned whites, who were aroused into action by the 1908 Springfield riot.

Mary White Ovington, a white social worker who had worked in black neighborhoods, was among these concerned individuals. She helped organize a national conference on the "Negro Question" to be held on Lincoln's birthday in 1909. Niagara Movement leaders attended. The following year, this interracial group founded the **National Association for the Advancement of Colored People (NAACP).**

By 1914 the NAACP had fifty branches and six thousand members. Its magazine, the *Crisis,* edited by Du Bois, reached more than thirty thousand readers. The organization worked primarily through the courts. It won its first major victory when the Supreme Court declared grandfather clauses unconstitutional in 1915. In the decades ahead, the NAACP would remain a vital force in the fight for civil rights.

African American Achievement African American mutual aid and benefit societies

Lynching of African Americans, 1886–1920

Years	Number of Persons Lynched
1886–1890	392
1891–1895	639
1896–1900	493
1901–1905	407
1906–1910	345
1911–1915	279
1916–1920	275

Source: *Historical Statistics of the United States*

Interpreting Tables
Violence against African Americans was an alarmingly frequent phenomenon in the late 1800s. In spite of vocal protests like the one shown below, mobs had killed more than 3,000 African Americans by the 1920s. *In which five-year period did the most lynchings occur?*

also multiplied in this period. Social workers and church groups founded settlement houses in black neighborhoods. The Young Men's and Young Women's Christian Associations developed separate recreational and guidance programs for African American youth. The National Urban League (1911) improved job opportunities and housing for blacks.

Also during this period, African American intellectuals began to publish literature, history, and path-breaking sociological studies. Black-owned businesses appeared everywhere. To help them, Booker T. Washington founded the National Negro Business League in 1900. By 1907 it had 320 branches.

Thanks to the determination and support of many individuals and institutions, African Americans survived the difficult post-Reconstruction era. Some, such as Madam C. J. Walker, actually thrived.

Madam C. J. Walker

In 1912 **Madam C. J. Walker** (1867–1919) asked Booker T. Washington to put her on the program of the annual meeting of the Negro Business League. He refused. But on the last day of the assembly, she spoke to the group anyway, saying:

I am a woman who came from the cotton fields of the South. I was promoted from there to the washtub. Then I was promoted to the cook kitchen, and from there I promoted myself into the business of manufacturing hair goods and preparations. . . . I have built my own factory on my own ground.

Madam C. J. Walker was an inspiration to many African American women.

The mostly male audience was so impressed that they invited Walker back the next year as a keynote speaker.

Madam C. J. Walker is a stunning example of African American achievement in the turn-of-the-century era. Born Sarah Breedlove—the name *Walker* would come from a husband—she was the daughter of ex-slaves and share-croppers. Her first seven years were spent on a Louisiana cotton plantation. Then, after the death of her parents, she moved to Vicksburg, Mississippi, to work as a domestic servant. She later moved to St. Louis, where she worked for seventeen years laundering clothes.

"I got myself a start by giving myself a start," Walker would later say. She did so by deciding in her late thirties to develop her own preparations to style and strengthen the hair of African American women, many of whom suffered hair loss from poor diet, stress, scalp diseases, and damaging hair treatments. After experimenting with different formulas and trying them out on friends, Walker sold her products door to door.

Walker moved to Denver, Colorado, in 1905, where she married C. J. Walker, a newspaper sales agent. There she set up a prosperous mail-order business for her hair products. She also established a string of beauty parlors and training schools for "hair culturists."

Her business a great success, Walker bought property in Harlem, New York, an area that had begun to attract African American residents. Her Harlem town house and later her estate in Irvington-on-Hudson, New York, became gathering places for the country's African American leaders. Walker supported black welfare, education, and civil rights work with large contributions and made many speeches for the antilynching drives of the NAACP and for African American women's organizations.

Walker also created job opportunities for African Americans. In her keynote speech to the National Negro Business League in 1913, Walker summed up her life's work as having "made it possible for many colored women to abandon the washtub for a more pleasant and profitable occupation." By 1916 her company claimed twenty thousand employees.

"The girls and women of our race must not be afraid to take hold of business endeavor," she said in her 1913 speech. "I want to say to every Negro woman present, don't sit down and wait for the opportunities to come. . . . Get up and make them!"

SECTION 3 REVIEW

Key Terms, People, and Places
1. Define (a) poll tax, (b) literacy tests, (c) grandfather clause, (d) lynching.
2. Identify Madam C. J. Walker.

Key Concepts
3. How do Jim Crow laws and de facto discrimination differ?
4. How did African Americans respond to the growing repression following Reconstruction?
5. What are some examples of African American achievement and perseverance during this period?

Critical Thinking
6. **Distinguishing False from Accurate Images** To what extent did the end of slavery and the official granting of political rights bring freedom to African Americans? Explain.

Reading a Political Cartoon

Political cartoons can tell you a great deal about the past. For many years, cartoonists have tried to influence public feeling about important issues. To do so, they use visual images to exaggerate or highlight certain details about the facts. This is one reason why cartoons often can make a point more strongly than words alone can.

Study the cartoon below, which was published in 1892. Ask yourself what point about Jim Crow laws the cartoonist was trying to make. Then answer the following questions.

1. Identify the symbols used in the cartoon. Cartoons often use symbols, visual images that stand for some other idea or event. For exam-

ple, a skull and crossbones is a commonly used symbol for death. A dove is a symbol for peace. To understand a cartoon, you must be able to identify the symbols it uses.

Decide what the symbols in this cartoon stand for. (a) What is the figure on the left holding in his right hand? What are the men on the right holding? (b) What is the building at the right meant to be? (c) What is the significance of the cannon and the date printed on it? (d) Based on these symbols, what groups do these people represent?

2. Analyze the meaning of the symbols. Use your reading of this chapter and the cartoon to decide what the symbols refer to. (a) What

do the signs on the building say? (b) What practice is being referred to in this cartoon? (c) Based on your answers to a and b above, how would you interpret the meaning of the other symbols in the cartoon, which you identified earlier?

3. Interpret the cartoon. Draw conclusions about the cartoonist's point of view. (a) What do you think the cartoonist thought of Jim Crow laws? Give evidence to support your answer. (b) How is the cartoonist trying to influence the public's attitude toward the practice? (c) How does the cartoonist portray the white figures? Is this a sympathetic portrayal?

The Woman Question

Much had changed for women in the late 1800s—new jobs, new educational opportunities, new roles in the home. Yet much stayed the same, including continued economic and political inequality. This contradiction fueled great debate at the turn of the century.

Key Concepts

- Americans held conflicting attitudes about the status of women in society in the late 1800s.
- Women's lives were changing rapidly as a result of changes in technology, the workplace, and society in general.
- Many women demanded economic and political equality and promoted changes in women's lifestyles.

Key Terms, People, and Places

woman question

Many women at the turn of the century began seeking change in their traditional roles—and in their traditional clothing, such as the restrictive corsets advertised above.

W omen hain't no business a votin'," pronounced Josiah Allen, a fictional creation of the popular turn-of-the-century humorist Marietta Holley; "they had better let the laws alone, and tend to their housework. The law loves wimmin and protects 'em." Replied his wife, Samantha, "If the law loves wimmin so well, why don't he give her as much wages as men get for doin' the same work?"

Most Americans around 1900 would have known exactly what Samantha and Josiah were arguing about. They would have called it the **woman question,** a wide-ranging debate about the social role of women that grew out of several major developments of the era. As a result of technological change, industrialization, the expansion of education, and the movement of people into the cities, women's lives were undergoing rapid change. Yet many Americans were unwilling to acknowledge these changes and expand their view of women's status in society.

What Was the Woman Question?

For women like Samantha Allen, the woman question boiled down to a few key demands: Women should be able to vote. They should be paid the same as men for doing the same work. They should be able to control their own property and income. They should have equal access to higher education and professional jobs. And, they should be free from domestic violence.

Women's rights advocates were countered by traditionalists, who insisted that giving women economic and political power equal to that of men would upset the social order. Some argued that allowing women any public roles would destroy their femininity. As the reality of women's lives changed, however, such arguments against women's rights became increasingly difficult to justify.

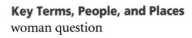

MAKING CONNECTIONS

To what extent does the woman question still exist? What aspects of it continue from the past? What are some new features of today's woman question?

Women in the Economy and Society

What was the reality of women's lives at the turn of the century? Women worked in most sectors of the economy and in many areas of public life. Their unpaid work at home continued to be essential. At the same time, because new technologies such as running water and washing machines decreased the time spent doing housework, a growing number of women were earning advanced degrees and entering professions. Others were building voluntary organizations that took leading roles in reforming education, labor relations, public health, and other areas of society.

Women's Work in the Home As they had for centuries, women continued to perform most of the jobs in the home. Thanks to the era's technological revolution (see Chapter 8), some aspects of this work became less time-consuming. Though technology was not available to all people, it did free many women for wage work, careers, and voluntary activity.

By 1900, fewer women were making their own bread or butchering and preserving their own meat. The number of foods available in tin cans increased fourfold between 1870 and 1880. Almost no one produced clothing from start to finish anymore. Patent medicines replaced remedies previously prepared at home. Even nursing the sick, once a special skill of women, was moving to the hospital and becoming professionalized.

Women still had much to do. In working-class households that could not afford the benefits of technology, housework continued to be strenuous. Many homes were without indoor plumbing. Even as late as 1917, only one quarter of American homes had electricity.

Working Outside the Home In 1870 nearly two million women—one in every eight over the age of ten—worked outside the home. Women worked in each of the 338 occupations listed in the United States census. Most of these women were single. But, in the decades that followed, a rising proportion of married women would go to work.

Most single female workers were between the ages of sixteen and twenty-four. Employers assumed they would leave upon marriage and rarely gave them supervisory jobs or advanced training. They also paid women three to five dollars a week less than men—about 30 to 60 percent less, on average.

Domestic work was an important source of income for many women. In 1900 about one in fifteen American homes employed live-in servants. Most were of foreign or African American origin. Working dawn to bedtime, six-and-a-half

New technologies, such as this washing machine, helped lessen women's burdens. But women also had new responsibilities as household consumers as suggested in the ad above.

days a week, these women cooked, cleaned, washed and ironed, and cared for children. Many supported their own families who lived elsewhere.

American society accepted the stereotype that women did not have the mental capacity for professional training. In 1873 retired Harvard Medical School professor Edward H. Clarke warned in his famous book *Sex in Education* that young women could not study and learn

and retain uninjured health and a future secure from [sickness], hysteria, and other derangements of the nervous system.

Three years before Clarke made this warning, the United States had 525 physicians, 67 ministers, and 5 lawyers who were women.

During this era, women in growing numbers moved out of the home and into the workplace. Some, such as the telephone operators (top), worked in the new industries that came with industrialization. Domestic work employed many immigrants and minorities such as those in the bottom photograph.

Still, most Americans believed that careers and married life were incompatible. Self-supporting women were allowed to train for professions but discouraged from entering fields that put them in competition with men. Women professionals found opportunities mostly in female-dominated institutions, such as women's colleges, hospitals, and settlement houses.

Volunteering for a Larger Role in Society

Women in both the North and South had performed exemplary voluntary service during the Civil War. Afterward, there was an explosion of interest among middle-class women in voluntary associations.

Women joined these organizations primarily for intellectual stimulation and sociability. They studied subjects of common interest, gave talks on selected topics, or heard lectures by distinguished guests. Some, such as the New England Woman's Club, founded in 1868, pursued specific causes such as temperance and girls' education. Others founded libraries or playgrounds. African American club women in Atlanta studied a national adult education program. The Chicago Woman's Club read Karl Marx's writings.

Whatever their focus, clubs gave women invaluable experience in speaking, writing, and financial skills. They helped women increase their self-confidence and take their first steps toward public life.

As the number of clubs for women expanded, the idea of forming them into national associations took hold. In 1873 the Association for the Advancement of Women came into being, and in 1890 the General Federation of Women's Clubs was formed. These groups took on increasingly ambitious and far-reaching projects, including suffrage and the correction of political abuses. In doing so, they joined with other groups founded to pursue specific reforms, such as the Woman's Christian Temperance Union, formed in 1874, and the National American Woman Suffrage Association, formed in 1890. This last group would carry the cause of woman suffrage to victory some thirty years later.

New Women, New Ideas

During this period of change, women struggled to agree on a proper focus for their activities. By the early 1900s, the woman question had grown to include a number of issues besides economic and political rights.

One issue was the question of lifestyle: How should women dress and behave? As more women entered the work force or went to college, they took this matter into their own hands. In search of more convenient hair styles, they began to "bob" or shorten their hair. They raised hemlines and wore more practical skirts and blouses. The New England Woman's Club even opened a store where women could buy sensible clothing.

Courting and marriage customs also changed. For example, instead of entertaining a man at home, many women now went out on dates without supervision. New women, as they were sometimes called, still hoped to marry. Yet they seemed to have higher expectations of fulfillment in marriage. This expectation was evidenced by the divorce rate, which rose from one in twelve in 1900 to one in nine by 1916. Many married new women began to push for the legalized spread of information about birth control, a campaign led by New York nurse Margaret Sanger. Such developments were shocking to Americans who held on to Victorian morals.

What was the consensus among women on the woman question? At the turn of the century, most women rejected ideas for drastic social change, such as the demand of some that women be freed from all household duties. Though the majority agreed with the principle of greater rights, middle-class women still saw domestic

fulfillment as their chief goal. Working-class women seldom had the time to debate the issue.

Voting rights was another matter. The issue of the vote prompted huge numbers of women to campaign or support the movement in some way. Even female workers got caught up in the suffrage movement. Soon the vote would be the one issue on which women from many walks of life would unite.

Viewpoints
On the Woman Question

In the late 1800s and early 1900s, debate over the social, political, and economic roles of women raged in the United States. *Summarize the arguments presented in the viewpoints below.*

For Women's Rights

"These things the women want to do and be and have are not in any sense masculine. They do not belong to men. They never did. They are departments of our social life, hitherto monopolized [until now controlled] by men, but no more made masculine by that use than the wearing of trousers by Turkish women makes trousers feminine. . . .

Charlotte Perkins Gilman, "Are Women Human Beings?" *Harper's Weekly*, May 25, 1912

Against Women's Rights

"So I say deliberately that the so-called woman movement is an attempt to escape the function of woman, a revolt against the fact that woman is not a man, an attempt to enter the field of effort in which man's powers are properly exercised. It is a rising against nature. It is a revolt against God."

Dr. Cyrus Townsend Brady, from a sermon given October 17, 1915

SECTION 4 REVIEW

Key Terms, People, and Places
1. Define the woman question.

Key Concepts
2. What arguments were used by those Americans who did not want to expand women's roles in the economy and society in the late 1800s?
3. What were the main characteristics of women's work outside the home in this period?

4. Describe women's involvement in volunteer work.
5. What was the general consensus among American women on the woman question?

Critical Thinking
6. **Determining Relevance** How did the growth in women's employment and volunteer activity outside the home support the demands by women for greater political and social roles?

The Decision to Rule Against Women's Suffrage

Time Frame:	1869–1875
Places:	St. Louis, Missouri; Washington, D.C.
Key People:	Virginia L. Minor and Francis Minor, Chief Justice Morrison R. Waite, and the Supreme Court
Situation:	Women's rights advocates believed the post-Civil War period to be right for winning the vote. Virginia Minor believed the Fourteenth Amendment made Missouri's ban against woman voters unconstitutional. She asked the Supreme Court to rule for women's suffrage.

In the reform-minded atmosphere immediately after the Civil War, many women became more determined than ever to achieve woman suffrage, for which they had been fighting for decades. After all, new laws and the Fourteenth and Fifteenth amendments to the Constitution were granting rights and privileges, including citizenship and suffrage, to formerly enslaved African Americans. In view of these changes, suffragists reasoned, the nation must be ready to give women the vote.

In 1874, advocates of women's suffrage saw an opportunity to advance their cause. The Supreme Court had agreed to hear the case *Minor* v. *Happersett*. Depending on its ruling, the Court could make women's suffrage a reality.

Women Make a Move for Suffrage

In the aftermath of the Civil War, Congress passed and the states ratified the Fourteenth and Fifteenth amendments to the Constitution. These amendments were designed to protect the rights of African Americans who had recently been released from slavery. The Fourteenth Amendment extended the rights of citizenship to all Americans, while the Fifteenth guaranteed all races the right to vote.

These amendments split the woman suffrage movement, which had been formed in 1848 at the Seneca Falls Women's Rights Convention in New York. One faction, the National Woman's Suffrage Association (NWSA), refused to endorse the Fifteenth Amendment because it ignored women's voting rights. They continued lobbying for voting and other rights at the federal level. The other faction, known as the American Woman Suffrage Association, supported the Fifteenth Amendment as a step toward winning the vote for women.

Virginia Minor, the president of the Missouri chapter of NWSA, was convinced that women's status in the United States would not be raised until suffrage was won. Her husband, lawyer Francis Minor, enthusiastically supported her endeavors toward this end. In 1869 the couple devised an ingenious argument. They claimed that, of the "rights and privileges" that the Fourteenth Amendment guaranteed to all American citizens, including women, "chief among [them] is the elective franchise"—the right to vote. The NWSA enthusiastically endorsed the Minors' reasoning that embodied in the Constitution itself was the right of woman suffrage.

During the national elections of 1872, NWSA waged a campaign to challenge the ban on women voting. One hundred and fifty of its members tried to vote in ten states. In Missouri, Virginia Minor demanded that the St. Louis registrar, Reese Happersett, register her to vote. When he refused, citing the Missouri constitution, she sued on the basis of the Fourteenth Amendment.

The Logic Behind Minor's Case

Because Missouri state law made it impossible for Minor to bring suit independently of her husband, the Minors jointly took their case to the circuit court at St. Louis and then to the Missouri supreme court. Minor lost her case in the Missouri courts and then appealed to the Supreme Court in 1874. Francis Minor was one of the attorneys who presented the case before the Court. He and the other attorneys asserted that the Constitution gave women the right to vote because women are United States citizens and "there can be no half-way citizenship.

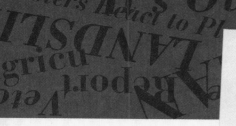

GOAL	Win women's suffrage	
POSSIBLE ACTIONS	The Supreme Court rules that under the Constitution the state of Missouri must allow Virginia Minor to vote	The Supreme Court rules that the state of Missouri has no obligation to allow Virginia Minor to vote
POSSIBLE RESULTS	• Women's suffrage is won under the Constitution.	• Women's suffrage can only be won through constitutional amendment.

Woman, as a citizen of the United States, is entitled to all the benefits of that position, and liable to all its obligations, or to none." Since citizens have the right to vote, and since the Fourteenth Amendment forbade the states from limiting the rights of citizens, then Missouri's ban on women voting was unconstitutional.

Supreme Court Chief Justice Morrison R. Waite, who sat listening to these arguments, was sympathetic to women's rights. Later, his personal physician would be a woman, and he would unsuccessfully argue for admitting women as members of the Supreme Court Bar. It seemed possible that Waite might be willing to embrace a broad reading of the Constitution, one that allowed him to infer women's suffrage from the vague wording of the Fourteenth Amendment.

Yet unfortunately for Minor and the NWSA, the Supreme Court had turned more cautious and respectful of precedent. The Court now tended to opt for more strict readings of the Constitution's language—readings that acknowledged only those rights specifically listed in the document. Realizing that their case had but a slim chance of victory, the Minors and the NWSA nevertheless remained hopeful that the Court would rule for women's suffrage.

The Response of the Supreme Court

The Supreme Court in 1875 decided unanimously that the state of Missouri had no obligation to allow Minor to vote. In the Court's opinion, written by Waite, the justices agreed that women were citizens entitled to the rights and privileges of citizenship, with or without the Fourteenth Amendment. Yet the Constitution and the Fourteenth Amendment never stated specifically that suffrage was one of those rights. Had that been so, they argued, the Fifteenth Amendment guaranteeing African Americans the right to vote would never have been necessary.

The Court further noted that the states always had determined the qualifications for voters. "When the Constitution of the United States was adopted," the justices continued, ". . . in no State were all citizens permitted to vote. Each State determined for itself who should have that power." If the framers of the Constitution meant all citizens to vote, the Court reasoned, they would have stated it explicitly. Waite's opinion concluded by remarking that the justices were not judging the merits of women's suffrage, but only determining the extent of women's constitutional rights.

After the Supreme Court's decision in *Minor* v. *Happersett,* those working for women's suffrage realized what a long road lay ahead. The only way to get a national vote for women would be through the long, difficult process of amending the Constitution. The two women's rights factions reunited in 1890 in the National American Woman Suffrage Association. Under a new generation of leaders, the group worked for thirty more years to achieve passage and ratification of the Nineteenth Amendment in 1920.

EVALUATING DECISIONS

1. (a) According to the Minors, how was women's suffrage implied in the Fourteenth Amendment?
(b) Why was this argument attractive to the NWSA?
2. (a) What was the Supreme Court's reasoning in unanimously ruling against the Minors? (b) Why was 1874 an unlikely time to expect the Minors to win?

Critical Thinking

3. **Recognizing Cause and Effect** Waite was said to believe that the people, acting through their elected representatives, knew their own best interest. Explain how such a belief might have led Waite to a make a more strict reading of the Constitution.

Chapter Review

Key Terms
1. vaudeville
2. yellow journalism
3. minstrel show
4. ragtime
5. jazz
6. Victorianism
7. poll tax
8. literacy tests
9. grandfather clause
10. Jim Crow
11. lynching
12. de facto discrimination
13. National Association for the

Advancement of Colored People (NAACP)
14. woman question

People
15. Booker T. Washington
16. W.E.B. Du Bois
17. Madam C. J. Walker

Terms For each term above, write a sentence that explains its relation to the cultural and social transformations of the late 1800s and early 1900s.

Matching Review the key terms in the list above. If you are not sure of a term's meaning, review its definition in the chapter. Then choose a term from the list that best matches each description below.
1. a system of legal segregation that degraded African Americans
2. a type of family entertainment consisting of comic sketches, song-and-dance routines, ventriloquists, jugglers, and trapeze artists
3. sensationalized news coverage
4. the wide-ranging debate about the social role of women that took place in the late 1800s

5. the beliefs associated with Britain's Queen Victoria, which include commitment to hard work, sobriety, and restraint in relations between men and women

True or False Determine whether each statement is true or false. If it is true, write "true." If it is false, change the underlined name to make the statement true.
1. Booker T. Washington was an African American who persevered through the post-Reconstruction era and established a successful business.
2. Madam C. J. Walker urged African Americans to win white acceptance by succeeding in occupations that whites needed them to fill.
3. W.E.B. Du Bois believed that the brightest African Americans had to step forward to seek advanced educations and lead their people.

Section 1 (pp. 334–357)
1. Why did public schools gain more students in the late 1800s?
2. Give evidence to show that opportunities for higher education increased for women during the late 1800s.
3. In what ways were the experiences of women and African Americans similar with regard to higher education?

Section 2 (pp. 338–342)
4. What kinds of amusements and entertainment were available for families to enjoy during the late 1800s?
5. Where and how did ragtime and jazz originate?
6. What did Victorians think of the new forms of entertainment that evolved during the late 1800s?

Section 3 (pp. 343–346)
7. In what ways did Jim Crow laws affect the daily lives of African Americans in the South?
8. How did the NAACP and the National Urban League help African Americans during the early 1900s?
9. What does the profile of Madam C. J. Walker reveal about the achievements of African Americans?

Section 4 (pp. 348–351)
10. What conflicting attitudes did Americans hold about the proper place of woman in the late 1800s?
11. How did women's lives change as a result of new technologies during this period?
12. Describe how women achieved greater social equality during the early 1900s.

1. **Drawing Conclusions** How might your education have been different if you had lived in the period immediately following the Civil War?
2. **Making Comparisons** As greater numbers of working-class people sought entertainment during the late 1800s, a commercial recreation industry emerged. How are the types of activities available today similar to the types of activities available during the late 1800s?
3. **Expressing Problems Clearly** Jim Crow required the segregation of whites and African Americans. Aside from the fact that facilities for African Americans were inferior, how might segregation have harmed African Americans?

1. **Evaluating Primary Sources** Review the primary source quotation on the bottom of page 338. Is Mathewson's assessment of the American public valid today? Give evidence to support your point of view.
2. **Understanding the Visuals** Review the quotations in the "Viewpoints" feature on page 351. Then, scan the chapter to find visuals that could be used to illustrate what each speaker believes is the proper role for women. Write a short paragraph explaining how each photograph supports the quotation.
3. **Writing About the Chapter** Imagine that you are living in the United States around the turn of the century. Write a letter to the editor of the local newspaper in which you take a stand on the woman question. Before you write your letter, draw up an outline of your argument. List several reasons for supporting or opposing expanded rights for women, and identify details or examples to support each of your reasons.

Next, write a draft of your letter. Begin by stating your position, and then present each of your reasons in a separate paragraph. Conclude by encouraging your readers to work for or against expanded women's rights. Read over your draft, carefully refining your arguments and correcting any errors. Then, make a final copy.

4. **Using the Graphic Organizer** This graphic organizer uses a tree map to organize information about the expansion of education in the late 1800s. (a) Based on what you have read in the chapter, how was the experience of higher education different for African Americans and minorities than it was for white males? (b) Describe the experience of higher education for women during the late 1800s. (c) On a separate sheet of paper, create your own graphic organizer about the changes in women's lives during the late 1800s.

The Expansion of Education, 1870–1915

Public Schools
- United States becomes more industrialized and urbanized, fueling need for more education, increased funding, child labor laws
- Immigrants in particular take advantage of public schools, although some resist Americanization
- Illiteracy rate drops to below 8 percent

Higher Education
- Wealthy philanthropists endow schools of higher education
- Between 1880 and 1900 college enrollment doubles, although still only a small percentage can afford costs or win scholarships

Women
- Women can attend some men's and co-ed colleges as well as colleges for women
- Women must still fight for equality at state schools
- Some parents fear college will harm their daughters

African Americans and Other Minorities
- Schools receive less money, are separate but unequal
- Very few African American women attend college
- Debate over how African Americans should use their education rages

THE GROWTH OF SPORTS

The great rise in sports at the turn of the century reflected many other changes that were taking place in America at the same time. If not for the country's growing wealth, most adults would not have been free from their constant labor to seek excitement in games. The popularity of sports also signaled a change in the way that Americans viewed health and "idle" entertainments. Before this time, many Americans shunned activities that did not create wealth or improve character. It was now morally acceptable to spend time pursuing interests because they were just plain fun. *How do you think changes taking place in society, technology, communications, and business affected the growth of sports?*

Padded football pants

◄ FOOTBALL AT THE TURN OF THE CENTURY This football card shows that players wore much less protection than modern players. Notice the lack of shoulder pads and helmet. The only protection came from padded pants (also worn by some basketball players of the time), which protected players from leg bruises. A century ago, the game was also less violent.

▼ SKIING Skiing, as we know the sport today, began in Norway in the mid-1800s when the addition of bindings made it possible for skiers to turn and jump. Norwegian immigrants then brought the sport to Minnesota, from where it spread to other snowy areas in the United States. Skiing, however, did not become widely popular until the 1930s with the introduction of the ski tow.

◀ EARLY BASEBALL Baseball achieved its status as the great American pastime in the last third of the 1800s. Many songs celebrated the game's heroes, such as the polka tune shown on this sheet-music cover. Fans of Georgetown University's baseball team dyed the ball (in the mitt on the right) dark blue and painted in the score to honor their team's victory over Yale in 1899.

ICE SKATING A common winter sport before the 1800s, ice skating became even more popular in the late 1800s. One reason for the sport's growth in popularity was the introduction of low-priced "store-bought" skates. ▶

◀ WOMEN CYCLISTS Before the late 1800s, outdoor sports activities for women were limited. But women's steady struggle for legal and social rights, as well as improvements in bicycles, contributed to a change. By the 1890s, women had joined the bicycle craze and entered into active, public sport. The athletic demands of riding a bicycle required new, more practical clothing for women, which outraged many people.

◀ On this 1870 bicycle, the pedals connect directly to the front wheels at the axle. The introduction of a chain and foot brakes in the 1890s made pedaling much easier and gave the cyclist more control.

The United States on the Brink of Change
1890–1920

"Whether they will or not, Americans must now begin to look outward. The growing production of the country demands it."
—Alfred T. Mahan, 1890

*T*he industrial boom at the turn of the century had far-reaching effects. In search of markets for its products, the United States joined the scramble for new territories, leading to international conflict and war. Meanwhile, the serious problems created by the boom inspired a reform movement known as progressivism. Both the ambitions of the imperialists and the ideals of the progressives contributed to the nation's growing role as a world power. This role eventually drew the United States into the horrors of World War I.

New York City's docks were teeming with activity in the early 1900s as the United States reached across the Atlantic Ocean in its quest to become an economic and political world power.

Becoming a World Power

1890–1913

*B*y the 1890s, farms and factories in the United States were producing more than the nation could consume. Soon, many business and political leaders began to pursue new markets abroad. Inspired by grand dreams of empire, some Americans pushed for new territory as well. As the nation grew into a world power, however, a troubling question arose in some citizens' minds: could a country born in a war for independence from colonial rule become a colonial power itself—without betraying the principles of liberty and equality on which it was founded?

Events in the United States

1890 Alfred Mahan publishes The Influence of Sea Power Upon History.	1893 American planters overthrow Queen Liliuokalani in Hawaii.	1896 William McKinley defeats William Jennings Bryan in presidential election.	1898 The Spanish-American War takes place. • The United States annexes Hawaii.
1890	**1893**	**1896**	**1899**

Events in the World

1885 Indian National Congress is founded.		1895 Japan defeats China in Sino-Japanese War. • Cubans rebel against Spanish rule.	1900 The Boxer Rebellion breaks out in China.

Pages 362–365
The Pressure to Expand

In the late 1800s, the United States began bursting at the seams with more goods than the nation could consume. Soon other parts of the world beckoned to government and business leaders eager to sell those extra goods. This economic expansion, however, increasingly led the United States into conflicts on foreign soil.

Pages 366–371
Foreign Entanglements, War, and Annexations

As the United States sought to increase its influence abroad, it frequently found itself feuding with other nations. A swift American victory in the Spanish-American War confirmed the nation's status as a world power, but it left some people arguing over how to govern newly acquired territories.

Pages 373–377
A Forceful Diplomacy

Whether people thought him a hero or a "wild man," most agreed that President Theodore Roosevelt conducted a vigorous foreign policy that suited the new status of the United States as a world power. Although President William Howard Taft continued Roosevelt's policies, he preferred a quieter, more subtle approach to influencing other nations.

Pages 380–383
The People's Response to Imperialism

After the Spanish-American War, the debate intensified over whether it was appropriate for the United States to continue to throw its net around other nations and drag them under American control. Anti-imperialists used a variety of arguments against the acquisition of territories.

1901 President McKinley is assassinated, and Theodore Roosevelt becomes President.

1908 William Howard Taft becomes President.

1910 Boy Scouts and Girl Scouts are introduced to the United States.

1914 Construction of the Panama Canal is completed.

1902	1905	1908	1911	1914	1917

1905 Japan defeats Russia in Russo-Japanese War.

1911 Revolution sweeps China.

1913 Second Balkan War erupts between Bulgaria, Serbia, and Greece.

The Pressure to Expand

SECTION PREVIEW

In the late 1800s, the United States began bursting at the seams with more goods than the nation could consume. Soon other parts of the world beckoned to government and business leaders eager to sell those extra goods. This economic expansion, however, increasingly led the United States into conflicts on foreign soil.

Key Concepts

- Overproduction of industrial and agricultural goods threatened the United States economy and created a pressing need for foreign markets.
- The need of the United States for economic expansion occurred at a time when the major European powers were scrambling to seize new territories around the globe.
- Americans who favored expansion used economic, moral, and social Darwinist arguments to justify their position.
- Economic expansion involved the risk of foreign entanglements.

Key Terms, People, and Places

imperialism, annexation, most-favored nation, banana republic; Alfred T. Mahan, Henry Cabot Lodge, Albert J. Beveridge; Hawaii

Business leaders eagerly sought new markets abroad in which to sell goods such as this American-grown fruit.

B y the late 1800s, the industrialists, inventors, and laboring forces of the United States had built a powerful industrial economy. But the nation could not consume food and goods fast enough to prevent harmful cycles of financial panic and depression. Labor and farmers protested their plight, helping to convince business and political leaders that the United States must secure new markets abroad. Some people also began to believe that the United States had a responsibility to carry democratic values and Protestant Christianity to others around the globe.

The Growth of Imperialism Around the World

Meanwhile, Europe had reached new heights in its quest for territories to rule as shown on the map on page 363. Under **imperialism,** stronger nations attempt to create empires by dominating weaker nations—economically, politically, or militarily. This type of policy also has been called expansionism. Although Spain's once-great empire in the Americas and the Pacific had shrunk considerably by 1890, it still held on to a few remaining outposts in Cuba, Puerto Rico, and the Philippines. Meanwhile, developments in transportation and communication made it easier for Great Britain, France, and Russia—nations with long imperialist traditions—to maintain and extend their grip on far-flung lands.

Great Britain, in particular, acquired so much new territory in Africa, Asia, and the Pacific that the saying "The sun never sets on the British Empire" became popular. Competition for new territory grew even more intense when the powerful new German state, unified in 1871, also showed expansionist ambitions in Africa and Asia.

By 1890 the United States was eager to join the international competition for new territories. That year James G. Blaine, secretary of state under President Harrison from 1889 to 1892, summarized the situation as follows:

> W e have developed a volume of manufactures which, in many departments, overruns the demands of the home market. . . . Our great demand is expansion . . . of trade with countries where we can find profitable exchanges.

Blaine denied that the United States was seeking "annexation of territory." But **annexation**—the addition of a new territory to an existing country—did take place.

The Tradition of Expansionism in the United States

Despite comments like Blaine's, the United States always had been an expansionist nation. In the 1840s, the concept of "manifest destiny" had captured the popular imagination. The seizure of new territories from Mexico and various Native American nations had followed.

As early as the 1820s, the chief principle of foreign policy in the United States had been the Monroe Doctrine. Under this doctrine, the United States had declared itself interested in anything that happened in the Western Hemisphere and warned European powers to keep out. United States secretaries of state continued to apply the principle after the Civil War. In 1866, for example, William H. Seward sent 50,000 federal troops, still in Texas after the Civil War, into Mexico. The display was meant to convince the French government to withdraw the puppet "emperor" they had placed on the Mexican throne. The following year, Seward bought Alaska from Russia. In addition to gaining more territory, Seward hoped that the presence of the United States on both sides of Canada would force the British out of that region.

Americans also had their eyes on the Pacific. By the 1860s, the United States had won **"most-favored nation"** status in China, which simply meant that it had the same access to trade with China as any other nation. The United States also had established a solid trading relationship with Japan. Now the United States government wanted control of some Pacific islands to use as refueling and repair stations for its naval vessels. To this end, Seward annexed the uninhabited Midway Islands in 1867. Eight years later, the United States government signed a treaty with **Hawaii,** an island nation in the Pacific, that allowed Hawaiians to sell sugar in the United States duty free, as long as they did not sell or lease territory to any foreign power.

Much closer to the United States, and therefore of greater concern, were the Caribbean islands and Latin America. In 1870 President Ulysses S. Grant announced that hereafter the Monroe Doctrine would protect all territories in these two regions from "transfer to a European power."

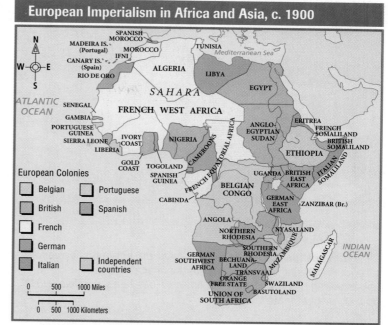

European Imperialism in Africa and Asia, c. 1900

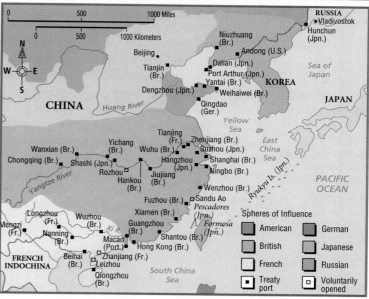

🌍 **Geography and History: Interpreting Maps**
By 1900, European imperialist nations controlled vast amounts of territory in both Africa and Asia, as the above maps illustrate. *Which African nations retained their independence from imperialist control?*

MAKING CONNECTIONS

In what sense were the expansionist policies of the United States in the late 1800s simply a continuation of the concept of manifest destiny?

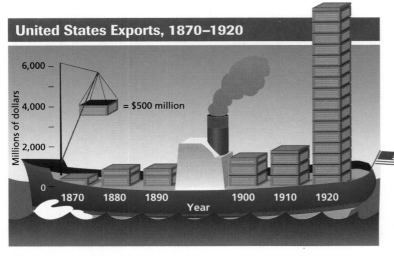

United States Exports, 1870–1920

= $500 million

Millions of dollars

6,000

4,000

2,000

0

1870 1880 1890 1900 1910 1920

Year

Interpreting Graphs
The expansion of American businesses into international markets in the late 1800s and early 1900s led to the rapid rise in United States exports during this period. *Why did American businesses wish to sell their goods outside of the United States?*

Americans Debate Expansionism

A debate arose in the 1890s over what foreign policy would best serve the United States in its various interests abroad. Some argued that the country should become even more involved in international economic affairs. Others replied that the country had enough problems of its own without risking foreign entanglements.

As this 1901 political cartoon suggests, the United States relied on the Monroe Doctrine to block European involvement in Latin America.

Voices Supporting Expansion Many business leaders believed that the economic problems of

the nation could be solved by expanding its markets. Some American businesses already dominated international markets. In the 1880s and 1890s, Rockefeller's Standard Oil, Mc-Cormick reapers, American Telegraph and Telephone, Singer Sewing Machine, Kodak Camera, and Sherwin-Williams Paint all became international corporations. Southern cotton farmers and western wheat growers also were involved heavily in overseas trade.

Other business leaders had gone a step farther, by investing directly in the economies of other countries. This step led steadily toward increased political influence in those countries. In Central America, for example, an American named Minor C. Keith won long-term leases for lands and railroad lines by providing financial services to the Costa Rican government. By 1913 Keith's United Fruit Company not only exported 50 million bunches of bananas a year to ports in the United States, but also dominated the political and economic institutions of Costa Rica, Guatemala, and Honduras. As a result, some people began to refer to the Central American nations as **banana republics.**

Lobbyists who favored a strong United States Navy formed a second force pushing for expansion. By the 1880s, United States warships left over from the Civil War were rusting and rotting. Naval officers joined with business interests to convince Congress to build modern steam-powered, steel-hulled ships to protect overseas trade. The most influential of these officers was Captain (later Admiral) **Alfred T. Mahan.** In his 1890 book, *The Influence of Sea Power Upon History, 1660–1783,* Mahan asserted that the economic future of the nation depended on gaining new markets abroad and that a powerful navy would be essential to protect these markets from foreign rivals. Influenced by Mahan's arguments, Congress authorized the building of nine cruisers, including the U.S.S. *Maine,* in the 1890s. Battleships, gunboats, torpedo boats, and more cruisers followed. By 1900, the United States had one of the most powerful navies in the world.

Political and cultural leaders also promoted expansionism. Among them were Massachusetts senator **Henry Cabot Lodge,** historian Frederick Jackson Turner, and a rising young politician from New York named Theodore Roosevelt. Although concerned about the need for new markets abroad, these men saw another purpose in expansionism. Worried about the effects of a closing frontier on the nation's spirit, they feared that the United States was on the brink of losing its vitality. They argued that a quest for empire might restore the country's pioneer spirit.

These and other leaders of the day also drew on the doctrine of social Darwinism to justify the conquest of new territories, just as they had done earlier to defend the treatment of Native Americans. In the opinion of such influential figures as Congregationalist minister Josiah Strong and Indiana senator **Albert J. Beveridge,** the "advanced" civilizations produced by Anglo-Saxon and Teutonic (Germanic) "races" were superior to the "primitive" societies they conquered. Thus, expansionism was not only inevitable but noble, for it introduced Protestant Christianity and modern civilization to those who might otherwise never have encountered such ideas. As Beveridge explained:

I t is elemental. It is racial. God has not been preparing the English-speaking and Teutonic peoples for a thousand years for nothing but vain and idle self-contemplation and self-admiration. No! . . . He has marked the American people as His chosen Nation finally to lead in the regeneration [rebirth] of the world. . . . American law,

ZULULAND

American order, American civilization, and the American flag will plant themselves on shores hitherto bloody and benighted [ignorant], but by those agencies of God henceforth to be made beautiful and bright.
— Albert J. Beveridge, *The Meaning of the Times and Other Speeches*, 1908

This postcard of African Zulus with a Singer sewing machine illustrates the spread of American products abroad in the late 1800s.

Public Opinion Leans Toward Expansion
Gradually public opinion warmed to the idea of expansionism. Most Americans did not see themselves as potential rulers of oppressed foreign peoples, but they did want new markets abroad and favorable trade relations. What they soon discovered was that political and military entanglements tended to follow. To maintain a territory's political stability, intervention—and sometimes war—became necessary. When annexation of that territory followed, governing those who resented American interference turned out to be difficult, bloody, and painful.

SECTION 1 REVIEW

Key Terms, People, and Places
1. Define (a) imperialism, (b) annexation, (c) most-favored nation, (d) banana republic.
2. Identify (a) Alfred T. Mahan, (b) Henry Cabot Lodge, (c) Albert J. Beveridge.
3. Identify Hawaii.

Key Concepts
4. Why did United States policy makers feel the need to secure new markets abroad in the late 1800s?

5. In addition to the potential economic benefits of expansion, what were some of the moral arguments that people who favored this policy used?
6. What risks did the United States take in attempting to find new foreign markets?

Critical Thinking
7. **Drawing Conclusions** How did the popular philosophy of social Darwinism make it easier for Americans to embrace imperialist policies in the late 1800s?

Foreign Entanglements, War, and Annexations

SECTION PREVIEW

As the United States sought to increase its influence abroad, it frequently found itself feuding with other nations. A swift American victory in the Spanish-American War confirmed the nation's status as a world power, but it left some people arguing over how to govern newly acquired territories.

Key Concepts
• The United States took advantage of several incidents in Latin America to reaffirm the validity of the Monroe Doctrine.
• A rebellion in Cuba and the pressure for expansion led the United States into war with Spain.
• While pursuing its interventionist policies, the United States acquired new territories and influence in the Pacific.

Key Terms, People, and Places
guerrilla, jingoism, sphere of influence, Open Door policy; William Randolph Hearst, Joseph Pulitzer, George Dewey; Cuba, Philippine Islands, San Juan Hill

In its drive to become a world power, the United States increasingly became involved in the affairs of Latin American nations.

T hose in the United States who dreamed of expansion looked to three main areas of the world in the late 1800s: Latin America, the islands of the Pacific, and China. In the 1890s, the United States established a pattern of intervention in these three areas that changed its status in world politics. In the process of expanding and becoming a world power, however, the United States increasingly found itself in conflict with other nations.

Stirrings in Latin America

During the 1890s, the United States played an active role in three diplomatic and military conflicts in Latin America. In the first of these incidents, in 1891, the United States government forced Chile to pay $75,000 to the families of United States sailors who were killed or injured by an angry mob during the sailors' shore leave in Valparaíso. Two years later, when a rebellion threatened the friendly republican government of Brazil, President Cleveland ordered naval units to Rio de Janeiro to protect United States shipping. This show of force broke the back of the rebellion.

In the third and most important incident of the era, the United States confronted the nation then considered the most powerful in the world, Great Britain. Since the 1840s, Britain and Venezuela had disputed ownership of a piece of territory located at the border between Venezuela and British Guiana. In the 1880s, the dispute intensified when rumors surfaced of mineral wealth in this border area. When President Cleveland's secretary of state, Richard Olney, warned Britain in July 1895 that the United States would enforce the Monroe Doctrine, the British government replied that the doctrine had no standing in international law. Two years later, however, Britain backed down. Concerned about the rising power of Germany in Africa, the British government realized that it needed to stay on friendly terms with the increasingly powerful United States.

The Spanish-American War

By the mid-1890s, therefore, the United States had not only reaffirmed the Monroe Doctrine but also forced the world's most powerful nation to bow to its will. Encouraged by

Sensational Newspapers

WOMAN TURNS INTO WILD DOG
WW2 BOMBER FOUND ON MOON
REAL AMERICAN MONSTERS AND DRAGONS
WONDERFUL RESULTS FROM MERELY
HOLDING TUBES OF DRUGS NEAR
ENTRANCED PATIENTS

Have you ever seen headlines like these while waiting in line at the supermarket? If so, you might be surprised to learn that the first two appeared in 1990, while the last two are from newspapers published in 1896.

Sensational newspapers are not a recent development. In the late 1800s, publishers engaged in fierce competition for the sale of popular daily newspapers. Yellow journalism attempted to attract customers by using sensational, though not necessarily true, photographs, stories, and headlines. If there was no startling news to report, editors would invent some.

One of William Randolph Hearst's editors described the logic behind the so-called "gee whiz" story: "We run our paper so that when the reader opens it, he says, 'Gee Whiz!'" Today's weekly tabloids refer to the same type of story as a "Hey, Martha."

It seems that many subjects are as popular today as they were one hundred years ago: miracle cures, harrowing escapes, gruesome crimes, controversial trials, tragic love stories, and supernatural occurrences. And as anyone can attest who has observed shoppers flipping through newspapers while waiting in today's supermarket lines, these stories still sell newspapers. *Can you think of any issues in the recent past that first surfaced in a tabloid like that described above?*

---

this development, expansionists soon spied an opportunity to make even more spectacular gains in Cuba.

The Cuban Rebellion An island nation off the coast of Florida, **Cuba** first rebelled against Spain in 1868. After ten years of fighting the rebels, Spain finally put in place a few meager reforms to appease the Cuban people. In 1895, after the island's economy had collapsed, Cubans who believed that Spanish rule was oppressive and incompetent rebelled again. This time Spain sent 150,000 troops and its best general, Valeriano Weyler, to put down the rebellion. Cuban exiles led by journalist José Martí urged the United States to intervene. Even though public support for the rebels was on the rise, both Presidents Cleveland and McKinley refused, unwilling to spend the money that intervention would require and fearing the United States would be saddled with colonial responsibilities it could not handle. Frustrated, Cuban **guerrillas**—soldiers who fight using surprise tactics—turned to the one tactic they knew would attract the United States government's attention: the destruction of American sugar plantations and mills in Cuba. As a result, business owners increased their pressure on the government to act. Newspaper publishers

William Randolph Hearst and **Joseph Pulitzer** vied with one another to publish horrifying stories of "Butcher" Weyler and his barbed-wire concentration camps. Their sensational headlines and stories, known as yellow journalism, whipped up the American public in favor of the rebels. The intense burst of national pride and the desire for an aggressive foreign policy that followed came to be known as **jingoism**. The name came from a line from a British song of the 1870s: "We don't want to fight, yet by Jingo! if we do, We've got the ships, we've got the men, and got the money too."

Pressure for War Builds Early in 1898, riots erupted in Havana, the capital of Cuba. In response, President McKinley moved the U.S.S. *Maine* into the city's harbor to protect American citizens and property. A few months later, in early February 1898, United States newspapers published an intercepted letter from the Spanish ambassador that described McKinley as "weak and a bidder for the admiration of the crowd." War fever mounted.

Then, on February 15, an explosion on the *Maine* killed more than 250 American sailors.

Morning Journal Sales	
1895	30,000
1897	400,000
1898	1,000,000

Source: *American Heritage,* February 1957

Interpreting Tables Sales of William Randolph Hearst's *Morning Journal* soared in 1898 thanks to sensational stories before and during the Spanish-American War.

the view of Theodore Roosevelt, then assistant secretary of the navy, the Philippines could become a key base from which the United States might protect its Asian trade. On February 25, while his boss, the secretary of the navy, was out of the office, Roosevelt cabled naval commanders in the Pacific to prepare for military action against Spain. When President McKinley discovered what Roosevelt had done, he ordered most of the cables withdrawn, but he made an exception in the case of the cable directed to Admiral **George Dewey.** Dewey was told to attack the Spanish fleet in the Philippines if war broke out with Spain.

Late in March, in a final attempt at a peaceful solution, McKinley sent a list of demands to Spain. These included compensation for the *Maine*, an end to the concentration camps, a truce, and Cuban independence. Although Spain accepted most of these demands and agreed to negotiate on the matter of Cuban independence, McKinley decided he could not resist the growing cries for war. On April 11, he sent a war message to Congress. A few days

Headlines and pictures like these stirred the American public's anger following the explosion on the U.S.S. *Maine* in early 1898.

Even though it probably had been caused by a fire that set off ammunition, an enraged American public blamed the Spanish for the disaster and called for war. Still, McKinley hesitated.

On the other side of the world, the people of another of Spain's last remaining possessions, the **Philippine Islands,** also were rebelling. In

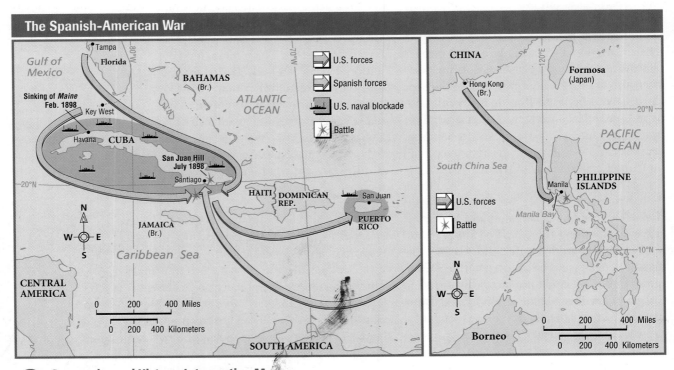

The Spanish-American War

Gulf of Mexico
Tampa
Florida
BAHAMAS (Br.)
ATLANTIC OCEAN
Sinking of *Maine* Feb. 1898
Key West
Havana
CUBA
San Juan Hill July 1898
Santiago
HAITI
DOMINICAN REP.
San Juan
PUERTO RICO
JAMAICA (Br.)
Caribbean Sea
CENTRAL AMERICA
SOUTH AMERICA

U.S. forces
Spanish forces
U.S. naval blockade
Battle

0   200   400 Miles
0   200   400 Kilometers

CHINA
Hong Kong (Br.)
Formosa (Japan)
PACIFIC OCEAN
South China Sea
Manila
Manila Bay
PHILIPPINE ISLANDS
U.S. forces
Battle
Borneo

0   200   400 Miles
0   200   400 Kilometers

Geography and History: Interpreting Maps
Although the Spanish-American War was fought in two locations on opposite sides of the world, the United States defeated Spain in just three months. *At what specific sites were the major battles of the war fought?*

later, rallying to the cry of "Remember the *Maine!*" Congress recognized Cuban independence and authorized force against Spain.

"A Splendid Little War" The war's first action took place, not in Cuba, but in the Philippines as shown on the map on page 368. On May 1, 1898, Admiral Dewey launched a surprise attack on Spanish ships anchored in Manila Bay, destroying Spain's entire Pacific fleet in just seven hours. In Cuba, meanwhile, United States warships quickly bottled up Spain's Atlantic fleet in the harbor at Santiago. Two months later, Theodore Roosevelt led a group of hastily organized volunteers called the "Rough Riders" in a charge up **San Juan Hill,** which became the most famous incident of the war. Several units of African American troops, known as the "Buffalo Soldiers," also performed superbly in the land war. A white soldier later wrote the *Washington Post* that "if it had not been for the Negro cavalry, the Rough Riders would have been exterminated."

The Spanish fleet made a desperate attempt to escape the harbor on July 3. In the ensuing battle, the United States Navy sank every Spanish ship, setting off wild Independence Day celebrations back in the United States.

It had all seemed quite simple. Although 2,500 Americans had died in the short war, fewer than 400 died in battle. The remainder died from food poisoning, yellow fever, malaria, and inadequate medical care. Future secretary of state John Hay captured the public mood when he wrote his friend Teddy Roosevelt that it had been "a splendid little war."

Dilemma in the Philippines In the treaty the United States signed with Spain in December 1898, the Spanish government recognized Cuba's independence. In return for a payment of $20 million, Spain also gave up the Philippines, Puerto Rico, and the Pacific island of Guam to the United States. The United States government called these territories "unincorporated," which meant that their residents would not become American citizens.

Although many Americans supported the treaty, others were deeply troubled by it. How could the United States become a colonial power without violating the nation's most basic principle—that all people have the right to liberty? Forced to justify this departure from American ideals, President McKinley explained that rebels in the Philippines were on the edge of war with one another and that the Filipino people were "unfit for self-government." If the United States did not act first, moreover, European powers might seize the islands. After a heated debate, the Senate ratified the treaty in February 1899.

Filipino rebels had fought with American troops in the war against Spain with the expectation that victory would bring independence. But when rebel leader Emilio Aguinaldo issued a proclamation in January 1899 declaring the Philippines a republic, the United States government ignored him. Mounting tensions between the rebel forces and American soldiers finally erupted into war in February. In the bitter three-year war that followed, 4,200 Americans were killed and 2,800 more wounded. Fighting without restraint—and sometimes with great brutality—American forces killed some 16,000 Filipino rebels and hundreds of thousands of Filipino civilians. Occasional fighting continued for years. The Philippines did not gain complete independence until 1946.

The Fate of Cuba and Puerto Rico Although the Teller Amendment, attached to Congress's

African American soldiers in the Tenth United States Cavalry are shown below. Wrote one soldier from this regiment: "If I die on the shores of Cuba my earnest prayer to God is that when death comes to end all, I may meet it calmly and fearlessly."

Filipino civilians suffered the highest casualty rates during the three-year war between the United States and the Philippines.

MAKING CONNECTIONS

In what ways was the Spanish-American War similar to the war between the United States and Mexico in 1846?

Other Gains in the Pacific

The United States government was intervening in other parts of the Pacific at the same time that the Spanish-American War was brewing. This intervention eventually brought about changes in the United States' relationship with Hawaii, Samoa, and China.

Annexation of Hawaii Hawaii had become increasingly important to United States business interests in the late 1800s. When Hawaii and the United States renegotiated their trade treaty in 1887, Hawaii leased Pearl Harbor to the United States as a coaling and repair station for naval vessels. That same year, white Hawaiian-born planters forced the Hawaiian king, Kalakaua, to accept a new constitution that, in effect, gave them control of the government.

When the king died in 1891, his sister Liliuokalani came to the throne. A strong nationalist, Queen Liliuokalani opposed United States control of the islands and sought to reduce the power of foreign merchants. In 1893, with the help of the United States Marines, pineapple planter Sanford B. Dole removed Queen Liliuokalani from power, proclaimed a republic, and requested that Hawaii be annexed by the United States. In 1896, when William McKinley was elected President, he supported the annexation. "We need Hawaii just as much and a good deal more than we did California. It is manifest destiny," McKinley said in early 1898. After briefly considering whether the Hawaiian people wished to be annexed, Congress was swayed by arguments that the United States needed naval stations in Hawaii in order to be a world power. In 1898 Congress approved the annexation of Hawaii.

Samoa The Polynesian islands of Samoa represented another possible stepping-stone to the growing trade with Asia. Back in 1878, the United States had negotiated a treaty with

1898 war resolution against Spain, promised Cubans their independence, United States involvement in Cuba did not end with the victory over Spain. In order to protect American business interests in the chaotic environment that followed the war, President McKinley installed a military government in Cuba that ruled for three years. This government organized a school system and restored economic stability. It also established a commission led by Major Walter Reed of the Army Medical Corps that found a cure for the deadly disease, yellow fever.

When Cubans began to draft a constitution in 1900, however, the United States government insisted that they include a document called the Platt Amendment. According to the provisions of this amendment, the Cuban government could not enter any foreign agreements, must allow the United States to establish two naval bases on the island, and must give the United States the right to intervene whenever necessary. The Platt Amendment remained in force until 1934.

Unlike Cuba, Puerto Rico never gained its independence. In an attempt to stem a growing independence movement, however, the United States government granted Puerto Ricans United States citizenship in 1917.

Samoa offering protection in return for a lease on their fine harbor at Pago Pago. When Britain and Germany began competing for control of these islands in the 1880s, tension between these European powers and the United States almost led to war. Eventually the three nations arranged a three-way protectorate of Samoa in 1889. The withdrawal of Great Britain from Samoa in 1899 left Germany and the United States to divide up the islands. A year after the annexation of Hawaii, the United States had acquired the harbor at Pago Pago as well.

Removed from power by American planters in 1893, Queen Liliuokalani was the last monarch of Hawaii.

An Open Door to China China's population was huge by the late 1800s, and its vast markets were increasingly important to American trade. But the United States was not the only nation interested in China. The Chinese monarchy was weakening, and many other countries—Russia, Germany, Britain, France, and Japan—were seeking **spheres of influence,** or areas of economic control, in China. In 1899 John Hay, now President McKinley's secretary of state, wrote notes to the major European powers trying to persuade them to keep an "open door" to China. He wanted to ensure through his **Open Door policy** that the United States would have equal access to China's millions of consumers.

Meanwhile, many Chinese resented foreign influence of any kind. A secret society called the Righteous and Harmonious Fists (the western press called them Boxers) started a rebellion in the spring of 1900 that led to the massacre of three hundred foreigners and Christian Chinese. Although the European powers eventually defeated the Boxers, Secretary Hay feared that these imperialist nations would use the rebellion as an excuse to seize more Chinese territory. Consequently, he issued a second series of Open Door notes. These notes reaffirmed the principle of open trade in China and made an even stronger statement about the intention of the United States to preserve it.

The Election of 1900

In the election of 1900, populist Democrat William Jennings Bryan and Republican William McKinley faced each other as they had in the election of 1896. McKinley named as his running mate Theodore Roosevelt, a man thoroughly identified with expansionism. American foreign policy had been so successful during McKinley's first term that the anti-imperialist Bryan had to drop the issue from his campaign speeches. Instead, he tried to emphasize the failures of Republican economic policies.

But by 1900, prosperity had returned to the nation. Bryan's complaints were ineffective, and McKinley won even more decisively than in 1896. A year later, however, he was dead—cut down by an assassin's bullet. Theodore Roosevelt, whom McKinley's friend Senator Marcus Hanna had once called a "wild man," was now President.

SECTION 2 REVIEW

Key Terms, People, and Places
1. Define (a) guerrilla, (b) jingoism, (c) sphere of influence, (d) Open Door policy.
2. Identify (a) William Randolph Hearst, (b) Joseph Pulitzer, (c) George Dewey.
3. Identify (a) Cuba, (b) the Philippine Islands, (c) San Juan Hill.

Key Concepts
4. What events led to the Spanish-American War?
5. What was the Open Door policy, and why was it important for the United States?

Critical Thinking
6. **Identifying Central Issues** What argument did anti-imperialists use to convince others that expansionism was wrong?

Using a Time Zone Map

Until the late 1800s, communities around the world calculated local time by the sun. When railroads began providing rapid long-distance train service between many communities—each with its own version of local time—this method began to cause scheduling nightmares.

In 1884 delegates from twenty-seven nations met in Washington, D.C., to discuss the problem. They eventually agreed on a system of worldwide standard time. Under this system, the world is divided into twenty-four time zones, shown by colored bands on the map below. Time is the same throughout each zone.

The prime meridian, which passes through Greenwich, England at 0° longitude, is the starting point for calculating the time in each zone. The International Date Line—located in the Pacific Ocean at 180° longitude—is where the date changes. The calendar date to the east of this line is one day earlier than that to the west.

Use the following steps to read the time zone map below.

1. Study the information on the map. The numbers at the bottom of the map indicate the number of hours each time zone differs from Greenwich time at the prime meridian. For example, a value of +3 means that the time in that zone is three hours *later* than Greenwich time; –3 means it is three hours *earlier.* The numbers at the top of the map provide examples of how this system works. (a) If it is 12:00 noon, Greenwich time, what time is it in Moscow? In Denver? (b) If it is 2:00 P.M. in Abidjan, Côte d'Ivoire, what time is it in the zone labeled +7? In the zone labeled –4? (c) If you flew west from Cairo, Egypt, to Lima, Peru, how many hours forward or back would you have to set your watch?

2. Compare the time in your zone with others. Find your time zone on the map. (a) If it is 1:00 A.M. in the time zone where you live, what time is it in Karachi, Pakistan? (b) If it is 12:00 noon in São Paolo, Brazil, what time is it where you live? (c) If it is 9:00 P.M. on Wednesday where you live, what time and day is it in Brisbane, Australia?

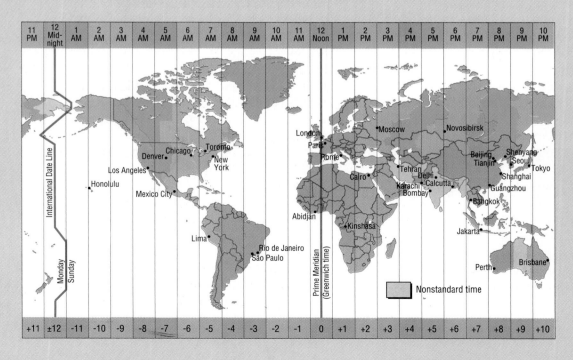

A Forceful Diplomacy

Whether people thought him a hero or a "wild man," most agreed that President Theodore Roosevelt conducted a vigorous foreign policy that suited the new status of the United States as a world power. Although President William Howard Taft continued Roosevelt's policies, he preferred a quieter, more subtle approach to influencing other nations.

Key Concepts

- The forceful and sometimes high-handed manner in which President Theodore Roosevelt conducted foreign policy had the effect of increasing the power of the presidency.
- Under Roosevelt, the United States secured a strip of land in Panama on which it built a canal linking the Atlantic and Pacific oceans.
- President Roosevelt asserted the right of the United States to use military force to preserve stability and order in neighboring countries.
- President William Howard Taft preferred economic pressure to military force in the conduct of American foreign policy.

Key Terms, People, and Places

Roosevelt Corollary, dollar diplomacy; Theodore Roosevelt, William Howard Taft; Isthmus of Panama, Colombia

B y 1900 the United States had emerged as a genuine world power, in control of territories overseas. Presidents Theodore Roosevelt and William Howard Taft acknowledged the change by developing a foreign policy to support the nation's new role in the world. Under their leadership, the United States continued to intervene in the domestic affairs of weaker countries of economic and strategic interest to the nation. Roosevelt did so in an independent and sometimes high-handed manner. Taft took a less aggressive approach, preferring economic pressure to military intervention.

AMERICAN PROFILES

Theodore Roosevelt

Was **Theodore Roosevelt** (1858–1919) really a "wild man"? He certainly was energetic. Before becoming President, he was a historian, politician, cowboy, buffalo hunter, crime fighter, reformer, and cavalryman. His active and colorful lifestyle made him famous the world over. The initials of his name were enough to identify him: TR.

The Shaping of a President Born into a wealthy merchant family in New York, TR was raised to be a leader. Although he had asthma as a child, his father insisted that he overcome his illness with rigorous physical exercise. Eventually, he developed a stocky body and fighter's stance.

TR was also studious. In 1876 he entered Harvard College, where he became increasingly interested in history. After graduation, TR married Alice Hathaway Lee and began to study law.

In February 1884, in the course of a single day, TR lost both his wife, who died in childbirth, and his mother, who died of typhoid. To recover from these twin blows, TR went west. Living on a ranch in the Dakota Territory, he hunted, rode, and studied history. There he started work on his most important and popular work, *The Winning of the West,* a glorification of the frontier myth and the "strenuous life." In TR's view, only strong-willed action would save the United States from physical and moral flabbiness.

Like many of his contemporaries, TR also believed in the superiority of the Anglo-Saxon race. He used arguments of racial superiority to justify the destruction of Native Americans. As he explained in his history of the West: "The man who puts the soil to use must of right dispossess the man who does not, or the world will come to a standstill."

This 1904 campaign pin for Teddy Roosevelt consists of a "teddy" bear holding a soldier's hat and sword.

After spending time on the western frontier as a young man (top), Teddy Roosevelt went on to become a war hero and President of the United States (bottom).

Soon after his return to New York City in 1886, TR remarried, this time to a childhood sweetheart, Edith Carow. When President McKinley named him assistant secretary of the navy, he worked hard to build a two-ocean fleet. Like Senators Henry Cabot Lodge and Albert Beveridge, TR was an unapologetic imperialist, who favored war with Spain and the acquisition of new territories abroad. When the Spanish-American War began, he resigned his position in the navy department to organize the First United States Volunteer Cavalry Regiment, made up in part of men he had met out west. The charge of his Rough Riders up San Juan Hill to take a Spanish garrison brought TR lasting fame.

That fall TR narrowly won the New York governorship. Although he ran an impressive administration, he infuriated the conservative bosses of the state Republican party. They were delighted when McKinley asked him to run as his vice-presidential candidate in 1900. The vice presidency was a post of such weakness that they were sure it would bury TR's political career for good. But their celebration proved premature. In September 1901, an assassin's bullet put Theodore Roosevelt in the White House.

Roosevelt as President Roosevelt called the presidency "a bully pulpit," by which he meant that it gave him a wonderful stage from which to win public support for change. Frequently restricted by Congress and other legal checks, Roosevelt still managed to expand the President's powers, especially in foreign affairs.

When Roosevelt was sworn in as President, he was forty-two years old, the youngest man ever to hold the office. Although today some people question his militaristic and racial beliefs, in his own time many people considered him a hero.

The Panama Canal

The Spanish-American War brought home to Americans the need for a quick route between the Pacific and Atlantic oceans. The **Isthmus of Panama** was an ideal location for such a route. At that time Panama was a province of **Colombia,** a country in South America. In 1879 a French company headed by Ferdinand de Lesseps had bought a twenty-five-year concession from Colombia to build a canal across Panama. Defeated by yellow fever and mismanagement, the company abandoned the project ten years later. It offered its remaining rights to the United States for $100 million. When in 1901 the price fell to $40 million, Congress accepted, but a lease on the land still had to be obtained from Colombia.

Colombia, on the other hand, was waiting for the French concession to expire in 1904 so that it could offer the isthmus at a higher price. Roosevelt was enraged by this attempt by Colombian "bandits" to "rob" the United States. As a result, he conspired with an official of the French company to organize a Panamanian "revolution" against Colombia.

The revolt took place in November 1903 with United States warships hovering offshore to provide support for the rebels. The United States immediately recognized an independent Panama and became its protector. In return, it

Cross-Section of the Panama Canal Zone

As a result of uneven elevation, the engineers who worked on the Panama Canal had to design a series of locks, pictured above, to raise and lower the ships that would pass through it. These locks added to the already considerable difficulty of constructing the canal. As the map at right shows, the Panama Canal cut thousands of miles off the sea journey from New York to San Francisco.

received a permanent grant of a ten-mile-wide strip of land for a Canal Zone.

Construction of the canal began in 1904. To complete this mammoth task, workers were brought in from several countries. Many of them had no construction experience whatsoever. Yet, after receiving proper training, the workers surpassed all expectations, finishing the canal in 1914, six months ahead of schedule and $23 million under budget.

Roosevelt's opponents did not appreciate the methods he had used to secure the Canal Zone. A newspaper published by William Randolph Hearst commented,

B esides being a rough-riding assault upon another republic over the shattered wreckage of international law . . . it is a quite unexampled instance of foul play in American politics.

Most Americans, however, approved of President Roosevelt's gaining of the Canal Zone in Panama. Two years after leaving office, Theodore Roosevelt gave a speech at the University of California at Berkeley in which he justified his methods in the Canal Zone.

I f I had followed traditional, conservative methods I would have submitted a digni-

fied State paper of probably 200 pages to Congress and the debates on it would have been going on yet; but I took the Canal Zone and let Congress debate; and while the debate goes on the canal does also.

Yet despite its success as a link between the Atlantic and Pacific oceans, the Panama Canal left a long heritage of ill will. In recognition of the illegal means used to acquire the Canal Zone, Congress voted a "guilt" payment of $25 million to Colombia in 1921, after TR had died.

Foreign Policy in the Early 1900s

In 1901 Roosevelt reminded an audience at the Minnesota State Fair of an old saying, "speak softly and carry a big stick; you will go far." In his view, the "big stick" was the American navy. Indeed, the threat of military force allowed Roosevelt to conduct an aggressive foreign policy. In December 1904, Roosevelt issued a message to Congress that became known as the **Roosevelt Corollary** to the Monroe Doctrine. In this corollary, or extension of a previously accepted idea, Roosevelt denied that the United States was interested in acquiring any more territory. It wanted only "to see neighboring countries stable, orderly, and prosperous," he

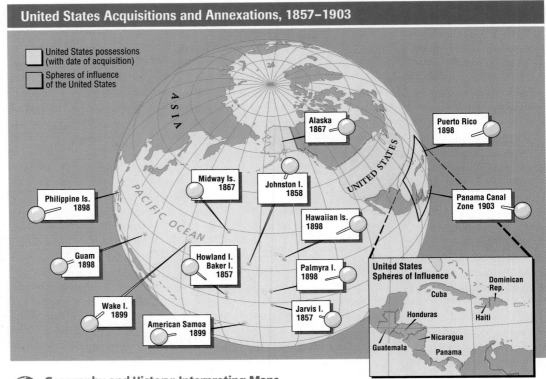

United States Acquisitions and Annexations, 1857–1903

United States possessions
(with date of acquisition)

Spheres of influence
of the United States

ASIA

PACIFIC OCEAN

UNITED STATES

Alaska
1867

Puerto Rico
1898

Midway Is.
1867

Johnston I.
1858

Panama Canal
Zone 1903

Philippine Is.
1898

Hawaiian Is.
1898

Guam
1898

Howland I.
Baker I.
1857

Palmyra I.
1898

Wake I.
1899

Jarvis I.
1857

American Samoa
1899

United States
Spheres of Influence

Dominican
Rep.

Cuba

Honduras

Haiti

Guatemala

Nicaragua

Panama

Geography and History: Interpreting Maps
Between 1857 and 1903, the United States acquired many new territorial possessions around the globe. *Why do you think so many of these new possessions were islands located in the Pacific Ocean?*

said. But if the countries engaged in activities harmful to the interests of the United States or if their governments collapsed, inviting intervention from stronger nations, then the United States would be forced to exercise "an international police power." In other words, the United States government would intervene to prevent intervention from other powers.

The first test of the Roosevelt Corollary concerned the small Caribbean island republic of Santo Domingo (now the Dominican Republic). When the island went bankrupt, European nations threatened to intervene to collect their money. Quickly Roosevelt made an "executive agreement" with Santo Domingo's president. Bankers in the United States took over the country's finances and paid its European debt.

Under Roosevelt, United States intervention in Latin America became common. This development angered Western Hemisphere countries. Congress also was displeased, for Roosevelt's interventionism meant that presidential powers grew while those of the legislature shrank.

THE WORLD CONSTABLE.

Published after the announcement of the Roosevelt Corollary, this political cartoon depicts Teddy Roosevelt as the world's police officer, using his "big stick" to maintain order and stability in Latin America.

Roosevelt as Peacemaker

Roosevelt's chief concern in Asia was to preserve China's "open door." In order for this to happen, Roosevelt believed that both Japan and Russia had to be kept in check. To achieve this, he supported Japan in its war with Russia over supremacy in Asia, but he did not let the war drag on. Roosevelt mediated a peace agreement in 1905 before Japan crushed Russia completely. In this way, he ensured a balance of power in Asia. When Japan accepted the Open Door policy, he invited delegates from the two nations to Portsmouth, New Hampshire, where he persuaded Japan to be satisfied with small grants of land and control over Korea instead of a huge payment of money. He also secured a promise from Russia to vacate Manchuria. Roosevelt's role as mediator won this "war maker" the Nobel Peace Prize.

MAKING CONNECTIONS

How were Teddy Roosevelt and Andrew Jackson similar in the way they used the power of the presidency to achieve their policy goals?

Taft and "Dollar Diplomacy"

William Howard Taft, who succeeded Roosevelt in the White House, was not as aggressive in pursuing foreign policy aims. A distinguished lawyer from Ohio, Taft had served as Roosevelt's secretary of war and headed the commission that governed the Philippines.

Taft's main goals were to maintain the open door to Asia and preserve stability in Latin America. As for the rest, he preferred "substituting dollars for bullets." By this he meant maintaining orderly societies abroad by increasing United States investment in foreign economies. Such an approach, he said, "appeals alike to idealistic humanitarian sentiments, to the dictates of sound policy and strategy, and to legitimate commercial aims." In other words, it pleased public opinion and made money for investors in the United States. Although some of Taft's contemporaries mocked his approach, calling it **"dollar diplomacy,"** Taft himself later used this term with pride.

Although President William Howard Taft shared Teddy Roosevelt's policy goals, he adopted a less aggressive approach to foreign policy.

A Mixed Legacy

Dollar diplomacy did not succeed as well as Taft had hoped. Although it increased the level of United States financial involvement abroad, the results were not always profitable. For example, when Taft's secretary of state, Philander Knox, persuaded bankers to invest in railroad projects in China and Manchuria, Russia and Japan united in an effort to block the influence of the Americans. In addition, many United States investments in China were lost when the country collapsed in revolution in 1911. Dollar diplomacy also created enemies in Latin America, especially in the Caribbean and Central America where local revolutionary movements opposed United States influence. Although the United States reached new heights as an international power under Roosevelt and Taft, anti-colonialism abroad and anti-imperialism at home provided a growing check to further expansion.

SECTION 3 REVIEW

Key Terms, People, and Places
1. Define (a) Roosevelt Corollary, (b) dollar diplomacy.
2. Identify (a) Theodore Roosevelt, (b) William Howard Taft.
3. Identify (a) Isthmus of Panama, (b) Colombia.

Key Concepts
4. What impact did Teddy Roosevelt have on the office of the presidency?

5. How did the United States secure the rights to build a canal through Panama?
6. What was the central message of the Roosevelt Corollary to the Monroe Doctrine?

Critical Thinking
7. **Making Comparisons** How was dollar diplomacy both similar to and different from the approach to foreign policy taken by Theodore Roosevelt?

The Building of the Panama Canal: A Geographic Perspective

On a world map, the Isthmus of Panama seems a mere thread of land. In reality, however, it is dozens of miles wide, formed of violent rivers, dense forests, and towering mountains. How did geographical issues affect the effort to build the canal?

When the United States set out to build the Panama Canal, three geographical factors affected the project. First, engineers had to decide where the canal should be located. Once construction began, the environment of the canal zone presented challenges to workers. Finally, to complete the project, massive amounts of earth had to be moved from one place to another.

Locating the Canal

When the construction team arrived in Panama in 1904, the end points of the canal already had been decided. It would begin at Colón on the Atlantic side and come out close to Panama City on the Pacific side, as the map on page 379 shows. In between lay two major obstacles. One was the Continental Divide, a ridge across Central America that separates rivers that flow west from rivers that flow east. The other obstacle was the wild and unpredictable Chagres River.

The French had never really solved the problem of how to tame the Chagres. The American solution, decided upon in 1906, was to "drown" the river. A vast earthen dam would be laid across the river valley at Gatún (see map opposite). The Chagres would then back up, creating the largest

artificial lake in the world at that time. The Chagres would become the only river in the world to cross a continental divide and flow into two oceans at once.

It was not hard to see where the canal should cross the divide. In the 1880s, a French company had scooped out 19 million cubic yards of dirt and rock from the divide near Culebra. Neither the French nor the Americans guessed that this excavation, the Culebra Cut, would require another 96 million cubic yards of digging before it was finished.

This plan for locating the canal meant that from the entrance at Colón Harbor, ships using the canal would sail 7 miles up a channel and ascend through three locks to a height of 85 feet above sea level. Then they would cross the new and sprawling Gatún Lake for 24 miles, pass through the 9 miles of the Culebra Cut, and descend by one lock to a smaller lake about 1 mile long. Another set of two locks would bring them to sea level and the final 8-mile leg of the canal to the open Pacific.

Against the Environment

While engineers and Congress were wrestling with the location of the canal, army physician

A Problem in Movement

When it came to actually digging the canal, the chief engineer, John F. Stevens, viewed the project as a simple problem of movement: dirt—lots of it—had to be moved. As an experienced builder of railroads, he knew that the cheapest, fastest way to move anything on land was by rail.

Within a week after his arrival, the new chief engineer had ordered double tracks laid. To get the dirt from the ditch to the train cars, Stevens brought in monster steam shovels. President Theodore Roosevelt, on an inspection visit to Panama, wrote, "Now we have taken hold of the job. . . . The huge steam shovels are hard at it, scooping huge masses of rock and gravel and dirt." The shovels were so efficient they filled five hundred trains with debris every day.

The highly efficient railway system could not solve another problem, however. Since Panama could not provide enough supplies to keep tens of thousands of workers fed and busy, ships traveled frequently between Colón and the United States. Ships brought in workers as well, some 45,000 of them, from 97 different nations.

When the canal was completed in 1914, the geographical obstacles of location, interaction with the environment, and movement had been overcome.

William Gorgas was wrestling with an insect. Medical science had learned only a few years before that two of the deadliest tropical diseases, yellow fever and malaria, were transmitted by mosquitoes. The secret of mosquito control, Gorgas found, was to cover, destroy, or drain every place where mosquitoes could lay their eggs—every tank, jar, hollow, and puddle, indoors or out. He divided the cities on the canal route into districts, each with an inspector who entered every house on a daily basis to check for uncovered or standing water. He also gave orders that any pools that could not be drained were to be covered with a film of oil or kerosene to kill the insects.

Gorgas's methods wiped out yellow fever before the end of 1905. Malaria, which was carried by a tougher mosquito, was not eliminated, but was much reduced.

GEOGRAPHIC CONNECTIONS

1. What two problems of movement did the building of the canal entail, and how were they solved?
2. How did Dr. Gorgas change the environment of Panama, and what effect did his work have?

Thinking Critically

3. **Making Comparisons** How was building the Panama Canal like building the transcontinental railroad?

The People's Response to Imperialism

SECTION PREVIEW

After the Spanish-American War, the debate intensified over whether it was appropriate for the United States to continue to throw its net around other nations and drag them under American control. Anti-imperialists used a variety of arguments against the acquisition of territories.

Key Concepts
- The annexation of the Philippines led to a spirited debate in the United States over imperialism.
- Anti-imperialists argued that taking over territories betrayed the principles on which the nation was founded.
- Economic benefits, pride in the nation's growing power, and the search for a new frontier made imperialism appealing to many Americans.

Key Terms, People, and Places
paradox of power; Juliette Low

This weathervane from about 1870 reflects national pride in the United States' emerging role as a world power.

Before the Spanish-American War, United States citizens already were debating the consequences of an expanded role in world affairs. Walter Gresham, President Cleveland's secretary of state in 1894, was one government official who worried about the issue. He cautioned against "the evils of interference in affairs that do not specially concern us." Until the annexation of the Philippines in 1898, however, most citizens supported the idea of overseas involvement.

The Anti-Imperialists

After the annexation, opposition to imperialism grew. In November 1898, opponents of United States policy in the Philippines established the Anti-Imperialist League. Most of its organizers were upper-middle-class professionals, such as the prominent Republican and former senator Carl Schurz, editor E. L. Godkin, Democratic politician William Jennings Bryan, settlement house leader Jane Addams, charity reformer Josephine Shaw Lowell, novelist Mark Twain, and Harvard philosopher William James. Steel industrialist Andrew Carnegie contributed thousands of dollars to the cause.

Moral and Political Arguments The anti-imperialists used a variety of arguments to support their position. The strongest of these were moral and political in nature. "Any nation," wrote Boston pacifist Lucia Mead in 1900,

whether it be monarchy or republic, which buys or takes by conquest another people, and dominates them without promise of granting them independence or . . . guaranteeing future Statehood, has adopted an imperialist policy.

Such behavior, the anti-imperialists asserted, was a rejection of the nation's foundation of "liberty for all."

As Carl Schurz explained in 1899:

We regret that it has become necessary in the land of Washington and Lincoln to reaffirm that all men, of whatever race or color, are entitled to life, liberty, and the pursuit of happiness.

Others said it more concisely: "The Constitution must follow the flag," by which they meant that the United States flag and United States laws went together, and that people in territories controlled by the United States should be entitled to the guarantees in the United States Constitution.

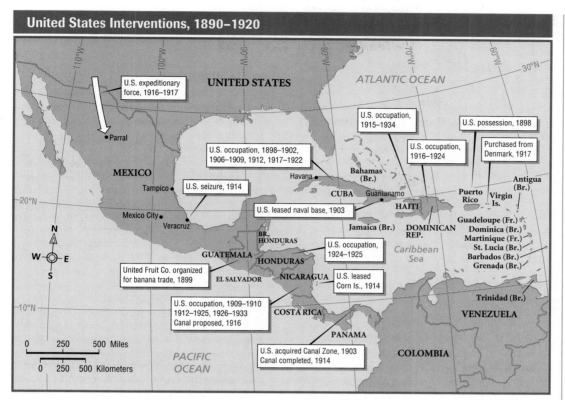

United States Interventions, 1890–1920

U.S. expeditionary force, 1916–1917

UNITED STATES

ATLANTIC OCEAN

30°N

• Parral

U.S. occupation, 1915–1934

U.S. possession, 1898

U.S. occupation, 1898–1902, 1906–1909, 1912, 1917–1922

U.S. occupation, 1916–1924

Purchased from Denmark, 1917

MEXICO

Havana •

Bahamas (Br.)

Antigua (Br.)

Tampico •

U.S. seizure, 1914

CUBA   Guantanamo

Puerto Rico   Virgin Is.

20°N

Mexico City •

U.S. leased naval base, 1903

HAITI

• Veracruz

Jamaica (Br.)

DOMINICAN REP.

Guadeloupe (Fr.)
Dominica (Br.)
Martinique (Fr.)
St. Lucia (Br.)
Barbados (Br.)
Grenada (Br.)

N W E S

BR. HONDURAS

GUATEMALA   HONDURAS

U.S. occupation, 1924–1925

Caribbean Sea

United Fruit Co. organized for banana trade, 1899

EL SALVADOR   NICARAGUA

U.S. leased Corn Is., 1914

Trinidad (Br.)

10°N

U.S. occupation, 1909–1910 1912–1925, 1926–1933 Canal proposed, 1916

COSTA RICA

VENEZUELA

0   250   500 Miles
0   250   500 Kilometers

PACIFIC OCEAN

PANAMA

U.S. acquired Canal Zone, 1903 Canal completed, 1914

COLOMBIA

Geography and History: Interpreting Maps
The above map illustrates how frequently the United States intervened in the affairs of Latin American countries in the early 1900s. The United States government defended these interventions as necessary for the protection of the nation's economic and political interests. *What economic interests were served by having influence in these nations?*

President of the American Federation of Labor Samuel Gompers objected to taking over countries in which United States labor laws did not apply. He pointed out that in Hawaii, half of the population consisted of "contract laborers, practically slaves," who did not benefit from the laws that protected American workers.

Expansionists replied that the people of the Caribbean and the Pacific were not ready for democracy and that the United States was preparing them for liberty. For example, Major General Arthur McArthur, military governor of the Philippines in 1900, said, "We are planting in those islands . . . the best traditions, the best characteristics of Americanism." The anti-imperialists responded that no people should be forced to wait to enjoy liberty.

Finally, anti-imperialists noted that imperialism endangered the nation's democratic institutions. Imperialist wars required large standing armies that could be used to crush dissent at home just as easily as to bring other nations under United States control.

A Race War? Other anti-imperialists saw racism at work in imperialism. Like Theodore Roosevelt, many Americans of this period believed that people of Anglo-Saxon heritage were superior to other races. The public officials who developed the country's imperialist policies shared these sentiments.

African Americans were at first torn about imperialistic issues. As United States citizens, they wanted to support their country in a time of war. But they recognized the racism that underlay imperialism. Bishop Alexander Walters of the A.M.E. Zion Church said in 1899,

H ad the Filipinos been white and fought as bravely as they have, the war would have been ended and their independence granted a long time ago.

Viewpoints
On the Race for Empire

The Spanish-American War heightened the debate between imperialist and anti-imperialist factions at home. **Which of the following viewpoints do you think best represents the political ideals of liberty and equality on which the United States was founded?**

Anti-Imperialist

"We assume that what we like and practice, and what we think better, must come as a welcome blessing to Spanish-Americans and Filipinos. This is grossly and obviously untrue. They hate our ways. They are hostile to our ideas. Our religion, language, institutions, and manners offend them.
William G. Sumner, Yale University professor, in an 1898 speech

Pro-Imperialist

"Think of the thousands of Americans who will pour into Hawaii and Puerto Rico when the republic's laws cover those islands with justice and safety! Think of the tens of thousands of Americans who will invade mine and field and forest in the Philippines when a liberal government, protected and controlled by this republic, if not the government of the republic itself, shall establish order and equity there!"
Albert J. Beveridge, leading imperialist and later United States senator, in an 1898 speech

Although most southern Democrats also opposed imperialism, they did so for different reasons. Many southern politicians feared the effects of having to absorb more people of different races into the United States. Consequently, southern Democrats led the movement in the Senate against ratifying the treaty with Spain.

A number of anti-imperialists outside the South, including William Jennings Bryan and Samuel Gompers, also opposed imperialist policies because of the fear that they would encourage people of different racial backgrounds to move to the United States. Reformer Carl Schurz wrote about these concerns:

> The prospects of the consequences which would follow the admission of the Spanish creoles and . . . the negroes . . . to participation in the conduct of our

government is so alarming that you instinctively pause before taking the step.

Practical Objections Finally, anti-imperialists raised practical objections to expansionist policies. In the view of these thinkers, it was not a good time for the United States to expand. First, expansion involved too many costs. Maintaining the necessary armed forces required more taxation, debt, and possibly even compulsory military service. Second, as African American leader Booker T. Washington said, the United States already had enough difficulties at home. "Until our nation has settled the Negro and Indian problems I do not believe that we have a right to assume more social problems," he argued.

Samuel Gompers raised a third point. He argued that laborers coming to the United States from annexed territories would compete with American workers for jobs. Since these immigrants would work for lower wages, their presence would drive all wages down. Industrialists also pointed out that goods produced cheaply in annexed countries could be imported to the United States without customs duties, which would hurt many American industries in the process.

Imperialism's Appeal to the American Imagination

Despite the strength of many anti-imperialist arguments, imperialism maintained a powerful hold on the American imagination. The director of the census had declared the frontier "closed" in the 1890 census. The America of explorers and pioneers, who bravely charted unknown territories, overcame great obstacles, and accomplished great deeds, was fast disappearing into the shadows of memory. What would keep Americans from growing too soft, from losing their competitive edge? Some looked to a new frontier abroad to answer this question.

The growth and popularity of youth scouting programs during this period shows that many middle-class Americans shared a "frontier mentality." Sir Robert Baden-Powell, an army officer of the British Empire, had used scouting techniques (tracking, woodcraft, and wilderness survival) to great success in a battle in South Africa. A few years after he returned to Britain as a war hero, Baden-Powell founded the Boy Scout movement. Scouting appeared in the United States in 1910 and soon became immensely popular. Two years later, **Juliette Low,** a close friend and admirer of Baden-Powell, founded the American Girl Scouts. Low hoped to use the program both to build moral character in girls and to teach them skills that would make them "hardy" and "handy."

In addition, the popular media glorified the accomplishments of imperialist frontier heroes. Theodore Roosevelt's book on his heroic charge, *The Rough Riders,* drew much praise. However, satirist Finley Peter Dunne's character, "Mr. Dooley," suggested the book should be called *Alone in Cuba* to emphasize Roosevelt's boastfulness. Another book of this era, *Conquest of the Tropics* (1914), describes the history of the United Fruit Company, portraying railroad entrepreneur Minor Keith as one of "the hardy American type which listens and responds eagerly to the call of the wild."

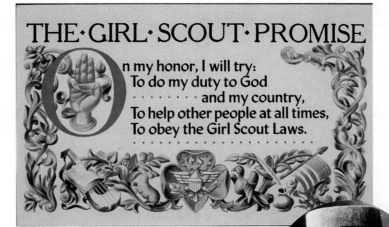

THE·GIRL·SCOUT·PROMISE

On my honor, I will try:
To do my duty to God and my country,
To help other people at all times,
To obey the Girl Scout Laws.

As "The Girl Scout's Promise" suggests, founder Juliette Low (bottom) saw scouting as a way of teaching moral character as well as frontier skills.

the United States discovered that these actions frequently took on a life of their own. Unforeseen difficulties arose. In the Caribbean and Central America, for example, the United States often had to defend governments that were friendly to its economic and political interests but unpopular with local inhabitants. In Latin America, the cry "Yankee, Go Home!" began to be heard.

On the other hand, because the United States was quickly becoming so powerful, other countries—even those fearful about maintaining their independence—increasingly were turning to the United States government for help. This state of affairs illustrated the **paradox of power.** Both admired and hated, welcomed and rejected, the United States would spend the rest of the century trying to decide the best way to reconcile its growing power and national interests with its relationships with other nations and peoples.

MAKING CONNECTIONS

How was the popular media's glorification of imperialist heroes such as Minor Keith similar to the often romantic portrayal of the men and women settlers of the American West?

The Paradox of Power

Having begun a pattern of international involvements, shown on the map on page 381,

---

shown on the map on page 381,

Key Terms, People, and Places
1. Define paradox of power.
2. Identify Juliette Low.

Key Concepts
3. Name some of the major arguments of the anti-imperialists.
4. Explain why imperialism was so appealing to many United States citizens.

5. What were some of the disadvantages of imperialism for the United States?

Critical Thinking
6. **Identifying Assumptions** Based on the arguments they used against imperialism, what kind of role do you think the anti-imperialists believed the United States should play in world affairs?

Chapter Review

Understanding Key Terms, People, and Places

Key Terms
1. imperialism
2. annexation
3. most-favored nation
4. banana republic
5. guerrilla
6. jingoism
7. sphere of influence
8. Open Door policy
9. Roosevelt Corollary

10. dollar diplomacy
11. paradox of power

People
12. Alfred T. Mahan
13. Henry Cabot Lodge
14. Albert J. Beveridge
15. William Randolph Hearst
16. Joseph Pulitzer
17. George Dewey
18. Theodore Roosevelt

19. William Howard Taft
20. Juliette Low

Place
21. Hawaii
22. Cuba
23. Philippine Islands
24. San Juan Hill
25. Isthmus of Panama
26. Colombia

Terms For each term above, write a sentence that explains its relation to the growth of the United States as a world power.

Matching Review the key terms in the list above. If you are not sure of a term's meaning, review its definition in the chapter. Then choose a term from the list that best matches each description below.
1. soldiers who fight using surprise tactics
2. the policy under which stronger nations attempt to create empires by dominating dominance over weaker nations
3. the addition of a new territory to an existing country

4. W. H. Taft's policy of "substituting dollars for bullets"
5. an intense burst of national pride and the desire for an aggressive foreign policy

Word Relationships Three of the terms in each of the following sets are related. Choose the term that does not belong and explain why it does not belong.
1. William Howard Taft, George Dewey, Philippine Islands, Cuba
2. William Randolph Hearst, Isthmus of Panama, Joseph Pulitzer, San Juan Hill
3. Alfred T. Mahan, Juliette Low, Henry Cabot Lodge, Theodore Roosevelt

---

Reviewing Main Ideas

Section 1 (pp. 362–365)
1. Describe the status of the United States economy in the late 1800s.
2. Why were the major European powers scrambling to seize new territory?
3. Briefly explain the arguments of Alfred T. Mahan, Henry Cabot Lodge, and Albert J. Beveridge regarding expansionism.

Section 2 (pp. 366–371)
4. Describe how the 1880 dispute between the United States and Great Britain reaffirmed the validity of the Monroe Doctrine.
5. Why did the American public favor war with Spain?
6. What new territories and influence did the United

States gain in the Pacific as a result of its interventionist policies?

Section 3 (pp. 373–377)
7. Describe Theodore Roosevelt's approach to foreign policy.
8. How did the Roosevelt Corollary affect United States policy in Latin America?
9. What were President Taft's main foreign policy goals and how did he plan to accomplish them?

Section 4 (pp. 380–383)
10. Explain why anti-imperialists believed that imperialism betrayed basic American principles.
11. What was the connection between imperialism and the closing of the American frontier?

1. **Distinguishing Fact from Opinion** Future secretary of state John Hay referred to the Spanish-American War as "a splendid little war." Can you think of any Americans, in addition to anti-imperialists, who might disagree with Hay?

2. **Demonstrating Reasoned Judgment** You have read that although some people today question Teddy Roosevelt's militaristic and racial beliefs, in his own time many people considered him a hero. How can you account for this change in public perception?

3. **Drawing Conclusions** During the late 1800s, the press fanned the flames of the Spanish-American War by publishing sensational stories about Spanish cruelties in Cuba. On what current issues do you think the press has played a major role in influencing public opinion? Has sensationalism played a part in influencing the public?

1. **Evaluating Primary Sources** Review the primary source quotation on the bottom of page 373. What does Roosevelt assume about Native American land use? Do you think that his assumption is accurate?

2. **Understanding the Visuals** Choose one visual from the chapter that provides an argument in favor of expansionism and one that provides an argument against expansionism. Explain how each visual argues its position.

3. **Writing About the Chapter** Imagine that you are living during the early 1900s. Write a letter to the editor of your local newspaper in which you argue either for or against an interventionist foreign policy. First, create a list of arguments that support your position. Note any opposing arguments to which you wish to reply. Next, write a draft of your letter in which you offer your ideas. Revise your letter, making sure that your opinions are well supported. Proofread your letter and draft a final copy.

4. **Using the Graphic Organizer** This graphic organizer uses a multi-flow map to show the causes and effects of American expansion during the late 1800s and early 1900s. (a) Based on the graphic organizer, what was the major negative effect of American expansion for Americans? (b) On a separate sheet of paper, create your own graphic organizer about the causes and effects of the Spanish-American War, using this graphic organizer as an example.

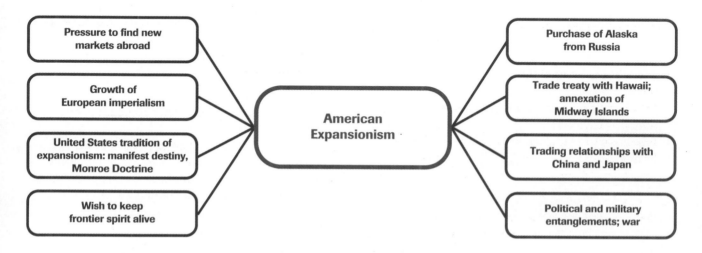

Pressure to find new markets abroad

Growth of European imperialism

United States tradition of expansionism: manifest destiny, Monroe Doctrine

Wish to keep frontier spirit alive

American Expansionism

Purchase of Alaska from Russia

Trade treaty with Hawaii; annexation of Midway Islands

Trading relationships with China and Japan

Political and military entanglements; war

The Era of Progressive Reform

1890–1920

*A*t the turn of the century, a spirit of reform known as progressivism took hold of many American people. Less a united movement than a loose collection of informal and unlikely alliances, progressivism targeted the massive problems of an urban, industrialized nation. In spite of opposition, progressives were able to redefine government's role in American life, make a serious run for the White House, and enact such lasting reforms as woman suffrage.

Events in the United States

1890 National American Woman Suffrage Association formed. • Yosemite declared a national park.	**1893** Illinois passes law prohibiting child labor. • A depression rocks the nation.		**1899** National Consumers League forms to investigate conditions under which goods are made.	**1903** Teddy Roosevelt proposes arbitration to end the United Mine Workers' strike.

1890	1893	1896	1899	1902

Events in the World

1890 Japan holds its first general elections. • Swiss government introduces social insurance.	**1894** Japan and Korea declare war on China. • British obtain control of Uganda.

1906 Upton Sinclair publishes The Jungle, *an exposé of the meat-packing industry.*

1908 The Supreme Court upholds an Oregon law limiting hours for women laundry workers.

1912 Massachusetts becomes the first state to adopt a minimum wage.
• Woodrow Wilson is elected President.

1919 State legislatures ratify the 18th Amendment, enacting prohibition.

1920 Women win the vote with the ratification of the 19th Amendment.

1905   **1908**   **1911**   **1914**   **1917**   **1920**

1904 Ten-hour work day established in France.

1907 Universal direct suffrage instituted in Austria.

1911 Turkish-Italian war begins.
• Mexican Civil War ends.

The Origins of Progressivism

In the twilight of the 1800s, many citizens could see that existing efforts to solve the massive problems of industrialization were failing. Could government heal the nation's ills?

Key Concepts

- The turn of the century brought a variety of new reform ideas.
- The many plans for reform fed into a stream of ideas that came to be called progressivism.
- Though progressives did not all share the same ideas and beliefs, they often used similar methods.

Key Terms, People, and Places

home rule, progressivism, social welfare program, muckraker; Henry George, Edward Bellamy, Florence Kelley

One popular cause in the early 1900s was the campaign for pure food and medicine, referred to in the magazine cover above.

By the end of the 1800s, many citizens were aware of the massive problems resulting from rapid industrialization. Unemployment, unsafe working conditions, and political corruption were just a few of these concerns, which have been discussed in earlier chapters. Citizens also realized that private efforts to address these issues, such as charity or settlement-house work, were inadequate. These concerned citizens—most of them educated middle- and upper-class men and women—began to argue that government had to become more actively involved in addressing the nation's ills. Their ideas soon redefined the United States government's role in society.

A Spirit of Reform in the late 1800s

The 1880s and 1890s were filled with lively debates about how to reform society. The ideas of journalists Henry George and Edward Bellamy were among the most popular. Socialists, unionists, and city government reformers also had many followers.

Two Visionaries In 1879 **Henry George** had written the book *Progress and Poverty* in an effort to explain why an advanced civilization seemed to increase rather than eliminate poverty. He concluded that poverty arose because private interests—speculators—bought and held land until its price went up. This practice prevented others from using land productively.

George proposed to solve this problem by ending taxes on improvements on land, such as houses and cultivation. State and local governments raised much of their income from these taxes. Instead, George proposed only a single tax—on the value of land itself. Such a tax would make speculation in land less attractive by increasing the cost of holding land without using it.

George's ideas had a powerful effect. "Single-tax" clubs sprang up everywhere. In 1894, club members from Iowa, Ohio, Minnesota, and Pennsylvania migrated to Fairhope, Alabama, to establish a single-tax colony.

In 1888 newspaper editor **Edward Bellamy** published a novel called *Looking Backward*. In it, a man undergoes hypnosis in 1887 and wakes up in the year 2000. He finds the United States transformed. The harsh working conditions, gaps between social classes, and political corruption of the late 1800s have disappeared. The reason for the change was that government had nationalized the great trusts and organized industrial management to meet human needs rather than to make profits. Writes Bellamy,

In a word, the people of the United States concluded to assume the conduct of their own business, just as one hundred odd years before they had assumed the conduct of their own government.

Bellamy's novel was a phenomenal best seller. In response to its vision, hundreds of "Nationalist" clubs formed.

Socialists Bellamy's views were related to the widely discussed ideas of socialism, an economic and political system featuring collective or government ownership of a nation's wealth. (See Chapter 8.) Many American socialists in this era wanted to end the capitalist system, distribute wealth more equally, and nationalize American industries—but through the ballot box, not through revolution. In 1901 they formed a Socialist Party of America, which by 1912 had won more than one thousand municipal offices. Although the party never became a political force on the national level, many reform-minded Americans gave consideration to its ideas at some time.

The Labor Movement Like members of the Socialist party, union members also hoped for economic change for the masses. Unions, however, concentrated on hours, wages, and conditions in the workplace. Reformers around the turn of the century supported many union goals.

The union movement grew in the 1890s, but slowly. Union membership was risky. Big business easily got the courts to prohibit strikes with court orders called injunctions.

Municipal Reform The spirit of social reform was also felt at the municipal, or city government, level. Municipal reformers opposed the influence that political bosses wielded and sought honest, cost-efficient government through a professional, nonpolitical civil service. They also worked for **home rule,** under which cities exercise a limited degree of self-rule. At that time, home rule helped cities escape domination by state governments, which often were controlled by political machines or rural interests.

Municipal reformers sometimes appeared naive in their belief that they could abolish corruption. Some of them also held negative views of immigrants, whom they felt were responsible for many city problems. Still, their ideas formed an important element of the era's spirit of reform.

Progressivism Takes Hold

Aspects of all the reform visions and programs discussed above influenced citizens at the end of the century. Other movements were also influential at this time—including nativism, prohibitionism, the purity crusade, charity reform, social gospel, and the settlement house movement, all discussed in Chapter 10. Together these fed into the stream of ideas that became known as **progressivism.** The Populist movement formed another, though less central, current in the progressive movement.

Progressives did not agree on all points. The movement was made up of a series of temporary alliances among diverse interests pursuing different but related goals. Yet many reformers identified themselves as progressives, and for a number of years, many progressives organized themselves into a formal political party.

The Views of Progressives As mentioned before, many progressives were well-to-do Americans. They recognized that the nation's free enterprise system often could be unfair, but they did not want to lose the high standard of living and personal liberty it had given them, and they deeply feared the violence of revolution. Thus, progressives were faced with the question of how to preserve what was good about the United States while reforming the bad.

In spite of the obstacles facing unions, the International Ladies Garment Workers Union (ILGWU) formed in 1900. After the 1909 strike shown below, which included 20,000 New York City women garment workers, the ILGWU won the right to bargain collectively.

Progressives argued that government must play a larger role in regulating economic activity. This regulation would prevent businesses from treating workers and competing enterprises unfairly. Progressives opposed government control of businesses, except of those companies that supplied essential services such as water, electricity, and transportation. They wanted to allow other businesses the freedom to operate independently—as long as society's needs came first.

Progressives also believed that government ought to increase its responsibility for human welfare. Capitalism, progressives argued, often forced workers into poverty through no fault of their own. Workers had no protection against substandard wages, unemployment, or workplace hazards. Progressives proposed that government protect workers from such miseries. They also wanted government to develop more **social welfare programs,** which would help ensure a basic standard of living for all Americans. These programs might include unemployment and accident and health insurance, as well as a social security system to cover disability and old age. Progressives expected that government would rely on trained experts and scientists to plan efficient programs, which professionals, not politicians, would manage.

Suffrage and Progressivism The cause of votes for women was important to many progressives. As social worker Jane Addams explained in a 1910 *Ladies Home Journal* article, women had a special interest in the reform of American society.

W omen who live in the country sweep their own dooryards and may either feed the refuse [trash] of the table to a flock of chickens or allow it innocently to decay in the open air and sunshine. In a crowded city quarter, however, if the street is not cleaned by the city authorities no amount of private sweeping will keep the tenement free from grime; if the garbage is not properly collected and destroyed a tenement house mother may see her children sicken and die of diseases.

In short, Addams argued, women in cities could not care for their families without government help—so government had to allow women to make known their needs through voting.

Women activists did not all agree on how to change society. Many focused on outlawing alcohol, others on reforming conditions in the workplace. But whatever their focus, it was widely agreed that women were powerless without political rights.

Progressive Regulation and Control In order to protect vulnerable citizens, progressives accepted an increased level of government control over areas once considered private, such as housing, health care, and the content of the movies people watched or the dancing styles they enjoyed. This aspect of progressivism aroused resistance, often among the very people progressives hoped most to help. For example, progressives saw child labor laws as critical to social progress. Naturally, employers who relied on cheap child labor opposed the laws. But poor people who could not survive without sending their children out to work also objected. Such disputes added to the perception that typically well-to-do progressives were insensitive to the plight of the poor.

LAD FELL TO DEATH IN BIG COAL CHUTE

Workers of all ages enjoyed little protection against workplace hazards— and few benefits when an accident befell them on the job. The fate of injured or killed workers aroused public sympathy and demands for reform.

Progressive Methods

Progressives worked for reforms in a systematic manner. First, relying heavily on scientific data and expert testimony, they investigated issues of concern, such as slum or sweatshop conditions. Next, they publicized the results of their investigations and put pressure on legislators to get laws passed and enforced. Women's organizations, such as clubs and charitable groups, were a key means of increasing grass roots support and pressuring officials to take some action.

Using the new mass-circulation publications, journalists also alerted the public to wrongdoing on the part of political bosses or big business. Theodore Roosevelt called such writers **muckrakers,** an allusion to a character in John Bunyan's 1678 book *Pilgrim's Progress* who was too busy raking filth to look to heaven. While TR disapproved of those who whitewashed wrongdoing, he condemned those who "earn their livelihood by telling . . . scandalous falsehoods about honest men."

Despite Roosevelt's criticism, the muckrakers included respected writers who identified and exposed real abuses. Lincoln Steffens, for example, exposed political corruption in St. Louis and other cities. Ida Tarbell revealed the abuses committed by the huge Standard Oil trust. *The Jungle* (1906), a novel by Upton Sinclair, laid bare the horrors of the meat-packing industry. Wrote Sinclair of the nation's corrupt and filthy canneries,

> I t seemed they must have agencies all over the country, to hunt out old and crippled and diseased cattle to be canned. . . . It was stuff such as this that made the "embalmed beef" that had killed several times as many United States soldiers as all the bullets of the Spaniards [in the Spanish-American War].

Although it was meant to promote socialism, Sinclair's book did little for workers. Its revelations, however, turned people's stomachs and thus led to a federal meat inspection program.

AMERICAN PROFILES

Florence Kelley

When you shop for clothing, do you ever wonder under what conditions it was made? When you buy medicines or a package of meat, do you worry about possible harmful effects to your health? At the turn of the century, issues such as these bothered many consumers. Because women tended to be the shoppers for their families, they were often the most vocal in asking such questions.

Florence Kelley (1859–1932) became a leader in the search for answers. She came from a prominent Pennsylvania family. Her father, William Darrah Kelley, was a fifteen-term member of Congress. Her great-aunt, Sarah Pugh, had a strong influence on her. An abolitionist and suffragist, Pugh had once refused to use cotton and sugar because slave labor produced them.

After completing her education at Cornell and at the University of Zurich in Switzerland, Kelley became a resident in Jane Addams's Hull House in Chicago. When federal officials asked Addams to investigate labor conditions in the neighborhood, Addams recommended Kelley for the job.

This cartoon shows that TR himself was willing to wield the muckrake to attack difficult problems. Here, TR tries to clean up the nation's meatpacking industry.

Florence Kelley led the way in several areas of progressive reform, including workplace and municipal reform.

Kelley's Early Career "Hull-House was . . . surrounded in every direction by home work carried on under the sweating system," Kelley wrote later, referring to a system of labor featuring poor conditions and pay. "From the age of eighteen months few children able to sit in high chairs at tables were safe from being required to pull basting threads." Once, Kelley reported, a public official who was supposed to visit a sweatshop refused to enter, fearing contamination from one of the many diseases, such as tuberculosis, that raged through the tenements at that time.

Largely through her efforts, in 1893 Illinois passed a law prohibiting child labor, limiting working hours for women, and regulating sweatshop conditions. The governor put Kelley in charge of enforcing it. She became so frustrated by the district attorney's refusal to prosecute cases that she earned a law degree in order to take legal action herself.

In 1897 a new governor replaced Kelley as factory inspector with a political friend who did nothing to enforce the 1893 law. It was this experience that drew Kelley into municipal reform. Only a civil service based on merit instead of favors, she realized, would keep unqualified political appointees out of important regulatory jobs.

Leading Consumer Action In 1899 a National Consumers' League (NCL) was organized to unite local consumers' leagues that had formed in the 1890s across the country. The NCL's board invited Florence Kelley to become general secretary, a post she held until her death. Through the consumers' leagues, women around the country investigated the conditions under which goods were made and sold. Local leagues urged women to patronize only those shops on a "White List"—that is, shops that did not employ children or require overtime. Leagues also insisted that factories obey state factory inspection laws and, later, pay a minimum wage.

Under Kelley's leadership, the NCL spearheaded national movements to outlaw child labor and protect workers, especially women. When criticized over this issue, Kelley would ask why "seals, bears, reindeer, fish, wild game in the national parks, buffalo" and numerous other creatures were worthy of government protection, "but not the children of our race and their mothers."

Kelley's legacy lasted long after her death. In 1954 Supreme Court justice Felix Frankfurter said that Florence Kelley "had probably the largest single share in shaping the social history of the United States during the first thirty years of this century."

SECTION 1 REVIEW

Key Terms, People, and Places
1. Define (a) home rule, (b) social welfare program, (c) muckraker.
2. Identify (a) Henry George, (b) Edward Bellamy, (c) Florence Kelley.

Key Concepts
3. What were some of the reform ideas at the turn of the century?

4. Who were the progressives and what did they want?
5. Describe the special role of women in the progressive movement.
6. Describe the methods of progressives.

Critical Thinking
7. **Recognizing Ideologies** What beliefs about the proper role of government lie at the heart of the progressive movement?

Progressivism: Its Legislative Impact

SECTION PREVIEW

Driven by the rising tide of public demand, a torrent of progressive reform programs flowed through local, state, and federal legislatures. Targets for the proposed reforms included politics, society, and the economy.

Key Concepts
- The progressive era produced several different kinds of reforms.
- Reform took place at the urban, state, and federal levels.
- Reformers found unlikely allies in political machines.

Key Terms, People, and Places
direct primary, arbitration, holding company

The unleashing of the progressive impulse led to a tremendous amount of legislation in the early 1900s. Reform took place at all levels of government—city, state, and federal.

Urban Reform

Much of the progressive reform began in the cities as opposed to the state or federal levels. In part this was because the less extensive the government, the easier it is to change that government. Also, cities were home to most of the settlement workers, club members, professionals, and business leaders who were pushing many of the reforms. Thus, they were on hand to maintain the pressure for change.

Attacking the Bosses Political machines and bosses sustained heavy criticism in the progressive period, but always seemed able to withstand such attacks. New York City provides a good example. In 1896 Columbia University president Seth Low ran for mayor, supported by municipal reformers and settlement work-

ers. To help his campaign against Tammany Hall's ward bosses, settlement houses sent out children with handbills to post in their neighborhoods. Low lost, but he tried again in 1901 and won, only to see the Tammany Hall machine return to power in the next election. Over the following decades, New York seesawed between turning to reform or sticking with the old political bosses. In some cities, voter support for reforms prompted machine politicians to work with reformers. Together they registered voters, improved city services, established public health programs, and enforced tenement codes. Such alliances could bring about astonishing improvements in urban life.

Cities Take Over Utilities Reformers made efforts to regulate or dislodge the monopolies that provided city utilities such as water, gas, and electricity. Reform mayors Hazen S. Pingree of Detroit (1889–1897), Samuel M. "Golden Rule" Jones of Toledo (1897–1904), and Tom Johnson of Cleveland (1901–1909) pioneered city control or ownership of utilities, thus providing residents with more affordable services. By 1915, nearly two out of three cities had some form of city-owned utilities.

Providing Welfare Services Some reform mayors led movements for city-supported welfare services. Hazen Pingree provided public baths, parks, and, to combat the 1893 depression, a work-relief program. "Golden Rule" Jones opened playgrounds and free kindergartens and built lodging houses for the homeless. "Nobody has a right to rule anybody else," he once said. In his view, all people would be good if social conditions were good.

Progressive-era legislation resulted in the regulation of the meatpacking industry. This stamp was used by federal officials who inspected meat for freshness.

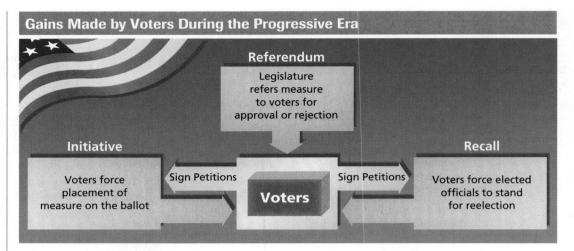

Gains Made by Voters During the Progressive Era

Referendum
Legislature refers measure to voters for approval or rejection

Initiative
Voters force placement of measure on the ballot

Sign Petitions

Voters

Sign Petitions

Recall
Voters force elected officials to stand for reelection

Interpreting Charts
Voters sought and won greater control over their state governments during the progressive era. By 1912, a dozen states had the initiative and referendum. Seven had recall. *Explain how these measures would help voters exert greater control over government.*

MAKING CONNECTIONS

Given what you read in Chapter 10 about political machines and immigrants, are you surprised to read about machines cooperating with progressive reformers? Explain.

Reforms at the State Level

Progressive governors and state legislators also were active. Governors Robert "Battling Bob" La Follette in Wisconsin and Hiram Johnson in California, among others, introduced reforms to make government more efficient and responsive to voters. They also championed state labor and factory legislation, motivated in part by the Triangle Shirtwaist Factory fire in New York City, in which inadequate and unenforced safety regulations contributed to 146 deaths (see "History Might Not Have Happened This Way," pages 398–399).

La Follette became a reformer out of disgust, after a Republican party boss offered him a bribe. In 1900 he won the Wisconsin governorship. By 1904 he had brought about a **direct primary**, an election in which voters cast ballots to select nominees for upcoming elections. Direct primaries replaced the handpicking of candidates by party leaders. By 1916 all but three states had direct primaries.

Reforms of the Workplace Activists also targeted the workplace. Applying the principle that employers and employees had to negotiate over differences, individual states established labor departments to provide information and dispute-resolution services to both sides.

States also worked toward ending exploitative and unsafe working conditions. They developed a workers' accident insurance and compensation system, and by 1920 all but five states had taken steps to make it easier for workers to collect payment for workplace accidents.

Government efforts to control working conditions met legal opposition at every turn. In a case known as *Lochner* v. *New York* (1905), for example, the Supreme Court struck down a law setting maximum hours for bakers on the ground that it "was an illegal interference with the rights of individuals . . . to make contracts."

Frustrated, reformers took another approach: they tried to convince the courts that government had to control conditions to protect women. This approach achieved a breakthrough in 1908, when in *Muller* v. *Oregon* the United States Supreme Court upheld an Oregon law that limited hours for women laundry workers to ten hours a day.

Labor reformers were successful on some other fronts as well. By 1907 the National Child Labor Committee had convinced some thirty states to abolish child labor—often defined as

Protecting Workers from the Workplace

During the progressive era (left), reformers sought to eliminate the dangerous conditions of factories. Today (above), workers are protected by strict guidelines established by the Occupational Safety and Health Administration (OSHA). These guidelines require the use of protective clothing and equipment in the workplace. *What other reforms might progressives try to implement in today's workplaces?*

employment of children under age fourteen. Minimum wage legislation for women and children also made headway. Florence Kelley led the national campaign, and after Massachusetts adopted a minimum wage in 1912, eight other states followed.

The Paradox of Protective Legislation Laws that singled out particular groups for protection had both positive and negative results. Maximum hour and minimum wage legislation for women led some employers to replace women with men, who were willing to work longer hours for lower wages. Special protection for women also fostered beliefs about female weakness, hurting women's case for voting and work rights equal to those of men. In the *Muller* decision, for example, Justice David J. Brewer had said that

> *continuance for a long time on her feet at work, repeating this from day to day, tends to injurious effects upon the body, and, as healthy mothers are essential to vigorous offspring, the physical well-being of woman becomes an object of public interest.*

Many progressives believed that laws protecting women would eventually break down the opposition to protection for all workers. This prediction came true: over the following decades, most protective legislation came to apply to both sexes.

Reforms at the Federal Level

Progressivism appeared at the federal level in labor and industrial relations, in the regulation of business and commerce, in the preservation of the environment, and in social legislation.

Theodore Roosevelt's "Square Deal" As President, Theodore Roosevelt was determined to use his powers vigorously. He got his chance in May 1902, when the United Mine Workers called a strike because of their low wages. As winter approached and mine owners continued to refuse to talk to the union, TR decided to intervene. Without coal, he realized, the nation would be without a key source of heating fuel.

TR insisted that both sides submit to **arbitration,** a process in which an impartial third party decides on a legally binding solution.

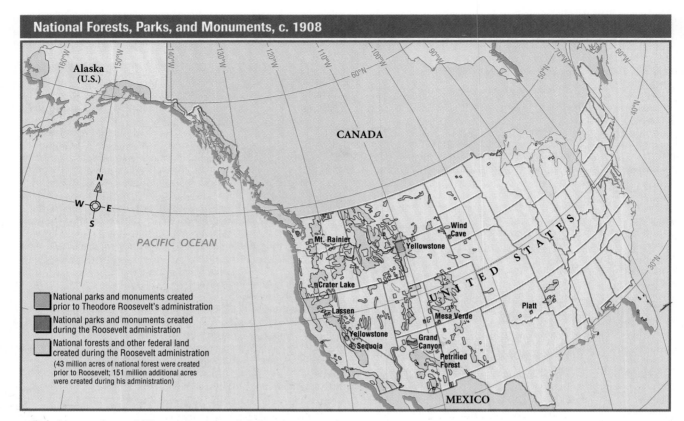

National Forests, Parks, and Monuments, c. 1908

Alaska (U.S.)

CANADA

PACIFIC OCEAN

UNITED STATES

MEXICO

Mt. Rainier
Crater Lake
Lassen
Yellowstone
Sequoia
Yellowstone
Wind Cave
Grand Canyon
Petrified Forest
Mesa Verde
Platt

■ National parks and monuments created prior to Theodore Roosevelt's administration

■ National parks and monuments created during the Roosevelt administration

■ National forests and other federal land created during the Roosevelt administration

(43 million acres of national forest were created prior to Roosevelt; 151 million additional acres were created during his administration)

Geography and History: Interpreting Maps
TR was convinced that "vigorous action must be taken" to save the nation's natural environment. Among the millions of acres of public land he set aside are sixteen national monuments and fifty-one wildlife refuges. *What do you notice about the location of the nation's parks, forests, and preserves?*

To encourage mine owners to accept this step, he threatened to use the army to seize and operate the mines. In 1903 arbitrators granted the miners a 10 percent raise and reduced their hours from ten to nine—but did not grant official recognition of their union. When TR called this a "square deal" for both sides, the phrase became a slogan of his presidency.

Reelected easily in 1904, TR focused on regulating railroads and food and drugs. In 1906 the Hepburn Act authorized the Interstate Commerce Commission to limit rates if shippers complained of unfair treatment. Also in 1906 the Pure Food and Drug Act and the Meat Inspection Act required accurate labeling of ingredients, strict sanitary conditions, and a rating system for meats.

Antitrust Activism Although the Sherman Antitrust Act (1890) was in place as a check on big business, it had never been vigorously enforced. Calling for an end to special privileges for capitalists, TR had his attorney general use the act to sue a huge holding company, the Northern Securities Company, which controlled railroads in the Northwest. **Holding companies** are corporations that hold the stocks and bonds of—and thus exert control over—numerous companies, thus achieving a monopoly. In 1904 the government won its case against Northern Securities in the Supreme Court.

By the time TR had completed his second term in 1909, the government had filed forty-two antitrust actions. The beef trust, Standard Oil, and the American Tobacco Company were either broken up or forced to reorganize. TR was not antibusiness. He did not wish to destroy trusts that he deemed "good," or not harmful to the public. But he believed that they should be supervised and controlled.

The Environment As settlement expanded into the West, people began to realize that the land, water, and forests there needed to be protected. At the urging of explorers and nature writers such as John Wesley Powell and John Muir, in 1872 Congress established Yellowstone in Wyoming as the nation's first national park and in 1890 made Yosemite in California a national park. Presidents Harrison and Cleveland preserved some 35 million acres of forest land.

In the early 1900s, reflecting the era's reliance on scientific data, the federal government called in experts to develop a workable policy for land and water use. In 1905 Roosevelt named Gifford Pinchot, a scientific forester, to head a new United States Forest Service. At his recommendation, TR set aside more than 200 million acres of land for national forests, mineral reserves, and water projects, shown on the map on page 396. A National Reclamation Act (1902) aimed at planning and developing irrigation projects aroused controversy between farmers and city residents in the Southwest over the use of scarce water resources that persist to this day.

Social Legislation Although most social legislation took place in the states, the federal government was active too. In response to pressure from women's clubs and labor organizations, in 1912 the government established a Children's Bureau within the Department of Labor, itself a new cabinet department. A Women's Bureau was formed in 1920. These two bureaus supported advocates of legislation that would benefit women and children. Both were headed by women, Julia Lathrop and Mary Anderson, the first female bureau heads at the federal level.

Progressive Era Amendments

Amendment	Result
16th Amendment Gives Congress power to levy an income tax	Allowed government to raise more revenue from wealthy people's incomes and less from tariffs that hurt the working poor
17th Amendment Provides for direct election of senators	By taking the election of senators out of the hands of the legislature, voters were able to play a more direct role in government

Interpreting Tables

By 1913, the progressive era had produced the Sixteenth and Seventeenth amendments. *How did the Seventeenth Amendment relate to the initiative, referendum, and recall that had passed in many states?*

National Prohibition Although not all progressives favored prohibition, many thought it would protect society from the poverty and violence associated with drinking. Women's support for it prompted brewery and liquor interests to oppose woman suffrage.

A number of states had passed prohibition laws in the 1800s, though most soon repealed them. The expansion of prohibition increased in the early 1900s, however. The states of the South and West (except for California) had outlawed the sale and manufacture of liquor by the time national prohibition arrived with the ratification of the Eighteenth Amendment in 1919. Until its repeal in 1933, Americans could not legally make, sell, or import liquor. They could still drink, however, and they proved very resourceful at obtaining alcohol illegally.

Prohibition is but one of the many distinct interests that came under the banner of progressivism in the early 1900s. Eventually supporters of many of those interests joined forces in a national political party.

SECTION 2 REVIEW

Key Terms, People, and Places
1. Define (a) direct primary, (b) arbitration, (c) holding company.

Key Concepts
2. What kinds of reforms took place at the city level and how did political machines become involved?
3. Briefly describe state-level reforms.

4. What is the "paradox of protective legislation"?
5. Briefly describe TR's progressive record.

Critical Thinking
6. **Testing Conclusions** Progressivism was not a single, unified movement, but a collection of distinct causes and concerns. Find evidence in this section to support this conclusion.

The Decision to Lock the Doors at the Triangle Shirtwaist Company

Time Frame:	1909—1911
Place:	The Asch Building in New York City's Greenwich Village
Key People:	Max Blanck and Isaac Harris, owners of the Triangle Shirtwaist Company; Triangle workers
Situation:	In New York's highly competitive garment manufacturing industry, the owners of the Triangle Shirtwaist Company had to decide how to cut spending in order to save money.

In the early 1900s, the Triangle Shirtwaist Company was one of the numerous garment manufacturing companies operating sweatshops in New York City. Seeking to boost profits, such manufacturers often tried to cut the costs involved in obeying the few existing fire safety laws. The Triangle Shirtwaist Company and others were able to take this approach in part because public officials failed to enforce safety and labor regulations adequately. The Triangle owners also tried to save money by preventing employees from leaving the workplace with materials supplied by the company—lace trims and fabric scraps, for example.

Sweatshop Conditions at Triangle

One of the largest garment manufacturers in New York, the Triangle company was also known as one of the hardest on its workers. Owners Max Blanck and Isaac Harris hired mostly immigrant women, who worked for less than men. Blanck and Harris also charged their workers for needles, the use of lockers and chairs, and any clothing that did not turn out right.

Avoiding the Costs of Meeting Fire Regulations

Aware that factories were hardly ever inspected for safety violations, the Triangle company routinely ignored local fire laws in an effort to save money. Like many of the sweatshops in downtown Manhattan, the ten-story Asch Building—and especially the top three floors that housed the Triangle Shirtwaist Company—was riddled with fire hazards. Blanck and Harris crammed as much equipment as possible into the factory, blocking access to fire hoses and stairways. They gave their employees no instruction in fire safety, nor did they hold fire drills.

Blanck and Harris were not alone in their willingness to avoid costs by ignoring fire safety standards. When the New York fire department tried to strengthen regulations and enforcement early in 1911, numerous local manufacturers blocked them at an emergency meeting on Wall Street. Claiming that the financial burden of the new regulations would be unreasonable, manufacturers convinced public officials that stricter fire laws should wait.

Locking Doors to Prevent Employee Theft Avoiding the costs of meeting fire regulations was not the only way Triangle's owners tried to save money. They also saved money by taking measures to prevent employee theft. According to

a newspaper report, the owners of the company ordered two hall doors and a single fire escape door on each floor to be locked "to safeguard employers from the loss of goods by the departure of workers through fire exits." Workers

The company

398

GOALS	Reduce business expenses and operating costs to save money and remain competitive in New York City's garment industry	
ACTIONS	Ignore fire safety standards or avoid the cost of meeting them.	Prevent employee theft of company goods.
OUTCOMES	• Block fire hoses and stairways with equipment. • Provide no fire drills or fire safety instruction. • Triangle employees are exposed to hazardous working conditions.	• Lock fire exits. • Have workers leave through one door. • Post a guard to check employees leaving work. • Triangle saves money.

left the company through one door, where a guard searched for stolen materials.

A Horrifying Disaster

Late in the afternoon on Saturday, March 25, 1911, tragedy struck. As about five hundred Triangle workers prepared to leave work, a carelessly tossed match or cigarette butt ignited some fabric cuttings on the eighth floor. Within seconds, a fire engulfed all three floors of the Triangle factory. A mere ten minutes later, more than 140 people lay dead.

The fire exposed the terrible potential of the Triangle company's violation of safety standards. As the flames spread, workers ran for the exits—and found most of them locked. A few dozen people made it to the elevator and reached the street before fire knocked the elevator out. There was one fire escape on the building, but those who were able to reach it found that the small, rusted structure could not support them. The fire escape collapsed to the ground, carrying people to their deaths. By the time firefighters could break down the factory's locked fire exits, scores of workers had burned to death, while many others had jumped to their deaths down the elevator shafts or out the windows. When it was all over, 146 workers were dead, and New York City had witnessed one of the most horrifying and tragic disasters in its history.

Response and Reform

The decision to lock the doors at Triangle was made without regard to the Triangle workers. The decisions that followed the blaze, however, helped to safeguard the lives, health, and welfare of workers throughout the state. The horror of the Triangle fire roused the public to immediate action. The day after the tragedy, the Women's Trade Union League and the Red Cross formed a committee to improve fire safety standards. It called on the city to appoint fire inspectors, to make fire drills compulsory, and to unlock and fireproof exits. The city building department declared the Asch Building unsafe, and fire officials began to improve the city's fire codes.

Labor unions demonstrated, calling on New York state to investigate factory conditions and enact stricter safety laws. In response, the state legislature formed a Factory Investigating Commission to look into working conditions. Its findings eventually prompted the state to redraft its entire labor code, making it the most ambitious in the nation.

EVALUATING DECISIONS

1. What actions did the Triangle Shirtwaist Company take that endangered its employees?
2. Why did the owners of the Triangle Shirtwaist Company decide to take those actions?

Critical Thinking

3. **Determining Relevance** The owners of the Triangle Shirtwaist Company were not alone in disregarding safety laws. How might this fact have affected their decisions?

Progressivism: Its Impact on National Politics

SECTION PREVIEW

In 1912 several of the loosely allied interests that made up progressivism joined forces in a new political party. Hitching their campaign wagon to a bull moose named TR, they set a course for the White House. Though they lost, the victors promoted many progressive ideas—until a distant war cast a shadow across the country.

Key Concepts

• Taft's presidency was marked by progressive legislation—and a rebel movement within his own party.
• Roosevelt abandoned Taft and led the "Bull Moose" movement.
• Wilson continued progressivism—until the movement came to an end with the approach of World War I.

Key Terms, People, and Places

New Nationalism, Bull Moose party, New Freedom

Many progressives joined forces in a new political party in 1912, taking as their symbol the mighty Bull Moose.

T he progressive movement had always been little more than a series of informal alliances. In 1912, however, a number of interests and groups associated with this movement came together into a formal political party. Though this party did not win the presidential election that year, its ideas continued to hold the attention of American voters and politicians—for a few more years, at least.

The Presidency After Roosevelt

The day after his election in 1904, TR announced he would not seek another presidential term. As the campaign of 1908 neared, he handpicked the next Republican presidential nominee—his secretary of war, William Howard Taft. On the Democratic side, William Jennings Bryan tried for a third (and last) time to win the office. Taft won easily.

President Taft had pledged to carry on TR's progressive program. He fulfilled that promise, pursuing some ninety antitrust cases and supporting numerous other reforms. Taft, however, had neither Roosevelt's energy nor strength of personality. He gave in to the Republican "old guard" that resisted many progressive programs. One such issue was tariff reduction, a favorite cause of progressives because tariffs favored business and hurt consumers. Taft's failure to reduce the tariff angered progressives in his own party, and an insurgent, or rebel, movement arose.

The Ballinger-Pinchot Affair A party crisis over conservation worsened matters for Taft. Ignoring the protests of conservationists, Taft's secretary of the interior, Richard A. Ballinger, allowed a private group to obtain several million acres of Alaskan public lands that contained rich coal deposits. Gifford Pinchot, TR's appointee to head the Forest Service, felt that Ballinger had shown special preference to the purchasing group and protested to a congressional committee. Taft fired Pinchot.

Upset over Taft's handling of the affair, insurgent House Republicans rebelled against their party leader. They joined with Democrats in a vote to investigate Ballinger. Although never found guilty of wrongdoing, Ballinger eventually resigned.

Insurgents also took action against the Republican old guard, who, by controlling the vital House Rules Committee, had blocked much reform legislation. The insurgents managed to change the committee's membership by making it elective and excluding powerful House Speaker, Joseph G. Cannon, a Republican reform opponent.

The Midterm Elections of 1910 TR returned from a hunting trip in Africa to find a storm of protest rising against Taft. At first he kept clear of it, but soon he began speaking out in support of insurgent Republican candidates in the 1910 midterm elections. He called for more federal regulation of business, welfare legislation, and progressive reforms such as stronger workplace protections for women and children, income and inheritance taxes, direct primaries, and the initiative, referendum, and recall. TR called this program the **New Nationalism.**

In the election, the Republicans lost seats as the Democrats captured the House of Representatives. A progressive group of Democratic and Republican insurgents dominated the Senate. Roosevelt, back in the political picture, announced by early 1912 that he would oppose Taft for the Republican presidential nomination.

Taft's Record Taft did not have a bad record on progressive causes. He had reserved more public lands and brought more antitrust suits in four years than TR had in seven. He also had supported the Children's Bureau, the Sixteenth and Seventeenth amendments, and the Mann-Elkins Act (1910), which placed telephone and telegraph rates under the control of the Interstate Commerce Commission rather than big businesses. In the end, however, Taft never recovered from the Ballinger-Pinchot affair.

MAKING CONNECTIONS

How influential are the opinions of former Presidents who are alive today? Do Americans listen to them or seek their views? Give examples.

The Election of 1912

As TR and Taft vied for the nomination in the primaries of 1912, TR's challenge began to succeed. Still, Taft controlled the central party machinery. When the Republican national convention met in Chicago in June, the Taft group disqualified the delegates TR had won in the primaries. Charging Taft's group with fraud, TR's supporters marched out, vowing to form their own party. In August they held their own

convention and formed the Progressive party. When TR was asked about his physical readiness for a campaign, he said, "I feel fit as a bull moose!" The **Bull Moose party** became the nickname of the Progressive party.

The Bull Moose platform included tariff reduction, woman suffrage, more regulation of business, an end to child labor, an eight-hour work day, a federal workers' compensation system, and the popular election of senators. Many women joined the party, campaigned for Progressive candidates, and in those states that already had won woman suffrage, ran for state and local offices. California's progressive crusader, Hiram Johnson, was TR's running mate.

TR ran a vigorous campaign that became legendary. For example, despite bleeding from a chest wound he suffered in an assassination attempt in Milwaukee, TR spoke for an hour and a half before seeking medical aid. "It takes more than this to kill a bull moose," he said as he showed the crowd his bloodstained shirt. Many Americans began to think of him as the people's champion and a hero.

A Four-Way Election Four men sought the presidency in 1912. Labor leader Eugene V. Debs ran on the Socialist ticket. Taft was the Republican candidate, and Roosevelt represented his Bull Moose progressives. Woodrow Wilson, a political newcomer and governor of New Jersey, headed the Democratic ticket. Wilson ran on a reform platform, too, but, unlike Roosevelt, he criticized both big business and big government.

Using Historical Evidence
In spite of his respectable record on progressive issues, Taft's presidency became entangled in controversy and conflict with Congress. *What does this cartoon suggest about TR's reaction to Taft's difficulties?*

Candidate and Party	Popular vote	Percent	Electoral vote
Woodrow Wilson/Democrat	6,296,547	41.8	435
Theodore Roosevelt/Progressive	4,118,571	27.4	88
William H. Taft/Republican	3,486,720	23.2	8
Eugene V. Debs/Socialist	900,672	6.0	–
Eugene Chafin/Prohibition	206,275	1.4	–
Arthur E. Reimer/Socialist Labor	28,750	0.8	–

Source: *Historical Statistics of the United States*

Interpreting Tables
In the 1912 election, progressive ideas played a part in the platforms of the Democrats, Progressives, Republicans, and Socialists. The button below shows Woodrow Wilson, the winner of the election. *What would have happened if TR had not run and Taft had received TR's votes?*

Calling his policy a **New Freedom,** he promised to enforce antitrust laws without threatening free economic competition.

Roosevelt trounced Taft, as the table above shows. But Wilson outdistanced them all, and the Democratic party took both houses of Congress.

Impact of the Wilson Victory An eloquent speaker and talented politician, Wilson could compromise when necessary—but also could hold unbendingly to his principles. As the governor of New Jersey, he had acquired a reputation as a reformer (see Section 2).

Wilson was not opposed to federal regulation, but he wanted to preserve as much free economic competition as possible. As he explained during the 1912 campaign, the world had become too interdependent for government to remain distant. "We used to think in the old-fashioned days," he said, "that all that government had to do was to put on a policeman's uniform, and say, 'Now don't anybody hurt anybody else.'" But life in the early 1900s had become so complex that Wilson believed government had "to step in and create new conditions."

Thus, following up on measures taken under TR, Wilson in 1914 created a Federal Trade Commission to be sure business complied with federal trade regulations. Also in 1914, the Clayton Antitrust Act spelled out specific activities big businesses could not do in restraint of trade, thus strengthening the nation's antitrust laws. Of great importance to labor unions, this act also exempted union activities from antitrust lawsuits, unless those activities led to "irreparable injury to property."

Wilson also lowered many tariffs and instituted major financial reforms. In 1913 he helped establish the Federal Reserve System. This system let banks borrow money to meet short-term demands, thus helping to prevent bank failures that occurred when large numbers of depositors withdrew funds during an economic panic. Such bank failures could cause widespread job loss and misery. Another Wilson financial reform was the establishment of the Federal Farm Loan Board in 1916, which made low-interest loans available to farmers.

Wilson was less active in social justice legislation. He allowed his cabinet officers to extend the Jim Crow practice of separating the races in federal offices—a practice that had begun under Taft. He also opposed a constitutional amendment on woman suffrage because his party platform had not endorsed it.

A Controversial Appointment Early in 1916 Wilson nominated progressive lawyer Louis D. Brandeis to the Supreme Court. Born in 1856 in Louisville, Kentucky, Brandeis was known for his brilliance and for fighting many public causes, often without fee. His work earned him the name "the people's lawyer."

Brandeis supported Wilson in 1912 and advised him during the campaign. When Wilson nominated him to the Supreme Court, the action drew a storm of protest. Opponents, who included former President Taft, accused Brandeis of being too radical. Anti-Semitism also played a part in opposition to Brandeis, as he was the first Jewish Supreme Court nominee. Nevertheless, Brandeis won his seat on the Court and served with distinction until 1939. His appointment marked the peak of progressive reform at the federal level.

Wilson Wins a Second Term Wilson ran for reelection in 1916. By then, the ties binding the Progressive party were weakening. TR did not want to run again. Instead, he endorsed Wilson's Republican opponent, Charles Evans Hughes, a former governor of New York and Supreme Court justice. Promising to keep the country out of war, Wilson won a narrow victory.

The Legacy of Progressive Reform

By the mid-1910s, progressives could take pride in the many changes they had helped bring about, such as redefining the role of government in business and politics.

This lithograph trumpets one of the few bright spots in relations between African Americans and whites during this era: Booker T. Washington's visit to Teddy Roosevelt's White House in 1901.

A Limited View of Progress Progressives so identified themselves because they believed they were working toward progress. Usually this term has a positive meaning. But what seems progressive to one class, race, or region might seem regressive, even repressive, to another.

For example, many African Americans felt ignored by progressives. Only a tiny group of progressives, those who helped found the NAACP, concerned themselves with the worsening race relations of the era. At the 1912 Progressive party convention, Roosevelt declined to seat southern African American delegates for fear of alienating white southern supporters. In addition, some white southern progressives who favored the women's vote did so with the racist argument that the white vote would double if suffrage passed. African Americans, on the other hand, would fall further behind because of their lower population and the effectiveness of voting restrictions in the South.

Progressives also focused narrowly on the problems of cities, ignoring the plight of tenant and migrant farmers and of nonunionized workers in general. Some supported immigration restriction and literacy tests.

Finally, many progressives uncritically supported the imperialistic adventures of the day. Just as they believed in the uplift of the slums and ghettos of American cities, they favored the "civilizing" of undeveloped nations, no matter what the residents of those countries wanted.

The End of the Progressive Coalition In August 1914, war began in Europe, and many nations began to assemble troops and supplies. Americans worried about how long they could remain uninvolved in the conflict. Soon, calls to prepare for war drowned out calls for reform in the United States. By the end of 1916 the reform spirit had sputtered out—with the exception of the drive for woman suffrage.

SECTION 3 REVIEW

Key Terms, People, and Places

1. Identify (a) New Nationalism, (b) Bull Moose party, (c) New Freedom.

Key Concepts

2. In what ways did President Taft support the progressive agenda?
3. Why did an insurgent movement arise during Taft's presidency?
4. Who ran for President in 1912?

5. In what ways did Wilson support progressivism?
6. Did the progressives deserve the name *progressive*? Explain.

Critical Thinking

7. **Recognizing Cause and Effect** Consider what you have read about the nature of the progressive movement in the early 1900s. How does this help explain the failure of the Bull Moose challenge in 1912?

Testing Conclusions

Testing conclusions means checking statements or opinions to see whether or not they are supported by known data. Data that is known to be valid can be used as criteria for testing a conclusion. If the data supports the conclusion, then you have reason to believe that the conclusion is sound. Use the following steps to test the validity of conclusions.

1. Study the conclusions to recognize the type of data that is necessary to verify them. If supporting data is provided, decide if it is useful for testing the conclusions. Read the conclusions at right, examine the data in the tables, and answer the following questions: (a) Upon what information are the conclusions based? (b) Is there a relationship between the conclusions and the evidence provided?

2. Decide on the criteria by which the conclusions could be tested most effectively. Some conclusions are based upon trends and must be tested against data that covers a period of time. Other conclusions are more specific and may need exact data for verification. (a) Does conclusion 1 deal with a trend or with a specific point in time? (b) Would data covering a period of time be needed to support conclusion 2?

3. Test the conclusions by comparing them with the data. Decide if the data supports or contradicts the conclusions and whether additional information is needed to determine the validity of some conclusions. (a) Do the facts support or contradict conclusion 3? (b) According to the data, is conclusion 5 valid or not? Why? (c) Do you agree with conclusion 4? Explain.

Conclusions:
1. The twenty-year period between 1900 and 1920 saw a steady and significant growth in union membership.
2. By 1920, union workers earned more money than nonunion workers while working fewer hours.
3. In terms of a percent of the work force, more workers were union members in 1910 than in 1920.
4. The reason why the vast majority of workers did not join labor unions in the early 1900s was that work stoppages led to pay stoppages and decreased earnings.
5. In 1900 builders claimed more union members than any other industry.

Work Force and Labor Union Membership			
Year	Total Workers	Total Union Membership	Percentage of Work Force in Unions
1900	29,073,000	868,000	3.0
1910	37,371,000	2,140,000	5.7
1920	42,434,000	5,048,000	11.9

Union Membership by Industry			
Year	Building	Textiles	Public Service
1900	153,000	8,000	15,000
1910	459,000	21,000	58,000
1920	888,000	149,000	161,000

Average Union and Nonunion Hours and Earnings in Manufacturing Industries				
	Union		Nonunion	
Year	Weekly Hours	Hourly Earnings	Weekly Hours	Hourly Earnings
1900	53.0	$0.341	62.1	$0.152
1910	50.1	$0.403	59.8	$0.188
1920	45.7	$0.884	53.5	$0.561

Source: *Historical Statistics of the United States*

Suffrage at Last: A Turning Point in History

SECTION PREVIEW

With a long, bitter campaign, women finally won the right to vote—and at the same time they demonstrated their skills as organizers and activists.

Key Concepts
- The quest for woman suffrage took more than seventy years and required great effort.
- The earliest victories for suffrage took place at the state level, and mostly in the western states.
- The campaign experienced internal division before finally achieving victory.

Key Terms, People, and Places
Carrie Chapman Catt, Alice Paul

I n August 1920, Tennessee's state legislature faced a tough issue. Thirty-five states had voted to ratify the Nineteenth Amendment, which established national woman suffrage. By the terms of the Constitution, the measure needed the approval of one more state in order to win ratification. Would Tennessee be the "perfect thirty-sixth"?

Gathered in the state capitol, the all-male Tennessee legislature made a rowdy spectacle. Despite prohibition, liquor flowed freely. Rumors of vote-buying circulated. Those on the suffrage side, the "suffs," wore yellow roses in their lapels. The "antis," or antisuffragists, wore red.

Both sides had supporters in hotels across the street. Suffrage leader Carrie Chapman Catt directed the lobbying effort for the suffs. "I've been here a month," she wrote a friend on August 15. "It is hot, muggy, nasty, and this last battle is desperate. . . . Even if we win, we who have been here will never remember it with anything but a shudder."

The Tennessee senate passed the amendment easily, voting 25 to 4. But the state house of representatives was bitterly divided. For day after sweltering day, the women and men who had fought for or against this moment anxiously followed every debate, every strategic move. Before learning the outcome, a review of the events preceding it will put the moment in perspective.

Suffrage at the Turn of the Century

Seventy-two years had passed since the 1848 meeting in Seneca Falls, New York, when activists formally demanded the vote for women. The struggle had cost a great deal of personal energy and money. People had grown old and died in the movement.

Divisions had plagued suffrage activists throughout. The movement had split in 1869 over different approaches to the goal. In 1890 a younger generation of leaders reconciled competing groups to form a united organization, the National American Woman Suffrage Association (NAWSA).

This deck of playing cards promotes the battle for woman suffrage—a battle that finally ended in 1920.

Women's Rights By the time of NAWSA's founding, women had won many rights. For example, married women could now buy, sell, and will property. Yet many challenges remained. Legal attempts to win suffrage had failed (see "History Might Not Have Happened This Way," a feature on *Minor* v. *Happersett*, pages 352–353). Perhaps more troubling to suffrage workers were the widely held attitudes about women and their proper social roles. When lawyer Myra Bradwell of Chicago was denied a state license to practice law in 1869, she took her case to the Supreme Court. In *Bradwell* v. *Illinois* (1873), the Court upheld the denial, reaffirming the "wide difference in the respective spheres and destinies of man and woman." Although Illinois had given Bradwell her license by 1890, for most Americans, woman's proper sphere remained the home, not the workplace.

By 1900, however, even larger numbers of traditional women were feeling justified in demanding the vote. Many women were participating in voluntary organizations that were investigating social conditions, publicizing their findings, suggesting reforms, lobbying officials, and monitoring enforcement of new laws. Working women were becoming more active in unions, picketing, and getting arrested. To many of these women, it seemed ridiculous to deny women the vote with arguments about "woman's proper sphere."

The Opposition Mobilizes As the suffrage movement became more energetic, an antisuffrage movement mobilized. Antis made two basic arguments. The first was that women were powerful enough without the vote. The second was the old notion that giving women the vote would blur the distinctions between the sexes and make women more masculine. Suffrage opponents also included liquor interests, who assumed that women voters would quickly establish prohibition.

MAKING CONNECTIONS

Consider what you read in Section 2 about the role of women in the progressive era. How does this information relate to the antisuffrage argument that women had enough power without the vote?

HUGGING A DELUSION

COPYRIGHTED BY LIFE PUBLISHING CO.

Using Historical Evidence Antisuffragists argued that suffragists were fooling themselves by expecting the vote to lead to fulfillment. *What does this cartoon suggest about how the vote would affect women?*

Suffragist Strategies

Suffragists followed two paths toward their goal. One path was to press for a constitutional amendment. The most commonly used method of amending the Constitution required two thirds of each house of Congress to pass a measure, which then had to be ratified by three fourths of the state legislatures.

The other path pursued by suffragists was to get individual states to permit women to vote. At first this approach was more successful (see the map on page 409), especially in the western states. There, survival on the frontier depended on the combined efforts of men and women—and thus encouraged a greater sense of equality.

Pushing for a federal amendment proved the more difficult approach. First introduced in Congress in 1868, a proposed amendment stalled. In 1878 it adopted the wording of suffrage leader Susan B. Anthony: "The right of citizens of the United States to vote shall not be denied or abridged by the United States or by any state on account of sex." With this language, the proposed amendment received its first committee hearing. Elizabeth Cady Stanton described the experience:

*I*n the whole course of our struggle for equal rights, I never felt more exasperated than on this occasion, standing before a committee of men many years my junior, all comfortably seated in armchairs.

The chair of the committee, Senator Wadleigh of New Hampshire, was a picture of "inattention and contempt." "He stretched, yawned, gazed at the ceiling, cut his nails, sharpened his pencil, changing his occupation and position every two minutes."

Stalled again, the bill was not debated until 1887. It was then defeated in the Senate by a vote of 16 for, 34 against, and 26 absent. Supporters reintroduced the "Anthony Amendment," as the bill came to be called, every year until 1896. Then it disappeared, and did not resurface again until 1913.

The Movement Heats Up in the 1910s At the turn of the century, the idea of votes for women had become more acceptable to a wider proportion of the population. Prominent and working women supported it. Increasing numbers of men supported it. But the suffrage movement itself was in the doldrums. New leadership and new techniques were desperately needed to give it added momentum.

One of these new leaders was **Carrie Chapman Catt,** a former high school principal and superintendent of schools in Mason City, Iowa. A talented speaker and organizer, she headed NAWSA from 1900 to 1904, and then again after 1915. Catt systematized NAWSA techniques, insisting on close, precinct-by-precinct political work.

Alice Paul also came on the scene. She had experienced the aggressive English suffrage movement while she was a student in England. In January 1913, she and a friend, Lucy Burns, took over the NAWSA committee that was supposed to work on congressional passage of the federal amendment.

Two months later, the two women had organized a parade of five thousand women in

Viewpoints
On the Nineteenth Amendment

Woman suffrage had been a subject of debate in the United States since the mid-1800s. In the early 1900s, that debate heated up. *Summarize the arguments presented in the viewpoints below.*

Pro-Woman Suffrage

"The great doctrine of the American Republic that 'all governments derive their just powers from the consent of the governed' justifies the plea of one-half of the people, the women, to exercise the suffrage. The doctrine of the American Revolutionary War that taxation without representation is unendurable justifies women in exercising the suffrage."
Robert L. Owen, senator from Oklahoma, 1910

Anti-Suffrage

"In political warfare, it is perfectly fitting that actual strife and battle should be apportioned [given out] to man, and that the influence of woman, radiating from the homes of our land, should inspire to lofty aims and purposes those who struggle for the right. I am thoroughly convinced that woman can in no better way than this usefully serve the cause of political betterment."
Grover Cleveland, "Would Woman Suffrage Be Unwise?"
Ladies' Home Journal, October 1905

Washington, D.C. Taking place on the day before Woodrow Wilson's inauguration, it drew so much attention that, when Wilson arrived at the train station, no crowd was there to greet him. Flushed with success, Paul transformed her committee into a new organization, the Congressional Union (CU).

A Collision over Strategy At this point, division tore the movement in two. Paul's CU called for an all-out national campaign for the constitutional amendment. She planned to enter different states, bypass the suffrage organizations there, and set up new ones.

The leadership of NAWSA felt that Paul's actions were premature, and in February 1914 expelled her group from the organization. When Paul adopted aggressive, militant protests—demonstrating in front of the White House, burning copies of President Wilson's speeches and even a life-size dummy made to look like Wilson—all attempts at smoothing

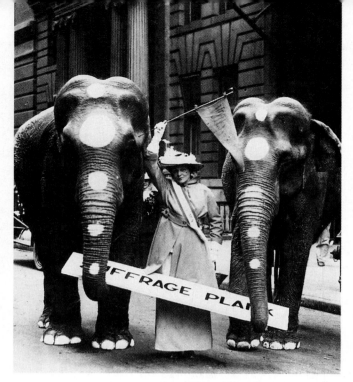

A journalist covering a suffrage march in New York City in 1912 described "women striding five abreast" up Fifth Avenue. Such colorful parades became a favorite technique of suffragists in the 1910s.

over their differences failed. When CU members ended up in jail for their demonstrations, went on hunger strikes over prison conditions, and then were force-fed, NAWSA condemned them, not their treatment.

NAWSA's state campaigns continued. Hopes had centered on four eastern states, New York, Pennsylvania, Massachusetts, and New Jersey. In 1915 the suffrage campaigns failed in all four. At that point, Catt was put back at NAWSA's helm and was given free rein to bring about victory. Out of this challenge came her "Winning Plan."

This plan consisted of developing a large troop of

"The question of woman suffrage is a very simple one," said Carrie Chapman Catt (left) in 1901. "The plea is dignified, calm, and logical."

totally committed, full-time leaders to work in "red-hot" campaigns for six years. The days of amateur dabbling were over. In addition, NAWSA decided to focus on getting Congress to propose the federal amendment.

By 1917, NAWSA had two million members. It was the largest voluntary organization in the country. In the fall, New York state finally voted in woman suffrage, raising to 172 the number of electoral votes from states with woman suffrage.

Impact of the War The United States entered World War I in April 1917. As women hastened to do their patriotic duty—volunteering for ambulance corps and medical work and taking up jobs left by men— their accomplishments came into the public eye. Talk about separate spheres for women and men seemed even more ridiculous. Moreover, in the spirit of national sacrifice inspired by the war, Congress adopted the prohibition amendment (the Eighteenth Amendment). Liquor interests no longer had reason to fight suffrage.

The Final Victory for Suffrage

In 1918 Congress formally proposed the suffrage amendment. Its members finally succumbed to the political forces of states that had passed suffrage and to the unrelenting work of NAWSA. They also had been keenly embarrassed and disturbed by the treatment the women of Paul's CU had received in jail.

Following the proposal of the amendment in Congress came the ratification battle. It would end in Tennessee.

Ratification Harry Burn, the Tennessee legislature's youngest member, had originally lined up with the antis. At the last moment he received a letter from his widowed mother. "Don't forget to be a good boy and help Mrs. Catt put the 'rat' in ratification," she wrote.

In deciding to vote "yes" for his mother, Burn broke a tie in the House. Realizing this, the speaker (an anti) voted *for* suffrage, and then called to reconsider the entire vote. (According to the legislature's rules, only by voting for a bill could a member move to reconsider it.) With this tactical move, the speaker hoped to gain time to rally the opposition.

The antis then took a daring step. They reasoned that if they left the capitol, the legislature would no longer have a quorum—the minimum number of members legally necessary to hold a vote. A large group of antis took a train to Alabama. The strategy backfired, however. When the house next met, the speaker claimed there was no quorum. But prosuffrage legislators held that the speaker was in violation of the rules and sent the suffrage bill to the governor.

On August 24, Tennessee's governor signed the suffrage bill. The news was rushed to Washington, D.C., and on August 26, the Nineteenth Amendment was declared ratified.

A Hard-Won Victory Woman suffrage was not granted to women. They fought for it, long and hard. When it was all over, Catt tried to calculate the effort. She counted

fifty-six campaigns of referenda to male voters; 480 campaigns to get Legislatures to submit suffrage amendments to voters; 47 campaigns to get State constitutional conventions to write woman suffrage into state constitutions; 277 campaigns to get State party conventions to include woman suffrage planks; 30 campaigns to get presidential party conventions to adopt woman suffrage planks in party platforms, and 19 campaigns with 19 successive Congresses.

Woman Suffrage Before the Nineteenth Amendment

- Full suffrage with effective date
- Presidential suffrage
- Primary suffrage
- No women's suffrage

WA 1910, OR 1912, ID 1896, MT 1914, ND, SD 1918, MN, WI, MI 1918, NY 1917, NH, VT, ME, MA, RI, CT, NJ, PA, DE, MD, NV 1914, UT 1896, WY 1890, CO 1893, NE, IA, IL, IN, OH, WV, VA, CA 1911, AZ 1912, NM, KS 1912, MO, KY, TN, NC, OK 1918, AR, SC, TX, LA, MS, AL, GA, FL

Geography and History: Interpreting Maps
Suffrage was already a reality in many states by the time of the Nineteenth Amendment's ratification. *What pattern do you notice in the locations of states that did and did not pass suffrage at the state level?*

Imagine the triumphant feelings after such an effort! Imagine, also, the bitterness at how long it had taken and the exhaustion of many women at its end. As Carrie Chapman Catt commented when the fight was all over, "It is doubtful that any man . . . ever realized what the suffrage struggle came to mean to women, . . . It leaves its mark on one, such a struggle."

The ratification of the Nineteenth Amendment marked the last major reform of the progressive era and was a turning point in American history. With suffrage finally won, women activists looked forward to a host of new battles in the long and difficult struggle to achieve true equality for women.

SECTION 4 REVIEW

Key Terms, People, and Places
1. Identify (a) Carrie Chapman Catt, (b) Alice Paul.

Key Concepts
2. What is the significance of the phrase "the perfect thirty-sixth"?
3. What were the two main strategies of the suffrage movement during the late 1800s and early 1900s?
4. On what grounds did people resist suffrage?

5. What factors finally turned the tide for suffrage?
6. Why is it incorrect to say that the vote was granted to women?

Critical Thinking
7. **Recognizing Ideologies** Recall what you have read about the reasons for the passage of suffrage in the West and at the national level. In the end, what seemed to "prove" women's fitness to vote?

The Lasting Impact of the Nineteenth Amendment

The passage of woman suffrage was a turning point not just for American women but for men as well. Women's admittance into full citizenship (or almost full—some important rights remained to be won) changed everyone's lives, forever. After suffrage, women did not bring about dramatic improvements in American political and social life, and they made few inroads into political office until many decades later. But at least women now had the dignity of individual citizenship. Thus, suffrage is a central part of the larger story of the nation's gradual achievement of its democratic promise.

Concrete Impact Of course, the women's vote did have more than a symbolic impact. Although many doors remained closed to women for years to come, the vote opened political and occupational opportunities previously unavailable to them. Women became eligible for posts within national party organizations, and public recognition and acceptance of women as professionals grew.

In addition, those who had been involved in the struggle were changed forever. Through participating in social reform movements, they had learned how to influence the making of social and public policy. The suffrage battle further honed their skills and made many of them even more aggressive in working for change. This experience helped women secure passage and state-by-state implementation of the Sheppard-Towner Act (1921), which allocated federal money for prenatal and infant health care. Later, women activists helped lead the fight for the repeal of prohibition.

1920 Suffragists celebrate ratification of the Nineteenth Amendment by painting in Tennessee on their suffrage map.

1933 Frances Perkins becomes the first woman to hold a cabinet post when Franklin Delano Roosevelt appoints her secretary of labor.

| 1900 | 1920 | 1940 |

1942 Women workers fill the nation's factories, making the planes, tanks, and other goods that help the United States win World War II.

Continuing Divisions Another legacy of the suffrage movement was conflict. Almost immediately following the passage of the Nineteenth Amendment, the divisions over tactics that had marked the final years of the suffrage battle surfaced again. Alice Paul was less interested in pursuing the reforms of the progressive era than in achieving complete legal equality with men. In 1923 her National Woman's party launched a new constitutional amendment campaign, this time for an Equal Rights Amendment (ERA) that would make women and men equal before the law.

Because of the potential of ERA to make illegal all the protective legislation for working women that progressive reformers had struggled for since the 1890s, many former suffragists opposed it. The League of Women Voters, the successor organization to NAWSA, led the opposition of many women's groups, including the Women's Trade Union League and Florence Kelley's Consumers' League.

The struggle over ERA tore apart what remained of the suffrage movement in the 1920s. Although the two sides cooperated on some legislation, such as winning the right to jury service for women, for the most part they stood on opposite sides for several decades. It was only with the renewed women's movement of the 1960s and 1970s that the issue was resolved among those who worked for feminist causes. Even then, however, the rest of the nation was opposed to an ERA and refused to ratify it.

REVIEWING THE FACTS

1. In what sense was the Nineteenth Amendment a *symbolic* victory for the American people?
2. In what sense was the Nineteenth Amendment a *concrete* victory?

Critical Thinking

3. **Making Comparisons** Compare the divisions of the women's movement before and after suffrage.

1972 Congress proposes the Equal Rights Amendment, touching off an unsuccessful ratification battle across the United States.

1992 Carol Mosely Braun becomes the first African American woman elected to the United States Senate. She is one of five women elected to the Senate that November.

1960 **1980** **2000**

1963 Feminist Betty Friedan's groundbreaking book The Feminine Mystique *helps inspire a new generation of women activists in the 1960s and beyond.*

The famous bestseller that ignited women's liberation

BETTY FRIEDAN

THE FEMININE MYSTIQUE

Chapter Review

Key Terms
1. home rule
2. progressivism
3. social welfare program
4. muckraker
5. direct primary

6. arbitration
7. holding company
8. New Nationalism
9. Bull Moose party
10. New Freedom

People
11. Henry George
12. Edward Bellamy
13. Florence Kelley
14. Carrie Chapman Catt
15. Alice Paul

Terms For each term above, write a sentence that explains its relation to the era of progressive reform.

Matching Review the key terms in the list above. If you are not sure of a term's meaning, review its definition in the chapter. Then choose a term from the list that best matches each description below.

1. Woodrow Wilson's policy in which he promised to enforce antitrust laws without threatening free economic competition
2. the system under which cities exercise a limited degree of self-government
3. a corporation that owns the stocks and bonds of numerous companies
4. an election in which voters cast ballots to select nominees for upcoming elections

5. a process in which an impartial third party decides on a legally binding solution to a dispute

True or False Determine whether each statement is true or false. If it is true, write "true." If it is false, change the underlined name to make the statement true.

1. Under the leadership of <u>Edward Bellamy,</u> the National Consumers' League spearheaded national movements to outlaw child labor and protect workers.
2. In <u>Henry George's</u> novel, a man undergoes hypnosis and wakes up in the year 2000 to find the United States transformed.
3. The National American Woman Suffrage Association believed that the tactics of <u>Alice Paul</u> in trying to win the vote for women were too extreme.

Section 1 (pp. 388–392)
1. What reform programs did Edward Bellamy envision and how were they similar to the widely discussed ideas of socialism?
2. What did progressives see as good about the United States? What did they want to reform?
3. What were the typical methods of progressive reformers?

Section 2 (pp. 393–397)
4. Briefly describe progressive reforms at the state and municipal levels.
5. What did the alliance of progressive reformers and political machines accomplish?
6. Briefly describe progressive reforms at the national level.

Section 3 (pp. 400–403)
7. Briefly describe the successes and failures of the Taft presidency.
8. Why did progressivism—with the exception of the suffrage movement—come to an end?

Section 4 (pp. 405–409)
9. After the victory for woman suffrage, Carrie Chapman Catt made a count of the campaigns that achieved passage of the Nineteenth Amendment. What does her tally reveal?
10. Where did campaigns to achieve suffrage first meet with success?
11. How did the Congressional Union (CU) and the National American Woman Suffrage Association (NAWSA) differ in their strategies?

1. **Drawing Conclusions** What does the profile of Florence Kelley reveal about progressive concerns and methods?
2. **Identifying Central Issues** What does the fate of Taft's presidency suggest about the nature of the presidency and presidential leadership?
3. **Demonstrating Reasoned Judgment** Progressives were sometimes criticized for being insensitive to the needs of the poor. Do you think that this criticism was justified?

1. **Evaluating Primary Sources** Review the primary source excerpts quoting Elizabeth Cady Stanton on page 407. What bias is revealed by the behavior of Senator Wadleigh and the other committee members?
2. **Understanding the Visuals** What visual evidence can you find in the chapter to indicate that the efforts of the progressive era have had a positive impact on the nation today?
3. **Writing About the Chapter** You are running for student council on the progressive ticket. Write a progressive campaign statement for your school. Before you begin, create a list of the goals of the progressive era. Decide which of them you can apply or adapt to your school. Consider any areas in which you feel progressivism failed, and suggest changes you think are necessary. Next, write a draft of your statement in which you explain your ideas. Revise your statement, making certain that each idea is clearly explained. Proofread your statement and draft a final copy.
4. **Using the Graphic Organizer** This graphic organizer uses a tree map to organize information about progressivism's legislative impact at the city, state, and federal levels. (a) What do the three levels of government have in common in terms of the types of reforms undertaken? (b) What were the four general areas of reform on the federal level? (c) On a separate sheet of paper, create your own tree map about the national political impact of progressivism (section 3), using this graphic organizer as an example.

Progressivism's Legislative Impact

City
- Improved city services
- City takeover of utilities
- Welfare services provided
- Alliance with political bosses in some cases

State
- State government becomes more efficient and responsive to voters
- Labor and factory legislation championed
- Direct primaries instituted
- Child labor abolished in some states
- Minimum wage laws for women and children

Federal
- TR negotiates Square Deal for miners
- Many antitrust actions filed
- Land and water policy initiated
- Children's Bureau and Women's Bureau established
- Prohibition passed

CHAPTER 14

The World War I Era
1914–1920

*T*he conflict began with a few shots fired by a single assassin. Within months, much of Europe was at war. Most Americans were reluctant to get involved, but powerful forces—including German submarines and American commercial interests—pulled the nation into the battle. By 1917 United States soldiers had joined Europeans in the trenches and terrors of the war. When the guns finally quieted, President Wilson launched a campaign for a treaty and a new international organization that would prevent such a tragedy from ever happening again. Meanwhile, the American people struggled to make peace in their own minds with the horrors of the war.

Events in the United States

1914 The United States declares itself officially neutral in World War I.

1915 Jane Addams and Carrie Chapman Catt organize the Woman's Peace party.

1916 Woodrow Wilson is reelected United States President on a peace platform.

1913	1914	1915	1916

Events in the World

1914 The assassination of Archduke Francis Ferdinand sets off World War I.

1915 German submarines sink the British Lusitania.
• The Panama Canal opens.
• The Republic of China forms.

1916 The Government of India Act gives Indians limited self-rule.

1917 The United States enters World War I. • Congress passes the Selective Service Act.	**1918** Congress passes the last of the Sedition and Espionage Acts. • President Wilson announces his peace plan.	**1919** The states ratify the Eighteenth Amendment, prohibiting the manufacture and sale of alcohol.	**1920** Warren G. Harding is elected United States President.	
1917	**1918**	**1919**	**1920**	**1921**
1917 The Russian Revolution ends the reign of the czars. • The Mexican Revolution ends.	**1918** Germany surrenders to the Allies. • Women over 30 win the right to vote in Britain.	**1919** The Versailles Treaty marks the official end of World War I. • The Allies establish the League of Nations.	**1920** Adolf Hitler helps organize the Nazi party in Germany. • Ibn Saud founds Saudi Arabia.	

The Road to War

SECTION PREVIEW

With the outbreak of war in Europe, Americans responded with claims of neutrality. Yet as the war dragged on, the need to defend American commercial and political interests drew the United States toward active involvement in the struggle.

Key Concepts
• World War I was a conflict of global origins and dimensions.
• The war saw the introduction of destructive new weapons and techniques.
• Americans responded with calls for neutrality and for war preparedness.

Key Terms, People, and Places
Central Powers, Allies; Kaiser Wilhelm, autocrat

Soldiers in World War I wore gas masks such as this to protect themselves from poison gas, a horrible new weapon introduced in the war.

By the early 1900s, war in Europe was hardly a new phenomenon. The Germans had fought often with France over Alsace-Lorraine, the coal- and iron-rich region near the border between the two countries. Austria-Hungary had fought to hold onto the many ethnic groups subject to its control. Russia's ancient quest for a warm-water port had led to frequent clashes on its frontiers. The French and British had warred repeatedly over territorial claims in Europe and in their colonies.

In 1914 all five of Europe's major powers went to war. The conflict—eventually known as World War I—divided them into two sides: Germany and Austria-Hungary made up the **Central Powers;** Russia, France, and Great Britain were called the **Allies.**

Archduke Francis Ferdinand: his assassination sparked the fighting.

Each side felt confident of swift victory. Six weeks, experts said, and it would all be over. The experts were wrong. Relatively equal in force and ability, the two sides quickly reached a bloody stalemate that would last more than four years and cost millions of lives.

What Caused World War I?

A complicated system of secret treaties had developed among the nations of Europe during the late nineteenth century. Designed to bolster each nation's security, the treaties bound the great powers to come to each other's aid in the event of attack. For many decades this system created a fragile balance of power that no nation dared disrupt. In 1914 the very system that had kept the peace led its creators into war.

The spark that ignited World War I was the June 28, 1914, assassination of the heir to the Austrian-Hungarian throne, Archduke Francis Ferdinand, and his wife, Sophie. They were gunned down during a visit to Sarajevo, the capital of Bosnia, a province within the Austrian-Hungarian Empire.

At the time of the assassinations, Bosnia was the focal point of a dispute between Austria-Hungary and the neighboring nation of Serbia. This dispute involved Serbia's efforts to achieve union with ethnic Serbs living in Bosnia by promoting Bosnian resistance to Austrian-Hungarian rule.

The Austrian-Hungarian government was convinced that Serbia was behind the assassinations, and used the event as an excuse to crush its small enemy. In late July Austria-Hungary insisted that Serbia apologize and made a number of other demands that interfered with Serbia's sovereignty. When Serbia refused to meet every one of the demands, Austria-Hungary declared war.

The Conflict Expands

The Austrian-Hungarian declaration of war set off a chain reaction that worked its way through Europe's complex web of alliances. Nation after nation became entangled. Serbia had the promise of protection from Russia, so Russia started amassing its troops. Two days later, Germany, Austria-Hungary's chief ally, demanded that Russia stop its mobilization. Russia refused. At that point, Russia's ally, France, began to ready its troops. Germany realized that soon it would be trapped between France attacking from the west and Russia from the east. So Germany too mobilized and, on August 1, declared war on Russia. Convinced that the French were ready to invade, Germany's military leaders decided to strike first. To reach France as fast as possible, however, they had to pass through Luxembourg and Belgium. This invasion brought Great Britain, Belgium's protector, into the conflict. A large proportion of the European continent was now at war.

Stalemate In earlier wars, a forceful offense led by a heroic cavalry often was enough to secure victory. Now, defensive forces could use modern firepower to stop such advances. In September 1914, German forces had advanced to within 30 miles of Paris. There, at the river Marne, a combined French and British force stopped their progress. Both sides then dug in. Holed up in a line of muddy, lice- and rat-infested trenches, the two sides faced each other across an empty "no man's land" (see the illustration on page 418). For months each side tried to reach the other's lines to destroy or at least push back the enemy. But neither side was able to gain more than a few miles, and that only at appalling human cost.

Meanwhile, an Austrian army was taking Belgrade, the Serbian capital. Combined German and Austrian-Hungarian forces were pushing the Russian lines back. At the end of 1914, the Ottoman Empire, centered in what is now Turkey, entered the war on the side of the Central Powers; and in the spring of 1915, Italy joined the Allies. Many more costly battles took place, but without significant gain for either side.

European Alliances in World War I

Allied Powers
Central Powers
Neutral nations

0   250   500 Miles
0   250   500 Kilometers

Geography and History: Interpreting Maps
Before the war, Europe was a land of empires and alliances. Thus when Austria-Hungary declared war on Serbia, much of the continent was drawn into the conflict. *Based on this map, which side, if any, had a geographical advantage in the war? Explain.*

Modern Warfare The number of soldiers killed or wounded was horrifying. Industrialization had produced new killing machines of terrible efficiency. In 1914 the youth of Europe had marched off to fight, eager for a chance at heroism. Ripped apart by machine guns, hand grenades, or artillery shells, and asphyxiated or disabled by poison gases, soldiers found that heroism came at a ghastly price.

"It was the machine gun that froze the front," one historian has written. If soldiers charging across no-man's land toward the enemy survived the shelling that rained down upon them, the enemy's machine guns, firing 450 rounds a minute, mowed them down. The generals, unaccustomed to the new weaponry, were confused. Again and again they gave the order to attack. But such tactics produced only a mounting pile of infantry dead. In one 1916 battle, for example, the British suffered 60,000 casualties in a single day of combat.

Morale sank. Desperate, troops began using any tactic available. They slaughtered prisoners of war. Erasing the distinction between soldier

Front-line Trench Warfare

No man's land	Support trench
XX Barbed wire	Reserve trench
Firing trench	Communications trench
Cover trench	

Interpreting Charts
Trench networks allowed armies to fire on the enemy, get supplies and reinforcements, and find cover from enemy fire. But soldiers leaving the trench to press the battle faced deadly machine gun fire. *How did trench warfare contribute to a stalemate in World War I?*

and civilian, they burned fields and poisoned wells. On the seas, German submarines struck any ship they believed to be carrying arms to the Allies. A British naval blockade slowly starved the German people. Soon the war was one of attrition—meaning that each side tried to wear down the enemy gradually by inflicting enormous losses.

MAKING CONNECTIONS

The United States today has many security alliances that are similar to those that drew so many countries into World War I. Do you think the United States should be willing to fight to protect the interests of its allies?

The American Response

July 29: AUSTRIA DECLARES WAR, RUSHES VAST ARMY INTO SERBIA; RUSSIA MASSES 80,000 MEN ON BORDER

August 2: GERMANY DECLARES WAR ON RUSSIA; FRANCE PREPARES TO JOIN HER ALLY

Americans read these 1914 headlines with mounting alarm. How could all these great countries of beauty, taste, and culture be at war with one another?

Some Americans felt personally involved. More than a third of the nation's 92 million people were first- or second-generation immi-

grants who still felt close ties to their old countries. About a quarter of these were German American, and another eighth were Irish American. Both groups harbored hostile feelings toward Great Britain due to past conflicts and the current war in Europe.

Most Americans favored the Allies, however. Germany, one of the Central Powers, was ruled by **Kaiser Wilhelm.** The Kaiser, or emperor, was an **autocrat**—a ruler with unlimited power. Americans saw the Germans as a people of frightening militarism and cold-blooded efficiency. Reporters who had rushed to Belgium in August 1914 to witness the German advance toward France fueled this view. Richard Harding Davis described the event for New York *Tribune* readers as "not men marching, but a force of nature like a tidal wave, an avalanche, or a river flooding its banks."

*A*t the sight of the first few regiments of the enemy we were thrilled. After, for three hours, they had passed in one unbroken steel-gray column, we were bored. But when hour after hour passed and there was no halt, no breathing time, no open spaces in the ranks, the thing became uncanny, unhuman.

Other Americans held a more neutral but cynical attitude. They looked at the European war as a great financial boon to the United States. One newspaper said that the war was "a supreme opportunity for American manufacturers to gain world-wide markets."

The United States Declares Neutrality In the end, the nation's business interests had a stronger impact on United States policy than the feelings of the American people. The war imperiled United States commercial investments overseas, which between 1897 and 1914 had increased fivefold, from $700 million to $3.5 billion. Now, German submarines and a British naval blockade of the North Sea were putting those investments at risk. To protect those investments, the United States declared itself officially neutral, protested the actions of both sides, and tried to act as peacemaker.

The Preparedness Movement At the same time that they pushed for neutrality, American business leaders who had strong commercial ties to Great Britain urged that the United States get ready for war. Their watchword was preparedness, and they wanted their country to be ready to aid Great Britain, if necessary. In December 1914, preparedness advocates organized a National Security League to "promote patriotic education and national sentiment and service among people of the United States."

By the late summer of 1915, the movement had won over President Wilson. The government set up camps to train American men for combat. By the summer of 1916, President Wilson and Congress had worked out an agreement for large increases in the armed forces.

The Peace Movement When world war broke out, a peace movement also swung into gear. In the early 1900s, peace advocates consisted primarily of former populists, midwest progressives, and social reformers.

Women were particularly active in the movement. On August 29, suffragists, dressed in black and carrying a banner of a dove, marched down New York City's Fifth Avenue to the slow beat of a muffled drum. In November 1915, a group of women and men social reformers founded the American Union Against Militarism.

Congress also had some peace advocates. Aiming to remind Americans of the costs of war, they insisted on paying for preparedness through a tax on the makers of arms and through higher income taxes. Claude Kitchin, member of Congress from North Carolina, predicted that when people discovered "that the income tax will have to pay for the increase in the army and navy, . . . preparedness will not be so popular with them as it now is."

Congress did increase taxes, but the preparedness movement remained strong. As you will read, the United States could not resist the forces pushing it toward entry into the conflict.

Jane Addams, second from the left in the front row, joined the delegation on this "peace ship," which journeyed to Europe in 1915 with hopes of ending the war.

SECTION 1 REVIEW

Key Terms, People, and Places
1. Define (a) Central Powers, (b) Allies.
2. Identify (a) Kaiser Wilhelm, (b) autocrat.

Key Concepts
3. Why did the dispute between Austria-Hungary and Serbia escalate?
4. For what reasons was this war so destructive?

5. What were the reactions in the United States to the outbreak of World War I?

Critical Thinking
6. **Checking Consistency** The alliance system in Europe in 1914 was designed to maintain peace. Yet it seemed to make the conflict worse once the fighting began. Explain this apparent inconsistency.

Identifying Alternatives

Identifying alternatives means finding one or more possible solutions to a problem. In the previous section, you read about the conflict in the United States over how to react to the war raging in Europe. The passages on this page make the case for two responses the United States might have made. Passage A presents the views of then President Woodrow Wilson, as stated in August 1914. Passage B, which was published in January 1915, presents the thoughts of former President Theodore Roosevelt.

Use the following steps to identify and analyze the alternatives presented in the passages.

1. Identify the nature of the problem under discussion. Before you can identify alternative solutions to a problem, you must understand what the problem is. (a) What is the issue that both passages address? (b) Does each passage present the same approach to the problem?

2. Identify the solutions proposed in the two passages. (a) What does Passage A suggest is the proper response of the United States to the war raging in Europe? (b) How does Passage B propose that the United States respond to the war? (c) In what ways are these two viewpoints similar or different?

3. Evaluate the potential effectiveness of each view. Consider the strengths and weaknesses of each proposal. For example, you might ask the following questions about Passages A and B: (a) What difficulties do you see in Wilson's suggestion that the United States not judge the actions of other nations? (b) What might happen if the United States acts in a "disinterested" way, as Wilson suggests? (c) Does Roosevelt make clear what he means when he refers to a nation that "does ill"? (d) Does Roosevelt explain the basis by which nations should be judged "highly civilized" or "well behaved"?

4. Consider other alternatives. Recall the nature of the problem under discussion. Then, using insights you gained above, think of other possible solutions. Ask: (a) What should be the goal of the United States in responding to the war in Europe? (b) What steps are most likely to achieve that goal?

Passage A

"My thought is of America. . . . [T]his great country of ours . . . should show herself in this time of peculiar trial a Nation fit beyond others to exhibit the fine poise of undisturbed judgment, the dignity of self-control, the efficiency of dispassionate [unemotional] action; a Nation that neither sits in judgment upon others nor is disturbed in her own counsels and which keeps herself fit and free to do what is honest and disinterested and truly serviceable for the peace of the world."

Woodrow Wilson, *Appeal for Neutrality,* August 19, 1914

Passage B

"Our true course should be to judge each nation on its conduct, unhesitatingly to antagonize every nation that does ill [at the point] it does ill, and equally without hesitation to act. . . .

One of the greatest of international duties ought to be the protection of small, highly civilized, well-behaved and self-respecting states from oppression and conquest by their powerful military neighbors. . . .

I feel in the strongest way that we should have interfered, at least to the extent of the most emphatic diplomatic protest and at the very outset—and then by whatever further action was necessary—[when Germany invaded Belgium]."

Theodore Roosevelt, *America and the World War,* 1915

The United States Declares War

SECTION PREVIEW

The United States struggled to avoid the horrors of World War I. But the nation could not prevent its slow slide into the conflict.

Key Concepts
- Germany's unrestricted submarine warfare had a powerful impact on American attitudes toward the war.
- Wilson won reelection in 1916 based on his success at keeping the United States out of the war.
- A series of events finally pushed Congress to declare war on the Central Powers—an act that was met with mixed reactions by the American people.

Key Terms, People, and Places
U-boat, *Lusitania*, Zimmerman note

From 1915 to 1917, growing conflict between the United States and Germany increased the popularity of the preparedness position and intensified the pressure for war. Ultimately, both Congress and the President were pushed toward entering World War I on the side of the Allies.

German Submarine Warfare

One factor pushing the United States toward war was the German use of submarine warfare. This tactic was effective militarily, but it cost the Germans dearly in terms of American public opinion.

The German **U-boat,** short for *Unterseeboot,* or submarine, was a terrifying new weapon that changed the rules of naval warfare. Submarine attacks depended on the element of surprise, so unlike other naval ships, U-boats issued no warning to their targets. This situation troubled many Americans. Though the British blockade threatened freedom of the seas and led to the slow starvation of the German people, the American public felt that such action was reasonable during wartime. In contrast, German attempts to break the blockade with submarines seemed unfair, even uncivilized.

The British encouraged such anti-German feeling. Shortly after the war began, the British cut the transatlantic cable connecting Germany and the United States. All news of the European front henceforth flowed through London. Its pro-Allied bias helped shape the opinion of the people in the United States in favor of punishing Germany for its alleged atrocities.

American public opinion of the Germans sank even lower on May 7, 1915, when a U-boat sighted the **Lusitania,** a British passenger liner, in the Irish Sea. Suspecting correctly that the ship carried weapons for the Allies, the U-boat fired on the liner. Eighteen minutes later the *Lusitania* disappeared beneath the waves along with its 1,198 passengers. Included among the dead were 128 Americans, who had boarded the *Lusitania* in spite of German warnings to stay off British ships. Nevertheless, the American press went wild over this German act of "barbarism."

Wilson counseled patience. He directed his secretary of state, William Jennings Bryan, to demand that Germany renounce unrestricted submarine warfare and make payments to the victims' survivors. Germany's reply that the ship carried small arms and ammunition did not quiet American anger.

Wilson ordered a second, stronger note. This time, however, Bryan refused to sign it, fearing it would lead to war. Bryan also insisted that Wilson send an equally strong note to

This German poster urges its U-boats on in their mission. The translation is, "Submarines: [come] out!"

American public opinion was extremely critical of Germany and its use of U-boats. The cartoon above right suggests that Germany felt no remorse for the loss of American lives. However, Germany did warn travelers—including passengers of the *Lusitania*—to stay out of the war zone (left).

Great Britain protesting its blockade. Wilson refused and Bryan resigned. His successor, Robert Lansing, signed the note to Germany. In response, Germany promised to stop sinking passenger ships without warning, as long as the ship's crew offered no resistance to German search or seizure.

Still, U-boats continued to sink British and French liners. The loss of American lives was small but infuriating. Wilson protested and, in response, Germany pledged restraint. Because Wilson could not threaten force without entering the war, however, he felt fairly powerless. But during this time, Wilson did embrace the concept of preparedness. He also authorized New York bankers to make a huge loan to the Allies. American neutrality was beginning to lose its meaning.

MAKING CONNECTIONS

Consider public feelings about Germany discussed in Section 1. How might these feelings explain public condemnation of U-boat warfare—and public acceptance of the British blockade?

Moving Toward the Brink of War

On February 1, 1917, Germany once again began unrestricted submarine warfare. Wilson had been reelected in November of 1916 with the slogan "He kept us out of war." Now his hope of maintaining freedom of the seas—and American neutrality—was dashed. Two days later, the United States broke off diplomatic relations with Germany, and Wilson asked Congress for permission to arm American merchant ships.

The Zimmerman Telegram In the Senate, a group of antiwar senators tried to prevent action on Wilson's request by using a filibuster. A filibuster is a tactic in which senators take the floor, begin talking, and refuse to stop talking to permit a vote on a measure. While this was taking place, the British revealed the contents of an intercepted German telegram to Mexico. In it, Arthur Zimmerman, Germany's foreign secretary, wrote:

W*e shall endeavor to keep the United States neutral. In the event of this not succeeding, we make Mexico a proposal of alliance. . . : Make war together, make peace together, . . . and . . . Mexico is to* *reconquer the lost territory in Texas, New Mexico, and Arizona.*

Neither Wilson nor Mexico took this telegram—the so-called **Zimmerman note**—seriously. Its release, however, scored another propaganda victory for Great Britain. War fever mounted.

Revolution in Russia By early 1917, Russia already had suffered enormous casualties in the war: 1.8 million killed, 2.4 million taken prisoner, and 2.8 million sick or wounded. Austrian and German forces had advanced deep into Russian territory. Ill-shod, ill-fed, and miserably equipped, the Russians fell back farther and farther into their interior.

Then, in March 1917, revolutionaries overthrew Czar Nicholas II, Russia's autocratic monarch, replacing him with a republican government. This event elated the prowar faction in the United States. Concern over being allied with the czar had helped slow the nation's move toward entry into the war. By overthrowing the czar, the Russian revolution removed a last stumbling block to a full American commitment to the Allies.

The War Resolution Meanwhile, between March 16 and March 18, Germany sank the United States ships *City of Memphis, Illinois,* and *Vigilancia.* On March 20 Wilson's cabinet voted unanimously for war. Casting the issue in idealistic terms, on April 2 Wilson told Congress that "The world must be made safe for democracy."

*I*t is a fearful thing to lead this great peaceful people into war, the most terrible and disastrous of all wars, civilization itself seeming to be in the balance. But the right is more precious than peace.

Antiwar forces were devastated. Social worker Jane Addams used her considerable prestige to appeal directly to the President, but to no avail. An Emergency Peace Federation was formed to pressure Congress not to say yes to war. But a war resolution passed 82 to 6 in the Senate and 373 to 50 in the House. On April 6, the President signed it.

The United States entry into World War I broke some long-standing alliances among progressives.

President Woodrow Wilson reluctantly led the nation into World War I.

| 1650 | 1700 | 1750 | 1800 | **Links Across Time** | 1850 | 1900 |

Making the World Safe for Democracy

According to President Wilson, the United States entered World War I to make the world safe for democracy. By fighting its enemies, Wilson said, the United States would "bring peace and safety to all nations and make the world at last free." On a number of occasions since that time, the United States has followed a similar policy—using military action as well as diplomatic means in an attempt to achieve peace, security, and democracy.

After World War II, the United States, acting under this policy, committed itself to strong resistance to communism. This policy contributed to American involvement in several wars and military actions. In July 1950, for example, the United Nations Security Council backed the use of military action to combat the communists in North Korea who were trying to conquer South Korea. Led by the United States, the South Koreans received "assistance to repel armed attack and restore international peace and security in the area."

In Vietnam a new government seized power in 1956, promising democratic elections—which were never held. A few years later, Presidents Kennedy and Johnson both tried to stop the spread of communism in Southeast Asia by committing thousands of troops to the Vietnam War.

More recently, President Bush echoed Wilson's policy in 1991 when he obtained Congress's approval to send American troops to liberate the Persian Gulf nation of Kuwait from an invasion by its neighbor Iraq. The action came after about six months of diplomatic pressures and economic sanctions against Iraq. *How successful do you think the United States has been in its policy of making "the world safe for democracy"?*

Jeannette Rankin of Montana, the first woman member of the House of Representatives, cast one of the few votes against the United States war resolution. She remained opposed to the war and lost her congressional seat in 1919.

Teddy Roosevelt pushed for war. La Follette favored peace. Settlement worker Lillian Wald resigned from the American Union Against Militarism, but Jane Addams stayed a member. Carrie Chapman Catt dedicated her suffrage association to serve the war effort, an act that prompted President Wilson to tell the Senate in 1918 that the passage of woman suffrage was "vital to the winning of the war."

Why Did the United States Go to War?

After years of reluctance, the United States was finally at war. Why? In the United States people believed that Germany's refusal to respect American claims to neutrality had forced the United States to retaliate. From Germany's perspective, however, its refusal was understandable. "Neutral noncombatant" hardly described the United States between 1914 and 1917. United States money and munitions had been flowing to the Allies long before its troops left for Europe.

The decision also can be seen as the result of long-standing commercial interests. As Jeannette Rankin, the first woman member of Congress, said in defense of her vote against the war, "I knew we were asked to vote for a commercial war." Indeed, in 1912, Wilson had announced, "Our industries have expanded to such a point that they will burst their jackets if they cannot find a free outlet to the markets of the world." In addition, British propaganda had helped promote anti-German feeling. Finally, many believed that the world *could* be made safe for democracy. If the United States hoped to benefit from a new world of peace and freedom, then the nation would have to be a player in the drama.

Political commentator Walter Lippmann saw the war as an opportunity for the United States to tap "new sources of energy" in its people that would make "the impossible . . . possible." "We can dare to hope for things which we never dared to hope for in the past," he wrote. Lippmann was convinced that democracy would be realized not just abroad but at home as well. "We shall turn with fresh interest to our own tyrannies—to our Colorado mines, our autocratic steel industries, our sweatshops and our slums."

In short, many Americans felt that the United States was on the brink of greatness. Its participation in World War I would hasten progress toward that goal.

SECTION 2 REVIEW

Key Terms, People, and Places
1. Define (a) U-boat, (b) *Lusitania*, (c) Zimmerman note.

Key Concepts
2. What was the impact in the United States of Germany's unrestricted submarine warfare?
3. State the reason for Wilson's reelection in 1916.
4. Why did the March 1917 revolution in Russia push the United States toward war?

5. How did the American people respond to the declaration of war?

Critical Thinking
6. **Identifying Alternatives** Consider the causes that brought the United States into World War I. What would the United States have had to do to avoid the conflict altogether? For what reasons did the United States not take such steps?

Americans on the European Front

SECTION PREVIEW

On entering the war, the United States saw itself merely as "associate" to the Allies. The Americans were quickly promoted to a leading role, however. Yankee soldiers and volunteers poured onto foreign battlefields and served nobly in many capacities.

Key Concepts

- At first, Americans envisioned a limited role for themselves in World War I.
- The role of the United States quickly expanded, and millions of draftees and volunteers, both women and men, became part of the effort.
- American military involvement helped turn the tide of the war.

Key Terms, People, and Places

American Expeditionary Force, armistice; doughboy

The United States was now at war. Would Americans achieve greatness in the mighty conflict? Pacifists looked to the future and saw European battlefields strewn with American corpses. Enthusiastic patriots, anxious for an unrestrained American commitment to the war, saw glory for the nation. United States officials, however, focused on the present and took a more cautious approach.

The United States Slowly Gets Involved

At first, President Wilson envisioned Americans as "associates" in the war, rather than equal partners with the Allies. Congress therefore authorized $3 billion in loans, naval support, supplies, and arms—but did not send troops.

For the Allies, this contribution was not enough. They insisted on an armed force, even a token one, to boost morale. Thus, in June 1917 the United States War Department, which had no formal plans for a European military operation, sent over General John J. "Black Jack" Pershing, a cold, tough veteran of the Spanish-American War, and a contingent of 14,500 men. Pershing quickly realized that he needed more troops.

Draftees and Volunteers At the time of Pershing's request, American troop strength fell far short of needs. When the United States entered World War I, the armed forces numbered only 120,000 enlisted men and 80,000 National Guardsmen. Thus, in May 1917 Congress passed a Selective Service Act, authorizing a draft of young men for military service.

During the Civil War, the draft had sparked riots. Now, however, the general feeling that this would be the "war to end all wars" resulted in wide acceptance for the program. By November 1918, over 24 million men had registered for the draft. From those, a lottery picked three million draftees. Volunteers and National Guardsmen made up the remainder of what was called the **American Expeditionary Force** (AEF).

Included in this American force was a new group of people—women. Eleven thousand women volunteered to serve in uniform as nurses, drivers, clerks, and telephone operators. Another 14,000 women served abroad as civilians working for the government or in private agencies. As Addie Hunton and Kathryn Johnson, two of the few African American women who made it to the front, later wrote: "We had the greatest opportunity for service that we have ever known."

The Convoy System In addition to building a fighting force, the War Department also had to worry about getting troops and supplies

In 1917 American soldiers began marching off to war, carrying items such as this trench shaving kit.

overseas. Toward this end, officials developed a system that protected merchant and troop ships from German U-boats by surrounding American ships with a convoy of small destroyers. The speed of the destroyers enabled them to mount counterattacks against U-boats or scare them off altogether. Between April and December 1917, merchant marine losses dropped by half.

American Soldiers in Europe "I don't know what the war's about, But I guess, by heck, I'll soon find out!" So went a popular World War I song that expressed the thoughts of the 2 million soldiers who eventually crossed the Atlantic Ocean. Infantrymen were called **doughboys**, a term that originated during the Civil War in reference to the dumpling-shaped buttons on Union infantry uniforms.

Once the American soldiers had arrived on foreign shores, Pershing did not integrate them with Allied troops, who in Pershing's view had become too accustomed to defensive action. He wanted to save his men's strength for offensive moves.

Segregation occurred not only between the American and Allied troops, but also within the American ranks. The more than 300,000 African Americans who volunteered or were drafted into service were kept separate from white troops. Though many African Americans fought with distinction and 3,925 died or were wounded, most never saw combat. The marines refused to accept African Americans

altogether, and the navy used them for menial tasks only. The army, too, used African Americans mostly for manual labor.

These assignments distressed many African Americans. The 369th Infantry Regiment, who came to be known as the Harlem Hell Fighters, was especially eager to fight. Its members convinced their white officers to loan them to the French, who did not practice segregation. Because of their distinguished service, the French awarded the entire regiment their highest combat medal, the *Croix de Guerre.*

MAKING CONNECTIONS

Consider Wilson's justification for entering the war, which was discussed in Section 2. Is the military's treatment of African Americans consistent with this justification? Explain.

AMERICAN PROFILES

Mary E. Gladwin

Many women did not wait for American entry into the war to find ways to serve. As early as the fall of 1914, women traveled to Europe as volunteers for the Red Cross, YWCA, or other service organizations. One such volunteer was Mary E. Gladwin.

Gladwin had become a nurse in her thirties after a career in teaching. She served as an American Red Cross volunteer in Georgia,

African American soldiers endured segregation overseas. But that did not keep the 369th Infantry, pictured here, from fighting valiantly and winning recognition for their bravery.

Puerto Rico, and the Philippines during the Spanish-American War, and in Hiroshima, Japan, during the Russo-Japanese War of 1905. After a major flood in Dayton, Ohio, in 1913, she supervised a staff of 110 nurses there.

Gladwin was fifty-three years old when she responded to a call to assist in Europe. As chief nurse in a unit of three doctors and twelve nurses, she set sail on a freighter on September 13, 1914. Her ultimate destination was Belgrade, the capital of Serbia. Awaiting an Austrian occupation, the city was almost deserted.

Gladwin's unit set itself up in a walled hospital complex that stood on a bluff overlooking the Danube and Sava rivers. Aside from the picturesque setting, the situation at the hospital was desperate. Every window had been blown out by the fighting. The volunteers arrived to find no food or equipment and 250 patients waiting for help. Gladwin threw herself into her rounds. With an interpreter, she worked her way through the confusing mixture of German, French, Serbian, and Russian tongues spoken by those at the hospital. Wrote Gladwin,

> I used to tumble into bed at two or three o'clock in the morning, and hear those men. They begged and prayed . . . for help. They swore, they tore their bandages and the nights when I got up (it took all my strength of mind to stay in bed), I knew exactly what I would find . . . the men in their agony tearing off the dressings, the dark streams of blood on the floor.

The hospital lacked blankets and coal for heat. Fleas and lice were everywhere. Pneumonia, pleurisy, scarlet fever, typhoid, and tetanus raged among patients and staff. In March 1915, three nurses and two physicians had to return home. Chief surgeon Dr. Edward Ryan contracted typhus.

The American Red Cross set a date for the recall of all its overseas medical units—October 1, 1915. As the date approached, however, Gladwin's unit was pinned down by fighting in the area and could not move. Although she finally left in November, a year later she was back on the eastern front. For the remainder of the war, she served with the Serbian Red Cross,

now from a station in Salonika, Greece. In 1920 the Red Cross awarded her the Florence Nightingale Medal.

Red Cross units had their critics. Before the United States entered the war, some asked what business American volunteers such as Gladwin had in a European war. By helping to heal soldiers and returning them to the front, were they not prolonging the conflict? But when the United States finally entered the war, the experience of people such as Gladwin would greatly assist the work of the Army Medical Corps in saving American lives.

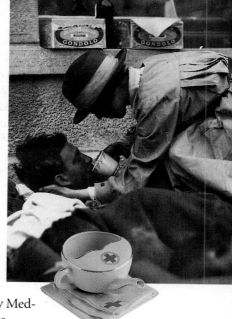

The efforts of American women like Mary Gladwin and the nurse shown above saved lives and contributed to the Allies' success. According to the Women's Overseas Service League, 348 women died during the war from bombardments or disease.

New Factors in the War

As the United States was expanding its involvement in the war, a major development occurred within the alliance. In November 1917, Vladimir Lenin led a new government to power in Russia.

Prior to his takeover, Lenin had been living in Switzerland and had promised to make peace with Germany if he ever gained control in Russia. Thus, Germany had helped arrange his return to Russia in April 1917. By November, Lenin had taken over the country.

Lenin's new regime immediately faced opposition from within the country. When civil war broke out, Lenin made peace with Germany on March 3, 1918.

Russia's exit from the war freed the Germans from the two-front war they had been forced to fight. From March through May 1918, German forces turned all their energies toward pounding at the French and British lines. They finally broke through, and by June 3, they were a mere 56 miles from Paris.

American forces came to the rescue. Marching out from Paris, the men received this word from their leader, Brigadier General James G. Harbord: "We dig no trenches to fall back on. The Marines will hold where they stand." And they did. At a loss of over half of their forces, they saved Paris, blunted the edge of the German advance, and began to turn the tide of the war.

Allied Counterattack The German command was astounded. "Nerves of the Americans are still unshaken," a general wrote to his headquarters. After turning back Germany at Paris, the Allied counteroffensive began in earnest in July. Using British tanks, a new machine that gave troops protection as well as mobility, the Allies began to break the German lines. On August 8, the battle of Amiens stopped the German advance once and for all. On August 11, German general Erich von Ludendorff sensed that the end was near. He advised Kaiser Wilhelm to seek terms for ending the war with the Allies.

The Allies, however, were not interested in any agreement in which Germany could win concessions from the Allies in return for peace.

They wanted total surrender. In September some 500,000 American troops, assisted by 100,000 French, began to hit the final German strongholds. Soon after the Germans were in full retreat.

The Allies also began to use airplanes to drop bombs. Aerial dogfights already had taken place. Each side had its "aces," such as the American captain Eddie Rickenbacker, who took down twenty-six enemy fighters. Now, Colonel Billy Mitchell organized a fleet of over 1,400 bomb-carrying planes. Although not very effective in this first attempt, aerial bombing raids would be devastating in future warfare.

Armistice The final Allied assault came on September 26. Over a million AEF troops began the drive to expel the Germans from France and cut their supply lines. Many individual acts of heroism shone during these final

World War I, 1917

Geography and History: Interpreting Maps
At the point of the United States entry into the war, the Central Powers had made gains in both the east and the west. Americans went immediately to work fighting against the Germans in France. *On which front had the Central Powers made the greatest gains?*

105-horsepower,
six-cylinder engine

Driver

Commander

One of four Lewis
machine guns

One of two 57-mm
pedestal-mounted
guns

Armor
plating

Pressed steel
track plate

months. Sergeant Alvin York of Tennessee, for example, saved an entire platoon by picking off machine gunners with his rifle and then, armed only with a pistol, captured 132 prisoners.

The Allies pressed on against their enemy. The German commanders begged for peace, but still hoped to dictate some terms. The Allies refused. Revenge was too sweet. By the time **armistice,** or a cease-fire, came, the Kaiser had fled. On November 11, the guns finally fell silent.

The War's Toll More than 50,000 American soldiers died in battle, and many more died of disease. The physical scars—and the mental scars—ran deep. Twenty-one-year-old Corporal Elmer Sherwood of Indiana wrote after one bloody battle in August 1918:

H undreds of bodies of our brave boys lie on Hill 212, captured with such a great loss of blood. We will never be able to *explain war to our loved ones back home even if we are permitted to live and return. It is too gigantic and awesome for expression through words.*

American losses were minute in comparison to those suffered by the Europeans. The total death toll of 8 million soldiers and sailors is only an estimate. The French alone suffered over 1 million war dead and 4,000 towns destroyed. Great Britain lost 900,000 troops and suffered 2 million wounded. As mentioned earlier, Russian deaths also were high. Across Europe, the war killed 20 million civilians during and immediately after the fighting, from starvation, disease, or related injuries.

This terrible slaughter took place on the battlefields of Europe. But the war also was "fought" on other fronts, as well. The next section discusses the impact of World War I on the American home front.

The tank was another new weapon introduced in World War I. The British and the Americans collaborated on designing and building tanks like the one shown above.

SECTION 3 REVIEW

Key Terms, People, and Places

1. Define (a) American Expeditionary Force, (b) armistice.
2. Identify doughboy.

Key Concepts

3. What were some of the military innovations introduced during World War I?
4. In what ways did American women serve in World War I?

5. How did American troops help turn the tide of the war on the battlefield?
6. How many people were killed and wounded as a result of World War I?

Critical Thinking

7. **Demonstrating Reasoned Judgment** The United States failed in its original plan to be a mere "associate" in the war. Do you think it is possible to be anything less than a "full partner" in a war? Explain.

On the Home Front

SECTION PREVIEW

World War I was fought at home, too. To win that war, the government took control of the economy—and of people's minds—to an extent never before attempted.

Key Concepts

• Waging World War I involved tremendous financial and managerial efforts on the home front.
• The atmosphere of war hysteria enabled the United States government to control and manipulate information and to repress free speech.
• The war spurred significant cultural and social changes.

Key Terms, People, and Places

Liberty Bond, Industrial Workers of the World

The United States government whipped up sentiment against the "Huns"—the Germans—with posters such as this.

Waging war required many sacrifices at home. Despite the efforts of the preparedness movement, the economy was not ready to meet the demands of modern warfare. In this era, war required huge amounts of money and personnel. As President Wilson explained, now "there are no armies . . . ; there are entire nations armed."

Financing the War

As those in Congress who had argued for peace had made clear, preparedness was costly. Taxes went up. Most of the money for the war, however, came from patriotic private citizens. The government launched a vigorous campaign to raise money from the American people, a plan created by Secretary of the Treasury William Gibbs McAdoo. By selling **Liberty Bonds** to enthusiastic Americans, McAdoo raised millions of dollars, which he then loaned to the Allies at low interest rates. People who purchased the bonds could later redeem them, collecting what they paid for the bonds plus interest.

Teams of salespeople across the country sold the bonds to the "patriotic people." Responding to the slogan "Every Scout to Save a Soldier," Boy Scouts and Girl Scouts set up booths on street corners and sold bonds. The government hired popular commercial artists to draw colorful posters and recruited famous screen actors to host bond rallies. An army of 75,000 "four-minute men" gave brief (four-minute) speeches before films, plays, and school or union meetings to persuade audiences to buy bonds.

Managing the Economy

The government also needed industry to convert to the production of war goods. In 1918 Wilson won authority to set up a huge bureaucracy to manage this process. Business leaders—so-called "dollar-a-year" men and women—gave their service for a token salary and flocked to Washington to take up posts in thousands of new agencies.

New Government Agencies A War Industries Board, headed by financier Bernard Baruch, oversaw the whole war effort. The board's control was almost dictatorial. It doled out raw materials, told manufacturers what and how much to produce, and even fixed prices. A Fuel Administration introduced gasless days and daylight saving time, which increased the number of daylight hours and thus lowered fuel consumption. A War Trade Board licensed foreign trade and punished firms suspected of dealing with the enemy.

A National War Labor Board, set up in April 1918 under former President Taft, mediated those labor disputes that might hinder the war effort. Labor leader Samuel Gompers promised to limit labor strife in war production industries. A separate War Labor Policies Board, headed by Harvard law professor Felix

Frankfurter, standardized wages, hours, and working conditions in the war industries. Labor unions won limited rights to organize and bargain collectively.

Regulating Food Consumption Using the slogan "food will win the war," the government began regulating food consumption. Under the leadership of engineer and future President Herbert Hoover, a Food Administration (1917) worked to increase agricultural output and reduce waste. Opposed to price controls and rationing, Hoover hoped that voluntary restraint and increased efficiency would accomplish these goals.

Women, assumed to be in charge of America's kitchens, were a key part of his program. Writing to women in August 1917, Hoover preached a "Gospel of the Clean Plate."

Stop, before throwing any food away, and ask "Can it be used?" . . . Stop catering to different appetites. No second helpings. Stop all eating between meals. . . . Stop all refreshments at parties, dances, etc. . . . One meatless day a week. One wheatless meal a day. . . . No butter in cooking: use substitutes.

"The American woman and the American home," he concluded, "can bring to a successful end the greatest national task that has ever been accepted by the American people." Eager for a chance to play a purposeful part in the war, women across the country responded to this patriotic challenge.

A Progressive Victory? Thanks to the war, some aspects of progressive-era visions had come to pass. Government now regulated American economic life to an extent most progressives had never dreamed possible. When regulation spilled over into more private areas of life, however, some progressives wondered if the growth in public power had become excessive. In addition, regulation had not lessened the power of the corporate world. Indeed, during the war, the government relaxed its pursuit of antitrust suits, the influence of business leaders grew, and corporate profits tripled.

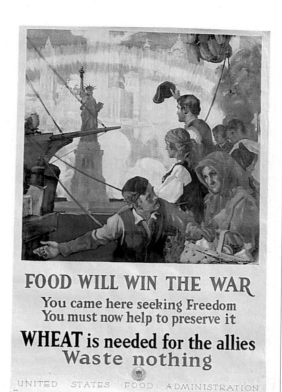

FOOD WILL WIN THE WAR
You came here seeking Freedom
You must now help to preserve it
WHEAT is needed for the allies
Waste nothing
UNITED STATES FOOD ADMINISTRATION

MAKING CONNECTIONS

How does the involvement of the federal government in the regulation of business during World War I differ from government policies toward business in the late 1800s? What factors account for this change?

Controlling Hearts and Minds

News and information also came under federal control during World War I. George Creel, a Denver journalist and former muckraker, headed a Committee on Public Information, the country's first propaganda machine. Creel's office coordinated the production of short propaganda films, pamphlets explaining war aims, and posters selling recruitment and Liberty Bonds. Study plans distributed to teachers from Creel's office put the entire blame for the war on Germany.

Enforcing Loyalty As in all wars, fear of spies and sabotage was widespread. A few months after the sinking of the *Lusitania*, a staff member of the German embassy left his briefcase on a train. In it were plans for undermining pro-Allied sentiment and disrupting the American economy. Henceforth, the government was on the alert for sabotage.

Once the United States declared war, this alertness approached hysteria. Nativism revived, this time more vigorously than before. Having won its battle for preparedness, the National Security League began to preach "100 Percent Americanism." In 1917 the League finally got Congress to pass, over Wilson's veto, a literacy test for immigrants. This test excluded those who could not read or write a language—relatively few immigrants, as it turned out. Limits on immigration would become more severe after the war.

"Hate the Hun!" The war also spurred hostility toward Germans, who were called Huns in reference to an Asiatic people who brutally invaded Europe in the fourth and fifth centuries. German composers and musicians were banned from symphony concerts. German measles became "liberty measles," a hamburger

"I am afraid we are going to have a good many instances of people roughly treated on very slight evidence of disloyalty," wrote Secretary of War Newton Baker. Indeed, as this 1917 photograph shows, anti-German feeling in the United States led to the arrest of many citizens of German descent.

a "liberty sandwich." The California Board of Education condemned German as a language that spread "the ideals of autocracy, brutality and hatred." Yet it was a brutal mob of Americans that, in April 1918, lynched German-born citizen Robert Prager near St. Louis, in spite of the fact that Prager had tried to enlist in the navy. This act was but one of numerous wartime attacks on people of German descent.

Repression of Civil Liberties Wilson had claimed that the United States was now fighting for liberty and democracy. Many Americans, including women still denied the vote, found the claim ironic. It was particularly galling to those who suffered from wartime restrictions on their civil liberties.

When Wilson addressed Congress on the war resolution, he had warned that disloyalty would be "dealt with with a firm hand of repression." Accordingly, Congress passed the Espionage Act (1917), which made it illegal to interfere with the draft. This was followed by the Sedition Act (1918), which made it illegal to obstruct the sale of Liberty Bonds or to discuss anything "disloyal, profane, scurrilous, or abusive" about the American form of government, the Constitution, or the army and navy.

The government imposed censorship on the press and banned some publications from the mails. It pursued more than 1,500 prosecutions and won over 1,000 convictions. Socialist and former presidential candidate Eugene Debs drew a ten-year jail sentence for criticizing the American government and business leaders and urging people to "resist militarism." From prison he ran again for President in 1920 and won nearly a million votes. The victor in that race, Warren G. Harding, pardoned him in 1921.

Controlling Political Radicals Socialists such as Debs argued that the war was merely a quarrel among imperialist capitalists. This view became a rallying point for antiwar sentiment. In the elections of 1917 in New York, Ohio, and Pennsylvania, socialists made impressive gains. The **Industrial Workers of the World,** a radical labor organization seeking the overthrow of capitalism, also gained new supporters. The IWW (also known as the "Wobblies") was founded in 1905. Unlike the labor movement Samuel Gompers led, the IWW focused on unskilled workers. It consisted mostly of western miners, lumbermen, migrant farm workers, and some eastern textile workers.

The views of socialists and the IWW distressed moderate labor leaders like Gompers, who had pledged union cooperation with the war effort. The police hounded the IWW. Raids in September 1917 led to the conviction of nearly two hundred members in trials held in Illinois, California, and Oklahoma. Vigilante groups, citizens who take the law into their own hands, lynched and horsewhipped others.

Cultural and Social Changes

Despite American criticism of Germany for its militarism, American patriotism and war fever made military styles and activities acceptable at home. Scouting programs, which for both boys and girls involved military-style uniforms, marching, and patriotic exercises, grew in popularity. Military drill became part of many school programs. By the summer of 1918, all able-bodied males in colleges and universities became army privates, subject to military discipline.

Social Mobility for Women and Minorities

Americans turned against militarism after the war. But other social changes had more lasting implications.

The war propelled certain people into higher paid work. As the war cut off the flow of immigrants from Europe, factories that used to discriminate against African Americans and Mexican Americans now actively recruited them. The Women's Land Army put women to work on farms. White women moved into jobs previously closed to them, such as telegraph messenger, elevator operator, and letter carrier. Middle-class white women moved into management positions.

As a result of the war, about 400,000 women joined the industrial work force for the first time. In 1917 a speaker for the Women's Trade Union League exulted, "At last, after centuries of disabilities and discrimination, women are coming into the labor and festival of life on equal terms with men." In 1919 a study appeared with the optimistic title, "A New Day for the Colored Woman Worker." These pronouncements, while premature, celebrated what seemed to be major change.

Prohibition Finally Passes

In 1917 the temperance movement was almost a century old. In that year, Congress proposed prohibition. The Eighteenth Amendment was passed less out of concern for the health of alcoholics and their families than to show patriotism. Because of the war, the grain that used to make alcohol would now make bread to meet needs at home and overseas. The states ratified the amendment in 1919.

The IWW gained strength during World War I. They also became the target of government crackdowns, part of a wider effort to control political radicals.

SECTION 4 REVIEW

Key Terms, People, and Places
1. Identify Industrial Workers of the World.

Key Concepts
2. How did the United States finance its involvement in World War I?
3. In what ways did the government try to control the economy?
4. By what means did the government try to convince Americans to support the war?

5. Whose civil liberties were sacrificed in this effort to win the war?
6. What were some social and cultural changes that took place as a result of the war?

Critical Thinking
7. **Recognizing Ideologies** The federal government went to great lengths to control public opinion. What do these actions suggest about government's view of public opinion and its role in the war effort?

Global Peacemaker

President Wilson's lofty vision for peace was brought back to earth by contentious allies and Congress. Meanwhile, many Americans experienced keen disappointment over postwar conditions at home.

Key Concepts

- At the postwar peace talks, Wilson's grand vision for peace was welcomed—but not wholeheartedly embraced.
- In the United States, reaction to the Versailles Treaty and to Wilson's proposal for a League of Nations was cool.
- The immediate postwar years in the United States were marred by disillusionment and economic disorder.

Key Terms, People, and Places

Fourteen Points, self-determination, League of Nations, reparations, Versailles Treaty

Enthusiasm for the war effort, demonstrated by this game board cover, gave way to despair in the postwar years.

With the fighting in Europe over, the nations involved in the conflict began the difficult task of shaping the peace. President Wilson, who feared that the failure to craft a treaty acceptable to all parties would lead to future wars, was determined to play a large role in this effort. But the postwar world—in Europe and at home—seemed almost as divided as before the war.

Wilson's Vision for Postwar Peace

On January 8, 1918, President Wilson delivered a peace program to Congress, which came to be called the **Fourteen Points** for the number of provisions it included. Among the program's key points were a call for an end to secret alliances, the restoration of freedom of the seas, and a reduction in armaments. The plan called for European colonial powers to handle all claims to each other's colonies with respect for the native populations. Wilson also demanded that Austria-Hungary allow its several ethnic groups to determine their own futures, a principle called **self-determination.** Finally, he called for an association of nations to join together in a single organization to secure world peace.

Wilson hoped that these points would form the basis of peace negotiations. At first, the Allies appeared to cooperate. After a while, as new political realities intervened, the fourteen points began to unravel.

The Paris Peace Conference In January 1919 an international peace conference met in Paris. Wilson decided to head the United States delegation himself. He also chose not to name any Republicans or senators to the group, a snub that would not be forgotten.

When Wilson arrived in Paris, Parisians threw flowers in his path and greeted the American President as a conquering hero. Wilson claimed he was not interested in gaining rewards for the United States, but sought only the establishment of a permanent agency to guarantee international stability. As he had said two years earlier, "There must be not a balance of power, but a community of power; not organized rivalries, but an organized common peace."

Wilson Is Forced to Compromise All would not go Wilson's way. First, the Allies *were* interested in reward. In particular, they wanted to divide up Germany's colonies. The French, determined never to be invaded again, wanted the total humiliation if not destruction of Germany. Russia, although absent from the conference, was on everyone's mind. In March, civil war had erupted there. British, French, and American forces had become involved in the fray on the side of Lenin's opponents. Would

Lenin's government collapse or prevail? Would it press for war claims?

From the start of the conference, Wilson was forced to compromise on his plans. He had to give up, for example, on the idea of self-determination for Germany's colonies, agreeing that the Allied powers could take them over.

Wilson did, however, get the other powers to postpone further discussion of Germany's fate and to move directly to his ideas for collective security. After ten days of hard work, he produced a plan for the **League of Nations,** an organization in which the nations of the world would join together to ensure security and peace for all members. Wilson then left for home, hoping to persuade Congress and the nation to accept his ideas.

Article 10 For Wilson, the heart of his proposal for the League of Nations was "Article 10." This provision pledged members to regard an attack on one as an attack on all. Since the League would not have any military power, the force of the article was moral only. Nevertheless, thirty-nine Republican senators or senators-elect signed a statement rejecting it, fearing the loss of American diplomatic independence.

MAKING CONNECTIONS

Were Wilson's goals for the peace process, as outlined in his Fourteen Points, consistent with his stated reasons for entering the war? Explain.

The Peace Treaty

In March, Wilson returned to the peace conference. The Big Four—Britain, France, Italy, and the United States—dominated the proceedings. Though the Allies accepted Wilson's plan for the League of Nations, French premier Georges Clemenceau used Wilson's embarrassment over American opposition to the League to exact harsh conditions against Germany. These included a fifteen-year French control of the mineral resources in Alsace-Lorraine. Wilson feared that this decision would lead to future wars, but he could not get Clemenceau to budge.

Viewpoints
On the League of Nations

Joining the League of Nations would involve a major commitment for the United States. The wisdom of making such a commitment was discussed from every angle. *On what basis does each speaker below support or oppose American entry into the League?*

For Joining the League of Nations
"The United States will, indeed, undertake . . . to 'respect and preserve as against external aggression the territorial integrity and existing political independence of all members of the League,' and that engagement constitutes a very grave and solemn moral obligation. But it is a moral, not a legal, obligation, and leaves our Congress absolutely free to put its own interpretation upon it."

President Woodrow Wilson, testifying before the Foreign Relations Committee, August 19, 1919

Against Joining the League of Nations
"Shall we go there, Mr. President, to sit in judgment, and in case that judgment works for peace join with our allies, but in case it works for war withdraw our cooperation? How long would we stand as we now stand, a great Republic commanding the respect and holding the leadership of the world, if we should adopt any such course?"

Senator William Borah (Idaho), testifying in the Senate, November 19, 1919

Wilson had to compromise elsewhere. Self-determination for the peoples of Austria-Hungary proved hard to apply. Central Europe was (and still is) an ethnic mixture of monumental complexity. As the map on page 436 shows, the conference created the new nations of Czechoslovakia and Yugoslavia, more nearly following ethnic lines than before the war. But these arrangements failed to resolve all ethnic tensions, which in the early 1990s contributed to the breakup of these nations.

War Guilt and Reparations Wilson met his greatest defeat when he gave in to French insistence on German war guilt and financial responsibility. The French wanted to cripple Germany. The British wanted **reparations**—payment from its enemy for the economic injury suffered in the war. In 1921 a Reparations

Europe After World War I

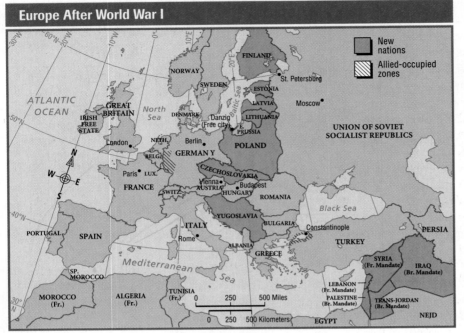

Legend:
- New nations
- Allied-occupied zones

Geography and History: Interpreting Maps
The peace process helped lead to the transformation of the map of Europe.
In what ways does this map of Europe differ from the map on page 417?

Committee ruled that Germany owed the Allies $33 billion, an amount far beyond its ability to pay. As Wilson had feared, Germany never forgot or forgave this humiliation.

Signing the Treaty The Allies presented the treaty to the Germans on May 7, 1919. Insisting that the treaty violated the Fourteen Points, the Germans at first refused to sign. They soon gave in, however, when threatened with a French invasion. On June 28 the powers signed the treaty at Versailles, the former home of the French kings outside of Paris. Thus, the treaty is known as the **Versailles Treaty.**

Seeking Approval at Home

On July 8, treaty in hand, Wilson returned home to great acclaim. But many legislators had doubts. Some senators, called the "irreconcilables," opposed the treaty because it included American commitment to the League of Nations. Irreconcilables argued that joining the League would weaken American independence.

Senator Henry Cabot Lodge, chair of the Foreign Relations Committee, led another group called the "reservationists." This group wanted to impose reservations on American participation in the League. In particular they wanted a guarantee that the Monroe Doctrine would remain in force. Wilson's point that compliance with League decisions was "binding in conscience only, not in law," failed to persuade them.

Wilson Barnstorms the Country Determined to win grass roots support for the League, Wilson took to the road. In twenty-three days he delivered three dozen speeches. In the midst of this tremendous effort, he suffered a stroke that paralyzed one side of his body. He would remain an invalid, isolated from his cabinet and visitors, for the rest of his term.

In his illness, Wilson grew increasingly inflexible. Congress would accept the treaty and the League as he envisioned it, or not at all. In November the Senate voted on the treaty with Lodge's reservations included. The vote was 39 for, 55 against. When the treaty came up without the reservations, it went down again, 38 to 53. In the face of popular dismay at this outcome, the Senate reconsidered the treaty in March, but once again the treaty failed to win approval.

A Formal End to Hostilities On May 20, 1920, Congress voted to declare the war officially over. Steadfast to his principles, Wilson vetoed it. Finally, on July 2, 1921, another joint resolution to end the war passed. By that time a new President, Warren Harding, was in office and signed it. Congress ratified separate peace treaties with Germany, Austria, and Hungary that October.

Difficult Postwar Adjustments

The biggest winners from the war were American business and financial interests. The United States was now the world's richest creditor. In 1922 a Senate debt commission calculated that Europe owed the United States $11.5 billion.

The return to peace caused problems for the general population, however. There was no plan for reintegrating returning troops into society. The federal agencies that had controlled the economy during the war abruptly cancelled war contracts. By April 1919, about 4,000 servicemen a day were being mustered out of the armed forces. But jobs proved scarce. The women who had taken men's places in factories and offices also faced readjustment. Late in 1918, Mary Van Kleeck, head of the Women in Industry Service, reported that "the question heard most frequently was whether women would now retire from industry." Many women did, either voluntarily or because they were fired.

Postwar Despair Many artists and intellectuals in the United States faced the postwar years with disillusionment. Some progressives had been encouraged by the government-business collaboration during the war. But for most other reformers, the war years marked the end of an era of optimism.

This disillusionment was not unique to artists and intellectuals. Wrote Alice Lord O'Brian, a military post exchange director from Buffalo who was twice decorated,

W*e all started out with high ideals . . . after being right up here almost at the front line . . . I cannot understand what it is all about or what has been accomplished by all this waste of youth.*

African American Troops at Home Like white troops, African American soldiers

Weariness and fear line the face of Corporal Johnson of the 58th Regiment as he rests during a pause in battle. The experience of war left deep scars in the bodies and minds of many Americans.

came home heroes. When the soldiers went to find jobs, however, the reception was quite different.

W.E.B. Du Bois, editor of the NAACP's magazine, the *Crisis,* had supported the war. In July 1918 he had written, "Let us, while this war lasts, forget our special grievances and close our ranks . . . with our white citizens and the allied nations that are fighting for democracy." A year later, after more lynchings of African Americans, including some still in uniform, his message became defiant. "This country of ours, despite all its better souls have done and dreamed, is yet a shameful land," he wrote in May 1919. "It **lynches**. . . . It steals from us. . . . It insults us. . . . We **return. We return from fighting. We return fighting**."

Du Bois's views, shared by many, heralded a new era in the struggle for equality. Indeed, the entire United States was on the threshold of a stormy era—the 1920s.

SECTION 5 REVIEW

Key Terms, People, and Places
1. Describe (a) self-determination, (b) League of Nations, (c) reparations, (d) Versailles Treaty.

Key Concepts
2. What were Wilson's Fourteen Points, and what were its key elements?
3. What factors forced Wilson to compromise on his plans at the Paris peace conference?

4. What was the American reaction to the Treaty of Versailles and the League of Nations?
5. What factors contributed to the difficult postwar adjustment in the United States?

Critical Thinking
6. **Expressing Problems Clearly** It is often said that Wilson won the war but "lost the peace." Explain your understanding of this statement.

Chapter Review

Understanding Key Terms, People, and Places

Key Terms
1. Central Powers
2. Allies
3. U-boat
4. *Lusitania*
5. Zimmerman note
6. American Expeditionary Force
7. armistice
8. Liberty Bond
9. Industrial Workers of the World
10. Fourteen Points
11. self-determination
12. League of Nations
13. reparations
14. Versailles Treaty

People
15. Kaiser Wilhelm
16. autocrat
17. doughboy

Terms For each term above, write a sentence that explains its relation to the outbreak of World War I, United States involvement in the war, or events that followed the conflict.

True or False Determine whether each statement is true or false. If it is true, write "true." If it is false, change the underlined term to make the statement true.
1. At the outbreak of World War I, the <u>Central Powers</u> consisted of Russia, France, and Great Britain.
2. The <u>American Expeditionary Force,</u> a radical labor organization, sought the overthrow of capitalism.
3. After the war, the European Allies demanded harsh <u>self-determination</u> from Germany.
4. Americans bought <u>Liberty Bonds</u> to help finance the war.
5. Wilson's peace program came to be called the <u>Zimmerman note</u>.

Section 1 (pp. 416 – 419)
1. How did the role of secret European treaties shift in 1914?
2. Why did troops fighting in the war resort to acts of desperation?
3. What position did businesses in the United States take regarding the war?

Section 2 (pp. 421 – 424)
4. For what reasons did many Americans develop an anti-German attitude?
5. Why was Wilson unable to keep his campaign promise to maintain neutrality?
6. In addition to Germany's refusal to respect American claims to neutrality, name two other reasons why the United States entered the war.

Section 3 (pp. 425 – 429)
7. Describe how Americans envisioned their role when they first entered the war. What led to the expansion of the American role in World War I?

8. What types of segregation occurred during the war?
9. Explain how the Allies were able to turn the tide of the war.

Section 4 (pp. 430 – 433)
10. Describe the changes in American life brought about by the War Industries Board, the National War Labor Board, and other new government agencies.
11. What was the result of news and media coming under government control during the war?
12. In what ways were people's civil liberties limited during the war?
13. Name some positive effects of the war.

Section 5 (pp. 434 – 437)
14. What was the response of the French and British to Wilson's peace plan?
15. Briefly describe congressional opposition to the League of Nations.
16. Describe the postwar adjustment for African Americans.

1. **Recognizing Ideologies** When the United States entered World War I, it hoped to play a supporting role as an "associate." What does this assumption suggest about the country's view of itself at the time?

2. **Identifying Central Issues** In what ways did World War I differ from previous wars involving the United States?

3. **Checking Consistency** Many members of Congress worried that the League of Nations would limit the independence of the United States. Based on what you have read about World War I, how independent was the United States from the affairs of Europe?

1. **Evaluating Primary Sources** Review the primary source excerpt on page 429. How would you expect such attitudes to affect soldiers returning from World War I?

2. **Understanding the Visuals** Examine the cartoon and the newspaper clippings on page 422. Do the cartoon and the clipping on the left support or refute each other? Explain your answer.

3. **Writing About the Chapter** Imagine that World War I has recently ended. Write a statement to Congress in which you express your opinion of President Wilson's proposal for the League of Nations. First, create a list of what you see as the positive aspects of Wilson's plan. Then, list the negative features. Note any suggestions you have for improvements. Next, write a draft of your statement in which you offer your ideas. Revise your statement, making certain that each idea is clearly explained. Proofread your statement and draft a final copy.

4. **Using the Graphic Organizer** This graphic organizer uses a modified flow map to organize information about the events leading to World War I and about early responses to the war on the part of Americans. Flow maps can show both a sequence of events or what happened as the result of an event. (a) Based on the chart, what was the cause of Americans becoming increasingly alarmed about the war? (b) What was the effect of American alarm? (c) On a separate sheet of paper, create your own flow map about American involvement in World War I in Europe and on the home front, using this graphic organizer as an example.

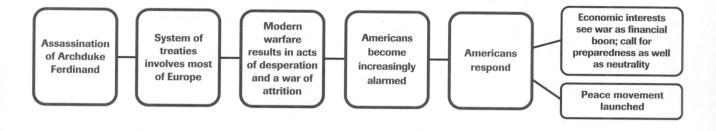

Assassination of Archduke Ferdinand → System of treaties involves most of Europe → Modern warfare results in acts of desperation and a war of attrition → Americans become increasingly alarmed → Americans respond → Economic interests see war as financial boon; call for preparedness as well as neutrality / Peace movement launched

FROM FIELD TO FACTORY

Beginning in 1915, hundreds of thousands of African Americans moved from the rural South to the cities of the North. Most African Americans made this "Great Migration" to take advantage of job opportunities in the North. Others, however, moved to escape the poverty and discrimination they faced in the Jim Crow South. This migration changed the lives of the African Americans who made the journey, and it changed the nature of race relations in the North.

How did the lives of African Americans change when they moved from the fields of the South to the factories of northern cities?

▲ HANDMADE DOLL
Cash-poor African Americans made or grew much of what they used in the South. This doll had its own handmade cradle and blankets.

▲ STORE OWNER'S RECORD BOOK The southern store owner kept track of sharecroppers' debts and payments in a ledger like this. Few African American sharecroppers ever made enough money to pay what they owed the store owner.

440

▲ PLOW More than two thirds of the African Americans living in the South were sharecropping farmers. Farming was back-breaking work for the whole family and seldom yielded more than survival. Farmers walked behind a mule-drawn plow like this one to break the land.

▼ SUITCASE AND BIBLES African Americans in the South had strong community ties, which centered around the local church. Leaving this community, even to escape hardships, was difficult.

LABORERS WANTED
AT
HOG ISLAND
GOVERNMENT SHIPBUILDING
35¢ AN HOUR
$3.85 A DAY
A CHANCE TO LEARN A GOOD TRADE AND GET
HIGHER WAGES

▲ JOB OPPORTUNITIES Because of World War I, industries could not get new laborers from Europe. Also, many native-born workers were drawn into the armed forces. African Americans streamed north to fill these open jobs.

◀ HOME SCHOOLING There were few schools for African Americans in the rural South, and the ones that existed were poor. Parents frequently were forced to be their children's teachers.

WORLD WAR I SOLDIERS ▶ Many African Americans learned about the opportunities in the North when they served as soldiers during World War I. For most soldiers, this was the first time they traveled more than a few miles from home.

Boom Times to Hard Times
1919–1938

"We in America today are nearer to the final triumph over poverty than ever before."
—Herbert Hoover, 1928

*W*hen President Herbert Hoover spoke these words, he expressed the optimism and faith in business and technology that characterized the United States in the 1920s. Following the stock market crash of October 1929, however, the fragile prosperity of the decade gave way to a period of severe economic distress known as the Great Depression. In the election of 1932, voters chose Franklin Delano Roosevelt for President, a choice that marked a turning point in the way Americans would view their Presidents.

During the Great Depression, poverty and suffering were constant traveling companions to families like the one above, forced to move from town to town to look for work.

A Stormy Era
1919–1929

"My candle burns at both ends . . . " wrote poet Edna St. Vincent Millay in 1920, a phrase that can be used to symbolize a divided nation during the entire decade. Some people wanted to put aside the horrible memories of war and so embraced anything new, be it product, attitude, or behavior. Others wanted to shield their eyes from the responsibility that came with being a new global power and tried to pull the nation back to attitudes and behaviors that were known and "safe."

Events in the United States

1919 Attorney General Palmer begins raids on suspected radicals.
• Chicago race riot occurs.

1920 Warren Harding elected President.
• The first commercial radio broadcast is made.

1922 T. S. Eliot publishes "The Wasteland."

1923 Harding dies; Calvin Coolidge takes office.
• Bessie Smith records her first jazz album.

| 1919 | 1920 | 1921 | 1922 | 1923 |

Events in the World

1920 The Treaty of Versailles ends World War I.
• The League of Nations is formed.

1921 Takashi Hara, Premier of Japan, is assassinated.

1923 Adolf Hitler fails in an attempted coup in Germany.

Pages 446 – 449

Postwar Adjustments

With the shadow of World War I finally lifting, some Americans hoped the way toward progressive-style reform would be relighted. Others, however, began to view such ideas for change with suspicion and fear.

Pages 452 – 456

Social and Political Developments

After the war, women and African Americans faced a world of new opportunities and old disappointments. In the political realm, Republicans won Americans' support—and votes.

Pages 457 – 460

New Manners, New Morals

From rising hemlines to the energetic sounds of jazz, the 1920s daringly broke with tradition. New social freedoms created opportunity—and dilemmas—for women. But beneath it all lay a nagging question: How much had really changed?

Pages 462 – 465

Creating a Shared Culture

People in city apartments, country farmhouses, and everywhere in between were connected in new ways in the 1920s. Such links allowed sweeping changes to envelop the entire nation.

Pages 466 – 469

Stemming the Tide of Change

Jazz music, moving pictures, fast cars—American life moved at a dizzying pace in the 1920s. All the motion left some people feeling queasy, and they sought to slow the pace of change.

1924	1925	1926	1927	1928	1929

1925 The Charleston becomes a dance craze.
• John Scopes is tried for teaching evolution.

1927 Charles Lindbergh flies solo across the Atlantic Ocean.
• Ford begins production of the Model A.

1928 Republican Herbert Hoover is elected President.

1929 Ten million families own radios.

1924 V. I. Lenin, founder of the Soviet Union, dies.
• France hosts the first Winter Olympics.

1926 Ibn Saud becomes king of Saudi Arabia.
• French painter Claude Monet dies.

1928 Chiang Kai-shek becomes president of China.

1929 The term apartheid is introduced in South Africa.

Postwar Adjustments

SECTION PREVIEW

With the shadow of World War I finally lifting, some Americans hoped the way toward progressive-style reform would be relighted. Others, however, began to view such ideas for change with suspicion and fear.

Key Concepts
- Postwar economic adjustments and labor unrest troubled the nation.
- Fears that the ideas of the Russian Revolution would spread led to a "red scare" in the United States.
- Efforts to limit immigration and foreign entanglements won wide support in the 1920s.

Key Terms, People, and Places
communist, red scare, general strike; Vladimir I. Lenin, Nicola Sacco, Bartolomeo Vanzetti

After the Russian Revolution, many Americans saw the Communist hammer and sickle as a symbol of a threat to the United States.

W orld War I was over. Now was the time, progressive reformers thought, to relaunch plans for economic and social change, such as unemployment insurance and housing initiatives, put on hold during the war.

The times, however, were less ripe for change than reformers hoped. The unprecedented brutality of the war had wounded the nation's spirit. Europe, once the model of enlightened civilization, was now viewed with disgust. Fear about the worldwide effects of revolution in Russia swept the country. And as the United States endured a bumpy transition back to peacetime, many Americans began to view proposals for changing society with suspicion and fear.

Postwar Economic Adjustments

During the war, American factories geared up to meet the demand for ships, guns, food, and other goods. When this demand dropped after the war, the economy entered a difficult period of adjustment. Returning veterans faced unemployment. When they got their jobs back, they did so by taking those that had been filled by women and minorities. In addition, food prices and rents shot up in the spring of 1919, and by 1920 the cost of living was more than double what it had been before the war. Farmers suffered as wartime orders declined and European farmers began producing crops again. Prices for wheat, corn, and hay dropped by half.

Labor unrest became increasingly common. From 1916 through 1920, the United States experienced between 3,350 and 4,450 strikes a year, most caused by disputes over wages and hours. When factory owners discovered that the absence of unions in the South helped make southern labor costs much lower than those in the North, many moved their businesses south, leaving northern mill towns to die. Union members responded with outrage.

The Russian Revolution Causes a Red Scare

Kerensky
Lenin
USSR
Communist
Intervention

The end of World War I did not bring an end to the turmoil overseas. As the fighting in Europe entered its final months, Russia erupted in revolution. Few foreign events would have as long-lasting an impact on the United States.

In March 1917, revolutionary forces overthrew the Russian monarchy headed by Czar Nicholas II and set up a representative form of government. Under the leadership of Aleksandr Kerensky, a lawyer who had defended opponents of the czarist regime, the new government pledged to continue in the European war. This pledge hurt Kerensky's standing with Russia's hungry workers and peasants, to whom the war seemed remote and unrelated.

Revolutionary leader **Vladimir I. Lenin** soon undermined Kerensky's power with promises of "peace, land, and bread." This message offered hope to Russia's weary people.

Although in the minority, Lenin and his followers believed that they represented all of Russia's workers. They therefore took the name *Bolsheviks*, the Russian word for *the majority*. They also adopted the red flag as their emblem.

In November 1917, the Bolsheviks overthrew Kerensky. Their new state, which eventually became the Union of Soviet Socialist Republics, made peace with Germany. It adopted socialism, a political and economic system in which all of society—represented by the government—jointly owns all property. Lenin also referred to his new regime as **communist**, a term that comes from the writings of German philosopher Karl Marx. It describes the revolutionary system that exists when workers have taken over a society and proclaimed an end to all differences between social and economic classes.

Lenin's ideas appealed to many poor Russians. But others resisted violently, and in early 1918, Russia erupted in civil war. Soldiers from Britain, France, Japan, and the United States intervened militarily on the side of Lenin's opponents to protect their countries' investments in the former Russia.

Lenin's "Reds" eventually won the civil war in 1920, and they resolved to fulfill Marx's ideology by spreading communism to other nations. From then on, the United States regarded the Bolshevik Reds as the world's villain.

National Unrest Is Blamed on the Reds In the United States, a rash of labor strikes and terrorist acts convinced many that the Reds were about to take over. A **red scare**—the fear of communism, socialism, or other so-called extreme ideas—gripped the nation.

One major strike took place in Seattle in January 1919. Shipworkers walked off their jobs and later were joined by workers in other industries. This action, one in which many unions participate as a show of worker unity, is known as a **general strike**. The Seattle strike paralyzed industry, trade, and the delivery of essential services in the area for five days. It also convinced many Americans that the United States was on the brink of revolution.

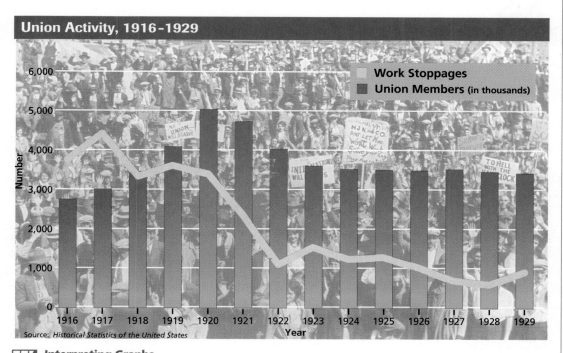

Union Activity, 1916–1929

Work Stoppages
Union Members (in thousands)

Source: *Historical Statistics of the United States*

Interpreting Graphs
The post–World War I years were stormy ones for labor and business. The number of annual strikes was high and union membership also rose slightly. *Based on this information, how would you summarize the condition of organized labor in the 1920s?*

Such fears set the stage for violent attacks on unions. In September, steelworkers in Gary, Indiana, and several other cities struck over hours, wages, shop conditions, and company recognition of their union. Claiming that the strike was the work of communists, the United States Steel Corporation used force to break it, killing eighteen and beating hundreds more.

Steel strike blamed; police walkout

Also that fall, Boston's police force tried to win their first pay raise since the start of World War I. When the police commissioner fired nineteen officers for union activity, the whole force voted to strike.

Many Bostonians were frightened and outraged by the police strike. But Massachusetts governor Calvin Coolidge responded quickly, proclaiming, "There is no right to strike against the public safety by anybody, anywhere, anytime." He received national attention for his firm response to the police walkout.

antiradical raids. people deported. NY case note. welfare supported

The Palmer Raids Convinced by the events of 1919 that the country was about to fall to radicals, many Americans grew anxious. Attorney General A. Mitchell Palmer, a man with political ambitions combined with a genuine fear of the communist threat, responded with enthusiasm. He set up an antiradical division to raid organizations suspected of so-called radical activity. These included communist and anarchist groups.

Thousands of individuals, mostly foreign-born and many innocent of any crime, were jailed as a result of the raids. Eventually, over five hundred people were deported without being formally charged with or convicted of any crimes. The army's chief of staff recommended that they be sent away on "ships of stone with sails of lead," and preacher Billy Sunday recommended a firing squad to save money on the ships.

The antiradical campaign then sputtered out, in part because some of its followers went too far. For example, in January 1920 the New York State Assembly voted to expel five socialist members, even though they had been legally elected and had violated no rules or laws. The assembly's defiance of the democratic process aroused wide protests.

Although the red scare faded, fear of revolution lingered. Indeed, these fears put a halt to reformers' postwar plans. Skillful use of terms such as *un-American* or *Bolshevik* by reform opponents was enough to denounce any proposal. Plans for state-supported housing initiatives, health and unemployment insurance, and a social-security system received little support.

MAKING CONNECTIONS

The United States Constitution is designed to protect expression of most ideas—even those that are unpopular. Did the Palmer raids violate this design? At what point is it acceptable to limit political speech?

their arrest   American outrage

The Sacco and Vanzetti Case

The red scare played a part in one of the most controversial events in United States history. The story began on April 15, 1920, when gunmen robbed and killed the guard and paymaster of a South Braintree, Massachusetts, shoe factory. A few weeks later, police arrested two Italian immigrants, shoemaker **Nicola Sacco** and fish peddler **Bartolomeo Vanzetti**, in connection with the crimes. Both were carrying guns at the time of their arrest, and Sacco's was the same model used in the crime. They were convicted and sentenced to die.

At the time, many Americans felt that the trial of Sacco and Vanzetti was unfair. The two admitted to being anarchists, and it seemed clear that their political views—as well as their

The case of Sacco and Vanzetti, who are pictured below, inspired much protest, including this piece of folk art.

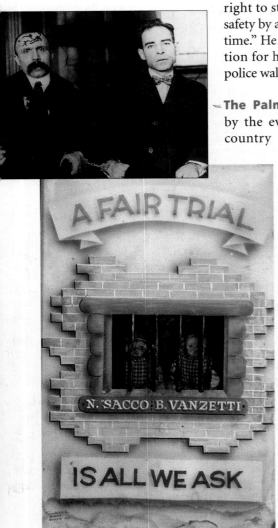

Italian heritage—had played a bigger role in their conviction than had any evidence against them. Appeals went on for years, but the original decision stood. In 1927, the two men were electrocuted.

The Sacco and Vanzetti case divided the country and provoked an international outcry. Some thought they were innocent. Others felt that, regardless of the pair's guilt or innocence, they had not been fairly tried. The two men, dignified to the end, went to their deaths comforted only by the thought that their fate would spark wider discussion of important issues. A writer who visited Vanzetti two days before his execution reported him as saying,

This is our career and our triumph. Never in our full life could we hope to do such work for tolerance, for justice, for man's understanding of man as we now do by accident.

Limit on Immigration
hostile environment

Renewed Isolationism and Nativism

Hostility to foreign people and ideas in the 1920s found expression in a renewed isolationism. The League of Nations was, as President Warren G. Harding said, "as dead as slavery." As for concerns about the security and safety of European countries, many Americans decided Europe would have to deal with them alone.

Nativism, a movement to limit immigration, first appeared in the 1800s. Not surprisingly, it revived after the war. Nativists now claimed that people from foreign countries could never be fully loyal to the United States.

When immigration swelled after the war, Congress reacted. In 1921, it limited annual immigration to 350,000 and set up quotas for certain nationalities. In 1924 it passed a law slashing immigration to 164,000. In addition to excluding Asians entirely, the law set quotas for each country at 2 percent of the total number of that country's immigrants living in the United States in 1890. The goal was to reduce immigration from southern and eastern Europe, for few immigrants from those countries had arrived in the United States before 1890. Nativists had long regarded these immigrants as undesirable, in part because of such cultural characteristics as their Catholic religion. (See Chapter 10.) As Washington congressman Albert Johnson declared in 1927,

The United States is our land. . . . We intend to maintain it so. The day of unalloyed [pure] welcome to all peoples, the day of indiscriminate acceptance of all races, has definitely ended.

Distrust of people and things "un-American," like the concerns over strikes and the spread of communism, contributed to a political climate that was hostile to reformers in the postwar years. But while the nation held firm against the invasion of ideas and people from abroad, individuals within the country were transforming the nation's political and social landscape.

This song, written in the 1920s, expressed the anti-immigration sentiment of the era.

SECTION 1 REVIEW

Key Terms, People, and Places
1. Define (a) communist, (b) general strike.

Key Concepts
2. How did the difficult postwar economic adjustments in the United States affect workers?
3. Who were the Bolsheviks?
4. What was the red scare?

5. Who were Sacco and Vanzetti, and why are they remembered?
6. Why did Congress restrict immigration in the 1920s?

Critical Thinking
7. **Expressing Problems Clearly** Summarize the obstacles facing those who wished to reintroduce reforms in the postwar United States.

The Decision to Restrict Immigration

Time Frame:	1917–1924
Place:	Washington, D.C.
Key People:	Members of United States Congress
Situation:	When some citizens strongly expressed their fear that new immigrants were threatening American character and institutions, Congress debated whether or not to control who would be allowed to enter the United States.

Congress has debated immigration policy every year since its first meeting in 1790. During World War I and in the years immediately after, the debate heated up. Congress faced strong pressure from the public to create an immigration policy that would severely restrict the numbers of newcomers from abroad.

Background to the Decision

Until the mid 1800s, most immigrants coming to the United States quickly blended in with old, established residents. Most of these immigrants to the United States came from western and northern Europe. They were culturally similar in many ways to the native-born descendants of America's first white settlers.

The "New" Immigrants Between 1880 and 1920 more than 23 million people left Europe to come to the United States. These "new" immigrants, as they were called, came from southern and eastern European countries such as Italy, Poland, and Russia. Their unfamiliar clothing, customs, and languages seemed "foreign" to many. Their religions were Catholicism, Orthodox Christianity, or Judaism—not Protestantism like most of the old immigrants. Many did not read or write any language, and few spoke English.

The new immigrants crowded into the cities. Some people blamed the growth of urban slums, the political corruption of cities, and other problems on the new immigrants. Others feared that they would take jobs away from "Americans."

The new immigrants, argued some, came from the most unstable parts of Europe—the places where the war had started and communism had been born. If newcomers did not already carry dangerous political ideas, many believed they were certainly vulnerable to these ideas. Furthermore, a number of respected scholars spread false notions that southern and eastern Europeans were inferior to other white people.

In Favor of Immigration Not everyone opposed immigration. To many, the United States was a "golden door" that all who wished to better themselves could enter.

THE ONLY WAY TO HANDLE IT.

Migration, jazz enjoyed a golden age. Singers Bessie Smith and Ma Rainey, pianist Duke Ellington, and trumpeter Louis "Satchmo" Armstrong became widely known performers.

Literary life among African Americans also flowered, part of a movement that came to be called the **Harlem Renaissance**. Publishers began printing novels and other writings by African American writers such as Countee Cullen, Zora Neale Hurston, Claude McKay, and Langston Hughes. Alain Locke's 1925 book titled *The New Negro* celebrated this development. Locke argued that being of both African and American heritage need not be a cause of conflict but rather of mutual enrichment.

The Garvey Movement New York City was home to another notable African American named **Marcus Garvey**. Garvey came to New York from his native Jamaica in 1916 to establish a new headquarters for his Universal Negro Improvement Association (UNIA). The UNIA sought to build up African Americans' self-respect. Its message of racial pride attracted masses of followers.

Garvey urged followers to return to "Motherland Africa." He also invested his followers' money in the Black Star steamship line. When Garvey oversold stock in this enterprise, he was jailed on fraud charges in 1925. The UNIA collapsed, but Garvey's ideas remained an inspiration to later "black pride" movements.

MAKING CONNECTIONS

Consider what you have read about postwar economic conditions in the United States. How might these conditions have contributed to the problems facing African Americans following their migration to the North?

A Decade of Republican Dominance

During the 1920s, the Republican party took a firm hold on the White House. One reason was that in the early 1920s, the economy began to rebound from the hard times that followed World War I. Industrial productivity soared, unemployment went down, and the number of strikes dropped. Voters gave the Republicans credit for the nation's recovery.

For the presidential election of 1920, Republican conservatives nominated **Warren G. Harding,** an Ohio senator. **Calvin Coolidge,** of the Boston police strike fame, was his running mate. The handsome, silver-haired Harding seemed the very picture of an American President, and many voters were attracted to his promise of a "return to normalcy." The Republicans overwhelmed the Democratic ticket of James Cox and Franklin D. Roosevelt.

A Scandal-Ridden Administration Harding, considered by many observers to be an "amiable second-rater," did make some good cabinet appointments, such as the highly regarded Herbert Hoover for secretary of commerce. Yet Harding also selected a number of unqualified friends for key posts. Some of these pals brought scandal down upon Harding's administration.

Harding himself did not have to deal with these troubles. He died on August 2, 1923, two-and-a-half years into his first term. By 1924, however, the full extent of the corruption in his administration was exposed. One Harding appointee had stolen government funds, others had taken payments in return for influence. Several other officials also were accused of wrongdoing, and two committed suicide.

The worst Harding scandal came to be known as **Teapot Dome**. It involved Harding's secretary of the interior, Albert B. Fall, who leased critical government oil reserves in Elk Hill, California, and Teapot Dome, Wyoming, to two private oil companies. In return, Fall received illegal payments and so-called loans that totaled over $300,000. Fall later went to jail for his role in the scandal.

The Democrats in 1924 tried to use public anger over the Teapot Dome affair to defeat the Republicans. The object below carried the Democratic message.

The Election of 1924 Voters apparently did not hold Vice President Calvin Coolidge responsible for these scandals. Following Harding's death, Coolidge completed the term. He then easily won his own election in 1924 over the Democratic ticket of John W. Davis and Charles Bryan and the Progressive candidate Bob La Follette.

YES, SIR, HE'S MY BABY!

Using Historical Evidence Calvin Coolidge, depicted here with a saxophone, was known for his support of big business. *What does this cartoon suggest about big business's reaction to Coolidge's policies?*

business, as the cartoon at left illustrates. "The chief business of the American people is business," he told a group of newspaper editors in 1925. Coolidge demonstrated his beliefs by raising tariffs. This helped American manufacturers by making foreign goods more expensive and American goods more attractive to buyers.

Coolidge was less willing to use the federal government to aid ordinary citizens. For example, he rejected aid for victims of a Mississippi River flood, saying that government had no duty to protect citizens "against the hazards of the elements."

The Election of 1928 As Coolidge neared the end of his first full term, he announced that he would not seek reelection in 1928. In his place, the Republicans nominated the well-respected **Herbert Hoover**. During and after World War I, Hoover achieved spectacular success running relief programs in Europe and the Food Administration in the United States. Later, he held cabinet posts in both the Harding and Coolidge administrations. Voters seemed to trust that he would provide sound leadership for the nation. Indeed, Hoover easily won election over the Democratic candidate, New York governor Al Smith.

In fact, the 1928 election returns did reveal some signs of weakness in the Republican armor, as you will read in Section 5. These political shifts, however, were subtle and hard to detect. Far more obvious were the dramatic changes in morals, manners, and fashion being flaunted by the energetic youth of the nation's growing urban centers.

"Silent Cal" Coolidge, as he was nicknamed, was a shy man known for using few words. His other memorable trait was an uncritical support for the interests of American

Key Terms, People, and Places
1. Define (a) Harlem Renaissance, (b) Teapot Dome.
2. Identify (a) Marcus Garvey, (b) Warren G. Harding, (c) Calvin Coolidge, (d) Herbert Hoover.

Key Concepts
3. What were some of the disappointments and successes of suffrage?
4. For what reasons did African Americans move north, and what was the result?
5. What factors helped lead to Republican success in the 1920s?

Critical Thinking
6. **Formulating Questions** What questions might you examine to determine whether or not African American migration in the early 1900s improved the lives of migrants generally?

New Manners, New Morals

SECTION PREVIEW

From rising hemlines to the energetic sounds of jazz, the 1920s daringly broke with tradition. New social freedoms created opportunity—and dilemmas—for women. But beneath it all lay a nagging question: How much had really changed?

Key Concepts

- Many American youth were eager for social changes after the war.
- The Jazz Age introduced many new tastes and manners, especially for women.
- The changes were not as widespread as presented in popular media.

Key Terms, People, and Places

Jazz Age, flapper

For many Americans, World War I was a watershed event. By bringing to a crashing close most of the monarchies of Europe, the war made the code of values and morals that they represented seem dreadfully old-fashioned. Many Americans longed to shed these old ideas and, with them, the horrors and disillusionment of World War I.

Young people were especially eager for change. They experimented with new social freedoms that took root first in the cities and then spread across the country. Yet, though the brash new ways of the urban youth became a symbol of the 1920s, many changes of the era turned out to be superficial.

Jazz Age Manners

Several factors contributed to the cultural changes taking place following World War I. As more youth finished high school and went on to college, they looked to each other rather than to their parents for standards of behavior. Soldiers returning home from the war brought new styles and habits to their hometowns. Advances in communications rapidly spread the emerging culture. (See Section 4.)

Along with the great postwar African American migration from the South to the North came jazz, blues, and Dixieland music, which quickly found a home in northern urban nightspots. The wide availability of phonograph records and record players meant that people could play the music wherever they gathered. Jazz had such a strong influence on the tastes and manners of the age that the 1920s became known as the **Jazz Age.**

The exciting rhythms of jazz captivated young people and blossomed on dance floors. Dance marathons—in which couples competed to see who could stay on the dance floor longest—became a popular fad. Young Americans let off steam in other zany ways as well: Flagpole sitting and goldfish eating became crazes during the 1920s.

Like jazz itself, most American dance rages of the early 1900s came from African American culture. As Carl Van Vechten, an admirer of black culture in the twenties, explained, the dances would start on street corners in African American communities, move into saloons and nightclubs, and from there onto the music-hall stage and into the larger culture. "This has been the history of the Cake-Walk, the Bunny Hug, the Turkey Trot, the Charleston, and the Black Bottom," he wrote, referring to several dances of the early 1900s.

Older generations mocked the new dances. A writer in 1920 sneered about how the youth of his day "trot like foxes, limp like lame ducks, . . . all to the barbaric yawp of strange instruments. . . ." But by mid-decade, critics celebrated

Jazz music, played on records and phonographs like these, lay at the heart of a dramatic change in fashion, manners, and morals.

During dance marathons in the 1920s, people frequently fainted from exhaustion. This 1928 marathon consisted of an 8-mile dance down the highway to a ballroom, where the marathon continued.

jazz as a positive force. Leopold Stokowski, a well-known symphony conductor, observed that jazz had "come to stay because it is an expression of the times, of the breathless, energetic, superactive times in which we are living."

Breaking Social Conventions in the Jazz Age

During the twenties, young men and women displayed growing freedom in their relations with one another. They dated without chaperones, talked slang, danced with their bodies touching, and in general defied the social conventions of the time. Poet Edna St. Vincent Millay voiced this youthful, some would say reckless, new spirit when she wrote:

My candle burns at both ends;
It will not last the night;
But ah, my foes, and, oh my friends—
It gives a lovely light.

"First Fig," 1920

Changes in fashion reflected the new morals and manners. Women's clothing became more revealing, exposing arms and knees. Makeup, once associated only with the stage and prostitutes, appeared on the faces of ordinary women for the first time.

The wider availability of cars in the 1920s shaped some aspects of youth behavior. Instead of meeting at a young woman's home, young men increasingly took their partners out on dates. In an automobile, they could escape all supervision. This development had far-reaching implications: Fearing a rise in sexually transmitted diseases and unwanted pregnancies, some teachers and social workers urged a more open discussion of sex.

The new freedoms, however, created a dilemma for many young women. In the twenties, women's behavior was still judged by stricter standards than men's. As a result, women were torn by conflicting social pressures that encouraged them both to adopt new standards of behavior and to adhere to old ones.

The Flapper The ultimate symbol of Jazz Age behavior was the youthful woman known as the **flapper**. The term came from a popular drawing of a dancing woman with her boots open and flapping. As author Preston Slosson observed in his 1930 work *The Great Crusade and After*, the flapper was

breezy, slangy, and informal in manner; slim and boyish in form; covered in silk and fur that clung to her as close as onion skin; with carmined [vivid red] cheeks and lips, plucked eyebrows and close-fitting helmet of hair; gay, plucky and confident.

Jazz Age men had their symbol, too—the "rake," with his careening automobile, reckless drinking, and irresponsible flirting. But the flapper became the more widely used symbol of the rebellious youth culture. Perhaps this was because standards of behavior for women had always been more constrained than for men. Thus, the new styles and manners seemed more startling when women adopted them.

MAKING CONNECTIONS

Compare the flapper to women from the suffrage or the abolition movements of the past or the feminist movement of recent years. In what ways are they similar and different?

How Widespread Was the New Youth Culture?

In reality, the urban youth culture represented by the flapper was not as widespread as the popular media suggested. Although the economy appeared healthy, deeply rooted problems, especially on the nation's farms, had many Americans worrying more about their economic survival than how to do the hottest new dance. Large numbers of young people did not rebel against traditional social and religious standards. Women everywhere experimented with cropped hair and short skirts, but many did so out of convenience rather than out of identification with flappers.

Reality for Women For women, especially, many of the new social freedoms turned out to be limited. Single women in large numbers moved into office, sales, and service jobs during the 1920s. Yet employers continued to assume that women were in the labor force only until they were married, and thus did not train them for advancement or pay them as well as men. Many hospitals and law firms refused to hire women physicians and lawyers.

Flappers defined a whole new style of dress and behavior.

| 1650 | 1700 | 1750 | 1800 | Links Across Time | 1850 | 1900 | 1950 | 2000 |

Women's Fashions

The flappers of the 1920s broke the mold of traditional dress for women. Over the course of history, women's clothing has undergone many such changes. In the late 1800s, for example, many women took pains to present an "hourglass" figure. Because few women possessed the desirable tiny waist naturally, they often wore restrictive corsets that were reinforced with whalebone for added stiffness. Usually, a helper was needed to pull the laces of the corset tight enough to reduce the waist as much as possible. These corsets restricted the abdomen so much that they were blamed by physicians for contributing to many kinds of internal health problems.

Within a few years, young women wanted to achieve just the opposite look—a boyish, straight silhouette. Fashion changes in the 1920s reflected new morals and manners among the nation's youth. Ankle-length dresses and cotton stockings gave way to short, tight dresses worn with silk stockings rolled down to the knees. Young women bobbed their long hair into short, boyish styles, often to the horror of their more traditional mothers.

Following World War II, the desire for stability in the 1950s home contributed to another fashion shift toward longer skirts and a return to the hourglass figure ideal. But then the social revolution of 1960s youth led again to a fashion revolution. For the first time, slacks were considered acceptable garb for women and hemlines rose again—this time to the previously unseen heights of the miniskirt. *What effects might accepted standards of beauty and fashion have on women?*

The number of married women combining work, careers, and family life also rose slowly during the 1920s. But married women's working lives remained restricted. Employers often fired white women when they became pregnant. African American women had different experiences. White employers expected—and their own economic need often required—that they work even after they became pregnant.

In spite of workplace inequalities, many women enjoyed the independence that came with a job. Yet many also felt the pull of traditional roles of wife and mother. Former suffragist Sue Shelton White expressed the dilemma as a choice "between the frying pan and the fire—both very uncomfortable."

The Impact of Technological Change For the majority of women, it was technological change more than flapperism or jazz that seemed to promise real liberation. Thanks to cars, women could more easily shop for food. As manufacturers lowered prices for electrical products and as merchants introduced installment-plan buying, more women bought sewing machines, vacuum cleaners, and other labor-saving devices.

These developments eased life, but by no means freed women from drudgery. In fact, they raised expectations of household work. Kitchens and clothes now could be—and thus had to be—spotless. "By Their Floors Ye Shall Judge Them," warned a floor-polisher ad. "It is written that floors are like unto a mirror, reflecting the character of the housewife."

Of course, technological change in the 1920s changed more than the ways women did housework. Enormous changes in communications technology helped to create a whole new culture.

Using Historical Evidence Thanks to new electrical appliances, the nature of housework changed, but the demands on women remained. *What does this ad suggest about the responsibilities of women?*

SECTION 3 REVIEW

Key Terms, People, and Places
1. Define flapper.

Key Concepts
2. What factors led many Americans to challenge existing social norms following World War I?
3. Why did the Jazz Age changes in manners appear to have a greater impact on women than on men?

4. How far-reaching were Jazz Age changes? Explain.

Critical Thinking
5. **Demonstrating Reasoned Judgment** "The developments of the 1920s, including the changing manners and the technological developments of the era, were a mixed blessing for women." Explain the meaning of this statement.

Analyzing Advertisements

Print advertisements—ads that appear as posters or in newspapers and magazines—offer important visual evidence about the consumer goods and services that were promoted during a historical period. Advertisements also can offer useful clues to the widely held ideas, attitudes, and values of the past. When using advertisements as historical evidence, however, it is important to bear in mind that advertisers rely on many different types of techniques in order to influence people's buying decisions. Ads may reflect certain lifestyles to which advertisers want consumers to aspire, rather than lifestyles that reflect reality for the majority of people during a certain historical period.

By the 1920s, the previously straightforward "what-it-is and what-it-does" mode of advertising was giving way to "situational" ads. These ads depicted not only the products, but also the ways in which those products might increase personal satisfaction or enhance the lives of typical consumers. One such advertisement from the 1920s appears at right.

Use the following steps to analyze the ad.

1. Identify the subject of the ad. (a) What product or service is being promoted? (b) What facts about the product does the ad provide? (c) What issue does this advertisement use to appeal particularly to men? To women?

2. Analyze the ad's reliability as historical evidence. (a) Do you think that the people depicted in the ad portray typical consumers of the 1920s? Explain. (b) What is the unstated message that the advertiser is using in this case to persuade people to buy the product?

3. Study the ad to learn more about the historical period. (a) What social or cultural values are being promoted in the advertisement? (b) In general, do you think that advertisements reflect consumers' desires for products or create the desire for such products? Explain.

—and he wonders why she said "NO!"

 Could he have read her thoughts he would not have lost her. A picture of neatness herself, she detested slovenliness. And not once, but many times, she had noticed his ungartered socks crumpling down around his shoe tops. To have to apologize to her friends for a husband's careless habits was too much to ask. So she had to say "NO"—and in spite of his pleading couldn't tell him WHY.

No SOX Appeal Without

 PARIS GARTERS
SINGLE GRIP — DOUBLE GRIP
NO METAL CAN TOUCH YOU
25c to $2
Dress Well and Succeed

Creating a Shared Culture

SECTION PREVIEW

People in city apartments, country farmhouses, and everywhere in between were connected in new ways in the 1920s. Such links allowed sweeping changes to envelop the entire nation.

Key Concepts
- Population movements and new developments in communications and transportation helped create a culture common to many Americans.
- Developments in radio, movies, advertising, and the automobile industry furthered the process of creating a national culture.

Key Terms, People, and Places
Charles A. Lindbergh, Henry Ford

Caps like this were worn by aviators in the 1920s. Heroes of aviation, as well as sports and movies, were products of the new entertainment media.

Change—resisted by some and welcomed by others—remained a constant force during the 1920s. During this decade, 14.6 million Americans moved from rural to urban areas and from one state to another. This included the migration of African Americans described in Section 2.

As people moved, they interacted with people in other regions to an extent never before possible. In addition, expanding mass media and advances in transportation led to a wider sharing of tastes, values, and experiences among people all across the country.

Americans at Leisure

Partly as the result of decades of union campaigns for shorter hours, the average factory workweek in the mid-1920s was just over fifty hours, down from nearly sixty hours in 1900. Men and women began exploring new ways to spend their growing leisure time. Industry and commerce stood ready to meet this need.

The Radio In 1920, only about twenty thousand people using homemade sets were receiving wireless radio messages. As an experiment, Frank Conrad of the Westinghouse Company in East Pittsburgh began to broadcast recorded music and baseball scores over the radio. The response was so great that the company began broadcasting new programs on a regular basis. By the fall of 1920, the country had its first radio station operated as a commercial enterprise, Pittsburgh's KDKA.

By 1922, over five hundred stations had formed, with newspapers controlling about a quarter of them. Listeners could now hear music, news, sports events, and religious services over the air. To reach more people, networks such as the National Broadcasting Company (NBC) brought together many individual stations, and each station in the network played the same programming. Soon much of the country was sharing the same jokes, commercials, and music.

The Movies By 1917, the movies had become big business. Luxury movie theaters began to replace storefront nickelodeons. As with radio, corporate giants took control. The studios of

Households with Radios, 1920–1930

Year	Number of Households with Radio Sets
1920	20,000
1922	60,000
1924	1,250,000
1926	4,500,000
1928	8,000,000
1930	13,750,000

Source: *Historical Statistics of the United States*

Interpreting Tables
Radio—once the hobby of a few dedicated enthusiasts—soon became a household fixture. *What industries probably benefited from the growth in the number of household radios?*

Metro-Goldwyn-Mayer, Warner Brothers, and Columbia dominated the field. Talkies—movies with sound—arrived in 1927 with *The Jazz Singer,* starring stage performer Al Jolson. By 1930, patrons were buying 100 million movie tickets a week.

MAKING CONNECTIONS

What leisure activities are important to young people today? In what ways are these activities similar to or different from the leisure activities of the 1920s?

The Worship of National Idols

The new entertainment media helped create national idols. The American people, eager for someone to look up to after the trauma of World War I, embraced them. From the movies, the ever-innocent Mary Pickford became America's Sweetheart; Clara Bow, the It Girl—a "good girl" who had "it," or sexual allure. Charlie Chaplin was the Little Tramp, and Rudolph Valentino, the Sheik.

Sports Heroes After the movie stars came sports figures. Among the most famous were Babe Ruth, the New York Yankee hitter of sixty home runs in 1927; prizefighters Jack Dempsey and Gene Tunney; and Gertrude Ederle, the first woman to swim the English Channel.

Lindbergh's Historic Flight The decade's ultimate hero, **Charles A. Lindbergh,** was from Minnesota. Lindbergh was a stunt flyer and air-mail pilot. In May 1927, the twenty-five-year-old competed for a $25,000 prize offered to the first aviator to fly nonstop across the Atlantic Ocean from New York to Paris. Except for a team of two flyers who landed in a sleepy Irish bog in 1919, everyone else attempting the crossing had crashed or disappeared.

Flying his *Spirit of St. Louis* with a dangerous overload of fuel, struggling through ice storms and fatigue, Lindbergh managed to cross the great ocean and land safely on May 21 at Le Bourget airfield near Paris. He became an instant hero. A poem in the *New York*

Sun ignored the industrial know-how that had made his flight possible and celebrated Lindbergh as the ultimate lone conqueror:

> *No kingly plane for him;*
> *No endless data, com-*
>   *rades, moneyed chums;*
> *No boards, no councils,*
>   *no directors grim—*
> *He plans ALONE and*
>   *takes luck as it comes.*

To many Americans, the tall, handsome, independent Lindbergh came to symbolize their national spirit. *The New Republic* declared, he is "ours. . . . He is no longer permitted to be himself. He is US personified. He is the United States."

Daring Charles Lindbergh, who was the first aviator to fly nonstop across the Atlantic Ocean, embodied the American ideal of the lone conqueror.

Selling New Products and Ideas

While many Americans were adoring the same heroes, other aspects of their daily lives also became increasingly similar. Chain supermarkets spread, along with products known mostly by brand names. The A&P grocery chain, which had 5,000 stores in 1922, had 15,500 by 1929. The nation's first shopping center (in Kansas City) and first fast-food chain (A & W Root Beer) appeared in the twenties. Soon people across the country were shopping in the same stores for the same goods.

The advertising industry boomed, rising to the challenge of selling the country's many new products. Agents and salesmen grew from 11,000 in 1910 to 25,000 in 1920. Through advertising, products became synonymous with brand names. Paper hankies became "Kleenex," record players became "Victrolas."

In aggressive campaigns, advertisers convinced people that they needed to buy new products. When the Lambert Company discovered it could sell more Listerine as a cure for bad breath than as a general antiseptic, its advertising agents introduced the term *halitosis*—a new

Cars were assembled by dozens of workers as they passed by on a conveyor.

Even the detailed and skillful work of upholstering seats was performed on an assembly line.

Model T bodies moved down a slide to be fitted on the chassis.

Each worker on the line performed the same step over and over.

Henry Ford's ingenious production methods were based on two key ideas: the assembly line and uniformity of product. The assembly line, shown above, broke down car production into precise steps. Uniformity of product held that each car should be identical—an idea never before applied to such complicated machinery.

"scientific" word for an age-old problem. "What secret is your mirror holding back?" ads asked. "Even your best friend won't tell you."

Manufacturers put huge amounts of money into advertising. In 1922 Lambert's advertising budget came to $100,000. By 1928, it was spending $5 million and still raking in huge profits.

An Affordable Automobile

The automobile, invented in the 1890s, came of age in the 1920s. Over the decade, the number of registered automobiles rose from 8 million to over 23 million.

By freeing individuals to set their own schedules, automobiles individualized travel. People who were not wealthy traveled more often and over greater distances. To accommodate them, the government built new road systems, parks, and beaches for everyone, not just the rich. These developments had a powerful impact on the economy, stimulating the construction, rubber, gasoline and petroleum, advertising, and tourist industries.

The United States owed much of the boom in the auto industry to one man. His genius helped revolutionize industry at the same time that it changed the face of the nation itself.

AMERICAN PROFILES

Henry Ford

Henry Ford was born on a Michigan farm in 1863. Early in life he showed an aptitude for

things mechanical, and he seemed destined for a career working with machines.

In the late 1880s, while an engineer at the Detroit Illuminating Company, Ford began working on a horseless carriage powered by an engine. In 1896 he produced a "quadricycle," the lightest of the current gasoline-driven models. Ford started his own company in 1903 to manufacture automobiles. By 1910, he was selling over thirty thousand of his Model T's.

Pioneering Production Methods Ford had even higher ambitions. He wanted to "democratize the automobile," producing more cars at prices ordinary people could afford. Toward this end, he developed the revolutionary assembly line illustrated above.

Ford's system worked. By making large numbers of identical automobiles in an identical way, Ford could take advantage of the economy of scale to lower his costs for producing each car. In 1914, the first year his assembly line was fully operational, his company sold 248,000 cars at $490 each, almost half of what a car had cost in 1910. The following year he dropped the price to $390. By the early 1920s he was producing 60 percent of the nation's automobiles. He led the world market as well.

Others improved upon Ford's success. In the mid-twenties, General Motors surpassed Ford by introducing the Chevrolet in colors. Ford had failed to grasp the growing impor-

Even small items such as wheels were assembled separately.

Henry Ford (above) began his career when horseless carriages like this were state of the art.

tance of style and color to the American people. He joked that his customers could get their "Tin Lizzies" in any color they liked, as long as it was black. But in 1927, Ford began producing a new car, the Model A, in colors.

Running the Business In 1914, Ford had won praise by introducing the five-dollar-a-day pay rate for many of his workers, double what other factories paid. Yet Ford was not always well regarded by his workers. He was notorious for authorizing the use of spies and violence in an effort to combat unions in his plants.

Ford ruled his business like a dictator. "We expect the men to do what they are told," he explained in his 1922 book, *My Life and Work.*

The organization is so highly specialized and one part is so dependent upon another that we could not for a moment consider allowing men to have their own way. . . . Anyone who does not like to work in our way may always leave.

Ford's reputation also suffered when, in 1920, he allowed his newspaper, the *Dearborn Independent,* to engage in an anti-Semitic campaign. The attacks on Jews upset many people.

Ford's outbursts were a symptom of the age. Upset by social and moral changes of which he disapproved, Ford found a scapegoat in the Jews. As the next section discusses, he was not the only person to reach out for such simplistic solutions.

SECTION 4 REVIEW

Key Terms, People, and Places

1. Identify (a) Charles A. Lindbergh, (b) Henry Ford.

Key Concepts

2. How did commerce and industry respond to the increase in leisure time in the twenties?
3. How did the expanded advertising industry affect the American consumer?

4. What was the impact of easily available automobiles on American society?
5. What were the key features of Ford's assembly line?

Critical Thinking

6. **Recognizing Cause and Effect** How did the growth of mass media, such as radio and movies, lead to the creation of national heroes?

Stemming the Tide of Change

SECTION PREVIEW

Jazz music, moving pictures, fast cars—American life moved at a dizzying pace in the 1920s. All the motion left some people feeling queasy, and they sought to slow the pace of change.

Key Concepts

- Prohibition, censorship, the growth of the Ku Klux Klan, and other developments reflected a desire to slow the changes in morals and manners in the 1920s.
- Some artists responded to the changes in the nation with despair and self-exile.
- The 1928 election dramatically demonstrated the social and political divisions in the United States.

Key Terms, People, and Places

speakeasies, bootlegging, fundamentalism, Scopes trial; T. S. Eliot, F. Scott Fitzgerald

Prohibition forced many beer companies to find new beverages to brew. Above are labels from such products.

T he social and cultural changes taking place in the United States in the 1920s were exhilarating to many people. Other Americans, however, were quite alarmed at what they saw as the nation's moral and intellectual decay.

Moral Controls

Throughout United States history, various groups had worked for the prohibition of alcoholic beverages. In 1919, prohibitionists finally achieved their goal with the ratification of the Eighteenth Amendment to the Constitution. The amendment outlawed the making, selling, transporting, importing, or exporting of any intoxicating beverages.

Prohibition's supporters believed that the Eighteenth Amendment would stop people from drinking alcohol. They thought some of the most undesirable features of modern urban life might thus be curbed. As preacher Billy Sunday declared,

> T he reign of tears is over. The slums will soon be only a memory. We will turn our prisons into factories and our jails into storehouses and corncribs. Men will walk upright now. Women will smile and children will laugh. Hell will be forever for rent.

Prohibition in Practice The use of alcohol did decrease for a few years after 1919, especially among the poor. Prohibition, however, proved impossible to enforce. Congressman Thomas Spencer Crago of Pennsylvania had predicted that the attempt to enforce prohibition would breed "a discontent and disrespect for law in this country beyond anything we have ever witnessed before." He was right. For many, openly defying prohibition was almost fun. Others only pretended to comply, sneaking liquor into their homes or slinking off to **speakeasies,** bars where liquor was served illegally.

During prohibition, many crooks made fortunes **bootlegging**—smuggling liquor across the border from Canada, shipping it from the West Indies or Mexico, or distilling their own moonshine. Organized gangs, the most famous of which was Al Capone's in Chicago, fought to gain control over the illegal but highly profitable traffic in liquor. Designed to wipe out crime, prohibition created new ones. By decade's end, many people began to call for reform.

Morality at the Movies In an effort to draw bigger audiences, filmmakers in the early 1920s began to include more sexually explicit content. This development prompted a movement to control the industry. To avoid censorship from outside the movies, filmmakers decided to censor themselves. In 1922, they set up their own organization, which devised a production code for movies that limited the amount of love-making, bare skin, and crime a film could show.

Laws for the Dance Floor Considered a sign of the decay of modern morals, dancing to that "Unspeakable Jazz" aroused widespread criticism in the early 1920s. "Anyone who says that 'youths of both sexes can mingle in close embrace'—with limbs intertwined and torso in contact—without suffering harm lies," accused a writer in the *Ladies Home Journal* in 1921.

To discourage close dancing, respectable dance halls required couples to remain six inches apart and ceased moonlight dances—those with the lights turned low. By 1929, cities and states across the country had passed over three hundred laws to control dancing and dance halls. Most were easily evaded.

MAKING CONNECTIONS

Consider some of the laws that regulate behavior today. Do you think these laws will still be enforced in one hundred years? Explain.

Controls on Beliefs

During the early twentieth century, the rising prestige of science, changing social roles for women, and social gospel reform movements challenged many traditional religious beliefs. In reaction, religious traditionalists published a series of pamphlets called *The Fundamentals.* These tracts, which appeared between 1909 and 1914, insisted that every word in the Bible was inspired by God, and that every biblical story was literally true. The pamphlets gave birth to a religious movement called **fundamentalism.**

The Scopes Trial In 1923 and 1924, fundamentalist legislators in at least twelve states introduced laws to ban the teaching of evolution in the public schools. *Evolution* is the name for Charles Darwin's theory, put forward in 1859, that holds that humans and all other species developed over time from lower to more complex forms. Fundamentalists argued that the theory of evolution contradicted biblical accounts of the creation of the world.

Viewpoints
On the Eighteenth Amendment

Flagrant violations of prohibition led to loud cries for reform, or repeal of the Eighteenth Amendment. The speakers below are addressing a Senate committee investigating violations of the law. *What basic value underlies each argument?*

For Reform or Repeal of the National Prohibition Act
"It is impossible to tell whether prohibition is a good thing or a bad thing. It has never been enforced in this country. . . . I will concede that the saloon was odious [offensive], *but now we have delicatessen stores, pool rooms, drug stores, millinery shops, private parlors, and 57 other varieties of speakeasies selling liquor and flourishing."*
New York congressman Fiorello La Guardia, 1926

Against Reform or Repeal of the National Prohibition Act
"Permit me to show another side of the picture, and propose that instead of lowering our standards, we urge that the law be strengthened. . . . The closing of the open saloon . . . has resulted in better national health, children are born under better conditions, homes are better, and the mother is delivered from the fear of a drunken husband."
Ella A. Boole, president of the
National Woman's Christian Temperance Union, 1926

Several states passed an antievolution law. The American Civil Liberties Union (ACLU), however, felt that the laws violated the Constitution. In 1925, the ACLU announced that it would defend any teacher willing to challenge the statutes. John T. Scopes, a young high school biology teacher from Dayton, Tennessee, accepted. He read to his class a description of Darwin's theory. His arrest followed.

Thanks to radio, the **Scopes trial** became a national sensation. Famed lawyer Clarence Darrow headed the ACLU defense team. Former presidential candidate William Jennings Bryan defended the antievolution law. The climax came when Bryan insisted that everything in the Bible was literally true. Darrow got Bryan to admit that even he interpreted figuratively some biblical stories and ideas. Bryan, widely ridiculed, died soon after the trial.

Because Scopes had violated the law, the trial jury convicted him and imposed a one-hundred

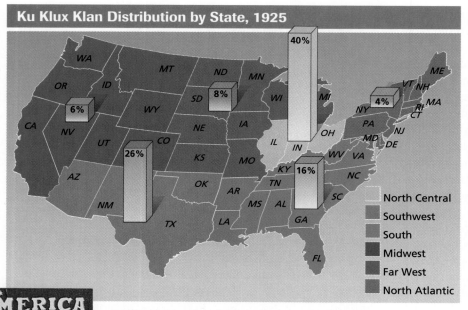

Ku Klux Klan Distribution by State, 1925

40%
8%
6%
4%
26%
16%

North Central
Southwest
South
Midwest
Far West
North Atlantic

AMERICA for Americans

🌐 **Geography and History: Interpreting Maps**
The resurgence of the Ku Klux Klan in the 1920s occurred in all corners of the country. *In which regions was the Klan the strongest? The weakest?*

dollar fine. The Tennessee Supreme Court threw out the fine—and a chance to test the law's constitutionality—on a technicality. The United States Supreme Court has since ruled, however, that similar laws violate the Constitution by promoting certain religious views. Nevertheless, debate over the proper place of evolution theory in American education continues today.

A Campaign of Political Action and Terror
In June 1920, the Ku Klux Klan (KKK), which had revived in 1915, launched a recruitment campaign using mass-marketing techniques of the advertising age. By October 1921, it had 85,000 new recruits. At its high point in the 1920s, the Klan boasted membership of between three and five million.

The Klan's political power extended across the country. In Oklahoma, Klan votes removed an anti-Klan governor. In Oregon, they dealt a blow to Catholic schools by getting a law passed requiring all children to attend public schools. In the South, they terrorized African Americans, and in the Southwest, pursued violators of prohibition. In the Northeast and West, they targeted Jews. They also went after Catholics, then 36 percent of the population and pre-

sumed by the Klan to be more loyal to their Pope than to the United States.

The Klan's goal was to restore white Protestants to a dominant place in American society and to halt the nation's so-called moral decline. According to the KKK's Imperial Wizard Hiram Wesley Evans, the Klan by 1926 was well on its way toward success. "When the Klan first appeared," he wrote, "the invasion of aliens and alien ideas" had brought about the destruction of cherished moral values. "After ten years of the Klan [the nation] is in arms for defense," Evans boasted.

The Klan movement of the 1920s collapsed suddenly under the weight of its violent nature. In 1928 the Grand Dragon of Indiana, David Stephenson, was jailed on second-degree murder charges. Stephenson took revenge on the politicians who failed to get him released by revealing the extent of Klan influence and political corruption in the state. Stephenson's revelations caused a scandal that broke the movement, at least for a time.

A Different Form of Social Protest

Efforts at moral, intellectual, and political control were not the only responses to the changes taking place in the United States in the 1920s. Some rebellious spirits were critical of their times for completely different reasons.

Before World War I, in urban artistic colonies such as New York City's Greenwich Village, artists and intellectuals had created hotbeds for discussion of new ideas in politics, theater, art, literature, and music. These thinkers felt themselves to be on the brink of artistic and intellectual triumph over nineteenth-century values and ideals. Then came World War I, a conflict of such brutality that belief in human progress seemed impossible to these artists. Following that came a period in which unconventional ideas were denounced as radical. Disillusioned, a whole group of artists turned against their culture, depicting it in biting satires or choosing, instead, to flee from it altogether.

Poet Ezra Pound wrote of "a botched civilization." **T. S. Eliot's** "The Waste Land" became the symbolic poem of the generation. Novelist **F. Scott Fitzgerald** wrote of the youth of his times as "the beautiful and the damned." His 1925 masterpiece, *The Great Gatsby*, exposed what he saw as the shallow self-involvement and illusions of the Jazz Age rich.

To these disillusioned artists, old ideals no longer inspired faith. Progressivism and related reform ideas now seemed dull. "If I am convinced of anything," journalist H. L. Mencken wrote, "It is that Doing Good is in bad taste."

Rejecting the American mass culture and ethic of success, some artists went into self-exile, many to Paris. Soon, they found it just as hard to live there. Ironically, when they came back, some got jobs in advertising or the book trade, the very businesses they had earlier despised.

The Election of 1928 Reflects the Conflicts of the Era

No single event more dramatically reflected the divisions of the era than the presidential election of 1928. On the Democratic side was New York governor Al Smith, a Roman Catholic from a family of recent immigrants, and a "wet," or opponent of prohibition. Smith's formal education had ended at the eighth grade. But after New York's Democratic political machine, Tammany Hall, got him a seat in the New York State Assembly, Smith educated himself and became a champion of workers' rights. Because of his record in New York, Smith in 1928 had the support of many progressives—even though he was a product of Tammany Hall, which progressives despised.

The Republicans ran Herbert Hoover, a Protestant Quaker from West Branch, Iowa; a Stanford-educated friend of big business; and a "dry," or supporter of prohibition. In contrast to Smith, who was a fiery campaigner, Hoover was dull but polished. He was especially popular among women voters.

For the first time, radio played an extensive role in an election. Over the airwaves, Hoover came across as moderate, sensible, and trustworthy. In contrast, Smith's thick New York City accent made him sound uneducated and brash to many audiences. Smith also suffered the effects of an anti-Catholic propaganda campaign that sought to raise fears among voters about Smith's loyalty to the United States.

These factors—combined with the widespread though not entirely accurate belief that the economy was strong—gave Hoover a landslide victory. Yet Hoover's win did hide some dark clouds on the Republican horizon. Smith carried the nation's twelve largest cities, an important development in the increasingly urban United States. He also broke into the midwestern belt of unhappy, indebted farmers, who were experiencing economic hard times in spite of the nation's apparent prosperity.

From the vantage point of 1928, however, Hoover's victory seemed decisive. Indeed, with the election over, the roar of the 1920s seemed to quiet down. Yet it would not be long before it would rise again—this time driven by panic.

SECTION 5 REVIEW

Key Terms, People, and Places
1. Define (a) speakeasy, (b) bootlegging, (c) fundamentalism.

Key Concepts
2. For what reasons did Prohibition fail?
3. What attempts were made in the 1920s to control morals, and how successful were they?
4. Explain the facts and significance of the Scopes trial.

5. What were some of the goals of the Ku Klux Klan in the 1920s?
6. What group do T. S. Eliot and F. Scott Fitzgerald represent?

Critical Thinking
7. **Demonstrating Reasoned Judgment** In what ways did the 1928 election reflect the social and political divisions of the era?

Chapter Review

Key Terms
1. communist
2. red scare
3. general strike
4. Harlem Renaissance
5. Teapot Dome
6. Jazz Age
7. flapper
8. speakeasies
9. bootlegging
10. fundamentalism
11. Scopes trial

People
12. Vladimir I. Lenin
13. Nicola Sacco
14. Bartolomeo Vanzetti
15. Marcus Garvey
16. Warren G. Harding
17. Calvin Coolidge
18. Herbert Hoover
19. Charles A. Lindbergh
20. Henry Ford
21. T. S. Eliot
22. F. Scott Fitzgerald

Terms For each term above, write a sentence that explains its relation to the social and technological changes that took place in the 1920s.

Matching Review the key terms in the list above. If you are not sure of a term's meaning, review its definition in the chapter. Then choose a term from the list that best matches each description below.
1. bars where liquor was served illegally
2. youthful woman symbolizing the spirit of the 1920s
3. smuggling or distilling liquor illegally
4. period when artistic life flowered among African Americans

True or False Determine whether each statement is true or false. If it is true, write "true." If it is false. change the underlined person or place to make the statement true.
1. <u>Warren G. Harding</u> sought to build up African Americans' self-respect and racial pride.
2. Many people believed that shoemaker <u>Nicola Sacco</u> had been unfairly tried because of his Italian heritage and political views.
3. <u>T. S. Eliot</u>'s novel *The Great Gatsby* exposed what he saw as the self-involvement of the Jazz Age.
4. <u>Bartolomeo Vanzetti</u> became a national hero after his solo flight across the Atlantic Ocean.

Section 1 (pp. 446 – 449)
1. Briefly describe conditions in the American economy in the first few years following World War I.
2. What events of 1919 led many Americans to fear that the Russian Revolution would spread to the United States? How did politicians respond?
3. How did Congress limit immigration in the 1920s?

Section 2 (pp. 452 – 456)
4. Why did women's votes fail to change politics as much as suffragists had hoped?
5. Describe the general experience of African American migrants to the North in the postwar years.
6. In what sense was the 1920s a "Republican decade"?

Section 3 (pp. 457 – 460)
7. In what ways did young people defy social conventions after World War I?

8. How did changes in fashion for women reflect the new morals and manners of the Jazz Age?
9. How were new social possibilities still limited for women during the Jazz Age?

Section 4 (pp. 462 – 465)
10. How did the growth of leisure time help lead to the creation of a national culture?
11. What role did chain supermarkets, advertisers, and fast-food chains play in creating a common culture?
12. How did Henry Ford "democratize the automobile"?

Section 5 (pp. 466 – 469)
13. Briefly describe some of the efforts to control Americans' morals and beliefs in the 1920s.
14. Why were many writers disillusioned in the 1920s?
15. In what ways did the election of 1928 reflect the divisions of the era?

1. **Recognizing Ideologies** During the 1920s, terms such as "un-American" and "Bolshevik" were used to ignite people's fears and obscure complex issues. Describe terms that play a similar role today.

2. **Demonstrating Reasoned Judgment** "For many African Americans, the migration to the North was a mixed success." Explain the meaning of this statement.

3. **Distinguishing False from Accurate Images** The flapper was a popular image of the 1920s that, in fact, represented only a small number of American women. Are there symbols that represent the present era? If so, what are they? What role does the media play in promoting this image? Who does the image truly represent?

1. **Evaluating Primary Sources** Review the primary source excerpt on page 465. If you were a business manager, what would be your opinion of this method of running a business? If you were a worker? If you were running a business, would you emphasize creativity or efficiency? What are the benefits and drawbacks of each approach?

2. **Understanding the Visuals** Write a short paragraph explaining how the information in the graph on page 447 and the photo of sheet music on page 449 are related.

3. **Writing About the Chapter** You are a newspaper editor in the early 1920s. Write an editorial in which you offer your opinion about the outcome of the Sacco and Vanzetti case. Before you begin, review the chapter for details about the red scare and the treatment of immigrants, and consider how these factors might have influenced the trial. As you write a draft of your editorial, consider the following questions: Is there any valid reason to consider Sacco and Vanzetti's political beliefs in their trial? What if Sacco and Vanzetti are in fact guilty—does it matter whether they received a fair trial? Proofread your work and draft a final copy.

4. **Using the Graphic Organizer** This graphic organizer uses a web to organize information about the changes in technology and culture that took place in the 1920s. Webs often can show connections between seemingly unconnected ideas. In this web, dotted lines are used to show these connections.
(a) Based on what you have read in the chapter, what is the connection between increased leisure time and the rise in popularity of the radio and movies?
(b) According to the graphic organizer below, what did chain stores and the auto industry have in common in the 1920s? (c) On a separate sheet of paper, create your own graphic organizer about the new manners and social freedoms that arose during the Jazz Age.

THE JAZZ AGE

No music was more important to an era than jazz was to the 1920s. This unique American music grew from the culture of southern African Americans and traveled north with them. Jazz was more than mere music, however. Much of the country's youth—African American and white—saw jazz as the symbol of their new generation. *Compare the importance of jazz in the 1920s with the importance of "rock and roll" to later generations.*

▲1930s RADIO Radio, more than any other medium, made jazz familiar to the American public. The jazz heard on the radio was adapted by all-white bands to appeal to largely white audiences.

▲ DUKE ELLINGTON The jazz clubs of Harlem and Chicago were one of the few places where African American musicians could perform their music for white audiences. Duke Ellington, pictured on the sheet music of one of his famous compositions, became a Harlem headliner in 1923.

DIZZIE GILLESPIE'S ▶ TRUMPET Jazz musicians developed their own playing styles and unique signatures. Dizzy Gillespie, whose bent horn distinguished him from other trumpet players, pioneered the modern jazz and bebop styles. His career, which began in the 1930s, spanned seven decades.

472

◀ HYMIE SHERTZER
The well-known sax-
ophonist worked
with many bands
as well as in
recording
studios and
in radio.

FLAPPER'S DRESS ▶
AND BEADS The symbol of
the Jazz Age was the flapper
with her "jazz style" clothes. The
flapper's short skirts, silk stockings, and fake jewelry were new
and daring, shocking many in the
older generation. Flapper clothes
were a must for doing the newest
dances to jazz music.

◀
SHERTZER'S
SAXOPHONE
The saxophone
was invented in
Europe in 1840
but never became
a popular orchestral
instrument. Musicians
like Shertzer, however, made the sax's
smooth, easily blended sound one of the
major voices of the jazz band.

◀BENNY GOODMAN'S
CLARINET Known as the "King of
Swing," Goodman began his jazz career in
1926. His "big band" helped make jazz
popular with white audiences, but he preferred small groups. Goodman's 1936
trio with African American musicians
Lionel Hampton and Teddy Wilson
was the first popular racially
mixed jazz group. Goodman
was also a classical performer
who made recordings with
leading symphony
orchestras.

◀ 1920s JAZZ BAND
Most jazz artists strug-
gled to earn a living and
remained anonymous.
This band, which was
photographed in St. Louis
in the 1920s, is unidenti-
fied. The band played the
New Orleans style jazz.

473

Crash and Depression
1929–1933

*T*he surface prosperity of the late 1920s hid deep faults in the American economy. When stock prices began to fall in October 1929, panic brought the economy crashing down. The United States sank into a long-lasting depression that brought widespread suffering. President Hoover's policies proved ineffective in turning the economy around, so Americans were eager to hear presidential candidate Franklin D. Roosevelt's proposals. In the 1932 election, voters chose Roosevelt, marking a major turning point in American history.

Events in the United States

1928 The automobile, steel, rubber, glass, and housing industries are in recession.

1929 Stock market hits record high in September, then crashes in October.

1931 Empire State Building opens in New York, becoming the world's tallest skyscraper.

1928	1929	1930	1931

Events in the World

1928 Fifteen nations sign the Kellogg-Briand Pact renouncing war.

1930 U.S., Britain, Japan, France, and Italy sign naval disarmament treaty.

1931 Japanese troops occupy Manchuria.
• Spain is declared a republic.

1932 Veterans in the Bonus Army protest in Washington, D.C.

1933 Prohibition is repealed.
• Franklin D. Roosevelt is inaugurated as President.

1934 Farm families leave drought-stricken Great Plains and move west to California.

1932   **1933**   **1934**   **1935**

1932 Amelia Earhart is the first woman to fly solo across the Atlantic.

1934 Nationalists force communists under Mao Zedong into "Long March" across China.

The Economy in the Late 1920s

SECTION PREVIEW

Optimism and faith in business continued throughout the 1920s. But while many were buying goods on credit and investing in the booming stock market, millions more had no share in the country's prosperity.

Key Concepts
- Voters believed Herbert Hoover's administration would continue the good times.
- The government and many people believed that business prosperity served national interests.
- People went into debt to buy products and to invest in the stock market.
- Farmers and many industrial workers did not share in the general prosperity of the 1920s.

Key Terms, People, and Places

real wages, welfare capitalism, installment buying, speculation, buy on margin

During the 1920s catalogs brimming with new goods tempted consumers to buy on credit.

T he mood of most Americans in the late 1920s was optimistic, and for good reason. Medical advances had greatly reduced deaths from whooping cough, diphtheria, and other serious diseases. Since 1900, the number of infant deaths had declined, and life expectancy had lengthened more than 10 years, to 59 years for men and 63 years for women.

The brightest hopes seemed to come from the economy. In his final message to Congress, President Calvin Coolidge said that the country could "regard the present with satisfaction and anticipate the future with optimism." His successor, Herbert Hoover, predicted that "poverty will be banished from this nation."

The Economy Inspires Trust

Coolidge chose not to run in 1928, but years of prosperity under the Republicans made victory easy for Hoover. A self-made millionaire, Hoover was widely admired for the way he had organized food relief in Europe during and after World War I. He had also been an effective secretary of commerce for Presidents Harding and Coolidge. People expected that the good times would get even better under Hoover.

"Wonderful Prosperity" The United States economy seemed to be in fine shape. In 1925, the market value of all stocks was $27 billion. Over the next few years, it soared: in 1928 alone, stock values rose by almost $11.4 billion. Because the stock market was widely regarded as the nation's economic weathervane, the *New York Times* could describe the year as one "of unprecedented advance, of wonderful prosperity." By early October 1929, stock values hit $87 billion.

Working people also seemed better off. Since 1914, **real wages**—what money could actually buy—had increased more than 40 percent. Although some industries were troubled, and some workers lost jobs to assembly-line machinery, unemployment in general averaged below 4 percent.

Even critics of capitalism made optimistic predictions. In 1928, former muckraker Lincoln Steffens wrote:

B ig business in America is producing what the Socialists held up as their goal: food, shelter and clothing for all. You will see it during the Hoover administration.

"Everybody Ought to Be Rich" People had unusually high confidence in the business world during the 1920s. For some, business success became almost a religion. One of the

This car advertisement from 1927 reflects the apparent prosperity and optimism of those years.

decade's best-selling books was *The Man Nobody Knows* (1925). Written by Bruce Barton, an advertising executive, it told Jesus' life story in business terms. Barton portrayed Jesus as a managerial genius who "picked up twelve men from the bottom ranks of business and forged them into an organization that conquered the world."

Similarly, Americans trusted the advice of corporate leaders such as John J. Raskob. In a 1929 article, "Everybody Ought to Be Rich," he stated that savings of only $15 a week over twenty years could bring a $400-a-month income from investments. "And because income can do that," Raskob said, "I am firm in my belief that anyone not only can be rich, but ought to be rich."

The three Republican Presidents of the 1920s equated the interests of the nation with the interests of the business world. They, too, expressed great confidence in business. Although people in the late 1920s were wildly buying stocks with borrowed money, the Hoover administration did nothing to discourage such borrowing.

Welfare Capitalism Partly because workers' standard of living seemed to be improving, organized labor lost members during the 1920s. To counter moves by outside union organizers and keep workers contented, companies met some of their workers' needs without prompting by unions. This new approach to labor relations was known as **welfare capitalism**. Employers raised wages and provided benefits such as paid vacations, health plans, and even English classes for recent immigrants.

MAKING CONNECTIONS

Although vacations and health plans were unusual benefits in the 1920s, more and more working people today expect them. What does this change show about the relative status of workers in the 1920s and 1990s?

Signs of Trouble

Despite the apparent prosperity, all was not well. Only later, however, did many people recognize the warning signs of an unsound economy.

Uneven Riches In reality, the economy of the 1920s was seriously out of balance. Despite some stock market success stories, it was mainly the rich who got richer. Huge corporations, rather than small businesses, dominated American industry. In 1929, 200 large companies controlled 49 percent of American industry.

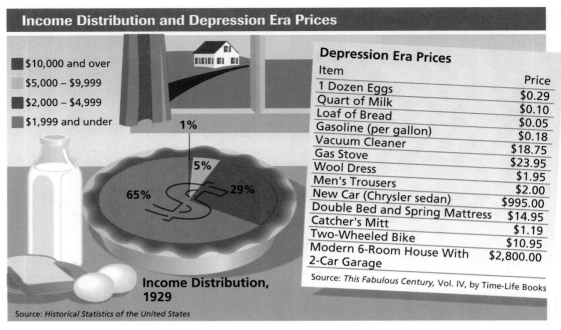

Income Distribution and Depression Era Prices

Income Distribution, 1929

- $10,000 and over
- $5,000 – $9,999
- $2,000 – $4,999
- $1,999 and under

1%
5%
65%
29%

Source: *Historical Statistics of the United States*

Depression Era Prices

Item	Price
1 Dozen Eggs	$0.29
Quart of Milk	$0.10
Loaf of Bread	$0.05
Gasoline (per gallon)	$0.18
Vacuum Cleaner	$18.75
Gas Stove	$23.95
Wool Dress	$1.95
Men's Trousers	$2.00
New Car (Chrysler sedan)	$995.00
Double Bed and Spring Mattress	$14.95
Catcher's Mitt	$1.19
Two-Wheeled Bike	$10.95
Modern 6-Room House With 2-Car Garage	$2,800.00

Source: *This Fabulous Century*, Vol. IV, by Time-Life Books

Interpreting Graphs

The pie graph shows how unevenly the country's wealth was distributed in the 1920s. *What percentage of Americans earned less than $2,000 a year? Looking at the list of prices and assuming that you didn't buy on credit, find what you could have bought with that income—a monthly income of $165 or less.*

This political cartoon, symbolic of the stock market frenzy, shows greedy brokers "fishing" for new clients from the top of the New York Stock Exchange building.

Similarly, personal wealth was concentrated in a tiny percentage of American families. (See the graph above.) In 1929, the richest Americans—24,000 families, or just 0.1 percent of the population—had incomes of more than $100,000. They also held 34 percent of the country's total savings. Of those families, 513 were millionaires.

By contrast, 71 percent of American individuals and families earned less than $2,500 a year. About 21.5 million households—nearly 80 percent of all families—had no savings. Many people earned so little that almost everyone in a family, including children, had to work just to get by.

Buying on Credit Another sign of trouble was an increase in personal debt. Traditionally, Americans feared debt and resisted buying goods unless they had the cash to pay for them. In the 1920s, however, assembly-line production lowered the cost of many consumer items, making them affordable for more people. People also were eager to forget World War I. They flocked to buy radios, vacuum cleaners, refrigerators, and other exciting new products, whether or not they could afford them.

Advertising made new goods irresistible. Store owners also had enough confidence in the economy to let people buy goods "on time." **Installment buying** let people purchase expensive items such as automobiles and furniture and pay for them (with interest) over many months.

"Get Rich Quick" A "get-rich-quick" attitude prevailed during the 1920s. Stock prices were on a dizzy climb, and the press quickly reported success stories of ordinary people who had made fortunes.

Before World War I, only the wealthy played the stock market. Now, with stock prices rising, **speculation**—taking chances in the stock market—became widespread. Small investors entered the market, often with their life savings. If they could not afford to buy stocks at face value, stockbrokers let them **buy on margin**.

They paid a fraction of the price (10 to 50 percent) and borrowed the rest.

Brokers charged high interest and could demand payment of the loan at any time. But if the price of the stocks went up, the borrower could sell at a price high enough to pay off the loan and interest charges and still make money.

Too Many Goods, Too Little Demand By the late 1920s, the country's warehouses held piles of unbought consumer goods. Wages had risen, but not as fast as production. People could not afford to buy goods as fast as they were made.

Although the stock market kept rising, overproduction caused some industries to slow in the late 1920s. The automobile industry, which had helped create American prosperity, slumped after 1925. Industries that depended on it—steel, rubber, and glass—also were in recession. Housing construction fell by 25 percent between 1928 and 1929.

Hard Times Most farmers never shared in the 1920s prosperity. New machinery enabled them to grow more crops, but the huge postwar demand for food ended as European farmers recovered. As a result, crop prices in the United States fell so low that farmers could not pay what they owed for land and machinery. Rural banks suffered when loans were not repaid, and about 6,000 failed. "We were in the Depression before 1929, we just didn't call it that," recalled a rural Tennessean.

Outside agriculture, factory workers faced low wages and long hours. Conditions were especially bad in coal mines and southern

Farm families faced hard times in the 1920s. Many had to watch while their homes, land, and animals were sold at auction.

textile mills. In the rayon mills of Elizabethton, Tennessee, for instance, women worked 56-hour weeks, earning 16 to 18 cents an hour—about $10 a week.

To some observers, these factors—uneven wealth, rising debt, speculation in the stock market, overproduction, and hard times for many workers—clearly signaled trouble in the economy. In 1928, Belle Moskowitz, who had managed Al Smith's losing presidential campaign that year, predicted that "growing unemployment, business depression or some false step" would soon trigger a reaction against Hoover and his policies. Although the collapse did not come till the next year, she soon was proved right.

SECTION 1 REVIEW

Key Terms, People, and Places
1. Define (a) real wages, (b) welfare capitalism, (c) installment buying, (d) speculation, (e) buy on margin.

Key Concepts
2. Why was there so much optimism in the United States in the late 1920s?
3. How did most Americans regard the business world in the 1920s?

4. In what ways had many Americans gone deeply into debt? Why?
5. Which groups were experiencing hard times in the 1920s despite the general prosperity in the United States?

Critical Thinking
6. **Identifying Central Issues** Why did most people not realize that the economy in the 1920s was not as healthy as it seemed?

The Stock Market Crash

In 1929 the foundation of the seemingly prosperous economy was so unstable that the stock market crash in October led to a severe depression whose effects spread worldwide.

Key Concepts

- A sudden fall in stock prices in late October 1929 brought a wave of panic selling.
- The crash contributed to a severe decline in the overall United States economy.
- The results of the stock market crash were felt worldwide.

Key Terms, People, and Places

Dow Jones industrial average, Gross National Product (GNP), collateral

The Long and the Short of it

Ticker-tape machines, which report stock market activity, brought both good news and bad to investors, as this drawing from a 1930 *Life* cover shows.

After Herbert Hoover's 1928 election, stock prices continued to climb. Early that year, the **Dow Jones industrial average**, an average of stock prices of leading industries, was 191. By inauguration day, March 4, 1929, it had risen another 122 points. Prices faltered in April, but brokers said, "Buy!" On September 3, the Dow Jones reached an all-time high of 381.

The Market Crashes

The rising stock market dominated the news. Keeping track of prices was almost as popular as counting Babe Ruth's home runs. Eager, nervous investors filled brokerage houses around the country to catch the latest news coming in on the ticker tape or posted on blackboards. Prices for many stocks soared far above their real value, in terms of the company's earnings and assets.

Black Thursday, Black Tuesday After the peak in September, stock prices fell slowly. Some brokers began to call in loans, but others loaned even more. Business leaders such as Charles E. Mitchell, head of the National City Bank of New York, assured the nervous public: "Although in some cases speculation has gone too far, . . . the markets generally are now in a healthy condition."

As the stock market closed on October 23, the Dow Jones average dropped 21 points in an hour. The next day, Thursday, October 24, worried investors began to sell, and stock prices fell. Falling prices panicked others, who also sold quickly—at any price. Investors who had bought General Electric stock at $400 a share sold it for $283 a share. U.S. Steel stock fell from 261 3/4 to 193 1/2.

Again, business and political leaders told the country not to worry. Colonel Leonard P. Ayres, a banking executive, said that only a nation as rich as the United States could "withstand the shock of a $3 billion paper loss on the Stock Exchange in a single day without serious effects to the average citizen." President Hoover announced: "The fundamental business of the country . . . is on a sound and prosperous basis."

To stop the panic, a group of bankers pooled their money to buy stock. Banker Richard Whitney, a Stock Exchange official, went to the floor and, in a few minutes, made offers for $20 to $30 million worth of stock. This action stabilized prices, but only for a few days. By Monday prices were falling again. Investors all over the country raced to get out of the stock market. On October 29, known as Black Tuesday, a record 16.4 million shares were sold, compared with 4 to 8 million shares a day, earlier in the year.

The collapse continued. By November 13, the Dow Jones had fallen from its September high of 381 to 198.7. Overall losses amounted to $30 billion.

Coming to Terms It took time for people to recognize the extent of the disaster caused by the crash. Arthur Crew Inman, a wealthy Boston resident, lost heavily in the market. He wrote in his diary, "The profit in my little book melted yesterday to seven thousand. It is probably nil today. . . . My dreams of a million—where are they?" Inman, however, had a secure income of $12,000 a year. Although upset, he viewed the situation with wry humor, adding this mock prayer:

> O *Stock Market, God of American gamblers, be merciful to me, a petty and insignificant worshipper at your shrine! If I have been greedy, forgive me! Leave me my remnants, O Stock Market!*

For people like Inman, whose entire wealth did not depend on the stock market, life went on much as before, with perhaps a few cutbacks. Others, even wealthy families, lost everything. Brokers and banks called in their loans, but people did not have cash to pay them.

When the stock market crashed, many investors—large and small—stockbrokers, bankers, and manufacturers fell too. As the economic slide got steeper, it took more and more ordinary people down with it. The graph below shows the fluctuations in the stock market from 1925 to 1933.

MAKING CONNECTIONS

Many people today use credit cards and charge accounts to buy on credit. Is it as dangerous now as it was in 1929? Why or why not?

The Crash Affects Millions

By 1929, about 4 million people, out of a population of 120 million, had invested in the stock market. They were the first to suffer from the crash, but it soon affected millions who had

As stock market prices fell, the ticker tape could not report market activity fast enough. Nervous investors crowded into Wall Street, hoping to hear the latest news.

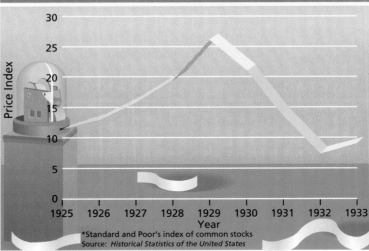

Stock Prices,* 1925–1933

*Standard and Poor's index of common stocks
Source: *Historical Statistics of the United States*

Interpreting Graphs
With only a few pauses, stock market prices climbed steadily during the 1920s. *According to this graph, when did market prices reach their lowest point before starting to rise again?*

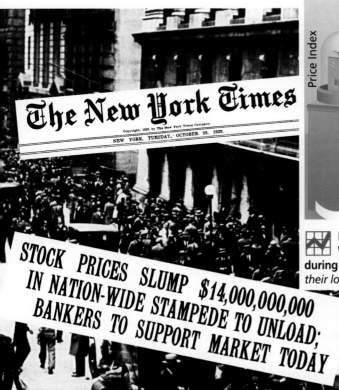

The New York Times

NEW YORK, TUESDAY, OCTOBER 29, 1929.

STOCK PRICES SLUMP $14,000,000,000 IN NATION-WIDE STAMPEDE TO UNLOAD; BANKERS TO SUPPORT MARKET TODAY never owned a single share of stock. Eventually, like ripples from a stone thrown into a pond, its effects spread beyond the United States. The Great Depression had begun.

Workers and Farmers Lose Out As income and profits fell, American factories began to close. Week after week, thousands of workers lost their jobs or had their pay cut. In August 1931, Henry Ford shut down his Detroit automobile factories, putting at least 75,000 people out of work.

In several European countries, workers had government unemployment insurance, but the United States had no such program. By 1932, nearly 13 million were unemployed, about a quarter of the labor force (see graph on page 483). Others worked only part time or had their wages cut. The **Gross National Product (GNP)**—the total annual value of goods and services a country produces— was $103 billion in 1929. By 1933 it was only $56 billion.

The effects of the crash spread. Restaurants and other small businesses closed because customers could no longer afford to patronize them. Once-wealthy families dismissed household workers. Farm prices, already low, fell even more, bringing final disaster to many families (see graph below). In 1929, a bushel of wheat had sold at the low price of $1.04; in 1932 it brought 38 cents. Cotton dropped from 17 to 6.5 cents a pound. In 1930 a severe drought parched farmlands in the Great Plains, a foretaste of the weather that would turn the area into a dust bowl. (See "Time and Place: The Black Blizzards," pages 484–485.)

Banks Close Unpaid farm loans already had ruined many rural banks. Now city banks were in trouble. Banks exist on the interest they earn from lending out their deposits. They assume that not everyone will claim their deposits at once. After the stock market crash, people with loans to repay as well as nervous depositors rushed to withdraw their money.

Thousands of banks closed their doors when they could not return their depositors' money or sell foreclosed properties. In just a few years, more than 5,500 banks failed. By 1933, the money from nine million savings accounts had vanished.

Worldwide Repercussions The crash would have been serious even if it had hurt only the United States. But by the 1930s, international banking, manufacturing, and trade had made nations interdependent. When the world's leading economy fell, the global economic system began to crumble.

After World War I, the United States had insisted that France and England, its wartime allies, repay their war debts. At the same time, Congress kept import taxes high, making it hard for European nations to sell goods in the United States. With economies weakened by the war and little chance of selling goods in the United States, the Allies had to rely on Germany's reparations payments for income.

As long as United States companies invested in Germany, reparations payments continued. But with the Depression, investments fell off. German banks failed, Germany suspended reparations, and the Allies in turn stopped

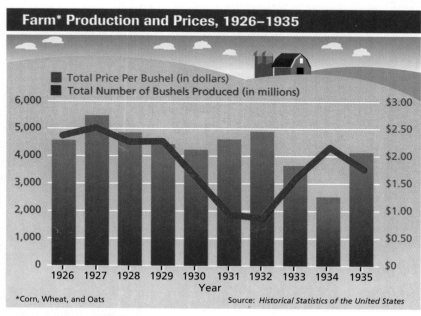

Farm* Production and Prices, 1926–1935

■ Total Price Per Bushel (in dollars)
■ Total Number of Bushels Produced (in millions)

*Corn, Wheat, and Oats

Source: *Historical Statistics of the United States*

Interpreting Graphs
American farmers invested heavily to meet the postwar need for food, but demand suddenly fell—and crop prices dropped as a result. *In what year did farm prices drop the most?*

Unemployment, 1926–1933

Number Unemployed (in thousands)

12,000

8,000

4,000

0

1926 1927 1928 1929 1930 1931 1932 1933

Year

Source: *Historical Statistics of the United States*

Interpreting Graphs
The number of people without jobs increased each year after the crash. *What caused unemployment to rise sharply after 1929?*

paying their debts. Europeans no longer could afford to buy American-made goods. Thus the American stock market crash started a downward cycle in the global economy.

What Caused the Great Depression?

The stock market crash of 1929, though devastating to investors, was only the final push that toppled the fragile structure of the American economy. Deeper problems were the real underlying causes of the Great Depression.

Overspeculation During the 1920s, speculators bought stocks with borrowed money, then pledged those stocks as **collateral,** or security, for loans to buy more stocks. Brokers' loans went from under $5 million in mid-1928 to

$850 million in September 1929. Based on borrowed money and optimism instead of real value, the stock market boom was as unsteady as a house of cards. When investors lost confidence, it collapsed, taking them with it.

Government Policies Short-sighted government economic policies were also to blame. Throughout the 1920s, most politicians believed, like President Coolidge, that "the chief business of America is business." Not wanting to interfere in that business, the government took no action against unwise speculation. Congress passed high tariffs that protected American industries but hurt American farmers and international trade.

An Unstable Economy Overall, the seemingly prosperous economy lacked a firm base. National wealth was unevenly distributed, with the most money in the hands of a few families, who tended to save or invest rather than buying goods. Industry produced more goods than most consumers wanted or could afford. While some people profited, most felt that their incomes had not kept up with prices. Farmers and many workers had not shared in the economic boom. The unevenness of the 1920s prosperity made rapid recovery impossible.

SECTION 2 REVIEW

Key Terms, People, and Places
1. Define (a) Dow-Jones industrial average, (b) Gross National Product, (c) collateral.

Key Concepts
2. What were the main events leading up to Black Tuesday in 1929?
3. Who were the first to feel the effects of the crash?
4. Why did banks fail?

5. What effect did the United States stock market crash have on the world economy?

Critical Thinking
6. **Identifying Assumptions** In the 1930s, the United States did not provide any type of unemployment insurance. What beliefs support the idea that government should provide workers with unemployment insurance?

The Black Blizzards

Between 1933 and 1940, so much earth blew out of the central and southern Great Plains that the area became known as the Dust Bowl. What factors contributed to this environmental disaster?

The Great Plains is famous the world over as "America's breadbasket." Deep, fertile soils, a growing season long enough for most crops, and flat land give the region its farming advantage. But because the region is dry, farming on the plains is a risky undertaking.

The Plow that Broke the Plains

It was the dryness of the region that early settlers noticed first. For this reason, maps in the early 1800s referred to the Great Plains as the Great American Desert. By the late 1800s, however, farmers discovered the truth of the Great American Desert—when there was water, the Great Plains was one of the world's best farming regions.

Early farmers faced a major obstacle. The soils of the Great Plains were protected by a thick layer of native grasses with roots that were difficult to cut. To break the roots required expensive steel plows and months of hard labor. Yet, from the time that hard winter wheat was first introduced in central Kansas in the mid 1870s, farmers in the plains sank their plow blades into the sod and turned it over to make wheat fields.

In the early years of the twentieth century, wheat brought good prices, and farmers continually increased the acres of plowed land at the expense of the native grasses. In 1917 prices went even higher, spurred upward by the great demand caused by World War I. The price increases stimulated an even greater fervor to plow more land to grow wheat: "Plant more wheat! Wheat will win the war!" was the slogan. By 1919 farmers plowed under nearly 4 million acres of grassland. Even after the war ended, the big plow-up continued.

It was new technology that allowed so much land to be plowed. Plowing with tractors allowed farmers to turn over far more acres in a day than they ever could have without those machines. When prices for wheat began to fall in the early 1920s, farmers responded by growing even more wheat. In the five years between 1925 and 1930 alone, more than 5 million additional acres of grassland disappeared, converted to wheat fields by the relentless plow blades.

Interaction: Drought and Human Activity Led to Dust Storms

At the time the first dust storms occurred in the early 1930s, farmers blamed them on the severe and lengthy drought that began and lasted until the end of the decade. While drought was a major factor in creating the Dust Bowl, it was not the only factor. Farming practices contributed as much as the weather to the disaster.

The plains region experiences great variations. Hot and humid tropical air masses move into the region from the Gulf of Mexico and cold polar air masses push southward from above the Arctic Circle. When these two air masses collide, powerful storms with fierce updrafts are created.

Violent winds picked up the dark, nutrient-rich topsoil and carried it eastward, sometimes for hundreds of miles, leaving behind barren, shifting dunes of grit and sand.

Legend:
- Severe wind erosion
- Slight wind erosion
- Dust Bowl

Area of main map

Great Plains

Severe weather could not harm the environment as long as the thick layer of prairie grasses protected the topsoil. But when farmers stripped the soil of its natural protection by plowing the land, they opened the door to a major disaster.

Not Enough Rain

The most severe storms of the dry years were dubbed "black blizzards." Violent winds picked up the dark, nutrient-rich topsoil and carried it eastward, sometimes for hundreds of miles, leaving behind barren, shifting dunes of grit and sand. The map above shows the extent of soil erosion across the plains.

Time after time, dirt was sucked up off the parched plains and dropped by the ton over states and cities to the east. The dirt darkened the sky in New York City and Washington, D.C. It stained the snows of New England red and dropped on ships hundreds of miles off the Atlantic coast. The drought and winds persisted for more than seven years, bringing ruin to farmers.

The combination of terrible weather and very low prices for farm products caused 60 percent of the people in the Dust Bowl to lose their farms. Relief did not come until the early 1940s when the rains finally arrived and World War II drove farm prices up. By that time the damage was done. Driven by their need to grow more wheat to pay their growing debts, Dust Bowl farmers were the agents of their own destruction in the "Dirty Thirties."

GEOGRAPHIC CONNECTIONS

1. What caused the black blizzards of the 1930s?
2. (a) What features of land and climate make the Great Plains a good farming region? (b) What features make it a poor farming region?

Critical Thinking

3. **Identifying Alternatives** What might the farmers of the Great Plains do to prevent another Dust Bowl?

485

Social Effects of the Depression

SECTION PREVIEW

Most people were not immediately affected by the 1929 stock market crash, but by the early 1930s, wage cuts and growing unemployment brought widespread suffering.

Key Concepts
- Wage cuts and unemployment affected all levels of society, making many people homeless.
- Those groups already experiencing economic difficulty, such as farmers, faced harder times.
- The Depression affected people's mental and physical health.
- Conditions for African Americans worsened during the Depression.

Key Terms, People, and Places
Hooverville; Father Divine, Scottsboro Boys

"Apples 5 cents" became a familiar sign in many cities in the 1930s, as out-of-work people struggled to make a living.

Not everyone felt the impact of the crash immediately. Many thought the depression that followed would not last. For them, reality hit in 1931 or 1932. As hard times spread to all levels of society, a song from a 1932 Broadway revue became a theme song of the times:

Once I built a railroad, made it run,
Made it race against time.
Once I built a railroad, now it's done.
Brother, can you spare a dime?

Brother, Can You Spare A Dime?

Imagine that the bank where you had a savings account suddenly closed. Your money was gone. Or your parents lost their jobs and could not pay the rent. One day you came home to find your furniture on the sidewalk—you had been evicted.

People at all levels of society faced these situations. Professionals and white-collar workers, who had felt more secure than laborers, were laid off suddenly with no prospects of finding another job. Those whose savings disappeared found it hard to understand why banks no longer had the money they had deposited for safekeeping.

"Hoovervilles" The hardest hit were those at the bottom of the economic ladder. Some unemployed laborers, unable to pay their rent, moved in with relatives. Others drifted. In 1931, census takers estimated the homeless in New York City alone at 15,000.

Homeless people sometimes built shanty towns, with shacks of tar paper, cardboard, or scrap material. These homes for the homeless came to be called **Hoovervilles,** mocking the President whom people blamed for the crisis. A woman living in Oklahoma visited one Hooverville:

Here were all these people living in old, rusted-out car bodies. . . . There were people living in shacks made of orange crates. One family with a whole lot of kids were living in a piano box.

"On The Bum" Many homeless and jobless people became drifters, hitchhiking from one "hobo jungle" to another. Thousands rode the rails—mostly men and boys, but also women and girls wearing men's clothing. They slept in boxcars or open freight cars. By early 1933, a million people were estimated to be on the move, risking jail, injury, or death.

Farm Distress Farm families suffered as low food prices cut their income. When they could not pay their mortgages, they lost their farms to the banks, which sold them at auction. In the South, landowners expelled tenant farmers and sharecroppers. Folksinger Woody Guthrie, then

Makeshift huts were homes for homeless and the unemployed in this Hooverville in downtown New York.

a teenager, later told about trying to sell food in an almost-deserted town:

> W ho's gonna buy what I grow? I don't wanta bum nobody for my nickels. I wanta grow me a garden. But, gosh, who'd eat it? Few people driftin' across the streets now an' then, but most of them look like they ain't eatin' very much.

In protest against low farm prices, farmers dumped thousands of gallons of milk and destroyed other crops. These desperate actions shocked a hungry nation.

Hardships Create New Problems

As it wore on, the Depression had a serious physical and psychological impact on the entire nation. Unemployment and fear of losing a job caused great anxiety. People became depressed; many considered suicide, and some took their own lives.

Impact on Health "No one has starved," President Hoover declared, but some did, and thousands more went hungry. Those who could not afford food or shelter got sick more easily. Children suffered most from the long-term effects of poor diet and inadequate medical care. One boy tramp recalled:

> A ll last winter we never had a fire except about once a day when Mother used to cook some mush or something. When the kids were cold they went to bed. I quit high school of course.

In the country, people grew food and ate berries and other wild plants. In cities, they sold apples and pencils, begged for money to buy food, and fought over the contents of restaurant garbage cans. Families who had land planted "relief gardens" to feed themselves or to barter food for other items.

Family Problems Living conditions declined as families moved in together, crowding into small houses or apartments. The divorce rate dropped because people could not afford separate households. Other couples postponed wedding plans. People gave up even small pleasures like an ice cream cone or a movie ticket.

Men who had lost jobs or investments often felt like failures because they could no longer provide for their families. If their wives or children were working, men thought their own status had fallen. It embarrassed them to be seen at home during normal work hours. They were ashamed to apply for relief or ask friends for help.

Women faced other problems. Those who worked at home and were used to depending on a husband's paycheck worried about feeding their hungry children. Working women were accused of taking jobs away from men. Even in the better times of the 1920s, Henry Ford had fired 82 married women. "We do not employ married women whose husbands have jobs," he explained. In the Depression, this practice became common. In 1931, the American Federation of Labor endorsed it. Most school districts would not hire married women teachers, and many fired those who got married.

Many women continued to find work, however, because poor-paying jobs such as domestic service, typing, and nursing were considered "women's work." The greatest job losses of the Depression were in industry and other areas that seldom hired women. Even on the same job, however, women usually were paid less than men.

MAKING CONNECTIONS

Depression attitudes and policies discriminated against working women. Have attitudes toward working women today changed? If so, how?

Discrimination Increases

African Americans continued to leave the South, though not as many as in the 1920s. They worked as janitors or porters in northern cities but soon lost even those jobs to whites. Black unemployment soared—56 percent of black Americans were out of work in 1932. Photographer Gordon Parks, who rode the rails to Harlem, later wrote:

> To most blacks who had flocked in from all over the land, the struggle to survive was savage. Poverty coiled around them and me with merciless fingers.

Because relief programs discriminated against African Americans, black churches and organizations like the National Urban League gave private help. The followers of M. J. Divine, a Harlem evangelist known as **Father Divine,** opened soup kitchens that fed hungry thousands every day.

Discrimination increased for African Americans in the South. Some white Americans declared openly that African Americans had no right to a job if whites were out of work. African Americans were denied civil rights such as access to education, voting, and health care. Lynchings increased.

The justice system often ignored black rights. In March 1931, near Scottsboro, Alabama, nine African American youths who had been riding the rails were arrested and accused of raping two white women on the train. Without being given the chance to hire a defense lawyer, eight of the nine were quickly convicted by an all-white jury and sentenced to die.

| 1650 | 1700 | 1750 | 1800 | **Links Across Time** | 1850 | 1900 | 1950 | 2000 |

Homelessness

So many homeless young men and women were riding freight trains and searching for work in 1933, that railroad officials often hired people to search the cars and remove the homeless they found there—by force, if necessary. Homelessness has become a growing problem in the 1990s as it was during the 1930s.

The economic conditions that brought about widespread unemployment during the Depression were a clear cause of homelessness. People point to a variety of reasons for the rapid increase in the number of homeless in the 1990s—unemployment, a decline in low-rent housing for the poor, changes in qualifications for government disability payments, and the premature release of many patients from mental-health facilities. Experts estimate that about 20 percent of homeless people have jobs, 33 percent are families with children, and 10 percent are single women. *What assistance for the homeless is available in the 1990s that was not available in the 1930s?*

Poverty was especially hard on sharecroppers in the South, who had to live in improvised camps after being evicted from their farms by landowners.

Like the Sacco and Vanzetti case a few years earlier, saving the so-called **Scottsboro Boys** became a national cause. Eventually the Supreme Court decided the youths had not had a fair trial and ordered new trials.

AMERICAN PROFILES

Wilson Ledford

Americans survived the Depression in many ways. Here, Wilson Ledford, who was then a teenager in rural Tennessee, remembers the early years.

Wilson first felt the effects of the Depression in March 1930 when he was fifteen, living in Chattanooga with his mother and younger sister. Wilson had worked part time and after school in a grocery store since he was eleven. By 1930, his family could no longer afford Chattanooga. They moved back to Cleveland, Tennessee, a nearby small town where one of Wilson's brothers had left a house when he moved West. Like many farmhouses then, it had no running water or electricity.

Wilson's mother owned another house and 15 acres of land, which brought in $6 a month rent—except when the tenants were out of work. After taxes and insurance, the family had about a dollar a week to live on.

Wilson "swapped work with neighbors." He looked after the family horse and cow, chopped wood for the fireplace, tended the garden that provided family food, and raised corn to feed the animals:

W*e had to raise most of what we ate since money was so scarce. . . . Sometimes I plowed for other people when I could get the work. . . . I got 15 cents an hour for plowing and I furnished the horse and plow.*

Nothing was wasted. His mother kept chickens and traded eggs at the store for things they could not raise. Overalls cost 98 cents; shoes were $2. She bought a pig for $3 and raised it for meat, and made jelly from wild blackberries. Despite the family's own poverty, Wilson's mother gave extra milk and butter to

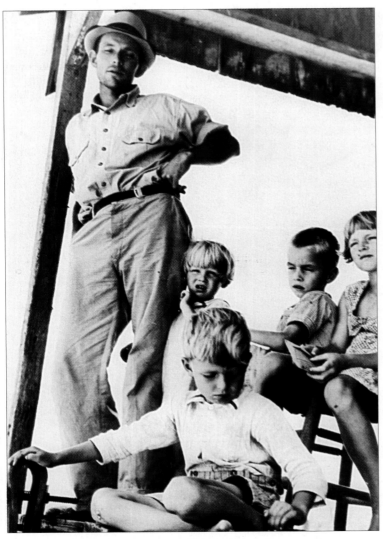

"If they come to take my farm, I'm going to fight. I'd rather be killed outright than die by starvation." Although farm families were hard hit by the Depression, the fighting spirit represented by this quote was seen across the country.

"some poor people, a woman with three small children who lived in a one-room shack with a dirt floor."

Wilson never got to high school, "as survival was more important then than getting an education was, and I had to work to survive." The Ledfords had no radio, but he and his neighbors made their own entertainment. Wilson and some other boys cleaned the rocks off a field, graded it, and made a baseball diamond. Baseballs were precious. "You could buy a pretty good baseball for a quarter and a real good one for 50 cents. . . . If we lost a ball during the game, everyone had to go hunt for it."

In the summer of 1932, when he was seventeen, Wilson got a job in Chattanooga with another brother, delivering ice. At the end of the summer, the brother bought him a 1924 Model T Ford for $25. The next summer, too, Wilson hauled ice: "I worked twelve hours a day, six days a week and made $3.00 a week."

When the icehouse closed in the fall, Wilson hitchhiked throughout the Southeast looking for work, but never had any success. "I pumped up so many tires for people I rode with, I had blisters all in my hands. Finally I got back home."

In the next few years, Wilson bought a truck to haul coal, cotton, and oranges, then worked nights in a woolen mill while carrying ice during the day. Finally, "I got a call from Chickamauga Dam and I went to work there. That was a good job working on the dam, I made 60 cents an hour. Times were better by then, but did not start booming until World War II started."

SECTION 3 REVIEW

Key Terms, People, and Places
1. Define Hoovervilles.
2. Identify (a) Father Divine, (b) Scottsboro Boys.

Key Concepts
3. What were the earliest social effects of the Depression?
4. How did the Depression affect farmers?

5. How did the Depression affect family life?
6. How did conditions for African Americans change during the Depression?

Critical Thinking
7. **Determining Relevance** What can you learn about the Depression from Wilson Ledford's experiences?

Distinguishing False from Accurate Images

Distinguishing false from accurate images means examining widely held beliefs about a person, a thing, or an event to determine whether or not those beliefs are based in fact. When studying history, you may uncover source materials such as newspaper and magazine articles that use stereotypes or that put forth misleading ideas. Learning to recognize the differences between false and accurate images will help you to reach your own conclusions about a statement.

The letter excerpted below was written to President Herbert Hoover during the early years of the Depression. Practice distinguishing between false and accurate images by using the following steps.

1. Summarize the main message of the passage. The first step in evaluating a piece of information is to understand what its central message is. Read the excerpt below and answer the following question: What is the main point of the letter?

2. Look for generalizations and overstatements in the passage. Generalizations are broad and oversimplified statements about people, events, or issues that are presented as being accurate in all cases. Overstatements exaggerate or stretch the truth. These techniques often signal claims that are unsupported by facts and, therefore, may indicate the use of false images. (a) What generalizations can you find in the letter? (b) What overstatements or unsupported claims do you find?

3. Look for supporting facts or evidence. Accurate statements are usually backed up by statistics, quotations, or other verifiable evidence. Facts can be fabricated and used in misleading ways, however, so always check them for accuracy. (a) What verifiable facts, if any, are given in the letter below? (b) Based on the use of facts in the letter, what can you conclude about the accuracy of its message?

Annapolis, Maryland
September 10, 1931

My dear Mr. Hoover,

In these days of unrest and general dissatisfaction it is absolutely impossible for a man in your position to get a clear and impartial view of the general conditions of things in America today. But, of this fact I am very positive, that there is not five per cent of the poverty, distress, and general unemployment that many of your enemies would have us believe. It is true, that there is much unrest, but this unrest is largely caused . . . by the excessive prosperity and general debauchery through which the country has traveled since the period of the war. The result being that in three cases out of four, the unemployed [person] is looking for a very light job at a very heavy pay, and with the privilege of being provided with an automobile if he is required to walk more than four or five blocks a day.

National Relief Director, Walter S. Gifford, and his committee are entirely unnecessary at this time, as it has a tendency to cause communities to neglect any temporary relief to any of their people, with the thought of passing the burden on to the National Committee. . . .

. . . Believe me to be one of your well wishers in this ocean of conflict.

Yours sincerely,
W. H. H.

491

Surviving the Great Depression

Living through the Great Depression was an unforgettable experience. Despite the hard times, many Americans learned to face troubles together with courage and humor.

Key Concepts

- The Great Depression left a lasting impression on those who lived through it.
- People had good memories of working together and helping each other.
- The Depression ended the era of the 1920s.

For the homeless of the Depression, this "kind-hearted woman" symbol on a sidewalk or fence in front of a house meant that the family inside would help provide food or clothing.

Key Terms, People, and Places

Socialists, Twenty-first Amendment; Norman Thomas; Empire State Building

N o one who lived through the Great Depression ever forgot it. It changed people's feelings about banks, business, government—and money. Even after the economy recovered, the "Depression generation" would continue to pinch and save before buying anything.

Working Together for Change

Not all the memories of the Depression were bad or despairing. Writing in 1932, reporter Gerald W. Johnson noted:

T he great majority of Americans may be depressed. They may not be well pleased with the way business and government have been carried on, and they may not be at all sure that they know exactly how to remedy the trouble. They may be feeling dispirited. But there is one thing they are not, and that is—beaten.

People pulled together to help each other. Tenant groups formed to protest rent increases and evictions. Religious, political, and charitable groups set up soup kitchens and breadlines to feed the hungry. In some farm communities, people agreed to keep bids low when foreclosed farms were auctioned. Buyers then returned the farms to their original owners.

Many individual acts of kindness shone as people helped those they saw as worse off than themselves. One woman, Kitty McCulloch, remembered:

T here were many beggars, who would come to your back door, and they would say they were hungry. I wouldn't give them money because I didn't have it. But I did take them in and put them in my kitchen and give them something to eat.

She also gave one beggar a pinstripe suit belonging to her husband, who, she explained, already had three others.

Moves to the Political Left As bad as conditions were, only a few called for radical political change. In Europe, economic problems had brought riots and political upheaval, but in the United States most citizens trusted in the democratic process to solve them. As writer William Saroyan observed in 1936:

T en million unemployed continue law-abiding. No riots, no trouble, no multi-millionaires cooked and served with cranberry sauce, alas.

For some Americans, however, radical and reform movements offered new solutions to the country's problems, promising a fairer distribution of wealth. Membership in the Communist party, consisting mainly of intellectuals and labor organizers, was 14,000, and in the 1932 election, the Communist candidate polled just over 100,000 votes. More people than the numbers suggest, however, also believed that the new Communist government in the Soviet Union might have the right answers.

Socialists, who called for gradual social and economic changes rather than revolution, did better politically. Their presidential candidate, **Norman Thomas,** won 881,951 votes in 1932, about 2.2 percent of the total vote. Others who might have supported Thomas voted for Franklin D. Roosevelt simply to defeat Hoover.

Voting figures and party membership do not reflect the widespread interest in radical and reform movements in the 1930s. Those who were part of those movements remember the decade as a high point of cooperation among different groups of Americans—students, workers, writers, artists, and professionals of all races. They worked together for social justice in cases such as that of the Scottsboro Boys.

MAKING CONNECTIONS

Third-party candidates, such as the Socialists, have almost no chance of winning presidential elections. Why, then, do they present candidates? What influence do minor parties have?

Looking Ahead

For the most part, Americans gritted their teeth and waited out the hard times. They looked for change and signs of hope.

Depression Humor Wry jokes and cartoons kept people laughing through their troubles. The term "Hooverville" was at first a joke. People who slept on park benches huddled under "Hoover blankets"—old newspapers. Empty pockets turned inside out were termed "Hoover flags." When Babe Ruth was criticized for requesting a salary of $80,000—higher than President Hoover's—he joked, "I had a better year than he did."

People fought despair by laughing at it. In 1929 humorist Will Rogers quipped, "When Wall Street took that tail spin, you had to stand in line to get a window to jump out of." A cartoon that showed two men jumping out of a

Above: To get a warm meal, many people—even those who had once been relatively prosperous—had to stand in breadlines or outside soup kitchens run by churches and community groups. *Below:* Showing the darker side of Depression humor, an end-of-the-year cartoon in *Life* magazine summed up the hopes and disasters of 1929.

window arm-in-arm was captioned "The speculators who had a joint account."

Prohibition Is Repealed In February 1933, Congress voted to repeal the ban on alcoholic beverages. The **Twenty-first Amendment** was ratified by the end of the year. Some people, including President Hoover, regretted the end of this social experiment limiting the sale of alcohol, but most welcomed repeal as an end to national hypocrisy and as a curb on gangsters who prospered from bootlegging.

Despite the economic hardships of the 1930s, American architects and developers raced to build the world's tallest building. Workers like the man shown above looked out over the rest of New York City as they labored to complete the Empire State Building.

The end of prohibition and return of legalized alcohol stimulated parts of the economy—grain growing, breweries and distilleries, even the pretzel industry. Control of alcohol returned to the states, eight of which chose to continue the ban on liquor sales.

The Empire State Building For many, a dramatic symbol of hope was the new **Empire State Building,** begun in 1930. John J. Raskob, the developer of the gleaming new skyscraper, won the race to build the world's tallest building.

One hundred and two stories high, the Empire State Building soared 1,250 feet into the sky and was topped with a mooring mast for blimps. Sixty-seven elevators, traveling 1,000 feet per minute, brought visitors to its observation deck. On the first Sunday after it opened, over 4,000 people paid a dollar each to make the trip.

The End of An Era By 1933, it was clear that an era was ending. One by one, symbols of the 1920s faded away. Gangster Al Capone went to prison for tax evasion. Boxer Jack Dempsey was defeated. Babe Ruth retired. The Depression-era labor policies of car-maker Henry Ford, once admired for his efficiency, made him labor's prime enemy.

In 1932 the nation was shocked when the infant son of aviation hero Charles Lindbergh and Anne Morrow Lindbergh was kidnapped and murdered. Somehow this tragedy seemed to echo the nation's woeful condition and its fall from the energy and heroism of the 1920s. Finally, eight weeks before Roosevelt's inauguration in 1933, former President Calvin Coolidge, a symbol of the age of prosperity, died.

SECTION 4 REVIEW

Key Terms, People and Places
1. Define (a) Socialists, (b) Twenty-first Amendment.
2. Identify (a) Norman Thomas, (b) Empire State Building.

Key Concepts
3. Why did radical political groups gain support in the early 1930s?

4. What Depression memories might some people remember as good?
5. What were signs that the 1920s era had ended?

Critical Thinking
6. **Formulating Questions** What questions could you ask people who lived in the Depression era in order to understand its effects on both their lives and their attitudes?

The Election of 1932: A Turning Point in History

SECTION PREVIEW

As the Depression worsened, people came to blame Hoover and the Republicans for their misery. The 1932 presidential election brought a sweeping victory for Democrat Franklin D. Roosevelt, and a new direction for American government.

Key Concepts
- President Hoover hoped to use voluntary action to end the Depression.
- Federal government action and funds for relief were inadequate under Hoover.
- Promising a "new deal," the Democratic candidate, Franklin D. Roosevelt, won an overwhelming victory in the presidential election of 1932.

Key Terms, People, Places
Hawley-Smoot tariff, Reconstruction Finance Corporation; John Maynard Keynes, Bonus Army, Franklin Delano Roosevelt, Eleanor Roosevelt

F or a few months after the stock market crash, President Hoover, along with business leaders, insisted that the key to recovery was confidence. Hoover blamed the Depression on "world-wide economic conditions beyond our control"—not on problems in the United States economy.

Hoover Tries to End the Crisis

Taking Hoover's advice, business and government leaders tried to maintain public confidence in the economy. Even as factories closed and breadlines formed, Hoover administration officials insisted that things would get better soon.

Voluntary Action Fails Hoover believed deeply that voluntary controls in the business world were the best way to end the economic crisis. He quickly organized a White House conference of business leaders and got their promise to maintain wage rates. At first, many firms kept wages up. By the end of 1931, however, many quietly cut workers' pay.

Hoover meant well, but he held rigidly to this principle of voluntary action. A shy man, successful in business but inexperienced in politics, he could not make his plan attractive to the American people. After a year of misery, they began to blame him and the Republicans for the crisis.

The Government Acts Hoover then took more action. To create jobs, the government spent more on new public buildings, roads, parks, and dams. Boulder Dam (later renamed Hoover Dam) was begun in 1930. A President's Emergency Committee on Employment advised local relief programs.

Trying to protect domestic industries from foreign imports, in 1930 Congress passed the **Hawley-Smoot tariff,** the highest import tax in history. The tariff backfired. European countries raised their own tariffs, bringing a sudden slowdown in international trade. Hoover suspended the Allies' payments of their war debts, but Europe's economies grew weaker.

In 1932, Hoover set up the **Reconstruction Finance Corporation** (RFC), which gave government credit to banks so that they could extend loans. The RFC reflected the theory that prosperity at the top would help the economy as a whole. To many people, however, it seemed that the government was helping bankers while ordinary people went hungry.

The Democrats in 1932 based their campaign on the promise that Franklin Roosevelt would end the Depression.

President Hoover's apparent inaction made people everywhere eager to blame him for their troubles, as this cartoon from 1931 shows.

Some government efforts helped, but not enough. Hoover wanted state and local governments to handle relief, but their programs never had enough money. Despite the RFC, banks continued to fail.

Hoover's Unpopularity Grows Many people blamed Hoover—not always fairly—for all their problems. "The 1932nd Psalm" was a popular take-off on Psalm 23:

Hoover is my Shepherd, I am in want,
He maketh me to lie down on
park benches,
He leadeth me by still factories,
He restoreth my doubt in the
Republican Party.

Hoover argued that direct federal relief would destroy people's self-respect and create a large bureaucracy. His refusal to help brought bitter public reaction and negative publicity.

Although his World War I relief work had made him the "Great Humanitarian," Hoover's attitude toward Depression relief made him seem cold and hard-hearted. While people went hungry, newspapers showed a photograph of him feeding his dog on the White House lawn. People booed when he said such things as "Our people have been protected from hunger and cold."

Private charities and local officials could not meet the demands for relief, as Hoover wanted. Finally in 1932, Hoover broke with tradition and let the RFC lend the states money for unemployment relief. But it was too little and too late.

As the Depression deepened, some economists backed the ideas of British economist **John Maynard Keynes.** He said that massive government spending could help a collapsing economy and encourage more private spending. This economic theory was not yet widely accepted, however.

Veterans March on Washington A low point for Hoover came in the summer of 1932, when 20,000 jobless World War I veterans and their families encamped in Washington, D.C. They wanted immediate payment of a pension bonus that had been promised for 1945. The House of Representatives agreed, but the Senate said no. Most of the **Bonus Army** then went home, but a few thousand stayed, living in shacks.

Although the bonus marchers were generally peaceful, a few violent incidents prompted Hoover to call in the army. General Douglas MacArthur decided to use force to drive the marchers out of Washington. Armed with bricks and stones, the Bonus Army faced guns, tanks, and tear gas. Many were injured. Hoover was horrified but took responsibility for MacArthur's actions. In the next election, the lingering image of this ugly scene would help defeat him.

MAKING CONNECTIONS

In recent decades, the government has actually helped protesters to hold marches in Washington. What reasons can you give for this difference in treatment?

World War I veterans from all parts of the country demonstrated on the steps of the Capitol in Washington, D.C., in 1932, hoping that their promised bonus would help them survive unemployment and homelessness.

A "New Deal" for America

"I pledge myself to a new deal for the American people," announced presidential candidate **Franklin Delano Roosevelt** as he accepted the Democratic party's nomination at its Chicago convention in July 1932. Delegates cheered, and an organ thundered out the song "Happy Days Are Here Again."

The Republicans, in June, had again named Hoover. As the presidential campaign took shape, the differences between the two candidates became very clear.

The Roosevelts In Franklin and **Eleanor Roosevelt,** the Democrats had a remarkable political couple to bring them victory. Franklin, nicknamed "FDR" by the press, was born in 1882. He graduated from Harvard University and took a job in a law firm, although his main interest was politics. He was elected twice to the New York State Senate, then became assistant secretary of the navy in President Woodrow Wilson's cabinet.

In 1920, FDR ran for Vice President but lost. The following summer, he came down with polio and he never walked without help again. He spent much of the 1920s recovering at Warm Springs, Georgia, but kept up his political interests.

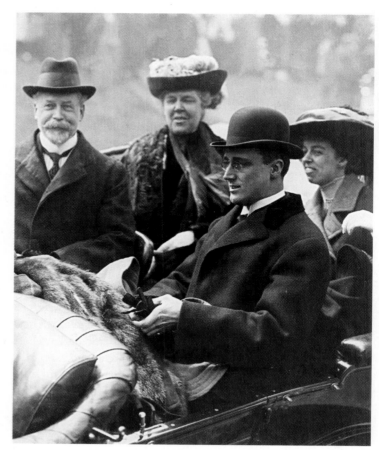

Franklin and Eleanor Roosevelt (at right)—seen here a few years after their marriage—followed a family tradition of political and social activism.

Eleanor Roosevelt, a niece of Theodore Roosevelt, was born in 1884 into a wealthy family. Educated in an English boarding school, she later worked at a social settlement house in New York City. She married her distant cousin Franklin in 1905 and they had six children.

By the 1920s, the marriage was shaky, but the couple stayed together. In New York state, Eleanor worked for legislation about public housing, state government reform, birth control, and better conditions for working women. By 1928, when FDR was persuaded to run for governor of New York, she was an experienced political worker and social reformer.

After FDR's success as governor of New York (1929–1932), his supporters believed him ready to try for the presidency. With his broad smile and genial manner, he represented a spirit of optimism that the country badly needed.

Unlike Hoover, FDR was ready to experiment with governmental roles. Though from a wealthy background, he had genuine compassion for ordinary people, in part because of his own struggle with illness. He was also moved by the great gap between the nation's wealthy and the poor.

As governor of New York, he had worked vigorously for Depression relief. In 1931, he set up an unemployment commission and a relief administration, the first state agencies to aid the poor in the Depression era. When, as a presidential candidate, FDR promised the country a "new deal," he had similar programs in mind.

Roosevelt and Hoover The two candidates and their proposed programs contrasted sharply. In October 1932, Hoover said:

Viewpoints
On Ending the Depression

Sharp philosophical differences characterized the presidential campaign of 1932. *How do both viewpoints below support what you know about the approach of Hoover and Roosevelt to ending the Depression?*

Against Drastic Measures
We are told by the opposition that we must have a change, that we must have a new deal. It is not the change . . . to which I object but the proposal to alter the whole foundations of our national life which have been built through generations of testing and struggle.
Herbert Hoover, speech at Madison Square Garden, October 31, 1932

For Drastic Measures
I have recounted to you in other speeches, and it is a matter of general information, that for at least two years after the crash, the only efforts made by the [Hoover administration] to cope with the distress of unemployment were to deny its existence.
Franklin D. Roosevelt, campaign address, October 13, 1932

This campaign is more than a contest between two men. . . . It is a contest between two philosophies of government.

Still arguing for voluntary aid, Hoover attacked the Democratic platform. If its ideas were adopted, he said, "this will not be the America which we have known in the past." He sternly resisted the idea of giving the national government more power.

Roosevelt, by contrast, called for "a reappraisal of values" and controls on business:

I feel that we are coming to a view through the drift of our legislation and our public thinking in the past quarter century that private economic power is . . . a public trust as well.

While statements like this showed FDR's new approach, probably any Democratic candidate could have beaten Hoover in 1932. Even long-time Republicans deserted him. Reserved by nature, Hoover became grumpy and isolated.

This *New Yorker* cover drawn for the inauguration clearly shows how people saw Roosevelt, the new President, in contrast with Hoover.

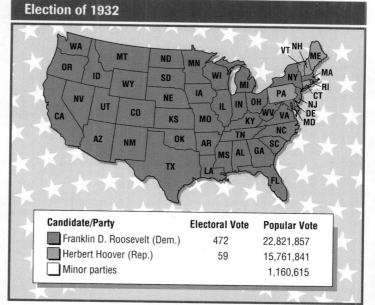

Election of 1932

Candidate/Party	Electoral Vote	Popular Vote
Franklin D. Roosevelt (Dem.)	472	22,821,857
Herbert Hoover (Rep.)	59	15,761,841
Minor parties		1,160,615

Geography and History: Interpreting Maps
Franklin D. Roosevelt and the Democratic party won the popular vote in 1932 as well as a huge margin of electoral votes. *Which states' electoral votes did Hoover win?*

He gave few campaign speeches. Crowds jeered his motorcade.

FDR won the presidency by a huge margin—seven million popular votes. (See the map above.) Much of his support came from groups that had begun to turn to the Democrats in 1928: urban workers, coal miners, and immigrants of Catholic and Jewish descent. Some people did not really vote for Roosevelt, they simply voted *against* Hoover and the Republican policies. Still, the words of FDR's inaugural address gave most of the country renewed hope:

S o first of all let me assert my firm belief that the only thing we have to fear is fear itself.

With these words, Roosevelt reassured a frightened nation and began a journey into a new era of government involvement and presidential activism.

SECTION 5 REVIEW

Key Terms, People, and Places
1. Define (a) Hawley-Smoot tariff, (b) Reconstruction Finance Corporation.
2. Identify (a) John Maynard Keynes, (b) Bonus Army, (c) Franklin Delano Roosevelt, (d) Eleanor Roosevelt.

Key Concepts
3. How did President Hoover hope to end the Depression and its hardships?

4. What was the intent of the Hawley-Smoot tariff?
5. In the 1932 election, what groups supported Roosevelt?

Critical Thinking
6. **Distinguishing False from Accurate Images**
   Was Hoover's great unpopularity justified, or would the economic crisis have defeated anyone?

The Lasting Impact of the Election of 1932

O n a rainy day in 1933, FDR stood before a Depression-weary crowd and took the oath of office of President of the United States. As reporter Thomas Stokes observed, a stirring of hope moved through the crowd when Roosevelt began, "This nation asks for action and action now."

Phrases like this foreshadowed a sweeping change in the style of presidential leadership and government response to its citizens' needs. Ultimately, such changes altered the way many Americans viewed their government and its responsibilities.

A Revolutionary Change

In the depths of the Great Depression, many Americans had to give up cherished traditional beliefs in "making it on their own." They turned to the government as their only hope. Thus, the Roosevelt years saw the beginning of many programs that changed the role of the government in American society.

Presidential Activism In general, the Presidents since FDR—whatever their politics and personality—have carried on the tradition begun by Roosevelt and responded actively to people's needs. Harry Truman inherited the presidency when Roosevelt died in 1945. His domestic program extended the social welfare commitments that Roosevelt had made, such as social security and unemployment insurance. He also argued that government should provide medical care programs to its citizens.

Even supposedly nonactivist Presidents such as Dwight Eisenhower have acted when necessary. For example, in 1957 Eisenhower sent army troops to Little Rock, Arkansas, to protect black students entering a formerly all-white high school.

Government Involvement Continues In the 1960s, President Lyndon Johnson was even more successful at working with Congress than FDR had been. Johnson's proposal of programs like Medicare

1933 Roosevelt's inauguration begins a new age of activist Presidents.

1957 President Dwight Eisenhower sends troops to integrate Arkansas high school.

	1930		1940		1950

1948 President Truman bans racial segregation in the military.

and Medicaid, which offered health care benefits to the elderly and the poor, extended the ideas of social welfare.

Attempts at a More Limited Role Fail

During the 1970s and 1980s, several Presidents attempted to take a more limited role in social welfare. President Richard Nixon sought to scale back involvement in social issues, but because the American public had come to expect this commitment, he failed. At the same time, people began to complain about the "imperial presidency" as Nixon acted aggressively to maintain law and order at home.

Presidents Ford and Carter, too, fashioned a more modest role for themselves and the government during their presidencies, but found that without strong leadership, the American government could not operate effectively.

When Ronald Reagan took office in 1981, he waged a campaign against "entitlements"—those programs that provide basic support for elderly, unemployed, or impoverished people. Because these programs were taking the largest share of the federal budget, Reagan argued that they should be cut back, maintaining that the government should not be so involved in the social welfare of its citizens. But he still acknowledged the need for a basic

safety net that would catch those who were unable to help themselves.

The People Choose Social Intervention

After such attempts to reduce government's role in people's lives, voters elected a President in 1992 who argued that the government has a responsibility to help citizens. President Bill Clinton acted on this belief often during his first year in office. When rain-swollen rivers flooded the Midwest in 1993, he authorized federal disaster funds and—as people expected—personally visited flooded towns and farmlands. He also presented a plan to Congress for a national health care program.

REVIEWING THE FACTS

1. How did Roosevelt's election affect people's expectations of the role of the President?
2. What actions has President Clinton taken that follow in President Roosevelt's footsteps?

Critical Thinking

3. **Expressing Problems Clearly** What are possible consequences of both a large government role in social welfare and a limited government role?

1971 President Richard Nixon imposes a freeze on wages and prices.

1984 President Reagan introduces programs to aid farmers.

| 1960 | 1970 | 1980 | 1990 |

1965 President Lyndon Johnson signs bills on Medicare and aid to education into law.

1993 President Bill Clinton visits flood-damaged areas in the Midwest.

Chapter Review

Understanding Key Terms, People, and Places

Key Terms
1. real wages
2. welfare capitalism
3. installment buying
4. speculation
5. buy on margin
6. Dow Jones industrial average
7. Gross National Product (GNP)
8. collateral
9. Hooverville
10. Socialists
11. Twenty-first Amendment
12. Hawley-Smoot tariff
13. Reconstruction Finance Corporation

People
14. Father Divine
15. Scottsboro Boys
16. Norman Thomas
17. John Maynard Keynes
18. Bonus Army
19. Franklin Delano Roosevelt
20. Eleanor Roosevelt

Places
21. Empire State Building

Terms For each term above, write a sentence that explains its relation to the economy of the late 1920s and the Great Depression.

Matching Review the key terms in the list above. If you are not sure of a term's meaning, review its definition in the chapter. Then choose a term from the list that best matches each description below.
1. what money can actually buy
2. the total annual value of goods and services a country produces
3. taking chances in the stock market
4. agency that gave government credit to banks so that they could extend loans

True or False Determine whether each statement is true or false. If it is true, write "true." If it is false, change the underlined name to make the statement true.
1. Herbert Hoover opened soup kitchens in Harlem during the Depression.
2. The Scottsboro Boys marched on Washington in the summer of 1932 to demand immediate payment of their pension bonuses.
3. Franklin Delano Roosevelt won the 1932 election by a huge margin.
4. In 1932 John Maynard Keynes ran for President on the Socialist ticket.
5. Father Divine supported massive government spending to revive the economy.

Reviewing Main Ideas

Section 1 (pp. 476 – 479)
1. Why did the economy of the 1920s inspire trust?
2. How did the rising stock market affect the way wealth was distributed in the United States?
3. Why did farmers fail to share in the 1920s prosperity?

Section 2 (pp. 480 – 483)
4. What were the results for investors when the Dow Jones average dropped suddenly?
5. Explain how the stock market crash started a downward cycle in the global economy.

Section 3 (pp. 486 – 490)
6. How did the Depression affect those at the bottom of the economic scale?

7. Why were farm families hit particularly hard by the Depression?
8. In what ways did the Depression affect African Americans more severely than white Americans?

Section 4 (pp. 492 – 494)
9. What were some ways in which people pulled together to help each other during the Depression?
10. In what ways did the end of Prohibition mark the end of an era?

Section 5 (pp. 495 – 499)
11. What government actions did Hoover finally take to try to end the Depression? Why did his program fail?
12. What programs had Roosevelt set up as governor of New York that foreshadowed his "new deal"?

1. **Predicting Consequences** If you had lived during the 1920s, what evidence would you have had of the coming Depression?

2. **Determining Relevance** During the Depression, some economists turned to the ideas of British economist John Maynard Keynes, who argued that massive government spending could help a collapsing economy. Do you agree with Keynes's approach? To what extent are Keynes's views still at work in the United States economy today?

3. **Recognizing Cause and Effect** Looking back, the stock market speculation and installment buying of the late 1920s may seem irresponsible. What reasons can you find for the way people were behaving at that time?

1. **Evaluating Primary Sources** Review the first primary source quotation on page 498. Do you agree with Hoover's assessment that the election of 1932 was a contest between two different philosophies of government? Explain your answer.

2. **Understanding the Visuals** Much of the "humor" of Depression jokes and cartoons is bitter rather than funny, like the cartoon on page 493. Look at the cartoons on pages 478 and 496 and answer the following questions: (a) What issues do they address? (b) What is the tone of the humor in each case?

3. **Writing About the Chapter** It is 1932. You want to preserve this period in history in a letter that your grandchildren can read in the 1990s. First list the main points you wish to make about events leading up to the Depression, daily life in difficult economic times, and the upcoming election. Note how your life has been permanently changed by the Depression. Then write a draft of a letter in which you explain your experiences and those of the people around you. Revise your letter, making sure that you have used enough detail to bring your experiences to life. Proofread your letter and draft a final copy.

4. **Using the Graphic Organizer** This graphic organizer uses a tree map to organize information about the social effects of the Depression. (a) Based on the graphic organizer below, what were the five social effects of the Depression? (b) According to the graphic organizer, which groups suffered increased discrimination due to the Depression? (c) On a separate sheet of paper, create your own graphic organizer about signs of trouble in the 1920s economy, using this graphic organizer as an example.

Social Effects of the Depression

- **Homelessness**
  - Hoovervilles
- **Farmers suffer**
  - Many lose farms
- **Poor diet and inadequate medical care**
  - Children especially hard hit
- **Family problems**
  - Families move in together
  - Men feel sense of failure
  - Women face job discrimination
  - Divorces and marriages both decline
- **Increased discrimination against African Americans**
  - Civil rights violations worsen
  - Unemployment soars to 56 percent for African Americans

The New Deal
1933–1938

*F*ranklin Roosevelt breezed into the White House, raising people's hopes with a promise to change the relationship between government and the economy. When the dust from FDR's first flurry of programs settled, critics were quick to point out the President's failures. Indeed, though the New Deal did help millions of Americans, it left many people out and failed to end the Depression. Still, the New Deal left permanent marks on American political, social, and cultural life—and on citizens' attitudes about their government.

Events in the United States

1932 Franklin Delano Roosevelt is elected President of the United States.

1933 Frances Perkins becomes the first woman cabinet member.

1934 Congress passes the Indian Reorganization Act.

1935 Congress passes the Social Security Act.

| 1932 | 1933 | 1934 | 1935 |

Events in the World

1932 Bolivia and Paraguay begin a three-year territorial war in which more than 100,000 people die.

1933 Hitler and the Nazis take over Germany.
• The Philippines gain independence from the United States.

1934 Stalin launches the Great Purge in the Soviet Union.

1935 Italy invades Ethiopia.
• German Jews lose citizenship under Nuremburg Laws.

1936 President Roosevelt wins reelection in a landslide.
• Auto workers strike in Michigan.

1937 Roosevelt's attempt to pack the Supreme Court fails.

1938 The Fair Labor Standards Act bans child labor.
• Orson Welles's radio production of H. G. Wells's War of the Worlds causes national panic.

1939 Author John Steinbeck publishes The Grapes of Wrath.
• Hollywood releases The Wizard of Oz.

1936	1937	1938	1939	1940

1936 The Spanish Civil War begins.
• Olympic Games held in Berlin.

1937 Japan launches a full-scale war against China.

1938 Mexico nationalizes its oil fields.

1939 Germany and the Soviet Union sign the Nazi-Soviet Pact.
• World War II begins.

Forging a New Deal

FDR came to office with a breezy confidence—and no detailed plan of action. But act he did, pushing program after program to spur recovery and reduce misery. Not all of his ideas worked as planned, but they did manage to give the nation hope.

Key Concepts
• The Roosevelt administration restored the optimism of the American people.
• After achieving mixed results with his New Deal, Roosevelt launched the Second New Deal.

Key Terms, People, and Places
New Deal, hundred days, public works program, Wagner Act, Social Security Act; Frances Perkins, Mary McLeod Bethune

Many victims of the Depression found work and relief through such government programs as the Civilian Conservation Corps—the CCC.

When Franklin Roosevelt took office in 1933, he had big plans for the country—the so-called **New Deal**. Even Roosevelt himself, however, was not sure exactly how the New Deal would work. Nevertheless, the new President's personality and willingness to experiment won him the support of the American people. As humorist Will Rogers said, "The whole country is with him, just so he does something. If he burned down the capital we would cheer and say, 'Well, we at least got a fire started anyhow.' "

Restoring the Nation's Hope

Shortly after FDR took office, World War I veterans staged a second Bonus March on Washington. This time, the new administration provided campsites for the veterans. Even more astounding, Eleanor Roosevelt paid them a visit.

When she drove up, "They looked at me curiously and one of them asked my name and what I wanted," she recalled. By the time she left an hour later, the veterans were waving and calling out, "Good-by and good luck to you!" The First Lady later told reporters how polite the marchers had been. By this act she both soothed popular fears about renewed radical agitation and demonstrated the new administration's approach to unrest.

FDR also soothed the public. In his inaugural address of March 4, 1933, he tried to restore confidence: "Let me assert my firm belief that the only thing we have to fear is fear itself." The first Sunday after taking office, Roosevelt spoke to the nation over the radio in what became regular "fireside chats." His easy manner and confidence calmed his listeners. His words contained little of substance, but they made people feel better.

The First Hundred Days In campaigning for the White House, FDR had promised "bold, persistent experimentation." No one knew exactly what that experimentation would entail, only that someone was going to do something. As reporter Arthur Krock expressed it, Washington "welcomes the 'new deal,' even though it is not sure what the new deal is going to be."

Americans soon found out. From March to June 1933, during a period known as the **hundred days,** FDR feverishly pushed program after program through Congress to provide relief, create jobs, and stimulate economic recovery. Some of these programs were based on federal agencies that had controlled the economy during World War I, or on programs started under Hoover or by state governors. Former progressives figured prominently, inspiring New Deal legislation or administering programs.

Closing the Banks FDR's first step was to restore public confidence in the nation's banks. On March 6 he ordered all banks to close. He then pushed Congress to pass the Emergency

Banking Act, which authorized the government to inspect the financial health of all banks. Congress also established a Federal Deposit Insurance Corporation (FDIC) to insure deposits up to $5,000.

These acts reassured the American people, many of whom had been terrified by the prospect of losing all their savings in a bank failure. Government inspectors found that most banks were healthy, and two thirds had reopened by March 15. After the brief "bank holiday," deposits at last exceeded withdrawals.

Providing Relief and Creating Jobs FDR's next step was to replenish badly depleted local relief agencies. Harry Hopkins, a former social worker, directed a Federal Emergency Relief Administration (FERA) that sent funds to these agencies. He was in office barely two hours before he had given out $5 million. At the same time, Hopkins professed a strong belief in helping people find work. He said,

> Give a man a dole [handout], *and you save his body and destroy his spirit. Give him a job and pay him an assured wage and you save both the body and the spirit.*

The government also put federal money behind **public works programs**—government-funded projects to build public facilities. Its

first such effort along these lines was the Civil Works Administration (CWA), which gave the unemployed jobs building or improving roads, parks, airports, and other facilities. The CWA was a tremendous morale booster to its 4 million employees. As a former insurance salesman from Alabama remarked, "When I got that [CWA identification] card it was the biggest day in my whole life. At last I could say, 'I've got a job.'"

FDR believed fervently in conservation of the environment. For this reason, the Civilian Conservation Corps (CCC), which put 2.5 million unmarried male workers into forest, beach, and

President Roosevelt's manner both radiated and inspired confidence. At Hilltop Cottage in Hyde Park, New York, FDR chats with the caretaker's granddaughter in 1941.

1650   1700   1750   1800

Links Across Time

1850   1900   1950   2000

Putting People to Work

When President Roosevelt took office in 1933, at least one of every four American workers was unemployed. Among FDR's first initiatives were programs to provide work—programs similar to ones Bill Clinton proposed during his presidential campaign in 1992.

New Deal programs created a variety of work agencies, such as the Civilian Conservation Corps (CCC), the Public Works Administration (PWA),

and the National Youth Administration (NYA). These organizations provided work to people who would otherwise have had none.

In 1993 Bill Clinton responded to high unemployment figures by proposing to invest $100 billion dollars in building and repairing roads, bridges, sewers, airports, and communication systems. He also proposed spending federal money on a job-training program that would

include classes and apprenticeships. Clinton hoped that his spending programs would provide work for unemployed Americans.

Roosevelt was able to put his plans into action. President Clinton hoped to use similar programs to help people learn skills and earn a living. ***Based on what you know about reactions to the New Deal, what do you think were the reactions to President Clinton's plan?***

The CCC gave young people jobs and preserved the nation's natural resources. This worker is planting seedlings in Montana.

NRA participants displayed the blue eagle label shown below.

NRA
MEMBER

U.S.

WE DO OUR PART

park maintenance and restoration projects, was his favorite program. CCC workers earned only $1 a day but were boarded in camps and received job training. One participant commented that CCC work "gives a fellow self-confidence and teaches them how to get along by themselves." Thanks to Eleanor Roosevelt's intervention, from 1934 to 1937 the CCC funded similar programs for young women, though only 8,500 women benefited.

Public works programs also helped Native Americans. John Collier, FDR's commissioner of Indian affairs, used New Deal funds and Native American workers to build schools, hospitals, and irrigation systems. Native Americans also benefited from the Indian Reorganization Act of 1934, which ended the sale of tribal lands begun under the Dawes Act (1887) and restored ownership of unallocated lands to Native American groups.

A Helping Hand to Business The sharp decline of industrial prices in the early 1930s had caused many business failures—and also much unemployment. The National Industrial Recovery Act (NIRA) of June 1933 sought to bolster those prices and thus help businesses and individuals.

The NIRA allowed trade associations in many industries to draw up codes to regulate wages, working conditions, production, and even prices. The act also set a minimum wage and gave organized labor collective bargaining rights.

For a brief time, the codes stopped the tailspin of industrial prices. But by the fall of 1933, when higher wages went into effect, prices rose, too. Consumers stopped buying. The cycle of overproduction and underconsumption returned, and many businesses failed. Businesses soon complained that the codes were too complicated and that control by the National Recovery Administration (NRA) was too rigid. Critics joked that NRA really stood for "National Run Around" or "No Recovery Allowed."

The best part of the NIRA may have been its Public Works Administration (PWA). Directed by Secretary of the Interior Harold Ickes, the PWA launched projects ranging from the Grand Coulee Dam on the Columbia River in the state of Washington, to the causeway connecting Key West to the Florida mainland, to New York's Triborough Bridge.

Another New Deal act was less pleasing to business. A Federal Securities Act (May 1933) required full disclosure of information about stock offered for sale. The next year, Congress set up the Securities and Exchange Commission (SEC) to regulate the stock market. Congress also gave the Federal Reserve Board power to regulate the purchase of stock on margin—a practice that had contributed heavily to the crash.

Saving Homes and Farms The New Deal helped people keep their homes and farms. The Home Owners' Loan Corporation (HOLC) refinanced mortgages of middle-income home owners. An Agricultural Adjustment Administration (AAA) tried to raise farm prices. The AAA used proceeds from a new tax to pay farmers not to raise certain crops and animals. Lower production, it was hoped, would raise prices.

Under this program, some farmers also destroyed animals and plowed under growing crops. Many Americans, however, could not understand how the federal government could encourage the destruction of food while so many Americans were hungry.

Improving the Quality of Life One public works project proved especially popular. The Tennessee Valley Authority (TVA), created in May 1933, helped farmers and created jobs in one of the country's least modernized regions. By

The Tennessee Valley Authority

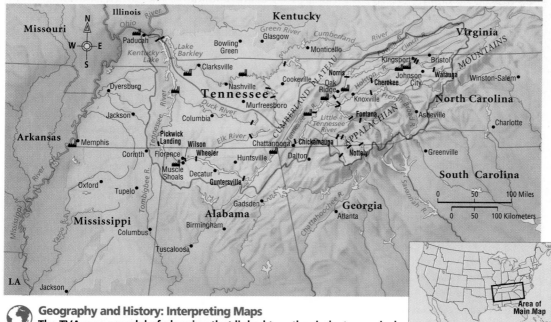

Geography and History: Interpreting Maps
The TVA was a model of planning that linked together industry, agriculture, forestry science, and flood prevention. To many critics, however, the TVA was also the emblem of big government. *In how many states did the TVA provide service and benefits?*

reactivating a hydroelectric power facility started during World War I, the TVA provided cheap electric power, flood control, and recreational opportunities to the entire Tennessee River valley, as shown on the map above.

MAKING CONNECTIONS

What are the major differences between FDR's approach to the Depression and Hoover's?

New Deal Personnel

FDR surrounded himself with eager and hardworking advisers. Some, like Hopkins and Ickes, went directly into his cabinet or headed one of the new agencies. Others, such as Raymond Moley, Adolf A. Berle, and Rexford G. Tugwell, were part of a so-called brain trust, an informal group of intellectuals who helped Roosevelt devise policies. For the first time, a woman held a cabinet post. **Frances Perkins** became secretary of labor, a job she held until 1945. Perkins was one of almost thirty women who held key New Deal positions.

Eleanor Roosevelt Among FDR's most important colleagues was his wife, Eleanor Roosevelt. She threw herself into supporting New Deal programs and traveled widely for her husband, visiting coal mines, sewing rooms, and housing projects. She held her own press conferences, and in 1935 started her own newspaper column, "My Day," in which she drummed up support for the New Deal.

At times, ER took stands that embarrassed her husband. For example, in 1938 at a Birmingham, Alabama, meeting of the Southern Conference for Human Welfare, an interracial group, she knew she had to obey local Jim Crow laws that required African Americans and whites to sit in separate parts of the auditorium. In protest, she sat in the center aisle between the divided races. Her act

Eleanor Roosevelt surprised many Americans with her activism. In 1933 alone, she traveled 40,000 miles. Here, the First Lady emerges from an inspection of an Ohio coal mine.

received wide publicity, and no one missed its symbolism.

Many Americans were confused by ER's activities. In their view, a First Lady should take care of her husband and serve graciously at state dinners. Gradually, the public got used to ER, and many came to admire her for her idealism and humanity.

AMERICAN PROFILES

Mary McLeod Bethune

FDR's administration broke new ground by hiring African Americans to more than one hundred policy-making posts. One of Roosevelt's key appointments was **Mary McLeod Bethune** (1875–1955), who held the highest position of any black woman in the New Deal.

The President was not the first to recognize Bethune's talents. From the mid-1920s on, she had been one of the country's most influential spokespersons for African American concerns. Bethune achieved this status through her efforts in three areas: education, women's voluntary associations, and government.

Improving African American Education Born near Mayesville, South Carolina, Bethune was the fifteenth of seventeen children born to for-

"Your road may be somewhat less rugged because of the struggles we have made." So stated Mary McLeod Bethune of efforts in the New Deal era to further the interests of women and African Americans.

merly enslaved parents. With the help of a scholarship and money she earned by ironing, cooking, and cleaning, she received an education at the Scotia Seminary in Concord, North Carolina. Bethune's opportunity did not come without sacrifice. For example, during one period at Scotia, Bethune owned only one dress, which she washed out each night and wore again the next day.

In 1895 Bethune began training for missionary work in Africa, only to discover a year later that her church sent out only white missionaries. Undaunted, she turned her missionary spirit toward teaching, and in 1904 moved to Daytona Beach, Florida, determined to open a school for African American girls. Describing how she started this enterprise, Bethune later wrote:

> On October 3, 1904, I opened the doors of my school, with an enrollment of five little girls, aged from eight to twelve, whose parents paid me fifty cents weekly tuition. . . . Though I hadn't a penny left, I considered cash money as the smallest part of my resources. I had faith in a living God, faith in myself, and a desire to serve.

Later, Bethune moved her school to the site of an old dumping ground. She purchased the land with a five-dollar down payment, which she raised by selling ice cream and sweet-potato pies to local laborers.

That was how the Daytona Normal and Industrial Institute got started. Despite its humble beginnings, the school prospered. By 1918 Bethune had added a four-year high school. In 1923 it merged with Cookman Institute, a coeducational school in Jacksonville. This institution was renamed Bethune-Cookman College in 1929, and Bethune became its president.

Volunteerism Bethune was also active in voluntary groups, including the NAACP, National Urban League, and National Association of Colored Women. Assuming the presidency of this last group in 1924, Bethune developed international contacts to forge "a significant link between the peoples of color throughout the world." In 1935 she founded the National Council of Negro Women, which represented thirty African American women's organizations.

Serving in Government Also in 1935, the New Deal's National Youth Administration made her a consultant to its advisory council. This work eventually earned her an appointment to the post of director of the Division of Negro Affairs.

In her government posts, Bethune encouraged programs that aided African Americans. She also sought a share of New Deal posts for African Americans. "The White man has been thinking for us too long," she said, expressing her belief that African American officeholders would be more sensitive to African American concerns. She forged a united stand among black officeholders by organizing a Federal Council on Negro Affairs in August 1936. This unofficial group, known as the black cabinet, met weekly to hammer out priorities and to increase African American support for the New Deal.

At a time when no governmental commitment to the improvement of the lives of African Americans existed, Bethune helped create one. Recipient in 1935 of the NAACP's most prestigious award, the Spingarn Medal, and twelve honorary degrees, Bethune reached an extraordinary level of influence for women and for African Americans. Speaking about Bethune, Roosevelt once remarked, "I believe in her because she has her feet on the ground; not only on the ground but deep down in the plowed soil."

The End of the Honeymoon

The zeal and energy with which New Dealers attacked the Depression pleased most observers. But when the new programs failed to bring about significant economic improvement, criticism began to mount. Many worried about the increasing power that New Deal agencies were giving to the federal government. Former President Hoover warned against "a state-controlled or state-directed social or economic system. . . . That is not liberalism; it is tyranny," he said. Other criticisms of the New Deal are discussed in Section 2.

In 1935 the Supreme Court declared the NRA unconstitutional because it gave the President law-making powers and regulated local, rather than interstate, commerce. The following year, the Court ruled that the tax that funded AAA subsidies to farmers was also unconstitutional. The New Deal's most important programs had crumbled. It was time to reassess.

A Second New Deal

Meanwhile, most of the public remained behind Roosevelt. The midterm elections of 1934 showed stunning nationwide support for FDR's administration. In 1935 he launched a new, even bolder burst of legislative activity. Some have called this period the Second New Deal. In part, it was a response to his various critics. The Second New Deal included more social welfare benefits, stricter controls over business, stronger support for unions, and higher taxes on the rich.

New and Expanded Agencies New agencies attacked joblessness even more aggressively than before. The Works Progress Administration (WPA), an agency set up in 1935 and lasting eight years, provided work for more than eight million citizens. The WPA constructed or improved more than 20,000 playgrounds, schools, hospitals, and airfields, and supported the creative work of many artists and writers (see Section 3).

The Second New Deal responded to the worsening plight of agricultural workers. The original AAA had ignored many of the farm workers who did not own land. In the Southwest, for example, Mexican American farm workers struggled to survive. Many were forced to return to Mexico; others tried to form unions, inspiring fierce resistance from farmer associations. In the South, landlords had pocketed AAA subsidies, taken land out of production, and left tenants and sharecroppers to shift for themselves.

In May 1935 Rexford Tugwell set up a Resettlement Administration that loaned money to owners of small farms and helped resettle tenants and sharecroppers on productive land. In 1937 a Farm Security Administration (FSA) replaced Tugwell's agency. It loaned more than $1 billion to farmers and set up camps for migrant workers.

New Labor Legislation Labor unions had liked the NIRA provision—known as 7a—that granted them the right to organize and bargain collectively. When the NIRA was declared unconstitutional, however, workers began to demand new legislation to protect their rights.

In July 1935, Congress responded. It passed a National Labor Relations Act, called the **Wagner Act** after its leading advocate, New York senator Robert Wagner. The Wagner Act legalized practices allowed only unevenly in the past, such as closed shops—in which only union members can work—and collective bargaining. It also outlawed spying on union activities and blacklisting—a

A major Second New Deal program was the Social Security Act, which provided a variety of benefits to many retired, disabled, and unemployed workers. The original social security program did not cover agricultural or domestic workers.

practice in which employers agreed not to hire union leaders. The act also set up a National Labor Relations Board (NLRB) to enforce its provisions.

In 1938 a Fair Labor Standards Act banned child labor and established a minimum wage for all workers covered under the act. This law was a long-awaited triumph for progressive-era social reformers.

Social Legislation Congress also passed the **Social Security Act,** establishing a system that provided old-age pensions for workers; survivors' benefits for victims of industrial accidents; unemployment insurance; and aid for dependent mothers and children, the blind, and the physically disabled. The act was based

in part on models from European welfare states, and it was funded through contributions from employers and workers, which were then later paid out to people covered by the system who were not earning a wage.

Though the original Social Security Act did not cover many farm and domestic workers, it did help millions of beneficiaries feel more secure. Its importance to the American people has continued to grow, and its success has helped inspire numerous other social welfare programs.

The 1936 Election

No one expected the Republican presidential candidate of 1936, Kansas governor Alfred M. Landon, to beat FDR. But few predicted the extent of FDR's landslide. FDR carried every state except Maine and Vermont. Although Depression conditions had increased support for radical movements, no effective third party emerged to challenge the capitalist system. FDR buried Socialist Norman Thomas, who received fewer than 200,000 votes, and Communist candidate Earl Browder, who won only 80,000 votes.

Indeed, a broad cross section of the country's population supported the New Deal. Forming a new Democratic majority were farmers, recent immigrants, skilled and unskilled workers, northern African Americans, and women. Democrats also received support from the unions. Yet the New Deal was not without its critics, as the next section discusses.

SECTION 1 REVIEW

Key Terms, People, and Places
1. Describe (a) New Deal, (b) hundred days, (c) Wagner Act, (d) Social Security Act.
2. Identify Frances Perkins.

Key Concepts
3. What were some of the ways in which the Roosevelt administration restored hope to the nation?
4. What were some of the first New Deal programs?

5. In what ways did Mary McLeod Bethune seek to help African Americans?
6. What were the most important features of the Second New Deal?

Critical Thinking
7. **Drawing Conclusions** How do you explain the popularity of FDR with American voters?

The New Deal's Critics

SECTION PREVIEW

For millions of Americans, the New Deal meant survival, security, and even opportunity. Others, including many women and minorities, noted its failures with bitterness. As the New Deal continued to disappoint, its critics accumulated large followings across the political spectrum.

Key Concepts
• New Deal programs often treated women and minorities unfairly.
• The New Deal was criticized both for what it did and for what it did not do.

Key Terms, People, and Places
political right, political left, demagogue; Father Charles E. Coughlin, Huey Long

Franklin Roosevelt's success at the polls in 1936 suggests overwhelming approval of his New Deal. Indeed, vast numbers of Americans benefited from the relief and employment programs of the New Deal. Letters thanking the President poured into the White House. One example read:

> I'm proud of our United States and every time I hear the "Star-Spangled Banner" I feel a lump in my throat. There ain't no other nation in the world that would have sense enough to think of WPA and all the other A's.

Yet the New Deal had its failures—and inspired its share of critics. Another letter to Roosevelt read:

> If you could get around the country as I have and seen the distress forced upon the American people, you would throw your darn NRA and AAA, and every other . . . A into the sea.

The Limits of the New Deal

For all its success, the New Deal fell short of expectations. The Fair Labor Standards Act, for example, covered fewer than one quarter of all gainfully employed workers and set the minimum wage at twenty-five cents an hour—well below what most covered workers already made. New Deal agencies also were generally less helpful to women and minority groups than they were to white men.

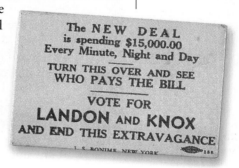

Women Many aspects of New Deal legislation put women at a disadvantage. The NRA codes, for example, permitted lower wages for women's work in almost a fourth of all cases. In relief and jobs programs, men and boys received strong preference. Jobs went to male "heads of families," unless the men were unable to work. No New Deal provision protected domestic service, the largest female occupation. In 1942 an African American domestic worker in St. Louis pleaded with the President to ask the "rich people" to "give us some hours to rest in and some Sundays off and pay us more wages." Working fourteen-hour days, she earned only $6.50 per week. An official matter-of-factly wrote back,

> State and Federal labor laws, which offer protection to workers in so many occupations, have so far not set up standards for working conditions in domestic situations. There is nothing that can be done . . . to help you and others in this kind of employment.

African Americans In the South, federal relief programs reinforced racial segregation. No person of color received a job at a professional level. Segregation prevailed on public works

Millions of Americans benefited from the New Deal. But critics, including FDR's 1936 opponent Alf Landon, were quick to point out the program's problems and shortcomings.

WORLD'S HIGHEST STANDARD OF LIVING

There's no way like the American Way

Using Historical Evidence This picture, taken at a relief center in Louisville, Kentucky, highlights the struggle of African Americans to overcome both the Depression and the effects of prejudice. *What elements of this picture contribute to its ironic effect?*

projects, and African Americans received lower pay than whites and were kept from skilled jobs on dam and electric power projects. Because the Social Security Act excluded both farmers and domestic workers, it failed to cover nearly two thirds of working African Americans.

African Americans in the North had not supported FDR in 1932. By 1936 they had joined his camp. Often the last hired and first fired, they had experienced the highest unemployment rates of any group during the Depression. They therefore appreciated many New Deal programs.

Yet the New Deal did nothing to end distressing discriminatory practices in the North. Especially troubling was the employment of only whites in white-owned businesses in black neighborhoods. In the absence of help from the federal government, African Americans took matters into their own hands. Protesters picketed and boycotted such businesses with the slogan "Don't shop where you can't work."

The early Depression also had seen an alarming rise in the number of lynchings. The federal government again offered no relief. In 1935 and 1938, bills to make lynching a federal crime went down to narrow defeat. NAACP head Walter White recalled in 1948 that FDR had given this explanation for his refusal to support these measures:

Southerners, by reason of seniority rule in Congress, are chairmen or occupy strategic places on most of the Senate and House committees. If I come out for the anti-lynching bill now, they will block every bill I ask Congress to pass to keep America from collapsing. I just can't take that risk.

Of course, FDR's record with African Americans was not all bad. FDR appointed more than a hundred African Americans to policy-making posts. The Roosevelts also conveyed an apparently genuine concern for the fate of African Americans. These factors help to explain FDR's wide support among black voters.

Criticism of the New Deal

African Americans may have supported FDR. But many others, at each end of the political spectrum, criticized the New Deal.

Criticism from the Right The **political right**—typically made up of those who want to preserve a current system or power structure—opposed Roosevelt. These critics included many wealthy people, who regarded FDR as their enemy. Early in the New Deal, they had disapproved of programs such as the TVA, which they considered to be socialistic. The Second New Deal gave them even more to hate, as FDR pushed through a series of higher taxes aimed at the rich.

The Social Security Act also aroused opposition from the right. Some people felt that it penalized successful, hardworking people. Other critics saw the assignment of social security numbers as the first step toward a militaristic, regimented society. They predicted that soon people would have to wear metal dog tags engraved with their social security numbers.

A group called the American Liberty League (1934) spearheaded much right-wing opposition to the New Deal. It was led by former Democratic presidential candidate Alfred E. Smith, the National Association of Manufacturers, and business figures such as John J. Raskob and the Du Pont family.

The league charged the New Deal with limiting individual freedom in an unconstitutional, "un-American" manner. To them, programs such as compulsory unemployment insurance smacked of "Bolshevism." They advised instead that people take responsibility for themselves and practice "thrift and self-denial."

Socialists and Progressives Others attacked the New Deal from the left. The **political left** generally seeks governmental change—sometimes radical change—as a means of helping the common people. These critics accused the New Deal of not going far enough in addressing the nation's ills.

In 1934 muckraking novelist and socialist Upton Sinclair ran for governor of California on the Democratic ticket. His platform, "End Poverty in California" (EPIC), called for a new economic system in which the state would take over factories and farms. EPIC clubs formed throughout the state, and Sinclair won the primary. Terrified, opponents used dirty tricks to discredit Sinclair. They produced fake newsreels showing people speaking in a Russian accent and endorsing Sinclair. Associated unfairly with Soviet communism, Sinclair lost the election.

The limited success of the New Deal in eliminating poverty helped lead to a revival of progressivism in Minnesota and Wisconsin. Running for the United States Senate, Wisconsin progressive Robert La Follette, Jr., argued that "devices which seek to preserve the unequal distribution of wealth . . . will halt the progress of mankind and, in the end, will retard or prevent recovery." His brother, Philip, also took a radical stand, calling for the redistribution of income. Philip's ideas persuaded the state Socialist party to join his progressives after he won the Wisconsin governorship in 1934.

MAKING CONNECTIONS

Consider what you have read about the poverty caused by the Depression. Do you agree with the criticisms of the political left or the political right? Explain why.

Using Historical Evidence The artist who created this cartoon had little faith that FDR's New Deal programs were in the country's best interest. *What is it that has put the "patient" to sleep? What does the cartoon imply will happen when the "patient" wakes up?*

Other New Deal Critics

Some New Deal critics were **demagogues**—charismatic leaders who manipulate people with half-truths, deceptive promises, and scare tactics. One such demagogue was **Father Charles E. Coughlin,** who used the radio to broadcast his message. In the early 1930s, the so-called Radio Priest was holding national audiences spellbound.

Coughlin achieved popularity in spite of the fact that his ideas were not consistent. Sometimes he advocated nationalizing the banks and redistributing wealth. At others, he defended the sanctity of private property. After first endorsing the New Deal, in 1934 he formed a "National Union for Social Justice," which denounced it. His increasing attacks on FDR grew reckless. In 1936 he called Franklin "Double-crossing" Roosevelt a "great betrayer and liar."

By the end of the 1930s, Coughlin was issuing openly anti-Semitic statements and showering praise on Adolf Hitler and Benito Mussolini, two menacing leaders who were then rising to power in Europe. Coughlin's actions alarmed many, and he lost some of his support. In the early 1940s, Roman Catholic officials ordered him to cease his broadcasts.

Huey Long—also known as the Kingfish—was a different type of demagogue. A country lawyer, he won the governorship of Louisiana in 1928 and became a United States senator in 1932. Unlike many other southern Democrats, Long never used racial attacks as the basis of his power. Instead, he worked to help the underprivileged, improving education, medical care, and public services. He also built an extraordinarily powerful and ruthless political machine.

Huey Long (below) achieved great popularity in the 1930s with his motto, "Every man a king." He had his eye on the presidency before his assassination.

Originally a supporter of FDR, he broke with him early in the New Deal. "Unless we provide for redistribution of wealth in this country, the country is doomed," he said. Calling his program "Share Our Wealth" (SOW) and using the motto "Every man a king," Long in 1934 proposed high taxes on large fortunes and inheritances, and grants of $5,000 to each American family.

Long's overly simplistic plan for helping all Americans achieve wealth attracted many followers. His success helped push FDR to propose new taxes on wealthy Americans in the Second New Deal. Meanwhile, Long began to eye the presidency. But in September 1935, the son-in-law of one of his political enemies shot and killed him.

Long and Coughlin never seriously threatened FDR or the New Deal. But their popularity warned Roosevelt that if he failed to spread the country's wealth more widely, he risked losing popular support.

The Court-Packing Scheme

Roosevelt received criticism not only for his programs, but also for his actions. No act aroused more opposition than his attempt to pack the Supreme Court.

Throughout the early New Deal, the Supreme Court had caused FDR his greatest frustration. The Court, which included four conservative justices, had invalidated the NRA, the AAA, and many state laws from the progressive era. In February 1937, FDR proposed a major court reform bill.

The Constitution had not specified the number of Supreme Court justices. Congress had last changed the number in 1869. But by Roosevelt's time, the number nine had become well established. Arguing dishonestly that he wanted to lighten the burden of the aging justices, FDR asked Congress to pass his reform, enabling him to appoint as many as six additional justices, one for each justice over seventy years of age. Most people understood Roosevelt's real intention. He wanted to "pack" the Court with judges favorable to the New Deal.

Negative reaction came swiftly from all sides. The President, critics raged, was trying to inject politics into the judiciary and was attacking the constitutional principle of separation of powers. With Hitler, Mussolini, and Stalin ruling as dictators in Germany, Italy, and the Soviet Union, the world seemed already to be tilting toward tyranny. If Congress let FDR reshape the Supreme Court, critics worried, the United States might follow. Sam E. Roberts of Kansas wrote his representative in Congress:

O ur liberty is much more important than any whim of the President's. He might be a kind dictator himself, but after the stage is set the next President might be a Hitler or Mussolini.

California's aging senator Hiram W. Johnson expressed the views of many legislators when he said:

S hall the Congress make the Supreme Court subservient to [subject to] the presidency? The implications of this are so grave and far-reaching, I can do but one thing, and that is, . . . oppose this extraordinary legislation.

FDR was forced to withdraw his reform. He also suffered much political damage. Southern Democrats and conservative Republicans united against further New Deal legislation. This alliance remained a force for years to come.

FDR did wind up with a liberal majority on the Court. Some older justices retired, allowing FDR to appoint his own justices. Even earlier, the Court had begun to uphold measures from

Viewpoints
On The New Deal

FDR's promise to improve life for all Americans with a New Deal did not win approval from all quarters. **Why, according to the viewpoints below, were some people pleased and some displeased with the New Deal?**

For the New Deal

"Roosevelt is the only President we ever had that thought the Constitution belonged to the pore [poor] man too. . . . Yessir, it took Roosevelt to read in the Constitution and find out them folks way back yonder that made it was talkin' about the pore man right along with the rich one. I am a Roosevelt man."
Testimony by mill worker George Dobbin, 1939. Collected in *These Are Our Lives,* Federal Writers Project of the Works Progress Administration (1939).

Against the New Deal

"All the prosperity he had brought to the country has been legislated and is not real. Nothing he has ever started has been finished. My common way of expressing it is that we are in the middle of the ocean like a ship without an anchor. No good times can come to the country as long as there is so much discrimination practiced. . . . I don't see much chance for our people to get anywhere when the color line instead of ability determines the opportunities to get ahead economically."
Testimony by Sam T. Mayhew, 1939.
Collected in *Such As Us* (1978).

the Second New Deal, including the Wagner Act—perhaps because the laws had been better thought out and drafted.

SECTION 2 REVIEW

Key Terms, People, and Places
1. Define (a) political right, (b) political left, (c) demagogue.
2. Identify (a) Father Charles E. Coughlin, (b) Huey Long.

Key Concepts
3. How did New Deal programs discriminate against or neglect women and minorities?
4. Why did people criticize FDR and the New Deal?

5. What was Franklin Roosevelt's attitude toward African American concerns about lynching?

Critical Thinking
6. **Checking Consistency** The text says that Roosevelt had critics at both ends of the political spectrum during the New Deal. Yet Roosevelt was easily reelected in 1936. How do you explain these two apparently conflicting facts?

Distinguishing Fact from Opinion

When you read historical materials—such as speeches, letters, and diaries—you will find that their authors express both facts and opinions. A fact is something that can be proved to be true by checking other sources. An opinion is a judgment that reflects beliefs or feelings—it may or may not be true.

To determine the soundness of an author's ideas, you need to be able to distinguish between fact and opinion. The ability to do so will help you evaluate what you read and reach your own conclusions about historical events.

Use the following steps to distinguish between fact and opinion in Herbert Hoover's criticism of the New Deal, excerpted from his speech to the Republican National Convention in 1936.

1. Determine which statements are facts. Remember that facts can be checked and confirmed by other sources. (a) For what reason is Hoover's first statement, about the Supreme Court, easily recognizable as a fact? (b) Choose two other statements of fact in the excerpt. Explain how you might prove that each statement is a fact.

2. Determine which statements are opinions. Sometimes authors signal opinions with phrases such as "I believe" or "I think," but often they do not. Other clues that indicate opinions are sweeping generalizations and emotion-packed words. (a) What indicates that the final sentence of the first paragraph is an opinion rather than a fact? (b) Choose two other statements of opinion, and explain what tells you that they are opinions.

3. Separate facts from opinions as you read. Generally, an opinion is more reliable when an author gives facts to support it. (a) How does Hoover support his opinion that many New Deal acts "were a violation of the rights of men and of self-government"? (b) Does he present any facts to support his statement that the Congress has "abandoned its responsibility"? (c) In your opinion, how good a job has Hoover done in supporting his opinions? Explain your answer.

"The Supreme Court has reversed some ten or twelve of the New Deal major enactments. Many of these acts were a violation of the rights of men and of self-government. Despite the sworn duty of the Executive and Congress to defend these rights, they have sought to take them into their own hands. That is an attack on the foundations of freedom.

More than this, the independence of the Congress, the Supreme Court, and the Executive are pillars at the door of liberty. For three years the word "must" has invaded the independence of Congress. And the Congress has abandoned its responsibility to check even the expenditures [spending] of money. . . .

We have seen these gigantic expenditures and this torrent of waste pile up a national debt which two generations cannot repay. One time I told a Democratic Congress that "You cannot spend your way into prosperity." You recall that advice did not take then. It hasn't taken yet.

Billions have been spent to prime the economic pump. It did employ a horde of paid officials upon the pump handle. We have seen the frantic attempts to find new taxes on the rich. Yet three-quarters of the bill will be sent to the average man and the poor. He and his wife and his grandchildren will be giving a quarter of all their working days to pay taxes. Freedom to work for himself is changed into a slavery of work for the follies of government. . . .

We have seen the building up of a horde of political officials. We have seen the pressures upon the helpless and destitute to trade political support for relief. Both are a pollution of the very fountains of liberty."

—Herbert Hoover, excerpted from *American Ideals Versus the New Deal*

518

Enduring Legacies of the New Deal

SECTION PREVIEW

The New Deal attacked the Great Depression with a barrage of programs and agencies. The Depression withstood this onslaught and refused to loosen its grip on the economy. Yet the New Deal was not without effect; it left a legacy that endures to this day.

Key Concepts
- The New Deal did not resolve the economic problems of the Depression.
- The New Deal did leave a significant legacy that has affected the presidency, labor unions, and American cultural life.

Key Terms, People, and Places
national debt, Congress of Industrial Organizations, sit-down strike

T he New Deal did not attempt truly radical solutions to the problems of the American economy in the 1930s. Neither did it end the nation's suffering. It did, however, lead to some profound and lasting changes in American politics and social life.

FDR and the New Deal increased the public's expectations of the presidency. Voters began to expect a President to formulate programs and solve problems. Government now was authorized to intervene in major ways, and business could no longer resist regulation—or unionization—with claims about the sanctity of private property.

In addition to its effects on the economy, the New Deal also helped enhance American cultural life. Americans of the 1930s—and of future generations—were entertained and enriched due to programs aimed at helping artists.

The Recession of 1937

The New Deal did not put an end to the Great Depression. As predicted by economist John Maynard Keynes (see Chapter 16), the New Deal's massive government spending did lead to some economic improvement. But the economy collapsed again in August 1937, as you can see on the graph on page 520.

Reductions in consumer income from social security payroll deductions were partly to blame. Americans had less money in their pockets, and so bought fewer goods. Consumers also had less money because FDR had cut back on programs such as the WPA. The President—who campaigned in 1932 with a promise to balance the budget—had become distressed at the rising **national debt.** This is the total amount of money the federal government has borrowed and has yet to pay back. Because the government spent more than it took in, the debt rose from $21 billion in 1933 to $43 billion by 1940.

After 1937, Harry Hopkins and others convinced FDR to start up the suspended programs in 1938. Joblessness and misery slowly decreased. Still, hard times lasted well into the 1940s, until the nation's entry into World War II.

The Triumph of the Labor Unions

By legalizing unions, the New Deal permanently changed the relations between workers and employers in America. Union membership rose from 3 million in 1933 to 10.5 million by 1941, a figure representing 28 percent of the nonagricultural work force. By 1945, 36 percent were unionized, the high-water mark for unions in the United States.

A New Labor Organization Activism by powerful union leaders helped to increase membership. The cautious and craft-based American Federation of Labor (AFL) had done

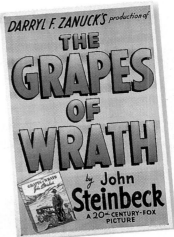

DARRYL F. ZANUCK'S production of THE GRAPES OF WRATH by John Steinbeck A 20th CENTURY-FOX PICTURE

The Depression era produced many lasting works of art, including the novel *The Grapes of Wrath* and the movie that was based on it.

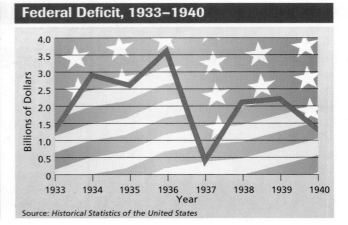

Federal Public Debt, 1933–1940

Source: *Historical Statistics of the United States*

Federal Deficit, 1933–1940

Source: *Historical Statistics of the United States*

Interpreting Graphs
The New Deal was paid for by huge increases in government spending. Because of yearly deficits, the national debt expanded greatly during the Depression. *In which year was the deficit the greatest? The lowest?*

little to attract unskilled industrial workers during its half-century of existence. In 1935 United Mine Workers president John L. Lewis, whose bushy eyebrows made him a familiar front-page figure, joined with other AFL unions to create a Committee for Industrial Organizations (CIO) within the AFL. Though the AFL did not support its efforts, the CIO sought to organize the nation's unskilled workers. It sent organizers into steel mills, auto plants, and southern textile mills and welcomed all workers regardless of sex, color, or skill. The AFL suspended the CIO unions in 1936. Nevertheless, by 1938 the CIO had two million members. The group then changed its name to the **Congress of Industrial Organizations** and in November of that year it formed a new union.

An Era of Strikes The Wagner Act legalized collective bargaining and told management it had to bargain in good faith with certified union representatives. But the act could not force a company to accept union demands. Although the Wagner Act was designed to bring about industrial peace, in the short run it led to a wave of some of the country's most spectacular strikes.

Many of these work stoppages were known as **sit-down strikes,** in which workers stopped work and refused to leave the premises. Supporters outside then organized picket lines. Together the strikers and the picket line prevented the company from bringing in scabs, or substitute workers, and the business was paralyzed.

Sit-down strikes began in the rubber tire plants in Akron, Ohio. The most famous took place in the winter of 1936 to 1937 in Flint, Michigan. In this strike, workers associated with the United Auto Workers (UAW) occupied General Motors' Fisher body plants. GM executives turned off the heat and blocked entry to the plants so that the workers could not receive food. They also sent in police against picketers outside. Violence erupted. The wife of a striker then grabbed a bullhorn and urged other wives to join the picketers. The group became so large that the police could not control them. Women later organized food deliveries to supply the strikers, set up a speakers' bureau to present the union's position to the public, and formed a Women's Emergency Brigade to take up picket duty. Governor Frank Murphy of Michigan and President Roosevelt refused to use the militia against the strike. By

Thanks in part to the Wagner Act and the efforts of the CIO, union membership soared in the 1930s. By 1939, nearly 30 percent of nonagricultural workers belonged to unions.

early February, General Motors had given in.

Not all strikes were as successful. Henry Ford continued to resist unionism. In 1937 at a Ford plant near Detroit, his men viciously beat UAW officials when the unionists tried to distribute leaflets. Walter Reuther, a beating victim and future president of the UAW later testified,

> They picked me up about eight different times and threw me down on my back on the concrete. While I was on the ground they kicked me in the face, head, and other parts of my body. . . . I never raised a hand.

The successful sit-down strike at the Fisher body plant in the winter of 1936–37 demonstrated the effectiveness of the new technique. Here, workers guard a window during the strike.

Like the Ford Company, Republic Steel Company refused to sign with steelworkers' unions until war loomed in 1941. At one bloody strike at Republic Steel on Memorial Day 1937, Chicago police killed ten picketers. Southern textile workers and clerical workers, both made up primarily of women, also remained unorganized in spite of New Deal efforts.

Cultural Life in the Thirties

Hard times stimulated a great release of creative energy in the United States during the Depression. In addition, Congress allocated federal funds to support the popular and fine arts. As a result, despite general unemployment among professionals, the arts not only thrived but created some enduring cultural legacies for the nation.

Literature Works of literature destined to become classics emerged during this period. Three examples are Pearl Buck's *The Good Earth* (1931), a saga of peasant struggle in China; John Steinbeck's *The Grapes of Wrath* (1939), a powerful tale about dust-bowl victims who travel to California; and Margaret Mitchell's fictional re-creation of the Old South, *Gone With the Wind* (1936). In 1936 Tennessee writer James Agee and photographer Walker Evans lived for a few weeks with sharecropper families in Alabama and produced a masterpiece of nonfiction literature, *Let Us Now Praise Famous Men* (1941). Folklorist Zora Neale Hurston wrote the classic *Their Eyes Are Watching God* (1937), a novel about an African American woman in Florida.

Radio and Movies Radio became the major medium of entertainment for most American families. In particular, comedy shows peaked in the thirties, producing stars such as Jack Benny, Fred Allen, George Burns, and Gracie Allen. The first soap operas—so called because they often were sponsored by soap companies—emerged in this period. These fifteen-minute stories designed to promote strong emotional responses were aimed at women who remained at home during the day. Symphony music and opera also thrived over the radio. By 1939 the country boasted 270 symphony orchestras.

By 1933 the movies had recovered from the initial setback caused by the early Depression. For a quarter, customers could see a double feature (introduced in 1931) or take the whole family to a drive-in (1933). Federal agencies used motion pictures to publicize their work. The Farm Security Administration, for example, produced classic documentaries of American agricultural life.

Some Hollywood studios concentrated on optimistic films about common people who triumphed over evil, such as Warner Brothers' *Mr. Smith Goes to Washington* (1939). In this era, the zany Marx Brothers produced such comic classics as *Monkey Business* (1931) and *Duck Soup* (1933). The greatest box-office hits were escapist, such as the gangster films that memorialized the prohibition era and the musicals featuring large orchestras and exquisitely choreographed dancers in luxurious costumes. No one understood the needs of Depression-era audiences better than Walt Disney, whose Mickey Mouse cartoons delighted moviegoers everywhere. Classics such as *Snow White and the Seven Dwarfs* (1937) and *The Wizard of Oz* (1939) came out in this period, as well as Charlie Chaplin's satire of capitalist society and its efficiency, *Modern Times* (1936).

In spite of the poverty of the Depression, cultural life bloomed in the 1930s. Charlie Chaplin's classic *Modern Times*, a satire about work in a modern factory, was released in 1936.

The WPA and the Arts FDR believed that the arts were not luxuries that people should give up in hard times. He thus earmarked WPA funds to support unemployed artists, musicians, historians, theater people, and writers. The Federal Writers' Project assisted more than six thousand writers, such as Richard Wright, Saul Bellow, Margaret Walker, and Ralph Ellison. Historians surveyed the nation's local government records, wrote state guidebooks, and collected life stories from about two thousand former slaves. Without this project, their stories would have been lost.

Other projects supported music and the visual arts. The Federal Music Project started community symphonies, organized free music lessons, and sent musicologists to lumber camps, prisons, and small towns to record a fast-disappearing folk heritage. The Federal Art Project hired artists to paint murals in the nation's public buildings.

The Federal Theatre Project (FTP), directed by Vassar College professor Hallie Flanagan, was the most controversial. Flanagan used drama to create awareness of social problems. Her project launched the careers of many actors, play-wrights, and directors who later became famous including Burt Lancaster, Arthur Miller, John Houseman, and Orson Welles.

Accusing the FTP of being a propaganda machine for international communism, the House of Representatives' Un-American Activities Committee (HUAC) investigated the project in 1938 and 1939. In July 1939 Congress killed the FTP appropriation.

MAKING CONNECTIONS

Americans still debate the role of government in funding the arts. In your opinion, should government pay to support art that criticizes it or offends certain taxpayers? Explain.

Lasting New Deal Monuments

The great public works of the Depression era—the bridges, dams, tunnels, public buildings, sewage systems, port facilities, and hospitals—remind us of this extraordinary period of government support for the national welfare. Constructed with great efficiency and durability, they stand to this day. In national and state parks and on mountain trails and oceanfront walks, Americans still reap advantages from the restoration and conservation work of the Civilian Conservation Corps.

Some of the federal agencies from the New Deal era have endured. The Tennessee Valley Authority remains a model of government planning. The Federal Deposit Insurance Corporation still guarantees bank deposits. The Securities and Exchange Commission continues to monitor the workings of the stock exchange. And in rural America, farmers still plant according to federal crop allotment strategies, which were put in place to conserve soil and reduce acreage after the Supreme Court struck down AAA crop reduction plans.

Social Security Almost everyone in the United States has come to depend on the social security system. Few people today seriously question its place in American society.

Over the years, however, social security has had many critics. You read about some of these critics in Section 2. Others attacked social security because, at first, payments were very low, and the program excluded millions of farmers, domestic workers, and the self-employed. For a long time the system discriminated against women. It assumed, for example, that the male-headed household was typical. A mother could lose benefits for her children if a man, whether providing support for her or not, lived in her house. Women who went to work when their children started school rarely stayed in the work force long enough or earned high enough wages to receive the maximum benefits from the system.

In addition, unlike every other industrialized country in the world except South Africa, the American social security system did not guarantee health insurance for all citizens. For decades this omission prompted calls for further legislation. Only recently has the executive branch of the government begun to tackle this problem.

A Legacy of Hope

In August 1939, Mrs. Renee Lohrback of San Antonio, Texas, wrote a sad letter to Eleanor Roosevelt. Lohrback was a typist who could not find work. Four children depended on her. The WPA had rejected her work application because she had a three-month-old baby to care for. The entire family lived in one damp basement room. Wrote Lohrback:

M*rs. Roosevelt, I'm begging you with all my heart to please help me if you can. I love my babies dearly and won't sub-*

mit to them being put in a home away from me. I would simply die apart from them.

This letter was typical of thousands both Eleanor and Franklin Roosevelt received daily in the late Depression era. As the letter indicates, personal suffering continued in the late 1930s, and people still despaired. But as the above letter also suggests, in their desperation people were now looking to their government for support. Indeed, government programs did mean the difference between survival and starvation for millions of Americans.

Shortly after Mrs. Lohrback wrote her letter, the event that would ultimately bring a lasting recovery to the United States was set in motion on the battlefields of Europe. Several years would pass before that recovery would reach the United States. When it did arrive, it came in the form of another tremendous test of the character of the United States: world war.

Government support for the arts led to many lasting works, including this mural painted by Thomas Hart Benton in 1930 for the New School of Social Research in New York City. Audrey McMahon, New York director of the WPA, said: "We did the best we could, and that best was very good."

SECTION 3 REVIEW

Key Terms, People, and Places
1. Define (a) national debt, (b) Congress of Industrial Organizations, (c) sit-down strike.

Key Concepts
2. What effect did the New Deal have on the American economy?
3. What factors contributed to the economic collapse of 1937?

4. In what sense did labor unions triumph in the thirties?
5. What was the impact of the New Deal on American cultural life?

Critical Thinking
6. **Identifying Central Issues** In your opinion, was the New Deal a success or a failure? Explain, citing information from the chapter.

Chapter Review

Key Terms
1. New Deal
2. hundred days
3. public works program
4. Wagner Act
5. Social Security Act

6. political right
7. political left
8. demagogue
9. national debt
10. Congress of Industrial Organizations

11. sit-down strike

People
12. Frances Perkins
13. Mary McLeod Bethune
14. Father Charles E. Coughlin
15. Huey Long

Terms For each term above, write a sentence that explains its relation to the New Deal or the legacies of the New Deal.

True or False Determine whether each statement is true or false. If it is true, write "true." If it is false, change the underlined term to make the statement true.
1. People on the <u>political right</u> accused Roosevelt's social programs of not going far enough in addressing the nation's problems.
2. The first <u>Congress of Industrial Organizations</u> employed the jobless to build or improve roads, parks, airports, and other public facilities.
3. Some critics of Roosevelt's programs were <u>demagogues</u> who manipulated people's emotions.
4. The <u>Social Security Act</u> legalized closed shops and collective bargaining.

5. President Roosevelt's <u>New Deal</u> programs provided jobs and improved the quality of life for some Americans.

Matching Review the key people in the list above. If you are not sure of a person's importance, review his or her significance in the chapter. Then choose a person from the list who best matches each description below.
1. a southern Democrat, known as the Kingfish, who called for the redistribution of wealth
2. the first woman to hold a cabinet post
3. the person who held the highest position of any African American woman in the New Deal
4. the radio broadcaster who first supported and then opposed the New Deal

Section 1 (pp. 506–512)
1. What characteristics of FDR's personality helped inspire hope in the American people?
2. Briefly describe the New Deal's public works programs and their purpose.
3. Explain how the Second New Deal differed from the original New Deal.

Section 2 (pp. 513–517)
4. For which groups in particular was the New Deal of limited success?
5. What was the basis of the political right's opposition to the New Deal?

6. Why did FDR want to pack the Supreme Court? Describe the consequences of his plan, citing details to support your statements.

Section 3 (pp. 519–523)
7. What did the Recession of 1937 indicate about the success of the New Deal?
8. What was the impact of the New Deal on the public's expectations of the presidency?
9. What permanent changes occurred for labor unions as a result of the New Deal?
10. Briefly describe the cultural impact of the New Deal, citing examples to support your description.

1. **Recognizing Ideology** What does the endurance and success of the Social Security Act suggest about the current attitudes of Americans toward government's role in their lives?

2. **Demonstrating Reasoned Judgment** You have read that voters were willing to follow the "bold, consistent experimentation" of the New Deal. What does this willingness suggest about the mood of the country when FDR was elected? Do you think that people would vote for bold experimentation today?

3. **Making Comparisons** Describe how Eleanor Roosevelt perceived her role as First Lady. How have the roles of more recent first ladies been similar to or different from that of Eleanor Roosevelt?

1. **Evaluating Primary Sources** Review the second primary source excerpt on page 517. Explain how the balance of power among the branches of government would be affected if Congress made the Supreme Court subject to the presidency.

2. **Understanding the Visuals** Skim through the chapter and find photographs, artwork, or other illustrations that both support and oppose the New Deal. Explain how each visual conveys its message of approval or disapproval.

3. **Writing About the Chapter** The New Deal tried to solve the nation's economic and social problems during the Depression. Write a proposal for a New Deal kind of program that would help end a social or economic problem today. First, choose a contemporary issue that you would like to see addressed. Then, jot down ideas for a government program that could help solve the problem. Include your ideas about how the program is to be financed. Next, write a draft of your proposal in which you explain your ideas. Revise your proposal, making certain that your solution is clearly explained, with as many details as possible about its implementation. Proofread your proposal and draft a final copy.

4. **Using the Graphic Organizer** This graphic organizer uses a tree map to organize main ideas and supporting details about the effects of the New Deal. (a) What were three main sources of entertainment during the 1930s, and what role did the government play in funding the arts? (b) If you were to travel throughout the United States today, what evidence of New Deal programs listed on the graphic organizer might you encounter? (c) On a separate sheet of paper, create your own tree map about the New Deal's critics, using this graphic organizer as an example.

Effects of the New Deal			
Economic Effects	**Labor Unions**	**Cultural Life**	**Permanent Monuments**
• Growing national debt • Joblessness decreases but lasts until World War II	• Union membership rises • Unions gain many new rights • Era of strikes	• Radio • Movies • Books • WPA support for arts	• Public works (bridges, dams, tunnels) • Federal agencies (TVA, FDIC, SEC) • Social Security • People look to government for support

Hot and Cold War
1939–1960

"We have to face the fact that either all of us are going to die together or we are going to learn to live together, and if we are to live together we have to talk."

—Eleanor Roosevelt, 1960

*M*any *Americans were determined to stay out of another European conflict, but Japan's attack on Pearl Harbor finally shattered their resolve and American isolationism ended forever. After the war, the nation barely had time to enjoy its hard-won peace before a "cold war" developed between the United States and the Soviet Union. That conflict and the threat of nuclear destruction cast a long shadow across the postwar era.*

Weary American infantrymen line up in the cold for a meal. Despite the fatigue of the soldiers and the world, World War II would rage in Europe for another four months after this January 1945 photograph was taken.

World War II
1939–1945

*I*n the 1930s a frightening series of events overseas showed that
the world war Americans had fought from 1917 to 1918 had
not succeeded in making the world "safe for democracy."
As ruthless dictators devoured whole nations in Europe,
northern Africa, and Asia, many Americans fervently
hoped that the United States could remain uninvolved.
This proved impossible, and in December 1941 the nation fully
committed its material and human resources to a second global
conflict that would end United States isolationism forever.

Events in the United States

1935 To keep
the United
States out of
war in Europe,
Congress passes
Neutrality Acts.

1938 Severe
recession
hits the
United States
economy.

1935	1936	1937	1938	1939

Events in the World

1936 Spanish
Civil War
begins.

1939 German
invasion of
Poland sets off
World War II.

528

1940	1941	1942	1943	1944	1945
	1941 The United States enters World War II after Japanese attack on Pearl Harbor.	*1942* Japanese Americans are relocated to internment camps.	*1943* Nearly 400,000 coal miners go on strike. • Race riots break out in Detroit.	*1944* Roosevelt wins unprecedented fourth term as President.	*1945* President Roosevelt dies. • Harry S Truman becomes President.
1940 Germany, Italy, and Japan sign the Tripartite Pact.	*1941* Germany invades the Soviet Union.		*1943* The Allies invade Italy.	*1944* The Allies invade France at Normandy on D-Day.	*1945* Germany surrenders. • Japan surrenders after United States drops atomic bombs.

Prelude to War

SECTION PREVIEW

World War I had left deep scars in Europe. Wounded national pride and devastated economies laid the foundation for the rise of fascist dictators and a second global conflict.

Key Concepts

- In Europe and Asia, aggressive nations were rapidly bringing neighboring states under their power.
- The United States at first struggled to stay out of the fighting abroad, while supporting the Allies with economic aid.
- The Japanese attack on Pearl Harbor finally dragged the United States into the war.

Key Terms, People, and Places

fascism, Nazi party, anti-Semitism, appeasement, Lend-Lease Act; Benito Mussolini, Adolf Hitler, Winston Churchill; Rhineland, Manchuria, Pearl Harbor

Nazis singled out Jews for persecution by forcing them to wear yellow Stars of David like this one.

Throughout the 1930s, Americans watched warily as dictators in Germany, Italy, and Japan sought to extend their power around the globe. Even so, most Americans wanted to stay out of the conflict. World War I had not made the world a better place; why, then, should they be eager to enter another foreign war? Besides, the American people had enough trouble at home, as the Depression stubbornly kept a grip on the economy. Yet as the struggle unfolded, it became clear that democracy everywhere was threatened by the dictators.

Fascism and Nazism in Europe

By the mid-1930s, Italian and German dictators had ruthlessly established their authority on the European continent. They took advantage of the humiliation felt by many Italians and Germans after World War I by promising to restore their nations to a position of glory.

Benito Mussolini was an Italian schoolteacher, journalist, and political activist who had been wounded in World War I. Along with many Italians, Mussolini felt that his country had been shortchanged in the peace settlement after the war. The few small territories Italy received from the former German and Turkish empires paled in comparison to those claimed by its fellow Allies, Britain and France. In 1919 Mussolini banded together with a group of war veterans, who also were dissatisfied, to found the revolutionary Fascist party.

The term *fascism* refers to a political philosophy that values the nation or the race above the individual. During World War II, Italy, Germany, and Japan all were ruled by fascist governments that wielded absolute power. The fascist powers each looked back in history to their nation's great and glorious past—a crucial difference between them and the communists, who looked forward to a transformation of society for a glorious new future.

Mussolini Becomes "the Leader" In 1922 Mussolini threatened a march on Rome unless his authority was recognized. King Victor Emmanuel III, who feared the disruption that could occur, asked him to become prime minister. Three years later, calling himself *Il Duce* ("the leader"), Mussolini declared a dictatorship that extended throughout the country.

Mussolini and the Fascists attempted to promote Italian power, in spite of the serious political and economic instability following World War I. Claiming that efficiency and order were necessary to make Italy as great as they felt it had been in the past, Mussolini and his party suspended elections, centralized the economy under state control, and began modernizing the armed forces. In order to supply colonies for his modern-day Roman Empire, he pursued an aggressive foreign policy. Under his direction, Italy invaded Ethiopia in 1935, and by the next year, it dominated that East African nation.

Hitler's Rise to Power At the same time, **Adolf Hitler,** a poorly educated Austrian who supported himself as a painter, rose to power in Germany. Hitler had been wounded and temporarily blinded in World War I. The war left him feeling enraged by Germany's defeat and by the degrading terms of the Treaty of Versailles.

In 1919 Hitler joined the forty-member German Workers' party. With his powerful public speaking, he soon became a leader in the growing party. In 1920 the group changed its name to the National Socialist German Workers' party, or **Nazi party**. In November 1923, by which time the party's membership had swelled to 55,000, Hitler and the Nazis attempted to seize power in the city of Munich.

Although many citizens of Munich supported Hitler, the rebellion was put down quickly. Hitler was found guilty of high treason and spent nine months in jail. During this time he began writing an autobiography titled *Mein Kampf* ("My Struggle"), in which he described his diagnosis of Germany's problems and how he planned to cure them.

Hitler and the Nazis continued their crusade throughout the 1920s and 1930s. They appealed to Germans ravaged by the Great Depression. Saddled with insurmountable war debts from World War I, Germany also faced terrible unemployment and massive inflation. Hitler promised to stabilize the country, rebuild the economy, and revive the German empire that had been shattered in the war.

As a result of such promises, Hitler won a large following. In addition, his tremendous personal magnetism swayed many to his views. One witness who observed Hitler speaking later recalled:

> I cannot remember in my entire life such a change in the attitude of a crowd in a few minutes, almost a few seconds. There were certainly many who were not converted yet. But the mood of the majority

Adolf Hitler was once described as looking rather ordinary, "like a waiter in a railway station restaurant" (right). When he spoke, however, his passion and charisma electrified audiences.

> abruptly changed. Hitler had turned them inside out, as one turns a glove inside out, with a few sentences. It had almost something of hocus-pocus, or magic about it.
> Karl Alexander von Müller,
> German historian

Hitler Becomes *Der Führer* In January 1933, the Nazi party was the largest group in the Reichstag (the German parliament), and Hitler was named chancellor. The next month he squelched his opposition in the Reichstag and suspended civil liberties. An act of parliament gave him dictatorial powers in the new government, known as the Third Reich. He was now *Der Führer* ("the leader").

Hitler appealed to a form of prejudice with a long and deep-rooted history in Western civilization: **anti-Semitism**, or the hatred of Jews. Hitler blamed Jews for Germany's problems and preached that so-called Aryans—blond, blue-eyed Germans—belonged to a dominant "master race." Anti-Semitism became a cornerstone of Hitler's program. He soon ordered the boycott of Jewish shops, the burning of books written by Jewish authors, and the imprisonment of Jews in concentration camps.

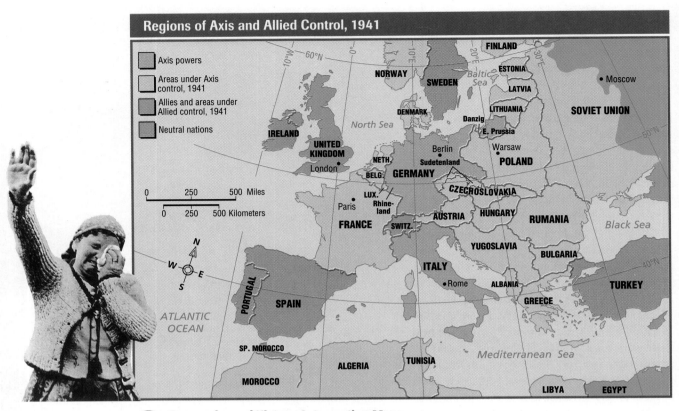

Regions of Axis and Allied Control, 1941

Axis powers

Areas under Axis control, 1941

Allies and areas under Allied control, 1941

Neutral nations

FINLAND
NORWAY
SWEDEN
ESTONIA
Baltic Sea
LATVIA
Moscow
DENMARK
LITHUANIA
Danzig
E. Prussia
SOVIET UNION
IRELAND
UNITED KINGDOM
London
NETH.
Berlin
Warsaw
BELG.
GERMANY
POLAND
Sudetenland
LUX.
CZECHOSLOVAKIA
Paris
Rhine-land
AUSTRIA
HUNGARY
RUMANIA
Black Sea
FRANCE
SWITZ.
YUGOSLAVIA
BULGARIA
ITALY
ALBANIA
TURKEY
Rome
GREECE
ATLANTIC OCEAN
PORTUGAL
SPAIN
Mediterranean Sea
SP. MOROCCO
ALGERIA
TUNISIA
MOROCCO
LIBYA
EGYPT
North Sea

0   250   500 Miles

0   250   500 Kilometers

N W E S

Geography and History: Interpreting Maps
Millions of people like this Czechoslovakian woman, shown reluctantly saluting the Nazis in 1938, saw their homelands conquered by the Axis powers. *How does this map illustrate the dire situation of the Allies in 1941?*

Like Mussolini, Hitler saw foreign policy as a way to bolster national pride. He, too, was determined to return Germany to a dominant position in the world. In 1936 he marched troops into the **Rhineland**—a section of western Germany from which the Treaty of Versailles had excluded German forces since the end of World War I. (See the map above.) In that same year, Hitler formed an alliance with Mussolini, and Italy and Germany became known as the Axis Powers.

The German Empire Grows German aggression continued as the decade of the 1930s drew to a close. Early in 1938 Hitler annexed Austria. Later that year, he demanded possession of the Sudetenland, a section of Czechoslovakia inhabited by an ethnic German population.

The League of Nations, which had been organized after World War I to try to maintain international peace, proved powerless to resist German aggression. England and France, reluctant to become involved in another conflict after the devastation of World War I, adopted a policy known as **appeasement**. To *appease* means to "keep the peace by giving in to someone's demands." Over and over England and France allowed Hitler to seize control of European territories, on the assumption that he finally would be satisfied.

Their assumption was wrong. Hitler's appetite proved insatiable, and he moved relentlessly to take over all of Czechoslovakia. Then, in September 1939, after signing a nonaggression pact with the Soviet Union so he would not have to fear a Soviet assault, Germany invaded Poland. Two days after this attack, leaders in England and France decided they would appease Hitler no longer. Angry and frustrated over his steady encroachment on the European continent, they finally declared war on Germany.

Japan Builds an Empire

In Asia in the 1930s, Japan was every bit as eager as Germany and Italy to establish itself as a world power. Japan consisted of a chain of small islands in the Pacific and lacked the raw materials needed for a booming industrial economy. Military leaders who dominated the government resented their dependence on the United States and other nations for such necessary resources as iron, coal, and petroleum. High tariffs prevented Japan from enjoying a profitable export trade with the United States and led to a prolonged economic depression in Japan. To make Japan self-sufficient, its leaders were determined to incorporate part of the Asian mainland into what they called the Greater East Asia Co-Prosperity Sphere.

In 1931 Japan attacked **Manchuria**, a region in northern China rich in minerals. By the next year, Japan controlled Manchuria. It quickly established a puppet government and renamed the area Manchukuo. Despite condemnation by the League of Nations, Japan continued its aggression in China. In 1937 Japanese troops launched an attack and seized Shanghai, Nanjing, Beijng, and other Chinese cities.

Japanese aggression continued over the next few years. Ever hungry for more resources, raw materials, and markets, Japan also sought control of Southeast Asia, as the map below shows. In 1940 the island nation signed an alliance with Germany and Italy, known as the Tripartite Pact. Now all three of the world's major fascist powers were partners. Secure in that alliance, the Japanese invaded southern Indochina—then ruled by France—in the middle of 1941.

MAKING CONNECTIONS

How do you think different groups of Americans reacted to German and Japanese aggression? How might their memories of World War I have affected their responses? Compare your answers to the information that follows.

The American Response to Axis Aggression

The United States watched the storm clouds rising in Europe and Asia but hoped to remain uninvolved. Most Americans remained

Regions of Japanese Control, 1941

Areas under Japanese control, 1941

Geography and History: Interpreting Maps
The terrified baby at right somehow escaped harm during the 1937 bombing of a Shanghai train station by the Japanese. *Judging from this map, what regions in 1941 appear to have been in the greatest danger of being attacked next by Japan?*

People opposed to the United States entering World War II voiced their opinions on bumper stickers such as the one above, or wore pins that read "America First" (below). Those who favored United States involvement in the war urged "Bundles [of supplies] for Britain" (below).

disillusioned by World War I; they had fought to make the world safe for democracy, but questioned later whether their actions had made any difference at all. Many Americans wanted to follow a policy of isolationism, believing that American interests could best be served by staying out of the quarrels of other nations entirely. Isolationists formed the America First Committee to denounce any move by the government toward involvement in the war.

Congress responded to isolationist sentiment in the 1930s by passing a series of three neutrality acts. Taken together, these laws declared that the United States would withhold weapons and loans from all nations at war and would sell other goods to warring powers only if they paid cash and picked up the goods themselves, a policy known as "cash and carry." The third and last of these acts was passed in 1937, thus completing American neutrality policy. In early 1941 a Gallup poll revealed that 88 percent of the American people still opposed entering the war.

Challenges to Neutrality Despite most Americans' desire for noninvolvement, the ominous events of the war convinced other Americans that the United States should help the Allies. Between September 1939 and June 1940, the Axis Powers in Europe defeated Poland, Norway, Denmark, Belgium, Luxembourg, and France. In Asia, Japan was swallowing up French and Dutch colonies. Unless something was done quickly, England—which was single-handedly resisting the Axis in Europe—might not survive. In May 1940, journalist William Allen White organized the Committee to Defend America by Aiding the Allies,

which worked vigorously to enlist the support of the American people.

The Arsenal of Democracy That same year, while seeking and winning a third presidential term, Roosevelt moved to help Great Britain directly. When British prime minister **Winston Churchill** asked for American destroyers to convoy supplies across the Atlantic, Roosevelt agreed to trade fifty old American ships in return for sites on which to build eight naval and air bases on British territory in the Western Hemisphere.

The next year, Roosevelt helped push the **Lend-Lease Act** through Congress. Britain desperately needed economic help to continue its struggle against the Axis. Under Lend-Lease, the United States would provide war supplies to Britain and worry about payment later. It was like lending a garden hose to a neighbor whose house was burning, Roosevelt said. You loaned it to him, and he returned it when the fire was out. With that commitment, the United States became, in FDR's words, "the great arsenal of democracy."

The Attack on Pearl Harbor

As the war in Europe unfolded, tensions between the United States and Japan increased. In 1940 the United States stopped selling airplanes to Japan, then moved to terminate a long-standing trade agreement. By mid-1940, the United States had ceased selling other crucial items, such as scrap metal and oil, to Japan. After Japan's attack on Indochina, it froze all Japanese financial assets in the United States. Desperate for oil in particular, Japan was determined to do whatever was necessary to attain its militaristic aims. The United States naval fleet based in Hawaii stood directly in the way of Japan's plans to dominate eastern Asia and the Pacific.

The Japanese took matters into their own hands. Hoping to knock out the United States Pacific Fleet before an all-out military conflict could begin, Japan launched a surprise attack on the American naval base at **Pearl Harbor**, Hawaii, on December 7, 1941. The attack destroyed five battleships, three cruisers, and several smaller vessels, while wiping out almost 200 airplanes. Nearly 2,400 people died. Fortunately, the Pacific Fleet's aircraft carriers were on a mission elsewhere in the Pacific and so were spared destruction.

The attack stunned the American people. Then, in the wake of the initial shock, came a feeling of determination. A college student recalled hearing the news:

> I n an incredibly short time— it seemed to be almost a matter of moments—a wave of patriotism swept the country. As we drove home we felt, This is our country, and we're going to fight to defend it. When we got home that evening we were glued to the radio. "The Star-Spangled Banner" was played, and everyone in the room automatically rose. And we were disillusioned college students— the 1940s version of the 1960s kids.
>
> Dellie Hahne, a student at Santa Barbara State College, California

In recent years Roosevelt had come to believe that the United States could not avoid involvement in World War II. The attack on Pearl Harbor meant that the nation could hesitate no longer. The day after the raid, in one of his most stirring speeches, the President told the Congress and the American people that December 7, 1941, was "a date which will live in infamy." He called on Congress to declare war against Japan. Congress quickly

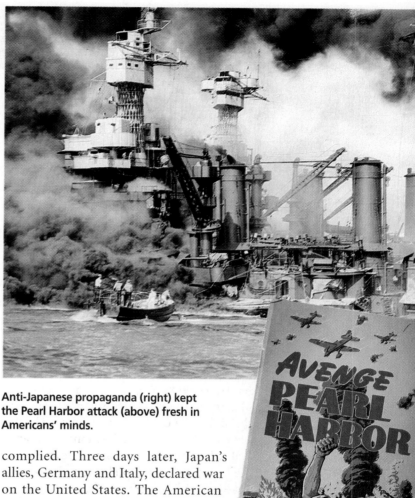

Anti-Japanese propaganda (right) kept the Pearl Harbor attack (above) fresh in Americans' minds.

complied. Three days later, Japan's allies, Germany and Italy, declared war on the United States. The American people now were committed to this war. Their contributions would make the difference between victory and defeat for the Allies.

SECTION 1 REVIEW

Key Terms, People, and Places
1. Define (a) fascism, (b) Nazi party, (c) anti-Semitism, (d) appeasement, (e) Lend-Lease Act.
2. Identify (a) Benito Mussolini, (b) Adolf Hitler, (c) Winston Churchill.
3. Identify (a) Rhineland, (b) Manchuria, (c) Pearl Harbor.

Key Concepts
4. What steps did Italy, Germany, and Japan take early in 1935 to extend their power?

5. How did the United States respond to international upheaval in the 1930s?

Critical Thinking
6. **Testing Conclusions** "In the years leading up to the attack on Pearl Harbor, the United States was gradually becoming more and more involved in the war. Even if the attack had never happened, the United States would eventually have become involved in the fighting." Explain why you agree or disagree with this conclusion.

The Military Struggle

SECTION PREVIEW

By December 1941, only an exhausted Britain stood between the Nazis and their dream of dominating the European continent. The United States finally cast its lot with the British—but was it already too late?

This helmet was worn by General George Patton, whose brilliant use of tanks helped sweep the Germans out of France in 1944.

Key Concepts

- American military strength turned the tide of the war in favor of the Allies.
- The Allies decided to concentrate first on winning the war in Europe and North Africa and then focus on the Pacific.
- At the end of the war in Europe, the American public discovered the horrors of the holocaust.

Key Terms, People, and Places

blitzkrieg, Battle of the Bulge, holocaust; Douglas MacArthur, Dwight D. Eisenhower, Chester Nimitz, Joseph Stalin; Midway Island, Guadalcanal, Normandy

W orld War II was a global war in an even greater sense than World War I. With campaigns occurring on many fronts at the same time, the war required enormous coordination of people and resources. If they hoped to defeat their Axis foes, Allied military strategists had to look at the "big picture" formed by a mosaic of smaller objectives.

Allied War Aims

While the immediate objective was to win the war, the United States was from the start planning to shape the postwar peace. Months before the United States entered the war, Roosevelt had shared his vision of what the world should be like. In a speech to Congress in early 1941, the President spoke of the "four essential human freedoms"—freedom of speech, freedom of worship, freedom from want, and freedom from fear. That summer, he met with British prime minister Winston Churchill off the coast of Newfoundland, and the two leaders issued the Atlantic Charter. This document described their notion of a free and democratic postwar world. It demanded self-determination for all nations, so that people everywhere could decide what kind of government they wanted; equal trading rights for all, so that every country could share in the world's riches; and a system of general security to help keep peace.

While the four freedoms and the Atlantic Charter defined the United States' formal aims in the war, most Americans fought for more personal reasons. As soldiers huddled in filthy foxholes overseas, they dreamed of home and a cherished way of life. War correspondent John Hersey once asked a young marine on the Pacific front what he was fighting for. After reflecting for a moment, the soldier just sighed, "What I'd give for a piece of blueberry pie."

Early Danger

The Allies were in deep trouble by the time the United States entered the war. With fighting occurring around the globe, they found themselves on the defensive on virtually every front. To have any chance of victory, they had to determine military priorities. Soon after Pearl Harbor, Roosevelt and Churchill decided that they would concentrate on defeating Germany and its European supporters first, while waging a defensive war against Japan in the Pacific. Only after the Nazis had been defeated would they devote full attention to the Asian front.

The European and North African Fronts
The situation was desperate in Europe and North Africa. The German **blitzkrieg** ("lightning war")—a series of sudden military attacks

by land and air—had extended Germany's control across Europe. England had survived the Battle of Britain, a relentless air attack that lasted from July 1940 to June 1941, but the German bombings of cities like London had taken a heavy toll. Suspicious of Soviet intentions in eastern Europe, Hitler broke his nonaggression pact with the Soviet Union in early 1942. German troops drove deep into the Soviet Union, gaining substantial territory. In North Africa, a German army led by Field Marshal Erwin Rommel, known as the "Desert Fox" for his shrewd tactics, was equally successful.

The Pacific Front Conditions for the Allies were not much better in the Pacific. The attack on Pearl Harbor had destroyed much of the American fleet, although not its aircraft carriers. Japan already controlled a large part of eastern

and southern Asia. After years of fighting, China had been ground down. India, a British colony, was threatened from east and west, and Australia, part of the British Commonwealth, was expecting a Japanese invasion soon.

After Pearl Harbor, Japan moved successfully against the Pacific islands of Guam and Wake and against the British colony of Hong Kong in China and the British naval base at Singapore, just south of the Malay Peninsula. (See the map below.) In the spring of 1942, Japanese forces defeated Filipino and American troops in the Philippines and drove General **Douglas MacArthur** from the islands. After the defeat on March 10, 1942, MacArthur promised the Filipinos and American soldiers: "I shall return."

Turnaround The situation began to improve toward the end of 1942. Despite initial German

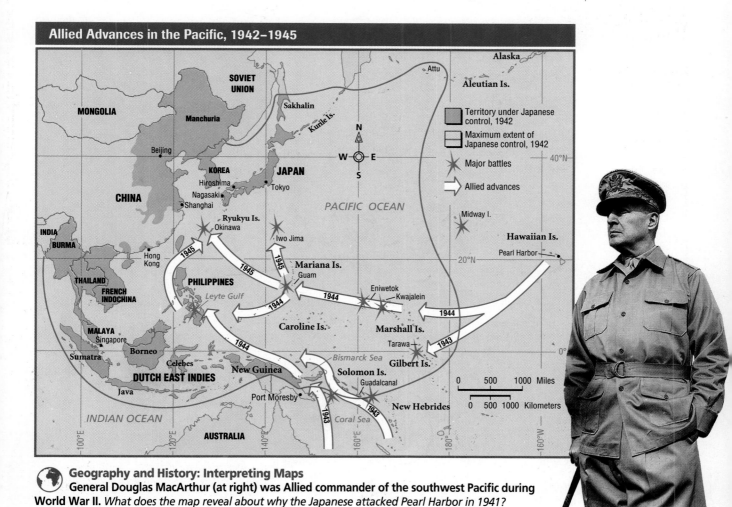

Allied Advances in the Pacific, 1942–1945

Geography and History: Interpreting Maps
General Douglas MacArthur (at right) was Allied commander of the southwest Pacific during World War II. *What does the map reveal about why the Japanese attacked Pearl Harbor in 1941?*

triumphs in the Soviet Union, the Soviets were helped by the fact that Hitler repeated the same mistake made by the French emperor Napoleon more than a hundred years earlier. German troops advanced into the Soviet Union far beyond their country's ability to support them, and they were not equipped to deal with harsh Russian winters. The Soviets managed to withstand a long and costly attack on the city of Stalingrad. In September 1942, the Germans began bombing the city, while 300,000 German soldiers waited to attack. The Soviets took up positions in the rubble left by the bombing. When the Germans advanced, the Soviets engaged them in bitter house-to-house fighting for the next four months. At the end of that time, the Germans had been repulsed. In the process of defending Stalingrad, however, the Soviet Union suffered more casualties than the United States experienced in the entire war.

In the Atlantic, the Allies used radar (which had been crucial in the Battle of Britain) and sonar to find and destroy German submarines. Without that ability, troops would have been left without weapons or food, for the Germans had sunk 125 Allied ships in May 1942 alone.

Meanwhile, the Allies took the offensive in North Africa (see the map below). In early 1943, Roosevelt and Churchill met at Casablanca, in the North African nation of Morocco, to decide where to strike back. The Soviet Union, which was fighting alone on the eastern front, desperately wanted the other Allies to open up a second front in western Europe. Churchill, however, was determined not to launch a frontal invasion until he felt Germany was likely to fall.

Allied Advances in Europe and Northern Africa, 1942–1945

Geography and History: Interpreting Maps
General Dwight Eisenhower (at right) commanded many Allied initiatives in Europe, including the D-Day landing at Normandy in 1944. *Which arrow on the map represents this landing? Which arrows show the strategy of attacking the "soft underbelly" of the Axis?*

Instead, he persuaded Roosevelt to attack what he called the "soft underbelly" of the enemy, moving from North Africa to Sicily and Italy. The Soviets felt that by postponing the attack in western Europe, Britain and the United States "sacrificed" the Soviets in order to pursue their own war aims. Many thousands of Soviet soldiers died—and the German army was weakened—in the following months. Bitterness over this strategic decision would affect United States-Soviet relations in the postwar years.

Operation Torch, as the North African campaign was called, began in November 1942. It was a combined Anglo-American operation under the command of General **Dwight D. Eisenhower**. The Allied forces landed first in Morocco and Algeria, controlled by German puppet governments. The Allies easily triumphed, then moved east to Tunisia, where they encountered Rommel's Afrika Corps. In May 1943, the Axis forces in that region surrendered.

After their victory in North Africa, the Allies turned toward Italy. In July 1943, paratroopers of the 82nd Airborne Division jumped into Sicily, the island just off the "toe" of Italy; the invasion was a success. Next, Allied forces assaulted the Italian mainland and pushed toward Rome. The Italians overthrew Mussolini after the Sicily invasion and surrendered in September. German soldiers stationed in Italy dug in, though, and contested every mile of territory as the Allies moved up the Italian peninsula. In early 1944, the Allies landed, via sea, on the beaches of Anzio, and six months later they liberated the nearby city of Rome. The war was hardly over, but in the Italian campaign, the Allies had taken a major step forward. (See the map on page 538.)

MAKING CONNECTIONS

What are some of the differences between fighting a war on your own soil and going somewhere else to fight?

Midway and Guadalcanal At about the same time, battles over two small but highly strategic islands in the Pacific shifted the balance of power between the Allies and Japan. Japanese admiral Isoroku Yamamoto wanted to engage the United States Navy at **Midway Island**, near Hawaii, in an attempt to destroy the aircraft carriers that the Pearl Harbor bombing had missed. When, in April 1942, Colonel James Doolittle launched a successful air raid on Tokyo from the carrier USS *Hornet*, which had departed from Midway, Japanese officials approved Yamamoto's plan.

Before the attack on Midway, the Japanese intended to secure their position around Australia by landing troops at Port Moresby in New Guinea. (See the map on page 537.) The United States had broken the Japanese military code, so American officials were aware of this strategy. In May 1942, in the Battle of the Coral Sea, planes launched from the American carriers *Lexington* and *Yorktown* fought a Japanese fleet for four days, finally forcing the enemy to turn back. This Allied victory slowed the Japanese drive toward Australia.

Americans again intercepted Japanese code messages and were prepared for the attack on Midway on June 4, 1942. Even so, the battle did not go well for the American forces at first. Most of the planes that Admiral **Chester Nimitz** sent from the island to attack the Japanese fleet were quickly shot down, as were those launched from American carriers. It was a bit of sheer luck that finally favored the Americans. At about 10:25 A.M., when the Japanese believed they had seen the last of the American fighter planes and were refueling for a final attack on the island, a group of dive-bombers that had gotten lost suddenly found their target. Three of the four Japanese carriers were swiftly demolished as fuel hoses and bombs on the Japanese ships exploded. The fourth was later destroyed while trying to escape. As a result of this tremendous blow to Japan's naval power, Midway would be the last Japanese offensive operation in the war.

At this point, the Allies took the offensive in the Pacific. Their first goal would be to secure the island of **Guadalcanal**, in the Solomon Islands. (See the map on page 537.) United States marines landed on the island beginning on August 7, 1942. Japanese leaders deemed Guadalcanal "the fork in the road which leads

Americans wore pins like this one of General Eisenhower to show their support of the Allied military effort.

Periscopes

Radio tower

Escape hatch

Anchor

Showers & toilets

Conning tower

Bunks

Galley

Engineers' room

Electric engines

Diesel engines

Radio room

Ammunition

Batteries

Torpedoes

Control room

Officers' quarters

In the early years of the war, submarines—especially German U-boats—were able to terrorize surface ships with sneak attacks. They could approach other ships undetected, with their sailors viewing targets through the periscope (left). Later in the war, however, Allied aircraft equipped with radar were able to detect a submarine replenishing its supply of fresh air at the surface and alert destroyer ships to the submarine's location.

to victory for them or for us," so they made an all-out effort to recapture it.

Months of heavy fighting followed. In mid-November, the naval Battle of Guadalcanal ended with American control of the waters around the island, cutting off Japanese supply lines. In February 1943, American marines finally secured the island. From Guadalcanal, American forces would begin their strategy of "island-hopping," moving north through the Pacific by selectively attacking a few Japanese-held islands, their final objective being the Japanese homeland. The last two major battles in the Pacific war were fought on the small islands of Iwo Jima and Okinawa. The Japanese defended them fiercely, and both sides suffered heavy casualties before the Allies prevailed.

The Road to Victory in Europe The Allies were ready to tighten the noose. In Europe they now looked to liberate Germany itself from the Nazis. Toward the end of 1943, Churchill, Roosevelt, and Soviet leader **Joseph Stalin** met together for the first time in Tehran, Iran. They

agreed that an invasion across the English channel should come next.

Air attacks throughout 1943 and 1944 softened German resistance. Yet even though the Allies destroyed military, industrial, and transportation facilities, the Nazis fought on.

Then came Operation Overlord, which aimed to drive the Germans out of France and defeat the Third Reich itself. D-Day began before dawn on June 6, 1944. It was the largest amphibious invasion—a landing by sea—in history. More than 150,000 Allied soldiers in 600 warships and 4,000 other vessels crossed the English channel and came ashore along 60 miles of the **Normandy** coast in northern France. (See the map on page 538.) The Germans knew an attack was coming, but they expected it near Calais, where the English channel was narrowest. Despite the advice of his generals to counterattack, Hitler hesitated, for he still feared a larger invasion at Calais. The Allies, under the command of General Dwight Eisenhower, were thus able to land safely on the beach. In the course of the first week, they placed 326,000 soldiers, 50,000 vehicles, and

100,000 tons of supplies on the French coast. By the time the invasion of Normandy was over in July, the Allied forces had landed more than a million men.

Bitter fighting followed as the Allies pushed toward Paris. At the end of August, they liberated the French capital, then freed Brussels and Antwerp in Belgium a few days later.

The Germans launched a counterattack in Belgium and Luxembourg in December 1944, called the **Battle of the Bulge** because it caused a large bulge in the Allied line. When it sputtered out after one month, the way into Germany was clear. As Allied bombers continued to hammer major German cities, the Soviets pushed into Germany from the east, while American forces crossed the Rhine River and drove in from the west.

The Holocaust

As the Allies moved toward final victory, they discovered the horrors of what Hitler called the "Final Solution"—his effort to exterminate all Jews and other people he considered enemies of the Aryan state. For the duration of the war, the Nazis had engaged in a systematic campaign to liquidate the entire

Jewish population of Europe. The extermination camps of Auschwitz, Maidanek, and Treblinka were located in Poland; Buchenwald and Dachau were in Germany. In these and other camps, the Nazis killed 6 million Jews in what we now call the **holocaust**, from the Greek term for "total destruction by fire." They also murdered another 5 million Slavs, Gypsies, and other people they considered undesirable—political enemies (especially communists), homosexuals, and the physically and mentally disabled.

Nazi doctors performed cruel experiments on their victims, often as an excuse to torture them as much as for any scientific purpose. Many victims were told to remove all their clothing and report to a bath house, which was actually a lethal gas chamber. Their bodies were then stripped of gold teeth, rings, and other valuables and burned in large ovens.

In liberating the concentration camps, American troops found the gaunt survivors who had somehow escaped death in the gas chambers and crematoriums. Second Lieutenant Dick Winters from Pennsylvania recorded the following impressions when he first saw Dachau:

| 1650 | 1700 | 1750 | 1800 | **Links Across Time** | 1850 | 1900 | 1950 | 2000 |

The "Final Solution" and "Ethnic Cleansing"

As Hitler and the Nazi party rose to power in Germany in the 1930s, they blamed Germany's recent economic and social troubles on the Jewish people and other minority groups.

Eventually, the Nazis decided on the "Final Solution" to what they termed the "Jewish problem." Their solution amounted to genocide, or systematic extermination of an entire ethnic group. When the realities of the "final solution" came to light, a horrified world community promised, "Never again."

In 1992 long-standing conflicts between Serb, Croat, and Muslim ethnic groups intensified in the former country of Yugoslavia. The Serbs wanted the areas they controlled to be the home of Serbians only, although Muslims had lived there for centuries. To bring about their aims, the Serbs followed a policy of "ethnic cleansing," including camps for the torture, rape, starvation, and execution of thousands of Slavic Muslim and ethnic Croat civilians. The United States State Department asserted that the Serbian

abuse "dwarfs anything seen in Europe since the Nazis."

In 1993 the International Court of Justice in The Hague (in the Netherlands) implied that Serb aggression in Bosnia was "tantamount to genocide." The United Nations Security Council voted unanimously to establish a war crimes tribunal to bring to justice anyone found guilty of atrocities. *What do you think are the responsibilities of the United States when faced with strong evidence of genocide in another country?*

The memory of starved, dazed men, who dropped their eyes and heads when we looked at them through the chain-link fence, in the same manner that a beaten, mistreated dog would cringe, leaves feelings that cannot be described and will never be forgotten. The impact of seeing those people behind that fence left me saying, only to myself, "Now I know why I am here!"

Survivors of the Nazi holocaust were a chilling sight. Their bodies were emaciated from lack of food, and their eyes appeared haunted by memories of horrible torture.

The End of the War in Europe

In early 1945, Roosevelt, Churchill, and Stalin met again, this time at Yalta, a city in the Soviet Union near the Black Sea. After the "Big Three" Allied leaders had decided to split Germany into peacekeeping zones and to reorganize the government of Poland, the Soviets agreed to enter the war in the Pacific three months after the defeat of Germany.

The end of the European war was not far off. The Third Reich was in shambles. Hitler fulfilled a vow he had made in 1939: "I shall stand or fall in this struggle. I shall never survive the defeat of my people." On April 30, 1945, he committed suicide in a Berlin bunker. On May 8, Germany's unconditional surrender took effect, and the European war came to a close. American soldiers rejoiced, and civilians celebrated at home. But Japan still had to be defeated.

In the Pacific, the United States was embarking on a relentless drive toward the Japanese home islands. (See the map on page 537.) Pushing north from Australia and west through the islands of the central Pacific, American troops slowly gained control. Marines, with help from naval forces, took the islands of Tarawa, Kwajalein, and Guam. Meanwhile, MacArthur returned to the Philippines, as he had promised, with a dramatic landing on the island of Leyte. By the end of 1944, American bombers were close enough to attack the Japanese islands themselves and dropped hundred of tons of explosives on Japanese cities.

In one final meeting of the Big Three, Allied leaders met at Potsdam, Germany, in mid-1945. By this time Roosevelt was dead, and his successor, Harry S Truman, had to oversee the end of the war. The three heads of state warned the Japanese to surrender or face "prompt and utter destruction."

Around the same time, a meeting of delegates from fifty nations met in San Francisco to plan for an international organization to keep the peace. That conference created and approved the charter of the United Nations. While the conference was going on, however, there was still work to be done on the battlefields, carried out by the men and women who actually fought and won the war.

SECTION 2 REVIEW

Key Terms, People, and Places
1. Define (a) blitzkrieg, (b) Battle of the Bulge.
2. Identify (a) Douglas MacArthur, (b) Dwight D. Eisenhower, (c) Chester Nimitz, (d) Joseph Stalin.
3. Identify (a) Midway Island, (b) Guadalcanal, (c) Normandy.

Key Concepts
4. What was the holocaust?

5. How did the United States entry into the war affect the Allied position?

Critical Thinking
6. **Formulating Questions** Imagine that you are responsible for deciding Allied military strategy at the point when the United States entered World War II. Develop a list of questions that you would ask your military advisers before firming up your strategy.

Americans on the Battle Fronts

SECTION PREVIEW

The grim reality of combat far from home was tough on all soldiers. Discrimination in the armed forces made the experience even more painful for many Americans.

Key Concepts

- Life for American soldiers on the war fronts was brutal and frightening.
- Several groups—including women, African Americans, Latino Americans, and Native Americans—served in the armed forces despite discrimination.
- While their families were interned at home, Japanese Americans bravely defended their country overseas.

Key Terms, People, and Places

GI, WAC

World War II changed the lives of the men and women who were uprooted from home and sent far away from loved ones to provide the military muscle that won the war. The 15 million Americans who served as soldiers, sailors, and aviators made their way through distant deserts, jungles, swamps, turbulent seas, and forbidding skies. Anxious to engage the enemy, fearful of what would happen when they did, for them the war was often a desperate struggle just to stay alive.

The GI War

American soldiers called themselves **GIs**, after the "Government Issue" stamp on all shoes, clothes, guns, and other equipment provided by the military. Thousands entered the service when they received their official draft notices: "Greetings. You are hereby ordered for induction into the Armed Forces of the United States. . . ." Even more rushed to volunteer after the attack on Pearl Harbor.

In the field, the war was hardly the romantic struggle portrayed in some books and films. The miserable conditions were described in the newspaper columns of Ernie Pyle, the popular war correspondent who lived with the enlisted men on the battle fronts and wrote about the war from their perspective. Pyle sent reports back to the United States six times a week until he died from a sniper's bullet in the Pacific campaign in 1945. He characterized the life of a typical soldier as follows:

> *The front-line soldier has lived like an animal for months and is a veteran of the cruel fierce world of death. Everything has been abnormal and unstable in his life for months. He has been filthy dirty, has eaten if and when, has slept on the hard ground without cover. His clothes have been greasy, he has lived in a constant haze of dust, pestered by flies and the heat, moving constantly, deprived of all the things that once meant stability. Things such as walls, chairs, floors, windows, faucets, shelves, Coca-Colas and the greatly important little matter of knowing you'll go to bed tonight in the same place you got up in this morning.*
>
> Written aboard a navy ship in the Allied invasion fleet headed for Sicily, July 16, 1943

The army Medal of Honor (above) paid tribute to gallantry in action above and beyond the call of duty. Fatigues (below) were standard wear for American soldiers.

AMERICAN PROFILES

Charles Rigaud

Ernie Pyle's description of combat life would have been all too familiar to Charles Alfred Rigaud. Marine Captain Rigaud was responsible for leading his men into battle against the Japanese on the island of Guadalcanal. John Hersey, another well-known war correspondent, was with Rigaud and his unit during the Third Battle of the Mataniko River. While this battle was not among the most famous of the war, Hersey's vivid account reveals that it was fraught with terror, death, heartache—and remarkable courage.

Rigaud's mission in the Third Battle was to push the Japanese, who were advancing toward the American camp, back across the Mataniko River. To reach the river, Rigaud's unit would have to pass through a jungle valley filled with Japanese snipers. Once there, they would face machine gun and mortar fire from established Japanese battle positions. Rigaud, the veteran marine in charge of this operation, looked to Hersey "like anything except a killer who took no prisoners. He had a boy's face. . . . His mustache was not quite convincing."

Charles Rigaud had grown up in Oriskany Falls, New York, almost ten thousand miles from the jungles of Guadalcanal. Back home he played the violin, both in orchestras and at square dances. Rigaud also loved the outdoors and he often went on hunting and trapping trips with a close friend.

Rigaud attended Syracuse University, where he joined ROTC (Reserve Officers' Training Corps) and graduated with a commission as a second lieutenant. He joined the marines just as the war began. In command in the field, he was responsible for his company. He had led them through other battles on Guadalcanal and on the nearby island of Tulagi. Success had come at no small cost—twenty-two of his men were dead.

Now, on October 8, 1942, Rigaud and his unit were slowly making their way through the jungle into another perilous situation. They walked single file down a narrow path, keeping five paces between them so that any snipers in the area would not have a big target. Before they reached the river, one marine lay dead in the path, killed by a Japanese sharpshooter.

After hours of difficult marching, the trees began to thin and the river was in sight. Then a single "high flat snap [that] was easily recognizable as a Japanese sound" broke the silence. Within seconds the air was filled with sniper fire, followed quickly by machine gun and mortar fire from across the river. Rigaud's company had walked right into a Japanese trap.

Marines carrying machine gun parts came together in bunches to set them up. Under heavy fire from the Japanese, however, no more than two guns were ever assembled. As his men took cover and tried to fight back, Rigaud rushed about checking on all of them. The Japanese fire was terrifying, and before long, a desperate rumor began to circulate that the order to withdraw had been given. As his men headed back toward the jungle, Rigaud stood up and shouted, "Who . . . gave that order? . . . Where do you guys think you're going? . . . Get back in there." Soon, however, he did give the order for withdrawal. He knew they could not hold their position.

Rigaud and most of his men survived to fight another day. The Third Battle of the Mataniko River was won by other companies of marines who forced a Japanese retreat on October 9. John Hersey, when preparing to leave Guadalcanal, asked if he could do anything for Rigaud when he got back to the United States. Rigaud answered, "Well, if you go through a place called Oriskany Falls, wish you'd tell my folks you saw me."

Women in the Armed Forces

Not all soldiers were men. By the war's end, over 300,000 American women had served in the military. Faced with serious personnel needs, officials were willing to use women's help in virtually all areas except combat.

Oveta Culp Hobby, director of the Women's Army Auxiliary Corps (WAAC—later shortened to **WAC**, Women's Army Corps), told potential recruits, "This is *your* war." Women

Marine Captain Charles Rigaud was recommended for decoration after his brave fighting on the island of Tulagi in the Pacific.

worked as typists and clerks, but also as control tower operators, radio operators, parachute riggers, and mechanics. The navy had a similar organization, the WAVES (Women Accepted for Volunteer Emergency Service). One quarter of all WAVES served in naval aviation. Women Air Force Service Pilots (WASPs) ferried planes around the country, and they towed targets for antiaircraft gunnery practice missions as well.

MAKING CONNECTIONS

How has the role of women in the United States military changed since World War II?

Equality in the Armed Forces

Although the military discriminated against African Americans, their participation as soldiers helped win the war. The all-African American 92nd Infantry Division, known as the Buffaloes, fought in the bloody Italian campaign of 1943 and 1944. The 333rd Field Artillery Battalion served with distinction with General George Patton's Third Army in France. These are only a few examples.

According to official policy, African Americans were not allowed to join either the air force or the marines. In the navy, they could only enlist in the messman's branch, which provided food services for the troops. The army, like the Red Cross, separated the blood plasma donated by African Americans.

Near the end of the war, however, shortages of soldiers led military officials to bend the

Using Historical Evidence *How does this 1943 magazine cover demonstrate the new opportunities women had during World War II?*

To defeat the Japanese in the Pacific, United States marines had to keep their strategies from the enemy. Navaho code talkers, using their native language for secret military communications, allowed the Allies to stay one step ahead of the Japanese.

Viewpoints
On the Integration of the Military

Discussion about desegregating the armed forces during World War II aroused strong feelings on both sides. Below are two opposing viewpoints. **What arguments does each side use to support its viewpoint?**

Against Integration

"In this hour of national crisis, it is much more important that we have the full-hearted co-operation of the thirty million white southern Americans than that we satisfy the National Association for the Advancement of Colored People. . . . If they be forced to serve with Negroes, they will cease to volunteer; and when drafted, they will not serve with that enthusiasm and high morale that has always characterized the soldiers and sailors of the southern states."

W. R. Poage, Texas state representative, 1941

For Integration

"Though I have found no Negroes who want to see the United Nations lose this war, I have found many who, before the war ends, want to see the stuffing knocked out of white supremacy. . . . If freedom and equality are not vouchsafed [granted] the peoples of color, the war for democracy will not be won. . . . We demand the abolition of segregation and discrimination in . . . [all] branches of national defense."

A. Philip Randolph, "Why Should We March?" November 1942

the navy organized twenty-five supply ships with integrated crews. The marines finally invited African Americans to enlist in the corps in 1945.

Nearly 350,000 Mexican Americans served in the military during World War II, most enlisting in the army. Mexican American soldiers made up a quarter of the combat troops defending Bataan in the Philippines shortly after Pearl Harbor. They faced Erwin Rommel in North Africa and played a major role in the D-Day invasion of 1944. Guy Gabaldón, who had been raised by a Japanese American family in Los Angeles, earned the Silver Star for his actions in the Battle of Saipan, an island in the Marianas in the western Pacific. Using his language skills, he persuaded more than a thousand Japanese soldiers to surrender to the Allies. By the end of the war, seventeen Mexican Americans had earned the Congressional Medal of Honor.

Though Native Americans were denied the right to vote in three states, they were still eligible for the draft, and eventually 25,000 served in the army and other branches of the military. Ira Hayes, a Pima from Arizona, was one of three survivors at Mount Suribachi on Iwo Jima. Some Navahos worked as code talkers in the marines, using their unique language as a means of transmitting messages by radio and phone.

While tens of thousands of Japanese Americans were interned in camps in the United States (see Chapter 19, Section 4), others seized the opportunity offered them to fight. The 442nd Regimental Combat Team eventually fought in Italy under General Mark Clark and then moved into France. There, they took almost ten thousand casualties and became the most decorated unit in the war.

rules. An army program begun in January 1945 allowed 20,000 volunteers—including over 4,500 African Americans—to train for infantry duty. From March until the end of the war in Europe, African Americans fought alongside whites in these volunteer combat units. In 1944

SECTION 3 REVIEW

Key Terms, People, and Places

1. Define (a) GI, (b) WAC.

Key Concepts

2. What does the profile of Charles Rigaud reveal about the soldiers who fought in the war?

3. Describe the roles that women played during World War II.

4. What contributions did African Americans make in the military during World War II?

Critical Thinking

5. Checking Consistency Were the goals the United States was fighting for in World War II consistent with its treatment of women and minorities? Explain why you answered yes or no.

Examining Photographs

Photographs are a form of visual evidence that can provide valuable information about an event or historical period. They can show what people or places in recent history looked like and can document momentous occasions. Photographers, however, like other observers of events, have their own points of view. Therefore, you must analyze their photographs carefully.

By their choice of subject, lighting, and camera angle, photographers can influence what is seen and how it is perceived. They may choose to photograph a scene that strikes them as particularly interesting, dramatic, or revealing but that, in reality, is not typical or representative. Photographers may also distort the appearance of objects in their pictures to create an illusion or convey a particular mood. By making these choices, photographers affect what is learned from their pictures.

The photograph at right was taken during World War II on a Pacific island southeast of the Philippines that was the scene of bitter fighting during the fall of 1944. Use the following steps to analyze the photograph.

1. Study the photograph to identify the subject. Look at the photograph as a whole, then study the details. (a) What do you see in the picture? (b) What broad subject or issue does the photograph address? (c) Was the photograph likely taken before, during, or after a tough battle? Explain.

2. Analyze the reliability of the photograph as a source of information. (a) What mood or emotion is captured in this photograph? (b) What aspects of the photograph capture this mood? (c) Does the photograph look as if it has been altered in any way by the photographer? Explain. (d) Does it seem as if the soldier posed or was unaware that he was being photographed?

3. Study the photograph to learn more about the historical period. Refer to the photograph and what you have read about World War II to answer the following questions. (a) What could you learn about the Pacific front if this photograph was your only source of information? (b) What can photographs such as this one contribute to a person's knowledge about an event that written sources cannot? (c) From what you have read in this chapter about the fighting on the Pacific islands during World War II, do you think this photograph presents a realistic picture of the war? Explain.

Dropping the Atomic Bomb: A Turning Point in History

SECTION PREVIEW

A collaboration of the top scientists in the world put a devastating secret weapon in American hands. Desperate to end the war as quickly as possible, the United States decided to unleash the terrible force of the atomic bomb on two unsuspecting Japanese cities.

Key Concepts

- The top secret Manhattan Project, which began before the United States entered the war, took years to develop the atomic bomb.
  - Alternatives to using the bomb on Japan were considered, but President Truman believed that the bomb would actually save many lives.
  - Two atomic bombs demolished Hiroshima and Nagasaki; the long-term effects on survivors were unpredictable.

Key Terms, People, and Places

Manhattan Project, Interim Committee; Albert Einstein, J. Robert Oppenheimer, Harry S Truman; Hiroshima, Nagasaki

This watch was stopped and partially melted when an atomic bomb exploded over Hiroshima, Japan, in 1945.

W orld War II was a technological war. Aircraft were now more maneuverable and could fly longer distances without refueling. The aircraft carrier introduced a new type of naval battle at Midway: one in which the opposing vessels were never in sight of one another. Specialized landing craft and dive-bombers made amphibious landings such as the Normandy invasion possible. But the world could scarcely imagine the destructive capacity of the new bomb being secretly developed in the United States.

The Manhattan Project

A letter written by physicist **Albert Einstein** in August 1939 helped set in motion the process of developing this new kind of bomb in the United States. Einstein was known worldwide for developing the theory of relativity, which describes how time and space function in the universe. He speculated that enormous energy might be released if atoms could be split in a particular way. In his letter to President Roosevelt, he wrote, "It is conceivable . . . that extremely powerful bombs of a new type may . . . be constructed," and he hinted that the Germans were already trying to build such a weapon. Einstein's letter reached Roosevelt just as World War II was starting in Europe.

Intrigued with the possibility of a new weapon and concerned that Germany might develop it first, Roosevelt established an Advisory Committee on Uranium to look into the matter. After the United States entered the war, the venture was reorganized and became known as the **Manhattan Project**.

The Manhattan Project developed into one of the greatest engineering enterprises of all time. During the final three years of the war, this top secret undertaking involved the building of thirty-seven installations in the United States and Canada. It employed 120,000 people and cost $2 billion—an unimaginable sum at the time. Scientists already had succeeded in splitting the nucleus of the uranium atom. Now they needed to produce a self-sustaining atomic chain reaction, in which particles released from the splitting of one atom would cause another atom to break apart, and so on. In December 1942, a physicist working with Italian scientist Enrico Fermi at the University of Chicago placed a phone call including a coded message to be relayed to President Roosevelt:

"You'll be interested to know," the physicist said, "that the Italian navigator [Fermi] has just landed in the New World. The earth was not as large as he had estimated, and he arrived in the New World sooner than he had expected."

"Is that so?" he was asked. "Were the natives friendly?"

"Everyone landed safe and happy." The message meant that the chain reaction had been accomplished without blowing up the laboratory in the process. Next, scientists had to find ways to gather enough of a special kind of uranium—or produce a new element, plutonium—to mold into a bomb.

On July 16, 1945, they tested their effort. In the desert at Alamogordo, New Mexico, scientists detonated the world's first atomic device. It left a huge crater in the earth's floor and shattered windows 125 miles away. As he watched the first blast, physicist **J. Robert Oppenheimer**, who had spearheaded the entire project, remembered the words of the *Bhagavad Gita*, the Hindu holy book: "Now I am become Death, the destroyer of worlds."

The Decision to Drop the Bomb

Once the bomb was ready, American policymakers had to decide if and when to use it. The war in Europe was over, but the Pacific struggle still ground on. There were other courses of action besides dropping the bomb that might end the war. Allied planners had already worked out the details of a massive invasion of the Japanese islands. But this was a frightening prospect. Art Rittenberg, who joined the marines after he graduated from high school in 1942, described the prospect of invading Japan from the point of view of an enlisted soldier:

M*ake no mistake about it, the Japanese were great fighters and everyone respected . . . them and feared them. They fought like [crazy] for Iwo [Jima] . . . , a two-and-a-half-mile long piece of volcanic sand and rock. What are they going to fight like in the home islands?*

The estimated cost of the invasion in American lives was as high as one million.

Using Historical Evidence This painting by Jacob Lawrence depicts a Hiroshima family after the atomic blast. *Why has the artist made the people's faces and the furniture look as they do?*

A naval blockade or continued bombing might also help defeat Japan. A demonstration on a deserted island might show the Japanese the bomb's awesome power. Some diplomats believed that Japan might surrender more quickly if the United States simply softened its insistence on "unconditional surrender" and guaranteed that the emperor could keep his throne.

American officials debated these possibilities in the **Interim Committee**, a group that included both government leaders and scientists. In the end, they were unwilling to choose any of the alternatives to dropping the bomb. They did not want to incur further casualties or let the long war drag on still longer. They did not want to suffer the embarrassment of a failed demonstration. Besides bringing Japan to its knees, some historians have speculated that the new bomb offered a dramatic display of

Allied might and served as an example of American power to the Russians. Although they were allies during the war, the United States and the Soviet Union had very different ideas about the shape of the postwar world. The deployment of a new atomic weapon allowed the United States to flex its muscles before the eyes of its communist rival.

The Interim Committee therefore recommended dropping the new bomb. **Harry S Truman**, President for barely four months after Franklin Roosevelt's death in April 1945, would have had a difficult time arguing against using the weapon that had consumed so many resources over the past five years. Truman, however, had no intention of arguing. He recorded in his memoirs that he "regarded the bomb as a military weapon and never had any doubt that it should be used."

Not all American officials shared this view. General Eisenhower, looking back on this moment in history in a 1963 *Newsweek* interview, said,

I told [Secretary of War Henry Stimson] I was against [dropping the bomb] on two counts. First, the Japanese were ready to surrender, and it wasn't necessary to hit them with that awful thing. Second, I hated to see our country be the first to use such a weapon.

But the final decision rested with the commander in chief. Truman decided to follow the advice of the Interim Committee.

MAKING CONNECTIONS

Do you think Truman would have been more reluctant to use the atomic bomb on Germany or Italy, if they had not yet surrendered in August 1945, than he was to use it on Japan? Why or why not?

The Bombs in Japan

On August 6, 1945, an American plane dropped "Little Boy," a uranium bomb, on the Japanese city of **Hiroshima**. It killed 70,000 people immediately or soon thereafter and injured 70,000 more. Three days later, another plane dropped "Fat Man," a plutonium bomb, on the city of **Nagasaki**, killing 40,000 people and injuring a like number.

The bombs were a terrifying experience for those people who managed to escape instant death. Novelist Masuji Ibuse recalled the Hiroshima blast: "I saw a ball of blindingly intense light, and simultaneously I was plunged into total, unseeing darkness." Then followed the screams of pain as the city descended into chaos. The black cloud of dust that had instantly turned day into night soon formed a mushroom cloud over the region. People wandered around in confusion looking for friends and family or simply in shock.

Hiroshima was ablaze after the explosion. The bomb ignited fires near where it had detonated, and more fires began as hot wires were exposed in crumbling buildings. People suffering from terrible burns—many of whom would die within a few days—rushed to plunge themselves into one of Hiroshima's seven rivers. The white-hot blast had burned people's clothes off their bodies; some people had designs from their kimonos scorched into their flesh. Author Tatsue Urata pictured a victim in Nagasaki:

The skin was peeling off his face and chest and hands. He was black all over—I suppose it was dirt that had stuck to him where the skin had peeled off; his whole body was coated with it and the blood trickling from his wounds made red streaks in the black.

People who survived the fires still had much to endure. Schoolchildren who had been outside when the bombs hit were so badly disfigured that they became social outcasts. Radiation poisoning—an effect that few people had even considered before the bomb was actually dropped—continued to produce unpredictable symptoms and to claim more victims in the years that followed.

Bombs in both cities demolished buildings, too. Hiroshima and Nagasaki were little more than mounds of rubble near where the bombs had hit. Similar damage had been done in

A moment before "Little Boy" leveled Hiroshima, the American GI above would have been standing in the midst of a thriving city. The photo at left shows the mushroom cloud that formed over Nagasaki when "Fat Man" exploded.

Tokyo and other cities by hundreds of conventional weapons, but this destruction had been caused by just one bomb.

The Japanese were dazed by the blasts. They were already considering surrender when the Soviet Union entered the war on the Chinese front two days after Hiroshima. Following the Nagasaki explosion, they sought to end the conflict any way they could. On August 14, 1945, Japanese leaders accepted American terms. The island nation formally surrendered on September 2, bringing the long and destructive war to a final end.

SECTION 4 REVIEW

Key Terms, People, and Places
1. Define Interim Committee.
2. Identify (a) Albert Einstein, (b) J. Robert Oppenheimer, (c) Harry S Truman.
3. Identify (a) Hiroshima, (b) Nagasaki.

Key Concepts
4. What was the purpose of the Manhattan Project, and what resources were required to accomplish this purpose?
5. What were some alternatives to dropping the atomic bomb on Japan?

Critical Thinking
6. **Demonstrating Reasoned Judgment** World War II veteran Art Rittenberg recalls that war propaganda "heavily influenced the way we viewed the Japanese. I never thought of them as people like myself who had gone to high school, who had gone to a dance, who had friends, who had parents. They were 'the Japs.' " List three reasons that such attitudes may have affected the decision to drop two atomic bombs on Japan and three reasons they may not have.

The Lasting Impact of the Atomic Bomb

The atomic bomb did more than simply end the war. The nuclear technology developed by the Manhattan Project launched a wide range of political and economic changes in the postwar world. The Soviet Union tested its first atomic weapon in 1949, and the specter of nuclear war between the superpowers cast a dark shadow over international affairs.

The Arms Race

The arms race was on. The United States tested a new and even more destructive nuclear weapon, the hydrogen bomb, in 1952. The Soviets soon had their own hydrogen bomb. Besides increasing tension and fear between the superpowers, tests in the 1950s and 1960s produced large quantities of fallout, radioactive dust in the atmosphere that drifted down to earth and contaminated every-thing it touched. Water, milk, and all kinds of foods could become toxic. In response, the United States, the Soviet Union, and Great Britain—now also a member of the "nuclear club"—signed a treaty in 1963 banning above-ground testing of nuclear devices.

Both the United States and the Soviet Union continued to produce many thousands of nuclear devices. By 1983 the United States possessed about 26,000 nuclear warheads, a number closely matched by the Soviet stockpile. Despite the proliferation of weapons, however, leaders were in no hurry to spark a nuclear conflict. The possibility of "mutually assured destruction" acted as a strong deterrent. This situation meant that a country could not win a nuclear war because it would be destroyed by its opponent's defensive weapons.

The Soviet Union and the United States, as well as other countries, continued to devote much of

1945 Physicist J. Robert Oppenheimer and General Leslie R. Groves oversee first atomic bomb test in New Mexico desert.

| 1900 | 1920 | 1940 |

1939 Albert Einstein informs President Roosevelt that atomic weapons are possible.

their defense budgets to the development of conventional (nonnuclear) weapons. Atomic weapons were a deterrent against atomic weapons, but "limited" wars employing conventional weapons still played a central role in the postwar world. The war between the United States and Iraq in 1991, called the Persian Gulf War, is a good example. This brief conflict introduced the sophisticated new Patriot missile, which is capable of seeking out and destroying incoming missiles in midair.

Peaceful Applications

Nuclear technology has other applications besides the machinery of war. In 1953 Britain harnessed the power of the atom to produce electricity, completing the first nuclear power plant. By 1957 the United States had an operating nuclear plant in Shippingport, Pennsylvania. Many more were to follow. But in the late 1960s and early 1970s, some citizens began to question the safety of nuclear power. The possibility of radiation leaks and the risks involved in storing atomic waste, which remains dangerously radioactive for tens of thousands of years, frightened many people. By 1978 orders for new nuclear power plants had dropped to zero, and many plants under construction in the 1980s were abandoned before they were finished.

New technologies that have grown out of nuclear research have been useful in the medical field. For example, methods of isotope separation developed by the Manhattan Project have given birth to nuclear medicine, in which small amounts of radioactive chemicals can be injected into and traced throughout the body to diagnose certain diseases. The atom contains an awesome and terrifying force, but it can also be tamed for human benefit.

REVIEWING THE FACTS

1. Did nuclear weapons make conventional war obsolete? Explain your answer.
2. What are some of the peaceful applications of nuclear technology?

Critical Thinking

3. **Formulating Questions** If your local utility company were planning to build a nuclear power plant in your community, what questions would you want to ask a nuclear scientist about the plant?

1952 United States tests first megaton-class hydrogen bomb on Pacific island of Eniwetok.

1982 Nearly one million people join an antinuclear demonstration in New York City.

1990s A bone scan using radioisotope tracers can determine whether cancer in one part of the body has spread to the bones.

1960   1980   2000

1950s American companies market backyard fallout shelters to families fearful of nuclear war.

1957 First American light-water nuclear power plant begins generating electricity in Shippingport, Pennsylvania.

553

Chapter Review

Key Terms
1. fascism
2. Nazi party
3. anti-Semitism
4. appeasement
5. Lend-Lease Act
6. blitzkrieg
7. Battle of the Bulge
8. holocaust
9. GI
10. WAC
11. Manhattan Project
12. Interim Committee

People
13. Benito Mussolini
14. Adolf Hitler
15. Winston Churchill
16. Douglas MacArthur
17. Dwight D. Eisenhower
18. Chester Nimitz
19. Joseph Stalin
20. Albert Einstein

21. J. Robert Oppenheimer
22. Harry S Truman

Places
23. Rhineland
24. Manchuria
25. Pearl Harbor
26. Midway Island
27. Guadalcanal
28. Normandy
29. Hiroshima
30. Nagasaki

Terms For each term above, write a sentence that explains its relation to World War II.

Matching Review the key terms in the list above. If you are not sure of a term's meaning, review its definition in the chapter. Then choose a term from the list that best matches each description below.
1. a policy of keeping the peace by giving in to someone's demands
2. a series of sudden military attacks by land and air
3. the German counterattack in Belgium and Luxembourg in December 1944
4. the nickname for an American soldier

5. the group of American officials who studied alternative methods of ending the war in the Pacific

Word Relationships Three of the terms in each of the following sets of terms are related. Choose the term that does not belong, and explain why it does not belong.
1. (a) Albert Einstein, (b) Benito Mussolini, (c) J. Robert Oppenheimer, (d) Harry S Truman
2. (a) Chester Nimitz, (b) Douglas MacArthur, (c) Winston Churchill, (d) Dwight D. Eisenhower
3. (a) Pearl Harbor, (b) Rhineland, (c) Guadalcanal, (d) Midway Island

Section 1 (pp. 530–535)
1. What did Japan hope to gain by invading Manchuria and other parts of the Asian mainland?
2. How did the United States support the Allies with economic aid while staying out of the fighting?
3. Why did Japan attack Pearl Harbor?

Section 2 (pp. 536–542)
4. What events helped turn the tide of war in favor of the Allies?
5. What was Hitler's "Final Solution"?

Section 3 (pp. 543–546)
6. While some Japanese Americans were fighting the

enemy overseas, what was happening to many of their families in the United States?
7. In what ways did the United States government discriminate against African Americans during World War II?
8. What unique contribution were Native Americans able to make to the American military effort?

Section 4 (pp. 548–551)
9. Why did the United States government reject the idea of invading Japan in order to end the war?
10. What were the immediate effects of using the atomic bomb on Hiroshima and Nagasaki?

1. **Expressing Problems Clearly** What situation often motivated the armed forces to relax their discrimination against women and African Americans?
2. **Expressing Problems Clearly** The Soviet Union fought alongside the Allies during World War II, yet soon after became a bitter enemy of the United States. Give evidence to show that the seeds of conflict between the United States and the Soviet Union were already present during World War II.
3. **Distinguishing False from Accurate Images** Many popular video games deal with war. Do you think that the images of war presented in such games accurately portray the real experience of fighting in a war? Why or why not?

1. **Evaluating Primary Sources** Review the first primary source excerpt on page 550. Dwight Eisenhower disagreed with President Truman's decision to end the war by using the atomic bomb. Are Eisenhower's reasons convincing? Explain why or why not.
2. **Understanding the Visuals** Look through the chapter to find visuals that reveal the attitude of the United States toward the war before and after Pearl Harbor. Write a paragraph to accompany your choice of visuals, explaining what the attitude was and what change, if any, it underwent.
3. **Writing About the Chapter** Imagine that you are living in London during the Battle of Britain, the devastating German air attack that was most intense during the summer and fall of 1940. Write a letter to a relative in the United States, explaining your fears and uncertainties. First, review the chapter for details about the war. Next, write a draft of your letter, adding details from your imagination as you picture yourself living with the relentless bombing and the knowledge that much of Europe is under Nazi control. Revise your letter, making sure that it is written from the point of view of someone who does not know how the conflict will end. Proofread your letter and draft a final copy.
4. **Using the Graphic Organizer** This graphic organizer uses a multi-flow chart to organize information about the causes and effects of Britain and France's declaration of war on Germany in September 1939. Causes of that event appear in the boxes at left. Effects of the event are listed to the right. (a) According to the graphic organizer, what were two major causes of this event? (b) On a separate sheet of paper, create your own multi-flow chart. In the center box, write "Japanese bombing of Pearl Harbor draws U.S. into war." Add three causes and three effects of this event to the appropriate boxes.

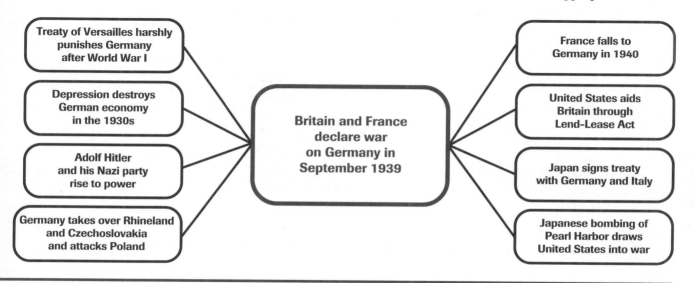

Treaty of Versailles harshly punishes Germany after World War I

Depression destroys German economy in the 1930s

Adolf Hitler and his Nazi party rise to power

Germany takes over Rhineland and Czechoslovakia and attacks Poland

Britain and France declare war on Germany in September 1939

France falls to Germany in 1940

United States aids Britain through Lend-Lease Act

Japan signs treaty with Germany and Italy

Japanese bombing of Pearl Harbor draws United States into war

World War II at Home
1941–1945

AIR RAID PRECAUTIONS HAVE BEEN TAKEN HERE

Signed by_____

Auxiliary Defense Manual

*A*s war clouds gathered over Europe and Asia in the late 1930s, the United States government faced an enormous challenge. How would it convert a depressed peacetime economy and a public that still remembered the horrors of World War I into an efficient war production machine? This massive organizational project required not only mobilizing American businesses but also "selling" the American public on the war. Families who had known terrible hardship during the Depression and who were sending their loved ones into combat would have to be convinced to sacrifice still more. With slogans such as "Remember Pearl Harbor" and "Don't You Know There's A War On?" the government launched a massive campaign that reminded people at every turn to conserve, participate, and sacrifice.

Remember PEARL HARBOR

Events in the United States

1939 Robert de Graff starts the Pocket Books company.

1940 Roosevelt asks Congress to approve the production of 50,000 airplanes per year.

1941 A. Philip Randolph suggests a march on Washington to end discrimination.

1938	1939	1940	1941

Events in the World

1939 First evacuation of women and children from London.

1940 Rationing begins in Britain.

1942	1943	1944	1945	1946
1942 Popular movies such as Casablanca glorify the war effort and inspire troops.	**1943** Race riots in Los Angeles. • Congress passes Smith-Connally Act limiting strikes.	**1944** The number of working women rises to over 19 million, up from 14.6 million in 1941.	**1945** Japanese Americans are released from internment camps.	
1942 Great Britain produces 23,671 aircraft, 8,611 tanks, and 173 major vessels.	**1943** Germans give up after 900-day siege of Stalingrad.	**1944** Anne Frank and her family arrested by Nazis in Amsterdam.	**1945** Hitler commits suicide in an underground bunker in Germany.	

The Shift to Wartime Production

SECTION PREVIEW

Despite its horrors, World War II did bring an end to the Depression in America. Millions of workers streamed back into the factories to produce airplanes, tanks, and guns—and to receive a welcome paycheck.

Key Concepts

- During World War II, the American economy converted to producing materials for the war.
- World War II ended the Great Depression as millions joined the wartime labor force and, after the United States joined the war, the military.
- The war was paid for with taxes and by government borrowing.

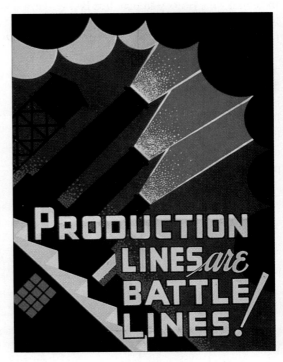

Many advertisements linked their products to wartime patriotism.

Key Terms, People, and Places

cost-plus system, wildcat strike, deficit spending; John L. Lewis

A t the start of World War II, supplying goods to the Allied forces helped boost the American economy. With the cloud of the Depression finally beginning to lift, companies were eager to start making cars, refrigerators, and washing machines again, and consumers were eager to buy them. The government would have to campaign vigorously to convince Americans to continue to sacrifice such items for the sake of the war effort.

Mobilizing the War Economy

President Roosevelt understood that the outcome of the war would ultimately depend on America's ability to produce war materials such as bombers, tanks, and uniforms. He knew that the government would have to take a firm hand in coordinating the production efforts of hundreds of American businesses used to pursuing their own interests. In May 1943 FDR organized the Office of War Mobilization under the direction of James F. Byrnes. A former Supreme Court justice, Byrnes was a skillful negotiator whose guidance made wartime production run smoothly.

Conversion of the Auto Industry After the bombing of Pearl Harbor, the nation was convinced of the need to produce large amounts of war materials. The automobile industry responded to this need by converting its factories to produce bombers. On February 10, 1942, as the last cars rolled off the assembly lines, workers began taking apart automobile machinery and packing it for storage.

The government used posters such as this one, designed by Ches Cobb, to remind people on the home front of their responsibility to the war effort.

Passenger Car and Military Aircraft Production, 1939–1946

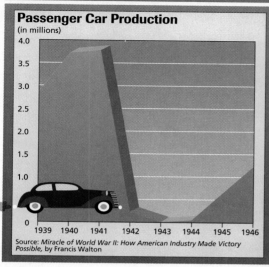

Passenger Car Production
(in millions)

Source: *Miracle of World War II: How American Industry Made Victory Possible,* by Francis Walton

Military Aircraft Production
(in thousands)

Source: *Historical Statistics of the United States*

Interpreting Graphs
What overall trends in auto production and military aircraft production do these graphs show? Do you think the effect of assembly-line production on the aircraft industry can be judged from the information in the graph on the right? Explain your answer.

While many existing plants were being converted, Henry Ford was planning to build an immense new factory to produce B-24 Liberator bombers. Ford wanted to use assembly-line techniques, which had never before been applied in the aircraft industry, to produce planes faster and more efficiently. To achieve his goal, Ford conceived the huge Willow Run bomber plant near Ann Arbor, Michigan. Willow Run covered 975 acres with an assembly line that stretched a full mile across a flat meadowland. When operating at full capacity, the plant employed more than 42,000 people.

MAKING CONNECTIONS

How do you suppose the government encouraged businesses to undertake the expensive process of wartime conversion? Compare your response to the information that follows.

New Opportunities for Profit Secretary of War Henry L. Stimson understood that "if you are going to try to go to war, or to prepare for war, in a capitalist country, you have to let business make money out of the process or business

won't work." To that end, the government established the **cost-plus system,** in which the government paid all development and production costs plus a percentage of those costs as profit on anything a company made for the war.

Thousands of business executives went to Washington to work in war agencies responsible for coordinating production. Many accepted token salaries of one dollar from the government while remaining on their own companies' payrolls. From inside war agencies, these "dollar-a-year men" helped to decide which firms would receive profitable contracts.

New Markets and Methods Entrepreneurs prospered during World War II. Some succeeded in creating profitable new markets for their products. Robert Woodruff, head of Coca-Cola, declared in December 1941: "We will see that every man in uniform gets a bottle of Coca-Cola for five cents wherever he is and whatever it costs [the company]." By the time the war was over, American troops had drunk five billion bottles of Coca-Cola. At the same time, Woodruff's company had established a new "army" of civilian consumers who had enjoyed the drink while in uniform.

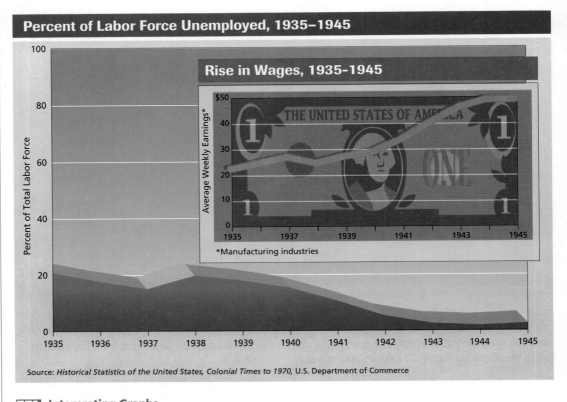

Percent of Labor Force Unemployed, 1935–1945

Rise in Wages, 1935–1945

*Manufacturing industries

Source: *Historical Statistics of the United States, Colonial Times to 1970*, U.S. Department of Commerce

Interpreting Graphs
The conversion of the United States economy during the war brought businesses huge profits from government contracts. According to these graphs, in what two ways did workers benefit during the war?

Welder Benny Chan gives the "V for Victory" sign.

Other entrepreneurs pioneered modern production methods. Henry J. Kaiser, for example, introduced mass production techniques to shipbuilding. The vessels that made him famous were called Liberty ships. In 1941 it took 355 days to build one Liberty ship. By the end of the war, Kaiser's shipyard located in Portland, Oregon, could assemble a ship in just 14 days.

Workers, the War, and Unions

Business owners were not the only group to benefit from war production. War production brought an end to the devastating unemployment of the 1930s. As the graph shows, by 1943 unemployment had fallen dramatically. Average weekly wages in manufacturing, adjusted for inflation, rose 27 percent in a little over three years.

With more people working, union membership rose. Between 1940 and 1941, the number of workers belonging to unions increased by 1.5 million. Union membership continued to rise sharply once the United States entered the war, from 10.5 million in 1941 to 14.8 million in 1945.

Two weeks after the attack on Pearl Harbor, labor and business representatives agreed to refrain from strikes and lockouts—a tactic in which an employer "locks" employees out of their jobs to avoid meeting their demands. The no-strike agreement became hard to honor, however, as the cost of living rose during the war and Pearl Harbor faded from memory. The government had to remind citizens continually of the importance of the agreement. Leonard Williamson, a superintendent for a large construction company, recalled the government's involvement in the building of a military base in New Jersey:

They started at one time to develop a strike there, and some big guy from the Pentagon came down, and he just laid the cards on the table: "There'll be no strikes." Everybody kind of buckled down, and we finished the thing in record time.

Still, the number of strikers doubled between 1942 and 1943, and it continued to rise in the last two years of the war. Some of the strikes were **wildcat strikes**—that is, they were organized by the workers themselves and not endorsed by the unions.

The most serious confrontations organized by unions occurred in the coalfields, where **John L. Lewis,** head of the United Mine Workers union, called strikes on four different occasions in 1943. Lewis and the miners, seeing industry profits soar while their wages stayed the same, demanded a pay raise to compensate for the rising cost of living. Secretary of the Interior Harold J. Ickes finally negotiated an agreement with Lewis. Meanwhile, Congress passed the Smith-Connally Act in June 1943 to place limits on future strike activity.

Financing the War

In World War II, the United States government was willing to spend whatever it cost to energize war production and maintain a "fighting" mentality at home. Federal spending increased from $9.4 billion in 1939 to $95.2 billion in 1945, and the gross national product more than doubled in that time.

A raise in taxes paid for approximately 41 percent of the cost of the war. The Revenue Act of 1942 increased the number of Americans who paid income taxes, levying a flat 5 percent tax on all incomes over $624 a year. The rest of the money was borrowed from banks, private investors, and the public. The United States Treasury launched a series of bond drives to borrow money from individual Americans, raising a total of $135 billion.

Massive wartime spending ended the Great Depression. In the 1930s most economists believed that the economy would fix itself if the government did not interfere. English economist John Maynard Keynes, on the other hand, argued that **deficit spending**—government spending of borrowed money—should be used to get a depressed economy moving again. Deficit spending during World War II turned the economy around overnight. Unfortunately, it also catapulted the nation into a habit of deficit spending, causing economic problems that continue to this day.

The results of wartime spending were stupendous. Each year the United States raised its production goals for military materials, and each year it met them. By the middle of 1945, the nation had produced 80,000 landing craft, 100,000 tanks and armored cars, 300,000 airplanes, 15 million guns, and 41 billion rounds of ammunition. The country had indeed become, in Franklin Roosevelt's words, the "arsenal of democracy."

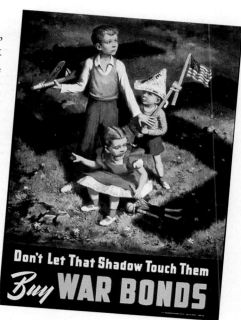

Don't Let That Shadow Touch Them
Buy WAR BONDS

This poster, designed to appeal to people's emotions, encouraged Americans to sacrifice and helped raise money for the war.

SECTION 1 REVIEW

Key Terms, People, and Places
1. Define (a) cost-plus system, (b) wildcat strike.
2. Identify John L. Lewis.

Key Concepts
3. What were the major problems involved in mobilizing the American economy in World War II?
4. How did World War II end the Great Depression?

5. How did deficit spending help the war effort?

Critical Thinking
6. **Formulating Questions** Imagine that you are a business owner in 1942, and that the government has asked you to produce materials for the war. Develop a list of questions that you would want to ask before you agreed to cooperate.

Daily Life on the Home Front

SECTION PREVIEW

While American soldiers crouched in foxholes overseas, friends and families supported their struggle on the home front. Rationing and conserving resources like gasoline, scrap metal, and rubber drew most of the country into the war effort.

Key Concepts

- The mood on the American home front was one of cooperation and determined optimism.
  - American consumers had money in their pockets for the first time in years, and they looked for ways to spend it.
    - Shortages of many basic items, such as sugar, meat, and gasoline, plagued the wartime economy.
    - The government sought to maintain morale at home through various public relations campaigns.

Key Terms, People, and Places

rationing

Rationing coupons set limits on the amount of scarce items each family could buy during the war.

T he daily life of most Americans during World War II was filled with constant reminders of the war. To escape, many used the first extra cash they had earned since the Depression to purchase paperback books and go to the movies or baseball games, among other popular diversions. Rubber and aluminum drives, encouraged by the government, were designed to make most Americans feel part of the war effort.

Prosperity and Popular Culture

In the middle of the war, seven out of ten Americans felt that they had not had to make any "real sacrifices" because of the war. Morale was quite high as the Depression subsided. In 1941, 34 percent of all American families had incomes of less than $1000 a year, but new jobs created by the war brought that figure down below 20 percent by 1945. One measure of people's optimism was an increase in the birthrate. The population grew by 7.5 million between 1940 and 1945, nearly double the rate of growth for the 1930s. The so-called postwar baby boom that extended through the 1950s really began during the war.

Money to Burn As the wartime economy gathered speed, many Americans who had gone without steady paychecks for years suddenly found themselves earning more money than they needed just for basic necessities. They were hungry for ways to spend this extra income—they wanted new cars and trucks and appliances. Unfortunately, wartime conversion meant that most of these goods were unavailable, so they had to look for other ways to spend their money.

Among the items that people did buy were books. The new Pocket Books company, founded by Robert de Graff in 1939, developed a market for paperback books. De Graff believed that more Americans would read if books were more widely available and at lower prices. His instinct proved correct when he sold 34,000 copies of the first Pocket Book, titled *How to Win Friends and Influence People*, in two months. Soldiers carried Pocket Books with them into combat, and when the war was over, these men joined a sizeable new market for paperbacks.

Approximately 85 million Americans, or 62 percent of the population, went to the movies each week during the war. Many of these films were in the "escapist" category: love stories, adventure tales, or light comedies that took audiences' minds off the serious business of war. Others dealt with the war directly and promoted themes of patriotism and American victory. Hollywood, too, was "doing its part" to contribute to the war effort.

Baseball and Popular Music Though more than 4,000 of the 5,700 major and minor league players were in the military services, Americans still flocked to baseball games during the war. Ball clubs had to scramble to make up for the losses in their ranks. To fill their rosters, many had to place want ads in newspapers:

I f you are a free agent and have previous professional experience, we may be able to place you to your advantage on one of our clubs. We have positions open on our AA, B, and D classification clubs. If you believe you can qualify for one of these good baseball jobs, tell us about yourself.
Sporting News, February 25, 1943

Women ball players also took to the fields to lift the spirits of war-weary Americans. In 1943 Philip Wrigley founded the All-American Girls' Softball League, which became the All-American Girls' Baseball League in 1945. Women who played for teams such as the Rockford (Illinois) Peaches and the South Bend (Indiana) Blue Sox had to attend charm school and wear impractical skirted uniforms. But they endured such inconveniences for the chance to play professional ball, and they attracted scores of devoted fans.

As in World War I, many popular songs during World War II were written to inspire hope and patriotism. Frank Loesser's "Praise the Lord and Pass the Ammunition"—based on a true story—told of a navy chaplain who took over an anti-aircraft gun at Pearl Harbor after several of his fellow sailors had been killed. "There's a Star-Spangled Banner Waving Somewhere" was one of the best-selling records of 1942 and 1943. "White Christmas," from the 1942 film *Holiday Inn,* was the sentimental favorite, both for soldiers overseas and for civilians at home.

Shortages and Controls

The war brought its share of problems along with increased prosperity and a high-spirited popular culture. Although they had money to spend, Americans had to live with shortages and disruptions throughout the war.

Pete Gray, a one-armed outfielder, did his part for the war effort by playing for the St. Louis Browns and giving the "troops" at home a lift.

Some consumer items were simply unavailable. Metal to make zippers was used for guns; rubber for girdles went into tanks and trucks; fabric for dresses became military uniforms instead. In an effort to save cloth, government regulations required the elimination of vests, patch pockets, and cuffs in men's suits. They also limited the length and width of women's skirts, which grew shorter and narrower during the war period. Two-piece bathing suits for women—considered somewhat shocking in the 1920s and 1930s—could now be justified on the basis of military need because they required less fabric.

Some foods were also in limited supply during the war. Sugar became scarce when the major source of American imports, the Philippines, fell to the Japanese and shipping lanes from other countries were closed. Coffee could not be transported easily from Brazil. Meat and countless other items were likewise scarce.

Worried that shortages would lead to price increases, the government used tough measures to head off inflation.

VICTORY SPEED 35 MILES

Children, too, did their part for the war effort. These boys in New York City used their powers of persuasion—and noisemaking—to urge their neighbors to contribute to an aluminum drive.

President Roosevelt created the Office of Price Administration (OPA) in mid-1941, and the following year he gave the agency the authority to freeze prices. In the middle of 1942, OPA began **rationing,** or distributing goods in a fixed amount by using coupons. It assigned point values to scarce items such as sugar, coffee, meat, butter, shoes, and gasoline. Consumers were issued coupons worth a certain number of points. Once they had used up their points, they were not allowed to buy any more of the rationed items until additional coupons were issued.

MAKING CONNECTIONS

What effect do you think wartime shortages and rationing had on people's morale? Do you suppose it made people feel angry at the government or more patriotic?

Campaigns at Home

The government understood the need to maintain morale. While making rationing seem fun was not an easy task, the government had to create a sense of patriotism and participation in the war effort while convincing citizens to conserve precious resources.

| 1650 | 1700 | 1750 | 1800 | Links Across Time | 1850 | 1900 | 1950 | 2000 |

Taking Care of the Troops

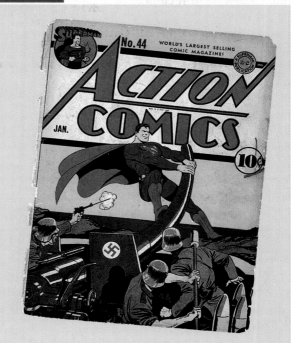

During wartime, America's businesses have always played their part by producing items designed specifically to boost the morale of those on the front lines. During World War II, special editions of certain comic books, such as Action Comics, were printed and sent to cheer up the soldiers overseas. Similarly, Hershey Foods developed a nonmelting chocolate bar for the troops in the Persian Gulf War of 1991 that was specially formulated "for desert or tropical conditions." *What product would you develop for our troops? Explain your reasoning.*

In one campaign, Americans were asked to save scrap metal and other materials that could be used for war machinery. Huge drives collected tin cans, pots and pans, razor blades, old shovels, and even old lipstick tubes. In Virginia, collectors raised sunken ships from the James River; in Wyoming they took apart an old steam engine to use the parts. When rubber was in short supply, people collected rubber hoses, raincoats, and bathing caps. Americans were asked to save kitchen fats because the glycerin could be used to make powder for bullets or shells. Some historians have questioned whether the items collected were ever really used for their intended purpose. Whether they were or not, the collection process served another important purpose: it was another way the government kept the American public's attention focused on the war effort.

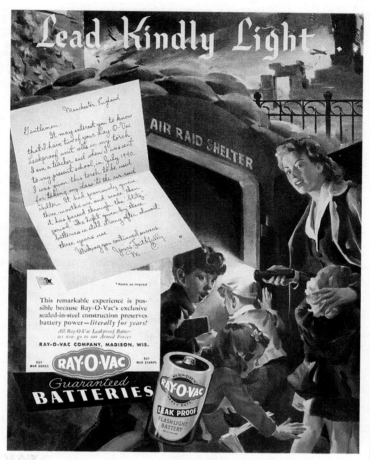

Using Historical Evidence Besides emphasizing quality and value, advertisers used a war-related setting and emotion to sell their products during the war. *How are all of those used in this ad?*

Another campaign encouraged Americans to buy savings bonds to finance the war. In the spring of 1941, Secretary of the Treasury Henry Morgenthau, Jr., decided "to use *bonds* to sell the *war,* rather than *vice versa.*" Morgenthau realized that selling war bonds would give people "a financial stake in American democracy—an opportunity to contribute toward the defense of that democracy."

"Play your part." "Conserve and collect." "Use it up, wear it out, make it do or do without"—these refrains echoed throughout the United States, constantly reminding Americans of their patriotic duty in the wartime campaign.

SECTION 2 REVIEW

Key Terms, People, and Places

1. Define rationing.

Key Concepts

2. What items were in short supply during the war, and how did the government respond to these shortages?

3. How did the scarcity of cloth during World War II affect clothing fashions?

4. What was the purpose of government campaigns such as the war bond campaign?

Critical Thinking

5. **Identifying Assumptions** What underlying beliefs was the United States government acting upon when it waged its massive effort to "sell" the war to Americans at home?

Women and the War

During World War II, thousands of American women rolled up their sleeves and went to work in defense plants and shipyards. Adapting quickly to work usually done by men and overcoming a sometimes cold welcome from fellow male employees, they helped satisfy the Allies' urgent need for military goods.

Key Concepts

- During World War II, American women of all ages went to work.
- Women were successful in their new jobs despite the hardships and discrimination they faced.
- At the end of the war, women were strongly encouraged to leave their jobs, whether they wanted to or not.

Key Terms, People, and Places

Rosie the Riveter

The motto of the women's Auxiliary Reserve Pool (ARP) during World War II was "Prepared and Faithful."

A popular song during World War II paid tribute to a fictional young woman named **Rosie the Riveter,** who worked in a defense plant while her boyfriend Charlie served in the marines. The government used images of Rosie the Riveter in posters and propaganda films of the 1940s to attract women to the work force. In general, the Rosie created by the government was young, white, and middle class. Patriotism was her main motive for taking a war job—she wanted to do her part on the home front while her brother, husband, or boyfriend fought on the military front. In reality, the wartime economy made it essential for American women of all ages and ethnic and economic backgrounds to work. And, despite the ideals that the government set before them, they worked for a variety of reasons beyond patriotism.

Shifting Patterns of Employment

Before the war, most women who worked for wages were single and young. Even during the hard times of the Depression, most people disapproved of a married woman working outside the home to earn money. This social opposition was reinforced by the fear that working women took jobs away from unemployed men. According to a poll taken in 1936, 82 percent of Americans believed that a married woman should not work if her husband had a job. Nevertheless, by 1940 about 15.5 percent of all married women were working.

Women often worked as sales clerks and household servants because many other fields were closed to them. Men dominated the machinery, steel, and automobile industries, while women more commonly worked in industries that produced clothing, textiles, and shoes. In the jobs they did hold, women usually earned much less than men.

Like World War I, World War II brought many women into the work force. As men were drafted into the armed forces, a large number of factory jobs fell vacant. News of these well-paying job openings brought women who were already working in traditional women's jobs to take over these positions. But these women were not enough. So the Office of War Information launched a propaganda campaign to fill the rest of the positions with women who normally would not have considered working outside the home: older, married women.

Posters and advertisements told women that it was their patriotic duty to work for their country. "An American homemaker with the strength and ability to run a house and raise a family . . . has the strength and ability to take her place in a vital War industry," declared one government advertisement. As a result of this campaign, the number of working women rose from 14.6 million in 1941 to about 19.4 million in 1944. (See the graph on page 568.)

More than half of all American women were employed at some point during the war; at its peak, women made up 36 percent of the total civilian labor force.

Along with growing numbers of women in the work force, the type of women who worked changed significantly during the war. Married women accounted for almost three quarters of the increase; for the first time in American history, they outnumbered single working women. More than two million women over the age of thirty-five found jobs, and by the end of the war, half of all women workers were over age thirty-five.

An even more striking change occurred in the kind of work women did. Increasingly they moved out of domestic service and into manufacturing, particularly the defense industries. Now women worked in airplane plants and shipyards as steelworkers, riveters, and welders. Rosie the Riveter—strong, determined, and capable—became the ideal to which American women were supposed to aspire.

MAKING CONNECTIONS

Rosie the Riveter was the image of the working woman promoted by the government. Why did the government have to create a character such as Rosie the Riveter?

The Wartime Working Experience

Despite resistance in the past, employers were usually pleased to have women workers—although often for reasons many Americans find misguided today. Employers believed, for instance, that women could do certain welding tasks better than men, for they could squeeze into smaller places. They also made assumptions about women's mental abilities that led them to think that women could do simple, repetitious tasks more effectively than men.

Working Conditions for Women of Color
African American women had long worked in greater proportion than married white women, but they had been largely restricted to domestic work. In addition to gender stereotyping,

This war worker is assembling one part of an aircraft in a California factory.

African American women often faced racial discrimination when they applied for defense jobs. Wanita Allen, who wanted to work at Murray Auto Body in Detroit, Michigan, described her experience this way:

> I didn't have any problem getting in the training program. They said you have to have 300 hours to get a job in the plant, and I got my 300, 400, going on 500 hours, and was learning blueprint and everything else, but still no job. They would come in from the plant proper to pick women who'd maybe been there just a couple of days on the training program, and they would put them to work. But they were white women.

Allen later helped gather evidence for a lawsuit against the plant, and she and many other African American women were eventually hired at Murray Auto. Through lawsuits and other forms of protest, African American women changed their profile in the work force. Between 1940 and 1944, the proportion of African American women in industrial jobs

These women welders at the Kaiser shipyard in Richmond, California, are working on the Liberty ship S.S. *George Washington Carver.*

Shipyards to pay for her family's home. Other women simply found the work more exciting than what they had done before. Evelyn Knight described why she left a position as a cook to work in a navy yard: "After all, I've got to keep body and soul together, and I'd rather earn a living this way than to cook over a hot stove." Still other women took jobs for patriotic reasons. One rubber plant worker declared, "Every time I test a batch of rubber, I know it's going to help bring my three sons home quicker."

Many women also were eager to prove that they could do whatever their jobs required. Adele Erenberg left a position as a Los Angeles cosmetics clerk to work in a machine shop when the war began. The noisy atmosphere was intimidating at first, and it was two weeks before fellow employees spoke to her. Her response was: "Okay, . . . I'm going to prove to you I can do anything you can do, and maybe better than some of you."

increased from 6.8 percent to 18 percent, while the number working in domestic service dropped from 59.9 percent to 44.6 percent.

Benefits of Employment On the whole, women were delighted to be employed. To many, the money they earned made a difference in their lives. Josephine McKee, a Seattle mother of nine who worked at the Boeing Aircraft Company, was able to pay off debts from the Depression. Leola Houghland, also from Seattle, used her earnings at Associated

AMERICAN PROFILES

Beatrice Morales Clifton

Beatrice Morales Clifton never imagined herself as Rosie the Riveter. In 1942 she was living in Pasadena, California, with her husband Julio and four children. Her teenage niece wanted to get a job, so Clifton took her to apply for work in the aircraft industry.

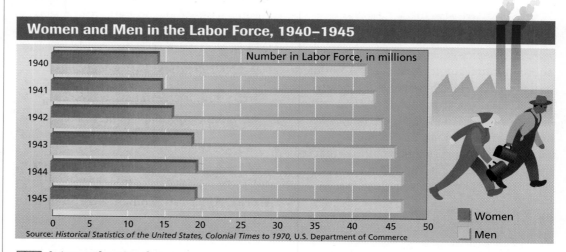

Women and Men in the Labor Force, 1940–1945

Number in Labor Force, in millions

	Women	Men

Source: *Historical Statistics of the United States, Colonial Times to 1970,* U.S. Department of Commerce

Interpreting Graphs
What was the overall trend in women's employment during World War II, according to this graph? Why did the ratio of women to men in the labor force remain about constant during the war?

Clifton was surprised when the man in the employment office suggested that she herself fill out an application; she had been married at age fifteen and had never considered looking for work outside the home. "But," she later explained, "the more I kept thinking about it, the more I said, 'That's a good idea.'" Her husband was initially opposed to her plan, but Clifton was determined. She told him, "I've made up my mind. I'm going to go to work."

Clifton was hired by Lockheed Aircraft in Los Angeles. When she arrived for her first day of work, she found the factory "exciting and scary at the same time." The male worker assigned to teach Clifton her job resented working women. When she made a slight slip with the rivet gun, he told her, "You're not worth the money Lockheed pays you."

With the support of her female co-workers, however, Clifton soon learned to enjoy her work. Her confidence grew as she mastered one skill after another. She later explained:

I felt proud of myself and felt good [because] I had never done anything like that. I felt good that I could do something, and being that it was war, I felt that I was doing my part.

I went from 65 cents to $1.05 [an hour]. That was top pay. It felt good and, besides, it was my own money. I could do whatever I wanted with it.

After leaving her wartime job for several years, Clifton returned to Lockheed in 1951. By the time she retired in 1978, she was a supervisor for about fifty other workers, half of them men. Asked how her work experiences affected her life, Clifton said,

My life, it was changed from day to night. . . . The changes started when I first started working. They started a little bit, and from then on it kept on going. Because after I quit . . . at Lockheed, I wasn't satisfied. I started looking for ways of getting out and going to work. See, and before, I had never had that thought of going out.

Problems for Working Women

For all the positive aspects of employment, working women experienced a number of problems. Some faced hostile reactions from other workers, particularly in jobs previously held only by men. Restrictions imposed by managers who worried about mixing the sexes in their plants irritated other women. General Motors, for example, fired male supervisors and female employees found "fraternizing," or socializing with one another.

Many working women worried about leaving their children. More than half a million women with children under ten worked during the war, and day-care centers were scarce. Even when the government provided such facilities, most women preferred to have their children cared for by family members or friends, and this often required making complicated arrangements. Women were encouraged to work, but at the same time they continued to bear complete responsibility for both their children and for many of the chores in the home.

Women also earned significantly less than men doing the same jobs. Although the National War Labor Board declared in the fall of 1942 that women who performed "work of the same quality and quantity" as men should receive equal pay, the policy often was ignored. Women began at the bottom, with the lowest-paying jobs. Because they had less seniority, they frequently advanced more slowly. Their wages reflected these patterns. At the Willow Run plant in 1945, women earned a yearly average of $2,928, compared with $3,363 for men. Conditions improved toward the end of the war, but the gap never closed.

Beatrice Morales Clifton worked at Lockheed Aircraft during World War II.

MAKING CONNECTIONS

Women were encouraged to enter the work force and provided essential labor for the war effort, but they were never paid the same as men. What do you predict happened to these workers when the war ended?

Sisters under the apron—Yesterday's war worker becomes today's housewife.

What's Become of Rosie the Riveter?

Government propaganda aimed at women did an about-face once the war was over. Posters such as this one now urged women to give up their factory jobs and return to full-time homemaking.

The Postwar Push to "Demobilize" Women

The government propaganda campaign that urged women to report to the defense plants also assumed that when the war was over, women would leave their jobs and return to their homes. The following script excerpt from the recruitment film *Women of Steel*, produced by the Office of War Information, demonstrates this assumption.

> NARRATOR: *Women make good drivers, too. American girls raised to drive the family car have no trouble at all handling trucks and tractors. Edith Stoner's husband is in Alaska. She took this job for the duration. . . . How do you like your job, Mrs. Stoner?*

EDITH STONER: *I love it.*
NARRATOR: *How about after the war? Are you going to keep on working?*
EDITH STONER: *I should say not. When my husband comes back, I'm going to be busy at home.*
NARRATOR: *Good for you!*

At the war's end, many women in fact wanted to continue working, but the pressures to return home were intense. Servicemen wanted "their" jobs back, and they longed to return to the familiar family arrangements they had known before the war. A new campaign by industrialists and government officials now encouraged women to leave their jobs. Articles in women's magazines changed their tune after the war, too. Ammunitions worker Margaret Wright recalled:

> Y ou know, during the war they [were] telling you to cook dishes that you could cook quick and get on to work. Now, they were telling you how to cook dishes that took a full day. There were more articles in there about raising your child. . . .

During demobilization, twice as many women as men lost factory jobs.

Some women were tired of their defense jobs—which in many cases were not very fulfilling once the war's sense of urgency had ended—and looked forward to their work at home. Others, like Beatrice Clifton, would never again feel satisfied being full-time homemakers. After the war, many women continued to work part-time to supplement their families' incomes.

SECTION 3 REVIEW

Key Terms, People, and Places
1. Identify Rosie the Riveter.

Key Concepts
2. How did the profile of women in the work force change during World War II?
3. How did the government use Rosie the Riveter to accomplish its wartime goals?
4. What problems did women encounter as they worked?

5. What options did women defense workers have at the war's end?

Critical Thinking
6. **Recognizing Bias** At the end of the war, government and business responded to the need to provide jobs for returning soldiers by pressuring women to leave their jobs. What underlying beliefs does this response suggest?

Identifying Assumptions

Identifying assumptions means recognizing the unstated beliefs that may underlie a statement or action. An assumption is an idea that a person takes for granted as true. In fact, it may prove either true or false, but in order to determine the accuracy of an assumption, you must first be able to recognize it as such.

Editorials, opinion pieces, and illustrations frequently contain many assumptions. Magazine covers, such as the one shown here, are often excellent sources of information about public attitudes toward historical events. At the same time, illustrations may be drawn in such a way that they also reveal assumptions of the artist.

By the time artist Norman Rockwell's portrayal of "Rosie the Riveter" appeared on the cover of *The Saturday Evening Post* in 1943, American women by the thousands were already making history. They were working in nontraditional factory jobs, assembling ships and airplanes for the country's war effort.

To examine the accuracy of the image portrayed in this painting, use the following steps to identify and evaluate the assumptions on which it may be based.

1. Determine the subject of the cover illustration. Study the illustration carefully and answer the following questions. (a) What is the woman in the illustration doing? (b) Who is "Rosie the Riveter" supposed to represent? (c) What general subject or issue does the illustration address? (d) What is the overall message of the illustration?

2. Define the artist's point of view. To help determine if the artist is presenting a particular viewpoint,

answer the following questions. (a) What seems to be the artist's purpose in creating this illustration? (b) How would you describe the artist's attitude toward the subject? (c) What aspects of the illustration clearly express this point of view? (d) Are there any elements in the illustration that contrast with each other? If so, what might the artist be trying to convey through these contrasts?

3. Identify the assumptions on which the artist's viewpoint is based and decide whether they are valid. To help decide if the artist's assumptions can be supported by facts, answer the following questions. (a) What assumptions, if any, does the artist make about the nature of the work performed by the woman in the illustration? Does the artist make any assumptions about why she holds this job? (b) What assumptions, if any, does the artist make about the women who work in nontraditional jobs? (c) Can any aspects of a person's physical appearance, such as clothes or posture, be reliably linked to his or her occupation? Explain. (d) How can you find out if the artist's apparent assumptions are valid?

571

The Struggle for Justice at Home

SECTION PREVIEW

For many Americans, the war broke down racial barriers in the job market. Japanese Americans, however, fell victim to bitter prejudice at home as the United States battled Japan abroad.

Key Concepts

- Events on the home front helped stimulate the movement for equal rights for African Americans.
- Mexican Americans and Native Americans battled discrimination at home and entered the work force in greater numbers during the war.
- A large number of Japanese Americans were forced into internment camps by the United States government during the war, while others served courageously in the military.

Key Terms, People, and Places

"Double V" campaign, bracero, internment camp; A. Philip Randolph

Clinging to her most precious belongings, this little girl waits to be moved to an internment camp.

P resident Roosevelt, in his 1942 Columbus Day speech, expressed the need to set aside bigotry for the sake of the wartime effort:

> I n some communities employers dislike to hire women. In others they are reluctant to hire Negroes. We can no longer afford to indulge such prejudice.

In fact, the war did bring greater opportunities for a number of groups in America. But racial prejudice did not disappear during the war years. On the contrary, the war fanned the flames of many conflicts that had been smoldering for decades.

The Wartime Struggle Against Jim Crow

Although the effort to end discrimination toward African Americans had long been under way by the time the United States entered World War II, the Jim Crow system—which provided for the rigid separation of the races—remained firmly in place in the South. In the North, fewer laws enforcing segregation were on the books, but African Americans still were discriminated against in employment, education, and housing patterns. During the 1940s, over two million African Americans migrated from the South to northern and western cities (see map on page 573). There they found new opportunities, but they also found themselves concentrated in urban ghettos, or sections of a city in which many members of a particular minority group live due to economic pressure or discrimination. A survey taken in 1941 showed that 50 percent of all African American homes were substandard, versus only 14 percent of white homes.

When the war began, African American unemployment remained high—one out of five potential workers was unemployed. The United States Employment Service, a government agency created during the Depression to provide unemployed Americans with job counseling and placement, continued to honor employers' requests for "whites only," thereby continuing existing patterns of discrimination.

The war turned a spotlight on the injustice of racism in the United States. Alexander J. Allen, who worked for the Baltimore Urban League during the war, remarked, "It made a mockery of wartime goals to fight overseas against fascism only to come back to the same kind of discrimination and racism here in this country." One poignant example of this "mockery" occurred when a group of African American GIs was refused service by the owner of a lunch counter:

African American Migration, 1940–1950

States that had significant loss of African American population

States that had significant gain in African American population

2% Gain or loss of African Americans as a percentage of a state's total population

Map labels: WA, OR, MT, ND, MN, ID, SD, WI, MI +3%, VT, ME, NY +3%, NH, MA, RI, PA +2%, CT, NJ +1%, DE, MD, NV, UT, CO, IA, IL +3%, IN +1%, OH +2%, WV, CA, NE, KS, MO +3%, KY -2%, VA -5%, AZ, NM, OK -1%, AR -4%, TN -2%, NC -3%, SC -7%, MS -5%, AL -4%, GA -6%, TX -2%, LA -4%, FL -7%

Geography and History: Interpreting Maps
All of their possessions loaded into the family car, these young people are moving north. *According to this map, what states lost the greatest percentage of their African American populations in the 1940s? How do you think the wartime economy affected African American migration?*

> Y ou know we don't serve coloreds here," the man repeated. . . .
>
> We ignored him, and just stood there inside the door, staring at what we had come to see—the German prisoners of war who were having lunch at the counter. . . .
>
> We continued to stare. This was really happening. It was no jive talk. The people of Salina would serve these enemy soldiers and turn away black American GIs.

Lloyd Brown, an American soldier stationed in Salina, Kansas

African Americans and others experienced discrimination not only at lunch counters. In the United States military, where men were risking their lives to defend their country, white and African American troops were strictly segregated.

Many white Americans, however, saw no problems in these racial practices. A 1942 poll revealed that six out of ten whites felt that African Americans were satisfied with existing conditions and needed no additional opportunities. Mirroring the lack of concern felt by much of white America, the government did not seem eager to improve the situations of African Americans. Franklin Roosevelt, preoccupied with military matters, was not willing to disrupt the war effort to promote social equality. "I don't think, quite frankly," he said in late 1943, "that we can bring about the millennium [a period of human perfection] at this time."

African Americans disagreed with the President and began organizing for change on their own. The Pittsburgh *Courier*, an African American newspaper, launched a **"Double V" campaign:** *V* for victory in the war against the Axis powers, *V* for victory in the struggle for equality at home. **A. Philip Randolph**—head of the Brotherhood

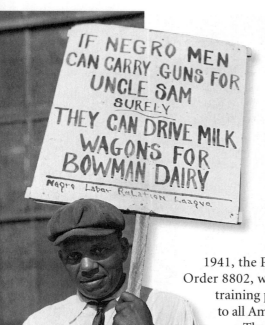

of Sleeping Car Porters, a labor union with a largely African American membership—proposed a massive march on Washington in early 1941 to demand an end to discrimination in all areas of American society. Worried about the possibility of violence in the nation's capital, Roosevelt tried to talk Randolph out of the march. Randolph agreed only when, on June 25, 1941, the President signed Executive Order 8802, which opened jobs and job training programs in defense plants to all Americans regardless of race.

The order also created the Fair Employment Practices Committee (FEPC) to hear complaints about job discrimination in defense industries as well as in the government. While the FEPC was only moderately successful, it did highlight the issue of discrimination, and it opened the way for employers to fill their job openings by hiring African Americans.

Using Historical Evidence This man is protesting outside a Chicago milk company in 1941. *How does the injustice the man is protesting conflict with the issues being fought for abroad during World War II?*

Meanwhile, African Americans were beginning to take direct action to promote equality. The Congress of Racial Equality (CORE), committed to using nonviolent techniques to end racism, was founded in Chicago in 1942. In May 1943 CORE organized its first sit-in at a restaurant called the Jack Spratt Coffee House. Groups of CORE members, each including at least one African American, filled the restaurant's counter and booths and refused to leave until everyone was served. They succeeded in ending Jack Spratt's discriminatory policies, and the sit-in technique quickly spread to CORE groups in other cities. These efforts paved the way for later civil rights activity but could not head off major race riots during the summer of 1943. Thirty-four people died in Detroit on June 16, and New York City was the scene of another riot on August 1 and 2.

MAKING CONNECTIONS

In what ways did the war speed up, and in what ways did it retard, the movement toward equal rights for African Americans?

Mexican Americans and Braceros During World War II

Like African Americans, Mexicans working in the United States and Mexican American citizens faced discrimination during the war. At the same time, the war did bring new employment opportunities for Mexican Americans. Planning for future needs, the Labor Department's Office of Education established vocational schools in a number of southwestern cities and provided training for rural Americans—including Mexican Americans—that eased the transition to war work.

Mexican Americans made major gains on the industrial front during World War II. By 1944, 17,000 were employed in the Los Angeles shipyards, where none had worked three years before. Mexican Americans also found jobs in shipyards and aircraft factories elsewhere in California and in Washington, Texas, and New Mexico. Some headed for other war production centers in places such as Detroit, Chicago, Kansas City, and New York.

The Bracero Program On the agricultural front, a shortage of farm laborers led the United States to seek help from Mexico. In 1942 an agreement between the two nations provided for transportation, food, shelter, and medical care for thousands of **braceros** (Spanish for "workers"), Mexican farm laborers brought to work in the United States. Between 1942 and 1947, more than 200,000 braceros participated in the program. When their contracts expired, however, they were quickly transported back to Mexico.

Despite their vital contributions to the war effort, Mexicans and Mexican Americans continued to suffer discrimination. Braceros endured miserable working conditions, and employers sometimes withheld their wages. Industrial workers occasionally received lower wages for the same work done by people of other ethnic backgrounds. Crowded cities often bred racial tensions. In Los Angeles, where many Mexican Americans lived, those tensions erupted in a bloody race riot in mid-1943.

Zoot Suit Riots Los Angeles was a popular city for sailors on leave from nearby military bases. In April and May 1943, street fighting broke out between sailors and residents of Mexican descent. Many Mexican American men wore a popular style of clothing known as the "zoot suit," which had baggy pants and a long jacket. Gangs of sailors roamed the streets looking for men wearing such suits, whom they attacked and humiliated. Although one Spanish newspaper, *La Opinión,* encouraged the victims not to respond with more violence, some Mexican American youths took revenge on the sailors when they had the chance.

The fighting turned into a full-scale riot during the first weeks of June 1943. Local newspapers usually blamed Mexican Americans for the violence. Police often arrested the victims rather than the sailors who had initiated the attacks. Finally, army and navy officials intervened by restricting soldiers' off-duty access to Los Angeles. By mid-June the riots had subsided.

Native Americans and the War at Home

Despite their history of oppression by the United States government, Native Americans behaved patriotically during World War II. Thousands enlisted in the armed forces or migrated to urban centers to work in defense plants. Government propaganda held up these Native Americans as models of loyal service.

Nearly fifty thousand Native Americans worked in war industries around the country. Over two thousand Navaho helped build a large supply depot in New Mexico. Iroquois worked in aluminum plants and mining operations in New York state. Other Native Americans constructed airplanes on the West Coast and made tanks and ships in other war production centers.

Thousands of Native Americans who left reservations to take military or industrial jobs

had to adapt quickly to white culture. At the end of the war, Native Americans who had served abroad or worked in industrial centers in the United States were less likely to return home. For some Native Americans, the cultural transition brought a sense of alienation and rootlessness that left lasting scars.

The Japanese American Internment

Japanese Americans suffered the worst discrimination during the war. In late 1941, they comprised a tiny minority in the United States. Numbering but 127,000—or one tenth of one percent of the entire population—they were concentrated on the West Coast, where prejudice against them had been festering for decades. About two thirds of the Japanese Americans had been born in the United States and were therefore American citizens, but their citizenship mattered little in the heat of war.

Anti-Japanese sentiment grew stronger after Japan attacked Pearl Harbor. Rumors of sabotage on the West Coast spread quickly. One report that reached President Roosevelt's desk, while noting that the Japanese Americans there were almost all loyal citizens, went on to say that "there are still Japanese in the United States who will tie dynamite around their waist and make a human bomb out of themselves." The report also suggested that "dams could be blown and half of California could actually die of thirst."

Mexican American "zoot suiters" were the target of attacks in 1943, but they themselves were often blamed by police for the violence.

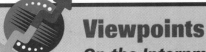

Viewpoints
On the Internment of Japanese Americans

The forced internment of Japanese Americans produced strong feelings on both sides of the issue. Two views are given below. *How does each of these viewpoints address the issue of constitutional rights?*

For Internment

"It is a fact that the Japanese navy has been reconnoitering [investigating] the Pacific Coast. . . . It is [a] fact that communication takes place between the enemy at sea and enemy agents on land. The Pacific Coast is officially a combat zone: some part of it may at any moment be a battlefield. Nobody's constitutional rights include the right to reside and do business on a battlefield."

Walter Lippmann, American columnist,
February 12, 1942

Against Internment

"Racial discrimination in any form and in any degree has no justifiable part whatever in our democratic way of life. . . . All residents of this nation are kin in some way by blood or culture to a foreign land. Yet they are primarily and necessarily a part of . . . the United States [and are] . . . entitled to all rights and freedoms guaranteed by the Constitution."

Supreme Court Justice Frank Murphy's dissenting opinion,
Korematsu v. United States, 1944

The press capitalized on people's fears. Headlines such as "Jap Boat Flashes Message Ashore" and "Japanese Here Sent Vital Data to Tokyo" gave newspaper readers the feeling that Japanese spies were everywhere. *Time* and *Life* magazines told readers how to tell the Chinese, who were allies, from the Japanese, who were enemies: "The Chinese expression is likely to be more placid, kindly, open; the Japanese more positive, dogmatic, arrogant."

As a result of these fears and prejudices, the government decided to remove all Japanese from the West Coast. On February 19, 1942, President Roosevelt signed Executive Order 9066 authorizing the secretary of war to establish military zones and to remove "any or all persons" from such zones. The War Relocation Authority (WRA) was created to move 110,000 Japanese Americans—citizens and noncitizens alike—to ten **internment camps** in remote areas across the country.

The relocation process took place hastily, and Japanese Americans had little time to secure their property before they left for the camps. Many lost their businesses, homes, and other property. Henry Murakami, a resident of California, remembers losing the $55,000 worth of fishing nets that had been his livelihood:

> When we were sent to Fort Lincoln [in Bismarck, North Dakota] *I asked the FBI men about my nets. They said, "Don't worry. Everything is going to be taken care of." But I never saw the nets again, nor my brand-new 1941 Plymouth, nor our furniture. It all just disappeared. I lost everything.*

Japanese Americans had no idea where they were going when they boarded the buses for the internment camps. Monica Sone, who lived in Seattle before the war, imagined her camp would be "out somewhere deep in a snow-bound forest, an American Siberia. I saw myself plunging chest deep in the snow, hunting for small game to keep us alive." She and her family packed winter clothes, only to end up in Camp Minidoka, on the sun-baked prairie of central Idaho. The average summer temperature there was 110 degrees.

All of the internment camps were located in desolate areas. They consisted of wooden barracks covered with tar paper and were protected by barbed wire and armed guards. Rooms inside the barracks had only cots, blankets, and a light bulb. Toilet, bathing, and dining facilities were communal.

Despite these injustices, more than 17,000 Japanese Americans served in the armed forces. About 1,200 of the Japanese Americans who volunteered for service did so from relocation centers. Many more volunteers came from Hawaii, where no internment had taken place. The 442nd Regimental Combat Team, composed entirely of Japanese Americans, won more medals for bravery than any other unit in United States history.

Although the vast majority of Japanese Americans abided by the policy of internment, a few did challenge it in the courts. Four cases eventually reached the Supreme Court, which in each case upheld the constitutionality of the wartime relocation. In one case, California resident Fred Toyosaburo Korematsu was convicted of violating Executive Order 9066 because he failed to report to an assembly center for relocation. The Supreme Court ruled in *Korematsu* v. *United States* (1944) that "Korematsu was not excluded from the Military Area because of hostility to him or his race," but that "the military urgency of the situation demanded that all citizens of Japanese ancestry be segregated from the West Coast temporarily." The dissenting opinion, however, labeled the policy "an obvious racial discrimination."

Finally, early in 1945, all Japanese Americans were allowed to leave the camps. Some were able to return to their homes and resume their lives. Others, finding that their property had been seized, had no place to go. It was not until 1988 that the United States government took responsibility for this gross violation of civil liberties. At that time Congress passed and President Ronald Reagan signed a law awarding each surviving Japanese American internee a tax-free payment of $20,000. These monetary reparations could not undo the damage that had been done decades earlier, but the law at least acknowledged the injustice.

Using Historical Evidence Tags with family identification numbers were attached to each piece of luggage and each family member at assembly centers for Japanese Americans. Permitted to take only a few possessions with them, many tried to sell their belongings but were forced to abandon what they could not carry or sell. *How do you think each person in this photo is feeling about the situation?*

SECTION 4 REVIEW

Key Terms, People, and Places
1. Define (a) "Double V" campaign, (b) bracero, (c) internment camp.
2. Identify A. Philip Randolph.

Key Concepts
3. What strategies did African Americans use in their struggle for equal rights during World War II?
4. What were the major effects of World War II on the lives of Mexican Americans?
5. What impact did World War II have on the lives of Native Americans?

6. What fears and prejudices led to the internment of Japanese Americans during World War II?

Critical Thinking
7. **Recognizing Cause and Effect** Although some German Americans and Italian Americans were relocated from the West Coast during the war, this action was on a much smaller scale than the internment of Japanese Americans. What do you think caused the harsher treatment of Japanese Americans?

Chapter Review

Key Terms

1. cost-plus system
2. wildcat strike
3. deficit spending
4. rationing
5. "Double V" campaign
6. bracero
7. internment camp

People

8. John L. Lewis
9. Rosie the Riveter
10. A. Philip Randolph

Terms For each term above, write a sentence that explains its relation to World War II in the United States, from 1941 to 1945.

True or False Determine whether each statement is true or false. If it is true, write "true." If it is false, change the underlined term to make the statement true.

1. During World War II, Japanese citizens and noncitizens alike were sent to <u>internment camps</u> in remote areas of the country.
2. <u>Braceros</u> are organized by workers themselves and not endorsed by the union.
3. A government program called <u>rationing</u> distributed scarce goods among consumers by using a point value system and issuing coupons.
4. In 1942 a shortage of farm labor led the United States to seek help from Mexican <u>wildcat strikes.</u>
5. African Americans launched the <u>cost-plus system</u>, with the goals of victory against the Axis powers and victory in the struggle for equality.

True or False Determine whether each statement is true or false. If it is true, write "true." If it is false, change the underlined name to make the statement true.

1. <u>Rosie the Riveter</u> was a fictional defense plant worker in World War II.
2. <u>A. Philip Randolph</u> called strikes in 1943 to demand pay raises.
3. <u>John L. Lewis</u> proposed a massive march on Washington in 1941 to demand an end to discrimination.

Section 1 (pp. 558–561)

1. How did the United States government help businesses convert to wartime production?
2. Give examples to show how entrepreneurs were able to profit during the war.
3. What effect did the increased work force during the war have on union membership?
4. Describe the positive and negative effects of deficit spending during World War II.

Section 2 (pp. 562–565)

5. What factors accounted for the mood of optimism on the home front?
6. Name several new ways in which people spent their free time and newly earned money during the war.
7. How did the government deal with wartime shortages?
8. What campaigns did the government undertake to encourage Americans to participate in the war effort?

Section 3 (pp. 566–570)

9. What changes took place in the kinds of jobs women held before and during World War II?
10. How did their new jobs benefit women?
11. Why did government campaigns strongly encourage women to return home after the war?

Section 4 (pp. 572–577)

12. Explain how the war turned a spotlight on the injustice of racism in American society.
13. Describe some of the opportunities and some of the problems encountered by Mexican Americans during the war.
14. How did the war speed the process of assimilation for Native Americans?
15. What factors influenced the government's decision to intern Japanese Americans on the West Coast during World War II?

1. **Making Comparisons** Many entrepreneurs prospered during the war. What did Robert de Graff's Pocket Books company have in common with Robert Woodruff's Coca-Cola company?
2. **Predicting Consequences** At the end of the war, government propaganda urged women to resume their traditional roles as homemakers. How do you think this campaign influenced family patterns and women's self-perception in the postwar years?
3. **Identifying Assumptions** Explain the assumptions underlying the 1942 poll that revealed that six out of ten whites felt that African Americans were satisfied with existing conditions and opportunities (page 573).

1. **Evaluating Primary Sources** Review the primary source excerpts on page 569. What long-term effects did joining the work force during the war have for some women?
2. **Understanding the Visuals** Write a short paragraph explaining the contradiction demonstrated by the poster on page 558 and the photos on page 574 and 577. Find a primary source excerpt in Section 4 that supports your explanation.
3. **Writing About the Chapter** Write a letter from the viewpoint of an American teenager in the early 1940s to a soldier who is serving in World War II. In your letter explain how your life and the lives of people around you have changed because of the war, including the lives of women, minorities, and local entrepreneurs. First, make a list of the changes that are affecting your life such as shortages and rationing. Note new ways in which you spend your leisure time. Write a draft of your letter, in which you describe your present life. Revise your letter, making sure that you have presented a detailed and interesting picture of life on the home front. Proofread your letter and draft a final copy.
4. **Using the Graphic Organizer** This graphic organizer uses a tree map to organize information about daily life on the home front during the war. Tree maps can help classify main ideas and supporting details. (a) According to the tree map, what are two factors that contributed to the mood of optimism and cooperation on the home front? (b) What supporting details could be included under a new main idea on the tree map: "Entrepreneurs profited from the war"? (c) On a separate sheet of paper, create your own graphic organizer about the struggle for justice among minorities during the war, using this graphic organizer as an example.

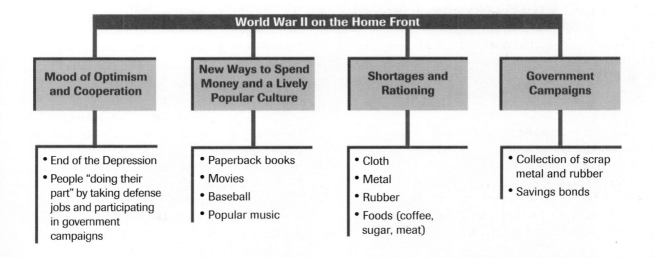

World War II on the Home Front

Mood of Optimism and Cooperation
- End of the Depression
- People "doing their part" by taking defense jobs and participating in government campaigns

New Ways to Spend Money and a Lively Popular Culture
- Paperback books
- Movies
- Baseball
- Popular music

Shortages and Rationing
- Cloth
- Metal
- Rubber
- Foods (coffee, sugar, meat)

Government Campaigns
- Collection of scrap metal and rubber
- Savings bonds

BRINGING THE WAR HOME

Americans living and working "stateside" seldom forgot about the war overseas. Almost everyone had relatives and close friends who faced constant danger from the fighting. Besides, the government wouldn't let Americans forget about the war. Rationing, pleas for conservation, a steady stream of patriotic messages, even requests to donate the family dog to the army—all this and more reminded Americans that their country was in a life-and-death struggle against totalitarian dictatorships. *What effect do you think these reminders had on the morale of soldiers and on Americans living in the United States?*

▲ LABEL ON MILK BOTTLE This label conveyed the message that conserving resources was every American's patriotic duty. The recycling effort included hundreds of products, especially those made with metal or rubber.

◀ "E" BUTTON The army and navy awarded these "E" (for excellence) pins to civilian workers who met production quotas or did outstanding work.

◀ RATION CARDS AND STAMPS Shoppers during the war needed their ration books to purchase many items that were either in short supply or needed by the armed forces. Notice the initials OPA, which stood for the Office of Price Administration. This agency distributed the ration books and also had the authority to set prices for items in short supply.

▲ HITLER AND UNCLE SAM
This button used gallows humor to ask everyone to "pull" together to win the war. The need to put aside disagreements among Americans was a common government message.

◀ WAR RELIEF EFFORT While the American economy boomed during the war, Europe and Asia were devastated. Americans proudly wore pins like this one to indicate that they had contributed money to help people in other countries.

VICTORY ▶ BUTTON The letter *V*, for victory, was the most common symbol of the war effort. Many businesses used the *V* and the American flag to send a patriotic and a promotional message.

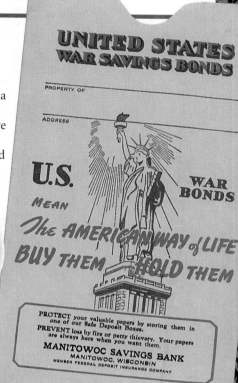

SAY IT WITH FLYERS

UNITED STATES WAR SAVINGS BONDS

PROPERTY OF

ADDRESS

U.S. WAR BONDS

MEAN

The AMERICAN WAY of LIFE

BUY THEM HOLD THEM

PROTECT your valuable papers by storing them in one of our Safe Deposit Boxes.
PREVENT loss by fire or petty thievery. Your papers are always here when you want them.

MANITOWOC SAVINGS BANK
MANITOWOC, WISCONSIN
MEMBER FEDERAL DEPOSIT INSURANCE COMPANY

◀ DOGS FOR DEFENSE
The armed forces needed dogs for sentry duty, to sniff out explosives, and for many other tasks. Citizens who donated dogs to the military could proudly wear this button.

SLEEVE FOR U.S. WAR BONDS ▲
The government borrowed an incredible 135 billion dollars from individual Americans to finance the war effort. These War Savings Bonds not only helped finance the war, but they gave thousands of Americans a personal and financial stake in the outcome of the war and preserving "the American way of life."

PROPAGANDA POSTERS No matter where they went—at work, on the street, at the movies—Americans saw wonderfully creative posters reminding them that their way of life depended on the outcome of the war. The posters shown at right encouraged people to work hard at their jobs to win the war. The posters used images of happy families to stir up even more support for the war effort. ▶

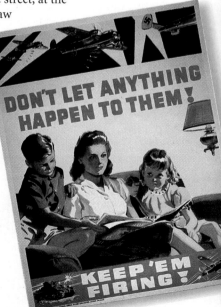

DON'T LET ANYTHING HAPPEN TO THEM!

KEEP 'EM FIRING!

MORE
MORE
MORE
MORE
MORE
PRODUCTION

The Cold War and American Society

1945–1960

*T*he United States and the Soviet Union temporarily ignored their differences during World War II. After the war, however, these differences began to pull the two nations apart again. Soon the world was divided into two camps, formed around communist and capitalist beliefs. The bitterness of the conflict affected both international relations and relations among Americans at home. In its desperate attempt to counteract communism around the world, the United States government created a frenzied mood of fear and suspicion within its own borders.

Events in the United States	**1945** Fifty nations adopt the United Nations charter in San Francisco.	**1946** Winston Churchill gives his famous "iron curtain" speech in Fulton, Missouri.	**1948** George Orwell's frightening novel 1984 is published.	**1949** North Atlantic Treaty Organization (NATO) is established.		**1952** Dwight D. Eisenhower is elected President.
	1945	**1947**	**1949**		**1951**	
Events in the World			**1948** The Berlin airlift begins. • Israel is founded.	**1949** Communists seize control of China. • Soviet Union tests its first atomic bomb.	**1950** The Korean War begins.	

1953 The Rosenbergs are executed for espionage.

1954 Nationally televised McCarthy hearings lead to Joseph McCarthy's downfall.

1957 President Eisenhower formulates a plan to protect the Middle East from communism.

1959 The United States cuts diplomatic ties with Cuba after Fidel Castro seizes power.

1953	1955	1957	1959	1961

1954 The Vietnamese defeat the French at Dien Bien Phu.

1956 The Soviet Union crushes a popular uprising in Hungary.

1957 The African nation of Ghana wins independence.

1959 Revolutionary leader Fidel Castro overthrows dictatorship in Cuba.

1960 The Soviet Union shoots down a United States spy plane.

Origins of the Cold War

During World War II, a common enemy forced communist and democratic nations together in a shaky alliance. Once the shooting stopped, however, political and economic differences divided the globe along new lines.

Key Concepts
- The Soviet Union and the United States suppressed their disagreements during World War II.
- Diplomatic relations between the United States and the Soviet Union quickly broke down after the war.
- The beliefs of communism and capitalism created different goals for the two superpowers in the postwar period.

Key Terms, People, and Places

cold war, proletariat, totalitarian, iron curtain

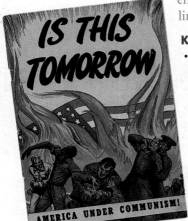

The mass media helped spread terror during the cold war years. This 1947 comic book described how the Soviets might be planning to conquer and enslave the people of the United States.

T he **cold war** was the bitter state of indirect conflict that existed between the United States and the Soviet Union for more than four decades after the end of World War II. This conflict developed out of long-standing disagreements between the two nations. After the Russian Revolution of 1917, the United States had refused to extend formal diplomatic recognition to the new communist nation until 1933. Americans were angered when the Soviet Union signed a nonaggression pact with Germany in 1939, but found themselves on the same side as the Soviets when Hitler broke the agreement and attacked the Soviet Union in 1941. The Allies pulled together to defeat the Axis powers, but by the end of the war, relations between the United States and Britain on the one hand and the Soviet Union on the other became increasingly tense.

Wartime Problems

At Tehran in 1943 and at Yalta in 1945, President Franklin Roosevelt had met with British prime minister Winston Churchill and Soviet leader Joseph Stalin to work out disagreements about the future of Germany and Poland. The three leaders had finally agreed to partition Germany into four zones—one American, one British, one French, and one Soviet. They also had agreed that in Poland a government sympathetic to the Soviet Union should control postwar policy. This new Polish government should, however, include representatives sympathetic to the West, and democratic elections should be held in the future. In diplomatic fashion, these agreements were left vague so that everyone could agree to them. Their imprecise terms, however, left room for disputes in the future.

Adding to this tension over Germany and Poland, the Soviet Union blamed the United States for delaying the opening of a western front in Europe during the war. While the Allies attacked the "soft underbelly" of the Axis Powers in southern Europe, the Soviets sustained heavy losses fighting the Germans alone on the eastern front. The Soviets were on their own for two years before Operation Overlord finally took some of the pressure off in June 1944.

Tension also arose during the development of the atomic bomb. The United States had relied on British help in the Manhattan Project while consciously excluding the Soviet Union. President Truman, Stalin, and Churchill had met at the Berlin suburb of Potsdam in 1945 to discuss ending the war in Japan and postwar plans for Europe. At that time, Truman hinted to Stalin that the United States had a new weapon of extraordinary force, but he said nothing more about it. Stalin, who knew about the bomb from Soviet spies in New Mexico, simply nodded and said that he hoped it would be put to good use. Stalin's casual manner hid, for the moment, the Soviets' resentment over being left out of the atom bomb project.

The Allies Follow Separate Postwar Paths

Americans became increasingly disillusioned with the Soviet Union as the war drew to a close. During the struggle, they had viewed the Soviets sympathetically. Newspapers and magazines encouraged support for the Americans' long-suffering ally. Journalist Joseph Goulden, who grew up in Texas during the war, recalled how he and his friends had played war games and pretended to be Soviet soldiers:

> We assembled new sabotage devices with fingers stiffened by the subzero temperatures of Mother Russia—old soup cans hand-packed with dirt and cinders—and climbed back up the embankment. . . . Another successful sabotage by Russian guerrillas. Under cross-examination none of the band could have distinguished a Communist from a logarithm. But we did know from movies that the Russians were brave and skilled partisans; in our minds their heroic stand at Stalingrad was equal to the defense of the Alamo.

Franklin Roosevelt affectionately referred to Stalin as "Uncle Joe." *Time* magazine even chose the Soviet leader as "Man of the Year" in 1940. But near the end of the war, the gaping divide between the two nations' postwar goals could be ignored no longer.

American Aims The United States fought in World War II to protect its vision of the American dream. The nation hoped to share with the world the essential elements of a democratic life—liberty, equality, and representative government. The United States also sought to create a world in which its own economic interests would be served by worldwide markets for its products. As a major contributor to victory in the war, the United States was determined to see its vision survive in the postwar world.

HOLLYWOOD'S FIRST DRAMA OF RUSSIA'S YOUNG HEROES!

THE BOY FROM STALINGRAD

with BOBBY SAMARZICH · CONRAD BINYON · MARY LOU HARRINGTON
SCOTTY BECKETT · STEVEN MULLER · Screen Play by Ferdinand Reyher
Produced by COLBERT CLARK · Directed by SIDNEY SALKOW
A COLUMBIA PICTURE

The 1943 film advertised in this poster promoted a heroic image of our Soviet allies. When World War II was over, however, Hollywood portrayed the "Commies" as sly and dangerous enemies.

MAKING CONNECTIONS

How would communism, a system in which private property does not exist and resources are shared by everyone, present a threat to American capitalism?

The Soviet Stance The Soviets approached the postwar world very differently from the United States. Communism predicted that through a process of class struggle, the workers of the world would eventually triumph. The first step toward that triumph involved removing the resources necessary for production from the hands of private business owners. If this happened, then members of the **proletariat**—working-class men and women—would join together for the common good, sharing resources equally among themselves.

Until the proletariat established a true communist state, however, a strong central government would control the society's resources. In practice, the Soviet state under Stalin was vastly different from the ideal state under communism. He created a **totalitarian** dictatorship in which the central government ruled by terror and held absolute control over its citizens' lives.

The Cold War in Europe

0   200   400 Miles
0   200   400 Kilometers

Legend:
- "Iron curtain"
- Communist nations
- Capitalist nations
- ⊛ Capital cities

ATLANTIC OCEAN

NORWAY
Oslo ⊛

FINLAND
Helsinki ⊛

North Sea

Baltic Sea

Stockholm ⊛
SWEDEN

Moscow ⊛

Dublin ⊛
IRELAND

DENMARK
⊛ Copenhagen

SOVIET UNION

UNITED KINGDOM
London ⊛

The Hague ⊛
NETH.

Berlin ⊛
EAST GERMANY

POLAND
⊛ Warsaw

Brussels ⊛
BELGIUM
⊛ Bonn

Paris ⊛ LUX.

WEST GERMANY

Prague ⊛
CZECHOSLOVAKIA

N
W   E
S

FRANCE

Bern ⊛
SWITZ.

Vienna ⊛
AUSTRIA

⊛ Budapest
HUNGARY

ROMANIA
Bucharest ⊛

Black Sea

PORTUGAL
Lisbon ⊛

⊛ Madrid
SPAIN

ITALY

Belgrade ⊛
YUGOSLAVIA

BULGARIA
Sofia ⊛

⊛ Rome

Tiranë ⊛
ALBANIA

Adriatic Sea

Mediterranean Sea

GREECE
⊛ Athens

🌐 Geography and History: Interpreting Maps
This map shows the territories controlled by communist and capitalist countries. After World War II, the Soviet Union was every bit as concerned about protecting its national security as was the United States. *How does this map illustrate the policy pursued by the Soviet Union to protect itself from its capitalist rivals in Europe?*

After losing twenty million people—about as many as live in New York state today—and suffering the destruction of cities such as Stalingrad in the war, the Soviet Union was determined to rebuild on its own terms. One part of that rebuilding required having friendly nations along the western borders of the Soviet Union. Several times in the past century and a half, the Soviet Union had faced attack from the west. Having repelled first Napoleon and then Hitler, the Soviets wanted regimes in Eastern Europe sympathetic to their own aims.

Postwar Clashes The United States and the Soviet Union clashed first over Poland. The loosely worded Yalta agreement called for a new Polish government influenced strongly by the Soviet Union but including a few representatives sympathetic to the West. President Truman met with Soviet foreign minister Vyacheslav Molotov on April 23, 1945, and told him that "the United States Government . . . could not agree to be a party to the formation of a Polish government which was not representative of all Polish democratic elements." Truman insisted that the Soviets were not keeping their part of the Yalta agreement, and he demanded bluntly that the Soviets do exactly as they were told. Molotov protested, "I have never been talked to like that in my life." "Carry out your agreements and you won't get talked to like that," Truman retorted.

The next evening President Truman received an answer from Molotov's boss. Stalin sent a message in which he emphasized that because Poland bordered the Soviet Union, the Soviets must be allowed to have a strong influence there. He said that securing friendly neighbors along Soviet borders was "demanded by the blood of the Soviet people abundantly shed on the fields of Poland," and he concluded:

> I am ready to fulfill your request and do everything possible to reach a harmonious solution. But you demand too much of me. In other words, you demand that I renounce the interests of security of the Soviet Union, but I cannot turn against my country.

It was clear from the determined tone of Stalin's message that there was to be no such "harmonious solution" to the Poland problem.

American and British officials were not the only ones grappling with the alarming actions of their former ally. Polls reflected the American public's shifting views of the Soviet Union. A poll in September 1945 found that 54 percent of the respondents trusted the Soviets to cooperate with Americans in the postwar period. Two months later, the number fell to 44 percent, and by February 1946, it had dropped still further to 35 percent.

As they soured on the Soviet Union, Americans began to transfer their wartime hatred of Nazi Germany to the communist Soviet Union. Both nations, according to authors, journalists, and government officials, were totalitarian regimes whose leaders had absolute control and the ability to eliminate any opposition. George Orwell's haunting novel *1984*, published in the United States in 1949, described a frightening future world in which a totalitarian state, represented by the ever-present face of "Big Brother," monitors and controls every aspect of people's lives. *Life* magazine called Big Brother a mating of Hitler and Stalin. Truman himself declared the next year that "there isn't any difference between the totalitarian Russian government and the Hitler government."

Using Historical Evidence Winston Churchill (right) is shown making the 1946 speech in which he introduced the idea of the iron curtain. *In the cartoon (left), why is United States secretary of state James Byrnes portrayed as a determined suitor? Whom is he courting? How does the cartoonist rate his chances of success?*

Declaration of the Cold War While there was no formal declaration of war, two speeches marked the onset of the struggle. In 1946 Stalin declared his confidence in the ultimate triumph of the Soviet system. The Soviet Union would strengthen its military forces and do whatever was necessary to ensure its survival in a struggle with the West.

Winston Churchill, now out of office, responded that same year. Speaking in Fulton, Missouri, Churchill said that "from Stettin in the Baltic to Trieste in the Adriatic, an iron curtain has descended across the [European] Continent." This so-called **iron curtain**, the new battlefront of the cold war, sharply divided the capitalist West from the communist East. The map on page 586 shows these divisions. In his speech, Churchill stressed that the English-speaking peoples had to work together to stop the Soviet Union from closing the iron curtain around any more nations.

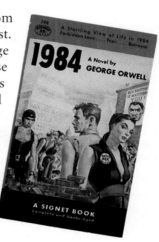

Orwell's *1984*—a story of "forbidden love and terror in a world many of us may live to see"— painted a dismal picture of life under a communist dictatorship.

SECTION 1 REVIEW

Key Terms, People, and Places
1. Define (a) cold war, (b) proletariat, (c) totalitarian, (d) iron curtain.

Key Concepts
2. What wartime issues paved the way for the cold war?
3. How did American aims and Soviet aims for the postwar period differ?

4. How did American public opinion about the Soviet Union change after World War II?

Critical Thinking
5. **Identifying Central Issues** What are the main points that separate the capitalist from the communist vision of society?

Recognizing Cause and Effect

History is more than a list of events; it is a study of the relationships among events. Recognizing cause and effect means examining how one event or action brings about others. If you can understand how events or ideas relate to and affect each other, you can begin to formulate workable solutions to problems.

Follow the steps below to practice recognizing cause and effect.

1. Identify the two parts of a cause-effect relationship. A cause is an event or action that brings about an effect. As you read, look for key words that signal a cause-effect relationship. Words such as *because, due to,* and *on account of* signal causes. Words such as *so, thus, therefore,* and *as a result* signal effects. Read statements A through C at right, and answer the following questions. (a) Which statements contain both a cause and an effect? (b) Which is the cause and which is the effect in each statement? (c) What words, if any, signal the cause-effect relationship?

2. Remember that an event can have more than one cause and more than one effect. Several causes can lead to one event. So, too, can a single cause have several effects. Read statement D at right, and respond to the following. (a) Find an example of a cause that has more than one effect. (b) Find an example of an effect that has more than one cause.

3. Understand that an event can be both a cause and an effect. A cause can lead to an effect, which in turn can be the cause of another event. In this way, causes and effects can form a chain of related events. You can diagram the following statements to show such a chain: The United States feared Soviet expansion in Europe. → The United States began a military buildup. → The Soviet Union began a military buildup. → An arms race between the two countries began. Now read statement D below, and using arrows, draw a diagram of the causes and effects that shows the chain of related events.

Statements

A Because President Roosevelt believed that postwar cooperation with the Soviet Union was necessary, he viewed Stalin as a partner—if not an ally—in formulating a peace.

B Unlike Roosevelt, President Truman was persuaded by advisers that the Soviet Union would become a "world bully" after the war. As a result, he adopted a "get tough" policy whose aim was to block any possibility of Soviet expansion.

C The Soviets, for their part, believed that the United States was intent on global domination and meant to encircle the Soviet Union with anticommunist states.

D Due to mounting distrust between the United States and the Soviet Union, each power came to view the postwar peace negotiations as an opportunity to test the other's global objectives. Thus, negotiating the status of Poland became the first such test. Other tests included the plans for former German satellite states and the policies for the occupation of Germany. Each power regarded its own positions in these negotiations as essentially defensive, but each viewed the other's stances as aggressive and expansionist. Together these tests and stances produced the cold war, an armed and dangerous truce that lasted for forty-five years.

Containment

The United States government viewed Soviet communist influence as a disease that was rapidly spreading around the globe. Foreign policy in the postwar years focused on preventing any more capitalist nations from becoming "infected."

Key Concepts

- American foreign policy in the postwar years was summed up by the term *containment,* which meant preventing nations around the world from adopting communism.
- Containment was spelled out in a series of speeches, plans, and documents.
- Despite talk of liberating the nations dominated by the Soviet Union during the 1950s, containment continued to shape American foreign policy under President Eisenhower.

Key Terms, People, and Places

United Nations, containment, Truman Doctrine, Marshall Plan, Berlin airlift, NATO, NSC-68, satellite nation; George C. Marshall, Mao Zedong

T he founding of the United Nations in 1945 ignited new hope for international peace and understanding. Deep differences between Western democracy and communism, however, made it difficult for the UN to fulfill its great promise. Afraid of Soviet communist expansion, American leaders developed programs aimed at preventing the Soviets from extending their influence any further.

The United Nations

Near the end of World War II, diplomats hoped to create a new international peacekeeping organization. The League of Nations, founded at the end of World War I, had failed, largely because the United States had refused to join. This time, American policymakers succeeded in securing the support of the United States Congress for the **United Nations.**

In April 1945, delegates from fifty nations met in San Francisco to adopt a charter, or document setting down official rules, for the new organization. The United Nations charter pledged that member countries would seek to settle their disagreements peacefully. It also committed them to try to stop wars from occurring and to end those that did break out. All member nations belonged to the General Assembly. Eleven countries sat on the Security Council. Five of those—the United States, the Soviet Union, Great Britain, France, and China—had permanent seats and a chance to veto any policies under consideration. This veto power, exercised by both communist and capitalist powers, limited the UN's ability to take action in the early postwar years and led the United States to explore other approaches to controlling the Soviet Union.

On June 26, 1945, after the UN charter had been signed by representatives from all fifty nations, Harry Truman delivered a speech to the assembly. He said,

> T he Charter of the United Nations which you have just signed is a solid structure upon which we can build a better world. History will honor you for it. Between the victory in Europe and the final victory in Japan, in this most destructive of all wars, you have won a victory against war itself.

The Policy of Containment

Despite the hopeful sentiments expressed in Truman's speech to the UN and the fact that the Soviet economy was in ruins following World War II, American leaders still perceived a serious threat to United States interests from the Soviet Union. To address their concerns, officials developed a policy known as **containment.**

After World War II, the Marshall Plan provided United States aid to European nations. Some of this aid went to purchase food, such as this load of sugar.

At its birth, the United Nations was hailed by President Harry Truman as "a victory against war itself." In this photograph, Truman and representatives from other member nations look on as Secretary of State Edward Stettinius signs the UN charter in June 1945.

The definition of containment came from George Kennan, a top-ranking American diplomat stationed in Moscow. In early 1946, he sent an eight-thousand-word telegram back to the State Department analyzing Soviet policy. The Soviet Union was not going to yield, he believed, and the United States needed to remove any opportunities for its enemy to establish communist governments in other countries.

The Truman Doctrine Truman was an unassuming man, with a straightforward approach to the job he inherited from Franklin Roosevelt. He had a chance to apply the policy of containment in early 1947. When Great Britain informed the United States that it could no longer continue to provide Greece and Turkey with economic and military aid, Truman was afraid that those two nations might embrace communist strategies to ease their economic troubles. The State Department therefore developed a program for American assistance and then had to sell the plan to Congress. Undersecretary of State Dean Acheson told congressional leaders that "like apples in a barrel infected by one rotten one, the corruption of Greece would infect Iran and all to the east."

Meanwhile, Truman followed the advice of Senator Arthur Vandenberg of Michigan. The President, a

This sign, which sat on Truman's desk, expressed his belief that the President of the United States cannot "pass the buck"—or shirk responsibility for tough decisions.

Democrat, was determined to enlist Republicans in his foreign policy initiatives, and Vandenberg was the ranking Republican in this area. Vandenberg told Truman that if he wanted his program passed to assist Greece and Turkey, he had to generate public support—and that meant he had to "scare the hell out of the country." In his speeches, Truman warned the American people about the serious threat to national security posed by Soviet influence abroad. In a statement to Congress that came to be called the **Truman Doctrine,** he said, "I believe that it must be the policy of the United States to support free peoples who are resisting attempted subjugation [conquering] by armed minorities or by outside pressures." Responding to his plea, Congress appropriated $400 million for Turkey and Greece.

MAKING CONNECTIONS

In the 1980s, President Ronald Reagan referred to the Soviet Union as "the evil empire." How does this compare to Arthur Vandenberg's advice to President Truman?

The Marshall Plan By 1947, Communist parties were growing stronger in a number of countries, and American policymakers were afraid that the Soviet Union might intervene to support local communist movements. At the same time, they were eager to open new markets for American goods. That year, Secretary of State **George C. Marshall** carried containment a step further with a plan to address both concerns.

Marshall unveiled his plan in a speech at Harvard University in June 1947. The **Marshall Plan** called for the nations of Europe—including the Soviet Union and other communist countries—to draw up a program for economic recovery from the war. The United States would then support the program with financial aid.

The Soviet Union and its Eastern European neighbors (under Soviet pressure) did not participate. Soviet foreign minister Molotov called the plan "nothing but a vicious American scheme for using dollars to buy its way" into European affairs. Sixteen Western European nations, however, hammered out a plan requesting $17 billion over a four-year period. In 1948 Congress approved the Marshall Plan, also called the European Recovery Program. The United States sent over $13 billion in aid to Europe over the next four years. The Western European economy was quickly restored to health, and the United States was rewarded with strong trading partners in that region of the world.

One of the nations to benefit from the Marshall Plan was West Germany. At the end of World War II, Germany had been split into four zones occupied by the Soviet Union, France, Britain, and the United States. The city of Berlin, located in the Soviet zone, was likewise divided among the four Allies. When the Western powers united the French, British, and American zones to form West Germany and introduced a West German currency in the western part of Berlin, the Soviets reacted by blockading all ground and water routes to West Berlin in June 1948.

Truman did not want to risk starting a war with the Soviet Union by forcing open the transportation routes; nor did he want to give up West Berlin to the Soviets. Instead he began the **Berlin airlift,** moving supplies into West Berlin by plane. Food, coal, and other vital supplies were flown into the city every day for over a year. The Soviets finally ended the blockade in May 1949, and the airlift ended the following September. By this time the Marshall Plan had resulted in progress toward economic stability in the capitalist nations of Western Europe, including West Germany. Nevertheless, the tension that resulted from the airlift helped convince the Western powers that they needed to form a peacetime alliance for security against the Soviet threat.

NATO In 1949 the United States helped to establish the North Atlantic Treaty Organization—**NATO**—shown on the map on page 726. The twelve nations in the alliance—Belgium, Britain, Canada, Denmark, France, Iceland, Italy, Luxembourg, the Netherlands, Norway, Portugal, and the United States—vowed that an attack against one would be viewed as an attack against all. Dropping its opposition to military treaties with Europe for the first time since the American Revolution, the United States was now actively involved in European affairs.

Two disturbing events in 1949 prompted more drastic action from the United States. In April of that year, Chinese nationalists led by General Chiang Kai-shek lost control of their country to **Mao Zedong** and his communist followers. Civil war between these two factions had torn China since the early part of the century, and not even the need to fight off a common enemy—Japan—during World War II could unite the nation.

Despite support from the United States in the postwar years, Chiang was unable to stop Mao from steadily taking over control of China. Now, in mid-1949, Roosevelt's intended "anchor" of democracy in East Asia had turned into a communist dictatorship. Chiang was forced to retreat to the island of Taiwan off the southeast coast of China. The United States continued to

Viewpoints
On Joining NATO

Debates over whether or not the United States should join the North Atlantic Treaty Organization (NATO) were held in Congress and in the press. *What fears underlie the following arguments for and against the United States joining this peacetime alliance?*

For Joining NATO

"From now on, no one will misread our motives or underestimate our determination to stand in defense of our freedom. . . . The greatest obstacle that stands in the way of complete recovery [from World War II] is the pervading and paralyzing sense of insecurity. The treaty is a powerful antidote to this poison. . . . With this protection afforded by the Atlantic Pact, western Europe can breathe easier again."
Senator Tom Connally (Texas), Chairman, Committee on Foreign Relations, address before the United States Senate, 1949

Against Joining NATO

"This whole program in my opinion is not a peace program; it is a war program. . . . We are committing ourselves to a policy of war, not a policy of peace. We are building up armaments. We are undertaking to arm half the world against the other half. We are inevitably starting an armament race. . . . The general history of armament races in the world is that they have led to war, not to peace."
Senator Robert A. Taft (Ohio), address before the United States Senate, 1949

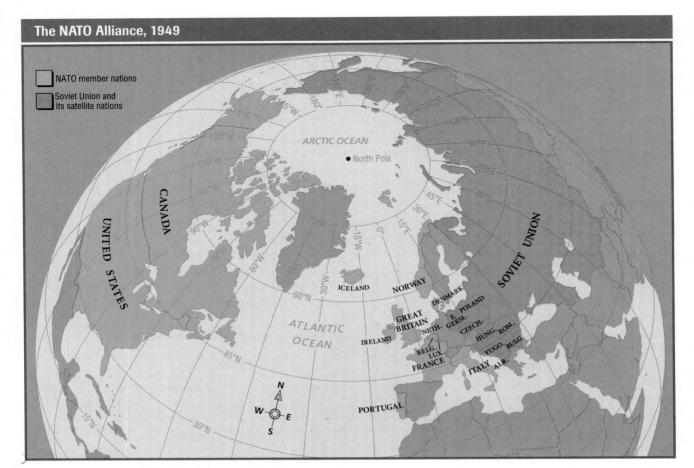

The NATO Alliance, 1949

NATO member nations

Soviet Union and its satellite nations

ARCTIC OCEAN
• North Pole

CANADA
UNITED STATES
SOVIET UNION

ICELAND
NORWAY
DENMARK
GREAT BRITAIN
E. POLAND
NETH. GERM.
CZECH.
IRELAND
HUNG. ROM.
BELG.
LUX.
YUGO. BULG.
FRANCE
ITALY ALB.

ATLANTIC OCEAN

PORTUGAL

Geography and History: Interpreting Maps
This map shows the nations that sided with the United States during the cold war and those that aligned with the Soviet Union. *How does the map illustrate the new global perspective gained by American leaders after World War II?*

recognize Chiang's government (now located on Taiwan) as the official government of all China, but Chiang would never regain control from the communists. The "loss of China" would become, in the minds of many Americans, a stain on the record of the Truman administration. The desire to prevent other nations in Asia from following the same path would be used to justify many future cold war policies, including involvement in the Korean and Vietnam wars.

More bad news surfaced later in 1949. On September 23, Truman made a brief but terrifying announcement to the nation: "We have evidence that within recent weeks an atomic explosion occurred in the USSR." Years sooner than some officials expected, the Soviet Union had broken the West's monopoly on nuclear weapons.

NSC-68 In response to these events, the National Security Council spelled out American policy in a document known as **NSC-68.** The National Security Council had been created in 1947 to develop broad policy concepts on which the President could build specific strategies.

NSC-68 outlined several policies that the United States might adopt in light of the current state of international affairs. The paper said, however, that only one of these policies could be seriously considered. It stated that the United States should triple its defense budget—and some leaders suggested quadrupling it from about $13 billion to $50 billion annually. This unprecedented level of peacetime defense spending was justified by NSC-68 and its supporters on the basis of the new demands of global security. According to this policy, only a vigorous defense effort could keep communism in check and ensure the survival of the free world.

Containment in the 1950s

When Dwight Eisenhower succeeded Harry Truman in 1953, the Republican party redefined American foreign policy. Secretary of State John Foster Dulles was a deeply religious person who hated communism because it denied the existence of God. Containment, he believed, was too cautious an approach to the communist threat. Instead, he proposed a policy of liberation, to roll back communism where it had already taken hold.

This approach proved impossible to put into practice. Eisenhower, who had helped keep the Allies together during World War II, understood the need for caution in dealing with the Soviet Union. Less rigid than his secretary of state, he recognized that the United States could not change the governments of Soviet **satellite nations**—countries controlled politically and economically by the Soviet Union—in Eastern Europe. When East Germans demonstrated against the Soviet Union in 1953, the United States merely stood back and watched. Three years later, when freedom fighters in Hungary rose up against Soviet domination, the United States again kept its distance as Soviet soldiers crushed the uprising. President Eisenhower recognized that any other response by the United States might have led to a larger war, and he wanted to avoid that at all costs.

On November 4, 1956, newspaper headlines announced that Soviet tanks had attacked Budapest and other cities in Hungary to squash the resistance of anticommunist rebels. Hungarian premier Imre Nagy was taken prisoner; Joseph Cardinal Mindszenty, the Roman Catholic bishop of Hungary, took refuge with the American diplomatic staff in Budapest.

Throughout the 1950s, despite talk of liberating Soviet satellite nations, the policy of containment remained in effect. Containment itself proved difficult enough. Before long the United States would be putting to use some of the weapons NSC-68 had recommended it build.

SECTION 2 REVIEW

Key Terms, People, and Places

1. Define (a) containment, (b) Truman Doctrine, (c) Marshall Plan, (d) Berlin airlift, (e) NATO, (f) satellite nation.
2. Identify (a) George C. Marshall, (b) Mao Zedong.

Key Concepts

3. (a) What were the goals of the United Nations in 1945? (b) What prevented the UN from achieving these goals?
4. How were the Truman Doctrine and the Marshall Plan expressions of the containment policy?

5. What did NSC-68 recommend that the United States do to defend against the communist threat?
6. Why did President Eisenhower not follow the advice of John Foster Dulles and attempt to "roll back communism" in Germany and Hungary?

Critical Thinking

7. **Recognizing Cause and Effect** In 1946 George Kennan described "the traditional and instinctive Russian sense of insecurity" on which the Soviet view of world affairs was based. What events in Russian history may have caused such insecurity?

The Cold War in Asia, the Middle East, and Latin America

The policy of containment had been created with the aim of maintaining European stability. As communist movements developed in Asia, the Middle East, and Latin America, however, the United States extended the policy to meet challenges around the world.

Key Concepts
- Both the Korean War and early American involvement in Vietnam stemmed from cold war tension.
- The United States juggled oil interests and political sympathies in the Middle East while trying to control communist influence there.
- In Latin America, the United States and the Soviet Union struggled for control in unstable countries.

Key Terms, People, and Places
38th parallel, domino theory, 17th parallel; Ho Chi Minh, Fidel Castro; Indochina

This cover illustration from a 1959 *Newsweek* magazine shows that the fate of the world hung on the uneasy balance of power between Khrushchev and Eisenhower, each of whom commanded many nuclear warheads.

The policy of containment soon was broadened to apply not only to Europe but also to Asia, the Middle East, Latin America—in short, anywhere United States government and military officials perceived a communist threat. Political struggles in countries that had seemed to have little impact on the United States before 1945, such as Korea, Vietnam, Iran, and Cuba, became vital issues of national security when viewed through the lens of the cold war. Each "minor" war in which the United States took part reflected the delicate balance between its two major foreign policy objectives: avoiding another world war and keeping a tight lid on communism.

The Korean War

The policy followed by the Allies at the very end of World War II created the context for the Korean War. Korea, which had been occupied by Japan for decades, hoped for its independence once the Japanese finally were defeated. The war ended, however, before careful plans could be worked out, and the Allies resorted to a short-term solution. Soviet soldiers accepted the surrender of Japanese troops north of the **38th parallel,** the latitude line that runs through Korea at 38°N; American forces did the same south of the parallel. While the dividing line was never intended to be permanent, the Soviet Union set up and supported a government in the north, and the United States did the same in the south. The major powers left Korea but continued to support the regimes they had created.

Both North and South Korea hoped to unify the country, but each wanted to do so on its own terms. In June 1950, the North Korean army moved across the 38th parallel intending to bring about this unification. The United States felt certain—wrongly, it turned out—that the maneuver had been directed by the Soviets. Faced with what he viewed as a clear case of aggression, Truman was determined to respond. He recalled in his memoirs:

I n my generation, this was not the first occasion when the strong had attacked the weak. I recalled some earlier instances: Manchuria, Ethiopia, Austria. I remembered how each time that the democracies failed to act it had encouraged the aggressors to keep going ahead. . . . If this was allowed to go unchallenged, it would mean a third world war, just as similar incidents brought on the second world war.

Rather than respond alone, the United States went to the UN Security Council. With the new People's Republic of China excluded and the Soviet delegation absent in protest of that exclusion, the United States gained unanimous approval for resolutions branding North Korea the aggressor and calling on UN member states to assist in restoring peace.

General Douglas MacArthur planned a bold strategy to drive the North Koreans out of South Korea. In September 1950, while most North Korean troops were fighting near Pusan in the southeast, marines landed at the western port city of Inchon. The landing allowed UN forces to cut off North Korean supply lines through Inchon and to sandwich enemy troops between MacArthur at Inchon and the other UN troops at Pusan.

MacArthur's strategy was an overwhelming success. UN troops pushed the North Koreans back across the 38th parallel and continued into the north. With these early victories behind them, they hoped to unify the country on South Korea's terms. As they approached China's border, however, the Chinese warned them against going any farther. MacArthur ignored the warning, and in October 1950 Chinese troops entered the war. In fierce fighting, the Chinese and North Koreans pushed the UN forces back into the south (see the map at right).

As the war bogged down, Truman found himself in conflict with his most colorful general. MacArthur wanted to teach the Chinese a lesson, and proposed using atomic weapons or blockading the Chinese mainland. Truman wanted to do everything he could to keep the conflict limited and refused to expand the war.

MacArthur would not back down, however. In March 1951 he sent a letter to Joseph W. Martin, the minority leader of the House of Representatives, that contained a thinly veiled attack on the Truman administration's failure to see the gravity of the situation in Asia. After Martin read the letter in the House on April 5, Truman fired MacArthur for insubordination.

MacArthur returned home to a hero's welcome. When he addressed a joint session of Congress on April 19, his speech was often interrupted by bursts of applause. Finally, he said an emotional farewell:

*S*ince I took the oath at West Point, the hopes and dreams [of youth] have all vanished. But I still remember the refrain of one of the most popular barracks ballads of that day, which proclaimed most proudly that old soldiers never die, they just fade away.

And like the old soldier of that ballad, I now close my military career and just fade away, an old soldier who tried to do his duty as God gave him the light to see that duty.

Good-bye.

Once tempers had cooled, MacArthur did, in fact, fade from view, and Truman was able to proceed with his plan to keep the war limited. The struggle dragged on for two more years. Finally, a truce was signed in 1953, leaving the

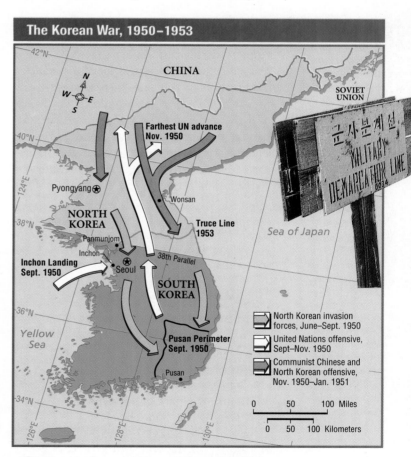

The Korean War, 1950–1953

CHINA
SOVIET UNION
Farthest UN advance Nov. 1950
Pyongyang
Wonsan
NORTH KOREA
Truce Line 1953
Sea of Japan
Panmunjom
Inchon
38th Parallel
Inchon Landing Sept. 1950
Seoul
SOUTH KOREA
Yellow Sea
Pusan Perimeter Sept. 1950
Pusan

North Korean invasion forces, June–Sept. 1950
United Nations offensive, Sept.–Nov. 1950
Communist Chinese and North Korean offensive, Nov. 1950–Jan. 1951

0   50   100 Miles
0   50   100 Kilometers

Geography and History: Interpreting Maps
This map shows the major battles of the Korean War. The sign shown above marked the final truce line in Korea, near the 38th parallel. *How does the map illustrate the back-and-forth nature of the war? What did MacArthur accomplish by landing his troops at Inchon rather than Pusan?*

In this oft-repeated scene from the war, South Korean civilians flee from North Korean invaders while United States troops advance to meet the enemy.

country divided at almost exactly the same place as before the war, near the 38th parallel.

The Korean War caused enormous frustration at home. Americans wondered why 54,000 of their soldiers had been killed, and far more had been wounded, for such limited results. They also wondered whether their government was serious about wanting to stop the spread of communism. Meanwhile, the war also led to an ever-larger defense budget, just as NSC-68 had demanded. By 1950 the military took up one third of the total federal budget. Ten years later, it consumed one half.

The Early War in Vietnam

At the same time, another war was unfolding in **Indochina.** France had long controlled this part of Southeast Asia, which had fallen to the Japanese during World War II. Vietnam, one part of Indochina, now sought independence in a struggle led by **Ho Chi Minh,** the leader of the Indochina Communist party. Although Ho was sympathetic to the principles of communism, he was really more of a Vietnamese nationalist than a

Soviet sympathizer. In his battle for Vietnamese independence, he used the American Revolutionary War as his model for independence. Ho and his political organization, the Viet Minh, established the Democratic Republic of Vietnam in 1945. He then had to fight France, which was determined to reclaim its empire.

An ugly war unfolded and attracted the attention of American officials. The United States needed the assistance of France for its policy of containment in Europe. American leaders doubted that France could survive a long colonial war in Asia without help. While Ho Chi Minh did not have close ties with the Soviet Union, he was still dedicated to the ideas of Karl Marx, and Americans were persuaded that communism was the same everywhere and had to be resisted wherever it surfaced. The United States therefore provided France with large amounts of economic aid for reconstruction at home, and that assistance allowed France to use its own resources in Vietnam. By 1954 the United States was giving France aid amounting to more than three fourths the cost of the war.

Even so, the war was not going well. France's position deteriorated at about the time Eisenhower took over the presidency, and in 1954 the Vietnamese defeated France in a major battle at Dien Bien Phu, an outpost in northern Vietnam. This worried Eisenhower, who believed in the **domino theory.** This theory

ON BEHALF OF VIETNAM GOVERNMENT AND PEOPLE I BEG TO INFORM YOU THAT IN COURSE OF CONVERSATIONS BETWEEN VIETNAM GOVERNMENT AND FRENCH REPRESENTATIVES THE LATTER REQUIRE THE SECESSION OF COCHINCHINA AND THE RETURN OF FRENCH TROOPS IN HANOI STOP MEANWHILE FRENCH POPULATION AND TROOPS ARE MAKING ACTIVE PREPARATIONS FOR A COUP DE MAIN IN HANOI AND FOR MILITARY AGGRESSION STOP I THEREFORE MOST EARNESTLY APPEAL TO YOU PERSONALLY AND TO THE AMERICAN PEOPLE TO INTERFERE URGENTLY IN SUPPORT OF OUR INDEPENDENCE AND HELP MAKING THE NEGOTIATIONS MORE IN KEEPING WITH THE PRINCIPLES OF THE ATLANTIC AND SAN FRANCISCO CHARTERS
RESPECTFULLY

HOCHIMINH

Hochiminh

Ho Chi Minh (left) sent this urgent telegram to President Truman in October 1945 asking for United States support of Vietnamese independence. Not wanting to jeopardize relations with France, Truman ignored Ho's plea.

French Indochina, 1954

ASIA

CHINA

BURMA

Tonkin

Dien Bien Phu
Haiphong
Hanoi

Luang Prabang
LAOS

Vientiane

VIETNAM

17th Parallel
Hue

Gulf of
Tonkin

South
China Sea

THAILAND

Annam

CAMBODIA

Gulf of
Siam

Phnom
Penh

Cochin-
China

Saigon

☐ Areas of
French control

☐ Areas of
Viet Minh control

0   100   200 Miles

0   100   200 Kilometers

Geography and History: Interpreting Maps
Reread Ho Chi Minh's telegram on page 596. *What did
the French demand in 1945? According to this map, how many of
their objectives had the French achieved by 1954?*

compared countries to dominos and held that
"you have a row of dominos set up, you knock
over the first one, and what will happen to the
last one is the certainty that it will go over very
quickly." Thus, if one country in Indochina fell to
communism, other countries in the area would
soon follow. Still, Eisenhower did not want the
United States to become further involved.

Instead, an international conference in
Geneva decided to draw a dividing line, similar
to the ones drawn in Germany and Korea following World War II. Vietnam would be
divided along the **17th parallel,** with Ho Chi
Minh holding power in the north and an anticommunist government in charge in the south.

For the time being, the United States provided military aid to the South Vietnamese
government but resisted greater involvement.
That course would change in the next decade.

The Middle East

The cold war was also played out in the
Middle East. This area had strategic importance because of its large supplies of oil. During

World War II, the Allies had occupied Iran, a large nation just south of
the Soviet Union. After the war, the
United States and Britain departed;
the Soviet Union did not. The United
States became increasingly concerned
as Soviet tanks rumbled toward the
Iranian border, and threatened vigorous American action unless the Soviets pulled back. In the face of that
determined stance, the Soviets withdrew.

Two years later, in 1948, the UN
divided Palestine into an Arab state
and a Jewish state. Zionist Jews had
for years hoped to establish a Jewish
nation in Palestine, but it was not
until World War II, when thousands
of European Jews immigrated to the
region, that the Jewish population
was large enough to form a new
state. Tensions between Palestinian
Jews and Arabs erupted with the UN
announcement of the new Jewish
state, called Israel, on May 14, 1948.
The United States and the Soviet Union immediately recognized Israel, but Israel was soon
invaded by surrounding Arab states. Israel
defeated those states and annexed most of the
Palestinian territory, as shown on the map on
page 598. While sympathetic to Israel, the
United States tried to maintain ties with the oil-
rich Arab nations of the region and to prevent
them from falling into the Soviet orbit.

MAKING CONNECTIONS

What conflicts over oil-rich Middle East
nations has the United States been drawn into
in recent years?

The Cold War in Latin America

The cold war likewise affected United States
policy in Latin America. For decades the
United States had dominated economic affairs
in this part of the world. By the mid-1920s, the
United States had gained control over the
economies of ten Latin American countries.

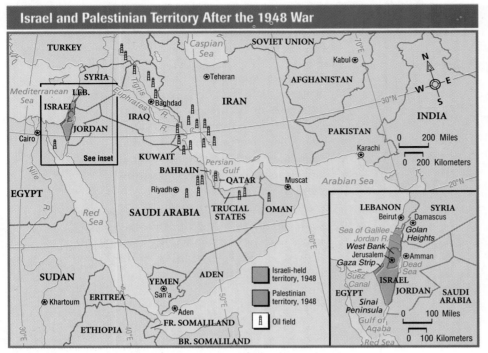

Israel and Palestinian Territory After the 1948 War

Israeli-held territory, 1948

Palestinian territory, 1948

Oil field

Geography and History: Interpreting Maps
After the 1948 war, Palestinian-held territory was annexed by Egypt and Jordan. *How might the location of the Soviet Union in relation to that of Middle Eastern countries have fueled concerns in the United States?*

overthrow Jacobo Arbenz Guzmán, a reform-minded leader, on the grounds that he was sympathetic to radical causes. The CIA takeover restored the property of an American corporation called the United Fruit Company, which had been seized by the government in Guatemala. This action also demonstrated that where it sensed a communist threat, the United States would do almost anything to restore stability and to install leadership it found more sympathetic. Such actions also fueled the Soviet perception that the United States was escalating the cold war.

In 1959 another crisis occurred as revolutionary leader **Fidel Castro** overthrew a long-standing dictatorial regime in Cuba. Although some Americans recognized the need for social reform in Latin America, others were more shortsighted. When Castro seized American property in Cuba, the United States responded by severing diplomatic ties and cutting off exports. In response, Cuba turned to the Soviet Union for economic and military support. Even when Soviet aid dried up several decades later, the United States refused to deal more closely with its Caribbean neighbor because Cuba remained a communist nation.

American troops also had invaded Honduras and Nicaragua to prop up leaders who supported United States interests. After World War II, the fear of Soviet communist influence led the United States government to protect Latin American nations where United States corporations had large financial investments.

In 1954 the United States feared possible communist activity in Guatemala. As a result, the Central Intelligence Agency (CIA) helped to

---

SECTION 3 REVIEW

Key Terms, People, and Places
1. Define (a) 38th parallel, (b) 17th parallel.
2. Identify (a) Ho Chi Minh, (b) Fidel Castro.
3. Identify Indochina.

Key Concepts
4. How were the seeds of the Korean War planted at the end of World War II?
5. What was the connection between the war in Vietnam and the cold war in Europe?

6. Why was the United States especially concerned about the possibility of communist control in the Middle East?
7. What economic factors led the United States to intervene in Guatemala and Cuba?

Critical Thinking
8. **Determining Relevance** Explain how Eisenhower's "domino theory" expressed the basic assumptions of American cold war policy.

The Cold War in the United States

SECTION PREVIEW

The effort to contain communism abroad made Americans fear subversion at home. The nation became swept up in an ugly campaign to expose suspected communists among its own citizens.

Key Concepts

- The fear of subversion by communist sympathizers in the United States led President Truman to create the Federal Employee Loyalty Program.
- A congressional committee investigated "un-American activity" in the late 1940s and 1950s.
- Senator Joseph McCarthy led a vicious crusade against American radicals that destroyed the careers and lives of many citizens.

Key Terms, People, and Places

House Un-American Activities Committee (HUAC); Alger Hiss, Julius and Ethel Rosenberg, Joseph R. McCarthy

D uring the Great Depression, tens of thousands of Americans had joined the Communist party, which was a legal organization. They were looking for answers to the question of why the American economic system no longer seemed to work. After World War II, some of these citizens were still Communist party members, although most had withdrawn. Now, in an atmosphere of cold war fears, their past came back to haunt them.

In the administrations of both Harry Truman and Dwight Eisenhower, concern over the growing appeal of communism around the world led to wholesale violations of civil liberties at home. The fear of subversion, or conspiracy to overthrow the government, launched a crusade that persecuted not only people who had ties to the Communist party but also anyone whose views leaned toward the left. The political left is made up of people who generally want to see the existing political system changed—sometimes radically—to benefit the common person. The political right is composed of people who generally wish to preserve the current system. During the late 1940s and 1950s, people were afraid to make statements that could in any way identify them with the political left. The government's loyalty program removed the left from power while effectively silencing any real political debate in the United States.

Truman's Loyalty Program and HUAC

As the Truman administration pursued support for its containment program, it pictured the cold war struggle in life-or-death terms. In his speeches, the President declared that the issue facing the world was whether "tyranny or freedom" would win out. Godless communism was a "threat to our liberties and to our faith," Truman said. It had to be stopped at all costs.

Administration officials feared that communism was infiltrating the United States. Exposure of a number of wartime spy rings in 1946 increased American anxiety. When the Republican party made significant gains in the midterm congressional elections that year, Truman became concerned that his political opponents would use the loyalty issue for their own ends. He therefore began his own investigation. He established a Federal Employee Loyalty Program in early 1947.

Under the terms of this program, the FBI was to check its files for individuals who might be engaged in suspicious activity. Cases would then move to a new Loyalty Review Board. While civil rights were supposed to be safeguarded, in fact those accused of disloyalty to

Anticommunist films like *The Red Menace* (1949) played on Americans' fear of communist activity in the United States. Such films also gave Hollywood studios a chance to prove their loyalty and patriotism.

I'M NO COMMUNIST

Red Channels

Actor Humphrey Bogart (top) flew to Washington, D.C., in 1947 to protest the congressional committee's actions against other actors. He then had to launch a public relations campaign to clear his own name. *Red Channels* (bottom), an index of blacklisted actors, was published in 1950.

their country often found themselves under attack with little chance to defend themselves. Rather than being innocent until proven guilty, they found that the accusation alone made it difficult for them to clear their names.

Although the Truman loyalty program examined several million employees, it only dismissed several hundred. Still, it helped create a dangerous climate of suspicion throughout the country.

Meanwhile, Congress began its own loyalty program. The **House Un-American Activities Committee (HUAC)**, which had been established a decade earlier to investigate disloyalty on the eve of war, now began a probe of the motion picture industry. It argued that films had tremendous power to corrupt the American public and suggested that numerous Hollywood figures had left-wing inclinations that compromised their work.

Many stars protested the procedures. Singer Judy Garland urged Americans to "write your Congressman a letter" denouncing the campaign. Actor Frederic March asked Americans to consider the question: "Who's next? . . . Is it you, who will have to look around nervously before you can say what's on your mind? . . . This reaches into every American city and town!" But HUAC pressed on.

AMERICAN PROFILES

The Hollywood Ten

In October 1947, HUAC called nineteen Hollywood figures to testify. According to rumors, all were either members of, or had close associations with, the Communist party. These Hollywood personalities—writers, directors, producers, actors—were a distinguished lot. Ring Lardner, Jr., had shared an Academy Award for writing *Woman of the Year* in 1942; Howard Koch had coauthored *Casablanca* that same year. Others too were responsible for some of the best films of the previous ten years.

Facing the committee, the celebrities who stood accused had no chance to defend themselves. Chairman J. Parnell Thomas first called friendly witnesses (those whose views were in line with the committee's), allowing them to make accusations and to slander whomever they chose. Then he turned his attention to the Hollywood activists themselves. Over and over the committee asked, "Are you now or have you ever been a member of the Communist party?" When some of the writers attempted to make their own statements, Thomas denied them the floor. Ten of the accused refused to answer his question by invoking rights guaranteed by the First Amendment. This amendment protects individuals, as the Supreme Court recently had ruled in *West Virginia Board of Education* v. *Barnette* (1942), against government officials who try to "prescribe what shall be orthodox in politics, nationalism, religion, or other matters of opinion." The committee responded by threatening prison terms if the Hollywood Ten failed to testify, but they held their ground. When the committee likewise stood firm, the Ten went to jail for contempt of Congress and served sentences ranging from six months to a year.

Worse still, Hollywood gave in totally to the committee. The day Congress voted the contempt citations, fifty motion picture executives held a meeting at the Waldorf-Astoria Hotel in New York. They announced that the Hollywood Ten had "been a disservice to their employers" and had "impaired their usefulness to the industry." They were discharged without compensation until they had "purged" themselves, or demonstrated their loyalty in some undefined way. So began the blacklist—a list of persons who would not be allowed to work. The blacklist included not only the Hollywood Ten but also many others who seemed in some way "subversive."

The hearings had a powerful impact on American films. In the immediate postwar years, the industry had been willing to make movies dealing with controversial subjects such as racism and anti-Semitism. Now studios resisted all films dealing with social problems and emphasized "pure entertainment" instead.

Spy Cases Inflame the Nation

Several spy cases at the start of the cold war helped fuel suspicion of a communist conspiracy in the United States. In 1948, HUAC investigated **Alger Hiss,** who had been a high-ranking State Department official before he left government service. Whittaker Chambers, a former Communist who had become a successful *Time* magazine editor, accused Hiss of having been a Communist in the 1930s. Hiss denied the charge and sued Chambers for libel. Chambers then went one step further and declared that Hiss had been a Soviet spy.

After two trials, Hiss was convicted of perjury—too much time had passed for the espionage charge to be pressed—and in 1950 he went to prison for four years. Not all Americans were convinced he was guilty—indeed, even today Americans still debate the Hiss case—but for most people at the time the case seemed to prove that there was a real communist threat in the United States.

Several months after Hiss's conviction, **Julius and Ethel Rosenberg,** a husband and wife who held radical views, were accused of passing atomic secrets to the Soviets during the war. While opinion about the Rosenbergs' guilt was split, they were nonetheless convicted of espionage and executed in the electric chair in 1953. Like the Hiss case, the Rosenberg trial focused attention on a possible internal threat and inflamed anticommunist passions.

The McCarthy Era

Joseph R. McCarthy, a Republican senator from Wisconsin, took the anticommunist crusade even further. Through his skillful use of the media and his willingness to make wild accusations about almost anyone, he quickly landed himself on center stage.

McCarthy's Rise to Power McCarthy attracted attention in early 1950 with a speech in Wheeling, West Virginia. He would be up for reelection in two years, and he figured that he could gain support by identifying himself as a leader in the fight against communism in the United States government. So he claimed he

held in his hand a list with the names of 205 known Communists in the State Department. In fact he had no such list, simply names of people accused of disloyalty under the Federal Employee Loyalty Program and still in their jobs. But such minor complications never stopped McCarthy. When pressed for details, he declared that he would show his list to the President; then he reduced the number from 205 to 57.

McCarthy soon took on other targets. He lashed out at Dean Acheson, the current secretary of state, calling him a "pompous diplomat in striped pants," and at George Marshall, a former secretary of state, referring to him as "a man steeped in falsehood" for his inability to prevent the fall of China to the communists. Marshall was a national hero and a man of unquestioned integrity, but McCarthy made the incredible claim that he was involved in "a conspiracy so immense and an infamy so black as to dwarf any such previous venture in the history of man."

McCarthy gained support through these tactics because Truman's loyalty program had planted fears in the minds of many Americans about the supposed communist threat at home. But McCarthy also succeeded because he knew how to give journalists what they needed for newspaper stories. He knew when their deadlines

To this day there is no agreement on whether Ethel and Julius Rosenberg—shown above just after her conviction in 1951—were heads of a Soviet spy ring or tragic victims of anticommunist hysteria.

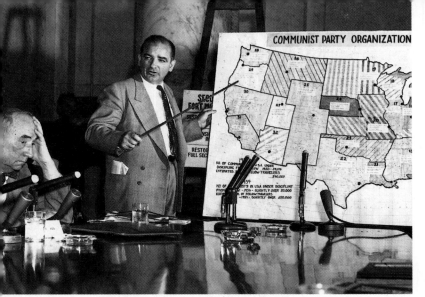

The public responded favorably to McCarthy's attacks. By the end of 1953, 50 percent of the sample in one Gallup poll had a positive opinion of McCarthy, with only 29 percent holding an unfavorable view.

MAKING CONNECTIONS

McCarthy had the power to ruin a person's reputation with a mere accusation. What people or institutions today have a similar power?

McCarthy's Fall McCarthy finally overreached himself when he took on the United States Army. In 1953 the army drafted McCarthy's assistant G. David Schine. When the military refused the request of Roy Cohn, another influential McCarthy assistant, to give Schine special treatment, McCarthy decided to investigate army security. Congress then began to examine the complaint.

The Army-McCarthy hearings began in April 1954, were televised nationally, and lasted for thirty-six days. They reached a climax when McCarthy charged that Fred Fisher, an assistant to army counsel Joseph Welch, had been a member of an organization sympathetic to the

Using Historical Evidence Army counsel Joseph Welch (seated at table) listens to Senator McCarthy discuss communist infiltration with the aid of a giant map. *How does this photo show Welch's reaction to McCarthy's tactics?*

occurred and recognized that they needed stories for their editors. He provided material at just the right time. When he had nothing to report, he would call a press conference to announce that new disclosures would be coming soon.

Some Republican politicians, who hoped McCarthy's campaign would damage the reputation of the Democratic administration in the eyes of voters, encouraged McCarthy. Robert Taft, a senator from Ohio, told his colleague, "If one case doesn't work, try another." McCarthy did.

| 1650 | 1700 | 1750 | 1800 | **Links Across Time** | 1850 | 1900 | 1950 | 2000 |

The Hunt for Witches and Communists

Between June and September of 1692, fourteen women and five men were hanged in Salem, Massachusetts, as witches. Those who "confessed" to witchcraft were spared; many who maintained their innocence were hanged. Historians today compare Salem in 1692 to the United States in the 1950s. The Puritans had recently resisted hostile Native Americans in King Philip's War and outlasted all challenges to their religious beliefs. Instead of feeling secure, however, the Puritans suddenly saw the devil in the very heart

of their community. Similarly, the United States in the 1950s had just defeated its enemies in World War II and recovered from the Depression. Yet, many Americans feared that evil forces within their community posed a grave threat. Senator Joseph R. McCarthy seized upon this fear to start a "witch-hunt" of his own.

The stress of the cold war with the Soviet Union frightened Americans. On very little evidence, they began to suspect a strong communist conspiracy to take over the United States. In what has been called "the

McCarthy terror," thousands of innocent people were accused of being communists or communist sympathizers. At numerous public hearings, those who refused to answer questions were treated as guilty.

In 1954, after being condemned by the Senate for his activities, McCarthy's reign of terror ended. As in Salem more than two centuries earlier, the witch-hunt was over. *What emotion seems to have allowed both the Salem witch trials and the McCarthy hunt for communists to happen?*

Communist party. Welch, an eloquent Boston lawyer, was furious:

> Until this moment, Senator, I think I never really gauged your cruelty or your recklessness. . . . If it were in my power to forgive you for your reckless cruelty, I would do so. I like to think I am a gentleman, but your forgiveness will have to come from someone other than me. . . . Let us not assassinate this lad [Fisher] further, Senator. You have done enough. Have you no sense of decency, sir, at long last? Have you left no sense of decency?

The Senate, once frightened by McCarthy's power, now condemned him for his reckless attacks. Although he remained in office, his strength was gone. He died three years later, a broken man.

McCarthy's Impact In his peak years in power, though, McCarthy had a powerful impact on American society. He, and the others who participated in the anticommunist crusade, generated a sense of fear and suspicion that filtered down to all levels. In the late 1940s and early 1950s, it seemed impossible to dissent in the United States. Civil servants, government workers, teachers, and writers all came under attack and found their right to defend themselves restricted. Often an accusation alone was enough to end a person's career.

Examples of abuse extended throughout American life. Subway workers in New York were fired for refusing to answer questions about their political beliefs and actions. A fire department officer in Seattle was dismissed just forty days before reaching twenty-five years of service (and gaining retirement benefits) because, although he denied that he was a current member of the Communist party, he declined to speak about his past involvement. Investigations of university faculties in 1952 and 1953 led to dismissals of professors who refused to cooperate with hostile congressional committees. Navaho in Arizona and New Mexico were denied all government assistance during one brutal winter on the grounds that their communal way of life was un-American. Latino workers sometimes faced deportation for belonging to unions that seemed radical.

Eventually, this second red scare, like the first one following World War I, subsided. But for a time it created widespread fear and confusion in the United States. Some of the victims were fortunate enough to reclaim their careers. Others suffered for years to come. The entire nation suffered from the era's suppression of free speech and honest debate.

These demonstrators show the depth of anticommunist feeling among many Americans in the postwar period.

SECTION 4 REVIEW

Key Terms, People, and Places

1. Identify (a) Alger Hiss, (b) Julius and Ethel Rosenberg, (c) Joseph R. McCarthy.

Key Concepts

2. Why did Harry Truman launch his Federal Employee Loyalty Program?
3. What was the HUAC and why did it make Hollywood a specific target of its investigations?

4. How did Senator McCarthy create an atmosphere of suspicion and paranoia in the United States?

Critical Thinking

5. **Identifying Assumptions** HUAC forced Americans to answer the question "Are you now or have you ever been a member of the Communist party?" What assumptions was this question based on?

Chapter Review

Key Terms
1. cold war
2. proletariat
3. totalitarian
4. iron curtain
5. United Nations
6. containment
7. Truman Doctrine
8. Marshall Plan
9. Berlin airlift
10. NATO
11. NSC-68
12. satellite nation
13. 38th parallel
14. domino theory
15. 17th parallel
16. HUAC

People
17. George C. Marshall
18. Mao Zedong
19. Ho Chi Minh
20. Fidel Castro
21. Alger Hiss
22. Julius and Ethel Rosenberg
23. Joseph R. McCarthy

Places
24. Indochina

Terms For each term above, write a sentence that explains its relation to the post–World War II period.

Matching Review the key terms in the list above. If you are not sure of a term's meaning, review its definition in the chapter. Then choose a term from the list that best matches each description below.
1. division line between North and South Korea
2. belief that if one country falls to communism, neighboring countries will fall as well
3. state of indirect conflict between the United States and the Soviet Union after World War II
4. division between the capitalist West and the communist East in Europe

True or False Determine whether each statement is true or false. If it is true, write "true." If it is false, change the underlined name to make the statement true.
1. After two trials, <u>Joseph R. McCarthy</u> went to prison for four years on perjury charges.
2. <u>George C. Marshall</u> rose to power by accusing people of disloyalty to the United States.
3. <u>Fidel Castro</u> led the struggle for independence in Vietnam.
4. After their conviction on charges of espionage, <u>Julius and Ethel Rosenberg</u> were executed in 1953.

Section 1 (pp. 584–587)
1. Describe the relationship between the United States and the Soviet Union during World War II.
2. How did the issue of Poland's government cause diplomacy between the United States and the Soviet Union to break down after World War II?
3. Why did the United States and the Soviet Union have different goals for the postwar period?

Section 2 (pp. 589–593)
4. Summarize the policy of containment pursued by the United States during the cold war.
5. How were the Truman Doctrine, the Marshall Plan, and NSC-68 expressions of containment policy?
6. How did President Eisenhower and Secretary of State Dulles differ in their views of foreign policy?

Section 3 (pp. 594–598)
7. What two foreign policy objectives did Presidents Truman and Eisenhower have to balance in their handling of the Korean War and the early Vietnam War?
8. What conflicts did the United States face in shaping foreign policy in the Middle East?
9. How did the cold war affect United States policy in Latin America?

Section 4 (pp. 599–603)
10. What were the purpose and effects of Truman's Federal Employee Loyalty Program?
11. What accusations did HUAC make against the nineteen Hollywood figures that it called in to testify?
12. What impact did Senator McCarthy's anticommunist crusade have on American society?

1. **Making Comparisons** You have read about the different political and economic ideas that motivated the United States and the Soviet Union during the cold war. How were the foreign policy aims of the two countries similar?

2. **Drawing Conclusions** During the cold war, fear and hostility toward communism were the driving forces behind many of the social and foreign policies in the United States. How much of this fear actually was grounded in reality?

3. **Identifying Alternatives** Imagine that you are an adviser to President Eisenhower. The President has asked you to draw up a list of alternatives to help him decide on his policy about the emerging conflict in Vietnam. What alternatives can you propose? Which alternative will you advise the President to use?

1. **Evaluating Primary Sources** Review the statement of the Truman Doctrine on page 590. Create four questions that, if answered, would help explore what Truman's statement meant for foreign policy in the future.

2. **Understanding the Visuals** Look at the image in the section preview showing Khrushchev and Eisenhower on page 594, and then at the photograph on page 593. Write a short paragraph explaining how the illustration of the two cold war leaders explains one reason why the United States was reluctant to become involved in the event shown in the photograph on page 593.

3. **Writing About the Chapter** You have been accused by HUAC of participating in a communist conspiracy. Write a statement in which you defend yourself against these charges. First create a list of the reasons why the accusation is false. Note ways in which the anticommunist hysteria of the times has

contributed to your false accusation. Then write a draft of your statement in which you respectfully but firmly defend yourself. Revise your statement, making certain that each point is clearly explained. Proofread your statement and draft a final copy.

4. **Using the Graphic Organizer** This graphic organizer uses a modified flow map to outline developments on the policy of containment during the 1940s and 1950s. Large boxes show main developments; smaller boxes add details. (a) Based on your reading of the chapter and this graphic organizer, explain how the Marshall Plan implemented the Truman Doctrine and took it a step further. (b) According to the flow map, what events led to the NSC-68 recommendation for a massive increase in defense spending? (c) On a separate sheet of paper, create your own graphic organizer about the origins of the cold war, using this graphic organizer as an example.

The Postwar Years at Home

1945–1960

*A*mericans had dreamed of peace and prosperity through sixteen grueling years of economic depression and world war. After the war, they expected to enjoy the benefits of their new standing as a military and economic superpower. People embraced a wide array of technological developments that promised to make their lives easier, and they relished the chance to live more comfortably than their parents had. While not all groups shared in the prosperity, most Americans now were able to buy the homes, cars, and other items that they had once only imagined owning.

Events in the United States

Events in the World

1947 Jackie Robinson becomes the first African American to play major league baseball.

1948 Scientists invent the transistor.
• President Truman desegregates the armed forces.

1951 J. D. Salinger publishes his novel The Catcher in the Rye.

1945	1947	1949	1951

1945 The British Labour party nationalizes major industries after winning power.

1947 India is divided into India and Pakistan.
• Japan adopts a new constitution.

1948 South African Alan Paton's Cry the Beloved Country examines racial segregation in his country.

1951 United States occupation of Japan ends.

1953 Two thirds of all families in the United States own televisions.

1954 Supreme Court issues Brown v. Board of Education ruling desegregating schools.

1955 Ray Kroc opens his first McDonald's fast-food restaurant.
• Montgomery bus boycott begins.

1957 First commercial nuclear power plant opens in Shippingport, Pennsylvania.

1960 Gross National Product reaches $504 billion, more than double that of 1945.

1953   **1955**   **1957**   **1959**   **1961**

1953 Soviet leader Joseph Stalin dies.

1955 Juan Perón is deposed as dictator of Argentina.
• Soviet Union forms Warsaw Pact.

1957 The Soviet Union launches Sputnik satellite.

1960 Organization of Petroleum Exporting Countries (OPEC) is formed.

The Postwar Economy

SECTION PREVIEW

The American Dream—a home in the suburbs, a car in the garage—materialized for many people in the postwar years.

Even some children's games in the 1950s reflected the ideal middle-class life. These game pieces are from "Merry Milkman," in which players delivered milk, eggs, and butter to suburban homes.

Key Concepts
- After World War II, the American economy grew rapidly. People could buy more with their money and created new ways of organizing businesses.
- Technological advances such as atomic energy and computers altered American life.
- The economy was increasingly driven by the needs and wants of affluent consumers.

Key Terms, People, and Places
per capita income, real purchasing power, diversified conglomerate, franchise, agribusiness, baby boom, GI Bill; William J. Levitt

When American soldiers returned from the battlefields, they wanted nothing more than to put the horrors of the war behind them and enjoy the comforts of home and family. As large numbers of young people married and started families, they wanted homes, furniture, and other household items. During the war, when most items were rationed or not produced at all, many people had simply put their money into savings. Now most Americans were eager to acquire everything the war—and before that, the Depression—had denied them.

Thus the United States embarked on one of the greatest periods of economic expansion in its history. The Gross National Product (GNP) more than doubled, jumping from $212 billion in 1945 to $504 billion in 1960. During the same period, **per capita income**—the average income per person—increased from $1,526 to $2,788. **Real purchasing power**—what people actually could buy with their money—grew by about 22 percent. The United States was now the richest nation in the world.

Corporations Create New Jobs

Major corporate expansion accompanied economic growth. In the 1950s, a few huge firms dominated many industries. General Motors, Ford, and Chrysler overshadowed all competitors in the automobile industry; General Electric and Westinghouse enjoyed similar positions in the electrical business. Giant corporations, fearful after the Depression of investing all their resources in one business, became **diversified conglomerates.** They acquired companies that produced entirely different goods and services, so that if one area of the economy failed, their investments in another area would be safe. International Telephone and Telegraph, for example, purchased Avis Rent-a-Car, Sheraton Hotels, Hartford Fire Insurance, and Continental Baking.

At the same time, another kind of expansion took place. In 1954 Ray Kroc, who sold milkshake machines called Multimixers, was amazed when two brothers who owned a restaurant in San Bernardino, California, ordered their tenth Multimixer. With ten machines, the restaurant could make fifty milk shakes at once. Because of the restaurant's fast, efficient service and its prime location along a busy highway, it was enjoying great success. Intrigued by the possibilities, Kroc purchased the two brothers' idea of assembly-line food production. He also acquired the name of the brothers' restaurant: McDonald's. Kroc took his fast food nationwide by selling **franchises**—the right to open McDonald's restaurants using the same system—to other eager entrepreneurs. Hundreds of other restaurant franchises, such as Burger King and Kentucky Fried Chicken, followed.

The franchise system flourished in the 1950s. It worked so well that it was applied to other kinds of businesses, such as clothing stores and automobile muffler shops. The system's advantage lay in the fact that an individual with only a few thousand dollars could own a small business that enjoyed the support—especially in terms of national advertising—of a multimillion-dollar parent company. The system also created countless low-paying jobs across the nation. But with the growth of the franchise system, many small, unique stores with ties to the local community were replaced by nationwide chains that were the same everywhere in the country.

Technology Transforms Life

New developments in technology also spurred industrial growth. An entirely new industry—the generation of electrical power through the use of atomic energy—resulted from the research that had produced the atomic bomb. In 1956 film producer Walt Disney voiced Americans' hopes and fears about atomic power in his book and film *Our Friend the Atom*. Disney began with a story about a fisherman who found a sealed bottle. When the fisherman opened the bottle, a genie escaped and threatened to kill him. The fisherman got the genie back into the bottle and would only open it again when the genie promised to grant him three wishes. "The story of the atom is like that tale," Disney explained:

T*he fable . . . has a happy ending; perhaps our story can, too. Like the Fisherman we must bestir our wits* [think carefully before we act]. *We have the scientific knowledge to turn the Genie's might into peaceful and useful channels.*

The next year, Navy captain Hyman G. Rickover oversaw the development of the first commercial nuclear power plant in Shippingport, Pennsylvania. The new plant promised the peaceful use of atomic energy that Walt Disney had imagined.

The Computer Industry At the same time that Americans were looking forward to inexpensive energy from nuclear reactors, they reached out to embrace the computer industry. Wartime research led to the development of ever more powerful calculators. Grace Hopper, a research fellow at Harvard University's computation laboratory, led the way in the creation of the software that runs computers. She also introduced the term *debugging*, which was born when she removed a moth caught in a relay switch that had caused a large computer to shut down. Today the term means "ridding a computer program of errors."

In 1947 scientists at Bell Laboratories invented the transistor, a tiny circuit that did the work of a much larger vacuum tube. Because of the transistor, giant machines that once filled whole rooms could now fit on a desk. Calculations that had taken hours could now be computed in fractions of a second. The Census Bureau purchased one of the first computer systems to tally the 1950 census. Soon hotels, airlines, and countless other industries used computers to keep track of their customers.

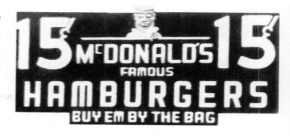

This sign at the original fast-food restaurant in San Bernardino, California, advertised the McDonald brothers' mass-produced hamburgers.

MAKING CONNECTIONS

Today the government and many businesses use computers to create files with information on every American. How might this use of computers threaten people's right to privacy?

Television Americans fell in love with another invention in the 1950s: television. Developed in the 1930s, television became enormously popular after World War II. By 1953 two thirds of all American families owned TVs.

In 1955 the average American family watched television four to five hours a day. Children grew up on such programs as "Howdy Doody Time" and "The Mickey Mouse Club." Teenagers danced to the rock-and-roll music played on "American Bandstand," a predecessor of today's MTV. Other viewers followed situation comedies like "I Love Lucy" and "Father Knows Best."

Television networks raised the money to broadcast these shows by selling advertising

The Incredible Shrinking Computer

In their early days, computers filled entire rooms and performed calculations at a snail's pace (left). Over the years, improvements in technology have reduced the size of computers—such as the laptop model above—to fit almost anywhere. Computers now have the power to do many complex operations at lightning speed. *How has the computer revolution increased the pace of life for all Americans?*

Situation comedies like "Leave It to Beaver" (TV inset) entertained audiences while promoting the family values of the 1950s. Frozen foods allowed TV viewers to cook dinner during commercial breaks.

time. Television commercials gave Americans constant exposure to products they supposedly needed to live a comfortable life. Children grew up singing lyrics to commercials, which they sometimes knew even better than popular songs. Companies got their money's worth from advertising dollars: millions of viewers were persuaded to buy the items they saw on television commercials.

Changes in the Work Force

Using the nearly miraculous technology of the post–World War II years, Americans invented their way out of their manufacturing jobs and into new ones. In earlier years, most Americans made a living as blue-collar workers, or those who produce goods. After the war, however, new machines performed many of the jobs previously done by people. By 1956 a majority of all American workers held white-collar jobs, in which they no longer produced goods but instead performed services for others, working at counters or in offices.

The new white-collar workers felt encouraged by the working conditions they found: clean, bright offices rather than the dark, often dangerous factories of the recent past. But they soon realized that office jobs had drawbacks as well. Work in large corporations was often impersonal. White-collar workers sometimes never saw the products that their companies made. Employers might pressure employees to dress, think, and act alike. Some workers felt they sacrificed individuality for the sake of the corporation. Sociologist C. Wright Mills had this scathing comment: "When white-collar people get jobs, they sell not only their time and energy but their personalities as well."

For those who kept their blue-collar jobs, working conditions and wages improved during the 1940s and 1950s. Labor unions continued to work for change, and their strength reached an all-time high as the war ended. In 1955 the two largest unions, the American Federation of Labor (AFL) and the Congress of Industrial Organizations (CIO) merged. The AFL-CIO, a new and more powerful organization, remains a major force today. Workers won gains that we now take for granted, such as guaranteed cost-of-living increases.

Changes in Farm Work and Life

The world of American agriculture was also transformed in the postwar period. Technological improvements made planting and harvesting easier. Fertilizers, fungicides, and pesticides promoted and protected plant growth. As farming became more profitable, it underwent the same kind of consolidation experienced by industry.

Once again, Americans had invented themselves out of their old jobs. Hundreds of thousands of small farmers who could no longer compete with farms using high-tech machinery abandoned rural America in search of new lives in the cities and suburbs. They left their farms behind to be bought up by big businesses. Americans called this new industry **agribusiness.**

Americans Move to the Suburbs

With so many people working and making a better living than ever before, the **baby boom** that had begun during World War II continued. The birthrate, which had fallen to 19 births per one thousand people during the Depression, soared to more than 25 births per thousand in its peak year of 1947. (See the graph at right.)

Large families seeking new houses and wanting to enjoy the benefits of a booming economy retreated from the aging cities to suburbs that ringed the urban areas. World War II veterans enjoyed the benefits of the Servicemen's Readjustment Act of 1944, commonly known as the **GI Bill,** which gave them low-interest mortgages to purchase their new homes.

Developers like **William J. Levitt** built new communities in the suburbs. He pioneered mass-production techniques in home building by buying precut and preassembled materials and building houses in weeks instead of

months. Proud of his creations, Levitt gave his name to the new towns. Soon there was a Levittown in New York, another in Pennsylvania, and a third in New Jersey. Others quickly adopted Levitt's techniques, and new communities sprang up all over the United States.

The houses were affordable, but they all bore a monotonous resemblance to one another. Folk singer Malvina Reynolds expressed her revulsion for the new communities with these words from "Little Boxes," a popular song of the era:

> Little boxes on the hillside
> Little boxes made of ticky-tacky
> Little boxes on the hillside
> Little boxes all the same.
> There's a green one and a pink one
> And a blue one and a yellow one
> And they're all made out of ticky-tacky
> And they all look just the same.

Suburban growth depended on automobiles and roads. To meet the demand, auto makers produced up to 8 million new cars each year in the 1950s. The 1956 Interstate Highway Act provided $26 billion to build an interstate highway

As reported in a 1953 article in *Life* magazine, "Every day, including Saturdays and Sundays, is moving day in Los Angeles." Four hundred people a day moved into the suburbs around that city in the 1950s.

Birth Rate, 1930–1960

Source: *Historical Statistics of the United States*

Interpreting Graphs
What was the overall trend in the birth rate after World War II? How might the lack of consumer goods during the war have contributed to this trend?

Estimated Outstanding Consumer Credit, 1945–1958

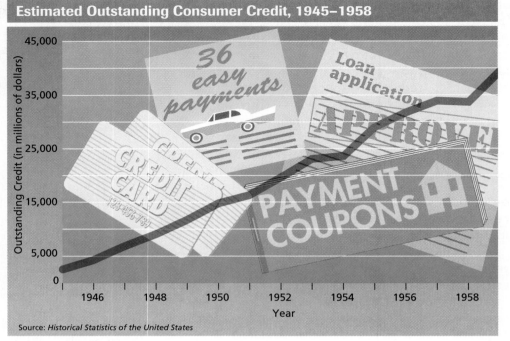

Source: *Historical Statistics of the United States*

Interpreting Graphs
The consumer credit shown in this graph includes automobile and home loans as well as credit card debts. *By approximately what factor did consumer credit increase between 1945 and 1950? How many more dollars worth of consumer credit was accumulated between 1950 and 1958?*

Consumer Credit Finances Growth

The postwar American economy required enormous consumption of goods to remain healthy. The increase in real purchasing power helped pay for some consumer goods but not all. After years of depression and war, Americans willingly went into debt to make up the difference, as the graph at left shows. Lending agencies created new ways to make borrowing easy, such as the credit card. The Diner's Club credit card appeared in 1950, followed at the end of the decade by the American Express card, and then by the BankAmericard (later called Visa).

system more than 40,000 miles long. The project provided a national web of new roads and allowed the evacuation of major cities in the event of nuclear attack. As President Eisenhower noted,

> The total pavement of the system would make a parking lot big enough to hold two thirds of all the automobiles in the United States. The amount of concrete poured to form these roadways would build . . . six sidewalks to the moon.

Advertisers persuaded consumers that only by buying new products could they attain status and success. Americans responded by using their credit to purchase washing machines, vacuum cleaners, and television sets. The United States had become, in the words of economist John Kenneth Galbraith, "the affluent society."

A decade before, the nation had faced the problems of scarcity and want. Now it would have to deal with the consequences of abundance.

SECTION 1 REVIEW

Key Terms, People, and Places
1. Define (a) per capita income, (b) real purchasing power, (c) baby boom, (d) GI Bill.
2. Identify William J. Levitt.

Key Concepts
3. How did the diversified conglomerate, the franchise system, and agribusiness each change the American economy after World War II?

4. What technological advances had an important impact on Americans in the decade after World War II?
5. What factors contributed to suburban development from 1945 to 1960?

Critical Thinking
6. **Recognizing Cause and Effect** In what ways did the Depression and World War II contribute to the postwar economic boom of the 1950s?

Making Comparisons

Making comparisons means examining two or more ideas, objects, events, or people to discover ways that they are alike and ways they are different. When studying history, being able to make comparisons allows you to evaluate more fully historical periods and specific events or viewpoints.

One way to evaluate an event, idea, or historical period is to compare statistics about a subject. Beginning in the 1950s, the popularity of television soared and had a great impact on the daily lives of Americans. Below are two tables noting the number of television sets per household, the percentage of households with television sets, and the amount of money spent on television advertising between 1950 and 1990. Use the following steps to compare the data and draw conclusions about the impact of television in the United States.

1. Identify the basis on which you will make the comparison. It is not possible to compare two or more items that are fundamentally different. Making a comparison is possible only when items share a common concept or characteristic. Look over the tables, then answer the following questions. (a) What subject do the data have in common? (b) What period of time is covered by the data? (c) What purpose would a comparison of these data serve?

2. Determine the ways in which the data on the two charts are alike. Making comparisons includes finding similarities between two or more items. What relationship can you see between the rapid increase in the number of television sets in the United States and the spiraling amount of money spent on television advertising?

3. Determine the ways in which the data are different. Making comparisons also includes finding any differences that may exist between items. In what fundamental way do the data differ?

4. Summarize and evaluate your comparison of the data. Complete the comparison based on similarities and differences. (a) In your opinion, did the increase in the number of households with television sets drive up the amount of money spent on advertising or visa versa? (b) Why did the *percent* of households with television sets stay about the same between 1970 and 1990, while the *number* of households with television sets continued to increase? (c) In your opinion, will the amount of money spent on television advertising continue to increase? How much do you think will be spent in the year 2000?

U.S. Households with Television, 1950–1990

Year	Households with Television	Percent of U.S. Households with Television
1950	3,800	9%
1960	45,200	86%
1970	60,100	96%
1980	77,800	98%
1990	92,000	98%

Source: *The Universal Almanac,* 1993

Television Advertising Expenditures

Year	Estimated Expenditures (in millions of dollars)
1950	171
1960	1,627
1970	3,596
1980	11,469
1990	28,405

Sources: *Statistical Abstract of the United States,* 1992; *Historical Statistics of the United States.*

The Mood of the 1950s

SECTION PREVIEW

After World War II, many Americans were blessed with wealth, success, and leisure. Conformity seemed the order of the day, although some groups made it their business to avoid the popularly accepted lifestyles of the 1950s.

Key Concepts

• Middle-class Americans valued comfort and security during the 1950s.

• Expectations about the proper roles for men and women were fostered by the media and society.

Key Terms, People, and Places

beatniks; Benjamin Spock, Betty Friedan, J. D. Salinger

In the 1950s, the "happy house-wife" portrayed in the media used state-of-the-art appliances to cook and clean, and she looked glamorous while doing so. Poodle skirts (below) were part of the uniform for teenage girls.

Middle-class Americans were comfortable during the 1950s. Most did not question whether the images of prosperous, suburban white families frequently seen on television represented "typical" American experiences. They valued the apparent harmony that minimized differences between individuals and groups in the United States. Compromise, rather than conflict, was the way disagreements could be settled. After the deprivations of depression and war, people wanted to enjoy their newly won prosperity and provide even better opportunities for their children.

Americans Value Conformity

The 1950s were years of conformity in the United States. Throughout the country, members of middle-class society seemed to want to imitate those around them rather than search out unique experiences. Even the descendants of the immigrants of the early 1900s seemed to value American middle-class culture above their own diverse cultural heritages.

In the past, sociologist David Riesman observed, Americans had valued individuality. Now they strained to conform. Riesman cited *Tootle the Engine*, a children's story in the popular Little Golden Book series. Tootle, a young train engine, found it was more fun to play in the fields than it was to stay on the tracks. His fellow citizens in "Engineville" worked hard to break him of the habit. Tootle finally absorbed the lesson of his peers: "Always stay on the track no matter what." The story, Riesman believed, was a powerful parable for the young people of the 1950s.

Some called the middle-class youth of the 1950s the "silent generation." The silent generation seemed to have little interest in the problems and crises of the larger world; its members were content to let other people worry about such issues. Instead, many middle-class young people appeared to devote their energies to joining fraternities and sororities, organizing parties and pranks, and generally pursuing entertainment and fun.

Movies generally portrayed the girls of the silent generation in poodle skirts and bobby socks and the boys in letter sweaters. The image of 1950s youth as cheerleaders and football heroes was not entirely accurate, however. Many young people rejected the values of their parents and felt misunderstood and alone. A few films, such as *Rebel Without a Cause* in 1955, captured these feelings of alienation.

Religion Revives in the United States In the 1950s Americans who had drifted away from religion in earlier years flocked back to their churches or synagogues. Evangelists like Billy Graham used radio and television to spread

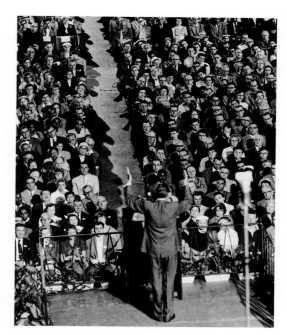

Thousands gathered to hear evangelist Billy Graham preach. He conducted large-scale crusades in major American cities, including this one in New York in 1957.

their messages to more people than ever before. The new interest in religion stemmed in part from the cold war struggle against "godless communism," in part from an effort to find hope in the face of the threat of nuclear war, and in part from a desire to do what everyone else seemed to be doing.

Evidence of the newfound commitment to religion was everywhere. In 1954 Congress added the words "under God" to the Pledge of Allegiance, and the next year it required the phrase "In God We Trust" to appear on all American currency. Religion also became commercial. Those in need could Dial-a-Prayer for the first time, and new slogans such as "The family that prays together stays together" became commonplace. By the end of the 1950s, 95 percent of all Americans felt linked to some formal religious group, even if they never attended services.

Women's and Men's Roles Americans in the post-World War II years were keenly aware of the roles that they were expected to play as men and women. Men were supposed to go to school and then find jobs to support wives and children. Theirs was the public sphere, the world away from home where they earned money and made important political, economic, and social decisions. Men of this time often judged themselves and others by what they could buy with the money they earned.

Women in the 1950s were expected to play a supporting role for their husbands' lives in the public sphere. They kept house, cooked meals, and raised children. Many women had enjoyed working outside the home during World War II and were reluctant to give up good jobs. But propaganda from both employers and the government made it clear that women were expected to give their jobs to returning soldiers. In 1947 *Life* magazine recorded women's frustration in a photo essay titled "The American Woman's Dilemma."

By the 1950s the dilemma seemed solved. Most middle-class women settled into the demands of raising children and decorating their suburban homes. In 1956 *Life* produced a special edition on women that carried a very different message from the issue of nine years before. In a story entitled "Busy Wife's Achievements," *Life* profiled Marjorie Sutton, a happy housewife who had married at the age of sixteen, had four children, and now kept busy with the PTA, Campfire

These Chicago-area commuters may have identified with the characters in *The Man in the Gray Flannel Suit.* The 1955 novel told the story of a couple who seemed to be living the American dream but who felt strangely discontented with their lives.

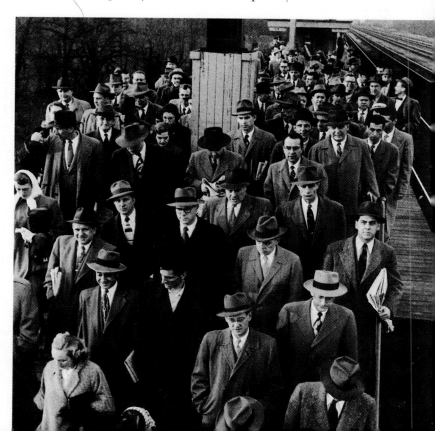

Girls, and charity causes. She served as "home manager, mother, hostess, and useful civic worker," and even found time to exercise twice a week "to help preserve her size 12 figure."

Pediatrician **Benjamin Spock** assured American families that mothers should stay home with their young children. In his *Common Sense Book of Baby and Child Care*, published in 1946 and still selling today (though in revised form), he advised a mother to remain with her children if she wanted them to grow up stable and secure. Adlai Stevenson, Democratic candidate for President in 1952 and 1956, reinforced this message when he told a group of female college students that "the assignment for you, as wives and mothers, you can do in the living room with a baby in your lap or in the kitchen with a can opener in your hand."

Despite such expectations, more women than ever before—many of them married with children—held paying jobs in the 1950s. Besides the satisfaction of earning their own money, women wanted to be able to buy the items that were part of the media image of "the good life"—automobiles, electric appliances, and so on.

In 1950, 22 percent of all married American women had jobs; by 1960 the figure had risen to 31 percent. Married women with jobs had first begun to outnumber unmarried women with jobs near the end of World War II; in the postwar years, the gap grew even larger. The graph below shows these trends.

In 1963 **Betty Friedan** published an explosive critique of the 1950s ideal of womanhood. Friedan had graduated with top honors from Smith College in 1942 but had given up her career as a journalist to become a full-time homemaker and mother. In her book *The Feminine Mystique*, Friedan lashed out at the culture that denied creative roles to women:

I t was unquestioned gospel [in the 1950s] that women could identify with nothing beyond the home—not politics, not art, not science, not events large or small, war or peace, in the United States or the world,

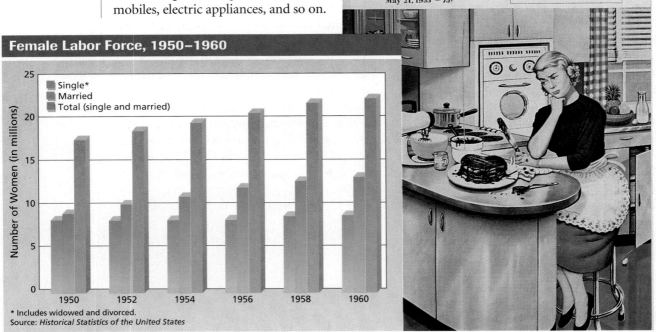

Female Labor Force, 1950–1960

Number of Women (in millions)

Single*
Married
Total (single and married)

1950   1952   1954   1956   1958   1960

* Includes widowed and divorced.
Source: *Historical Statistics of the United States*

Interpreting Graphs

As the *Post* cover (above right) suggests, women in the 1950s were encouraged to link their self-esteem to their success in the kitchen and home. *According to the graph, what was actually happening to American women during this period? How many women joined the work force between 1950 and 1960?*

unless it could be approached through female experience as a wife or mother or translated into domestic detail!

Millions of women, Friedan charged, were frustrated with their roles in the 1950s.

MAKING CONNECTIONS

In what ways are women and men today pressured to conform to social standards?

Pockets of Nonconformity Appear

Occasional challenges to the rigid expectations of 1950s society did erupt. Holden Caulfield, the main figure in **J. D. Salinger's** 1951 novel *The Catcher in the Rye,* was troubled by the hypocrisy of the "phonies" he saw at boarding school and in the world at large. His effort to preserve his own integrity despite the fierce pressure to conform was an experience to which many readers could relate.

Members of the "Beat Generation," called **beatniks** by middle-class observers, launched a different kind of challenge. Beatniks, some of them writers, some artists, some simply participants in the movement, stressed spontaneity and spirituality instead of apathy and conformity. They challenged traditional patterns of respectability and shocked other Americans with their more open sexuality and their use of illegal drugs.

Author Jack Kerouac, the spiritual leader of the beatniks, gathered with others in coffee houses in San Francisco, California, where they shared ideas and experiences. The unconven-

Viewpoints
On Rock-and-Roll Music

When the defiant beat of rock and roll burst onto the American scene in the mid-1950s, few people remained impartial about its sound or its impact. *What does each viewpoint below say about the relationship between rock music and delinquency?*

Against Rock and Roll

"Rock 'n' roll . . . is sung, played and written for the most part by [mentally deficient] goons and by means of its almost imbecilic repetition and sly, lewd, in plain fact, dirty lyrics . . . it manages to be the [warlike] music of every sideburned delinquent on the face of the earth."
   Singer Frank Sinatra, The *New York Times,* January 12, 1958

For Rock and Roll

"If my kids are home at night listening to my radio program, and get interested enough to go out and buy records and have a collection to listen to and dance to, I think I'm fighting delinquency."
   Radio disc jockey Alan Freed, The *New York Times,* January 12, 1958

tional Kerouac typed his best-selling novel *On the Road,* published in 1957, on a 250-foot roll of paper. The novel's lack of standard punctuation and paragraph structure was meant to reflect an open approach to life.

Such challenges to conformity were not the norm. Most Americans were willing to seize the comfort offered by the postwar economy and preferred to live their lives in the relative safety of the suburbs. Many people pleased with this lifestyle eventually began to expect the government to ensure that the "good life" continued.

SECTION 2 REVIEW

Key Terms, People, and Places
1. Define beatniks.
2. Identify (a) Benjamin Spock, (b) Betty Friedan, (c) J. D. Salinger.

Key Concepts
3. In what aspects of American life was conformity most visible during the period between 1945 and 1960?

4. What social and economic roles were men and women expected to play in the 1950s?

Critical Thinking
5. **Making Comparisons** In what ways was the "Beat Generation" of the 1950s similar to or different from the rebellious youth of the 1920s?

The Suburban Explosion

After World War II, American cities rapidly expanded outward as people moved into suburbs that first housed them and then became major centers for shopping, working, and recreation. What factors contributed to this suburban explosion?

Both nature and people can change a place. Changes in the landscape, such as those caused by a hurricane or drought, often are dramatic. The changes that people make in the environment can be just as striking. At no time in United States history were these changes more evident than in the decades following World War II.

Movement: Railroads and Streetcars Lead to Suburban Growth

The largest cities in the United States in the 1700s were commercial centers situated at key waterfront locations. This was because goods and people could move much more rapidly and easily on water than over land. Workplaces in these cities were clustered near the waterfront, while residences crowded nearby, so working people could walk between their homes and jobs.

These compact, circular-shaped cities began to expand when railroads first cut paths outward from the centers. In the decades before and after the Civil War, small residential communities sprouted around railroad stations that were situated six or more miles from the central cities, as the map of Newport in 1775 shows. These small communities provided quiet, pastoral settings for those with sufficient money to afford daily rail trips to and from their jobs in the city.

Even more urban residents could consider moving away from the city centers after the late 1880s, when electric-powered streetcar lines reached into the surrounding countryside. Many of the newer dwellings accessible by streetcar were larger than city homes and sat in the middle of pleasant yards. By World War I, some of the larger cities extended out as far as ten miles from their centers, where most people still worked and shopped. Because streetcar lines did not extend as far in some directions as in others, the overall shape of the cities were star-like, shown in the map of Detroit in 1920.

Population Growth, Automobiles, and Highways Continue the Trend

The Great Depression and World War II required most Americans to defer their desire for new, larger houses in pleasant settings. Once the war ended, however, millions of people returned to the nation's cities, where they married, produced children in record numbers, and searched for bigger homes. Available housing within cities filled quickly, but the automobiles that many veterans purchased permitted them to consider locations outside cities. The GI Bill made money readily available for housing. The result was construction at a rate unprecedented in the nation's history. Between 1947 and 1965, at least 1.25 million new houses were built each year, with more than one half of those units in the expanding suburbs.

In the first decade after the war ended, the number of automobiles owned by city dwellers increased dramatically. In 1956 the federal government established an interstate highway system to connect

After the nation's first enclosed, climate-controlled shopping center opened in 1956, the suburban mall became the new mecca for American consumers.

Newport, 1775

Narragansett Bay

N
W • E
S

■ Buildings

0   50   100 Feet

0   100 Meters

Detroit, 1920

Detroit city limits

Developed areas

Streetcar and bus lines

0   1   3 Miles

0   1   3 Kilometers

N
W • E
S

Detroit R.

major cities. In addition to highways radiating out from city centers, engineers constructed "beltways" that circled cities at distances ranging from six to twenty miles from the core. The result was a dramatic reshaping of metropolitan areas.

Stores and Jobs Follow

As suburban neighborhoods grew, traveling to stores in the city center was no longer convenient. Store owners soon recognized this and built new establishments in suburban locations. Starting in the early 1950s, groups of stores began to cluster together in shopping centers surrounded by large parking lots. After the nation's first enclosed, climate-controlled shopping center opened in 1956, the suburban mall became the new mecca for American consumers.

A major reason for the success of suburban shopping malls was their easy access from freeways. Such locations also were recognized as ideal sites for offices, factories, service providers, and many other forms of economic activity. These businesses grouped themselves in dozens of low buildings straddling heavily traveled freeways and streets and formed what journalist Joel Garreau has called "edge cities."

The growth of edge cities was not without its difficulties. As suburbs became more densely settled, they began to experience the same pollution, crime, and other problems formerly associated with central cities. Of greatest concern to the people who worked, shopped, and lived in edge cities was the increasing traffic congestion. The easy access that attracted so many people to the suburbs was becoming a distant memory. Urban observers today wonder what new forms of transportation will evolve to move people and goods more quickly and easily—and how those new forms once again will transform the geography of American cities.

GEOGRAPHIC CONNECTIONS

1. Why did the earliest large cities develop in waterfront locations?
2. What factors contributed to the boom in suburban housing construction after World War II?

Critical Thinking

3. **Predicting Consequences** Many cities have considered banning cars from downtown streets. How would this affect both cities and suburbs?

619

Domestic Politics and Policy

SECTION PREVIEW

The postwar period created many challenges for American leaders—including the conversion back to a peacetime economy and the debate over the proper role of government in the nation's economic and social affairs. Presidents Harry Truman and Dwight Eisenhower used two very different styles of leadership to meet these challenges.

Key Concepts

- Truman's main task as President was converting a powerful wartime economy to peacetime production.
- Truman wanted to advance the principles of the New Deal through his own Fair Deal.
- In 1952 Americans favored Dwight Eisenhower's modern republicanism, which encouraged expansion without destroying the economic and social programs of the 1930s.

Key Terms, People, and Places

Taft-Hartley Act, modern republicanism, *Sputnik;* Adlai Stevenson, Richard M. Nixon

Enthusiastic Eisenhower supporters during the 1952 election campaign could add this colorful scarf to their wardrobe.

I n the postwar years, political events reflected the economic and social patterns of the country. Middle-class Americans, who grew more numerous all the time, pressured the government to help maintain the nation's newly won prosperity. Democrat Harry S Truman first struggled with the problems of reconversion to a peacetime economy, then fought for a reform program blocked repeatedly by Congress. Republican Dwight D. Eisenhower took a more low-key approach to the presidency. His genial, reassuring manner made him one of the most popular Presidents in the years following World War II.

Reconversion and the Fair Deal

Harry Truman wanted to follow in Franklin Roosevelt's footsteps, but he often appeared ill-prepared for the presidency. He seemed to have a scattershot approach to governing, offering a different batch of new proposals in every speech. People wondered where his focus lay.

Truman's first priority was reconversion—the social and economic transition from wartime to peacetime. Soldiers wanted to return home, and politicians were flooded with messages that warned, "No boats, no votes." Truman responded quickly and got most soldiers home by 1946.

Lifting the economic controls that had kept wartime inflation in check proved a more difficult challenge. Americans had done without thousands of consumer goods during World War II. Now they wanted those goods, and they wanted them right away. The government eased the controls, and prices soared, in the words of one political cartoonist, "over the moon!" Since wages failed to keep up with prices, many people still could not enjoy the fruits of their years of sacrifice.

Meanwhile, angry workers demanded wage increases that they had forgone for the sake of the war effort. In 1946, 4.6 million workers went on strike, more than ever before in the United States. Strikes hit the automobile, steel, electrical, coal, and railroad industries and affected nearly everyone in the country.

Though Truman agreed that workers deserved high wages, he thought that their demands were inflationary—that is, he believed that such increases would push the prices of goods still higher. In his view, workers failed to understand that big wage increases might destroy the health of the economy.

Angry at the disruptions, Truman threatened to draft some striking workers and order them as soldiers to stay on the job. Truman's White House took other steps as well. When

John L. Lewis and his United Mine Workers defied a court order against a strike, the Truman administration asked a judge to serve Lewis with a contempt of court citation. The court fined Lewis $10,000 and his union $3.5 million.

Congress went even further than Truman. In 1947 it passed the **Taft-Hartley Act.** This act allowed the President to declare an eighty-day cooling-off period, during which strikers in industries that affected the national interest had to return to work while the government conducted a study of the situation. Reflecting the widespread anticommunist paranoia gripping the United States at the time, the measure also required union officials to sign noncommunist oaths. Furious union leaders complained bitterly about the measure, and Truman vetoed it. Congress passed the act over Truman's veto.

MAKING CONNECTIONS

Why might Congress have been especially concerned about possible communist ties among union officials?

Truman's Fair Deal Truman had supported Roosevelt's New Deal, and now, playing on the well-known name, he devised a program he called the Fair Deal. The Fair Deal extended the New Deal's goals.

Truman agreed with FDR that government needed to play an active role in securing economic justice for all American citizens. As the war ended, he introduced a twenty-one point program that included legislation designed to promote full employment, a higher minimum wage, greater unemployment compensation for workers without jobs, housing assistance, and a variety of other items. Over the next ten weeks, Truman added more proposals. By early 1946 he had asked for a national health insurance program and legislation to control atomic energy.

In attempting to promote his program, Truman ran into tremendous political opposition. A coalition of conservative Democrats and Republicans opposed him at every turn.

As the 1946 midterm elections approached, Truman seemed little more than another bungling bureaucrat. Some people commented,

"You just sort of forget about Harry until he makes another mistake." Others adapted a well-known saying: "To err is Truman." Truman's support in one poll dropped from 87 percent just after he assumed the presidency to 32 percent in November 1946. In the 1946 elections, Republicans won majorities of both houses of Congress.

The 80th Congress battered the President for the next two years. Under the leadership of conservative Republican senator Robert A. Taft of Ohio, commonly known as "Mr. Republican," the Republican party did whatever it could to reduce the size and the power of the federal government, to decrease taxes, and to stymie Truman's liberal goals.

The Election of 1948 Truman decided to seek another term as President in 1948. He had no reason to expect victory, however, because even in his own party, his support was disintegrating. The southern wing of the Democratic party, protesting a moderate civil rights plank in the party platform, split off from the main party. These segregationists formed the States' Rights, or Dixiecrat, party and nominated

Some supporters of the Truman-Barkley ticket in 1948 attached this sign to their cars' license plates.

In 1948 Truman became the first President ever to campaign in Harlem. The button at left announced his commitment to the civil rights cause.

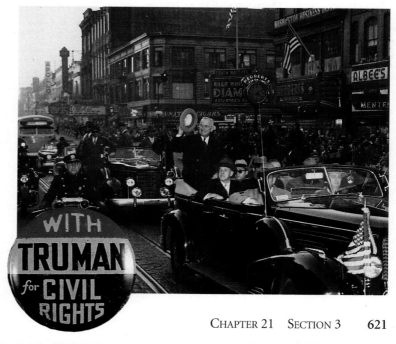

Governor J. Strom Thurmond of South Carolina for President.

Meanwhile, the left wing of the Democratic party deserted Truman to follow Henry Wallace, who had been Roosevelt's third Vice President. Many Democrats believed that Wallace was the right person to carry on the ideas begun by Franklin Roosevelt. Most recently Wallace had served as Truman's secretary of commerce. Wallace had resigned, however, because he did not support Truman's cold war policies.

Running against Republican Thomas E. Dewey, governor of New York, Truman crisscrossed the country by train, campaigning not so much against Dewey as against the Republican Congress, which the President repeatedly mocked as the "do-nothing" 80th Congress. Truman's campaign style was electrifying. In off-the-cuff speeches, he challenged all Americans: "If you send another Republican Congress to Washington, you're a bigger bunch of suckers than I think you are." "Give 'em hell, Harry," the people yelled as Truman got going. And he did.

Among other things, Truman vehemently attacked Congress's farm policy. In the past, a federal price-support program permitted farmers to borrow money to store surplus crops until someone bought the produce. Recently, however, Congress had failed to provide additional storage bins, just as a good harvest loomed on the horizon. Truman told the farmers:

*T*he Republican Congress has already stuck a pitchfork in the farmers' backs. . . . When you have to sell your grain below the support price because you have no place to store it, you can thank this same Republican Congress.

On election day, although virtually all experts and polls picked Dewey to win, Truman scored an astounding upset. He now stepped out of FDR's shadow to claim the presidency in his own right, with a chance to push further for his liberal legislative goals. But over the next four years, the Fair Deal scored only occasional successes, and on balance was disappointing compared to the New Deal the decade before. Truman decided not to run for reelection in 1952. Instead, the Democrats chose **Adlai Stevenson,** governor of Illinois, as their presidential candidate.

Dwight Eisenhower and the Republican Approach

Running against Stevenson for the Republicans was Dwight Eisenhower. As a public figure, Eisenhower's approach to politics differed from Harry Truman's. Whereas Truman was a scrappy fighter, Ike—as the people affectionately called Eisenhower—had always been a talented diplomat. During World War II, Eisenhower forged agreements among Allied military commanders; now his easy-going charm gave Americans a sense of security.

By 1952, Americans across the land chanted, "I Like Ike." The Republicans used a "K_1C_2" formula for victory, which focused on the three problems of Korea, communism, and corruption. Eisenhower promised to end the Korean War, and the Republican party guaranteed a tough approach to the communist challenge. Eisenhower's vice-presidential running mate, Californian **Richard M. Nixon,** hammered on the topic of corruption in government.

The Checkers Speech In spite of his overwhelming popularity, Eisenhower's candidacy hit a snag in September 1952. Newspapers accused Richard Nixon of having a special fund, set up by rich Republican supporters.

The *Chicago Tribune* was so certain of Truman's defeat that it printed this edition before the final election results were tallied. Truman was delighted to see the headline proved wrong.

"Secret Nixon Fund!" and "Secret Rich Man's Trust Fund Keeps Nixon in Style Beyond His Salary," screamed typical headlines. In fact, Nixon had done nothing wrong, but the accusation that he had received illegal gifts from political friends was hard to shake.

Soon, cries arose for Eisenhower to dump Nixon from the ticket. Eisenhower decided to allow Nixon to save himself, if he could. On September 23, Nixon went on television to explain the situation in his own words. With Ike joining a national audience, Nixon delivered one of the most memorable speeches in recent political history. He emotionally denied wrongful use of campaign funds. He gave a detailed account of his personal finances, including his $4,000 life insurance policy and the $38,500 debt on his house and other items. In response to the charge that he was living above his means, he described his wife, Pat, as wearing a "good old Republican cloth coat."

The emotional climax of the speech came when Nixon admitted that he had, in fact, received one gift from a political supporter:

It was a little cocker spaniel dog. . . . Black and white spotted. And our little girl—Tricia, the six-year-old—named it Checkers. And you know the kids love that dog and I just want to say this right now, that regardless of what they say about it, we're going to keep it.

At the end of his speech, Nixon requested that the American people contact the Eisenhower campaign headquarters to register their opinions as to whether or not he should stay on the Republican ticket. The response was overwhelming. People from all across the nation called, wired, and wrote to Eisenhower, demanding that Nixon continue as his running mate. Nixon had turned a political disaster into a public relations bonanza.

In the election, Democratic candidate Adlai Stevenson never had a chance. Ike got 55 percent of the popular vote and swept into office with a Republican Congress as well.

Four years later, despite a number of serious illnesses during his first term in office, the American people wanted Ike back. Eisenhower won reelection—again over Stevenson—with almost 58 percent of the vote. After 1952, however, the Democrats regained control of Congress.

Modern Republicanism

In domestic matters, the President was determined to slow the growth of the federal government. He also wanted to limit the President's power and raise the legislature's and the courts' authority.

Ike's priorities included cutting spending, reducing taxes, and balancing the budget. He called this approach to government "dynamic conservatism" or **"modern republicanism."** He intended to be "conservative when it comes to money, liberal when it comes to human beings."

Ike's natural inclination was to work behind the scenes. One writer has described his style as the "hidden hand." "I am not one of those desk-pounding types that likes to stick out his jaw and look like he is bossing the show," Eisenhower said. Critics misinterpreted his apparent lack of leadership, joking about an Eisenhower doll—you wound it up and it did nothing for eight years. But the American people approved of Ike's style. Eisenhower defended his approach, declaring,

Now, look, I happen to know a little about leadership. I've had to work with a lot of nations, for that matter, at odds with each other. And I tell you this: you do not lead by hitting people over the head. . . . I'll tell you what leadership is. It's persuasion—and conciliation—and education—and patience. It's long, slow tough work. That's the only kind of leadership I know or believe in—or will practice.

Using Historical Evidence Richard Nixon thanked the voters who had shown their support after his "Checkers" speech with this postcard. *What image of Nixon does the photograph promote?*

The "I Like Ike" message was seen everywhere in 1952, even on women's compacts.

House

Control panel (water, electricity, air)

Geiger counter

550-gallon water tank

Water heater

Hot plates

Air blower and filter

5 feet

Wall (16-inch cement)

Earth

Earth

Toilet

Television Radio

Tool storage

Fire extinguisher

Food storage

Oil burner

Generator

Escape hatch

Oxygen cylinders

Battery charger and battery

Sputnik sparked real fears of nuclear attack. Many Americans hoped they could survive a nuclear war in a basement fallout shelter. After an atomic explosion, radioactive particles attach themselves to dust in the atmosphere, which continues to rain down upon the earth for as long as two weeks. In the shelter shown above, an air filter protects people from breathing radioactive dust, and a Geiger counter tells them when the radioactivity outside has returned to a safe level.

In the tradition of past Republican Presidents such as Coolidge and Hoover, Eisenhower favored big business. His cabinet was composed mostly of successful businessmen, plus one union leader, which prompted critics to charge that the cabinet consisted of "eight millionaires and a plumber." For secretary of defense he chose Charles E. Wilson, former president of General Motors, who believed that "what was good for our country was good for General Motors, and vice versa."

Modern republicanism did everything possible to aid corporate America. It transferred control of about $40 billion worth of offshore oil lands from the federal government to the states so that the states could lease oil rights to corporations. The administration also tried to end government competition with big business. For example, Eisenhower sought to eliminate the Tennessee Valley Authority, the New Deal enterprise that provided electrical energy to the public at low cost. Though he failed, in this effort Ike revealed his preference for private power companies.

Ike's attempt to balance the budget backfired. His cuts in government spending caused the economy to slump. When that happened, tax revenues dropped, and the deficit grew larger instead of smaller. Economic growth, which had averaged 4.3 percent between 1947 and 1952, fell to 2.5 percent between 1953 and 1960. The country suffered three economic recessions during Eisenhower's presidency, from 1953 to 1954, from 1957 to 1958, and again from 1960 to 1961.

Eisenhower's Achievements Despite economic troubles, Eisenhower remained enormously popular. And though he tried to cut back on the size of the federal government, he accepted the basic direction it had followed since the Roosevelt days. He believed the government's authority should be reduced, but he understood that the welfare state—in which the government accepts responsibility for providing basic economic security for all Americans—was here to stay.

Sputnik Shocks Americans In 1957 the Soviet Union launched **Sputnik,** the first artificial satellite to orbit the earth. *Sputnik* sped around the world every 96 minutes at a rate of 18,000 miles per hour. The United States, which had viewed itself as the world's foremost scientific power, was mortified. Worse yet, the United States' own rocket, rushed to the launching pad before it was ready, rose only a foot before crashing to the ground.

Critics charged that the apparent stability and security of the United States was, in fact, only smugness and self-satisfaction. Perhaps the institutions most vulnerable to critics' attacks were the nation's schools. Americans questioned whether their children were learning to read, write, and calculate well enough to succeed in an increasingly competitive world.

Another fear prompted by *Sputnik* was the possibility of nuclear attack. The Soviet rocket that launched the satellite might also be used to send a hydrogen bomb to American shores. In one response to anxiety about a nuclear attack, millions of Americans constructed bomb shelters in their basements. The art on page 624 shows a typical bomb shelter of the 1950s.

Less than a year after the launching of *Sputnik* shredded Americans' confidence, Congress passed and President Eisenhower signed into law the National Defense Education Act of 1958. The act provided millions of dollars in low-cost loans to college students and significant reductions in repayments if they ultimately became teachers. The federal government also granted millions to state schools for building science and foreign language facilities.

Besides the jolt to their confidence caused by *Sputnik,* Americans had other reasons to doubt the health of the nation in the postwar years. Some people began to wonder whether the inequalities in American society might be just as dangerous to the United States as threats from foreign nations. The people still liked Ike, but deep troubles were becoming more and more visible.

The blow that *Sputnik* delivered to American self-assurance is reflected in this "Space Race" card game from the 1950s, in which those dealt the *Sputnik* card would lose two turns.

SECTION 3 REVIEW

Key Terms, People, and Places
1. Define (a) Taft-Hartley Act, (b) modern republicanism.
2. Identify (a) Adlai Stevenson, (b) Richard M. Nixon.

Key Concepts
3. What problem did Harry Truman face in reconverting the nation to a peacetime economy after World War II?

4. What were some of the goals of Harry Truman's Fair Deal program?
5. What was *Sputnik,* and what impact did it have in the United States?

Critical Thinking
6. **Recognizing Ideologies** How did Truman's and Eisenhower's approaches to the role of the federal government in solving domestic problems differ?

The Continuing Struggle for Equality

SECTION PREVIEW

The events of World War II—including the fight against fascism abroad and the African American migration at home—breathed new life into the civil rights movement. The actions of many courageous Americans brought significant results in the postwar years.

Key Concepts

- World War II caused changes in American society that led African Americans to demand more equality between the races.
- African Americans used the courts and a protest movement to wage their battle for racial justice.
- Other minorities began to follow the example set by the African American movement.

Key Terms, People, and Places

termination policy; Jackie Robinson, Thurgood Marshall, Martin Luther King, Jr.

The NAACP was one organization devoted to fighting racial injustice in the United States. In the South, African Americans had to use separate facilities at all public places.

Before and during World War II, African Americans were not treated as equals by a large portion of American society. After the war, however, the campaign for civil rights began to accelerate. Thousands of African Americans had served their country during the war and felt this service was a mockery if they were not allowed equal rights in their own country. Hundreds of thousands had moved to northern cities during the war and experienced a new sense of freedom there, in spite of poor living conditions. Millions more simply believed that the time had come to demand that the nation live up to its creed that all are equal before the law.

President Truman, while holding in private many of the racial prejudices he had learned growing up in the South, recognized that as President he had to take action. In 1948 he wrote in a letter to a friend,

I am not asking for social equality, because no such things exist, but I am asking for equality of opportunity for all human beings, and, as long as I stay [in the White House], I am going to continue that fight.

In July 1948 Truman banned discrimination in the hiring of federal employees. He also ordered an end to segregation and discrimination in the armed forces. Real change came slowly, however. Only with the onset of the Korean War in 1950 did the armed forces make significant progress in ending segregation.

AMERICAN PROFILES

Jackie Robinson

The battle against racial segregation was taken up not only in the military but on the professional baseball diamond as well. For years, major league baseball had banned African Americans, forcing them to play in the separate Negro Leagues. In 1946 Branch Rickey, general manager of the Brooklyn Dodgers, decided to challenge the ban. (See "History Might Not Have Happened This Way," page 630.)

Rickey selected **Jackie Robinson** (1919–1972) to be the first African American to break the color line. Robinson had grown up in Pasadena, California, and attended the University of California in Los Angeles. In college Robinson earned letters in football, basketball, baseball, and track and was also a superb golfer, swimmer, and tennis player.

Robinson had a record of standing up against racial injustice. While he was in the army during World War II, a bus driver had snarled at him, "Get in the back where you belong or there'll be trouble." Robinson knew that buses on the army post were not segregated, so he stood his ground. Although he had not broken any rules, Robinson had to undergo a court-martial before clearing his name.

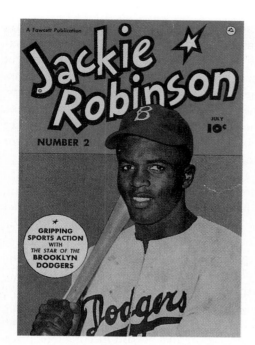

After his brilliant first season with the Brooklyn Dodgers, Jackie Robinson was featured in baseball magazines such as the one above, issued in 1951.

The mental toughness that Robinson acquired from such experiences and his ability to rise above the injustices he encountered served him well during his baseball career. He faced prejudice from fans, opponents on the field, and even his own teammates. Robinson later recalled his first interview with Branch Rickey:

I am a normal man with the feelings of any normal man. If anything, my competitive instincts are so sharp that I will eagerly challenge any man who challenges me. But Mr. Rickey made entirely clear to me that day that I could not behave normally. . . . On my ability to measure up to the challenge would depend not only my future but the future of my race in baseball.

Despite many instances of prejudice, Robinson behaved with dignity and had a sparkling first season. He was Rookie of the Year in 1947 and kept improving with time. Just as important, Robinson fostered pride in African Americans around the country and opened the way for other African Americans to follow him into professional sports.

MAKING CONNECTIONS

In the 1990s Charles Barkley, an African American professional basketball player, insisted, "I am not a role model!" How might the American public have reacted if Jackie Robinson had made that statement in 1947?

Brown v. Board of Education

Beginning in the 1930s, the National Association for the Advancement of Colored People, NAACP, launched a series of court cases aimed at overturning the 1896 *Plessy* v. *Ferguson* Supreme Court decision. *Plessy* v. *Ferguson* held that segregation of the races in public institutions and accommodations was constitutional as long as facilities were "separate but equal."

In 1951 Oliver Brown sued the Topeka, Kansas, Board of Education to allow his eight-year-old daughter Linda to attend a school that only white children were allowed to attend. She passed the school on her way to the bus that took her to a distant school for African Americans. After appeals, the case reached the Supreme

Linda Brown (inset) was at the center of the landmark *Brown* v. *Board of Education* case. African American students like Elizabeth Echford of Little Rock, Arkansas, (below) still had to endure the insults of white students who disagreed with the Court's decision.

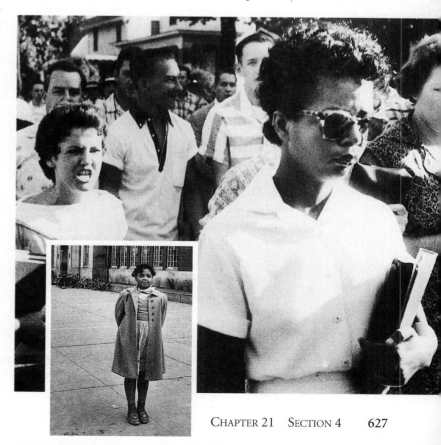

Court. There a brilliant African American lawyer named **Thurgood Marshall** argued on behalf of Brown and against segregation in America's schools.

On May 17, 1954, in *Brown* v. *Board of Education of Topeka, Kansas,* the Supreme Court issued its ruling. It declared unanimously that "separate facilities are inherently unequal." The "separate but equal" doctrine was no longer permissible in public education. President Eisenhower, who privately disagreed with the *Brown* ruling, refused to take a stand, saying only that "the Supreme Court has spoken and I am sworn to uphold the constitutional processes in this country; I will obey." A year later, the Court ruled that local school boards should move to desegregate "with all deliberate speed."

The ruling in *Brown* v. *Board of Education* caused fear and angry resistance in many southern whites. The worst confrontation came at Central High School in Little Rock, Arkansas. Just before the start of the 1957 school year, Governor Orval Faubus declared that he could not keep order if integration occurred. He posted the Arkansas National Guard at the school, and guardsmen turned away nine African American students who tried to enter.

Eisenhower could no longer avoid the issue of segregation. Faubus's actions were a direct challenge to the Constitution and to his own authority as President. Eisenhower therefore placed the National Guard under federal command. With paratroopers and other soldiers on guard in Arkansas to protect the nine African American children, the long, slow process of school integration began.

The Montgomery Bus Boycott

In December 1955, in Montgomery, Alabama, Rosa Parks, a seamstress who had been secretary of the Montgomery NAACP for twelve years, took a seat in the middle section of a bus, where both African Americans and whites usually were allowed to sit. When a white man got on at the next stop and had no seat, however, the bus driver ordered Parks to give up hers. She refused. Even when threatened with arrest, she held her ground. At the next stop, police seized her and ordered her to stand trial for violating the segregation laws.

African American civil rights officials in Montgomery made the most of the incident. Fifty African American leaders met and, after Jo Ann Robinson of the Women's Political Council (WPC) suggested the idea, decided to organize a boycott of the entire bus system. Robinson and other members of the WPC wrote and distributed leaflets announcing the boycott. **Martin Luther King, Jr.,** the twenty-six-year-old minister of the Baptist church where the original boycott meeting took place, eventually became the spokesperson for the protest movement. He proclaimed:

T*here comes a time when people get tired . . . tired of being segregated and humiliated, tired of being kicked about by the brutal feet of oppression. We have no alternative but to protest.*

Using Historical Evidence These participants in the Montgomery bus boycott seemed not to mind getting a little wet as they walked to work. *How did the boycott demonstrate the effectiveness of applying economic pressure to promote social change?*

The morning of the first day of the boycott, King prowled the streets of Montgomery anxiously to see how many African Americans would participate. Here are excerpts from his account of that morning:

During the rush hours the sidewalks were crowded with laborers and domestic workers, many of them well past middle age, trudging patiently to their jobs and home again, sometimes as much as twelve miles. They knew why they walked, and the knowledge was evident in the way they carried themselves. And as I watched them I knew that there is nothing more majestic than the determined courage of individuals willing to suffer and sacrifice for their freedom and dignity.

Over the next year, fifty thousand African Americans in Montgomery walked, rode bicycles, or joined car pools to avoid the city buses. Despite losing money, the bus company refused to change its policies. Finally, the Supreme Court ruled that bus segregation, like school segregation, was unconstitutional.

The Montgomery bus boycott produced a new generation of leaders in the African American community, particularly Martin Luther King, Jr. In addition, it introduced nonviolent protest as a means of achieving equality for minority groups in the United States.

Other Voices of Protest

Mexican Americans also demanded equal rights after World War II. A court case in Texas involving a funeral home that refused to bury a Mexican American war casualty led to the soldier's burial in Arlington National Cemetery in Washington, D.C. Groups like the Community Service Organization and the Asociación Nacional México-Americana found that peaceful protest could slowly bring about some of the results Mexican Americans desired.

Native Americans faced discrimination unique to their situation. The federal government managed the reservations where most Native Americans lived. In 1953, however, the government adopted a new approach, known as "termination," which sought to eliminate Native American reservations altogether. The administration used its **termination policy** to promote assimilation of Native Americans into the mainstream of American life.

Such assimilation did more harm than good. A 1954 Seminole petition to President Eisenhower eloquently stated the Native Americans' pride in their heritage:

We are not White Men but Indians, do not wish to become White Men but wish to remain Indians, and have an outlook on all things different from the outlook of the White Man.

In time the federal government discarded the termination policy. Yet the problems of the Native Americans remained: poverty, discrimination, and little real political representation. For Native Americans, the civil rights advances of the 1950s were mere tokens of the real gains that were needed.

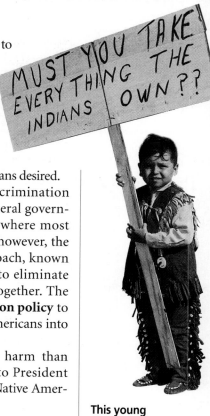

This young protester was part of a 1958 Tuscarora picket in New York. The Native Americans were attempting to block a state power project on their reservation.

Key Terms, People, and Places
1. Define termination policy.
2. Identify (a) Jackie Robinson, (b) Thurgood Marshall, (c) Martin Luther King, Jr.

Key Concepts
3. (a) For what reasons did the civil rights movement accelerate after World War II? (b) What avenues of protest did civil rights activists use in their struggle?

4. What was the principle behind the Supreme Court's ruling in *Brown* v. *Board of Education?*
5. How did Mexican Americans and Native Americans assert their rights in the 1950s?

Critical Thinking
6. **Determining Relevance** Why did Eisenhower feel bound to respond to the use of the National Guard to prevent school integration in Little Rock?

History Happened This Way
might not have
Key Decisions and Decision Makers

The Decision to Integrate Major League Baseball

Time Frame	1945
Place	New York City
Key People	Branch Rickey, general manager of the Brooklyn Dodgers baseball team, and Jackie Robinson, an African American athlete
Situation	Branch Rickey wanted to hire the first African American baseball player in the major leagues and prove that integration was possible. His decision could further African American civil rights in sports and other areas.

Unbelievable as it may seem today, in 1945 African American baseball players were not allowed to play in the major leagues. Many people at the time were beginning to fight for African American civil rights, and the situation in professional baseball attracted their attention. African Americans pointed with pride to athletes like Joe Louis, who was the world heavyweight boxing champion, and Jesse Owens, who won an unprecedented four gold medals in track and field in the 1936 Olympic games. Civil rights activists wanted to see the integration of baseball as well. Branch Rickey, the general manager of the Brooklyn Dodgers, recognized the possibilities integration offered to baseball. Jackie Robinson, a spectacular African American athlete from California, was the man Rickey identified as he considered his options. Rickey began to wonder whether the time had come to end segregation in baseball. As he considered the sensitive issue of integration, Rickey could have chosen any one of several possible avenues.

To Integrate or Not, and If So, How?

One possible avenue Rickey could have chosen was to drop the idea of integrating the major leagues altogether. Although baseball commissioner Kenesaw Mountain Landis declared in 1942 that "There is no rule, formal or informal, or any understanding—unwritten, subterranean, or sub-anything—against the hiring of Negro players by the teams of organized ball," baseball remained rigidly segregated. Most owners and other leaders of the game wanted to keep it that way. Many white Americans agreed.

Another option was to try to enlist the support of other teams before attempting to hire an African American player. Rather than working alone, Rickey knew that persuading other important baseball figures of the merits of opening the major leagues to African Americans would make it more likely that integration would succeed.

A third option was to find a superb African American athlete, such as Robinson, who could endure the taunts and jeers he was certain to receive when he took the field, and to work with him to show other teams—and American society as a whole—that integrated baseball could work.

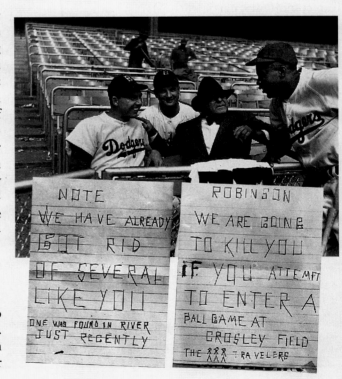

NOTE WE HAVE ALREADY GOT RID OF SEVERAL LIKE YOU ONE WAS FOUND IN RIVER JUST RECENTLY

ROBINSON WE ARE GOING TO KILL YOU IF YOU ATTEMPT TO ENTER A BALL GAME AT CROSLEY FIELD THE ☒☒☒ TRAVELERS

Possible Repercussions

Rickey knew that the safest course was to leave the situation alone and abandon the idea of integration. Major league baseball was prospering, and many people were reluctant to rock the boat. African American players had their own Negro Leagues, such people reasoned, so they had a chance to play. Taking no action was the best way to ensure stability on the field.

Seeking support from other teams, Rickey believed, would backfire. Baseball commissioner Landis and other top officials already had derailed the efforts of Bill Veeck, Jr., the bold young son of the former president of the Chicago Cubs, to buy the Philadelphia Phillies and hire black players. The more people who were involved, the more likely any integration plan was to fail.

Rickey also realized that the final option, simply hiring Jackie Robinson, might well erupt in violence both on and off the field. White ballplayers might refuse to play with Robinson. Fans might stay away from the game. Robinson himself might be hurt.

Rickey's Decision

Rickey decided that he would take what was in some ways the riskiest option: he would hire Jackie Robinson to play for the Brooklyn Dodgers.

Rickey called Robinson into his office on August 28, 1945 and told the ballplayer of his plan. Then, in a calculated move to test how Robinson would respond to the pressure he was likely to face, Rickey acted the part of those who might try to discourage him. He roared insults at Robinson, abused him, and threatened him with violence. "Mr. Rickey," Robinson finally said, "do you want a ballplayer who's afraid to fight back?" Rickey answered, "I want a player with guts enough not to fight back."

Rickey's decision paid off. Robinson played first for the Montreal Royals, a minor league team, then joined the Brooklyn Dodgers to become the first African Ameri-

Goal	To integrate major league baseball		
Possible Actions	**Do nothing and hope integration would eventually take place**	**Enlist the support of other baseball teams**	**Hire an African American player**
Possible Results	• Continue the tradition of segregated baseball, as integration was not likely to occur without some major impetus	• Unlikely to succeed in integrating the major leagues, because strong resistance to integration existed in the baseball community	• Might convince baseball leaders and society in general that integration could work, but might lead to violence both on and off the field

can to play in the major leagues. The photograph at left shows Rickey, seated and wearing a suit, and Robinson (far right). At first, he did have to endure much abuse, including threatening letters like the one on page 630. Robinson's wife, Rachel, worried about him:

A t the end of his first season in baseball, I became extremely worried about Jack. I knew nobody could go along day after day, week after week, month after month bottling up his emotion. . . . He couldn't eat, and at night he'd toss constantly in his sleep. . . . But Jack wouldn't give it up.

Robinson's bravery and Branch Rickey's willingness to take a chance paved the way for future African American baseball players.

EVALUATING DECISIONS

1. Why did Branch Rickey choose not to work with other teams in bringing African Americans into major league baseball?
2. What did Rickey want Jackie Robinson to do when taunted by other players and fans?

Critical Thinking

3. **Predicting Consequences** What do you think Rickey hoped would happen if Jackie Robinson proved to be a success? What might have happened if he had failed?

Chapter Review

Key Terms
1. per capita income
2. real purchasing power
3. diversified conglomerate
4. franchise
5. agribusiness
6. baby boom
7. GI Bill
8. beatniks
9. Taft-Hartley Act
10. modern republicanism
11. *Sputnik*
12. termination policy

People
13. William J. Levitt
14. Benjamin Spock
15. Betty Friedan
16. J. D. Salinger
17. Adlai Stevenson
18. Richard M. Nixon
19. Jackie Robinson
20. Thurgood Marshall
21. Martin Luther King, Jr.

Terms For each term above, write a sentence that explains its relation to the postwar years in the United States.

True or False Determine whether each statement is true or false. If it is true, write "true." If it is false, change the underlined term to make the statement true.
1. The <u>Taft-Hartley Act</u> sought to eliminate Native American reservations.
2. Ray Kroc started the first <u>diversified conglomerate</u>.
3. The launching of *Sputnik* embarrassed the United States, which viewed itself as the world's greatest scientific power.
4. <u>Per capita income</u>, what people actually could buy with their money, grew by about 22 percent in the postwar period.
5. President Eisenhower called his approach to government <u>agribusiness</u>.

Matching Review the key people listed above. If you are not sure of a person's significance, review his or her importance in the chapter. Then choose a name from the list that best matches each description below.
1. African American lawyer who argued on the side of Oliver Brown in *Brown* v. *Board of Education*
2. Democratic candidate for President in 1952 and 1956
3. accused of receiving illegal gifts from political friends
4. pioneered mass-production techniques in home building
5. author of a book that criticized society for limiting the roles of women

Section 1 (pp. 608–612)
1. Why did the United States economy grow so rapidly after World War II?
2. What changes occurred in American business after the war?
3. What changes took place in the work force after World War II? What accounts for this change?

Section 2 (pp. 614–617)
4. What values did middle-class Americans cherish most during the 1950s?
5. Give examples showing how the media fostered expectations about the proper role of women.
6. What challenges to the rigid expectations of the period arose during the 1950s?

Section 3 (pp. 620–625)
7. What was President Truman's first priority after World War II?
8. Why did Truman oppose the demand of labor for higher wages?
9. What were Eisenhower's goals for the presidency? How successful was he in achieving these goals?

Section 4 (pp. 626–629)
10. What steps did President Truman take that helped African Americans achieve racial justice?
11. How did African Americans use the courts and non-violent protest in their battle for equality?
12. Why did Native Americans protest against the federal government's termination policy in the 1950s?

1. **Demonstrating Reasoned Judgment** Which technological advance of the 1950s—atomic energy, computers, or television—do you think has had the most far-reaching impact on the way Americans live? Explain why you think so.

2. **Drawing Conclusions** During the 1950s the United States became, in the words of economist John Kenneth Galbraith, "the affluent society." What might be some of the consequences, both positive and negative, of this abundance?

3. **Making Comparisons** During the 1990s many politicians, religious leaders, and ordinary citizens have called for a return to "family values." What do these family values have in common with the values of the 1950s?

4. **Predicting Consequences** In 1957, the launch of the Soviet satellite *Sputnik* jolted Americans' sense of stability and security. Do you think that a major scientific breakthrough by another nation would have the same effect today?

1. **Evaluating Primary Sources** Review the primary source excerpt on page 629. What assumptions did the federal government make when it created the termination policy to promote Native American assimilation into mainstream American culture?

2. **Understanding the Visuals** Examine the visuals on pages 608, 611, and 612 and describe how the issues represented may have contributed to the dilemma faced by women in the 1950s.

3. **Writing About the Chapter** You have read that in 1956, *Life* magazine published a photo essay titled "Busy Wife's Achievements" about a happy full-time mother of four. Write the text for a *Life* magazine photo essay about a working mother's life in the 1990s. First make a list describing some of the activities in a typical working mother's day, noting her job, number of chil-

dren, and responsibilities. Next, write a draft of your essay in which you describe the typical working mother today, including her achievements and the challenges she faces. Revise your essay, making certain that each idea is clearly explained. Proofread your essay and draft a final copy. If you wish, you may include ideas for photos and captions to accompany the text.

4. **Using the Graphic Organizer** This graphic organizer uses a double web to compare and contrast the presidencies of Harry Truman and Dwight Eisenhower. (a) Based on the information in the web, how were Truman and Eisenhower similar as Presidents? (b) How does the web contrast Truman's personality with Eisenhower's? (c) Create your own graphic organizer comparing and contrasting the concerns of men and women in the 1950s.

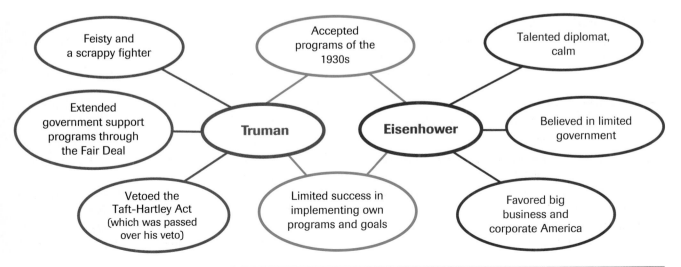

The Upheaval of the Sixties
1960–1975

"Today our concern must be with the future. For the world is changing. The old era is ending. The old ways will not do."
—John F. Kennedy, 1960

When John F. Kennedy became President in 1961, Americans sensed a new era was dawning. Buoyed by the promise of change, African Americans pushed hard to end a century of inequality. Inspired by the civil rights movement, women, Latinos, Native Americans, and others also pressed for equality. Although much progress was achieved in the sixties, the promise that began this turbulent decade was shattered by a series of assassinations, a wave of urban riots, and a controversial war in Southeast Asia.

Inspired by the righteousness of their cause, civil rights workers march toward a better future in this 1965 voter registration drive in Selma, Alabama.

The Kennedy and Johnson Years

1960–1968

*B*old phrases such as "the New Frontier" and "the Great Society" captured the spirit of optimism that energized the United States in the early 1960s. John F. Kennedy, the youngest President ever elected, promised vigorous leadership. His focus on cold war politics and problems with an uncompromising Congress, however, left little room for domestic reform. Kennedy's successor, Lyndon Johnson, did more to help Americans at home. He rallied Congress and the country behind the most ambitious social program since the New Deal of the 1930s. Johnson's foreign policy, based on the assumption that communists were determined to take over the world, led the nation into conflicts with other countries.

Events in the United States

1960 John F. Kennedy and Richard Nixon appear in the first televised presidential debates.

1961 President Kennedy establishes the Peace Corps.
• Bay of Pigs invasion in Cuba fails.

1962 The Cuban missile crisis occurs.

1963 President Kennedy is assassinated.
• Lyndon Johnson becomes President.

1960 | **1961** | **1962** | **1963**

Events in the World

1960 The Soviets shoot down U.S. spy plane.
• The Congo gains independence from Belgium.

1961 The Soviets build the Berlin Wall.
• Soviet cosmonaut is first to orbit the earth.

636

Pages 638 – 641
The New Frontier

President John F. Kennedy's first years in office did not bear the legislative fruit he promised in his inspiring campaign speeches. More interested in foreign affairs than in affairs at home, Kennedy did not shepherd his proposals along the legislative path. Congress, which fought him at every step, contributed to the lack of progress.

Pages 643 – 647
The Great Society

Lyndon Johnson picked up the domestic agenda after John Kennedy's death. In the greatest triumph of social legislation since Franklin Roosevelt's New Deal, he launched a remarkable reform program that offered something for everyone and for a time promised to ease the inequalities in American life.

Pages 650 – 657
Foreign Policy in the 1960s

The drama and seriousness of events on the world stage beckoned Kennedy more than did the problems at home. He performed boldly on several foreign policy issues, with decisions grounded in familiar cold war assumptions about the intentions of the Soviet Union. When Johnson took office, he saw foreign affairs as something of a nuisance, but continued Kennedy's policies.

1964 Congress passes the Civil Rights Act.

1965 Congress passes the Voting Rights Act and establishes Medicare and Medicaid.

1966 Miranda v. Arizona *ruling establishes that suspects must be informed of their rights before questioning.*

1964	1965	1966	1967	1968

1964 Khrushchev is removed from power in the Soviet Union.
• *The military leads coup in Brazil.*

1965 Ferdinand Marcos becomes president of the Philippines.

1966 Chinese Cultural Revolution begins.
• *Indira Gandhi becomes Indian prime minister.*

1967 Israel defeats Arab states in Six-Day War.
• *Civil war breaks out in Nigeria.*

1968 Student uprising shakes France.
• *The Soviet Union invades Czechoslovakia.*

The New Frontier

SECTION PREVIEW

President John F. Kennedy's first years in office did not bear the legislative fruit he promised in his inspiring campaign speeches. More interested in foreign affairs than in affairs at home, Kennedy did not shepherd his proposals along the legislative path. Congress, which fought him at every step, contributed to the lack of progress.

Key Concepts

- The youthful President Kennedy created a popular image that appealed to Americans eager for change.
- Kennedy's program included the space program, a tax cut to restore prosperity, and, near the end of his presidency, direct aid to the poor.
- Kennedy's legislative proposals on domestic policy suffered defeat in Congress.

Key Terms, People, and Places

liberal consensus, mandate, New Frontier, Warren Commission; John F. Kennedy, Earl Warren

Images of the new President and his family flooded popular culture in the early 1960s, appearing even in board games such as the one shown above.

President Eisenhower had steered the nation along a moderate course through the 1950s. In an era of conformity, the popular Eisenhower had presided over a consensus, or general agreement, within the government that the United States was in good shape.

When **John F. Kennedy** took office, he adopted this **liberal consensus** view. According to this view, held by many in government and the public, capitalism was the best economic system and the United States was threatened more by communism abroad than by domestic problems such as poverty and racial injustice. Only at the end of his time in office, when he could no longer ignore the signs that the fabric of American society was being torn apart, did Kennedy earnestly move toward addressing these domestic problems.

The Election of 1960

Kennedy, a Massachusetts Democrat who had served in the United States House of Representatives and Senate, faced serious obstacles in his quest for the presidency. He was only forty-three years old, and many questioned whether he had the experience needed for the nation's highest office. His Roman Catholic religion also seemed a potential problem to some. No Catholic had ever been elected President, and some feared he would be controlled by the Catholic church in Rome. Kennedy defused the religion issue in the primary campaign, when he won in the largely Protestant state of West Virginia. With that hurdle behind him, he campaigned hard, with promises to spur the sluggish economy. During the Eisenhower administration, the Gross National Product (GNP) had grown very slowly, and the economy had suffered several recessions. Kennedy proclaimed that it was time to "get America moving again."

Television played a key role in the election. Kennedy and Republican candidate Richard Nixon, who was Eisenhower's Vice President, squared off in the first televised debates ever held. Television sets now glowed in a majority of American households, and the debates made a major difference in the outcome of the election. Both candidates expressed their views well, but Kennedy, who had hired professional television consultants to help him with makeup and clothes, looked more polished and relaxed. While Nixon looked out at the studio audience, Kennedy looked directly at the camera and thus into the eyes of every television viewer. At the end of the first debate, momentum had shifted Kennedy's way. A CBS poll estimated that 57 percent of the people voting in November felt that the debates had affected their choice.

In the election, Kennedy won by an extraordinarily close margin. Though the electoral vote was 303 to 219, Kennedy won by only 120,000 popular votes out of more than 34 million cast. If but a few thousand voters in Illinois or Texas had cast ballots for Nixon, the Republicans would have won. The razor-thin victory would affect policy decisions when Kennedy took office. With only borderline support, he did not have a **mandate,** or the backing of voters, to push his more controversial measures through Congress.

Jacqueline and John Kennedy dazzled the nation with their beauty, glamour, and youth.

The Promise of Camelot

No matter how slim his margin of victory, Kennedy was now President. In ringing phrases he declared in his inaugural address that "the torch has been passed to a new generation of Americans." He pledged the United States to defend the interests of western democracies at any cost:

L*et every nation know, whether it wishes us well or ill, that we shall pay any price, bear any burden, meet any hardship, support any friend, oppose any foe to assure the survival and the success of liberty.*
Inaugural Address, January 20, 1961

The new administration was buoyant and energetic. Jacqueline Kennedy, the President's attractive young wife, charmed the country with her grace. Nobel Prize winners visited the White House. The Kennedys and their friends loved to play touch football on the lawn or take long hikes. The administration, which seemed full of idealism and youth, earned the nickname Camelot after a 1960 Broadway musical that portrayed the legendary kingdom of the British king Arthur. Arthur dreamed of transforming medieval Britain from a country in which "might makes right"—or the strong always get their way—into one where might, or power, would be used to achieve right. The sentimental idealism of Broadway's *Camelot* seemed the perfect image for President Kennedy.

MAKING CONNECTIONS

In what ways might an image of youthful energy help—and hurt—a new President?

Kennedy's Economic Program

In a speech early in his administration, Kennedy said that the nation was poised at the edge of a **New Frontier,** and the name stuck to the reform programs he proposed. The proposals focused on the economy, aid to the poor, and the space program.

Concerned about the continuing recession, Kennedy hoped to work with the business community to restore prosperity to the nation. Often, however, he faced resistance from executives who were suspicious of his plans. The worst fears of business leaders were realized in the spring of 1962. When the U.S. Steel Company announced that it was raising the price of steel by $6 a ton, other firms did the same. Worried about inflation, Kennedy called the price increase unjustifiable and charged that it showed "utter contempt for the public interest." He ordered a federal investigation into the possibility of price-fixing. Under that pressure, U.S. Steel and the other companies backed down. But business

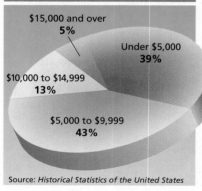

Distribution of Families, by Annual Income, 1962

- $15,000 and over: **5%**
- Under $5,000: **39%**
- $10,000 to $14,999: **13%**
- $5,000 to $9,999: **43%**

Source: *Historical Statistics of the United States*

Interpreting Charts
What percentage of American families in 1962 had an annual income of $10,000 or more? How does the pie chart support what Michael Harrington wrote in The Other America?

leaders remained angry, and the stock market fell in the steepest drop since the Great Crash of 1929.

On the larger issue of ending the economic slump, Kennedy proposed cutting taxes. In 1963 the President called for a $13.5 billion cut in taxes over three years. The measure would reduce government income and create a budget deficit at first, but Kennedy believed that the extra cash in taxpayers' wallets would stimulate the economy and bring added tax revenues in the end. Many people, both conservative and liberal, vigorously opposed the policy. Economist John Kenneth Galbraith claimed that the deficit would cause frivolous spending without addressing serious national problems:

> I am not sure what the advantage is in having a few more dollars if the air is too *dirty to breathe, the water too polluted to drink, the commuters are losing out on the struggle to get in and out of the cities, the streets are filthy, and the schools are so bad that the young, perhaps wisely, stay away, and hoodlums roll citizens for some of the dollars that they save in taxes.*

The tax-cut proposal, like many others Kennedy made, was soon bottled up in a congressional committee and stood little chance of passage.

Kennedy also was eager to take action against poverty. In his first two years in office, Kennedy hoped that he could help the poor simply by stimulating the economy. With his privileged background, Kennedy was out of touch with the brutal realities of poverty. In 1962 author Michael Harrington publicized this problem in a book he called *The Other America*. Harrington revealed that while middle-class Americans were enjoying the prosperity of the 1950s, a shocking one fifth of the population was living below the poverty line. The chart at left shows income distribution in the United States in 1962. Kennedy, who had seen poverty firsthand during the 1960 campaign, read Harrington's book and realized that the situation demanded direct aid to the poor. Despite his concern, however, Kennedy acted to address the poverty problem too late in his presidency, and he never succeeded in pushing legislation through Congress.

Kennedy was more successful in his effort to breathe life into the space program. As astronaut Alan Shepard was launched 115 miles into space in 1961, Kennedy committed the United States to landing a man on the moon before the end of the decade. As the graph at left shows, Congress increased National Aeronautics and Space Administration (NASA) funding for this project.

Camelot in Perspective

Kennedy energized the country with his eloquent call for action, but his legislative record was mixed at best. Foreign policy, covered in Section 3, really concerned Kennedy the most, and his domestic vision was not as focused. He also wanted to avoid making enemies in Congress by pushing unpopular programs; such enemies might refuse to give him the votes he

Federal Funding of NASA* Research and Development, 1950–1965

Millions of Dollars (y-axis): 0, 1,000, 2,000, 3,000, 4,000, 5,000, 6,000

Year (x-axis): 1950, 1953, 1956, 1959, 1962, 1965

Launching of *Sputnik*, 1957

*National Aeronautics and Space Administration
Source: *Historical Statistics of the United States*

Interpreting Graphs
Approximately how much federal funding did NASA receive in 1961, the year Alan Shepard flew in space? How does the graph illustrate the influence of the Soviet Union's Sputnik *on United States policy?*

needed to progress on foreign policy. Kennedy's lack of experience as a legislative leader further eroded his effectiveness. Finally, the Congress, though Democratic, was determined to follow its own agenda and seemed to thwart Kennedy at every turn. For all these reasons, most of Kennedy's proposals died in Congress. Measures that did finally work their way into law, like a modest increase in the minimum wage, barely made a dent in the nation's problems.

The Nation Mourns Still, Kennedy pressed on. On November 22, 1963, as he looked ahead to reelection the following year, he went to Texas to mobilize support. As he rode through Dallas in an open car, shots rang out. Fatally wounded, President Kennedy was pronounced dead soon after his arrival at a nearby hospital.

The country was shattered. Jimmy Carter, a Georgia farmer who later became President, had just gotten down from his tractor when he heard the news: "I wept openly for the first time in ten years, for the first time since my own father died." Millions of Americans remained glued to their television sets for the next four days as the impact of the tragedy sank in. Just as members of an earlier generation remembered where they had been when the Japanese attacked Pearl Harbor, Americans would always recall vividly what they were doing in 1963 when they learned that their President had been shot.

The Assassination Debate Shortly after Kennedy's death, a commission headed by Chief Justice **Earl Warren** was formed to investigate the crime. Despite the fact that the prime

suspect, Lee Harvey Oswald, was himself gunned down two days after Kennedy was killed, the **Warren Commission** declared that Oswald had worked alone in shooting the President. Since then, however, some people have argued that Oswald was involved in a larger conspiracy, and that he was killed in order to protect others who had helped plan Kennedy's murder.

For a time the assassination embellished the Kennedy myth. The myth began to fade with time, but Lyndon Johnson, who succeeded Kennedy as President, made good use of the spirit of hope and the desire for change that Kennedy had inspired. He saw enacted much of the legislation that his predecessor had failed to push through Congress.

Millions of Americans watched President Kennedy's funeral on television. *Inset:* A *Life* magazine cover shows Jacqueline Kennedy and her children during the funeral.

SECTION 1 REVIEW

Key Terms, People, and Places
1. Define (a) liberal consensus, (b) mandate, (c) New Frontier, (d) Warren Commission.
2. Identify (a) John F. Kennedy, (b) Earl Warren.

Key Concepts
3. How did President Kennedy hope to stimulate the economy?
4. Why was the Kennedy administration nicknamed Camelot?

5. (a) What did Kennedy try to accomplish in his domestic program? (b) How successful was he?

Critical Thinking
6. **Drawing Conclusions** Kennedy remarked that in the 1960 election, "it was TV more than anything else that turned the tide." Do you think that television may have given Kennedy an unfair advantage over Nixon, or did it provide voters with information they needed to make an intelligent decision?

GEOGRAPHY

GRAPHS & CHARTS

HISTORIAN'S
TOOLBOX

CRITICAL THINKING

HISTORICAL EVIDENCE

Exploring Oral History

Oral history is made up of people's verbal accounts and recollections of former times and events. As historical evidence, it is one of the oldest and most universal methods by which people have acquired information about the past.

Historians preserve oral history by interviewing people and recording their words on audio- or videotape or in written transcripts. Historians may gather oral history at the time an event takes place or at some later date, perhaps years or even decades later.

Historians often seek out oral histories because they give a unique perspective on the past. Oral histories are a type of primary source and therefore are more valuable to historians than secondary sources. Oral histories record not only facts about the past, but also people's opinions, feelings, and impressions—all important to a historian in putting together a picture of the past.

The excerpt at right is taken from a 1983 interview with John Lewis, an Atlanta city council member, on the twentieth anniversary of President Kennedy's death. In 1963 Lewis was chairperson of the Student Nonviolent Coordinating Committee and one of the leaders of the civil rights March on Washington.

Read the oral account at right and then use the following steps to analyze its content.

1. Identify the nature of the oral account. (a) Who was interviewed? (b) When did the interview take place? (c) What was Lewis's attitude toward Kennedy at the time of his death? (d) Did that attitude change in any way over time?

2. Determine the reliability of the evidence. (a) How might Lewis's role in the events being recollected affect his interpretation of those events? (b) How might events after Kennedy's death have affected the account? (c) What do Lewis's views reveal about his political perspective?

3. Study the evidence to learn more about the historical event. (a) What impact does Lewis think Kennedy's presidency had on government policy and the nation? (b) What can you learn about Kennedy's presidency from Lewis's account?

An Interview with John Lewis:
Remembering President Kennedy's Assassination

"I was living in Atlanta then, but I had gone back to Nashville for a trial. I was getting into a car to go to the Nashville airport when I heard it on the radio. And to me, it was the saddest moment in my life. I had grown up to love and to admire President Kennedy. I remember crying on the plane.

I saw him as a sort of guy that listened. Sincere. Caring. People argue and say that he didn't really do anything. But he did listen, and during that period from 1961 to 1963, I'll tell you, I think probably for the first time in modern American history, we felt, "Well, we have a friend in the White House." On some things we disagreed. We'd call them up and argue and debate with them on some issue, and we said a lot of different things, and sometimes it was harsh. But we saw the Kennedy administration during that period as a sympathetic referee in the whole struggle for civil rights.

His campaign had created a sense of hope, a sense of optimism for many of us. When someone asked him about the civil rights sit-ins that year, he said, 'By sitting down, these young people are standing up for the very best in American tradition.' "

—*Newsweek,* November 28, 1983

The Great Society

SECTION PREVIEW

Lyndon Johnson picked up the domestic agenda after John Kennedy's death. In the greatest triumph of social legislation since Franklin Roosevelt's New Deal, he launched a remarkable reform program that offered something for everyone and for a time promised to ease the inequalities in American life.

Key Concepts

- Lyndon Johnson was a skillful politician who used his forceful personality to get measures passed in Congress.
- Johnson's Great Society included a tax cut, a "war on poverty," health-care legislation, aid to education, and other proposals.
- Supreme Court decisions in the 1960s supported the Great Society, but the program also had many critics.

Key Terms, People, and Places

Great Society, Volunteers in Service to America (VISTA), Medicare, Immigration Act of 1965; Lyndon B. Johnson

L yndon B. Johnson succeeded where Kennedy had failed. Vice President under JFK, Johnson found himself elevated to the presidency when Kennedy was assassinated. Once in office, he used all the talents he had developed as Senate majority leader to push through Congress an extraordinary program of reforms on domestic issues.

LBJ's Path to the White House

Lyndon B. Johnson arrived in Congress in 1937 as a New Deal Democrat from Texas. Johnson took a conservative stance in order to appeal to more Texas voters during his quest for a Senate seat. He won the seat in 1948 by a tiny margin of only eighty-seven votes and was promptly dubbed "Landslide Lyndon"—a nickname that stuck for the rest of his career. In the Senate, Johnson demonstrated both his talent and his ambition by winning leadership posts. In the six years from 1954 to 1960, he became famous for his ability to manipulate the political system to accomplish his goals.

Johnson was a forceful, energetic man. He was "not a very likable man," as former Secretary of State Dean Acheson once told him, but Johnson was more concerned with accomplishment than popularity, and his single-minded intensity enabled him to get his way. Other senators marveled at the "Johnson treatment," in which he carefully researched a bill, then approached in a hallway or office the legislator whose vote he needed. If he thought it was the best way to persuade the legislator, he would attack, "his face a scant millimeter from his target, his eyes widening and narrowing, his eyebrows rising and falling," according to columnists Rowland Evans, Jr., and Robert Novak. He might grab his victim by the lapels or by the shoulders, flattering, cajoling, shouting in turn. And without fail he got the vote.

Johnson was a master of behind-the-scenes dealing in the Senate, but John Kennedy knew more about how to win a presidential nomination. When Johnson's bid for the Democratic nomination failed in 1960, he accepted Kennedy's invitation to run for the vice presidency. Once in office, however, Johnson suffered miserably. He was uncomfortable with the Kennedy crowd, whose Ivy League educations made him feel intellectually inferior. He also was frustrated with the powerlessness of the vice presidency and upset at being away from Congress, where he had been so effective. Then came the assassination, and suddenly he was President.

Johnson sensed the profound shock gripping the nation. He knew that millions of Americans viewed him as the wrongful heir to the Kennedy tradition. He also was aware that he had less than a year to convince the American

The fiberglass sculpture above, which was a gift to President Johnson, portrays him as a rough-and-ready Texan.

When Lyndon Johnson was elected President in 1964, he renewed his pledge to follow through on Kennedy's programs.

Despite strong publicity efforts, including advertising on bars of soap, Republican candidate Barry Goldwater's run for the presidency in 1964 was unsuccessful. It did signal the beginnings of a conservative movement in the United States, however.

people of his competence before running for the presidency in 1964.

Speaking to the nation for the first time after Kennedy's death, Johnson expressed his grief at the loss. "All I have," he declared in this address, "I would have given gladly not to be standing here today." He went on to convey his determination to carry on where the slain President had left off. Johnson's theme was "Let us continue," and he asked Congress to pass the measures that Kennedy had sought.

The Great Society

Congress, also aware that the American people needed some action that would heal the wound caused by the loss of their President, responded to Johnson's appeal. Swift passage of Kennedy's civil rights and tax-cut bills followed. Soon Johnson branched out and sought laws to aid public education, provide medical care for the elderly, and eliminate poverty. By the spring of 1964, he had begun to use the phrase **"Great Society"** to describe his goals. In a speech at the University of Michigan in May 1964, he told students:

Your imagination, your initiative, and your indignation will determine whether we build a society where progress is the servant of our needs, or a society where old values and new visions are buried under unbridled [unrestrained] growth. For in your time we have the opportunity to move not only toward the rich society and the powerful society, but upward toward the Great Society.

Johnson's early successes paved the way to a true landslide victory over Republican Barry Goldwater in the election of 1964. Goldwater, a senator from Arizona, held views that seemed frighteningly radical to many Americans. For example, he

opposed civil rights legislation, and he believed that military commanders should be allowed to use nuclear bombs as they saw fit on the battlefield. The Johnson campaign capitalized on voters' fears of nuclear war and aired a television commercial in which a little girl's innocent counting game turned into the countdown for a nuclear explosion. Johnson received 61 percent of the popular vote and an overwhelming 486 to 52 tally in the Electoral College. Democratic majorities were established in both houses of Congress: 295 to 140 in the House of Representatives and 68 to 32 in the Senate. Landslide Lyndon now had the mandate to move ahead even more aggressively.

The Tax Cut Johnson accepted the idea that had been supported by Kennedy that carefully controlled budget deficits could bring about prosperity. To gain conservative support for Kennedy's tax-cut bill, he agreed to cut spending. Once that was done, the measure passed, and it worked just as planned. As the tax cut went into effect, the Gross National Product (GNP) rose 7.1 percent in 1964, 8.1 percent in 1965, and 9.5 percent in 1966. The deficit, which many people feared would grow, shrank, while the revival of prosperity generated new tax revenues. Unemployment fell, and inflation remained in check.

The War on Poverty Next, LBJ pressed for the poverty program that Kennedy had begun to consider. In his 1964 State of the Union message he vowed, "This administration today, here and now, declares unconditional war on poverty in America." The Economic Opportunity Act, passed in the summer of 1964, created **Volunteers in Service to America (VISTA)**, which sent volunteers to help people in poor communities. The act also set up "community action programs" to give the poor a voice in defining housing, health, and education policies in their own neighborhoods. Poor people were to participate in decisions about the distribution of government money and resources.

Medicare Johnson also focused attention on the increasing cost of medical care. Twenty years before, Harry Truman had proposed a

Federal Dollars to Public Schools,* 1959–1971

Millions of Dollars (y-axis): 0, 500, 1,000, 1,500, 2,000, 2,500, 3,000, 3,500, 4,000

School Year (x-axis): 1959–60, 1961–62, 1963–64, 1965–66, 1967–68, 1969–70, 1970–71

* Elementary and secondary
Source: *Digest of Education Statistics*

Interpreting Graphs
Congress passed President Johnson's Elementary and Secondary Education Act in 1965. *How does the graph illustrate the overall effect of this legislation? By how much did the federal education budget increase between the 1963–1964 and 1965–1966 school years?*

medical assistance plan as part of his Fair Deal program, but it had never been passed into law. Johnson provided the necessary leadership by tying **Medicare**—which would provide health care for the elderly—to social security and confining the new approach to people over the age of sixty-five. "No longer will older Americans be denied the healing miracle of modern medicine," Johnson declared. "No longer will illness crush and destroy the savings that they have so carefully put away." Another program, called Medicaid, met the needs of poor Americans of any age who could not afford their own private health insurance. This broad-based health care program was the most important piece of social welfare legislation since the passage of the Social Security Act in 1935. It demonstrated the government's commitment to provide help to those Americans who needed it.

Aid to Education Johnson was equally successful in his effort to provide funds for elementary and secondary education. Kennedy had fought for a bill to aid public education but

was defeated when Catholics insisted on equal support for parochial, or private Catholic, schools. Bending over backwards to prove that his own Catholicism was not influencing policy decisions, Kennedy had opposed the Catholics, saying that such a provision would be a violation of the separation of church and state. In the process he had lost the entire bill. Johnson endorsed a measure to provide aid to states based on the number of children from low-income homes. That money could then be distributed to public as well as private schools, including parochial schools. The bill passed, and Johnson signed it into law in the small Texas school he had attended as a child. The graph above shows federal aid to schools from 1959 to 1971.

Other Measures As a result of White House prodding, Congress passed a measure to give rent supplements to the poor. It created a new Department of Housing and Urban Development, thus elevating the importance of housing issues. It provided substantial aid to colleges

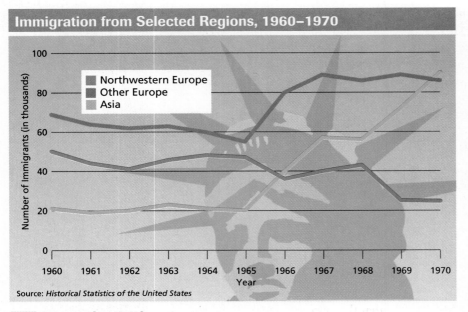

Immigration from Selected Regions, 1960–1970

Number of Immigrants (in thousands)

- Northwestern Europe
- Other Europe
- Asia

Source: *Historical Statistics of the United States*

Interpreting Graphs
What general trends in immigration during the 1960s are shown by the graph? How did the Immigration Act of 1965 contribute to these trends?

and universities. It offered grants to artists through a new National Endowment for the Arts and to scholars through a similar National Endowment for the Humanities. This was the first assistance for such groups since the Works Progress Administration of the New Deal.

The Great Society also reformed the restrictive immigration policy that had been in place since 1924. The **Immigration Act of 1965** eliminated the quotas that had discriminated against all immigrants from areas outside northern and western Europe. It now had a much more flexible limit of 170,000 people from the Eastern Hemisphere and 120,000 from the Western Hemisphere. Family members of United States citizens were exempted from the quotas, as were political refugees. In the 1960s approximately 350,000 immigrants entered the United States each year; in the 1970s the number rose to more than 400,000 a year.

Supreme Court Support

The Supreme Court under Chief Justice Earl Warren supported the actions of Johnson's Great Society in the 1960s. The 1954 *Brown* v. *Board of Education* decision outlawing school

segregation signaled that the Warren Court was prepared to play an active role in politics. As the Johnson administration made good on its promise to promote civil rights, the Court backed up this program. It upheld all measures aimed at guaranteeing African American rights and demonstrated that discrimination would no longer be tolerated.

The Supreme Court handed down several decisions protecting the rights of persons accused of crimes. In the *Gideon* v. *Wainwright* case in 1963, the Court ruled that suspects in criminal cases who could not afford a lawyer had the right to free legal aid. In *Escobedo* v. *Illinois,* 1964, the justices said that accused individuals had to be given access to an attorney while being questioned. In 1966 the Court ruled, in *Miranda* v. *Arizona,* that a suspect must be warned of his or her rights before being questioned. Police must now read all suspects a Miranda warning, which informs accused persons that they have the right to remain silent and that anything they do say may be used against them in court.

In 1965 the Court struck down a Connecticut law that prohibited the use of birth control devices and prevented doctors from sharing information about contraceptives, even with married couples. *Griswold* v. *Connecticut* held that such a law violated a couple's right to privacy. Although the Constitution does not explicitly mention a right to privacy, the Court ruled that such a right was implied because without it, the rights that are specifically guaranteed would be meaningless.

In *Baker* v. *Carr,* 1962, the Court declared that congressional districts had to be apportioned on the basis of "one person, one vote." This prevented the party in power from gerrymandering electoral districts—drawing the lines that established the districts in unfair ways to give themselves more votes. In another area, the Court ruled that religious prayer in public schools was unconstitutional according to the First Amendment principle of separation of church and state. In yet another significant decision, the Court decreed that obscenity laws could not restrict material that might have some "redeeming social value."

The Supreme Court's decisions in the 1960s were controversial. Some conservatives argued that the justices had gone too far and began a long struggle to turn back the new decisions.

MAKING CONNECTIONS

Is the Supreme Court any less political—any less affected by its members' liberal or conservative views—than Congress? Should it be?

Challenges to the Great Society

At first the Great Society seemed enormously successful. Soon, however, criticisms began to surface. New programs raised expectations, and disillusionment followed when not all demands could be met. Middle-class Americans complained that too many of their tax dollars were being spent on poor people. Other critics argued that Great Society programs put too much authority in the hands of the federal government, which could not possibly respond well to the particular needs of local communities across the nation.

At the same time, radicals complained that the Great Society did not fundamentally alter the distribution of wealth and power in a capitalist economy. Tom Hayden, a student leader who was one of the most influential radical critics, charged that Johnson's programs sought simply to maintain the middle class and to provide the poor with middle-class values—but not middle-class incomes—in the process. Hayden declared in 1966 that the Great Society was a failure:

*T*he 1965 antipoverty program *should evoke little optimism. The amount of money allotted is a pittance* [a small amount]. . . ; *its main thrust is to shore up sagging organizational machinery, not to offer the poor a more equitable share of income and influence.*

Michael Harrington, who had helped focus attention on poverty with his book *The Other America,* argued that the amount of money the government spent was not nearly enough: "What was supposed to be a social war turned out to be a skirmish and, in any case, poverty won."

Before his death, John Kennedy had been more concerned about foreign affairs than domestic; when Johnson took office, he placed the emphasis on the latter. The next section describes Kennedy's actions on the world stage and, after his death, the beginnings of a conflict in Southeast Asia that began to consume the resources that Johnson had hoped to spend on his programs at home. His inability to keep that conflict under control undermined and finally ended the Great Society.

Johnson was both criticized and praised for his Great Society but to him, the programs were all good—"major accomplishments without equal or close parallel in the present era."

SECTION 2 REVIEW

Key Terms, People, and Places
1. Define (a) VISTA, (b) Medicare, (c) Immigration Act of 1965.
2. Identify Lyndon B. Johnson.

Key Concepts
3. How did Lyndon Johnson mobilize support for his domestic programs when he became President?
4. What were the key elements of the Great Society?

5. What were some criticisms of the Great Society?

Critical Thinking
6. **Determining Relevance** What role did the principle of judicial interpretation—the power of the courts to interpret the law—play in the 1965 Supreme Court case *Griswold* v. *Connecticut*? Would the case have been decided differently if the Court did not have this power?

Kennedy's Decision to Send an American to the Moon

Time Frame:	November 1960—May 1961
Place:	Washington, D.C.
Key People:	President John F. Kennedy, physicist Jerome Wiesner, NASA head James Webb
Situation:	When John F. Kennedy was elected President, the Soviet Union was rapidly widening its lead in space exploration. The United States needed to find a way to catch up and, if possible, surpass the Soviets in space.

When the Soviet Union launched *Sputnik*, the first artificial satellite, in 1957, a shocked American public worried that the Soviets were gaining a dramatic lead in space. Senator Henry Jackson captured the dismay of many Americans when he declared that *Sputnik* represented "a devastating blow to the prestige of the United States as the leader of the scientific and technical world."

When Kennedy took office in 1960, he assigned a task force, headed by MIT physicist Jerome Wiesner, to evaluate the future direction of the space program. Wiesner's team concluded that the potential scientific payoffs of sending astronauts into space were not worth the enormous costs. They recommended that NASA concentrate on exploratory missions without human crews.

In April 1961, however, Soviet Yuri Gagarin became the first person to complete an orbital flight around the earth. Gagarin's flight rekindled Americans' fears that the United States was falling behind the Soviet Union. Under fire for neglecting his campaign promise to revitalize the space program, the President began to press his advisers for ways to beat the Soviets in space.

Lunar Politics

In the early 1960s, many experts remained skeptical about the scientific merits of sending human beings into space. Sending a person to the moon seemed particularly foolish, both because the moon held little scientific interest and because robots and other instruments could explore it without risking human life.

Financial considerations made the goal of landing a person on the moon even more problematic. Estimates placed the cost of a 10-year project to send an American to the moon at $30 billion to $40 billion. Opponents of the plan questioned the wisdom of diverting so much money and energy to a high-stakes project of questionable scientific value. They pointed to the nation's need for greater spending on public education and social welfare programs. As President Eisenhower bluntly put it, "Anybody who would spend $40 billion in a race to the moon for national prestige is nuts."

Yet a growing number of politicians and scientists—including Vice President Lyndon Johnson and NASA head James Webb—supported sending a person to the

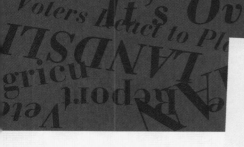

GOALS	Prevent the Soviets from taking control of space; protect American prestige and security		
POSSIBLE ACTIONS	Continue current uncrewed program of space exploration	Begin crewed space program to land an American on the moon within 10 years	Begin crewed program to land on the moon when space technology makes it safe to do so
POSSIBLE RESULTS	• Enable NASA to emphasize scientific discovery at a much lower cost • United States will have more money to spend on domestic problems • Soviet Union may increase lead in space, thus winning greater international prestige	• Project will fail, causing great embarrassment and, possibly, loss of life • Project will succeed, keeping Soviets from dominating space • Project will prove more costly and less scientifically valuable than an uncrewed space program	• Domestic problems will worsen as funds go to space program • Project will lose momentum and never be completed • Project will succeed, putting American space program ahead and advancing scientific knowledge

moon. They believed that the risks could be addressed by careful engineering and that a human could gather much more information than a robot.

The supporters of a crewed space program believed that the race to the moon represented an important battle in the cold war. If the Soviets won in space, the rest of the world might see it as a victory of communism over capitalism. The United States would have to resign itself, as the Vice President put it, "to going to bed each night by the light of a Communist moon."

People who favored a crewed flight to the moon also believed that there were economic benefits to this approach. The race to the moon meant huge contracts and thousands of new jobs for the aerospace industry. In the view of those who supported such a race, science, industry, and education also would profit from technological advances made by a crewed space program.

Some scientists who supported sending people into space favored a third approach. They believed that NASA should wait until space technology was further advanced before attempting to send a person to the moon. They recognized that this emphasis on safety meant it might take several decades to land an American on the moon rather than the relatively short space of ten years.

Kennedy's Decision

Despite the objections, President Kennedy came to believe that a highly visible space program would distract attention from problems at home and abroad. "I am tired of the headlines," he told an aide. "All they describe is crisis, and they give the impression that we have our backs against the wall everywhere in the world." A successful lunar program could erase that impression.

On May 5, 1961, as part of Project Mercury, Alan Shepard became the first American to travel in space. The public's enthusiastic response convinced Kennedy that it was time to submit the moon launch proposal.

In his May 25 special message to the Congress, the President issued a bold challenge to the nation. Rather than continuing an uncrewed space program or taking a go-slow approach in the moon race, he said, the United States "should commit itself to achieving the goal, before this decade is out, of landing a man on the moon." Kennedy's decision finally yielded results on July 20, 1969, when astronaut Neil Armstrong became the first person to set foot on the moon.

EVALUATING DECISIONS

1. What were some reasons in favor of starting a project to put an American on the moon?
2. Why did some people oppose the moon program?

Critical Thinking

3. **Determining Relevance** Lyndon Johnson said that "control of space means control of the world." To what extent was this idea behind Kennedy's decision to send an astronaut to the moon? What other factors contributed to his decision?

Foreign Policy in the 1960s

SECTION PREVIEW

The drama and seriousness of events on the world stage beckoned Kennedy more than did the problems at home. He performed boldly on several foreign policy issues, with decisions grounded in familiar cold war assumptions about the intentions of the Soviet Union. When Johnson took office, he saw foreign affairs as something of a nuisance, but
• continued Kennedy's policies.

Key Concepts
- Kennedy promoted a new program called the Peace Corps.
- Kennedy's commitment to the cold war and his inexperience in foreign affairs showed in his handling of an invasion of Cuba and in his dealings with the Soviet Union.
- The Cuban missile crisis brought the United States and the Soviet Union perilously close to nuclear war.
- President Johnson continued the cold war against communism abroad.

Key Terms, People, and Places
Peace Corps, Berlin Wall, Cuban missile crisis, Limited Test Ban Treaty; Nikita Khrushchev; Bay of Pigs

Long-range missiles capable of carrying nuclear explosives heightened cold war tension. The Soviet Union and the United States could launch nuclear attacks against each other with the push of a button.

W hile Presidents Kennedy and Johnson promised to seek a "new frontier" and a "great society" in domestic affairs, their foreign policy stayed strictly within the limits of the cold war. Communist challenges and the Presidents' reactions to them led to confrontations that seriously threatened world peace.

Kennedy's Approach to Foreign Policy

The rhetoric of Kennedy's inaugural address proclaimed that the United States would do anything to uphold its version of freedom throughout the world. By this, the new President was referring to defending United States interests against the Soviet Union and its allies.

The Alliance for Progress One focus of Kennedy's foreign policy was the promotion of "peaceful revolution" in developing countries around the world. In other words, he wanted to promote changes in foreign countries that would serve the capitalist interests of the United States in order to prevent those countries from aligning with the Soviet Union. To counter procommunist revolutionary movements, the United States wanted to help countries in Latin America, Asia, and Africa. To do so, Kennedy believed that modern transportation and communication systems and stable governments sympathetic to the United States were necessary. Two months after taking office, Kennedy called on

all the people of the hemisphere to join in a new Alliance for Progress—Alianza para Progreso—a vast cooperative effort, unparalleled in magnitude and nobility of purpose, to satisfy the basic needs of the American people for homes, work and land, health and schools.

Address to Latin American diplomats, March 13, 1961

The administration devoted $100 billion to public and private funding to promote economic development and social reform and to sidetrack revolution before it occurred. All citizens in the Western Hemisphere, Kennedy declared, had "a right to social justice," and that included "land for the landless, and education for those who are denied education." Soon, however, Latin Americans began to question whether what was good for the United States was necessarily good for their countries. Because of such doubts, the Alliance for Progress never lived up to Kennedy's expectations.

One answer to such charges that the United States was more interested in its own agenda than it was in helping other countries was the **Peace Corps.** This new program of JFK's would send volunteers abroad to help developing nations around the world. It would, aide Arthur M. Schlesinger, Jr., declared,

replace protocol-minded, striped-pants officials [with] reform-minded missionaries of democracy who mixed with the people, spoke the native dialects, ate the food, and involved themselves in local struggles against ignorance and want.

AMERICAN PROFILES

Paul Cowan

Paul Cowan was one such "reform-minded missionary." After college in 1963 he worked in the civil rights movement tutoring African American children in Maryland. In 1965 Cowan and his wife, Rachel, joined the Peace Corps and prepared to work in Ecuador in South America. After a training program at the University of New Mexico, they went to the city of Guayaquil to do community development work. Their task would be to raise the standard of living in poor areas by pressuring local governments to provide services such as garbage disposal and clean water.

The job turned out to be far more complicated and frustrating than the Cowans had anticipated. An inefficient bureaucracy constantly hampered their work. The local government was almost as poor as the people it served, and its lack of funds made it essentially powerless. "From the day we moved into the *barrio* [neighborhood]," Paul Cowan later recalled, "the question we were most frequently asked by the people we were supposed to be organizing was whether we would leave them our clothes when we returned to the States."

The Peace Corps bureaucracy, which was too often insensitive to the local culture in which the volunteers were

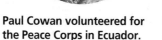

Paul Cowan volunteered for the Peace Corps in Ecuador.

immersed, also frustrated the couple. Cowan returned home upset, like so many students of his generation, with the slow pace and the twisted path toward progress. Yet, as he looked back on his experience, he wrote:

After all the tragedies and frustrations of this past decade, I still believe that someday we will create an America which realizes, with the great Cuban revolutionary José Martí, that "los niños son la esperanza del futuro del mundo" [the children are the hope of the future of the world] and create a society based on that homily.

A Series of Global Crises

The Peace Corps program was one for which Kennedy was, in general, praised. Other actions of his on the foreign scene were viewed less positively. Kennedy's first serious problem arose in Cuba, an island approximately 90 miles off the Florida coast.

The Bay of Pigs The United States had worried about Cuba ever since revolutionary leader Fidel Castro had seized power there in 1959.

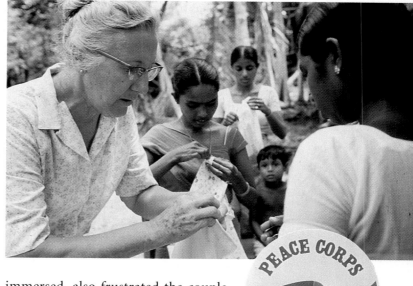

The executive order that created the Peace Corps stated, "They will live at the same level as the citizens of the countries which they are sent to, doing the same work, eating the same food, speaking the same language." The Peace Corps volunteer above is teaching sewing skills to women in Sri Lanka.

Many Cubans had supported Castro because he promised to improve the lives of poor people who were being exploited by wealthy Cubans and by United States companies operating in Cuba. Castro had taken over private property, including that of the United States corporations that had dominated the Cuban economy for decades. He also developed ties to the Soviet Union, particularly after the United States broke diplomatic relations and refused to accept him as the legitimate leader of Cuba. United States officials feared that he could become a model for revolutionary upheaval throughout Latin America.

When Kennedy became President, he learned that President Eisenhower had approved a plan in 1960, in which the Central Intelligence Agency (CIA) was providing military training for Cuban opponents of Castro in Guatemala, a nearby Central American country. When training was complete, an invasion of Cuba at a place called the **Bay of Pigs** was planned. With the expectation that when the invasion began, the Cuban people would use the opportunity to overthrow Castro, Kennedy gave the CIA the go-ahead.

Resistance to the plan soon surfaced, however. When Senator J. William Fulbright, Democratic chairman of the Foreign Relations Committee, learned of the scheme, he called it an "endless can of worms" and declared:

> To give this activity even covert [secretive] support is of a piece with the hypocrisy and cynicism for which the United States is constantly denouncing [condemning] the Soviet Union in the United Nations and elsewhere. This point will not be lost on the rest of the world—nor on our own consciences. . . . The Castro regime is a thorn in the flesh; but it is not a dagger in the heart.
>
> Memorandum to President Kennedy, March 29, 1961

Despite such reservations and those of some military leaders, Kennedy accepted the advice of the Joint Chiefs of Staff to push ahead.

| 1650 | 1700 | 1750 | 1800 | **Links Across Time** | 1850 | 1900 | 1950 | 2000 |

Intervention in Latin America

When the United States invaded Cuba at the Bay of Pigs in 1961, it was neither the first time nor the last that the United States invaded a Latin American country. The United States has often intervened militarily in Latin America to protect its own interests.

Plans for the invasion of Cuba were, in fact, modeled on an invasion of Guatemala, in Central America, that took place in 1954 during the Eisenhower administration. The CIA had backed a group of guerrillas who opposed the elected, procommunist president, Jacobo Arbenz Guzmán. Concerned that Guatemala would become a communist foothold in Latin America, the United States funded a military coup that overthrew the government. Only later did people learn of the CIA's role in the coup.

More recently, the United States invaded both Grenada, an island nation off the coast of Venezuela, and Panama, in Central America. After Grenada's leader, Maurice Bishop, was killed by procommunist members of his own party in October 1983, President Ronald Reagan sent a force of 6,000 United States troops and 300 from several Caribbean countries to Grenada. They removed the leaders of the coup and returned power to the country's original anticommunist government.

Six years later, in 1989, the United States launched an invasion of Panama to oust Manuel Noriega, the head of the Panamanian military. Noriega was indicted in the United States in 1988 on charges of drug trafficking. Although Noriega lost an election in 1989, he disregarded election results and declared himself "maximum leader." At first the United States supported Panamanians who wanted to overthrow Noriega. When their attempt failed, President George Bush ordered an invasion. Noriega surrendered to United States authorities early in 1990, after 24,000 United States troops invaded Panama to ensure his arrest. *How did the reasons for the invasion of Panama differ from those in Cuba, Guatemala, and Grenada?*

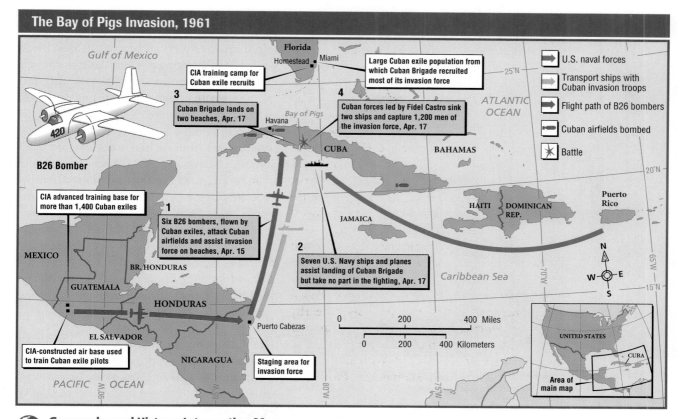

The Bay of Pigs Invasion, 1961

B26 Bomber

CIA training camp for Cuban exile recruits

Large Cuban exile population from which Cuban Brigade recruited most of its invasion force

3 Cuban Brigade lands on two beaches, Apr. 17

Cuban forces led by Fidel Castro sink two ships and capture 1,200 men of the invasion force, Apr. 17 **4**

CIA advanced training base for more than 1,400 Cuban exiles

1 Six B26 bombers, flown by Cuban exiles, attack Cuban airfields and assist invasion force on beaches, Apr. 15

2 Seven U.S. Navy ships and planes assist landing of Cuban Brigade but take no part in the fighting, Apr. 17

CIA-constructed air base used to train Cuban exile pilots

Staging area for invasion force

U.S. naval forces
Transport ships with Cuban invasion troops
Flight path of B26 bombers
Cuban airfields bombed
Battle

Geography and History: Interpreting Maps
This map outlines the ill-fated Bay of Pigs invasion authorized by President Kennedy in 1961. *How were Guatemala and Nicaragua involved in the plan? How does the map show why the United States would want to maintain friendly governments in Latin American nations?*

The invasion, depicted in the map above, took place on April 17, 1961, and was a total disaster. An air strike failed to destroy Cuba's air power. Castro was therefore able to stop the United States–supported troops from coming ashore. When advisers urged Kennedy to use United States planes to provide air cover for the soldiers, he refused. Rather than continue a hopeless effort, he chose simply to cut his losses and accept defeat.

The United States lost a great deal of prestige in the disastrous attack. The nation's illegal effort to overthrow a legitimate government was exposed to the world. The United States faced anger from other countries in Latin America for violating agreements not to interfere in the rest of the Western Hemisphere. And the invasion itself was clumsy and incompetent. European leaders, who initially had high hopes for the new President, were concerned about the kind of leadership he planned to provide.

The Berlin Crisis Upset by the experience at the Bay of Pigs, Kennedy was now even more determined to respond firmly to what he perceived as a growing communist threat. Unfortunately, his first meeting with Soviet leader **Nikita Khrushchev** was another disaster.

This time the issue was Germany. After World War II, the Allies had divided Germany into zones, with the United States, Great Britain, the Soviet Union, and France each controlling one sector of the country. While the original intention was that the zones would be temporary, the lines had hardened as cold war tensions pitted the former Allies against each other. In time the western regions had been combined into one, creating the nation of West Germany, while the sector controlled by the Soviet Union became East Germany. The city of Berlin, lying inside East Germany, had been likewise divided. The Soviet effort to cut off access to Berlin in 1948 had failed as a result of President Truman's

Using Historical Evidence A West Berlin resident walks along his side of the Berlin Wall. *Why was the wall an appropriate symbol of the cold war?*

successful Berlin airlift. Now the Soviets made another effort to resolve problems in Berlin on their own terms. They demanded a peace treaty that would make the division of the city permanent and cut off the flow of East Germans into West Germany, particularly through Berlin.

Kennedy feared that the Soviet effort in Germany was part of a larger plan to take over the rest of Europe. Despite his need to establish himself as a leader in the international community, Kennedy's first conversation with Khrushchev in Vienna, Austria, in June 1961 went poorly. Kennedy felt bullied by the Soviet leader, and he knew he came off second best.

Upon returning home, Kennedy decided to show the Soviets that the United States would not be intimidated. He asked Congress for a huge increase of more than $3 billion for defense. He requested more men for the army, navy, and air force. He doubled the number of young men being drafted into the armed services, and he called up reserve forces for active duty. At the same time, he sought over $200 million for a program to build fallout shelters across the country, with the argument that the United States had

to be prepared if the confrontation over Berlin led to a nuclear war. Kennedy appeared on television to tell the American people that West Berlin was "the great testing place of Western courage and will, a focal point where our solemn commitments . . . and Soviet ambitions now meet in basic confrontation." The United States, he said, would not be pushed around: "We do not want to fight—but we have fought before." This address, strategic analyst Michael Mandelbaum later declared, was "one of the most alarming speeches by an American President in the whole, nerve-wracking course of the cold war."

The Soviets responded by building a wall in Berlin. It effectively sealed East Berliners in their region of the city (and in East Germany) and so ended the immediate crisis. The **Berlin Wall** became an enduring symbol of East-West conflict for the next three decades.

The Cuban Missile Crisis Kennedy had a chance to regain his prestige in another confrontation in Cuba. The Soviet Union, disturbed by the attempted invasion at the Bay of Pigs, had pledged to support Cuba. In October 1962, photographs taken from a United States spy plane revealed that the Soviets were placing offensive missiles on Cuban soil. Khrushchev may have been trying to bolster Soviet standing in the international community by positioning missiles so close to the United States. He may have been trying to show that the Soviets would not allow their Cuban allies to be shoved around. In any event, the missiles did not alter the overall strategic balance, for the Soviets could already inflict serious damage on the United States from missile bases within their own country. But Kennedy was convinced that the missiles in Cuba presented a direct challenge to which he must respond.

The President quickly convened his top advisers in a series of secret meetings. His brother Robert, serving as the nation's attorney general and his most influential adviser, argued against an air strike to knock out the missiles. It seemed, he said, too much like the Japanese attack on Pearl Harbor that had started World War II. Nonetheless, President Kennedy ordered United States forces on full alert. Bombers and missiles were armed with nuclear weapons. The fleet was ready to move. Soldiers were prepared to invade Cuba at a moment's notice.

Kennedy's advisers in the National Security Council realized the dangerousness of the situation in this **Cuban missile crisis,** especially with nuclear warheads poised ready for use. At one point former Secretary of State Dean Acheson joined the deliberations and declared that the United States had to knock out the Soviet missiles. He was then asked what would happen next. The following conversation records his response.

> ACHESON: *I know the Soviet Union well. I know what they are required to do in the light of their history and their posture around the world. I think they will knock out our missiles in Turkey.*
> AN NSC ADVISER: *Well, then what do we do?*
> ACHESON: *I believe under our NATO treaty . . . we would be required to respond by knocking out a missile base inside the Soviet Union.*
> ANOTHER ADVISER: *Then what do they do?*
> ACHESON: *That's when we hope that cooler heads will prevail, and they'll stop and talk.*

After preparing his forces, Kennedy went on television to tell the public about the missiles and to demand that the Soviets remove them. The United States, he said, would not shrink from the risk of nuclear war. He then announced a naval "quarantine" around Cuba to prevent the Soviets from bringing in more missiles. He was careful not to call the action a "blockade," because a blockade is an act of war.

For two days the two most powerful nations in the world stood teetering on the brink of disaster. Soviet ships steamed toward the quarantine line. United States forces were ready to respond as soon as the line was crossed. Then Khrushchev called the ships back, though work on the missile sites inside Cuba continued. A few days later Khrushchev sent Kennedy a long letter in which he pledged to remove the missiles if Kennedy promised that the United States would end the quarantine and stay out of Cuba. A second letter demanded that the United States remove its missiles from Turkey

Viewpoints
On the Cold War

The fear of Soviet communist expansion continued to concern the United States and its allies in the decades following World War II. *How does each of the speakers below propose to battle communism?*

For Coexistence with the Soviet Union
"*Some may object that, as a practical matter, the fire spread by communism can be fought effectively only with fire. I disagree. . . . Our duty is to show that between communism and the flickering old order, the United States recognizes a third choice—permissive societies whose central purpose is to embody [represent and act on] the peoples' will and the peoples' needs.*"
Senator J. W. Fulbright of Arkansas in an address to the United States Senate, June 29, 1961

For Aggression Against the Soviet Union
"*It is our purpose to win the cold war, not merely wage it in the hope of attaining a standoff. . . . [I]t is really astounding that our government has never stated its purpose to be that of complete victory over the tyrannical forces of international communism. . . . We need a declaration that our intention is victory. . . . And we need an official act, such as the resumption of nuclear testing, to show our own peoples and the other freedom-loving peoples of the world that we mean business.*"
Senator Barry Goldwater of Arizona in an address to the United States Senate, July 14, 1961

in exchange for the withdrawal of Soviet missiles in Cuba. The United States accepted the terms of the first note and ignored the second. With that, the crisis was over. As Secretary of State Dean Rusk observed to President Kennedy, "We have won a considerable victory. You and I are still alive."

In the Cuban missile crisis, the world was closer than ever before to nuclear war. Far more powerful hydrogen bombs had replaced the first atomic weapons, and this was the closest the superpowers had come to using them. For a time, Kennedy emerged from the confrontation as a hero. He had stood up to the Soviets and shown that the United States would not be pushed around. His reputation, and that of the Democratic party, improved, and popular support

The tongue-in-cheek slogan on this bumper sticker refers to the Soviet missiles in Cuba, which marked the presence of the enemy only 90 miles off the Florida coast.

helped with mid-term congressional elections just weeks away. In time, however, critics came to suggest that what Kennedy felt was his finest hour was actually a rash and extreme response to a situation that could have been handled more rationally. Kennedy had not used traditional diplomatic channels to try to defuse the crisis, but rather had proclaimed his willingness to move to the brink of nuclear war and even beyond. He avoided disaster, Dean Acheson later observed, by "plain dumb luck."

The Cuban missile crisis did lead to a number of efforts to reduce the risk of nuclear war. Once the confrontation was over, Kennedy and Khrushchev established a "hot line" between their two nations to allow for immediate discussion in the event of a future crisis. In the summer of 1963, they also signed the first nuclear treaty since the development of the atomic bomb. The **Limited Test Ban Treaty** banned nuclear testing above the ground, and so eliminated the radioactive fallout that was threatening to contaminate human, animal, and plant life. It still permitted underground testing, and scientists proved

resourceful in creating bigger and better bombs that way, but it was nonetheless, as Kennedy noted, "an important first step toward peace, a step toward reason, a step away from war."

Yet despite such steps, turmoil still afflicted the relationship between the United States and the Soviet Union. In Southeast Asia, conflict between communist North Vietnam and United States–backed South Vietnam was escalating. In the years ahead, it would lead the United States into war.

MAKING CONNECTIONS

Do you agree with Robert Kennedy that for the United States to strike Soviet missile sites in Cuba would have been similar to the Japanese attack on Pearl Harbor? Explain your answer.

LBJ and Foreign Affairs

Whereas Kennedy had been passionately concerned with the world abroad, President Johnson was preoccupied with domestic policy. Johnson was convinced that he could cajole foreign leaders with the same ease with which he controlled policymakers at home. His dismissive attitude toward smaller countries led the United States into some large and costly conflicts.

Trouble in Panama Johnson was frustrated by what he called those "piddly little" countries in Latin America. Soon after he had assumed the presidency, Panama asked for a renegotiation of the treaty Theodore Roosevelt had signed in 1903 guaranteeing the United States access to the Canal Zone. The symbolic issue of which flag—the United States or the Panamanian—should fly in the zone led to a riot and loss of life. Johnson phoned the Panamanian leader and helped cool the situation, then authorized discussions that eventually led to a new treaty.

Invasion of the Dominican Republic In the Dominican Republic, Johnson acted more aggressively. In 1965 he heard that the military rulers in this Caribbean nation close to Cuba had been attacked by rebels, and that the

After coming close to war with the Soviets early in his presidency, Kennedy signed the Limited Test Ban Treaty in 1963. In a nationwide television address following the signing, Kennedy said, "Let us, if we can, step back from the shadows of war and seek out the way of peace."

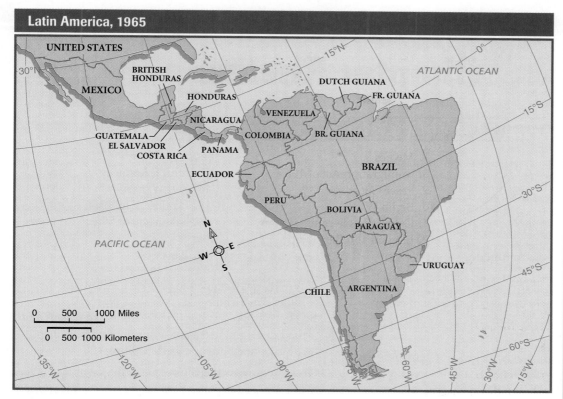

Latin America, 1965

UNITED STATES
30°N
MEXICO
BRITISH HONDURAS
HONDURAS
GUATEMALA
EL SALVADOR
COSTA RICA
NICARAGUA
PANAMA
VENEZUELA
COLOMBIA
ECUADOR
PERU
BOLIVIA
PARAGUAY
CHILE
ARGENTINA
URUGUAY
DUTCH GUIANA
FR. GUIANA
BR. GUIANA
BRAZIL
15°N
0°
15°S
30°S
45°S
60°S
ATLANTIC OCEAN
PACIFIC OCEAN

0   500   1000 Miles
0   500 1000 Kilometers

135°W 120°W 105°W 90°W 60°W 45°W 30°W 15°W

Geography and History: Interpreting Maps
President Johnson often felt annoyed when faced with problems in Latin America that took his attention away from domestic policy. *In the context of the cold war, why did United States leaders consider it important to maintain a strong presence in this part of the world?*

disruption might endanger United States citizens living there. LBJ was livid. Arguing (wrongly, it turned out) that communist elements were causing the disruption, he sent 22,000 marines to the Dominican Republic. The presence of the United States forces tipped the balance away from the rebels. Johnson's action promoted stability in the Dominican Republic, but only at the cost of supporting a repressive military government.

Meanwhile, the Vietnam War began and soon consumed more and more resources. Johnson tried to take the same approach in Vietnam as he had in the Dominican Republic. As will be discussed in Chapter 25, his policy there had much more disastrous results.

SECTION 3 REVIEW

Key Terms, People, and Places
1. Define (a) Peace Corps, (b) Berlin Wall, (c) Limited Test Ban Treaty.
2. Identify Nikita Khrushchev.
3. Identify Bay of Pigs.

Key Concepts
4. What was the significance of Kennedy's confrontation with Khrushchev over Berlin?
5. What was the Cuban missile crisis, and how did it end?

6. Was President Johnson's approach to foreign affairs similar to or different from Kennedy's? Explain your answer.

Critical Thinking
7. **Demonstrating Reasoned Judgment** Dean Acheson called Kennedy's success in the Cuban missile crisis a result of "plain dumb luck." Do you agree or disagree with this opinion? Give reasons to support your answer.

Chapter Review

Key Terms

1. liberal consensus
2. mandate
3. New Frontier
4. Warren Commission
5. Great Society
6. Volunteers in Service to America

7. Medicare
8. Immigration Act of 1965
9. Peace Corps
10. Berlin Wall
11. Cuban missile crisis
12. Limited Test Ban Treaty

People

13. John F. Kennedy
14. Earl Warren
15. Lyndon B. Johnson
16. Nikita Khrushchev

Places

17. Bay of Pigs

Terms For each term above, write a sentence that explains how it relates to domestic and foreign policy during the presidencies of John F. Kennedy and Lyndon B. Johnson.

True or False Determine whether each statement is true or false. If it is true, write "true." If it is false, change the underlined term to make the statement true.

1. Lyndon Johnson's <u>New Frontier</u> focused on domestic policy.
2. President Kennedy's <u>Medicare</u> program sent American volunteers abroad to help people in developing countries.
3. The <u>Warren Commission</u> prohibited above-ground nuclear testing.

4. <u>VISTA</u> was designed to provide medical care for older Americans.
5. <u>The Limited Test Ban Treaty</u> eliminated quotas that had discriminated against immigrants from areas outside northern and western Europe.

Matching Review the key people in the list above. If you are not sure of a person's significance, review that person in the chapter. Then choose a name from the list that best matches each description below.

1. the head of the group that investigated the Kennedy assassination
2. the leader who ordered United States forces on full alert during the Cuban missile crisis
3. the creator of the Great Society

Section 1 (pp. 638 – 641)

1. Explain why the Kennedy administration was compared to the Broadway musical *Camelot*.
2. What domestic programs did Kennedy propose?
3. Why was Kennedy's domestic policy largely unsuccessful?
4. (a) How did the nation react to Kennedy's assassination in 1963? (b) What later actions were taken to investigate his death?

Section 2 (pp. 643 – 647)

5. How did Lyndon Johnson's personality help him advance his political career?
6. Explain Johnson's statement to University of Michigan students that they had the opportunity to move "upward toward the Great Society."

7. Describe three Supreme Court decisions of the 1960s that supported the ideals of the Great Society.
8. What criticisms of the Great Society surfaced?

Section 3 (pp. 650 – 657)

9. For what reasons did President Kennedy initiate the Peace Corps?
10. What did the invasion at the Bay of Pigs and the Berlin crisis reveal about President Kennedy's foreign policy?
11. How did President Kennedy interpret the presence of Soviet missiles in Cuba?
12. What was Johnson's approach to foreign policy?
13. How did foreign affairs affect Johnson's Great Society programs?

1. **Making Comparisons** Describe the programs you would implement if you were to create a Great Society today. In what ways would they be similar to the programs of Johnson's Great Society?

2. **Predicting Consequences** How did the beliefs of Kennedy and Johnson about the spread of communism abroad lead to United States involvement in the Vietnam War?

1. **Evaluating Primary Sources** Review the first primary source excerpt on page 655. What does this conversation reveal about the way in which ideologies—fundamental political beliefs—determined the actions of the United States and Soviet governments during the cold war?

2. **Understanding the Visuals** Look at the tables on page 640. How might the facts illustrated in the table on income distribution have affected President Kennedy's ability to influence Congress to change NASA spending, as shown in the second table?

3. **Writing About the Chapter** You are a top adviser to President Kennedy when photos from a United States spy plane reveal the presence of Soviet missiles in Cuba. Write a memo advising the President on how to handle the situation. First, make a list of the various actions that the President might take. Note both the positive and negative aspects of each. Next, write a draft of your memo in which you offer each possibility, describe its pros and cons, and finish with your recommendation for the best course of action. Revise your memo, making certain that each possible course of action is clearly explained. Proofread your memo and draft a final copy.

4. **Using the Graphic Organizer** This graphic organizer uses a tree map to organize information about foreign policy in the 1960s. (a) Based on the information in the tree map, what earlier event may have caused President Kennedy to need to regain the respect of the international community during the Cuban missile crisis? (b) What was the Soviet response to Kennedy's declaration that West Berlin was a testing ground for Western resolve? (c) On a separate sheet of paper, create your own tree map about the Great Society, using this tree map as an example.

Foreign Policy in the 1960s

Kennedy Inaugural Address
- JFK pledges to defend United States interests against the Soviet Union
- He promotes "peaceful revolution" in developing countries

Bay of Pigs
- Castro stops United States–backed troops from coming ashore
- United States loses prestige

Berlin Crisis
- JFK sees Berlin as testing ground for United States resolve
- Soviets build Berlin Wall

Cuban Missile Crisis
- JFK tries to regain respect
- United States and Soviet Union come to brink of nuclear war; Soviets back down

LBJ in the Cold War
- LBJ sends marines to Dominican Republic
- United States becomes more deeply involved in Vietnam conflict

The Civil Rights Movement
1960–1968

*A*fter scoring major legal victories through the 1950s, the civil rights movement enjoyed a groundswell of popular support in the 1960s. African Americans and others focused their attention on ending segregation and securing voting rights in the South. The battle against inequality was a bitter and often violent one, but it yielded significant results by the middle of the decade. Once desegregation was under way, the movement began to address the more subtle issues of economic injustice that plagued the nation's urban centers.

we shall overcome

register-vote

1962 James Meredith becomes the first African American student to attend the University of Mississippi.

1963 Martin Luther King writes his "Letter from a Birmingham Jail."
• The March on Washington takes place.

1961 Freedom Riders challenge segregation on interstate buses.

Events in the United States

1960	1961	1962	1963

Events in the World

1960 Congo and Nigeria win independence.
• South Africa bans the African National Congress.

1961 Mao Zedong's economic plan, the Great Leap Forward, ends in China.

1962 Algeria and Uganda win independence.
• The Soviet Union removes missiles from Cuba.

1963 The Organization of African Unity is founded.

1964	1965	1966	1967	1968
1964 Congress passes the Civil Rights Act. • Three young civil rights activists are killed in Mississippi.	**1965** Congress passes Voting Rights Act. • Malcolm X is assassinated. • Watts riot occurs.	**1966** The militant Black Panther party is founded. • Splits develop in civil rights movement.		**1968** The Kerner Commission publishes its report on civil disobedience.
1964 The Beatles achieve international fame as rock musicians. • Palestine Liberation Organization is founded.		**1966** The Cultural Revolution begins in China.	**1967** First successful human heart transplant takes place in South Africa. • Israel defeats Arabs in Six-Day War.	**1968** Japanese novelist Kawabata Yasunari wins Nobel Prize in literature.

Leaders and Strategies

SECTION PREVIEW

Civil rights groups in the 1960s were as diverse as the people in the movement. Each group had its own priorities, but all spoke up against violence and unfair treatment of African Americans with a clear, strong voice that said, "No more."

The Congress of Racial Equality was one of many civil rights groups committed to improving the status of African Americans. This hat was designed to be worn at the 1963 March on Washington.

Key Concepts
- The civil rights movement consisted of many separate groups, each with a slightly different aim within the larger goal of social equality.
- Martin Luther King, Jr., was a Southern Baptist minister who became a leader in the civil rights movement through his powerful speaking and commitment to nonviolent resistance.

Key Terms, People, and Places
interracial, Congress of Racial Equality (CORE), Southern Christian Leadership Conference (SCLC), Student Nonviolent Coordinating Committee (SNCC)

The civil rights movement was composed of ordinary citizens whose courage and determination to end racial injustice in the United States brought remarkable changes to the nation. As in all grassroots movements, the motivation for change came from the experiences and beliefs of a large number of people at the local level, not from a central organization directing activities. Several groups did form, however, out of the need to share information and coordinate activities within the movement. Each of the groups described in this section had its own goals and concerns, but all of them helped to focus the energies of thousands of Americans committed to securing civil rights for all citizens.

The NAACP Focuses on Legal Issues

By the time the civil rights movement began to make its impact felt in the 1960s, the National Association for the Advancement of Colored People (NAACP) was one of the oldest civil rights organizations in the United States. It had been founded in 1910 to promote equality, remove obstacles to voting for all Americans, and secure full legal equality. W.E.B. Du Bois, a prominent African American scholar who had been one of the founding members, summarized the NAACP's goals in a memo to its board of directors: +local level

> The main object of this association is to secure for colored people, and particularly for Americans of Negro descent, free and equal participation in the democracy of modern culture. This means the clearing away of obstructions to such participation, effort toward fitting these people for this participation, and it means also the making of a world democracy in which all men may participate.

The NAACP was **interracial**—it consisted of both African Americans and white Americans working together for the common goal of equality. Du Bois, who was the first African American to receive a doctoral degree from Harvard University, served as director of publicity and research. He also edited the NAACP magazine, the *Crisis*.

One major focus of NAACP activity was to put an end to lynching. The organization's efforts succeeded in getting two antilynching bills passed by the House of Representatives in the 1930s. Southern leaders in the Senate prevented these bills from becoming law, but the NAACP kept the issue of lynching in the public eye.

The NAACP was more successful in its court battles. In the 1920s and 1930s, it had won a number of legal battles in the areas of

Using Historical Evidence The NAACP was committed to stopping the practice of lynching. In the photo at left, taken in 1930, a crowd in Marion, Indiana, witnesses the lynching of two African American men. The men were dragged from jail by a mob after being accused of killing a white man. *How would you describe the attitude of the people in the crowd?*

housing and education and scored a major victory in the 1954 *Brown* v. *Board of Education* decision. (See Chapter 21, Section 4.)

Although the NAACP appealed primarily to middle- and upper-class African Americans, it also welcomed the support of whites in the effort to end social and political discrimination. Sometimes, in its emphasis on achieving legal equality for all races, the organization appeared out of touch with the more basic issues of economic survival faced by many African American citizens.

Other organizations emerged to fill that gap. The National Urban League, founded in 1911, sought to assist people moving to major American cities. It helped African Americans moving out of the South find homes and jobs and made sure that they received fair treatment at work. Urban League workers looked for migrant families on ship docks and at train stations. They placed them in apartments they had inspected, and they insisted factory owners and union leaders teach African American workers the skills that could lead to better jobs. Urban League activities complemented those of the NAACP.

CORE Continues Its Fight

The **Congress of Racial Equality (CORE)** took another approach. It had been founded in 1942 by pacifists dedicated to bringing about change through peaceful confrontation. It too was interracial, including both African American and white members. During World War II, CORE had organized demonstrations against segregation in cities including Baltimore, Chicago, Denver, and Detroit.

In the years after World War II, CORE director James Farmer worked without pay in order to keep the organization alive. The growing interest in civil rights in the 1950s gave him a new base of support and allowed him to turn CORE into a national organization. It would soon play a major role in the confrontations that lay ahead.

SCLC: A Southern Group Emerges

Another key organization in the civil rights movement was the **Southern Christian Leadership Conference (SCLC)**. It was founded in 1957 by Martin Luther King, Jr.,

Viewpoints
On School Integration

In parts of the Deep South, the battle for equal rights continued to be fought at the nation's schoolhouse doors each September, even after the Supreme Court ordered schools to desegregate in 1954. *How do the viewpoints below reflect the course of the civil rights movement of the 1960s?*

For School Integration
"Nearly nine years have elapsed since the Supreme Court ruled that state laws requiring or permitting segregated schools violate the Constitution. That decision represented both good law and good judgment—it was both legally and morally right. Since that time it has become increasingly clear that neither violence nor legalistic measures will be tolerated as a means of thwarting court-ordered desegregation."

President John F. Kennedy,
message to Congress, February 28, 1963

Against School Integration
"I draw the line in the dust and toss the gauntlet before the feet of tyranny and I say segregation today, segregation tomorrow, segregation forever."

Governor George Wallace (Alabama),
inaugural address, January 14, 1963

It was SCLC that shifted the focus of the civil rights movement to the South. Other civil rights organizations had been dominated by northerners. Now southern African American church leaders moved into the forefront of the struggle for equal rights.

Martin Luther King Leads a Movement
King used his post at SCLC to become a leader in the national civil rights movement. He had been born in Atlanta and raised in a prominent Baptist family. Both his father and his grandfather were ministers, and he followed in their footsteps. King grew up memorizing biblical passages and watching members of his family fight for African American rights. He went to Morehouse College in Atlanta, then received a divinity degree from the Crozer Theological Seminary in Pennsylvania. He later earned his Ph.D. from Boston University. He preached to his first congregation in Montgomery, Alabama. Before he was thirty years old, King was playing a central role in the civil rights movement as a result of his articulate leadership of the bus boycott.

King was influenced by the beliefs of Mohandas Gandhi. Gandhi was a great Indian leader who had won a fierce struggle to gain his country's independence from Great Britain in 1947. Gandhi preached that nonviolence was the only way to achieve victory against much stronger foes. It would not help to fight violence with violence. Rather, those who fought for justice must peacefully refuse to obey unjust laws and must remain nonviolent—regardless of the violent reaction such peaceful resistance might provoke.

Nonviolence Training As the Montgomery boycott came to a successful conclusion, King began training followers for what they might expect in the months ahead. Films describing Gandhi's activities were shown regularly in African American congregations. Songs and theatrical skits served to underscore the success of passive resistance in India. A leaflet urged bus boycotters to follow seventeen rules for maintaining a nonviolent approach as they prepared to ride newly desegregated vehicles. Among those rules were:

and other African American clergymen after their success in the Montgomery bus boycott (see Chapter 21). Initially, sixty African Americans from ten states convened in Atlanta, Georgia, and agreed that they needed to coordinate their efforts. They urged African Americans "to assert their human dignity" and to refuse "further cooperation with evil." A month later, one hundred African American ministers took the next step they had agreed on and met in New Orleans, Louisiana. Later they elected King president of what came to be called the Southern Christian Leadership Conference. In its first official statement, SCLC called on African Americans

to understand that nonviolence is not a symbol of weakness or cowardice, but as Jesus demonstrated, nonviolent resistance transforms weakness into strength and breeds courage in the face of danger.

*P*ray for guidance and commit yourself to complete nonviolence in word and action as you enter the bus. . . . Be loving enough to absorb evil and understanding enough to turn an enemy into a friend. . . . If cursed, do not curse back. If pushed, do not push back. If struck, do not strike back, but evidence love and goodwill at all times. . . . If another person is being molested, do not arise to go to his defense, but pray for the oppressor and use moral and spiritual force to carry on the struggle for justice. . . . Do not be afraid to experiment with new and creative techniques for achieving reconciliation and social change. . . . If you feel you cannot take it, walk for another week or two [rather than ride the bus].

Nonviolent protest was a practical strategy in the civil rights struggle, but it also represented a moral philosophy. "To accept passively an unjust system is to cooperate with that system; thereby the oppressed become as evil as the oppressor," King said. "Noncooperation with evil is as much a moral obligation as is cooperation with good." King's message, eloquently delivered, told African Americans that they would be victorious in the end. At the same time, it forced whites to confront the difficulties African Americans faced and persuaded many of them to offer their support to the movement for change.

MAKING CONNECTIONS

What do you think are some of the strengths and weaknesses of nonviolent protest as a means to bring about social change? Do you think this approach would be effective in the 1990s?

SNCC Breaks Away

The **Student Nonviolent Coordinating Committee (SNCC,** pronounced "snick") was originally part of SCLC. In the spring of 1960, as the movement was heating up, SCLC executive director Ella Baker organized a conference

for students active in the struggle. Baker believed that the NAACP and SCLC had not kept up with the demands of young African Americans, and she wanted to provide a way for them to play an even greater role in the movement. More than two hundred students showed up for her meeting in North Carolina. Most came from southern communities, but some northerners attended as well.

Baker delivered the opening address. "The younger generation is challenging you and me," she told the adults present. "They are asking us to forget our laziness and doubt and fear, and follow our dedication to the truth to the bitter end." Martin Luther King spoke next and called the civil rights movement

a revolt against the apathy and complacency of adults in the Negro community; against Negroes in the middle class who indulge in buying cars and homes instead of taking on the great cause that will really solve their problems; against those who have become so afraid they have yielded to the system.

At the end of the meeting, the participants organized a temporary coordinating committee. A month later, fifteen student leaders met with Baker and other SCLC and CORE leaders and

On the night of April 26, 1960, burning crosses—the symbol of the Ku Klux Klan—appeared in the front yards of many African American residents of Atlanta. Above, Martin Luther King, Jr., removes a cross from his lawn as his young son looks on.

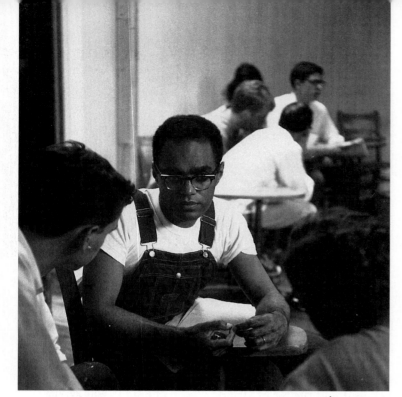

Robert Moses helped train SNCC volunteers in Ohio in 1964. His low-key style was well suited to SNCC, which strove for democracy rather than rigid leadership. SNCC member Jane Stembridge summed up the philosophy: "Finally it all boils down to human relationships. . . . Love alone is radical. Political statements are not."

American students to come to SNCC meetings. While Martin Luther King spoke with eloquence and passion, Moses was much more soft spoken. He took time to gather his thoughts, and then he spoke slowly. Todd Gitlin, a white student activist leader, later noted that Moses was loved and trusted "*precisely because* he seemed humble, ordinary, accessible." Gitlin went on to describe Moses's style:

> H*e liked to make his points with his hand, starting with palm downturned, then opening his hand outward toward his audience, as if delivering the point for inspection, nothing up his sleeve. The words seemed to be extruded* [thrust forth], *with difficulty, out of his depths. What he said seemed earned. . . . To teach his unimportance, he was wont* [accustomed] *to crouch in the corner or speak from the back of the room, hoping to hear the popular voice reveal itself.*

AMERICAN PROFILES

Anne Moody

Anne Moody was one of the many young Americans who became involved in the civil rights movement in the 1960s. As a child in the rural Mississippi town of Centreville, Moody grew up wondering what "the white folks' secret" was. "Their homes were large and beautiful with indoor toilets and every other convenience that I knew of at the time," she observed. "Every house I had ever lived in was a one- or two-room shack with an outdoor toilet." When fourteen-year-old Emmett Till, visiting from Chicago, was killed in Mississippi, supposedly because he had whistled at a white woman, Moody was horrified. She became increasingly disturbed as she noticed how the African Americans she knew passively accepted constant humiliation by white southerners. "I began to look upon Negro men as cowards," she said. "I could not respect them for smiling in a white man's face, addressing him as Mr. So-and-So, saying yessuh and nossuh when after they were

voted to maintain their independence from other civil rights groups. By the end of the year, the Student Nonviolent Coordinating Committee was a permanent and separate organization.

SNCC filled its own niche in the civil rights movement. It gave young African Americans a chance to make decisions about priorities and tactics, and it shifted the focus away from church leaders alone. SNCC was also more militant, or willing to resort to more extreme measures to achieve immediate change, than were most of the older organizations committed to gradual change.

Robert Moses was one of the most influential leaders of SNCC. He had been a mathematics teacher in Harlem, a largely African American section of New York City, as the civil rights movement developed. Like many others, he wanted to be involved. He first went to work for SNCC in Atlanta, and later headed for Mississippi to encourage other African

One focus of SNCC activities was African American voter registration in the South. Those involved were jailed, beaten, and even killed for their efforts.

home behind closed doors" they would curse that same man.

Because she was bright and did well in school, Moody became the first member of her family to go to college. She completed her sophomore year at a small school called Natchez Junior College, then spent her last two years at Tougaloo College near Jackson, Mississippi. At Tougaloo she became involved in the civil rights movement. She joined the NAACP and also worked with CORE and SNCC. The professor who coordinated NAACP activities at Tougaloo asked Moody to take part in the first sit-ins in Jackson in 1963. She agreed to lead groups of students in still more sit-ins to desegregate local businesses, and she gave self-defense workshops for demonstrators.

Moody was amazed at the violent reaction she and other demonstrators—both African American and white—provoked when they sat down at a Woolworth's lunch counter in Jackson. (See photo on page 670.) After three hours of being humiliated—screamed at, beaten, and smeared with ketchup and mustard—Moody went back to the NAACP office. She sat there and reflected on her experience:

*A*ll *I could think of was how sick Mississippi whites were. They believed so much in the segregated Southern way of life, they would kill to preserve it. . . . Before the sit-in, I had always hated the whites in Mississippi. Now I knew it was impossible for me to hate sickness. The whites had a disease, an incurable disease in its final stages.*

Like so many other students in the 1960s, Moody was jailed for taking part in civil rights demonstrations. The jail cells in Jackson were segregated, and she and her African American friends were separated from their white colleagues. Facilities for the African Americans were crude, with no curtain around the shower.

Worse was the reaction from her family at home. Her mother, afraid for the lives of her relatives, begged Moody to end her involvement with the civil rights movement. The local sheriff had warned that Moody should never return to her hometown. Her brother had been beaten up and almost lynched by a group of white boys. Moody's sister angrily told her that her activism was threatening the life of every African American in Centreville.

Against all that resistance, Moody persevered. She participated in demonstrations, helped force the desegregation of facilities, and remained determined to do everything she could to make the South a better place for African Americans. But it was never easy, and the gains came at tremendous personal cost. Like many other Americans committed to changing their society through nonviolent means, Moody learned that challenging white supremacy often provoked an ugly and violent reaction.

Anne Moody joined a SNCC voter registration drive during her first year at Tougaloo College. She said of her fellow SNCC workers, "I had never known people so willing and determined to help others."

SECTION 1 REVIEW

Key Terms, People, and Places
1. Define (a) interracial, (b) CORE, (c) SCLC, (d) SNCC.

Key Concepts
2. What function did the National Urban League perform for African Americans?
3. What was Martin Luther King, Jr.'s, contribution to the civil rights movement?
4. What role did SNCC play in the movement?

Critical Thinking
5. **Demonstrating Reasoned Judgment** Martin Luther King, Jr., said, "To accept passively an unjust system is to cooperate with that system; thereby the oppressed become as evil as the oppressor." Drawing on your knowledge of the section, give a concrete example of what this statement means, and explain why you do or do not agree with it.

Using Autobiography and Biography

Autobiography and biography are two major sources of evidence about a historical period. An autobiography is an account of a person's life as written by that person. A biography is an account of a person's life written by someone else. Both sources offer clues—revealed in the narrative—of what society was like at the time the person lived. As well as describing the person's life, an autobiography or biography also describes the kind of conditions under which people lived, how they reacted to those conditions, and the attitudes and values prevailing at that time.

An autobiography can be especially helpful in capturing a moment in time because it is a firsthand account. But both autobiography and biography must be judged on their reliability. How objective is the writer about the facts presented? Do the facts seem colored by the writer's desire to cast the person profiled in a good or bad light? Or do the facts seem straightforward and believable?

Use the following steps to analyze an excerpt from *And the Walls Came Tumbling Down,* by Ralph Abernathy. Abernathy was a civil rights leader who worked with Martin Luther King, Jr., in organizing the Montgomery bus boycott and who later founded the SCLC with King.

1. Identify the kind of account and the subject of the profile. (a) Is the excerpt from an autobiography or a biography? How can you tell? (b) What events is Abernathy describing? How can you tell?

2. Analyze the source's reliability as historical evidence. (a) How well acquainted is the writer with the facts he describes? (b) What is his point of view toward them? (c) How accurate do you judge his report to be? Explain why.

3. Search for clues that tell what the historical period was like. (a) What groups are in conflict and why? (b) What can you learn about the level of violence that exists in some parts of society? (c) What is the attitude of certain whites to the struggle? (d) What is the attitude of the African Americans involved?

Though we knew that our people could follow the path of nonviolence while in control of themselves, we also knew that in moments of sudden anger almost anybody could be tempted to strike back—and one injured policeman could nullify the work of weeks. So we took particular care to teach our people to count to ten before they responded in any way to verbal or physical abuse.

We also showed them how to march along bent over, elbows guarding their stomachs and hands covering their ears and temples. We devised this technique for use in the event that we were bombarded with rocks and bottles while demonstrating. We also taught a modified version of the same maneuver for use while being beaten with fists or billy clubs.

Then, too, we told everyone to go limp when anyone laid hands on them during an arrest. In the first place, it signaled to the arresting officer that he would encounter no active resistance; hence there was no need for excessive force. But equally important, a limp body was harder to handle, took more time to haul into a paddy wagon, and therefore limited the efficiency of the police. . . .

It is surprising how many of the situations we would later face were actually anticipated and discussed in these Saturday workshops. By the time we reached the end of our years together, Martin and I had seen people assaulted with fists, clubs, bottles, and rocks and were moved by the manner in which they endured such abuse. Almost without exception they behaved exactly as we taught them to behave. They protected themselves from the full force of blows, but they didn't strike back, even when their lives were endangered; and for the most part they replied with courtesy and charity.

—From *And the Walls Came Tumbling Down,* by Rev. Ralph David Abernathy, 1989

Nonviolent Confrontation: A Turning Point in History

SECTION PREVIEW

"We Shall Overcome," sang civil rights protesters, revealing both their spirit of nonviolence and their steadfast commitment to the cause. Acts such as sitting at "whites only" lunch counters brought vicious responses, but also showed the courage and determination of the protesters.

Key Concepts

- The sit-in technique, pioneered by CORE in the 1940s, became a popular and effective tool among civil rights activists in the 1960s.
- Nonviolent protest took the form of Freedom Rides in 1961, when activists bravely desegregated the interstate bus system.
- The violence that erupted during peaceful marches in Birmingham, Alabama, shocked the nation and created sympathy for the civil rights movement.

Key Terms, People, and Places

sit-in, Freedom Rides, Albany Movement

B uilding on the success of the Montgomery bus boycott, African American students took the next step in the campaign for equal rights. With quiet dignity, they insisted on fair treatment in facilities that had been segregated for decades. When their peaceful protests caused angry whites to strike back violently, they refused to respond with violence. Throughout the early 1960s, they maintained their commitment to passive resistance and in the process generated nationwide support for their goals.

Sit-Ins Test the Limits of Inequality

The Congress of Racial Equality (CORE) created the **sit-in** in 1943 when it desegregated the Jack Spratt Coffee House in Chicago. (See Chapter 19, Section 4.) The sit-in technique meant that African American CORE members, often accompanied by white members, simply sat down in a segregated establishment and refused to leave until they were served or accommodated. By testing the limits of segregation policies and putting business owners' profits at risk by causing a disruption, CORE brought an end to segregation in the facilities it targeted. Sit-ins became common practice for many groups participating in the civil rights movement.

On January 31, 1960, Ezell Blair, Jr., an African American freshman at the Agricultural and Technical College in Greensboro, North Carolina, asked his parents if they would be troubled if he caused a disturbance in the community. They were puzzled by the strange question and wanted to know why. "Because," he said, "tomorrow we're going to do something that will shake up this town."

The next day, Blair and three other African American students from the college walked into a Woolworth's store in Greensboro and purchased a few items. Then they sat down at a lunch counter reserved for "whites only." When a surprised waitress wanted to know what they were doing, one of them answered, "We believe since we buy books and papers in the other part of the store, we should get served in this part."

The manager refused to allow them to be served. Rather than leave, Blair and his friends simply remained where they were until the store closed. The next day, twenty students returned to participate in a sit-in at the store. Members of the press poured into Greensboro, and the publicity led to other sit-ins across the state.

John Lewis, an African American activist who participated in sit-ins in Nashville, Tennessee, reflected on his experience in a similar store:

This student picketed a restaurant in Georgia that refused to serve African Americans unless they stood up at the lunch counter.

John Salter, Jr., Joan Trumpauer, and Anne Moody (left to right) held a sit-in at a Jackson, Mississippi, lunch counter in May 1963. A hostile crowd registered their response by mocking and pouring food on the three activists.

I*t was a Woolworth in the heart of the downtown area, and we occupied every seat at the lunch counter, every seat in the restaurant. . . . A group of young white men came in and they started pulling and beating primarily the young women. They put lighted cigarettes down their backs, in their hair, and they were really beating people. In a short time police officials came in and placed all of us under arrest, and not a single member of the white group, the people that were opposing our sit-in, was arrested.*

But the students persisted, and soon thousands were involved in the campaign. The sit-ins gained the support of SCLC. Martin Luther King told students that arrest was a "badge of honor." In the next year, some 70,000 students participated in the sit-ins, and 3,600 served time in jail. The protests failed to change southern customs immediately, but they began a process of change that could be contained no longer.

MAKING CONNECTIONS

What groups in recent times have used non-violent protests such as sit-ins to affect public policy? Have their tactics been effective?

Freedom Rides

In the spring of 1961, CORE led an effort to test a recent Supreme Court decision. In *Boynton* v. *Virginia,* 1960, the Court had expanded on an earlier ruling that prohibited segregation on buses traveling across state lines. As a result of the *Boynton* decision, waiting rooms and dining facilities that served interstate travelers now could not be segregated, either. The **Freedom Rides,** organized by CORE with aid from SNCC, placed groups of African American and white activists on interstate buses heading south and stopping at terminals on the way, as the map on page 671 shows.

At first the Freedom Riders encountered little trouble. When they reached the Deep South, however, they faced a ferocious response. In Anniston, Alabama, a bus was met by a mob of white men at the terminal. They carried weapons—guns, knives, blackjacks, chains—all clearly visible and meant to intimidate. The Freedom Riders decided not to test the facilities there and prepared to move on. James Farmer described what happened next:

B*efore the bus pulled out, however, members of the mob took their sharp instruments and slashed tires. The bus* got to the outskirts of Anniston and the tires blew out and the bus ground to a halt. Members of the mob had boarded cars and followed the bus, and now with the disabled bus standing there, the members of the mob surrounded it, held the door closed, and a member of the mob threw a firebomb into the bus, breaking a window to do so. Incidentally, there were some local policemen mingling with the mob, fraternizing with them while this was going on.

The riders escaped before the bus burst into flames, but many were beaten by the mob as they stumbled, choking on the smoke, out of the vehicle. They had anticipated trouble, and indeed, their strategy was meant to provoke a confrontation. But the level of violence took them by surprise.

As a result of the savage response, CORE director James Farmer contemplated calling the project off. But SNCC leaders begged to be allowed to continue. When Farmer warned,

"You know that may be suicide," student activist Diane Nash answered, "If we let them stop us with violence, the movement is dead! . . . Your troops have been badly battered. Let us pick up the baton and run with it."

Photographs of the charred and battered bus in Anniston, with flames and black smoke rising from its smashed windows, horrified the country. Burke Marshall, Assistant Attorney General, expressed astonishment "that people—presumably otherwise sane, sensible, rational—would have this kind of reaction simply to where people were sitting on a bus." His boss, Attorney General Robert Kennedy, who initially had been reluctant to lend federal support to the protest, finally assigned federal marshals to protect the Freedom Riders. Kennedy and the Justice Department also pressured the Interstate Commerce Commission to issue a ruling prohibiting segregation in interstate transportation, and the federal government forced local communities to follow the new regulations.

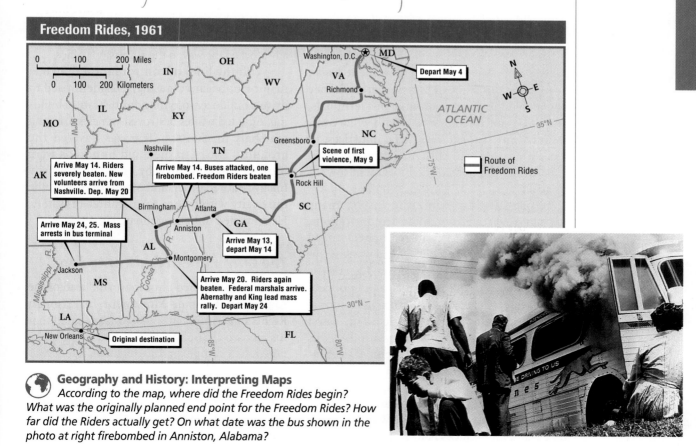

Freedom Rides, 1961

Depart May 4

Arrive May 14. Riders severely beaten. New volunteers arrive from Nashville. Dep. May 20

Arrive May 14. Buses attacked, one firebombed. Freedom Riders beaten

Scene of first violence, May 9

Arrive May 24, 25. Mass arrests in bus terminal

Arrive May 13, depart May 14

Arrive May 20. Riders again beaten. Federal marshals arrive. Abernathy and King lead mass rally. Depart May 24

Original destination

Route of Freedom Rides

Geography and History: Interpreting Maps
According to the map, where did the Freedom Rides begin? What was the originally planned end point for the Freedom Rides? How far did the Riders actually get? On what date was the bus shown in the photo at right firebombed in Anniston, Alabama?

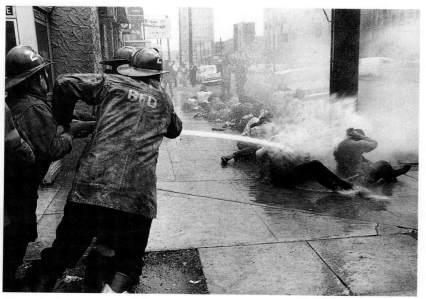

Police in Birmingham, Alabama, used high-powered hoses to break up civil rights marches in 1963. Television coverage of this brutal treatment of peaceful demonstrators prompted widespread sympathy for the movement.

The Albany Movement

The Freedom Rides exacted a heavy toll from civil rights workers, but the campaign did lead to significant gains in the desegregation of interstate bus travel. A campaign that began soon after the Freedom Rides did not fare so well.

In October 1961, African Americans in Albany, Georgia, who had joined together and called themselves the **Albany Movement,** began a year-long campaign of protest marches. They demanded the desegregation of bus terminals, and they wanted to open talks with white community leaders to address racial injustices. In December, Martin Luther King arrived in Albany, hoping to lead the movement toward its goals.

While King's presence did inspire many African Americans to join the demonstrations, it also irritated some local civil rights leaders, who resented the way King seemed to swoop in and take charge of the movement. The Albany police chief, Laurie Pritchett, also did not help the movement. He shrewdly kept the national press from seeing and reporting on the worst violations of civil rights committed by his forces. Once he even joined a group of demonstrators in prayer before they were carted off to jail. His tactic of "nonviolent" opposition to the civil rights protests kept the Albany Movement from stirring up the same nationwide sympathy that the Freedom Rides had created.

King was jailed at one point but promptly released when Albany authorities learned that volunteers were mobilizing to protest the arrest. As the campaign seemed to be failing, King began to turn his attention elsewhere. The Albany Movement had largely fizzled out by the end of 1962, with few real accomplishments to show for a difficult year.

The Integration of Ole Miss

In September of 1962, James Meredith had better success in his personal quest for civil rights. The African American air force veteran was a student at Jackson State College but wanted to transfer to the all-white University of Mississippi (known as Ole Miss). When he was denied entrance on racial grounds, he sued and carried his case to the Supreme Court, which upheld his claim. Mississippi governor Ross Barnett had other ideas. He declared that Meredith would not be allowed to enroll, whatever the Court declared, and at one point personally blocked the way to the admissions office.

With the lines of confrontation drawn, a major riot began. One angry resident tried to drive a bulldozer into the administration building. Agitated whites destroyed vehicles bringing marshals to campus. Tear gas covered the grounds. Two men died and hundreds were hurt. Army troops sent by President Kennedy finally restored order, and Meredith entered the university with troops to guarantee his safety. He remained until he graduated in 1963.

The Birmingham Confrontation

In late 1962 Fred Shuttlesworth, head of the Alabama Christian Movement for Human Rights in Birmingham, Alabama, decided that his city would be the perfect site for another nonviolent campaign. Birmingham, which was 40 percent African American, was rigidly segregated. Victory there could serve as a model for future resistance elsewhere. Shuttlesworth therefore invited Martin Luther King to visit the city in April 1963.

Local business leaders, afraid of the money they would lose if King's visit touched off demonstrations throughout the city, tried to negotiate with Shuttlesworth to call off the plan. These negotiations did not go very far, however, and King arrived on schedule.

Civil rights activists faced Eugene "Bull" Connor, the Birmingham police commissioner who was committed to crushing the protest. When reporters wanted to know how long King planned to stay, King drew on a biblical story and told them he would remain until "Pharaoh let his people go." Bull Connor replied, "I got plenty of room in the jail."

Activists, still committed to their peaceful approach, challenged discriminatory hiring practices and segregated public facilities. City officials declared that protest marches violated a regulation prohibiting parades without a permit and arrested King. When a group of white clergy criticized the campaign as an ill-timed threat to law and order, King responded from his cell. In his "Letter from a Birmingham Jail," he defended his tactics and his timing:

> For years now I have heard the word "Wait!" It rings in the ear of every Negro with a piercing familiarity. . . . But when you have seen vicious mobs lynch your mothers and fathers at will and drown your sisters and brothers at whim; when you have seen hate filled policemen curse, kick, brutalize and even kill your black brothers and sisters with impunity; . . . when you have to concoct an answer for a five-year-old son who is asking in agonizing pathos: "Daddy, why do white people treat colored people so mean?" . . . then you will understand why we find it difficult to wait.

After more than a week, King posted bail and emerged from jail. Soon after, he decided to allow children to participate in the campaign to test the conscience of the Birmingham authorities and the nation. As they marched with the adults, Bull Connor arrested more than 900 of the children. Police turned high-pressure fire hoses, able to tear the bark from trees, on the demonstrators. They also brought out trained police dogs that attacked the arms and legs of marchers. When protesters fell to the ground, policemen beat them with clubs and took them off to jail.

Television cameras recorded the scenes of appalling violence for people around the country. Even those unsympathetic to the civil rights movement were revolted. As reporter Eric Sevareid observed, "A newspaper or television picture of a snarling police dog set upon a human being is recorded in the permanent photo-electric file of every human brain."

In the end, the protesters won. A compromise arranged by Assistant Attorney General Burke Marshall led to desegregation of city facilities, fairer hiring practices, and organization of a biracial committee to keep channels of communication open. The success of the Birmingham marches was just one example that proved the effectiveness of nonviolent protest. While the technique did not always work—or worked only slowly—nonviolent confrontation as a means to social change had earned itself a place of honor in the history of civil rights in the United States.

SECTION 2 REVIEW

Key Terms, People, and Places
1. Define (a) sit-in, (b) Freedom Rides, (c) Albany Movement.

Key Concepts
2. What was the significance of the sit-in movement?
3. What was the point of the Freedom Rides?
4. What was the aim of the Birmingham campaign?

Critical Thinking
5. **Drawing Conclusions** In May 1961, an article in *The New York Times* encouraged the Freedom Riders to call off their program, arguing, "Non-violence that deliberately provokes violence is a logical contradiction." Explain why you agree or disagree with this statement as it applies to the Freedom Rides.

The Lasting Impact of Nonviolent Confrontation

The nonviolent, direct-action campaigns of the early 1960s marked the beginning of a new chapter in the African American struggle for equal rights. The sit-ins, the Freedom Rides, and the marches forced a shift in American attitudes and created a climate within which reform could take place.

Prior to the movement, most Americans had taken white supremacy for granted. Most white southerners were not significantly different from Melton McLaurin, who grew up in the rural town of Wade, North Carolina, in the 1950s. "Like many such families in small southern towns," he later recalled, "we assumed that the blacks of the village were in residence primarily to serve us, and we used their labor to support our comfortable lifestyle." The civil rights movement of the 1960s, however, brought a shift in perspective that made McLaurin

different from his parents. Returning home for a visit in 1984, he watched his father deliver a gift to an African American family at Christmas. It was a gracious gesture from a 65-year-year-old man who accepted changes without fully understanding them. At the same time, McLaurin observed, his father "remained, spiritually, emotionally, a resident of the Wade I had left and to which I could never return."

African Americans themselves experienced even more dramatic changes. In the late 1960s, Henry Louis Gates, a high school student from West Virginia, applied for admission to Yale University in Connecticut. In his application, which earned him a spot at the school, he described how the civil rights movement had brought changes in his own life: "My grandfather was colored; my father was Negro; and I am black." In other words, the movement

1960s African American students around the nation demand that their colleges create Black Studies programs.

1965	1970	1975

1960s African Americans' pride in their heritage is shown in the popularity of traditional African clothing.

brought a shift in African Americans' sense of identity and in the way they wanted to be viewed by the larger culture. African Americans looked back toward their African roots, and with that rediscovery came a powerful pride in their ethnic identity. Some African American students began wearing *dashikis*—brightly colored African shirts—while others stopped straightening their hair and wore it longer in a style called the Afro.

Those were surface changes, to be sure, but they reflected larger cultural shifts. In the course of the next several decades, as you will read in the following chapters, the civil rights movement itself shifted course. African Americans refused to accept the second-class citizenship that had been forced upon them for the past one hundred years. They discovered that beyond segregation lay more subtle forms of discrimination, and they continued the fight to secure their full rights.

In time, however, their efforts sparked an opposing reaction on the part of previously sympathetic whites, who felt that change was coming too quickly and often at their expense. For example, Americans were divided on the issue of affirmative action programs, which sought to make up for past discrimination by requiring employers to make a special effort to hire African Americans. The civil rights movement, so passionate in the 1960s, has today lost some of its steam. But the results remain visible. And the struggle to attain equality continues, especially in the economic sphere.

REVIEWING THE FACTS

1. How did the civil rights movement change the way some African Americans perceived their own identity?
2. What obstacles did the movement toward full equality for African Americans face after the 1960s?

Critical Thinking

3. **Formulating Questions** Imagine that you are conducting a study on how far the civil rights movement has come as of the 1990s. Create a list of questions that your study would seek to answer. Some of the questions may involve statistics, while others may deal with how African Americans and others perceive the situation today.

1970s The women's rights movement employs nonviolent protests like those of the civil rights movement.

1992 Spike Lee's film Malcolm X *marks a renewed interest in the slain civil rights leader.*

| 1980 | 1985 | 1990 |

1980s Multicultural curriculums reflect the growing diversity in American classrooms.

The Political Response

When President Kennedy avoided committing himself to the politically charged civil rights struggle, students demanded leadership from the White House.

SECTION PREVIEW

For politicians in the early 1960s, taking a firm stand in favor of civil rights was a risky business. As the decade wore on, however, the rising voice of protest no longer could be ignored in Washington.

Key Concepts

• At the start of his presidency, John F. Kennedy was hesitant to embrace the civil rights cause.
• Kennedy finally took a moral stand for civil rights but was unable to secure passage of his bill.
• Lyndon Johnson succeeded in gaining passage of the Civil Rights Act of 1964 and the Voting Rights Act of 1965.

Key Terms, People, and Places

March on Washington, Civil Rights Act of 1964, Voting Rights Act of 1965

The protest activities of the early 1960s forced a political response. At first President John F. Kennedy, worried about his narrow electoral victory, hoped to avoid getting involved in the struggle. Finally, when the violence became extreme, he provided the moral leadership that President Eisenhower had not and committed himself to full support for a civil rights bill. The bill remained bottled up in a congressional committee when he died late in 1963, however. Kennedy's successor, Lyndon B. Johnson, harnessed a wave of popular sympathy after Kennedy's assassination and made the cause his own. Through LBJ's efforts, the civil rights movement reached its high point in the middle of the decade.

John Kennedy's Reaction

Kennedy had sought to straddle the fence at the start of his presidency. As a member of Congress, he had voted for civil rights measures but never embraced the cause wholeheartedly. In his presidential campaign, he had sought and won many African American votes with bold rhetoric. In 1960 he proclaimed, "If the President does not himself wage the struggle for equal rights—if he stands above the battle—then the battle will inevitably be lost." He also declared that a "stroke of the pen" could eliminate racial discrimination in federal housing.

In October 1960, just weeks before the election, Kennedy had an opportunity to make a powerful gesture of goodwill toward African Americans. Martin Luther King had been arrested in Alabama and sentenced to four months of hard labor. His family feared for his life in the prison camp. Kennedy called Coretta Scott King, Dr. King's wife, and said, "If there is anything I can do to help, please feel free to call on me." Then Robert Kennedy called the Alabama judge who had sentenced King and persuaded the judge to release him on bail. Word of the Kennedys' actions spread quickly through the African American community, and many switched their votes from Nixon to Kennedy. These votes were crucial in Kennedy's slim margin of victory in the election.

Once in office, though, Kennedy moved slowly. He did not want to alienate southern senators, whose votes he would need to achieve his foreign policy goals, by taking a strong stand on civil rights. He appointed a number of African Americans to prominent positions. Thurgood Marshall, for example, joined the United States Circuit Court and later became the first African American Supreme Court justice. But at the same time, Kennedy named a number of segregationists to federal courts. He also conveniently forgot about his pledge to end housing discrimination.

But Kennedy was deeply disturbed by the scenes of violence in the South that were flooding the media. The race riots surrounding the Freedom Rides in 1961 had been an embarrassment to Kennedy when he met with Nikita Khrushchev in Vienna. To observers around the world, the upheaval in Birmingham looked even more like the beginning of a revolution. Aware that he had to do something, Kennedy spoke to the American people on nationwide television. He called the quest for equality "a moral issue" and underscored the need for action:

> We preach freedom around the world, and we mean it, and we cherish our freedom, here at home, but are we to say to the world, and much more importantly, to each other that this is a land of the free except for the Negroes? . . . The time has come for this nation to fulfill its promise.

Several months earlier, Kennedy had proposed a modest civil rights bill to help support African American voting rights and to aid schools beginning to desegregate. The Birmingham crisis pushed him further. He introduced a far stronger bill that would prohibit segregation in public places, ban discrimination wherever federal funding was involved, and advance the effort to desegregate schools. It was the most comprehensive civil rights measure ever endorsed by a United States President. The public stood behind Kennedy; a Gallup poll soon after his televised speech showed that 61 percent of the nation approved of the way he was doing his job. But Congress, still dominated by white southerners, proved resistant and kept the bill from coming up for a vote.

The March on Washington

Civil rights leaders proposed a march on Washington to lobby for passage of Kennedy's civil rights bill. Like Franklin Roosevelt when he was faced with a similar march in 1941, Kennedy tried to sidetrack the proposal. He feared it would simply alienate Congress and might result in serious racial violence in the United States capital. But his efforts to get organizers to call off the demonstration failed. Vice President Johnson warned civil rights leaders that the march might

backfire, and that it was time instead for political deal making in Congress. But Martin Luther King noted, "I have never engaged in any direct action movement which did not seem ill-timed." In the end, Kennedy bowed to the inevitable and supported the march.

The **March on Washington** took place in August 1963. More than 200,000 people came from all over the country to call for jobs and freedom. Prominent African American celebrities were present: government official Ralph Bunche, author James Baldwin, entertainer Sammy Davis, Jr., singer Harry Belafonte, baseball player Jackie Robinson. Many of the leading folk singers of the early 1960s were also there. Peter, Paul, and Mary; Joan Baez; and Bob Dylan all sang songs like "Blowin' in the Wind" and "We Shall Overcome," which had become the unofficial anthem of the struggle. The leaders of the major civil rights organizations all addressed the crowd.

At the march, Martin Luther King delivered what was to become his best-known address. With power, eloquence, and passion, he spoke to the demonstrators and to the nation at large:

> I have a dream that one day this nation will rise up and live out the true meaning

"Jobs and Freedom" was the official slogan for the March on Washington in 1963. Thousands like the young woman in the inset turned out to show their support for the civil rights movement.

of its creed, "We hold these truths to be self-evident, that all men are created equal." I have a dream that one day on the red hills of Georgia, sons of former slaves and the sons of former slave owners will be able to sit down together at the table of brotherhood. . . . I have a dream that my four little children will one day live in a nation where they will not be judged by the color of their skin, but by the content of their character. . . . When we allow freedom to ring, when we let it ring from every village and every hamlet, from every state and every city, we will be able to speed up that day when all of God's children, black men and white men, Jews and Gentiles, Protestants and Catholics, will be able to join hands and sing in the words of the old Negro spiritual: "Free at last. Free at last. Thank God Almighty, we are free at last."*

King's words echoed around the country. President Kennedy, watching the speech on television, was impressed with King's skill. But still the civil rights bill remained stalled in Congress.

MAKING CONNECTIONS

Why do you think Vice President Johnson preferred to use politics to get the civil rights bill passed rather than relying on demonstrations?

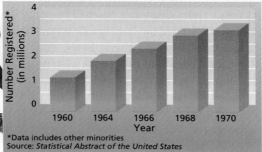

African American Voter Registration in the South, 1960–1970

Number Registered* (in millions) — vertical axis: 0, 1, 2, 3, 4

Horizontal axis (Year): 1960, 1964, 1966, 1968, 1970

*Data includes other minorities
Source: *Statistical Abstract of the United States*

Interpreting Graphs
Civil rights workers like the woman at left had already begun registering African Americans years before the Voting Rights Act of 1965. *How many new African American voters registered between 1960 and 1970?*

Lyndon Johnson's Role

Three months after the March on Washington, President Kennedy was dead and his civil rights bill was not much closer to passage. Lyndon Johnson was finally able to move the legislation along. Although he had voted against civil rights measures early in his congressional career, as Senate majority leader Johnson had worked to get a civil rights bill passed in 1957. Upon becoming President, he was eager to use his political skills to build support for Kennedy's bill. In his first public address, he told Congress and the country that nothing "could more eloquently honor President Kennedy's memory than the earliest possible passage of the civil rights bill." Johnson promised African American leaders that he would push for the measure "with every energy [he] possessed," and he made good on that commitment.

Johnson let Congress know that he would accept no compromise on civil rights. After the House of Representatives passed the bill, the Senate became caught in a lengthy filibuster, in which southern members exercised their privilege of unlimited debate. Johnson finally enlisted his old colleague, Republican minority leader Everett Dirksen, to support cloture—a two-thirds vote to cut off debate. Never before had such a procedure been used for a civil rights measure. In June 1964 the Senate voted for cloture. Soon after, it passed the bill.

The **Civil Rights Act of 1964** banned discrimination in all public accommodations and gave the Justice Department authority to act more vigorously in school segregation and voting rights cases. It also included an equal-opportunity provision that prohibited discriminatory hiring on the basis of race, sex, religion, or national origin in companies with more than twenty-five employees, as shown in the chart on page 679.

Johnson was satisfied, but the struggle moved on with a momentum of its own. In 1964 leaders of the major civil rights groups organized a voter registration drive in Mississippi. About a thousand African American and white volunteers, most of them college students, went to Mississippi to participate in what came to be called Freedom Summer. The

Civil Rights Act of 1964

Title I	Prohibits different registration standards for white and African American voting applicants
Title II	Prohibits discrimination in the use of public accommodations
Title III	Guarantees equal access to and treatment in all public-owned and -operated facilities
Title IV	Authorizes the federal government to provide technical and financial aid to all school districts in the process of desegregation
Title V	Extends tenure of Civil Rights Commission until January 31, 1968
Title VI	Guarantees that no individual will be subjected to racial discrimination in any program that is receiving federal financial aid
Title VII	Prohibits discrimination by employers or unions with more than 100 employees or members during the first four years the Act is in effect, and thereafter for more than 25 employees or members Establishes a commission to investigate and to mediate charges of discrimination
Title VIII	Directs the Census Bureau to compile voting statistics by race in regions designated by the Civil Rights Commission
Title IX	Allows higher federal courts to prevent lower federal courts from remanding a civil rights case to a state or local court
Title X	Establishes a Community Relations Service in the Department of Commerce to mediate racial disputes at the local level
Title XI	Guarantees the right of jury trial in criminal contempt cases that grow out of any part of the Act, except for Title I Provides that the Civil Rights Act cannot be invalidated as a whole even if a single portion of it is invalidated

Source: *The Negro Almanac: A Reference Work on the Afro American*

Interpreting Tables
One of the landmark achievements of the Johnson administration was the passage of the Civil Rights Act of 1964. *Which provision of the act allows the federal government to assist in school desegregation with money or other forms of aid?*

STUDENT NONVIOLENT COORDINATING COMMITTEE
WE SHALL OVERCOME

Ku Klux Klan held rallies to intimidate the volunteers. In August FBI agents found the bodies of three civil rights workers—James Chaney, Andrew Goodman, and Michael Schwerner—who had been murdered by opponents. This violence was only part of the turbulence seen that summer. Civil rights leaders reported three deaths, thirty-five shootings, thirty firebombings, and eighty mob attacks. A thousand volunteers were arrested.

In order to claim their full political rights, newly registered Mississippi voters, along with members of SNCC, organized the Mississippi Freedom Democratic party. The MFDP sent delegates to the Democratic National Convention in the summer of 1964. These delegates argued that they, rather than segregationist politicians, were the rightful representatives of the state.

Fannie Lou Hamer, a timekeeper on a cotton plantation who had lost her job when she tried to register to vote, addressed the convention in a speech carried on national television. She related the treatment she had received in one voter drive:

> I began to scream, and one white man got up and began to beat me on my head and tell me to "hush." . . . All of this on account we want to register, to become first class citizens. [If] the Freedom Democratic Party is not seated now, I question America.

Lyndon Johnson offered a compromise to the Freedom party: he would seat two MFDP delegates of his own choosing, and he promised that the rules of the convention would be

When Fannie Lou Hamer registered to vote in her home state of Mississippi, the owner of the plantation where she lived promptly evicted her. She told her story at the 1968 Democratic National Convention (right), reaching a television audience of millions.

of your fellow Americans the right to vote in this country."

At one point in his speech, Johnson paused, raised his arms, and repeated the words that had become the marching song of the civil rights movement: "And . . . we . . . shall . . . overcome." Johnson got the response he wanted. After turning back another filibuster, Congress passed the **Voting Rights Act of 1965.**

The Voting Rights Act authorized the attorney general to appoint federal examiners to register voters where local officials prevented African Americans from exercising their constitutional right. The act singled out the South, for six states and part of another did not pass the test of having 50 percent of the voting-age population registered in 1964. In the year following passage, over 400,000 African Americans registered to vote in the Deep South, as shown by the chart on page 678. By 1968 the number reached 1 million. This act changed the nature of southern politics. It created an entirely new voting population, and it led to African American representation at local, state, and national levels.

The Civil Rights Act and the Voting Rights Act were landmarks in the history of civil rights in the United States, and they had a real impact. For some African Americans, however, these legislative accomplishments were not nearly enough. Impatient with the slow pace of progress, many African Americans turned a receptive ear to radical leaders who voiced the fury born of centuries of oppression. Pride and power, rather than peaceful resistance, were the watchwords for this new outgrowth of the civil rights movement.

changed in 1968 so there would be no more discrimination in the Mississippi delegation. The MFDP rejected the compromise. Johnson went on to win reelection in a landslide, but he knew he had to do something about the issue of voting rights for African Americans.

In early 1965 Johnson addressed a joint session of Congress and a national television audience. He was at his most eloquent as he spoke about the right to vote: "The command of the Constitution is plain. There is no moral issue. It is wrong—deadly wrong—to deny any

SECTION 3 REVIEW

Key Terms, People, and Places

1. Define (a) March on Washington, (b) Civil Rights Act of 1964, (c) Voting Rights Act of 1965.

Key Concepts

2. Why was Kennedy initially reluctant to support civil rights wholeheartedly? How did his position change?

3. What role did Lyndon Johnson play in the passage of civil rights legislation?

Critical Thinking

4. **Demonstrating Reasoned Judgment** Reflect on the struggle for civil rights up to 1965. Then explain why you agree or disagree with the following statement: "If A. Philip Randolph had gone ahead with his plans for the 1941 March on Washington, legislation such as the Civil Rights Act and the Voting Rights Act would have been passed twenty years earlier."

The Challenge of Black Power

During the civil rights movement, change happened slowly and at times appeared to have ground to a halt. The response from some African Americans was a call for self-defense—even if it meant using violence.

Key Concepts

• The anger felt by many African Americans was expressed in the words of writer James Baldwin, activist Malcolm X, and others.

• Malcolm X preached that African Americans could expect nothing from white society in the United States and therefore needed to create a separate society.

• Street riots erupted in some cities in the late 1960s.

Key Terms, People, and Places

de jure segregation, de facto segregation, Nation of Islam, Black Power; James Baldwin, Malcolm X

Son, a collection of essays published in 1955, he told of the damaging effects of segregation in the United States. He attacked not simply **de jure segregation**— the rigid pattern of separation dictated by law in the South—but also **de facto segregation**—the separation that resulted from the ghetto conditions in many northern cities. This pattern is shown on the map below. In 1963, in his best seller *The Fire Next Time,* Baldwin argued that these conditions could not continue. African American anger was ready to erupt. In one essay he described the horrors of the recent past—

this past, the Negro's past, of rope, fire, torture, castration, infanticide, rape; death and humiliation; fear by day and night; fear as deep as the marrow of the bone; doubt that he was worthy of life, since everyone around

A raised fist became the symbol of the Black Power movement, a militant outgrowth of the earlier civil rights movement.

After passage of the two civil rights acts in 1964 and 1965, the movement shifted course. Racial discrimination continued, both in the North and in the South. African Americans became frustrated at the slow and sometimes halting pace of change. Their growing anger found expression in the speeches and essays of a number of critics, who challenged the nonviolent approach that had guided the movement in the early 1960s. More militant calls for reform changed the nature of the struggle and led to increasing division in the movement and in the United States as a whole.

African American Anger

James Baldwin was a gifted writer who described the African American experience in his works and became a spokesperson for the civil rights movement. In his *Notes of a Native*

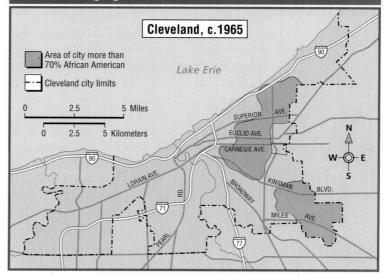

De Facto Segregation in the North, c. 1965

Cleveland, c.1965

Area of city more than 70% African American

Cleveland city limits

0   2.5   5 Miles

0   2.5   5 Kilometers

Lake Erie

SUPERIOR AVE.
EUCLID AVE.
CARNEGIE AVE.
LORAIN AVE
BROADWAY
KINSMAN BLVD.
MILES AVE.
PEARL RD.
90
71
77

Geography and History: Interpreting Maps
This map shows the areas of Cleveland, Ohio, with the highest concentrations of African Americans in the 1960s. *What social and economic factors may have contributed to this pattern of settlement?*

Equal Rights Movements

The civil rights movement of the 1960s resulted in federal laws that forbade discrimination against African Americans. The success of the civil rights movement has inspired other minority groups to fight for equal rights. Latinos, Asian Americans, women, children, the elderly, and people with disabilities are among those groups who have also used demonstrations and sit-ins, court challenges, and legislative pressure to demand their constitutional guarantee of equal rights.

Victory was gained by one group when President Bush, in his 1990 State of the Union message, spoke of the need for a "better America" where "for the first time, the American mainstream includes all our disabled citizens." In July 1990 the Americans with Disabilities Act was finally approved by both houses of Congress. This law was the result of a long struggle by physically or mentally disabled people to ensure equal access to employment, transportation, telecommunications, and public accommodations.

Businesses that employ twenty-five or more workers are now forbidden to refuse to hire or promote a qualified disabled job applicant. In addition, nearly all businesses are required to provide access for people with disabilities. For example, aisles in stores must be wide enough for a wheelchair.

Railroads, bus lines, mass transit systems, and public school bus companies are required to ensure that all new vehicles are accessible to disabled persons. Telephone companies must provide services so that hearing- or voice-impaired people can use their systems. *What facilities and programs in your school ensure equal access for disabled students?*

---

him denied it; sorrow for his women, for his kinfolk, for his children, who needed his protection, and whom he could not protect; rage, hatred, and murder, hatred for white men so deep that it often turned against him and his own, and made all love, all trust, all joy impossible.

In this essay and others published in the popular press, Baldwin warned Americans that unless change occurred soon, the nation could expect uncontrollable violence.

Malcolm X

Another leader who expressed the deeply felt anger of many African Americans was **Malcolm X.** He was born Malcolm Little in Omaha, Nebraska, in 1925. His father, a Baptist minister, spread the "back-to-Africa" message of Marcus Garvey but died when Little was a child. Little was raised in ghettos in Detroit, Boston, and New York, where he spent his youth involved in various criminal activities. At age twenty, he was arrested for an attempted burglary and served seven years in prison. While in jail he read widely and became interested in a group called the **Nation of Islam.**

The Nation of Islam was founded in 1933 in Chicago by Elijah Muhammad. He taught that Allah, the God of Islam, would bring about a "Black Nation" composed of all the nonwhite peoples of the world. According to Elijah Muhammad, one of the keys to self-knowledge was knowing one's enemy, and the enemy of the Nation of Islam was the white man and white supremacy. Members of the Nation of Islam did not seek change through political means but waited for Allah to create the Black Nation. In the meantime, they led a righteous life and worked hard to become economically self-sufficient.

Released from prison in 1952, Malcolm Little converted to the Nation of Islam, changed his name to Malcolm X, and became a disciple of Elijah Muhammad. He spent the next twelve years spreading the gospel of his new faith.

Malcolm X disagreed with both the tactics and the goals of the early civil rights movement. He called the March on Washington the "Farce on Washington" and voiced his irritation at "all of this non-violent, begging-the-white-man kind of dying . . . all of this sitting-in, sliding-in, wading-in, eating-in, diving-in, and all the rest." He preached that integration would not work and that African Americans had to take their destiny into their own hands:

No sane *black man really wants integration! No* sane *white man really wants integration! No sane black man really believes that the white man ever will give the black man anything more than token integration. No! The Honorable Elijah Muhammad teaches that for the black man in America the only solution is complete* separation *from the white man . . . . The American black man should be focusing his effort toward building his own businesses, and decent homes for himself. As other ethnic groups have done, let the black people, wherever possible, however possible, patronize their own kind, hire their own kind, and start in those ways to build up the black race's ability to do for itself. That's the only way the American black man is ever going to get respect.*

Before long Malcolm X had attracted a wide following. By 1963 Elijah Muhammad had become increasingly jealous of the attention that Malcolm X was receiving. When Elijah Muhammad objected to a remark Malcolm X had made about the Kennedy assassination, Malcolm X left the Nation of Islam and formed his own religious organization, called Muslim Mosque, Inc. He then made a pilgrimage to Mecca, the holy city of Islam in Saudi Arabia. When he returned, he proclaimed that he had been wrong to preach the hatred of white people. Malcolm X was assassinated in February 1965; three members of the Nation of Islam were charged with the murder. But his message lived on, and it attracted the attention of many of the young workers in SNCC.

MAKING CONNECTIONS

The Nation of Islam had its historical roots in the ideas of Marcus Garvey's "back-to-Africa" movement. How were the ideas behind each movement related to each other?

Black Power Rages

One of the SNCC leaders influenced by Malcolm X was Stokely Carmichael. He had been born in Trinidad, in the West Indies, and came to the United States at the age of eleven. He grew up interested in political affairs and involved in African American protest. At Howard University in Washington, D.C., he and other students took over the Washington chapter of SNCC. He was beaten and jailed for his participation in demonstrations and finally got tired of civil disobedience. Carmichael called on SNCC workers to carry guns for self-defense. He also argued that African Americans should cease deferring to whites and make SNCC into an exclusively African American organization. His election as head of the organization in 1966 was a reflection of SNCC's growing radicalism.

A turning point in the civil rights movement came in June 1966, at a march that took place in Greenwood, Mississippi. As Martin Luther King's followers sang "We Shall Overcome," Carmichael's supporters drowned them out by singing "We Shall Overrun." Then Carmichael, just out of jail, jumped into the back of an open truck to address the group:

This is the twenty-seventh time I have been arrested, and I ain't going to jail no more! . . . The only way we gonna stop them white men from whuppin' us is to take over. We been saying freedom for six years—and we ain't got nothin.' What we gonna start saying now is "Black Power!"

Elijah Muhammad (above left) called African Americans "the lost-found Nation of Islam in the wilderness of North America." Malcolm X (above right) was a leading minister of the Nation of Islam until 1963.

As he repeated "We . . . want . . . Black . . . Power!" the audience responded with the same words in a thunderous echo. Carmichael's idea of **Black Power** called on African Americans "to unite, to recognize their heritage, to build a sense of community . . . to begin to define their own goals, to lead their own organizations and support those organizations."

In the fall of 1966, a number of African American militants founded a new political party—the Black Panthers. The Panthers wanted African Americans to lead their own communities and demanded that the federal government rebuild the nation's ghettos in repayment for years of discrimination. Huey Newton, one of the founders of the group, repeated the words of Chinese leader Mao Zedong: "Power flows from the barrel of a gun." At the same time, the organization had a gentler side and developed day-care centers, health-care facilities, and free breakfast programs in communities where it took hold.

Black Power gave rise to the "Black Is Beautiful" slogan that helped foster a sense of racial pride. It also led to a serious split in the civil rights movement, as radical groups like SNCC and the Black Panthers moved away from the NAACP and other more conservative organizations.

Riots in the Streets

Riots in a number of American cities were symptoms of the continuing poor conditions under which many African Americans were forced to live in the mid-1960s. There were no "whites only" signs above water fountains in northern cities, but more subtle forms of discrimination kept African Americans living in poverty. African Americans were kept out of well-paying jobs, job training programs, and suburban housing. Police officers assigned to ghetto neighborhoods were viewed by African American residents as dangerous oppressors rather than upholders of justice. James Baldwin remarked that a white police officer in one of these neighborhoods was "like an occupying soldier in a bitterly hostile country."

Riots ravaged Rochester, New York; New York City; and several cities in New Jersey in 1964. One of the most violent riots began in the Watts neighborhood of Los Angeles on August 11, 1965. On that steamy summer day, police pulled over a twenty-one-year-old African American man for drunk driving. At first the interaction was friendly between the police, the suspect, and the crowd of Watts residents that had gathered around. When the suspect resisted arrest, however, one police officer panicked and began swinging his riot baton. The crowd was outraged, and the scene touched off six days of rioting. Thousands of people filled the streets, burning cars and stores, stealing merchandise, and sniping at fire fighters. When the national guard and local police finally gained control, thirty-four people were dead and more than a thousand were injured.

Violence spread to other cities in 1966 and 1967. Cries of "Get Whitey" and "Burn, Baby, Burn" replaced the gentler slogans of the earlier civil rights movement. The

Members of the Black Panther party marched through the streets of New York City in 1968 to protest the trial of one of their leaders, Huey P. Newton.

National Advisory Commission on Civil Disorders, known as the Kerner Commission, noted in a report in 1968: "The nation is rapidly moving toward two increasingly separate Americas."

The Legacy of the Movement

African Americans and whites both wondered at times whether progress in civil rights was possible. Anne Moody felt frustrated when the movement failed to bring the quick change activists sought. As she listened to others sing civil rights songs during one demonstration, she found herself unable to forget the suffering that continued. "We Shall Overcome" echoed around her, but all she could think was, "I wonder. I really wonder."

Lyndon Johnson was devastated by the violence that exploded near the end of his presidency. "How is it possible," he asked, "after all we've accomplished? How could it be? Is the world topsy turvy?" While the measures passed by his administration had brought good results, they were not nearly enough.

Despite the need for further progress, the movement had brought tremendous change. Segregation was now illegal. African Americans were assured the right to vote, and the power they wielded changed the nature of American political life. Between 1970 and 1975, the number of African American elected officials rose by 88 percent. African Americans served as mayors in large cities like Atlanta, Detroit, Los Angeles, and Newark and served in Congress in larger numbers as well. Black studies courses

began to appear in high schools and colleges. African Americans had a new sense of identity and pride in their ethnic heritage.

African American congresswoman Barbara Jordan noted the impact of the movement:

> The civil rights movement called America to look at itself in a giant mirror. . . . Do the black people who were born on this soil, who are American citizens, do they really feel that this is the land of opportunity, the land of the free. . . . America had to say no.

The response to that question was the first step toward making the United States a fairer society for all.

The rallying cry "Burn, Baby, Burn" became a nightmarish reality in the streets of Los Angeles in 1965. After fire fighters quenched the flames in buildings all over Watts, crowds of looters moved in to carry off the spoils.

SECTION 4 REVIEW

Key Terms, People, and Places
1. Define (a) de jure segregation, (b) de facto segregation, (c) Nation of Islam, (d) Black Power.

Key Concepts
2. How did James Baldwin give voice to African American anger?
3. When Malcolm X belonged to the Nation of Islam, what did he preach about the future of race relations in the United States?

4. Why was there rioting in many cities across the United States in the late 1960s?

Critical Thinking
5. **Drawing Conclusions** The Nation of Islam and the Black Power movement both taught that African Americans should seek to establish their own communities separate from white Americans. Explain why you do or do not believe that such a goal is possible.

Chapter Review

Key Terms
1. interracial
2. Congress of Racial Equality
3. Southern Christian Leadership Conference (SCLC)
4. Student Nonviolent Coordinating Committee (SNCC)
5. sit-in
6. Freedom Rides
7. Albany Movement
8. March on Washington
9. Civil Rights Act of 1964
10. Voting Rights Act of 1965
11. de jure segregation
12. de facto segregation
13. Nation of Islam
14. Black Power

People
15. James Baldwin
16. Malcolm X

Terms For each term above, write a sentence that explains its relation to the civil rights movement.

Matching Review the key terms in the list above. If you are not sure of a term's meaning, review its definition in the chapter. Then choose a term from the list that best matches each description below.
1. bus trips on which groups of African American and white activists traveled south to protest segregation on interstate transportation facilities
2. an organization that grew out of a conference for students active in the civil rights struggle
3. the legislation that banned discrimination in all public accommodations
4. a religious group whose members believed that Allah would create a Black Nation
5. a group of African Americans who joined together in Georgia for a year-long campaign of protest marches

Matching Review the key people in the list above. Then choose a name from the list that best matches each description below.
1. an author who wrote about the damaging effects of segregation in his book *Notes of a Native Son*
2. a member of the Nation of Islam who preached that neither African Americans nor whites wanted integration

Section 1 (pp. 662–667)
1. How did CORE differ from the NAACP in its approach?
2. What methods did Martin Luther King, Jr., favor to achieve equality, and where did these methods originate?
3. How did SNCC differ from SCLC?

Section 2 (pp. 669–673)
4. Why was the sit-in strategy effective in ending segregation policies?
5. How did activists desegregate the interstate bus system?
6. Describe the effect of the violence that erupted during the 1963 Birmingham marches, explaining both its local and national impact.

Section 3 (pp. 676–680)
7. In what ways did President Kennedy straddle the fence in his civil rights policies?
8. What role did Martin Luther King, Jr., play in the March on Washington?
9. How did Lyndon Johnson secure passage of major civil rights legislation during his presidency?

Section 4 (pp. 681–685)
10. What did author James Baldwin warn might happen if change in the area of civil rights did not occur quickly?
11. What message for African Americans did Malcolm X preach as a member of the Nation of Islam?
12. What were the underlying causes of the riots that occurred in many cities in the mid- to late 1960s?

1. **Formulating Questions** Create four questions to ask civil rights activist Anne Moody that would, if answered, lead to a deeper understanding of what participating in the civil rights movement of the early 1960s was like.

2. **Identifying Alternatives** What issues could provoke a sit-in or other nonviolent protest in your community? What other options for effecting change are available to members of your community?

3. **Distinguishing Fact from Opinion** Malcolm X once said that for African Americans, "The only solution is complete separation from the white man." Explain why you think this statement is a fact or an opinion.

1. **Evaluating Primary Sources** Review the primary source excerpt on pages 677–678. In what ways has Martin Luther King's dream come closer to being a reality? In what ways is it still a dream for the future? Use as many specific examples as possible, from both your personal experience and your knowledge of current events, to support your conclusions.

2. **Understanding the Visuals** In the primary source excerpt on page 673, Martin Luther King says, "For years now I have heard the word 'Wait!'" Find visuals in the chapter that illustrate why the people who fought for civil rights found it impossible to "wait" any longer to be treated fairly.

3. **Writing About the Chapter** It is the spring of 1960. SCLC executive director Ella Baker has asked you, a young African American, to attend a meeting of a new organization, the Student Nonviolent Coordinating Committee (SNCC). Write a letter in which you reply to Baker's invitation, explaining why you will or will not attend this meeting. First, create a list of what you see as the potential benefits of SNCC. Then list its possible negative features. Note any suggestions you have for the new organization. Next, write a draft of your reply to Baker's invitation in which you offer your ideas. Revise your letter, making sure that each idea is clearly expressed. Proofread your letter and draft a final copy.

4. **Using the Graphic Organizer** This graphic organizer uses a tree map to organize information about nonviolent confrontation during the civil rights movement. A tree map shows how details support a main idea. On this tree map, blue entries show the results of various events. (a) What was the result of each of the protests mentioned on the chart? (b) Which method of protest listed was the most effective as a nonviolent protest? (c) On a separate sheet of paper, create your own tree map about the challenge of Black Power, using this graphic organizer as an example.

Nonviolent Confrontation During the Early Civil Rights Movement				
Sit-ins	**Freedom Rides**	**Albany Movement**	**Integration of Ole Miss**	**Birmingham Confrontation**
• Test limits of segregation policies • Put business profits at risk • Become an effective way to integrate restaurants and stores	• Activists travel on interstate buses • Violence erupts in Deep South • Segregation prohibited on interstate transportation	• Activists plan a year of protests • Local leaders angered when Martin Luther King, Jr., takes charge • Movement fizzles	• Lines of confrontation drawn when James Meredith tries to gain admission to Ole Miss • Violence erupts • Ole Miss becomes integrated	• Activists challenging discriminatory hiring practices and segregated city facilities met with violence • Protesters win desegregated city facilities, fairer hiring practices, biracial committee

Continuing Social Revolution
1960–1975

*C*hange. Upheaval. Action. These words describe the social revolution of the 1960s and early 1970s. Far from occurring in a vacuum, the 1960s civil rights movement breathed new life into other issues. Women, Latinos, Asian Americans, and Native Americans adapted civil rights tactics to achieve their own goals of equality. Similar tactics helped launch movements to protect the environment and improve the quality and safety of certain consumer goods.

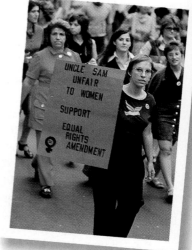

Events in the United States

1960 Asian Americans represent Hawaii in Congress.

1962 Biologist Rachel Carson publishes Silent Spring.

1963 Feminist Betty Friedan publishes The Feminine Mystique.

1965 César Chávez organizes farm workers.
• Ralph Nader publishes Unsafe at Any Speed.

1966 The National Organization for Women is founded.

1960	1962	1964	1966

Events in the World

1961 The Berlin Wall is built to divide East and West Berlin.

1964 Jomo Kenyatta becomes president of independent Kenya.

1966 Indira Gandhi becomes prime minister of India.

Pages 690 – 695

1 The Women's Movement

For generations, many American women had realized they were being treated as second-class citizens. Encouraged by the gains of the civil rights movement, women united behind the goal of ending discrimination based on gender.

Pages 697 – 701

2 Ethnic Minorities Seek Equality

Inspired by the civil rights movement, Latinos and Asian Americans launched their own movements to overcome racial discrimination. Each group faced different obstacles in its struggles for equal treatment.

Pages 702 – 706

3 Native American Struggles

Most Native Americans in the 1960s were living under conditions that were the result of centuries of discrimination and constantly changing government policies. They too took their cue from the civil rights movement to work for self-determination.

Pages 707 – 709

4 Environmental and Consumer Movements

The mood of protest in the 1960s energized movements to preserve the environment and challenge the safety of certain consumer products.

	1968 Activists found American Indian Movement (AIM).	1970 The federal government sets up the Environmental Protection Agency.	1972 Ms. magazine is founded.	1973 Native Americans stage a protest at Wounded Knee, South Dakota.	1975 Congress passes the Indian Self-Determination and Education Assistance Acts.
1968	**1970**		**1972**	**1974**	**1976**
	1969 Golda Meir becomes prime minister of Israel.	1970 Salvador Allende is elected president of Chile.	1972 Bangladesh becomes an independent nation.	1974 Haile Selassie is deposed as ruler of Ethiopia.	1975 Margaret Thatcher becomes head of Britain's Conservative party.

The Women's Movement

For generations, many American women had realized they were being treated as second-class citizens. Encouraged by the gains of the civil rights movement, women united behind the goal of ending discrimination based on gender.

Key Concepts
- American society in the 1950s discriminated against women economically and socially.
- From the civil rights movement, women learned legal and political techniques to fight discrimination.
    - Feminist leaders organized groups to advocate women's rights.
    - The feminist movement produced a backlash among some who wanted to preserve traditional roles.

Key Terms, People, and Places
feminism, feminist, National Organization for Women (NOW), Equal Rights Amendment (ERA); Gloria Steinem, Phyllis Schlafly

The new women's movement chose symbols for its cause that represented power.

The African American struggle for civil rights made other citizens keenly aware of inequalities in American life. Women, though not a minority in numbers, recognized certain disadvantages they had accepted for years and were determined to do something about them. From working in civil rights and other movements, many women had learned techniques that would help them gain a more equal role in American life.

The women's movement of the 1960s, although influenced by the civil rights movement, was not a new development in the nation's history. In the 1800s, particularly, women had worked for the right to vote and for equality in education and in jobs. The term **feminism** first came into recorded use in 1895 as a word to describe the theory of political, economic, and social equality of men and women. **Feminists** were those who believed in or acted on behalf of this theory.

Social Conditions Set the Stage for the Feminist Movement

The women's movement of the 1960s sought to change the style of American life that had been accepted for decades. Society expected women always to put home and family first.

During and after World War II, however, more and more women entered the labor force. As described in Chapter 21, the popular image of the 1950s put women at home, married, and raising children, but in fact more and more married women were employed. By the beginning of the 1960s, about half of all women held jobs.

Working women, however, earned less than working men doing similar or even the same jobs. In 1963, for example, women, on average, were paid only 63 cents for each dollar that men earned. By 1973 this figure had dropped to 57 cents. This financial inequality created a growing sense of frustration among women and led to demands for change.

In those same years, more and more women were going to college. In 1950 only 25 percent of all Bachelor of Arts degrees had gone to women. Twenty years later, in 1970, it was 41 percent. Better-educated women had high hopes for the future but often were discouraged by the discrimination they faced when they looked for jobs or tried to advance in their professions. Many employers, for example, acting under the belief that home and family should be a woman's only responsibility, denied women job opportunities for which they were qualified. Women who did enter the work force often found themselves underemployed, performing jobs and earning salaries far below their abilities. The graph on page 691 shows median incomes of men and women from 1950 to 1975. Now this generation of women was ready to act to change these conditions.

The Impact of the Civil Rights Movement

While social conditions set the scene for the women's movement, the civil rights movement provided a model for techniques and an inspiration for action. Black and white women joined in the struggle for civil rights, but they often found that they were expected to make coffee and do clerical work while men made most of the policy decisions.

At the same time, women gained valuable skills from their work in the movement. They learned the value of direct action and the usefulness of political pressure in making society respond. They saw the importance of strong publicity in making others understand the conditions they were trying to change.

The civil rights movement also provided women with legal tools to fight discrimination. One important piece of legislation was the 1964 Civil Rights Act (see Chapter 23).

Originally, the section of the act called Title VII prohibited discrimination based on race, religion, or national origin. When Congress debated the bill, however, some opponents of civil rights added an amendment to outlaw discrimination on the basis of gender. This action was a strategy to make the entire bill look ridiculous, so that it would fail in the final vote. To the dismay of its opponents, both the amendment and the bill passed. The new Civil Rights Act now had a provision that gave women a legal framework to use to fight discrimination.

Even with the added boost of the new legislation, progress took time. Women soon discovered that the Equal Employment Opportunity Commission (EEOC) set up by the bill took women's claims less seriously than those of African Americans. Nevertheless, Title VII would be tremendously important as the women's movement gained steam.

Women's Groups Raise "Consciousness"

As the 1960s unfolded, women began to meet together to compare experiences. Civil rights workers met to look for ways in which they could play a larger role in the struggle.

Median Incomes of Men and Women, 1950–1975

(Bar graph showing Annual Income in dollars for Men and Women from 1950 to 1975, with values ranging from 0 to $7,000)

Source: *Statistical Abstract of the United States*

Interpreting Graphs
Women's incomes continued to lag behind men's earnings, partly because many low-paying fields were traditionally considered "women's work." *Did the gap increase or decrease between 1950 and 1975?*

Soon they went beyond politics, exploring other aspects of their lives. The growing movement drew women who were active in other forms of protest and reform—student radicals, opponents of the draft, and workers for welfare rights and other social issues.

Another important influence was Betty Friedan's 1963 book *The Feminine Mystique* (see Chapter 21). Friedan described the cultural patterns that prevented women from achieving their full potential. Many readers recognized what she called "the problem that has no name"—the despair that came from trying to be the perfect wife and mother, the only roles society granted women.

Meeting in kitchens and living rooms, women in "consciousness-raising" groups began to talk about their lives in new ways. One participant, Nancy Hawley, a community activist in Boston, Massachusetts, was troubled by patterns she saw in her work for other social issues. "Though many of us were working harder than the men," she noted, "we realized we were not listened to and often ignored."

Betty Friedan voiced many women's feelings in her influential book *The Feminine Mystique.*

Women from different backgrounds shared their stories in informal meetings and found they had common experiences.

Women Organize NOW

In 1966 a small group of women decided to form an organization to pursue their goal of achieving equality. These women were frustrated that existing women's groups were unwilling to pressure the Equal Employment Opportunity Commission to take women's grievances more seriously. Twenty-eight professional women, including Betty Friedan, established the **National Organization for Women (NOW)** "to take action to bring American women into full participation in the mainstream of American society *now*."

NOW sought fair pay and equal job opportunities. It attacked the "false image of women" in the media, such as advertising that used sexist slogans or photographs. In one such ad in the 1960s, for example, an oven manufacturer asked, "Can a woman ever feel right cooking on a dirty range?" thus reinforcing the popular notion that a woman's sole contribution was to be a homemaker. NOW also called for more balance in marriages, with men and women sharing parenting and household responsibilities. A year after NOW was founded, it had 1,000 members.

Throughout the country, more and more women recognized the negative attitudes directed toward them. In New Orleans, Louisiana, civil rights activist Cathy Cade mentioned that her boyfriend had made fun of her for going to a "women's meeting." Others in her group began to tell stories of being teased or ridiculed for coming to a women's group. Such lack of support outside the group made their bond stronger within the group. As Cade put it:

> One thing became clear: that in the black movement I had been fighting for someone else's oppression and now there was a way that I could fight for my own freedom, and I was going to be much stronger than I ever was.

In San Francisco, Mimi Feingold, also a veteran of the civil rights and draft resistance movements, felt the same sense of exhilaration at her group's first meeting:

> It was something that we had all been waiting for, for a long time. It was a really liberating experience for all of us. . . . This was finally permission to look at our own lives and talk about how unhappy we were.

MAKING CONNECTIONS

What is the popular image of women today, and how does it differ from the image of women in the 1950s?

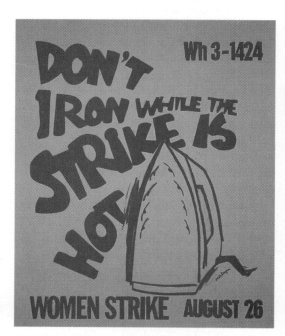

On August 26, 1970, the anniversary of the passage of the constitutional amendment on women's suffrage, thousands of women left jobs and household chores to observe "Women's Equality Day."

Four years later there were 15,000. Today, about 280,000 women belong to NOW.

For some women, NOW seemed too extreme; for others it was not extreme enough. Some saw NOW—and the women's movement in general—as mainly for the benefit of white, middle-class women. Nonetheless, NOW served as a rallying point in the movement to end sex discrimination and promote greater equality for all women.

The Impact of Feminism

The women's movement came of age in the early 1970s. Songs were one expression of the energy of the struggle. In 1971 pop singer Helen Reddy recorded a song that was soon broadcast on radio stations around the country. Delivered in the ringing, forceful style of an anthem, Reddy's hit song proclaimed:

> *I am woman, hear me roar*
> *In numbers too big to ignore,*
> *And I know too much to go back*
>   *and pretend. . . .*
>
> *Yes, I've paid the price*
> *But look how much I gained.*
> *If I have to, I can do anything.*
> *I am strong, I am invincible,*
> *I am woman.*

Reddy's lyrics reflected a new sense of women's self-confidence and a strength that drove the movement on.

Books and magazines likewise promoted the cause. *Our Bodies, Ourselves,* a handbook published by a women's health collective in Boston, encouraged women to understand their own health issues. It sold 200,000 copies in the first several years after its publication and three million by 1990. In 1972 journalist **Gloria Steinem** and several other women founded *Ms.* magazine, which was devoted to feminist issues and provided women with viewpoints that were decid-

The cover at left from the first edition of *Ms.* magazine, begun by Gloria Steinem (above), shows the many roles women had to fill.

edly different from those in *Good Housekeeping, Ladies' Home Journal,* and other women's magazines of the day. The preview issue of 300,000 copies sold out in eight days, and by 1973 *Ms.* had nearly 200,000 subscribers. While not all readers considered themselves feminists, they became familiar with the arguments of the movement from the magazine.

Slowly the women's movement brought a shift in attitudes. For example, a survey of first-year college students revealed a significant change in career goals. In 1970, men interested in fields such as business, law, engineering, and medicine outnumbered women by eight to one. Five years later, the margin had dropped to three to one. More women entered law school and medical school. They were finally admitted to military academies and trained as officers. The graph on page 694 clearly illustrates this trend in women's career paths.

Feminist Issues on the National Stage

Despite many shared concerns, the women's movement continued to be divided on its goals. In 1972 *Time* magazine observed, "The aims of the movement range from the modest, sensible amelioration [betterment] of the female condition to extreme and revolutionary visions." The more radical feminists emphasized the need to end male domination, sometimes rejecting men, marriage, and childbearing.

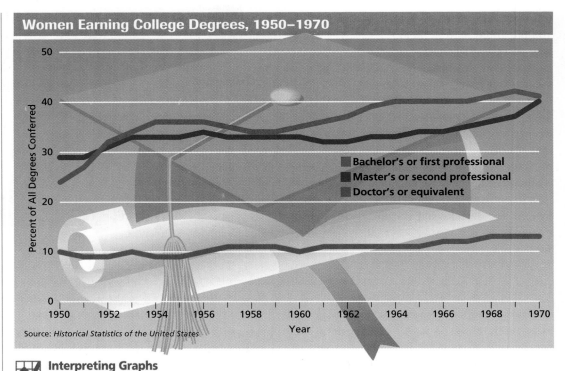

Women Earning College Degrees, 1950–1970

Percent of All Degrees Conferred

- Bachelor's or first professional
- Master's or second professional
- Doctor's or equivalent

Year

Source: *Historical Statistics of the United States*

Interpreting Graphs
As women's educational levels rose, so did their expectations of good jobs and fair salaries. *At which degree level—bachelor's, master's, or doctoral—did women gain the least?*

The Equal Rights Amendment NOW and other groups pressed for equal employment opportunities and facilities like day-care centers to make life more manageable for working parents. An even wider group took part in the campaign for constitutional change. In 1972 Congress passed the **Equal Rights Amendment (ERA)** to the Constitution:

E*quality of rights under the law shall not be denied or abridged by the United States or by any State on account of sex.*

To become law, the amendment had to be ratified by thirty-eight states. Thirty states complied quickly, then a few others, and approval at first seemed certain. Strong opposition surfaced, however, and the struggle for ratification went on until 1982 and then died.

Roe* v. *Wade NOW also worked to reform the laws governing a woman's right to choose an abortion instead of continuing an unwanted

pregnancy. Many states outlawed or severely restricted access to abortion. Women who could afford to travel to another state could usually find legal medical services, but poorer women turned to abortion methods that were not only illegal but frighteningly unsafe. A landmark social change came in 1973, when the Supreme Court legalized abortion in the controversial *Roe* v. *Wade* decision. The justices based their decision on a constitutional right to personal privacy, but they still allowed states to restrict abortions.

Backlash Against the Women's Movement

Many men at first were hostile to the feminist movement, which became known as "women's liberation" or "Women's Lib." Nor were all women sympathetic. Some responded by stressing their desire to remain at home and raise children and their satisfaction with traditional roles.

Marabel Morgan, a housewife from Florida, was one of those who argued that a woman's highest purpose in life should be to stay home and help her husband. In her book *The Total Woman*, published in 1973, she said:

> It is only when a woman surrenders her life to her husband, reveres and worships him, and is willing to serve him, that she becomes really beautiful to him. She becomes a priceless jewel, the glory of femininity, his queen!

Morgan suggested the "4A" approach: accept, admire, adapt, appreciate. She advised women readers how to make their marriages move from "fizzle to sizzle." Her tactic of defining a woman's self-worth in terms of beauty won her an approving audience. Two years after publication, her book had sold 500,000 copies.

Conservative political activist **Phyllis Schlafly** led a national campaign to block ratification of the ERA, saying:

> It won't do anything to help women, and it will take away from women the rights they already have, such as the right of a wife to be supported by her husband, the right of a woman to be exempted from military combat, and the right . . . to go to a single-sex college.

Schlafly also helped spread false ideas about the supposed effects of the ERA, such as coed bathrooms and the end of alimony. Women already had legal backing for their rights, she argued. Eventually, such arguments would prevent the ERA from being ratified within the time limit.

Viewpoints
On Working Mothers

The paragraphs below are from two of the books most widely read by women in the years from 1950 to 1975. *What argument does each author use to support his or her opinion?*

Against Working Mothers

"To work or not to work? *Some mothers* have *to work to make a living. Usually their children turn out all right, because some reasonably good arrangement is made for their care. But others grow up neglected and maladjusted. . . . It doesn't make sense to let mothers go to work making dresses in a factory or tapping typewriters in an office, and have them pay other people to do a poorer job of bringing up their children."*

Benjamin Spock, M.D., *Baby and Childcare,* 1957 edition, first published in 1945

For Working Mothers

"*At the present time, one can say anything—good or bad— about children of employed mothers and support the statement by some research finding. But there is no definitive evidence that children are less happy, healthy, adjusted, because their mothers work. The studies that show working women to be happier, better, more mature mothers do not get much publicity. Since juvenile delinquency is increasing, and more women work or 'are educated for some kind of intellectual work,' there is surely a direct cause-and-effect relationship, one says. Except that evidence indicates there is not.*"

Betty Friedan, *The Feminine Mystique,* 1963

SECTION 1 REVIEW

Key Terms, People, and Places
1. Define (a) feminism, (b) feminist, (c) National Organization for Women (NOW), (d) Equal Rights Amendment (ERA).
2. Identify (a) Gloria Steinem, (b) Phyllis Schlafly.

Key Concepts
3. How did the civil rights movement influence the women's movement?
4. What were some goals of NOW?

5. What did Betty Friedan identify as "the problem that has no name"?
6. What opposition did the women's movement encounter?

Critical Thinking
7. **Identifying Assumptions** What beliefs prompted many women to join the women's movement and groups such as NOW in the 1960s?

GEOGRAPHY

GRAPHS & CHARTS

HISTORIAN'S
TOOLBOX

CRITICAL
THINKING

HISTORICAL
EVIDENCE

Recognizing Bias

Recognizing bias means being aware of information and ideas that are one-sided or that present only a partial view of a subject. Knowing how to recognize bias is important because this skill helps you to better understand not only historical events, but also current issues. Campaign speeches, debates on controversial topics, and opinions expressed in the media all contain elements of bias. The ability to spot bias will help you analyze information about the present and the past.

Bias often is attached to issues that have an impact on people's emotions. One such issue is the women's movement, which questions the role of women in American life. Both of the excerpts on this page were taken from articles written during the reappearance of the women's movement in the 1960s and early 1970s. Use the following questions to help you determine whether either of these writings is biased.

1. Decide whether the excerpt presents only one side of an issue, while suggesting it covers all sides. Writing from a single viewpoint signals imbalance—and bias. (a) What is the overall message of each excerpt? (b) Which presents only one side of the issue while suggesting that it is a complete picture?

2. Determine whether the issue as described is supported by opinions or verifiable facts. Sometimes what appear to be facts are actually opinions disguised as facts. (a) Which details presented in the excerpts can be checked for accuracy? (b) Are any opinions presented as though they were facts? Give an example from the excerpts.

3. Examine the excerpts for hidden assumptions or generalizations that are not supported by facts. What hidden assumptions or generalizations does excerpt A contain? Excerpt B?

4. Analyze the excerpts for bias. Which excerpt is the least biased? Explain your answer.

A "What do black women feel about Women's Lib? Distrust. It is white, therefore suspect. They don't want to be used again to help somebody gain power—a power that is carefully kept out of their hands. They look at white women and see them as the enemy—for they know that racism is not confined to white men. . . . The faces of those white women hovering behind that black girl at the Little Rock school in 1957 do not soon leave the retina of the mind."
—Toni Morrison, "What the Black Woman Thinks About Women's Lib,"
The New York Times Magazine, August 22, 1971

B "The 14th and 15th amendments, written in 1868 and 1870, said: "ALL PERSONS BORN OR NATURALIZED IN THE U.S. ARE CITIZENS AND HAVE THE RIGHT TO VOTE."
Susan B. Anthony, considering herself to be a person, registered and voted in 1872. She was arrested, brought to trial, convicted of the crime of voting—because she was a woman, and the word PERSONS mentioned in our Constitution *DID NOT MEAN WOMEN*. . . . If she were alive today, Susan B. Anthony might vote, but she would still see 1000 legal discriminations against women upon various state statute books. . . .
The solution of the problem of giving women 100 per cent protection of the Constitution . . . is the adoption of the Equal Rights for Women Amendment which reads: "EQUALITY OF RIGHTS UNDER LAW SHALL NOT BE DENIED OR ABRIDGED BY THE UNITED STATES OR BY ANY STATE ON ACCOUNT OF SEX."
—Marjorie Longwell, "The American Woman—Then and Now,"
Delta Kappa Gamma Magazine, Fall 1969

Ethnic Minorities Seek Equality

SECTION PREVIEW

Inspired by the civil rights movement, Latinos and Asian Americans launched their own movements to overcome racial discrimination. Each group faced different obstacles in its struggles for equal treatment.

Key Concepts

- Latinos used tactics from the civil rights movement to overcome discrimination.
- Education and cultural pride were the major goals of the Latino movement.
- The United Farm Workers, led by César Chávez, sought better conditions for Mexican American farm workers.
- Asian Americans faced racial discrimination, particularly during World War II and the cold war.
- Asian Americans made economic and political gains in the 1960s and 1970s.

Key Terms, People, and Places

Latino, Anglo, *barrio*, migratory farm workers, United Farm Workers, Japanese American Citizens League; César Chávez

---

The United States is home to many ethnic and racial groups. Throughout the country's history, each group has faced different kinds of prejudice and discrimination. Latinos and Asian Americans have lived in the United States for many years. Yet both have had to fight for equality in mainstream American society.

The Latino Population

Spanish-speaking Americans, or **Latinos,** come from many places, although they share the same language and some elements of culture. But whether they come from Puerto Rico, Cuba, Mexico, or other parts of the Americas, Latinos often have been seen as outsiders and denied equal opportunities in many aspects of life, including employment, education, and housing.

In the 1960s and early 1970s, more and more people arrived from Central America and South America. Between 1970 and 1980, census figures for people "of Spanish origin" rose from 9 million to 14.6 million. Different groups tended to settle in certain areas. Americans of Cuban descent concentrated in Florida, Puerto Rican in the Northeast, and Mexican in the West and Southwest. As their population grew, Latinos throughout the country found and expressed a new pride in their heritage.

Mexican American Protests

Mexican Americans, often known as Chicanos, always have been the most numerous Latinos in the United States. In the 1960s, they began to organize against discrimination in education, jobs, and the legal system, leading to *el Movimiento Chicano*—the Chicano movement.

Cultural Identity Activists began encouraging pride in Mexican American culture and its dual heritage from Spain and the ancient cultures of Mexico. In 1967 Rodolfo "Corky" Gonzales, a Denver activist, wrote a long poem that raised Mexican Americans' self-awareness nationwide. *Yo Soy Joaquin* ("I am Joaquin") expresses the importance of cultural identity in Mexican history and the modern world. It begins:

I am Joaquin
lost in a world of confusion
caught up in the whirl of a gringo [white]
  society,
confused by the rules,
scorned by attitudes,
suppressed by manipulation
and destroyed by modern society.

Nationwide boycotts made the United Farm Workers' symbol, the eagle, well known.

Gonzales emphasized that **Anglos**—English-speaking, non-Latinos—had undermined Mexican Americans' control over their lives. Gonzales said that Anglos had done this through economic pressure and through institutions such as the schools, the Roman Catholic church, and the media.

Education Many Chicanos wanted changes in education. Schools in the *barrios,* or Latino neighborhoods, were crowded and run-down, with high dropout rates. In March 1968, ten thousand Mexican American students walked out of five such Los Angeles high schools to protest their unequal treatment. Students in Colorado, Texas, and other parts of California followed their example. Students demanded better courses and facilities and Latino teachers and counselors.

AMERICAN PROFILES

César Chávez

César Chávez (1927–1993), founder of the United Farm Workers, became a hero to millions of Americans, both Latino and Anglo. He was born in Yuma, Arizona, where his family had farmed for three generations. During the Great Depression, they lost their adobe farmhouse because they could not afford the taxes. Moving to California, they became **migratory farm workers,** who make a living moving from farm to farm to provide the labor needed to plant, cultivate, and harvest crops.

Chávez later remembered how his family fostered a powerful sense of independence:

I don't want to suggest we were that radical, but I know we were probably one of the strikingest families in California, the first ones to leave the fields if anyone shouted "Huelga!" — which is Spanish for "Strike!"

As he grew up among farm workers, Chávez gradually came to believe that unions were a way to resist employers' economic power. Migratory farm workers were some of the most exploited workers in the country, spending long hours doing backbreaking work for little pay. In the 1960s Chávez began to organize Mexican field hands into what became the **United Farm Workers (UFW).** He and a group of loyal followers went from door to door and field to field. By 1965 the union had 1,700 members.

The UFW's first target was the grape growers of California. Chávez, like Martin Luther King, Jr., believed in nonviolent action. In 1967, when growers refused to grant more pay, better working conditions, and union recognition, Chávez organized a successful nationwide consumer boycott of grapes picked on nonunion farms. Later boycotts of lettuce and other crops also won consumer support.

Chávez's efforts created many angry enemies and even brought him death threats. He responded by saying:

It's not me who counts, it's the Movement. And I think that in terms of stopping the Movement—this one or other movements by poor people around the country—the possibility is very remote. . . . The tide for change now has gone too far.

In 1975 California passed a measure that required collective bargaining between growers and union representatives. Workers now had a legal basis to ask for better working conditions. Chávez's efforts not only made him a national hero but also brought migratory farm workers into the broader movement for civil rights.

Other Latino Protests

Mexican Americans had other heroes too. Some formed organizations that took a militant approach, while others used political action.

Brown Berets In East Los Angeles, David Sanchez and other young Mexican Americans formed a community action group that took

As leader of the United Farm Workers, César Chávez once said the "truest act of courage . . . is to sacrifice ourselves for others in a totally nonviolent struggle for justice."

A mural in Los Angeles illustrates Mexican American pride.

on a semi-military style. Known as the Brown Berets, they later started branches in other cities. The group regarded itself as "defensive," protecting Mexican Americans against police and other authorities and sometimes acting outside the law. Sanchez said:

> W e're not a violent or a nonviolent organization . . . we are an emergency organization. . . . If we see a cop beating up a Chicano, we move in and stop the cop, we try to be ready for every emergency.

Political Action Some Latinos worked within mainstream politics. In 1961 voters in San Antonio, Texas, elected Henry B. González to Congress. Another Texan, Elizo "Kika" de la Garza, went to the House of Representatives in 1964, while Joseph Montoya of New Mexico was elected to the Senate.

New political groups formed to support Latino interests. For example, José Angel Gutiérrez brought together Mexican American groups in Crystal City, Texas, leading to the formation of the political party *La Raza Unida* in 1970. The new party worked for better housing and jobs and backed Mexican American political candidates.

Another leader, Reies López Tijerina, argued that the Anglo culture had stolen the Chicanos' land and heritage. To call attention to broken treaties, in 1966 his *Alianza Federal de Mercedes* (Federal Alliance of Land Grants) marched on the New Mexico state capital. At about the same time, the Mexican American Legal Defense and Educational Fund (MALDEF), was founded. It has provided legal aid to help Mexican Americans gain civil rights and encouraged Mexican American students to become lawyers.

MAKING CONNECTIONS

Different regions of the United States are home to larger numbers of certain ethnic groups. What ethnic groups are prominent in your area and what discrimination do they face, if any?

Asian Americans Fight Discrimination

Ever since their arrival in the United States, Americans of Chinese and Japanese ancestry have faced racial discrimination. Prejudice against Japanese Americans reached a peak during World War II, and the communist takeover of China in 1949 influenced attitudes toward Chinese Americans. In general, the years after the war brought many hopeful and positive changes for Asian Americans.

Japanese Americans After the War A major issue for Japanese Americans was compensation for the losses they had suffered during their wartime internment in the 1940s. As discussed in Chapter 19, Japanese American citizens living along the West Coast were forced to relocate to internment camps after the government decided they were a risk to American security once the nation declared war on Japan. Not only had their lives been disrupted, but

they had lost hundreds of millions of dollars in homes, farms, and businesses. The main voice for Japanese Americans, the **Japanese American Citizens League** (JACL), in 1948 won passage of the Japanese American Claims Act, under which Congress eventually paid relatively small amounts for property losses. JACL also worked for changes in anti-Asian immigration laws.

About two thirds of Japanese Americans who had been relocated returned to the Pacific Coast, but others moved to cities east of the Rockies. Their new communities were more a part of mainstream society than the prewar *nihonmachis*—"Japantown"—had been.

Economic Changes Although Asian Americans as a group were well educated, in 1960 they earned less than white Americans. In California, for example, for each $51 a white male was paid, a Chinese man would earn $38 and a Japanese man, $43. College graduates faced prejudice in attempting to move into management jobs.

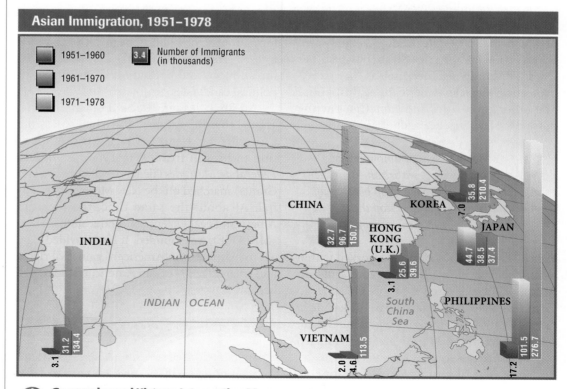

Asian Immigration, 1951–1978

1951–1960
1961–1970
1971–1978

3.4 Number of Immigrants (in thousands)

CHINA: 32.7 / 96.7 / 150.7
KOREA: 7.0 / 35.8 / 210.4
JAPAN: 44.7 / 38.5 / 37.4
HONG KONG (U.K.): 3.1 / 25.6 / 39.6
INDIA: 3.1 / 31.2 / 134.4
VIETNAM: 2.0 / 4.6 / 113.5
PHILIPPINES: 17.2 / 101.5 / 276.7

INDIAN OCEAN
South China Sea

Geography and History: Interpreting Maps
Patterns of immigration from Asia changed dramatically in the 1950s, 1960s, and 1970s. *Which two countries sent the greatest number of people in the 1950s? In the 1970s?*

Statehood for Hawaii created, for the first time, a state in which most voters were of Asian or part-Asian ancestry. Members of Congress from the new state, such as Daniel Inouye (above), reflected the islands' cultural diversity.

As a group, Asian Americans in the 1960s and 1970s were making economic gains faster than other minorities. Nonetheless, they still faced discrimination and relied on the example of the civil rights movement to push for gains. Some Chinese American community activists in the 1970s asked for federal help in overcoming problems of unemployment, health, and language barriers. Another development in the 1970s was an increase in immigration from other Asian countries, especially Korea, India, and Vietnam, as illustrated by the map on page 700.

Political Representation A major step forward for Asian Americans' self-image was the granting of statehood to Hawaii in 1959. The new state sent Hiram Leong Fong, a Chinese American, to the Senate, and Daniel K. Inouye, a Japanese American, to the House of Representatives. Other Asian American lawmakers have since been elected from Hawaii and California.

SECTION 2 REVIEW

Key Terms, People, and Places
1. Define (a) Latino, (b) Anglo, (c) *barrio*, (d) migratory farm workers, (e) United Farm Workers, (f) Japanese American Citizens League.
2. Identify César Chávez.

Key Concepts
3. What was the importance of the poem *Yo Soy Joaquin?*
4. What role did César Chávez play in the Chicano struggle for equal rights?

5. What were other forms of Chicano protest?
6. What world events influenced prejudice against Asian Americans?
7. Why was Hawaiian statehood significant for Asian Americans?

Critical Thinking
8. **Recognizing Bias** What factors might have made prejudice against Asian Americans last longer than discrimination against people of European ancestry?

Native American Struggles

Most Native Americans in the 1960s were living under conditions that were the result of centuries of discrimination and constantly changing government policies. They too took their cue from the civil rights movement to work for self-determination.

Key Concepts
- Native Americans faced unique problems in terms of poverty and discrimination.
- Many Native American activists worked to maintain their traditional culture and identity as a people.
- The American Indian Movement focused on urban problems and spearheaded protests.
- Protests and legal challenges won Native Americans more self-determination.

Key Terms, People, and Places
American Indian Movement (AIM); Dennis Banks, Russell Means; Alcatraz

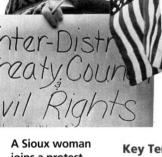

A Sioux woman joins a protest against federal policies for Native Americans.

N ative Americans were another minority who were inspired by the civil rights movement to seek equality and control over their own lives. Overall, Native Americans were perhaps the country's most troubled nonwhite group, in part because of government policies. Activists used legal challenges and direct action to reach their goals.

Native Americans Face Unique Problems

As the original inhabitants of North America, Native Americans have occupied a unique social and legal position. Although their cultures and languages are varied, white society has seen "Indians" as one group. The Constitution excluded them from citizenship, and Congress assumed the right to supervise them.

From the 1800s on, government agencies limited self-government for Native Americans and often worked to erase their traditional lifestyles. Until 1924, many Native Americans did not have full citizenship rights. Today they are citizens of both the United States and their own nations or tribal groups.

As a whole, Native Americans have routinely been denied equal opportunities. They have had higher rates of unemployment, alcoholism, and suicide, as well as a shorter life expectancy, than white Americans. Poverty and poor living conditions were once common in their communities. Like other nonwhite groups, Native Americans were the victims of centuries-old stereotypes, reinforced by the way movies and other media depicted them.

Native Americans also had some grievances that were unique. **Dennis Banks,** a Chippewa, explained why he became an activist:

I t was a question of this government being responsible to me, and not seeing to it that I had an opportunity to lead a decent life, or to own a piece of land, or to find a good job, like they had promised my ancestors in all these treaties. They broke all of those promises. They stole everything from them and wrecked their way of life—which was a good way.

Roots of Native American Activism

An important part of the Native Americans' way of life was their tie to the land and what it stood for. "Everything is tied to our homeland," declared D'Arcy McNickle, a Native American anthropologist, in 1961. Yet, many years after pioneers first moved onto Indian territory, state and federal governments continued to take over traditional tribal lands. Protecting what was left became a major goal of Native Americans.

Native American Pride and Sports Team Names

The Native American movement of the 1960s and early 1970s influenced changes in more areas than one might expect. One example of the effects of the reawakening of Native American pride can be found in the sports world, where Native American names and images often have been used as team names and mascots. Arguing that using Native American names in such a way is degrading and racially offensive and that other races are not used for the same purpose, Native Americans began to request that some teams change their names. In response,

in 1969 Dartmouth College, in New Hampshire, changed its team name from the Indians to the Big Green to avoid racial insensitivity. In 1972, Stanford University, in California, whose team name was also the Indians, likewise changed its name. Stanford chose the Cardinal to replace its previous name. Syracuse University followed suit not much later, abandoning its original mascot, the Saltine Warrior, for an orange with arms and legs.

The attitudes that prompted these changes have affected professional sports teams as well. In 1991

the Atlanta Braves sparked considerable debate over both their name and their rallying cry, the "Tomahawk Chop." The same year, controversy over the Washington Redskins reached fever pitch with the introduction of a bill before Congress. Senator Ben Nighthorse Campbell of Colorado proposed that no federal land be allotted for the Redskins' new stadium until the team changed its name. Thus far, the name change has not taken place. *What other popular names or symbols might some groups find offensive?*

Land Claims A government project in New York state triggered one early protest. According to a 1794 treaty, the Seneca Nation held the land on its Allegany reservation. The federal government, however, had long planned to build a dam there as part of a flood control project. The Kinzua Dam would affect 10,000 acres of hunting and fishing land, as well as homes and sacred sites.

In 1956 Congress held hearings, which did not include the Seneca, and appropriated funds for the dam. After legal appeals failed, the Seneca in 1961 went to President John Kennedy, but he supported the government claim. Once the dam was built, Congress agreed to pay $15 million in damages, but this did not restore the land.

Other Native Americans responded to this decision by bringing lawsuits for violations of treaty rights and failure to make promised payments. Court rulings supported many claims. For example, in 1967 the Court of Claims ruled that the federal government had forced the Seminole to give up Florida lands in 1823 for an unreasonably low price. The court directed the government to pay more to the Seminole community.

The American Indian Movement One of the leading activist movements began in Minneapolis in 1968, led by Dennis Banks and George Mitchell, both Chippewa. At a meeting of 250 people representing twenty Native American organizations, Banks set forth the goals: "Let's get a new organized effort going, a new coalition that will fight for Indian treaty rights and better conditions and opportunities for our people."

The new organization came to be called the **American Indian Movement (AIM).** It originally focused on the special problems of Native Americans living in cities. Following the example of militant black groups, AIM set up Indian patrols to monitor street activity. It also began survival schools to encourage racial and cultural pride in young people.

Many people, both white and Native American, criticized AIM's militant approach. On the group's second anniversary, however, Banks repeated its goals:

We must commit ourselves to changing the social pattern in which we have been forced to live. . . . The government and churches have demoralized, dehumanized, massacred, robbed, raped, promised, made treaty after treaty, and lied to us. . . . We must now destroy this political machine that man has built to prevent us from self-determination.

MAKING ✕ CONNECTIONS

One goal of Native American activists has been to force the federal government to honor treaties made in the 1800s. Why were so many treaties made—and then broken?

Echoes of past history surrounded the Sioux village of Wounded Knee, where AIM members, led by Russell Means (left) and others, protested past and present federal government actions against Native Americans.

Confronting the Government

Trying to call attention to issues long ignored, Native Americans staged several standoffs with the federal government. In 1972, demonstrators formed the Broken Treaties Caravan, traveled to Washington, D.C., and occupied the federal government's Bureau of Indian Affairs' offices for six days. Other protests were even more dramatic.

The Occupation of Alcatraz In November 1969, seventy-eight protesters from several Native American groups landed on Alcatraz, an island in San Francisco Bay on which stood an abandoned federal prison. They claimed the 13-acre rock under the terms of the Fort Laramie Treaty of 1868, which allowed male Native Americans to file homestead claims on federal lands. The occupation also was a protest against the policies and methods of the Bureau of Indian Affairs.

Others joined the original group, planning to turn the deserted island into an educational and cultural center. In March 1970, author Vine Deloria, Jr., a Standing Rock Sioux, wrote hopefully about the project in the *New York Times*:

> *B*y making Alcatraz an experimental Indian center operated and planned by Indian people, we would be given a chance to see what we could do toward developing answers to modern social problems. Ancient tribalism can be incorporated with modern technology in an urban setting. Perhaps we would not succeed in the effort. . . . It just seems to a lot of Indians that this continent was a lot better off when we were running it.

The occupation failed to achieve the desired results. Federal marshals eventually removed

AIM leader Dennis Banks leads a protest march at Mount Rushmore, South Dakota.

the last protesters after a year and a half. But the episode dramatized Native American grievances and gained important national exposure.

Confrontation at Wounded Knee An even more dramatic confrontation came in 1973 at the Oglala Sioux village of Wounded Knee, South Dakota. There, in 1890, the army's Seventh Cavalry had massacred more than two hundred Sioux men, women, and children.

The Pine Ridge reservation around the village was one of the country's poorest, with half its families living on welfare. In February 1973, AIM leaders **Russell Means** and Dennis Banks and some two hundred AIM members took over the village. AIM sought to draw attention to conditions on the reservation and to the 371 treaties it said the government had broken over the years.

Other Native American leaders came out in support of the occupation. Onondaga Chief Oren Lyons, speaking for the Iroquois, said:

W e support the Oglala Sioux Nation or any Indian Nation that will fight for its sovereignty. . . . The issue

here at Wounded Knee is the recognition of the treaties between the United States Government and the sovereign nations that were here before.

Federal marshals and FBI agents then surrounded the village, allowing only occasional shipments of supplies. From time to time, gunfire broke out. As the siege went on, agents arrested some three hundred people, including news reporters and outside supporters.

By the time the standoff finally ended in May, two AIM members had been killed and about a dozen people hurt, including two federal marshals. The government agreed to re-examine treaty rights.

The Government Responds Native American activism brought some responses from the government. The Kennedy and Johnson administrations in the 1960s tried to bring jobs and income to some reservations by encouraging industries to locate there and leasing reservation lands to energy and development corporations. But many Native Americans worried about the effects

Many Native American groups went to court to win back land and other rights. Wearing traditional ceremonial dress, George Crows Fly High and Martha Grass, along with civil rights leader Ralph Abernathy, seek a meeting with Supreme Court justices.

these projects would have on the land. In the 1970s, the Navaho, Crow, Northern Cheyenne, and others sought to renegotiate or cancel many of the leases.

Pressure by Native Americans also led to their inclusion in "Great Society" programs dealing with housing, health, and education. Government agencies made resources available and let Native Americans plan and run their own programs and, in some places, their own schools.

A number of laws passed in the 1970s favored Native American rights. The Indian Education Act of 1972 gave parents and tribal councils more control over schools and school programs. The Indian Self-Determination and Education Assistance Acts of 1975 upheld Native American autonomy and let local leaders administer federally supported social programs for housing and education.

Native Americans also continued to win legal battles to regain land, mineral, and water rights. For example, in 1971 the Alaska Federation of Natives was given $1 billion and 40 million acres of land. In 1970, after rejecting a cash settlement, the Taos in New Mexico won back Blue Lake, a religious shrine, as well as 48,000 acres of land. A Taos representative said:

> We don't have gold temples in this lake, but we have a sign of a living God to whom we pray—the living trees, the evergreen and spruce . . . and the lake itself. . . . We are taking that water to give us strength so we can gain in knowledge and wisdom.

SECTION 3 REVIEW

Key Terms, People, and Places
1. Define American Indian Movement.
2. Identify (a) Dennis Banks, (b) Russell Means, (c) Alcatraz.

Key Concepts
3. What problems were typical of Native American communities in the 1960s?
4. How did the African American civil rights movement influence the tactics of Native American groups?

5. What group was the original focus of the American Indian Movement?
6. What did Native Americans hope to accomplish by lawsuits?

Critical Thinking
7. **Making Comparisons** How was the social and political situation of Native Americans different from that of African Americans?

Environmental and Consumer Movements

SECTION PREVIEW

The mood of protest in the 1960s energized movements to preserve the environment and to challenge the safety of certain consumer products.

Key Concepts

• The activism of minorities in the 1960s spurred environmentalists and consumers to take action.
• The modern environmental movement was triggered by Rachel Carson's *Silent Spring*.
• Ralph Nader was a major figure in beginning the movement for consumers' rights.

Key Terms, People, and Places
Environmental Protection Agency (EPA);
Rachel Carson, Ralph Nader

In the 1960s and early 1970s, the mood of protest surrounding the civil rights movement inspired a number of other movements. Environmentalists demanded actions that would preserve and restore the earth's environment and resources. Similarly, consumers and vigilant consumer advocates used proven protest techniques to ensure that American industries would be accountable to their customers and workers. Their efforts brought changes in public attitudes and public policy—changes that affect the lives of Americans to this day.

The Environmental Movement

Like the women's movement, the environmental movement did not spring up in the 1960s but had roots in the American past. In the late 1890s and early 1900s, progressives had worked to make public lands and parks available for the people. New Deal programs of the 1930s included tree-planting projects in an effort to put people back to work—as well as to conserve forests and farmlands.

Rachel Carson The modern environmental movement stemmed even more directly, however, from the work of marine biologist **Rachel Carson.** She had once hoped to become a writer but initially followed her interest in zoology. In the 1930s and 1940s, however, she combined her talents and began to write about scientific subjects for general audiences. In 1951 Carson published *The Sea Around Us*, which was an immediate best seller. Her major—and most influential—book was *Silent Spring*, published in 1962. In *Silent Spring*, Carson attacked the use of chemical pesticides, particularly DDT, which had increased agricultural productivity but killed various plants and animals other than the insect pests that were its target:

Environmental activists battled for a variety of issues in the 1960s.

> The most alarming of all man's assaults upon the environment is the contamination of air, earth, rivers, and sea with dangerous and even lethal materials. This pollution is for the most part irrecoverable. . . . In this now universal contamination of the environment, chemicals are the sinister and little-recognized partners of radiation in changing the very nature of the world.

As Carson explained, chemicals sprayed on crops entered into living organisms and moved from one to another in a chain of poisoning and death. Specifically, the lingering effects of DDT threatened to destroy many species of birds and fish, including the national symbol, the bald eagle.

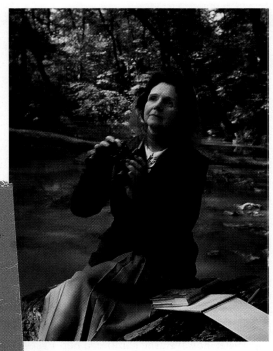

Disturbed by the changes she saw in her environment, biologist Rachel Carson sounded a trumpet call to action in her book *Silent Spring,* inspiring others to join a strong environmental movement.

Nuclear Power Another issue arose toward the end of the 1960s, as environmentalists focused on the problems of nuclear power plants built to generate electricity. While nuclear plants caused less air pollution than coal-burning plants, they produced steam that was then discharged into local waterways. The steam raised water temperatures, killing fish and plant life. People also worried about the possibility of nuclear plant accidents.

Public Response Grassroots environmental movements sprang up in many places, supporting conservation efforts and opposing actions such as the building of new nuclear plants. In 1970 Americans celebrated the first Earth Day, which would become a yearly observance aimed at heightening awareness of environmental issues and marked by day-long activities to clean up pollution and litter. Besides Rachel Carson, other scientists were alarmed by environmental problems. For example, in his 1971 book *The Closing Circle,* biologist Barry Commoner warned about rapid increases in pollution.

The efforts of the environmentalists helped spur the federal government to create new policies. Responding to public concerns about air and water pollution, in 1970 Congress passed the Water Quality Improvement Act and the Clean Air Act. Also in 1970, President Richard Nixon's administration established the **Environmental Protection Agency (EPA).** The EPA combined existing federal agencies concerned with air and water pollution. As the nation's watchdog against polluters, the EPA today monitors and reduces air and water pollution and regulates the disposal of solid waste and the use of pesticides and toxic substances.

Silent Spring was a bombshell. The chemical industry fought back vigorously, arguing that Carson confused the issues and left readers "unable to sort fact from fancy." The public was not persuaded by this attack. So great was national concern that a special presidential advisory committee was appointed. It called for continued research and warned against the widespread use of pesticides. Eventually DDT was banned in the United States, and other chemicals were controlled more strictly. For more information about the impact of *Silent Spring,* see the feature "Time and Place: A Geographic Perspective" on page 710.

It was not only DDT that worried people. They became more conscious of poisonous fumes in the air, oil spills on beaches, and toxic wastes buried in the ground. In the mid-1960s, President Lyndon Johnson's administration addressed environmental concerns as part of the "Great Society." Johnson hoped for "an environment that is pleasing to the senses and healthy to live in." Environmental legislation was part of his broader reform program.

MAKING CONNECTIONS

Do you think that concern for the environment has increased or decreased since the 1970s? What evidence have you seen?

The Consumer Movement

The consumer movement was yet another outgrowth of the 1960s protests. It too had roots in earlier years. The Pure Food and Drug Act of 1906, for example, was one early effort to maintain standards and protect the public. In the 1960s and early 1970s, however, the movement grew far stronger and involved more people.

Attorney **Ralph Nader** spearheaded the new consumer effort. Nader had been a serious activist all his life. While a student at Princeton University in the early 1950s, Nader protested the spraying of campus trees with DDT. His interest in automobile safety began at Harvard Law School and continued into his law practice in Hartford, Connecticut. In 1964 Daniel Patrick Moynihan, then assistant secretary of labor, hired Nader as a consultant on the issue of automobile safety regulations.

The government report Nader wrote soon became a book, *Unsafe at Any Speed: The Designed-in Dangers of the American Automobile.* It began:

> For over half a century the automobile has brought death, injury, and the most inestimable sorrow and deprivation to millions of people. With Medea-like intensity, this mass trauma began rising sharply four years ago reflecting new and unexpected ravages by the motor vehicle. A 1959 Department of Commerce report projected that 51,000 persons would be killed by automobiles in 1975. That figure will probably be reached in 1965, a decade ahead of schedule.

Like the muckrakers of the Progressive era, Nader used facts to support his passionate argument that car manufacturers would be responsible for many of these deaths. He called many cars "coffins on wheels," pointing to dangers such as a tendency to flip over. The industry, he charged,

knowingly continued to build over one million cars before confronting the safety problems.

Nader's book was a sensation, and in 1966 he testified before Congress about automobile hazards. That year, Congress passed the National Traffic and Motor Vehicle Safety Act. The *Washington Post* noted that, "Most of the credit for making possible this important legislation belongs to one man—Ralph Nader. . . . A one-man lobby for the public prevailed over the nation's most powerful industry."

Nader broadened his efforts and investigated the meatpacking business, helping to secure support for the Wholesome Meat Act of 1967. He next looked into consumer problems in other industries. Scores of volunteers, called "Nader's Raiders," signed on to help. They turned out report after report and inspired consumer activism. As ordinary Americans began to stand up for their rights, consumer protection offices had to respond to a flood of complaints.

Concern for the earth and its health prompted Earth Day rallies and clean-ups, including such events as a roadway "lie-down" by 5,000 people to protest car fumes in Italy and a Cheyenne ceremony at dawn outside Bozeman, Montana.

SECTION 4 REVIEW

Key Terms, People, and Places
1. Define Environmental Protection Agency.
2. Identify (a) Rachel Carson, (b) Ralph Nader.

Key Concepts
3. What was the target of Rachel Carson's book *Silent Spring?*

4. What role did Ralph Nader play in the consumer movement?

Critical Thinking
5. **Recognizing Cause and Effect** What were some of the results of Rachel Carson's book *Silent Spring?*

After *Silent Spring*

Although many of her concerns were shared by other scientists, Rachel Carson's book Silent Spring *was a landmark in the environmental movement. Why did Carson's book have such an impact?*

The publication of Rachel Carson's book *Silent Spring* in 1962 is usually described as a landmark event in the history of the environmental movement. Carson, concerned about the disappearance of songbirds from America's towns and cities, blamed the immensely successful and widely used pesticide DDT. Scientists already were beginning to weigh the environmental costs of DDT against its proven benefits in controlling insects. Their voices, however, tended to be overridden by the chemical companies and the agricultural lobby, both of which favored continued DDT use.

What Carson did was to plant in the mind of the general public an important concept: that humans are a part of a living ecological system, not outside of it or dominant over it. Geographers and other scientists had long been interested in the concept that people, plants, and animals are all part of the same ecosystem. After *Silent Spring*, however, a growing awareness of the theme of interaction between humans and the environment led to a national movement that continues to this day.

> What Carson did was to plant in the mind of the general public an important concept: that humans are a part of a living ecological system, not outside of it or dominant over it.

some time, at first in Europe, and much later in the United States. This was the concern that "progress" in science and technology was a two-edged sword. Such progress, people worried, might bring about negative as well as positive outcomes, and unintended as well as intended consequences. One such worry focused on the massive increase in the number of automobiles. While cars made it possible for many Americans to live outside of the cities where they worked, their use also brought increased air pollution. By the end of the 1960s, cars and trucks were identified as being the sources of more than half the air pollution in the United States.

It was into this troubled decade that Rachel Carson brought the environmental movement in 1962. During the 1960s, the environmental movement grew to a mass movement, partly because of court cases against the use of DDT brought late in the decade by the Environmental Defense Fund, one of many activist groups. At the close of the decade, the movement won official government recognition with the founding of the Environmental Protection Agency in 1970.

Human and Environmental Interaction: Background to a Movement

By pointing out that DDT not only poisoned insects, but also killed birds that ate the poisoned insects, Carson questioned humankind's relationship with the natural world. Her views were part of a much larger concern that had been building for

DDT: A Case Study of a Shift in Ideology

Until the 1960s, most Americans generally accepted the idea that humans should use the natural world for their own ends. Science and technology were the tools that let them do so. A case in point was the use of DDT by large-scale commercial farmers. Many important and profitable American

A Shift in Public Opinion: The Environment

"Which of these problems would you like to see government devote most of its attention to in the next two years? — Gallup Poll question

Issue	Percent of Public Mentioning Item		
	1965	1970	Five-Year Change
Reducing amount of crime	41	56	15%
Reducing pollution of air and water	17	53	36%
Improving public education	45	31	-14%
Helping people in poor areas	32	30	-2%
Conquering "killer" diseases	37	29	-14%
Improving housing, clearing slums	21	27	6%
Reducing racial discrimination	29	25	-4%
Reducing unemployment	35	25	-10%
Improving highway safety	18	13	-5%
Beautifying America	3	5	2%

Source: *The Politics of Environmental Concern*, by Walter A. Rosenbaum

farm crops came originally from Europe and Asia, bringing their own insect pests with them. By the early 1900s, farmers were ready to use any easy-to-use, inexpensive method to kill insects that gobbled up corn, wheat, and other crops.

Farmers turned enthusiastically to chemical insecticides, but many of these poisons contained metals such as lead or arsenic that were deadly to humans. Against this background, DDT—which was apparently not toxic to humans even in massive doses—seemed like a wonderful solution.

By the 1960s, however, new research findings caused some people to question the assumption that humans should freely exploit nature. Rachel Carson brought some of that new research to light. She based her book on observations of the negative effect of DDT caused by massive spraying in American urban areas in an attempt to protect Dutch Elm trees from insect pests. As it turned out, DDT was a poison that remained in the ecosystem long after it had destroyed insect pests. It built up in the fatty tissues of birds and fish that ate the poisoned insects, and its long-term effects could be fatal. In birds, for example, DDT weakened shell formation so that young birds did not hatch. Predator birds

high in the food chain, such as hawks and eagles, reached the crisis stage first because they ate smaller birds, fish, and rodents.

Silent Spring sparked a debate that in 1972 resulted in the banning of almost all uses of DDT in the United States. Even more significantly, by questioning the popular ideology that nature exists for the benefit of humanity, Carson and other scientists and historians helped introduce a new ideology. Within a decade, environmentalism grew from something that interested only a small number of geographers and scientists to a nationwide movement embraced by a majority of citizens.

GEOGRAPHIC CONNECTIONS

1. Why were American crops such as wheat and corn susceptible to insect pests?
2. How did farmers' use of DDT affect other parts of the environment?

Critical Thinking

3. **Recognizing Ideologies** How did people's beliefs about their relationship with the natural environment change during the 1960s?

Chapter Review

Key Terms
1. feminism
2. feminist
3. National Organization for Women (NOW)
4. Equal Rights Amendment (ERA)
5. Latino
6. Anglo
7. *barrio*
8. migratory farm workers
9. United Farm Workers (UFW)
10. Japanese American Citizens League
11. American Indian Movement (AIM)
12. Environmental Protection Agency (EPA)

People
13. Gloria Steinem
14. Phyllis Schlafly
15. César Chávez
16. Dennis Banks
17. Russell Means
18. Rachel Carson
19. Ralph Nader

Places
20. Alcatraz

Terms For each term above, write a sentence that explains its relation to citizen activism and the social revolution of the l960s and early 1970s.

Matching Review the key terms in the list above. If you are not sure of a term's meaning, review its definition in the chapter. Then choose a term from the list that best matches each description below.
1. the theory of the political, economic, and social equality of men and women
2. a Latino neighborhood
3. the nation's watchdog against polluters
4. English-speaking, non-Latino Americans
5. people who make a living moving from place to place to plant, cultivate, and harvest crops

True or False Determine whether each statement is true or false. If it is true, write "true." If it is false, change the underlined name to make the statement true.
1. <u>Gloria Steinem</u> began the environmental movement by writing *Silent Spring*.
2. <u>César Chávez</u> spearheaded the consumer effort by attacking automobile safety.
3. In *The Feminine Mystique,* <u>Dennis Banks</u> described the cultural patterns that prevented women from reaching their full potential.
4. The American Indian Movement leader <u>Russell Means</u> helped take over the village of Wounded Knee as a protest against the American government.

Section 1 (pp. 690 – 695)
1. Describe how society in the 1950s discriminated against women.
2. What political skills did women learn from their work in the civil rights movement?
3. Name at least three of the ways in which women tried to fight discrimination during the l960s and early 1970s.
4. Describe the beliefs and fears that eventually prevented ratification of the ERA.

Section 2 (pp. 697 – 701)
5. Describe the goals of the Chicano movement.
6. What does the profile of César Chávez reveal about the tactics used by Latinos to overcome discrimination?
7. What positive changes did the years after World War II bring for Asian Americans?

Section 3 (pp. 702 – 706)
8. How did the United States government contribute to the discrimination faced by Native Americans?
9. What was the major issue over which Native American activists confronted the federal government?
10. Describe some of the tactics used by the American Indian Movement.
11. How successful was Native American activism in achieving its goals?

Section 4 (pp. 707 – 709)
12. What were the goals of the consumer movement?
13. Describe how Rachel Carson's *Silent Spring* initiated the environmental movement.
14. What were two of the targets of Ralph Nader's consumer movement?

1. **Drawing Conclusions** During the l960 and l970s, César Chávez's United Farm Workers organized boycotts of grapes, lettuce, and other crops. Explain the purpose of these boycotts. What issues might lead you to join in a boycott?

2. **Demonstrating Reasoned Judgment** Think of a local concern that affects your community, such as a new housing development that threatens to destroy your favorite patch of trees or the need for increased recycling in your neighborhood. Following the examples of any of the activists you have read about in the chapter—such as Gloria Steinem, César Chávez, Rachel Carson, or Ralph Nader—what could you do to champion your cause?

1. **Evaluating Primary Sources** Review the second primary source excerpt on page 695. What assumptions is Phyllis Schlafly making when she explains her arguments against the ERA?

2. **Understanding the Visuals** Look at the graph of median incomes for men and women on page 691. What does this graph tell you about the legitimacy of the drive for passage of the Equal Rights Amendment?

3. **Writing About the Chapter** Choose one of the following characters: a woman, a Chicano, a Native American, or an Asian American during the 1960s. As your chosen character, you are to testify to a congressional subcommittee regarding the discrimination faced by you and your group. First, create a list of examples illustrating the discrimination you face. Note any historical explanations for this discrimination and any suggestions you have for improving the situation. Next, write a draft of your testimony in which you explain your experiences and those of your group. Revise your testimony, making sure that each example, explanation, and suggestion is clearly explained. Proofread your testimony and draft a final copy.

4. **Using the Graphic Organizer** This graphic organizer uses a tree map to organize information about the women's movement. (a) According to the graphic organizer, how did the women's movement benefit from legal action? (b) What was the connection between consciousness-raising and women's groups? (c) On a separate sheet of paper, create your own graphic organizer about Native American struggles against discrimination, using this graphic organizer as an example.

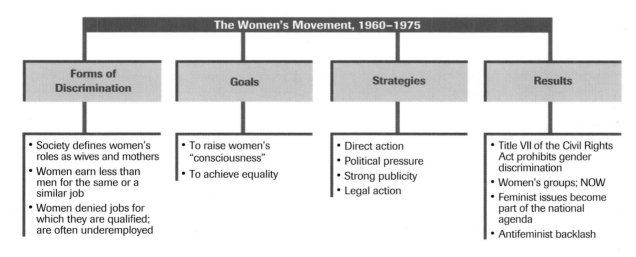

The Women's Movement, 1960–1975

Forms of Discrimination	Goals	Strategies	Results
• Society defines women's roles as wives and mothers • Women earn less than men for the same or a similar job • Women denied jobs for which they are qualified; are often underemployed	• To raise women's "consciousness" • To achieve equality	• Direct action • Political pressure • Strong publicity • Legal action	• Title VII of the Civil Rights Act prohibits gender discrimination • Women's groups; NOW • Feminist issues become part of the national agenda • Antifeminist backlash

The Vietnam War and American Society

1960–1975

*T*he Vietnam War was one of the most tragic events of the cold war. United States Presidents from Eisenhower to Nixon spent billions of dollars and sent half a million soldiers to Vietnam. Over time, as the war consumed more and more resources, many Americans questioned whether the United States should remain involved in this faraway conflict. The Vietnam War was only one of many issues that divided American society in the 1960s, but it cut deep and left lasting scars.

Events in the United States

1960 Student activists establish Students for a Democratic Society (SDS).

1963 President Kennedy is assassinated.
• The Bob Dylan song "The Times They Are A-Changin' " is a hit.

1964 Lyndon Johnson wins reelection to the presidency.

1965 President Johnson rapidly increases the number of American troops in Vietnam.

1967 Antiwar protesters march on the Pentagon.

1960	1962	1964	1966

Events in the World

1963 South Vietnamese leader Diem is assassinated.
• Kenya wins independence.

1964 Civil war escalates in Vietnam.
• United Nations troops restore order in the Congo.

1965 European Common Market nations eliminate industrial tariffs.

1967 Israel defeats the Arabs in the Six-Day War.
• Civil war begins in Nigeria

1968 Richard Nixon is elected United States President.

1970 Rock stars Janis Joplin and Jimi Hendrix die of drug overdoses.
• Four students are shot at Kent State.

1972 Nixon is reelected.

1973 The United States withdraws final troops from Vietnam.

1968	1970	1972	1974	1976

1969 Golda Meir becomes prime minister of Israel.

1970 The Aswan Dam is completed in Egypt.

1971 East Pakistan becomes the independent nation of Bangladesh.

1972 Ferdinand Marcos declares martial law in the Philippines.

1974 Argentinian dictator Juan Perón dies.

1975 The South Vietnamese government surrenders to North Vietnam.

The War in the 1960s

SECTION PREVIEW

Determined to defeat Ho Chi Minh's communist forces, Presidents Kennedy and Johnson supported dictatorships and sent thousands of American soldiers to fight and die in Vietnam.

Key Concepts

- Fearing that communist forces would take over Vietnam, the United States supported the repressive government of Ngo Dinh Diem in southern Vietnam.
- President Kennedy increased American involvement in the early 1960s by sending military advisers to South Vietnam.
- President Johnson used the Gulf of Tonkin incident as an excuse to begin bombing North Vietnam and sending thousands more American troops to the country.

Key Terms, People, and Places

Viet Cong, Gulf of Tonkin Resolution, escalation, Tet Offensive; Ngo Dinh Diem; Saigon

The fates of three nations—Vietnam, the United States, and France—became interwoven in the struggle for control over Vietnam.

By the mid-twentieth century, Vietnam had a history of nationalism that extended back nearly 2,000 years. Two Vietnamese sisters, Trung Trac and Trung Nhi, organized the first major revolt against Chinese oppressors in A.D. 39. The Vietnamese continued to resist Chinese domination for centuries afterward. In the 1800s, France established itself as a new colonial power in Vietnam. Ho Chi Minh, the leader of the Vietnamese independence movement after World War II, continued his country's tradition of nationalism in his resistance to Chinese and French control. Policy makers in the United States, however, saw Ho merely as a communist and therefore an enemy in the cold war. As the independence movement in Vietnam turned into a civil war in the 1960s, the United States was determined to support the anticommunist government it had helped create in the south.

Background of the War

The United States became involved in Vietnam because of the demands of the cold war. As discussed in Chapter 20, American policy makers supported the French effort to crush Ho Chi Minh's independence movement because they needed French support to make the policy of containment work in Europe. The French attempt to reestablish control over its former colony failed in 1954. After the French were defeated at Dien Bien Phu, a conference was held in Geneva, Switzerland, to discuss the situation in Indochina. The conference included representatives of Ho Chi Minh, Vietnamese emperor Bao Dai, Cambodia, Laos, France, the United States, the Soviet Union, China, and Britain.

As a result of the Geneva Conference, Vietnam was divided into two separate nations in 1954. Ho Chi Minh, a nationalist leader sympathetic to communist ideas, controlled North Vietnam. **Ngo Dinh Diem,** a former official in Bao Dai's government who had been living in exile in the United States and Europe, became the premier of South Vietnam, with the support of the United States. In 1955, Diem became the president. France and North Vietnam agreed that elections would be held in 1956 to unify the country. Diem and his United States supporters, however, did not commit to the elections, which they feared would remove Diem from power. The elections never took place.

John Kennedy's Policy in Vietnam

President Eisenhower gave his firm support to Diem's South Vietnamese government, providing some 675 United States military advisers to assist in the continuing struggle against the north. When President Kennedy took office, he decided to do even more.

Using Historical Evidence Ngo Dinh Diem (left) "always dressed in white and looked as if he were made out of ivory," according to one journalist. While he paced the halls of his presidential palace, Buddhist monks protested his government by burning themselves to death on the streets of Saigon. *How do these photographs illustrate the basic weakness of the Diem government?*

Kennedy was a cold warrior, like most other United States leaders after World War II. He was determined to prevent the spread of communism at all costs. Early in his term, Kennedy sent Vice President Lyndon Johnson to Vietnam to assess the situation. Referring to the great British leader of World War II, Johnson called Diem "the Winston Churchill of Southeast Asia." He argued that if South Vietnam was to survive, it needed even more aid. In response, Kennedy increased the number of American military advisers to Vietnam. By the end of 1963, that number had grown to more than 16,000.

But military aid by itself could not ensure success. The problem was that Diem lacked support in his own country. He imprisoned people who criticized his government in "re-education centers." He filled many powerful government positions with members of his own family. United States aid earmarked for economic reforms went instead to the military and into the pockets of corrupt officials. Diem launched an enormously unpopular program to move peasants from their ancestral lands to "strategic hamlets"—government-run farming communities that isolated the peasants from communist influences seeping into South Vietnam. On top of everything else, Diem was a Catholic in a largely Buddhist country, and he often dismissed the religious concerns of others.

When Diem insisted that Buddhists obey Catholic religious laws, serious opposition developed. In June 1963, a Buddhist monk doused himself with gasoline and burned himself to death. Photographs showing his silent, grisly protest appeared on the front pages of newspapers around the world. Other monks followed the example, but their martyrdom did not budge Diem. Kennedy finally realized that Diem would never reform and acknowledged that the struggle against communism in Vietnam could not be won under Diem's rule.

United States officials told South Vietnamese military leaders that the United States would not object to Diem's overthrow. With that encouragement, Vietnamese troops struck in early November 1963, assassinated Diem, and seized control of the government.

Lyndon Johnson's War

Three weeks after Diem's assassination, Kennedy himself was dead, and the new military government in South Vietnam was already in trouble. While the ruling generals bickered among themselves and failed to direct the South Vietnamese army effectively, communist guerrillas in the south, known as **Viet Cong,** gained control over more territory and earned the loyalty of an increasing number of South Vietnamese. Throughout the struggle, the Viet Cong received assistance from Ho Chi Minh and the North Vietnamese.

Lyndon Johnson, the new United States President, was as much of a cold warrior as Kennedy, and he was equally suspicious of the communist sympathies of Ho Chi Minh. He commented about the continuing need for containment:

> The Communists' desire to dominate the world is just like the lawyer's desire to be the ultimate judge on the Supreme Court or the politician's desire to be President. You see, the Communists want to rule the world, and if we don't stand up to them, they will do it. And we'll be slaves. Now I'm not one of those folks seeing Communists under every bed. But I do know about the principles of power, and when one side is weak, the other steps in.

Just after he assumed office, Johnson met with Henry Cabot Lodge, United States ambassador to South Vietnam. Lodge told the new President that if he wanted to save Vietnam, he faced some tough choices. Johnson was determined to do whatever necessary to win the war. "I am not going to lose Vietnam," he said. Referring to the communist takeover of China in 1949, he went on: "I am not going to be the President who saw Southeast Asia go the way China went."

In his campaign for reelection as President in 1964, Johnson posed as a man of peace. "We are not about to send American boys nine or ten thousand miles away from home to do what Asian boys ought to be doing for themselves," he declared. He called Barry Goldwater, his Republican opponent in the election, a warmonger. He attacked critics who suggested using American bombs in Vietnam.

President Johnson vowed not to let Vietnam "go the way China went." What do you think Johnson believed the Truman administration should have done in 1949?

Intensifying the War Meanwhile, however, war planning was under way. During the election campaign, LBJ cleverly secured congressional authorization for deepening American involvement in Vietnam. He did so in August 1964 by announcing that North Vietnamese torpedo boats had attacked United States destroyers in the international waters of the Gulf of Tonkin, thirty miles from North Vietnam. He did not mention that the United States ships appeared to the North Vietnamese to be participating in combat raids against North Vietnam, nor that the commander of one United States ship was not sure that an attack really had taken place. Despite the confusion over these details, Johnson asked for and obtained a resolution giving him authority to "take all necessary measures to repel any armed attack against the forces of the United States and to prevent further aggression."

Congress passed this **Gulf of Tonkin Resolution** by a vote of 416 to 0 in the House of Representatives and 88 to 2 in the Senate. Johnson had been waiting for some time for an opportunity to propose the resolution, which, he noted, "covered everything." The President now had nearly complete control over what the United States did in Vietnam—without Congress ever officially declaring war.

After his reelection, Johnson began a drastic military **escalation,** or expansion, of the war by devoting more and more American money and personnel to the conflict. In February 1965, after a Viet Cong attack at Pleiku in South Vietnam killed eight Americans and wounded 126, Johnson authorized retaliatory bombing of North Vietnam. Two weeks after the Pleiku attack, General William Westmoreland, the commander of United States forces in Vietnam,

General William Westmoreland (below) believed he could win the war with enough American troop strength, but he and President Johnson vastly underestimated the determination of the communist forces operating throughout Vietnam.

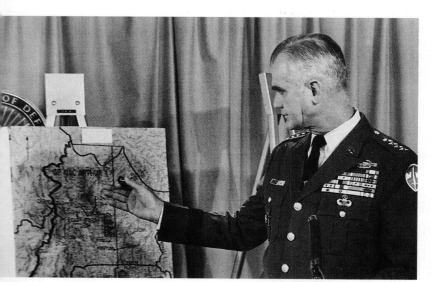

asked Johnson to send two battalions of marines to protect the American airfield at Danang. Johnson heeded the request, beginning a rapid buildup of American troops. At the start of 1965, nearly 25,000 American soldiers were stationed in Vietnam; by the end of the year, the number rose to 184,000. That number had climbed to 385,000 by 1966, to 485,000 by 1967, and to 543,000 by 1968.

Initially, United States soldiers had gone to Vietnam to advise the South Vietnamese. Now they took responsibility for trying to prop up the South Vietnamese government. Led by military men Nguyen Van Thieu and Nguyen Cao Ky, the new government was more effective than Diem's but remained dictatorial. Despite the large United States presence in Vietnam, the communist forces only intensified their efforts.

The Tet Offensive On January 30, 1968, the North Vietnamese mounted a major offensive during Tet, the Vietnamese new year. The **Tet Offensive,** shown in the map at right, included strikes on numerous provincial and district capitals and other towns in South Vietnam. In **Saigon,** the South Vietnamese capital, the Viet Cong attacked the American embassy, Tan Son Nhut air base, and the presidential palace. Even though they were turned back, the Viet Cong won a psychological victory. In contrast to official reports that claimed the North Vietnamese were on the verge of surrender, the Tet Offensive dramatically demonstrated that the Viet Cong could launch a massive attack on targets throughout South Vietnam. Furthermore, as images of

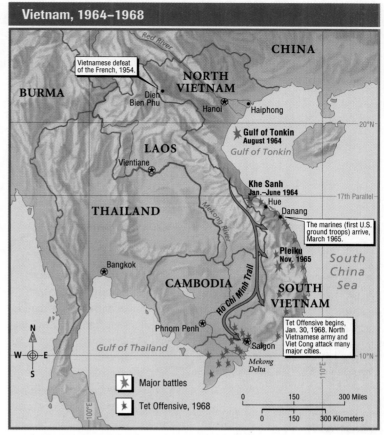

Vietnam, 1964–1968

Vietnamese defeat of the French, 1954.

The marines (first U.S. ground troops) arrive, March 1965.

Tet Offensive begins, Jan. 30, 1968. North Vietnamese army and Viet Cong attack many major cities.

★ Major battles

★ Tet Offensive, 1968

Geography and History: Interpreting Maps
The Ho Chi Minh Trail, shown in the map above, was a supply route from North Vietnam through Laos and Cambodia into South Vietnam. *How might the Ho Chi Minh Trail have contributed to the execution of the Tet Offensive?*

the fighting flooded American television, many people at home began to express reservations about United States involvement in Vietnam.

SECTION 1 REVIEW

Key Terms, People, and Places
1. Define (a) Viet Cong, (b) Gulf of Tonkin Resolution, (c) escalation, (d) Tet Offensive.
2. Identify Ngo Dinh Diem.
3. Identify Saigon.

Key Concepts
4. Why did the United States support the government of Ngo Dinh Diem in South Vietnam?
5. How did President Kennedy increase United States involvement in Vietnam's civil war in the early 1960s?

6. How did President Johnson use the Gulf of Tonkin incident to further his goals in the Vietnam conflict?

Critical Thinking
7. **Checking Consistency** Based on what you have read about Ngo Dinh Diem's government in South Vietnam, do you think that supporting this government was consistent with the stated aim of United States foreign policy: to defend freedom around the world? Explain why or why not.

The Brutality of the War

SECTION PREVIEW

Vietnam was the first war that Americans witnessed on their television screens. They were not prepared for the awful violence they saw, but neither were those who experienced the war firsthand.

Images of brutality and bloodshed, such as this one of a Vietnamese child wounded in the war, made American television viewers question United States involvement in Vietnam.

Key Concepts

• Many American soldiers went to Vietnam eager to do their patriotic duty, but they quickly learned that fighting the Viet Cong was a cruel and nerve-wracking ordeal.

• Vietnamese civilians were under constant attack from the air and the ground by United States troops, who could not distinguish them from Viet Cong or North Vietnamese soldiers.

• The massacre at My Lai brought the horrifying reality of the war home to many Americans.

Key Terms, People, and Places

My Lai massacre

The Vietnam War was a long, brutal struggle. American soldiers were fighting a guerrilla war against a hidden enemy, and so they were often unable to tell friendly South Vietnamese peasants from Viet Cong soldiers waiting for an opportunity to attack them. As buddies fell before sniper bullets, land mines, and booby traps, GIs grew increasingly frustrated by the demands of a war that seemed to be accomplishing few clear objectives. Meanwhile, Vietnamese civilians in both the north and the south suffered heavy casualties in the ferocious destruction of their land and way of life.

The American Soldiers' War

Many American soldiers went to war enthusiastic about the job they were being asked to do. Many, like Ron Kovic of Long Island, had dreamed of being heroes when they grew up. Television characters such as the Lone Ranger and the Cisco Kid—rugged heroes of the American West—shaped their ideas about what it meant to be an American. They learned patriotism by watching actor John Wayne perform daring deeds in his movie roles.

Kovic, like many Americans, worried about the communist threat and was afraid that communists "were infiltrating our schools, trying to take over our classes and control our minds." After high school, he joined the marines to do his part to defend his country. He proudly served a tour in Vietnam and signed up for a second tour. This second tour of duty would take a terrible toll on Kovic's body and mind.

He and other soldiers were finding the war confusing and disturbing. They were trying to defend the freedom of the South Vietnamese, but the population, reared in an altogether different political tradition, seemed indifferent to their effort. "We are the unwilling working for the unqualified to do the unnecessary for the ungrateful," Kit Bowen of the First Infantry Division wrote to his father in Oregon.

Fighting conditions were also different from those they had seen in films. Carrying sixty-pound packs, they had to walk through jungles of ten-foot-tall elephant grass and across flooded rice paddies. Much of the time they fought leeches, fever, and jungle rot—a tropical fungus that infected the skin. Racial tensions within the American ranks destroyed morale. Death always lurked around the corner. American troops never knew what to expect next, and they never could be sure who was a friend and who was an enemy. The Vietnamese woman selling soft drinks by the roadside might be a Viet Cong ally, counting enemy soldiers as they passed. A child peddling candy might be concealing a live grenade.

The Viet Cong lacked the sophisticated equipment of the United States troops, so they avoided head-on clashes. Instead they used guerrilla warfare tactics, working in small groups to launch sneak attacks and practice sabotage. They were skilled in setting clever traps. For example, they might bury a land mine in a path that they expected a platoon of marines to take. When a soldier stepped on the mine, platoon leaders and others would gather around the wounded man, and Viet Cong snipers would have their guns aimed at the spot, ready to kill them.

Angel Quintana, an American soldier, described life in Vietnam:

An infantryman almost never sleeps. Even if you have time to sleep, you can't because you have all these memories in your head. If you're near a fire-support base, then you sleep even less with the noise of the cannons—the 155s, the 105s, the 4.2s, all firing at the same time. It's like an earthquake. And when you're in the jungle, you're afraid. As macho as you may be, you feel it. You know that death is behind you. You don't know whose turn it is. There are times when you lose the fear because something happens, like they kill a friend of yours. For five or six days it goes away because you're so shook up from losing your friend that life means nothing to you. Then it passes, and you start to be interested in life again.

Ron Kovic confronted his fears by making an aggressive effort to be a good soldier. But the horrors of war came to haunt him after he accidentally killed a United States corporal. Later, he shot at shadowy figures in a village hut, only to learn that his unit had killed and wounded innocent children. The final blow came when a sniper's bullet entered his spine. As his spinal column was severed and he lost all sensation in his legs, all he could feel was "the worthlessness of dying right here in this place at this moment for nothing." He was paralyzed from the chest down, after which he felt, in his words, "like a big clumsy puppet with all his strings cut."

MAKING CONNECTIONS

In what ways were the experiences of American soldiers who served in Vietnam and in the Pacific theater during World War II similar? How were they different?

Vietnamese Civilians and the War

The war was even more devastating for Vietnamese civilians in both the north and the south. Because American soldiers were never sure who might be sympathetic to the Viet Cong, civilians suffered as much as soldiers. As the struggle intensified, the destruction worsened. Saturation bombing—air raids that dropped thousands of tons of explosives over large areas—tore North Vietnam apart. The fragmentation bombs used in these raids, which threw pieces of their thick metal casings in all directions when they exploded, were not confined to the north alone; they were also used in the south, where they killed and maimed countless civilians.

United States forces also used chemical weapons against the Vietnamese. In order to expose Viet Cong hiding places, an herbicide known as Agent Orange was dropped on jungle landscapes, causing the leaves to fall off trees. Agent Orange also killed crops, and later it was discovered to cause health problems in humans and livestock. (See "History Might Not Have Happened This Way," pages 794–795.) Another destructive chemical used in Vietnam was called napalm. This jellylike substance, dropped from planes, burned uncontrollably as it stuck to people's bodies and seared off their flesh.

The war touched everyone in Vietnam. As Le Thanh, a North Vietnamese child in the 1960s, recalled,

Nobody could get away from the war. It didn't matter if you were in the countryside or the city. While I was living in the country I saw terrible things. . . . I saw children who had been killed, pagodas and churches that had been destroyed, monks and priests dead in the ruins, schoolboys who were killed when schools were bombed.

Although death was a constant presence in the war, few could harden their hearts against it. From the medic trying in vain to save a dying comrade, to the marine finally giving in to anguished tears in a lonely barracks, the war left few untouched.

The situation was similar in the south. Near the village of My Thuy Phuong, one peasant remembered this incident:

> One day I was walking back home from the ricefield, carrying tools on my shoulder. Then behind me I heard a large, loud noise. A very bad noise. I looked back and saw an American helicopter following me, shooting down the path toward me. I was very scared, so [I] jumped into the water by the side. Just one moment later, the bullets went right by. So scary.

AMERICAN PROFILES

Le Ly Hayslip

Born in a tiny village in the northern part of South Vietnam, Le Ly Hayslip now lives in the United States and is an American citizen. Like other Vietnamese, as a child she learned "to love God, my family, our traditions, and the people we could not see: our ancestors." Then, when she was twelve years old, American helicopters came to Ky La, and the war intruded on her life.

For the next three years Le Ly fought for the Viet Cong. She and others were taught to follow Uncle Ho—Ho Chi Minh—in the struggle against the South Vietnamese government. For them, " 'Western culture' meant bars, brothels, black markets, and *xa hoi van minh*—bewildering machines—most of them destructive."

Life for Le Ly was never safe. Because she had ties to the Viet Cong, she always had to be alert to the moves of South Vietnamese soldiers. They often "took out their frustration on us: arresting nearby farmers and beating or shooting them on the spot, or carting anyone who looked suspicious off to jail." Captured by the South Vietnamese, she was questioned and then released. Later she was detained again, and this time tortured. Though she was fortunate enough to be freed once again, she now found herself suspected by the Viet Cong, since they could not understand why she had been released twice. She was caught in the middle. "If the [South

Le Ly Hayslip endured both physical and emotional pain during the Vietnam War.

Vietnamese] were like elephants trampling our village," she observed, "the Viet Cong were like snakes who came at us in the night."

After the Viet Cong sentenced her to death, Le Ly's life was filled with the terror of being discovered. She realized she could not stay in Ky La. She also realized that her life had changed forever: "From now on, I promised myself, I would only flow with the strongest current and drift with the steadiest wind—and not resist."

Determined to leave Vietnam, Le Ly began to spend time with American soldiers and civilians. Eventually she met Ed Hayslip, a civilian contractor, who wanted to marry her and take her and her son back to the United States.

Le Ly accepted his proposal and became an immigrant to the United States. Still a young woman, she had seen more than most people see in a lifetime. For her, the war would never go away, and she devoted her life to trying to break down the barriers between the old world where she had been raised and the new world where she now lived.

The My Lai Massacre

In March 1968, the brutality of the war came into sharp focus in a massacre at My Lai, a small village in South Vietnam. In response to word that the community was sheltering 250 members of the Viet Cong, a United States infantry company moved in to clear out the village. Rather than enemy soldiers, the company found women, children, and old men. The American troops already had suffered heavy combat losses. They were worn down by the uncertainties and terrors of fighting a guerrilla war. Some lost control.

Lieutenant William L. Calley, Jr., was in charge. He first ordered, "Round everybody up," and then gave the order for the prisoners to be killed. One soldier, Private Paul Meadlo, later described what happened:

> We huddled them up. We made them squat down. . . . I poured about four clips [about 68 shots] into the group. . . . The mothers kept hugging their children. . . . Well, we kept right on firing. . . . I still dream about it. About the women and children in my sleep. . . . Some nights, I can't even sleep. I just lay there thinking about it.

Stories of the horrible **My Lai massacre,** in which more than a hundred Vietnamese were slaughtered, shocked Americans at home. This was more than the nation had bargained for when it went to war.

SECTION 2 REVIEW

Key Terms, People, and Places
1. Define My Lai massacre.

Key Concepts
2. Why was the war so hard on American troops?
3. How did the war affect Vietnamese civilians?
4. What happened at My Lai, and how did it affect Americans' perception of the war?

Critical Thinking
5. **Making Comparisons** Le Ly Hayslip and her fellow Viet Cong were willing to fight and die to keep "Western culture" out of Vietnam. How did their perception of American values differ from that of the GIs who grew up watching the Lone Ranger on television?

Student Protest

SECTION PREVIEW

"The times they are a-changin'," folksinger Bob Dylan sang in the 1960s. Student activists demanded many changes during this period, but the Vietnam War took center stage in the protest movement.

This 1969 poster advertised one of many antiwar demonstrations that shook the nation during the Vietnam War era.

Key Concepts
- The United States was ripe for change in the early 1960s, and students began to challenge the foundations of American life.
- The Vietnam War became the focus of the protest movement in the 1960s.
- Student protesters used peaceful demonstrations, teach-ins, educational campaigns, and sometimes violence to voice their opinions.

Key Terms, People, and Places
Students for a Democratic Society (SDS), New Left, teach-in, conscientious objector

I n June 1971, the *New York Times* published the first in a series of articles based on a classified government study of United States involvement in the Vietnam War. The Pentagon Papers, as the study came to be called, revealed that government officials, including President Johnson, had lied to Congress and the American public about the war. Although many were shocked by these revelations, others had long suspected that there were ugly truths hiding behind the optimistic statements of politicians and military leaders. In fact, opposition to the war had been growing steadily since the early 1960s.

Students were in the forefront of the antiwar movement, and their activism undermined support for the war in the population at large. Still, many Americans remained patriotically devoted to their country's involvement in Vietnam, and the issue created deep rifts within the United States.

Student Activism and Changing Times

Student activism began in the early 1960s. When members of the baby boom generation graduated from high school, college and university enrollments swelled with more students than ever before. Unlike previous generations of students, who needed to work after high school, members of this generation had time to experiment before they went out into the world.

Change was in the air. Even in the conformist years of the 1950s, popular culture—including rock-and-roll music and rebellious youths on the movie screen—had indicated that many young Americans were not satisfied with the values of their parents. The early 1960s saw a widening of this generation gap. In 1963 folksinger Bob Dylan captured the new mood in a song entitled "The Times They Are A-Changin' ":

Come mothers and fathers
Throughout the land
And don't criticize
What you can't understand
Your sons and your daughters
Are beyond your command
There's a battle
Outside and it's ragin'
It'll soon shake your windows
And rattle your walls . . .
For the times they are a-changin'.

The civil rights movement, discussed in Chapter 23, was a stepping-stone to other movements for change. Civil rights activists were among those who organized **Students for a Democratic Society (SDS)** in 1960. Its manifesto, the Port Huron Statement, appeared in 1962. It was written largely by Tom Hayden, a student at the University of Michigan. The statement declared:

> We are people of this generation, bred in at least modest comfort, housed now in universities, looking uncomfortably at the world we inherit.
>
> When we were kids the United States was the wealthiest and strongest country in the world. . . . As we grew, however, our comfort was penetrated by events too troubling to dismiss. . . . We would replace power rooted in possession, privilege, or circumstance by power and uniqueness rooted in love, reflectiveness, reason, and creativity. As a social system we seek the establishment of a democracy of individual participation.

Although it was but a tiny organization at the start, SDS was a major force in the development of a new political movement that came to be called the **New Left**. Members of the New Left believed that radical changes were the only way to solve problems such as poverty and racism in the United States.

MAKING CONNECTIONS

The Port Huron Statement rejected a system of "power rooted in possession, privilege, or circumstance." What other social movements have you read about that criticized similar aspects of American society?

The Free Speech Movement The first blow of the student revolution came at the University of California at Berkeley in September 1964. Civil rights workers became angry when the university refused to allow them to distribute leaflets outside the main gate of the campus. The students, who had fought for equal rights in the South, argued that their right to free speech was being challenged, and they resisted the university's effort to restrict their political activity. When police came to arrest one of their leaders, students surrounded the police car and kept it from moving. The free speech movement was under way.

Eventually the administration tried to find a compromise. Then, however, the governing board that had the final word over university policy decided to hold student leaders responsible for their actions and filed charges against some. Irate students took over Sproul Hall, the main administration building. Student leader Mario Savio declared that the university was no more than a vast, impersonal bureaucracy:

> There comes a time when the operation of the machine becomes so odious [hateful], makes you so sick at heart, that you can't take part, you can't even tacitly [silently] take part. And you've got to put your bodies upon the gears and upon the wheels, upon the levers, upon all the apparatus, and you've got to make it stop.

Students wore buttons echoing the instructions on their university registration cards and protesting the impersonal treatment they received from the school. "I am a U.C. Student," the buttons read. "Do not Fold, Bend, or Mutilate." Folksinger Joan Baez came to the school and sang "We Shall Overcome," the marching song of the civil rights movement. When police arrested students in Sproul Hall, other students, supported by the faculty, went on strike and stopped attending classes to show their support for the free speech demonstrators.

Berkeley remained the most radical campus, but the agitation there spread to other campuses across the United States. In the spring of 1965, activists challenged regulations they felt unfairly curbed their freedom, such as restrictions on the hours when women and men could visit each others' dorms. Students also sought greater involvement in college

In October 1964, Berkeley student Mario Savio stood atop a police car to address a crowd of protesters demanding free speech (above). The building in the background is Sproul Hall.

United States Military Forces in Vietnam, 1965–1972

Military Forces (in thousands)

600
500
400
300
200
100
0

1965 1966 1967 1968 1969 1970 1971 1972

Year

Source: *Statistical Abstract of the United States*

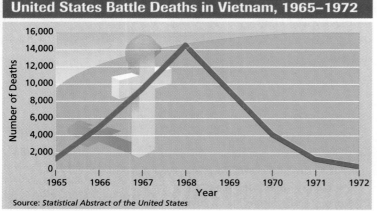

United States Battle Deaths in Vietnam, 1965–1972

Number of Deaths

16,000
14,000
12,000
10,000
8,000
6,000
4,000
2,000
0

1965 1966 1967 1968 1969 1970 1971 1972

Year

Source: *Statistical Abstract of the United States*

Interpreting Graphs
How many United States soldiers were in Vietnam in 1965? In 1967? How do the graphs show some reasons for antiwar protest, especially among students? Explain how the top graph might relate to the Tet Offensive (January 1968) and its effect on public opinion in the United States.

affairs. SDS recruited some of these discontented students to work in campaigns to improve conditions in the cities of the United States.

The Teach-in Movement Then the Vietnam War intervened. As escalation began, students were among the first to protest American involvement in the war. Some opposed what they regarded as American imperialism. Others questioned American interests in a civil war. All called for withdrawal. The Tet Offensive in early 1968 finally turned a majority of Americans against the war, but the student protest movement had been registering many young people's disapproval for years. The graphs above give some indication of the statistics students found disturbing.

The first **teach-in** took place at the University of Michigan in March 1965. When a small group of faculty members planned a strike to protest the war, the Michigan legislature threatened to fire them. Instead, an even larger group decided to make a public statement. Fifty or sixty professors decided to teach a special night session in which issues concerning the war could be aired. To their surprise, several thousand people showed up and made the evening a monumental success. Soon other teach-ins followed at colleges around the country. Both supporters and opponents of the war appeared at the early teach-ins, but soon antiwar voices dominated the proceedings.

Resistance to War

At about the same time that the first teach-ins were taking place, resistance to the military draft was beginning to sweep the country. A selective service act allowing the government to draft men between the ages of eighteen and twenty-six had been in place since 1951. As more and more young men were being called into service and sent to fight in Vietnam, Americans began to question the morality and fairness of the draft. College students could receive deferments, which meant they did not have to go to war, but those who could not afford college did not have this avenue open to them. Many other young men tried to avoid the draft by leaving the country or by claiming that they were **conscientious objectors**—they opposed fighting in the war on moral grounds.

SDS grew by leaps and bounds as it embarked on a campaign against the draft. Leaders encouraged men to refuse to report for duty. The organization also launched attacks on campus units of the Reserve Officers' Training Corps (ROTC), on CIA recruiters, and on companies producing napalm and other tools of destruction. "Hey, hey, LBJ. How many kids did you kill today?" marchers chanted during demonstrations around the country. In 1967 some 300,000 opponents of the war marched in New York City, while 100,000 tried to close down the Pentagon, home of the Defense Department, near Washington, D.C. In 1969 the National Chicano Moratorium Committee staged its own antiwar demonstrations. These protesters argued that Vietnam was a racial war, with black and brown Americans being used against their brothers and sisters in developing nations.

Protest became a way of life. In the first six months of 1968, more than 200 major demonstrations erupted at colleges and universities around the country. The most dramatic confrontation came at Columbia University in New York. There the issues of civil rights and the war were closely related. An SDS chapter sought to get the university to cut its ties with a research institute that did work for the military. At the same time, an African American students' organization tried to halt construction of a gymnasium that would encroach upon an adjacent neighborhood. Together, these two groups took over the president's office. Finally the president called the police, and hundreds of students were arrested. A student sympathy strike followed, and the university closed early that spring.

Sometimes the radical movement turned violent. Activists in one SDS faction called themselves the Weathermen, after a line in a Bob Dylan song—"You don't need a weatherman to know which way the wind blows." They were determined to bring about a revolution immediately. In October 1969, the group converged on Chicago. Members dressed in hard hats, boots, and work gloves rampaged through the streets wielding pipes, clubs, rocks, and chains. They tangled with police (as they had planned), regrouped, and came back for still another confrontation.

Bo Burlingham, a participant from Ohio, explained why he had joined in the attack:

This antiwar protest took place in San Francisco in 1967.

W hy did we do it? The status quo meant to us war, poverty, inequality, ignorance, famine and disease in most of the world. To accept it was to condone and help perpetuate it. We felt like miners trapped in a terrible poisonous shaft with no light to guide us out. We resolved to destroy the tunnel even if we risked destroying ourselves in the process.

The violent measures of groups like the Weathermen represented the extreme expression of youthful discontent in the 1960s. The spirit of change led most members of the counterculture to work for reforms in peaceful ways, but that same spirit led others simply to "drop out" of the traditional culture they were rejecting.

SECTION 3 REVIEW

Key Terms, People, and Places

1. Define (a) SDS, (b) New Left, (c) teach-in, (d) conscientious objector.

Key Concepts

2. What were the roots of student activism in the 1960s?

3. What was the role of SDS in the growing protest movement?

4. How did the Vietnam War affect the student protest movement?

5. What did activists hope to accomplish, and what methods did they use?

Critical Thinking

6. Distinguishing False from Accurate Images Mario Savio described the university as a huge machine with gears and wheels. Explain why you think that this image does or does not accurately reflect the nature of any large institution.

Checking Consistency

Checking consistency means determining whether ideas that should agree—or follow logically one from the other—actually do. Government actions, for example, should always agree with the Constitution. Where no such overriding rules apply—in the creation of foreign policy, for instance—policy objectives are expected to be consistent with past decisions on similar issues. Checking for consistency will help reveal whether the government is in fact operating as it should.

Use the following steps and what you have read about the Vietnam era to check for consistency in the examples at right.

1. Identify the principle or other factor to be used as the baseline for checking consistency. You should expect certain facts, ideas, or actions to agree—either with one another or with an overriding principle. Read the information in Items A and B at right. (a) What rule or principle serves as the baseline for checking consistency in Item A? (b) In Item B, what did Johnson's description of the North Vietnamese in 1965 suggest about the goals of his policy in Vietnam at the time? (c) How can Johnson's statement serve as the baseline for checking his consistency in other statements about Vietnam?

2. Note the corresponding action or idea to be checked for consistency. (a) In Item A, what action did the Supreme Court take? (b) What probably happened as a result of this action? (c) In Item B, what did Johnson's description of the North Vietnamese (the "Communists") in 1966 suggest about the goals of his policy in Vietnam at the time?

3. Check for consistency between the principle or baseline factor and the corresponding action or idea. In the examples below, compare the second action or idea against the baseline you have identified to see if the two ideas are consistent with or contradict each other. (a) In Item A, did the action taken by the Supreme Court agree or conflict with the constitutional requirement of the First Amendment? Explain your answer. (b) In Item B, was Johnson's statement of his policy objective in 1966 consistent with the statement he had made in 1965? Explain your answer.

A "Congress shall make no law . . . abridging the freedom of speech, or of the press. . . ."

—First Amendment, United States Constitution

In 1971 the United States Supreme Court denied the government's request to prohibit two newspapers from publishing "The Pentagon Papers," a highly classified documentary history of United States involvement in Vietnam through May 1968.

B "This war, like most wars, is filled with terrible irony. For what do the people of North Vietnam want? They want what their neighbors also desire: food for their hunger, health for their bodies, . . . an end to the bondage of material misery. . . . Neither independence nor human dignity will ever be won by arms alone. It also requires the works of peace."

—President Lyndon B. Johnson, address at Johns Hopkins University (April 7, 1965)

"Aggression is on the march and the enslavement of free men is its goal. . . . If we allow the Communists to win in Vietnam, it will become easier and more appetizing for them to take over other countries in other parts of the world. . . . That is why it is vitally important to every American family that we stop the Communists in South Vietnam."

—President Lyndon B. Johnson, Honolulu Conference (February 6, 1966)

The Counterculture

SECTION PREVIEW

In the 1960s, a youth culture that stressed freedom and individuality created for some people a promising new "space" in which to explore themselves. At the same time, it filled others with fear and disgust.

Key Concepts
- Rejecting the conventional lifestyles of older Americans, many young people in the 1960s became part of a counterculture that sought to promote freedom and creativity.
- The counterculture advanced new attitudes about personal relationships, drugs, and music.
- Many Americans were shocked by the new values of the counterculture.

Key Terms, People, and Places
counterculture, hippie, psychedelic drug, Woodstock

I n the 1960s, many Americans began to look for alternatives to traditional patterns of living. Young people in particular were involved in what became known as the **counterculture.** Drawing on the example of the Beat Generation of the 1950s, members of the counterculture rejected conventional customs. They experimented with new forms of dress, different attitudes toward sexual relationships, and the use of drugs. Some members of the counterculture were politically involved; most were not. But their challenge to traditional norms was visible both in the political protests of the 1960s and in the changing social patterns of American life.

Reflections of the Counterculture

People's appearances reflected the changes that were taking place. The **hippies** of the 1960s—men and women who self-consciously rejected conventional norms—tried to look different. Women chose freer fashions, such as miniskirts and loose-fitting dresses. Men let their hair grow long and wore beards. Many hippies adopted the dress of working people, which seemed somehow more "authentic" than the school clothes of middle-class youth. Therefore, men and women wore jeans, muslin (plain-woven cotton) shirts, and other simple garments that were intended to look handmade.

The Sexual Revolution The new views about sexual behavior advanced by the counterculture were labeled "the sexual revolution." The young people who led this revolution demanded more freedom to make personal choices. Some argued that sex should be separated from its traditional ties to family life. Lynn Ferrin, who moved to San Francisco to become part of the counterculture in California, remembered her feelings at the time:

> I was among the women in that whole vanguard of sexual freedom who were very excited by being free women. . . . In my circles, you wouldn't think of getting married, settling down with one person. The suburbs and the station wagon full of Cub Scouts became something you didn't want anything to do with.

The sexual revolution in the counterculture led to more open discussion of sexual subjects. Newspapers, magazines, and books published articles that might not have been printed, even in the recent past. The 1962 book by Helen Gurley Brown, *Sex and the Single Girl*, became a best-seller. In 1966 William H. Masters and Virginia E. Johnson shocked many people when they published *Human Sexual Response*, a report on their scientific studies of sexuality.

One way in which 1960s youth expressed themselves was by turning everyday objects into works of art. Country Joe McDonald of the popular rock group Country Joe and the Fish decorated his guitar (above) with antiwar symbols. Others decorated their clothing with colorful embroidery.

This group of hippies lived together in the New Buffalo Commune. They turned out for the 1968 Fourth of July parade in El Rito, New Mexico, in their outrageously painted bus.

Novels like D. H. Lawrence's *Lady Chatterly's Lover,* which had been banned in the United States since 1928 for being too explicit, now became available.

Many men and women also experimented with new living patterns. Some hippies rejected traditional relationships and lived together in communal groups. More and more people simply lived together as couples, without getting married.

The Drug Scene Also part of the 1960s counterculture were **psychedelic drugs,** which are drugs that cause the brain to behave abnormally. As a result, the brain produces hallucinations and other altered perceptions of reality. The beatniks had experimented with drugs a decade before, but they had been in the minority. Now drug use became more widespread among the nation's youth.

One early proponent of psychedelic drug use was researcher Timothy Leary, who worked at Harvard University with Richard Alpert on the chemical compound lysergic acid diethyl amide, commonly known as LSD. The two men were fired from their research posts for using undergraduates in experiments with the drug. Leary then began to preach that drugs could help free the mind. He advised listeners, "Tune in, turn on, drop out."

Soldiers who had used drugs in Vietnam brought them home when their tours of duty were completed. Marijuana became common among middle-class college students. Todd Gitlin, a radical activist who became president of SDS, explained that "the point was to open up a new space, an *inner* space, so that we could *space out,* live for the sheer exultant point of living."

On the other side of the drug issue, however, was serious danger. Overdoses and deaths from accidents that occurred while under the influence of drugs caused concern in many quarters. Three leading musicians—Janis Joplin, Jim Morrison, and Jimi Hendrix—died of complications from drug overdoses. They were not the only ones. Their deaths represented the tragic excesses to which some people were driven by their reliance on drugs as an escape.

MAKING CONNECTIONS

What might some young people in the 1960s have been trying to escape by seeking a spiritual "inner space"? In what ways do young people today seek similar escapes?

The Music World

Music likewise reflected and contributed to the cultural changes. The rock and roll of the 1950s and the folk music of the early 1960s gave way to a new kind of rock. The Beatles, a group of performers from England, heavily influenced the music of this period, taking first England and then the United States by storm. Mick Jagger of the Rolling Stones was an aggressive, sometimes violent showman on stage. Janis Joplin was a hard-driving, hard-drinking singer whose powerful interpretations of classic blues songs catapulted her to super-stardom before her death in 1970.

Woodstock The diverse strands of the counterculture all came together at the Woodstock Music and Art Fair in upstate New York in August 1969. About 300,000 people gathered for several days in a large pasture in Bethel, New York, to listen to the major bands of the rock world. Despite brutal heat and bursts of rain, those who attended **Woodstock** recalled the festival with something of a sense of awe for the fellowship they experienced there. Tom Law, one participant at Woodstock, commented on the mood:

> The music had very little to do with it. The music was great and it was there and kept everybody focused on that. But the event was so much bigger than the music. It was a phenomenon. It was absolutely a phenomenon. And it was also the most peaceful, civilized gathering that was probably happening on the planet at the time.

The weekend was trouble-free. Police avoided confrontations with those attending by choosing not to enforce drug laws. The crowd remained under control. After the festival, many supporters spoke about the "Woodstock Nation" as a model for the new and better world to come.

Other Americans, however, viewed both the festival and the mood it reflected with distaste. Even as older people began growing their hair

Links Across Time

1650   1700   1750   1800   1850   1900   1950   2000

Music: The Sound of Rebellion

The 1960s were not the first time that Americans were shocked by the music their children were listening to. In the 1920s, the jazz sound of Louis Armstrong and the Hot Five (left) was too hot for many older listeners—but the young flappers and rakes loved it. The performances of rock bands in the 1960s (above) were similarly lost to the older generation. **Does any of the music you listen to today leave the older people you know baffled?**

Altamont The fears of those who criticized Woodstock came true at another rock festival that took place at the Altamont Speedway in California in December 1969. There, 300,000 people gathered for a concert concluding an American tour by the Rolling Stones. When promoters of the concert failed to provide adequate security, the Stones hired a band of Hell's Angels, the infamous and lawless motorcycle gang, to keep order. The cyclists battered any people who annoyed them and ended up beating one man to death when he ventured on stage.

The violence at the Altamont concert was not the only sign of contradictions within the counterculture. Despite their celebration of simple lifestyles, most hippies were children of the comfortable middle class, and they melted right back into it

The young people who attended the Woodstock Music and Art Fair in 1969 reflected the new fashions and social values of their times.

longer and wearing more colorful clothes, they were not interested in the more fundamental changes they saw occurring around them. Some young people also disliked these changes. In particular, opponents deplored the drugs, sex, and nudity they saw at the Woodstock festival and around the country. To them, the counterculture represented a rejection of morals and honored values and seemed a childish reaction to the problems of the era.

when the counterculture fell apart. American corporations seized on the opportunity to market items such as blue jeans and stereo equipment to members of the counterculture, who eagerly bought the products. By the 1980s, many baby boomers who had protested the capitalistic values of the 1950s and 1960s would be holding executive positions in the same corporations they had once denounced.

SECTION 4 REVIEW

Key Terms, People, and Places
1. Define (a) hippie, (b) psychedelic drug, (c) Woodstock.

Key Concepts
2. Describe the values that were rejected and those that were embraced by the counterculture of the 1960s.
3. How was the counterculture reflected in the sexual values, drug use, and music of its members?
4. How did Americans outside the counterculture view the movement?

Critical Thinking
5. **Identifying Assumptions** Lynn Ferrin recalled being part of a group of women in the 1960s "who were very excited by being free women" and "wouldn't think of getting married, settling down with one person." What assumptions about marriage are revealed in this statement? Explain why you think these assumptions are or are not valid.

The End of the War

SECTION PREVIEW

The antiwar movement finally convinced politicians in Washington that it was time to pull out of Vietnam, but American troops withdrew very slowly, and the fighting was far from over.

Key Concepts

- Growing opposition to the war convinced Lyndon Johnson not to run for reelection and helped Richard Nixon to become President in 1968.
- Nixon gradually replaced American troops with South Vietnamese, but at the same time he began a new bombing assault on Cambodia that enraged antiwar protesters.
- A cease-fire was finally signed in 1973, but by 1975 North Vietnamese leaders had taken control of the entire country.
- The war left permanent scars in the Vietnamese countryside as well as in the hearts of Vietnamese and Americans.

Key Terms, People, and Places

Vietnamization; Kent State University

T he antiwar movement created serious opposition to American involvement in Vietnam. It also polarized the United States. Deep rifts in the Democratic party and in the country as a whole forced Lyndon Johnson to leave the presidency at the end of his term and paved the way for the election of Republican Richard Nixon in 1968. Nixon made good on a pledge to withdraw the United States from the Southeast Asian struggle, but only after expanding the war outside Vietnam and creating even more violent protest at home.

Mounting Opposition

By 1968 the antiwar movement was in full swing. Political activists drew on all of their resources to mount the most extensive resistance campaign in American history. Marchers took to the streets, while artists, authors, and musicians contributed their talents to the antiwar crusade.

Years of protest and a growing list of American casualties had steadily increased public opposition to the war. In a 1965 Gallup poll, 62 percent of those interviewed felt that the United States was handling the war in Vietnam "as well as could be expected." In 1966 only 41 percent approved of Johnson's Vietnam policy; that figure dropped to 35 percent in 1968. At the same time, disapproval of Johnson's actions increased from 37 percent in 1966 to 50 percent in 1968. In 1968, 49 percent of those polled felt that the United States had made a mistake in sending troops into the war. Details on these statistics can be found in the table on page 734.

Johnson finally succumbed to the opposition. As resistance to the war mounted, his own popularity fell accordingly. After the Tet Offensive, when the North Vietnamese demonstrated that they still had the resources to carry out a broad-based attack in South Vietnam, Johnson recognized that American public opinion had shifted in such a way that he could not win another election.

The Vietnam Women's Memorial in Washington, D.C., shows two nurses helping a wounded soldier. The memorial sculpture was erected in 1993 to honor the thousands of women who had served in the war.

Public Opinion of United States Involvement in Vietnam

"Do you approve or disapprove of the way President Johnson is handling the situation in Vietnam?"

	Approve	Disapprove	No opinion
December 1965	56%	26%	18%
May 1966	41%	37%	22%
April 1967	43%	42%	15%
July 1967	33%	52%	15%
December 1967	39%	49%	12%
February 1968*	35%	50%	15%

* During Tet Offensive

"In view of the developments since we entered the fighting in Vietnam, do you think the United States made a mistake sending troops to fight in Vietnam?"

	Yes, made mistake	No, did not	No opinion
May 1966	36%	49%	15%
April 1967	37%	50%	13%
July 1967	41%	48%	11%
February 1968†	49%	41%	10%

† After Tet Offensive

Source: *The Gallup Poll: Public Opinion 1935–1971*, by George H. Gallup

Interpreting Tables

What percentage of those polled in 1965 approved of Lyndon Johnson's handling of the war? What percentage approved in 1968? Between 1966 and 1968, what happened to the percentage of people who thought the United States should never have entered the war?

Johnson rarely left the White House near the end of his presidency for fear of being assaulted by angry, shouting crowds of protesters. He felt like "a jackrabbit in a hailstorm, hunkering up and taking it."

After watching the campaign of antiwar candidate Eugene McCarthy gain momentum in the Democratic primaries, President Johnson declared dramatically in a nationally televised speech that he would not run for another term as President. He knew that he had lost his base of support. He hoped that by ordering a pause in the relentless bombing of Vietnam he could encourage peace talks to end the war and so restore unity in the United States as he left public life.

The media—especially television—strongly influenced public opinion during the Vietnam War. What are the major issues facing the people of the United States today, and how are people's opinions on these issues affected by the media?

Richard Nixon's Approach

Eugene McCarthy's campaign faltered, and Robert Kennedy, who likewise challenged Johnson, was assassinated (see Chapter 26). Another candidate, Hubert Humphrey, eventually was nominated by the Democrats. For the Republicans, Richard Nixon ran for the presidency with the claim that he had a secret plan to end the war in Vietnam. He never divulged the details, and critics doubted that a plan really existed, but his pledge still helped secure his election over Humphrey. Once in the White House, Nixon dedicated himself to a policy of **Vietnamization,** which involved removing American forces and replacing them with South Vietnamese soldiers. Between 1968 and 1972, American troop strength dropped from 543,000 to 39,000, and opposition to the war among people in the United States declined.

Even as he moved to bring American soldiers home, Nixon himself became caught up in the war. As much as he wanted to defuse antiwar sentiment at home, he was determined not to lose the war, either. And so, as he withdrew American troops, he resumed bombing raids, keeping his actions secret from his critics. The map on page 735 shows the major targets of those bombing raids.

President Nixon also widened the war beyond the borders of Vietnam. In April 1970, he announced that United States and South Vietnamese forces were moving into neighboring Cambodia to clear out communist camps there, from which the enemy was mounting attacks on South Vietnam. The United States, he asserted, would not stand by like "a pitiful helpless giant" while the Viet Cong attacks from Cambodia went on:

We take this action not for the purpose of expanding the war into Cambodia but for the purpose of ending the war in Vietnam and winning the just peace we all desire. We have made and we will continue to make every possible effort to end this war through negotiation at the conference table rather than through more fighting on the battlefield.

His actions belied his words, however, and the move brought chaos and civil war in Cambodia and a fresh wave of protests at home.

Renewed Protests

Nixon's invasion of Cambodia in 1970 reignited the protest movement on college campuses in the United States. At **Kent State University** in Ohio, students reacted angrily to the President's action. On the weekend following his speech, they broke windows in the business district downtown and burned the army ROTC building on campus, which had become a hated symbol of the war.

In response, the governor of Ohio ordered the National Guard to Kent State. Tension mounted. When students threw rocks and empty tear gas canisters at them, the soldiers loaded their guns and donned gas masks. They knelt down and aimed their rifles at the students, as if warning them to stop. Then the guardsmen retreated to another position. At the top of a hill, they suddenly turned and began firing on the students below.

Tom Grace was a sophomore crossing campus just before the outburst. He was more than 150 feet away and thought he was keeping a safe distance from the disturbance. He was wrong:

When the National Guardsmen got to the top of the hill, all of a sudden there was just a quick movement, a flurry of activity, and then a crack, or two cracks of rifle fire, and I thought, Oh my God! I turned and started running as fast as I could. I don't think I got more than a step or two, and all of a sudden I was on the ground. It was just like somebody had come over and given me a body blow and knocked me right down. The bullet had entered my left heel and had

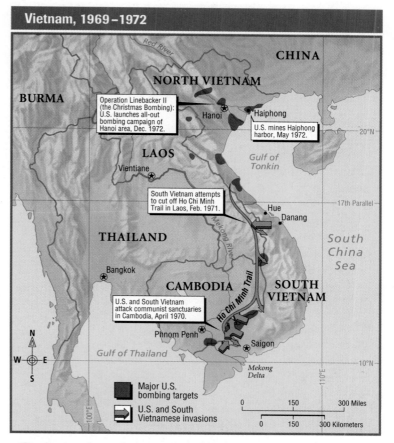

Vietnam, 1969–1972

Operation Linebacker II (the Christmas Bombing): U.S. launches all-out bombing campaign of Hanoi area, Dec. 1972.

U.S. mines Haiphong harbor, May 1972.

South Vietnam attempts to cut off Ho Chi Minh Trail in Laos, Feb. 1971.

U.S. and South Vietnam attack communist sanctuaries in Cambodia, April 1970.

Major U.S. bombing targets

U.S. and South Vietnamese invasions

🌍 **Geography and History: Interpreting Maps**
According to this map, in what areas were United States bombing raids concentrated during the later years of the war? What do you think these bombing raids were supposed to accomplish?

literally knocked me off my feet. I tried to raise myself, and I heard someone yelling, "Stay down, stay down! It's buckshot!" . . . The bullet blew the shoe right off my foot, and there was a bone sticking through my green sock. It looked like somebody had put my foot through a meat grinder.

Grace was relatively lucky. After just thirteen seconds of firing, four students lay dead, with nine others wounded. Two of the dead had been demonstrators more than 250 feet away from the soldiers. The other two were bystanders, almost 400 feet away.

A similar attack occurred at Jackson State University in Mississippi. Policemen and highway patrolmen fired into a women's dormitory there without warning. Two people were killed, and more were wounded.

Viewpoints
On the Tragedy of Kent State

In May 1970, four students were killed at Kent State University when the National Guard opened fire on a crowd of antiwar protesters. *How do the following viewpoints reflect the issues that tore apart American society at that time?*

From the mother of a student
"President Nixon wants people to believe Jeff turned to violence. That is not true. What kind of sympathy is this? When four kids are dead he gave no comfort. Nixon acts as if the kids had it coming. But shooting into a crowd of students, that is violence. They say it could happen again if the Guard is threatened. They consider stones threat enough to kill children. I think the violence comes from the government."

Mother of Jeffrey Glenn Miller, one of four students killed at Kent State, quoted in *Life* magazine, May 15, 1970

From the wife of a Guardsman
"They didn't go to Kent State to kill anyone. I know he'd rather have stayed home and mowed the lawn. He told me so. He told me they didn't fire those shots to scare the students off. He told me they fired those shots because they knew the students were coming after them, coming for their guns. People are calling my husband a murderer; my husband is not a murderer. He was afraid."

Wife of a member of the National Guard, quoted in *Newsweek* magazine, May 18, 1970

Americans were horrified by these attacks. They had hoped that the rifts of the past few years between the youth of the United States and those in positions of power were starting to heal. Now the wounds were opened even wider than before.

The United States Withdraws

The war dragged on as Nixon ran for a second term as President in 1972, and South Vietnam refused to accept a proposed settlement. To reassure the South Vietnamese of continuing American concern, Nixon ordered the most intense bombing campaign of the war in the spring of 1972. The United States bombed Hanoi, the North Vietnamese capital, and mined North Vietnamese harbors. Just days before the election, National Security adviser Henry Kissinger announced, "Peace is at hand." In January 1973, after Nixon was reelected, a cease-fire was finally signed, and United States involvement in the war came to an end.

But the civil war continued for another two years in Vietnam. After the withdrawal of United States forces, South Vietnamese soldiers steadily lost ground to their North Vietnamese enemies. In the spring of 1975, the North Vietnamese launched a campaign of strikes against strategic cities throughout South Vietnam, the final objective being the seat of government in Saigon. South Vietnamese forces crumpled in the face of this campaign. On April 29, with communist forces surrounding Saigon, the United States carried out a dramatic last-minute evacuation. More than 1,000 Americans and nearly 6,000 Vietnamese were taken from the city by helicopter to aircraft carriers waiting offshore. On April 30, the Saigon government officially surrendered to the North Vietnamese.

Legacy of the War

The Vietnam War was the longest and least successful war in which the United States had ever participated. It resulted in 58,000 Americans dead and about 300,000 wounded. It cost more than $150 billion and disrupted the American economy in the process. The costs of the war were even higher in Vietnam itself. The Vietnamese were bombarded by more bombs than had fallen on all Axis powers during World War II. The number of dead and wounded Vietnamese soldiers ran into the millions, with countless civilian casualties. The landscape itself would long reveal the scars of war.

In the United States, the war also fractured the liberal consensus that had guided the nation during and after World War II. Americans had believed that they could defend the world from communism anywhere, at any time. American technology and money, they assumed, could always bring victory. That assumption was proved false in Vietnam, and the United States now had to reassess its global mission.

The legacy of the war lingered on long after the last bomb had been dropped. Soldiers came home to a different reception than their fathers and grandfathers had in World War II. The war had been so unpopular that some of the outrage felt by antiwar Americans was transferred to the GIs who had fought in Vietnam. It was often hard for returning soldiers to rationalize their participation in Vietnam, and it was harder still to integrate themselves back into American life. Ron Kovic, who was paralyzed in the war, summed up his feelings about his smashed dreams and body in a haunting poem. He had been born on the fourth of July, a date that had once underscored his patriotism. Now it seemed a bitter joke.

In 1975 Nha Trang in South Vietnam was evacuated just before communist troops took over. The man above was punched by an American official as he tried to board the last plane out, which was already overcrowded with fleeing refugees.

> I *am the living death*
> *the memorial day on wheels*
> *I am your yankee doodle dandy*
> *your john wayne come home*
> *your fourth of july firecracker*
> *exploding in the grave*

The Vietnam Veterans Memorial in Washington, D.C., was created to recognize the courage of American GIs during the Vietnam ordeal and to help heal the wounds the war had caused. An open competition, announced in 1980, specified that the memorial should be a quiet, contemplative structure that included a list of the war dead. It was won by Maya Ying Lin, a twenty-two-year-old Chinese American architecture student.

The memorial is a starkly beautiful structure, elegant in its simplicity. It consists of two long black marble slabs, intersecting in a V shape, with all the names of the known dead inscribed chronologically according to date of death. In 1993 a Vietnam Women's Memorial was unveiled near the wall to honor the more than 11,000 women who served in Vietnam.

SECTION 5 REVIEW

Key Terms, People, and Places
1. Define Vietnamization.
2. Identify Kent State University.

Key Concepts
3. What were the political effects of growing public disapproval of the war in 1968?
4. What was Richard Nixon's approach to the war in Vietnam?
5. How did the war in Vietnam finally end?

6. What was the lasting impact of the war in Vietnam and in the United States?

Critical Thinking
7. **Determining Relevance** The counterculture of the 1960s was despised by many Americans who saw it as a senseless rejection of time-honored values. Explain how such feelings might have played a part in the violence that erupted at Kent State University in 1970.

Chapter Review

Key Terms
1. Viet Cong
2. Gulf of Tonkin Resolution
3. escalation
4. Tet Offensive
5. My Lai massacre
6. Students for a Democratic Society (SDS)
7. New Left
8. teach-in
9. conscientious objector
10. counterculture
11. hippie
12. psychedelic drug
13. Woodstock
14. Vietnamization

People
15. Ngo Dinh Diem

Places
16. Saigon
17. Kent State University

Terms For each term above, write a sentence that explains its relation to the Vietnam War or to American society during the 1960s.

True or False Determine whether each statement is true or false. If it is true, write "true." If it is false, change the underlined term to make the statement true.
1. People who attended <u>Woodstock</u> remembered the sense of fellowship they experienced there.
2. After his reelection, Johnson began the <u>Vietnamization</u> of the war.
3. Members of a new political movement called the <u>Viet Cong</u> believed that radical change was the only way to solve poverty and racism in the United States.
4. <u>The Gulf of Tonkin Resolution</u> included strikes on provincial and district capitals and other towns in South Vietnam.
5. The use of <u>psychedelic drugs</u>, which alter perceptions of reality, was part of the 1960s counterculture.

Matching Review the key people and places in the list above. If you are not sure of their significance, review the information given in the chapter. Then choose a person or place from the list that best matches each description below.
1. the site of major strikes during the Tet Offensive
2. the site of violent protests against the American invasion of Cambodia
3. the repressive prime minister of South Vietnam

Section 1 (pp. 716 – 719)
1. Describe the government of Ngo Dinh Diem.
2. What was President Kennedy's policy toward Vietnam in the early 1960s?
3. Describe how the Vietnam War escalated under President Johnson.

Section 2 (pp. 720 – 723)
4. Explain why many American soldiers were eager to go to Vietnam. Why did many feel different once they actually began to fight?
5. Why was the war so devastating for Vietnamese civilians?
6. Explain how the My Lai massacre affected the attitudes of Americans at home toward the Vietnam War.

Section 3 (pp. 724 – 727)
7. What was the source of the 1960s "generation gap"?
8. What were some of the changes that student activists demanded during the 1960s?

Section 4 (pp. 729 – 732)
9. How did the styles of dress in the 1960s reflect counterculture values of freedom and individuality?
10. Why did many Americans view the counterculture with shock and dismay?

Section 5 (pp. 733 – 737)
11. Why did Lyndon Johnson decide not to run for reelection in 1968?
12. Why did Richard Nixon authorize the invasion of Cambodia in 1970?
13. What happened in Vietnam after the United States withdrew?
14. What is the purpose of the Vietnam Veterans Memorial in Washington, D.C.?

1. **Demonstrating Reasoned Judgment** If you had been a student during the Vietnam War, do you think that your views of the conflict would have changed or remained the same throughout the course of the war? What factors might have influenced your views?

2. **Expressing Problems Clearly** Since the end of the Vietnam War, government officials have advised caution in global affairs so that the United States does not get involved in "another Vietnam." Explain what is meant by this warning.

3. **Formulating Questions** Create three questions that you might ask a soldier who fought in Vietnam that, if answered, would give some idea of what participating in the war was like.

1. **Evaluating Primary Sources** Review the primary source excerpt on page 718. What underlying beliefs are revealed in Johnson's statement? Did history prove his beliefs to be correct?

2. **Understanding the Visuals** A protest sign carried in a 1967 antiwar demonstration in San Francisco read, "No war on children." Find an image in the chapter that might have inspired such a slogan. In general, how do the visuals in the chapter support the idea that the 1960s were a turbulent and confusing era?

3. **Writing About the Chapter** It is 1968. Write a letter to the editor of your school newspaper explaining why you will or will not participate in the upcoming student demonstration against the Vietnam War. First, create a list of the reasons why you do or do not support the war. Note your opinion about peaceful demonstrations as a way to effect change. Next, write a draft of your letter in which you explain your point of view. Revise your letter, making certain that each idea is clearly explained. Proofread your letter and draft a final copy.

4. **Using the Graphic Organizer** This graphic organizer uses a flow map to show the sequence of events leading to the end of the Vietnam War. (a) According to the map, what was one result of Nixon's bombing of Cambodia? (b) What contradiction in Nixon's policy toward Vietnam is shown by the flow map? (c) On a separate sheet of paper, create your own flow map about the beginnings of the Vietnam War, using this graphic organizer as an example.

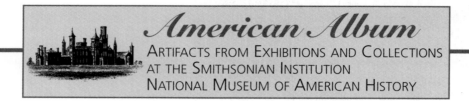

American Album
ARTIFACTS FROM EXHIBITIONS AND COLLECTIONS
AT THE SMITHSONIAN INSTITUTION
NATIONAL MUSEUM OF AMERICAN HISTORY

PERSONAL LEGACY

The V-shaped Vietnam Veterans Memorial, unlike most other monuments in Washington, D.C., is built on a small, human scale. Visitors find themselves drawn to its two polished black-granite walls, on which are inscribed more than 58,000 names of Americans killed and missing in the war. When this memorial opened in 1982, something unusual and unexpected began to occur: visitors left personal tokens at the base of the walls to honor and remember the soldiers who fought the war. The usual gifts of flowers, wreaths, and small American flags mix with the most common items of a soldier in Vietnam—helmets, combat boots, and dog tags. Some mourners leave the items that gave soldiers comfort, such as favorite magazines, beverages, and items of clothing. A few visitors leave things, such as notes, jewelry, and stuffed animals, that carry memories of the bond between soldier and mourner. This practice continues today, and the National Park Service collects and preserves the artifacts. *What do the objects shown here tell you about the life of a combat soldier in Vietnam?*

▲ The photo above shows one of the thousands of personal memorials left beside the Vietnam Veterans Memorial in Washington, D.C.

Republican Revival and Decline 1968–Present

"In this present crisis, government is not the solution to our problem; government is the problem."

—Ronald Reagan, 1981

By 1968 many Americans were tired of the turmoil of the sixties. The election of Richard Nixon as President that year marked the emergence of a Republican majority that lasted, with one brief exception, for more than twenty years. A long recession following the election of George Bush in 1988, however, created growing dissatisfaction with Republican policies. When Democrat Bill Clinton defeated Bush in the 1992 presidential election, Americans seemed ready to head in a new direction.

With a handshake and a smile, presidential power passed from Republican George Bush to Democrat Bill Clinton on a sunny day in January 1993.

The Nixon Years
1968–1974

*A*merican politics shifted dramatically in 1968, as violence and confrontation divided the country. Republican Richard Nixon capitalized on the disruption to gain the presidency. In office, Nixon was conservative in domestic affairs, but he took bold steps in changing relations with China and the Soviet Union. The Watergate scandal, involving Nixon's 1972 reelection campaign, angered Americans and forced Nixon to an action never before taken by a United States President.

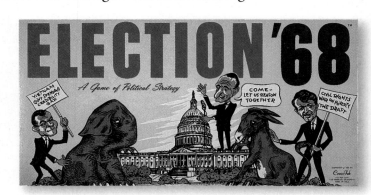

ELECTION '68
A Game of Political Strategy

Events in the United States

1968 Martin Luther King, Jr., and Robert Kennedy are assassinated.
• Violence disrupts the Democratic National Convention.

1969 Richard Nixon is sworn in as President.
• United States astronauts land on the moon.

1970 Four Kent State University students are killed by the Ohio National Guard at an antiwar protest.

1971 The Supreme Court allows school busing for desegregation.

1968	1969	1970	1971

Events in the World

1968 Pierre Trudeau is elected prime minister of Canada.

1969 Civil war continues in Nigeria.

1971 China is admitted to the United Nations.
• Idi Amin seizes power in Uganda and begins a reign of terror.

MR. PRESIDENT:
**RELEASE
the
TAPES!**

1972 Nixon visits China. • Break-in at Democratic headquarters sets off the Watergate scandal.	**1973** The Senate begins investigating the Watergate affair. • Spiro Agnew resigns as Vice President.	**1974** Nixon resigns the presidency. • Vice President Gerald Ford becomes President.	**1975** White House aides go to jail for Watergate crimes.	
1972	**1973**	**1974**	**1975**	**1976**
1972 SALT I treaty between the United States and the Soviet Union limits nuclear weapons.	**1973** The fourth Arab-Israeli war begins on Yom Kippur. • OPEC places embargo on oil shipments.	**1974** Writer Alexander Solzhenitsyn is exiled from the Soviet Union.	**1975** Civil war begins in Lebanon. • Mozambique wins independence from Portugal.	

1968: A Turning Point in History

SECTION PREVIEW

A crisis-filled year of assassinations, antiwar protest, and violence polarized the country in 1968. The turmoil paved the way for the election of Richard Nixon and the emergence of a Republican majority in national politics.

LBJ's political career is crushed in "The Time Machine," shown in this 1967 British cartoon.

Key Concepts
- The Tet Offensive increased protests over American involvement in Vietnam.
- The assassinations of Dr. Martin Luther King, Jr., and Robert Kennedy increased divisions in the country.
- Violence at the Democratic presidential convention polarized people politically and caused disunity in the party.
- Reaction against violence helped Republican Richard Nixon win the presidency.

Key Terms, People, and Places
Poor People's Campaign; Robert F. Kennedy, Eugene McCarthy, Hubert Humphrey, George C. Wallace, Richard M. Nixon, Spiro Agnew

I n the troubled decade of the 1960s, perhaps the most shattering year was 1968. A series of tragic events hit with such force that, month by month, the nation seemed to be coming apart. In the midst of the turmoil—and, in part, as a result of it—the way was paved for the election of Richard Nixon and the emergence of a Republican majority in national politics that would last for the next twenty years. The nation experienced an emotional shift as well as a political one. Against a backdrop of domestic violence, chaos, and confrontation, many Americans saw as hopeless the chance of achieving peaceful social change through political activism.

The Tet Offensive Increases Antiwar Sentiment at Home

The Vietnam War continued to rage in 1968. One encounter during the war had a profound effect on the American people and made 1968 a turning point in the conflict.

Beginning on January 30, the Viet Cong launched a massive three-week surprise attack against South Vietnam. While the Tet Offensive, as this attack was called, ended in military defeat for North Vietnam, it caused more and more Americans to question whether winning the Vietnam War was possible. After three years of escalation under the Johnson administration, many Americans wondered what had been achieved if the enemy could mount such a blistering offensive. Television news coverage of Tet increased the impact the attack had on the American public. Millions watched as news anchor Walter Cronkite, known for his objective viewpoint, said in February, "It now seems more certain than ever that the bloody experience in Vietnam is to end in stalemate."

After Tet, public opinion polls showed that a majority of Americans opposed the war. From a military perspective, Tet was a major defeat for the Viet Cong. But from a political perspective, it was a major defeat for the United States—and for the Johnson administration.

Popular Leaders Fall to Violence

For many Americans, the memory of President John F. Kennedy's assassination in 1963 was still vivid and haunting five years later. They looked to other leaders to carry on the spirit and idealism of the Kennedy years. But in 1968, people's hopes were again shattered by the burst of bullets from assassins' guns.

Tragedy Strikes The major spokesperson for African Americans in the decade after 1955 was Martin Luther King, Jr. By the mid-1960s,

King, convinced that poverty bred violence, broadened his crusade to attack all economic injustice.

In 1968 King began the **Poor People's Campaign,** planning a march on Washington like that in 1963. Traveling around the United States to mobilize support, he went to Memphis, Tennessee, in early April to support striking garbage workers seeking better working conditions. On April 3, King spoke eloquently, referring to threats made against his life:

W*e've got some difficult days ahead. But it doesn't matter with me now, because I've been to the mountain top. And I don't mind. Like anybody, I would like to live a long life. . . . But I'm not concerned about that now. I just want to do God's will. And He's allowed me to go up to the mountain. And I've looked over. And I've seen the promised land.*

The next day, as King stood on the balcony of his motel, a shot from a high-powered rifle ripped through his jaw. An hour later, King was dead.

King's assassination sparked violent reactions across the nation. In an outburst of rage and frustration, some African Americans rioted, setting fires and looting stores in 124 cities. Riots and police responses left forty-five people dead. President Johnson ordered flags on federal buildings to be flown at half-mast to honor King, but it took more than 5,500 troops to quell the violence. For many Americans of all races, the death of King eroded faith in the idea of nonviolent change.

Another Leader Falls Robert F. Kennedy, who had served his brother John as attorney general, was now running for President himself. Earlier in the year, in March, Senator **Eugene McCarthy** of Minnesota had come out against the war and challenged Lyndon Johnson in the New Hampshire Democratic primary. When McCarthy did well—42 percent to the President's 49 percent—Kennedy saw that

Seconds after shots ring out, Martin Luther King lies mortally wounded, while companions point frantically to the direction from which the shots were fired.

Johnson was vulnerable and entered the campaign himself. Kennedy's bid received a critical boost later that month when, on March 31, LBJ addressed the American people on television. After announcing that he had ordered a reduction in the bombing of North Vietnam as a step toward furthering peace negotiations, Johnson stunned the nation by saying he would not run for a second term as President.

In the years since his brother's death, Bobby Kennedy had reached out to many Americans—Chicanos in the California fields, Native Americans in the Southwest, African Americans in the Mississippi delta, poor white families in New York tenements. Morally and politically opposed to the Vietnam War, he condemned the killing of both Americans and Vietnamese. And he criticized the Johnson administration for financing a war instead of the programs needed to help the poor and disadvantaged at home.

Kennedy spent the spring of 1968 battling McCarthy in the Democratic primary elections. In June he won a key victory in California's primary. But on the evening of the primary, after giving his victory speech, Robert Kennedy was shot by an assassin and died a day later.

When the shooting was reported, several campaign workers who had watched the speech

Busboy Juan Romero was the first to reach Robert Kennedy after he was shot in a hotel kitchen just after winning the California primary.

on TV were waiting for Kennedy in his Los Angeles hotel room. One of them, civil rights leader John Lewis, later said, "We all just fell to the floor and started crying. To me that was like the darkest, saddest moment." In a 1987 statement, Lewis also described the funeral journey to Arlington National Cemetery and reflected on the killings that had shattered the country:

*A*ll along the way, you saw people coming up to the train crying and these hand-made signs saying, "We love you, Bobby," "Goodbye, Bobby," "God bless you, Bobby," and so forth. . . . Something was taken from us. The type of leadership that we had in a sense invested in, that we had helped to make and to nourish, was taken from us.

Kennedy's death ended many people's hopes for reform or reconciliation.

MAKING CONNECTIONS

Many people who lived through the 1960s would agree with John Lewis that the country lost its sense of hope after the assassinations. Do you think that people in the United States today have regained a sense of hope?

The 1968 Democratic Convention

By the time the Democrats convened in Chicago that summer, the party was in shreds. Eugene McCarthy was still a prominent antiwar candidate, but party regulars thought he was too far from the mainstream. They supported Vice President **Hubert Humphrey,** who had long been a strong advocate of social justice and civil rights.

Humphrey, however, was hurt by his support of administration policies on Vietnam. In the face of growing antiwar protest, he hardly seemed the one to bring the party together. Robert Kennedy, the one candidate who might have succeeded, was dead.

"The Whole World Is Watching" The prospect of thousands of demonstrators at the Democratic convention—radicals, peace marchers, hippies—enraged Chicago mayor Richard J. Daley. He had the convention hall protected by barbed wire and chain-link fencing. He also ordered police to clear out protesters gathered in Lincoln Park along the lake shore. As the police went in with tear gas and clubs, several violent confrontations took place.

The climax came as the delegates voted down a peace resolution and seemed ready to nominate Humphrey. As thousands of protesters gathered for a rally near the convention hotel, the police moved in, using their nightsticks to club anyone on the street, including passersby, hotel guests, and reporters.

Todd Gitlin, onetime president of Students for a Democratic Society, recorded the scene this way:

*W*ho beat whom? In brief, again and again, the police came down like avenging thugs. They charged, clubbed, gassed, and mauled—demonstrators, bystanders, and reporters. They did it when there were minor violations of the law, like the curfew; they did it when there were symbolic provocations, like the lowering of an American flag; they did it when provoked . . . ; in crucial instances, like the assault outside the Hilton Hotel Wednesday evening, they did it when unprovoked.

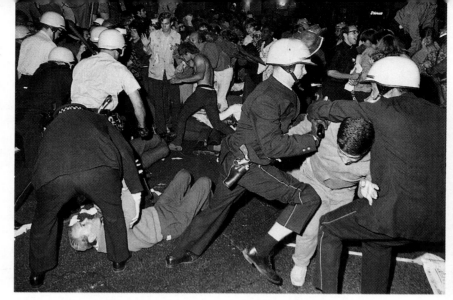

Much of the violence took place in front of television cameras, while crowds chanted "The whole world is watching." As convention delegates voted, Senator Abraham Ribicoff of Connecticut denounced the "Gestapo tactics on the streets of Chicago," provoking an angry scene with Daley. Humphrey was nominated, but the party had been torn apart.

Wallace Woos Voters Adding to the Democrats' problems was a third-party candidate in the race. Alabama governor **George C. Wallace** had gained national fame for playing on racial tensions among southerners. Now he turned to blue-collar voters in the North who resented campus radicals and liberal antiwar forces. Wallace won support by attacking "left-wing theoreticians, briefcase-totin' bureaucrats, ivory-tower guideline writers, bearded anarchists, smart-aleck editorial writers and pointy-headed professors."

The Election of 1968

The Republicans chose **Richard M. Nixon,** who had narrowly lost to John Kennedy in 1960. In his campaign, Nixon backed law and order and claimed to have a secret plan to end the war in Vietnam. Earlier, Nixon had often seemed harsh and angry, but this time he let his running mate, Governor **Spiro Agnew** of Maryland,

Determined to stop protests at the 1968 Democratic Convention, Chicago police and National Guardsmen used nightsticks, tear gas, and rifles against demonstrators and others who were caught up in the violence.

deliver nasty rhetoric, such as calling Humphrey "squishy soft" on communism.

Nixon's campaign was well run and well financed. Late in the campaign, Humphrey began to catch up. But even though President Johnson stopped the bombing of North Vietnam on October 31, it was too late. Many disillusioned Democrats stayed home on election day, voting for no one.

In the popular vote, Nixon squeaked by with only 43.4 percent—less than one percentage point ahead of Humphrey's 42.7 percent. Wallace won the rest. Although Democrats kept control of both houses of Congress, the Republicans were back in the White House.

SECTION 1 REVIEW

Key Terms, People, and Places
1. Define Poor People's Campaign.
2. Identify (a) Robert F. Kennedy, (b) Eugene McCarthy, (c) Hubert Humphrey, (d) George C. Wallace, (e) Richard M. Nixon, (f) Spiro Agnew.

Key Concepts
3. How did the Tet Offensive contribute to the turbulence of 1968?

4. What were some aftereffects of the assassination of Martin Luther King, Jr.?
5. From what groups did Wallace try to attract support?
6. What issues did Nixon emphasize in his campaign?

Critical Thinking
7. **Recognizing Cause and Effect** How did the assassination of Robert Kennedy affect the chances of the Democrats in the 1968 presidential election?

The Lasting Impact of the Year 1968

The year 1968 was a turning point in American political life, bringing a shift in the direction of both foreign and domestic policies. The turmoil of the year also had a psychological impact on many people.

Foreign Policy Attitudes

The turbulence sparked by Vietnam, which reached a peak in 1968, destroyed the nation's consensus on foreign policy. Now many Americans wondered whether they could—or should—support the aims of the United States around the world. Questions about Vietnam would haunt the country for decades.

Presidential War Powers Opposition to the war also brought a challenge to the President's powers as commander in chief. Many Americans were disturbed by the way Lyndon Johnson had maneuvered the United States into Vietnam and by Nixon's order to bomb Cambodia, thereby escalating the war. The War Powers Act, passed over Nixon's veto in 1973, required the President to notify Congress quickly if troops were sent overseas. The act then required congressional approval of such troop movements.

The war powers issue continued to cause controversy. In the Reagan administration, for example, members of Congress filed lawsuits to stop military actions in Central America and on the island of Grenada. The question arose again in 1990 when President George Bush sent American troops to Kuwait after the Iraqi invasion. Bush finally asked for—and got—Congress's approval of the Persian Gulf War.

1977 When Jimmy Carter won the presidency, he served as a lone Democrat in the midst of over twenty years of Republicans in the White House.

1980	1982	1984

1984 Despite protests from members of Congress, President Reagan orders military action in Grenada.

Changes at Home

In domestic affairs, the events of 1968 brought significant change, both political and social. As the war eroded many "Great Society" programs, conservative Americans challenged the entire liberal approach toward government assistance for those in need. Since Franklin Roosevelt's New Deal in the 1930s, the range of social programs had grown. Few people wanted to eliminate programs like social security or Medicare, but Republicans were committed to cutting back the role of government. Winning the White House in 1968 gave them the chance to do so. Their successors went even further—in particular, the Reagan administration in the 1980s drastically cut funds for social programs.

The 1968 election also brought an end to the Democratic domination of national politics that had lasted for more than thirty years. Joined together by President Roosevelt in 1936, the party included working-class Americans, first- and second-generation immigrants, and African Americans. The events of 1968 split that group. What followed was seen by some analysts as an emerging Republican majority. Although a Democrat won the White House in 1976, Republicans won the presidency in every other election from 1980 to 1988. In congressional politics, Republicans encouraged the growth of a new conservative movement, reflected in legislation and in several significant decisions by the Supreme Court.

Emotionally, the violence of 1968 also left its mark on the nation, ending what for many had been an era of idealism. After Bobby Kennedy's death, civil rights worker John Lewis said:

> There are people today who are afraid, in a sense, to hope or to have hope again, because of what happened in 1963, and particularly what happened in 1968.

REVIEWING THE FACTS

1. What groups were included in the old Democratic party?
2. What was the significance of Richard Nixon's victory in 1968?

Critical Thinking

3. **Identifying Assumptions** Why did Congress believe it was necessary to pass the War Powers Act in 1973?

1980s Republicans continued their push for a new conservative movement with Supreme Court nominations that moved the Court to the right.

1991 The question of presidential war powers arose again when President George Bush sent troops to the Persian Gulf.

1986   1988   1990

1989 As social programs were cut back during the years of Republican government, homelessness and other local problems increased.

751

The Nixon Administration

SECTION PREVIEW

Having gained the presidency, Richard Nixon was determined to maintain his power at all costs. He kept tight control of his administration and took a conservative direction on the national front.

Key Concepts
• Nixon's reserved, secretive personality influenced his staff and his style of governing.
  • Nixon tried to take a more conservative stance in dealing with the economy and with issues such as law and order.
  • Nixon slowed the advancement of civil rights with his policies, aimed in part at winning support in the South.

Key Terms, People, and Places
imperial presidency, Organization of Petroleum Exporting Countries (OPEC), embargo, busing; Henry A. Kissinger, H. R. Haldeman, John Ehrlichman, John Mitchell

This crocheted replica of the presidential seal was sent to President Nixon by a well-wisher early in his presidency.

R ichard Nixon had struggled hard during a twenty-year political career mixed with setbacks and successes. He suffered a number of bitter defeats but came back to national politics each time. Having worked hard to gain the presidency, he was determined to maintain strict control over his administration.

Nixon in Person

Richard Nixon was a shy and remote man. Although uncomfortable with people, he put up a front when he campaigned, and he used new techniques such as television to good advantage. He often seemed stiff and lacking in humor and charm, however. Many Americans respected Nixon for his abilities and his skillful handling of the vice presidency under Eisenhower, but many others neither trusted nor liked him.

Nixon's family was poor, and he never got over his sense of being an outsider. In 1963 he described how that feeling drove him to achieve:

W *hat starts the process really are laughs and slights and snubs when you are a kid. Sometimes it's because you're poor or Irish or Jewish or Catholic or ugly or simply that you are skinny. But if you are reasonably intelligent and if your anger is deep enough and strong enough, you learn that you can change those attitudes by excellence, personal gut performance.*

According to Pat Buchanan, then a Nixon speech writer, there was "a mean side to his nature." He was willing to say or do anything to defeat his enemies. Adlai Stevenson, who ran

Despite his shy personality, Nixon knew how to play a crowd and often put on an "imperial" aspect when appearing in public.

unsuccessfully for the presidency twice in the 1950s, spoke of a place called "Nixonland—a land of slander and scare, of sly innuendo, of a poison pen, the anonymous phone call, and hustling, pushing, shoving—the land of smash and grab and anything to win."

Nixon had few close friends, insulating himself from people and the press. He took support and security from his family—his wife, Pat, and their two daughters. Away from the White House, he secluded himself at his estates in Florida and California, both lavishly redone at government expense. He dreamed of what historian Arthur Schlesinger, Jr., has called an **imperial presidency,** meaning an executive branch that dominates the branches of government to an extreme degree. By his own choice, his administration reflected a closed, secretive style.

Nixon's Top Staff People

Nixon's staff gave him support and loyalty. His cabinet members were all wealthy, white, male Republicans, sympathetic to his views. Yet Nixon generally worked around his cabinet and more often relied on a few other key appointees for advice.

One was **Henry A. Kissinger,** a Harvard government professor, who joined the Nixon administration as head of the National Security Council and in 1973 became Nixon's secretary of state. He played a major role in shaping foreign policy, both as an adviser to the President and in behind-the-scenes diplomacy.

Two influential staff members shielded Nixon from the outside world and carried out his orders. **H. R. Haldeman,** an advertising executive who had campaigned tirelessly for Nixon, became chief of staff. He once observed, "I get done what he wants done and I take the heat instead of him."

The Oval Office in the White House saw many meetings of Nixon and his inner circle of close advisers—here, left to right, are Kissinger, Ehrlichman, the President, and Haldeman.

Lawyer **John Ehrlichman** served first as legal counselor, then rose to the post of chief domestic adviser. He and Haldeman framed issues and narrowed options for the President. Together they became known as the "Berlin Wall" for the way they protected Nixon's privacy.

Finally, there was **John Mitchell,** a lawyer who had worked with Nixon in New York and then managed his campaign. He was named attorney general and wielded great influence, speaking with Nixon several times a day. White House staff members called Mitchell "El Supremo" for his stature as a top aide.

MAKING CONNECTIONS

A President's personality can greatly affect the style and actions of an administration. What kind of personalities have recent Presidents such as Reagan, Bush, and Clinton had?

Domestic Policy Issues: A Different Direction

The Vietnam War and domestic issues had both been important in the 1968 political campaigns. Domestically, Nixon took a different course than his Democratic predecessors.

Economic Problems The economy was shaky when Nixon took office. Largely because of spending for the Vietnam War, inflation had doubled between 1965 and 1968. At the same time, unemployment continued to grow. Nixon's first priority was to halt inflation. He felt that federal spending had gotten out of control and wanted to cut back, even if it led to further unemployment.

At the same time, he was determined to avoid economic controls. He had seen such controls in action while working for the Office of Price Administration during World War II. "I will not take the nation down the road of wage and price controls, however politically expedient they may seem," he said in 1970.

During his first few years in office, however, controlling spending proved difficult. Both unemployment and inflation continued to rise. Lawrence O'Brien, head of the Democratic National Committee, called the new situation "Nixonomics":

*A*ll the things that should go up—the stock market, corporate profits, real spendable income, productivity—go down, and all the things that should go down—unemployment, prices, interest rates—go up.

Although Republicans traditionally aimed for a balanced budget, Nixon began to consider deficit spending—spending beyond the budget in order to stimulate the economy. This was the approach that English economist John Maynard Keynes had called for during the Depression and that many Democrats had supported. "I am now a Keynesian in economics," Nixon announced in 1971, to the surprise of many.

To slow the high rate of inflation, shown in the graph below, he imposed a ninety-day freeze on wages, prices, and rents, but then pressure from business and labor led him to lift controls. Inflation soared again.

Unrest in the Middle East brought more disruptions to the troubled economy. Americans depended on cheap, imported oil for about a third of their energy needs. But in 1973, Israel and the Arab nations of Egypt and Syria went to war. When the United States backed its ally Israel, the Arab members of the **Organization of Petroleum Exporting Countries (OPEC)** angrily responded by imposing an **embargo,** or restriction, on oil shipped to the United States. OPEC, a group of nations that sets oil prices and production, also quadrupled its prices. Oil prices soared, even after the embargo ended in 1974. The map on page 755 shows the nations that belong to OPEC.

The oil crisis affected everyone. A loaf of bread that had cost twenty-eight cents earlier in the 1970s now was eighty-nine cents. Americans

Because Americans depended so heavily on oil from the Middle East for gasoline and heating fuel, Arab oil producers had an effective weapon in the threat of raising prices.

Rate of Inflation, 1968–1976

(Graph: Percent Annual Price Increase, y-axis 0 to 60; x-axis Year 1968 to 1976)

Legend:
- All consumer item prices
- Food prices
- Fuel prices

Source: *Statistical Abstract of the United States*

Interpreting Graphs
Rising oil prices in the 1970s had a strong impact on all parts of the American economy. *When did oil prices reach their peak? How long did high prices last?*

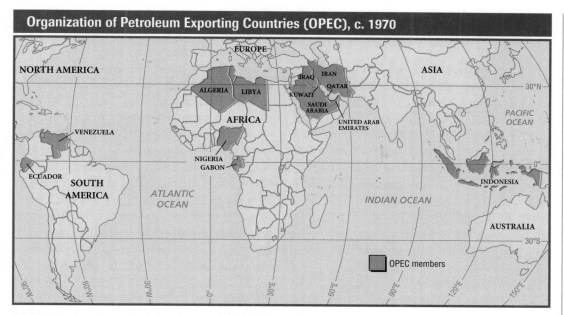

Organization of Petroleum Exporting Countries (OPEC), c. 1970

OPEC members

Geography and History: Interpreting Maps
OPEC brought together the world's major oil producers. *In what region of the world are many of these nations concentrated? What political effects did this have? What oil-producing nations are located in the Americas?*

who were used to paying twenty-five cents a gallon for gas now paid sixty-five cents. Higher energy prices fueled inflation, which in turn led consumers to cut back on spending. The result was another recession. Unemployment reached 9 percent, the highest rate since the 1930s.

Social Programs Meanwhile, Nixon was trying to stop the growth of government spending on social programs that were part of Lyndon Johnson's Great Society. Critics claimed that the programs were wasteful, encouraged "welfare cheaters," and discouraged people from seeking work.

Nixon had exploited that frustration in his campaign, but he now faced a dilemma. On the one hand, he wanted to please conservative voters in the South who demanded cutbacks. On the other hand, he hoped to appeal to traditionally Democratic blue-collar voters, who wanted to keep the programs that benefited them.

The administration suggested a work-incentive program that would give families a basic minimum income, while requiring them to register for job training and accept a job when one was found. The Family Assistance

Plan failed to pass the Senate but did gain Nixon political points with some voters.

Law and Order Another important campaign issue had been the need to restore "law and order" in the country. President Nixon recognized that a strong backlash had developed against student radicals, antiwar protesters, and the youth counterculture in general. Many older working-class and middle-class Americans held those groups responsible not only for demonstrations in the streets but also for rising crime, growing drug use, and permissive attitudes toward sex.

To strengthen his position on law and order, Nixon's strategy was to discourage any kind of protest. In speeches, he lashed out at all demonstrators, once calling students "bums." After National Guardsmen shot and killed student protesters at Kent State University, Nixon implied that the students themselves had caused the tragedy. Speaking at Kansas State University later in 1970, he said:

The time has come for us to recognize that violence and terror have no place in a free society. Whatever the purported [supposed] *cause of the perpetrators may be . . . no cause justifies violence.*

Other members of the administration backed him up. Attorney General Mitchell stepped up the Justice Department's campaign against crime. Using his gift for colorful rhetoric, Vice President Spiro Agnew called student protesters and professors an "effete corps of impudent snobs," *effete* meaning they were weak and *impudent* meaning they were rude and disrespectful. Unhappy with press coverage of the White House, Agnew also accused television reporters and producers of distorting administration actions.

The "Southern Strategy" Nixon felt that he had little to gain by supporting advances in civil rights. Few African Americans had voted for him in the 1960 race against John Kennedy, and in 1968 he had gotten just 12 percent of the black vote. Besides, he reasoned, any attempt to court the black electorate could threaten the white southern vote in a reelection bid. Thus, while there were some civil rights gains in the Nixon years, the record was generally weak.

Explaining his position, Nixon once observed that "there are those who want instant integration and those who want segregation forever. I believe that we need to have a middle course between those two extremes." Given the strong resistance to change that persisted in many places, this meant a slowdown in desegregation.

Nixon's aim was to find the proper "southern strategy" to win over the Democratic white South. Senator Strom Thurmond of South Carolina, who had left the Democratic party in 1948, was now a Republican and became Nixon's strongest southern supporter. To keep him and his colleagues happy, Nixon sought to reduce the appropriation needed for enforcing fair housing, and he eased guidelines for desegregation.

The Justice Department, headed by John Mitchell, tried to prevent the extension of the Voting Rights Act of 1965, which had greatly increased the number of African Americans who could vote in the South. Congress went ahead with the extension, but Nixon had made his point to white southern voters.

Another controversial issue was the use of **busing** to end school segregation. In several cities, federal courts ordered school systems to

1650   1700   1750   1800   **Links Across Time**   1850   1900   1950   2000

To Coin a Phrase

The language of American politics gained a new entry when Spiro Agnew uttered the phrase "effete corps of impudent snobs" in a speech he made in 1969. American political language has had a long and colorful past. Since the early republic, American politicians have invented their own words and phrases or borrowed them from other people, such as journalists or members of the military. Some of the terms and phrases coined by politicians from the past to the present include:

silk stocking A wealthy person; dates back to colonial times when

only the rich could afford to wear silk stockings.

cookie pusher A diplomat who spends time attending social teas rather than doing any real work; dates from the 1940s.

fishing expedition An investigation with no specific goal, usually made by one political party into the business of another; popularized in the 1940s.

pooh-bah A self-important high official; a popular term in American politics since the 1950s.

nervous Nellies People who become easily disturbed or upset; popularized by President Johnson,

who used the term to describe some critics of his policy in Vietnam.

waxworks The honored guests at a political dinner who sit on a raised platform, so named because of the frozen, or waxen, smiles they keep on their faces; dates from the late 1960s.

break all the china To obey an order regardless of the obstacles; a favorite Nixon phrase.

FOB Friend of Bill's; a phrase meant to describe a personal friend of President Clinton, popularized in the press since Clinton's inauguration.

How might a term or a phrase coined by a politician become commonly used by Americans?

bus students to other schools to end the pattern of all-black or all-white schools. Particularly in northern cities, such as Detroit and Boston, some white students and their parents met incoming black students with boycotts or violent protests.

In 1971 guidelines for busing were laid down by a Supreme Court decision that went against Nixon's views. A federal judge in North Carolina had ruled that voluntary integration efforts were not working. In *Swann v. Charlotte-Mecklenburg Board of Education,* the Court agreed, saying that busing was one possible option for ending school desegregation.

Nixon had long been opposed to busing. He now went on national television to say that he would ask Congress to halt it. He also allowed the Department of Health, Education, and Welfare to restore federal funding to school districts where segregation persisted. Although busing continued in some places, Nixon's position was clear to voters in the South.

Nixon and the Supreme Court

During the campaign, Nixon had criticized the Supreme Court as too liberal and soft on criminals. In his first term, four justices died, resigned, or retired, giving him the extraordinary opportunity to name four new justices and thus reshape the Court. He first named Warren Burger as Chief Justice, replacing Earl Warren. Burger was a moderate who was easily confirmed by the Senate.

Later nominations reflected Nixon's southern strategy and conservative views. The Senate rejected his first nominees from the South: Clement Haynsworth of South Carolina and G. Harrold Carswell of Florida. Opponents

These demonstrators expressed their unhappiness with busing by burying a school bus and erecting the following epitaph nearby: "Here lies a school bus/No mourning from us./No more fuming/No more fussing/May this be the end of busing."

charged that both choices showed racial bias. Haynsworth was also suspected of conflict of interest in some court rulings, while Carswell was seen as intellectually mediocre. Bitterly, Nixon told the press, "I cannot successfully nominate to the Supreme Court any federal appellate judge from the South who believes as I do in the strict construction of the Constitution." Eventually Nixon appointed Harry A. Blackmun, Lewis F. Powell, Jr., and William H. Rehnquist, all qualified jurists, who generally tilted the Court in a more conservative direction.

While Nixon developed domestic policies to "bring Americans together again," as he said in his inaugural speech, he took a greater interest in what he could do to shape foreign policy. The outcome of his plans to play an important role in world affairs is discussed in the next section.

SECTION 2 REVIEW

Key Terms, People, and Places
1. Define (a) imperial presidency, (b) OPEC, (c) embargo, (d) busing.
2. Identify (a) Henry A. Kissinger, (b) H. R. Haldeman, (c) John Ehrlichman, (d) John Mitchell.

Key Concepts
3. What steps did Nixon take to fix the economy?

4. Why did Nixon strongly advocate law and order?
5. What was Nixon's "southern strategy"?

Critical Thinking
6. **Determining Relevance** How did Nixon's background and philosophy influence his style of governing?

Nixon's Foreign Policy

SECTION PREVIEW

Nixon's main interest was in foreign affairs, where he made significant changes. Working closely with Henry Kissinger, he took dramatic steps toward new relationships with both China and the Soviet Union.

Key Concepts
- Henry Kissinger played an important role in shaping the foreign policy of the Nixon administration.
- Nixon took bold steps in relaxing international tensions.
- Nixon reversed American policy in relations with the People's Republic of China.
- The United States and the Soviet Union moved toward arms control.

Key Terms, People, and Places
realpolitik, détente, Strategic Arms Limitation Talks (SALT)

This giant panda was one of two given to the people of the United States from the People's Republic of China on the occasion of President Nixon's visit there in 1972.

A s President, Nixon's greatest achievements were in the field of foreign policy. "I've always thought this country could run itself domestically without a President," he once observed. He understood the implications of strategic planning and diplomacy in foreign affairs, and took a creative approach that helped ease the tensions of the cold war. Aided by the skillful diplomacy of Henry Kissinger, Nixon opened the way to establishing relations with China and crafted a better relationship with the Soviet Union.

AMERICAN PROFILES

Henry Kissinger

While Nixon had an astute grasp of foreign policy, he still relied heavily on Henry Kissinger in charting his course. The German-born Kissinger quickly gained the President's confidence and became a dominant figure in the administration.

Henry (originally Heinz) Kissinger came from a Jewish family that fled Nazi Germany in 1938 when he was fifteen. The Kissingers settled in New York City that same year. In New York, Kissinger worked during the day at a shaving brush company, finished high school at night, and then attended City College. He was drafted in 1943, and an army teacher and historian encouraged him to go to Harvard University at the end of the war. There he completed both undergraduate and graduate degrees and wrote his doctoral dissertation on Klemens von Metternich, a nineteenth-century Austrian statesman and diplomat who helped maintain stability in Europe in the face of liberal change. Kissinger's studies gave him an admiration for *realpolitik,* a German term for "practical politics" based on achieving power.

On the faculty at Harvard, Kissinger rose quickly through university positions, gaining a reputation for being brilliant but arrogant and abrasive. By 1962 he was a full professor of government.

Outside the university, Kissinger soon became a recognized expert on foreign relations. His first book, *Nuclear Weapons and Foreign Policy,* published in 1957, argued that President Eisenhower's doctrine of massive retaliation was a mistake, and that a limited nuclear war could be fought successfully. He also worked with Nelson Rockefeller, governor of New York, who recommended him to Nixon.

Kissinger understood how to deal with the insecure President. Nixon needed to be flattered, and he liked people who could talk tough. Kissinger was willing to accommodate him and soon became the man Nixon talked to most. "Henry, of course, was not a personal friend," Nixon later said, but the two spoke five

Henry Kissinger was a major architect of American foreign policy in the 1970s.

Kissinger also had a remarkable ability to manipulate the press. Journalists depended on him for stories and were wary of antagonizing him. A *Time* magazine reporter noted how Kissinger worked: "You know you are being played like a violin, but it's still extremely seductive."

His efforts in ending the Vietnam War and easing cold war tensions made Kissinger a celebrity. He shared the 1973 Nobel Peace Prize with North Vietnam's Le Duc Tho (who refused it), appeared on twenty-one *Time* covers, and in 1973 was first in a Gallup Poll listing the most-admired Americans. He left a lasting mark on American foreign policy.

or six times a day, sometimes in person, sometimes by phone, and often for hours at a time.

Kissinger's actual influence in shaping American foreign policy was broader than his official roles—first as national security adviser and then as secretary of state. He knew how to frame questions in ways the President wanted. He could distill foreign policy issues into briefing papers that gave Nixon options for making decisions. In his memoirs, Kissinger wrote:

N*ixon could be very decisive. Almost invariably during his Presidency his decisions were courageous and strong and often taken in loneliness against all expert advice. But wherever possible Nixon made these decisions in solitude on the basis of memoranda or with a few very intimate aides.*

Kissinger saw to it that he was with the President when such decisions were made.

Both men were suspicious and secretive. Together, they took an almost conspiratorial approach to foreign policy. "They tried not to let anyone else have a full picture, even if it meant deceiving them," Lawrence Eagleburger, a State Department official, observed.

Superpower Tensions Relax

Nixon's greatest accomplishment was in bringing about **détente,** a relaxation in the tensions between the superpowers. This role was ironic, for in the 1950s Richard Nixon had been one of the most bitter and active anti-communists in government. He had made his reputation as someone willing to demand extraordinary action in response to the communist threat. As President, however, Nixon dealt imaginatively with both China and the Soviet Union. Bypassing Congress, and often bypassing his own advisers, he and Kissinger reversed the direction of postwar American foreign policy.

Nixon drew on Kissinger's understanding that foreign affairs were more complex than a simple standoff between the United States and the threat of communism. Kissinger pointed out that there were deep rifts in the communist world itself, noting, "The deepest international conflict in the world today is not between us and the Soviet Union but between the Soviet Union and Communist China."

A New Approach to China

The most surprising policy shift was toward China. When the communist revolution ended in 1949, establishing the People's Republic of China, Americans saw all communists in Asia

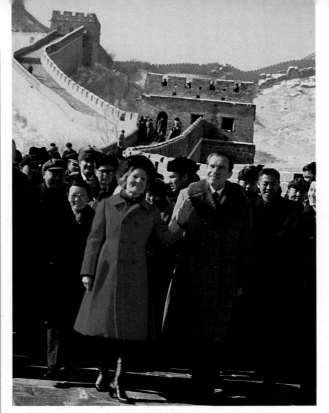

The President and First Lady Pat Nixon head a group touring the Great Wall of China on this historic first visit to the People's Republic of China.

as part of a united plot to dominate the world. Ignoring reality, the United States did not extend formal diplomatic recognition to the new Chinese government—in effect, officially pretending instead that it did not exist. Even when a Chinese-Soviet alliance crumbled, the United States clung to its rigid position. It insisted that the government of Chiang Kai-shek, set up on the island of Taiwan when the Nationalists fled the Chinese mainland, was the rightful government of all China.

Quietly, Nixon began to prepare the way for change. In his inaugural address in 1969, he referred indirectly to China when he declared, "We seek an open world . . . a world in which no people, great or small, will live in angry isolation." His first foreign policy report to Congress in 1970 began:

T*he Chinese are a great and vital people who should not remain isolated from the international community. . . . United States policy is not likely soon to have much impact on China's behavior, let alone its ideological outlook. But it is certainly in our interest, and in the interest of peace and stability in Asia and the world, that we take what steps we can toward improved practical relations with Peking [Beijing].*

The next year, the administration relaxed some regulations toward China. Then the Chinese invited an American table-tennis team to visit the mainland, and the United States began to ease some trading restrictions. In July 1971, after extensive secret diplomacy by Kissinger, Nixon made the dramatic announcement that he planned to visit China the following year. He would be the first United States President to travel to that country.

Nixon understood that the People's Republic was an established government and would not simply disappear. Other nations had recognized the new government, and it was time for the United States to do the same. Similarly, other countries wanted to give China's seat in the United Nations to the People's Republic, and the United States could no longer muster international opinion against this change.

Nixon had other motives as well. He recognized that he could use Chinese friendship as a bargaining chip in his negotiations with the Soviet Union. Press coverage of the trip would give him a boost at home. Also, he believed that he could take the action without political damage, because of his past reputation as a strong anticommunist.

Nixon traveled to China in February 1972. He met with Mao Zedong, the Chinese leader who had spearheaded the revolution in 1949. He spoke with Premier Zhou Enlai about international problems and ways of dealing with them. He and his wife, Pat, toured the Great Wall and other Chinese sights, all in front of television cameras that sent historic pictures home. When he returned to the United States, he waited in his plane until prime time so his return would be seen by as many television viewers as possible. Formal relations were not yet restored—that would take a few more years—but the basis for diplomatic ties had been established.

Strengthening Ties with the Soviet Union

At the same time that he was dealing with China, Nixon turned his attention to the Soviet Union. He and Kissinger hoped to play off one communist state against the other. In 1971 he outlined his aim for East-West relations in Europe:

E*ast-West conflict in Europe springs from historical and objective causes, not transient [changing] moods or personal misunderstandings. For 25 years Europe has been divided by opposing national interests and contrary philosophies. . . . To relax tensions means a patient and persistent effort to deal with specific sources and not only with their manifestations [obvious appearances]. . . . We in the West are convinced by the history of the postwar period that a détente that does not apply equally to Eastern and Western Europe will be inherently [basically] unstable.*

Several months after his China trip, Nixon visited the Soviet Union. He was welcomed as warmly in Moscow as he had been in Beijing. In a series of cordial meetings with Premier Leonid Brezhnev, the two nations negotiated a weapons pact, agreed to work together to explore space, and eased long-standing trade limits.

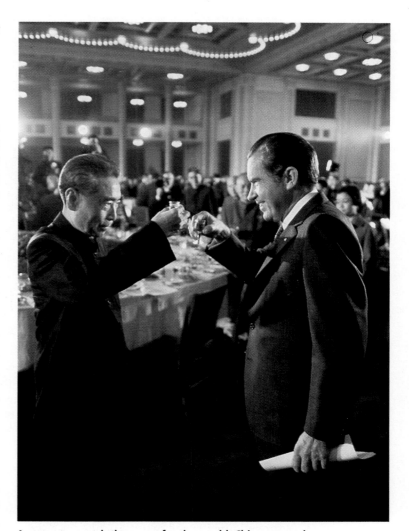

As reporters catch the event for the world, Chinese premier Zhou Enlai and President Richard Nixon congratulate each other on the new ties between their nations.

MAKING CONNECTIONS

What are the relations between the United States and Russia today? How have they changed since the 1970s?

The Superpowers Agree to Limit Weapons

Nixon saw arms control as part of the process in tying the various strands of his foreign policy program together. Like many Americans, he was worried about the wide-spread proliferation of nuclear weapons. The Limited Test Ban Treaty of 1963 had ended atmospheric testing of new bombs, but underground testing continued. Bigger and better bombs were being made all the time, and some people feared that the world might be destroyed unless these weapons were brought under control.

Nixon was determined to address the nuclear threat and to deal creatively with the Soviet Union at the same time. He had entered office intent on achieving superiority over the Soviet Union, but came to recognize that superiority made little sense in an era in which each nation had more than enough weapons to

The Cold War warmed slightly as Soviet premier Leonid Brezhnev and President Nixon met and SALT I was signed.

Kissinger kept tight control of the negotiating process. In 1971 Nixon noted:

> *Perhaps for the first time, the evolving strategic balance allows a Soviet-American agreement which yields no unilateral* [one-sided] *advantages. The fact [that] we have begun to discuss strategic arms with the USSR is in itself important. Agreement in such a vital area could create a new commitment to stability, and influence attitudes toward other issues.*

Thirty months of talks culminated in an important pact to limit offensive nuclear weapons, ready to be signed when Nixon went to Moscow.

The SALT I treaty included a five-year interim agreement that held the number of intercontinental ballistic missiles (ICBMs) and submarine-launched ballistic missiles at 1972 levels. The treaty also included an agreement restricting the development and deployment of defensive antiballistic missile systems.

SALT I was a diplomatic triumph and an important step forward. But it did little to limit the number of warheads the two nations possessed or to stop them from improving nuclear weapons systems in other ways. The practical Kissinger called for respecting the limits imposed while improving defenses. "The way for us to use this freeze is for us to catch up," he said soon after the summit. "If we don't do this we don't deserve to be in office." Still, SALT I showed that arms control agreements were possible, paving the way for more progress in the future.

destroy their enemies many times over. This ability is known as overkill. Balance between the superpowers was what the nuclear age demanded. The United States and the Soviet Union therefore began **Strategic Arms Limitation Talks,** known as SALT. Once again,

---

SECTION 3 REVIEW

Key Terms, People, and Places
1. Define (a) *realpolitik,* (b) détente, (c) Strategic Arms Limitation Talks (SALT).

Key Concepts
2. What were Henry Kissinger's official and actual roles in the Nixon administration?
3. What was Kissinger's relationship with the press?
4. How did Nixon alter American relations with the People's Republic of China? Why did he believe it was important to effect such changes?
5. What actions did President Nixon take toward the Soviet Union?

Critical Thinking
6. **Demonstrating Reasoned Judgment** Considering its weaknesses, how important was the SALT I treaty?

The Watergate Scandal

SECTION PREVIEW

Richard Nixon was willing to use presidential power to do whatever was necessary to remain in the White House. Eventually this approach compromised the presidency itself. The resulting Watergate scandal angered the nation and moved Nixon to take drastic steps.

Key Concepts
- The Nixon White House operated in an atmosphere of suspicion.
- Nixon and his supporters were willing to take extreme measures to win the 1972 election.
- When the Watergate break-in was traced to the White House, the President himself became involved in trying to cover it up.
- Nixon's involvement in Watergate made his impeachment likely, causing him to resign.

Key Terms, People, and Places
Watergate, Pentagon Papers, perjury; Plumbers, Daniel Ellsberg, John J. Sirica

L ooking toward the 1972 election, Nixon was determined to win an overwhelming mandate for a second term. Fiercely loyal aides were prepared to do anything for him, even if it meant breaking the law. When Nixon tried to hide their actions, he implicated himself in what became known as **Watergate,** a scandalous series of events that ended his presidency and threatened the foundations of American government.

Suspicion and Deceit at the White House

Reflecting Nixon's suspicious mind, the White House operated as if it was in a state of siege, surrounded by enemies. Nixon's staff responded to the President's attitude by trying to protect him at all costs from anything that might weaken his position.

One result of this mind-set was what became known as the "enemies list." Special counsel Charles W. Colson helped develop a list of prominent people unsympathetic to the administration. It included politicians such as Senator Edward Kennedy, members of the media such as reporter Daniel Schorr, and a number of outspoken performers including comedian Dick Gregory and actors Jane Fonda and Steve McQueen. Aides then considered how to harass these White House "enemies." One idea, for example, was to arrange income tax investigations of people on the list.

Despite his dedication to a domestic policy of law and order, Nixon was sometimes willing to take illegal actions more serious than the activities they were meant to control. For example, when he suspected that news stories were being leaked by the National Security Council, he ordered Kissinger to wiretap the phones of his own staff. When stories began to circulate about the secret bombing of Cambodia, Nixon had reporters' phones tapped, too.

At the same time, he sought tighter coordination of American intelligence activities. Both the FBI and the CIA were already illegally monitoring radical activists by tapping their phones and opening mail. In mid-1970 Nixon's staff proposed a plan for wiretaps and other investigations that was so far outside the law that even FBI director J. Edgar Hoover rejected the plan.

The White House then organized its own unit—nicknamed the **Plumbers**—to stop government security leaks. The group included E. Howard Hunt, a spy novelist and former CIA agent, and G. Gordon Liddy, once an FBI agent. In the spring of 1971, **Daniel Ellsberg,** a

MR. PRESIDENT: RELEASE the TAPES!

After persistent public demands for the release of the tapes containing information about Watergate, President Nixon finally complied—then resigned three days later. His resignation letter is shown above.

former Defense Department official, had given the *New York Times* the **"Pentagon Papers"**—a huge, secret Pentagon study of the Vietnam War. The *New York Times* began to publish the Pentagon Papers in June 1971. The documents showed that the executive branch often had deceived the Congress and American people about the real situation in Vietnam and had deliberately escalated the conflict. Intent on stopping further leaks, Nixon approved the plan to create the Plumbers. With approval from White House chief domestic adviser John Ehrlichman, the undercover unit broke into the office of Ellsberg's psychiatrist in an effort to discover damaging information about Ellsberg's private life.

MAKING CONNECTIONS

Other than its illegality, what problem can you see with a President assuming as much power as did Nixon?

Nixon's Campaign for Reelection

Determined to ensure Nixon's victory in 1972, the Committee to Reelect the President—known as CREEP—used other questionable tactics. Headed by John Mitchell, CREEP launched a fund-raising campaign to collect as much money as possible before a new law made it necessary to report such contributions. The money would fund both routine campaign activities and "dirty tricks" kept hidden from the public.

CREEP funded a variety of questionable actions. For example, people on its payroll leaked a fabricated letter to a conservative New Hampshire newspaper to discredit presidential contender Edmund Muskie, a Democratic senator from Maine. Charging Muskie with making insulting remarks about French Canadians living in the state, the letter was timed to arrive two weeks before the New Hampshire primary. The normally calm and composed Muskie responded by breaking down in tears in front of television cameras, which seriously damaged his reputation. Other "dirty tricks" carried out by CREEP included sending hecklers to disrupt Democratic campaign meetings and assigning

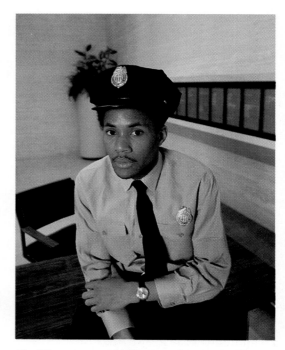

The Watergate scandal began when security guard Frank Willis (above) discovered a door left ajar by CREEP "burglars" trying to break in and install wiretaps in the Democratic party headquarters.

undercover "spies" to join the campaigns of major candidates.

"Dirty Tricks" at the Watergate Complex An intelligence branch within CREEP, which included "Plumbers" Liddy and Hunt, masterminded outlandish plans. One elaborate scheme called for the wiretapping of top Democrats to try to compromise them at their convention. Twice Mitchell refused to go along, not because the plan was illegal, but because it was too risky and expensive. Finally in 1972 he approved another idea: tapping the phones at Democratic National Committee headquarters in the Watergate apartment complex in Washington, D.C.

The first break-in to install illegal listening devices failed. A second attempt, on the night of June 16, 1972, ended with the arrest of the five men involved. One suspect was James McCord, a former CIA officer working for CREEP as a security officer. The Watergate "burglars" carried money that could be traced to CREEP and thus implicated Nixon's reelection campaign.

Top officials, including Nixon himself, had to decide what to do to conceal the incident. When the FBI traced the money carried by the Watergate burglars to CREEP, Nixon authorized the CIA to call off the FBI on the grounds that the matter involved "national security." Though he had not been involved in planning the break-in, the President was now part of the illegal cover-up.

As the Watergate case went on, the White House became more deeply involved. Nixon authorized the payment of hush money to keep Hunt and others quiet. Top officials, including Mitchell, committed **perjury**—lying under oath—in court to shield the President and others.

The 1972 Presidential Election Still, Watergate had barely reached the public's notice. In the 1972 presidential election, the Democrats ran George McGovern, a liberal senator from South Dakota, who lost to Nixon by a landslide. Nixon won a popular majority of 47 million to 29 million votes and swamped the Electoral College by a tally of 520 to 17. He had the mandate he wanted, though he did not get a Republican majority in either house of Congress.

The Watergate Story Continues

Despite Nixon's victory, the Watergate case refused to disappear. Nixon himself had proclaimed publicly that "no one in the White House staff, no one in this administration, presently employed, was involved in this very bizarre incident." At the trial in early 1973, the Watergate burglars either pleaded guilty or were found guilty. At sentencing time, however, Judge **John J. Sirica** was not convinced that he had gotten to the bottom of the matter. Criticizing the prosecution, he said:

> I have not been satisfied, and I am still not satisfied that all the pertinent facts that might be available—I say might be available—have been produced before an American jury. . . . I would hope that the Senate committee is granted the power by Congress . . . to try to get to the bottom of what happened in this case.

To prompt the burglars to talk, Sirica sentenced them to long prison terms.

Meanwhile, *Washington Post* reporters Bob Woodward and Carl Bernstein were following a trail of leads. Even before the election, they had learned about the secret funds at CREEP and had begun to write about the political intelligence effort and the sabotage campaign. As they began to realize who was involved, they called Mitchell and asked him to verify their story. He denied it angrily.

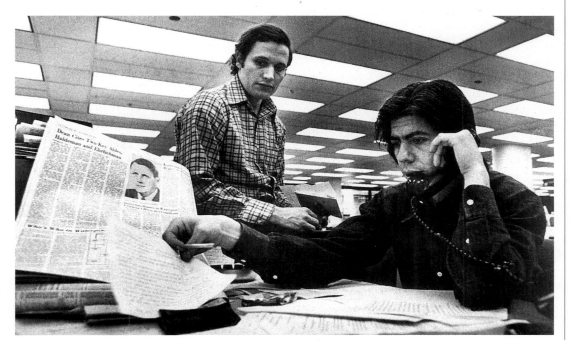

Investigative reporters Bob Woodward (left) and Carl Bernstein (right) persisted in tracking down information to uncover the Watergate story.

1972

June Five members of CREEP are arrested for breaking into Democratic National Committee headquarters in the Watergate Office Building. Two former Nixon aides are also arrested.

1973

January All seven men arrested plead or are found guilty.

April Nixon denies knowledge of the break-in.

May Nixon appoints special prosecutor Archibald Cox. The Senate establishes a Select Committee on Presidential Campaign Activities, which begins Watergate hearings.

June John Dean tells the Select Committee that Nixon authorized a cover-up.

July The Select Committee learns that Nixon had been secretly recording presidential conversations since 1971 and asks Nixon to release certain tapes. Nixon refuses.

Dean testifies before the Select Committee.

August Cox sues Nixon for the tapes. Judge John J. Sirica orders Nixon to release the tapes. Nixon appeals, but the appeals court supports Sirica.

October Nixon offers summaries of the tapes, which Cox rejects. Nixon has Cox fired, setting off a series of firings and resignations known as the "Saturday Night Massacre." The House of Representatives begins steps to impeach Nixon. Nixon finally releases the tapes, but investigators find two are missing.

The tapes become the center of the controversy.

November An eighteen-and-a-half minute gap is found on one of the tapes. The White House blames accidental erasure, but later investigation proves that the tape was deliberately erased.

1974

January Nixon claims "executive privilege."

April Attorney Leon Jaworski, the new special prosecutor, and the House Judiciary Committee subpoena Nixon to surrender tapes and related documents. Nixon supplies 1,254 pages of edited transcripts. Jaworski sues Nixon for the originals.

July The Supreme Court orders Nixon to give Jaworski the tapes and documents. The House Judiciary Committee recommends three articles of impeachment.

August Nixon releases additional transcripts, which show that he learned of the break-in as early as June 23, 1972 and ordered the cover-up. Nixon resigns August 9.

Nixon leaves Washington, D.C.

The Senate Investigates At the same time, a Senate Select Committee on Presidential Campaign Activities began to investigate the Watergate affair. James McCord, one of the convicted Watergate burglars, responded to his lengthy prison sentence by testifying before the committee, giving members a sense of what had gone on. The newspaper stories by Woodward and Bernstein helped the investigation, while leads from the Senate committee in turn aided the reporters.

As rumors grew that the White House was involved, Nixon tried to protect himself. In April 1973 he fired Haldeman and Ehrlichman, his two closest aides. On national television, he proclaimed that he would take final responsibility for the mistakes of others, for "there can be no whitewash at the White House."

Still the investigation ground on. In May 1973 the Senate committee, chaired by Senator Sam Ervin of North Carolina, began televised public hearings on Watergate. Millions of Americans watched, fascinated, as the story unfolded like a mystery thriller. John Dean, seeking to save himself, testified that Nixon knew about the cover-up. Other staffers described the various illegal activities undertaken in the White House.

The most dramatic moment came when one aide revealed the existence of a secret taping system in the President's office that recorded all meetings and telephone conversations—supposedly to provide a historical record of Nixon's presidency. Now those tapes could show whether or not Nixon had actually been involved in the cover-up.

The "Saturday Night Massacre" In an effort to prove his honesty, Nixon agreed to the appointment of a special Watergate prosecutor in the Justice Department. Archibald Cox, a Harvard law professor, took the post and immediately asked for the tapes. Nixon refused to release them. When Cox persisted, Nixon ordered him fired during the weekend of October 20, 1973, triggering a series of resignations and firings that became known as the "Saturday Night Massacre."

An Administration in Jeopardy By this time, Nixon was in serious trouble. His public approval rating plummeted. After Cox's firing, *Time* magazine declared "The President Should Resign."

Nixon appointed another special prosecutor, Leon Jaworski of Texas, who also asked for the tapes. Nixon then tried to show his innocence by releasing edited transcripts of some of his White House conversations. He carefully excised the most damaging evidence, but many people were angry and disillusioned when they read the actual words of some of the conversations in the Oval Office.

There was a subplot in the troubled White House. Vice President Spiro Agnew, accused of evading income taxes and taking bribes, resigned in disgrace early in October 1973, just ten days before the "Saturday Night Massacre." To succeed him, Nixon named Gerald R. Ford, the House minority leader. For nearly two months, until the Senate confirmed Ford, the nation had a President in trouble—and no Vice President.

Impeachment Ahead? Nixon had to do something. After the "Saturday Night Massacre," Congress had begun the process that could lead to impeachment—bringing charges and holding a trial to determine whether he should remain in office. In July 1974, the House Judiciary Committee, which included twenty-one Democrats and seventeen Republicans, began to hold hearings to determine if there were adequate grounds for impeachment.

This debate, like the earlier hearings, was televised nationally. The country watched anxiously as even Republicans deserted the President. Representative M. Caldwell Butler of Virginia spoke for many of them when he said:

> For years we Republicans have campaigned against corruption and misconduct. . . . But Watergate is our shame. Those things have happened in our house and it is our responsibility to do what we can to clear it up. . . . It is a sad chapter in American history, but I cannot condone what I have heard; I cannot excuse it; and I cannot and will not stand for it.

By sizable tallies, the House Judiciary Committee voted to impeach the President on

Viewpoints
On Nixon's Impeachment

In July 1974, the House Judiciary Committee conducted its televised debate on the possible impeachment of President Richard Nixon. *What attitudes about Nixon's impeachment are expressed in the two statements below?*

For Impeachment

"My faith in the Constitution is whole, it is complete, it is total. I am not going to sit here and be an idle spectator to the diminution [lessening], the subversion [overthrow], the destruction of the Constitution. . . . The Framers confided in the Congress the power if need be to remove . . . a President swollen with power and grown tyrannical."

Representative Barbara Jordan, Democrat (Texas)

Against Impeachment

"As the trust is placed in Congress to safeguard the liberties of the people through the awesome and extraordinary powers to remove a President, so must Congress's vigilance be fierce in seeing that the trust is not abused. . . . Not only do I not believe that any crimes by the President have been proved beyond a reasonable doubt, but I do not think the proof even approaches the lesser standards of proof which some of my colleagues, I believe, have injudiciously [with poor judgment] suggested we apply."

Representative Edward Hutchinson, Republican (Michigan)

Americans were fascinated but dismayed by the conversations taped in the Oval Office. This cartoonist saw Nixon as a man trapped by his own plots.

In the midst of the Watergate hearings, a worn Nixon finds the energy to shake hands with some sightseers at the White House.

charges of obstruction of justice, abuse of power, and refusal to obey a congressional order to turn over his tapes. To remove him from office, the full House of Representatives would have to vote for impeachment, and the Senate would have to hold a trial. The outcome seemed obvious in this case.

Nixon Resigns from Office On August 5, after a brief delay, Nixon finally obeyed a Supreme Court ruling and released the tapes. Despite a disturbing gap of eighteen and a half minutes where the conversation had been mysteriously erased, the tapes gave clear evidence of Nixon's involvement in the cover-up. Three days later, Nixon appeared on national television and painfully announced that he would resign the office of the President the next day. On August 9, Nixon resigned, the first President ever to do so. In a smooth constitutional transition, Vice President Gerald Ford was sworn in, telling the country "our long national nightmare is over."

Why Watergate?

Watergate raised many questions about the use and abuse of power. Richard Nixon was committed to winning in 1972 at any cost. He had gone further than his predecessors in creating an "imperial presidency," surrounding himself with subordinates who believed he could do no wrong. Though many of them were lawyers, they did not let the law stand in their way. They paid a high price, for most of them spent time in prison because of the Watergate cover-up. Nixon himself was never indicted and remained free by virtue of a presidential pardon granted by Gerald Ford.

SECTION 4 REVIEW

Key Terms, People, and Places
1. Define (a) Watergate, (b) Pentagon Papers, (c) perjury.
2. Identify (a) Plumbers, (b) Daniel Ellsberg, (c) John J. Sirica.

Key Concepts
3. Why did the White House undertake illegal wiretaps?
4. How was the Watergate break-in linked to the White House?

5. How did Richard Nixon become involved in the Watergate cover-up?
6. What was the ultimate reason for Nixon's resignation?

Critical Thinking
7. **Determining Relevance** In what way did the ending of the Watergate affair demonstrate the strength of the Constitution?

Analyzing Presidential Records

Presidential papers record a President's time in office. Letters, memorandums, notes on meetings, speeches, transcripts of press conferences—nearly every word the President utters seems to find its way into these papers. Thus, they provide a good source of information when trying to piece together historical evidence about the past.

In more recent times, technology has added new forms of "papers" as historical evidence—audio- and videotapes. President Nixon's audiotapes, recorded in the Oval Office, loomed large in the Watergate affair. In fact, it was a tape that finally ended the affair—a recording of a conversation that took place just a few days after the Watergate break-in on June 16, 1972. Not released until August 5, 1974, it proved that Nixon knew of the cover-up all along.

Use the following steps to analyze excerpts from this tape.

1. Identify the source by asking who, when, where, and what.
(a) Who are the speakers on the tape? (b) Who else is mentioned in it? (c) When did the conversation take place? (d) Where? (e) What is the major topic?

2. Identify the main points of information in the excerpts.
(a) Why is Haldeman concerned about the FBI? (b) What recommendation does he put forward about using the CIA to end the investigation? (c) How does President Nixon respond to the recommendation?

3. Study the tape to find clues to the historical period. (a) What can you infer about the extent of the powers that Nixon believed he had over FBI and CIA operations? (b) What can you infer about Nixon's sense of priorities at the time the recording was made? (c) What can you infer about the extent of Haldeman's influence?

CAST OF CHARACTERS
PRESIDENT NIXON
H. R. HALDEMAN, *Chief of Staff*
PAT GRAY, *Acting FBI Director*
JOHN MITCHELL, *Chairman of CREEP*
VERNON WALTERS, *Deputy CIA Director*

June 23, 1972

HALDEMAN Now, on to the investigation, you know the Democratic break-in thing. We're back in the problem area because the FBI is not under control, because Gray doesn't exactly know how to control it and . . . their investigation is now leading into some productive areas—because they've been able to trace the money. . . . Mitchell's recommendation [is] that the way to handle this now is for us to have Walters call Pat Gray and just say, "Stay . . . out of this—this is ah, business here we don't want you to go any further on it." That's not an unusual development, and ah, that would take care of it.

NIXON What about Pat Gray—you mean Pat Gray doesn't want to?

HALDEMAN Pat does want to. He doesn't know how to, and he doesn't have any basis for doing it. Given [Walters' call], he will then have the basis.

NIXON Yeah.

HALDEMAN [Gray will] say, "We've got this signal from across the river [the CIA] to put a hold on this." And that will fit rather well because the FBI agents who are working the case, at this point, feel that's what it is.

NIXON They've traced the money [the money that was found on the Watergate burglars]? Who'd they trace it to?

[Haldeman describes various people who contributed to CREEP and Nixon wonders if these people will say that the burglars, not CREEP, asked for the money.]

HALDEMAN Well, if they will. But then we're relying on more and more people all the time. That's the problem and they'll stop if we could take this other route.

NIXON All right.

HALDEMAN And you seem to think the thing to do is get [the FBI] to stop?

NIXON Right, fine.

Excerpted from *The New York Times,* Tuesday, August 6, 1974

Chapter Review

Understanding Key Terms, People, and Places

Key Terms
1. Poor People's Campaign
2. imperial presidency
3. Organization of Petroleum Exporting Countries (OPEC)
4. embargo
5. busing
6. *realpolitik*
7. détente
8. Strategic Arms Limitation Talks (SALT)
9. Watergate
10. Pentagon Papers
11. perjury

People
12. Robert F. Kennedy
13. Eugene McCarthy
14. Hubert Humphrey
15. George C. Wallace
16. Richard M. Nixon
17. Spiro Agnew
18. Henry A. Kissinger
19. H. R. Haldeman
20. John Ehrlichman
21. John Mitchell
22. Plumbers
23. Daniel Ellsberg
24. John J. Sirica

Terms For each term above, write a sentence that explains its relation to the events of 1968 or to the Nixon years.

True or False Determine whether each statement is true or false. If it is true, write "true." If it is false, change the underlined term to make the statement true.
1. In the spring of 1971, newspapers published the <u>Pentagon Papers,</u> a huge, secret government study of the Vietnam War.
2. Henry Kissinger was an admirer of <u>détente,</u> or politics based on achieving power.
3. In 1968 Martin Luther King, Jr., began the <u>Strategic Arms Limitation Talks.</u>
4. Because the United States supported Israel in the war in the Middle East, Saudi Arabia imposed a <u>perjury</u> on oil shipments.
5. Oil prices soared when members of <u>OPEC</u> quadrupled their prices.

Word Relationships Three of the people in each of the following sets are related in terms of their activities and accomplishments. Choose the person who does not belong and explain why he does not belong.
1. (a) Hubert Humphrey, (b) Henry A. Kissinger, (c) Richard M. Nixon, (d) George C. Wallace
2. (a) Eugene McCarthy, (b) John Ehrlichman, (c) John Mitchell, (d) H. R. Haldeman
3. (a) Plumbers, (b) Daniel Ellsberg, (c) Robert F. Kennedy, (d) John J. Sirica

Reviewing Main Ideas

Section 1 (pp. 746 – 749)
1. How did the assassinations of Martin Luther King, Jr., and Robert Kennedy affect Americans?
2. Why was the Democratic party in such a state of disunity and disarray at the 1968 convention?
3. How did Nixon's law and order stance help him win the presidency?

Section 2 (pp. 752 – 757)
4. Describe Nixon's relationship to the key members of his staff.
5. How did Nixon differ from his predecessors on issues of the economy and social programs?
6. Describe Nixon's civil rights policies and their effect on the civil rights movement.

Section 3 (pp. 758 – 762)
7. Explain why Henry Kissinger left a lasting mark on American foreign policy.
8. Describe how Nixon reversed United States policy toward China.
9. What was the result of Nixon's negotiations with the Soviet Union on arms control?

Section 4 (pp. 763 – 768)
10. What measures did the Committee to Reelect the President take to win the 1972 election?
11. Describe Nixon's involvement in the Watergate cover-up.
12. What were the impeachment charges brought against Nixon? Why was he not impeached?

1. **Testing Conclusions** Some commentators have observed that only a Republican veteran of the cold war like Richard Nixon would have been able to reestablish relations with China. Do you agree, or do you feel that a Democratic President might have been equally successful?

2. **Demonstrating Reasoned Judgment** Should Nixon have been pardoned? Explain your reasoning.

3. **Predicting Consequences** What kind of President do you think Americans were looking for after Watergate and the Nixon resignation?

4. **Distinguishing False from Accurate Images** Adlai Stevenson described "Nixonland" as a place where the President would do "anything to win." Do you agree or disagree with Stevenson's observation? Explain your answer.

1. **Evaluating Primary Sources** Review the primary source excerpt on page 752. What does this statement reveal about Nixon's motivations? What other possible responses might someone have to being an outsider? Can you think of anyone with whom you are familiar in your personal life or from your reading whose ambition stems from anger?

2. **Understanding the Visuals** On page 752, Nixon is described as a shy and remote man who put up a front when he campaigned for office. The picture on page 752 shows Nixon on the campaign trail. Based on this picture, what conclusions can you make about the public side of Nixon's personality?

3. **Writing About the Chapter** You have been asked to write a preface to a new biography of Richard Nixon, in which you evaluate his presidency. First,

make a list of the positive accomplishments of the Nixon administration. Then, make a list of the negative aspects of Nixon's presidency. Note which events you think have had the most lasting impact. Next, write a draft of your preface in which you summarize your conclusions. Revise your preface, making sure that each idea is clearly explained. Proofread your preface and draft a final copy.

4. **Using the Graphic Organizer** This graphic organizer uses a flow map to show the sequence of events in 1968. (a) What was the result of the 1968 Democratic convention? (b) List three factors that contributed to Nixon's victory in the 1968 election. (c) On a separate sheet of paper, create your own flow map about the Watergate scandal, using this graphic organizer as an example.

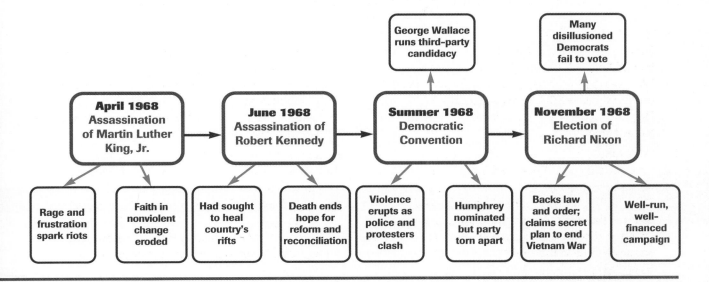

771

The Post-Watergate Period
1974–1980

*T*he upheaval from the Watergate scandal continued to disrupt American society even after Richard Nixon resigned. People wondered whether any President could heal the rifts that tore the country apart. Gerald Ford, the man who took Nixon's place, tried to revive the confidence that had sustained the United States through past troubles. But after two years in office, he lost the presidency to a little-known Democrat, Jimmy Carter, who promised the country honesty and morality.

Events in the United States

	1973	1974	1975	1976
	1973 Henry Kissinger wins the Nobel Peace Prize. • Congress enacts the War Powers Act.	**1974** Gerald Ford becomes President after Nixon resigns.		**1976** Americans celebrate their bicentennial. • Jimmy Carter is elected President.

Events in the World

	1973	1974	1975	1976
	1973 President Allende of Chile is killed in a military coup.	**1974** Giscard d'Estaing becomes president of France.	**1975** The Khmer Rouge takes power in Cambodia.	**1976** Chinese leader Mao Zedong dies.

The New York Times

LATE CITY EDITION

"All the News That's Fit to Print"

VOL.CXXIII...No.42,597 NEW YORK, MONDAY, SEPTEMBER 9, 1974 25 CENTS

FORD GIVES PARDON TO NIXON, WHO REGRETS 'MY MISTAKES'

1977 *President Carter establishes the Department of Energy.*
• *The Panama Canal treaties are signed.*

1978 *President Carter visits Nigeria and Liberia.*
• *Egyptian and Israeli leaders meet at Camp David.*

1979 *Americans are taken hostage in Iran.*
• *A nuclear accident occurs at Three Mile Island in Pennsylvania.*

1980 *Jimmy Carter loses the presidency to Ronald Reagan.*

1977 **1978** **1979** **1980** **1981**

1977 *South Africa declares the black homeland of Bophuthatswana independent.*

1978 *Civil war begins in Nicaragua.*

1979 *Egypt and Israel sign a peace treaty.*
• *Margaret Thatcher becomes British prime minister.*

1980 *War begins between Iran and Iraq.*

The Ford Administration

SECTION PREVIEW

Gerald Ford faced difficulties with the presidency he inherited. Although he wanted to help the nation recover from the Watergate affair, he never managed to step forward as a strong leader or deal effectively with problems that dogged the economy.

Key Concepts

- Gerald Ford had long experience in Congress, but some critics thought he was not qualified to be President.
- Neglected during Watergate, the economy was in trouble by the mid-1970s.
- Ford continued the foreign policies initiated under Nixon.

Key Terms, People, and Places

stagflation, Helsinki Accords; Gerald R. Ford, Nelson Rockefeller

This ornate soup tureen was a gift from Queen Elizabeth II of Great Britain to President Ford to commemorate the American bicentennial.

The new President, **Gerald R. Ford,** was a decent man who faced a difficult job. He had to help the United States emerge from its worst political scandal at a time when the economy was in trouble and the war in Vietnam was ending in defeat. Ford began on the wrong foot, with a well-meant pardon for Richard Nixon that outraged many. In the months that followed, he never managed to provide the leadership the country needed.

"A Ford, not a Lincoln"

Gerald Ford was one of the most popular politicians in Washington when he was appointed Vice President in October 1973, after Spiro Agnew resigned in disgrace for accepting bribes. In a long career in Congress, Ford had risen to become minority leader of the House of Representatives, where he was well-liked by members of both parties. He was an unassuming, midwestern Republican from Michigan, who believed in traditional American virtues such as hard work and self-reliance. His stands on the issues of the day reflected these beliefs. Over the years, he had opposed federal aid to education, the antipoverty program, and government funds for mass transit. He supported measures for law and order and defense spending.

Nixon chose Ford as a noncontroversial figure who might bolster his own support from Congress. When Ford was confirmed, Congress and the public were interested mainly in his honesty and stability, not his qualifications for the presidency. In fact, during his years in Washington, Ford had often been the target of jokes. One was attributed to President Lyndon Johnson, who could be cruel when fighting political opponents. Knowing that Ford had played football on the University of Michigan championship team in the 1930s, Johnson remarked that perhaps he had played too long without a helmet.

While the choice of Ford as Vice President was generally well received, it brought new criticism of the man from those concerned about his qualifications for taking over the presidency should the need arise. Journalist Richard Rovere wrote in *The New Yorker*:

That he is thoroughly equipped to serve as Vice President seems unarguable; the office requires only a warm body and occasionally a nimble tongue. However . . . neither Richard Nixon nor anyone else has come forward to explain Gerald Ford's qualifications to serve as Chief Executive. He altogether lacks administrative experience. If his knowledge of foreign affairs exceeds that of the average literate citizen, the fact has yet to be demonstrated.

Ford acknowledged his own limitations when he was sworn in, saying, "I am a Ford, not a Lincoln."

When Nixon resigned eight months later, Ford became the first nonelected President. Other Vice Presidents who had moved into the White House had at least been elected to the vice presidency as part of the national ticket. To fill the vice-presidential vacancy, Ford named former New York governor **Nelson Rockefeller**—creating the unique situation of having both a President and a Vice President who had been appointed, but not elected.

MAKING CONNECTIONS

The Twenty-fifth Amendment to the Constitution, which allows the President to appoint a replacement when the vice presidency is vacant, was passed in 1967, only a few years before Watergate. Is this the best way to fill such a high office? What other method would you suggest?

The New York Times

"All the News That's Fit to Print"

VOL. CXXIII..No. 42,597

NEW YORK, MONDAY, SEPTEMBER 9, 1974

LATE CITY EDITION

20 CENTS

FORD GIVES PARDON TO NIXON, WHO REGRETS 'MY MISTAKES'

The Nixon Pardon

Ford became President in the midst of what he called "our long national nightmare." The nation was embittered by Watergate and did not look forward to the prospect of an impeachment trial—which would be only the second in United States history. Many Americans wondered whether the Constitution would survive such seeming disrespect from the nation's leaders. When Ford assumed the presidency, the nation needed a leader who could take it beyond the ugliness of Watergate.

In response to this public mood, President Ford declared that it was a time for "communication, conciliation, compromise and cooperation." Americans were on his side. *Time* magazine noted "a mood of good feeling and even exhilaration in Washington that the city had not experienced for many years."

All too quickly, however, Ford lost that popular support. Barely a month after Nixon had resigned, Ford pardoned the former President for "all offenses" he might have committed, preventing further prosecution. On national television, Ford explained that he had looked to God and his own conscience in deciding "the right thing" to do about Nixon and "his loyal wife and family":

> Theirs is an American tragedy in which we have all played a part. It could go on and on and on, or someone must write the end to it. I have concluded that only I can do that, and if I can I must. . . . My conscience tells me that only I, as President, have the constitutional power to firmly shut and seal this book. My conscience tells me that it is my duty not merely to proclaim domestic tranquillity but to use every means that I have to ensure it.

Ford knew critics would surface, but he thought, "Most Americans will understand." He was wrong. While many of Nixon's loyalists

Betty Ford described her husband as "an accidental Vice President, and an accidental President, and in both jobs he replaced disgraced leaders." One of Ford's first presidential acts—pardoning Richard Nixon—stirred up a storm of controversy.

faced prison for their role in Watergate, the former President walked away without a penalty. Ford's generous gesture backfired, making people wonder what kind of bargain had been made when Nixon resigned. They questioned the new President's judgment and ability as he tried to move ahead. Ford found himself booed when he made public speeches, just as Johnson and Nixon had been. He, too, had to leave speaking engagements from back doors to avoid angry demonstrators.

Ford Tries to Move Ahead

Recovery from Watergate was not the only difficult issue Ford had to face. While focused on the scandal, the nation seemed to have stood still, but some conditions had grown worse. Now, at a time when the country needed direction, the new administration seemed unclear about what course to take.

Problems with inflation and unemployment prompted one cartoonist to send President Ford this comment on the issue.

The Economy Stagnates Preoccupation with Watergate had hurt Nixon's ability to deal with the economy, and it was still in sorry shape. Inflation hovered around 11 percent a year, significantly higher than it had been in the past, while unemployment climbed to 5.3 percent, as the graph on page 777 shows. Home building, usually a sign of a healthy economy, stalled as interest rates rose. The fears of worried investors brought a drop in stock prices.

In the past, economists had believed that a moderate rise in inflation could help control the rate of unemployment. Conversely, rising unemployment would counterbalance an increase in inflation. Federal policy makers had sought to strike a satisfactory balance between the two. Now, however, inflation and unemployment both rose, while the economy remained stalled and stagnant. Economists named this new situation **stagflation,** but giving it a name did not make it go away. Nixon's preoccupation with Watergate had compromised his effort to deal with economic difficulties. By the time Ford assumed the presidency, the situation had reached crisis levels. Not since Franklin Roosevelt took office during the Great Depression had a new President faced such harsh economic troubles.

Ford's approach—like Herbert Hoover's in the early 1930s—was to try to restore public confidence. The centerpiece of his economic program was the "Whip Inflation Now," or "WIN," campaign. The President asked Americans to wear red and white "WIN" buttons, to save a portion of their incomes, and to plant vegetable gardens to challenge rising prices in the stores. This effort to manage the economy by coordinating the everyday actions of millions of people was doomed from the start. The plan had no real incentives and soon faded away.

Eventually, Ford's administration recognized that the government must act, but its initial attempts backfired. A policy to curb inflation by controlling the money supply led to the worst recession since the 1930s, with widespread job layoffs. Unemployment soared to 9 percent in 1975. Congress then backed an antirecession spending program, and Ford, reversing his previous course, backed an increase in unemployment benefits and a multibillion dollar tax cut. The economy recovered slightly, but inflation and unemployment remained high and the deficit increased.

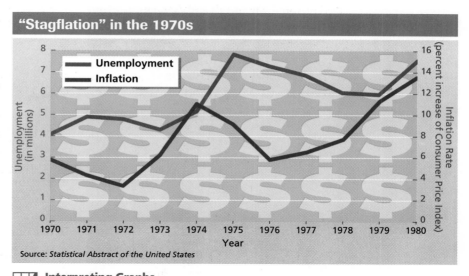

"Stagflation" in the 1970s

Source: *Statistical Abstract of the United States*

Interpreting Graphs
Upon assuming office, President Ford declared war on inflation, calling it "Public Enemy No. 1." Ford's administration, however, saw the worst economic slump in the United States since the Great Depression. *In what year did the highest consumer prices coincide with the second highest level of unemployment in the decade?*

Conflicts with Congress In spite of having served many years in the House of Representatives, President Ford was often locked in combat with the Democratic Congress. His basic dilemma was that he believed in limited government at a time when strong executive leadership was needed to get the nation on its feet. Jerold F. terHorst, his first press secretary, once noted how Ford's own sense of decency came into conflict with his view of presidential power:

> If he saw a schoolkid in front of the White House who needed clothing, he'd give him the shirt off his back, literally. Then he'd go right in the White House and veto a school-lunch bill.

Ford vetoed bills to create a consumer protection agency and to fund programs for education, housing, and health care. Congress responded by overriding a higher percentage of presidential vetoes than it had since the presidency of Franklin Pierce in the 1850s.

Foreign Policy Actions In foreign policy, Ford followed the basic outlines of Nixon's approach, keeping Henry Kissinger on as secretary of state. During the Ford years, the United States continued forging ties with China, freeing the country from its involvement in Vietnam, and refocusing its attention on Europe.

Congress asserted itself on foreign policy as it did on domestic policy. Irritated at the growth of the "imperial presidency," it had passed the War Powers Act in 1973 over Nixon's veto. This law let Congress either approve or disapprove the President's sending troops overseas and bringing forces home. Congress now used its power to stop new United States military action in Southeast Asia as the North Vietnamese strengthened control over all Vietnam in 1975. It also refused to become involved in political unrest in Turkey and Angola.

Despite Congress's effort to play a greater role in foreign affairs, the Ford administration did initiate some foreign policy actions. In mid-1975, soldiers from communist Cambodia captured the *Mayaguez*, an American merchant ship cruising in Cambodian waters. When protests went unanswered, Ford sent 250 marines to rescue the ship's crew. The rescue succeeded, but 41 Americans were killed—probably needlessly, as later investigations showed that the Cambodian government apparently was preparing to return both ship and crew. For Ford and Kissinger, however, the incident was a chance to counteract the impression that Vietnam had weakened the United States internationally.

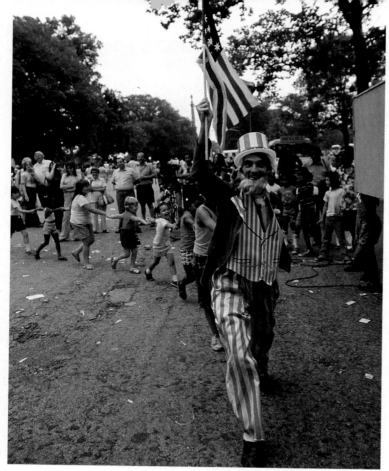

"Uncle Sam" leads a joyful parade in honor of the 200th anniversary of the Declaration of Independence. All across the country, bicentennial celebrations drew people together and stirred up feelings of national pride.

On other foreign policy fronts, Ford's record was stronger. Ford continued Strategic Arms Limitation Talks (SALT) and held out hope for further nuclear disarmament. He also signed the **Helsinki Accords**, a series of agreements made at a summit meeting in Finland. There, thirty-five nations, including the Soviet Union, pledged to cooperate economically and to promote human rights. As revolutions in Africa and elsewhere around the world toppled colonial governments, the administration took steps toward developing relationships with the new regimes.

Foreign policy in the Ford years was mainly a reaction to outside events. Still, the United States remained at peace, avoided major confrontations, and continued the difficult process of redefining its role abroad.

The Country Celebrates a Birthday

Amidst lingering recession and the memory of Watergate, Americans seized the chance to forget their problems at a nationwide birthday party. July 4, 1976, marked the bicentennial, or two hundredth anniversary, of the Declaration of Independence. Across the country, people in small towns and great cities celebrated with parades, concerts, air shows, political speeches, and fireworks.

The climax of the national party was the Fourth of July itself. In New York City, more than two hundred sailing ships, including majestic "tall ships," sailed into the harbor while millions watched from the shore. Other cities competed to have the most spectacular fireworks display or the longest parade. Many observers saw the bicentennial mood as an optimistic revival after years of gloom.

SECTION 1 REVIEW

Key Terms, People, and Places
1. Define (a) stagflation, (b) Helsinki Accords.
2. Identify (a) Gerald R. Ford, (b) Nelson Rockefeller.

Key Concepts
3. What were Ford's strengths and weaknesses as President?
4. What problems did the economy face during the Ford administration? How did President Ford attempt to address those problems?

5. What was the direction of Ford's foreign policy?
6. What was the relationship like between President Ford and Congress?

Critical Thinking
7. **Demonstrating Reasoned Judgment** Should Gerald Ford have pardoned Richard Nixon? Why or why not? Consider both the explanations that Ford gave and your own assessment of what the pardon did and did not accomplish.

The Carter Transition

SECTION PREVIEW

The Watergate scandal continued to influence the nation's political decisions as the people chose a Democrat, Jimmy Carter, for President in 1976. Carter tried to bring a new spirit of trust and honesty to Washington.

Key Concepts

- Gerald Ford did not appear "presidential" to many voters in the 1976 election.
- Jimmy Carter's campaign emphasized his trustworthiness and his status as a Washington outsider.
- Carter's small-town background and deep religious beliefs influenced his style and policies as President.

Key Terms, People, and Places

James Earl Carter, Jr.

I n a reaction against the Watergate scandal and economic woes, voters elected a Democrat, Jimmy Carter, as President in 1976. **James Earl Carter, Jr.,** a businessman and former naval officer who had been governor of Georgia, promised to bring a fresh approach to the White House. At first Carter enjoyed his status as a "Washington outsider," but in time that position lessened his ability to lead effectively.

The Election of 1976

Although Gerald Ford initially said that he would not seek election to the office he had inherited, by 1976 he had changed his mind. But as he campaigned to win the nation's approval, a number of personal liabilities continued to hurt his chances for success.

In the public's perception, Ford did not appear "presidential," and while people liked him, he never completely captured their confidence. He was a wooden speaker, and, as

described by the English journalist Alistair Cooke, "always seemed to be battling gamely with a language he had only recently acquired." At the Republican convention, Ford narrowly won the nomination against a strong challenge from Ronald Reagan, a former actor and governor of California, who represented the conservative wing of the party.

Ford faced Jimmy Carter, who, as governor of Georgia, had worked against racial discrimination in his state. Nationally, Carter began as a virtual unknown, with a broad smile and soft southern accent. In addition to his political activities, he also owned a successful peanut farm in Georgia. In a skillful primary campaign, he appealed to a wide audience and easily won the Democratic nomination. His running mate was Walter Mondale, a progressive senator from Minnesota.

Carter played on the backlash that followed Watergate. Over and over, he stressed that he was not part of the Washington establishment and so would bring a different perspective to the nation's capital. He distanced himself from many involved in the scandal by pointing out that he was not a lawyer but just "a peanut farmer."

Carter presented himself as honest and straightforward. In *Why Not the Best?*—an autobiography published in 1975—he said, "There is no need for lying. Our best national defense is the truth." In a later memoir, he recalled his campaign approach:

I ran as though I would have to govern—
always careful about what I promised,
and determined not to betray those who
gave me their support. Sometimes I irritated my opponents and the news reporters
by firmly refusing to respond to questions
to which I did not know the answers. And

Jimmy Carter's smile was famous. One writer described it as "the biggest grin of any President since TR."

repeatedly I told supporters, "If I ever lie to you, if I ever make a misleading statement, don't vote for me. I would not deserve to be your President."

Carter's appeal succeeded. The basic issue in 1976 was trust, and he used it superbly. Patrick Caddell, a public opinion pollster, noted:

W*ithout the trust thing, he couldn't have made it. . . . Most people would really rather trust other people than distrust them, except in politics; most people have a reason to distrust most candidates. Jimmy was a stranger in town. They had no reason to distrust him and he didn't give them one.*

Carter began the campaign with a lead, then nearly lost it as voters wondered whether he could really govern. Ford hurt his own cause with a number of embarrassing mistakes, such as declaring in a television debate that the Soviets did not dominate Eastern Europe. One observer commented that the campaign was like the Indianapolis 500, the nation's largest auto race, with people watching to see who would crash next.

In the end, Carter gained the support of most elements of the old Democratic coalition. He was successful with blue collar, African American, and some Catholic voters. He also won most of the South. Though Democrats in races for Congress and local contests generally swept the election, Carter's own margin was narrow: he won 50 percent of the popular vote to Ford's 48 percent. The electoral vote, 297 to 240, was also close. The map below left shows these election results.

MAKING CONNECTIONS

Like Jimmy Carter, candidates for Congress and the presidency often point out that they are "Washington outsiders," not part of the establishment. Why do you think this argument appeals to some voters?

The President from Plains, Georgia

Jimmy Carter—a southerner with a short career in politics—*was* different from his recent predecessors in the White House. His family had lived for generations in the rural South; the population of his hometown of Plains was six hundred. After graduating in 1946 from the United States Naval Academy, where he was trained as an engineer, he served on nuclear submarines. Later he took over management of his family's prosperous peanut farm and warehouse. He did not enter Georgia state politics until 1962.

Carter's deeply felt religious faith dominated his view of the world and led to considerable curiosity and questioning from reporters. He was a born-again Baptist, who noted that his life had been "shaped in the church." He relied on the Bible and read it daily—often in Spanish to improve his skill with the language. His faith, he believed, would keep him from taking on "the same frame of mind that Nixon or Johnson did—lying, cheating and distorting the truth."

On the other hand, Carter believed strongly in personal freedom. In Georgia, for instance, he had rejected calls for prayer in the public

Presidential Election of 1976

Candidate/Party	Electoral Vote	Popular Vote	% Popular Vote
Jimmy Carter (Dem.)	297	40,827,394	49.9
Gerald R. Ford (Rep.)	240	39,145,977	47.9

Geography and History: Interpreting Maps
This map shows that Ford captured the vote of most of the Midwest. *What do you know about Ford's background that might help to explain this?*

schools. Despite his strong religious beliefs, he would not use the presidency as a "pulpit" to promote them.

Personal Abilities Carter was thoughtful, able, and precise. Alistair Cooke called him the "most intelligent" and "best-informed" President the nation had known in years. Yet, Cooke said, Carter

unfortunately used his intelligence to identify, and articulate, 12 sides to every question. . . . He wound up bearing a distressing resemblance to a stalled centipede. All the feelers were wiggling, but the body itself was immobile.

Approach to the Presidency In the first months of Carter's presidency, he appeared to be a reform Democrat. When he accepted his party's nomination, he demanded "an end to discrimination because of race or sex," challenged the established "political and economic elite," and suggested new welfare and health-care programs.

He began by appointing significantly more women and minorities to his staff than previous administrations had done. Of 1,195 full-time appointees, 12 percent were women, 12 percent were African American, and another 4 percent were Hispanic. In nominating federal judges, he chose four times as many women as had all previous Presidents combined.

In other areas, however, Carter began to look more conservative. As a result, his support from his own party gradually began to dwindle. He had won in 1976 by a narrower margin than other Democratic candidates, who consequently felt that they owed him less than if he had won a sweeping victory that carried them into office as well. The press, too, became more critical as the Carter presidency seemed to lose its momentum.

Staff Problems The "outsider" role became a disadvantage in the White House, too. Carter surrounded himself with southern, mostly Georgian, advisers, who had little sense of how crucial it was for the President to work with Congress. Carter himself was uneasy with congressional expectations and demands, and found it difficult to bargain effectively to pass legislation. Without any congressional experience, he lacked the kind of ability that Lyndon Johnson had to wheel and deal and win over reluctant politicians.

Carter also suffered from hints of scandal in an administration that took pride in being pure. Banker Bert Lance, the director of the Office of Management and Budget, was an old friend from Georgia on whom the President relied. When Lance was accused of allowing large bank overdrafts and other irregularities in

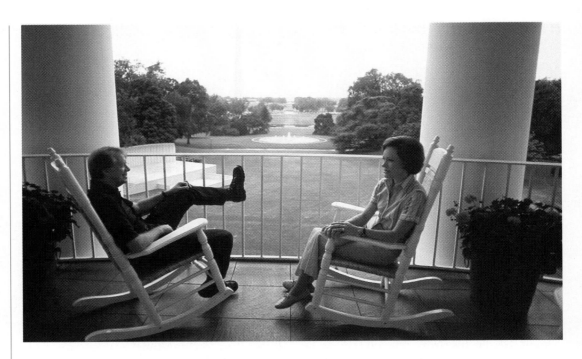

The Carters brought a folksy style to the presidency, a style some people criticized as undignified. In spite of the President's low-key image, he was known among friends as a "super-achiever." One friend called Carter "the most disciplined person I've ever seen."

his bank in the past, Carter came strongly to his defense but finally had to conclude that Lance must resign.

Carter's brother Billy posed other problems. He was a flamboyant, irreverent character who relished the attention he received as part of the presidential family. His careless, sometimes anti-Semitic, comments were embarrassing, and his acceptance of $200,000 in "loans" from friends in Libya made it look as if family business was entwined with foreign affairs.

A Question of Style Finally, Carter's image suffered from his attempt to discard the aloof, ceremonial style of the presidency for one of greater simplicity. At first, people responded warmly to his informal, "down home" approach. They loved it when he and his wife, Rosalynn, dismissed the limousine and strolled down Pennsylvania Avenue after the inauguration. Carter wore jeans in the White House and spoke to the nation on television wearing a cardigan sweater instead of a business suit. Critics, however, soon complained about the lack of dignity and ceremony.

Carter finally discarded his low-key approach. After a few months, he let the band play "Hail to the Chief" on "special occasions," noting, "I found it to be impressive and enjoyed it." The honesty that prompted the President to make this comment also influenced his decisions in foreign policy, as the next section shows.

SECTION 2 REVIEW

Key Terms, People, and Places
1. Identify James Earl Carter, Jr.

Key Concepts
2. What problems during Ford's first term plagued him in the 1976 election?
3. How did Carter's "outsider" image hurt his effectiveness in office?

4. What was Carter's presidential style? How did the American people react to this style?

Critical Thinking
5. **Determining Relevance** How might Carter's outspokenness about his religious beliefs have affected the 1976 election?

Carter's Foreign Policy

SECTION PREVIEW

Carter's religious beliefs led him to emphasize peacemaking and human rights in foreign affairs, resulting in some outstanding successes. Those same beliefs also played a part in preventing his reelection.

Key Concepts
- Carter's peacemaking efforts helped bring some stability to the Middle East.
- Carter's beliefs also guided his actions in Latin America and Africa.
- Relations with the Soviet Union worsened because of Carter's stand on certain issues.
- A hostage crisis in Iran gravely damaged the Carter presidency.

Key Terms, People, and Places
shuttle diplomacy, Camp David Accords, dissident; Anwar el-Sadat, Menachem Begin, Cyrus Vance, Shah Mohammad Reza Pahlavi, Ayatollah Ruholla Khomeini

P resident Carter achieved his greatest successes in foreign policy. Although he had little diplomatic experience when he took office, he brought the standards that governed his personal life into foreign affairs. While that approach brought notable achievements, it also complicated the relationship of the United States with some nations and ultimately hurt his chance for reelection.

Human Rights Diplomacy

Carter was unwilling to compromise his powerful sense of morality. This trait guided his approach to foreign policy. In his inaugural speech, he declared, "Our commitment to human rights must be absolute. . . . We can never be indifferent to the fate of freedom elsewhere." Support for human rights became the cornerstone of his foreign policy.

Carter later wrote, "Our country has been strongest and most effective when morality and a commitment to freedom and democracy have been most clearly emphasized in our foreign policy." But since the Truman era, he went on, the country had not kept to that standard:

> I nstead of promoting freedom and democratic principles, our government seemed to believe that in any struggle with evil, we could not compete effectively unless we played by the same rules or lack of rules as the evildoers. . . . When I announced my candidacy in December 1974, I expressed a dream: "That this country set a standard within the community of nations of courage, compassion, integrity, and dedication to basic human rights and freedoms."

MAKING CONNECTIONS

Jimmy Carter set certain standards for foreign policy. Do you think foreign policy today is based on some or all of those principles? Should it be? Why or why not?

A Step Toward Middle East Peace

Carter's commitment to finding ethical solutions to prickly problems was most visible in the Middle East question, and there he had the greatest success. In that unstable region, conflicts between Israel and the Arab nations had existed for nearly thirty years, most recently in 1967 and 1973. After the last Arab-Israeli war, Henry Kissinger had undertaken **shuttle diplomacy**, moving back and forth between nations in an attempt to arrange peace in the region, but conflicts continued.

At first, Carter hoped to call an international conference on the Middle East. Then leader

Yellow ribbons became the symbol of hope for the safe return of the Americans held hostage in Iran. The ribbons seemed to decorate every available space when the hostages finally were freed.

Anwar el-Sadat of Egypt made a historic visit to Israel, beginning negotiations with Prime Minister **Menachem Begin.** The two men had such different personalities, however, that they had trouble compromising. Carter intervened, sending Secretary of State **Cyrus Vance** to invite them to Camp David, the rustic presidential retreat in the Maryland hills. In such a setting, he hoped that he could smooth their differences and move the peace process forward.

Carter knew it was a bold step. In his diary entry for July 31, 1978, he wrote, "We understand the political pitfalls involved, but the situation is getting into an extreme state." He and the two Middle Eastern leaders maintained tight secrecy about the coming conference.

At Camp David in September 1978, Carter assumed the role of peacemaker and practiced highly effective personal diplomacy to bridge the gap between Sadat and Begin. They finally agreed on a framework for peace that became known as the **Camp David Accords.** Under the resulting peace treaty, Israel would withdraw from the Sinai peninsula, which it had occupied in 1967. Egypt, in return, became the first Arab country to recognize Israel's existence as a nation.

The Camp David Accords, of course, did not solve all the problems of the Middle East. Foremost was the question of what to do about the Palestinians, many of whom had fled their homes when Arab nations declared war on Israel immediately after that country was established in 1948. Still, as Secretary of State Vance noted:

T *he Camp David Accords rank as one of the most important achievements of the Carter administration. First, they opened the way to peace between Egypt and Israel, which transformed the entire political, military, and strategic character of the Middle East dispute. Genuine peace between Egypt and Israel meant there would be no major Arab-Israeli war, whatever the positions of [other Arab groups].*

Moreover, Vance pointed out, the agreement also let negotiators focus on the Palestinian question and established a process for future talks.

Foreign Policy Takes New Directions

Carter's foreign policy team took new steps in other parts of the world as well. Often these reflected the President's own philosophy.

The Panama Canal Another diplomatic milestone was Carter's successful fight to have the Senate ratify treaties returning the Panama Canal to Panama by the year 2000. Once again, his morality guided his approach to foreign policy.

In the early 1900s, President Theodore Roosevelt was proud of the way he had gained control of Panamanian land for the canal. Now Panama and other Latin American countries were increasingly unhappy with the continuing United States presence. It was time to give up some control over that region.

Returning the canal caused bitter debate in Congress, but the Senate finally accepted the pacts by a close margin of one vote. While agreeing to return the canal, the United States reserved the right to intervene militarily, if necessary, to keep it open. The pacts gave the United States security while improving relations with Latin America.

Recognition of China Building on Nixon's initiative in Asia, Carter took the next step and established diplomatic relations with the People's Republic of China as of January 1979. The Chinese wanted American technology and expertise in modernizing their country, while the United States hoped that closer ties with China would keep the Soviet Union on guard. Businesses in the United States also were eager to open the Chinese market of nearly a billion people.

A jubilant President Carter congratulates Egypt's President Sadat (left) and Israeli prime minister Begin (right) on the signing of the Camp David Accords, a historic step toward peace in the Middle East.

New African Nations Great changes were taking place in Africa, as countries that had been dominated by colonial powers revolted and became independent nations. Under Carter, relations with many nations in Africa improved, guided by Andrew Young, United States ambassador to the United Nations.

Young, a minister and civil rights leader who had served in Congress, shared many of Carter's views. He convinced the President that the United States should not interfere with African leaders as they shaped new governments. When Carter visited Nigeria and Liberia in March 1978, the popularity of this approach was shown as thousands cheered him in the streets.

Soviet-American Relations

Several issues complicated the relationship between the United States and the Soviet Union. Détente—a relaxation of the tensions between the superpowers—was at a high point when Carter took office. In his first year, he declared optimistically that the United States would forge even closer ties with the Soviet Union.

Then Carter's commitment to human rights alienated Soviet leaders, undermining efforts to work together. The Soviets were annoyed when the President verbally supported **dissidents,** Soviet writers and other activists who opposed the actions of their government.

SALT II In particular, this situation slowed efforts to reach further agreement on arms control. Negotiations were already underway for a second Strategic Arms Limitation Treaty (SALT II). Misjudging the Soviets, Carter offered new weapons reduction proposals that went further than earlier agreements. The Soviets, already suspicious of Carter because the United States had recognized China and was vocally supporting human rights, balked at the proposals.

Finally, Carter and Soviet president Leonid Brezhnev signed the new treaty in Vienna in June 1979. More complicated than SALT I, it limited the number of nuclear warheads and missiles each power retained. SALT II still had to be ratified by the Senate, however.

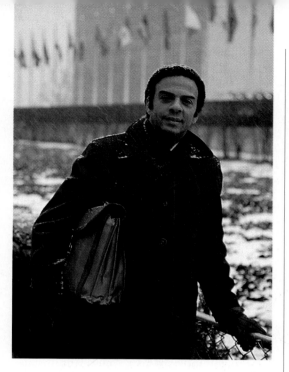

Andrew Young (left) believed strongly in black majority rule in Africa. In 1981 he would be elected mayor of Atlanta, Georgia.

Afghanistan SALT II seemed to have little chance of passage when the Soviet Union invaded Afghanistan, a country on its southern border. To end agitation against the Soviet-supported government there, Soviet troops invaded in December 1979.

Carter reacted by calling Brezhnev on the "hot line," the open telephone line between Washington and Moscow, and telling him that the invasion was "a clear threat to the peace." He also added, "Unless you draw back from your present course of action, this will inevitably jeopardize the course of United States–Soviet relations throughout the world."

Carter took other steps to emphasize United States disapproval of Soviet aggression. Realizing that SALT II surely would be turned down, he postponed sending it to the Senate. He also imposed a boycott on the summer Olympic Games scheduled to be held in Moscow in 1980. Eventually, some sixty other nations joined the boycott. Détente was effectively dead.

Iran Holds Americans Hostage

The worst foreign policy crisis that Carter faced occurred in Iran, on the Persian Gulf. For years the United States had supported the rule of **Shah Mohammad Reza Pahlavi,** who had taken many steps to modernize Iran.

Americans overlooked the corruption and harsh repression of the shah's government because he was a reliable supplier of oil and a pro-Western force. Carter himself praised the shah in a visit to Tehran, Iran's capital, in late 1977.

In January 1979, revolution broke out in Iran, led by Muslim fundamentalists who wanted to bring back old ways, and liberal critics who wanted political and economic reform. The shah fled the country and was replaced by an elderly Islamic leader, the **Ayatollah Ruholla Khomeini,** who had been in exile. Khomeini and his followers were aggressively anti-Western, determined to make Iran a strict Islamic state.

In October, in what was intended as a humanitarian gesture, Carter let the exiled shah enter the United States for medical treatment. Many Iranians were outraged. On November 4, angry students seized the American embassy in Tehran and took sixty-six Americans hostage. Though a few were soon released, more than fifty were held for over a year, creating bitter animosity between the United States and Iran.

AMERICAN PROFILES
Kathryn Koob

One of the American hostages was Kathryn Koob, a diplomat. The eldest of six daughters

President Carter and Soviet president Leonid Brezhnev sign SALT II in Vienna, Austria. Carter believed that the arms limitation agreement would "make the world a safer place for both sides."

who grew up on an Iowa farm, she loved to travel. After graduating from Wartburg College in Iowa and earning a master's degree at the University of Denver, she joined the Foreign Service. She became a diplomat, working to promote American aims abroad.

Kate Koob arrived in Iran in July 1979, when the revolution was in full swing. She was director of the Iran-American Society, which promoted cultural exchange. On November 4, her staff heard that students had occupied the American embassy. The next day, she herself was taken hostage.

It was a brutal experience. During the day, zealous young women revolutionaries were her guards, while the "brothers" came at night with threats and questions. "The next day passed, and the next, and the next," she later wrote, "with more interrogations, more comings and goings. And always, the ever-present chanting of the mob outside the gates."

Sometimes imprisoned alone, sometimes with other women, she never knew whether any of them would survive:

The biggest fear was not knowing what the future held and not knowing what was happening to my colleagues. And then there was the undercurrent: threats of trials and executions.

Usually she could maintain her resolve:

A they're-not-going-to-get-us attitude began to set in. . . . Each day we survived was to our benefit. I decided the challenge each morning was to get through the day.

Sometimes, though, fear broke through, intensified by thoughts of her worried family and by constant stress:

And the sounds outside the embassy were nerve-wracking. . . . There seemed to be a continuous crowd of people shouting anti-American slogans, listening to the exhortations [cries] of the students and mullahs [clergymen] who were always on hand. In addition to the crowd noises, there were three or four loud-speakers blaring newscasts. . . . As I sat confined in my chair I thought, I can't take this, I just can't take this.

The Hostage Crisis Ends

The ordeal of Kate Koob and the other hostages continued for 444 days. They were blindfolded and moved from place to place. Some were tied up and beaten. Others spent time in solitary confinement and faced mock executions intended to keep them constantly afraid. Meanwhile, the American public became increasingly frustrated and impatient for the hostages' release. Nightly newscasts made the crisis a national issue.

People expected the President to secure the hostages' freedom. When his efforts failed, his hopes for reelection were doomed. Carter broke diplomatic relations with Iran and froze all Iranian assets in the United States. Khomeini held out, insisting that the shah be sent back. Under pressure, Carter finally authorized a daring commando rescue mission, but it ended in disaster when several helicopters broke down in the desert sands and eight American soldiers were killed. The government was humiliated, and Carter's popularity dropped even further.

Carter was torn apart by the crisis. At one point, just weeks after the Americans had been taken prisoner, he confided his feelings to Hamilton Jordan, one of his closest aides:

*Y*ou know, I've been worried all week about the hostages as a problem for the country and as a political problem for me. But it wasn't until I saw the grief and hope on the faces of their wives and mothers and fathers that I felt the personal responsibility for their lives. It's an awesome burden.

After months of secret talks, in early 1981 the Iranians agreed to release the 52 hostages. Not until the day Carter left office, however, were they allowed to come home. Buses carried them, blindfolded, to the airport where—almost in disbelief—they saw the airplanes that would take them out of Iran. Because Carter was not reelected, however, it was his successor, Ronald Reagan, who greeted them as they arrived on American soil.

In spite of the sentiments of anti-American Iranians (left), personnel from the United States embassy in Tehran, Iran, reach freedom after being held as hostages for more than a year (above). Among them is Kathryn Koob (second from bottom).

SECTION 3 REVIEW

Key Terms, People, and Places

1. Define (a) shuttle diplomacy, (b) Camp David Accords, (c) dissident.

2. Identify (a) Anwar el-Sadat, (b) Menachem Begin, (c) Cyrus Vance, (d) Shah Mohammad Reza Pahlavi, (e) Ayatollah Ruholla Khomeini.

Key Concepts

3. What was the significance of the Egypt-Israel agreements made at Camp David?

4. How did Carter's personal beliefs affect his actions in Latin America and Africa?

5. What factors led to the worsening of relations with the Soviet Union?

6. How did Carter respond to the Iran hostage crisis?

Critical Thinking

7. Making Comparisons How did Carter's commitment to acting on moral principles compare with Nixon and Kissinger's emphasis on *realpolitik*?

Recognizing Ideologies

An ideology might be defined as the beliefs that underlie the actions or statements of a person, a group, or a culture. An important critical thinking skill is being able to identify such beliefs. If you can recognize ideologies, you can better understand why certain actions are taken or statements are made.

Use the following steps to help you recognize the ideologies that underlie two opposing statements made during the debate over the Panama Canal treaties.

1. Identify the main topic of the statements and the people who made them. (a) What is the subject under debate in these statements? (b) Who made each statement? (c) In which branch of government does each speaker serve? (d) To what party does each belong?

2. Locate the major points that each speaker makes. (a) What reasons does Speaker A give for rejecting the proposed change? (b) What reasons does Speaker B give for accepting it?

3. Identify the beliefs that underlie the reasons given. (a) What does Speaker A believe about the rights of property with regard to the Panama Canal? (b) What attribute of the national character does he believe should guide United States foreign policy on this issue? (c) What does Speaker B believe about the role of fairness with regard to the canal? (d) What attributes of national character does he think should guide United States foreign policy?

Passage A

The case for rejecting the proposed treat[ies] . . . begins with one crucial point: The Panama Canal is United States property, and the Canal Zone is United States territory. According to the terms of the 1903 treaty with Panama, we acquired sovereign rights over the Canal Zone "in perpetuity" [forever]. The Supreme Court upheld our exercise of sovereignty in 1907. . . . Moreover, the maps of the world show the Canal Zone as part of the United States.

Thus, it is clear that the burden of proof rests on those who favor the treaties; those who oppose them are merely standing up for American rights. Proponents must show that it is in the national interest to dispose of American property which, in addition to its strategic and economic value, represents a cumulative investment of roughly $7 billion.

. . . Would we give up Alaska to the Russians if they were suddenly to demand it? Such weakness is entirely contrary to our national character and heritage.

—Strom Thurmond, Republican (South Carolina), "Why the U.S. Should Keep the Panama Canal," *The Christian Science Monitor*, September 13, 1977

Passage B

The most important reason, the only reason, to ratify the treaties is that they are in the highest national interest of the United States and will strengthen our position in the world. Our security interest will be stronger; our trade opportunities will be improved. We will demonstrate that as a large and powerful country we are able to deal fairly and honorably with a proud but smaller sovereign nation.

. . . We Americans want a more humane and stable world. We believe in goodwill and fairness as well as strength. This agreement with Panama is something we want because we know it is right.

. . . If Theodore Roosevelt were to endorse the treaties, as I'm quite sure he would, it would be mainly because he could see the decision as one by which we are demonstrating the kind of great power we wish to be. . . . In this historic decision, he would join us in our pride for being a great and generous people with a national strength and wisdom to do what is right for us and what is fair to others.

—President Jimmy Carter, televised speech, February 1, 1978

Carter's Domestic Problems

SECTION PREVIEW

In addition to crises overseas, domestic issues brought more trouble for the Carter presidency. The administration could not effectively create and pass legislation, dooming Carter's energy program and efforts to stabilize the economy.

Key Concepts

- The Carter administration had trouble getting its domestic programs through Congress.
- Economic policy under Carter was inconsistent and ineffective.
- Congress blocked Carter's ambitious energy conservation goals.
- Carter gave stronger support to civil rights than Nixon or Ford had done.

Key Terms, People, and Places

Nuclear Regulatory Commission, deregulation, amnesty; Allan Bakke; Three Mile Island

While Jimmy Carter had several triumphs in foreign affairs, he had little success in programs at home. He could not find a way to work effectively with Congress and its leaders, which stalled his plans in many areas, especially energy and the economy. Looking back, he wrote, "I quickly learned that it is a lot easier to hold a meeting, reach a tentative agreement, or make a speech than to get a controversial program through Congress."

That was not the only problem. As *New York Times* columnist Tom Wicker observed, Carter "never established a politically coherent administration." His strategies were not clearly defined. Public support, which had been with him at first, faded as his programs floundered.

The Economy Wobbles

Carter inherited an unstable economy and had trouble finding a way to balance inflation and growth. Inflation also had been a problem for Ford, but had seemed under control after the recession that lasted from 1974 to 1976. To prevent another recession, Carter tried to stimulate growth with government deficit spending. As deficits grew, the Federal Reserve Board increased the money supply, but inflation then rose to about 10 percent.

To stop inflation, Carter tried to slow the economy and reduce the deficit by cutting spending. Cuts fell mostly on social programs, angering reform-minded Democrats. At the same time, the slowdown in the economy increased unemployment and the number of business failures.

Things got worse in 1980, when the new federal budget showed continued high spending. In reaction, bond prices fell and interest rates soared. Borrowers were angry at having to pay high interest rates—sometimes over 20 percent, which is about 3 times higher than they are today—for mortgages and other loans.

People lost confidence in Carter and his economic advisers. The administration's vacillating efforts—trying first one approach, then another—gave the impression that it had no idea what was happening or how to fix it. When Carter left the White House, economist Robert J. Samuelson commented:

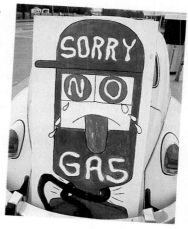

> What was most consistent about the Carter administration was its inability to make a proposal in January that could survive until June. . . . The Carter administration never projected a clear economic program or philosophy because it never had one.

When a revolution in Iran caused oil shortages at home, American drivers faced long lines at the gas pumps—when gas was available at all.

A Carter Crusade: Saving Energy

Carter made energy conservation a major goal, but he had trouble winning support from Congress and the public. Despite earlier embargoes and shortages, Americans still depended heavily on imported oil. In the late 1970s, more than 40 percent of the oil used in the United States was imported. Some thought the country should be energy self-sufficient instead of depending on supplies from other countries.

OPEC, the Organization of Petroleum Exporting Countries, had been raising oil prices steadily since 1973. People grumbled about rising prices, shortages, and long lines at the gas station. Although Carter was not responsible for oil prices or shortages, he often was the focus of people's complaints.

In April 1977, Carter presented his comprehensive energy program to Congress and the people. He asked people to save fuel by driving less and keeping homes and offices cooler. He also created a new cabinet department, the Department of Energy, to bring together a variety of federal programs promoting conservation and looking for new energy sources. But when he called the need for conservation the "moral equivalent of war," critics seized on the acronym MEOW (from the first letter of each word) to make fun of it.

The energy proposals bogged down in Congress for months, opposed fiercely by representatives from states that produced oil and gas. Eventually, however, the National Energy Act taxed "gas-guzzling" cars, required utilities to use coal rather than oil, removed price controls on domestic oil and natural gas, and allowed tax credits and research funds for alternative energy sources such as solar energy and synthetic fuels.

Three Mile Island Nuclear power seemed one exciting alternative energy source, but serious questions persisted about its costs and safety. Since the 1960s, grassroots activists and some scientists had been criticizing the nuclear power industry. In March 1979, people's doubts and fears seemed to be confirmed by an accident at the nuclear power plant at **Three Mile Island,** near Harrisburg, Pennsylvania.

A small leak through a faulty seal in the cooling system stopped the pumps that circulated the coolant. Temperatures in the reactor core rose, but plant operators misread the symptoms and shut down an emergency cooling system. A partial meltdown of the core occurred, releasing some radiation.

| 1650 | 1700 | 1750 | 1800 | Links Across Time | 1850 | 1900 | 1950 | 2000 |

Carter's Commitment to Public Service

Jimmy Carter had entered public service years before he became President in 1976 (near right). After he lost the presidency to Ronald Reagan in 1980, Carter remained committed to public service. Among other activities, Carter is a leading member of Habitat for Humanity (far right), which volunteers its members' time and energy to build houses for the homeless. *Can you think of any Presidents since Carter who have continued their involvement in public life?*

Nuclear energy generates enormous amounts of heat, which then is used to make steam. The steam then produces electricity. To make heat, the reactor splits the nuclei of uranium or plutonium in half. Despite the strides made in understanding such reactions, scientists have not yet been able to make use of the full potential of nuclear energy, which could supply the world's electricity for millions of years.

People near the plant were terrified by the idea of a radioactive leak, and 140,000 people fled their homes. Panic increased when the film *The China Syndrome*—in which the plot centers on a fictional reactor meltdown—opened in town. As reporters flocked to Three Mile Island, the story made headlines around the world.

The Future of Nuclear Power Carter named a commission to investigate the accident at Three Mile Island. Its report identified operator errors that had made the initial problem worse. In his response to the report, Carter noted "very serious shortcomings in the way that both the Government and the utility industry regulate and manage nuclear power." He proposed reorganizing the **Nuclear Regulatory Commission,** the

agency in charge of nuclear power, and called on utility companies to improve standards:

> The steps that I am taking today will help to assure that nuclear power plants are operated safely. Safety, as it always has been and will remain, is my top priority. . . . I challenge our utility companies to bend every effort to improve the safety of nuclear power.

In spite of Carter's efforts, the nuclear industry fell on hard times. People were angry at cost overruns in building new plants, often reflected in their electric bills. Protesters blocked building sites. Orders for new plants were canceled, and some construction was halted.

Viewpoints
On Nuclear Energy

The need to reduce the dependence of the United States on foreign oil prompted viewpoints strongly for and against nuclear power. *What concerns do the following viewpoints address?*

For Nuclear Energy

"When you debate the issue of nuclear energy, you are actually debating the issue of growth. Growth will be the key issue for the remainder of this century, and it is the resolution of that issue which will determine the lifestyles of most Americans for generations to come. . . . Economic growth has been inextricably linked to the growth of the supply of energy throughout history."

Senator James A. McClure (Idaho), address before the National Conference on Energy Advocacy, February 2, 1979

Against Nuclear Energy

"If this country . . . continues to rely more and more on nuclear power a meltdown disaster is almost predictable, and when it does occur, disaster and chaos from the medical and psychological effects as well as the shutdown of electricity from all nuclear power plants will be the result. For years now, the utilities and nuclear power industry have refused to listen to scientific logic and reasoning concerning the dangers of this technology. . . . Perhaps it is time for emotion and for passion and for commitment to stir our souls and our hearts and our minds once again into action."

Dr. Helen Caldicott, in *Nuclear Madness, What You Can Do!* 1980

MAKING CONNECTIONS

Carter tried to emphasize the importance of using energy wisely and conserving oil. Are many Americans today concerned about this issue? What examples can you give?

Steps Toward Deregulation

Carter also moved toward **deregulation,** or reducing or removing government controls, in several industries. In the late 1800s and early 1900s, agencies such as the Interstate Commerce Commission had been established to regulate rates and business practices in certain industries. Over the years, regulations had multiplied, and now Carter argued that they hurt competition and increased consumer costs.

Carter's energy plan included proposals to take controls off oil and natural gas prices. He also took steps to deregulate railroads, trucking, and airlines.

Many liberal Democrats and consumer groups were upset. They argued that regulation was a way of assuring that businesses would be accountable to the public. Critics also worried that companies would not maintain safety standards and that airlines and railroads, for example, would cut service to less profitable areas of the country. Deregulation continued during the next two administrations, both Republican, though not always with the promised benefits to consumers.

Other Domestic Issues

Concern for moral values influenced the President's approach to domestic questions as well as foreign policy. Some of his actions were controversial. Once in office, for example, Carter carried out his promise to grant **amnesty**—a general pardon—to those who had evaded the draft during the Vietnam War. Because the war still divided Americans, reactions were mixed.

Civil Rights Carter was more sympathetic to the goal of equal rights than either Ford or Nixon had been. During the 1976 campaign, he had won African American support with what columnist David Broder called "an eloquence, a simplicity, a directness that moved listeners of both races."

Carter also tried to move beyond the civil rights battles of the 1950s and 1960s. As a white southerner himself, he understood the South's need to overcome the negative images of the past decades:

> The most important [message] was that we in the South were ready for reconciliation, to be accepted as equals, to rejoin the mainstream of American political life. This yearning for what might be called political redemption was a significant factor in my successful campaign.

Carter won the approval of African Americans with his staff appointments, particularly to visible, prestigious posts such as the United Nations ambassadorship for Andrew Young. On the other hand, African Americans were disappointed by his weak support of social programs and his concentration on economic problems and foreign affairs instead of on civil rights.

The Bakke Case In 1978 the Supreme Court ruled on a case that had important implications for civil rights and affirmative action policies. **Allan Bakke,** who was white, applied to the medical school at the University of California at Davis in 1973 and 1974. After being turned down twice, he sued the school for "reverse discrimination." Bakke charged that the policy of reserving sixteen of one hundred class spaces for minority group applicants violated both the Civil Rights Act of 1964 and the Constitution.

In a complex ruling in *Regents of the University of California* v. *Bakke,* the justices wrote six separate opinions. While the Court ordered Bakke's admission to the California medical school, it also upheld the consideration of race as one factor in admission decisions, though it did not allow actual quotas. The decision supported the concept of affirmative action, but the case signaled the start of a white backlash against the policy.

Evaluating the Carter Presidency

Historians continue to assess Jimmy Carter's presidency. Some explain it as mainly a reaction to Watergate, a brief period of Democratic rule in a long period of Republican dominance. They also find serious flaws in the administration itself, mainly in its inability to create and stick

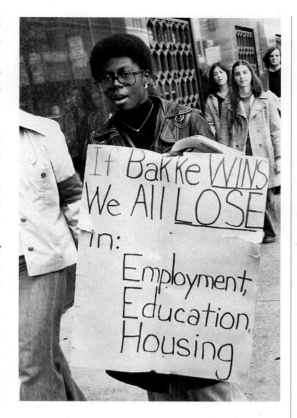

Allan Bakke took his case against affirmative action all the way to the Supreme Court when he claimed to be a victim of reverse discrimination. People argued both sides of the issue and some marched to voice their views.

with a consistent policy or to display strong leadership. After Carter's defeat in 1980, economist Robert J. Samuelson observed that Charles Schultze, retiring head of the Council of Economic Advisers, was typical of the entire team:

*I*n many ways, Schultze symbolizes the puzzle of the departing Carter administration: that a lot of good people went into government four years ago, and a government of good people didn't produce a good government.

SECTION 4 REVIEW

Key Terms, People, and Places

1. Define (a) Nuclear Regulatory Commission, (b) deregulation, (c) amnesty.
2. Identify Allan Bakke.
3. Identify Three Mile Island.

Key Concepts

4. What were the problems with Carter's economic policy?

5. What were Carter's energy goals?
6. What developments in civil rights took place during the Carter administration?

Critical Thinking

7. **Recognizing Cause and Effect** Carter won the presidency on the strength of being a Washington "outsider." How did this ultimately hurt his administration?

History might not have Happened This Way

Key Decisions and Decision Makers

The Decision to Reveal the Effects of Agent Orange

Time Frame:	1977–1978
Place:	Chicago, Illinois
Key People:	Maude de Victor, Ethel Owens, Bill Kurtis
Situation:	Veterans Administration counselor Maude de Victor found evidence that mysterious illnesses among Vietnam veterans were due to exposure to the chemical Agent Orange, but had to decide what to do about her discovery.

During and after the Vietnam War, the federal Veterans Administration (the VA) was faced with helping a new generation of veterans who were troubled by the physical and psychological aftereffects of a confusing and unpopular war. Many Vietnam veterans could not find work or resume a normal life, for they had come home emotionally shattered, alcoholic, or addicted to drugs. In addition, many developed mysterious ailments. Some blamed these health problems on exposure to Agent Orange, a chemical used by the American military to destroy vegetation in Vietnam. The photograph at right shows a before-and-after shot of one area in Vietnam that was treated with the chemical. The VA rejected the claims against Agent Orange, but one dedicated VA employee became convinced that it had harmed many soldiers.

Looking for the Truth

Maude de Victor was a benefits counselor at the VA in Chicago. She had been a corpsman at a naval hospital from 1959 to 1961, then joined the VA. Perhaps because of her work on an experimental program in radiation therapy while in the navy, she contracted breast cancer in 1976. She was still recovering from treatment when she began to hear complaints about Agent Orange from Vietnam veterans.

In 1977 Ethel Owens called de Victor to say that her husband Charlie, a thirty-year air force veteran, was dying of cancer. Charlie, Ethel said, had once told her that if he died of cancer, "it was because of the chemicals used in Vietnam." De Victor sent Owens's file to Washington but was told the illness had nothing to do with Vietnam. When Owens died, the VA did not pay full benefits, saying his death was not service related.

De Victor began to track down military and chemical company records. She learned about Operation Ranch Hand, the program to defoliate Vietnamese forests and crops by spraying chemical herbicides from the air. One chemical, Agent Orange, contained a type of dioxin considered highly toxic. Between 1965 and 1970, nearly 12 million gallons of Agent

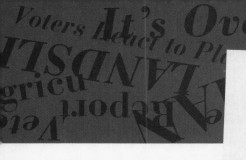

GOALS	Get medical and financial help for Vietnam veterans suffering from the results of exposure to Agent Orange			
POSSIBLE ACTIONS	**Drop the investigation as ordered by superiors**	**Apply pressure for action within the VA**	**Take the information outside the VA**	**Publicize the situation through the news media**
POSSIBLE RESULTS	• Victims of Agent Orange will be ignored, and VA policy will not change. • The VA will eventually recognize the claims of Agent Orange victims and help them.	• The VA will not change its position, and veterans will not receive help. • The VA will, in time, take responsibility for helping Agent Orange victims.	• Officials will protect the military's image. • Some politicians may take up the cause of Agent Orange victims but fail to change VA policy. • Sympathetic politicians will act to change the VA policy.	• The media will not pursue the story. • The media will publicize, but the public will not respond. • Publicity will prompt public outrage, but no results. • Publicity and outrage will bring help for victims.

Orange were sprayed on Vietnam. Soldiers in helicopters flew through clouds of the defoliant, while chemical fog drifted down onto troops and Vietnamese civilians on the ground.

De Victor talked to veterans who had a variety of bizarre illnesses—rashes, headaches, strange lumps and sores, mood swings, or cancers. Others told her of their children's birth defects or their wives' miscarriages. Mapping the use of Agent Orange in Vietnam, she found that these ailing veterans had served in the areas sprayed with the chemical.

By early 1978, she had more than fifty case histories showing a link between Agent Orange and medical problems. She also had evidence that the government knew the dangers of Agent Orange. She showed her data to her superiors at the VA, but the they dismissed her findings and ordered her to stop her investigation.

Disobeying Orders

At that point, Maude de Victor could have dropped the investigation as she had been told to do. She understood why the VA would not admit the dangers of Agent Orange—the government feared a flood of disability claims and lawsuits from sick veterans and Vietnamese survivors, as well as condemnation from the world community. But she decided that getting help for sick veterans and their families was important.

Again, there were choices. She could go on applying pressure within the VA. Or she could risk her job and go to officials elsewhere in government. Both courses could be slow—and possibly useless. She wanted the world to know the story—so she turned to the news media.

Bill Kurtis, a Chicago news anchor, put on an hour-long documentary about her findings. "Agent Orange: The Deadly Fog" aired on March 23, 1978, and drew a torrent of calls from journalists, politicians, and Vietnam vets. The VA did not let de Victor take the calls and transferred her to another department, but she continued to discuss the issue. Claims related to Agent Orange began to pour into the VA, which still denied its harmful effects.

De Victor quit the VA in disgust in 1981, but she had started a movement. Veterans formed lobbying organizations and filed a class action suit against chemical companies. They turned up evidence that the government and manufacturers had known the risks of using Agent Orange. In 1985 Vietnam veterans injured by Agent Orange were awarded millions of dollars in compensation.

EVALUATING DECISIONS

1. Why did Maude de Victor go to the media with her findings?
2. What was the impact of de Victor's decision to publicize the harmful effects of Agent Orange?

Critical Thinking

3. **Determining Relevance** What element of de Victor's personal life may have contributed to her commitment to the Agent Orange cause?

Chapter Review

Key Terms
1. stagflation
2. Helsinki Accords
3. shuttle diplomacy
4. Camp David Accords
5. dissident
6. Nuclear Regulatory Commision
7. deregulation
8. amnesty

People
9. Gerald R. Ford
10. Nelson Rockefeller
11. James Earl Carter, Jr.
12. Anwar el-Sadat
13. Menachem Begin
14. Cyrus Vance
15. Shah Mohammad Reza Pahlavi
16. Ayatollah Ruholla Khomeini
17. Allan Bakke

Places
18. Three Mile Island

Terms For each term above, write a sentence that explains its relation to the events of the Ford or Carter administrations.

Matching Review the key terms in the list above. If you are not sure of a term's meaning, review its definition in the chapter. Then choose a term from the list that best matches each description below.
1. a general pardon
2. a writer or other activist who opposes the actions of his or her government
3. a condition in which the economy remains stalled during a period of high inflation and rising unemployment
4. a series of agreements in which thirty-five nations pledged to cooperate economically and to promote human rights
5. the process of reducing or removing government controls

True or False Determine whether each statement is true or false. If it is true, write "true." If it is false, change the underlined name to make the statement true.
1. In 1978 <u>Nelson Rockefeller</u> sued the University of California at Davis for "reverse discrimination."
2. <u>Menachem Begin</u> took many steps to modernize Iran, but his government was corrupt and repressive.
3. Egyptian leader <u>Anwar el-Sadat</u> made a historic visit to Israel to try to establish peace between the two countries.

Section 1 (pp. 774 – 778)
1. Briefly describe Gerald Ford's beliefs and his voting record in Congress. Why did some critics feel that he was not qualified to be President?
2. Describe two major challenges that Ford inherited when he took office.
3. Briefly describe the successes and failures of Ford's foreign policy.

Section 2 (pp. 779 – 782)
4. Why did Jimmy Carter's candidacy appeal to voters eager to recover from the Watergate scandal?
5. Describe Carter's personal beliefs, his personal style, and his special abilities.

Section 3 (pp. 783 – 787)
6. What was President Carter's role in establishing the Camp David Accords?

7. Describe President Carter's policy toward Africa.
8. In Carter's first year, he said that the United States would forge closer ties with the Soviet Union. Why did his statement prove to be premature?
9. Why did the Iran hostage crisis damage Carter's presidency?

Section 4 (pp. 789 – 793)
10. What problems did Carter experience in his dealings with Congress?
11. You have read columnist Tom Wicker's observation that Carter "never established a politically coherent administration." How can this observation be applied to Carter's economic policies?
12. Explain why Americans faced oil shortages and high prices in the late 1970s. Why was Carter unable to reach his energy conservation goals?

1. **Testing Conclusions** Both Ford and Carter were branded as ineffective leaders by their critics. Yet both inherited serious economic and social problems from previous administrations. To what extent do you think the ineffectiveness of these Presidents was due to inherited problems and to what extent was it due to inadequate leadership?

2. **Demonstrating Reasoned Judgment** Do you think that Jimmy Carter would have been a more effective or a less effective President if he had been less concerned with moral values? Give evidence from the chapter to support your point of view.

3. **Checking Consistency** Although people complained about gas lines and fuel shortages during the 1970s, many did not back Carter's energy policies. How do you account for this discrepancy?

4. **Identifying Central Issues** You have read that in the election of 1976 the most important issue was trust. What do think is the most important issue for voters today when electing a President?

1. **Evaluating Primary Sources** Review the primary source excerpt on page 783. Based on your reading of the chapter, to what extent was Carter able to live up to his ideals in his foreign and domestic policies?

2. **Understanding the Visuals** Look at the map on page 780. How did your state vote in the 1976 election? Is this consistent with its voting pattern today?

3. **Writing About the Chapter** You are running as a third-party candidate in the presidential election of 1976. You want to combine the best aspects of both Carter and Ford while avoiding their weaknesses. Write a speech in which you announce your candidacy and the reasons why you should be elected. First, create a list detailing Ford's and Carter's positions on important issues. Note how your positions will improve upon theirs. Next, write a draft of your speech in which you explain your positions. Revise your speech, making sure that your ideas are clearly explained, then proofread and draft a final copy.

4. **Using the Graphic Organizer** This graphic organizer uses a tree map to organize main ideas and supporting details about Carter's foreign policy. (a) One reason for the breakdown of détente in the Carter years was due to Carter's commitment to human rights. According to the map, what was a second reason? (b) According to the map, what events led to the capture of American hostages in Iran? (c) Create your own tree map about Carter's domestic policy, using this graphic organizer as an example.

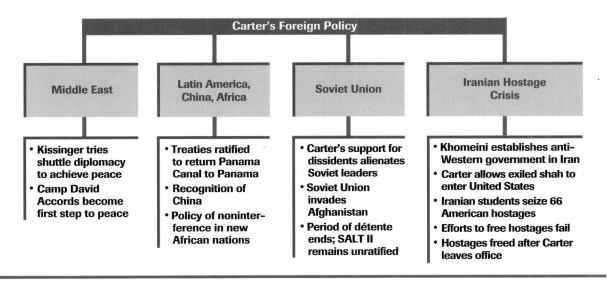

Carter's Foreign Policy

Middle East
- Kissinger tries shuttle diplomacy to achieve peace
- Camp David Accords become first step to peace

Latin America, China, Africa
- Treaties ratified to return Panama Canal to Panama
- Recognition of China
- Policy of noninter-ference in new African nations

Soviet Union
- Carter's support for dissidents alienates Soviet leaders
- Soviet Union invades Afghanistan
- Period of détente ends; SALT II remains unratified

Iranian Hostage Crisis
- Khomeini establishes anti-Western government in Iran
- Carter allows exiled shah to enter United States
- Iranian students seize 66 American hostages
- Efforts to free hostages fail
- Hostages freed after Carter leaves office

High Tide of the Conservative Movement 1980–1992

*I*n 1980 the Republican party—now controlled by conservatives—scored a major electoral victory. Under the leadership of Ronald Reagan and then George Bush, the Republicans rolled back the liberal agenda that had shaped national policy ever since the New Deal of Franklin D. Roosevelt. The Republicans' main thrust was an attempt to revive the moral values of the nation, which conservatives felt had eroded in an increasingly permissive society.

Building on America's Strength
GEORGE BUSH
PRESIDENT

Events in the United States

1979 Religious conservatives found the Moral Majority.

1980 Republican Ronald Reagan defeats Democrat Jimmy Carter for the presidency.

1982 The Equal Rights Amendment fails to win ratification.

1984 Democrat Geraldine Ferraro becomes the first woman to run for the vice presidency on a major party ticket.

1978	1980	1982	1984

Events in the World

1979 The Soviet Union invades Afghanistan.

1980 Rhodesia, in Africa, is renamed Zimbabwe.

1982 Britain and Argentina engage in the Falklands War.

1984 South African archbishop Desmond Tutu receives the Nobel Peace Prize.

Pages 800 – 804
The Conservative Revolution

The elections of 1980 brought a conservative President to the White House and a Republican majority to the Senate. Behind these changes was a well-organized union of several diverse groups who sought to reverse many of the policies and programs of the preceding decades.

Pages 805 – 809
Republican Policies at Home

The 1980s were years in which the rich became even richer, while the poor and many of those in the middle saw few benefits from the nation's apparent prosperity. Presidents Reagan and Bush cut back on social programs and followed a conservative agenda.

Pages 811 – 815
The Halting Pace of Reform

The movement toward greater equality for women and minority groups slowed during the administrations of Presidents Reagan and Bush. Because many conservatives opposed extending more rights to such groups, the government sometimes adopted policies that reversed earlier gains.

Pages 818 – 821
The United States in a New World

After more than forty years of the cold war, in the early 1990s the United States watched as communist governments crumbled. The foreign policies of Reagan's first years in office became outdated as the nation faced new possibilities and problems.

1986 The Iran-contra affair becomes public.	1987 The Senate rejects Robert Bork's nomination to the Supreme Court.	1988 Vice President George Bush wins the presidential election.		1990 A severe economic recession deepens.	1991 The United States and United Nations troops defeat Iraq in the Persian Gulf War.	
1986		**1988**		**1990**		**1992**
1986 Corazon Aquino is elected president of the Philippines.	1987 Syrian troops invade Lebanon. • Riots break out in Israel's West Bank territory.	1988 Civil wars sweep Ethiopia and the Sudan. • Pakistan elects Benazir Bhutto president.	1989 The Berlin Wall is torn down. • Japanese emperor Hirohito dies.	1990 Violetta Chamorro is elected president of Nicaragua. • Namibia becomes an independent state.		1992 Somalia is torn by war and famine.

The Conservative Revolution

SECTION PREVIEW

The elections of 1980 brought a conservative President to the White House and a Republican majority to the Senate. Behind these changes was a well-organized union of several different groups who sought to reverse many of the policies and programs of the preceding decades.

Key Concepts

- The new conservative movement had its roots partly in the anticommunist politics of the 1950s.
- Groups with conservative economic, social, and religious views worked together to overturn the liberal programs of the New Deal and the Great Society.
- Conservatives used television and other techniques very effectively to promote their views.

Key Terms, People, and Places

New Right, coalition, televangelism; Ronald Reagan, George Bush

With this 1980 campaign poster, Ronald Reagan appealed to the patriotism of many American voters who felt that President Carter had not provided strong guidance in managing the economy or foreign affairs.

I n the presidential election of 1964, the Republicans nominated Senator Barry Goldwater, an extreme conservative. This nomination signaled the growing influence of a new conservative movement. By 1980 this movement had created an alliance of various special-interest groups to form what became known as the **New Right.** Not only had conservatives gained influence within the Republican party; they had, through the effective use of the media, found supporters elsewhere as well. By the early 1980s, members of the New Right had succeeded in electing many conservative candidates in state, local, and national elections.

Foremost among these conservative politicians was **Ronald Reagan,** who was elected to the presidency in 1980. A former movie and television actor, Reagan was an ideal New Right candidate. Likable, photogenic, genial—and committed to conservative ideals—Reagan as President had little trouble winning support for cutbacks in many liberal social programs created by previous administrations.

Background of the "New" Conservatives

The New Right had its political roots in the anticommunism of the 1950s, although many conservative Americans also looked back to earlier social values. In the late 1940s and early 1950s, as the cold war began and Soviet power increased, fear of communism was widespread. Some conservatives viewed federal social programs—even popular ones such as social security—as evidence of communist influence within the United States government. Moderate Republicans like President Dwight D. Eisenhower accepted most of these programs, but others in the party did not.

After Lyndon Johnson's crushing defeat of Barry Goldwater in 1964, some analysts concluded that conservative views could never succeed in United States politics. Goldwater had, for example, opposed federal civil rights and antipoverty efforts and supported a buildup of weapons against an expected Soviet attack. But his candidacy did show that anticommunist fear, combined with conservative views, still persisted. In 1968 Richard Nixon, who had begun his political career with a "tough-on-communism" stance in the 1940s and 1950s, was able to bring the Republicans back to the White House.

After the Watergate scandal ended Nixon's administration in disgrace, Democrat Jimmy Carter won the presidency in 1976. Four years later, spiraling inflation and a frustrating hostage situation in Iran made Carter appear ineffective. The Republican party was ready to take over again.

The Conservative Coalition

The New Right derived its power from the support of many groups with a wide range of political, economic, and social concerns. These groups formed a **coalition**—a union of several groups that work together to achieve a common goal. The groups in the new conservative coalition did not always agree with one another, but they all contributed to the broadbased strength of the movement.

Some in the conservative coalition were most concerned with the role of government in the economy. These conservatives argued that the nation was faced with enormous inefficiency and waste. Productivity was falling while prices were rising. They believed it was time to reduce the size of government, cut taxes, and get rid of the regulations that limited economic competition. They charged that liberal policies that spent large sums of money on social problems had failed.

Ronald Reagan, who would bring this ideology to the White House in the 1980s, revealed its spirit in his own slogan: "Government is not the solution to our problem. Government is the problem." The answer, he said, was traditional American free enterprise:

> The competitive free enterprise system has given us the greatest standard of living in the world, produced generation after generation of technical wizards who consistently lead the world in invention and innovation, and has provided unlimited opportunities enabling industrious Americans from the most humble of backgrounds to climb to the top of the ladder of success.

Some groups in the conservative movement wanted to restore what they considered Christian values to society. They objected to attitudes and ways of behaving that had become more widely accepted in the 1970s, including sexual freedom, legalized abortion, "Women's Lib," some forms of rock music, and the movement for gay and lesbian rights. The Moral Majority, a group led by a Baptist minister from Virginia named Jerry Falwell, was founded in 1979 to focus the efforts of religious conservatives.

Other conservatives demanded an end to many government-supported social programs.

Jimmy Swaggert, known for his charismatic preaching, was one of several Christian evangelists who used television to promote the conservative agenda.

Those who were part of the backlash against civil rights activism (Chapter 26) criticized the policy of affirmative action. This program, in order to make up for past discrimination, required employers to give special consideration to the hiring of women and people from minority groups. Some conservatives called affirmative action a form of "reverse discrimination," favoring one group over another on the basis of race or gender. This issue was one that attracted some traditionally Democratic blue-collar workers to the new conservatism.

MAKING CONNECTIONS

In what ways did the New Right resemble the progressive movement of the early 1900s? In what ways was it different?

Conservatives Find Effective Tactics

Conservatives used the latest political techniques to win over new supporters. Jerry Falwell and a number of other evangelists used the power of television brilliantly to reach millions of people. In a format that became known as **televangelism,** they appealed to viewers to contribute money to their campaign against sin.

Televangelists delivered fervent sermons on specific political issues and used the money they raised to back conservative politicians.

Conservative strategists also used television effectively, with brief, powerful television images that conveyed their message visually. Speeches were crafted to contain "sound bites"—short, memorable statements that would be repeated on the evening news. Strategists also pioneered in using "spin doctors" to give a candidate's comments the best possible interpretation for the public. For example, conservative columnist George Will helped Ronald Reagan prepare for a debate with President Carter in the 1980 campaign. In the TV coverage immediately following the debate, Will appeared as a political analyst. Hoping to influence viewers who might not have made up their own minds yet, Will declared Reagan the winner in the debate.

Similarly, conservatives led the way in using direct mail to raise huge sums of money for conservative candidates. Mass mailings of requests for donations were sent to individuals who were likely to support conservative causes. This effort reached out to people who might ignore generalized appeals such as television ads.

AMERICAN PROFILES

Richard Viguerie

Richard A. Viguerie (1933–) was at the cutting edge in developing the conservative coalition's new fund-raising techniques. Originally from near Houston, Texas, Viguerie had graduated from college but dropped out of law school before the end of his first year. His real interest was politics, especially conservative politics, and he spent much of his spare time working for the Republican party. He was a campaign worker for Eisenhower in 1952 and 1956, and he served as a county chairman in the Young Republicans organization.

Viguerie's big break came in 1961, when he responded to an advertisement in the prominent conservative magazine *National Review*. He was hired as executive secretary of Young Americans for Freedom, a conservative youth group. Viguerie began to approach wealthy contributors for funds to pay off the group's huge debt, but he soon found that he was more comfortable writing them letters. This experience led him to start his own direct-mail organization in 1964.

Viguerie began by going to the office of the clerk of the House of Representatives, where he copied down the names and addresses of contributors who had given fifty dollars or more to Barry Goldwater's presidential campaign. His first list of 12,500 conservative contributors was the basis for later lists with millions of names.

Next, Viguerie began to sell his services to conservative political candidates. Using his list to run direct-mail campaigns, he helped Robert Griffin win a Senate race in Michigan in 1966. In 1969 he assisted Phil Crane in an upset victory in an Illinois congressional race. After the Watergate scandal, tighter limits were imposed on campaign contributions. Now it was even more important to be able to tap small contributors, and Viguerie's services were in great demand. The graph on page 803 shows the results of these new methods.

Viguerie firmly believed that the country was ready for a conservative revival. "The plain truth is that more and more Americans are sick of liberalism—and aren't afraid to say so," he argued. He believed that the real job for conservatives

Conservative activist Richard Viguerie recognized the enormous potential of direct mail as a political fund-raising tool.

Political Campaign Spending,* 1952–1988

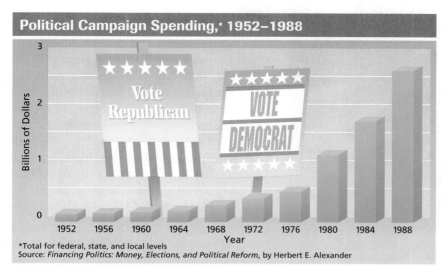

*Total for federal, state, and local levels
Source: *Financing Politics: Money, Elections, and Political Reform,* by Herbert E. Alexander

Interpreting Graphs
In what year shown on the graph did campaign spending first increase significantly? How might the activities of Richard Viguerie and other conservatives have affected these statistics?

was to seize control of the Republican party, and he devoted all his energies to that goal.

Reagan Brings Conservatism to the White House

Ronald Reagan, who came to politics late in life, became the most influential spokesperson for the conservative cause. He began as a radio broadcaster and then embarked on a career as a movie actor in Hollywood. When he stopped acting in films, he served as a spokesperson for General Electric. Adopting the conservative point of view, he made speeches praising capitalism and corporate leaders and criticizing government regulation.

Reagan's personality, visibility, and skill in articulating conservative ideas helped him become governor of California in 1966. In 1976, with the support of Republican conservatives, he challenged Gerald Ford for the presidential nomination but lost by a narrow margin. By 1980, however, the growing strength of conservatives in the party gave Reagan the nomination.

In his campaign, Reagan attacked the incumbent Jimmy Carter, saying he offered little more than a "litany of broken promises." He entertained voters with his down-to-earth humor while criticizing Carter's economic record: "A recession is when your neighbor loses his job. A depression is when you lose yours. A recovery is when Jimmy Carter loses his."

The continuing hostage crisis in Iran, as well as other issues, worked against Carter, and Reagan won a landslide victory. He gained 51 percent of the popular vote to Carter's 41 percent. (John Anderson, member of Congress from Illinois, ran as a third-party candidate.) The Republicans gained control of the Senate for the first time in twenty-five years.

Reagan Seeks a Second Term Four years later, Reagan ran for a second term. This time the Democrats picked Senator Walter Mondale, who had been Carter's Vice President. In an unusual move, Mondale chose Geraldine Ferraro, a member of Congress from New York, as his running mate. Ferraro was the first woman ever to be nominated on a major party's presidential ticket. While the nomination appealed to many voters, it also created a backlash among some voters who believed women should remain in traditional roles.

The ticket was not strong enough to overcome Reagan's popularity and an economy that appeared strong despite growing deficits. Reagan won 59 percent of the popular vote, and Mondale won the electoral votes of only the District of Columbia and his home state of Minnesota.

While hosting the popular "G. E. Theater" in the 1950s, young Ronald Reagan sharpened his communication skills and gained valuable exposure to the American television audience.

When debating Democratic challenger Michael Dukakis (right) in the 1988 presidential campaign, George Bush raised questions in voters' minds about Dukakis's plans for the economy.

In his second term, Reagan continued to win over the country. He was a skillful communicator who used television the way Franklin Roosevelt had used radio fifty years before, talking soothingly about concerns everyone shared. He was a talented storyteller, often using anecdotes to make his points.

In spite of problems during his presidency, Reagan enjoyed enormous popularity. One critic gave him the name "Teflon President" because, like pans with a nonstick coating, nothing stuck to him. He made mistakes and misstatements, often seemed uninterested in governing, and occasionally fell asleep during meetings. He delegated a great deal of authority to others and sometimes was unclear about policy decisions made in his name. A number of his aides and associates were charged and convicted of illegal and unethical actions. None of these blunders lessened his personal approval ratings, however. In 1989, when Reagan left office, 63 percent of the American people approved of his overall performance.

Bush Continues the Agenda

The conservative movement seemed safe when Reagan's Vice President, **George Bush,** sought the presidency. The son of a well-to-do Connecticut senator, Bush had begun his career in the Texas oil industry, then served in government as a member of Congress, as an envoy to China, and as head of the CIA. The public initially saw him as a weak candidate, without Reagan's charm, but the prosperity of the Reagan years was on his side. The candidate for the Democrats, Governor Michael Dukakis of Massachusetts, was at a disadvantage as he tried to convince voters of the need for a change. The campaign was marked by personal attacks and negative advertising.

Although Bush and his running mate, Senator Dan Quayle, won nearly 54 percent of the popular vote, Bush still lacked the mandate Ronald Reagan had enjoyed eight years earlier. Moreover, many Republican congressional candidates lost in the elections, giving Democrats control of both the Senate and the House of Representatives.

As President, Bush projected an image of cheerful energy and optimism, calling for cooperation and an end to dissension between Congress and the White House. While people were aware of problems in his handling of many issues, they generally felt that he was trying to do his best. Bush's personal approval rating remained at a remarkably high 67 percent after his first year and a half and rose even higher during the Persian Gulf War in 1991 (see Section 4 of this chapter). His popularity began to drop only when the economy faltered late in his term.

SECTION 1 REVIEW

Key Terms, People, and Places

1. Define (a) New Right, (b) coalition, (c) televangelism.

2. Identify (a) Ronald Reagan, (b) George Bush.

Key Concepts

3. What roots did the conservative movement have in the 1950s?

4. What groups formed the conservative coalition?

5. What techniques did the conservative movement use to promote its ends?

Critical Thinking

6. Recognizing Cause and Effect How did new fund-raising techniques help the conservative movement to achieve political power in the 1980s?

Republican Policies at Home

SECTION PREVIEW

The 1980s were years in which the rich became even richer, while the poor and many of those in the middle saw few benefits from the nation's apparent prosperity. Presidents Reagan and Bush cut back on social programs and followed a conservative agenda.

Key Concepts
- Reagan's economic plan reduced government spending, except in the area of defense.
- Reagan and Bush's Supreme Court appointments made the Court more conservative.
- Although the economy prospered in the 1980s, the gap between rich and poor increased.

Key Terms, People, and Places
supply-side economics, S & L, new federalism; Sandra Day O'Connor, Clarence Thomas

R epublican administrations in the 1980s took a three-part approach to domestic policy. First, they hoped to revive the economy. Second, they wanted to cut back on costly social welfare programs. Third, they sought to restore the traditional values held by conservative Christians.

Reagan's Domestic Program

Reagan was most concerned with promoting economic recovery. Achieving this goal, he believed, meant reforming tax policy, cutting back on the role of government, and shifting responsibility for many programs from the federal government to city and state governments. At the same time, however, he greatly increased spending for defense.

Tax Reform Reagan's recovery program, which became known as "Reaganomics," rested on the theory of **supply-side economics.** This theory reversed earlier policies, based on the ideas of John Maynard Keynes, which argued that it was necessary to increase people's purchasing power to improve the economy. This meant giving them more money, whether through jobs, grants, or lower taxes. By contrast, "supply-siders" wanted to lower taxes to put more money in the hands of businesses and investors—those who supplied the goods for consumers to buy. The theory assumed they would then hire more people and produce more goods and services, making the economy grow. Prosperity would "trickle down" from the top to those at the lower levels of the economy.

In February 1981 Reagan presented to Congress his proposals to cut spending, lower taxes, and eliminate unnecessary government regulations. The administration pushed through the new tax policy. A 5 percent tax cut went into effect in October 1981, followed by 10 percent cuts in 1982 and 1983. The new cuts benefited wealthy Americans the most.

Then, in 1986, Congress passed the most sweeping tax reform measure in American history. It closed loopholes in the law that had allowed some Americans to avoid paying their fair share of taxes, and it expanded the tax base. Yet it still benefited the rich most of all, cutting the maximum tax rate—the rate on the highest incomes—from 70 percent to 28 percent.

This doll suggests that while Reagan's economic policies benefited the very rich, many other Americans "lost their shirts"—along with their jobs—in the 1980s.

MAKING CONNECTIONS

How was Reaganomics similar to the economic policies of Presidents Harding and Coolidge in the 1920s?

Cuts in Social Programs Both philosophy and practicality guided Reagan's efforts to cut back social programs. He challenged the assumption held since the New Deal that the federal government had the responsibility to assist people directly. While he said that his administration would maintain a "safety net" for truly needy people, he also was committed to the idea that *anyone* who really tried could succeed in the United States.

Reagan's economic policy also dictated saving money at the federal level wherever possible. The federal government was collecting less in taxes and, as the graph below shows, spending more on defense. To make up the difference, he cut back public service jobs, unemployment payments, welfare benefits, and food stamp allocations. Elderly Medicare patients had to pay a larger share of their own medical bills. College students had to take out loans instead of getting federal grants. Spending for social welfare programs dropped by billions of dollars.

Deregulation Reagan, like President Jimmy Carter before him, was in favor of removing government regulations that stifled competition in the free-market economy. While Carter had begun deregulation by focusing on the oil and transportation industries, Reagan sought to remove government controls from virtually all areas of the economy.

The Reagan approach to deregulation removed both rules that limited competition and those that protected the public. It targeted agencies like the Environmental Protection Agency and the Occupational Health and Safety Administration, which enforced standards for controlling pollution or maintaining safe workplaces. Always the emphasis was on eliminating regulations that the administration believed were inefficient and expensive, but that others saw as protecting workers, consumers, and the environment.

The S & L Scandal One crucial area of deregulation was banking and finance, particularly the "thrift institutions" or savings and loan banks, often called **S & Ls.** These generally small, stable banks historically had concentrated on making home mortgage loans to individuals. The aim of deregulation was to allow these banks to make riskier but more profitable investments.

Officials at a number of unregulated S & Ls took advantage of the new laws to make huge fortunes for themselves while driving their banks into failure. When the banks failed, it was not the bank officials or even most depositors who lost money. Because bank accounts are insured by the federal government, taxpayers had to make up the millions of dollars in bad investments. Although a number of banking officials were indicted for their dishonest actions, the money was gone.

The New Federalism While he moved to cut back the role of the federal government, Reagan sought to give more responsibility to state and local governments. Borrowing a term from the Nixon administration, Reagan called this plan the **new federalism.** By eliminating funding for federal programs and instead giving the states sizable grants that they could spend as they chose, he hoped to

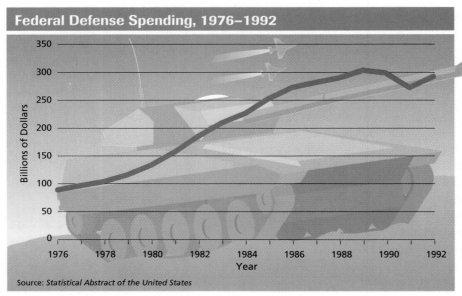

Federal Defense Spending, 1976–1992

Billions of Dollars (y-axis): 0, 50, 100, 150, 200, 250, 300, 350

Year (x-axis): 1976, 1978, 1980, 1982, 1984, 1986, 1988, 1990, 1992

Source: *Statistical Abstract of the United States*

Interpreting Graphs
Notice the change in defense spending in the early 1980s. *By how much did the defense budget increase during Reagan's two terms in office? What happened to defense spending during the Bush administration?*

encourage local governments to take the lead in meeting community needs.

Unfortunately, the policy did not work as planned. A recession early in Reagan's presidency left a number of cities and states nearly bankrupt, for they now had responsibility but not enough money for programs formerly funded from Washington.

Social Issues Reagan also took a conservative approach to social issues, endorsing the goals of such groups as the Moral Majority. He spoke out on issues like the need for prayer in public schools, which the Supreme Court had earlier ruled unconstitutional.

Bush Continues Conservatism

When he challenged Reagan for the Republican nomination in 1980, George Bush criticized Reagan's economic plan, calling it "voodoo economics." But after he lost his own bid for the presidency and accepted the vice-presidential slot, Bush adhered to Reagan's approach. While running for the presidency himself in 1988, he played on voters' fears that his Democratic opponent, Michael Dukakis, would raise taxes. Bush became known for his own promise: "Read my lips: no new taxes." As President, however, he went back on that promise when the budget deficit soared out of control.

Bush also continued to cut spending for social programs. Democratic majorities in both houses of Congress passed measures to assist people caught in a serious recession—such as one extending benefits for unemployed workers—but Bush used his veto power again and again to defeat these bills.

Bush was even more outspoken than Reagan in his support for conservative social goals. Conservatives once had questioned Bush's commitment to their program for moral renewal. As President, he reassured them by coming out directly against abortion. He tried to further their other demands as well.

The Supreme Court

Conservative ideals got further help from a series of Republican appointments to the

Supreme Court. As justices retired, Reagan and Bush had the chance to nominate five new justices—more than half the Court. In 1981 Reagan appointed **Sandra Day O'Connor,** the first woman justice on the Supreme Court. Her conservative views led her to vote often with other conservatives, such as William Rehnquist and Warren Burger. Rehnquist, the most conservative member of the Court, became Chief Justice when Burger retired in 1986. Reagan chose another conservative, Antonin Scalia, to take the spot on the Court that Rehnquist had vacated.

Reagan's next choice, judge and former law professor Robert Bork, displayed a narrow view of civil liberties and civil rights that worried many members of Congress as well as the public. The Senate rejected his nomination in 1987. Reagan then nominated Douglas Ginsberg, but Ginsberg soon withdrew himself from consideration amid charges of having used marijuana in the past. Finally, Reagan nominated Anthony Kennedy, a moderate conservative who was quickly approved by the Senate.

The Thomas Hearings George Bush made two appointments to the Court. The first, in 1990, was David Souter of New Hampshire, a relative unknown who proved to be fairly moderate. The second, in 1991, was **Clarence Thomas,** who became one of the Court's most conservative justices. Although Thomas was approved by the Senate, his confirmation hearings brought a storm of public debate.

When Thomas first appeared before the Senate Judiciary Committee, questions arose about

Sandra Day O'Connor became the first woman on the United States Supreme Court in 1981. President Reagan took her conservative views into account when selecting her as a nominee.

his commitment to civil liberties and his stand on crucial issues such as abortion rights and affirmative action. By the time Thomas was to be considered by the full Senate, however, these matters were overshadowed by charges made against him by a former co-worker. In a surprise statement, University of Oklahoma law professor Anita Hill alleged that Thomas had sexually harassed her when he was her supervisor at the Equal Employment Opportunity Commission (EEOC).

During several days of televised Senate hearings, committee members questioned Thomas, Hill, and numerous witnesses for each side. Millions of Americans watched and made their own judgments. Although Hill's charges did not prevent Thomas's confirmation, the hearings brought the issue of sexual harassment into the spotlight, sparking dialogue across the nation.

Attacks on *Roe* v. *Wade* While not all Republican choices for the Supreme Court were equally conservative, they clearly created a different consensus. Gone was the liberal Court of the 1950s and 1960s. The new Court was far less likely to take such an active role in social policy and far more likely to reconsider and limit rights granted in the past. One area in which the Court showed its

Anita Hill (below left) faced a panel of white male senators in October of 1991 to testify that she had been sexually harassed by Supreme Court nominee Clarence Thomas (inset). The scene itself—along with the senators' ultimate rejection of her testimony—symbolized for many Americans the continuing problem of sexism.

more conservative nature was in its rulings on abortion. After the Court made abortion legal in the 1973 *Roe* v. *Wade* decision, antiabortion forces concentrated their efforts on overturning the ruling. While the Court continued to uphold the basic principle of *Roe* v. *Wade,* in several later cases, it allowed states to impose some restrictions. In a 1989 Missouri case, *Webster* v. *Reproductive Health Services,* the Court said that state legislatures could impose rather severe restrictions on the right to abortion. In *Planned Parenthood* v. *Casey,* in 1992, the Court reaffirmed the essential right to choose an abortion, but it allowed the state of Pennsylvania to impose certain restrictions, such as a twenty-four-hour waiting period and a requirement that minors have permission from a parent or judge before ending a pregnancy.

Impact of the Reagan-Bush Era

Republican policies on the domestic front brought an end to the recession that Reagan had inherited when he first took office and ushered in the prosperous, materialistic decade of the 1980s. While the United States experienced an economic boom from 1983 to 1990, however, the next decade began with another devastating recession. Corporate profits dropped, and large companies began to lay off workers. In mid-1991, the unemployment rate reached 7 percent, the highest rate in almost five years.

A small group of people prospered in the 1980s. Political analyst Kevin Phillips described this new class of "upper America."

T*he 1980s were the triumph of upper America—an ostentatious* [showy] *celebration of wealth, the political ascendancy of the rich and a glorification of capitalism, free markets and finance. . . . No parallel upsurge of riches had been seen since the late 19th century, the era of the Vanderbilts, Morgans and Rockefellers. It was the truly wealthy, more than anyone else, who flourished under Reagan. . . . The truth is that the critical concentration of wealth in the United States was developing at higher levels—decamillionaires, centimillionaires, half-billionaires and* *billionaires. Garden variety million-aires had become so common that there were about 1.5 million of them by 1989.*

Meanwhile, less fortunate Americans were hurting. Unemployment rose both at the beginning and end of the decade, as the graph on this page shows. Farmers watched banks foreclose on their farms. Blue-collar workers witnessed high-paying industrial jobs disappear as periodic recessions reflected the loss of economic strength. The wealth that seemed to flow so easily into the pockets of "upper America" during the 1980s did not trickle down far enough to reach the majority of Americans.

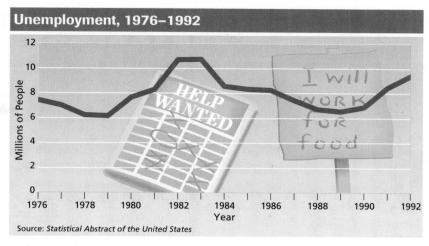

Unemployment, 1976–1992

Source: *Statistical Abstract of the United States*

Interpreting Graphs
Examine the graph above showing unemployment statistics from 1976 to 1992. *What was the general trend in unemployment during Bush's term? What effect might these statistics have had on his campaign for reelection in 1992?*

Poverty The Republican approach widened the gap between rich and poor. By the end of the 1980s, wealth was more unevenly shared than at any time since the end of World War II. Average family incomes were higher because of the number of two-income families, but individual salaries actually declined. For the poorest one fifth of the population, even total family income dropped.

Real poverty increased, hitting women and children the hardest. One of every five American children was living in poverty at the end of the 1980s. Particularly in the cities, a permanent "underclass" of those who could never escape poverty seemed to be developing. Homeless people living on the street, once unusual except in large cities, became a common and distressing sight.

The Deficit Soars Despite the apparent prosperity of the Reagan era, Republican policies had a disastrous effect on the federal budget deficit—the amount by which the government's spending exceeds its income in a given year. Reagan, like most Republicans, favored a balanced budget. But though he made deep cuts in spending for social programs, the huge increase in military spending, combined with his tax-cutting policies, had the opposite result.

The annual deficit soared out of control, from $60 billion in 1980 to a peak of $221 billion in 1986. Reflecting these yearly shortfalls, the national debt rose from $914 billion in 1980 to $3.1 trillion in 1990. Future generations would have to bear the monumental interest payments on this debt, while later administrations would have to try to reduce the deficit.

SECTION 2 REVIEW

Key Terms, People, and Places
1. Define (a) supply-side economics, (b) S & L, (c) new federalism.
2. Identify (a) Sandra Day O'Connor, (b) Clarence Thomas.

Key Concepts
3. How did the appointments made by Reagan and Bush change the character of the Supreme Court?

4. Describe Reagan's economic plan.
5. What were the results of the economic policies followed by the federal government in the 1980s?

Critical Thinking
6. **Expressing Problems Clearly** Explain how Reaganomics created enormous deficits and a mounting national debt that would burden future generations of taxpayers.

Demonstrating Reasoned Judgment

Making connections between ideas is the basis for reasoned judgment. This critical thinking skill enables you to analyze the merits of a statement or opinion and so to reach your own conclusions about its validity.

During the Reagan and Bush administrations, the use of illegal drugs in the United States reached historic highs, and both Presidents sought to end drug abuse. In September 1989, President Bush declared an all-out "War on Drugs." The administration's major weapon in this war, he declared, would be strengthened law enforcement—more police, more prisons, more and longer prison sentences for drug offenders—and military intervention in stopping the shipment of drugs into the United States from other countries. The passage at right represents one person's response to this plan.

Read the passage. Then use the following steps to analyze the response and to test the reasonableness of both the writer's judgment and your own.

1. Examine the source and nature of the evidence by asking *who, when, where,* and *what*.
(a) Who wrote the response?
(b) When? (c) Where did the response appear? (d) What are the writer's qualifications for knowing about the subject he is addressing? (e) Might the writer have any personal biases that affected his view of the drug policies pursued by Reagan and Bush?

2. Identify the major points in the response. (a) Why does the writer of this passage think that expanded legal measures will not work? (b) Why does he think that military action is doomed to failure as well? (c) What evidence does he offer that both are bound to fail? (d) What steps does he think should be taken to solve the problem?

3. Evaluate the evidence offered and the writer's reasoning.
(a) How convincing do you find his arguments? Explain why. (b) How possible do you think it is to achieve the solution he suggests? Explain why. (c) What grade—from A down to F (failing)—would you give the writer on how well he demonstrates reasoned judgment? Why?

Police, prosecutors, courts and prison, not to mention the military, can do little to prevent crime, including drug abuse.

. . . Expenditures for law enforcement have been increasing at a rate four times greater than those for education. Only recognition of the truth and effective action based on it can free us from the human tragedy of drug abuse. A first truth in the war on drugs, as on crime generally, is that the enemy is us, or more precisely, our children, hence our future.

The population of our prisons is already greater than that of Washington, D.C. Inmates are overwhelmingly young, male and from minorities. Is it possible that a country that talks of freedom, equality and justice and claims any sense of responsibility, decency or a degree of intelligence would offer more prisons as a solution to anything . . . ?

. . . The Vietnam War should have taught us the impossibility of controlling foreign conduct by military intervention. This includes the impossibility of stopping the production of cocaine, heroin and other drugs in foreign countries by military action. . . .

In a real fight against drugs, we must work with our young people. To reduce crime and drug abuse we must work for adequate housing and assistance to families; good health care; an education for a full life, including the truth about drugs; meaningful jobs and commitment to freedom, equality and justice. Children born and raised healthy, in loving families among people aspiring to those ideals, will rarely abuse drugs, or hurt one another.

—Ramsey Clark, U.S. attorney general under President Johnson, 1967–1969, quoted in *The Nation* magazine, October 16, 1989

The Halting Pace of Reform

SECTION PREVIEW

The movement toward greater equality for women and minority groups slowed during the administrations of Presidents Reagan and Bush. Because many conservatives opposed extending more rights to such groups, the government sometimes adopted policies that reversed earlier gains.

Key Concepts

• More African Americans voted and were elected to public office during the 1980s than in previous years, but the conservative agenda did not generally support extending civil rights.
• The women's movement faced a backlash from conservatives but still pressed forward.
• Latinos became a more visible presence in politics in the 1980s.
• Native Americans became more involved and influential in their own businesses and educational institutions.

Key Terms, People, and Places

acquired immunodeficiency syndrome (AIDS); Henry Cisneros

years. These new voters, helped by a greater openness in people's attitudes, elected an increasing number of African American candidates to office.

Voters in some of the nation's largest cities, including those in New York, Los Angeles, Chicago, and Cleveland, elected African American mayors. In 1989 Douglas Wilder of Virginia became the first African American to be elected governor of a state. Thousands of other African Americans served in state legislatures and other state offices.

At the national level, the number of African American representatives in Congress doubled from twelve in 1971 to twenty-four in 1989. In the 1984 and 1988 elections, the Reverend Jesse Jackson, once an aide to Martin Luther King, Jr., ran for the presidency. At first, Jackson found himself on the fringe of the Democratic party. The second time around, he moved into the mainstream and dominated the primary campaign. He received 7 million votes and won nearly 1,200 delegates. While he did not win the nomination, he demonstrated that an African American candidate could be a serious contender at the national level.

Yet at the same time, administration policies opposed many of the programs that had helped to achieve these gains. Reagan, like Nixon, opposed the policy of busing students to achieve

I n the 1980s and early 1990s, minority groups continued to push for equality in American life. But progress came more slowly than in the past. The economic climate, with its periodic downturns, made life more difficult for many middle-class Americans, who began to think that enough had been done already to assist minority groups. Meanwhile, the Reagan and Bush administrations did little to encourage change.

Civil Rights in the 1980s

Real gains in civil rights were visible as the 1980s began. The federal commitment to extend voting rights had given the vote to millions of African Americans who had been denied it for

Jesse Jackson (at the Democratic Convention in Atlanta, below) tried to build a "Rainbow Coalition" of supporters from differing backgrounds in his bids for the presidential nomination in 1984 and 1988.

Viewpoints
On the Legacy of the Civil Rights Movement

Decades after the civil rights movement demanded racial justice in the United States, problems persisted. **What does each of the viewpoints below say about the impact of the movement on race relations in the early 1990s?**

Substantial Progress

"Before the civil rights movement, there was a very wide separation between blacks and whites. I don't think the separation is as great today. There has been more speaking out. Blacks now let themselves open up and say how they feel in no uncertain terms. I think there are friendships between blacks and whites that didn't exist before. In spite of everything, I think the racial situation is healthier than it was before. Blacks are no longer invisible."

Eileen Barth, retired social worker and child care professional, quoted in Studs Terkel, *Race,* 1992

Little or No Progress

"The country is more segregated today than it was when [Martin Luther] King and [Robert] Kennedy were alive. What Dr. King and Bobby were fighting was segregation and discrimination imposed by law, by the state. . . . All of that has changed. . . . But in the North, everybody knows what's happened in the cities. At universities, there's much more black withdrawal into separate communities. I grew up thinking we were going to have an integrated society, not just an end to official racism."

Anthony Lewis, columnist for the *New York Times,* quoted in *Life,* April 1993

---

the spring of 1992, the Supreme Court's decision in the *Freeman* v. *Pitts* case released a suburban Atlanta school board from a desegregation order. The Court argued that it was not permissible to use federal policy to undo the effects of population shifts.

Many African Americans were troubled by the changes they saw taking place. Joseph Lattimore, a fifty-year-old insurance broker from Chicago, reflected on what he had seen in the years since he had moved north from Mississippi. "Some things are better today and some things are worse," he told author Studs Terkel in the early 1990s. Lattimore felt frustrated with the slow pace of change:

> As far as integrating with you [white Americans]—we have sang "We Shall Overcome," we have prayed at the courthouse steps, we have made all these gestures, and the door is not open. I'm just tired. Pretty soon I'll have grandkids and they will want to sing "We Shall Overcome." I will say, "No, we have sang that long enough." We should not make a lifetime of singing that song. I refuse to sing it anymore.

MAKING CONNECTIONS

Why might the song "We Shall Overcome," which had inspired civil rights activists in the 1960s and 1970s, cause a feeling of disappointment for African Americans in the 1990s?

---

racial balance in public schools, and his position signaled a general shift in direction. The administration worked to end some affirmative action programs. Reagan tried to prevent the extension of the Voting Rights Act of 1965, which had sparked African American political gains, and only backed off when faced with intense criticism from both Democrats and Republicans. He also weakened the Civil Rights Commission by appointing members who did not support its major goals.

As federal judges appointed by Reagan and Bush took office, the federal courts did less in the area of civil rights. The courts stopped pressing for school desegregation and in some cases approved patterns of racial separation. In

The Women's Movement Meets a Backlash

The women's movement, too, had made progress but now occasionally met with setbacks. Conditions had clearly improved in the two decades during which the movement had been under way. In 1982, in the tenth anniversary issue of *Ms.* magazine, founding editor Gloria Steinem noted, "Now, we have words like 'sexual harassment' and 'battered women.' Ten years ago it was just called 'life.'"

The women's movement, however, had also met with a backlash, or counterreaction. One focus of the backlash was the Equal Rights

Women's Occupations, 1986

- **1%** Farming, forestry, fishing
- **9%** Operators, fabricators, laborers
- **2%** Precision production, craft, and repair
- **24%** Managerial and professional
- **18%** Service occupations
- **46%** Technical, sales, administrative support

Source: *The 1988 Information Please Almanac,* edited by Otto Johnson

Interpreting Charts
The chart above shows a one-year snapshot of occupations held by women. *What percentage of women in 1986 held managerial or professional jobs? What kinds of jobs were held by the largest share of women? How do you think a pie chart for men's occupations would be different?*

Amendment to the Constitution, which banned discrimination on the basis of gender. Though its ratification seemed assured after Congress passed the amendment in 1972, its momentum faltered and opposition increased—both from women who felt threatened by social changes and from conservative members of Congress who were similarly uncomfortable with the women's movement. Conservative activist Phyllis Schlafly organized a letter-writing campaign to legislators, claiming that passage of the ERA would lead to such changes as the drafting of women into the armed forces and the decline of the traditional family. By mid-1982 it was clear that too many state legislatures would reject the amendment, and the ERA died.

Economically, more women gained access to good jobs and the professions, but most remained concentrated in lower-paying, traditionally "female" jobs—secretaries, nurses, waitresses, or cashiers. The graph above shows the percentage of women in various occupations in 1986. Even when they got jobs formerly reserved for men, they faced barriers to promotions and executive positions. Wage differences continued: in 1985 full-time working women still earned only about sixty-four cents for every dollar earned by men.

In early 1992 Gloria Steinem reflected on both the problems and the prospects of the women's movement.

> We are only 25 years into what by all precedent is a century of feminism. But once you get a majority consciousness change, you also get a backlash. It's both an inevitable tribute to success and a danger. The future depends entirely on what each of us does every day. After all, a movement is only people moving.

Thus, despite all challenges, the women's movement continued to flourish. The hard-won victories of the 1960s and 1970s paved the way for future progress.

The Gay and Lesbian Rights Movement

In the progressive climate of the 1960s and 1970s, some homosexual men and women became more open about their sexual orientation and about the discrimination they often encountered. One crucial event was a 1969 riot following a police raid on the Stonewall Inn, a gay bar in New York City, which sparked a new sense of activism. The movement to secure rights and protection for gay men and lesbian women took many forms, from quiet political action to deliberately outrageous behavior. But, even more than the women's movement, it brought an emotional backlash from people who were uncomfortable with the challenge to traditional sexual norms.

The appearance of **acquired immunodeficiency syndrome (AIDS)** in 1981 contributed to the backlash. Caused by a virus that attacks the body's immune system, AIDS as yet has no cure. At first, most of its victims were intravenous drug users and gay men. Some conservatives therefore viewed AIDS as a curse that punished certain people for their habits and lifestyles. By the early 1990s, however, the number of cases in the United States had reached 200,000, and the disease had spread into the larger community. AIDS could no longer be viewed as strictly a gay issue—it was an epidemic, nationally and internationally.

preparing them for college. Of those who went on to higher education, only 7 percent completed their course of study. In many cases, these figures were due to lack of encouragement in school, combined with discrimination in counseling and class assignments.

Native Americans Take Action

On their own, Native Americans made considerable gains in the 1980s and early 1990s. They gave particular attention to increasing their education and to developing their business and legal skills.

Many tribal communities founded their own colleges. In the decade after Congress passed the Tribally Controlled Community College Assistance Act in 1978, twenty tribally controlled colleges received financial support. In the early 1960s, only a few hundred Native Americans in the entire country attended college, but in the 1980s, the number rose to the tens of thousands.

Another approach involved the development of business skills, although many business values and ethics contradict traditional Native American attitudes. Dale Old Horn, department head at Little Big Horn College in Montana, explained the problem of clashing values:

The Crow Indian child is taught that he is part of a harmonious circle of kin relations, clans and nature. The white child is taught that he is the center of the circle. The Crow believe in sharing wealth, and whites believe in accumulating wealth.

Nonetheless, a number of Native American groups started business ventures in an effort to improve their communities' prosperity. Iola Hayden, executive director of Oklahomans for

The AIDS quilt is a personal memorial to Americans who have died of the disease. Friends and family members contribute patches that celebrate the lives of their loved ones. In 1992 the quilt was displayed before the Capitol. It contained 26,000 panels—only one sixth of the total number of Americans who had succumbed to AIDS by that time.

"Time and Place," on pages 816 – 817, contains a full discussion of the AIDS epidemic.

The Movement for Latino Rights

Latinos continued to make political gains in the 1980s and 1990s. **Henry Cisneros** was elected mayor of San Antonio, Texas, while Federico Peña was elected to the same post in Denver, Colorado. In New Mexico, Governor Toney Anaya referred to himself as the nation's highest elected Hispanic American. Nationwide, more and more Latinos won elective office, and more Latino administrators were appointed at all levels of government. In 1988 Lauro Cavazos was named secretary of education, becoming the first Latino to serve in the President's cabinet.

Outside government, the number of Latino college and university faculty members more than doubled in the decade ending in 1980. Appointments to prestigious positions, like that of Manuel T. Pacheco as president of the University of Arizona in 1991, promised to lead to future gains for Latinos.

Yet Latinos also faced continuing problems in the United States. In 1987 only 60 percent of all Latino high school students graduated, and only 31 percent were enrolled in courses

Henry Cisneros was one of many Latinos elected to prominent government positions in the 1980s and 1990s.

Indian Opportunity, described a new willingness to be involved in commercial ventures:

I grew up with the liberal thinking that big business was bad, and we had been treated in such a way that kept us out of the enterprise arena. Now we're beginning to realize that, if we want to be self-sufficient, we're going to have to become entrepreneurs ourselves. It's a painfully slow process because we . . . don't have a generation of entrepreneurs to look back on as an example. We are the generation to develop that.

The Choctaw in Mississippi are an example of one group that made an aggressive effort to develop skills as entrepreneurs. By the middle of the 1980s, they owned all or part of three businesses on their reservation. They employed a thousand people and cut their unemployment rate in half.

Native Americans continued to fight in the courts for their land and their rights. An Office of Economic Opportunity program established in 1968 helped the University of New Mexico Law School start a Native American scholarship program that educated thirty-five to forty Native American lawyers each year. Graduates of this program, along with other attorneys, successfully argued for tribal jurisdiction in cases concerning reservations. Court cases around the country upheld long-ignored treaty rights.

SECTION 3 REVIEW

Key Terms, People, and Places
1. Define AIDS.

Key Concepts
2. How did President Reagan try to curtail some of the civil rights gains of the 1960s and 1970s?
3. By the 1980s, what had the women's movement achieved, and what obstacles did women still face?
4. Who was Henry Cisneros, and why was his career in public office significant?

5. How did Native Americans use economics and the law to promote their interests?

Critical Thinking
6. **Formulating Questions** Imagine that you are preparing a report entitled "How Much Have Women Gained Since the 1960s?" Create a list of questions on which you would base your investigation before writing the report.

The AIDS/HIV Pandemic

With no cure and no vaccine, the only strategy to curb the spread of the deadly disease of AIDS and the HIV virus is through prevention. But what patterns can we detect in the movement of the disease? How can we use that information to prevent the disease from spreading further and to find a cure?

With its enormous impact on our society today, it is hard to imagine that little more than ten years ago, acquired immunodeficiency syndrome (AIDS) was unknown. The first cases of AIDS were reported at the Centers for Disease Control (CDC) in June 1981. During the 1980s, more than 65,000 people died from the disease. As of September 1993, a total of 328,392 AIDS cases had been reported to the CDC, of which 201,775 had died. Globally, reliable statistics are difficult to obtain, but estimated numbers of AIDS cases range from 400,000 to 1 million. With no cure and no vaccine in sight, the number of people with AIDS continues to rise. Moreover, it is no longer an epidemic confined to certain limited populations. AIDS has become a pandemic—a disease that threatens the lives of the entire human population around the world.

AIDS is caused by a virus called HIV (Human Immunodeficiency Virus). HIV is found in the blood and other bodily fluids of infected people, and it is transmitted by sexual intercourse, intravenous drug use, exposure to contaminated blood, or from mother to fetus. So far, the only way to halt further spread of the pandemic is to change the behaviors that transmit the virus.

Education, especially of teenagers, about AIDS and its prevention is critical to controlling the pandemic.

Movement of AIDS and the HIV Virus

The origins and spread of a disease are important in understanding the disease. Thus, examining the geographic theme of movement in relation to AIDS is important in uncovering clues in the search for cures and prevention strategies.

The AIDS pandemic in the United States went through three phases in the 1980s. The years before 1985 represent an initial phase when the occurrence of AIDS was mainly confined to large urban areas and to certain risk groups such as homosexual men and intravenous drug users. San Francisco, New York, the District of Columbia, and Miami were the major epicenters in this early phase. About 2,500 new cases were reported nationally each year during this period.

The second phase, from 1985 to 1987, was characterized by a rapid increase in AIDS cases along with greater public awareness. AIDS incidence increased significantly both in the epicenters themselves and in the counties surrounding these epicenters. About 17,000 new cases were added each year in this period. During the third phase, from 1988 to 1990, the number of new AIDS cases rose to 33,000 each year. More important, the pattern of the pandemic changed. Urban areas in the Midwest and West Virginia began reporting cases. But smaller counties close to big cities experienced the fastest growth in AIDS, most of them in the Midwest, West Virginia, and rural Florida. Additionally, a steady increase in AIDS in the heterosexual population, low-income classes, and ethnic minority groups was reported.

The map on page 817 is a three-dimensional perspective on AIDS incidence rates for the period 1981 to 1990. The geographical pattern is shaped like

Higher peaks indicate
greater incidence of AIDS
cases. Every 1 cm equals 310
cases per 100,000 people.

a horseshoe, with high AIDS rates on the East and West coasts and in the South, forming a ring around the United States on three sides. High concentrations occur in metropolitan areas; the interior section of the country generally has much lower AIDS rates. San Francisco and New York continue to be the dominant epicenters. Chicago and a number of midwestern cities, by contrast, have lower rates than might be expected for urban areas of their size. In 1990 Florida became the third-highest infected state, following New York and California.

Controlling the Pandemic: A Continuing Challenge

The HIV/AIDS pandemic will continue to pose a serious threat to society in the twenty-first century. It is important to remember that the disease is no longer confined to certain groups; the entire population is at risk. More and more cases are found in rural areas and among poor people, ethnic minorities, women, children, and heterosexual people.

Education, especially of teenagers, about AIDS and its prevention is critical to controlling the pandemic.

Scientists are working together to find a vaccine and a cure. Systematic collection of HIV/AIDS data will be crucial in the 1990s. By carefully examining this data and learning about the movement of the disease, we can predict future trends and allocate limited health resources more efficiently.

GEOGRAPHIC CONNECTIONS

1. Where in the United States did the fastest growth in AIDS occur in the late 1980s?
2. How is the disease spread? What geographic patterns has the spread of AIDS followed?

Critical Thinking

3. **Identifying Alternatives** What do you think the government should do to control the pandemic effectively, given the country's limited health resources?

The United States in a New World

SECTION PREVIEW

After more than forty years of the cold war, in the early 1990s the United States watched as communist governments crumbled. The foreign policies of Reagan's first years in office became outdated as the nation faced new possibilities and problems.

Key Concepts
- The collapse of the Soviet Union brought an end to the cold war.
- The United States and Iraq went to war after Iraq invaded its neighbor Kuwait.
- The United States intervened in countries in Latin America and the Caribbean.

Key Terms, People, and Places
Strategic Defense Initiative (SDI), Intermediate-Range Nuclear Forces (INF) Treaty, Persian Gulf War, Iran-contra affair; Mikhail Gorbachev, Boris Yeltsin, Saddam Hussein, Sandinista, contras

American poet Robert Frost once wrote, "Something there is that doesn't love a wall," and the people of East Germany would no doubt agree. This concrete slab came from the dismantling of the hated Berlin Wall in 1989.

I n the 1980s and early 1990s, the world changed dramatically. Ronald Reagan was intent on defending the United States against what he termed an "evil empire"—the Soviet Union. Yet by the end of George Bush's term, the cold war that had dominated international politics for more than forty years was over. American policy makers had to rethink traditional assumptions and learn to operate in what George Bush called a "new world order."

Reagan's Defense Policies

Ronald Reagan took office in 1981 determined to defend United States interests in the cold war. He believed in a tough approach toward the Soviet Union and wanted not only to strengthen conventional military forces but also to increase the supply of nuclear weapons.

The costs of such a buildup were enormous, contributing to the growing budget deficit. Over a five-year period, the administration sought a military budget of $1.5 trillion, an amount far higher than ever before.

In March 1983 Reagan proposed an altogether new program of missile defense. The **Strategic Defense Initiative (SDI)**, popularly called "Star Wars," involved a satellite shield in outer space that would intercept incoming Soviet missiles. It would cost an estimated $30 billion and, according to many scientists, might never work. Still, Reagan remained committed to funding research on the initiative.

While proposing increased spending for defense, the Reagan administration continued arms control discussions. It abandoned SALT II, the arms reduction plan negotiated but never ratified under Jimmy Carter. As new negotiations bogged down, the arms race escalated and military budgets soared.

The Cold War Comes to an End

Surprising events in the Soviet Union changed the direction of American foreign policy. **Mikhail Gorbachev,** who became the new Soviet leader in 1985, made daring reforms in his country. He proposed a program of *perestroika*—restructuring the economy—and *glasnost*—political openness. These new policies paved the way toward better relations with the United States. Summit meetings led to the **Intermediate-Range Nuclear Forces (INF) Treaty** in 1987. Under the INF treaty, 2,500 Soviet and American nuclear missiles in Europe would be destroyed.

Later, talks between Bush and Gorbachev in 1989 and 1990 brought agreements limiting the buildup of both nuclear and chemical weapons. The two leaders signed the Strategic Arms Reduction Treaty (START) in 1991. START dramatically decreased the number of long-range weapons that the superpowers had stockpiled.

Post–Cold War Europe, 1994

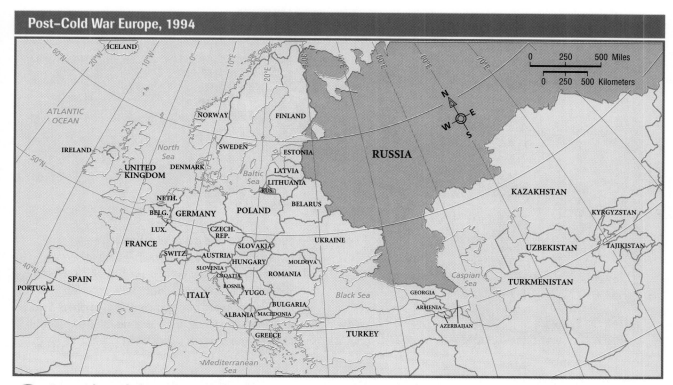

Geography and History: Interpreting Maps
In the late 1980s the Eastern bloc shattered into a jigsaw puzzle of diverse republics. *What kinds of problems do you think might follow the break-up of such a large nation as the Soviet Union?*

Upheaval in Russia The arms control agreements were one indication that the cold war was ending. Changes accelerated within the Soviet Union, where Gorbachev began moves toward democracy, including free elections. He faced opposition on both sides, however—from conservatives in the Soviet government and from those who wanted faster reforms.

Boris Yeltsin had been elected president of Russia, the largest and most heavily populated of the Soviet republics. He now emerged as the new Soviet leader. With a speed that shocked the world, the Soviet Union itself fell apart, as reformers pressed for more gains. The various republics, shown in the map above, proclaimed their autonomy. Most joined Russia in a loose Commonwealth of Independent States (CIS).

Eastern Europe The changes in the Soviet Union echoed throughout Eastern Europe. In November 1989 the Communist party leader in East Germany suddenly announced that people could travel freely to West Germany. As the border guards—who in the past had shot people

trying to leave—stepped aside, East Germans flooded into West Berlin.

The fall of the Berlin Wall was heard all over Eastern Europe. In Poland, Lech Walesa's ten-year-old Solidarity movement finally triumphed over the communist government and assumed power. In Czechoslovakia, the forces of freedom were similarly victorious, and playwright Vaclav Havel became president. New regimes took charge in Bulgaria, Hungary, Romania, and Albania as well.

The transition was not always easy. Czechoslovakia soon broke into two states, the Czech Republic and Slovakia. A brutal civil war broke out in Yugoslavia when the central government collapsed and rival ethnic groups went to war with each other. The map above shows Europe in the aftermath of these changes.

World Trouble Spots

The end of the cold war did not bring peace outside Europe either. Conflict broke out in many places, and terrorism brought unexpected

The Wall: Its Rise and Fall

Begun in 1961, the Berlin Wall was still being reinforced by East German workers—under the watchful eyes of armed border patrols—in 1967 (left). When the border finally opened in 1989, Berliners celebrated with a joyous all-night party (above). *Do you think it would be possible for a barrier such as the Berlin Wall to keep a city permanently divided?*

tragedies. The Middle East remained a place of religious tension and chaos.

Lebanon Some of the problems in the Middle East centered in Lebanon, a country caught up in the hostilities between Israel and the Palestine Liberation Organization (PLO). In 1982 President Reagan sent several thousand marines into Beirut, the capital, as part of a peacekeeping force. Early in 1983, an explosive-filled truck blew up the American embassy in Beirut, killing more than sixty people.

Then, on a Sunday morning in October 1983, another terrorist truck loaded with explosives crashed through the gates of a marine barracks, killing 241 Americans. Many Americans demanded an immediate withdrawal from Lebanon, and by the following February, all the troops left.

The Persian Gulf War In August 1990, **Saddam Hussein,** the dictator of Iraq, invaded neighboring Kuwait, a small nation rich in oil. Now Americans worried that Iraq's action might threaten the flow of oil to the West. They also were shocked by the open aggression.

Bush responded strongly. In an open letter to college students, he declared:

There is much in the modern world that is subject to doubts or questions—washed in shades of gray. But not the brutal aggression of Saddam Hussein against a peaceful, sovereign nation and its people. It's black and white. The facts are clear. The choice unambiguous—right vs. wrong.

Working through the United Nations, the United States mobilized an alliance of twenty-eight nations. When the UN deadline for Iraqi withdrawal passed in mid-January 1991, an international army of half a million troops struck at Iraq in "Operation Desert Storm."

The **Persian Gulf War** was over quickly. Iraqi rockets fell on cities in nearby Saudi Arabia, Israel, and Bahrain, while the UN forces struck back from the air. Despite Hussein's promise of victory, UN forces overwhelmed the Iraqis in just forty-two days. Iraqi casualties numbered in the tens of thousands, while only 240 UN troops were killed. Bush's approval rating in the United States soared to an unprecedented 91 percent.

Though compelled to leave Kuwait, Hussein remained in power. His ruthless armies continued to crush opponents within his own country. Fearful of getting involved in another situation like Vietnam, Bush was unwilling to send in more United States forces. Public opinion also favored bringing American troops home.

MAKING CONNECTIONS

Reread the excerpt from Bush's letter. How does his description of Saddam Hussein echo the cold war speeches of earlier Presidents?

Policy in Latin America

Like earlier administrations, Reagan and Bush often intervened in the internal struggles in neighboring Latin America. The policies of these two Presidents reflected the fear that left-wing or Marxist governments would gain power in the Americas. As a result, the United States, as in the past, sometimes supported repressive dictators as a way of opposing communism.

In El Salvador the United States aided a repressive conservative regime in resisting guerrillas, some of whom were Marxists. In neighboring Nicaragua, the administration tried to undermine the Marxist **Sandinista** government. Working through the CIA, the United States armed and trained guerrilla fighters known as **contras** (from the Spanish for "counterrevolutionaries"). The official reason for this aid was that the contras would stop the flow of weapons from Cuba to the guerrillas in El Salvador.

Congress, however, thought that Reagan also wanted to help the contras overthrow the Sandinistas. In 1982 Congress forbade using federal funds for this purpose, and in 1984 it

voted to stop the CIA or any other agency from giving the contras any military aid.

Some members of the Reagan administration still believed that aid to the contras was justified to prevent communist forces from controlling Latin America. When the contras' war floundered, some members of the National Security Council sent money from the illegal sale of weapons to Iran to the contras.

When this action became public in the fall of 1986, Oliver North, the marine colonel who had made the arrangements, took the blame. Most Americans realized, however, that North was not acting on his own. Investigations of the **Iran-contra affair,** as the incident came to be called, suggested that both President Reagan and Vice President Bush had known more about the plan than they admitted. The Iran-contra scandal brought the most serious criticism faced by the Reagan administration.

Using Historical Evidence
Women soldiers, like the two Americans above, played a significant role in the Persian Gulf War. *How do you think a World War II soldier in the 1940s would have reacted to this photograph?*

SECTION 4 REVIEW

Key Terms, People, and Places

1. Define (a) SDI, (b) INF treaty, (c) Persian Gulf War, (d) Iran-contra affair.
2. Identify (a) Mikhail Gorbachev, (b) Boris Yeltsin, (c) Saddam Hussein, (d) Sandinista, (e) contras.

Key Concepts

3. How did the cold war end?
4. Why did the United States become involved in the Persian Gulf War?

5. Why did the Reagan administration's support for Nicaraguan rebels lead to scandal?

Critical Thinking

6. **Demonstrating Reasoned Judgment** "The cold war could not have lasted long after 1990. If the Soviet economic and political system had not failed when it did, the United States economy would have collapsed under the weight of the soaring defense budget." Explain why you agree or disagree with this statement.

Chapter Review

Key Terms

1. New Right
2. coalition
3. televangelism
4. supply-side economics
5. S & L
6. new federalism
7. acquired immuno-deficiency syndrome (AIDS)
8. Strategic Defense Initiative (SDI)
9. Intermediate-Range Nuclear Forces (INF) Treaty
10. Persian Gulf War
11. Iran-contra affair

People

12. Ronald Reagan
13. George Bush
14. Sandra Day O'Connor
15. Clarence Thomas
16. Henry Cisneros
17. Mikhail Gorbachev
18. Boris Yeltsin
19. Saddam Hussein
20. Sandinista
21. contra

Terms For each term above, write a sentence that explains its relation to the social and political changes that took place during the conservative movement.

Matching Review the key terms in the list above. If you are not sure of a term's meaning, review its definition in the chapter. Then choose a term from the list that best matches each description below.

1. the theory that predicts lower taxes will stimulate the economy by putting more money in the hands of businesses and investors
2. a satellite shield intended to intercept incoming missiles
3. generally small, stable banks that historically made home mortgage loans to individuals
4. the policy of shifting the focus of government from the federal to the state level

True or False Determine whether each statement is true or false. If it is true, write "true." If it is false, change the underlined name to make the statement true.

1. A former actor, <u>George Bush</u> was tremendously popular during his two terms as President.
2. <u>Sandra Day O'Connor's</u> nomination hearings brought a storm of public controversy when charges were filed by a former co-worker.
3. Brutal dictator <u>Henry Cisneros</u> remained in power after the Persian Gulf War.
4. <u>Boris Yeltsin</u> emerged as the new Russian leader after the break-up of the Soviet Union.

Section 1 (pp. 800 – 804)

1. What were the roots of the conservative movement?
2. Describe three goals of the conservative coalition.
3. What techniques did conservatives use to win support for their political agenda?

Section 2 (pp. 805 – 809)

4. Explain President Reagan's theory that prosperity would "trickle down" from the top of the economy.
5. What conservative goals did Reagan and Bush support?
6. How did the policies of Reagan and Bush affect the distribution of wealth in the United States?

Section 3 (pp. 811 – 815)

7. How did conditions for African Americans change under Reagan and Bush?

8. Describe the backlash against the women's movement during the 1980s.
9. Give evidence to show that Latinos continued to make political gains during the 1980s and 1990s.
10. What changes occurred for Native Americans during the Reagan and Bush era?

Section 4 (pp. 818 – 821)

11. What was Reagan's defense policy when he took office in 1980?
12. What events in the Soviet Union and Eastern Europe changed the direction of American foreign policy during the 1980s and early 1990s?
13. What was the outcome of the Persian Gulf War?

1. **Demonstrating Reasoned Judgment** You have read that Ronald Reagan enjoyed a 68 percent approval rating when he left office, despite his many mistakes and misstatements. How do you account for Reagan's popularity?

2. **Making Comparisons** Native Americans experienced some positive changes during the 1980s and early 1990s. From what you have read about the experience of African Americans at the time, do you think that Native Americans were helped in their efforts by the Reagan and Bush administrations?

3. **Predicting Consequences** What opportunities and challenges for the United States do you think were created by the end of the cold war?

4. **Determining Relevance** If Reagan and Bush had attended the Constitutional Convention in 1787, how might they have advised the Framers as to the proper role of the federal government?

1. **Evaluating Primary Sources** Review the primary source excerpt on page 801. What does Reagan assume about the free enterprise system? Are there factors that can hinder an individual's success even if he or she is industrious?

2. **Understanding the Visuals** Reread the Kevin Phillips quotation on pages 808 to 809. How does the Reaganomics doll on page 805 illustrate what Phillips calls "upper America"? How does it illustrate what is on the other side of the prosperity of the 1980s?

3. **Writing About the Chapter** It is 1990. *Time* magazine has asked you to write a retrospective essay about the 1980s, focusing on either the social, political, or economic changes that occurred in the United States during the decade. First, review the chapter and make a list of the points you plan to cover. Next,

write a draft of your essay in which you describe life in the 1980s. Revise your essay, making certain that each idea is clearly explained. Proofread your essay and draft a final copy.

4. **Using the Graphic Organizer** This graphic organizer uses a web map to organize information about Republican policies during the 1980s and early 1990s. In this web, dotted lines are used to show connections between seemingly unconnected ideas. (a) What is the connection between tax reform, increased spending for defense, and cuts in social programs? (b) How do both deregulation and the new federalism demonstrate a similar view of the role of the government? (c) On a separate sheet of paper, create your own web map about the conservative movement using this graphic organizer as an example.

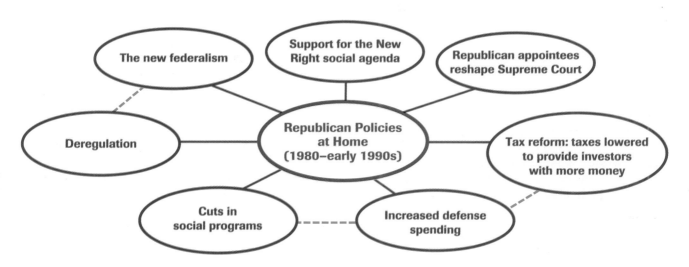

The Promise of Change
1992–Present

*I*n 1993 Democrat Bill Clinton ended twelve years of Republican rule in the White House when he became the forty-second President of the United States. The 1990s would present a unique set of challenges to the new administration. With the end of the cold war abroad and a rapidly changing cultural climate at home, President Clinton and the American people would need to find creative solutions to many complex problems.

Events in the United States

1990 Congress passes the Immigration Act of 1990.

1992 Democrat Bill Clinton defeats Republican George Bush in the presidential election.

| 1989 | 1990 | 1991 | 1992 |

Events in the World

1991 Yugoslavian republics of Slovenia and Croatia declare their independence.
• The Haitian president is overthrown.

1992 The European Community drops many trade barriers between members.
• Boris Yeltsin is elected president of Russia.

Pages 826 – 831
The Clinton Administration

After twelve years of Republican rule, the American public cast a vote for change in 1992. Democrat Bill Clinton promised a plan for universal health care and help for the ailing economy. As President, he made a quick start at tackling these complex and deep-rooted problems.

Pages 832 – 837
The United States and the World in the 1990s

The end of the cold war in the 1990s left the Clinton administration struggling to find its way through uncharted waters in international relations. The collapse of communism and the increase in ethnic tensions in various parts of the world created new problems for the nation.

Pages 838 – 842
American Society in the 1990s

By the 1990s, the face of the United States had changed. With an increase in the number of immigrants and a rise in minority birth rates, a much larger percentage of the population than ever before was African American, Latino, Asian American, or Native American. The United States needed to find new ways to deal with this ethnic and cultural diversity.

1993 President Clinton appoints Ruth Bader Ginsburg to the Supreme Court.
• Congress passes the North American Free Trade Agreement.

1994 President Clinton pushes for reform of the health-care and welfare systems.

1993	1994	1995	1996	1997

1993 Israel and the Palestine Liberation Organization sign a peace treaty.

1994 War continues between Serbia and Bosnia-Herzegovina.
• The Winter Olympics are held in Lillehammer, Norway.

The Clinton Administration

SECTION PREVIEW

After twelve years of Republican rule, the American public cast a vote for change in 1992. Democrat Bill Clinton promised a plan for universal health care and help for the ailing economy. As President, he made a quick start at tackling these complex and deep-rooted problems.

Key Concepts
- Bill Clinton, elected President in 1992, promised to revive the economy and renew the nation's sense of community.
- Hillary Rodham Clinton, the new First Lady, was a trusted adviser to the President and headed a task force to devise a national health insurance plan.
- President Clinton made an effort to appoint members of underrepresented groups to his cabinet and the Supreme Court.

Key Terms, People, and Places
Bill Clinton, Hillary Rodham Clinton, Al Gore

Democratic nominees Bill Clinton and Al Gore went "on the road to change America" in 1992, making a bus tour of the country to win voters' support.

In November 1992, voters faced an unusual choice among three major presidential candidates. The current President had presided over the third term of a Republican era, and he hoped to extend it another four years. His Democratic challenger, the youthful governor of Arkansas, proposed a more active role for the government in solving the nation's economic and social problems. The third candidate, a billionaire businessman, promised to shun traditional party politics and bring common-sense thinking to Washington.

The Election of 1992

The election of 1992 reflected transformations both at home and abroad. As the cold war came to an end, voters wanted the government to address the huge federal deficit and related economic difficulties with the same intensity it had shown in resisting communism since the end of World War II.

On the Republican side, George Bush sought a second term as President. Conservative journalist Patrick Buchanan, who had worked as a speech writer for Richard Nixon and Ronald Reagan, challenged Bush for the Republican nomination. Bush survived that test, but Buchanan's popularity among many voters in the primary campaign persuaded Bush that he had to take a more conservative stance in order to win broad support.

On the Democratic side, **Bill Clinton** was the surprise victor in a crowded field of candidates. During the campaign, he had to overcome a label that some journalists in Arkansas had used to describe his political style: "Slick Willie." The name suggested that Clinton would say whatever he needed to say—regardless of the complete truth—to get what he wanted. His statements to the press about his avoidance of the draft during the Vietnam War seemed evasive, and critics saw Slick Willie at work. Despite such criticisms, Clinton managed to regain his control over the primary elections, and he gave himself a new nickname: the "Comeback Kid."

Clinton reached out to the large population of voters who had been born during the postwar baby boom. A baby boomer himself who had reached maturity during the 1960s, Clinton argued that it was time for a new generation to take over. At the age of forty-six, he provided a stark contrast to the sixty-eight-year-old Bush, who had come of age during World War II.

The third candidate was Ross Perot, a wealthy Texan who had made his fortune in computer data processing. Perot offered to use his business skills to cut the budget, revive the economy, and give the country leadership. He organized a large network of volunteers who collected the necessary signatures from all fifty states to get his name on the ballot.

The campaign was fought largely on television. Presidential and vice-presidential debates gave the candidates formal exposure to the voters. Far more important for molding public opinion, however, were informal appearances on talk shows and interview programs. Ross Perot was a frequent guest on "Larry King Live." Bill Clinton played his saxophone on the "Arsenio Hall Show" and appealed to younger voters with appearances on MTV.

On election day, Clinton won 43 percent of the popular vote, versus 38 percent for Bush and 19 percent for Perot. In the Electoral College, Clinton gained 357 votes, versus 168 votes for Bush and none for Perot. The Democrats kept control of both houses of Congress, with more women and minority members than ever before.

Bill Clinton's Early Years

Bill Clinton was born in the small town of Hope, Arkansas, in 1946. He attended public schools in Arkansas, where he was a hardworking and competitive student. As a high school senior, he participated in Boys State, a summer camp in which students learn about politics. From there, Clinton was elected as one of Arkansas's delegates to Boys Nation. He traveled to Washington, D.C., and met his idol, President John Kennedy. The experience convinced him that he should pursue a career in politics.

Wanting to spend more time in the nation's capital while preparing himself for a political career in Arkansas, Clinton attended Georgetown University in Washington. After earning a bachelor's degree in international government, he spent two years studying at Oxford University in England on a Rhodes scholarship. Then he accepted a scholarship to Yale Law School, where he earned his law degree in 1973.

Clinton won his first political campaign in 1976, when he was elected Arkansas state attorney general. Two years later, at age thirty-two, he became the youngest governor in the United States. One of Clinton's top priorities was education reform. He appointed his wife, **Hillary Rodham Clinton,** to chair an Education Standards Committee of the Arkansas State Board of Education. This committee recommended a

Bill Clinton loved music as much as he loved politics. After meeting President Kennedy at age seventeen, however, he was swayed toward politics. Arkansas newspaper columnist John Brummet has mused, "One can only wonder what might have happened if young Billy . . . had met Elvis Presley instead of JFK that summer." In 1992 Clinton demonstrated on the "Arsenio Hall Show" that his skills on the saxophone were still sharp.

new set of requirements for high school graduation so that students in the state would be better prepared when they left the public school system. Improving Arkansas's schools would remain high on Clinton's agenda throughout his time as governor.

Before his run for the presidency, Clinton had heard political science professor William A. Galston speak about the need for citizens to balance rights and responsibilities. It was not enough for people to wait for government to provide things for them; they had obligations to fulfill as well. When he won the presidency in 1992, Clinton embraced Galston's approach. He spoke about the need for the nation to operate on the basic principle that both individuals and government have responsibility to each other. President Clinton called this philosophy a "New Covenant."

President Kennedy, in his inaugural address, encouraged Americans to "ask not what your country can do for you—ask what you can do for your country." How did Bill Clinton's "New Covenant" reflect Kennedy's influence?

AMERICAN PROFILES

Hillary Rodham Clinton

Clinton was aided immeasurably in his political career by his wife, Hillary Rodham Clinton. She had grown up in Park Ridge, Illinois, a suburban community not far from Chicago. After graduating from high school, she attended Wellesley College, just outside Boston. She majored in political science, developed a reputation for her ability to analyze problems clearly, and in her senior year, served as president of the college government.

Rodham attended law school at Yale University, where she met Bill Clinton. Following graduation, she worked for the Children's Defense Fund in Boston for a few months, and then took a job with the House Judiciary Committee in Washington, which was investigating the possible impeachment of President Nixon during the Watergate affair. When Nixon resigned in 1974, she decided to join Clinton in Arkansas. She taught at the University of Arkansas Law School in Fayetteville and then joined a law firm in Little Rock when Clinton, now her husband, was elected state attorney general.

From 1983 to 1987, Hillary Rodham Clinton chaired the Arkansas Education Standards Committee. For this job, she traveled to each of the state's seventy-five counties, attending public meetings to discuss education reform. She also helped create a program in which the state sent aides into the homes of preschool children whose parents did not have the resources to prepare them for success in school. Many conservatives objected to this program, believing that the state should not interfere in family life.

Hillary Rodham Clinton was often criticized for her outspoken stance. Columnist

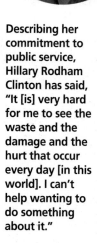

Describing her commitment to public service, Hillary Rodham Clinton has said, "It [is] very hard for me to see the waste and the damage and the hurt that occur every day [in this world]. I can't help wanting to do something about it."

Anna Quindlen noted that, to some observers, "Hillary Clinton was seen as abrasive, power-hungry and unfeminine when to some of us she seemed merely smart, outspoken and hard-working." During the 1992 campaign, she carefully played a more subdued role in order to avoid drawing such criticism. Once Bill Clinton was in office, however, it became clear how much he relied on her judgment and advice.

Hillary Rodham Clinton was more than an informal adviser. Her husband asked her to head the effort to define a new approach to national health care. Drawing on her experience with education reform in Arkansas, she led a task force of five hundred people and traveled throughout the country to speak with all concerned groups. Her work led to the development of the Clinton administration's massive health-care reform package, which she and her husband hoped would extend medical benefits to all American citizens.

Clinton's White House Team

As he assembled his political team, President Clinton vowed that his cabinet appointees would "look like the rest of America." (See the chart on page 829.) In 1993 Clinton chose four women, four African Americans, and two Latinos to be part of his cabinet. He chose Janet Reno as the first woman attorney general. He appointed African Americans Jesse Brown in Veterans Affairs, Ronald Brown in Commerce, and Mike Espy in Agriculture. Henry Cisneros in Housing and Urban Development and Federico Peña in Transportation gave Latinos more representation than ever before.

Clinton's first appointment to the Supreme Court also reflected his commitment to diversity. Ruth Bader Ginsburg became the second woman justice in 1993, joining Sandra Day O'Connor and the seven male justices.

Clinton's First Year in Office

Clinton swept into office on a wave of positive feelings. Maya Angelou, a prominent

African American poet, reflected the optimism in a poem she wrote especially for his inauguration:

H*ere, on the pulse of this*
  new day,
You may have the grace to
  look up and out
And into your sister's eyes
  and into
Your brother's face, your
  country,
And say simply,
Very simply,
With hope,
Good morning.

Clinton was committed to acting quickly. He and his aides wanted to move aggressively at the start, as Franklin Roosevelt had done in 1933, and create enough momentum to continue to the end of his term. "I know I can pass a sweeping package of legislation during the first 100 days of my administration," Clinton had declared before the election. "It will be the most productive period in modern history." Clinton's statement reflected a very optimistic view of what he could achieve as President. Once in office, he found the going a bit tougher and slower than he had imagined.

Economic Initiatives The economy clearly needed help. The recession that had struck near the end of George Bush's term lingered. The massive deficit, meanwhile, was squelching new initiatives, which required increased spending. During the campaign, Clinton's proposed solution was to cut the deficit and stimulate the economy at the same time. Over and over, he spoke of the need to "grow the economy" to get the country moving again. All too soon, however, his economic stimulus package went down to defeat at the hands of Congress.

He was more successful with his first budget, but even this plan just barely squeaked by Congress. Budget cuts, along with tax increases, were necessary to reduce the deficit. Yet neither cuts nor taxes were popular with the public. The

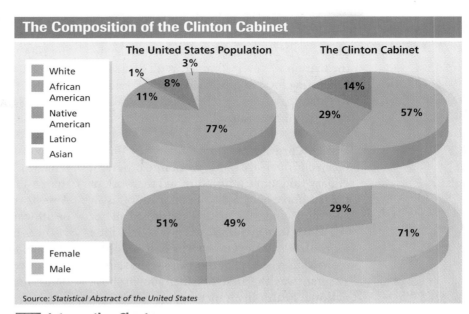

The Composition of the Clinton Cabinet

The United States Population
- White
- African American
- Native American
- Latino
- Asian

3%
1%
8%
11%
77%

The Clinton Cabinet
14%
29%
57%

51% 49%

- Female
- Male

29%
71%

Source: *Statistical Abstract of the United States*

Interpreting Charts
Clinton pledged to appoint a cabinet that "looked like the rest of America." *According to the pie charts, how well did Clinton succeed in this plan—in terms of both ethnicity and gender?*

gas tax that was finally proposed—4.3 cents per gallon—was the result of a difficult compromise and continued to cause some complaints. New income taxes and taxes on social security benefits were met with similar discontent. The tax increases fell most heavily on the wealthiest Americans but still caused irritation among people who had to pay anything more. As they sought to gauge public opinion, legislators in both houses of Congress were reluctant to approve cuts that affected their own constituents.

Bill Clinton asked Maya Angelou to compose an official inaugural poem. She read her poem, "On the Pulse of Morning," at the January 1993 ceremony, as Vice President Al Gore (bottom right) looked on.

The final votes could not have been closer. In the House of Representatives, the budget passed by a 218 to 216 margin. In the Senate, the margin was even slimmer. With fifty senators voting for and fifty against, Vice President **Al Gore,** the presiding officer, had to break the tie to pass the measure.

Health-Care Reform As President Clinton pushed for passage of his economic program, Hillary Rodham Clinton directed the work of the task force on health-care reform. It was an enormous undertaking that consumed all her attention in the administration's first nine months. For years Americans had sought a more comprehensive health-care system. Harry Truman was the first President to propose national health insurance as part of his Fair Deal program at the end of World War II. Like much of his program, however, it failed to gain passage partly because of Republican resistance to extending social welfare goals.

In the 1950s and early 1960s, as other nations experimented with national health programs, the American Medical Association led the opposition to any plan that limited doctors' independence. Meanwhile, health care grew increasingly expensive and was often out of reach of the poorest Americans. Lyndon Johnson finally broke the logjam with the passage of Medicare, for the elderly, and Medicaid, for the poor, in 1965. These efforts helped for a time. But by the 1990s, the system was more expensive and less efficient than ever before. Approximately 37 million Americans lacked even the most limited health-care coverage.

In September 1993, Clinton appeared on national television and spoke on behalf of his administration's new health-care package. He told Congress and the entire country:

T*his health-care system of ours is badly broken, and it is time to fix it. Despite the dedication of literally millions of talented health-care professionals, our health care is too uncertain and too expensive, too bureaucratic and*

Clinton's Health-Care Plan, 1994

Basic Provisions	Types of Care	Costs	Administration	Financing of Reform
• Doctors' services • Preventive care • Ambulance services, hospitalization • Long-term care, home health care, hospice care • Eye and ear care, dental care (children) • Laboratory work • Physical therapy • Prescription drugs • Mental health/substance abuse care • Health education	• Health maintenance organizations (HMOs) offer a variety of services under one roof for a monthly fee • Fee-for-service plans require full payment for each particular service (20% paid by the individual, 80% by the insurer) • "Hybrid," or "blended" plans offer features of both	• Businesses will pay at least 80% of the costs; employees will pay remainder. The federal government will subsidize costs for small businesses. • The self-employed will pay 100%, but that cost will be 100% tax-deductible. • The unemployed will have their costs paid by the government.	• Health alliances, formerly known as "health-insurance purchasing cooperatives," will pool the purchasing power of consumers, defined by region or state, enabling them to purchase insurance at bulk rates. Large businesses may form their own alliances.	• Medicare savings • Medicaid savings • Revenue gains • Sin taxes • Medicare and Medicaid recipients who would join health alliances • Other federal program savings

Interpreting Tables
Hillary Rodham Clinton traveled around the country gathering information, opinions, and ideas for national health-care reform. At right, she meets an elderly woman who would be affected by the reforms. *How would the new plan help unemployed workers?*

too wasteful. It has too much fraud and too much greed. At long last, after decades of false starts, we must make this our most urgent priority: giving every American health security, health care that can never be taken away, health care that is always there.

Clinton stated that all citizens would be covered by the new program, outlined in the table on page 830. Each state would create health alliances to pay health claims. Health plans, consisting of networks of doctors, hospitals, and insurers, would work with the alliances to provide health care.

Many people, including Republican leaders, criticized Clinton's health-care package. Following Clinton's State of the Union Address in January 1994, in which the President vowed to veto any health-care legislation that did not guarantee coverage for all Americans, Senate minority leader Bob Dole appeared on television to respond to the address. Voicing the concerns of many Americans, Dole said that the Clinton plan would "put a mountain of bureaucrats between you and your doctor" and lead to "more cost . . . less choice . . . more taxes . . . less quality . . . more government control." Republicans argued that the administration had not come up with a way to finance the costly plan, which they estimated would create a deficit of at least $918 billion in its first six years. These were serious criticisms, which Clinton would need to address. Still, his proposal had forced serious debate on the future of health care in the United States.

Viewpoints
On Health-Care Reform

In November 1993, as he presented his detailed health-care plan to Congress, President Clinton promised he would sign only a law that "guarantees every single American a comprehensive package of health benefits . . . that can never be taken away." **Compare and contrast the following statements on the subject.**

Against the Clinton Plan
"There is good reason to believe the Clinton plan will dilute health-care delivery in the United States. . . . Based on past performance, neither the federal government nor the insurance industry can be trusted to be solely responsible for America's health coverage. That's why the only solution to the crisis lies in a public-private partnership, one that maintains and enhances a high level of quality health care, that transcends partisan differences and special interests and keeps pace with technological advances and clinical skills. Unfortunately, on this Thanksgiving day that kind of solution lies somewhere between Plymouth Rock and the Congress of the United States."
Benjamin Lipson, insurance agent and editor of The Lipson Letter, a column in the *Boston Globe*, November 25, 1993

For the Clinton Plan
"There are moral, ethical, social, political, and economic reasons why we must ask to take on this [health-care] system, to fix what is broken and to preserve and enhance what does work so well for those of us able to access the system. . . . The status quo is unacceptable and . . . marginal changes are also unacceptable as to what the basic building blocks of health care reform must be. . . . Individuals have to take more responsibility for their own health. And . . . we have to responsibly fund our health-care system."
Hillary Rodham Clinton, address to a forum on health care at the World Trade Center, December 1993

SECTION 1 REVIEW

Key Terms, People, and Places
1. Identify (a) Bill Clinton, (b) Hillary Rodham Clinton, (c) Al Gore.

Key Concepts
2. What part did television have in the 1992 presidential election?
3. What role did Hillary Rodham Clinton have in the new administration?
4. What did President Clinton mean when he pledged to appoint a cabinet that "looked like the rest of America"? How did he fulfill this pledge?
5. What were the two main goals of the Clinton administration at the beginning of his presidency?

Critical Thinking
6. **Determining Relevance** Did Bill Clinton receive a clear mandate from voters in the 1992 election? How might the election results have affected his ability to pass his legislative measures in Congress?

The United States and the World in the 1990s

SECTION PREVIEW

The end of the cold war in the 1990s left the Clinton administration struggling to find its way through uncharted waters in international relations. The collapse of communism and the increase in ethnic tensions in various parts of the world created new problems for the nation.

Key Concepts

- The Clinton administration supported Russian president Boris Yeltsin in his efforts to bring reform to the former Soviet Union.
- Israel and the Palestine Liberation Organization signed a peace agreement in 1993, officially ending nearly fifty years of fighting in the Middle East.
- While South Africa moved toward justice for its African majority population, the United States became involved in civil war in Somalia.
- An agreement signed by Mexico, the United States, and Canada in 1993 promised more open trade between these North American neighbors.

Key Terms, People, and Places

apartheid, sanctions, North American Free Trade Agreement (NAFTA); Slobodan Milosevic, Yitzhak Rabin, Yasir Arafat, Frederik W. de Klerk, Nelson Mandela

In a mission dubbed Operation Restore Hope, the United States helped distribute truckloads of food and other vital supplies in the famine-stricken East African country of Somalia.

I n the 1990s, the United States faced a radically different world. The cold war was now over, but the collapse of communism and the rise of religious, racial, and ethnic tensions around the globe created new problems. The United States struggled to support the efforts of many nations to create more democratic societies. At the same time, American leaders tried to keep the United States on top of a changing world economy.

The United States and the Former Soviet Union

As the Soviet empire crumbled, United States leaders tried to promote the move toward Western-style democracy in the former republics. Boris Yeltsin was elected president of Russia, the largest of the republics. American policy makers quickly voiced their support for his initiatives. The United States, Clinton declared, "supports the historic movement toward democratic political reform in Russia. President Yeltsin is the leader of that process."

Yet Yeltsin faced serious difficulties. The transition to a free market economy, after decades of rigid controls, could not happen overnight. The United States offered a $2.5 billion aid package to help ease the process, but even that was not enough. Goods were still in short supply, and the economy remained unstable. In the fall of 1993, when the Russian parliament resisted reforms that Yeltsin argued were necessary, he dissolved the parliament and called for a new legislature to be chosen in December elections. A group of one hundred legislators resisted Yeltsin's move and continued to meet in the parliament building. Two weeks later, in early October, government tanks stormed the building. More than 150 people were killed in the process, and more than 1,500 people, including the legislators, were placed under arrest. Yeltsin meanwhile strengthened his own authority by increasing censorship and removing his opponents from the government.

The December elections, however, did not provide Yeltsin with the popular mandate he wanted for his reforms. Instead of filling the new parliament with representatives who favored reform, Russians cast nearly 25 percent of their votes for the right-wing party headed by Vladimir Zhirinovsky. Yeltsin's party received less than 15 percent. Voters approved a new constitution granting President Yeltsin wider powers, but Yeltsin would face an uphill battle against antireform leaders.

Zhirinovsky's success in the election was a sign of trouble to many observers around the world. Like the fascist leaders of the 1930s, Zhirinovsky appealed to voters by promising an end to economic hardship and a return to national greatness. He also blamed many of Russia's woes on "foreigners" and Jews. When asked if he would run for president in 1996, when Yeltsin's term expired, Zhirinovsky replied, "Certainly."

The United States and the Former Yugoslavia

The fragmentation of the Soviet Union was felt throughout Eastern Europe. Former satellite nations threw off communist rule. Poland, Czechoslovakia, Bulgaria, Hungary, Romania, and Albania all established new regimes. In Yugoslavia, ethnic hostilities that had been suppressed for years resurfaced when the nation's central government collapsed.

Yugoslavia, shown in the map on page 834, had long been a powder keg. A political spark there had ignited World War I almost eighty years before. After World War II, only a strong communist dictatorship bound together the various republics, composed of different ethnic groups.

During the 1980s, political leaders with strong nationalist feelings rose to power in each of Yugoslavia's republics. **Slobodan Milosevic—** a leader of the largest ethnic group, the Serbs— wanted to preserve the union of Yugoslavia and ensure that Serbs had a powerful voice in governing the country. When the republics of Slovenia and Croatia declared their independence in 1991, many ethnic Serbs living in those regions feared repression by the new governments. Fighting soon broke out among Serbs, Croats, and Muslims. The powder keg had been ignited, and violence quickly spread to the neighboring republic of Bosnia-Herzegovina.

1650   1700   1750   1800   **Links Across Time**   1850   1900   1950   2000

Sarajevo Then and Now

Before the breakup of Yugoslavia, Sarajevo was a bustling modern city (above). With the outbreak of civil war in 1991, however, Sarajevo found itself under siege by Serbian forces. Much of the city was reduced to rubble, including the Bosnian National Library—where an undaunted Sarajevo Orchestra rehearsed in 1993 (left). *What might such destruction mean for the people of a city?*

The Former Yugoslavia, 1994

Boundary of the former Yugoslavia

Portion of Bosnia Herzegovina under Muslim control

Portion of Bosnia Herzegovina under Serbian control

Portion of Bosnia Herzegovina under Croatian control

0   50   100 Miles

0   50   100 Kilometers

Geography and History: Interpreting Maps
This map shows the regions of Bosnia-Herzegovina controlled by various groups in 1994. *How does it demonstrate the problems in many former communist nations after their governments collapsed in the late 1980s and early 1990s?*

When the Muslim and Croatian majority in Bosnia-Herzegovina decided to secede from Serbian-dominated Yugoslavia in 1992, Serbian forces in those regions were ready to resist. Backed by Milosevic and the republic of Serbia, these forces began a siege of the city of Sarajevo. They also embarked on a vicious "ethnic cleansing" campaign to eliminate Croatian and Muslim inhabitants from Serb-controlled areas of Bosnia-Herzegovina. Killing took place on both sides of the conflict, as Croat and Muslim forces mercilessly slaughtered Serbs.

The world watched in horror as the violence in Bosnia-Herzegovina worsened. In the spring of 1993, Clinton pledged to send American troops as part of a peacekeeping force, but when the American public proved reluctant to become involved, he backed off from his

pledge. Meanwhile, negotiators plunged into the complex process of trying to craft a peace treaty that could provide some balance among the warring groups. In March 1994, Croats and Muslims signed a pact that would politically unite their territories in Bosnia-Herzegovina and, it was hoped, encourage Bosnian Serbs to agree to a peaceful settlement.

The United States and the Middle East

More progress in the quest for stability came in the Middle East. The patient diplomacy of the Bush administration had failed to bring the long-sought peace settlement to the region. Then, in September 1993, the world learned that the Palestine Liberation Organization (PLO) and Israel had been engaged in secret negotiations of their own and were almost ready to sign a peace treaty recognizing Israel's right to exist and ending more than fifty years of hostility.

The agreement provided for Palestinian self-rule in the Gaza Strip, between Israel and the Sinai Peninsula, and in the town of Jericho, on the West Bank of the Jordan River. (See the map on page 835.) Israel had seized both regions from the Palestinians in the Six-Day War of 1967 and controlled them ever since. Over the years, violence between Palestinians and Israeli occupying forces had made the regions into virtual war zones. Weary of the constant fighting, PLO and Israeli leaders finally committed themselves to negotiating a workable solution.

Peacemaking was a prickly process, particularly between people who had been enemies for so long. But, as Israeli prime minister **Yitzhak Rabin** observed, "Peace is not made with friends. Peace is made with enemies." As events moved quickly forward, the United States joined the peace process. On September 13, 1993, in a ceremony held on the White House lawn, PLO head **Yasir Arafat** and Yitzhak Rabin shook hands after signing the agreement.

In the months that followed the historic handshake, radical Palestinian groups and some Israelis showed their disapproval of the accord with renewed violence. Arafat's authority was challenged by radicals within the PLO who killed a number of Israelis in terrorist attacks.

In February 1994, a Jewish settler in the West Bank walked into a crowded mosque in the town of Hebron and opened fire on the Palestinians who were kneeling in prayer there. More than forty people were killed and many others wounded, and riots that followed the massacre led to more casualties.

In addition to the problems caused by violence, the accord had left many issues unsettled. Arafat and Rabin argued over who would control border crossings around the new Palestinian territories. Months after the deadline for withdrawal of Israeli troops had passed in December 1993, the future of Israeli-Palestinian relations hung in a highly uncertain balance.

The United States and Africa

Meanwhile, the United States became more involved in Africa. Americans, like people around the world, hailed the effort to overturn **apartheid**—the systematic separation of the races—in South Africa. Throughout the twentieth century, the white minority (which was only 15 percent of the population) had segregated and suppressed the African majority. In the mid-1980s, the United States Congress voted to impose economic **sanctions** to try to topple the repressive regime. Economic sanctions are actions taken by one or more countries against another country to restrict that nation's trade by boycotting, blockading shipping, or other means. The sanctions against South Africa included a rule prohibiting new American investments in the country. In 1990 South African prime minister **Frederik W. de Klerk** recognized that he

Israel, 1994

Final status of West Bank and Gaza Strip to be negotiated within three years of 1993 agreement

1993 agreement between Israel and the Palestine Liberation Organization calls for Israeli military withdrawal from the Gaza Strip and gradual takeover of administration by Palestinians

1993 agreement between Israel and the Palestine Liberation Organization turns Jericho over to Palestinian administration

Land occupied by Israel following the 1967 war

Major Israeli settlements in the West Bank

Geography and History: Interpreting Maps
President Clinton presided over the signing of the 1993 peace accord between Israel's Yitzhak Rabin (above left) and the PLO's Yasir Arafat (above right). *How did the accord affect the West Bank and Gaza Strip?*

could not control the forces of change; he released seventy-one-year-old **Nelson Mandela,** a leader in the struggle to end apartheid, who had spent the last twenty-seven years in jail.

Mandela made a triumphant tour of the United States and the world. His organization, the African National Congress (ANC), spearheaded the negotiations with the ruling white regime to create a smooth transition to a biracial democracy.

Mandela and de Klerk both received the 1993 Nobel Peace Prize, an honor that reflected their common commitment to ending apartheid in South Africa. In 1993 Mandela called for an end to international economic sanctions in South Africa, in recognition of the country's new beginning. But the legacy of apartheid continued to cause serious problems. President de Klerk had called for the country's first multiracial elections to be held in April 1994. The ANC registered to become a political party in February, but more radical white and African groups planned to boycott the elections.

The Freedom Alliance, which included both proapartheid whites and African nationalists, feared the ANC would win the elections and impose a communist dictatorship. The alliance demanded changes in the constitution that would ensure greater independence for regions within South Africa. As the April elections approached, negotiations between the government and the various political groups followed a twisting and uncertain path. Violence continued to flow from conflict between the ANC and African nationalist groups, leading to many deaths.

At the same time, the United States became embroiled in East Africa. Following a severe drought, the nation of Somalia suffered from a terrible famine. After thousands of people had starved to death and many more were in danger of starving, President Bush sent American troops into Somalia as part of a United Nations relief effort. By June 1993, when food and medicine had been successfully distributed to many Somalis, the number of United States troops had dwindled from 28,000 to 5,000.

That June, however, the situation took a turn for the worse. A number of American soldiers were killed or taken hostage. The UN envoy to Somalia offered a reward for the capture of Mohammed Farrah Aidid, the leader believed to be behind the increased violence toward UN troops. As the hunt for Aidid went on, the American public recalled how the United States gradually had been drawn deeper and deeper into the Vietnam War. They demanded withdrawal from Somalia before it was too late. In October 1993, President Clinton increased the number of American troops but vowed that they would all return home by the following April.

MAKING CONNECTIONS

How does the Vietnam War continue to affect United States foreign policy in the 1990s?

The United States in the Western Hemisphere

The 1990s saw a mixture of hope and frustration in the dealings of the United States with its Western Hemisphere neighbors. In

Using Historical Evidence A group of Haitian children stands in front of the shantytown where they live. *What does this photograph tell you about the effects of political instability in Haiti?*

Haiti, located on a Caribbean island 600 miles off the Florida coast, the United States supported exiled president Jean-Bertrand Aristide. This democratically elected president was forced out of power in 1991 by a military coup. The United States helped negotiate a plan for military leaders to step down and allow Aristide to resume control, but then found it impossible to enforce the agreement. Guerrilla hit men terrorized the nation, assassinating officials from the Aristide government and others who opposed military rule. Neither diplomacy nor economic sanctions by the United States seemed to help the situation, and the people of Haiti suffered from vicious terrorism and stifling poverty.

One reflection of the effort to foster cooperation in the Western Hemisphere was the **North American Free Trade Agreement (NAFTA),** which sought to promote free trade between Canada, Mexico, and the United States. The table above shows the provisions of NAFTA. The agreement inspired heated debate in the United States between groups that predicted the different effects NAFTA might have on the economy.

NAFTA was negotiated during the Bush administration, but Clinton had to get it ratified by Congress. He threw his support behind the pact, only to face sustained opposition from labor unions that feared NAFTA might lead to the loss of American jobs. Despite the opposition, the Senate finally approved the NAFTA treaty in November 1993.

The next month, representatives from the United States and 116 other nations agreed to expand the General Agreement on Tariffs and Trade (GATT). Pending approval by Congress and other legislatures, GATT would eliminate a broad range of international tariffs, thus removing long-standing barriers to world trade. The new agreement also would create a new World Trade Organization (WTO), which would enforce GATT rules and settle trade disputes between countries. President Clinton praised GATT, expressing his belief that it would boost the global economy: "No wealthy country in the world today can hope to . . . raise incomes unless there are more customers for its goods and services."

The North American Free Trade Agreement (NAFTA), 1994

The Agreement	The Result	The Controversies
The United States, Canada, and Mexico will remove tariffs and most other mutual trade restrictions over the next 15 years.	The resulting free-trade zone will form a single market similar to, but much larger than, the European Community.	Despite NAFTA's "side agreements" and other provisions, concern remains over its potential effects on the environment and on the United States job market.

Interpreting Tables
President Clinton called NAFTA "more than a trading bloc—it's a building block in our efforts to assert America's global leadership on behalf of American jobs and opportunity." *According to the table, what new trading opportunities does NAFTA provide?*

SECTION 2 REVIEW

Key Terms, People, and Places
1. Define (a) apartheid, (b) sanctions, (c) NAFTA.
2. Identify (a) Slobodan Milosevic, (b) Yitzhak Rabin, (c) Yasir Arafat, (d) Frederik W. de Klerk, (e) Nelson Mandela.

Key Concepts
3. How did the United States respond to the disintegration of the Soviet Union?
4. What role did the United States play in helping to further peace in the Middle East?

5. What changes occurred in South Africa in the first part of the Clinton administration?
6. What was the purpose of the North American Free Trade Agreement?

Critical Thinking
7. **Making Comparisons** Israel and the former Yugoslavia were two regions that experienced ethnic violence in the early 1990s. In what ways were the circumstances of this violence similar and different in these two places?

American Society in the 1990s

SECTION PREVIEW

By the 1990s, the face of the United States had changed. With an increase in the number of immigrants and a rise in minority birth rates, a much larger percentage of the population than ever before was African American, Latino, Asian American, or Native American. The United States needed to find new ways to deal with this ethnic and cultural diversity.

Key Concepts

• In the 1980s and 1990s, more immigrants came to the United States from parts of the world other than Western Europe.
• Several factors combined to change the ethnic and cultural composition of the United States.
• Many Americans supported the attempt to include all groups in the definition of the nation, but others worried that this effort could be taken to extremes.

Key Terms, People, and Places

bilingual education, multiculturalism

Though known as a "nation of immigrants," the United States still had problems dealing with the many people who sought to immigrate in the 1990s. This California road sign warns drivers to be on the lookout for undocumented aliens who might have crossed the border from Mexico.

A s the United States shifted course in both domestic and foreign affairs, the makeup of the nation itself changed. Although the 1990 census revealed that during the 1980s the population had increased from 228 million to about 250 million, the growth rate was one of the lowest in United States history. More important was the changing composition of the population. By the early 1990s, the number of Americans with non-European roots had risen dramatically. This increased ethnic diversity forced the United States to take a fresh look at itself as a nation of immigrants.

New Immigration Patterns and Policies

Immigration patterns changed in the 1980s and 1990s. The Immigration Act of 1965, which was part of Lyndon Johnson's Great Society, altered quotas that favored Western Europeans and allowed the freer acceptance of people from all parts of the world. The Immigration Reform and Control Act of 1986 sought to curb illegal immigration while permitting aliens who had lived in the United States since 1982 to register to become citizens. The Immigration Act of 1990 went even further. This law increased immigration quotas by 40 percent and eased restrictions that had denied entrance to many people in the past.

In the 1980s, 37 percent of all legal immigrants came from Asia and 47 percent came from Mexico, the Caribbean, and Latin America. (See the pie chart on page 839.) The same patterns continued in the 1990s. The so-called Sun Belt, stretching from Florida to California, felt the impact of this immigration most of all. In cities such as Los Angeles, numerous new arrivals—Koreans, Vietnamese, Cambodians, Filipinos, Samoans, Taiwanese—competed for jobs and apartments with Mexicans, African Americans, and Anglos. This was the same kind of competition found among different groups in New York City a century before.

The adjustment was not always easy for the recent immigrants. The new arrivals often strained public services. "We just can't keep up," declared Los Angeles board of education president Jackie Goldberg:

O *ften we get the child without the parent. How do they come? I think most come on a bus, after walking a long time. They come with whatever money their parents can spare and a piece of paper with a name and address. We get kids of 11 or 12 who have never been to school.*

Language posed a particular problem for the nation's schools. The pros and cons of **bilingual education,** in which students are taught in both their native language and English, were hotly debated. Amelia McKenna, director of Los Angeles's bilingual education program, observed, "We have between 84 and 90 languages in our district. Nearly 40 percent of our students—242,000 children—are limited in English."

As native-born Americans struggled with hard times, they became less sympathetic to new immigrants than they had been before. A *Newsweek* cover story in August 1993 noted that while a majority of those polled felt that immigration had been a good thing in the past, a mere 29 percent thought it was good in the present, and 60 percent said that it was harmful to the United States today. A poll in the newspaper *USA Today* that same summer found that 65 percent of the people questioned wanted to see immigration cut back.

Some people felt that immigrants took jobs from working Americans, drained taxpayer dollars, and threatened the stability of American culture. "They bring different values and that's why we have more crime and drug problems," declared Mary Goldsmith, a homemaker from Kentucky who was one of those surveyed by *USA Today*. Once again, as in the past, the United States had to deal with opposition to immigration.

MAKING CONNECTIONS

During what other periods of United States history have Americans disapproved of immigrants moving into their communities? Why did they object to immigration?

Ethnic and Cultural Diversity

In the 1980s and 1990s, as immigration increased and minority birth rates soared, the number of Americans with roots outside Europe rose dramatically. As the chart on page

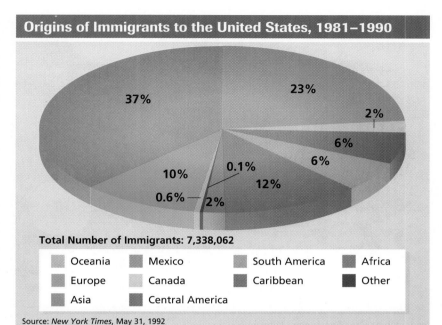

Origins of Immigrants to the United States, 1981–1990

37%   23%   2%   6%   6%   10%   0.1%   12%   0.6%   2%

Total Number of Immigrants: 7,338,062

Oceania   Mexico   South America   Africa
Europe   Canada   Caribbean   Other
Asia   Central America

Source: *New York Times*, May 31, 1992

Interpreting Charts
Which group comprised the largest percentage of immigrants to the United States in the 1980s? What was the second largest group? How would you expect these statistics to affect the overall ethnic composition of the United States over several decades?

842 shows, an all-time high of 23 percent of the population in 1990 was African American, Latino, Asian American, or Native American, up from 20 percent ten years before. Now the nation included 30 million African Americans (11 percent of the population), 22.4 million Latinos (8 percent of the population), 7.3 million Asian Americans (3 percent of the population), and 2 million Native Americans (just under 1 percent of the population). The United States was entering a new age. It was becoming, in the words of writer Ben J. Wattenberg, "the first universal nation."

African Americans continued to make major strides forward. They were increasingly visible in national politics as a result of the elections of 1992. Carol Moseley-Braun of Illinois became the first African American woman ever to serve in the United States Senate. In the House of Representatives, the number of African Americans rose from twenty-six to thirty-nine. In the field of education, Condoleezza Rice became the first African American woman to hold the position of provost, or chief academic officer, at Stanford University in California.

Using Historical Evidence *Whom does the man in the cartoon represent? In what ways has he climbed out of the pit of racial inequality? What new obstacle does he face as he emerges from the first pit? What circumstances in the United States of the 1990s does the cartoon reflect?*

Senator Ben Nighthorse Campbell (below) was elected to represent his home state of Colorado in the election of 1992.

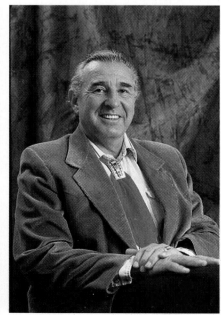

Latinos made similar gains. In Congress, the number of representatives rose from thirteen to nineteen in the election of 1992. This was the largest Latino delegation in United States history. In the past, most Latinos in Congress were Mexican Americans. Now Cubans, Puerto Ricans, and other groups were represented. They were ready to help the nation move in new directions. As Nydia M. Velázquez, a Puerto Rican member of Congress from New York, noted, "Many of the new members were elected on [the promise of] changing business as usual. The message and mandate from voters was clear. We have to change and put partisanship [party politics] aside."

Native Americans, too, became increasingly visible and vocal. Ben Nighthorse Campbell of Colorado became the first Native American in the Senate in more than sixty years

when he assumed his seat in 1993. Outside of Congress, some Native Americans pressed long-standing claims for land that had been taken from them years before. The Oglala Sioux, for example, struggled to regain possession of the Black Hills of South Dakota, and turned down a $300,000 cash settlement offered by the government in an effort to get them to drop their claim. Elsewhere, a number of Native American groups fought to keep the landscape from being despoiled. In 1991 the Hualapais in Arizona defeated plans to build a uranium strip mine near the lip of the Grand Canyon. A growing sense of pride and self-determination among Native Americans made it possible for them to fight such developments, even when some Native Americans viewed industrial growth as the way to overcome poverty and unemployment in their communities.

Women, too, contributed to increasing cultural diversity in the United States. In the 1992 Congress, the Senate included six women and the House forty-eight—both new records. Women who had demanded equal pay for equal work in the past now began to argue that they should receive equal pay for *comparable* work, so that employees in jobs traditionally relegated to women might still earn a fair wage. Legal cases dealing with this question of comparable work began to make their way through the courts.

Gay men and lesbians began to assert their identities and fight for their rights more aggressively in the 1990s. President Clinton, while compromising on a campaign promise to lift the ban on homosexuals in the military, supported homosexual rights and appointed an openly lesbian woman, Roberta Achtenberg, as an assistant secretary of housing and urban development. A few gay and lesbian characters began to appear on television and in movies, demonstrating a gradually increasing tolerance of and sensitivity to homosexuality in the mainstream culture.

In the spring of 1993, one of the largest marches in United States history took place in

Washington, D.C., where hundreds of thousands of Americans gathered to demand homosexual rights. The march was an inspiring experience for many gays and lesbians who were both happy to see the large turnout and astonished at the diversity of people within the homosexual community itself. Some Americans, on the other hand, were shocked by the same realizations, and continued to believe that a homosexual lifestyle was morally wrong.

The increasing diversity in the United States was reflected in still other ways. In the religious realm, many new houses of worship arose. The number of Muslim mosques in the New York area and in other cities around the country rose dramatically. Asian groups brought their own temples and shrines to the United States. Meanwhile, groups with long histories in the United States continued to grow.

In the 1993 march for gay and lesbian rights in Washington, D.C., some gay men and lesbians marched with their parents. Many others turned out to show their support—including Jesse Jackson (near center, holding banner).

Multiculturalism and Education

As various groups within the United States began to develop a greater sense of pride in their individual cultural identities, many people began to criticize the way that American history was written and taught. The perspective of history books and school curriculums, critics charged, was biased toward the cultural heritage of Western Europe while ignoring African American, Latino, Asian American, Native American, and other cultures. The desire to embrace rather than exclude minority cultures led to the concept of **multiculturalism.** "The key to multiculturalism," writes professor of education Jaime S. Wurzel, "is awareness"—awareness that one's own way of thinking is shaped by culture, and awareness that there are other, equally valid cultures in the world. Wurzel defines the goal of a multicultural education as follows:

The multicultural style of thinking and feeling is tolerant of cultural differences, the ambiguities of knowledge, and variations in human perspective. It rejects simple answers and fosters inquiry. The multicultural person questions the arbitrary nature of his or her own culture and accepts the proposition that others who are culturally different can enrich their experience. Thus, to be multicultural is to be aware and able to incorporate and synthesize different systems of cultural knowledge into one's own.

Some advocates of multicultural education took the definition of multiculturalism a step further than awareness and tolerance of other cultures. They insisted that for minority students to develop self-esteem, they needed historical role models from their own ethnic groups. Therefore, textbooks in the United States would need to recognize and celebrate the contributions of people from all groups in the shaping of the nation's history.

Others disapproved of this approach. One historian and former adviser to President

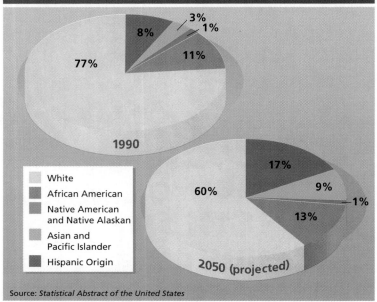

The Changing Ethnic Composition of the United States

1990
- 77%
- 8%
- 3%
- 1%
- 11%

2050 (projected)
- 60%
- 17%
- 9%
- 1%
- 13%

Legend:
- White
- African American
- Native American and Native Alaskan
- Asian and Pacific Islander
- Hispanic Origin

Source: *Statistical Abstract of the United States*

Interpreting Charts

According to the charts, which group in the United States will experience the most dramatic rate of growth between 1990 and 2050? What will happen to the white population as a percent of the total population?

Europe, and King's ideas about nonviolent resistance were shaped by the work of Indian leader Mohandas Gandhi.

Schlesinger and others worried that extreme interpretations of multiculturalism could work to undermine American society by emphasizing the differences between groups rather than the shared values and experiences of all Americans. Peggy Noonan, once a speech writer for President Reagan, declared that immigrants especially needed to be taught "the great unifying myths that define the dreams, characteristics, and special history of America." Schlesinger elaborated on this point:

> *Our task is to combine due appreciation of the splendid diversity of the nation with due emphasis on the great unifying Western ideas of individual freedom, political democracy, and human rights. These are the ideas that define the American nationality—and that today empower people of all continents, races, and creeds.*

Kennedy, Arthur M. Schlesinger, Jr., criticized what he called "ethnic cheerleading"—using history to make people feel good about themselves rather than to discover the truth about the past. In his book *The Disuniting of America,* Schlesinger pointed out that many great leaders had found inspiration in the lives and writings of people from other ethnic groups. Martin Luther King, Jr., for example, was named after the sixteenth-century monk Martin Luther, who sparked the Protestant Reformation in

The debate over multiculturalism was but a new wrinkle in the uniquely American question of how to create a unified society from a nation of diverse immigrants. As author Michael Dorris noted, "Our dynamic American landscape of fabulously interwoven ethnicities has struggled for generations to devise a workable definition of itself." The motto of the United States declared the nation's ongoing commitment to achieve that goal: *E pluribus unum—*"Out of many, one."

SECTION 3 REVIEW

Key Terms, People, and Places
1. Define (a) bilingual education, (b) multiculturalism.

Key Concepts
2. What changes occurred in immigration in the 1980s and 1990s?
3. How did the ethnic composition of the United States change in the 1980s and early 1990s?

Critical Thinking
4. **Predicting Consequences** The movement toward multiculturalism is an attempt to allow all groups to have a voice in American history and policy making. How might the movement actually have the opposite effect on some groups, for example by making it difficult or uncomfortable for some people to speak up?

Predicting Consequences

Many social scientists, especially those who work for the government, try to look into the future. They study what has happened in the past, and on the basis of that, they try to predict what might happen next.

Every ten years the government takes a census of the national population. Social scientists study the evidence from the census to see what they can predict from it. For example, what has been the rate of population growth over the past decades? What does this suggest about the rate of population growth we might expect in the next few years? Which groups are likely to grow faster and which slower?

The table at right focuses on census information on the changing number of families in three ethnic groups in the United States and family income in those groups over a fifteen-year period. Use the following steps to analyze the information in the table and draw on your understanding of history to predict possible trends in the 1990s and beyond.

1. Identify the kinds of information in the table. (a) What does this table tell you about the number of families in various ethnic groups in the United States? (b) By what percentage did the number of Latino families increase between 1975 and 1980? (c) The median income for a given group represents the center of the income distribution—in each group, exactly half of the families earn more

and half earn less than the median income. What does it mean if one group has a lower median income than another group?

2. Analyze the rate of change. (a) Which group of families is growing at the fastest rate? (b) Which group's median income has grown at the fastest rate? (c) Which group or groups seem the most economically vulnerable—that is, which have the least stable median incomes?

3. Use your knowledge of history to predict the consequences that your findings might have in the future. You have read in the chapter that the Immigration Act of

1965 allowed more people from places other than Western Europe to immigrate to the United States, and that the Immigration Act of 1990 further increased immigration quotas by 40 percent. (a) How might the table illustrate the consequences of the 1965 law? (b) What consequences might the 1990 law have by the year 2000? (c) If there were an economic recession or boom in the late 1990s, which group or groups might reflect such changes in their median incomes? How do you think the median incomes in the three groups might be affected in these scenarios? (d) What changes in the trends shown on the table would have to take place in order to alter your predictions?

Change in Number of Families and Median Income,* by Selected Ethnic Groups, 1975–1990

	Year	Number of Families (in thousands)	Percent Change (over past 5 years)	Median Income (dollars)	Percent Change (over past 5 years)
White Families	1975	49,873	—	34,662	—
	1980	52,710	+5.7	34,743	+0.2
	1985	54,991	+4.3	35,410	+1.9
	1990	56,803	+3.3	36,915	+4.3
African American Families	1975	5,586	—	21,327	—
	1980	6,317	+13.1	20,103	−5.7
	1985	6,921	+9.6	20,390	+1.4
	1990	7,471	+7.9	21,423	+5.1
Latino Families	1975	2,449	—	23,303	—
	1980	3,235	+29.5	23,342	+0.6
	1985	4,206	+30.0	23,112	−1.0
	1990	4,981	+18.4	23,431	+1.4

* In 1990 dollars
Source: *Statistical Abstract of the United States*

Chapter Review

Understanding Key Terms, People, and Places

Key Terms
1. apartheid
2. sanctions
3. North American Free Trade Agreement (NAFTA)
4. bilingual education

5. multiculturalism

People
6. Bill Clinton
7. Hillary Rodham Clinton
8. Al Gore
9. Slobodan Milosevic

10. Yitzak Rabin
11. Yasir Arafat
12. Frederik W. de Klerk
13. Nelson Mandela

Terms For each term above, write a sentence that explains its relation to the Clinton administration, American society in the 1990s, or the relationship of the United States to the rest of the world during the 1990s.

Matching Review the key terms in the list above. If you are not sure of a term's meaning, review its definition in the chapter. Then choose a term from the list that best matches each description below.
1. a systematic separation of the races
2. the treaty promoting free trade between Canada, Mexico, and the United States

True or False Determine whether each statement is true or false. If it is true, write "true." If it is false, change the underlined name to make the statement true.
1. Serbian leader <u>Yitzak Rabin</u> wanted to preserve the union of Yugoslavia.
2. Weary of constant fighting, PLO leader Yasir Arafat and Israeli prime minister <u>Nelson Mandela</u> committed themselves to negotiating peace in the Middle East.
3. <u>Al Gore</u> led the effort to define a new American health-care system.

Reviewing Main Ideas

Section 1 (pp. 826 – 831)
1. What issues did American voters want the federal government to address in 1992?
2. What public perception did Bill Clinton have to overcome in his race for the presidency?
3. What does the profile of Hillary Rodham Clinton reveal about her interests and abilities?
4. How did President Clinton's first appointment to the Supreme Court reflect his commitment to diversity?
5. What were President Clinton's objectives in reforming the health-care system?

Section 2 (pp. 832 – 837)
6. What challenges faced Boris Yeltsin in 1993?
7. Why were many people around the world concerned by the number of votes won by Zhirinovsky in elections held in Russia in 1993?
8. What caused fighting to break out in Yugoslavia in 1991?

9. What progress did Israel and the Palestinian Liberation Organization make toward peace in the early 1990s? What forces impeded this progress?
10. Explain why the United States became involved in the civil war in Somalia. What was the reaction of the American public to this involvement?
11. What arguments were made in favor of and in opposition to NAFTA?

Section 3 (pp. 838 – 842)
12. How was the Sun Belt affected by immigration during the 1980s and 1990s?
13. Describe the Immigration Act of 1990 and tell how it differed from the Immigration Reform and Control Act of 1986.
14. What factors led to change in the ethnic and cultural composition of the United States?
15. How have Americans responded to multiculturalism?

1. **Identifying Assumptions** Columnist Anna Quindlen commented that to some observers Hillary Rodham Clinton was seen as "abrasive, power-hungry and unfeminine" while to others she seemed "smart, outspoken and hard-working." How do you account for these opposing points of view?
2. **Identifying Central Issues** If President Clinton appointed you to head a task force to make recom- mendations about health-care reform, what steps would you take in order to investigate the issue?
3. **Determining Relevance** What changes, if any, have occurred in the ethnic and cultural composi- tion of your community in recent years? What factors might account for these changes? If your community has not experienced change, how do you explain the lack of change?

1. **Evaluating Primary Sources** Review the primary source excerpt on page 829. Why was the poem appropriate for Bill Clinton's inauguration? For what other twentieth-century President might this poem have been appropriate?
2. **Understanding the Visuals** Look at the pie charts on pages 839 and 842. How is the information in the two charts related? Explain how you might use one of the charts to predict the information shown in the other one.
3. **Writing About the Chapter** Write a television script entitled "The First Years of the Clinton Presi- dency in Review." First, create a list of what you see as the accomplishments of Clinton's presidency. Then make a list of the challenges that still remain and the ways in which the President might be able to meet them. Next write a draft of your script in which you explain your ideas and note what kinds of images—such as photographs or television news footage—could be used to illustrate your points. Revise your script, making certain that each idea is clearly explained. Proofread your script and draft a final copy.
4. **Using the Graphic Organizer** This graphic orga- nizer uses a web map to organize international events during the early years of the Clinton adminis- tration. (a) Which events show a trend toward peace and global unity? (b) Which regions present chal- lenges during the 1990s? (c) On a separate sheet of paper, create your own web map about American society in the 1990s using this graphic organizer as an example.

THE INFORMATION AGE

Ever since people began recording and exchanging information, they've asked four practical questions: What is the best way to store the information? How much information can be put in a space of a certain size? How can later users of the information retrieve it? How can the information be sent to people in other places? You hold one of the best and earliest answers to these questions in your hands—a book. Starting in the last century, people began to develop new forms of communication—the telegraph, the telephone, and the radio. In the last few decades, many more ways to store, retrieve, and transmit information have created an information explosion. *How does each object shown here help send or process information?*

▲ WATERGATE BUGS The burglars who broke into the Democratic National Committee headquarters carried these "bugs." The ability to listen in on private conversations and invade privacy is an unwelcome by-product of the information age.

▼ COMMUNICATIONS SATELLITE Telstar was the world's first communications satellite, relaying signals from one part of earth to another. On the day it was launched, July 10, 1962, it transmitted the first live television pictures from the United States to Europe.

◄ FIBER–OPTIC CABLE Hair-thin glass fibers can carry sound and data long distances using coded light pulses. Cables made of these optical fibers are lighter, cost less to use, and can carry much more information than metal cables.

▶ COMPUTER PIONEER
Grace Murray Hopper stands next to the UNIVAC, one of the earliest computers. Hopper pioneered the compiler—the link between a computer's circuits and the computer program. Her work also served as a foundation for COBOL, the most widely used computer language for business applications.

▲ LASER HEAD Theodore Maiman developed this early laser in 1960. Laser light can carry more information than radio waves. Laser light is used to decode information stored on CD-ROM and compact audio disks.

◀ HAND-HELD COMPUTER
The ability of a single silicon chip to store and process information has shrunk the size of the computer. A person can carry this computer anywhere and operate it at any time with a small stylus.

▶ SILICON CHIP
The miracle of the information age is this chip of impure silicon—a microprocessor. Computers with silicon chips are more complex, faster, and can handle many times more information than the original roomsize computers that used vacuum tubes and transistors.

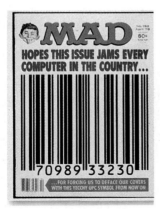

▲ BAR CODES *Mad Magazine* makes fun of bar codes—lines of varying thickness carrying information that can be read by laser light.

▶ EARLY COMPUTER
The very first computers had no keyboards to enter information, no screens to view what was entered, and no storage devices. The Osborne, shown here, was a personal computer that offered the user all these improvements.

A Nation Looks Ahead

In the 1990s, the United States is struggling with issues that have colored its history for hundreds of years. The campaign to deal with the budget deficit and revive the economy is part of an ongoing effort to promote national prosperity. The crusade to accommodate cultural diversity is the result of discussions in the past about how to integrate millions of immigrants into American society. The battle to better the lives of citizens who still face discrimination is rooted in the reform movements that have gradually extended the American dream.

On the foreign front, the need to adjust to an ever-changing world is likewise anchored in the past. The debate about how best to deal with the collapse of communism is related to discussions about the role of the United States in foreign affairs that began in the early days of the republic. These discussions and the decisions that follow from them will expand the scope of United States interests across the North American continent and then well beyond American shores.

As the nation heads toward the twenty-first century, it is trying to revive its sense of purpose. Many citizens are seeking to recover the sense of community that has sustained the United States at key points in the past. They hope that the fundamental values Americans hold in common will bring the nation together to work for a better future. But serious differences of opinion on many issues make consensus hard to come by. The United States, like other nations, has long grappled with the question of how best to deal with conflict over public policy. Sometimes disputes degenerate into violence. More often they are resolved in heated debates in Congress and other arenas where all competing groups can have their say.

In the 1990s Americans sometimes find themselves pitted against one another as they try to decide how to reform the health-care system; under what circumstances—if any—to permit abortion; and what to do about preserving the natural environment. The tone of debate often is shrill, but the discussion itself is a testament to the power of democracy as a means of settling disputes.

Despite the enduring value of democracy as a political foundation, the nation faces tough times as it looks ahead. The economy remains sluggish. Families sometimes cease hoping they can get ahead and resign themselves to trying not to fall behind. Children wonder whether they will be able to do as well as their parents did when they set off on their own.

Still, Americans in the 1990s look ahead with a sense of hope. In spite of its many problems, the United States has tremendous assets to use in confronting the challenges of the modern world. First among these assets are the American people themselves, who have proven themselves capable not only of economic miracles but also of acts of inspiring generosity. Both abilities will be needed as the world enters the twenty-first century.

The challenges that face the country in the 1990s seem both familiar and strange as we head into the future from our vantage point of knowing the past. And we know that, like the immigrants to Ellis or Angel islands in the late 1800s and early 1900s, like the ordinary citizens who struggled through the Great Depression, like the Native Americans rebuilding their communities in the late twentieth century, and like the politicians debating whether to send the country to war in 1990, our paths will be full of decisions and unexpected turns. As we choose our way among the paths of the present, we, too, are shaping the nation's future.

From Sea to Shining Sea by Jacqueline Paton, Merrimack, New Hampshire.

Reference Section

The Declaration of Independence

In Congress, July 4, 1776

THE UNANIMOUS DECLARATION OF THE THIRTEEN UNITED STATES OF AMERICA,

When in the Course of human events, it becomes necessary for one people to dissolve the political bands which have connected them with another, and to assume among the Powers of the earth, the separate and equal station to which the Laws of Nature and of Nature's God entitle them, a decent respect to the opinions of mankind requires that they should declare the causes which impel them to the separation.

We hold these truths to be self-evident, that all men are created equal, that they are endowed by their Creator with certain unalienable Rights, that among these are Life, Liberty and the pursuit of Happiness. That to secure these rights, Governments are instituted among Men, deriving their just powers from the consent of the governed, That whenever any Form of Government becomes destructive of these ends, it is the Right of the People to alter or to abolish it, and to institute new Government, laying its foundation on such principles and organizing its powers in such form, as to them shall seem most likely to effect their Safety and Happiness. Prudence, indeed, will dictate that Governments long established should not be changed for light and transient causes; and accordingly all experience hath shown, that mankind are more disposed to suffer, while evils are sufferable, than to right themselves by abolishing the forms to which they are accustomed. But when a long train of abuses and usurpations, pursuing invariably the same Object evinces a design to reduce them under absolute Despotism, it is their right, it is their duty, to throw off such Government, and to provide new Guards for their future security.—Such has been the patient sufferance of these Colonies; and such is now the necessity which constrains them to alter their former Systems of Government. The history of the present King of Great Britain is a history of repeated injuries and usurpations, all having in direct object the establishment of an absolute Tyranny over these States. To prove this, let Facts be submitted to a candid world.

He has refused his Assent to Laws, the most wholesome and necessary for the public good.

He has forbidden his Governors to pass Laws of immediate and pressing importance, unless suspended in their operation till his Assent should be obtained; and when so suspended, he has utterly neglected to attend to them.

He has refused to pass other Laws for the accommodation of large districts of people, unless those people would relinquish the right of Representation in the Legislature, a right inestimable to them and formidable to tyrants only.

He has called together legislative bodies at places unusual, uncomfortable, and distant from the depository of their Public Records, for the sole purpose of fatiguing them into compliance with his measures.

He has dissolved Representative Houses repeatedly, for opposing with manly firmness his invasions on the rights of the people.

He has refused for a long time, after such dissolutions, to cause others to be elected; whereby the Legislative powers, incapable of Annihilation, have returned to the People at large for their exercise; the State remaining in the mean time exposed to all the dangers of invasions from without, and convulsions within.

He has endeavored to prevent the population of these States; for that purpose obstructing the Laws for Naturalization of Foreigners; refusing to pass others to encourage their migration hither, and raising the conditions of new Appropriations of Lands.

He has obstructed the Administration of Justice, by refusing his Assent to Laws for establishing Judiciary powers.

He has made Judges dependent on his Will alone for the tenure of their offices, and the amount and payment of their salaries.

He has erected a multitude of New Offices, and sent hither swarms of Officers to harass our people and eat out their substance.

He has kept among us in time of peace, Standing Armies, without the Consent of our legislature.

He has affected to render the Military independent of and superior to the Civil power.

He has combined with others to subject us to a jurisdiction foreign to our constitutions, and unacknowledged by our laws; giving his Assent to their Acts of pretended Legislation:

For Quartering large bodies of armed troops among us:

For protecting them, by a mock Trial, from Punishment for any Murders which they should commit on the Inhabitants of these States:

For cutting off our Trade with all parts of the world:

For imposing taxes on us without our Consent:

For depriving us in many cases, of the benefits of Trial by Jury:

For transporting us beyond Seas to be tried for pretended offenses:

For abolishing the free System of English Laws in a neighbouring Province, establishing therein an Arbitrary government, and enlarging its Boundaries so as to render it at once an example and fit instrument for introducing the same absolute rule into these Colonies:

For taking away our Charters, abolishing our most valuable Laws, and altering fundamentally the Forms of our Governments;

For suspending our own Legislature, and declaring themselves invested with Power to legislate for us in all cases whatsoever.

He has abdicated Government here, by declaring us out of his Protection, and waging War against us.

He has plundered our seas, ravaged our Coasts, burned our towns, and destroyed the lives of our people.

He is at this time transporting large armies of foreign mercenaries to compleat the works of death, desolation and tyranny, already begun with circumstances of Cruelty and perfidy scarcely paralleled in the most barbarous ages, and totally unworthy the Head of a civilized nation.

He has constrained our fellow Citizens taken Captive on the high Seas to bear Arms against their Country, to become the executioners of their friends and Brethren, or to fall themselves by their Hands.

He has excited domestic insurrections amongst us, and has endeavored to bring on the inhabitants of our frontiers the merciless Indian Savages, whose known rule of warfare, is an undistinguished destruction of all ages, sexes, and conditions.

In every stage of these Oppressions We have Petitioned for Redress in the most humble terms. Our repeated Petitions have been answered only by repeated injury. A Prince, whose character is thus marked by every act which may define a Tyrant, is unfit to be the ruler of a free People.

Nor have We been wanting in attentions to our British brethren. We have warned them from time to time of attempts by their legislature to extend an unwarrantable jurisdiction over us. We have reminded them of the circumstances of our emigration and settlement here. We have appealed to their native justice and magnanimity, and we have conjured them by the ties of our common kindred to disavow these usurpations, which, would inevitably interrupt our connections and correspondence. They too have been deaf to the voice of justice and of consanguinity. We must, therefore, acquiesce in the necessity, which denounces our Separation, and hold them, as we hold the rest of mankind, Enemies in War, in Peace Friends.

We, therefore, the Representatives of the united States of America, in General Congress, Assembled, appealing to the Supreme Judge of the world for the rectitude of our intentions, do, in the Name, and by the Authority of the good People of these Colonies, solemnly publish and declare, That these United Colonies are, and of Right ought to be Free and Independent States; that they are Absolved from all Allegiance to the British Crown, and that all political connection between them and the State of Great Britain, is and ought to be totally dissolved, and that as Free and Independent States, they have full Power to levy War, conclude Peace, contract Alliances, establish Commerce, and to do all other Acts and Things which Independent States may of right do. And for the support of this Declaration, with a firm reliance on the protection of Divine Providence, we mutually pledge to each other our Lives, our Fortunes and our sacred Honor.

JOHN HANCOCK
President of the Continental Congress 1775–1777

NEW HAMPSHIRE
  Josiah Bartlett
  William Whipple
  Matthew Thornton
MASSACHUSETTS BAY
  Samuel Adams
  John Adams
  Robert Treat Paine
  Elbridge Gerry
RHODE ISLAND
  Stephan Hopkins
  William Ellery
CONNECTICUT
  Roger Sherman
  Samuel Huntington
  William Williams
  Oliver Wolcott
NEW YORK
  William Floyd
  Philip Livingston
  Francis Lewis
  Lewis Morris

NEW JERSEY
  Richard Stockton
  John Witherspoon
  Francis Hopkinson
  John Hart
  Abraham Clark
DELAWARE
  Caesar Rodney
  George Read
  Thomas McKean
MARYLAND
  Samuel Chase
  William Paca
  Thomas Stone
  Charles Carroll
  of Carrollton

VIRGINIA
  George Wythe
  Richard Henry Lee
  Thomas Jefferson
  Benjamin Harrison
  Thomas Nelson, Jr.
  Francis Lightfoot Lee
  Carter Braxton
PENNSYLVANIA
  Robert Morris
  Benjamin Rush
  Benjamin Franklin
  John Morton
  George Clymer
  James Smith
  George Taylor
  James Wilson
  George Ross

NORTH CAROLINA
  William Hooper
  Joseph Hewes
  John Penn
SOUTH CAROLINA
  Edward Rutledge
  Thomas Heyward, Jr.
  Thomas Lynch, Jr.
  Arthur Middleton
GEORGIA
  Button Gwinnett
  Lyman Hall
  George Walton

Source: Documents of American History, Volume I

The Constitution of the United States of America

PREAMBLE

We the people of the United States, in order to form a more perfect union, establish justice, insure domestic tranquility, provide for the common defense, promote the general welfare, and secure the blessings of liberty to ourselves and our posterity, do ordain and establish this Constitution for the United States of America.

The Preamble, or opening paragraph of the Constitution, establishes the fundamental assumption of American government: that government derives its power from the people. "We the people" are the most important words in the Constitution, as President Abraham Lincoln emphasized in 1863 when he called the United States a "government of the people, by the people, and for the people" in his Gettysburg Address. Presidents and other politicians today regularly invoke "the people" as the source of their power when making important speeches.

The Preamble also states, however, that the purpose of the Constitution is to create an orderly, stable, and just society. The authors of the Constitution were worried about the impact of too much democracy in the new American nation, fearing that what "We the people" wanted would not always lead to "a more perfect union" or insure "domestic tranquility." In fact, the tension between the desire for democracy and the wish for a stable social order is one of the most important and enduring themes in American history.

Article I
LEGISLATIVE BRANCH
Section 1 *Legislative Powers; The Congress*

All legislative powers herein granted shall be vested in a Congress of the United States, which shall consist of a Senate and House of Representatives.

SECTION 1 The Constitution outlines the legislative branch first, for this part of the federal government is the closest and most directly responsible to the people. The men who wrote the Constitution deliberately established a bicameral, or two-part, legislative branch, whose two houses would not only balance each other but also modify the impact of "the people." All legislation requires the approval of both the House of Representatives and the Senate.

Section 2 *House of Representatives*

1. Election of Members The House of Representatives shall be composed of members chosen every second year by the people of the several states, and the electors in each state shall have the qualifications requisite for electors of the most numerous branch of the state legislature.

CLAUSE 1 The Founding Fathers wanted the House of Representatives to be the part of the federal government most responsive to the will of the people. They made sure that voters could change the membership of the House frequently by requiring every member to run for office every two years. Today, the House is

After months of debate and differing opinions over the form of the new government, delegates signed the Constitution on September 17, 1787.

the only part of the federal government the people could change in one election; if the people wished, they could replace all 435 members of the House every two years.

2. Qualifications No person shall be a representative who shall not have attained to the age of twenty-five years, and been seven years a citizen of the United States, and who shall not, when elected, be an inhabitant of that state in which he shall be chosen.

CLAUSE 2 The purpose of these requirements was to make certain that representatives actually live among the people whom they represent. The authors of the Constitution wanted to avoid absentee legislators—representatives who did not actually live in their districts—something that happened frequently in the British Parliament. They wanted to ensure direct contact between the people and their representatives.

3. Apportionment Representatives and direct taxes* shall be apportioned among the several states which may be included within this Union, according to their respective numbers, which shall be determined by adding to the whole number of free persons, including those bound to service for a term of years and excluding Indians not taxed, three fifths of all other persons. The actual enumeration shall be made within three years after the first meeting of the Congress of the United States, and within every subsequent term of ten years, in such manner as they shall by law direct. The number of representatives shall not exceed one for every thirty thousand, but each state shall have at least one representative; and until such enumeration shall be made, the state of New Hampshire shall be entitled to choose three, Massachusetts eight, Rhode Island and Providence Plantations one, Connecticut five, New York six, New Jersey four, Pennsylvania eight, Delaware one, Maryland six, Virginia ten, North Carolina five, South Carolina five, and Georgia three.

CLAUSE 3 As a result of this provision, the United States government must conduct a census of the population every ten years. The primary purpose of the census is to determine how many members of Congress each state will have. The decision to count only three fifths of the total number of enslaved persons was a compromise between southerners, who wanted the total number to be counted in order to have more members in Congress, and northerners, who wanted southerners to have fewer representatives and consequently

---

* The black lines indicate portions of the Constitution altered by subsequent amendments to the document or that no longer apply.

Note: Spelling and capitalization have been modernized.

Source: Documents of American History, Volume I

Both the Senate and the House of Representatives are housed in the Capitol building in Washington, D.C. The building's impressive dome dominates the city's skyline.

less influence in the legislature. This clause became controversial in the 1800s when abolitionists and slaveholders began to argue about whether the Constitution sanctioned slavery. Notice that the language is very vague. The word *slaves* does not appear, just "other persons." The Thirteenth Amendment effectively repealed this clause when it made slavery illegal in 1865 following the Civil War.

4. Filling Vacancies When vacancies happen in the representation from any state, the executive authority thereof shall issue writs of election to fill such vacancies.

CLAUSE 4 This clause allows the governor of each state to call special elections to replace members of Congress who die or resign in the middle of their terms.

5. Officers; Impeachment The House of Representatives shall choose their speaker and other officers; and shall have the sole power of impeachment.

CLAUSE 5 Both the British Parliament and the colonial legislatures had fought long and hard to obtain the right to control their own affairs, meaning that the members rather than a king or president would choose their officers. Imagine how much more power the President of the United States would have in Congress if he or she could simply appoint the Speaker of the House and other officials. Another cherished right was the power to impeach, or accuse, government officials of committing crimes or abusing their offices. Impeachment proceedings against a federal official or judge must always begin in the House.

Section 3 *Senate*

1. Composition; Term The Senate of the United States shall be composed of two senators from each state chosen by the legislature thereof, for six years; and each senator shall have one vote.

CLAUSE 1 By giving each state two senators, the authors of the Constitution sought to prevent large states with bigger populations from dominating smaller states. To make the Senate less directly responsive to the people's wishes, senators were to have six-year terms and be chosen by state legislators. The people did not directly elect senators until the Seventeenth Amendment was ratified in 1913.

2. Classification; Filling Vacancies Immediately after they shall be assembled in consequence of the first election, they shall be divided as equally as may be into three classes. The seats of the senators of the first class shall be vacated at the expiration of the second year, of the second class at the expiration of the fourth year, and of the third class at the expiration of the sixth year, so that one third may be chosen every second year; and if vacancies happen by resignation, or otherwise, during the recess of the legislature of any State, the executive thereof may make temporary appointments until the next meeting of the legislature, which shall then fill such vacancies.

CLAUSE 2 This clause ensures that the membership of the Senate, unlike that of the House, cannot be changed in one election. In the Senate, terms are staggered, so it would take three elections and six years to replace all 100 senators. Longer terms tend to make the Senate a more independent body than the House; its members are a little more likely to vote the way they wish rather than the way they think people might want them to vote.

3. Qualifications No person shall be a senator who shall not have attained to the age of thirty years, and been nine years a citizen of the United States, and who shall not, when elected, be an inhabitant of that state for which he shall be chosen.

CLAUSE 3 This clause is meant to ensure that senators will not be absentees, that they will represent the people and places they know. When politicians who have grown up in one state run for the Senate in another state, they are often accused of being outsiders. Massachusetts native Robert F. Kennedy overcame this charge when he was elected senator from New York in 1964, but Connecticut-born George Bush could not do so when he ran for the Senate from Texas and lost in 1970.

4. President of the Senate The Vice President of the United States shall be president of the Senate, but shall have no vote, unless they be equally divided.

CLAUSE 4 During the first few decades of the republic, the Vice President generally attended the meetings of the Senate. Now he usually attends only on ceremonial occasions or when the Senate is equally divided over a bill.

5. Other Officers The Senate shall choose their other officers, and also a president pro tempore, in the absence of the Vice President, or when he shall exercise the office of the President of the United States.

CLAUSE 5 This sentence ensures that no other officials, such as the President, can exercise undue influence in the Senate by controlling the selection of its officers.

6. Impeachment Trials The Senate shall have the sole power to try all impeachments. When sitting for that purpose, they shall be on oath or affirmation. When the President of the United States is tried, the Chief Justice shall preside: and no person shall be convicted without the concurrence of two thirds of the members present.

CLAUSE 6 If the House votes to impeach, or indict, a federal official, the Senate becomes a court to try that person. The senators are like members of a jury. They listen to lawyers present evidence for and against the accused and then vote to convict or acquit. To make sure that an official is not impeached for frivolous or partisan reasons, the Constitution requires a two thirds vote in the Senate in order to convict someone. In 1974 President Richard Nixon resigned the presidency when he realized that more than 67 senators would vote to convict him.

7. Penalty on Conviction Judgment in cases of impeachment shall not extend further than to removal from office, and disqualification to hold and enjoy any office of honor, trust or profit under the United States: but the party convicted shall nevertheless be liable and subject to indictment, trial, judgment and punishment, according to law.

CLAUSE 7 Under the Constitution, the only punishment for officials who are impeached and convicted is that they can no longer be part of the United States government. The regular criminal court system must determine all jail terms, fines, and other punishments. In 1974 President Gerald Ford pardoned Richard Nixon for all illegal acts he may have committed as President, even though Nixon was never actually convicted of any specific crime.

Section 4 *Elections and Meetings*

1. Election of Congress The times, places and manner of holding elections for senators and representatives, shall be prescribed in each state by the legislature thereof; but the Congress may at any time by law make or alter such regulations, except as to the places of choosing senators.

CLAUSE 1 The states decide how and when to choose members of Congress, although Congress reserves the right to change the ways in which they do it. In 1842 Congress

Congress has often been the scene of heated debates among the country's legislators. Here, Henry Clay speaks to his colleagues about their inability to compromise on proposed legislation regarding slavery in February 1850.

with the concurrence of two thirds, expel a member.

CLAUSES 1 AND 2 These clauses were also designed to ensure that Congress would maintain control of its activities. They protect the integrity of the people's representatives from interference by the President or judges.

3. Record Each house shall keep a journal of its proceedings, and from time to time publish the same, excepting such parts as may in their judgment require secrecy; and the yeas and nays of the members of either house on any question, shall, at the desire of one fifth of those present, be entered on the journal.

CLAUSE 3 The Founders recognized that the people needed some sort of record of what their representatives said and how they voted in order to hold them accountable for their actions. Although the Constitution requires Congress to maintain a journal—today published as the *Congressional Record*—it also gives Congress the power to keep some matters secret. For example, representatives might not want to publish their debates on an issue involving national security.

4. Adjournment Neither house, during the session of Congress, shall, without the consent of the other, adjourn for more than three days, nor to any other place than that in which the two houses shall be sitting.

CLAUSE 4 Some of the Constitution's clauses may seem strange today. Why, for example, would the men who wrote the Constitution care about adjournments? The answer lies in colonial and British history. Sometimes one house of Parliament or a colonial legislature would leave or adjourn in order to prevent some legislation from passing or to hold up proceedings. This clause guarantees that, while they may not always agree with each other, the two houses of Congress must deal with each other. One house cannot adjourn unless the other agrees to an adjournment.

required that elections be held on the first Tuesday after the first Monday in November in even-numbered years.

2. Sessions The Congress shall assemble at least once in every year, and such meeting shall be on the first Monday in December, unless they shall by law appoint a different day.

CLAUSE 2 This clause guarantees that Congress will meet on a regular basis. A few decades before the American Revolution, kings and royal governors had called legislatures into session and dismissed them at their pleasure. In the 1630s, King Charles I refused to call Parliament and tried to govern England without a legislature. The Constitution makes certain that this cannot happen in the United States. Congress, not the President, decides when it will meet. In 1933 the Twentieth Amendment set the annual opening date as January 3, rather than the first Monday in December.

Section 5 *Legislative Proceedings*

1. Organization Each house shall be the judge of the elections, returns and qualifications of its own members, and a majority of each shall constitute a quorum to do business; but a smaller number may adjourn from day to day, and may be authorized to compel the attendance of absent members, in such manner, and under such penalties, as each house may provide.

2. Rules Each house may determine the rules of its proceedings, punish its members for disorderly behavior, and,

Section 6 *Compensation, Immunities, and Disabilities of Members*

1. Salaries; Immunities The senators and representatives shall receive a compensation for their services, to be ascertained by law, and paid out of the treasury of the United States. They shall, in all cases, except treason, felony and breach of the peace, be privileged from arrest during their attendance at the session of their respective houses, and in

going to and returning from the same; and for any speech or debate in either house, they shall not be questioned in any other place.

CLAUSE 1 Imagine what would happen if members of Congress could be arrested for what they say. This idea may seem ridiculous now, but it actually happened in the 1600s and 1700s. If Presidents or judges could arrest members of Congress, they could directly interfere with their proceedings. This clause essentially guaranteed that members of Congress did not have to worry about arbitrary interference by the executive and judicial branches.

2. Restrictions on Other Employment No senator or representative shall, during the time for which he was elected, be appointed to any civil office under the authority of the United States, which shall have been created, or the emoluments whereof shall have been increased during such time; and no person holding any office under the United States shall be a member of either house during his continuance in office.

CLAUSE 2 In Great Britain and in some of the American colonies, government officials had also held seats in Parliament or in legislatures. The authors of the Constitution feared that this practice encouraged corruption and discouraged independent decisions. If cabinet officers or presidential appointees were members of Congress, they would probably vote the way the President wanted them to. They might be more beholden to the President than to their constituents. Today, no federal officer may also be a member of Congress. In Great Britain, on the other hand, the prime minister and other cabinet officers are all members of Parliament.

Section 7 *Revenue Bills, President's Veto*

1. Revenue Bills All bills for raising revenue shall originate in the House of Representatives; but the Senate may propose or concur with amendments as on other bills.

CLAUSE 1 Because the House of Representatives is the body closest to the people, the Constitution requires that all legislation regarding taxes must begin there. The idea is that the people's representatives are the most appropriate guardians of the people's pocketbooks. Even today, if the President of the United States wants to raise taxes, the bill must begin in the House, not the Senate.

2. How a Bill Becomes a Law; the Veto Every bill which shall have passed the House of Representatives and the Senate, shall, before it become a law, be presented to the President of the United States; if he approve he shall sign it, but if not he shall return it, with his objections to that house in which it shall have originated, who shall enter the objections

at large on their journal, and proceed to reconsider it. If after such reconsideration two thirds of that house shall agree to pass the bill, it shall be sent, together with the objections, to the other house, by which it shall likewise be reconsidered, and if approved by two thirds of that house, it shall become a law. But in all such cases the votes of both houses shall be determined by yeas and nays, and the names of the persons voting for and against the bill shall be entered on the journal of each house respectively. If any bill shall not be returned by the President within ten days (Sundays excepted) after it shall have been presented to him, the same shall be a law, in like manner as if he had signed it, unless the Congress by their adjournment prevent its return, in which case it shall not be a law.

3. Resolutions Passed by Congress Every order, resolution, or vote to which the concurrence of the Senate and House of Representatives may be necessary (except on a question of adjournment) shall be presented to the President of the United States; and before the same shall take effect, shall be approved by him, or being disapproved by him, shall be repassed by two thirds of the Senate and House of Representatives, according to the rules and limitations prescribed in the case of a bill.

CLAUSES 2 AND 3 These two clauses carefully regulate the balance of power between the legislative and executive branches while trying to maintain the independence of both. Thus, the President has the right to reject any bill the Congress passes, but only if one third of the members agree with him after further deliberation. A presidential veto—when a President refuses to sign a bill into law—makes the President equally powerful with Congress but not completely independent of it. The President cannot veto a bill without some congressional support. These clauses prevent either the Congress or the President from acting arbitrarily or impulsively.

Section 8 *Powers of Congress*
The Congress shall have power

1. To lay and collect taxes, duties, imposts and excises, to pay the debts and provide for the common defense and general welfare of the United States; but all duties, imposts and excises shall be uniform throughout the United States;

CLAUSE 1 This clause gives the federal government power it did not have under the Articles of Confederation, specifically, the right to tax. It is one of the most important provisions of the Constitution, for without the power to raise revenues, the government would not have the money to operate itself or fund programs. This clause also ensures that the government must tax every part of the country

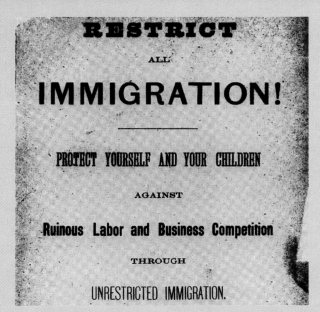

RESTRICT
ALL
IMMIGRATION!

PROTECT YOURSELF AND YOUR CHILDREN

AGAINST

Ruinous Labor and Business Competition

THROUGH

UNRESTRICTED IMMIGRATION.

American citizens have not always welcomed newcomers with open arms. This poster reflects the objections of some to unrestricted immigration in the 1880s.

equally. For example, federal taxes must be the same in Arizona as in Maine.

The phrase "provide for the common defense and general welfare of the United States" is one of the vague phrases in the Constitution that Presidents, Congress, and judges have often interpreted very broadly in order to take actions not specifically mentioned in the Constitution. Because Congress theoretically has the power to act for the "general welfare," it can take any steps it deems necessary to guarantee the defense and welfare of the nation as a whole.

2. To borrow money on the credit of the United States;

CLAUSE 2 The power to borrow money allows Congress to spend money beyond the amount it is able to tax. Secretary of the Treasury Alexander Hamilton's financial program in the 1790s, most wartime spending, and many of the social programs of the 1900s would have been impossible without this clause.

3. To regulate commerce with foreign nations, and among the several states, and with the Indian tribes;

CLAUSE 3 As a result of this clause, Congress possesses the power to supervise all commerce, both among the various states and between the United States and foreign nations. Without this provision, the states might have established tariffs on imports and exports, and trade in the United States would have become a complex patchwork of regulations and taxes. Imagine, for example, if states in the middle of the

country taxed or regulated trade between the eastern and western halves of the United States. Congress did not have the power to regulate commerce under the Articles of Confederation. This clause was designed to create a clear, uncomplicated system of trade that would advance the economic interests of the nation.

4. To establish an uniform rule of naturalization, and uniform laws on the subject of bankruptcies throughout the United States;

CLAUSE 4 Only Congress, not the states, can regulate the way in which immigrants become citizens of the United States. In addition, only Congress can regulate the handling of bankruptcies, another attempt to create uniform economic regulations throughout the United States.

5. To coin money, regulate the value thereof, and of foreign coin, and fix the standard of weights and measures;

6. To provide for the punishment of counterfeiting the securities and current coin of the United States;

CLAUSES 5 AND 6 These two clauses ensure that there is only one kind of money in the United States. Without such regulation, the states or private institutions could issue their own money. The members of the Constitutional Convention included these clauses to create a stable and predictable medium of exchange throughout the United States.

7. To establish post offices and post roads;

CLAUSE 7 Just as Congress has the power to regulate commerce—the exchange of goods—so, too, it has the power to regulate the exchange of information and news through the mails. Without this power, Americans might have to contend with fifty different postal services in the United States.

8. To promote the progress of science and useful arts, by securing for limited times to authors and inventors the exclusive right to their respective writings and discoveries;

Inventions such as this Singer sewing machine were regulated and protected by patents issued by the United States Congress.

CLAUSE 8 This clause gives Congress the power to regulate the exchange of knowledge in the United States. Congress, not the states, issues patents and copyright protection to people who come up with new ideas or technology.

9. To constitute tribunals inferior to the Supreme Court;

CLAUSE 9 This brief clause grants Congress an important power—the right to create the federal court system below the level of the Supreme Court. Because the Constitution itself does not explain the judicial system in great detail, Congress has had enormous leeway in the creation of this system.

10. To define and punish piracies and felonies committed on the high seas and offenses against the law of nations;

11. To declare war, grant letters of marque and reprisal, and make rules concerning captures on land and water;

CLAUSES 10 AND 11 Congress also has the power to regulate international relations, particularly any matters concerning war.

12. To raise and support armies, but no appropriation of money to that use shall be for a longer term than two years;

CLAUSE 12 Although Congress can form armies to defend American interests, it can only pay for them for two years at a time. This clause reflects the deep fear the Founders and other former colonists had about standing, or professional, armies. They worried that government officials might use permanent armies to stifle opposition and take away liberties, as kings had done in the past.

13. To provide and maintain a navy;

CLAUSE 13 Following a British constitutional tradition, the delegates at the Constitutional Convention felt no need to

Although the Framers probably could not have envisioned it, women soldiers have played significant roles in the country's armed forces. These women served in the Persian Gulf War.

restrict naval expenditures to two years. They viewed the navy as far less of a threat to civil authority than the army.

14. To make rules for the government and regulation of the land and naval forces;

CLAUSE 14 These rules are spelled out in the Uniform Code of Military Justice, passed by Congress in 1950.

15. To provide for calling forth the militia to execute the laws of the Union, suppress insurrections and repel invasions;

16. To provide for organizing, arming, and disciplining, the militia, and for governing such part of them as may be employed in the service of the United States, reserving to the states respectively, the appointment of the officers, and the authority of training the militia according to the discipline prescribed by Congress;

CLAUSES 15 AND 16 The National Defense Act of 1916 made each state's militia part of the National Guard. Under normal circumstances, each state's governor is in charge of that state's National Guard; however, the President has the power to call into federal service any or all National Guard units when necessary, as President George Bush did during the 1991 Persian Gulf War.

17. To exercise exclusive legislation in all cases whatsoever, over such district (not exceeding ten miles square) as may, by cession of particular states, and the acceptance of Congress, become the seat of the government of the United States, and to exercise like authority over all places purchased by the consent of the legislature of the state in which the same shall be, for the erection of forts, magazines, arsenals, dockyards, and other needful buildings; and

CLAUSE 17 This clause provides for what would become the nation's capital, Washington, D.C., and for federal establishments in the states. Without this provision, Philadelphia or some other large city might have become the nation's permanent capital.

18. To make all laws which shall be necessary and proper for carrying into execution the foregoing powers, and all other powers vested by this Constitution in the government of the United States, or in any department or officer thereof.

CLAUSE 18 No other clause in the Constitution has been used more often by judges and federal officials to increase the power of the federal government. Read loosely, the "necessary and proper," or "elastic," clause says that Congress may take any steps not otherwise prohibited by the Constitution to guarantee that the other provisions of the Constitution are carried out.

Section 9 *Powers Denied to Congress*

1. The Slave Trade ~~The migration or importation of such persons as any of the states now existing shall think proper to admit, shall not be prohibited by the Congress prior to the year one thousand eight hundred and eight, but a tax or duty may be imposed on such importation, not exceeding ten dollars for each person.~~

CLAUSE 1 Although the Constitution outlawed the importation of enslaved persons into the United States, this provision did not take effect until two decades after the ratification of the document. Notice again how careful the language is. The word "slave" does not appear, only "such persons as any of the States now existing shall think proper."

2. Writ of Habeas Corpus The privilege of the writ of habeas corpus shall not be suspended, unless when in cases of rebellion or invasion the public safety may require it.

CLAUSE 2 The writ of habeas corpus directs a sheriff, public official, or other person who is holding citizens against their will to produce them so that the legality of their detention can be determined. This clause protects American citizens from being held in prison without being formally charged with a crime. Without the writ, the government could simply put people it did not like in jail and hold them there without explanation. President Abraham Lincoln, who called the Civil War a rebellion, did suspend the writ of habeas corpus and imprison people without showing cause.

3. Bills of Attainder; *Ex Post Facto* Laws No bill of attainder or ex post facto law shall be passed.

CLAUSE 3 A bill of attainder is a legislative act that punishes a person without a trial in court. An ex post facto law is a retroactive one; it declares that an action is a crime after it has been committed. These important provisions prevent the government from arresting and punishing people without due process of law.

4. Apportionment of Direct Taxes No capitation, ~~or other direct,~~ tax shall be laid, unless in proportion to the census or enumeration herein before directed to be taken.

CLAUSE 4 This provision outlawed all direct taxes on individuals until the Sixteenth Amendment (1913) gave Congress the power to tax personal incomes.

5. Taxes on Exports No tax or duty shall be laid on articles exported from any state.

CLAUSE 5 Congress cannot tax anything sent out of a state, although it does have the power to tax imported goods.

6. Special Preference for Trade No preference shall be given by any regulation of commerce or revenue to the ports of one state over those of another: nor shall vessels bound to, or from, one state, be obliged to enter, clear, or pay duties in another.

CLAUSE 6 These specific restrictions on the states keep them from trying to regulate trade outside their own boundaries. Interstate trade is solely the business of the national government.

7. Spending No money shall be drawn from the treasury, but in consequence of appropriations made by law; and a regular statement and account of the receipts and expenditures of all public money shall be published from time to time.

CLAUSE 7 Like many other parts of the Constitution, this paragraph reflects eighteenth-century fears about corruption and power. The purpose of the clause was to prevent Presidents or other officials from thwarting the will of Congress and the people by spending money in secret on projects prohibited by Congress. It is a significant check on presidential power. The Iran-contra scandal involved government officials who attempted to raise and spend money in support of the contras in Nicaragua, an activity that Congress had made illegal.

8. Titles of Nobility No title of nobility shall be granted by the United States: and no person holding any office of profit or trust under them, shall, without the consent of the Congress, accept of any present, emolument, office, or title, of any kind whatever, from any king, prince or foreign state.

CLAUSE 8 The Founders included this provision to prevent the establishment of an aristocracy in the United States. The clause was also designed to discourage foreign nations from attempting to bribe or otherwise corrupt government officials. Today, exceptions are made, usually in the case of retired officials. Presidents Ronald Reagan and George Bush, for example, received formal recognition from the government of Great Britain after their public careers were over.

Section 10 *Powers Denied to the States*

1. Unconditional Prohibitions No state shall enter into any treaty, alliance, or confederation; grant letters of marque and reprisal; coin money; emit bills of credit; make any thing but gold and silver coin a tender in payment of debts; pass any bill of attainder, ex post facto law, or law impairing the obligation of contracts, or grant any title of nobility.

2. Powers Conditionally Denied No state shall, without the consent of the Congress, lay any imposts or duties on

imports or exports, except what may be absolutely necessary for executing its inspection laws: and the net produce of all duties and imposts, laid by any state on imports or exports, shall be for the use of the treasury of the United States; and all such laws shall be subject to the revision and control of the Congress.

3. Other Denied Powers No state shall, without the consent of Congress, lay any duty of tonnage, keep troops, or ships of war in time of peace, enter into any agreement or compact with another state, or with a foreign power, or engage in war, unless actually invaded, or in such imminent danger as will not admit of delay.

CLAUSES 1, 2, AND 3 These three clauses specifically prohibit the states from getting involved in foreign affairs or interstate commerce. Their purpose is to limit the power of the states to internal affairs. Anything that affects more than one state, economically or militarily, is properly the business of the national government.

Article II
EXECUTIVE BRANCH
Section 1 *President and Vice President*

1. Chief Executive; Term The executive power shall be vested in a President of the United States of America. He shall hold his office during the term of four years, and, together with the Vice President, chosen for the same term, be elected, as follows:

CLAUSE 1 The Founders deliberately left the duties of the President vague. During the past century, Presidents have assumed great power, in part because the Constitution does not put many specific restrictions on the office. Although the presidential term is four years, many members of the Constitutional Convention expected incumbents to be reelected more than once. In fact, they thought most Presidents would serve for a long time. But after Franklin Roosevelt was elected to four terms between 1932 and 1944, the Twenty-second Amendment (1951) restricted Presidents to two terms. There is no such limit on Vice Presidents.

2. Electoral College Each state shall appoint, in such manner as the legislature thereof may direct, a number of electors, equal to the whole number of senators and representatives to which the state may be entitled in the Congress: but no senator or representative, or person holding an office of trust or profit under the United States, shall be appointed an elector.

CLAUSE 2 This clause establishes what we call the Electoral College, the group of people who elect the President. State legislatures decide how electors for that state will be

Members of the Constitutional convention knew that George Washington was likely to be the nation's first President.

chosen. The number of electoral votes each state has is equal to the number of its senators and representatives added together.

3. Former Electoral Method ~~The electors shall meet in their respective states, and vote by ballot for two persons, of whom one at least shall not be an inhabitant of the same state with themselves. And they shall make a list of all the persons voted for, and of the number of votes for each; which list they shall sign and certify, and transmit sealed to the seat of the government of the United States, directed to the president of the Senate. The president of the Senate shall, in the presence of the Senate and House of Representatives, open all the certificates, and the votes shall then be counted. The person having the greatest number of votes shall be the President, if such number be a majority of the whole number of Electors appointed; and if there be more than one who have such majority, and have an equal number of votes, then the House of Representatives shall immediately choose by ballot one of them for President; and if no person have a~~

majority, then from the five highest on the list the said House shall in like manner choose the President. But in choosing the President, the votes shall be taken by states, the representation from each state having one vote; a quorum for this purpose shall consist of a member or members from two thirds of the states, and a majority of all the states shall be necessary to a choice. In every case, after the choice of the President, the person having the greatest number of votes of the electors shall be the Vice President. But if there should remain two or more who have equal votes, the Senate shall choose from them by ballot the Vice President.

CLAUSE 3 The Twelfth Amendment (1804) replaced this paragraph, which is no longer in force.

4. Time of Elections The Congress may determine the time of choosing the electors, and the day on which they shall give their votes; which day shall be the same throughout the United States.

CLAUSE 4 Congress has established the Tuesday after the first Monday in November every fourth year as the time to choose electors. By law, the electors cast their ballots on the Monday after the second Wednesday in December.

5. Qualifications for President No person except a natural-born citizen, or a citizen of the United States at the time of the adoption of this Constitution, shall be eligible to the office of President; neither shall any person be eligible to that office who shall not have attained to the age of thirty-five years, and been fourteen years a resident within the United States.

CLAUSE 5 This provision ensures that the President of the United States will be a mature person, who is not only a natural-born citizen of the United States but has also lived in the nation for at least fourteen years.

6. Presidential Succession In case of the removal of the President from office, or of his death, resignation, or inability to discharge the powers and duties of the said office, the same shall devolve on the Vice President, and the Congress may by law provide for the case of removal, death, resignation or inability, both of the President and Vice President, declaring what officer shall then act as President, and such officer shall act accordingly, until the disability be removed, or a President shall be elected.

CLAUSE 6 The Twenty-fifth Amendment (1967) supersedes the first half of this provision, more clearly explaining when and how a Vice President becomes President.

7. Salary The President shall, at stated times, receive for his services, a compensation, which shall neither be increased nor diminished during the period for which he shall have been elected, and he shall not receive within that period any other emolument from the United States, or any of them.

CLAUSE 7 This clause prohibits Congress from changing a President's salary while he or she is in office. The authors of the Constitution were afraid that Congress might use its power to corrupt or punish a President. Without this clause, for example, Congress could threaten to lower a President's salary to prevent him or her from vetoing a bill. Today, the President of the United States is paid $200,000 a year, plus $50,000 in a taxable expense account. Additional benefits include residence in the White House, Secret Service protection, and means of transportation. Congress cannot give a President a valuable gift ("an emolument") while he or she is in office.

8. Oath of Office Before he enter on the execution of his office, he shall take the following oath or affirmation:—"I do solemnly swear (or affirm) that I will faithfully execute the office of the President of the United States, and will to the best of my ability, preserve, protect and defend the Constitution of the United States."

Bill Clinton swore to uphold the Constitution of the United States when he took office on January 20, 1993.

President Carter signed an arms limitation agreement with Soviet president Leonid Brezhnev in 1979. The Constitution gives the President the power to enter into such treaties with foreign governments.

CLAUSE 8 Note that the President swears to uphold the Constitution, not the United States. When Presidents take the oath of office, they commit themselves to the form of government outlined in this document. Remember that people in the 1780s and 1790s did not assume that the Constitution would be permanent; after all, the Articles of Confederation had lasted only a decade. The oath commits the President to this Constitution and no others.

Section 2 *Powers of the President*

1. Military Powers The President shall be commander in chief of the army and navy of the United States, and of the militia of the several states, when called into the actual service of the United States; he may require the opinion, in writing, of the principal officer in each of the executive departments, upon any subject relating to the duties of their respective offices, and he shall have power to grant reprieves and pardons for offenses against the United States, except in cases of impeachment.

CLAUSE 1 Even though the President is a civilian, he or she is the supreme commander of the military. The phrase "require the opinion, in writing" is one of the few places in which the Constitution refers to what is called the cabinet, the heads of the executive departments. The President's power to grant pardons is limited to federal crimes.

2. Treaties; Appointments He shall have power, by and with the advice and consent of the Senate, to make treaties, provided two thirds of the senators present concur; and he shall nominate, and by and with the advice and consent of the Senate, shall appoint ambassadors, other public ministers and consuls, judges of the Supreme Court, and all other officers of the United States, whose appointments are not herein otherwise provided for, and which shall be established by law: but the Congress may by law vest the appointment of such inferior officers, as they think proper, in the President alone, in the courts of law, or in the heads of departments.

CLAUSE 2 To make major agreements with foreign countries or to appoint major public officials, the President has to seek the advice and consent of the Senate. The aim of this provision is to prevent the President from conducting personal diplomacy, committing the United States to something only he or she wants, and from appointing only his or her friends to judgeships and federal offices.

3. Temporary Appointments The President shall have power to fill up all vacancies that may happen during the recess of the Senate, by granting commissions which shall expire at the end of their next session.

CLAUSE 3 This clause simply allows the President to make temporary appointments when Congress is not in session.

Section 3 *Duties of the President*

He shall from time to time give to the Congress information of the state of the Union, and recommend to their consideration such measures as he shall judge necessary and expedient; he may, on extraordinary occasions, convene both houses, or either of them, and in case of disagreement between them, with respect to the time of adjournment, he may adjourn them to such time as he shall think proper; he shall receive ambassadors and other public ministers; he shall take care that the laws be faithfully executed, and shall commission all the officers of the United States.

SECTION 3 This paragraph lists the specific duties and responsibilities of the President. He must give a State of the Union address occasionally (usually once a year). In addition, he may call special sessions of Congress, adjourn Congress if the two houses are divided about it, receive ambassadors, and commission officers. Finally, he must see "that the laws [of the United States] be faithfully executed." These are important duties. But notice how general they are and how few in number. Compare them with the lengthy list of specific things the Congress can and cannot do. The members of the Constitutional Convention were not as sure of what the office of the presidency would be as they were of Congress. Much of the job has been defined by the men who have held the office.

Section 4 *Impeachment*
The President, Vice President and all civil officers of the United States, shall be removed from office on impeachment for, and conviction of, treason, bribery, or other high crimes and misdemeanors.

SECTION 4 If the President goes too far in assuming powers and breaks the law in the opinion of a majority of the members of the House of Representatives, he can be impeached and tried by the Senate. This event has happened once in American history. President Andrew Johnson was impeached by the House of Representatives in 1867. Although a majority of senators voted that he was guilty, more than a third had doubts, so Johnson remained in office. In 1974 the House Judiciary Committee voted to recommend the impeachment of President Richard Nixon, but he resigned before the full House was able to vote on the recommendation.

Article III
JUDICIAL BRANCH
Section 1 *Courts, Terms of Office*
The judicial power of the United States, shall be vested in one Supreme Court, and in such inferior courts as the Congress may from time to time ordain and establish. The judges, both of the Supreme and inferior courts, shall hold their offices during good behavior, and shall, at stated times, receive for their services, a compensation which shall not be diminished during their continuance in office.

SECTION 1 Although the Constitution makes provisions for a federal court system to hear and decide cases, it only specifically creates the Supreme Court. Acts of Congress have created all other federal courts, as well as established the number of Supreme Court justices. In order to preserve the integrity and independence of judges from both the executive and legislative branches, federal judges serve "during good behavior," which basically means as long as they live, and cannot have their salaries reduced.

Section 2 *Jurisdiction*
1. Scope of Judicial Power The judicial power shall extend to all cases, in law and equity, arising under this Constitution, the laws of the United States, and treaties made, or which shall be made, under their authority;—to all cases affecting ambassadors, other public ministers and consuls;—to all cases of admiralty and maritime jurisdiction;—to controversies to which the United States shall be a party;—to controversies between two or more states;— between a state and citizens of another state; —between citizens of different states;—between citizens of the same state claiming lands under grants of different states, and between a state, or the citizens thereof, and foreign states, citizens or subjects.

CLAUSE 1 This paragraph lists the kinds of cases federal courts can hear and decide on. They have jurisdiction over cases relating to the Constitution, federal laws, treaties, and diplomatic officials. They also have jurisdiction over cases involving disputes between the United States and someone else, between two states, or between citizens of different states. The Eleventh Amendment (1795) substantially restricted the jurisdiction of federal courts in cases involving states.

2. Supreme Court In all cases affecting ambassadors, other public ministers and consuls, and those in which a state shall be a party, the Supreme Court shall have original jurisdiction. In all the other cases before mentioned, the Supreme Court shall have appellate jurisdiction, both as to law and fact, with such exceptions, and under such regulations as the Congress shall make.

CLAUSE 2 Under this clause, the Supreme Court has both original and appellate jurisdiction. That is, the Court is first to hear and decide cases involving foreign ambassadors and individual states. But it also has appellate jurisdiction, meaning people can appeal the decisions of lower courts to the Supreme Court.

Clarence Thomas's appointment to the Supreme Court was approved after lengthy hearings in the Senate.

Many Americans thought that Sacco and Vanzetti did not receive a fair trial, a right that is protected by the Constitution.

3. Trial by Jury The trial of all crimes, except in cases of impeachment, shall be by jury; and such trial shall be held in the state where the said crimes shall have been committed; but when not committed within any state, the trial shall be at such place or places as the Congress may by law have directed.

CLAUSE 3 In reaction to cases in English constitutional history, the members of the Constitutional Convention guaranteed American citizens the right to trial by jury in federal cases and the right to have the trial in the place where the crime supposedly occurred. The Founders feared the power of government to take defendants to distant places to try them quickly and without a jury.

Section 3 *Treason*
1. Definition Treason against the United States shall consist only in levying war against them, or in adhering to their enemies, giving them aid and comfort. No person shall be convicted of treason unless on the testimony of two witnesses to the same overt act, or on confession in open court.

CLAUSE 1 The definition of treason is very specific because the authors of the Constitution wanted to make certain

that people were not imprisoned or punished simply for criticizing the government. The crime of treason can apply only to citizens or resident aliens, and even then only in time of war.

2. Punishment The Congress shall have power to declare the punishment of treason, but no attainder of treason shall work corruption of blood, or forfeiture except during the life of the person attained.

CLAUSE 2 Although the United States has never executed anyone for treason, death remains the maximum punishment for someone convicted of this charge. The minimum punishment, by act of Congress, is five years in prison and/or a $10,000 fine. The phrase "corruption of blood, or forfeiture" means that punishment for treason affects only the person convicted of it; neither the traitor's family nor descendants can be punished.

Article IV
RELATIONS AMONG THE STATES
Section 1 *Full Faith and Credit*
Full faith and credit shall be given in each state to the public acts, records, and judicial proceedings of every other state. And the Congress may by general laws prescribe the manner in which such acts, records and proceedings shall be proved, and the effect thereof.

SECTION 1 In this clause, the authors of the Constitution were again asserting the supremacy of the federal government. Congress would have responsibility for making sure that each state respected the legal actions of the others.

Section 2 *Privileges and Immunities of Citizens*
1. Privileges The citizens of each state shall be entitled to all privileges and immunities of citizens in the several states.

CLAUSE 1 The Constitution ensures that states cannot discriminate against people from other states. The federal government will make certain that citizens of the United States enjoy their full rights in every part of the nation.

2. Extradition A person charged in any state with treason, felony, or other crime, who shall flee from justice, and be found in another state, shall on demand of the executive authority of the state from which he fled, be delivered up, to be removed to the state having jurisdiction of the crime.

CLAUSE 2 The legal term for this process is *extradition*. If someone commits a crime in Minnesota, for example, and then flees to Montana, the governor of Montana must arrange to transport the alleged criminal back to Minnesota for trial if the governor of Minnesota requests this action.

Although governors sometimes delay complying with such requests for political reasons, the federal government has the power to force governors to comply.

3. Fugitive Slaves ~~No person held to service or labor in one state, under the laws thereof, escaping into another, shall, in consequence of any law or regulation therein, be discharged from such service or labor, but shall be delivered up on claim of the party to whom such service or labor may be due.~~

CLAUSE 3 This clause was nullified by the Thirteenth Amendment in 1865, which made slavery illegal throughout the United States.

Section 3 *New States and Territories*
1. New States New states may be admitted by the Congress into this Union; but no new states shall be formed or erected within the jurisdiction of any other state, nor any state be formed by the junction of two or more states, or parts of states, without the consent of the legislatures of the states concerned as well as of the Congress.

CLAUSE 1 Only the federal government can create new states. Congress decides on the rules and procedures for admitting new states to the Union. It cannot, however, make new states out of old ones unless the legislature of a particular state agrees to this course of action. Since 1789 Congress has created thirty-seven states. Five of these—Vermont, Kentucky,

John Muir and President Theodore Roosevelt led an effort to conserve land in the West, sparking the birth of the National Park system.

Tennessee, Maine, and West Virginia—were originally parts of other states. One—Texas—was an independent republic. One—California—was part of Mexico before it became a state. The other thirty states have become parts of the United States after first being territories. The Northwest Ordinance of 1787 outlines the process by which a territory becomes a state.

2. Federal Lands The Congress shall have power to dispose of and make all needful rules and regulations respecting the territory or other property belonging to the United States; and nothing in this Constitution shall be so construed as to prejudice any claims of the United States, or of any particular state.

CLAUSE 2 Simply put, this clause gives Congress the power to govern all federal territory and other property as it sees fit. In theory, state governments have no say when it comes to the regulation or disposal of federal lands. This clause led to controversy in the 1800s because Congress had the power to abolish slavery on federal property if it wished. Controversy has continued in the 1900s because of the question of how to handle the vast acreage in national parks and other preserves owned and operated by the federal government, particularly in western states.

Section 4 *Protection Afforded to States by the Nation*
The United States shall guarantee to every state in this Union a republican form of government, and shall protect each of them against invasion; and on application of the legislature, or of the executive (when the legislature cannot be convened) against domestic violence.

SECTION 4 The federal government is the most powerful government in the United States. Not only will it protect the states from all enemies, foreign and domestic, it will ensure that each state has a "republican form of government." Officials and judges today assume that "republican" means a representative government. But the Constitution leaves it up to Congress to decide what is "republican" and what is not.

Article V
PROVISIONS FOR AMENDMENT
The Congress, whenever two thirds of both houses shall deem it necessary, shall propose amendments to this Constitution, or, on the application of the legislatures of two thirds of the several states, shall call a convention for proposing amendments, which, in either case, shall be valid to all intents and purposes, as part of this Constitution, when ratified by the legislatures of three fourths of the several states, or by conventions in three fourths thereof, as the

one or the other mode of ratification may be proposed by the Congress; provided ~~that no amendment which may be made prior to the year one thousand eight hundred and eight shall in any manner affect the first and fourth clauses in the ninth section of the first Article; and~~ that no state, without its consent, shall be deprived of its equal suffrage in the Senate.

ARTICLE V One of the most democratic features of the Constitution is its ability to be changed. Amendments to the Constitution are essentially revisions of the original document.

While the authors of the Constitution wanted the people to be able to change this document, they did not want it changed for frivolous reasons. Consequently, they made sure that the process of amending the Constitution would take a great deal of consensus as well as time. Proposing an amendment to the Constitution requires either a two thirds vote in each house of Congress or the approval of a national convention called by two thirds of the state legislatures. After an amendment has been proposed, either the legislatures or special conventions of three fourths of the states must approve the amendment before it can become law. All twenty-seven amendments to the Constitution have originated in Congress.

Article VI
NATIONAL DEBTS, SUPREMACY OF NATIONAL LAW, OATH
Section 1 *Validity of Debts*
All debts contracted and engagements entered into, before the adoption of this Constitution, shall be as valid against the United States under this Constitution, as under the Confederation.

SECTION 1 One of the major reasons some Americans supported the Constitution was because this document would enable the new nation to pay off the huge debts contracted during the American Revolution. Under the Articles of Confederation, Congress had lacked the power to tax; to pay for the war effort, it had been forced to borrow millions of dollars. Once the Constitution went into effect, this clause promised creditors of the United States that the new government would pay all bills contracted under the Articles of Confederation.

Section 2 *Supremacy of National Law*
This Constitution, and the laws of the United States which shall be made in pursuance thereof; and all treaties made, or which shall be made, under the authority of the United States, shall be the supreme law of the land; and the judges in every state shall be bound thereby, anything in the constitution or laws of any state to the contrary notwithstanding.

SECTION 2 This is the "supremacy clause." In very general terms, it says that federal laws rank above state or local laws. No other government in the United States can make or enforce any law that is in conflict with the Constitution, acts of Congress, diplomatic treaties, or orders issued by the executive branch. In other words, the federal government is supreme in the United States.

After coming dangerously close to nuclear war with the Soviets, President Kennedy signed the Limited Test Ban Treaty in 1963.

Section 3 *Oaths of Office*
The senators and representatives before mentioned, and the members of the several state legislatures, and all executive and judicial officers, both of the United States and of the several states, shall be bound by oath or affirmation, to support this Constitution; but no religious test shall ever be required as a qualification to any office or public trust under the United States.

SECTION 3 This clause simply reinforces the supremacy clause. It requires that everyone holding office within the borders of the United States swear to uphold the Constitution.

The Framers of the Constitution specifically forbid the exclusion of anyone from government office for religious reasons. Americans take this right for granted today, but in the 1700s it was a relatively novel idea. In Great Britain, people who were not members of the Church of England could not hold office until the 1800s; Catholics, Jews, and Protestant Dissenters were effectively barred from government service.

Article VII
RATIFICATION OF CONSTITUTION

The ratification of the conventions of nine states shall be sufficient for the establishment of this Constitution between the states so ratifying the same:

ARTICLE VII The Framers required only nine of thirteen states to approve the Constitution, in large part because they knew it would be extremely difficult to win unanimous approval. Because they also had doubts about whether state legislatures would approve their new government, they provided for specially elected conventions to make the decision.

Done in convention by the unanimous consent of the states present the seventeenth day of September in the year of our Lord one thousand seven hundred and eighty-seven, and of the independence of the United States of America the twelfth. *In Witness* whereof we have hereunto subscribed our names.

United we stand—Divided we fall

The pillars in this cartoon symbolize the nine states that had to ratify the Constitution before it could become law.

ATTEST:
  William Jackson, SECRETARY
  George Washington, PRESIDENT
  and deputy from Virginia
NEW HAMPSHIRE
  John Langdon
  Nicholas Gilman
MASSACHUSETTS
  Nathaniel Gorham
  Rufus King
CONNECTICUT
  William Samuel Johnson
  Roger Sherman
NEW YORK
  Alexander Hamilton

NEW JERSEY
  William Livingston
  David Brearley
  William Paterson
  Jonathan Dayton
PENNSYLVANIA
  Benjamin Franklin
  Thomas Mifflin
  Robert Morris
  George Clymer
  Thomas Fitzsimons
  Jared Ingersoll
  James Wilson
  Gouverneur Morris
DELAWARE
  George Read
  Gunning Bedford, Jr.
  John Dickinson
  Richard Bassett
  Jacob Broom
MARYLAND
  James McHenry
  Dan of St. Thomas Jennifer
  Daniel Carroll

VIRGINIA
  John Blair
  James Madison, Jr.
NORTH CAROLINA
  William Blount
  Richard Dobbs Spaight
  Hugh Williamson
SOUTH CAROLINA
  John Rutledge
  Charles Cotesworth Pinckney
  Charles Pinckney
  Pierce Butler
GEORGIA
  William Few
  Abraham Baldwin

AMENDMENTS

The supporters of the Constitution had to agree to several changes in order to win the approval of the required nine states. The first ten amendments to the Constitution—or the Bill of Rights—incorporate most of the revisions called for by critics of the Constitution. Basically, the Bill of Rights protects the hard-won rights of citizens from a powerful national government. These amendments were originally meant to restrict only the federal government; however, the Supreme Court on occasion has held that most of them also apply to the states. The justices have based this extension on the due process clause of the Fourteenth Amendment. The amendments in the Bill of Rights were proposed by Congress on September 25, 1789, and ratified by December 15, 1791.

FIRST AMENDMENT (1791) *Freedom of Religion, Speech, Press, Assembly, and Petition*

Congress shall make no law respecting an establishment of religion, or prohibiting the free exercise thereof; or abridging the freedom of speech, or of the press; or the right of the people peaceably to assemble, and to petition the government for a redress of grievances.

Newspaper reporters Bob Woodward and Carl Bernstein uncovered and wrote about the Watergate scandal that led to the downfall of President Nixon.

FIRST AMENDMENT The First Amendment prohibits Congress from restricting five basic liberties—the right of the people to practice their religion as they wish; the right of the people to speak, publish, and express their views; and the right of the people to join together publicly with others to discuss issues and to petition, or ask, their government to change laws they think are unfair. Although most Americans now take these basic rights for granted, they are a vital part of the democratic system of government established by the Founders.

SECOND AMENDMENT (1791) *Bearing Arms*

A well-regulated militia being necessary to the security of a free state, the right of the people to keep and bear arms shall not be infringed.

SECOND AMENDMENT Although Congress must allow each state to maintain a militia, or national guard, for its protection, all state governments regulate the possession and use of firearms by private citizens. In the eighteenth century, when people were very distrustful of powerful governments, the right to bear arms was a cherished liberty. After all, the American Revolution began in April 1775 when men grabbed muskets and rifles to resist a British army marching from Boston to Concord, Massachusetts. Today, however, this amendment is more controversial. Some Americans continue to think of the right to bear arms as an essential right; others argue that because our times are so different from the late 1700s, the amendment is outdated.

THIRD AMENDMENT (1791) *Quartering of Troops*

No soldier shall, in time of peace be quartered in any house, without the consent of the owner, nor in time of war, but in a manner to be prescribed by law.

The protection of the First Amendment allowed thousands of Americans to demand equal rights for African Americans during the Civil Rights movement.

THIRD AMENDMENT It was a common practice for governments in the 1700s to house troops in private homes in order to save money on food and shelter. Before the American Revolution, the British government frequently quartered, or housed, troops in the homes of Americans. The colonists resented the practice, and it was one of the major grievances with Great Britain listed in the Declaration of Independence. Determined to prevent the practice in the United States, many Americans demanded and won this amendment to the Constitution. As a result, the United States government cannot quarter troops in private homes.

FOURTH AMENDMENT (1791) *Searches and Seizures*

The right of the people to be secure in their persons, houses, papers, and effects, against unreasonable searches and seizures, shall not be violated, and no warrants shall issue, but upon probable cause, supported by oath or affirmation, and particularly describing the place to be searched, and the persons or things to be seized.

FOURTH AMENDMENT This amendment protects another "right of the people" from a potentially intrusive government. No one can search for or seize evidence in an American citizen's house or arrest a citizen without a court order issued for "probable cause." The Supreme Court has reinforced this right with the "exclusionary rule," which holds that illegally obtained evidence cannot be used against a person in a court of law.

FIFTH AMENDMENT (1791) *Criminal Proceedings; Due Process; Eminent Domain*

No person shall be held to answer for a capital, or otherwise infamous crime, unless on a presentment or indictment of a grand jury, except in cases arising in the land or naval forces, or in the militia, when in actual service in time of war or public danger; nor shall any person be subject for the same offense to be twice put in jeopardy of life or limb; nor shall be compelled in any criminal case to be a witness against himself, nor be deprived of life, liberty, or property, without due process of law; nor shall private property be taken for public use, without just compensation.

FIFTH AMENDMENT This amendment, like the others in the Bill of Rights, provides people with protection from a powerful government. It outlines the ways in which the United States government must treat its citizens, even when it suspects them of criminal activity. For example, people cannot be tried unless they have been formally indicted, or accused, by a grand jury. They cannot be tried twice for the same crime. They cannot be required to give evidence against themselves. And they are entitled to "due process of law." If

the government takes their property, it must pay them for what it took. In other words, government officials cannot behave in an unfair or arbitrary manner. By respecting due process in dealing with alleged criminals, the Constitution respects and protects the rights of all Americans.

SIXTH AMENDMENT (1791) *Criminal Proceedings*

In all criminal prosecutions, the accused shall enjoy the right to a speedy and public trial, by an impartial jury of the state and district wherein the crime shall have been committed, which district shall have been previously ascertained by law, and to be informed of the nature and cause of the accusation; to be confronted with the witnesses against him; to have compulsory process for obtaining witnesses in his favor, and to have the assistance of counsel for his defense.

SIXTH AMENDMENT This amendment guarantees that even citizens who stand accused of a crime have rights when dealing with their government. They have the right to a relatively quick and open trial before a jury of their peers. They also have the right to be represented by an attorney, to know the charges against them, to examine witnesses, and to present evidence in their own defense.

SEVENTH AMENDMENT (1791) *Civil Trials*

In suits at common law, where the value in controversy shall exceed twenty dollars, the right of trial by jury shall be preserved, and no fact tried by a jury shall be otherwise reexamined in any court of the United States, than according to the rules of the common law.

SEVENTH AMENDMENT This amendment applies only to civil cases—that is, cases heard in federal courts that involve the rights of private individuals and involve no criminal behavior. People have a right to a jury trial in cases involving more than twenty dollars, a fairly large amount of money in the 1700s, unless both parties agree to waive, or give up, that right.

EIGHTH AMENDMENT (1791) *Punishment for Crimes*

Excessive bail shall not be required, nor excessive fines imposed, nor cruel and unusual punishments inflicted.

EIGHTH AMENDMENT Bail is the sum of money that a person accused of a crime may be required to post, or deposit with the court, in order to guarantee his or her appearance before the court at the proper time. Governments in the United States may require bail. They may also punish people convicted of crimes. The purpose of this amendment is to make certain that both bail and punishments are reasonable and fair. For example, executing someone for stealing a small amount of money would be unreasonable; however, the question of what constitutes a fair and reasonable punishment is not always easy to determine. Today, for example, many Americans disagree about whether capital punishment, or the execution of a convicted criminal, is by definition a "cruel and unusual" punishment.

NINTH AMENDMENT (1791) *Unenumerated Rights*

The enumeration in the Constitution, of certain rights, shall not be construed to deny or disparage others retained by the people.

NINTH AMENDMENT The Constitution lists many, but not all, of the rights enjoyed by the people. In other words, because a right is not spelled out in the Constitution does not necessarily mean that the people do not have this right. The point of this amendment was to prevent governments from denying people a right simply because it was not specifically listed in the Constitution.

TENTH AMENDMENT (1791) *Powers Reserved to the States*

The powers not delegated to the United States by the Constitution, nor prohibited by it to the States, are reserved to the states respectively, or to the people.

TENTH AMENDMENT The states are free to exercise whatever powers are not specifically given to the federal government or denied the states by the Constitution. In other words, states can do whatever they wish, as long as the Constitution does not prohibit the activity or reserve it solely for the federal government.

ELEVENTH AMENDMENT (1798) *Suits Against States*

The judicial power of the United States shall not be construed to extend to any suit in law or equity, commenced or prosecuted against one of the United States by citizens of another state, or by citizens or subjects of any foreign state.

ELEVENTH AMENDMENT People from other states or from foreign countries may not sue a state in federal court. For example, a resident of Pennsylvania, a citizen of France, or the government of France may not sue the state of Ohio in federal court.

Proposed by Congress March 4, 1794; ratified February 7, 1795; officially announced January 8, 1798.

TWELFTH AMENDMENT (1804) *Election of President and Vice President*

The electors shall meet in their respective states, and vote by ballot for President and Vice President, one of whom, at least, shall not be an inhabitant of the same state with themselves; they shall name in their ballots the person voted for as President, and in distinct ballots the person voted for as Vice President, and they shall make distinct lists of all persons voted for as President, and of all persons voted for as Vice President, and of the number of votes for each, which lists they shall sign and certify, and transmit sealed to the seat of the government of the United States, directed to the president of the Senate; the president of the Senate shall, in the presence of the Senate and the House of Representatives, open all the certificates and the votes shall then be counted;—the person having the greatest number of votes for President shall be the President, if such number be a majority of the whole number of electors appointed; and if no person have such a majority, then from the persons having the highest numbers not exceeding three on the list of those voted for as President, the House of Representatives shall choose immediately, by ballot, the President. But in choosing the President, the votes shall be taken by states, the representation from each state having one vote; a quorum for this purpose shall consist of a member or members from two thirds of the states, and a majority of all the states shall be necessary to a choice. And if the House of Representatives shall not choose a President whenever the right of choice shall devolve upon them, before the fourth day of March next following, then the Vice President, shall act as President, as in the case of the death or other constitutional disability of the President.—The person having the greatest number of votes as Vice President, shall be the Vice President, if such number be a majority of the whole number of electors appointed, and if no person have a majority, then from the two highest numbers on the list, the Senate shall choose the Vice President; a quorum for the purpose shall consist of two thirds of the whole number of senators, and a majority of the whole number shall be necessary to a choice. But no person constitutionally ineligible to the office of President shall be eligible to that of Vice President of the United States.

TWELFTH AMENDMENT This amendment was a response to the election of 1800. Article II, Section 1, Clause 3 stated that each member of the Electoral College should vote for two people for President of the United States; the one with the most votes would win, and the person who finished second would become Vice President. In 1800, however, Thomas Jefferson and Aaron Burr ended up with the same number of electoral votes. To prevent another tie, the Twelfth Amendment separates the voting for the two offices. Each elector now casts one vote for President and another for Vice President.

The Twentieth Amendment (1933) changed inauguration day from March 4 to January 20, mainly because of the sense of national emergency during the Depression and the problems created by Franklin Roosevelt having to wait from November to March to become President.

When slavery was abolished after the Civil War, African Americans and white Americans shared new working relationships, as these cowhands illustrate.

Proposed by Congress December 9, 1803; ratified June 15, 1804.

THIRTEENTH AMENDMENT (1865) *Slavery and Involuntary Servitude*
Section 1 *Outlawing Slavery*
Neither slavery nor involuntary servitude, except as a punishment for crime whereof the party shall have been duly convicted, shall exist within the United States, or any place subject to their jurisdiction.

Section 2 *Enforcement*
Congress shall have power to enforce this article by appropriate legislation.

THIRTEENTH AMENDMENT With the addition of this amendment following the North's victory in the Civil War, the Constitution forbade the practice of slavery anywhere in the United States. American citizens may not be held against their will unless they have been convicted of a crime. Section 2 simply gave Congress the power to enforce the abolition of slavery.

Proposed by Congress January 31, 1865; ratified December 6, 1865.

FOURTEENTH AMENDMENT (1868) *Rights of Citizens*
Section 1 *Citizenship*
All persons born or naturalized in the United States, and subject to the jurisdiction thereof, are citizens of the United States and of the state wherein they reside. No state shall make or enforce any law which shall abridge the privileges or immunities of citizens of the United States; nor shall any state deprive any person of life, liberty, or property, without due process of law; nor deny to any person within its jurisdiction the equal protection of the laws.

SECTION 1 Until the Civil War, constitutional amendments had been directed primarily at restricting the power of the national government. The Fourteenth Amendment, on the other hand, protects citizens against the states. Congress passed this amendment during the Reconstruction era, when some northerners were angry about the attempts by southern states to evade or ignore legislation dealing with the rights of African Americans.

This section of the amendment defines citizenship. People are citizens of the United States if they are born within its territorial borders or if they have been naturalized through the legal process. States can neither deprive American citizens of any of their rights and privileges without "due process of law," nor discriminate against them. They are entitled to "equal protection of the laws" simply because they are citizens of the United States. The purpose of this amendment was to protect former enslaved persons from state governments, many of which were trying to restrict their rights. Here the federal government is no longer viewed as the potential enemy of the people, as it had been in most of the first thirteen amendments. Now it is an ally of the people against potentially oppressive state governments.

It would be difficult to overestimate the importance of this section of the Fourteenth Amendment in the history of the United States. Through the "due process" provision, the Supreme Court has extended to the state governments the restrictions on government action listed in the first eight amendments.

Section 2 *Apportionment of Representatives*
Representatives shall be apportioned among the several states according to their respective numbers, counting the whole number of persons in each state, excluding Indians not taxed. But when the right to vote at any election for the choice of electors for President and Vice President of the United States, representatives in Congress, the executive and judicial officers of a state, or the members of the legislature thereof, is denied to any of the male inhabitants of such state, being twenty-one years of age, and citizens of the

United States, or in any way abridged, except for participation in rebellion, or other crime, the basis of representation therein shall be reduced in the proportion which the number of such male citizens shall bear to the whole number of male citizens twenty-one years of age in such state.

SECTION 2 The first sentence replaces Article I, Section 2, Clause 3. From this point forward, all people were to be counted equally in the census.

Section 3 *Former Confederate Officials*
No person shall be a senator or representative in Congress, or elector of President and Vice President, or hold any office, civil or military, under the United States, or under any state, who, having previously taken an oath, as a member of Congress, or as an officer of the United States, or as a member of any state legislature, or as an executive or judicial officer of any state, to support the Constitution of the United States, shall have engaged in insurrection or rebellion against the same, or given aid or comfort to the enemies thereof. But Congress may, by a vote of two thirds of each house, remove such disability.

SECTION 3 This paragraph concerns the pardoning of the men who led the Confederate States of America during the Civil War. Many members of Congress were upset with President Andrew Johnson's liberal pardon policy. This provision essentially gave Congress the power to pardon former Confederates. Congress repealed this section in 1898.

Section 4 *Public Debt*
The validity of the public debt of the United States, authorized by law, including debts incurred for payment of pensions and bounties for services in suppressing insurrection or rebellion, shall not be questioned. But neither the United States nor any state shall assume or pay any debt or obligation incurred in aid of insurrection or rebellion against the United States, or any claim for the loss or emancipation of any slave; but all such debts, obligations and claims shall be held illegal and void.

SECTION 4 According to this section, the public debt of the United States, including that incurred in fighting the Civil War, was legal and would be paid. The public debt of the Confederate States of America, however, was illegal and would not be paid. No one could recover any money they loaned the Confederacy or any expense they had incurred in supporting the South during the Civil War. Nor could they receive compensation for the loss of enslaved persons. This section was simply a punishment designed to hurt those who had engaged in, or supported, rebellion against the Union.

Section 5 *Enforcement*
The Congress shall have power to enforce, by appropriate legislation, the provisions of this article.

SECTION 5 Congress may do what is necessary to make sure Americans obey the provisions of the Fourteenth Amendment.

Proposed by Congress June 13, 1866; ratified July 9, 1868.

FIFTEENTH AMENDMENT (1870) *Right to Vote—Race, Color, Servitude*
Section 1 *Extending the Right to Vote*
The right of citizens of the United States to vote shall not be denied or abridged by the United States or by any state on account of race, color, or previous condition of servitude.

Section 2 *Enforcement*
The Congress shall have power to enforce this article by appropriate legislation.

FIFTEENTH AMENDMENT Like the Fourteenth Amendment, the purpose of the Fifteenth Amendment was to protect African Americans from the attempts of southern states to restrict their rights. As a result of this amendment, no state could deny persons the right to vote on the basis of race or color or because they had once been enslaved.

Proposed by Congress February 26, 1869; ratified February 3, 1870.

SIXTEENTH AMENDMENT (1913) *Income Tax*
The Congress shall have power to lay and collect taxes on incomes, from whatever source derived, without apportionment among the several states, and without regard to any census or enumeration.

SIXTEENTH AMENDMENT This amendment gives Congress the right to collect an income tax. Both the United States and its government had grown larger and more expensive to run, and the purpose of the income tax was to ensure a fair and regular source of income. The amendment modified Article I, Section, 2, Clause 3 and Section 9, Clause 4.

Proposed by Congress July 12, 1909; ratified February 3, 1913.

SEVENTEENTH AMENDMENT (1913) *Popular Election of Senators*
Section 1 *Method of Election*
The senate of the United State shall be composed of two senators from each state, elected by the people thereof, for six years; and each senator shall have one vote. The electors in each state shall have the qualifications requisite for electors of the most numerous branch of the state legislatures.

SECTION 1 Repealing parts of Article I, Section 3, Clauses 1 and 2, this amendment provides for the direct election of United States senators. As a result, voters, rather than state legislatures, choose their senators. Any person who is qualified to vote for state representatives can vote for United States senators.

Section 2 *Vacancies*
When vacancies happen in the representation of any state in the Senate, the executive authority of such state shall issue writs of election to fill such vacancies: provided, that the legislature of any state may empower the executive thereof to make temporary appointments until the people fill the vacancies by election as the legislature may direct.

SECTION 2 If a senator dies or resigns while in office, the governor of that state may appoint someone to serve until an election can be held, if the legislature of his or her state grants the governor such power.

Section 3 *Those Elected Under Previous Procedure*
This amendment shall not be so construed as to affect the election or term of any senator chosen before it becomes valid as part of the Constitution.

SECTION 3 Anyone who was serving in the Senate when this amendment was passed by Congress could complete his or her term.

Proposed by Congress May 13, 1912; ratified April 8, 1913.

EIGHTEENTH AMENDMENT (1919)
Prohibition of Intoxicating Liquors
Section 1 *Ban on Alcohol*
After one year from the ratification of this article, the manufacture, sale, or transportation of intoxicating liquors within, the importation thereof into, or the exportation thereof from the United States and all territory subject to the jurisdiction thereof for beverage purposes is hereby prohibited.

The Eighteenth Amendment's ban on alcohol forced many beer companies to sell new products.

Women finally gained the right to vote in 1920 with the passage of the Nineteenth Amendment, thanks to suffragists such as this one.

Section 2 *Enforcement*
The Congress and the several states shall have concurrent power to enforce this article by appropriate legislation.

Section 3 *Method of Ratification*
This article shall be inoperative unless it shall have been ratified as an amendment to the Constitution by the legislatures of the several states, as provided in the Constitution, within seven years from the date of the submission hereof to the states by Congress.

EIGHTEENTH AMENDMENT Climaxing a long campaign against alcohol that had begun in the early 1800s, this amendment forbid the making, selling, transporting, importing, and exporting of alcoholic beverages in the United States. Called prohibition, it was later repealed by the Twenty-first Amendment.

Proposed by Congress December 18, 1917; ratified January 16, 1919.

NINETEENTH AMENDMENT (1920) *Women's Suffrage*
The right of citizens of the United States to vote shall not be denied or abridged by the United states or by any state on account of sex.

Congress shall have power to enforce this article by appropriate legislation.

NINETEENTH AMENDMENT Like the Thirteenth Amendment, which made slavery illegal, this amendment testifies to the Constitution's reputation as a "living document," one that can be revised to reflect major social changes. The authors of the Constitution could scarcely have imagined a world in which women could vote. By the early 1900s, however, many Americans believed women were entitled to a voice in their own government. This amendment gives them the right to vote. Notice how the language restricts both the federal and the state governments from denying someone the vote on the basis of their sex.

Proposed by Congress June 4, 1919; ratified August 18, 1920.

TWENTIETH AMENDMENT (1933) *Commencement of Terms; Sessions of Congress; Death or Disqualification of President-Elect*

Section 1 *Beginning of Terms*
The terms of the President and Vice President shall end at noon on the 20th day of January, and the terms of senators and representatives at noon on the 3d day of January, of the years in which such terms would have ended if this article had not been ratified; and the terms of their successors shall then begin.

Section 2 *Congressional Sessions*
The Congress shall assemble at least once in every year, and such meeting shall begin at noon on the 3d day of January, unless they shall by law appoint a different day.

TWENTIETH AMENDMENT Largely a housekeeping amendment, its purpose was to speed up the transfer of power from one President to another and to limit the time that a defeated or retiring member of Congress—"a lame duck"— could serve. This amendment was a response to the long delay between Franklin Roosevelt's election in 1932 and his assumption of the presidency in 1933 at a time when the nation was in crisis. The amendment changed inauguration day from March 4 to January 20.

Section 3 *Presidential Succession*
If, at the time fixed for the beginning of the term of the President, the President-elect shall have died, the Vice President-elect shall become President. If a President shall not have been chosen before the time fixed for the beginning of his term, or if the President-elect shall have failed to qualify, then the Vice President-elect shall act as President until a President shall have qualified; and the Congress may by law provide for the case wherein neither a President-elect nor a Vice President-elect shall have qualified, declaring who shall then act as President, or the manner in which one who is to

act shall be selected, and such person shall act accordingly until a President or Vice President shall have qualified.

SECTION 3 These provisions deal with hypothetical cases. No situation like the ones described in this paragraph has ever occurred.

Section 4 *Elections Decided by Congress*
The Congress may by law provide for the case of the death of any of the persons from whom the House of Representatives may choose a President whenever the right of choice shall have devolved upon them, and for the case of the death of any of the persons from whom the Senate may choose a Vice President whenever the right of choice shall have devolved upon them.

SECTION 4 Congress has never passed such a law, largely because the situation described in the section is an extremely unlikely one. Essentially, this section provides a procedure for replacing presidential candidates who die before a final choice of President can be made, assuming no one received a majority of Electoral College votes in the first place.

Section 5 *Date of Implementation*
~~Sections 1 and 2 shall take effect on the 15th day of October following the ratification of this article.~~

Section 6 *Ratification Period*
~~This article shall be inoperative unless it shall have been ratified as an amendment to the Constitution by the legislatures of three fourths of the several states within seven years from the date of its submission.~~

SECTIONS 5 AND 6 Beginning with the Eighteenth Amendment, Congress set a limit of seven years for the ratification process.

Proposed by Congress March 2, 1932; ratified January 23, 1933.

TWENTY-FIRST AMENDMENT (1933) *Repeal of Prohibition*

Section 1 *Repeal*
The eighteenth article of amendment to the Constitution of the United States is hereby repealed.

Section 2 *State Laws*
The transportation or importation into any state, territory, or possession of the United States for delivery or use therein of intoxicating liquors, in violation of the laws thereof, is hereby prohibited.

Section 3 *Ratification Period*
~~This article shall be inoperative unless it shall have been ratified as an amendment to the Constitution by conventions in the several states, as provided in the Constitution, within~~

~~seven years from the date of the submission hereof to the states by the Congress.~~

TWENTY-FIRST AMENDMENT This amendment, the only one submitted to state conventions rather than to legislatures, repealed the Eighteenth Amendment and marked the failure of prohibition. Section 2 does give states power to regulate the distribution and use of intoxicating beverages in ways that would be unconstitutional with any other commodity.

Proposed by Congress February 20, 1933; ratified December 5, 1933.

TWENTY-SECOND AMENDMENT (1951) *Presidential Tenure*
Section 1 *Two-Term Limit*
No person shall be elected to the office of the President more than twice, and no person who has held the office of President, or acted as President for more than two years of a term to which some other person was elected President shall be elected to the office of the President more than once. ~~But this article shall not apply to any person holding the office of President when this article was proposed by the Congress, and shall not prevent any person who may be holding the office of President, or acting as President, during the term within which this article becomes operative from holding the office of President or acting as President during the remainder of such term.~~

Section 2 *Ratification Period*
~~This article shall be inoperative unless it shall have been ratified as an amendment to the Constitution by the legislatures of three-fourths of the several states within seven years from the date of its submission to the States by the Congress.~~

TWENTY-SECOND AMENDMENT Written in reaction to Franklin Roosevelt's four terms as President, this amendment limited future Presidents (after President Harry Truman, who was in office at the time) to two terms. If a Vice President succeeded a President when the latter was more than halfway through his term, then that Vice President could run for two more terms. For example, Lyndon Johnson became President during President Kennedy's third year in office; Johnson ran for President in 1964 and won. He could have run again in 1968, if he had chosen to do so. But no President can serve more than ten years. In the nation's history, only Franklin Roosevelt has been President for more than eight years; he served a little more than twelve.

Proposed by Congress March 24, 1947; ratified February 27, 1951.

TWENTY-THIRD AMENDMENT (1961) *Presidential Electors for the District of Columbia*

Section 1 *Determining Number of Electors*
The district constituting the seat of government of the United States shall appoint in such manner as the Congress may direct:

A number of electors of President and Vice President equal to the whole number of senators and representatives in Congress to which the district would be entitled if it were a state, but in no event more than the least populous state; they shall be in addition to those appointed by the states, but they shall be considered, for the purposes of the election of President and Vice President, to be electors appointed by a state; and they shall meet in the district and perform such duties as provided by the twelfth article of amendment.

Section 2 *Enforcement*
The Congress shall have power to enforce this article by appropriate legislation.

TWENTY-THIRD AMENDMENT Until this amendment became law in 1961, residents of Washington, D.C., could not vote for President of the United States. The Twenty-third Amendment gives them that right. The District has three electoral votes; it cannot have more than any state. Residents of Washington still do not have voting representatives in the United States Senate or in the House of Representatives. In fact, Congress governed the capital city until 1968, when it granted residents the right to elect their own mayor and city council.

Proposed by Congress June 16, 1960; ratified March 29, 1961.

TWENTY-FOURTH AMENDMENT (1964) *Right to Vote in Federal Elections—Tax Payment*
Section 1 *Poll Tax Banned*
The right of citizens of the United States to vote in any primary or other election for President or Vice President, for electors for President or Vice President, or for senator or representative in Congress, shall not be denied or abridged by the United States or any state by reason of failure to pay any poll tax or other tax.

Section 2 *Enforcement*
The Congress shall have the power to enforce this article by appropriate legislation.

TWENTY-FOURTH AMENDMENT Some states used poll taxes in order to keep African Americans and poor Americans from voting in elections. This amendment made it illegal to require people to pay a tax in order to vote for a federal officeholder. Like the Reconstruction amendments (Thirteenth to Fifteenth), its purpose is to keep states from infringing on the rights of any of their citizens.

Proposed by Congress September 14, 1962; ratified January 23, 1964.

TWENTY-FIFTH AMENDMENT (1967) *Presidential Succession, Vice Presidential Vacancy, Presidential Inability*

Section 1 *President's Death or Resignation*

In case of the removal of the President from office or of his death or resignation, the Vice President shall become President.

SECTION 1 Written shortly after the assassination of President John F. Kennedy, this section simply clarified Article II, Section 1, Clause 6. It followed the precedent established by Vice President John Tyler when he became President upon the death of President William Henry Harrison in 1841.

Section 2 *Vacancies in Vice Presidency*

Whenever there is a vacancy in the office of the Vice President, the President shall nominate a Vice President who shall take office upon confirmation by a majority vote of both houses of Congress.

SECTION 2 The purpose of this paragraph was to outline a procedure for filling a vacancy in the office of Vice President. After the assassination of President Kennedy in November 1963, the United States did not have a Vice President until January 1965. The vacancy marked the sixteenth time in American history that such a situation had occurred. This section provided a procedure for choosing a new Vice President; it has been used only twice. The first time occurred in 1973, when Spiro T. Agnew resigned the vice presidency. President Richard Nixon nominated and Congress confirmed Gerald R. Ford as Vice President. In 1974, when President Nixon resigned, Ford became President and chose Nelson Rockefeller to be the Vice President.

Section 3 *Disability of the President*

Whenever the President transmits to the president pro tempore of the Senate and the Speaker of the House of Representatives his written declaration that he is unable to discharge the powers and duties of his office, and until he transmits to them a written declaration to the contrary, such powers and duties shall be discharged by the Vice President as acting President.

SECTION 3 This section provides for a situation in which a President is too sick, too mentally incapacitated, or too gravely wounded to carry out the duties of his office.

Section 4

Vice President as Acting President

Whenever the Vice President and a majority of either the principal officers of the executive departments or of such other body as Congress may by law provide, transmit to the

The resignation of President Nixon placed Vice President Gerald Ford into the nation's highest office, giving him the power to pardon his predecessor.

president pro tempore of the Senate and the Speaker of the House of Representatives their written declaration that the President is unable to discharge the powers and duties of his office, the Vice President shall immediately assume the powers and duties of the office as acting President.

Thereafter, when the President transmits to the president pro tempore of the Senate and the Speaker of the House of Representatives his written declaration that no inability exists, he shall resume the powers and duties of his office unless the Vice President and a majority of either the principal officers of the executive department or of such other body as Congress may by law provide, transmit within four days to the president pro tempore of the Senate and the Speaker of the House of Representatives their written declaration that the President is unable to discharge the powers and duties of his office. Thereupon Congress shall decide the issue, assembling within forty-eight hours for that purpose if not in session. If the Congress, within twenty-one days after receipt of the latter written declaration, or, if Congress in not in session, within twenty-one days after Congress is required to assemble, determines by two thirds vote of both Houses that the President is unable to discharge the powers and duties of his office, the Vice President shall continue to discharge the same as acting President; otherwise, the President shall resume the powers and duties of his office.

SECTION 4 This section creates the procedure whereby somebody other than the President determines whether he or she is incapable of performing his or her duties. Initiating such an action requires the agreement of the Vice President and a majority of the cabinet. This procedure has never been used.

Proposed by Congress July 6, 1965; ratified February 10, 1967.

TWENTY-SIXTH AMENDMENT (1971) *Right to Vote—Age*
Section 1 *Lowering of Voting Age*
The right of citizens of the United States, who are eighteen years of age or older, shall not be denied or abridged by the United States or by any state on account of age.

Section 2 *Enforcement*
The Congress shall have the power to enforce this article by appropriate legislation.

TWENTY-SIXTH AMENDMENT In response to the size and influence of the "baby boom" generation, Congress lowered the minimum age to eighteen for voting in elections in the United States. A state could, if it wished, make the minimum age even lower.

Proposed by Congress March 23, 1971; ratified July 1, 1971.

TWENTY-SEVENTH AMENDMENT (1992) *Congressional Pay*
No law, varying the compensation for the services of the senators and representatives, shall take effect until an election of representatives shall have intervened.

TWENTY-SEVENTH AMENDMENT Congress can vote an increase in the pay of its members, but that increase may not take effect until after the next election. In other words, it gives "the people" a chance to express their opinion on the subject before it becomes law.

Proposed by Congress September 25, 1989; ratified May 18, 1992.

Illustrated Data Bank

T he maps, tables, and graphs that make up this Illustrated Data Bank are designed as reference materials to help you in your study of United States history. The first eight pages present data that is organized chronologically. This page and the facing page show a demographic picture of the nation in 1790. A table on pages 882 and 883 presents a summary of selected wars between Native American groups and the United States government. Pages 884 and 885 show three maps that describe the United States population in 1890 and territorial growth. Page 886 compares birth rate and median age over time and page 887 presents a demographic picture of the United States in 1990. The last five pages of the Illustrated Data Bank contain a physical-political map of the United States, a world political map, and a table of the fifty states.

Wherever possible, maps, tables, and graphs present data on three years: 1790, 1890, and 1990. This makes it possible to make comparisons among the different sets of data. For example, you can compare the population density maps to see how the nation's population changed from 1790 to 1890 to 1990. You can also compare data presented for the same year; for example, you can compare the map on this page with the table on the next page.

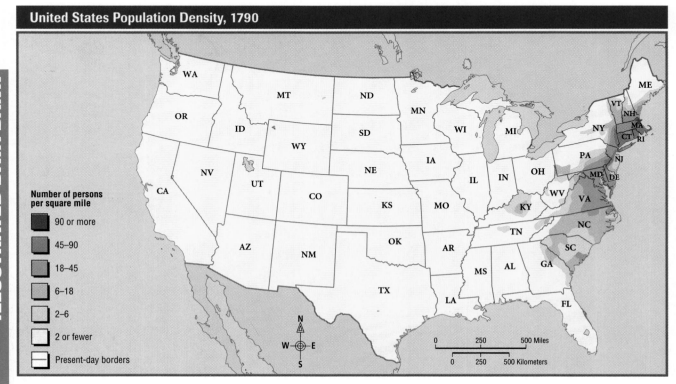

United States Population Density, 1790

Number of persons per square mile

- 90 or more
- 45–90
- 18–45
- 6–18
- 2–6
- 2 or fewer
- Present-day borders

United States Ethnic Groups, 1790

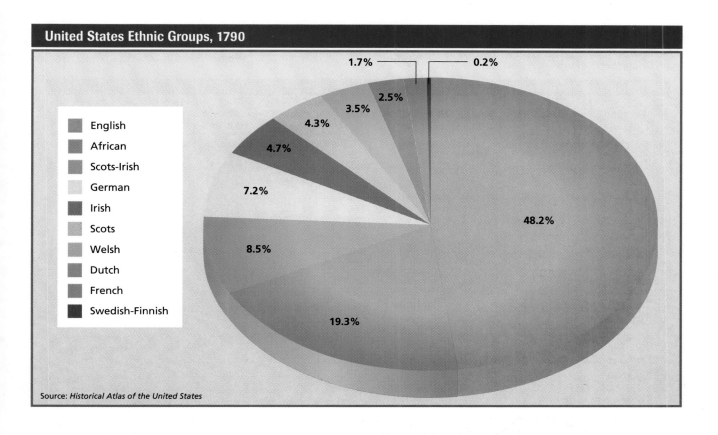

Legend:
- English
- African
- Scots-Irish
- German
- Irish
- Scots
- Welsh
- Dutch
- French
- Swedish-Finnish

48.2%
19.3%
8.5%
7.2%
4.7%
4.3%
3.5%
2.5%
1.7%
0.2%

Source: *Historical Atlas of the United States*

Enslaved Population of the United States, 1790

State	Total Population	Enslaved Population	Percent Enslaved
Connecticut	237,946	2,648	1.11
Delaware	59,096	8,837	14.95
Georgia	82,548	29,624	35.89
Maryland	319,728	103,036	32.33
Massachusetts	475,307	0	0.00
New Hampshire	141,885	157	0.11
New Jersey	184,139	11,423	6.20
New York	340,120	21,193	6.23
North Carolina	393,751	100,783	25.60
Pennsylvania	434,373	3,707	0.85
Rhode Island	68,825	958	1.39
South Carolina	249,073	107,094	43.00
Virginia	747,600	292,627	39.14

Source: *Historical Statistics of the United States*

Selected Major Indian Wars, 1794–1890

In the first column, states in parentheses refer to present-day states.
All casualty figures are estimates.

Old Northwest Territory

Battle of Fallen Timbers, 1794 (Ohio)	General Anthony Wayne and his 2,000 soldiers defeated a force of nearly 2,000 Miami led by Chief Little Turtle near what is now Toledo, Ohio. Wayne's victory forced the Native Americans to give up land in present-day Ohio and Indiana.
Battle of Tippecanoe, 1811 (Indiana)	A 1,000-man army led by William Henry Harrison defeated Shawnee chief Tecumseh and his alliance of Native Americans at present-day Battle Ground, Indiana.
War of 1812	During the war, many Native American groups joined the British to fight against the Americans.
Battle at River Raisin, 1813 (Ohio)	On the River Raisin, Tecumseh's alliance and British forces attacked and defeated the Kentucky militia.
Black Hawk's War, 1832 (Illinois, Wisconsin)	Led by Chief Black Hawk, Sauk and Fox resisted white demands, initiating a short war that consisted mainly of the outnumbered Native Americans trying to escape from the United States Army.
• Battle of Stillman's Run, 1832 (Illinois)	A force of about 40 Native Americans routed a 274-man militia commanded by Major Isaiah Stillman.
• Battle of Wisconsin Heights, 1832 (Wisconsin)	Fifty warriors held off 500 soldiers while the Sauk and Fox crossed the Wisconsin River.
• Bad Axe River, 1832 (Wisconsin)	The Army severely defeated Black Hawk's group, ending Native American resistance in the Northwest Territory. Hundreds of men, women, and children were shot or drowned as they crossed the Mississippi River.

Southeast

Creek War, 1813–1814 (Alabama, Georgia, Mississippi)	Moved to action by the encroachment of white settlers and the warnings of Shawnee leader Tecumseh, the Creek launched attacks in Alabama, Georgia, and Mississippi.
• Fort Mims Massacre, 1813 (Alabama)	In a surprise attack, the Creek attacked Fort Mims in Alabama and massacred more than 350 settlers.
• Battle of Horseshoe Bend, 1814 (Alabama)	General Andrew Jackson, aided by friendly Creek and Cherokee, virtually annihilated 1,000 Creek warriors. Jackson's victory forced the Creek to give up about two thirds of their land in Alabama.
First Seminole War, 1818 (Florida)	Seminole in northern Florida rose against whites, prompting General Jackson to invade Florida with a force of 3,000 men. Many Seminole were forced onto reservations.
Second Seminole War, 1835–1842 (Florida)	War began when the United States tried to move Seminole from Florida. Most of the Seminole surrendered in 1842.
• Dade's Massacre, 1835 (Florida)	Seminole warriors ambushed and defeated Major Francis Dade's force of 150 soldiers sent to reinforce Fort King. One soldier survived and 149 died.
• Battle of Okeechobee, 1838 (Florida)	About 400 Seminole ambushed General Zachary Taylor's 1,000-man army and were defeated by Taylor's superior numbers.
Third Seminole War, 1848–1858 (Florida)	Over ten years of raids and battles, the remaining Seminole were forced out of Florida and moved to reservations in Arkansas.

Northern Plains

Northern Plains Wars, 1854–1890	As white settlers spread farther into Native American territory, the Sioux, Cheyenne, and Shoshoni fought against American soldiers who sought to force the Indians to live on reservations.
• Minnesota Sioux War, 1862–1863	Angered over reservation conditions, the Sioux launch attacks in August 1862, on several settlements in Minnesota, including New Ulm and Fort Ridgely. The army put down the Sioux within a few months.

Selected Major Indian Wars, 1794–1890 (continued)

Northern Plains

• Colorado Cheyenne Wars, 1864–1869 (Colorado)	The Second Colorado Cavalry attacked a peaceful village of Cheyenne at Sand Creek in present-day Colorado. United States soldiers killed an estimated 450 men, women, and children, setting off the Colorado Cheyenne Wars.
• Fetterman Massacre, 1866 (Wyoming)	Crazy Horse and a group of Sioux successfully lured Caption William Fetterman and 80 troops out of Fort Kearny in present-day Wyoming. Fetterman's men rode directly into a force of 1,500 to 2,000 Sioux and were killed to a man.
Battle of the Rosebud, 1876 (Montana)	Led by Crazy Horse, a force of Sioux and Cheyenne defeated General George Crook and an army of about 1,100 men on the banks of the Rosebud River in present-day southern Montana.
Battle of Little Big Horn, 1876 (Montana)	General George Custer attacked a force of 2,000 to 3,000 Sioux and Cheyenne camped in the Little Big Horn valley. Custer and his regiment of over 260 men died.
Massacre at Wounded Knee, 1890 (South Dakota)	As the Seventh Cavalry attempted to disarm a Sioux village camped along the Wounded Knee River, an unidentified shot caused the soldiers to fire. More than 200 unarmed Sioux , including women and children, were killed.

Southern Plains

Pueblo Wars, 1847 (New Mexico)	The Taos Pueblo attacked Americans in present-day New Mexico, setting off a short-lived war. The army defeated the Pueblo within a few weeks, killing more than 160 and hanging six of the leaders.
Navaho Wars, 1846–1864 (New Mexico)	Navaho attacks on white settlers increased with the start of the Civil War. Kit Carson led an army that defeated a Navaho stronghold in Canyon de Chelly in present-day New Mexico and forced the Navaho onto reservations.
Meeker Massacre, 1879 (Colorado)	A Ute revolt began when Ute killed N. C. Meeker, a government agent. The fighting ended when Chief Ouray returned from a hunting trip and restrained his people. This was the last Ute war.
Red River War, 1874 (Texas)	In 1874, almost 4,000 Cheyenne, Kiowa, and Comanche left their reservations and moved into Texas. The army forced the Native Americans to return to their reservations in a campaign led by Lieutenant General Philip Sheridan.
Apache Wars, 1822–1890 (Texas, New Mexico, Arizona, and Mexico)	Leaders such as Mangas Coloradas and Geronimo led Apache raids against American Mexican settlements. After about 40 years of Apache hostilities, the government launched a campaign to kill Apache men and capture the women and children. Survivors were then forced onto reservations. Geronimo and his force surrendered at Skeleton Canyon, Arizona, in 1886, and were shipped to reservations.

Northwest

Cayuse War, 1847–1850 (Washington and Oregon)	Missionaries Marcus and Narcissa Whitman and eleven others were murdered by Cayuse in present-day Washington. The massacre sparked a bitter war. The local militia virtually destroyed the Cayuse as a people.
Rogue River War and Yakima War, 1855–1856 (Oregon)	The Rogue River Indians and Yakima both fought the movement of Americans into their territory and went to war in 1855. The army easily defeated both groups in separate wars, moving each to reservations.
Modoc War, 1872–1873 (Oregon, California)	The Modoc of southern Oregon and northern California left their reservation in northern California to return to their former hunting grounds. At the Battle of the Lava Beds at Tule Lake, California, a small group of Modoc warriors held off an army of 1,000 for months until the Modoc surrendered.
Nez Percé War, 1877 (Oregon, Idaho, Washington, Montana, Colorado)	The Nez Percé War started when a group of Nez Percé attacked white settlers in the Wallawa Valley. Chief Joseph of the Nez Percé led a retreat to Montana, but at Big Hole Basin, United States soldiers attacked. Chief Joseph later surrendered about 40 miles from the Canadian border.

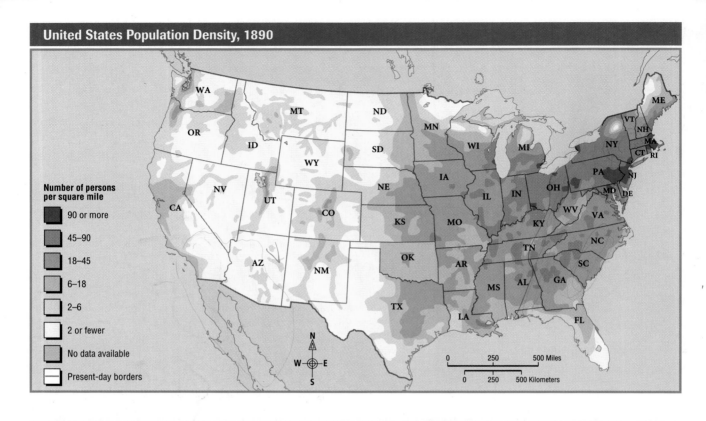

United States Population Density, 1890

Number of persons per square mile

- 90 or more
- 45–90
- 18–45
- 6–18
- 2–6
- 2 or fewer
- No data available
- Present-day borders

0   250   500 Miles
0   250   500 Kilometers

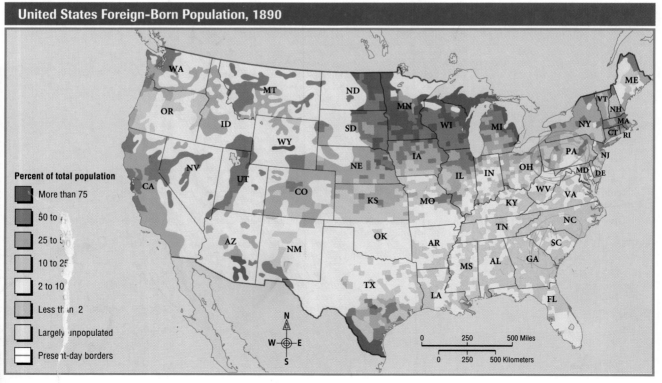

United States Foreign-Born Population, 1890

Percent of total population

- More than 75
- 50 to 7
- 25 to 5
- 10 to 25
- 2 to 10
- Less than 2
- Largely unpopulated
- Present-day borders

0   250   500 Miles
0   250   500 Kilometers

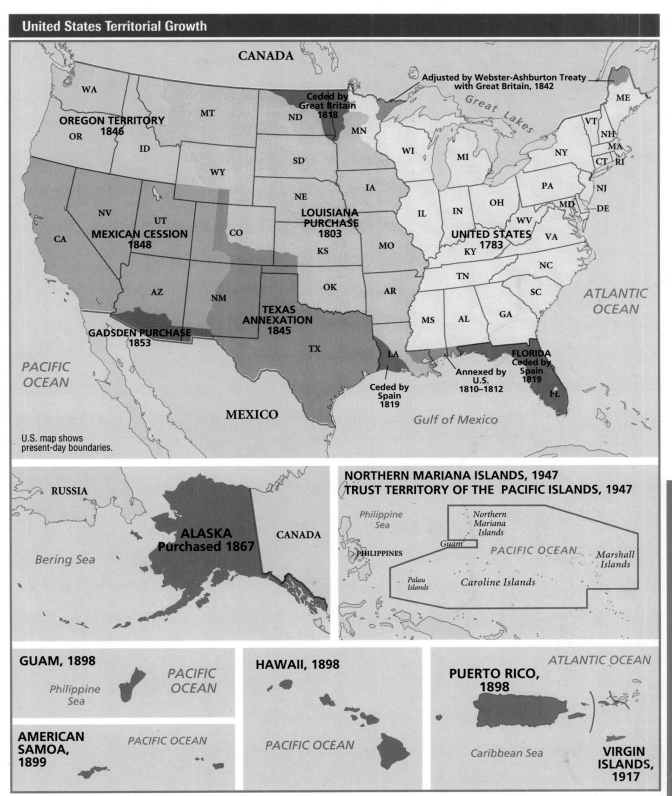

United States Territorial Growth

CANADA

WA

OREGON TERRITORY
1846

OR

ID

MT

ND

Ceded by
Great Britain
1818

Adjusted by Webster-Ashburton Treaty
with Great Britain, 1842

Great Lakes

ME

VT

NH

MA

CT RI

MN

WI

MI

NY

PA

NJ

SD

WY

NE

IA

NV

UT

CO

IL

IN

OH

MD

DE

WV

MEXICAN CESSION
1848

CA

KS

MO

UNITED STATES
1783

VA

KY

NC

TN

AZ

NM

OK

AR

SC

ATLANTIC
OCEAN

GADSDEN PURCHASE
1853

TEXAS
ANNEXATION
1845

MS

AL

GA

PACIFIC
OCEAN

TX

LA

Ceded by
Spain
1819

Annexed by
U.S.
1810–1812

FLORIDA
Ceded by
Spain
1819

FL

MEXICO

Gulf of Mexico

U.S. map shows
present-day boundaries.

RUSSIA

ALASKA
Purchased 1867

CANADA

Bering Sea

NORTHERN MARIANA ISLANDS, 1947
TRUST TERRITORY OF THE PACIFIC ISLANDS, 1947

Philippine
Sea

Northern
Mariana
Islands

Guam

PACIFIC OCEAN

Marshall
Islands

PHILIPPINES

Palau
Islands

Caroline Islands

GUAM, 1898

PACIFIC
OCEAN

Philippine
Sea

HAWAII, 1898

ATLANTIC OCEAN

PUERTO RICO,
1898

AMERICAN
SAMOA,
1899

PACIFIC OCEAN

PACIFIC OCEAN

Caribbean Sea

VIRGIN
ISLANDS,
1917

ILLUSTRATED DATA BANK

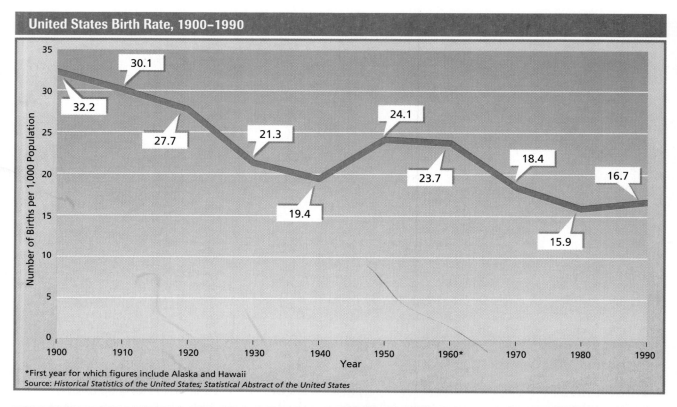

United States Birth Rate, 1900–1990

Number of Births per 1,000 Population

32.2
30.1
27.7
21.3
19.4
24.1
23.7
18.4
15.9
16.7

Year

*First year for which figures include Alaska and Hawaii
Source: *Historical Statistics of the United States; Statistical Abstract of the United States*

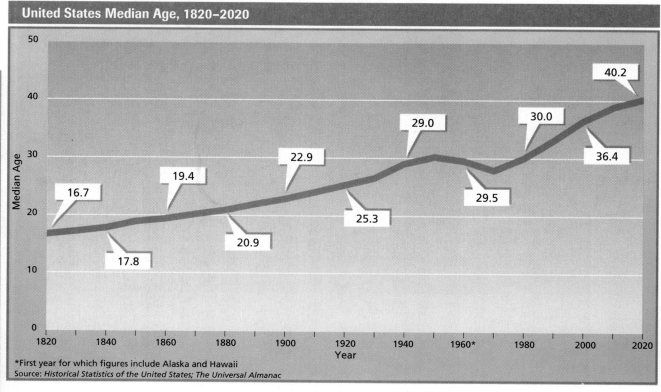

United States Median Age, 1820–2020

Median Age

16.7
17.8
19.4
20.9
22.9
25.3
29.0
29.5
30.0
36.4
40.2

Year

*First year for which figures include Alaska and Hawaii
Source: *Historical Statistics of the United States; The Universal Almanac*

United States Population by Race, 1990

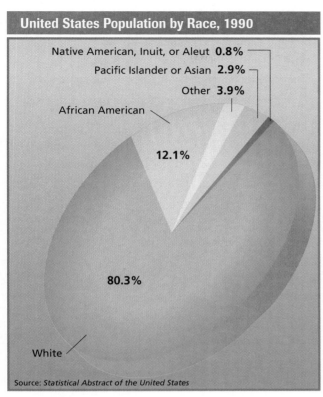

Native American, Inuit, or Aleut **0.8%**
Pacific Islander or Asian **2.9%**
Other **3.9%**
African American
12.1%
80.3%
White

Source: *Statistical Abstract of the United States*

United States Latino Population, 1990

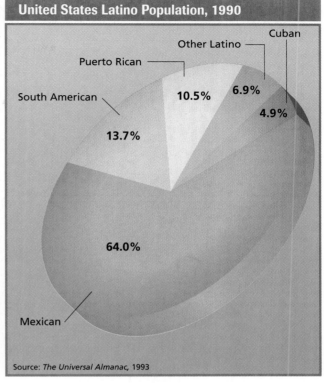

Other Latino
Cuban
Puerto Rican
South American
10.5%
6.9%
4.9%
13.7%
64.0%
Mexican

Source: *The Universal Almanac,* 1993

United States Population Density, 1990

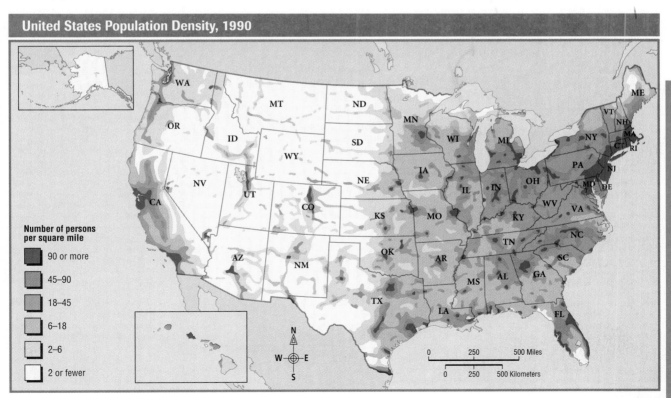

Number of persons per square mile

- 90 or more
- 45–90
- 18–45
- 6–18
- 2–6
- 2 or fewer

0   250   500 Miles
0   250   500 Kilometers

ILLUSTRATED DATA BANK

Elevations

Feet		Meters
13,120		4,000
6,560		2,000
1,640		500
656		200
0		0
Below sea level		Below sea level

⊛ National capital

★ State capitals

• Other cities

▲ Mountain peaks

UNITED STATES: PHYSICAL-POLITICAL

CANADA

Lake of the
Woods

Lake Superior

Presque Isle
Houlton

ME

Bangor

Augusta
Lewiston

BAHAMAS

ATLANTIC
OCEAN

Gulf of Mexico

ILLUSTRATED DATA BANK

THE WORLD: POLITICAL

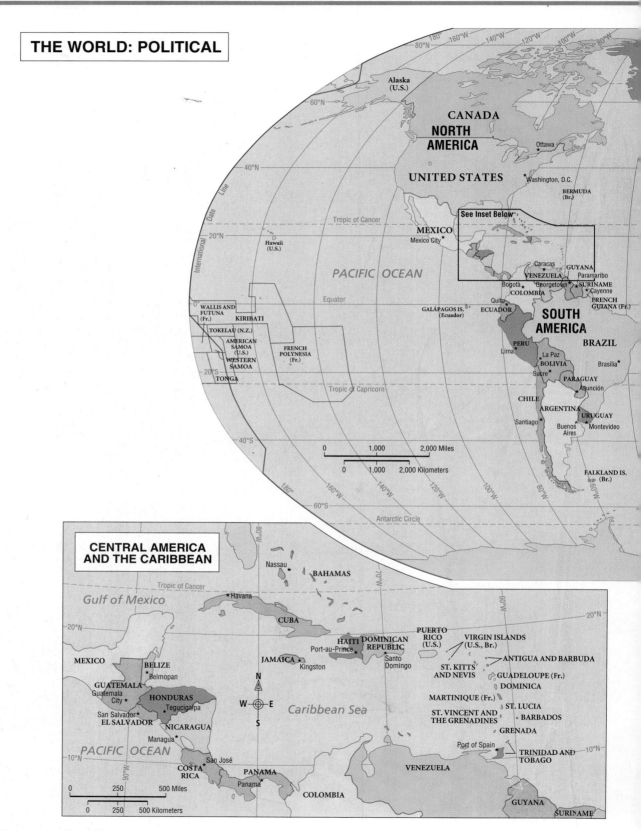

80°N 160°W 140°W 120°W 100°W 80°W

Alaska (U.S.)

60°N

CANADA
NORTH
AMERICA

Ottawa ★

40°N

UNITED STATES

★ Washington, D.C.

BERMUDA (Br.)

Tropic of Cancer

See Inset Below

20°N

MEXICO
Mexico City ★

Hawaii (U.S.)

Caracas ★
VENEZUELA   GUYANA
Bogotá ★   Georgetown ★ Paramaribo ★
COLOMBIA   SURINAME ★ Cayenne
Quito ★   FRENCH
GALÁPAGOS IS.   ECUADOR   GUIANA (Fr.)
(Ecuador)

International Date Line

PACIFIC OCEAN

Equator

0°

WALLIS AND
FUTUNA
(Fr.)   KIRIBATI

TOKELAU (N.Z.)

SOUTH
AMERICA

BRAZIL

AMERICAN
SAMOA
(U.S.)
WESTERN
SAMOA

FRENCH
POLYNESIA
(Fr.)

PERU
Lima ★

La Paz
★
BOLIVIA
Sucre ★

Brasília ★

20°S

TONGA

PARAGUAY
★ Asunción

Tropic of Capricorn

CHILE

ARGENTINA   URUGUAY
Santiago ★   Buenos ★ Montevideo
             Aires

40°S

0	1,000	2,000 Miles

0	1,000	2,000 Kilometers

FALKLAND IS.
(Br.)

180° 160°W 140°W 120°W 100°W 80°W 60°W

60°S

Antarctic Circle

CENTRAL AMERICA AND THE CARIBBEAN

Nassau ★
BAHAMAS

Tropic of Cancer

Gulf of Mexico

★ Havana

CUBA

70°W

20°N

HAITI DOMINICAN
       REPUBLIC

PUERTO
RICO
(U.S.)   VIRGIN ISLANDS
          (U.S., Br.)

MEXICO

BELIZE
★ Belmopan

JAMAICA ★
Kingston

Port-au-Prince ★
★ Santo
Domingo

ANTIGUA AND BARBUDA

ST. KITTS
AND NEVIS   GUADELOUPE (Fr.)

GUATEMALA
Guatemala
City ★

HONDURAS
★ Tegucigalpa

N

DOMINICA

MARTINIQUE (Fr.)

San Salvador ★
EL SALVADOR

NICARAGUA

W ◆ E

Caribbean Sea

ST. LUCIA
★ BARBADOS

ST. VINCENT AND
THE GRENADINES

Managua ★

S

GRENADA

PACIFIC OCEAN

10°N

COSTA
RICA ★
San José ★

PANAMA
★
Panama

VENEZUELA

Port of Spain ★
TRINIDAD AND
TOBAGO

10°N

90°W

0	250	500 Miles

0	250	500 Kilometers

COLOMBIA

GUYANA

SURINAME

ARCTIC OCEAN

GREENLAND
(Den.)

Arctic Circle

Reykjavik ★ ICELAND

RUSSIA

See Inset Below

EUROPE
★ Moscow

60°N

AZORES
(Port.)

KAZAKHSTAN

MONGOLIA
Ulan Bator

40°N

GEORGIA
ARMENIA
Tbilisi
Ankara
Yerevan
TURKEY

UZBEKISTAN
Bishkek
Alma-Ata
Tashkent
KYRGYZSTAN
TAJIKISTAN
TURKMENISTAN
AZERBAIJAN
Ashkhabad Dushanbe

NORTH
KOREA
Beijing
Pyongyang
Seoul
SOUTH
KOREA

JAPAN
Tokyo

PACIFIC OCEAN

CANARY IS.
(Sp.)

Algiers ★ Tunis
Rabat
TUNISIA

SYRIA
Damascus
IRAQ
Baghdad
Amman
ISRAEL
JORDAN
Cairo

Tehran
IRAN
Kabul
AFGHANISTAN
Islamabad

CHINA

TAIWAN
Taipei

Tropic of Cancer

W. SAHARA
(Morocco)

MOROCCO

ALGERIA
LIBYA
EGYPT

Tripoli

SAUDI
ARABIA
Riyadh
UNITED ARAB
EMIRATES
BAHRAIN
QATAR
KUWAIT
Abu Dhabi
Muscat
OMAN

PAKISTAN

New
Delhi
NEPAL
Kathmandu
Dhaka
BHUTAN

INDIA
BANGLADESH
MYANMAR
(BURMA)
Rangoon

LAOS
Hanoi
Vientiane
THAILAND
Bangkok
CAMBODIA
VIETNAM

HONG KONG (Br.)

NORTHERN MARIANA
ISLANDS (U.S.)

GUAM (U.S.)

MARSHALL
ISLANDS

20°N

CAPE
VERDE

See Inset Below

AFRICA

NIGER
CHAD
SUDAN

Khartoum

Asmara
ERITREA
N'Djamena
CENTRAL
AFRICAN REP.
Bangui
ETHIOPIA
Addis Ababa

YEMEN
Sana'a
DJIBOUTI

SRI
LANKA
Colombo

Phnom Penh

BRUNEI

Kuala Lumpur
MALAYSIA
SINGAPORE

PHILIPPINES
Manila

TRUST TERRITORY
OF THE PACIFIC
ISLANDS (U.S.)

FEDERATED STATES
OF MICRONESIA

Equator

0°

NIGERIA
Abuja

EQUATORIAL GUINEA
SÃO TOMÉ AND
PRINCIPE
Libreville
GABON
CABINDA
(Angola)
Brazzaville
CONGO
Luanda

CAMEROON
Yaoundé
RWANDA
Kinshasa
ZAIRE
BURUNDI

UGANDA
Kampala
KENYA
Nairobi
TANZANIA
Dar es Salaam

SOMALIA
Mogadishu

SEYCHELLES

INDIAN OCEAN

INDONESIA

Jakarta

PAPUA
NEW GUINEA

Port Moresby

NAURU

KIRIBATI

SOLOMON
ISLANDS

TUVALU

ATLANTIC
OCEAN

ANGOLA
ZAMBIA
Lusaka
ZIMBABWE
Harare

MALAWI
Lilongwe

MADAGASCAR
Antananarivo

COMOROS

MAURITIUS
RÉUNION
(France)

Tropic of Capricorn

AUSTRALIA

VANUATU

NEW CALEDONIA (Fr.)

FIJI

20°S

NAMIBIA
Windhoek
BOTSWANA
Gaborone
Pretoria
SOUTH
AFRICA
Cape Town

MOZAMBIQUE
Maputo
SWAZILAND
LESOTHO

N
W   E
S

Canberra

NEW
ZEALAND
Wellington

60°S

Antarctic Circle

ILLUSTRATED DATA BANK

WEST AFRICA

20°N

MAURITANIA
Nouakchott

MALI

NIGER

Dakar
SENEGAL
Banjul
GAMBIA
Bissau
GUINEA-
BISSAU

Bamako
BURKINA
FASO
Ouagadougou

Niamey

10°N

GUINEA
Conakry
Freetown
SIERRA LEONE
Monrovia
LIBERIA

CÔTE
D'IVOIRE
Yamoussoukro

BENIN

TOGO
GHANA
Accra
Lomé
Porto-Novo

NIGERIA

5°N

N
W   E
S

ATLANTIC OCEAN

Equator

0   250   500 Miles
0   250   500 Kilometers

EUROPE

NORWAY
Oslo
SWEDEN
FINLAND
Helsinki

North
Sea

IRELAND
Dublin
UNITED
KINGDOM

Stockholm
Tallinn
ESTONIA
Riga
LATVIA
Moscow

RUSSIA

50°N

London
The
Hague
NETHERLANDS
Amsterdam
BELGIUM
Brussels
Paris
LUXEMBOURG

Copenhagen

Berlin
GERMANY
Prague
Warsaw
POLAND

LITHUANIA
Vilnius
Minsk
BELARUS

Kiev
UKRAINE

ATLANTIC
OCEAN

FRANCE
SWITZERLAND
Bern

Vienna
AUSTRIA
SLOVAKIA
Bratislava
Budapest
HUNGARY

MOLDOVA
Chisinau

PORTUGAL
Lisbon
ANDORRA
MONACO
Madrid
SPAIN

SLOVENIA
Ljubljana
CROATIA
Zagreb
ITALY
SAN
MARINO
Rome

BOS. &
HERZ.
YUGO.
Sarajevo
Belgrade
Serbia
Montenegro

ROMANIA
Bucharest

Black Sea

GEORGIA

40°N

Sofia
BULGARIA

Tirané
ALBANIA
*The Former Yugoslav
Republic of Macedonia

F.Y.R. MAC.
Skopje
GREECE
Athens

TURKEY

SYRIA

GIBRALTAR (Br.)

Mediterranean Sea

MALTA

CYPRUS

LEBANON

0   250   500 Miles
0   250   500 Kilometers

N
W   E
S

State	Capital	Entered Union	Population (1990 Census)	Population Rank	Land Area (Square Miles)	Land Area Rank
Alabama	Montgomery	1819	4,040,587	22nd	51,705	29th
Alaska	Juneau	1959	550,043	49th	591,004	1st
Arizona	Phoenix	1912	3,665,228	24th	114,000	6th
Arkansas	Little Rock	1836	2,350,725	33rd	53,187	27th
California	Sacramento	1850	29,760,021	1st	158,706	3rd
Colorado	Denver	1876	3,294,394	26th	104,091	8th
Connecticut	Hartford	1788	3,287,116	27th	5,018	48th
Delaware	Dover	1787	666,168	46th	2,044	49th
Florida	Tallahassee	1845	12,937,926	4th	58,664	22nd
Georgia	Atlanta	1788	6,478,216	11th	58,910	21st
Hawaii	Honolulu	1959	1,108,229	41st	6,470	47th
Idaho	Boise	1890	1,006,749	42nd	83,564	13th
Illinois	Springfield	1818	11,430,602	6th	56,345	24th
Indiana	Indianapolis	1816	5,544,159	14th	36,185	38th
Iowa	Des Moines	1846	2,776,755	30th	56,275	25th
Kansas	Topeka	1861	2,477,574	32nd	82,277	14th
Kentucky	Frankfort	1792	3,685,296	23rd	40,409	37th
Louisiana	Baton Rouge	1812	4,219,973	21st	47,751	31st
Maine	Augusta	1820	1,227,928	38th	33,265	39th
Maryland	Annapolis	1788	4,781,468	19th	10,460	42nd
Massachusetts	Boston	1788	6,016,425	13th	8,284	45th
Michigan	Lansing	1837	9,295,297	8th	58,527	23rd
Minnesota	St. Paul	1858	4,375,099	20th	84,402	12th
Mississippi	Jackson	1817	2,573,216	31st	47,689	32nd
Missouri	Jefferson City	1821	5,117,073	15th	69,697	19th
Montana	Helena	1889	799,065	44th	147,046	4th
Nebraska	Lincoln	1867	1,578,385	36th	77,355	15th
Nevada	Carson City	1864	1,201,833	39th	110,561	7th
New Hampshire	Concord	1788	1,109,252	40th	9,279	44th
New Jersey	Trenton	1787	7,730,188	9th	7,787	46th
New Mexico	Santa Fe	1912	1,515,069	37th	121,593	5th
New York	Albany	1788	17,990,455	2nd	49,108	30th
North Carolina	Raleigh	1789	6,628,637	10th	52,669	28th
North Dakota	Bismarck	1889	638,800	47th	70,703	17th
Ohio	Columbus	1803	10,847,115	7th	41,330	35th
Oklahoma	Oklahoma City	1907	3,145,585	28th	69,956	18th
Oregon	Salem	1859	2,842,321	29th	97,073	10th
Pennsylvania	Harrisburg	1787	11,881,643	5th	45,308	33rd
Rhode Island	Providence	1790	1,003,464	43rd	1,212	50th
South Carolina	Columbia	1788	3,386,703	25th	31,113	40th
South Dakota	Pierre	1889	696,004	45th	77,116	16th
Tennessee	Nashville	1796	4,877,185	17th	42,144	34th
Texas	Austin	1845	16,986,510	3rd	266,807	2nd
Utah	Salt Lake City	1896	1,722,850	35th	84,899	11th
Vermont	Montpelier	1791	562,758	48th	9,614	43rd
Virginia	Richmond	1788	6,187,358	12th	40,767	36th
Washington	Olympia	1889	4,866,692	18th	68,138	20th
West Virginia	Charleston	1863	1,793,477	34th	24,231	41st
Wisconsin	Madison	1848	4,891,769	16th	56,153	26th
Wyoming	Cheyenne	1890	453,588	50th	97,809	9th

Source: *The Universal Almanac*, 1993

Key Events That Shaped the Nation

In addition to the eight "Turning Point" events discussed in detail in this book, the list that follows describes seventy-six events (arranged in chronological order) that have shaped the United States. Like all such lists, this one is biased—representing the personal opinions of this textbook's authors. The list is not intended to include every event of lasting importance. If it were, the result would be a list many times longer. You are invited to think about the events on this list, debate their significance with your classmates, and add events of your own.

1607 Jamestown and Tobacco

Jamestown, the first permanent English settlement in the Americas, teetered on the edge of ruin for the first decade of its existence. The colony was saved, however, when John Rolfe recognized that tobacco, which was highly prized in Europe, thrived in the climate and soil of Virginia. The lure of wealth from tobacco farming ensured the colony a steady stream of colonists. At the same time, Jamestown provided England with a foothold in North America and helped inspire further attempts at colonization.

1619 The Arrival of Enslaved Africans in North America

In 1619, Dutch traders sold twenty Africans to the English colonists in Jamestown. Unfamiliar with the concept of slavery, the colonists treated the Africans the same way they treated English indentured servants, who were freed after working off debts incurred in their passage to North America. It was not until the 1680s that the use of enslaved Africans became widespread. By 1760 about 325,000 enslaved Africans labored in England's North American colonies.

1651 The Navigation Acts

In the 1600s, England and the Netherlands clashed over which nation would control trade in Europe and the Americas. This economic competition caused the English government to enact a series of Navigation Acts beginning in 1651. These acts sought to cut the Dutch out of the profitable colonial trade by forcing the English colonies to limit their trade in certain goods to England alone. As the result of a series of wars between the two European powers, the English captured and retained the prosperous Dutch colony of New Amsterdam in 1664, renaming it New York. New York City became one of the most profitable commercial centers in the English colonies.

1670 The Founding of South Carolina

Planters from the island of Barbados founded Charleston in 1670, establishing what in 1701 would become the colony of South Carolina. These planters brought enslaved Africans with them, and, using the Africans' knowledge of rice farming, developed a plantation economy based upon rice cultivation. Slavery became so heavily established in South Carolina that by 1720 the African enslaved population outnumbered the white population by two to one. This lopsided ratio created an undercurrent of fear among white Americans that would lead to further repressive measures against the enslaved people.

1680 Popé's Rebellion

In an attempt to gain a firm hold on their colony in New Mexico, the Spanish ruthlessly exploited the native Pueblo people. Not only were the Pueblo forced into slavery, but they were also subject to the Spaniards' brutal attempts at destroying native religious practices. Popé, a Pueblo religious leader, led a rebellion in 1680. Under his leadership, the Pueblo drove the Spanish completely out of New Mexico. The Spanish returned twelve years later, but they never again attempted to enslave the Pueblos and gave some measure of respect to Pueblo cultural identity.

1720s–1760s The Great Awakening

A series of religious revivals swept through the colonies between 1720 and 1760, igniting religious fervor with an emphasis on achieving salvation. The so-called Great Awakening reached its peak in 1739, thanks to the preaching of George Whitefield. The twenty-four-year-old Whitefield, an Anglican priest, won converts by the thousands with his dramatic sermons. The Great Awakening helped shape the colonists' commitment to religious pluralism and equality, which later would help to shape their commitment to revolution against the British Empire.

1759 The Fall of Quebec

After five long years of defeat in the French and Indian War, the British finally turned the tides in 1759. Brigadier General James Wolfe decided to attempt the capture of Quebec, the capital of New France. Wolfe surrounded the fortress, eventually drawing out the French commander, Montcalm, into open battle. When the conflict was over, Wolfe and Montcalm lay dead, and the British controlled Quebec. This victory foreshadowed an overall French defeat in the war and the loss of all the French holdings in North America.

1765 The Stamp Act

In an attempt to raise money and pay the cost of an army to protect the colonies, Parliament passed the Stamp Act in 1765. This law required colonists to buy official stamps—in effect, pay a tax—for items such as legal documents. The

British had had such a tax for 100 years, and Parliament felt justified requiring it in the colonies. But Parliament underestimated colonial reaction to the act. The direct taxation of the Stamp Act outraged and united the colonies. Colonial assemblies passed resolutions claiming the sole right to pass taxes, and riots broke out in numerous port cities. Colonial sentiment against Great Britain deepened.

1775   Lexington and Concord

As relations between colonists and the British worsened, colonists began collecting weapons in preparation for war. On April 19, 1775, General Thomas Gage, the British military commander in Boston, sent about 700 British soldiers on a raid to seize weapons in nearby Concord. Warned in advance, colonial militiamen assembled on the village green in Lexington, a town through which the British would pass on their way to Concord. Upon arriving in Lexington, the British ordered the colonials to disperse. An unknown person then fired a shot, and both sides began shooting. When the smoke cleared, eight colonials lay dead. Marching on to Concord, the British found a much larger force of armed colonists waiting. After a battle in Concord, the British retreated toward Boston. Along the way, colonists fired on the British from the roadside, inflicting 273 casualties. The Revolutionary War had begun.

1776   The Declaration of Independence

The Second Continental Congress established a committee of five men to write a declaration of American independence. The committee insisted that Thomas Jefferson, a young Virginian, write the original draft. The Continental Congress approved the document, with some revisions, and on July 4, the thirteen colonies declared their independence from Great Britain.

1787   The Northwest Ordinance

The United States faced a serious problem after the Revolutionary War: sorting out land claims in its huge territory west of the Appalachian Mountains. States with large land claims in this territory insisted they be given the land; states with no claims argued for congressional control of the territory. Congress passed the Northwest Ordinance to solve these problems. This act reduced tensions over land claims, granted settlers the right to form their own territorial governments, and provided for an orderly admission of the new territories into statehood. This act guaranteed Americans in the new states equal representation in government, which set the stage for the rapid expansion of the United States.

1787   The Constitutional Convention

The weak American government created under the Articles of Confederation had become a serious concern to a powerful group of American leaders. The very survival of the republic seemed at stake. So when Congress called a convention to reform the Articles, the delegates quickly decided to go beyond their assigned task and form an entirely new government. The

result of their efforts was the Constitution. In 1788 the Constitution was ratified, creating a new, powerful central government that would alter the nature of American democracy.

1793   The Invention of the Cotton Gin

Although it is a matter of some debate who invented the cotton gin, Eli Whitney gained credit for the machine. The simple box contraption separated seeds from cotton fifty times faster than could be done by hand. The gin helped make possible a great expansion in cotton production. Increasing cotton production led to an increase in the practice of slavery in the South. Cotton and cotton products were the most important American exports until 1839, helping to fuel the expanding American economy.

1803   Marbury v. Madison

In the final hours of his presidency, John Adams appointed William Marbury to a judicial post. When President Jefferson took office, however, he declared that Marbury's appointment would not be honored. Marbury sued, taking the case to the Supreme Court. Chief Justice John Marshall denied Marbury's argument on a technicality. In the process, Marshall held that the courts have the power to declare acts of Congress unconstitutional. This landmark decision established the principle of judicial review, which gave great authority to the Supreme Court.

1803   The Louisiana Purchase

President Jefferson and the Senate nearly doubled the size of the nation by purchasing the Louisiana territory from France. The Louisiana territory was an enormous area of land that extended from the Mississippi River to the Rocky Mountains and from the Louisiana coast to Canada. The United States paid about $15 million for more than 800 million acres of land, a cost of about 1.8 cents per acre. Territory from the Louisiana Purchase created all or part of thirteen states.

1820   The Missouri Compromise

In 1819 the United States consisted of eleven free states and eleven slave states. "Free" Maine and "slave" Missouri were seeking statehood. At this point, Representative James Tallmadge introduced an amendment providing for gradual emancipation in Missouri. This sparked off a round of bitter debate. Henry Clay offered a compromise. Missouri would be slave and Maine free. And, in cases of territories seeking statehood in the future, land north of latitude 36° 30' would be free, and land south of the line would be open to slavery. The compromise temporarily quieted congressional debate over slavery and preserved the balance between the opposing sides in Congress.

1825   The Opening of the Erie Canal

The Erie Canal opened in 1825 after seven years of construction. The canal was a marvel of engineering: 40 feet wide and 364 miles long. Its closest competitor was only 28 miles long.

The canal greatly improved shipping between the Great Lakes region and New York City. The Erie Canal encouraged commerce and economic growth all along its route, and it also made New York City a vital center for western trade. The Erie Canal's success represented the transportation revolution in the United States that accelerated the growth of the economy.

1830 The Indian Removal Act

President Andrew Jackson supported the Indian Removal Act, which made provisions for the relocation of Native Americans living in the Southeast to what is today Oklahoma. In spite of the act, however, most of the Cherokee people living within the borders of Georgia and other states remained in their homes. But in 1837 and 1838, the United States Army forcibly moved the Cherokee west. The event came to be known as the "Trail of Tears," because as many as one quarter of the 15,000 Cherokee who made the trek died. The removal opened up vast tracts of land in the Southeast for white settlement, but Native Americans paid a terrible price.

1831 Nat Turner's Revolt and Garrison's Liberator

In 1831 the southern slaveholding culture suffered two powerful attacks. William Lloyd Garrison made a fiery appeal for the immediate end to slavery in the first issue of his abolitionist publication, *The Liberator*. Eight months later, African American Nat Turner led a slave revolt that stunned southern white society. Turner presented himself as a prophet ordained by God to free his people. With a small band of followers, he launched a revolt that was quickly crushed. Shaken by the verbal attacks by Garrison and the physical attacks of Turner, white southerners sought to tighten their control over enslaved people and heightened sectional tensions.

1832 The Nullification Crisis

South Carolina grew increasingly fearful of the federal government's power in the wake of spreading abolitionist views. Vice President John C. Calhoun, a South Carolinian, developed the doctrine of nullification, which held that a state had the right to nullify any law harmful to its interests. This doctrine struck at the heart of the dispute over the rights of the states versus the power of the federal government. President Andrew Jackson threatened to use force if South Carolina defied federal law. Meanwhile, Congress worked out a compromise that temporarily ended the standoff. The debate over states' rights, however, remained unresolved and would be decided only by the Civil War.

1834 – early 1850s The Settlement of the Oregon Country

The Oregon Country, home to numerous Native American groups for centuries, extended from northern California to the southern border of Alaska. Ignoring the Native Americans who already lived there, the United States and Britain signed a treaty in 1818 agreeing to joint occupation. Starting off from Independence, Missouri, settlers traveled along the Oregon Trail, a 2,000-mile trek across the Great Plains and the Rocky Mountains. Between 1842 and 1848, approximately 11,500 pioneers migrated to Oregon. In 1846, the United States and Britain agreed to divide the Oregon Country along the 49th parallel.

1836 The Founding of the Texas Republic

In 1822 Stephen Austin founded a colony of about 300 settlers in Texas, which then belonged to Mexico. By 1835 more than 30,000 Americans and 3,000 enslaved African Americans lived in Texas. In March 1836, supporters of a Texas independence movement formally declared the founding of the Republic of Texas. Mexico's leader, General Santa Anna, led an army of several thousand men to subdue the rebellion. At the Alamo, a former mission in San Antonio, fewer than 200 Texans held off 4,000 Mexican troops but ultimately were defeated. At the Battle of San Jacinto in April 1836 the Texas rebels routed Mexican troops and later forced Santa Anna to sign a treaty recognizing the republic. With almost no help from the United States government, Texas settlers had succeeded in gaining a large piece of territory from Mexico.

1848 The Discovery of Gold at Sutter's Mill, California

No event was more important in attracting settlers to the West than the discovery of gold at Sutter's Mill near the city of Sacramento in California in 1848. Lured by the promise of gold, people rushed west by the thousands. California had 14,000 residents in 1848; within a year its population was 100,000, and by 1852 the number had reached 200,000. The gold rush had a tremendous impact on life in California. Native Americans were forced to work in the mines, and disease and forced labor greatly reduced their population. While the gold rush devastated the Native Americans, it also brought growth to Pacific coast cities.

1848 The Treaty of Guadalupe Hidalgo

The Treaty of Guadalupe Hidalgo ended the Mexican War, which took place between 1846 and 1848 over a dispute between the United States and Mexico about the southern border of Texas. Under the terms of the Treaty of Guadalupe Hidalgo, Mexico ceded the United States one third of its territory, including present-day California, New Mexico, Nevada, Utah, and Arizona. The territorial acquisition, however, once again sparked bitter controversy over the extension of slavery and the balance of slave and free states in Congress.

1857 Dred Scott v. Sandford

Dred Scott, an enslaved African American living in Missouri, filed suit against his owner. He argued that because he and his wife, Harriet, had once been taken into states and territories where slavery was illegal, the couple was in fact free. The case reached the Supreme Court, and, in one of its most controversial rulings, the justices ruled against the Scotts. The Court held that as an African American, Scott was not a citizen and could not sue anyone. The Court also held that, because enslaved persons were property, Congress had to protect the rights of the slave owner. This decision stayed in force until the passage of the Fourteenth Amendment, which in 1868 guaranteed citizenship to African Americans.

1861 The Secession of the South

The election of Republican Abraham Lincoln to the presidency in the 1860 election demonstrated to the white South that northerners had the ability to elect a purely regional— and antislavery—candidate. Within a matter of months, seven southern states seceded and formed the Confederate States of America. Calmer heads on both sides sought to avoid the crisis, but events had proceeded beyond their control. The decisive incident came on April 12, 1861, when Confederate forces bombarded and captured the federal garrison of Fort Sumter in South Carolina, starting the Civil War. The United States had run out of peaceful compromises, and as a result over 600,000 Americans would die.

1863 The Emancipation Proclamation

President Lincoln issued the Emancipation Proclamation on New Year's Day, 1863. Lincoln had long said that the purpose of the Civil War was to save the Union. But he now realized that the war must also be a crusade against slavery. Critics noted that the declaration did not physically free a single enslaved person. The proclamation changed the nature of the war for the Union, however, adding to the war's purpose the freeing of enslaved people. The pronouncement also helped the Union politically by reducing the likelihood that Great Britain, which hated slavery, would support the South.

1863 The Battle of Gettysburg

In the summer of 1863, General Robert E. Lee led a Confederate army into the North. Lee thought he could end the Civil War by defeating a Union army on its own soil, which would compel the war-weary Union to recognize Confederate independence. Lee's army met the Union forces under General George Meade at Gettysburg, a small Pennsylvania town. The bloody fighting ended with Lee withdrawing his mauled army. The three days of battle cost nearly 50,000 casualties on both sides. Lee's shattered Confederate army never recovered and Union victories mounted. America's most costly war ended in 1865, with the Confederacy's surrender.

1865 African American Higher Education

Reconstruction offered African Americans an era of new promise. The African American community saw a great need for a core of educated leaders. Responding to this need, the American Missionary Association, the African Methodist Episcopal Church, and numerous other religious groups and philanthropists founded educational institutions throughout the country. Out of these efforts emerged the nation's leading black institutions of higher education, including Howard, Fisk, Atlanta, Dillard, Tougaloo, Morehouse, and Spelman. These colleges and universities were invaluable to African Americans, nurturing future political and social leaders.

1865–1870 The Reconstruction Amendments

The Thirteenth, Fourteenth, and Fifteenth amendments to the Constitution represented the central efforts of the Radical Republicans to benefit African Americans in the post–Civil War era. The Thirteenth Amendment abolished forever the institution of slavery. The Fourteenth and Fifteenth amendments guaranteed African Americans full citizenship and stated that the right to vote could not be denied on the basis of color or creed. After 1877, however, northern apathy for the issue of African American rights enabled southern states to deny African Americans many protections of the Fourteenth and Fifteenth amendments. Not until the 1960s were these injustices remedied.

1867 The Purchase of Alaska

When Russia expressed its desire to sell Alaska to the United States, William H. Seward, President Andrew Johnson's secretary of state, persuaded Congress to appropriate the asking price of $7.2 million. Initially mocked as "Seward's Folly," the purchase was to prove its asking price many times over. Thirty years later, an Alaskan gold rush yielded millions of dollars worth of gold. With this acquisition of Alaska, Russian influence in North America was eliminated and the United States gained a huge new territory.

1869 The Founding of the Knights of Labor

Originally founded as a secret labor society in 1869, the Noble Order of the Knights of Labor became a national, public organization in 1879. Terrence Powderly, the Knights' leader, sought reforms such as an eight-hour day and better wages. The Knights also attempted to form a political party by running candidates for political office, though their attempts were largely unsuccessful. Although the organization faded from significance by the end of the 1900s, the Knights of Labor was the most important representative of American labor into the 1890s.

1869 The Transcontinental Railroad

During the Civil War, the Union government promoted the building of railroads by offering generous land grants. One such project was a railroad that would link the West Coast with the East. The line was to be built by two different companies: the Central Pacific and the Union Pacific. In 1869, the two lines linked up in Utah, completing the first transcontinental railroad. The railroads promoted settlement of the West and helped create a nationwide transportation system that sparked tremendous growth in the American economy.

1869 Women's Suffrage in the Wyoming Territory

Western territories, with their rugged life styles and small populations, depended on women to take roles in social and political life that were unavailable to them in the eastern United States. In 1869 the Wyoming Territory passed into law a bill that granted women the right to vote and fully participate in national politics. This set a trend followed by many of Wyoming's neighbors. By 1914 every state in the western third of the nation, except New Mexico, had passed women's suffrage bills. The trailblazing of these western states helped pave the way for the ratification of the Nineteenth Amendment, which guaranteed all women the right to vote, in 1920.

1876 The Invention of the Telephone

On March 10, 1876, Alexander Graham Bell uttered the words, "Mr. Watson, come here. I want you." These few words, transmitted over a Bell invention called the telephone, altered communications technology forever. In the years ahead, Bell's American Telephone and Telegraph Company (AT&T) organized telephone line service and made widespread use of the telephone practical. By 1899 about one million telephones were operating in the United States. That number had grown to ten million by 1915. The telephone created a reliable, nationwide communication system that would play a vital part in American economic expansion.

1882 The Opening of the First Power Plant

Thomas Edison opened the first electric power plant in 1882. The plant generated energy that made electric lights glow throughout the Wall Street district in New York City. The display so impressed the public that investors poured money into construction of new power plants. Within sixteen years, nearly 3,000 stations provided power to businesses and the public. By 1929 two thirds of American families had electricity, and electric generators supplied 80 percent of industrial power needs.

1886 AF of L Formed

As the Noble Order of the Knights of Labor foundered in the 1890s, a new organization emerged to replace it as the leading national labor union. In 1886 Samuel Gompers organized the American Federation of Labor (AF of L). Gompers and the AF of L focused on such issues as a shorter workday, better wages, and safer working conditions. By 1900 the AF of L had one million members, and was the most important national union.

1887 The Dawes Severalty Act

Native American people in the West suffered greatly as settlers moved onto their lands. Reformers concerned with the fate of the Native Americans believed strongly that only by adopting the customs and values of white civilization could Native Americans be saved. Toward this end, Congress passed the Dawes Severalty Act. The law broke up tribal lands and allotted land parcels to individuals. Government officials hoped that individual land ownership would encourage Native Americans to farm like white Americans. In reality, relatively few Native Americans were able or willing to farm on their individual plots. Many sold their land to whites. As a result, Native American land holdings dwindled.

1890 The Formation of the National American Woman Suffrage Association

As the drive for women's suffrage heated up in the late 1800s, two leading woman suffrage groups joined forces to form the National American Woman Suffrage Association (NAWSA). NAWSA coordinated the efforts of state suffrage groups and utilized pressure tactics to convince legislators to vote for suffrage bills. The group's efforts finally paid off in 1920, when the Nineteenth Amendment was ratified.

1893 The First Automobiles

Inventors first developed prototypes of automobiles in 1893. This mode of transportation did not become common, however, until the 1910s and 1920s. It was then that Henry Ford's car company began to mass-produce cars at a cost low enough for working people to afford. By 1929 there were almost 27 million registered cars in the United States. The automobile industry became a dominant force in the American economy. Cars, trucks, and buses revolutionized American transportation and helped to spur the continued growth of the suburbs.

1896 Plessy v. Ferguson

By the 1880s, the United States government clearly had retreated from its commitment to African American equality. Southern state and local governments passed laws that segregated public facilities. The Supreme Court ruled on the constitutionality of these laws in the landmark case *Plessy* v. *Ferguson*. In its ruling, the Court held that "separate but equal" facilities did not violate the Fourteenth Amendment. Until the 1950s, southern states continued their systematic segregation of southern society and denial of African American voting and civil rights.

1898 The Spanish-American War and the Annexation of Hawaii

A powerful group of Americans sought to expand United States' influence beyond its own shores in the late 1890s. The Cuban revolt from Spain provided an opportunity, as public sentiment turned against the Spanish. In addition to its alleged mistreatment of the Cuban people, Spain was blamed for the mysterious sinking of the American battleship *Maine* in Havana harbor. The Spanish-American War lasted for three months, and victory gave the United States control of Puerto Rico and Guam. The United States also annexed the Philippines. Meanwhile, in Hawaii, an 1893 coup by American planters led to the overthrow of the Hawaiian government, and the islands were annexed by the United States government in 1898.

1909 The Founding of the NAACP

A prominent group of white and African American reformers joined together in 1909 to form the National Association for the Advancement of Colored People (NAACP). This organization fought important battles for voting rights and against segregation and lynching. In 1915 the NAACP scored its first major victory when the Supreme Court declared so-called grandfather clauses unconstitutional. These laws had been used throughout the South as part of an effort to deny African Americans their voting rights. The NAACP continued to fight discrimination and white violence and remains a leading civil rights organization today.

1914 The Opening of the Panama Canal

The Isthmus of Panama was an ideal location for a quick route between the Atlantic and Pacific oceans. After supporting a Panamanian revolt against Colombia in 1903, the United States received a permanent grant of a 10-mile-wide Canal Zone across the isthmus. Construction began in 1904 and ended ten years later. At a cost of $400 million, the United States now had easy access between two oceans and a greater ability to extend its power to other parts of the world.

1917 The United States Entry into World War I

After several years of claiming neutrality in World War I, the United States finally entered the war on the side of the Allies in 1917. American forces delivered an Allied victory, but after the war, revenge-minded Allied leaders frustrated Wilson's visions for postwar peace and security, opting instead to humiliate the defeated Germans. The Germans never forgot nor forgave their treatment at the hands of the Allies. The treaty contained the seeds of future conflict between the powers of Europe.

1929 The Stock Market Crash

In October 1929, stock prices plummeted. The stock market crash helped push the American economy into a deep downward cycle that would come to be known as the Great Depression. Unregulated speculation on the stock market, overvalued stocks, bad government policy, and a decline in purchasing power all contributed to the downturn. The Depression caused thousands of banks to close. By 1932 median income had been cut in half. Unemployment remained high throughout the 1930s, ranging from 20 to 38 percent. More than

merely an economic crisis, the Depression shattered many Americans' faith in government and business.

1935 The Social Security Act

During the Depression, President Franklin Roosevelt initiated reforms to ensure that no future depression would have such a devastating effect on the nation. The Social Security Act grew out of these efforts. This act provided income for retired workers, compensation to the unemployed, and assistance for dependent children. The program was funded by joint employee-employer contributions. The Social Security Act was a landmark piece of legislation that helped to create the foundation for the modern welfare state.

1935 The Wagner Act

Prior to 1935, President Roosevelt had not been interested in extending labor protections through new legislation. But when the Supreme Court struck down existing legislation that included key protections for labor, Roosevelt gave his support to the National Labor Relations Act, commonly known as the Wagner Act. This act outlawed blacklisting—by which employers conspired not to hire certain workers—and guaranteed labor the right to organize and bargain collectively. After decades of outright hostility toward unions, the United States government now officially recognized the right of labor unions to exist and represent workers in their relations with employers.

1941 The Attack on Pearl Harbor

On December 7, 1941, a Japanese force launched a surprise attack upon the American naval base at Pearl Harbor, Hawaii. Japanese leaders believed that the United States was blocking Japanese expansion in the Pacific, and they decided a lightning thrust would disable the American navy. The attack killed over 2,335 American soldiers and 68 civilians and destroyed 19 ships and 150 planes. On December 8, Congress voted in favor of a declaration of war against Japan, and the United States entered World War II.

1944 The Normandy Invasion

The Normandy invasion was the beginning of the end of World War II. With a force of 175,000 soldiers, 600 warships, and 11,000 planes, combined American and British forces landed on the northern coast of German-controlled France in June 1944. Within one month, over a million Allied troops had moved into France, and the defeat of Germany took less than a year. The Soviet Union, the United States wartime ally, never forgave the late date of the invasion, because the Soviets had been suffering terribly at the hands of the Germans since 1942. This contributed to postwar American-Soviet hostility.

1944 The Serviceman's Readjustment Act

In gratitude for the service of World War II veterans, Congress passed the Serviceman's Readjustment Act, commonly known as the GI Bill, in 1944. The act granted returning veterans job guidance, priority for jobs, loans, mortgage assistance, technical training, and educational benefits. This bill contributed to the peacetime success of World War II veterans, who as a group earned 40 percent more than nonveterans. Few women and minorities, however, received full benefits under the act.

1945 The Formation of the United Nation

Near the end of World War II, diplomats hoped to create a new international peacekeeping organization. In April 1945, delegates from fifty nations met in San Francisco to adopt a charter for the new organization, called the United Nations (UN). Members pledged to settle their disagreements peacefully and to try to prevent wars from occurring and stop those that did break out. The formation of the UN provided new hope for an era of international peace and understanding.

1947 The Desegregation of Major League Baseball

After World War II, African Americans began to make louder demands for equality. Mild-mannered Jackie Robinson proved to be one of the trailblazers. In 1947 Robinson took the field for the Brooklyn Dodgers, thus ending the exclusion of African Americans from major league baseball. Within a few years, more African American players entered professional baseball, football, and basketball. In coming years, athletes such as Hank Aaron, Lawrence Taylor, and Michael Jordan would rise to the top of their respective sports.

1947 The Truman Doctrine

The years after World War II witnessed increasing hostility between the United States and the Soviet Union. Postwar American policy came to be dominated by the goal of resisting communist expansion. This policy was first expressed officially in the Truman Doctrine. In 1947, Truman announced that it was the duty of the United States to protect the "free peoples" of the world from "subjugation by armed minorities or outside pressures." If America failed in this duty, Truman warned, communism could take over the world. The Truman Doctrine helped shape a United States foreign policy that contributed to the tensions of the cold war.

1949 The Formation of the North Atlantic Treaty Organization

The United States committed its economic resources to rebuild war-torn Western Europe, partially in an effort to prevent communist gains there. To provide military protection for Western Europe, the United States created a military alliance known as the North Atlantic Treaty Organization (NATO) in 1949. Twelve nations joined NATO, pledging mutual military protection. The United Sates provided military aid to all the members. NATO ensured that Western

Europe would be protected from Soviet invasion and provided the United States with a cold war weapon that could be used to contain any threat of communist aggression.

1954 The Army-McCarthy Hearings

The tense cold war atmosphere of the 1950s in the United States produced a widespread, exaggerated fear of Soviet infiltration. In this atmosphere, Wisconsin senator Joseph McCarthy won fame with his wild accusations of communist infiltration of American government. His attacks continued for four years, while producing little evidence of communist activity in the government. McCarthy's accusations against the army led to televised hearings, in which Americans for the first time recognized the reckless and ruthless nature of his tactics. Defeated and censured by his colleagues in Congress, McCarthy lost his influence. His anticommunist crusade, however, contributed to the cold war fears in the United States.

1954 Brown v. Board of Education of Topeka

Civil rights leaders in the 1950s determined that they had to overturn the "separate but equal" doctrine established by *Plessy v. Ferguson* in 1896. The NAACP's Legal Defense Fund fought segregation in the courts, and in 1951 it helped Oliver Brown sue the Topeka, Kansas, school board for not allowing his daughter to attend a nearby white school. The Supreme Court ruled on May, 17, 1954, that "separate facilities are inherently unequal." A year later, the court ordered desegregation of public schools to begin "with all deliberate speed." Though the South resisted integration for years, the *Brown* decision proved to be a major legal victory for the civil rights movement.

1955 The Montgomery Bus Boycott

Life in racially segregated Montgomery, Alabama, was radically altered in December 1955 when Rosa Parks, a seamstress and NAACP secretary, refused to move from the "whites-only" section of a public bus. Parks' defiance led to her arrest and unified the city's black community. African Americans began a campaign to boycott the public bus system. The boycott reduced the bus system's gross revenue by 65 percent. Meanwhile, the NAACP tested the legality of bus segregation, and in 1956 the Supreme Court ruled it unconstitutional. This victory gave strength to a broader civil rights movement, and Martin Luther King, Jr., emerged as a leading spokesperson for civil rights.

1960 Kennedy-Nixon Debate on Television

In the first televised presidential debate, Democratic candidate John F. Kennedy debated Republican candidate Richard Nixon. Kennedy took advantage of the power of television, projecting a charismatic, vigorous image. Polls showed that those who listened to the debate on the radio thought Nixon had won, while those who watched the debate on television believed Kennedy had triumphed. In future political elections, candidates' television images would be groomed as carefully as their stands on issues.

1962 The Cuban Missile Crisis

In 1962 Cuban leader Fidel Castro secretly secured Soviet aid to install Soviet-made nuclear missiles in Cuba, well within striking distance of the United States. American officials learned of the missiles when American spy planes took pictures of the missile sites. After considering options that included a military attack on Cuba, President Kennedy opted to set up a blockade around the island to turn back any Soviet ships. Kennedy's strong stance placed the United States at the very brink of war with the Soviet Union. The Soviets however, pulled back, agreeing to remove the missiles. The event intensified the cold war and the arms race between the United States and Soviet Union.

1962 The Publication of Silent Spring

Marine biologist Rachel Carson almost singlehandedly started the environmental movement with the publication of her 1962 book, *Silent Spring*. The book claimed that while the chemical pesticide DDT increased crop production, it also released deadly chemicals into the food chain. *Silent Spring* rocked the nation, and public concern eventually led to a government ban against the use and sale of DDT. Carson had succeeded in encouraging an awareness in American society of the concept of human-environmental interaction.

1963 The Assassination of President John F. Kennedy

On November 22, 1963, President John F. Kennedy was struck by an assassin's bullets while riding through the streets of Dallas, Texas. The wounds were fatal and the stunned nation was plunged into mourning. Authorities arrested and charged Lee Harvey Oswald with the assassination, but two days later night-club owner Jack Ruby murdered Oswald. Despite the official government report of the Warren Commission that Oswald had acted alone in the assassination, many Americans continued to believe that the murder was the product of a conspiracy of some sort. The assassination of President Kennedy, who had invigorated the nation with his youth and enthusiasm, inflicted a serious blow to the spirit of the nation.

1963 The Publication of The Feminine Mystique

After World War II, the United States witnessed a strong resurgence of the ideal of the woman as domestic homemaker. Betty Friedan did as society expected: she gave up a career in psychology to raise a family. Unhappy with the role that society had defined for women, she wrote *The Feminine Mystique*. In her book, Friedan charged that women were expected to find total personal satisfaction from being housewives. She claimed that women needed other ways to gain fulfillment,

such as forming an identity separate from the home. The *Feminine Mystique* gave rise to a renewed women's movement that continues today.

1964 The Civil Rights Act

The 1964 Civil Rights Act outlawed discrimination in public places and in employment practices, and empowered the attorney general to bring suit against offenders. The Supreme Court upheld the legislation. The American government finally had taken strong action toward guaranteeing African Americans their civil rights.

1964 The Gulf of Tonkin Resolution

President Lyndon B. Johnson was determined not to allow South Vietnam to fall under the control of communist North Vietnam. Toward this end, he sought a way to strengthen the United States commitment to South Vietnam. Johnson saw his opportunity when American ships, in North Vietnamese waters to aid South Vietnamese raids, were attacked by North Vietnamese torpedo boats. Johnson described the incident as a confirmed example of North Vietnamese aggression. He persuaded Congress to pass the Gulf of Tonkin Resolution, which gave him broad powers in applying military force. Johnson eventually would use the resolution to send more than 500,000 troops to Vietnam.

1965 The Voting Rights Act

The Civil Rights Act of 1964 had gaps that made possible the continued disenfranchisement of African Americans by southern states. Further peaceful protest by civil rights activists helped force the federal government to address this issue. Congress passed the Voting Rights Act in 1965. The act outlawed devices, such as literacy tests, used to deny African Americans the vote. It also empowered the federal government to oversee elections. By 1968 one million African Americans had registered to vote, a force that would come to have a strong impact upon elections.

1966 The Formation of the National Organization for Women

A small group of professional women, dissatisfied with existing women's groups, formed the National Organization for Women (NOW) in 1966. NOW sought equal pay for equal work, partnership in marriage, and changes in the representation of women in the media. Within five years the organization had 15,000 members and served as a powerful voice for women disenchanted with their status in American society. NOW helped to revolutionize the way Americans thought about and treated women.

1969 The Moon Landing

The Soviet advantage in space technology in the early 1960s spurred President John F. Kennedy to invest heavily in an American space program. Throughout the 1960s the space program made rapid progress. On July 20, 1969, the Apollo 11 lunar module landed on the moon. The nation watched as Commander Neil Armstrong took the first steps outside the spacecraft. Humankind had made a giant stride in the exploration of space, the last great frontier.

1972–1974 *The Watergate Scandal*

The Committee to Re-Elect the President (CREEP) was determined to win the 1972 reelection of President Richard Nixon. Toward this goal, a group of men tried to break into the Democratic National Headquarters in the Watergate building in order to install a listening device. The break-in led to the burglars' arrest. President Nixon claimed to have had no prior knowledge of the break-in, but he did participate in a cover-up of the incident. Though Nixon was overwhelmingly reelected, the investigation of Watergate continued, and it became clear the President was involved. Facing certain impeachment, Nixon became the first President to resign from office.

1973 *Roe v. Wade*

The National Organization for Women (NOW) made the reform of abortion laws a priority in the early 1970s. Existing laws made it difficult for women to obtain abortions, and the procedure was illegal in many states. NOW argued that the individual woman, not the state, should have the right to decide if abortion was appropriate. The issue went before the Supreme Court, which held that a woman's right to privacy gave her the right to obtain an abortion and that the state could regulate abortions only after a certain point in the pregnancy. This decision was a major victory for women's rights activists, but it inspired strong opposition by antiabortion groups. In the years after *Roe* v. *Wade,* the abortion debate has become a leading political issue.

1973 *AIM Occupies Wounded Knee, South Dakota*

The American Indian Movement (AIM), organized in 1968, occupied the town of Wounded Knee, South Dakota, to protest reservation conditions and to bring public attention to the history of broken treaties between the United States and Native Americans. The government reacted to the armed occupation of the town with force, firing upon Native Americans who sought to bring supplies to AIM. The standoff ended with the government agreeing to examine treaty rights. Native American actions such as this pressured the government to reevaluate its policy toward Native Americans.

1975 *The United Farm Workers' Grape Boycott*

César Chávez and his union of migratory farm workers confronted the grape growers of California, demanding better wages, working conditions, and the right to collective bargaining. The growers refused the demands of the workers. In response, Chávez organized a nationwide consumer boycott of grapes. The boycott was successful, and several growers came to terms with Chávez's group, now called the United Farm Workers. In 1975 the California legislature passed a law that required growers to bargain collectively with the agricultural workers' unions.

1981 *The Appointment of Sandra Day O'Connor to the Supreme Court*

President Ronald Reagan appointed Sandra Day O'Connor to the Supreme Court in 1981. Following her confirmation by the Senate, she became the first woman to sit on the Supreme Court. Her appointment marked an important symbolic achievement for American women, who continued to make gains in their access to leadership positions at all levels of government. In 1993 O'Connor was joined on the Supreme Court bench by Ruth Bader Ginsberg, who was appointed by President Bill Clinton.

1981 *The Discovery of the AIDS Virus*

In 1981 medical researchers discovered a fatal new disease, known as acquired immunodeficiency syndrome (AIDS). The disease, scientists learned, was caused by a virus that damages the body's ability to fight infection. Research also showed that the disease is transmitted through sexual contact with an infected person or by the sharing of contaminated intravenous needles. As yet, no cure for the disease nor means of immunization against the virus has been found. By March 1994, about 200,000 Americans had died of AIDS-related complications.

1987 *The Intermediate-Range Nuclear Forces Treaty*

After meeting several times to discuss arms control, President Ronald Reagan and Soviet premier Mikhail Gorbachev signed a treaty to limit the number of intermediate-range nuclear weapons. The INF treaty helped pave the way for the Strategic Arms Reduction Talks in 1991, which decreased the number of long-range nuclear missiles. These two treaties marked a significant warming in the relationship between the United States and the Soviet Union.

1991 *The Collapse of the Soviet Union*

Mikhail Gorbachev could not control the forces he had unleashed in the Soviet Union through his democratic, *perestroika* reforms. In the closing days of 1991, the Soviet Union dissolved, and the republics that once made up the Soviet Union became independent countries. In 1991, Boris Yeltsin leader of the Russian republic, declared a final end to the cold war, which had dominated American and Soviet foreign policy for over forty years.

KEY EVENTS

Glossary

This Glossary defines all key terms listed in section previews. The page number at the end of each entry indicates the text page on which the term appears in boldface. Key people are defined in the Biographical Dictionary on pages 912–918.

abolition Movement to ban, or abolish, slavery; began in the early 1800s and continued through the Civil War (p. 126)

acquired immunodeficiency syndrome (AIDS) Incurable, fatal disease that appeared in 1981; transmitted through the bodily fluid of an infected individual (p. 813)

administration A President's term in office, or the group of officials that makes up the executive branch, including the President (p. 80)

agribusiness Method of producing agricultural goods in which corporations run large farms using high-tech machinery (p. 611)

Albany Movement Largely unsuccessful protests against racial inequality in Albany, Georgia, in 1961 and 1962; led by Martin Luther King, Jr. (p. 672)

Allies The combination of Russia, France, Great Britain, and later the United States in World War I; opponents of the Central Powers (p. 416)

American Expeditionary Force (AEF) United States troops in World War I, including draftees, volunteers, and the National Guard (p. 425)

American Indian Movement (AIM) Native American rights group organized in 1968; organized protests and participated in the occupation at Wounded Knee in 1973 (p. 703)

American party Political party organized in 1854 by nativists to work against Catholics and immigrants; also called "Know Nothings" (p. 173)

American Revolution The war and the social and political changes that accompanied the creation of the United States of America (p. 48)

American System Economic policy proposed in 1825 by John Q. Adams and others under which the federal government would support business by passing protective tariffs and making internal improvements such as roads and canals (p. 114)

amnesty General pardon for those guilty of a certain crime; granted by President Jimmy Carter to draft evaders during Vietnam War (p. 792)

Anaconda Plan Civil War plan formed by the North to blockade the South and cut off its foreign trade (p. 194)

anarchist Political radical who opposes all government because it limits individual liberty and serves the wealthy, ruling classes (p. 272)

Anglo A white, non-Latino, English-speaking American (p. 698)

annexation Addition of a new territory to an existing country (p. 362) .

Anti-Federalist Those who opposed the new Constitution between 1787 and 1789 on the grounds that the central government it would create would be too powerful (p. 77)

anti-Semitism Hostility toward or discrimination against Jews (p. 531)

apartheid Systematic separation and inequality of races in South Africa enforced by whites during the 1900s (p. 835)

appeasement Act of giving in to someone's demands in order to keep the peace; unsuccessful policy of England and France toward Nazi Germany before World War II (p. 532)

arbitration Process of settling disputes in which both sides accept the legally binding decision of an impartial third party; often used in labor conflicts (p. 395)

armistice Cease-fire during a war, particularly at the end of World War I in 1918 (p. 429)

Articles of Confederation Agreement establishing a form of government among the states in 1781 (p. 62)

Atlantic World The encounter and exchange among the people of the Americas, Africa, and Europe that began in 1492 (p. 20)

autocrat Ruler with unlimited governing power (p. 418)

baby boom Increase in birth rate that began in World War II and continued into the 1950s (p. 611)

balance of trade Difference in value between a country's imports and exports over a given period of time (p. 32)

banana republic A Central American country in the early 1900s that depended upon banana exports and whose politics and economy were dominated by American business (p. 364)

barrio City neighborhood inhabited by Spanish speakers (p. 698)

Battle of the Bulge Battle fought from December 16, 1944 to January 16, 1945, between the Allies and Nazi forces in Belgium (p. 541)

beatnik Member of the "Beat Generation" in the 1950s who protested the pressure to conform through writing, art, and unconventional living (p. 617)

Berlin airlift The emergency program undertaken by the United States to deliver supplies to West Berlin in 1948 and 1949 after the Soviet Union blocked other access routes (p. 591)

Berlin Wall Barrier built by the Soviets in 1961 to keep people of East Berlin from escaping to the West; symbol of the cold war; torn down in 1989 (p. 654)

bicameral legislature Executive branch with two houses or groups of representatives, as in the United States Congress (p. 64)

bilingual education Education in which students with little knowledge of English are taught in both their native language and English (p. 839)

Bill of Rights The first ten amendments to the Constitution, which guarantee freedom of speech, religion, and other basic rights (p. 78)

Black Power An African American movement seeking unity, self-determination, and economic and political power (p. 684)

black codes Laws intended to keep African Americans under white authority, especially following the Civil War (p. 97)

blitzkrieg "Lightning war"; German tactic employed at the beginning of World War II, based upon overwhelming the enemy with a series of sudden attacks by land and air (p. 536)

blue laws Laws that regulate work, business, or entertainment on Sunday (p. 309)

bonanza farms Large farms owned by big businesses and managed by professionals (p. 289)

Bonus Army Group of World War I veterans who marched to Washington in 1932 asking to receive their pension bonus early (p. 496)

boomer Person wanting to settle in the West in the late 1880s, especially one of those who pressured Congress in 1889 to take over Native American land for this purpose (p. 287)

bootlegging Supplying liquor illegally during prohibition (1920–1933) by producing or smuggling it (p. 466)

boycott A means of protest based on refusing to buy products or use services (p. 50)

bracero Spanish term for "worker," particularly applied to the thousands of Mexican farm workers who migrated into the United States during World War II, most of whom were sent back after the war (p. 594)

Brooklyn Bridge Bridge completed in 1883 that connects Manhattan and Brooklyn (p. 257)

Bull Moose party Name for the Progressive party, organized to run Theodore Roosevelt for President in 1912 (p. 401)

busing Program begun in the 1960s to end racial segregation in schools by redistributing students (p. 756)

buy on margin Practice of buying stocks by paying 10 to 50 percent of the full price and borrowing the rest; common in the 1920s before the stock market crash of 1929 (p. 478)

cabinet Heads of the major departments of the United States government who advise the President (p. 79)

Camp David Accords Framework for peace between Israel and Egypt; signed in 1978 (p. 784)

canister Projectile used in a cannon that opens up after firing and sprays bullet-sized shot (p. 194)

capital Supply of wealth used to produce goods and profits (p. 102)

capitalism Economic system in which manufacturing is controlled by private corporations and individuals competing for profits (p. 102)

capitalist Person using capital to produce goods or services for profit (p. 107)

carpetbagger Northern Republican who moved to the South during Reconstruction to profit from unstable social conditions (p. 237)

cartel Loose association of businesses supplying the same product, often formed secretly; its members agree to limit supplies to keep prices high (p. 261)

cash crop Crop raised and sold for money, as opposed to a crop raised to supply food to the grower (p. 289)

Central Powers Combination of Germany and Austria-Hungary in World War I; opponents of the Allies (p. 416)

centralize To locate tasks or responsibilities so that they all happen in one place (p. 103)

Civil Rights Act of 1964 Law prohibiting discrimination in public accommodations and job opportunities (p. 678)

Civil War Armed conflict between the northern and southern states between 1861 and 1865 (p. 164)

clan Type of kinship network; consists of a group of families descended from a common ancestor (p. 14)

coalition Union of several groups who work together toward a common political, social, or economic goal (p. 801)

cold war Condition of indirect conflict that existed between the United States and the Soviet Union from World War II through the late 1980s (p. 584)

collateral Something pledged as security for a loan that can be claimed by the lender if the loan is not repaid (p. 483)

collective bargaining Negotiation between employers and workers, usually through a labor union (p. 270)

colony An area settled by immigrants who continue their ties with the parent country (p. 24)

commodity Something that can be bought and sold (p. 102)

communist Economic system in which manufacturing is controlled by the workers (p. 447)

Compromise of 1850 Agreement reached between northern and southern states in an effort to end dispute over the extension of slavery to the western territories (p. 170)

confederation An alliance of states formed to coordinate defense and their relations with foreign governments (p. 62)

congregacion Spanish colonial village where Native Americans were forced to worship as European Catholics and to farm (p. 25)

Congress of Industrial Organizations (CIO) Labor group that split off from the American Federation of Labor in 1938 and organized unskilled steel, auto, and other workers (p. 520)

Congress of Racial Equality (CORE) Civil rights organization started in 1942; active in sit-ins and demonstrations during the 1950s and 1960s (p. 663)

conquistador Spanish term for "conqueror" in North and South America during the period of conquest after the opening of the Atlantic World (p. 24)

conscientious objector Person who opposes fighting in a war on moral or religious grounds (p. 726)

Constitutional Union party Political party formed of moderates from the South and the border states in the election of 1860 (p. 185)

containment Cold war policy of the United States intended to prevent communist power from expanding beyond its geographical boundaries after World War II (p. 589)

contra Rebel fighting the Marxist Sandinista government of Nicaragua in the 1980s (p. 821)

contraband Property of the enemy seized during wartime; applied during the Civil War to enslaved African Americans set free by the Union army (p. 203)

Copperhead A Democrat during the Civil War who worked against the war and the antislavery policies of the Republicans (p. 202)

cost-plus system System devised during World War II to allow profits from war production, in which the government paid for basic manufacturing costs, plus a percentage for profit (p. 559)

counterculture A cultural movement in the 1960s formed mostly of young people who rejected conventions and experimented with new practices in dress, sexual relationships, and drug use (p. 729)

Crédit Mobilier A dummy corporation created by the stockholders of the Union Pacific Railroad, which allowed them to pay themselves with federal grants to build the railroad (p. 243)

Cuban missile crisis Dispute between the United States and the Soviet Union in 1962 over Soviet missile bases in Cuba (p. 655)

cult of domesticity The widespread belief in the early to mid-1800s in the importance of women's work in the home (p. 133)

currency policy The federal government's plan for the makeup and quantity of the nation's money supply (p. 295)

de facto discrimination Discrimination caused by conditions rather than by law; common in the North for African Americans after the Civil War (p. 344)

de facto segregation Segregation in the North and elsewhere caused by ghetto conditions rather than by law (p. 681)

de jure segregation Segregation enforced by laws; common in the South through the 1960s (p. 681)

debt peonage Labor system common in the South after the Civil War in which debt was used to keep farm workers on the land (p. 239)

Declaration of Independence Document published in 1776 declaring the independence of the United States from British rule (p. 53)

deficit spending Economic policy in which the government spends more than it receives in taxes, making up the difference by borrowing money (p. 561)

deflation Period of gradually dropping prices, generally brought on by the decrease in the supply of available money (p. 295)

demagogue Charismatic leader who manipulates people with half-truths, false promises, and scare tactics (p. 516)

Democratic party Political party descended from Jeffersonian Democrat-Republicans and Jacksonian Democrats (p. 172)

depression Severe economic slump during which stock values, business activity, and employment decline severely or remain at very low levels (p. 49)

deregulation Policy of reducing or removing government controls on industry (p. 792)

détente Relaxation of strained relations between nations, especially among the United States, the Soviet Union, and China in the 1970s and late 1980s (p. 759)

direct primary Election system in which voters rather than political bosses select nominees for elections (p. 394)

dissident An opponent of the established government, especially in the Soviet Union (p. 785)

diversified conglomerate Extremely large corporation formed of other corporations of many types (p. 608)

dollar diplomacy Policy of increasing United States investments abroad to keep foreign societies stable; adopted by President William Howard Taft in the early 1900s (p. 377)

domino theory Political theory common during the cold war that if one country fell to communism, countries nearby would also quickly become communist (p. 596)

"Double V" campaign Civil rights movement by African Americans during World War II, calling for victory both in the war and in the struggle for equality at home (p. 573)

doughboy Nickname for an infantryman in World War I (p. 426)

Dow Jones industrial average An average of the prices of the stock of leading industries that gauges the health of the stock market (p. 480)

draft Legal means of forcing people to serve in the armed forces (p. 199)

Dred Scott* v. *Sandford Supreme court case in 1857 that refused to recognize African Americans as citizens and overturned the Missouri Compromise (p. 178)

economy of scale Producing or buying an item on a very large scale so the price per item goes down (p. 263)

Electoral College Body of electors chosen by voters in each state to elect the President and Vice President (p. 73)

Emancipation Proclamation Declaration by President Abraham Lincoln that as of January 1, 1863, all enslaved people in areas in rebellion against the Union would be considered free by the North (p. 202)

embargo A policy of restricting trade with a nation (p. 754)

***encomienda* system** Social system in which Native Americans were required to work for an individual Spaniard, who was supposed to care for their well-being in return (p. 24)

entrepreneur Businessperson who takes risks for the sake of large profits (p. 102)

Environmental Protection Agency (EPA) Government agency established in 1970 to curb air and water pollution; now also regulates solid waste disposal, pesticides, and toxic substances (p. 708)

Equal Rights Amendment (ERA) Constitutional amendment to ensure equal rights for women; passed by Congress in 1972 but never ratified by the required number of states (p. 694)

escalation An increase or expansion, especially of war (p. 718)

evangelical movement Christian religious movement that emphasizes preaching instead of rituals, and stresses that salvation is possible only for those who believe in Christ (p. 99)

excise Tax on an item manufactured within a country (p. 89)

executive branch The part of a government that executes, or carries out, laws (p. 63)

Exoduster Member of a group of southern African Americans who participated in an exodus, or mass migration, to western lands in the late 1870s (p. 281)

fascism A political philosophy that values the nation or race over the individual, autocratic over democratic rule, and rigid control of society and the economy over a free society and market (p. 530)

Federalist Supporter of the new United States Constitution in the 1780s; also a member of a party that favored a strong federal government in the 1790s and early 1800s (p. 76)

feminism Theory of political, economic, and social equality of men and women (p. 690)

feminist Person who advocates the political, economic, and social equality of men and women (p. 690)

Fifteenth Amendment Constitutional amendment of 1870 guaranteeing all citizens the right to vote (p. 235)

first American party system Earliest political party system in the United States; composed of Jeffersonian Republicans and Federalists (p. 88)

flapper A type of young woman having a straight, slim silhouette and a fondness for dancing and brash actions; a symbol of the Jazz Age (p. 458)

Fourteen Points Peace program proposed by President Woodrow Wilson in 1918, intended to prevent wars like World War I (p. 434)

Fourteenth Amendment Constitutional amendment of 1868 that guarantees civil rights and equal protection of laws to all citizens (p. 234)

franchise The right to open a restaurant or other business using a system developed by and a name owned by a parent company (p. 608)

free soiler Settler in Kansas in the 1850s committed to an anti-slavery policy (p. 177)

Freedmen's Bureau Federal bureau in operation after the Civil War that helped former enslaved people and war refugees with food, medical, and other aid as well as schooling (p. 232)

Freedom Rides Campaign by African American and white civil rights workers in 1961 to protest segregated southern bus facilities by riding through the Lower South on buses (p. 670)

Fugitive Slave Act Part of the Compromise of 1850 requiring all states to return runaway slaves (p. 170)

fundamentalism Christian religious movement based on pamphlets issued between 1909 and 1914; holds that every word in the Bible was inspired by God and is literally true (p. 467)

Gadsden Purchase United States purchase of southern New Mexico and Arizona from Mexico for $10 million in 1853 (p. 150)

gag rule Rule passed in 1836 by southern representatives in Congress that prevented antislavery petitions from being considered by the House for eight years (p. 129)

general strike A strike in which many unions participate in order to show worker unity (p. 447)

gentry People, generally landowners, wealthy enough to afford others to work for them (p. 34)

Gettysburg Address Speech by President Abraham Lincoln at a Gettysburg cemetery dedication in 1863; redefined the meaning of the United States (p. 214)

ghetto Section of a city where de facto segregation limits residents to a certain ethnic or racial group (p. 322)

GI Bill Common name for Servicemen's Readjustment Act of 1944, which provided veterans' benefits such as low-interest mortgages (p. 611)

GI United States soldier serving during World War II (p. 543)

Gilded Age The period between 1877 and 1900; also called the Tragic Era and the Dreadful Decades (p. 308)

grandfather clause A part of a law that exempts a group from the law if they met certain conditions before the law was passed; used in the South in the late 1800s and early 1900s to ensure that white voting rights were not affected by literacy tests intended to screen out African American voters (p. 343)

Grange Farmer's group, also known as the Patrons of Husbandry, most popular during the 1860s and 1870s; formed farmers' cooperatives for buying large quantities of goods and pressured legislators to regulate railroads (p. 295)

Great Awakening Religious revival in the American colonies, 1730s–1740s (p. 36)

Great Compromise Agreement of 1787 that created a bicameral legislature in the Constitution; it established that representation in one house was to be proportional to population in one house and equal among states in the other (p. 70)

Great Society The legislative program proposed by President Lyndon Johnson in the 1960s; included civil rights laws, federal aid to education, elderly medical care, and poverty programs (p. 644)

greenback Paper money established during the Civil War; named for its color (p. 201)

Gross National Product (GNP) Total amount of goods and services a nation produces; used to gauge economic strength (p. 482)

guerrilla Soldier who fights irregular warfare, especially one using surprise tactics to harass and sabotage the enemy (p. 367)

Gulf of Tonkin Resolution Resolution passed by Congress in 1964 that gave the President authority to use "necessary" military force in Vietnam (p. 718)

gunboat Type of steam-driven boat used during the Civil War that was fitted with cannons and, sometimes, iron armor; it was able to navigate shallow rivers (p. 195)

Harlem Renaissance Period in the early 1900s during which the literary, musical, and artistic expression of African Americans blossomed in Harlem (p. 455)

Hawley-Smoot tariff Import tax levied in 1930, the highest in United States history; produced the opposite of its intended effect when international trade slowed (p. 495)

Helsinki Accords Agreement reached in the 1970s by a group of nations, including the United States and the Soviet Union, to cooperate economically and promote human rights (p. 778)

hierarchy Social system of many levels in which each level has power over the levels beneath it (p. 15)

hippie A member of the counterculture during the 1960s (p. 729)

holding company A corporation that controls other companies by holding their stocks (p. 396)

holocaust Nazi execution of six million Jews and five million others during World War II in extermination camps (p. 541)

home rule Municipal reforms in the late 1800s and early 1900s that gave cities limited self-rule, rather than state rule (p. 389)

Homestead Act Law passed in 1862 that offered certain settlers 160 acres of land if they built a house and farmed for five years (p. 280)

Hooverville Towns of makeshift houses built by homeless people during the Great Depression (p. 486)

horizontal consolidation Process of creating one giant business by bringing together smaller firms in the same field (p. 263)

House Un-American Activities Committee (HUAC) Committee of the House of Representatives active during the 1940s and 1950s that investigated supposed communist influence in the film and other industries (p. 600)

household economy Economic system common before the 1800s in which people's business consisted of maintaining households by growing food and making clothes and other necessities (p. 102)

hundred days First one hundred days of President Franklin D. Roosevelt's term of office (p. 506)

Immigration Act of 1965 A law that changed quotas favoring northern and western Europeans and expanded the number of people allowed to immigrate (p. 646)

impeach To formally charge a public official with misconduct; brought by the lower house in a legislative body (p. 235)

imperial presidency The type of presidency sought by President Richard Nixon, in which the executive branch would gain more power than allowed by the Constitution (p. 753)

imperialism A policy by which stronger nations attempt to create empires by dominating weaker nations economically, politically, or military; also called expansionism (p. 362)

indentured servant Person who contracts to work for another for a period of time (usually seven years), especially in return for travel costs or food and shelter (p. 27)

Industrial Revolution A period of major economic change that began during the late 1700s with the introduction of machines using sources of power other than humans or animals (p. 98)

Industrial Workers of the World (IWW) Radical labor organization of the early 1900s that sought the overthrow of the capitalist system; also known as the Wobblies (p. 432)

inflation A steady increase in prices and loss of value of currency that reduces people's ability to buy goods; usually results from an increase in the amount of money and credit available (p. 60)

installment buying A method of paying for an expensive item over many months in installments and including interest (p. 478)

Interim Committee Group of government leaders and scientists who studied the question of using the atomic bomb to force Japan's surrender during World War II (p. 549)

Intermediate-Range Nuclear Forces (INF) Treaty Nuclear arms reduction treaty signed by President Ronald Reagan and Soviet president Mikhail Gorbachev in 1987 (p. 818)

Internal Revenue Act of 1862 Law that created the Internal Revenue Service to manage collection of taxes (p. 201)

internment camp A camp in which people are confined or isolated, especially during a time of war (p. 576)

interracial Including two or more racial groups (p. 662)

Interstate Commerce Act Law passed in 1887 to curb rate-setting abuses by railroads and regulate other interstate business (p. 311)

Iran-contra affair A scandal during the administration of President Ronald Reagan in which money from illegal Iran arms sales was given to Nicaraguan contras to fight Sandinistas (p. 821)

iron curtain The imaginary line separating communist countries allied with the Soviet Union in eastern Europe and the allies of the United States in western Europe during the cold war (p. 587)

Jacksonian Democrats Name given to the Democratic party during the period from the 1820s to the 1850s; supported Andrew Jackson's policy of discouraging federal involvement in the United States economy (p. 114)

Japanese American Citizens League Organization that helped Japanese Americans after World War II (p. 700)

Jazz Age Term for the 1920s, a period marked by the great popularity of jazz music, which was linked to changes in manners, morals, and fashions (p. 457)

jazz Music that grew out of "raggy" rhythms and call-and-response forms for singers and instruments in New Orleans in the 1890s (p. 341)

Jeffersonian Republicans Name given to the Democratic party in the first American party system by historians seeking to distinguish it from the modern-day Republican party (p. 88)

Jim Crow System of laws in the late 1800s that segregated African Americans and forced them to use separate, inferior facilities (p. 343)

jingoism The swelling of national pride and desire for an aggressive foreign policy in late 1800s and early 1900s; resulted in the Spanish-American War and other expansionist activity (p. 367)

judicial branch The part of a government that decides if laws have been broken (p. 63)

Kansas-Nebraska Act Act of 1854 establishing that the people of a territory should decide whether slavery would be allowed there (p. 174)

kinship network Type of social organization consisting of relatives, or kin, such as parents, children, grandparents, aunts, uncles, cousins, and those who marry into the family (p. 13)

Know Nothings The American party, a nativist political party active in the 1850s (p. 173)

Ku Klux Klan Organization formed in the South in 1866, which used lynching and violence to intimidate and control African Americans and others (p. 240)

laissez-faire Economic policy under which government takes a hands-off approach to economic matters and plays a limited role in business (p. 308)

Latino People whose roots lie in Spanish-speaking lands to the south of the United States, including Mexico, Central and South America, and many islands of the Caribbean (p. 697)

League of Nations Organization proposed by President Woodrow Wilson after World War I in the hopes of joining nations together for peace and security (p. 435)

Lecompton constitution Proslavery Kansas constitution of 1857 (p. 179)

legislative branch The part of a government that makes the laws (p. 63)

Lend-Lease Act Law allowing United States loans to Great Britain early in World War II, without specified time of payment; helped Britain resist attacks before the United States entered the war (p. 534)

liberal consensus View widely held in the 1950s and 1960s that capitalism was the best economic system and that the United States was threatened more by communism abroad than by domestic issues like poverty (p. 638)

Liberty Bonds Certificates issued by the United States to raise money to loan to the Allies during World War I (p. 430)

Limited Test Ban Treaty Agreement reached by the United States and the Soviet Union in 1963 banning nuclear testing above ground (p. 656)

lineage Kinship network in which the members trace their descent from a common ancestor (p. 17)

literacy tests Tests in which would-be voters have to demonstrate certain knowledge before they can vote; once used in several states to prevent certain groups from voting (p. 343)

long drive Practice of moving cattle from distant grazing ranges to railroad centers for shipment; common in the West from the 1860s to the 1880s (p. 291)

low country Seaboard region of South Carolina and Georgia, excellent for growing rice and indigo (p. 40)

Loyalists American colonists who remained loyal to Britain during the American Revolution (p. 55)

Lusitania British passenger ship sunk by German U-boats in 1915 (p. 421)

lynching The illegal capture and execution of a person by a mob (p. 344)

mandate Wishes of constituents, as expressed in the election of a candidate by a large majority of voters (p. 639)

Manhattan Project Secret project that created the first atomic bomb in 1945 for use in World War II (p. 548)

manifest destiny Belief that the United States has a divine right to expand its territory; used to support imperialist expansion in the late 1800s (p. 149)

March on Washington Civil rights demonstration in Washington, D.C., led by Martin Luther King, Jr., in 1963 (p. 677)

Market Revolution Shift in the United States economy from home-based to market-based industries (p. 101)

Marshall Plan Program of European economic recovery after World War II, financed by the United States (p. 590)

Medicare Public health-care plan that funds medical care for the elderly (p. 645)

mercantilism European economic theory of the 1600s whereby a nation's economy can be strengthened by the use of protective tariffs, trade monopolies, and a balance of exports over imports (p. 32)

Middle Passage Section of the triangular trade from Africa to the Americas that transported enslaved persons (p. 38)

migratory farm workers Laborers who move from farm to farm planting, cultivating, and harvesting crops (p. 698)

Military Reconstruction Act of 1867 Legislation that divided the post–Civil War South into military districts governed by the North (p. 235)

minstrel show Theatrical show of the late 1800s in which white actors wore blackface and parodied African American music, dance, and humor (p. 340)

minutemen Colonists who fought British forces in the American Revolution; pledged to volunteer military service at a minute's notice (p. 48)

Missouri Compromise Agreement of 1820 that admitted Missouri into the Union as a slave state and Maine as a free state; set a precedent that continued until the Civil War (p. 97)

modern republicanism President Eisenhower's term for an approach to government that was "conservative when it comes to money, liberal when it comes to human beings" (p. 623)

monopoly Control of a commodity or service extending to the elimination of competition and the fixing of prices (p. 261)

Morrill Land-Grant Act Federal grant of 1862 that gave 140 million acres of western land to state governments, which then could sell the land to fund agricultural colleges (p. 280)

most-favored nation Trade status granting a nation the same trading privileges as other nations (p. 363)

muckraker Journalist of the late 1800s to early 1900s who tried to alert the public to alleged wrongdoing by politicians and big business (p. 391)

multiculturalism Social and educational movement that tries to embrace rather than exclude minority cultures (p. 841)

My Lai massacre The slaughter of more than a hundred unarmed Vietnamese peasants in March 1968 by United States forces during the Vietnam War (p. 723)

Nation of Islam African American religious group founded in 1933 that believes in the religion of Islam, self-sufficiency, self-discipline, and the creation of a black nation (p. 682)

National Association for the Advancement of Colored People (NAACP) African American civil rights organization founded in 1910; fought for civil rights through demonstrations, lawsuits, and other means throughout the 1900s (p. 345)

national debt Total debt of the federal government (p. 519)

National Organization for Women (NOW) Feminist group founded in 1966 to pursue equal rights for women (p. 692)

National Republicans Political party of the 1820s that favored strong federal government and a national bank; supported John Q. Adams and opposed the Jacksonian Democrats (p. 114)

Nationalist Member of a 1780s political group advocating strong national government to control the states (p. 64)

nativism Practice of favoring native-born citizens over immigrants (p. 173)

NATO North Atlantic Treaty Organization; alliance of ten European nations, the United States, and Canada that pledged mutual assistance in the event of an attack on any member nation (p. 591)

naturalization Process resulting in the citizenship of immigrants (p. 173)

Nazi party National Socialist Workers party; fascist political party that controlled Germany from 1933 until it was abolished in 1945; led by German dictator Adolf Hitler (p. 531)

New Deal Proposals and programs adopted by President Franklin Roosevelt in response to the Great Depression; included social and economic programs and changes in government regulation (p. 506)

new federalism Replacement of federal programs by federal grants to cities and states (p. 806)

New Freedom Political platform of Woodrow Wilson in the 1912 presidential election that criticized both big business and big government (p. 402)

New Frontier President John F. Kennedy's reform programs; included economic measures, aid to the poor, and the space program (p. 639)

New Jersey Plan Constitutional Convention proposal for a federal government having a unicameral legislature with equal representation for each state regardless of population (p. 70)

New Left Political movement of the 1960s advocating the need for radical change to solve the social problems of the United States (p. 725)

New Right Alliance of conservative special-interest groups in the Republican party from the 1960s to the 1990s (p. 800)

New Nationalism Program of progressive reforms proposed by President Theodore Roosevelt in 1910; included more regulation of business, welfare legislation, and other measures (p. 401)

nomad Person who migrates continually rather than living permanently in one place (p. 139)

North American Free Trade Agreement (NAFTA) International agreement in 1993 between Mexico, Canada, and the United States designed to promote free trade (p. 837)

NSC-68 National Security Council document of the cold war that suggested tripling the defense budget in an effort to contain communism (p. 592)

Nuclear Regulatory Commission Agency overseeing the operation of nuclear power plants in the United States (p. 791)

Open Door policy United States efforts to develop a trade relationship with China in the late 1800s to early 1900s; urged European nations with spheres of influence in China to not restrict trade in those areas (p. 371)

Organization of Petroleum Exporting Countries (OPEC) Group of Arab nations controlling prices and production of oil for export (p. 754)

Pacific Railroad Act of 1862 Legislation that allowed the federal government to offer public land and money to companies for construction of a transcontinental railroad (p. 201)

Panic of 1857 Economic depression that struck the North particularly hard before the Civil War and helped persuade the South to cut economic and political ties with the North (p. 181)

paradox of power Combination of contradictory attitudes toward a powerful country (p. 383)

pardon Official forgiveness of a person for a crime (p. 232)

patriarchal society Male-dominated social organization (p. 15)

Patriots American fighting forces in the War for Independence (p. 55)

Peace Corps Federal program that trains and sends volunteers to aid people of developing countries (p. 651)

Pendleton Act Legislation of 1883 that established a Civil Service Commission to control government hiring, ending the patronage system (p. 311)

Pentagon Papers Secret study by the Defense Department on the Vietnam War; leaked to the *New York Times* in 1971 (p. 764)

per capita income Average income per person; used to compare income of states, countries, etc. (p. 608)

perjury Lying under oath (p. 765)

Persian Gulf War War between Iraq and United Nations forces led by the United States over Iraq's annexation of oil-rich Kuwait in 1991 (p. 820)

Pickett's Charge Confederate attack led by General George Pickett at the Battle of Gettysburg in 1863 that resulted in severe Confederate losses; demonstrated the destructive powers of the new battle tactics and technology (p. 210)

piecework Work paid according to the number of finished units a worker produces (p. 265)

Pinkertons Private police force of the late 1800s and early 1900s; hired by companies to break strikes (p. 272)

Plumbers Secret White House group under President Richard M. Nixon; created to stop security leaks to the press (p. 763)

political boss Leader of a political machine (p. 324)

political left Those who wish to change the current social and political system or power structure (p. 515)

political machine Unofficial city organization designed to keep a particular party or group in power (p. 324)

political party Group actively involved in the political process; seeks to elect candidates to public office in order to control government policies (p. 88)

political right Those who wish to preserve the current social and political system or power structure (p. 514)

poll tax A tax (now unconstitutional) paid in some states before a person was allowed to vote (p. 343)

Poor People's Campaign Movement organized in 1968 by civil rights leader Martin Luther King, Jr., to attack economic injustice (p. 747)

popular sovereignty Belief that people can and should govern themselves (p. 53)

Populists Followers of the People's party of 1892 who sought radical reforms in United States economic and social policies; supported a silver standard, increased money supply, and a graduated income tax (p. 297)

precedent Custom arising from previous practice rather than a written law (p. 90)

presidio Spanish fort built in the American southwest to protect Spanish holdings and missions (p. 24)

progressivism Political and social reform movement of the late 1800s and early 1900s; included socialism, the labor movement, municipal reform, prohibitionism, the settlement house movement, and other reform movements (p. 389)

proletariat Members of the working class (p. 585)

psychedelic drug Drug that produces hallucinations and other altered perceptions of reality (p. 730)

public works programs Government-funded projects to build public facilities; central to President Franklin Roosevelt's New Deal job programs (p. 507)

Puritans Members of the Protestant Church of England of the 1600s and 1700s who wanted to reform, or purify, the church; some migrated to New England in the 1600s (p. 29)

Radical Republicans Wing of the Republican party of the 1860s made up of abolitionists and others hostile to the South; forced harsh Reconstruction laws through Congress (p. 202)

ragtime Style of music consisting of complex syncopated rhythms played over a steady beat; developed by African American musicians in the 1880s (p. 340)

ratify Formally approve a suggested action (p. 77)

rationing Distribution of goods in a limited amount in times of scarcity (p. 564)

real wages Value of income adjusted to account for inflation; used to compare wages in different time periods (p. 476)

real purchasing power Value of money adjusted to account for inflation; used to compare economic conditions in different time periods (p. 608)

realpolitik Foreign policy theory based on efficiency rather than ethics; from the German term for "practical politics" (p. 758)

Reconstruction Period from 1865 to 1877 when the states of the Confederacy were controlled by the federal government before being readmitted to the Union (p. 226)

Reconstruction Finance Corporation Government corporation set up by President Herbert Hoover in 1932 that gave government loans to banks (p. 495)

red scare Fear of communism, socialism, or other so-called extreme ideas (p. 447)

Reformation Religious movement in Western Europe in the 1500s originally aimed at reforming the Roman Catholic church; resulted in the formation of Protestant churches (p. 28)

religious toleration Idea that people of different religions should live together in peace (p. 29)

reparations Payments for economic injury exacted from a defeated enemy (p. 435)

Republican party Political party organized in the 1850s to oppose southern interests; gave rise to today's Republican party (p. 174)

Roosevelt Corollary Extension of the Monroe Doctrine by President Theodore Roosevelt whereby the United States would use force to prevent other foreign powers from intervening in the affairs of Western Hemisphere countries (p. 375)

Rosie the Riveter Fictional defense plant worker portrayed in government propaganda films and posters to attract women to the work force during World War II (p. 566)

S & L Savings and loan bank (p. 806)

salutary neglect Great Britain's colonial policy of not interfering in colonial politics and economy as long as such neglect served Britain's economic interests (p. 33)

sanction Coercive measure, such as a boycott, taken by a group to enforce demands (p. 835)

Sandinistas Marxist Nicaraguan revolutionaries who took control of the Nicaraguan government in 1979 (p. 821)

satellite nation Country controlled politically and economically by a powerful nation, especially by the Soviet Union during the cold war (p. 593)

scab Slang for a person hired to replace a striking worker (p. 272)

scalawag Southern white who became a Republican during Reconstruction to profit from unstable social conditions in that area (p. 237)

Scopes trial Tennessee trial of 1925 that challenged the law against teaching evolution in public schools (p. 467)

Scottsboro Boys Nine African American youths accused and unfairly tried and convicted of raping two white woman in Alabama in 1931; gained national support and received new trials by order of the Supreme Court (p. 489)

secede Formally withdraw from a political organization; southern states seceded from the United States to form the Confederacy in late 1860 and early 1861 (p. 117)

secessionist Southerner who wanted the South to secede from the Union before the Civil War (p. 185)

second American party system The political parties that developed out of the election of 1828; the National Republicans and Jacksonian Democrats (p. 114)

Second Great Awakening Wave of religious revivals in the United States during the early 1800s (p. 99)

section Region distinguished from others in United States geography by economic and cultural differences (p. 105)

secularize Transfer control from the church to the state (p. 144)

self-determination Freedom of a group of people to determine their own political status; proposed by President Wilson for ethnic groups in Austria-Hungary after World War I (p. 434)

separation of powers Constitutional provision that separates the powers of the federal government into legislative, executive, and judicial branches (p. 72)

17th parallel Latitude line established after World War II that divided North Vietnam from South Vietnam (p. 597)

sharecropper Farmer who grows crops on land owned by someone else and gives a share of the crops produced to the landowner in return for use of the land and supplies (p. 240)

shell Hollow cannon ball that explodes in the air or as it hits; developed during the Civil War (p. 193)

shuttle diplomacy Diplomatic negotiations conducted by an official mediator traveling frequently to the nations involved; used by Henry Kissinger in the 1970s to promote peace in the Middle East (p. 783)

siege Prolonged attack in which a city is surrounded and starved into surrender; used in the Civil War by General Ulysses S. Grant to capture Vicksburg, Mississippi (p. 210)

sit-down strike Work stoppage in which workers refuse to leave the premises until their demands are considered or met (p. 520)

sit-in Organized demonstration in which protesters seat themselves in segregated establishments to protest racial discrimination; became a common practice for many civil rights groups during the 1960s (p. 669)

Slave Power Name for the South used by opponents in the North before the Civil War (p. 174)

social Darwinism Application of Charles Darwin's "survival of the fittest" theory to human society; used by the great industrialists of the late 1800s to discourage government interference in business (p. 261)

social welfare program Government program that helps ensure a basic standard of living; includes unemployment, accident, and health insurance and social security programs (p. 390)

social gospel movement Social movement of the early 1900s that applied the Christian gospel to social problems (p. 328)

Social Security Act Legislation of 1935 that established a social welfare system funded by employee and worker contributions; included old-age pensions, survivor's benefits for victims of industrial accidents, and unemployment insurance (p. 512)

socialism The economic and political philosophy that advocates collective ownership of factories and property (p. 268)

socialist A person who advocates the principles of socialism (p. 493)

sooner Person who settled land in the newly opened Indian Territory before it was officially made available in 1889 (p. 287)

Southern Christian Leadership Conference (SCLC) Civil rights organization founded in 1957 by Martin Luther King, Jr.; employed nonviolent means of protest and helped shift the focus of the civil rights movement to the South (p. 663)

speakeasy Establishment that illegally sold and served liquor during prohibition (p. 466)

speculation Undertaking risk on stocks or real estate for the chance of profit (p. 478)

speculator Person who buys large areas of land hoping to sell it later for a profit (p. 280)

sphere of influence Area of economic control exerted by a foreign power, especially in China during the late 1800s (p. 371)

Sputnik First artificial satellite to circle Earth; launched by the Soviet Union in 1957, beginning the space race (p. 625)

squatter Person occupying public land in order to gain title to it (p. 287)

stagflation Slow economic growth coupled with high rates of inflation and unemployment (p. 776)

states' rights Theory that each state has the right to nullify acts of the federal government; advocated by 19th-century statesman John C. Calhoun to protect slavery and keep the North from gaining control of the federal government (p. 171)

steerage Large open area beneath a ship's deck where immigrants could travel cheaply but with few amenities (p. 314)

Strategic Defense Initiative (SDI) Satellite-operated defense system proposed by President Ronald Reagan in 1983; popularly called "Star Wars" (p. 818)

Strategic Arms Limitation Talks (SALT) Negotiations between the United States and the Soviet Union from 1971 to 1973 to limit offensive nuclear weapons (p. 762)

Student Nonviolent Coordinating Committee (SNCC) Student civil rights organization begun in 1960 to address the concerns of young African Americans; originally part of the Southern Christian Leadership Conference (p. 665)

Students for a Democratic Society (SDS) New Left political group organized in 1960 to work for radical change in United States society; heavily involved in Vietnam War protests (p. 724)

suburb Residential community on the outskirts of a city (p. 320)

suffrage The right to vote (p. 132)

supply-side economics Theory that the economy can be stimulated by increasing the availability of money for investments, achieved by reducing taxes on the rich; called "Reaganomics" in the 1980s (p. 805)

system of checks and balances United States system of government in which the power of each of the three branches of government is limited by that of the others (p. 73)

Taft-Hartley Act Legislation of 1947 that allows a President to order striking workers in crucial industries back to work while the government investigates the dispute (p. 621)

Tammany Hall Political machine controlling New York City politics from the 1860s to the 1920s (p. 324)

tariff Tax on imports or exports (p. 89)

teach-in Extended lecture on a controversial issue; arose in the 1960s to protest the Vietnam War (p. 726)

Teapot Dome Scandal during the administration of President Warren G. Harding involving the lease of public oil reserves to private companies in exchange for illegal payments (p. 455)

televangelism Television broadcasts conducted by evangelists; often used to raise money and support for churches and political movements (p. 801)

temperance movement Campaign against alcohol consumption; began as part of the middle-class reform movements of the 1800s (p. 125)

tenant farmer Farmer who pays cash for rental of land (p. 240)

termination policy United States government policy of the 1950s to eliminate reservations and assimilate Native Americans into mainstream American life (p. 629)

Tet Offensive Attack by the Viet Cong in South Vietnam in 1968 during Tet, the Vietnamese lunar new year; turned the

United States public against United States involvement in the Vietnam War (p. 719)

Thirteenth Amendment Constitutional amendment of 1865 outlawing slavery in the United States (p. 216)

Three-fifths Compromise Constitutional Convention agreement to count three fifths of a state's enslaved population when establishing state populations for representation in the House of Representatives (p. 71)

38th parallel Latitude line established after World War II that divided North Korea, which was allied with the Soviet Union, from South Korea, which was allied with the United States (p. 594)

Tories Majority party in the British Parliament during the American Revolution; also the name for American colonists still loyal to the crown (p. 55)

total war Warfare in which opponents attack civilians and the economic system of the enemy in addition to its soldiers (p. 211)

totalitarian Relating to a form of dictatorship or central government that has total control over all aspects of life and that suppresses all political and cultural expression of opposition (p. 585)

Trail of Tears Forced march of 15,000 Cherokee from their homes in the southeast to western reservations from 1837 to 1838 (p. 117)

Transcendentalism Intellectual and philosophical movement of the mid-1800s asserting that the nature of reality can be learned only by intuition rather than through experience (p. 124)

transcontinental railroad Railroad spanning North American continent; completed in 1869 (p. 254)

Treaty of Paris Agreement of 1783 that ended the War for Independence (p. 60)

triangular trade Trade between the Americas, Europe, and Africa in the 1700s; supported New England economies (p. 34)

Truman Doctrine Cold war policy, established by President Harry S Truman, pledging United States support for "free peoples" resisting communism (p. 590)

trust Combination of companies that turn over their assets to a board of trustees to control prices and competition in a particular industry (p. 262)

Twenty-first Amendment Constitutional amendment of 1933 repealing the Eighteenth Amendment, thus ending prohibition (p. 493)

U-boat Submarine of the German navy; introduced during World War I (p. 421)

unicameral legislature Government having a single legislative house (p. 64)

Union United States of America as a national unit, especially during the Civil War; the North and its forces in the Civil War (p. 164)

United Farm Workers (UFW) Group organized in the early 1960s to help migratory farm workers gain better pay and working conditions (p. 698)

United Nations International organization formed in 1945 to promote peace, security, and economic development among nations (p. 589)

United States Sanitary Commission Northern women's group in the Civil War that provided aid to soldiers (p. 244)

vaudeville Theatrical performances of the late 1800s characterized by slapstick and song-and-dance routines (p. 339)

Versailles Treaty Agreement in 1919 ending World War I; included huge war reparations to be paid by Germany (p. 436)

vertical consolidation Control of all phases of a product's development, from raw materials to delivery of the finished products (p. 263)

veto Overturn a law or decision by using the constitutionally granted power of one branch of government to block legislation made by another; the President can veto a bill passed by Congress (p. 70)

Victorianism Moral ideas associated with Britain's Queen Victoria in the nineteenth century; characterized by strict moral codes (p. 341)

Viet Cong Communist guerrillas of South Vietnam during the Vietnam War (p. 717)

Vietnamization Nixon's Vietnam War policy to replace United States troops in Vietnam with South Vietnamese troops (p. 734)

Virginia Plan Constitutional Convention proposal for a federal government having a bicameral legislature with representation based on population (p. 70)

Volunteers in Service to America (VISTA) Federal program that sends volunteers to aid poor communities in the United States (p. 644)

Voting Rights Act of 1965 Legislation that gave the federal government the power to register voters in areas where local officials prevented African Americans from voting (p. 680)

WAC Women's Army Corps; organization of women who volunteered for military service in World War II; a member of the Women's Army Corps (p. 544)

Wagner Act National Labor Relations Act of 1935; legalized union practices such as collective bargaining and the closed shop and outlawed certain antiunion practices such as blacklisting (p. 512)

War for Independence War fought between American colonists and Great Britain from 1775 to 1783, resulting in an independent United States of America (p. 48)

war of attrition Warfare in which a weaker army inflicts small but continuous losses of soldiers and material that gradually add up to an unbearable burden for the enemy (p. 194)

Warren Commission Group headed by Chief Justice Earl Warren; formed to investigate President John Kennedy's assassination (p. 641)

Watergate Scandal of President Richard M. Nixon's administration that began in 1972 when leading Nixon supporters burglarized Democratic National Party Headquarters at the Watergate office building in Washington, D.C. (p. 763)

welfare capitalism Industrial policy of meeting workers' needs with increased pay and benefits for the purpose of preventing labor union organization (p. 477)

Whiskey Rebellion Pennsylvanian revolt against a whiskey tax in 1794; demonstrated that the federal government would use force to make citizens obey federal law (p. 89)

wildcat strike A workers' strike not authorized by their union (p. 561)

Wilmot Proviso Proposal of 1846 that slavery not be allowed in territory acquired from the Mexican War; defeated by Congress, but opened debate between the North and South on slavery in the western territories (p. 151)

woman question Wide-ranging debate of the early 1900s on the social role of women (p. 348)

Woodstock Rock music festival of 1969 that became a symbol of counterculture music and behavior (p. 731)

writ of *habeas corpus* Court order requiring proof that a prisoner is being justly held (p. 200)

yellow journalism Newspaper coverage that sensationalizes stories to increase circulation; inflamed anti-Spanish sentiment in the United States before and during the Spanish-American War (p. 340)

Zimmerman note Telegram intercepted from a German official proposing an alliance with Mexico and offering to help Mexico regain Texas, New Mexico, and Arizona if the United States entered World War I; increased pressure on the United States to enter the war (p. 423)

Biographical Dictionary

The Biographical Dictionary identifies key people listed in section previews. The page number at the end of each entry indicates the text page on which the name appears in boldface.

Pronunciations given here are based on those given in *Webster's Biographical Dictionary*. To determine the pronunciation of the symbols used, compare them with the following examples.

ā	fāte	ī	īce
ă	chăotic	ĭ	ĭll
â	câre	ĭ	dĭrect
ă	făt	к	like *ch* in German *ich*
ă	ăccount	ō	ōld
ä	ärm	ŏ	ŏbey
á	ásk	ô	ôrb
á	sofá	ŏ	ŏdd
ē	ēve	oo	food
ē	ēvent	oo	foŏt
e	end	th	then
ĕ	silĕnt	ŭ	ŭp

´ accent

• syllable break

Stephen Austin

Adams, John Quincy Sixth President of the United States, 1825–1829; proposed greater federal involvement in the economy through tariffs and improvements such as roads, bridges, and canals (p. 112)

Adams, John Second President of the United States, 1797–1801; worked to relieve increasing tensions with France; lost reelection bid to Jefferson in 1800 as the country moved away from Federalist policies (p. 90)

Addams, Jane Cofounder of Hull House, the first settlement house, in 1889; remained active in social causes through the early 1900s (p. 329)

Agnew, Spiro Vice President under President Richard Nixon until forced to resign in 1973 for crimes committed before taking office; known for his harsh campaign attacks (p. 749)

Arafat, Yasir (är´ă•făt, yä´sir) Palestinian leader; gave up terrorist tactics and signed a peace agreement with Israelis in 1993 (p. 834)

Arthur, Chester A. Twenty-first President of the United States, 1881–1885; signed 1883 Pendleton Act, which instituted the Civil Service (p. 310)

Austin, Stephen Leader of first American group of Texas settlers in 1822; worked for Texan independence (p. 145)

Bakke, Alan Student who won a suit against the University of California in 1978 on the grounds that the affirmative action program had kept him out (p. 793)

Baldwin, James African American author and spokesperson for the civil rights movement during the 1960s (p. 681)

Banks, Dennis Native American leader in 1960s and 1970s; helped organize American Indian Movement (AIM) and the 1973 Wounded Knee occupation (p. 702)

Beecher, Catharine Author whose 1841 book *Treatise on Domestic Economy* supported the cult of domesticity (p. 132)

Beecher, Lyman Revivalist during the Second Great Awakening; feared the rise of individualism in the United States (p. 124)

Begin, Menachem (bĕ´gĕn´, mă•nä´hĕm) Israeli leader during the 1970s; began the Middle East peace process by reaching the 1978 Camp David Accords with Egypt (p. 784)

Bell, Alexander Graham Inventor; developed the telephone in 1876; one of the founders of American Telephone & Telegraph (AT&T) in 1884 (p. 256)

Bellamy, Edward Author of the novel *Looking Backward* (1888), which proposed nationalizing trusts to eliminate social problems (p. 388)

Bethune, Mary McLeod African American educator, New Deal worker; founded Bethune Cookman College in the 1920s, advised the National Youth Administration (p. 510)

Beveridge, Albert J. Indiana senator in the early 1900s; saw United States imperialism as a duty owed to "primitive" societies (p. 365)

Booth, John Wilkes Southern actor who assassinated President Abraham Lincoln in 1865 (p. 216)

Breckinridge, John C. Presidential candidate of the southern wing of the Democratic party in 1860 (p. 184)

Brown, John Abolitionist crusader who massacred proslavery settlers in Kansas before the Civil War; hoped to inspire slave revolt with 1859 attack on Virginia arsenal; executed for treason against the state of Virginia (p. 177)

Bryan, William Jennings Advocate of silver standard and proponent of Democratic and Populist views from the 1890s through the 1910s; Democratic candidate for President in 1896, 1900, and 1908 (p. 298)

Buchanan, James Fifteenth President of the United States, 1857–1861; supported by the South; attempted to moderate fierce disagreement over expansion of slavery (p. 175)

Bush, George H. W. Forty-first President of the United States, 1989–1993; continued Reagan's conservative policies; brought together United Nations coalition to fight the Persian Gulf War (p. 804)

Calhoun, John C. Statesman from South Carolina who held many offices in the federal government; supported slavery, cotton exports, states' rights; in 1850 foresaw future conflicts over slavery (p. 112)

Carnegie, Andrew Industrialist who made a fortune in steel in the late 1800s through vertical consolidation; as a philanthropist, he gave away over $350 million (p. 259)

Carson, Rachel Marine biologist, author of *Silent Spring* (1962), which exposed harmful effects of pesticides and inspired concern for the environment (p. 707)

Carter, James Earl, Jr. Thirty-ninth President of the United States, 1977–1981; advocated concern for human rights in foreign policy; assisted in mediating the Camp David Accords (p. 779)

Castro, Fidel (käs′trō, fe•thĕl′) Revolutionary leader who took control of Cuba in 1959; ally of Soviet Union through the 1980s (p. 598)

Catt, Carrie Chapman Woman suffrage leader in the early 1900s; helped secure passage of Nineteenth Amendment in 1920; headed National American Woman Suffrage Association (p. 407)

Chávez, César (chä′vāz, sä′sär) Latino leader from 1962 to his death in 1993; organized the United Farm Workers (UFW) to help migratory farm workers gain better pay and working conditions (p. 698)

Churchill, Winston Leader of Great Britain before and during World War II; powerful speechmaker who rallied Allied morale during the war (p. 534)

Cisneros, Henry Latino mayor of San Antonio; he was made head of Housing and Urban Development in 1993 under President Bill Clinton (p. 814)

Clark, William Leader, with Meriwether Lewis, of expedition through the West in 1804; brought back scientific samples, maps, and information on Native Americans (p. 138)

Clay, Henry Senator from Kentucky; accused by Jackson of giving votes to John Q. Adams in return for post as secretary of state; endorsed the American System to promote economic growth; advocate of Compromise of 1850 (p. 113)

Cleveland, Grover Twenty-second and twenty-fourth President of the United States, 1885–1889, 1893–1897; supported railroad regulation and a return to the gold standard (p. 311)

Clinton, Bill Forty-second President of the United States, 1993–; defeated George Bush after overcoming numerous political obstacles; advocated economic and health-care reform (p. 826)

Henry Cisneros

Clinton, Hillary Rodham First Lady, 1993– ; lawyer; head of United States health-care reform team (p. 827)

Columbus, Christopher Explorer whose voyage for Spain to North America in 1492 opened the Atlantic World (p. 19)

Coolidge, Calvin Thirtieth President of the United States, 1923–1929; promoted big business and opposed social aid (p. 455)

Coughlin, Father Charles E. "Radio Priest" who supported and then attacked President Franklin Roosevelt's New Deal; prevented by the Catholic church from broadcasting after he praised Hitler (p. 516)

Coxey, Jacob S. Populist who led Coxey's Army in a march on Washington, D.C., in 1894 to seek government jobs for the unemployed (p. 312)

Custer, George Armstrong General who directed army attacks against Native Americans in the 1870s; commanded army forces killed in 1876 at Little Bighorn in Montana (p. 285)

Davis, Jefferson President of the Confederate States of America; ordered attack on Fort Sumter, the first battle of the Civil War (p. 186)

De Klerk, Frederick W. Prime minister of South Africa who began the process of ending apartheid in the early 1990s (p. 835)

Dewey, George Officer in United States Navy, 1861–1917; led a surprise attack in the Philippines during the Spanish-American War that destroyed the entire Spanish fleet (p. 368)

Dinh Diem, Ngo (dǐn′zē′ĕm, nō′) Leader of South Vietnam, 1954–1963; supported by United States, but not by Vietnamese Buddhist majority; assassinated in 1963 (p. 716)

Dix, Dorothea Advocate of prison reform and of special institutions for the insane in Massachusetts before the Civil War (p. 126)

Douglas, Stephen Illinois senator who introduced the Kansas-Nebraska Act, which allowed new territories to choose their own position on slavery; debated Abraham Lincoln on slavery issues in 1858 (p. 173)

Douglass, Frederick African American abolitionist leader who spoke eloquently for abolition in the United States and Britain before the Civil War (p. 128)

Du Bois, W.E.B. (doo•bois′) African American scholar and leader in early 1900s; encouraged African Americans to attend colleges to develop leadership skills (p. 337)

Edison, Thomas A. Inventor; developed the light bulb, the phonograph, and hundreds of other inventions in the late 1800s and early 1900s (p. 253)

Ehrlichman, John Adviser on domestic policy to President Richard Nixon; deeply involved in Watergate (p. 753)

Einstein, Albert Physicist whose theory of relativity led to harnessing nuclear energy; proposed development of the atomic bomb in 1939 (p. 548)

Eisenhower, Dwight D. Thirty-fourth President of the United States, 1953–1961; leader of Allied forces in World War II; as President, he promoted business and continued social programs (p. 539)

Eliot, T. S. Poet; his work "The Waste Land" described the struggle of youth in the 1920s (p. 469)

Ellsberg, Daniel Defense Department official; leaked Pentagon Papers to the *New York Times* in 1971, showing government lies to public about Vietnam (p. 763)

Father Divine African American minister; his Harlem soup kitchens fed the hungry during the Great Depression (p. 488)

Fillmore, Millard Thirteenth President of the United States, 1850–1853; promoted the Compromise of 1850 to smooth over disagreements about slavery in new territories (p. 170)

Fitzgerald, F. Scott Novelist who depicted the United States and the world during the 1920s in novels such as *The Great Gatsby* (p. 469)

Betty Friedan

Fitzhugh, George Southern author who criticized northern industrialists for exploiting workers in his 1857 book *Cannibals All!* (p. 167)

Ford, Gerald R. Thirty-eighth President of the United States, 1974–1977; succeeded and pardoned Nixon; failed to establish strong leadership (p. 774)

Ford, Henry Manufacturer from the 1910s through the 1940s; made affordable cars for the masses using assembly line and other production techniques (p. 464)

Friedan, Betty Feminist author; criticized limited roles for women in her 1963 book *The Feminine Mystique* (p. 616)

Garfield, James A. Twentieth President of the United States, 1881; his assassination by a disappointed office seeker led to the reform of the spoils system (p. 310)

Garrison, William Lloyd White leader of radical abolition movement based in Boston; founded *The Liberator* in 1831 to work for an immediate end to slavery (p. 127)

Garvey, Marcus African American leader from 1919 to 1926 who urged African Americans to return to "motherland" of Africa; provided early inspiration for "black pride" movements (p. 455)

George III King of England during American Revolution (p. 49)

George, Henry Author of *Progress and Poverty* (1879) linking land speculation and poverty; proposed a single tax based on land value (p. 388)

Gorbachev, Mikhail (gôr´bä·chĕv, myĭ·kü·ēl´) Soviet leader whose bold reforms led to the breakup of the Soviet Union in the late 1980s (p. 818)

Gore, Al Senator from Tennessee; Vice President under President Bill Clinton, 1993– (p. 830)

Grant, Ulysses S. Eighteenth President of the United States, 1869–1877; commander of Union forces who accepted Lee's surrender in 1865 (p. 195)

Haldeman, H. R. Chief of staff under President Richard Nixon; deeply involved in Watergate (p. 753)

Hamilton, Alexander Officer in the War for Independence; delegate to the Constitutional Convention; Federalist and first secretary of treasury (p. 80)

Harding, Warren G. Twenty-ninth President of the United States, 1921–1923; presided over a short administration marked by corruption (p. 455)

Harrison, Benjamin Twenty-third President of the United States, 1889–1893; signed 1890 Sherman Antitrust Act later used to regulate big business (p. 312)

Harrison, William Henry Ninth President of the United States, 1841; died of pneumonia after only a month in office (p. 818)

Hayes, Rutherford B. Nineteenth President of the United States, 1877–1881; promised to withdraw Union troops from the South in order to end dispute over his election; attacked spoils system (p. 214)

Hearst, William Randolph Newspaper publisher from 1887 until his death in 1951; used "yellow journalism" in the 1890s to stir up sentiment in favor of the Spanish-American War (p. 367)

Hiss, Alger Former State Department official investigated as a possible communist spy by House Un-American Activities Committee after World War II; convicted of perjury in 1950 (p. 601)

Hitler, Adolf German leader of National Socialist (Nazi) party 1933–1945; rose to power by promoting racist and nationalist views (p. 531)

Ho Chi Minh (hō´ chē´ mĭn´) Leader of the Communist party in Indochina after World War II; led Vietnamese against the French, then North Vietnamese against the United States in the Vietnam War (p. 596)

Hoover, Herbert Thirty-first President of the United States, 1929–1933; worked to aid Europeans during World War I; responded ineffectively to 1929 stock market crash and Great Depression (p. 456)

Houston, Sam Leader of Texas troops in war for independence from Mexico in 1836; elected first governor of independent Texas (p. 146)

Humphrey, Hubert Democratic presidential candidate in 1968; lost narrowly to Nixon in an election bid hurt by support for the Vietnam War and by third-party candidate George Wallace (p. 748)

Hussein, Saddam (hoo·sĭn´, sȧd·dȧm´) Iraqi dictator; invaded Kuwait in 1990, setting off Persian Gulf War (p. 820)

Jackson, Andrew Seventh President of the United States, 1829–1837; supported minimal government and the spoils system; vetoed rechartering of the national bank; pursued harsh policy toward Native Americans (p. 95)

Jackson, Stonewall Confederate general known for his swift strikes against Union forces; earned nickname Stonewall by holding his forces steady under extreme pressure at the First Battle of Manassas (p. 193)

Jefferson, Thomas Third President of the United States, 1801–1809; main author of the Declaration of Independence; a firm believer in the people and decentralized power; reduced the federal government (p. 53)

Johnson, Andrew Seventeenth President of the United States, 1865–1869; clashed with Radical Republicans on Reconstruction programs; was impeached, then acquitted, in 1868 (p. 233)

Johnson, Lyndon B. Thirty-sixth President of the United States, 1963–1969; expanded social assistance with his Great Society program; increased United States commitment during Vietnam War (p. 643)

Chief Joseph

Joseph, Chief Leader of Nez Percé; forced to give up his home by United States army, fled toward Canada; captured in 1877 (p. 286)

Kelley, Florence Progressive reformer active from 1886 to 1920; worked in state and federal government for laws on child labor, workplace safety, and consumer protection (p. 391)

Kennedy, John F. Thirty-fifth President of the United States, 1961–1963; seen as youthful and inspiring; known for his firm handling of the Cuban missile crisis; assassinated in 1963 (p. 638)

Kennedy, Robert F. Attorney general under his brother, President John Kennedy, in the early 1960s; supported civil rights; assassinated while running for President in 1968 (p. 747)

Keynes, John Maynard British economist who believed that government spending could help a faltering economy; his theories helped shape New Deal legislation (p. 496)

Khomeini, Ayatollah Ruholla (kō•mā´nē, ĭ•yá•tŏl´lá rōō•hŏl´lá) Islamic fundamentalist leader of Iran after the 1979 overthrow of the Shah; approved holding of American hostages (p. 786)

King, Martin Luther, Jr. African American civil rights leader from the mid-1950s until his assassination in 1968; used nonviolent means such as marches, boycotts, and legal challenges to win civil rights (p. 628)

Kissinger, Henry Secretary of state under Presidents Richard Nixon and Gerald Ford; used *realpolitik* to open relations with China, to end the Vietnam War, and to moderate Middle East conflict (p. 753)

Khrushchev, Nikita (krōōsh´chôf, nyĭ´kyē´tŭ) Soviet leader from 1953 to 1964; opposed President Kennedy in the Cuban missile crisis (p. 653)

Lafayette, Marquis de (lä´fī•ĕt´, mär•kē´dĕ´) French officer who assisted American forces in the War for Independence (p. 59)

Lee, Robert E. Brilliant general of Confederate forces during the Civil War (p. 197)

Lenin, Vladimir I. Revolutionary leader in Russia; established a communist government in 1917 (p. 446)

Levitt, William J. Built new communities in the suburbs after World War II, using mass-production techniques (p. 611)

Lewis, John L. Head of United Mine Workers through World War II; used strikes during the war to win pay raises (p. 561)

Lewis, Meriwether Leader with William Clark of expedition through the West in 1804; brought back scientific samples, maps, and information on Native Americans (p. 138)

Lincoln, Abraham Sixteenth President of the United States, 1861–1865; known for his effective leadership during the Civil War and his Emancipation Proclamation declaring the end of slavery in Confederate-held territory (p. 180)

Lindbergh, Charles A. Aviator who became an international hero when he made the first solo flight across the Atlantic Ocean in 1927 (p. 463)

Lodge, Henry Cabot Massachusetts senator of early 1900s; supported United States imperialism (p. 365)

Long, Huey Louisiana politician in 1930s called the Kingfish; suggested redistributing large fortunes by means of grants to families; assassinated in 1935 (p. 516)

Low, Juliette Founder of American Girl Scouts in 1912 (p. 383)

MacArthur, Douglas United States general during World War II and Korean War; forced to resign by Truman in 1951 (p. 537)

Madison, James Fourth President of the United States, 1809–1817; called the Father of the Constitution for his leadership at the Constitutional Convention (p. 68)

Mahan, Alfred T. Author who argued in 1890 that the economic future of the United States rested on new overseas markets protected by a larger navy (p. 364)

Malcolm X African American leader during the 1950s and 1960s; eloquent spokesperson for African American self-sufficiency; assassinated in 1965 (p. 682)

Mandela, Nelson African anti-apartheid leader in South Africa beginning in the 1960s; imprisoned 1962–1989 (p. 835)

Mann, Horace School reformer and supporter of public education before the Civil War; devised an educational system in Massachusetts later copied by many states (p. 125)

Mao Zedong (mou´ dzŭ´ dŏong´) Leader of communists who took over China in 1949; remained in power until his death in 1976 (p. 591)

Marshall, George C. Secretary of state under President Harry Truman; assisted economic recovery in Europe after World War II and established strong allies for the United States through his Marshall Plan (p. 590)

Marshall, Thurgood First African American Supreme Court justice; as a lawyer, won landmark school desegregation case *Brown* v. *Board of Education* in 1954 (p. 628)

McCarthy, Eugene Candidate in the 1968 Democratic presidential race who opposed the Vietnam War; convinced President Lyndon Johnson not to run again through his strong showing in the primaries (p. 747)

McCarthy, Joseph R. Republican senator from Wisconsin in the late 1940s and early 1950s; led a crusade to investigate officials he claimed were communists; discredited in 1954 (p. 601)

McClellan, George Early Union army leader in the Civil War; careful organizer and planner who moved too slowly for northern politicians; ran against President Abraham Lincoln in the election of 1864 (p. 195)

McKinley, William Twenty-fifth President of the United States, 1897–1901; supported tariffs and a gold standard; expanded the United States by waging the Spanish-American War (p. 313)

Meade, George G. Union commander at Battle of Gettysburg in 1863; defended the high ground and forced Confederate army to attack, causing great casualties (p. 210)

Means, Russell Native American leader of 1960s and 1970s; helped organize American Indian Movement (AIM) and 1973 Wounded Knee occupation (p. 705)

Metacom Leader of Pokanokets in Massachusetts; also known by his English name, King Philip; led Native Americans in King

Philip's War, 1675–1676 (p. 29)

Milosevic, Slobodan (me•lôsh´ĕ•vĭk, slŏ´bă•dăn) Leader of Serbs in civil war that started in 1991 after the breakup of Yugoslavia; accused of genocide of Croats and Muslims (p. 833)

Mitchell, John Attorney general under President Richard Nixon; deeply involved in Watergate scandal (p. 753)

Mohammad Reza Pahlavi, Shah Leader of Iran, from 1941 until his overthrow in 1979; supported by the United States; brought modernization to his country along with repression and corruption (p. 785)

Monroe, James Fifth President of the United States, 1817–1825; acquired Florida from Spain; declared Monroe Doctrine to keep foreign powers out of the Americas (p. 112)

Mott, Lucretia Women's rights leader; helped organize first women's convention in Seneca Falls, New York, in 1848 (p. 133)

Mussolini, Benito (mōō´sŏ•lē´nĕ, bă•nē´tō) Italian fascist leader from 1925 through 1945; called *Il Duce* — "the leader"; known for his brutal policies (p. 530)

Nader, Ralph Consumer advocate; published *Unsafe at Any Speed* in 1965 criticizing auto safety and inspiring new safety laws (p. 709)

Nimitz, Chester Leader of United States troops in World War II battle of Midway Island, during which much of the Japanese navy was destroyed (p. 539)

Nixon, Richard M. Thirty-seventh President, 1969–1974; known for his foreign policy toward the Soviet Union and China and for illegal acts he committed in the Watergate affair that forced his resignation (p. 622)

Sandra Day O'Connor

O'Connor, Sandra Day First woman Supreme Court justice; appointed by Reagan in 1981 (p. 807)

Oppenheimer, J. Robert Physicist; headed Manhattan Project in World War II to develop first atomic bomb (p. 549)

Paine, Thomas Author of political pamphlets during 1770s and 1780s; wrote *Common Sense* in 1776 (p. 53)

Paul, Alice Woman suffrage leader of early 1900s; her Congressional Union used aggressive tactics to push the Nineteenth Amendment (p. 407)

Perkins, Frances Secretary of labor 1933–1945 under President Franklin Delano Roosevelt; first woman cabinet member (p. 509)

Pierce, Franklin Fourteenth President of the United States, 1853–1857; signed the Kansas-Nebraska Act, which renewed conflicts over slavery in the territories (p. 172)

Polk, James K. Eleventh President of the United States, 1845–1849; led expansion of United States to southwest through war against Mexico (p. 118)

Popé (pō•pa´) Medicine man who led Pueblos and Apaches against Spanish rule in the Revolt of 1680 (p. 25)

Powhatan Native American leader of Pamunkey people in Chesapeake Bay region of Virginia in late 1500s and early 1600s (p. 26)

Pulitzer, Joseph Early 1900s newspaper publisher; used "yellow journalism" to stir up public sentiment in favor of the Spanish-American War (p. 367)

Rabin, Yitzhak (rä•bēn´, yĭtz´ăk) Israeli prime minister who signed a peace agreement with Palestinians in 1993 (p. 832)

Randolph, A. Philip Civil rights activist from the 1930s to the 1950s; planned the Washington march that pressured President Franklin Delano Roosevelt into opening World War II defense jobs to African Americans (p. 573)

Jackie Robinson

Reagan, Ronald Fortieth President of the United States, 1981–1989; conservative leader who promoted supply-side economics and created huge budget deficits (p. 800)

Robinson, Jackie Athlete who in 1947 became the first African American to play baseball in the major leagues (p. 626)

Rockefeller, Nelson Vice President appointed by President Gerald Ford in 1974; the nation's only nonelected Vice President to serve with a non-elected President (p. 775)

Roosevelt, Eleanor First Lady 1933–1945; tireless worker for social causes, including women's rights and civil rights for African Americans and other groups (p. 497)

Roosevelt, Franklin D. Thirty-second President of the United States, 1933–1945; fought the Great Depression through his New Deal social programs; battled Congress over Supreme Court control; proved a strong leader during World War II (p. 497)

Roosevelt, Theodore Twenty-sixth President of the United States, 1901–1909; fought trusts, aided progressive reforms, built Panama Canal, and increased United States influence overseas (p. 373)

Rosenberg, Julius and Ethel Husband and wife convicted and executed in 1953 for passing atomic secrets to the Soviet Union; their guilt is still debated (p. 601)

Sacajawea (săk´á•já•wē•á) Shoshone woman who served as guide and translator for Lewis and Clark on their exploratory journey through the West in the early 1800s (p. 138)

Sacco, Nicola (săk´kō, nĕ•kô´lä) Immigrant and anarchist executed for a 1920 murder at a Massachusetts factory, though believed to be innocent by many (p. 448)

Sadat, Anwar el- (sá•dat´, ăn•wär´ ĕl) Egyptian leader in the 1970s; began the Middle East peace process by reaching the 1978 Camp David Accords with Egypt (p. 784)

Salinger, J. D. Author of 1951 novel *The Catcher in the Rye*, which criticized 1950s pressure to conform (p. 617)

Santa Anna, Antonio López de Mexican dictator who led government and troops in war against Texas; won the battle of the Alamo (p. 145)

Schlafly, Phyllis Conservative activist; led campaign during the 1960s and 1970s to block the Equal Rights Amendment (p. 695)

Seward, William Henry Republican antislavery leader during the 1860s; acquired Alaska in 1867 as secretary of state (p. 184)

Sheridan, Philip Union general in the Civil War who worked with Grant to cut off the retreat of Confederate forces after the fall of Richmond in 1865 (p. 216)

Sherman, William Tecumseh Union general in the Civil War; known for his destructive march from Atlanta to Savannah in 1864 (p. 208)

Sirica, John J. Washington judge who presided over the Watergate investigation in the 1970s; gave tough sentences to convicted participants and ordered President Richard Nixon to release secret tapes (p. 765)

Sitting Bull Chief Leader of Sioux in clashes with United States Army in Black Hills in 1870s (p. 285)

Smith, Joseph Founder of Church of Jesus Christ of Latter-day Saints, or Mormons, in New York in 1830; killed by a mob in Illinois in 1844 (p. 151)

Spock, Benjamin Pediatrician and author of *Common Sense Book of Baby and Child Care* (1946), which encouraged mothers to stay home with their children rather than work (p. 616)

Stalin, Joseph Leader of the Soviet Union from 1924–1953; worked with Roosevelt and Churchill during World War II but afterwards became an aggressive participant in the cold war (p. 540)

Stanton, Elizabeth Cady Women's rights leader in the 1800s; helped organize first women's convention; wrote the *Declaration of Sentiments* on women's rights in 1848 (p. 133)

Starr, Ellen Gates Cofounder of Chicago's Hull House, the first settlement house, in 1889 (p. 329)

Steinem, Gloria Journalist, women's rights leader since 1960s; founded *Ms.* magazine in 1972 to cover women's issues (p. 693)

Stevenson, Adlai Senator from Illinois and Democratic candidate for President in 1952 and 1956 against Eisenhower (p. 622)

Stowe, Harriet Beecher Author of the novel *Uncle Tom's Cabin* (1852), which contributed significantly to antisouthern feelings among northerners before the Civil War (p. 165)

Sumner, Charles Abolitionist and senator from Massachusetts; beaten badly in the Senate by a southern congressman after making an antislavery speech (p. 177)

Taft, William Howard Twenty-seventh President of the United States, 1909–1913; continued progressive reforms of President Theodore Roosevelt; promoted "dollar diplomacy" to expand foreign investments (p. 377)

Taney, Roger Chief Justice of the Supreme Court who wrote an opinion in the 1857 *Dred Scott* case that declared the Missouri Compromise unconstitutional (p. 179)

Taylor, Zachary Twelfth President of the United States, 1849–1850; tried to avoid slavery issues (p. 150)

Thomas, Clarence Conservative African American Supreme Court justice appointed in 1991; during his confirmation hearings he was charged with sexual harassment (p. 807)

Thomas, Norman Socialist party leader and candidate for President in the 1920 and 1930s; won 2 percent of the vote in 1932 (p. 493)

Thoreau, Henry David Transcendentalist author known for his work *Walden* (1854) and other writings (p. 124)

Travis, William Leader in Texas's bid for independence from Mexico in 1836; died at the Alamo after appealing to the United States for help (p. 145)

Truman, Harry S Thirty-third President of the United States, 1945–1953; authorized use of atomic bomb; signed Marshall Plan to rebuild Europe (p. 550)

Sojourner Truth

Truth, Sojourner Abolitionist and women's rights advocate before the Civil War; as a formerly enslaved person, she spoke effectively and authentically to white audiences on abolition issues (p. 134)

Tubman, Harriet "Conductor" on the underground railroad that helped enslaved persons escape to freedom before the Civil War (p. 128)

Turner, Frederick Jackson Historian who wrote an essay in 1893 emphasizing the western frontier as a powerful force in the formation of the American character (p. 300)

Turner, Nat African American preacher who led a slave revolt in 1831; captured and hanged after the revolt failed (p. 111)

Tweed, William Marcy Boss of Tammany Hall political machine in New York City; convicted of forgery and larceny in 1873 and died in jail in 1878 (p. 324)

Tyler, John Tenth President of the United States, 1841–1845; accomplished little due to quarrels between Whigs and Jacksonian Democrats (p. 118)

Van Buren, Martin Eighth President of the United States, 1837–1841; Jacksonian Democrat; was voted out of the executive office after the Panic of 1837 brought widespread unemployment and poverty (p. 118)

Vance, Cyrus Secretary of state under President Jimmy Carter; invited Israelis and Egyptians to Camp David in 1978 to begin Middle East peace process (p. 784)

Vanzetti, Bartolomeo (văn·zĕt´ĭ, bär´tō·lōmâ´ō) Immigrant and anarchist executed for a 1920 murder at a Massachusetts factory, though believed to be innocent by many (p. 448)

Vesey, Denmark African American who planned 1822 South Carolina slave revolt; captured and hanged after revolt failed (p. 110)

von Steuben, Baron Prussian officer who trained Washington's troops in the winter at Valley Forge (p. 59)

Walker, Madam C. J. African American leader and businesswoman in the early 1900s; she spoke out against lynching (p. 346)

Wallace, George C. Third-party candidate for President in 1968; focused his campaign on issues of blue-collar anger in the

North and racial tension (p. 749)

Warren, Earl Chief Justice of Supreme Court 1953–1968; led in many decisions that protected civil rights, rights of the accused, and right to privacy (p. 641)

Washington, Booker T. African American leader from the late 1800s until his death in 1915; founded Tuskegee Institute in Alabama; encouraged African Americans to learn trades (p. 337)

Washington, George First President of the United States, 1789–1797; led American forces in the War for Independence; set several federal precedents, including the two-term maximum for presidential office (p. 48)

Whitney, Eli Inventor; developed the cotton gin in 1793, which rapidly increased cotton production in the South and led to a greater need for slave labor (p. 98)

Wilhelm, Kaiser (vĭl´hĕlm, kī´zêr) Emperor of Germany during World War I; symbol to the United States of German militarism and severe efficiency (p. 418)

Wilson, Woodrow Twenty-eighth President of the United States, 1913–1921; tried to keep the United States out of World War I; proposed League of Nations (p. 401)

Yeltsin, Boris (yĕlt´sĭn, bŭ•ryēs´) Leader of Russia in late 1980s and early 1990s; took over from Mikhail Gorbachev as reforms continued and Communist party control ended (p. 819)

Young, Brigham Mormon leader who supervised migration to Utah beginning in the 1840s; first governor when Utah became a United States territory (p. 151)

Index

Note: Entries with a page number followed by a *c* indicate a chart or graph on that page; *m* indicates a map; and *p* indicates a picture.

constitution: state, 63–64
Constitution, United States, 854–871; arguments for and against, 78–79; Bill of Rights in, 78–79; ratification of, 77–78
Constitutional Convention, 68–69, 70*p;* delegates to, 71*p;* divisions and compromises at, 70
Constitutional Union party, 185
consumer movements, 392, 708–709
containment, policy of, 589–593
Continental Army, 59, 60
Continental Congress: First, 52; Second, 52–53, 62–63
Continental Divide, 138
Continental dollars, 60–61
Coolidge, Calvin, 455–456, 476; administration of, 456; death of, 494; in election of 1920, 455; as Massachusetts governor, 448
Copeland, John Anthony, 181
Copperheads, 202, 216
Cornwallis, Lord, 59
corruption: and big business, 308–309; and Crédit Mobilier scandal, 243–244; in Harding administration, 455; and political bosses, 324
Cortés, Hernán, 24
Costa Rica: United States' interests in, 364
cotton gin, 98, 98*p*
Coughlin, Charles E., 516
courts: in Constitution, 74. *See also* Supreme Court, United States; Supreme Court cases.
Cowan, Paul, 651, 651*p*
Cox, George B., 324
Coxey, Jacob S., 312–313
Coxey's Army, 312–313, 313*p*
Crawford, William H., 113
credit, buying on: in 1920s, 478
Crédit Mobilier scandal, 243–244
Creek people, 117
crime: and prohibition, 466
Crisis, The **(magazine),** 437, 662
Crisis The **(Paine),** 57
Critical Period, 65
critical thinking: analyzing political speeches, 176; checking consistency, 728; demonstrating reasoned judgment, 810; determining relevance, 119; distinguishing fact from opinion, 518; distinguishing false from accurate images, 491; drawing conclusions, 299; expressing problems clearly, 43; formulating questions, 153; identifying alternatives, 420; identifying assumptions, 571; identifying central issues, 75; predicting consequences, 843; recognizing bias, 696; recognizing cause and effect, 588; recognizing ideologies, 788; testing conclusions, 404
Croatia, 833–834
Crockett, Davy, 146
Crow people, 139
Crows Fly High, George, 706*p*
Cuba: and Bay of Pigs, 651–653, 653*m;* under Castro, 598, 651–653; and missile crisis, 654–656; and Platt Amendment, 370; Spanish-American War in, 367–370; and Teller Amendment, 369–370
Cuffe, Paul, 127
Cullem, Countee, 455
cult of domesticity, 133

Custer, George Armstrong, 285
Czechoslovakia: German aggression toward, 532; post–Soviet Union breakup, 833
Czech Republic, 819
Czolgosz, Leon, 313

Dachau, 541
da Gama, Vasco, 16
Daley, Richard J., 748
Darrow, Clarence: in Scopes trial, 467
Dartmouth College, 126
Darwin, Charles, 260, 467
"Daughters of Liberty," 51
Davis, Jefferson, 186, 194
Dawes Act (1887), 286, 508
D-Day, 540–541
DDT, 707–708, 710–711
Dean, John, 766
Debs, Eugene V.: in election of 1912, 401–402, 402*c;* in election of 1920, 432; and labor relations, 273, 273*p*
debt peonage, 239
de Champlain, Samuel, 27
Declaration of Independence, 53–54, 54*p,* 62, 851–853
Declaration of Sentiments, 134
Declaration of the Causes and Necessities of Taking Up Arms, A, 52–53
de facto segregation, 344, 681, 681*m*
defense spending, 806, 806*c,* 818
de jure segregation, 681
Delaware: and ratification of Constitution, 77
Delaware people, 36, 96
Deloria, Vine, Jr., 704
democracy: and western settlement, 301–302
Democratic party, 88; in 1850s, 172; in election of 1860, 184–185; in Gilded Age, 309, 311–313; 1968 convention for, 748–749
Democratic Societies, 89
Depression, 49; of 1893, 298. *See also* Great Depression.
deregulation: under Carter, 792; under Reagan, 806
détente, 759, 785
Dewey, Thomas E.: in election of 1948, 622
Dickinson, John, 51
Dien Bien Phu, 596, 716
direct primary, 394
discrimination: African American response to, 345; de facto, 344, 681, 681*m;* de jure, 681; post-Reconstruction, 343–344. *See also* civil rights movement.
disease: in cities, 322; impact on Native Americans, 20–21, 141, 152
District of Columbia, 80–81. *See also* Washington, D.C..
diversified conglomerates, 608
Divine, M. J. (Father), 488
Dix, Dorothea, 126, 126*p,* 132
Dixiecrat party: in election of 1948, 621–622
dollar diplomacy, 377
Dominican Republic: invasion of, 656–657
Doolittle, James, 539
Double V campaign, 573–574
doughboys, 426
Douglas, Stephen, 173–174, 180; in election of 1860, 184–185

Douglass, Frederick, 128, 128*p,* 134, 202, 205
draft: in Civil War, 199, 200, 425; in Vietnam War, 726, 792; in World War I, 425
Dred Scott **v.** *Sandford* **(1857),** 178–179, 182–183
Du Bois, W. E. B., 337, 337*p,* 345, 437, 662
Dukakis, Michael: in election of 1988, 804, 807
Dulles, John Foster, 593
Dust Bowl, 484–485, 485*m*
Dutch: settlements of, 21, 27–28, 27*p*

Earth Day, 708, 709*p*
Eastern Europe: creation of, 542, 584; impact of Soviet Union collapse on, 819, 819*m*
East Germany: Soviet domination of, 593
Economic Opportunity Act (1964), 644
economics: after collapse of Soviet Union, 832–833; capitalism in, 107–108; Keynesian approach to, 561, 754; *laissez-faire* policies in, 261, 308–309; Market Revolution in, 101, 103–104, 111, 114, 136; mercantilism as theory in, 32–33; slavery as issue of, 109–111; supply-side, 805
economy: under Bush, 807, 808–809; under Carter, 789; under Clinton, 829–830; conditions leading to Great Depression, 476–479, 478*c,* 478*p,* 479*p;* under Eisenhower, 623–624; under Ford, 776–777; Hamilton's program for, 88–89; household, 102–103; impact of Civil War on, 243–244; under Nixon, 754–755; post–Revolution, 64, 64*p,* 66–67; post–World War II, 608–612; under Reagan, 805–807, 808–809; in Reconstruction South, 238–239; role of banks in growth of, 103–104; in War for Independence, 60–61
Edison, Thomas A., 253
education: for African Americans, 228, 232, 233*p;* expansion of higher, 335–337; growth of public, 334–335; for immigrants, 334–335; impact of *Sputnik* on, 625; integration of, 663; under Lyndon Johnson, 645; for Mexican Americans, 698; for Native Americans, 706; problems of bilingual, 839; reforms for, 125–126*p;* and school enrollment, 126*c;* of women, 125–126, 135, 336–337, 690, 694*c*
Edwards, Jonathan, 37
Egypt: and Camp David Accords, 783–784, 784*p*
Ehrlichman, John, 753, 753*p,* 764, 766
Eighteenth Amendment, 397, 408, 433, 466
Eighth Amendment, 78*c*
Eisenhower, Dwight D.: administration of, 638; approach to presidency, 620; and civil rights movement, 628; communist concerns of, 599, 800; containment under, 593; domestic policies under, 612, 624–625; and domino theory, 596–597; economic policy under, 624; in election of 1952, 622–623; in election of 1956, 623; as general in World War II, 539, 540, 550; policy in Vietnam, 716; popularity of, 620, 625
elections: of 1776, 90; of 1800, 90–93, 91*p;* of 1824, 112–113; of 1828, 114; of 1832, 116; of 1840, 118, 118*p;* of 1848, 169; of 1852, 172; of 1856, 175; of 1860, 184–185; of 1864, 216; of 1868, 236; of 1876, 241, 241*m,* 309, 309*c;* of 1880, 309, 309*c,* 310; of 1884, 309, 309*c,* 311; of 1888, 312; of 1892, 297*m,* 298, 309, 309*c,*

33, 96

Massachusetts: and ratification of Constitution, 77

Massachusetts Bay Colony, 28

Mataniko River, Battle of, 544

Mayaguez, 777

Maya Ying Lin, 737

Maysville Road Veto (1830), 114

McCarthy, Eugene, 747, 748, 749

McCarthy, Joseph R., 601–603, 602*p*

McClellan, George: as Civil War general, 195, 197, 208; in election of 1864, 216

McCord, James, 764, 766

McCulloch v. Maryland, 115

McDowell, Irvin, 192, 193

McDowell, Mary, 329*p*

McGovern, George: in election of 1972, 765

McKay, Claude, 455

McKinley, William: assassination of, 313, 371, 374; domestic policies of, 298; in election of 1896, 297*m*, 298, 313; in election of 1900, 371; foreign policy under, 368–369, 370

McNickle, D'Arcy, 702

Meade, George G., 210

Means, Russell, 704*p*, 705

Meat Inspection Act (1906), 393*p*, 396

medical care in World War I, 426–427, 427*p*

Medicare, 644–645

Mein Kampf (Hitler), 531

Memphis: growth of, 94

men: roles of, in 1950s, 615–617

Mencken, H. L., 469

mentally ill: reforms for, 126

mercantilism, 32–33, 49

mercenaries: in War for Independence, 58

Meredith, James, 672

Metacom, 29

Mexican American Legal Defense and Educational Fund (MALDEF), 699

Mexican Americans: and civil rights, 629; education of, 335, 698; immigration to United States, 317; and New Deal, 511; protests of, 697–699; in World War II, 546, 574–575

Mexican Colonization Law (1824), 145

Mexican independence, 144

Mexican War, 124–125, 149–151, 149*m*

Mexico: and North American Free Trade Agreement, 837, 837*c*

Miami people, 96

Miamitown, 96

Middle Colonies, 27*m*, 33*m*; early settlement in, 34; slavery in, 41–42

Middle East, 834; Carter's policy toward, 783–784; cold war in, 597, 598*m*; oil crisis, 754–755; and OPEC, 790; peace talks in, 834, 835*m*; and Persian Gulf War, 750, 804, 820–821; trouble spots in, 820–821, 834; violence in, 834

Middle Passage, 38–39

Midway Islands, 539; United States annexation of, 363

migratory farm workers, 698

Military Reconstruction Act (1867), 235

Milosevic, Slobodan, 833–834

Milwaukee: immigrant settlements in, 316

mining: and Western settlement, 290, 290*p*

Minnesota: as state, 142

Minor v. Happersett, 352–353, 405–406

minutemen, 48

Miranda v. Arizona (1966), 646

Mississippi Freedom Democratic party, 679–680

Mississippi River: in Civil War, 196–197

Missouri: and Missouri Compromise, 97

Missouri Compromise of 1820, 97–98, 97*m*, 169, 174, 183

Mitchell, George, 703

Mitchell, John, 753, 756, 764, 765

Mitchell, Maria, 135

modern republicanism, 623–624

Molotov, Vyacheslav, 586*m*, 590–591

Mondale, Walter: in election of 1976, 779; in election of 1984, 804

money: gold standard for United States, 295; greenbacks as, 201; as issue in Gilded Age, 309–310; in War for Independence, 60–61

Monmouth Court House, 59

monopolies, 261; effects of, 312*p*

Monroe, James: administration of, 112

Monroe Doctrine of 1823, 112, 363, 364*p*, 366; Roosevelt Corollary to, 375–376

Montana: admission to Union, 300*c*

Monterey, 143

Montgomery bus boycott, 628–629, 628*p*, 664

Monticello, 89

Montoya, Joseph, 699

Moody, Anne, 666–667, 667*p*, 670*p*, 685

Moral Majority, 801, 807

Mormons, 151

Morrill Land-Grant Act (1862), 201, 280, 289

Morrison, Jim, 730

Morrison, Toni, 696

Morse, Samuel F. B., 256

Moses, Robert, 666, 666*p*

Moskowitz, Belle, 479

most-favored-nation status, 363

Mott, Lucretia, 133–134

mountain men, 148

Mount Vernon, 80

movies: morality in, 466–467; in 1920s, 462–463; in 1930s, 521; in 1950s, 614; in World War II, 562

Moynihan, Daniel Patrick, 709

Ms. magazine, 693

muckrakers, 391, 391*p*

mugwumps, 310

Muhammad, Askia, 17–18

Muhammad, Elijah, 682

Muir, John, 303*p*, 397

Müller, Karl Alexander von, 531

Muller v. Oregon (1908), 394, 395

multiculturalism, 841–842, 842*c*

Mun, Thomas, 32

municipal reform, 389

Munn v. Illinois (1877), 311

music: and free speech movement, 725; jazz in, 340–341, 454–455, 454*p*, 731; and the Negro spiritual, 340; and Rolling Stones, 731, 732; at Woodstock, 731–732, 732*p*; in World War II, 563

Muskie, Edmund, 764

Mussolini, Benito, 517, 530, 532

My Lai massacre, 723

Nader, Ralph, 709

Nader's Raiders, 709

Nagasaki, bombing of, 550–551, 551*p*

National Advisory Commission on Civil Disorders, 685

National Aeronautics and Space Administration (NASA), 640

National American Woman Suffrage Association (NAWSA), 350, 405, 407, 408

National Association for the Advancement of Colored People (NAACP), 345, 403, 510, 514, 662–663, 667

National Association of Colored Women, 510

National Broadcasting Company (NBC), 462

National Chicano Moratorium Committee, 726

National Child Labor Committee, 394–395

National Consumers League (NCL), 392

National Council of Negro Women, 510

National Defense Education Act (1958), 625

National Endowment for the Arts, 646

National Endowment for the Humanities, 646

National Energy Act, 790

National forests, parks and reservations, 396*m*

National Industrial Recovery Act (NIRA), 508, 512

Nationalists, 64–66

National Labor Relations Board (NLRB), 512

National Labor Union, 269

National Negro Business League, 345, 346

National Organization for Women (NOW): organization of, 692–693

National Reclamation Act (1902), 397

National Recovery Administration (NRA), 508, 516

National Republicans, 114, 116

National Security League, 419, 432

National Socialist German Workers party, 531

National Trades Union (NTU), 108

National Traffic and Motor Vehicle Safety Act (1966), 709

National Union for Social Justice, 516

National Urban League, 345, 488, 510, 663

National War Labor Board, 430, 569

National Woman's party, 452–453

National Youth Administration (NYA), 507, 511

Nation of Islam, 682

Native Americans: changing roles for men and women, 140–141; and civil rights, 629; in confronting government, 704–706, 704*p*, 705*p*, 706*p*; culture groups in, 13*m*; decline of village societies, 141; destruction of culture, 286; and early colonial settlements, 26–28; education of, 335, 706; effect of disease on, 141, 152; in French and Indian War, 49; gains made by, 840; impact of European encounter on, 20–21; impact of horse on, 139; land claims of, 703; and New Deal, 508; origin of, 14; rights for, 702–704, 814–815; second removal of, 284; social organization and spiritual life of, 12–14, 14*p*; Spanish treatment of, 25–26, 25*m*, 142–143; trade by, 14; and Trail of Tears, 117–118; unique problems of, 702; view of land use by, 14–15, 287; in War for Independence, 61, 61*p*; and Western settlement, 36, 96, 138–139, 152, 284–286, 301; in World War II, 545*p*, 546, 575. *See also specific*

Acknowledgments

Cover Design Martucci Studio, Alison Anholt-White, and L. Christopher Valente

Front Cover Engraving "The Brooklyn Bridge," engraving by the Shugg Brothers after the original by R. Schwartz, 1883. Museum of the City of New York.

Back Cover Photo Larry Fisher/Masterfile

Book Design DECODE, Inc.

Epilogue and Prologue Design Alan Lee

Picture Research Pembroke Herbert and Sandi Rygiel/Picture Research Consultants, Inc.

Time & Place Contributing Writers Carol Barrett, Department of Geography, University of Wisconsin at River Falls, River Falls, WI; Tom Baerwald, Program Director of Geography and Regional Science, National Science Foundation, Washington, D.C.; Peter Hugill, Department of Geography, Texas A&M University, College Station, TX; Nina Lam, Department of Geography and Anthropology, Louisiana State University, Baton Rouge, LA

Maps

GEO Systems, A Unit of R.R. Donnelly & Sons, Co.: 131, 146, 148, 149, 195, 197, 217, 363, 372, 375, 379, 409, 417, 428, 436, 509, 700, 872, 876, 877, 879, 800–801, 882-883

Horizon Design/Sanderson Associates: 13, 25, 33, 58, 97, 178, 186, 234, 241, 242, 255, 258, 285, 293, 297, 323, 368, 376, 381, 396, 453, 485, 499, 532, 533, 537, 538, 577, 586, 592, 595, 597, 598, 599, 653, 657, 671, 681, 755, 780, 813, 834, 835

Illustration

Peter Brooks: 50-51, 766

Function Thru Form: 22, 42, 63, 72, 95, 107, 125, 126, 137, 262, 264, 272, 288, 300, 310, 335, 336, 345, 364, 368, 447, 462, 468, 478, 481, 482, 483, 520, 560, 561, 562, 568, 570, 611, 616, 640, 645, 646, 678, 691, 694, 754, 777, 803, 806, 809, 816, 829, 839, 842, 873, 874-875, 878, 879, 884

Paul Gagnon: 22, 78, 83, 114, 119, 121, 151, 170, 175, 189, 194, 221, 236, 247, 277, 305, 325, 331, 344, 355, 367, 385, 394, 397, 402, 404, 413, 439, 471, 503, 525, 555, 579, 605, 633, 659, 679, 687, 711, 713, 771, 797, 819, 830, 837, 843, 845

Matthew Pippin: 14, 52, 98, 106, 209, 257, 282, 464-465, 594, 791

Photography

Abbreviation Key- LOC = Library of Congress; U/B = UPI/Bettmann Archives; RH/LS = photo by Rob Huntley/Lightstream; NA = National Archives; PRC = Picture Research Consultants, Inc.; FRENT = Collection of David J. and Janice L. Frent; BB = Brown Brothers; CP = Culver Pictures; WW = Wide World Photos; GL = Gamma Liaison; WC = Woodfin Camp & Associates; C&G = Chermayeff & Geismar/MetaForm photo by Karen Yamauchi; BS = Black Star; MP = Magnum Photos; SI = Smithsonian Institution; OPPS = Office of Printing and Photographic Services, Smithsonian Institution. NPS = Courtesy of the National Park Service

Prologue xxii, CP; **1 T,** Harper's Weekly, May 26, 1883; **1 B,** U/B; **2 TL, B,** Rensselaer Polytechnic Institute; **2 M,** The Metropolitan Museum of Art. The Edward W.C. Arnold Collection of New York Prints, Maps and Pictures. Bequest of Edward W.C. Arnold; **4 T,** Bernard Gotfryd/WC; **4 INSET,** Andy Levin/Photo Researchers; **6 T,** Missouri Historical Society. Block Brothers photograph; **6 INSET,** © Fredericks/The Image Works; **7,** Museum of Modern Art Film Still Archive.

Unit Openers Pages 8–9, "Election Day in Philadelphia" by John Lewis Krimmel, 1815. (detail) Courtesy, Winterthur Museum; **160-161,** Ruins of Richmond, Virginia, april 1865, Brady Studio. (detail) LOC; **248-249,** "Excursion Party at Devil's Gate Bridge, Utah" by A. J. Russell. (detail) Courtesy of the Oakland Museum History Department; **358–359,** New York & Cuba Mail Steamship Company Dock scene. (detail) U/B; **442-443,** "Mother and Child" by Dorothea Lange (detail). LOC; **526-527,** American Infantry, National Archives; **634-635,** "Selma March" March 1965 (detail) by James H. Karales; **742-743,** Clinton Inauguration, January 1993 (detail) U/B.

American Album Pages 84-85, Jug, Eric Long, SI; Gridiron, OPPS; Sampler, Eric Long, SI; Suit, Eric Long, SI; Respect, Library of Congress; Toys, OPPS; Dairying, Courtesy of Princeton University Library, Dept of Rare Books and Special Collections; Anvil & Hammer, Eric Long, SI; Gravestones, Dane Penland, SI; **222-223,** Shoulder Plate, Knife, Tins, Cutlery, Hard Tack, all by Rick Vargas and Richard Strauss, SI; Uniform, Dane Penland, SI; Flag, Alfred Harrell and Andrew Wynn, SI; Quinine, Dane Penland, SI; FIELD HOSPITAL, OPPS; Muskett, Rick Vargas, SI; **356-357,** Football Player, Baseball Music, Larry Gates, SI; Skiing, Football Pants, Baseball, all by Rick Vargas, SI; SKATING, Jim Wallace, SI; Bicycle, Alfred Harrell, SI; Cyclist, Collection of Sally Fox; **440-441,** Record Book, Dane Penland, SI; Doll, Eric Long, SI; Plow, Jeff Tinsley, SI; Suitcase, Eric Long, SI; Soldiers, Courtesy of the National Archives and Records Administration; Home Schooling, Library of Congress; Jobs, Jeff Tinsley, SI; **472-473,** Duke, Courtesy of John Hasse; Radio, Dane Penland, SI; Hymie, Danny Thompson, SI; Saxophone, Dane Penland, SI; Dress, Jeff Tinsley, SI; Clarinet, Dane Penland, SI; Trumpet, Jeffrey Ploskonka, SI; Band, Missouri Historical Society, Block Brothers Photo; **580-581,** Jeff Tinsley, SI all with the exception of; Propaganda Posters, Richard Strauss, SI; **740-741,** Boots, Helmet, Letter, Watch, Letter to Gary, Eric Long, SI, NPS; Dogtags, Rick Vargas, SI, NPS; Stuffed Animals, Richard Strauss, SI, NPS; Vietnam Memorial, Sandra Rogers, SI; **846-847,** Satellite, OPPS; Watergate, Margaret McCullough, SI, courtesy of the National Archives and Records Administration; Laser Head, OPPS, SI; Grace Hopper, Danny Thompson, SI; Hand Held Computer, Courtesy of Apple Computer, Inc.; Early Computer, Eric Long, SI; Barcodes, MAD's UPC symbol cover is © E.C. Publications, Inc., 1978. Used with permission from MAD Magazine. Chip, Copyright of Motorola, Inc. Used by permission. Fiber-Optic, Courtesy of Intel Corporation; Jeff Tinsley, SI.

Chapter 1 Page **10 L,** National Maritime Museum, Greenwich, England; **10 R,** Museum of Early Southern

Decorative Arts; **12 INSET,** Courtesy of the National Museum of the American Indian/ Smithsonian Institution #S:1514; **15,** Giraudon/Art Resource, NY; **17 T, B** Photograph by Jeffrey Ploskonka, National Museum of African Art, Eliot Elisofon Archive, Smithsonian Institution; **29,** Aldo Tutino; **18,** "Arrival at Tombocтоu from Barth", from Travels in Central Africa, 1857. Rare Book and Manuscripts Division, The New York Public Library, Astor, Lenox and Tilden Foundations; **19 (also 11),** National Maritime Museum. Photo © Michael Holford; **20,** "Portuguese Caravels" from America by Theodore De Bry 1594. (detail) Rare Book and Manuscript Division, The New York Public Library, Astor, Lenox and Tilden Foundations; **21 TR,** Aztec drawing of smallpox victim from the Flortine Codex, v. 4, Book 12 (detail). Courtesy of Biblioteca Medicea Laurenziana, Florence. Photo by Alberto Scardigli; **21 BL,** Courtesy of Magellan Systems Corporation; **21 BR,** London Science Museum. Photo © Michael Holford; **24 (also 11)** Courtesy of South Florida Science Museum, Photo by Randy Smith; **28,** "The Mason Children: David, Joanna, and Abigail" 1670 attributed to the Freake-Gibbs painter. Fine Arts Museums of San Francisco, Gift of Mr. & Mrs. John D. Rockefeller 3rd; **29,** Courtesy of the National Museum of the American Indian/ Smithsonian Institution, #4662, #4663; **30,** "Landing of Negroes at Jamestown, 1619" Free Library of Philadelphia; **32 (also 11),** Norwich textile sample book. Courtesy, The Winterthur Library: Joseph Downs Collection of Manuscripts and Printed Ephemera; **34 T,** John Lewis Stage; **34 B,** Colonial Williamsburg Foundation; **80,** Library Company of Philadelphia; **35,** "The First, Second, and Last Scenes of Mortality" by Prudence Punderson ca. 1783. Connecticut Historical Society; **37 T,** "Rev. George Whitefield" by J. Wollaston, 1742. Courtesy of the National Portrait Gallery, London; **37 B,** LOC. **38 (also 11),** Collection of Roddy and Sally Moore; **39 T,** "The Slave Deck" by Godfrey Meynall, (detail) 1846. National Maritime Museum; **39 B,** Mass. Historical Society; **40,** "The Old Plantation" artist unknown 1795. Abby Aldrich Rockefeller Foundation, Colonial Williamsburg; **42,** The Stagville Center, Division of Archives and History, North Carolina Dept. of Cultural Resources.

Chapter 2 **46 BR,** Independence National Historic Park, Philadelphia; **46TR,** National Archives. Photo © Rob Huntley/Lightstream; **48 (also 47),** Colonial Williamsburg Foundation; **49,** LOC; **50 BR,** North Wind Picture Archives; **50 B,** LOC; **51,** The Bostonian Society/Old State House; **52 INSET,** "Boston Massacre" engraving by Paul Revere. LOC; **54 R,** U/B; **54 L,** Independence National Historic Park, Philadelphia; **55 (also 47),** Lexington Historical Society. RH/LS; **56,** Courtesy Minuteman National Historic Park, RH/LS; **57,** "Attack on Bunker Hill, with the Burning of Charlestown" unknown artist. Gift of Edgar William and Bernice Chrysler Garbisch, ©1994, National Gallery of Art, Washington, D.C.; **58 both,** Courtesy Minuteman National Historical Park, RH/LS; **59,** "Tarleton's Cavalrymen after the Battle of Cowpers" by William Ranney. Collection of the State of South Carolina. Photo by Hunter Clarkeson, Alt Lee, Inc.; **60,** New York Historical Society; **61 T,** LOC; **61 B,** Independence National Historic Park, Philadelphia; **62 (also 47),** Yale University Art Gallery, Mabel Brady Garven Collection; **63,** "General Washington's Resignation" by Alonzo Chappel. Chicago Historical Society; **64,** Eric P. Newman Numismatic Education Society. RH/LS; **65,** Popular History of the United States by William Cullen Bryant, 1881 p. 98. LOC; **67,** CP; **68 (also 47),** Independence National Historic Park, Philadelphia (detail); **69,** "James Madison" by Charles Willson Peale, 1783. LOC; **70,** "Independence Hall" by William Birch, 1790. Rare Book Department, Free Library of Philadelphia; **71,** "Signing of the Constitution" by Thomas Prichard Rossiter, 1872. Independence National Historic Park, Philadelphia; **74,** "Washington at Verplancke's Point" by John Trumbull, 1790. Courtesy, Winterthur Museum; **76 (also 47),** "The Federal Ship Union" from AMERICAN MUSEUM, 1787, Philadelphia. Vol 4, p. 61. American Antiquarian Society; **77 B,** American Antiquarian Society; **79 T,** "Washington Taking the Oath" by H.A. Ogden. LOC; **79 B,** Museum of American Political Life; **81 TL,** LOC; **81 TR,** Fred J. Maroon.

Chapter 3 **86 L,** Shelburne Museum; **86 R,** West Virginia State Museum, photo by Michael Keller; **88 (also 87),** Henry Ford Museum and Greenfield Village; **90 B,** "John Adams" by John Trumbull, 1793. National Portrait Gallery, Smithsonian Institution, Washington, D.C./Art Resource N.Y.; **91,** U/B; **92 both,** Museum of American Political Life. Photo by Sally Anderson-Bruce; **93 both,** U/B; **94 (also 87),** Peabody and Essex Museum; **96,** The National Archives of the United States by Herman Viola. Publisher, Harry N. Abrams, Inc. Photo by Jonathan Wallen; **97,** "Slave Trader Sold to Tennessee" by Lewis Miller 1853. Colonial Williamsburg Foundation; **99,** "Religious Camp Meeting" 1839, watercolor by J. Maze Burbank. New Bedford Whaling Museum; **100,** Dukes County Historical Society, photo by Robert Schellhammer; **101 (also 87),** Lowell Historical Society; **102,** CP; **104,** Old Sturbridge Village; **105 (also 87),** Museum of American Textile History. Photo Rob Huntley/Lightstream; **109, 111,** LOC; **112 (also 87),** FRENT; **113,** The New York Historical Society; **115,** The New York Historical Society; **116,** "Webster's Reply to Haynes" by G.P.A. Healy. City of Boston Art Commission; **117,** Museum of the City of New York; **118,** FRENT.

Chapter 4 **122 TL,** New York State Historical Association; **122 BL,** Southwest Museum; **122 R,,** Henry Groskinsky; **124 (also 123),** Mass. Historical Society; **126 T,** "Daguerreotype of Emerson School" 1855 by Southworth and Hawes. The Metropolitan Museum of Art, Gift of I.N. Phelps Stokes, Edward S. Hawes, Alice Mary Hawes, Marion Augusta Hawes, 1937; **126 B,** Boston Athenaeum; **128,** National Portrait Gallery, Smithsonian Institution/ Art Resource, N.Y.; **129,** Sophia Smith Archives, Garrison Collection; **130,** ©Louis Psihoyos/Contact Press Images; **132 (also 123),** American Antiquarian Society; **133,** Schlesinger Library, Radcliffe College; **134 L,** "Elizabeth Cady Stanton" by Harriet Stanton de Forest, 1860. Schlesinger National Woman's Party, Washington, D.C. Photo by Jeff Mathewson; **134 R,** Women's Rights Collection, Sophia Smith Archives; **135,** Courtesy of Special Collections, Vassar College Library; **138 L (also 123),** Roberta Campbell Lawson Collection, Philbrook Museum of Art, Tulsa, OK; **138 B,** Rare Books and Manuscript Division, The New York Public Library, Astor, Lenox and Tilden Foundations; **139,** ©Jerry Jacka; **140,** "Migration of the Pawnees" by Alfred Jacob Miller, 1837. Collection of Western Americana, Beinecke Rare Book and Manuscript Library, Yale University; **141,** "Buffalo Chase, A Single Death" by George Catlin. National Museum of American Art, Smithsonian Institution. Gift of Mrs. Joseph Harrison, Jr./ Art Resource N.Y.; **142 (also 123),** Courtesy of The Oakland Museum History Dept.; **143 BL,** "Mission San Carlos Borremeo de Carmelo" by Oriana Day. Society of California Pioneers; **143 INSET,** Courtesy of the Texas Memorial Museum, Univ. of Texas at Austin. #41VV343; **144 TL,** Courtesy Museum of New Mexico, Neg. #11329; **144 TR,** Lowell Georgia Photography; **145,** "Stephen F. Austin" by Brand. Archives Div.-Texas State Library; **146,** Courtesy of the Texas Memorial Museum, Univer. of Texas at Austin; **147 (also 123),** Boot Hill Collection, photo by Henry Groskinsky; **152,** p 1983.20 California Forty-Niner c. 1850, 1/4 plate daguerreotype with applied color. Amon Carter Museum, Fort Worth, TX.

Chapter 5 **162 L,** Museum of American Political Life; **162 R,** FRENT; **164 (also 163) TL,** Museum of American Textile History. RH/LS; **165 T,** LOC; **165 B,** The Stow-Day Foundation, photo by Steve Laschevere; **166 BL,** Chicago Historical Society; **167,** "Lazell, Perkins and Co., Bridgwater, Ma." 1858 by J.P. Newell. The Corcoran Gallery of Art, Mary E. Maxwell, Fund; **168 TL,** Collection of PRC; **168 TR,** Grant Heilman; **169 (also 163),** Ontario County Historical Society; **170,** "The United States Senate, a.d. 1850" by R. Whitechurch. LOC; **171,** LOC; **173,** Milwaukee County Historical Society; **174,** "The Little Giant–in the Character of the Gladiator" 1858. Chicago Historical Society; **177 (also 163),** Courtesy of the Decorative and Industrial Arts Collection, Chicago Historical Society; **179,** "Arguments of Chivalry" by Winslow Homer. LOC; **180,** LOC, **181,** Boston

Athenaeum; **182**, "Dred Scott" by Louis Schultze, 1881. Missouri Historical Society; **184 (also 163)**, LOC; **187**, "Bombardment of Sumter" Harpers Weekly, 1861. LOC.

Chapter 6 **190 TL**, Museum of the Confederacy; **190 BL**, Confederate Memorial Hall, New Orleans. From ECHOES OF GLORY; ARMS & EQUIPMENT OF THE CONFEDERACY. Photo by Larry Sherer ©1991 Time-Life Books, Inc.; **190 TR**, Smithsonian Institution. From THE CIVIL WAR; TWENTY MILLION YANKEES. Photo by Larry Sherer ©1985 Time-Life Books, Inc.; **190 BR**, C. Paul Loane Collection, From ECHOES OF GLORY; ARMS & EQUIPMENT OF THE UNION. Photo by Larry Sherer ©1991 Time-Life Books, Inc.; **192 (also 191)**, Collection of David & Kevin Kyle; **195**, Collection of Michael J. McAfee. Courtesy William Gladstone. Photo by Seth Goltzer; **196**, LOC; **198**, "Last Meeting of Lee and Jackson" by Everett B.D. Julio. Museum of the Confederacy; **199 (also 191)**, West Point Museum Collections. Courtesy William Gladstone. Photo by Seth Goltzer; **200**, **202**, **203 T**, LOC; **203 INSET**, Collection of William Gladstone. Photo by Seth Goltzer; **204**, Moorland-Spingarn Research Center; **205**, Collection of William Gladstone. Photo by Seth Goltzer; **207**, Smithsonian Institution, From THE CIVIL WAR; WAR ON THE MISSISSIPPI. Photo by Larry Sherer © 1985 Time-Life Books, Inc.; **208 (also 191)**, The Beverly R. Robinson Collection, U.S. Naval Academy Museum; **210**, "Give Them Cold Steel" painting by Don Troiani. Photo courtesy Historical Art Prints, Southbury, CT 06488; **212 TL**, West Point Museum Collections. Courtesy of William Gladstone. Photo by Seth Goltzer; **212 BL, BR** U/B; **212 TR**, LOC; **213 BL**, P.J. Griffiths/MP; **213 M, BR**, Noel Quidu, Chip Hires/both GL; **214 (also 191)**, N.Y. State Dept of Military and Naval Affairs, Capitol Collection, Albany, NY. From ECHOES OF GLORY; ARMS & EQUIPMENT OF THE UNION. Photo by Larry Sherer ©1991 Time-Life Books, Inc.; **216**, "Sherman's March to the Sea" engraving after F.O.C. Darley. Photo by Ben Lourie. Collection of David M. Sherman, Washington, D.C.

Chapter 7 **224 L**, LOC; **224 TR, BR, 225 T, 226, 227, 228**, Collection of William Gladstone. Photo by Seth Goltzer; **230 BL**, Courtesy of the Arnold Rogers Collection; **230 INSET**, Drawing by Frederick Law Olmsted from *A Journey in the Seaboard States, 1856*; **231**, Collection of William Gladstone. Photo by Seth Goltzer; **225 MR, 232**, FRENT; **233 TL,TR**, Collection of William Gladstone; **225 ML, 237**, Collection of Nancy Gewirz, Antique Textile Resource, Bethesda, MD; **238, 239 TL**, LOC; **239 TR**, "Commercial Center of Atlanta, Georgia" by Horace Bradley. Courtesy Robert M. Hinklin Jr., Inc., Spartanburg, SC (detail); **240 BL**, Collection of State Historical Museum/Mississippi Department of Archives and History; **240 TL**, LOC; **225B, 243**, Courtesy of the Decorative and Industrial Arts Collection of the Chicago Historical Society; Acc No. 1920.53; Photographer: John Alderson; **244**, Collection of William Gladstone. Photo by Seth Goltzer; **245**, LOC.

Chapter 8 **250 L**, Division of Community Life, Smithsonian Institution; **250 R**, National Museum of American History, Smithsonian Institution. Photo by H. Brooks Walker; **252**, Division of Political History, Smithsonian Institution, **#89-6626**; **253**, Division of Community Life, Smithsonian Institution; **254**, Division of Community Life, Smithsonian Institution, **#86-2200**; **255**, Lightfoot Collection; **251 T, 256 L**, Div. of Political History, Smithsonian Institution, **#75-2343**; **256 R**, Courtesy Picture Tel; **251 TM, 259**, Museum of American Textile History; **260**, LOC; **261**, "The Protectors of Our Industries." Puck. Feb. 7, 1883. LOC; **264**, LOC; **251 BM, 265**, "The Gun Foundry" by John Weir. Putman County Historical Society, Cold Spring, N.Y.; **266**, Urban Archives, Temple Univ.; **267**, LOC; **268**, Collection of Ralph J. Brunke; **269 TR**, PRC; **269 TL**, "Underground Lodging for the Poor" by Paul Frenzeny. Harper's Weekly, Feb. 20, 1869. LOC; **251 B, 272**, "Haymarket Riot May 4, 1886" by Thure De Thulstrup (detail) Harper's Weekly, May 15, 1886. LOC; **273, BB; 274 BR**, Minnesota Historical Society/ St. Paul Daily News; **274 BL**, LOC; **274 M**, Franklin D. Roosevelt Presidential Library; **275 TL, U/B; 275 BR**, Courtesy International Brotherhood of Teamsters.

Chapter 9 **278 R**, Courtesy of the Panhandle-Plains Historical Society, Canyon, TX; **278 L**, ©Justin Kerr, 1989; **279 T, 280**, The Oakland Museum History Department; **281**, Denver Public Library, Western History Dept; **284**, Addison Doty. Morning Star Gallery, Santa Fe, NM; **286**, LOC; **288**, The Oakland Museum History Department; **289 BR**, State Historical Society of Wisconsin; **289**, Solomon D. Butcher Collection, Nebraska State Historical Society; **289 TR**, Grant Heilman; **279 LM, 290**, Western History Division, Denver Public Library; **291 TL**, "Jerked Down" by Charles Russell. Thomas Gilcrease Institute of American History & Art; **291 TR**, North Wind Picture Archives; **279 RM, 294**, The Oakland Museum History Dept.; **296 B**, Kansas State Historical Society; **296 T**, East Carolina Manuscript Collection, J.Y. Joyner Library, East Carolina Univ.; **298**, LOC; **300**, Boot Hill Museum, photo by Henry Grosinsky; **301**, "The Cowboy" by Remington, 1902. Amon Carter Museum of Western Art; **279 B, 302**, Buffalo Bill Historical Center, Cody WY; **303**, Theodore Roosevelt Collection, Harvard College Library.

Chapter 10 **306 TL**, C&G; **306 BL**, Collection of Picture Research Consultants, Inc., RH/LS; **306 R**, Museum of American Political Life. Photo by Sally Anderson-Bruce; **307 T, 308**, Division of Political History, Smithsonian Institution, **#93-3020; 310 BL, 310 INSET, 312, 313**, LOC; **314**, National Park Service, Gift of Angelo Forgione; **307 TM, 315, BB; 316**, LOC; **318 both, 319 INSET**, C&G; **319 T**, California Dept of Parks and Recreation, courtesy Fred Wasserman; **307 BM, 320**, Collection of PRC RH/LS; **321**, LOC; **322**, BB; **324**, FRENT; **326 BR**, Division of Political History, Smithsonian Institution, **#88-8676; 326 TL**, Collection of PRC RH/LS; **307 B, 327**, C&G; **328, 329 TR**, LOC; **329 INSET**, California Museum of Photography WX5266.

Chapter 11 **332 BL**, Collection of John Craig. RH/LS; **332 TL**, Radcliffe College Archives, Schlesinger Library; **332 R**, Museum of the City of New York, Gift of Aaron & Abby Shroeder; **333 T, 334**, Collection of Sue and Lars Hotham; **335**, Nebraska State Historical Society; **336**, Sophia Smith Collection; **337 both**, BB; **333 ML, 338**, Collection of Sally Fox; **339 TR**, LOC; **339 INSET**, California Museum of Photography #X55458; **340 TL**, Chicago Historical Society; **340 B**, UPI/Bettman; **340 INSETS**, Artwork from Wood River Gallery, Mill Valley, CA; **341 BL**, LOC; **341 BR**, Peter Menzel/Stock Boston; **342**, Chicago Historical Society; **343**, Old Court House Museum, Vicksburg, Mississippi; **333 MR, 345**, U/B; **346**, The Walker Collection of A'Lelia Perry Bundles, Alexandria, VA; **347**, Museum of American Political Life; **348, 333 B, 349 T**, Collection of PRC RH/LS; **349 INSET**, Courtesy Maytag Co.; **350 TR**, Kansas Historical Society; **350 INSET**, State Historical Society of Wisconsin; **357**, Collection of Sally Fox.

Chapter 12 **360 TR**, Granger Collection; **360 BR**, Museum of American Political Life. Photo by Sally Anderson-Bruce; **360 L**, Courtesy Deere & Company; **362**, The Oakland Museum History Dept.; **364, 361 T, 365**, LOC; **366**, Collection of PRC. Photo by Lightstream; **368 TL**, Chicago Historical Society; **368 INSET**, CP; **361 ML, 369**, NA; **370**, California Museum of Photography; **371**, Courtesy of the Liliuokalani Trust and the Bishop Museum (detail); **361 MR, 373**, Museum of American Political Life; **374 TL**, LOC; **374 INSET**, BB; **376**, "The World's Constable" by Dolrymple, JUDGE 1905, LOC; **377**, "William Howard Taft" (detail) White House Historical Assoc.; **378**, LOC; **361 B, 380**, "Goddess of Liberty Weathervane" by L.W. Cushing, 1870. Courtesy of Fred and Kathryn Giampietro; **383 both**, Courtesy Archives of the Girl Scouts of the U.S.A.

Chapter 13 **386 L**, Division of Political History, Smithsonian Institution, **#79-1002; 386 R**, Collection of PRC RH/LS; **387 TR, 388**, Boston Athenaeum; **389**, Labor-Management Documentation Center, Cornell University; **390 B**, International Museum of Photography, George Eastman House; **390 INSET**, LOC; **391**, CP; **392**, U/B; **387 TL, 393**, Courtesy of the Decorative & Industrial Arts Collection of the Chicago Historical Society: 1978.14.4; photo by John Alderson; **395 TR**, CP; **395 TM**, Bob Daemmrich/Stock Boston; **398 BR**, Museum of the City of New York; **398 INSET**, Stock Montage, Inc.; **387 M, 400**, Museum of American Political Life; **401**, "Goodness Gracious I Must Have Been Dozing" by Joseph Keppler from PUCK. Theodore Roosevelt Collection, Harvard College Library; **402, 403, 387 B, 405**, FRENT; **406**, Courtesy of the League of Women's Voters of the US; **408 T**, Sophia Smith College Archives; **408 B**, LOC; **410 BL**, Radcliffe College Archives, Schlesinger

Library; **410 BR**, The New York Historical Society; **410 M**, NA #44-2A-229; **411 T, B**, Collection of Bettye Lane. RH/LS; **411 BR**, U/B.

Chapter 14 **414 TL**, Collection of PRC RH/LS; **414 BL**, Collection of Sue and Lars Hotham. RH/LS; **412 TR, 414 BR, 415 TR, 416**, Collection of Colonel Stuart S. Corning, Jr. RH/LS; **416 B**, CP; **418**, Bayerisches Hauptstaatsarchiv; **419**, CP; **421**, Granger Collection; **415 TL, 422 TR**, Boston Athenaeum; **422 TL**, LOC; **423**, "Wilson" by Edmund Charles Tarbell, 1921. National Portrait Gallery, Smithsonian Institution/Art Resource, NY; **424**, U/B; **425**, Collection of Colonel Stuart S. Corning, Jr. RH/LS; **426, 415 MR, 427 T**, NA #111-SC-25026, #111-SC-14129; **427 INSET**, Collection of Colonel Stuart S. Corning, Jr. RH/LS; **415 ML, 430**, LOC; **431**, Collection of PRC; **432**, U/B; **433**, Wayne State University, Archives of Labor and Urban Affairs; **434**, The Michael Barson Collection/Past Perfect. RH/LS; **415 B, 437**, NA #111-SC-25026.

Chapter 15 **444 TL, FRENT; 444 R**, Courtesy Ford Archives; **444 BL**, Collection of Col. Stuart S. Corning, Jr. Photo by Lightstream; **446**, FRENT; **447**, Archives of Labor and Urban Affairs, Wayne State Univ.; **448 BL, FRENT; 448 TL**, U/B; **445 TR, 449**, C&G; **450, 451 BR**, LOC; **451 TL**, Collection of Frank Driggs; **445 TL, 454 B INSET**, U/B; **454 R INSET**, Beinecke Library, Yale University; **454 L INSET**, Cartier Bresson/MP; **455**, FRENT; **456 TL**, LIFE magazine December 10, 1925; **445 MR, 457**, Nipper's Choice Phonographs, Keene, NH. Photo by Wright Studio; **457 TR**, LOC; **458, 459**, U/B; **460**, Collection of PRC RH/LS; **461**, Saturday Evening Post, June 30, 1928, Curtis Archives; **462**, Nancy Gewirz, Antique Textile Resource, Bethesda, MD RH/LS. Collection of Joseph Benjamin Shuff; **463**, U/B; **445 ML, 465**, Courtesy Ford Archives; **445 B, 466**, Michael Barson Collection/Past Perfect RH/LS; **468**, C&G.

Chapter 16 **474 TL, FRENT; 474 R**, Detroit News; **475 T, 476**, Courtesy of Spiegel; **477**, Artwork from Wood River Gallery, Mill Valley, CA; **478**, Boston Athenaeum; **479**, U/B; **480**, LOC; **481 B**, U/B; **481 BL**, Copyright © 1929 by The New York Times Company; **486**, U/B; **487 T**, Museum of the City of New York. Photograph by Bernice Abbott, Federal Arts Project; **475 TM, 489**, U/B; **490 TL**, LOC; **488M, 493, 494 T**, U/B; **493 B**, CP; **475 B, 495**, FRENT; **496**, Reprinted from the Albany Evening News 6/7/31, with permission of the Times Union, Albany, N.Y.; **497 T**, U/B; **497 B**, CP; **499**, FDR Library; **500 BL**, U/B; **500 TL**, FRENT; **501 TL**, Nixon Presidential Materials; **501 BL**, Lyndon Baines Johnson Presidential Library; **501 TR, BR**, Roy Roper and Diana Walker/GL.

Chapter 17 **504 ALL, FRENT; 504 T, 506**, LOC; **507**, FDR Library; **508 T**, US Forest Service; **508 B**, U/B; **509**, BB; **510**, "Mary McLeod Bethune" by Betsy G. Reyneau (detail). National Portrait Gallery, Smithsonian Institution/Art Resource N.Y.; **512**, LOC; **508 B, 513**, FRENT; **614**, Margaret Bourke-White LIFE Magazine © Time Warner; **515**, FDR Library; **516**, U/B; **505 B, 519**, The Oakland Museum History Dept.; **520 B, 521**, LOC; **522**, Museum of Modern Art Film Still Archive; **523**, James Prigoff.

Chapter 18 **528 BL**, Collection of Chester Stott RH/LS; **528 BL**, Nancy Gewirz, Antique Textile Resource, Bethesda, MD RH/LS; **528 R**, Collection of Col. Stuart S. Corning Jr. RH/LS; **529 TL, 530**, US Holocaust Memorial Museum; **531 TL**, Bilderdienst Suddeutscher Verlag; **531 TR**, NA #242-HMA-2773; **532 INSET**, **533**, NA, *War & Conflict*, **#993, #1131; 534 T**, Herbert Hoover Presidential Library; **534 B**, Collection of Col. Stuart S. Corning, Jr. RH/LS; **535 TR**, US Navy; **535 INSET**, NA #179-WP-936; **529 TR, 536**, Collection of Major General George S. Patton RH/LS; **537, 538**, U/B; **539**, Collection of Col. Stuart S. Corning, Jr. RH/LS; **542**, US Holocaust Memorial Museum; **543 B**, Collection of Chester H. Stott. RH/LS; **543 T**, US Dept. of Defense; **544, 545 B**, NA #127-PX-227672, #127-GR-137; **545 T**, Peter Stackpole © Time Warner; **529 M, 547**, U/B; **529 B, 548**, NA; **549**, HIROSHIMA SERIES, 1983. No. 2: "The Family". Gouache on paper 23"x 17 1/2". Courtesy of Jacob Lawrence and Francine Seders Gallery Ltd.; **551 TL**, NA#127-GR-137; **551 TR, 552 TR**, U/B; **552 BL**, LOC; **552 BR**, Archive Photos; **553 TL**, Department of Energy; **553 M, BR**, Leif Skoogfors, Howard Sochurek/WC.

Chapter 19 **556 BL**, Collection of Chester Stott RH/LS; **556 TL**, Collection of Picture Research Consultants, Inc. RH/LS; **556 R**, Collection of Jeff Ikler RH/LS; **557 TR**, NA *War & Conflict* #830; **558 T**, Private Collection RH/LS; **558 B, 560, 561**, NA, #127-GR-137, #208-MP-1-DDD-5, #44-PA-124; **562, 557 TL**, National Museum of American History, Smithsonian Institution; **563 T**, U/B; **563 B**, LOC; **564 BR** Michael Barson Collection/Past Perfect © 1943, DC Comics RH/LS; **564 BL**, Courtesy Hershey Foods Corp.; **564 T**, WW; **565**, Collection of Jeff Ikler RH/LS; **557 MR, 566**, Collection of Col. Stuart S. Corning, Jr. RH/LS; **567**, LOC; **568**, NA #208-NP-1-HHH-5; **569**, Rosie the Riveter Revisited Project, Oral History Program, California State Univer. Long Beach; **570**, Ellen Kaiper Collection, Oakland; **571**, Courtesy of the Norman Rockwell Family Trust and Curtis Archives; **557B, 572, 573 T, 574, 575**, LOC; **573 B**, Collection of Jeff Ikler RH/LS; **577**, NA #210-GC-160.

Chapter 20 **582 ALL, 583 T, 584, 585, 587 B**, The Michael Barson Collection/Past Perfect. Photo by Rob Huntley/Lightstream; **587 TR**, U/B; **587 TL**, Courtesy of the J.N. Ding Darling Foundation; **589**, U/B; **590 T, B**, Harry S. Truman Presidential Library; **583 TM, 593 INSET**, Copyright © 1956 by The New York Times Company; **593 T**, ©Stern/BS; **583 BM, 594**, © 1959 Newsweek Inc. All rights reserved. Reprinted by permission; **595 INSET, 596 BR**, Reni Burri/MP; **596 INSET**, NA #210-GC-160; **596 T**, U/B; **599, 600 TL 583 &, INSET**, The Michael Barson Collection/Past Perfect RH/LS; **601**, BB; **602**, U/B; **603**, Elliot Erwitt/MP.

Chapter 21 **606**, Collection of PRC RH/LS; **606 R**, Bill Ray LIFE Magazine © Time Warner; **607 T, 608**, Collection of Robert and Bonnie Pope RH/LS; **609**, McDonald's Corp.; **610 TL**, Courtesy IBM Archives; **610 TR**, "Big Computers in Little Packages" ©1993 by Consumers Union of U.S. Inc., Yonkers, NY 10703-1057. Reprinted by permission from Consumer Reports, November 1993; **610 BL**, National Museum of American History, Smithsonian Institution. **#90-15751; 610 INSET**, Photofest; **610 BR**, Courtesy Campbell Soup Company; **611**, J.R. Eyerman LIFE Magazine © Time Warner; **613**, Collection of PRC RH/LS; **614 T**, The Michael Barson Collection/Past Perfect RH/LS; **607 T, 614 B**, Collection of Nancy Gewirz, Antique Textile Resource, Bethesda, MD RH/LS; **615 T**, Ralph Morse LIFE © Time Warner; **615 B**, Dan Weiner, Courtesy Sandra Weiner; **616**, Curtis Archives; **607 ML, 620**, Museum of American Political Life, photo by Steve Laschever; **621 T, FRENT; 621 B, 622** U/B; **607 MR, 621, INSET; 623 B**, Division of Political History, Smithsonian Institution, **#91-13778; 625 TR**, The Michael Barson Collection/Past Perfect RH/LS; **625 B**, Copyright © 1957 by The New York Times Company; **626 T**, Bob Adelman/MP; **626 INSET**, FRENT; **627 TL**, The Michael Barson Collection/Past Perfect RH/LS; **607B, 627**, INSET; Carl Iwasaki LIFE Magazine © Time Warner; **627 BR**, WW; **628**, Grey Vielet LIFE Magazine © Time Warner; **629**, WW; **630 ALL**, U/B.

Chapter 22 **636 TL, BL, 637 T, 638**, FRENT; **639**, JFK Presidential Library; **641 T**, © Charles Harbutt/Actuality Inc.; **641 INSET**, LIFE Magazine Cover December 6, 1963. Photo by Fred Ward/BS; **637 M, 643**, Lyndon Baines Johnson Presidential Library; **644 BOTH**, FRENT; **645**, © Bob Daemmrich; **647**, Lyndon Baines Johnson Presidential Library; **648**, NASA; **637 B, 650**, Courtesy Boeing Defense & Space Group; **651 T & INSET**, Courtesy of the Peace Corps; **651 B**, Fred W. McDarrah; **654**, U/B; **656 T**, FRENT; **656 B**, WW.

Chapter 23 **660 L**, Dan Budnick/WC; **660 R**, **661T, 662**, Art and Artifacts Division, Schomburg Center for Research in Black Culture. The New York Public Library, Astor, Lenox and Tilden foundations); **663**, 665, U/B; **666 T**, Steve Shapiro/BS; **666 B**, FRENT; **667**, Dial Juvenile Books, 1968, a Division of Penguin Books USA, Inc.; **661 ML, 669**, Don Uhrbrock LIFE Magazine © Time Warner; **670**, State Historical Society of Wisconsin; **671**, U/B; **672, 674 BL**, Charles Moore/BS; **674 BR**, Jack O'Connell/The Boston Globe; **675 M**, Nancy Pierce/BS; **675 BL**, Steve Northrup/TIME Magazine; **675 BR**, © Largo Int./Shooting Star International; **661 TR**, **676**, Robert Phillips LIFE Magazine ©Time Warner; **677 T**, Fred Ward, **677 INSET**, Steve Schapiro, both BS;

678, Eve Arnold/MP; **679**, FRENT; **680**, U/B; **661B, 681 TR**, WW; **683**, Eve Arnold/MP; **684**, U/B; **685**, Co Rentmeester LIFE Magazine © Time Warner.

Chapter 24 688 L, Museum of American Political Life. Photo by Sally Anderson-Bruce; **688 TR**, M. Abramson/BS; **688 BR**, Collection of Michael McCloskey; **689 TL, 690, 691 TR**, Al Freni LIFE Magazine © Time Warner; **691 B**, © 1993 Jill Krementz; **691 INSET**, FRENT; **692 T**, © Bettye Lane; **692 B**, Radcliffe College Archives, Schlesinger Library; **693 INSET**, Courtesy Lang Communications; **693 TR**, © Bettye Lane; **694**, Collection of PRC; **695 TR & BR**, Al Freni LIFE Magazine © Time Warner; **697 T & B**, FRENT; **689 TR, 698**, Paul Fusco/MP; **699**, Craig Aurness/WC; **701 TL**, George Bacon Collection, Hawaii State Archives; **701 TR**, WW; **689 M, 702**, Eddie Adams/TIME Magazine; **704 B & BL**, Dirck Halstead/TIME Magazine; **705 T**, Rick Smolan/Against All Odds; **705 B**, FRENT; **706**, U/B; **689 B, 707**, FRENT; **708 INSET**, Collection of PRC; **708 TR**, Alfred Eisenstaedt LIFE Magazine © Time Warner; **709 TR**, Ken Regan/Camera 5.

Chapter 25 714 R, Forest McMullin/BS; **714 L**, The Image Works Archive; **715 T, 716 TL**, Courtesy United Nations. RH/LS; **717 TL**, Howard Sorhurek LIFE Magazine © Time Warner; **717 TR**, U/B; **718**, WW; **720 INSET**, Philip Jones Griffiths/MP; **715 ML, 720 L**, Zenith Electronics Corporation; **721 TL**, Catherine Leroy/AP, print courtesy Time Inc. Picture Collection; **722 INSET**, Larry Burrows LIFE Magazine © Time Warner; **723**, Courtesy of Le Ly Hayslip; **715 MR, 724**, FRENT; **725**, The Bancroft Library, University of California; **727**, © Lisa Law/The Image Works; **715 BL, 729 TL & TR**, The Oakland History Department; **730**, © Lisa Law/The Image Works; **731 BL**, Frank Driggs Collection/MP; **731 BR**, Elliott Landy/MP; **732**, © Fredericks/The Image Works; **715 BR, 733**, Brad Markel/GL; **737**, Thai Khad Chuon/U/B.

Chapter 26 744 T & B, FRENT; **745 T, 746**, "The Time Machine" by Leslie Illingworth. Sept. 13, 1967 in *Punch*. Courtesy the Lyndon B. Johnson Presidential Library; **747**, Joseph Louw LIFE Magazine © Time Warner; **748**, Bill Eppridge LIFE Magazine © Time Warner; **749 B (ALL)**, FRENT; **749 T**, U/B; **750 BR**, Jean Louis Atlan/Sygma; **750 BL**, Arthur Grace/Sygma; **751 BR**, J. Langevin/Sygma; **751 M**, U/B; **751 BL**, Jim Pickerell; **752 TL**, Richard Nixon Library. Photo © Henry Groskinsky; **745 MR, 752 BR**, Roddey E. Mims/U/B; **753**, Nixon Presidential Materials Project; **754**, Courtesy Draper Hill, Memphis, Tenn © The Commercial Appeal, Memphis; **757**, Ted Cowell/BS; **758**, Courtesy National Zoological Park, photo by Jessie Cohen; **759**, Gerald R. Ford Presidential Library; **760**, Nixon Presidential Materials Project; **745 ML, 761**, John Dominis LIFE Magazine © Time Warner; **762**, J.P. Laffont/Sygma; **745 B, 763 INSET**, FRENT; **763 TR**, Nixon Presidential Materials Project; **764**, Dennis Brack/BS; **765**, U/B; **766 T**, Fred Ward/BS; **766 M**, "Watergate" by Tony Auth, 1973. Reprinted by permission: Tribune Media Services; **767**, "Nixon Caught in a Web of Tapes" by Robert Pryor. Courtesy of John Locke Studios, Inc.; **768**, Nixon Presidential Materials Project.

Chapter 27 772 L, Gerald R. Ford Presidential Library. Photo by Henry Groskinsky; **772 R**, Jimmy Carter Presidential Library. Photo by Henry Groskinsky; **774**, Courtesy Gerald R. Ford Presidential Library; **775 TR**, WW; **773 T, 775 INSET**, Copyright © 1974 by The New York Times Company; **776**, "Inflation" by Frank Interlandi. Courtesy Gerald R. Ford Presidential Library; **778**, Matthew Naythons/GL; **773 ML, 779, 780 BL & BR**, FRENT; **781**, Jimmy Carter Presidential Library; **782**, Dennis Brack/BS; **783**, FRENT; **773 MR, 784**, Jimmy Carter Presidential Library; **785**, Alex Webb/MP; **786**, U/B; **787 TR**, Peter Marlow/MP; **787 TL**, Alain Mingam/GL; **773 B, 789, 790 L & R**, Dennis Brack/BS; **793**, U/B; **794**, WW.

Chapter 28 798 L & R, 799 T, FRENT; **801**, Steve McCurry/MP; **802**, Dennis Brack/BS; **803**, U/B; **804**, Larry Downing/WC; **799 TM, 805**, FRENT; **807**, White House Photo/BS; **808 B & INSET**, Dennis Brack/BS; **799 BM, 811 T**, Division of Political History, Smithsonian Institution #2061-167; **811 B**, Wally McNamee/WC; **813**, © 1987 Matt Herron; **814**, Dennis Brack/BS; **799 B, 818, 820 TL & TR**, U/B; **821**, David Turnley/BS.

Chapter 29 824 L, Photograph by Mark Seliger from *Rolling Stone*, December 9, 1993. By Straight Arrow Publishers. 1993. All Rights Reserved. Reprinted by Permission. **824 R**, FRENT; **825 T, 826**, Dennis Brack/BS; **827 INSET**, John C. Sykes Jr.; **827 TR**, WW; **828**, Sygma; **829**, Jacques A. Chenet/GL; **830**, John Harrington/BS; **832**, © 1992 Klaus Reisinger/BS; **833 BL**, AFP Photo; **833 BR**, Leonard Freed/MP; **825 M, 835, 836**, Les Stone/Sygma; **825 B, 838**, JB Pictures Ltd.; **840 B**, Brad Markel/GL; **840 T**, David Horsey/Reprinted courtesy of the Seattle Post-Intelligencer; **841**, Porter Gifford/GL.

Epilogue 848, "From Sea to Shining Sea" Quilt by Jacqueline Paton. From the Permanent Collection of the Museum of American Folk Art.

Primary Source Bibliography

Chapter 1 Father Joseph Lafitau: *Customs of the American Indians Compared with the Customs of Primitive Times.* The Champlain Society, 1977, p. 184; **Chief Joseph:** McLuhan, T. C. *Touch the Earth: A Self-Portrait of Indian Existence.* Simon and Schuster, 1971, p. 54; **anonymous poet:** Furnivall, F. J., ed. *Ballads from Manuscripts, Vol. 1, 1868–1872.* Ballad Society Series, 1873; **Leo Africanus:** Bennett, Jr., Lerone. *Before the Mayflower: A History of the Negro in America.* Johnson Publishing Company, 1966, p. 18; **Christopher Columbus:** Morison, Samuel Eliot. *Admiral of the Ocean Sea: A Life of Christopher Columbus.* Little Brown, 1942, p. 231; **Inca Garcilaso:** Garcilaso de la Vega, El Inca. *The Royal Commentaries of Peru, La Florida Del Inca.* Fondo de Cultura Económica, 1956, pp. 220, 229; **Popé:** Gutiérrez, Ramón A. *When Jesus Came, the Corn Mothers Went Away.* Stanford University Press, 1991, p. 131; **Adriaen Van der Donck:** Jennings, Francis. *The Ambiguous Iroquois Empire.* W.W. Norton & Company, 1984, p. 47; **Miantonomo:** Cronin, William. *Changes in the Land: Indians, Colonists, and the Ecology of New England.* Hill and Wang, 1983, p. 139; **Thomas Mun:** Bruchey, Stuart, ed. *The Colonial Merchant: Sources and Readings.* Harcourt, Brace & World, 1966, p. 52; **Eliza Pinckney:** Ravenel, Harriott Horry. *Eliza Pinckney.* Charles Scribner's Sons, 1896, p. 6; **Jonathan Edwards:** Kupperman, Karen Ordahl, ed. *Major Problems in American Colonial History: Documents and Essays.* D.C. Heath, 1993, p. 369; **George Whitefield:** Gaustad, Edwin Scott. *The Great Awakening in New England.* Quadrangle Books, 1957, p. 27; **Olaudah Equiano:** Edwards, Paul, ed. *Equiano's Travels.* Heinemann Educational Books, 1967, p. 25; **Equiano:** Edwards, p. 32; **Charles Ball:** Bayliss, John F., ed. *Black Slave Narratives.* Macmillan, 1970, p. 52.

Chapter 2 John Dickinson: Greene, Jack P., ed. *Colonies to Nation, 1763–1789.* W.W. Norton & Company, 1975, p. 13; **Declaration of Independence; anonymous Englishman:** Wallace, Willard M. *Appeal to Arms: A Military History of the American Revolution.* Quadrangle/The New York Times Book Co., 1975, p. 43; **Michael Graham:** Dann, John C., ed. *The Revolution Remembered: Eyewitness Accounts of the War for Independence.* The University of Chicago Press, 1980, p. 50; **Thomas Paine:** Foot, Michael and Isaac Kramnick, eds. *Thomas Paine Reader.* Penguin Books, 1987, p. 116; **Sarah Osborn:** Dann, p. 245; **Joseph Plumb Martin:** Brown, pp. 223–224; **Fisher Ames:** Wood, Gordon S. *The Creation of the American Republic, 1776–1787.* W. W. Norton & Company, 1969, p. 411; **Richard Price:** Wood, p. 396; **Benjamin Rush:** Wood, p. 466; **United States Constitution; United States Constitution; Thomas Jefferson:** Kammen, Michael, ed. *The Origins of the American Constitution: A Documentary History.* Penguin, 1986, p. 91.

Chapter 3 Margaret Bayard Smith: Morris, Richard B. and James Woodress. *Voices from America's Past, Vol. 1: The Colonies and the New Nation.* E. P. Dutton, 1963, p. 194; **Thomas Jefferson:** Peterson, Merrill D., ed. **Thomas Jefferson.** Library of America, 1984, p. 494; **Morris Birkbeck:** Birkbeck, Morris. "Notes on a Journey from America from the Coasts of Virginia to the Territory of Illinois." Philadelphia, 1817, p. 34; **Mason Weems:** Weems, Mason. *The Life of George Washington.* The Belknap Press of Harvard University Press, 1962, p. xv; **From** *The Life of Washington*: Weems, p. 12; **Methodist women:** Davis, David Byron. *Antebellum*

American Culture: An Interpretive Anthology. D. C. Heath, 1979, p. 267; **Moses Grandy:** *Narrative of the Life of Moses Grandy Late a Slave in the United States of America.* Oliver Johnson Publishing Company, 1844, p. 11, quoted in Lerner, Gerda. *Black Women in White America, A Documentary History.* Vintage Books, 1973, p. 9; **Denmark Vesey:** Freehling, William W. *Prelude to the Civil War: The Nullification Controversy in South Carolina, 1816–1836.* Harper and Row, 1966, p. 54; **Edwin C. Holland:** Freehling, p. 59; **John Quincy Adams:** Wilentz, Sean, ed. *Major Problems in the Early Republic, 1778–1848.* D.C. Heath, 1992, p. 341; **President Jackson:** Wilentz, p. 388; **Cherokee:** Van Every, Dale. *Disinherited: The Lost Birthright of the American Indian.* William Morrow and Company, 1966, pp. 135–136.

Chapter 4 Abraham Lincoln: Davis, David Brion. *Antebellum American Culture: An Interpretive Anthology.* D. C. Heath, 1979, p. 407; **William Lloyd Garrison:** Wilentz, Sean, ed. *Major Problems in the Early Republic, 1787–1848.* D. C. Heath, 1992, p. 477; **Catharine Beecher:** *A Treatise on Domestic Economy.* T. H. Webb, 1842, pp. 26–34, 36–38; **Elizabeth Cady Stanton:** Stanton, Elizabeth Cady, et al. *History of Woman Suffrage, Vol. 1.* Fowler and Wells, 1889, pp. 58–59; **Sojourner Truth:** Ripley, Peter, ed. *Witness for Freedom: African Voices on Race, Slavery, and Emancipation.* University of North Carolina Press, 1993, p. 102; **James R. Walker:** Walker, James R. *Lakota Society.* University of Nebraska Press, 1982, p. 74; **Wilkis:** Grinnell, George Bird. *When Buffalo Ran.* University of Oklahoma Press, 1966, p. 46; **William Travis:** Ramsdell, Charles. "The Storming of the Alamo," *American Heritage*, Vol. XII, No. 2, February 1961, p. 91; **anonymous:** Unruh, John D., Jr. *The Plains Across.* University of Illinois Press, 1979, p. 414; **Reverend Walter Colton:** *Three Years in California.* S.A. Rollo, 1850, pp. 242–253.

Chapter 5 Harriet Beecher Stowe: *Uncle Tom's Cabin.* New American Library, 1981, p. 32; **Harriet Beecher Stowe:** p. 93; **George Fitzhugh:** Gorn, Elliot J., et al. *Constructing the American Past: A Source Book of a People's History, Vol. 1.* HarperCollins, 1991, p. 259; **John C. Calhoun:** Thomas, John L. *John C. Calhoun: A Profile.* Hill and Wang, 1968, p. vii; **John C. Calhoun:** Wiltse, Charles M. *John C. Calhoun: Sectionalist, 1840–1850.* The Bobbs-Merrill Company, 1951, p. 461; **John C. Calhoun:** Heffner, Richard D. *A Documentary History of the United States.* New American Library, 1965, pp. 119–120; **John C. Calhoun:** Heffner, p. 127; **Rutherford B. Hayes:** Holt, Michael F. *The Political Crises of the 1850's.* John Wiley and Sons, 1978, p. 120; **Know Nothings:** Holt, p. 163; **Stephen Douglas:** Holt, p. 145; **Charles Sumner:** Donald, David. *Charles Sumner and the Coming of the Civil War.* Alfred A. Knopf, 1960, p. 205; **Preston Brooks:** Donald, p. 295; **New York** *Evening Post:* Gienapp, William E. *The Origins of the Republican Party, 1852–1856.* Oxford University Press, 1987, p. 301; **Roger Taney:** Heffner, Richard D. *A Documentary History of the United States.* New American Library, 1976, p. 141; **Abraham Lincoln:** Angle, Paul M. *Created Equal? The Complete Lincoln-Douglas Debates of 1858.* The University of Chicago Press, 1958, p. 42; **Abraham Lincoln:** *Selected Speeches and Writings.* The Library of America, 1992, p. 131; **John Brown:** Oates, Stephen B. *To Purge This Land with Blood: A Biography of John Brown.* Harper Torchbooks, 1970, p. 351; **Republican:** Holt, p. 212; **newspaper editor:** Holt, Michael F. *The Political Crisis of the 1850's.* John Wiley and Sons, 1978, p. 241.

Chapter 6 editor of *Richmond Examiner:* Richmond Examiner, September 27, 1861; **Tennessee soldier:** McPherson, James. *Battle Cry of Freedom: The Civil War Era.* Oxford University Press, 1988, p. 413; **Mary Boykin Chesnut:** Woodward, C.Vann et al., eds. *Mary Chesnut's Civil War.* Yale University Press, 1981, pp. 326, 327, 330, 333, 339; **William Seward:** Bensel, Richard Franklin. *Yankee Leviathan: The Origins of Central State Authority in America, 1859–1877.* Cambridge University Press, 1990, p. 141; **Abraham Lincoln:** *Selected Speeches and Writings.* First Vintage Books, Library of America, 1992, p. 364; **New York Herald reporter:** *New York Herald*, July 18, 1863; **Frederick Douglass:** *Douglass' Monthly*, August, 1863; **Henry Harmon:** Redkey, Edwin S. *A Grand Army of Men: Letters from African-American Soldiers in the Union Army, 1861–1865.* Cambridge University Press, 1992, pp. 34–35; **Union officer:** Wheeler, Richard. *The Siege of Vicksburg.* Thomas Y. Crowell, 1978, p. xii; **James Autry:** Walker, Peter F. *Vicksburg, A People at War, 1860–1865.* The University of North Carolina Press, 1960, p. 91; **Grant's fellow officer:** Ketchum, Richard M. et al., eds. *The American Heritage Picture History of the Civil War.* American Heritage Publishing Company. Doubleday, 1960, p. 308; **Emma Balfour:** Walker, p. 135; **Josiah Gorgas:** McPherson, p. 665; **Abraham Lincoln's Gettysburg Address; Second Inaugural Address:** Lincoln, pp. 449-450; **William Sherman:** Foote, Shelby. *Civil War: A Narrative, Vol. 3.* Random House, 1974, p. 613.

Chapter 7 A.D. Lewis: Foner, Eric. *Reconstruction: America's Unfinished Revolution 1863–1877.* Harper and Row, 1988, p. 122; **African American/anonymous:** Foner, p. 80; **Charlotte Forten:** "Life on the Sea Islands," *Atlantic Monthly*, Vol. 13 (May and June) 1864, pp. 588–589, 591–594, 666–667; **white northerner:** Foner, Eric, p. 109; **Thomas Arnold:** Hoffmann, Charles and Tess. *North by South: The Two Lives of Richard James Arnold.* The University of Georgia Press, 1988, p. 256; **Fourteenth Amendment:** United States Constitution; **African American state convention:** Levine, Bruce et al, eds. *Who Built America? Working People and the Nation's Economy, Politics, Culture, and Society.* Pantheon Books, 1989, p. 477; **DeBow's Review:** *DeBow's Review*, Vol. V (February 1868), p. 136; **Thomas Allen:** Gorn, Elliott J. et al. *Constructing the American Past: A Source Book of a People's History.* HarperCollins Publishers, 1991, p. 321; **Lydia Child:** Foner, Eric, p. 473; **Ira Steward:** Levine, Bruce et al., p. 539.

Chapter 8 Cornelia Adair: Adair, Cornelia. *My Diary. August 30th to November 5th 1874.* University of Texas Press, 1965, pp. 105, 117; **From the folk tale "Railroads Ain't No Good":** Randolph, Vance, ed. "Railroads Ain't No Good" from *Sticks in the Knapsack and Other Folktales.* Columbia University Press, 1958, p. 84; **Finley Peter Dunne:** Filler, Louis, ed. *Mr. Dooley: Now and Forever.* Academic Reprints, 1954, p. 221; **Andrew Carnegie:** Carnegie, Andrew. *The Empire of Business.* Doubleday, 1902, pp. 138–140, quoted in Kirkland, Edward Chase. *Dream and Thought in the Business Community, 1860–1900.* Cornell, 1956, p. 156–157; **resident of Lynn, Massachusetts:** Bureau of Labor, *Fourth Annual Report*, 1873, p. 306; **Frederick Winslow Taylor:** Taylor, Frederick W. *The Principles of Scientific Management.* Harper and Row, 1911, p. 39; **factory manager:** Massachusetts Bureau of the Statistics of Labor. *Thirteenth Annual Report*, 1883; **Jacob Riis:** Riis, Jacob. *Children of the Poor.* Ayer Company Publishers, 1971; **Samuel Gompers:** Gompers, Samuel. *Labor and the Common People.* Ayer Company Publishers, 1971, p. 118; **George Baer:** Roy, Andrew. *A History of Coal Miners of the U.S.* J.L. Trauger, 1906, p. 424; **August Spies:** Kogan, B.R. "The Chicago Haymarket Riot," 1959 (a reproduction of the circular in the Chicago Historical Society collection).

Chapter 9 Dakota brochure: Billington, Ray A. *Westward Expansion: A History of the American Frontier.* Macmillan, 1982, p. 647; **preacher from Georgia:** Painter, Nell I. *Exodusters: Black Migration to Kansas After Reconstruction.* Knopf, 1977, p. 83; **Howard Ruede:** *Sod-House Days. Letters from a Kansas Homesteader, 1877–1878.* Columbia University Press, 1937, p. 28; **Elinore Pruitt Stewart:** *Letters of a Woman Homesteader.* University of Nebraska Press, 1961, pp. 214–215; **Chief Joseph:** Utley, Robert M. *The Indian Frontier of the American West, 1846–1890.* University of New Mexico Press, 1984, p. 193; **newspaper reporter:** Fite, Gilbert, *The Farmer's Frontier, 1865–1900.* University of New Mexico Press, 1974, p. 205; **newspaper report:** "Commercial and Financial Chronicle," September 21, 1879, quoted in Fite, p. 82; **Henry George:** *Progress and Poverty.* Phoenix Publishing, 1979; **rhyme:** Hicks, John D. *The Populist Revolt: A History of the Farmer's Alliance & the People's Party.* Greenwood, 1981, p. 204; **Tom Watson:** Woodward, C. Vann. *Tom Watson, Agrarian Rebel.* Oxford University Press, 1963, p. 220; **William Jennings Bryan:** Billington, p. 680; **Frederick Jackson Turner:** Billington, Ray, ed. *Frontier and Section: Selected Essays of Frederick Jackson Turner.* Prentice Hall, 1961, p. 61; **Edward L. Wheeler:** *Deadwood Dick, The Prince of the Road.* Garland, 1979, p. 16.

Chapter 10 anonymous: Kutler, Stanley I. *Looking for America: The People's History, Vol. 2.* W.W. Norton & Company, 1979, p. 178; **Fiorello LaGuardia:** *The Making of an Insurgent.* J.B. Lippincott Co., 1948, pp. 64–65; **newspaper reporter:** Swinton, John. *The New Issue: The Chinese American Question.* American News Co., 1870; **Sadie Frowne:** Adapted from "The Story of a Sweatshop Girl: Sadie Frowne," Katzman and Tuttle. *Plain Folk: The Life Stories of Undistinguished Americans.* Illinois, University of Illinois Press, 1982, pp. 75–95; **Eleanor McMain:** "Behind the Yellow Fever in Little Palermo: Housing Conditions Which New Orleans Should Shake Itself Free From Along with the Summer's Scourge," *Charities and the Commons,* Vol. 15, 1905, pp. 152–159; **Emily Dinwiddie:** "Some Aspects of Italian Housing and Social Conditions in Philadelphia," *Charities and the Commons,* Vol. 12, 1904, p. 490; **Martin Lomasney:** *Boston Globe,* December 2, 1923, quoted in Zink, Harold. *City Bosses in the United States. A Study of Twenty Municipal Bosses.* Duke University Press, 1930, p. 83.

Chapter 11 Pauli Murray: *Proud Shoes.* Harper and Row, 1956, pp. 269–270; **notice to performers:** Royle, Edwin Milton. "The Vaudeville Theatre," *Scribner's Magazine,* Vol. XXVI, October 1899, pp. 485–495; **Madam C. J. Walker:** Hine, Darlene Clark et. eds. *Black Women in America. An Historical Encyclopedia,* Vol. 2. Carlson Publishing, 1993, pp. 1209–1214; **Edward H. Clarke:** *Sex in Education; or a Fair Chance for the Girls.* Ayer Co. Publishers, 1972 (reproduction of the 1873 edition).

Chapter 12 James G. Blaine: LaFeber, Walter. *The New Empire: An Interpretation of American Expansion, 1860–1898.* Cornell University Press, 1963, p. 165; **Albert J. Beveridge:** *The Meaning of the Times and Other Speeches.* Books for Libraries Press, 1908, pp. 84–85; **Hearst newspaper:** LaFeber, p. 230; **Theodore Roosevelt:** Hart, Albert Bushnell and Herbert Ronald Ferleger, eds. *Theodore Roosevelt Cyclopedia.* Roosevelt Memorial Association, 1941, p. 407; **Lucia Mead:** Crapol, Edward P., ed. *Women and American Foreign Policy: Lobbyists, Critics, and Insiders.* Greenwood Press, 1987, p. 72; **Carl Schurz:** "The Policy of Imperialism," 1899 address by Carl Schruz to Anti-Imperialist Conference in Chicago, October 17, 1899; **Bishop Alexander Walters:** "Wisconsin Weekly Advocate," August 17, 1899, quoted in Gatewood, Willard B., Jr. *Black Americans and the White Man's Burden, 1898–1903.* University of Illinois Press, 1975, p. 200; **Carl Schurz:** Lasch, Christopher. "The Anti-Imperialists, the Philippines, and the Inequality of Man," *Journal of Southern History,* August 1958, p. 115.

Chapter 13 Edward Bellamy: *Looking Backward.* River City Press, 1888, p. 56; **Jane Addams:** "Why Women Should Vote." *Ladies Home Journal,* Vol. XXVII, January 1910, pp. 21–22; **Upton Sinclair:** *The Jungle.* Doubleday, 1906, pp. 96–97; **Justice David J. Brewer:** Muller v. Oregon, quoted in Kerber, Linda J., and Jane De Hart, eds. *Women's America: Refocusing the Past.* Oxford University Press, 1987, p. 541; **Elizabeth Cady Stanton:** Flexner, Eleanor. *Century of Struggle: The Woman's Rights Movement in the United States.* The Belknap Press of Harvard University Press, 1975, p. 177; **Carrie Chapman Catt:** Flexner, p. 176.

Chapter 14 Richard Harding Davis: New York *Tribune,* August 1914; **Arthur Zimmerman:** Leckie, Robert. *The Wars of America.* Harper and Row, 1968, p. 628; **Woodrow Wilson:** Cooper, John Milton, Jr. *Pivotal Decades: The United States, 1900–1920.* W.W. Norton and Company, 1990, p. 265; **Mary Gladwin:** Dock, Lavinia L., et al. *A History of American Red Cross Nursing.* Macmillan, 1922, p. 179; **Corporal Elmer Sherwood:** Berger, Dorothy and Josef, eds. *Diary of America.* Simon and Schuster, 1957, p. 536; **Herbert Hoover:** "Gospel of the Clean Plate" *Ladies Home Journal,* August 1917, p. 25; **Alice Lord O'Brian:** *No Glory: Letters from France, 1917–1919.* Airport Publishers, 1936, pp. 8, 141, 152–153.

Chapter 15 Bart Vanzetti: Stong, Phil. "The Last Days of Sacco and Vanzetti," in Leighton, Isabel, ed. *The Aspirin Age, 1919–1941.* Simon and Schuster, 1949, p. 188; **Albert Johnson:** Daniels, Roger. *Coming to America: A History of Immigration and Ethnicity in America.* HarperCollins, 1990, p. 284; **New Orleans citizen:** "Additional Letters of Negro Migrants of 1916–1918." *Journal of Negro History,* April 4, 1919, p. 451; **Edna St. Vincent Millay:** "First Fig." *Edna St. Vincent Millay: Selected Poems.* HarperCollins, 1991, p. 19; **Preston Slosson:** *The Great Crusade and After, 1914–1928.* Macmillan, 1929, p. 157; **New York Sun:** Ward, John William. "The Meaning of Lindbergh's Flight." *American Quarterly ,* Vol. X (Spring 1958), p. 1; **Henry Ford:** *My Life and Work.* Doubleday, 1923, p. 251; **Billy Sunday:** Sinclair, Andrew. *Era of Excess: A Social History of the Prohibition Movement.* Harper and Row, 1964, p. 248.

Chapter 16 Lincoln Steffens: Leuchtenberg, William. *The Perils of Prosperity, 1914–1932.* University of Chicago Press, 1958, p. 202; **Arthur Crew Inman:** Aaron, Daniel, ed. *The Inman Diary: A Public and Private Confession.* Harvard University Press, 1985, p. 401; **Broadway show tune:** Words by E. Y. Harburg, music by Jay Gorney. Harms, Inc., 1932. Renewed, permission from Warner Brothers Music. **Oklahoma woman:** Terkel, Studs. *Hard Times: An Oral History of the Great Depression.* Pantheon Books, 1970, p. 50; **Woody Guthrie:** *Bound for Glory.* E. P. Dutton, 1968, p. 189; **boy tramp:** Minehan, Thomas. *Boy and Girl Tramps of America.* Holt, Rinehart, and Winston, 1934, pp. 21–23, 53–54, 62–64; **Gordon Parks:** *Voices in the Mirror: An Autobiography.* Doubleday, 1990; **Wilson Ledford:** "How I Lived During the Depression." Interview taped and transcribed by Reuben Hiatt, November 7, 1982. Quoted in Snell, William R ed., *Hard Times Remembered: Bradley County and the Great Depression.* Bradley County Historical Society, 1983, pp. 117–121; **Gerald W. Johnson:** "The Average American and the Depression." Current History , February 1932; **Kitty McCulloch:** Terkel, Studs. *Hard Times: An Oral History of the Great Depression.* Pantheon Books, 1970; **William Saroyan:** *Inhale and Exhale.* Random House, 1936, p. 81; **The 1932nd Psalm:** E. J. Sullivan. Quoted in McElvaine, Robert S., ed. *Down and Out in the Great Depression: Letters from the Forgotten Man.* University of North Carolina Press, 1983, p. 34; **Herbert Hoover:** Myers, William S., ed. *The State Papers and Other Public Writings of Herbert Hoover.* Doubleday, Doran and Company, Inc., Vol. II, 1934, pp. 408–413; **Franklin D. Roosevelt:** *New York Times,* September 24, 1932; **Roosevelt:** Inaugural Address, March 4, 1933.

Chapter 17 Harry Hopkins: Dawley, Alan. *Struggles for Justice: Social Responsibility and the Liberal State.* Harvard University Press, 1991, p. 367; **Mary McLeod Bethune:** "Faith That Moved a Dump Heap." *Who, The Magazine About People,* January 3, 1941, pp. 31–35, 54; **Letters to Roosevelt:** Editors of Time Life. *This Fabulous Century: Sixty Years of American Life, 1930–1949.* Time Life Books, Vol. IV, 1969, p. 136; **federal official:** Markowitz, Gerald, and David Rosner, eds. "Slaves of the Depression." *Workers' Letters About Life on the Job.* Cornell, 1987, p. 154; **Walter White:** *A Man Called White: The Autobiography of Walter White.* Viking Press, 1948, pp. 179–180; **Sam E. Roberts:** Duram, James C. and Eleanor A. "Congressman Clifford Hope's Correspondence With his Constituents: A Conservative View of the Court-Packing Fight of 1937." *Kansas Historical Quarterly* 37/1 (Spring 1971), p. 71; **Hiram W. Johnson:** Barnes, William R., and A. W. Littlefield. *The Supreme Court Issue and the Constitution, Comments Pro and Con by Distinguished Men.* Barnes & Noble, 1937, p. 49; **Walter Reuther:** Madison, Charles A. *American Labor Leaders, Personalities and Forces in the Labor Movement.* Ungar, 1950, p. 382; **Mrs. Renee Lohrback:** Blackwelder, Julia Kirk. *Women of the Depression: Caste and Culture in San Antonio, 1929–1939.* Texas A&M Press, 1984.

Chapter 18 Karl Alexander von Müller: Flood, Charles Bracelen. *Hitler: The Path to Power.* Houghton Mifflin Company, 1989, p. 493; **Dellie Hahne:** Harris, Mark Jonathan et al. *The Homefront: America During World War II.* G. P. Putnam's Sons, 1984, p. 27; **Dick Winters:** Ambrose, Stephan. *Band of Brothers: E. Company, 506th Regiment, 101st Airborne: From Normandy to Hitler's Eagle's Nest.* Simon & Schuster, 1992, p. 270; **Ernie Pyle:** Nichols, David. *Ernie's War: The Best of Ernie Pyle's World War II Dispatches.* Random House, 1986, p. 141; **Art Rittenberg:** Lidz, Richard. *Many Kinds of Courage: An Oral History of World War II.* G. P. Putnam's Sons, 1980, p. 243; **Eisenhower:** Carroll, James. "The monster that adds a chill to the August air." *The Boston Globe,* August 17, 1993; **Tatsue Urata:** Winkler, Allan M. *Life Under a Cloud, American Anxiety About the Atom.*

Oxford University Press, 1993, p. 23.

Chapter 19 Leonard Williamson: Hoopes, Roy. *Americans Remember the Home Front: An Oral Narrative.* Hawthorn Books, 1977, p. 115; **Want ad:** *Sporting News,* February 25, 1943; **Wanita Allen:** Frank, Miriam, Marilyn Ziebarth, and Connie Field. *The Life and Times of Rosie the Riveter.* Clarity Educational Productions, 1982, p. 57; **Beatrice Clifton:** Gluck, Sherna Berger. *Rosie the Riveter Revisited: Women, the War, and Social Change.* Twayne Publishers, 1987, pp. 211, 219; **from the film Women of Steel:** Frank, Miriam, et al. *The Life and Times of Rosie the Riveter.* Clarity Educational Productions, 1982, p. 100; **Margaret Wright:** Frank et al., p. 94; **Roosevelt:** Columbus Day speech, 1942; **Lloyd Brown:** Blum, John Morton. *V Was for Victory: Politics and American Culture During World War II.* Harcourt Brace Jovanovich, 1976, p. 191; **Henry Murakami:** Harris, Mark Jonathan, ei al. *The Homefront: America During World War II.* G. P. Putnam's Sons, 1984, p. 113.

Chapter 20 Joseph Goulden: *The Best Years, 1945–1950.* Atheneum, 1976; **Joseph Stalin:** Truman, Harry S *Memoirs, Volume I: Year of Decisions.* Doubleday & Company, Inc., 1955, p. 86; **Harry Truman:** Truman, p. 289; **Truman:** Truman, *Memoirs, Volume I;* **MacArthur:** Phillips, Cabell. *The Truman Presidency: The History of a Triumphant Succession.* The Macmillan Company, 1966, p. 348; **Joseph Welch:** Lately, Thomas. *When Even Angels Wept: The Senator Joseph McCarthy Affair—A Story Without a Hero.* William Morrow & Company, Inc., 1973, pp. 587–588.

Chapter 21 Walt Disney: Winkler, Allan M. *Life Under a Cloud: American Anxiety About the Atom.* Oxford University Press, 1993, p. 140; **Malvina Reynolds:** Winkler, Allan M. *Modern America: The United States from World War II to the Present.* HarperCollins, 1985, p. 86; **Eisenhower:** *Mandate for Change, 1953–1956.* Doubleday and Company, Inc., 1963, p. 548; **Betty Friedan:** *The Feminine Mystique.* Norton, 1963; **Harry Truman:** Winkler, p. 70; **Richard Nixon:** Wicker, Tom. *One of Us: Richard Nixon and the American Dream.* Random House, 1991, p. 98; **Eisenhower:** Holbo, Paul S., and Robert W. Sellen, eds. *The Eisenhower Era.* Dryden Press, 1974, p. 113; **Jackie Robinson:** Henderson, Edwin B. *The Black Athlete: Emergence and Arrival.* Publisher's Agency under the auspices of the Association for the Study of Afro-American Life and History, 1976, p. xii; **Martin Luther King, Jr.:** Sitkoff, Harvard. *The Struggle for Black Equality: 1954–1980.* Hill and Wang, 1981, p. 50; **Martin Luther King, Jr.:** *Stride Toward Freedom: The Montgomery Story.* Harper and Row, 1958, pp. 53–55; **Seminole petition to Eisenhower:** Josephy, Alvin M., Jr. *Now That the Buffalo's Gone: A Study of Today's American Indians.* Alfred A. Knopf, 1982, p. 28.

Chapter 22 John F. Kennedy: Inaugural Address. January 20, 1961; **John Kenneth Galbraith:** Winkler, Allan M. *Modern America: The United States from World War II to the Present.* HarperCollins, 1985, p. 125; **Lyndon B. Johnson:** Speech at the University of Michigan, May 1964; **Tom Hayden:** Winkler, Allan M. *The Recent Past: Readings on America Since World War II.* Harper and Row,1989, p. 164; **John F. Kennedy:** Address to Latin American diplomats, March 13, 1961; **Arthur M. Schlesinger, Jr.:** Nash, Gary. *The American People. Volume Two, Since 1865: Creating a Nation and a Society.* Harper and Row, 1986, p. 963; **Paul Cowan:** *The Making of an Un-American: A Dialogue with Experience.* Viking Press, 1970, dedication page; **Senator J. William Fulbright:** Schlesinger, Arthur M. *A Thousand Days: John F. Kennedy in the White House.* Houghton Mifflin, 1965, p. 251; **Dean Acheson:** Winkler, Allan M. *Life Under a Cloud: American Anxiety About the Atom.* Oxford University Press, 1993, pp. 173–174.

Chapter 23 W. E. B. DuBois: Aptheker, Herbert, ed. *Pamphlets and Leaflets by W. E. B. DuBois.* Kraus-Thomason Organization Limited, 1986, p. 116; **Southern Christian Leadership Conference:** Sitkoff, Harvard. *The Struggle for Black Equality.* Hill and Wang, 1981, p. 65; **SCLC leaflet:** Sitkoff, p. 59; **Martin Luther King, Jr.:** Sitkoff, p. 92; **Todd Gitlin:** *The Sixties: Years of Hope, Days of Rage.* Bantam Books, 1987, pp. 148–149; **Anne Moody:** *Coming of Age in Mississippi.* Dell, 1968; **John Lewis:** Hampton, Henry, et al. *Voices of Freedom: An Oral History of the Civil Rights Movement from the 1950's Through the 1980's.* Bantam Books, 1990, p. 58; **James Farmer:** Hampton, p. 78; **Martin Luther King, Jr.:** "Letter From a Birmingham Jail." *Essay Series.* A. J. Muste Memorial Institute, p. 18; **John F. Kennedy:** Radio and Television Report to the American People on Civil Rights, June 11, 1963; **Martin Luther King, Jr.:** "I Have a Dream," Speech in Washington, D.C., August 1963. In Winkler, Allan M. *The Recent Past: Readings on America Since World War II.* Harper and Row, 1989, p. 275; **Fannie Lou Hamer:** Harley, Sharon, et. al. *The African American Experience: A History.* Globe Book Company, 1992, p. 336; **James Baldwin:** *The Fire Next Time.* Dial Press, 1963, p. 132; **Malcolm X:** *The Autobiography of Malcolm X.* Ballantine Books, 1990, pp. 245–246; **Stokely Carmichael:** Nash, Gary B., et al., eds. *The American People.* Harper and Row, 1986, p. 1001; **Barbara Jordan:** Harley, et al , p. 343.

Chapter 24 Cathy Cade: Evans, Sara. *Personal Politics: The Roots of Women's Liberation in the Civil Rights Movement and the New Left.* Alfred A. Knopf, 1979, p. 205; **Mimi Feingold:** Evans, p. 204; **Helen Reddy:** "I Am Woman." Words by Helen Reddy, music by Ray Burton. Irving Music, Inc. and Buggerlugs Music Co., 1971; **Equal Rights Amendment to the Constitution, 1972; Marabel Morgan:** *The Total Woman.* Simon and Schuster, 1973, pp. 96–97; **Phyllis Schlafly:** Nash, Gary B. *The American People: Creating a Nation and a Society.* Harper and Row, 1986, p. 1008; **Rodolfo Gonzales:** Hammerback, John C., Richard J. Jensen and Jose Angel Gutierrez. *A War of Words: Chicano Protest in the 1960's and 1970's.* Greenwood Press, 1985, p. 59; **César Chávez:** Levy, Jacques E. *César Chávez: Autobiography of La Causa.* W.W. Norton, 1975; **César Chávez:** Levy, p. 293; **David Sanchez:** Vigil, Maurilio. *Chicano Politics.* University Press of America, 1977, p. 173; **Dennis Banks:** Zimmerman, Bill. *Airlift to Wounded Knee.* Swallow Press, 1976, p. 117; **Dennis Banks:** Dewing, Rolland. *Wounded Knee: The Meaning and Significance of the Second Incident.* Irvington Publishers, Inc., 1985, p. 41; **Vine Deloria, Jr.:** "This Country Was a Lot Better Off When the Indians Were Running It." *New York Times Magazine,* March 8, 1970; **Onondaga Chief Oren Lyons:** *Voices from Wounded Knee: The People Are Standing Up.* Akwesasne Notes, 1974, p. 96; **a Taos representative:** Debo, Angie. *A History of the Indians of the United States.* University of Oklahoma Press, 1977, p. 419; **Rachel Carson:** *Silent Spring.* Houghton Mifflin, 1962, p. 6; **Ralph Nader:** *Unsafe at Any Speed: The Designed-in Dangers of the American Automobile.* Grossman Publishers, 1972, preface.

Chapter 25 Lyndon B. Johnson: Kearns, Doris. *Lyndon Johnson and the American Dream.* Harper and Row, 1976, p. 316; **Angel Qunitana:** Maurer, Harry. *Strange Ground: Americans in Vietnam, 1945–1975, An Oral History.* Henry Holt and Company, 1989, p. 171; **Le Thanh:** Chanoff, David, and Van Toai Doan. *Portrait of the Enemy.* Random House, 1986, pp. 62–63; **Vietnamese peasant:** Trullinger, James Walker, Jr. *Village at War: An Account of Revolution in Vietnam.* Longman, 1980, p. 118. **Private Paul Meadlo:** *New York Times,* November 25, 1969, p. 16; **Bob Dylan:** "The Times They Are A-Changin.' " Words and music by Bob Dylan. Warner Brothers, 1963; **Tom Hayden:** Students for a Democratic Society, *Port Huron Statement.* Quoted in Winkler, Allan. *The Recent Past: Readings on America Since World War II.* Harper and Row, 1989, pp. 218–219; **Mario Savio:** Winkler, Allan M. *Modern America: The United States from World War II to the Present.* Harper-Collins, 1985, p. 153; **Bo Burlingham:** Obst, Lynda Rosen, ed. *The Sixties: The Decade Remembered Now by the People Who Lived It Then.* Random House Rolling Stone Press, 1977, p. 300; **Lynn Ferrin:** Morrison, Joan and Robert K. *From Camelot to Kent State: The Sixties Experience in the Words of Those Who Lived It.* Times Books, 1987, p. 176; **Tom Law:** Makower, Joel. *Woodstock: The Oral History.* Doubleday, 1989, p. 333; **Richard Nixon:** Address to the Nation on the Situation in Southeast Asia. April 30, 1970; **Tom Grace:** Morrison, et al., pp. 332–333; **Ron Kovic:** *Born on the Fourth of July.* Pocket Books, 1989.

Chapter 26 Martin Luther King, Jr.: Kaiser, Charles. *1968 in America: Music, Politics, Chaos, Counterculture, and the Shaping of a Generation.* Weidenfeld and Nicolson, 1988, p. 144; **John Lewis:** Morrison, Joan, and Robert K. *From Camelot to Kent State: The Sixties Experience in the Words of Those Who Lived It.* Times

Books, 1987, pp. 34–35; **Todd Gitlin:** Obst, Lynda Rosen, ed. *The Sixties: The Decade Remembered Now by the People Who Lived It Then.* Random House Rolling Stone Press, 1977; **Richard Nixon:** Wicker, Tom. *One of Us: Richard Nixon and the American Dream.* Random House, 1991, p. 9; **Lawrence O'Brien:** Siegal, Frederick F. *Troubled Journey: From Pearl Harbor to Ronald Reagan.* Hill and Wang, 1984; **Richard Nixon:** Ambrose, Stephen E. *Nixon: Volume Two: The Triumph of a Politician, 1962–1972.* Simon and Schuster, 1989, p. 376; **Henry Kissinger:** *White House Years.* Little, Brown and Company, 1979, p. 45; **Richard Nixon:** *The Memoirs of Richard Nixon.* Grosset and Dunlap, 1978, p. 545; **Richard Nixon:** *Public Papers of the Presidents of the United States: Richard Nixon.* United States Government Printing Office, 1972, p. 237; **Richard Nixon:** *Public Papers of the Presidents of the United States: Richard Nixon,* p. 320; **John J. Sirica:** Bernstein, Carl and Bob Woodward. *All the President's Men.* Warner Paperback Books, 1975, p. 268; **M. Caldwell Butler:** Burns, James MacGregor. *The Crosswinds of Freedom.* Alfred A. Knopf, 1989, p. 507.

Chapter 27 Richard Rovere: Reeves, Richard. *A Ford, Not a Lincoln.* Harcourt Brace Jovanovich, 1975; **Gerald Ford:** *A Time to Heal: The Autobiography of Gerald R. Ford.* Harper and Row, 1979, pp. 177–178; J**erold F. terHorst:** "How Good a President?" *Newsweek,* October 18, 1976, p. 31; **Jimmy Carter:** *Keeping Faith: Memoirs of a President.* Bantam Books, 1982, p. 65; **Patrick Caddell:** Wooten, James. *Dasher: The Roots and the Rising of Jimmy Carter.* Weidenfeld and Nicolson, 1978, p. 356; **Alistair Cooke:** "On Language." *New York Times Magazine,* July 19, 1981; **Jimmy Carter:** Carter, pp. 142–143; **Cyrus Vance:** *Hard Choices: Critical Years in America's Foreign Policy.* Simon and Schuster, 1983, pp. 228–229; **Kathryn Koob:** *Guest of the Revolution.* Thomas Nelson Publishers, 1982, pp. 57, 64, 73; **Jimmy Carter:** Jordan, Hamilton. *Crisis: The Last Year of the Carter Presidency.* G. P. Putnam's Sons, 1982, p. 54; **Robert J. Samuelson:** "Good People, but Not Very Good Government." *The Eugene Register-Guard,* January 19, 1981; **Jimmy Carter:** Public address; **Jimmy Carter:** Carter, p. 22; **Robert J. Samuelson:** Samuelson, January 19, 1981.

Chapter 28 Ronald Reagan: *An American Life.* Simon and Schuster, 1990, p. 135; **Kevin Phillips:** "Reagan's America: A Capital Offense." *New York Times Magazine,* June 24, 1990; **Joseph Lattimore:** Terkel, Studs. *Race: How Blacks and Whites Think and Feel About the American Obsession.* The New Press, 1992, p. 138; **Gloria Steinem:** Gibbs, Nancy. "The War Against Feminism." *Time,* March 9, 1992, p. 57; **Dale Old Horn:** Sahagun, Louis. "Crow Tribe: Heavy Price of Tradition." *Los Angeles Times,* December 22, 1986; **Iola Hayden:** Gorman, Tom. "Choctaws Retain Culture as Their Business Thrives." *Los Angeles Times;* **George Bush:** "Open Letter to College Students on the Persian Gulf Crisis," January 9, 1991.

Chapter 29 Maya Angelou: Inaugural poem "On the Pulse of the Morning"; **Bill Clinton:** Address to Congress and the Nation on Health Care Reform. September, 1993; **Jackie Goldberg:** Gore, Rick. "L.A.'s Rainbow Road." *National Geographic,* June 1992, pp. 40–69; **Jaimie S. Wurzel:** *Toward Multiculturalism: A Reader in Multicultural Education.* Intercultural Press, Inc. 1988, p. 10; **Arthur M. Schlesinger, Jr:** *The Disuniting of America.* W.W. Norton and Company, 1992.